EIGHTEENTH EDITION

MODERN GUNS

IDENTIFICATION & VALUES

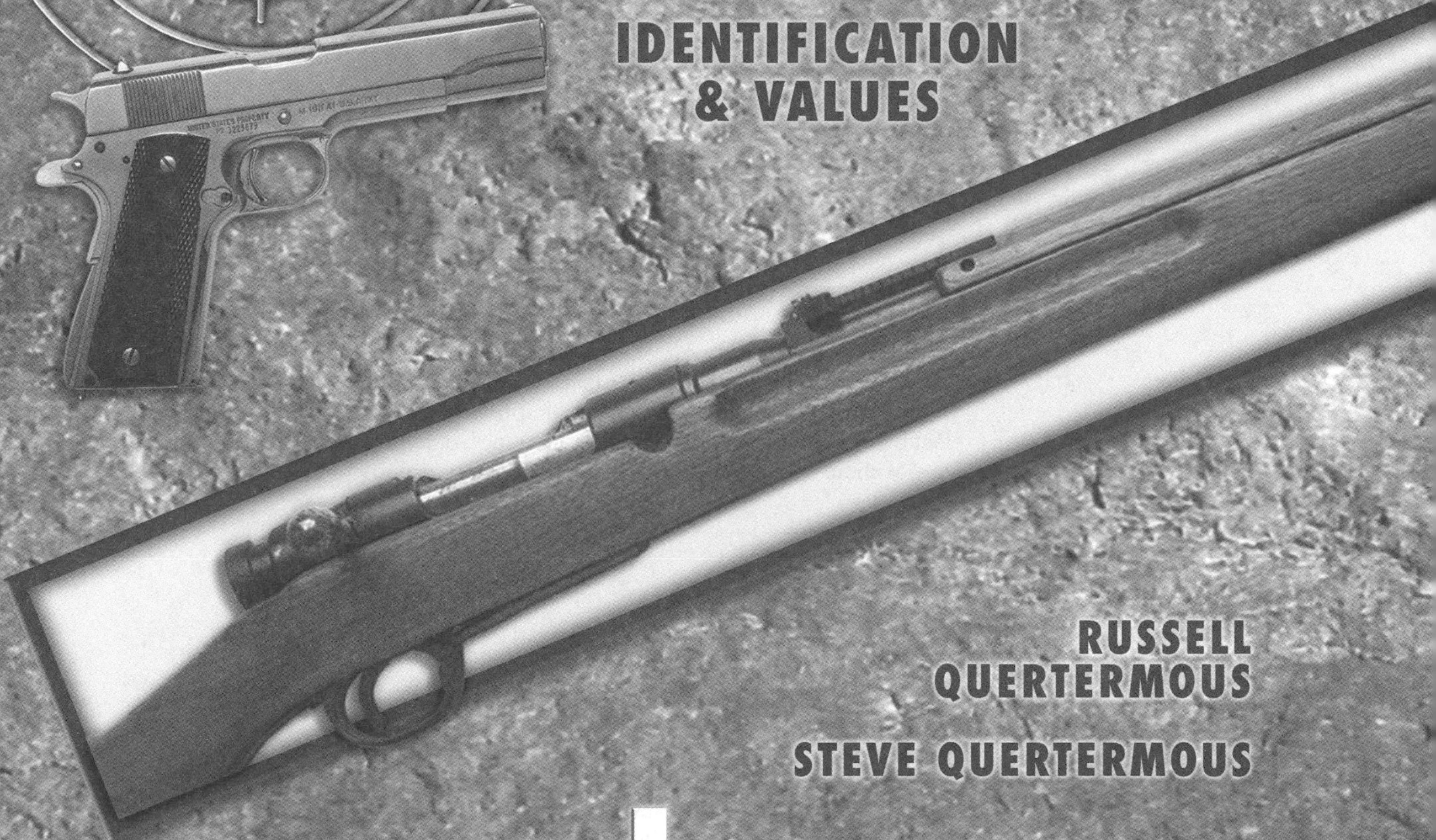

RUSSELL QUERTERMOUS

STEVE QUERTERMOUS

COLLECTOR BOOKS
A Division of Schroeder Publishing Co., Inc.

Front cover: Colt Model 1911A1, US Army handgun produced during World War II by the Ithaca Gun Co., nickel finish, $3,000.00+. From the Collection of Bob Rice. Japaneses Military Type 99 Service rifle, $420.00. Winchester Model 37A single-shot shotgun, $300.00.

Back cover: Colt Camp Perry single-shot handgun, $2,750.00. From the collection of Bob Rice. Ruger Single-Six revolver, $600.00. From the collection of Bob Rice.

Cover design: Terri Hunter
Book design: Beth Ray
Cover photography: Charles R. Lynch

COLLECTOR BOOKS
P.O. Box 3009
Paducah, Kentucky 42002–3009

www.collectorbooks.com

The current values in this book should be used only as a guide. They are not intended to set prices, which vary from one section of the country to another. Auction prices, as well as dealer prices, vary greatly and are affected by condition as well as demand. Neither the authors nor the publisher assumes responsibility for any losses that might be incurred as a result of consulting this guide.

Proudly printed and bound in the United States of America

CONTENTS

VALUES

For the purpose of estimating values, the firearm's condition is the first and foremost consideration. Conditions of guns evaluated in this guide are considered to be in accordance with the National Rifle Association (NRA) definitions, taken from its magazine, *The American Rifleman*. This evaluation system is generally accepted in the firearms trade.

New Discontinued – same as new, but discontinued model. The following definitions will apply to all second-hand articles.

Perfect – in new condition in every aspect.

Excellent – new condition, used little, no noticeable marring of wood or metal, bluing perfect (except at muzzle or sharp edges).

Very good – in perfect working condition, no appreciable wear on working surfaces, no corrosion or pitting, only minor surface dents or scratches.

Good – in safe working condition, minor wear on working surfaces, no broken parts, no corrosion or pitting that will interfere with proper functioning.

Fair – in working condition, but well worn, perhaps requiring replacement of minor parts or adjustments, no rust but may have corrosion pits which do not render article unsafe or inoperable.

Values in this guide are for guns in the following conditions:

New (retail) – suggested retail prices for models still in production.

Excellent, Very good, and Good – second-hand items.

The illustrations included are from gun manufacturers' promotional photos, advertisements, catalogs, and brochures. Since they are from a number of sources, relative size cannot be determined by comparing photos.

INTRODUCTION

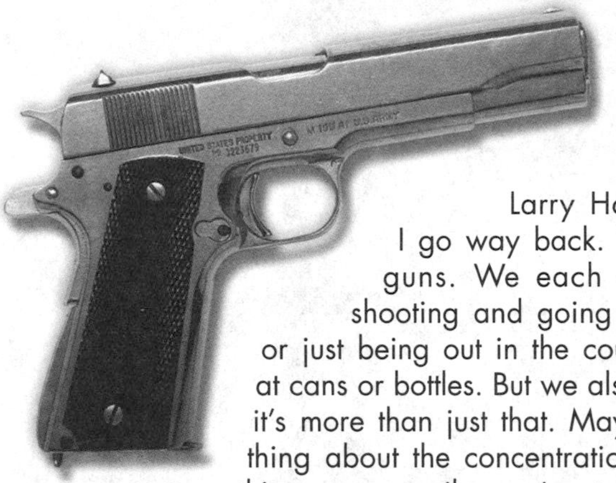

My buddy Larry Hammond and I go way back. We both like guns. We each enjoy target shooting and going to the range or just being out in the country plinking at cans or bottles. But we also realize that it's more than just that. Maybe it's something about the concentration and everything momentarily coming to a halt while you sight down the barrel at something in the distance. Sure, there is some kind of pleasure in zeroing-in on the bull's-eye and scoring a hit (or in my case at least hitting the paper). The noise is good and so is the smell of spent cordite after a few shots have been fired. But even if you never even load it, there is something alluring about a good gun. Maybe it is something about the smell of gun oil and wood.

Larry has always been a better shot than I have. He competed in the military with handguns and he still retains some of the insights and skills that made him a competitor, even if it has been a few years. He has always been the kind of guy you could count on, whether you need something big or small. He has let us use some of his guns, especially Smith & Wesson revolvers, over the years for the covers of *Modern Guns*. Larry and I were friends before we knew of our common interest in guns, but there is something about people interested in firearms that creates a community.

It was through one of our discussions about guns that Larry told me about another buddy of his, Bob Rice. He introduced me to Bob, and Bob's invitation to use some of his collection for the cover of the current edition of this book is an example of that community of gun owners. Bob has been a gun trader for years and has built a nice collection of short and long arms. Bob welcomed us into his home and offered anything we wanted to use from his holdings. On this edition's cover, the Colt Model 1911 A1 produced by Ithaca, the Colt Camp Perry, and the Ruger Single Six all came from Bob's collection. Community in action.

This eighteenth edition of *Modern Guns* is arranged in the same way as previous editions. It is divided into three broad categories: shotguns, rifles, and handguns. Within each category, manufacturers are listed alphabetically with a contents page at the beginning. Listings are grouped where possible into like kinds; that is, single-shots are grouped together, bolt action arms are together, lever actions are together, slide actions are together, and semiautomatics are together within each brand. In the case of handguns, single-shots are followed by semiautomatics, then revolvers.

The guns included in this guide are those firearms made from around 1900 to the present. You won't find extremely rare examples of exotic firearms or custom guns that demand tens of thousands of dollars. Hopefully, you will find a comprehensive overview of the firearms market today with examples of the majority of guns that can commonly be seen changing hands.

Prices will vary in different parts of the country. What is popular in one area might be slightly less so in another. Also keep in mind that, ultimately, the value of a gun, as with any item, is determined by the seller's eagerness to sell and the purchaser's willingness to buy. Changes in laws concerning firearms and modifications to guns to conform to government policies will affect value. As always, we encourage you to do more research on particular items that are of interest to you and to use this book as a guideline to establish the relative worth of your guns. There are no hard-and-fast rules, no absolutes.

Don't be afraid to use this book; take it along to auctions, garage sales, flea markets, and gun shows and use it as a guide. But don't let the figures in a book dictate whether or not you will make a trade on something you might really want.

SHOTGUNS

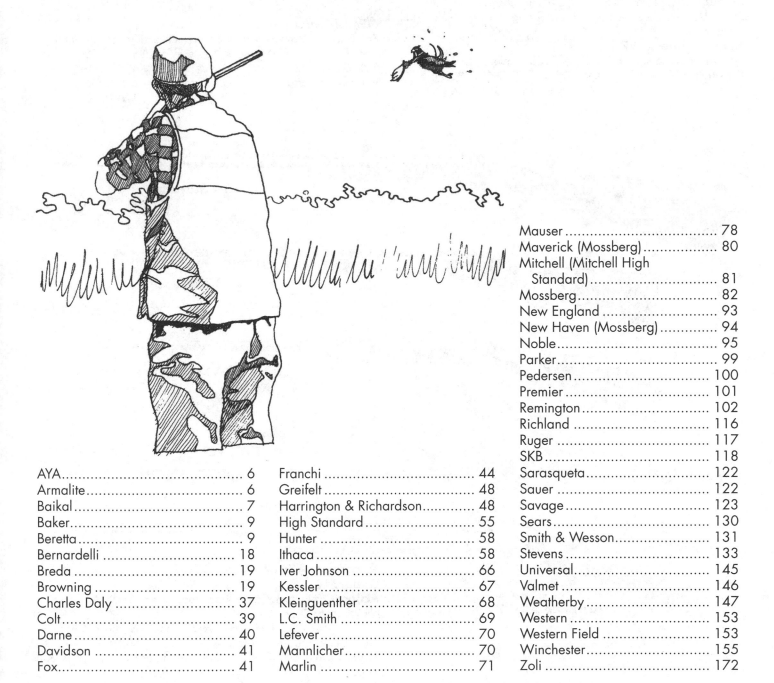

AYA

AYA Matador

Gauge: 10, 12, 16, 20, 20 magnum
Action: Box lock; top lever break-open; hammerless; selective single trigger and automatic ejector
Magazine: None
Barrel: Double barrel, 26", 28", 30" any choke combination
Finish: Blued; checkered walnut pistol grip stock and beavertail forearm
Approximate wt.: 7 lbs.
Comments: Made from 1953 until 1963. Replaced by Matador II.

Estimated Value:	**Excellent:**	**$500.00**
	Very good:	**$400.00**

AYA Matador II

Same as the Matador except ventilated rib. Produced from about 1963 to 1970.

Estimated Value:	**Excellent:**	**$550.00**
	Very good:	**$450.00**

AYA Bolero

Same as the Matador except non-selective single trigger and extractors; 28 and 410 gauges. Made from the mid-1950s until the 1980s.

Estimated Value:	**Excellent:**	**$475.00**
	Very good:	**$380.00**

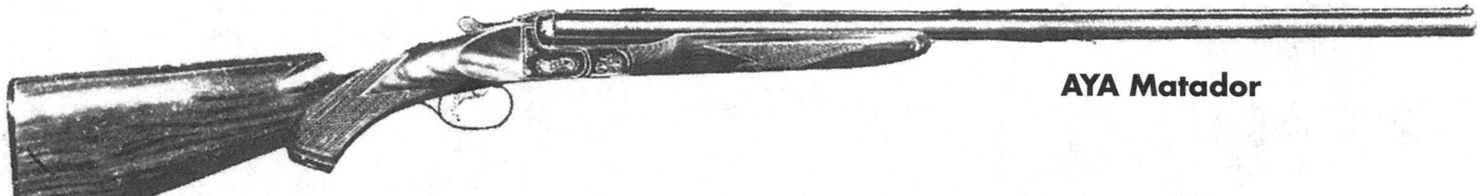

AYA Matador

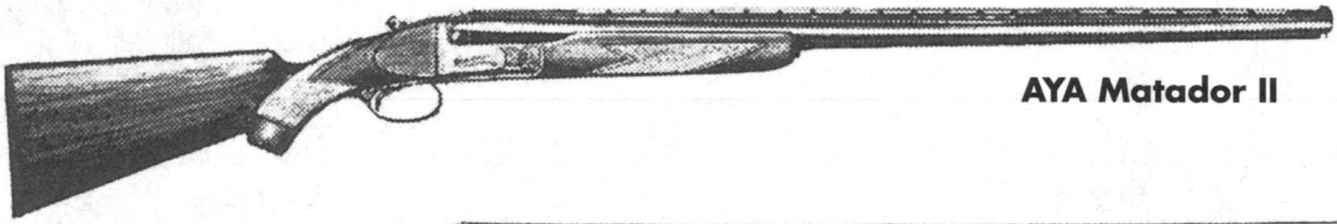

AYA Matador II

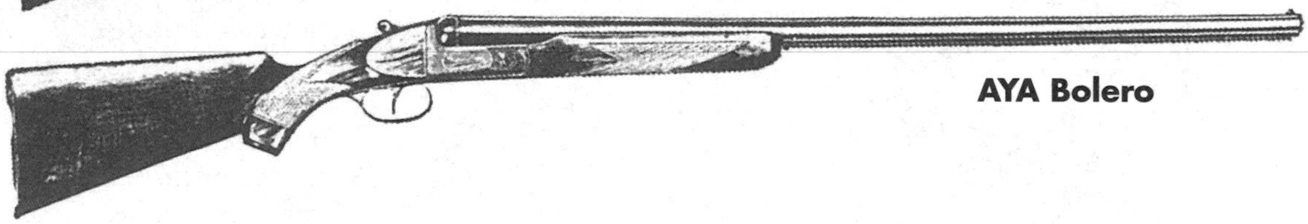

AYA Bolero

ARMALITE

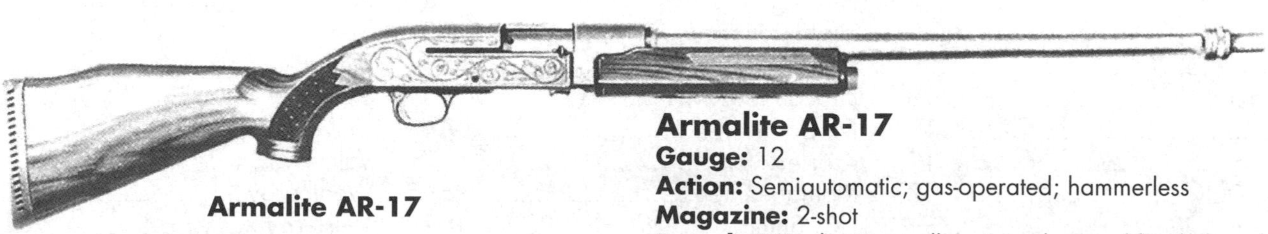

Armalite AR-17

Armalite AR-17

Gauge: 12
Action: Semiautomatic; gas-operated; hammerless
Magazine: 2-shot
Barrel: 24" aluminum alloy; interchangeable choke tubes; improved modified and full chokes
Finish: Gold anodized or black anodized; plastic stock and forearm
Approximate wt.: 5½ lbs.
Comments: Barrel and receiver housing made of high-tensile aluminum alloy. Made from about 1963 to 1965. Approximately 2,000 manufactured.

Estimated Value:	**Excellent:**	**$600.00**
	Very good:	**$480.00**

Baikal Models IJ-27 and IJ-27EIC

Gauge: 12
Action: Box lock; top lever break-open; hammerless; double trigger
Magazine: None
Barrel: Over and under double barrel; 26" or 28" improved cylinder and modified or modified and full chokes; ventilated rib
Finish: Blued; engraved receiver; hand-checkered walnut pistol grip stock and forearm
Approximate wt.: 7½ lbs.
Comments: Made in Soviet Union; IJ-27EIC has single trigger and automatic ejectors, add $40.00.

Estimated Value:	**Excellent:**	**$350.00**
	Very good:	**$280.00**

Baikal Model IJK-27EIC Silver

Same as the Model IJ-27EIC except: silver inlays and fancy engraving.

Estimated Value:	**Excellent:**	**$625.00**
	Very good:	**$500.00**

Baikal Model IJ-12

Less fancy but similar to the IJ-27. No engraving, no recoil pad; 28" barrel only. Imported in the early 1970s.

Estimated Value:	**Excellent:**	**$325.00**
	Very good:	**$260.00**

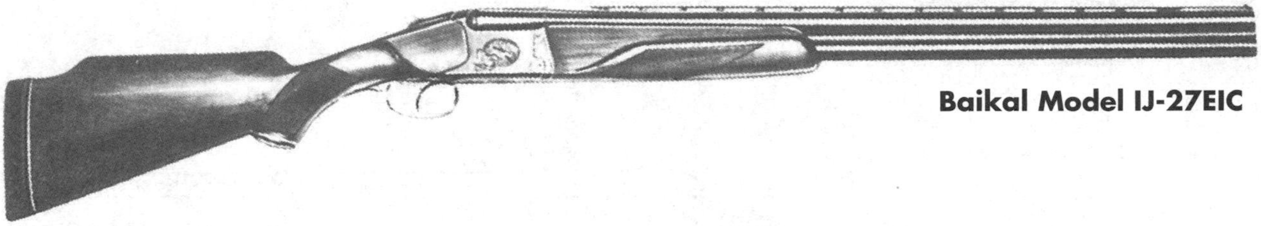

Baikal Model IJ-27EIC

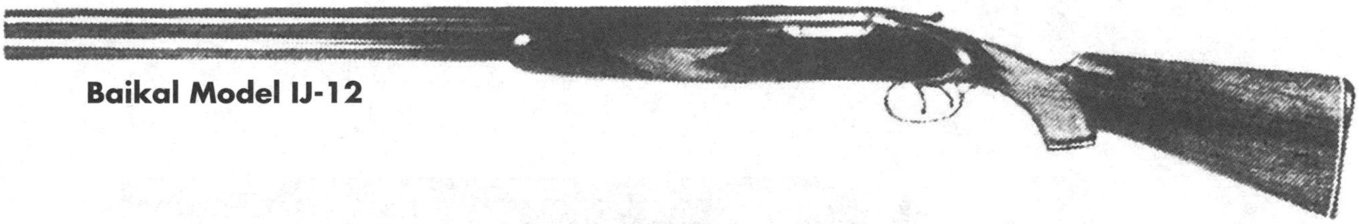

Baikal Model IJ-12

Baikal Model TOZ-66

Baikal Model TOZ-66

Gauge: 12
Action: Box lock; top lever break-open; exposed hammers
Magazine: None
Barrel: Side-by-side double barrel; 28" chrome lined, variety of chokes
Finish: Blued; checkered wood pistol grip stock and short tapered forearm; engraving
Approximate wt.: 8 lbs.
Comments: Imported during the 1970s.

Estimated Value:	**Excellent:**	**$225.00**
	Very good:	**$180.00**

Baikal Model TOZ-34E Souvenir

Gauge: 12, 20, 28
Action: Box lock; top lever break-open; hammerless
Magazine: None
Barrel: Over and under double barrel; 26" or 28" improved cylinder and modified or modified and full; ventilated rib on 12 and 20 gauge; solid rib on 28 gauge
Finish: Blued; select walnut, hand-checkered and pistol grip stock and forearm; engraved receiver
Approximate wt.: 7 lbs.
Comments: Imported from the Soviet Union. It features selective ejectors and cocking indicators.

Estimated Value:	**Excellent:**	**$410.00**
	Very good:	**$325.00**

Baikal Model IJ-18

Gauge: 12, 20, 410
Action: Box lock; top lever break-open; hammerless; single shot; cocking indicator
Magazine: None
Barrel: 26", 28" modified, 30" full choke
Finish: Blued; checkered walnut-stained hardwood, pistol grip stock and tapered forearm; engraved receiver
Approximate wt.: 6 lbs.
Comments: Imported from the Soviet Union.

Estimated Value:	**Excellent:**	**$125.00**
	Very good:	**$100.00**

Baikal Models IJ-58MA and IJ-58MAE

Gauge: 12, 20 magnum
Action: Box lock; top lever break-open; hammerless
Magazine: None
Barrel: Side-by-side double barrel; 26" improved cylinder and modified, 28" modified and full chokes; chrome lined
Finish: Blued; checkered walnut pistol grip stock and short tapered forearm; engraved receiver. IJ-58MAE has selective ejectors, add $25.00.
Approximate wt.: 7 lbs.
Comments: Imported in the 1970s.

Estimated Value:	**Excellent:**	**$300.00**
	Very good:	**$240.00**

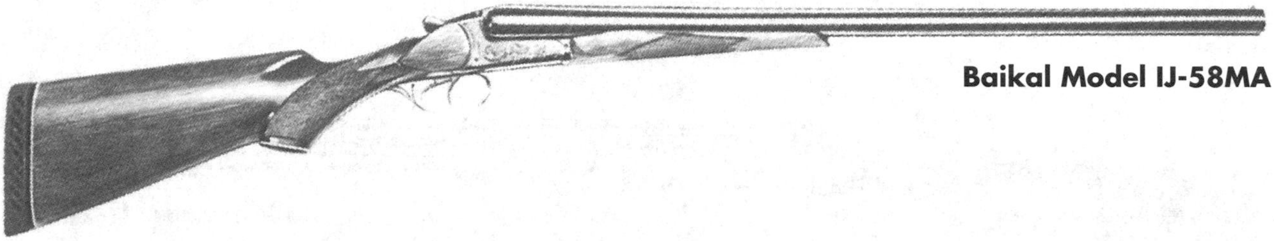

Baikal Model IJ-58MA

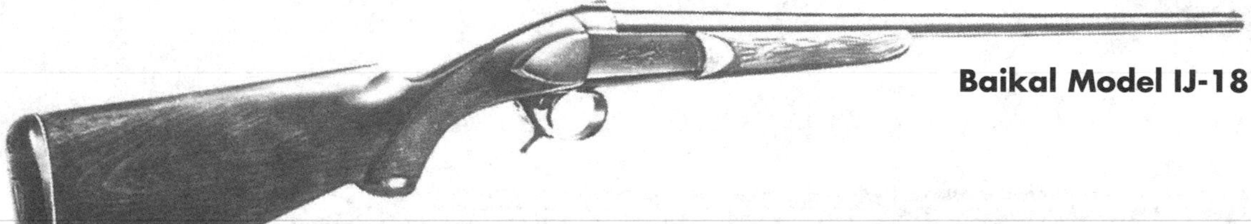

Baikal Model IJ-18

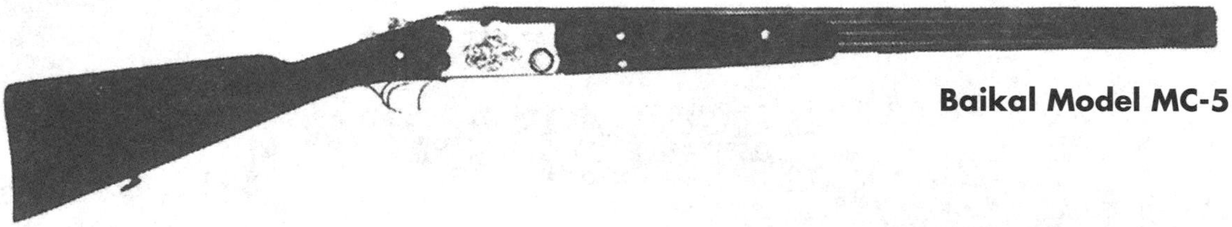

Baikal Model MC-5

Baikal Model IJ-43

Gauge: 12
Action: Box lock; top lever break-open; hammerless
Magazine: None
Barrel: Side-by-side double barrel; 20", 26," or 28" barrels
Finish: Blued; checkered walnut stock and forearm; engraved receiver
Approximate wt.: 8½ lbs.
Comments: Imported from the Soviet Union.

Estimated Value:	**Excellent:**	**$300.00**
	Very good:	**$240.00**

Baikal Model MC-5

Gauge: 20
Action: Box lock; top lever break-open; hammerless; double triggers
Magazine: None
Barrel: Over and under double barrel; 26" or 28" improved cylinder and modified or skeet chokes; ribbed
Finish: Blued; checkered walnut pistol grip or straight stock and forearm; engraved receiver
Approximate wt.: 5¾ lbs.
Comments: Imported during the 1970s.

Estimated Value:	**Excellent:**	**$1,000.00**
	Very good:	**$ 800.00**

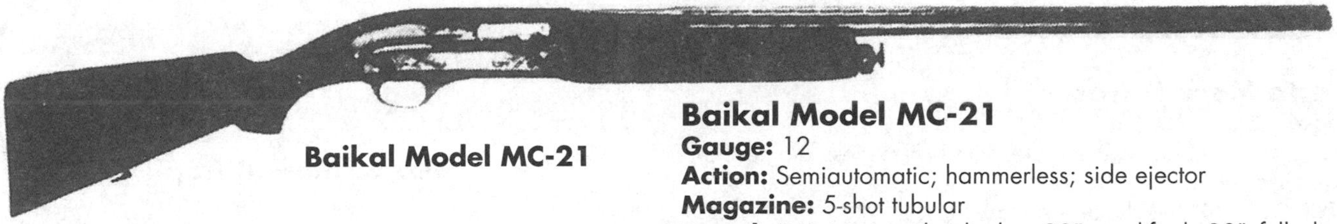

Baikal Model MC-21

Baikal Model MC-21
Gauge: 12
Action: Semiautomatic; hammerless; side ejector
Magazine: 5-shot tubular
Barrel: 26" improved cylinder; 28" modified; 30" full chokes; ventilated rib
Finish: Blued; checkered walnut, pistol grip stock and forearm; engraved receiver
Approximate wt.: 7½ lbs.
Comments: Imported in the 1970s.

Estimated Value:	**Excellent:**	**$375.00**
	Very good:	**$300.00**

BAKER

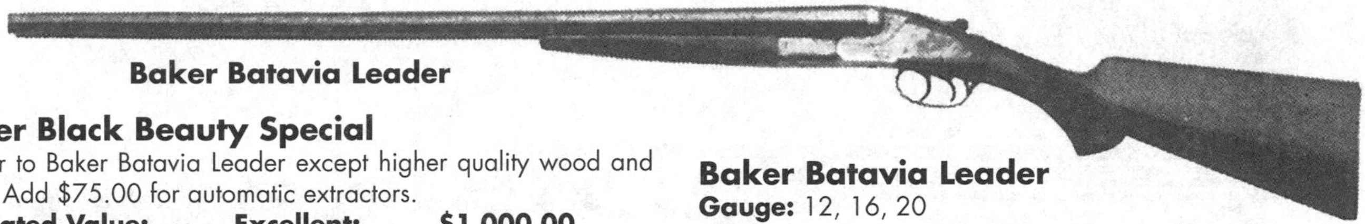

Baker Batavia Leader

Baker Black Beauty Special
Similar to Baker Batavia Leader except higher quality wood and finish. Add $75.00 for automatic extractors.

Estimated Value:	**Excellent:**	**$1,000.00**
	Very good:	**$ 800.00**

Baker Black Beauty Special

Baker Batavia Leader
Gauge: 12, 16, 20
Action: Box lock; top break-open; hammerless
Magazine: None
Barrel: 26", 28", 30", or 32" side-by-side double barrel; any standard choke combination
Finish: Blued; walnut pistol grip stock and forearm
Approximate wt.: 7 to 8 lbs.
Comments: Made from about 1900 to 1930. Add $75.00 for automatic extractors.

Estimated Value:	**Excellent:**	**$600.00**
	Very good:	**$480.00**

BERETTA

Beretta Companion FS-1
Gauge: 12, 16, 20, 28, 410
Action: Underlever; hammerless; single shot
Magazine: None
Barrel: 26", 28" full choke
Finish: Blued; checkered walnut pistol grip stock and forearm
Approximate wt.: 5 lbs.
Comments: A folding shotgun made from about 1960 to the late 1970s.

Estimated Value:	**Excellent:**	**$175.00**
	Very good:	**$140.00**

Beretta Model 412
Gauge: 12, 20, 24, 28, 32, 410
Action: Underlever, break-open, hammerless, single shot
Magazine: None
Barrel: 28" full or modified choke
Finish: Blued; checkered or smooth walnut semi-pistol grip stock and forearm
Approximate wt.: 5 lbs.
Comments: A lightweight folding shotgun designed for beginners, campers, and backpackers. Made from the early 1980s to the mid-1990s.

Estimated Value:	**Excellent:**	**$175.00**
	Very good:	**$140.00**

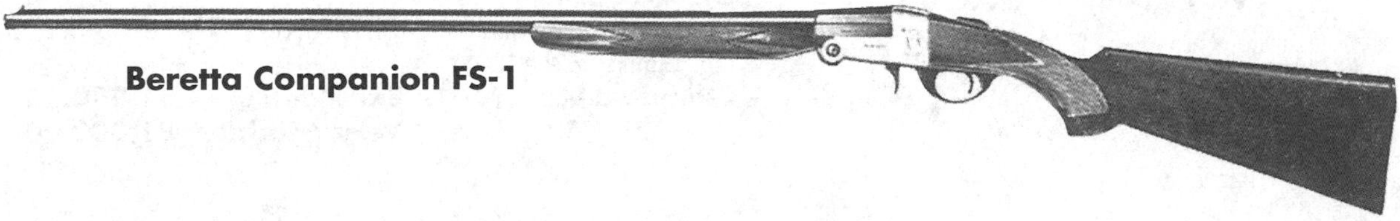

Beretta Companion FS-1

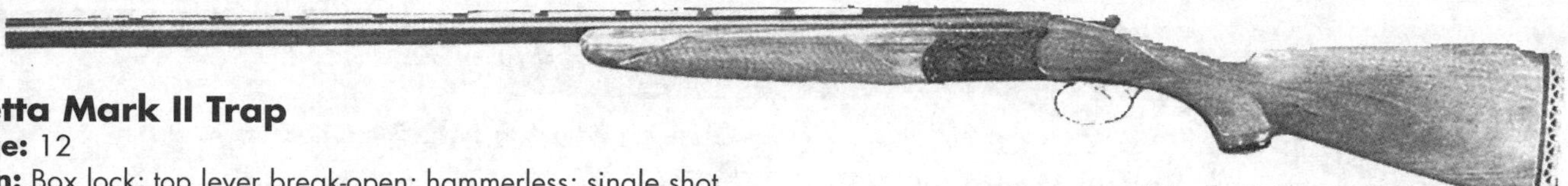

Beretta Mark II Trap

Beretta Mark II Trap

Gauge: 12
Action: Box lock; top lever break-open; hammerless; single shot
Magazine: None
Barrel: 32", 34" full choke; ventilated rib
Finish: Blued; checkered walnut Monte Carlo pistol grip stock and forearm; recoil pad; engraving
Approximate wt.: 8 lbs.
Comments: Made from the mid-1970s to the early 1980s.

Estimated Value:	**Excellent:**	**$750.00**
	Very good:	**$600.00**

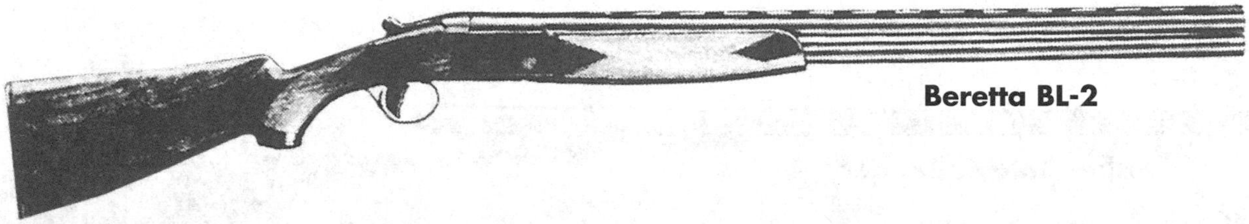

Beretta BL-2

Beretta BL-3

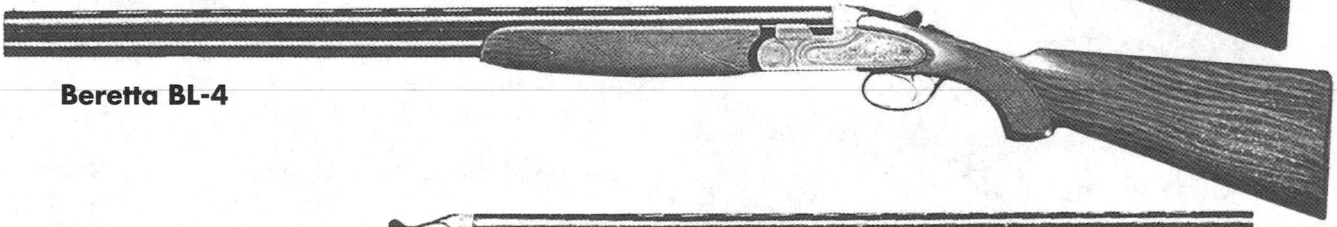

Beretta BL-4

Beretta BL-6

Beretta BL-1

Gauge: 12
Action: Box lock; top lever break-open; hammerless; double triggers
Magazine: None
Barrel: Over and under double barrel; chrome steel; 26" – 30" improved cylinder and modified or modified and full chokes
Finish: Blued; checkered walnut semi-pistol grip stock and forearm
Approximate wt.: 7 lbs.
Comments: Made from about 1969 to the early 1970s.

Estimated Value:	**Excellent:**	**$500.00**
	Very good:	**$400.00**

Beretta BL-2

Similar to the BL-1 except: selective single trigger.

Estimated Value:	**Excellent:**	**$435.00**
	Very good:	**$345.00**

Beretta BL-3

Similar to the BL-2 except: ventilated rib; engraving.

Estimated Value:	**Excellent:**	**$650.00**
	Very good:	**$520.00**

Beretta BL-4 and BL-5

Similar to the BL-3 except: deluxe engraving and checkering; automatic ejectors. Add $100.00 for BL-5.

Estimated Value:	**Excellent:**	**$825.00**
	Very good:	**$660.00**

Beretta BL-6

The finest of the BL line. Highest quality checkering and engraving. Similar to the BL-4.

Estimated Value:	**Excellent:**	**$1,250.00**
	Very good:	**$1,000.00**

Beretta Silver Snipe

Beretta Silver Snipe

Gauge: 12, 20, regular or magnum
Action: Box lock; top lever break-open; hammerless
Magazine: None
Barrel: 26" – 30" improved cylinder and modified, modified and full, full or skeet chokes; ribbed; over and under double barrel
Finish: Blued; nickel receiver; checkered walnut pistol grip stock and forearm
Approximate wt.: 7½ lbs.
Comments: Made from the mid-1950s to the late 1960s. Add $25.00 for single selective trigger.

Estimated Value:	**Excellent:**	**$625.00**
	Very good:	**$500.00**

Beretta Golden Snipe

Similar to the Silver Snipe except: ventilated rib; automatic ejectors. Discontinued in the mid-1960s.

Estimated Value:	**Excellent:**	**$800.00**
	Very good:	**$640.00**

Beretta Asel

Gauge: 12, 20
Action: Box lock; top lever break-open; hammerless; automatic ejector; single trigger
Magazine: None
Barrel: Over and under double barrel; 25", 28", 30" improved cylinder and modified or modified and full chokes
Finish: Blued; checkered walnut semi-pistol grip stock and forearm
Approximate wt.: 7 lbs.
Comments: Made from the late 1940s to the mid-1960s. Add 20% for 20 gauge.

Estimated Value:	**Excellent:**	**$3,500.00**
	Very good:	**$2,800.00**

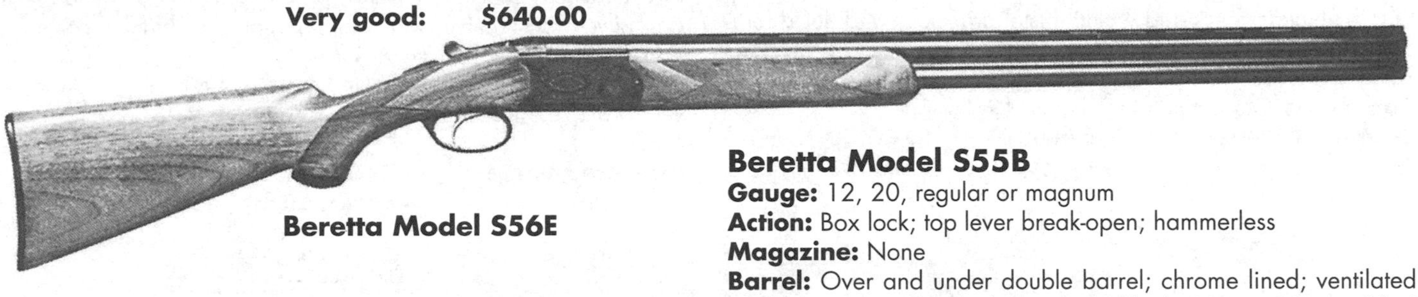

Beretta Model S56E

Beretta Model S56E

Similar to Model S55B except: scroll engraving on the receiver; selective automatic ejectors.

Estimated Value:	**Excellent:**	**$675.00**
	Very good:	**$540.00**

Beretta Model S55B

Gauge: 12, 20, regular or magnum
Action: Box lock; top lever break-open; hammerless
Magazine: None
Barrel: Over and under double barrel; chrome lined; ventilated rib; 26" improved cylinder and modified; 28" or 30" modified and full; 30" full in 12 gauge
Finish: Blued; checkered walnut pistol grip stock and beavertail forearm; recoil pad on magnum
Approximate wt.: 6 to 7 lbs.
Comments: Made from the late 1970s to the early 1980s.

Estimated Value:	**Excellent:**	**$650.00**
	Very good:	**$520.00**

Beretta Model 680 Trap

Beretta Model 680 Trap

Similar to the Model 680 Skeet except: Monte Carlo stock, recoil pad; 30" or 32" improved modified and full choke barrels.

Estimated Value:	**Excellent:**	**$1,650.00**
	Very good:	**$1,320.00**

Beretta Model 680 Mono Trap

Similar to the Model 680 Trap except: a single high-ventilated rib barrel; 32" or 34" full choke barrel.

Estimated Value:	**Excellent:**	**$1,700.00**
	Very good:	**$1,360.00**

Beretta Model 680 Competition Skeet

Gauge: 12
Action: Top lever break-open; hammerless; automatic ejector; single selective trigger
Magazine: None
Barrel: Over and under double barrel; 26" or 28" skeet choke barrels; ventilated rib
Finish: Blued; checkered walnut pistol grip stock and forearm; silver-gray receiver with engraving; gold-plated trigger
Approximate wt.: 7 lbs.
Comments: Interchangeable barrel; price includes luggage-style case.

Estimated Value:	**Excellent:**	**$1,775.00**
	Very good:	**$1,420.00**

Beretta Model 625

Gauge: 12, 20, regular or magnum
Action: Box lock; top lever break-open; hammerless; double barrel; mechanical extractor
Magazine: None
Barrel: 26" improved cylinder/modified; 28" or 30" modified/full; double barrel
Finish: Blued; gray receiver; checkered walnut pistol grip or straight stock and tapered forearm
Approximate wt.: 6 to 7 lbs.
Comments: Produced in the mid-1980s.

Estimated Value:	**Excellent:**	**$775.00**
	Very good:	**$625.00**

Beretta Model 685

Gauge: 12, 20, regular or magnum
Action: Top lever break-open; hammerless; single selective trigger
Magazine: None
Barrel: Over and under double barrel; 26" improved cylinder and modified, 28" or 30" modified and full, 30" full and full; ventilated rib
Finish: Blued; checkered walnut pistol grip stock and fluted forearm; silver-gray receiver with light engraving
Approximate wt.: 8 lbs.
Comments: Discontinued in the late 1980s.

Estimated Value:	**Excellent:**	**$700.00**
	Very good:	**$560.00**

Beretta Models 626 and 626 Onyx

Similar to the Model 625 except: selective automatic ejectors. Deduct 30% for Regular Model 626 (discontinued 1990). Produced from the late 1980s to the early 1990s.

Estimated Value:	**Excellent:**	**$950.00**
	Very good:	**$760.00**

Beretta Models 627EL and 627EELL

Similar to the Model 626 with higher grade finish and engraved sideplates. Add 70% for Model 627EELL.

Estimated Value:	**Excellent:**	**$2,000.00**
	Very good:	**$1,600.00**

Beretta Models 686 and 686 Essential

Gauge: 12, 20, 28, regular or magnum
Action: Top lever break-open; hammerless; single selective trigger; selective automatic ejectors
Magazine: None
Barrel: Over and under double barrel; 26" improved cylinder and modified, 28" or 30" modified and full, or 30" full and full; ventilated rib; multi-choke tubes
Finish: Blued; checkered walnut pistol grip stock and fluted forearm; silver-gray receiver with engraving or plain black receiver
Approximate wt.: 7 lbs.
Comments: Add 25% for Ultralight Onyx Model, 26% for Silver Perdiz, 6% for Sporting Clays Model, 30% for Silver Pigeon Model.

Estimated Value:	**Excellent:**	**$1,350.00**
	Very good:	**$1,075.00**

Beretta Model 685

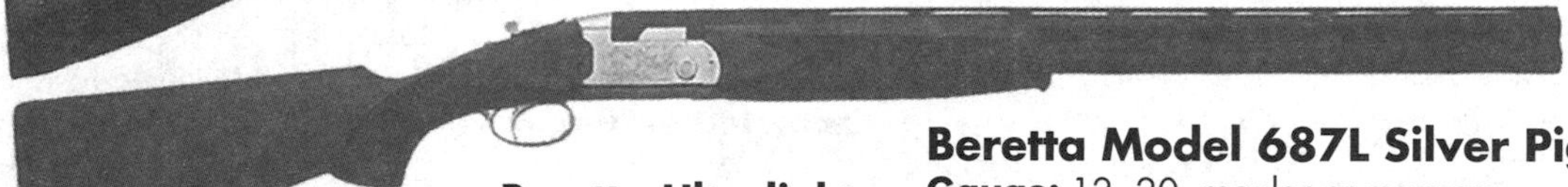

Beretta Ultralight

Beretta Ultralight

Gauge: 12 (2¾" chamber)
Action: Low profile, improved box lock; automatic safety; single selective trigger
Magazine: None
Barrel: Over and under double barrel; 28" with MC3 choke tube; ventilated rib
Finish: Blued with game scene engraved, nickel finish receiver; select walnut checkered pistol grip stock and schnabel forearm. A deluxe model is available; add 20%.
Approximate wt.: 6 lbs.
Comments: Introduced in the early 1990s.

Estimated Value:	**New (retail):**	**$2,450.00**
	Excellent:	**$1,835.00**
	Very good:	**$1,475.00**

Beretta Model 687L Silver Pigeon

Gauge: 12, 20, regular or magnum
Action: Top lever break-open; hammerless; selective automatic ejectors; single selective trigger
Magazine: None
Barrel: Over and under double barrel; 26" or 28" with interchangeable choke tubes; ventilated rib
Finish: Blued; grayed receiver with engraving; checkered walnut pistol grip stock and forearm
Approximate wt.: 6 to 6¾ lbs.
Comments: Add 25% for Golden Onyx Model; 20% for Sporting Clays Model.

Estimated Value:	**New (retail):**	**$2,450.00**
	Excellent:	**$1,835.00**
	Very good:	**$1,475.00**

Beretta Model 687EL Gold Pigeon

Similar to the Model 687L Silver Pigeon except: higher quality finish, extensive engraving on receiver and sideplate. Add 6% for Sporting Clays Model.

Estimated Value:	**Excellent:**	**$2,500.00**
	Very good:	**$2,000.00**

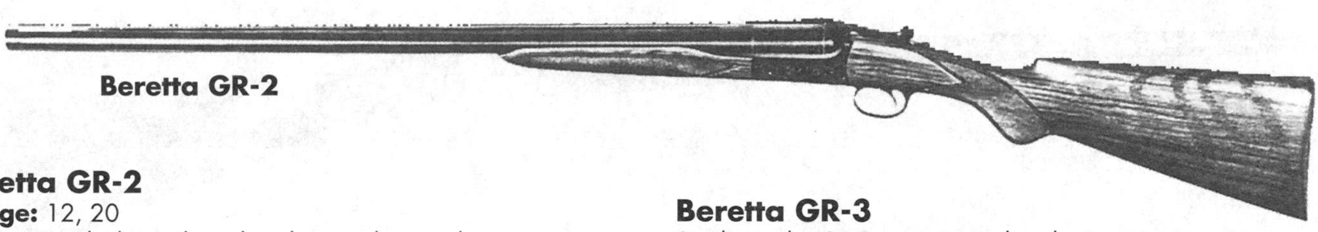

Beretta GR-2

Beretta GR-2

Gauge: 12, 20
Action: Box lock; top lever break-open; hammerless
Magazine: None
Barrel: Side-by-side double barrel; 26" – 30"; variety of choke combinations
Finish: Blued; checkered walnut semi-pistol grip stock and forearm
Approximate wt.: 6 to 8 lbs.
Comments: Made from the late 1960s to the mid-1970s.

Estimated Value:	**Excellent:**	**$800.00**
	Very good:	**$640.00**

Beretta GR-3

Similar to the GR-2 except: single selective trigger.

Estimated Value:	**Excellent:**	**$825.00**
	Very good:	**$660.00**

Beretta GR-4

Similar to the GR-3 except: automatic ejector engraving and deluxe woodwork.

Estimated Value:	**Excellent:**	**$950.00**
	Very good:	**$760.00**

Beretta Model 409PB

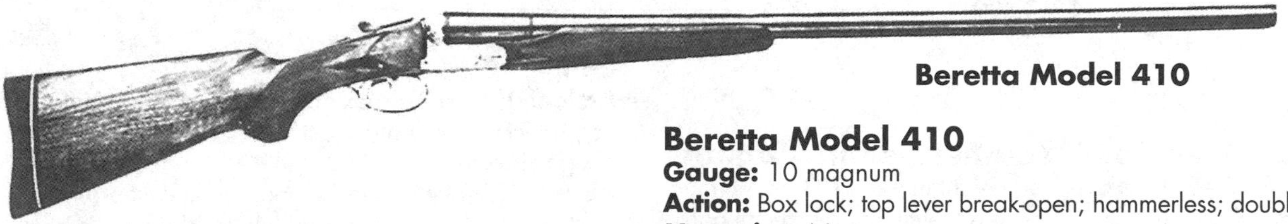

Beretta Model 410

Beretta Model 409PB

Gauge: 12, 16, 20, 28
Action: Box lock; top lever break-open; hammerless; double triggers
Magazine: None
Barrel: Side-by-side double barrel, 27½", 28½", 30", improved cylinder and modified or modified and full chokes
Finish: Blued; checkered walnut straight or pistol grip stock and small tapered forearm; engraved
Approximate wt.: 6 to 8 lbs.
Comments: Made from the mid-1930s to the mid-1960s.

Estimated Value:	**Excellent:**	**$750.00**
	Very good:	**$600.00**

Beretta Model 410

Gauge: 10 magnum
Action: Box lock; top lever break-open; hammerless; double triggers
Magazine: None
Barrel: Side-by-side double barrel; 27½", 28½", 30" improved cylinder and modified or modified and full chokes
Finish: Blued; checkered walnut pistol stock and short tapered forearm
Approximate wt.: 10 lbs.
Comments: Made from the mid-1930s to the early 1980s.

Estimated Value:	**Excellent:**	**$975.00**
	Very good:	**$780.00**

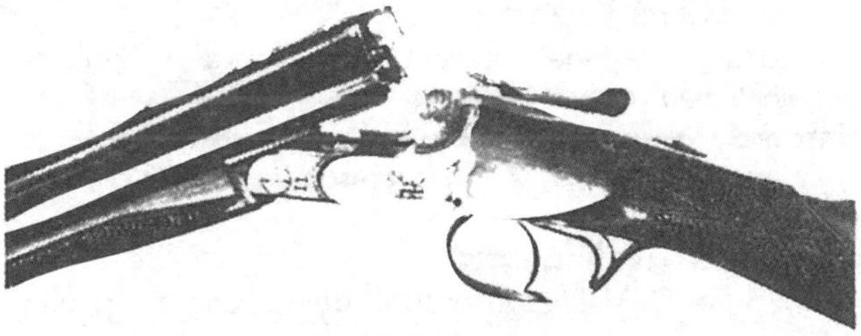

Beretta Model 410E

Beretta Model 410E

Similar to the Model 409PB except: higher quality finish and engraving; automatic ejector.

Estimated Value:	**Excellent:**	**$900.00**
	Very good:	**$720.00**

Beretta Model 411E

Similar to the Model 410E with higher quality finish.

Estimated Value:	**Excellent:**	**$1,250.00**
	Very good:	**$1,000.00**

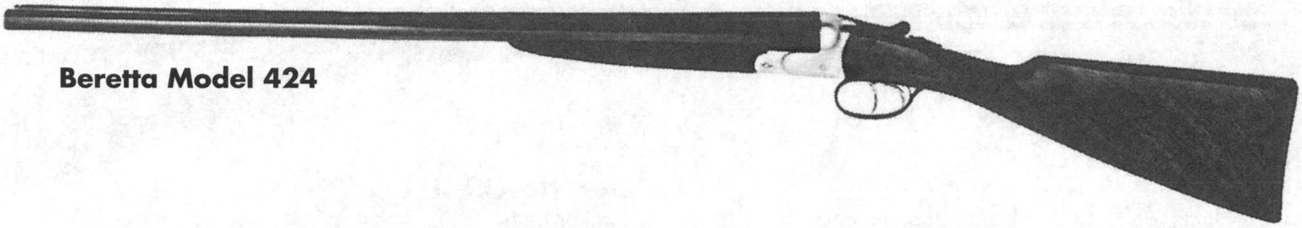

Beretta Model 424

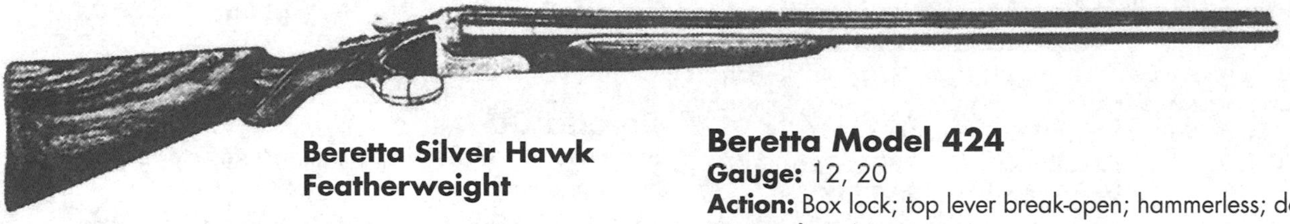

Beretta Silver Hawk Featherweight

Beretta Silver Hawk Featherweight

Gauge: 12, 16, 20, 28
Action: Box lock; top lever break-open; hammerless
Magazine: None
Barrel: Side-by-side double barrel; 26" – 32", variety of chokes; matted rib
Finish: Blued; checkered walnut pistol grip stock and forearm
Approximate wt.: 7¼ lbs.
Comments: Made from the mid-1950s to the late 1960s.
Estimated Value: **Excellent:** **$525.00**
Very good: **$420.00**

Beretta Silver Hawk Featherweight Magnum

Similar to the Silver Hawk Featherweight in 10 or 12 gauge magnum; chrome lined 30" or 32" barrels; ventilated rib; recoil pad.
Estimated Value: **Excellent:** **$675.00**
Very good: **$540.00**

Beretta Model 424

Gauge: 12, 20
Action: Box lock; top lever break-open; hammerless; double trigger
Magazine: None
Barrel: Side-by-side double barrel; chrome lined; matted rib; 26" or 28" improved cylinder and modified or modified and full chokes
Finish: Blued; checkered walnut straight grip stock and forearm
Approximate wt.: 6 lbs.
Comments: Produced from the late 1970s to the mid-1980s.
Estimated Value: **Excellent:** **$975.00**
Very good: **$780.00**

Beretta Model 426

Gauge: 12, 20, magnum
Action: Top lever break-open; hammerless; single selective trigger; selective automatic ejector
Magazine: None
Barrel: Side-by-side double barrel; 26" improved cylinder and modified or 28" modified and full; solid rib
Finish: Blued; checkered walnut pistol grip stock and tapered forearm; silver-gray engraved receiver; silver pigeon inlaid
Approximate wt.: 8 lbs.
Comments: Discontinued in the mid-1980s.
Estimated Value: **Excellent:** **$1,250.00**
Very good: **$1,000.00**

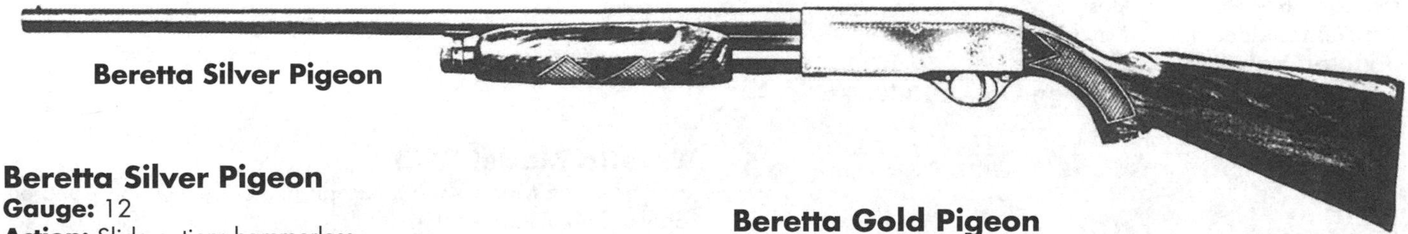

Beretta Silver Pigeon

Beretta Silver Pigeon

Gauge: 12
Action: Slide action; hammerless
Magazine: 5-shot tubular
Barrel: 26" – 32", various chokes
Finish: Blued; engraved and inlaid with silver pigeon; chrome trigger; checkered walnut pistol grip stock and slide handle
Approximate wt.: 7 lbs.
Comments: Made from about 1960 for six years.
Estimated Value: **Excellent:** **$325.00**
Very good: **$260.00**

Beretta Gold Pigeon

Similar to the Silver Pigeon except: heavy engraving; gold pigeon inlaid; ventilated rib; gold trigger.
Estimated Value: **Excellent:** **$425.00**
Very good: **$340.00**

Beretta Ruby Pigeon

Similar to the Gold Pigeon except: deluxe engraving and ruby eye in inlaid pigeon.
Estimated Value: **Excellent:** **$600.00**
Very good: **$480.00**

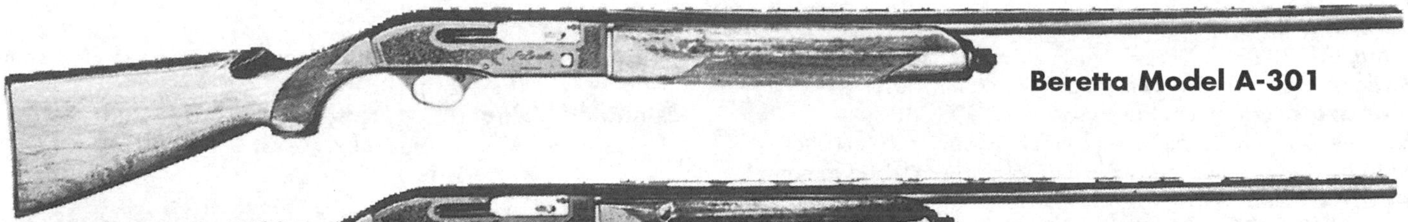

Beretta Model A-301

Beretta Model A-301 Trap

Beretta Model A-301

Gauge: 12, 20, regular or magnum
Action: Gas-operated, semiautomatic; hammerless
Magazine: 3-shot tubular
Barrel: 26" improved cylinder; 28" modified or full; 30" full in 12 gauge; ventilated rib; chrome molybdenum
Finish: Blued; checkered walnut pistol grip stock and forearm; decorated alloy receiver; recoil pad on magnum model
Approximate wt.: 6¼ to 7 lbs.
Comments: Made from the late 1970s to the early 1980s. Add 10% for magnum.

Estimated Value:	**Excellent:**	**$425.00**
	Very good:	**$340.00**

Beretta Model A-301 Trap

Similar to Model A-301 except: Monte Carlo stock, recoil pad and gold-plated trigger; 12 gauge only; 30" full choke barrel.

Estimated Value:	**Excellent:**	**$500.00**
	Very good:	**$400.00**

Beretta Model A-301 Skeet

Similar to the A-301 Trap except: 26" skeet choke barrel.

Estimated Value:	**Excellent:**	**$425.00**
	Very good:	**$340.00**

Beretta Model A-301 Deer Gun

Similar to Model A-301 except: 22" slug barrel; adjustable open sights.

Estimated Value:	**Excellent:**	**$400.00**
	Very good:	**$320.00**

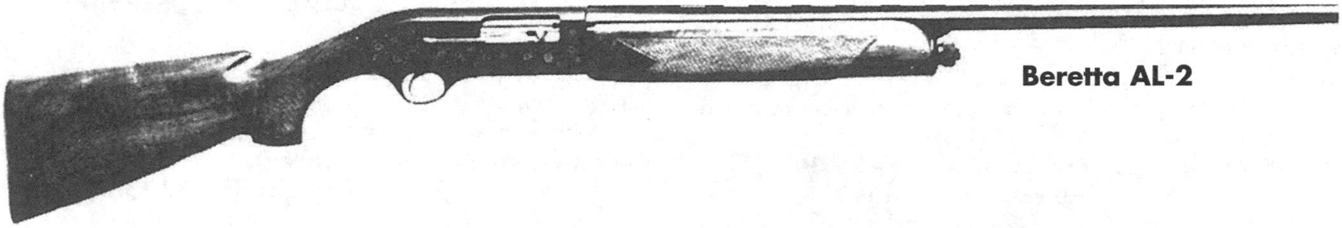

Beretta AL-2

Beretta AL-3

Beretta AL-1

Gauge: 12, 20, regular or magnum
Action: Gas-operated, semiautomatic; hammerless
Magazine: 3-shot tubular
Barrel: 26" – 30" skeet, improved cylinder, modified or full chokes; ventilated rib
Finish: Blued; checkered walnut pistol grip stock and forearm
Approximate wt.: 6½ to 7¾ lbs.
Comments: Made from the late 1960s to the mid-1970s.

Estimated Value:	**Excellent:**	**$425.00**
	Very good:	**$340.00**

Beretta AL-2

Similar to the AL-1 except: ventilated rib; recoil pad; chrome lined bores.

Estimated Value:	**Excellent:**	**$440.00**
	Very good:	**$355.00**

Beretta AL-3

Similar to the AL-2, with light engraving.

Estimated Value:	**Excellent:**	**$450.00**
	Very good:	**$360.00**

Beretta AL-391

Gauge: 12, 20
Action: Gas-operated, semiautomatic
Magazine: 3-shot
Barrel: 28" – 30"; full choke or interchangeable internal choke tubes; wide ventilated rib
Finish: Blued; satin finish receiver; checkered walnut, Monte Carlo pistol grip stock and forearm; recoil pad; gold trigger
Approximate wt.: 6½ lbs.
Comments: Introduced in the late 1990s. Additional models available at increased cost.

Estimated Value:	**New (retail):**	**$1,400.00**
	Excellent:	**$1,050.00**
	Very good:	**$ 840.00**

Beretta Silver Lark

Gauge: 12
Action: Gas-operated, semiautomatic; hammerless
Magazine: 5-shot tubular
Barrel: 26" – 32", improved cylinder, modified or full chokes
Finish: Blued; checkered walnut pistol grip stock and forearm
Approximate wt.: 7 lbs.
Comments: Made from the early to the late 1960s.
Estimated Value: **Excellent:** **$375.00**
Very good: **$300.00**

Beretta Gold Lark

Similar to the Silver Lark with high-quality engraving and ventilated rib.
Estimated Value: **Excellent:** **$450.00**
Very good: **$360.00**

Beretta Ruby Lark

Similar to the Silver Lark with deluxe engraving and a stainless steel barrel.
Estimated Value: **Excellent:** **$550.00**
Very good: **$440.00**

Beretta Model A302 Mag-Action

Beretta Model A302 Mag-Action

Gauge: 12, 20, regular or magnum
Action: Gas-operated, semiautomatic
Magazine: 3-shot tubular
Barrel: 26" improved cylinder; 28" modified or full; 30" full; ventilated rib
Finish: Blued; checkered walnut pistol grip stock and fluted forearm
Approximate wt.: 7 lbs.
Comments: Interchangeable barrel, 2¾" or 3" chambering. Produced from 1982 to 1987; add 5% for multi-choke model with four choke tubes.
Estimated Value: **Excellent:** **$425.00**
Very good: **$340.00**

Beretta Model A302 Skeet

Similar to the Model A302 Mag-Action except: 26" skeet choke barrel.
Estimated Value: **Excellent:** **$440.00**
Very good: **$350.00**

Beretta Model A302 Trap

Similar to the Model A302 Mag-Action except: Monte Carlo stock and 30" full choke barrel.
Estimated Value: **Excellent:** **$465.00**
Very good: **$375.00**

Beretta Model A302 Slug

Similar to the Model A302 Mag-Action except: 22" slug barrel; adjustable front sight; folding leaf rear sight; swivels.
Estimated Value: **Excellent:** **$440.00**
Very good: **$350.00**

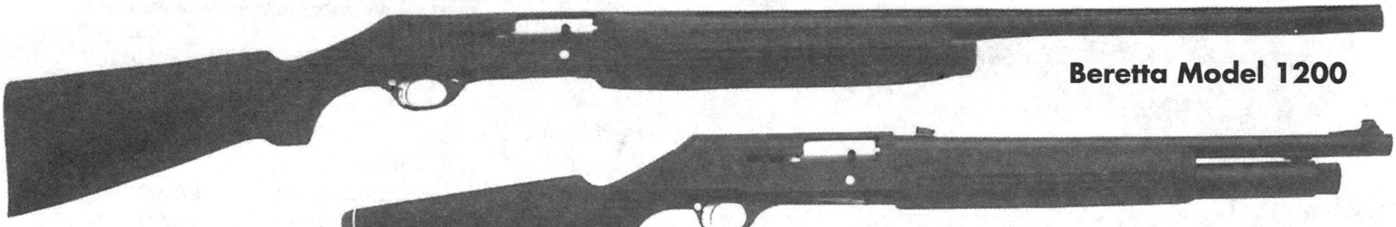

Beretta Model 1200

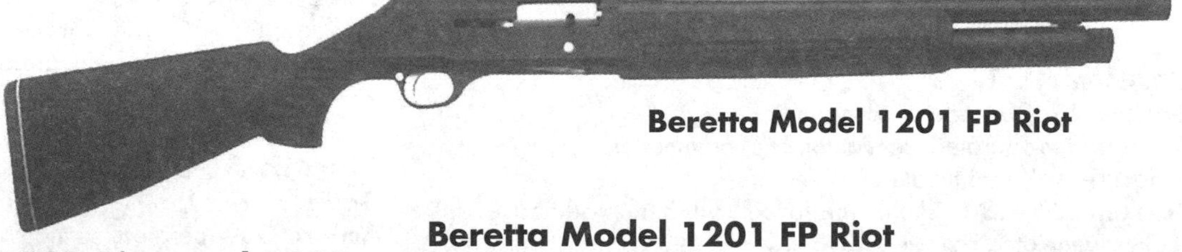

Beretta Model 1201 FP Riot

Beretta Models 1200, 1200 Riot, and 1201

Gauge: 12 and 12 magnum
Action: Inertia-operated, semiautomatic, short recoil
Magazine: 3-shot tubular; 7-shot in riot model
Barrel: 24", 26", 28" modified, full, or changeable choke tubes; 20" cylinder bore on Riot model
Finish: Blued; non-glare; synthetic stock and forearm
Approximate wt.: 7 lbs.
Comments: Made from 1988 to the mid-1990s. Add 5% for Riot model.
Estimated Value: **Excellent:** **$550.00**
Very good: **$440.00**

Beretta Model 1201 FP Riot

Gauge: 12 (3" chambers)
Action: Inertia-operated, semiautomatic, short recoil
Magazine: 5-shot (3" shells); 6-shot (2¾" shells); tubular magazine
Barrel: Matte black 18" or 20" barrel, chrome-plated interior; blade front sight and adjustable rear sight
Finish: Matte black polymer pistol grip stock and forearm
Approximate wt.: 6½ lbs.
Comments: Introduced in the early 1990s; available with optional pistol grip.
Estimated Value: **Excellent:** **$700.00**
Very good: **$560.00**

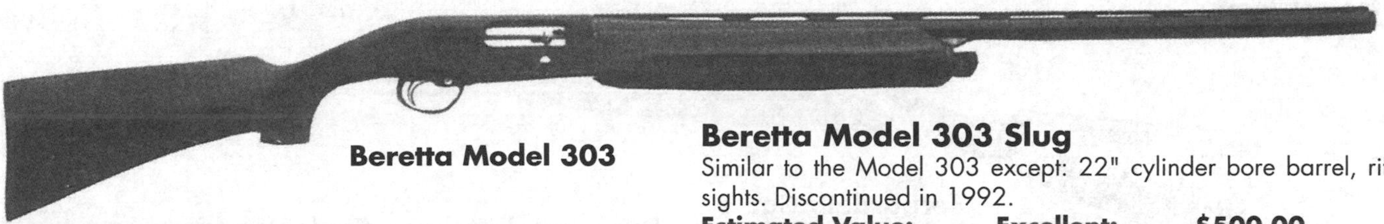

Beretta Model 303

Beretta Model 303

Gauge: 12, 20, regular or magnum
Action: Gas-operated, semiautomatic
Magazine: 3-shot tubular
Barrel: 26", 28", 30", or 32" in a variety of chokes or interchangeable choke tubes; 24" barrel on youth model
Finish: Blued; checkered walnut pistol grip stock and forearm; recoil pad on youth model
Approximate wt.: 6 to 7 lbs.
Comments: Replaced the 302 series in the late 1980s; discontinued in the late 1990s. Deduct 6% for shotguns without interchangeable choke tubes; add 10% for Sporting Clays Model.

Estimated Value:	**Excellent:**	**$550.00**
	Very good:	**$440.00**

Beretta Model 303 Slug

Similar to the Model 303 except: 22" cylinder bore barrel, rifle sights. Discontinued in 1992.

Estimated Value:	**Excellent:**	**$500.00**
	Very good:	**$400.00**

Beretta Model 303 Skeet

Similar to the Model 303 except: 26" skeet choke barrel.

Estimated Value:	**Excellent:**	**$600.00**
	Very good:	**$480.00**

Beretta Model 303 Trap

Similar to the Model 303 except: 30" or 32" full choke barrel or interchangeable choke tubes. Add 6% for interchangeable choke tubes.

Estimated Value:	**Excellent:**	**$500.00**
	Very good:	**$400.00**

Beretta Model 303 Slug

Beretta Model A304 Lark

Similar to the Model A390 Mallard except: 12 gauge, 2¾" only; doesn't use the self-compensating gas system; inertia operated only; made in the 1990s. Add 20% for gold lark.

Estimated Value:	**Excellent:**	**$475.00**
	Very good:	**$380.00**

Beretta Model A304 Slug

Same as A304 Lark except: 20" or 22" barrel with rifle sights (adjustable rear).

Estimated Value:	**Excellent:**	**$500.00**
	Very good:	**$400.00**

Beretta Model A390 Mallard

Gauge: 12, regular or magnum; 3" chamber
Action: Gas-operated, semiautomatic; self-compensating gas operating system performs with any 12 gauge factory load
Magazine: 3-shot tubular
Barrel: 24", 26", 28", or 30" with mobilchoke screw-in choke tubes; ventilated rib
Finish: Black; checkered walnut or synthetic pistol grip stock and forearm; a new stock drop system and cast-off spacer allows stock adjustment
Approximate wt.: 7 to 8 lbs.
Comments: Made from 1992 to the late 1990s. Add 20% for gold mallard; add 15% for ported sport trap.

Estimated Value:	**Excellent:**	**$675.00**
	Very good:	**$540.00**

Beretta Model A390 Slug

Same as Model A390 except: 20" or 22" barrel; fixed choke; plain barrel with hook-in bases for scope mounting; blade front sight and adjustable rear; made from 1992 to the late 1990s.

Estimated Value:	**Excellent:**	**$675.00**
	Very good:	**$540.00**

Beretta Pintail

Gauge: 12, regular or magnum; 3" chamber
Action: Inertia-operated, semiautomatic; falling block locking breech bolt
Magazine: 3-shot tubular
Barrel: 24", 26", or 28", nickel/chromium/molybenum steel with mobilchoke changeable tubes
Finish: Semi-matte black; checkered pistol grip stock and forearm
Approximate wt.: 7 lbs.
Comments: Introduced in 1994.

Estimated Value:	**Excellent:**	**$610.00**
	Very good:	**$490.00**

Beretta Model Pintail Slug

Same as Pintail except: 24" barrel with rifle sights (adjustable rear).

Estimated Value:	**Excellent:**	**$700.00**
	Very good:	**$550.00**

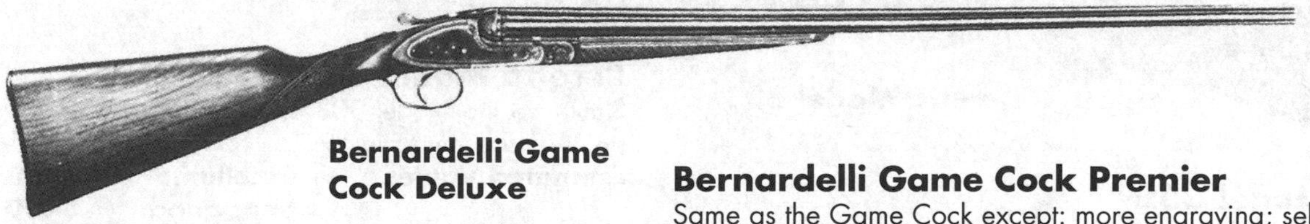

Bernardelli Game Cock Deluxe

Bernardelli Game Cock

Gauge: 12, 20
Action: Box lock; top lever break-open; double trigger; hammerless
Magazine: None
Barrel: Side-by-side double barrel, 25" improved and modified or 28" modified and full chokes
Finish: Blued; checkered walnut straight stock and forearm; light engraving
Approximate wt.: 6½ lbs.
Comments: Produced in the early 1970s.

Estimated Value:	**Excellent:**	**$1,000.00**
	Very good:	**$ 800.00**

Bernardelli Game Cock Deluxe

Same as the Game Cock except: light scroll engraving; single trigger; automatic ejector.

Estimated Value:	**Excellent:**	**$1,250.00**
	Very good:	**$1,000.00**

Bernardelli Game Cock Premier

Same as the Game Cock except: more engraving; selective single trigger; automatic ejector.

Estimated Value:	**Excellent:**	**$1,500.00**
	Very good:	**$1,200.00**

Bernardelli Roma

Gauge: 12, 16, 20, 28
Action: Anson and Deeley type; top lever break-open; hammerless; double trigger; automatic ejector
Magazine: None
Barrel: Side-by-side double barrel; 27½" or 29½" modified and full choke
Finish: Blued; checkered walnut straight or pistol grip stock and forearm
Approximate wt.: 5 to 7 lbs.
Comments: Imported in three grades from the mid-1940s to the late 1980s. Add $50.00 for single trigger.

Estimated Value:	**Roma 3**	**Roma 4**	**Roma 6**
Excellent:	**$1,000.00**	**$1,100.00**	**$1,300.00**
Very good:	**$ 800.00**	**$ 880.00**	**$1,040.00**

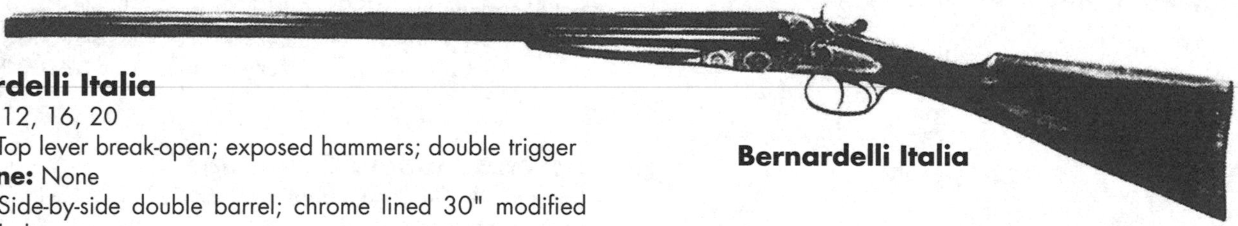

Bernardelli Italia

Gauge: 12, 16, 20
Action: Top lever break-open; exposed hammers; double trigger
Magazine: None
Barrel: Side-by-side double barrel; chrome lined 30" modified and full chokes
Finish: Blued; engraved receiver; checkered walnut straight grip stock and forearm
Approximate wt.: 7 lbs.
Comments: Produced from the early 1990s to the late 1990s.

Estimated Value:	**Excellent:**	**$1,325.00**
	Very good:	**$1,060.00**

Bernardelli Italia

Bernardelli Brescia

Similar to the Italia except: 28" barrels or 20 gauge in 26" barrels; modified and improved cylinder bore.

Estimated Value:	**Excellent:**	**$900.00**
	Very good:	**$720.00**

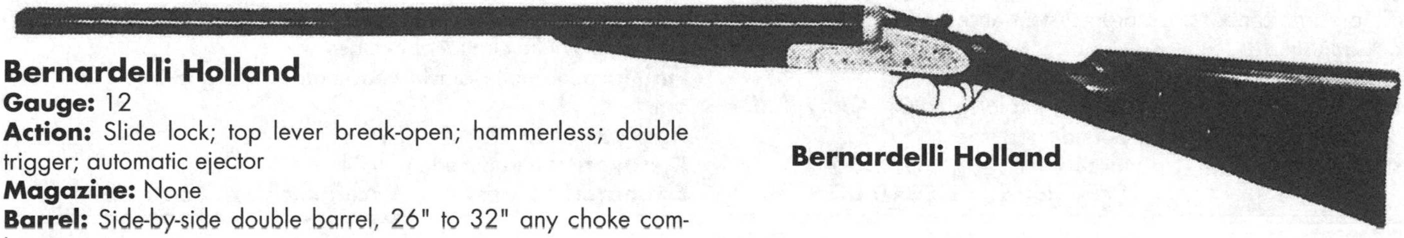

Bernardelli Holland

Gauge: 12
Action: Slide lock; top lever break-open; hammerless; double trigger; automatic ejector
Magazine: None
Barrel: Side-by-side double barrel, 26" to 32" any choke combination
Finish: Blued; straight or pistol grip stock and forearm; light engraving
Approximate wt.: 7 lbs.
Comments: Imported from the mid-1940s to the early 1990s.

Estimated Value:	**Excellent:**	**$4,750.00**
	Very good:	**$3,800.00**

Bernardelli Holland

Bernardelli Holland Deluxe

Same as the Holland but with engraved hunting scene.

Estimated Value:	**Excellent:**	**$5,000.00**
	Very good:	**$4,800.00**

Bernardelli St. Uberto 1

Gauge: 12, 16, 20, 28
Action: Box lock; top lever break-open; double triggers; hammerless
Magazine: None
Barrel: Side-by-side double barrel, 26" to 32", any choke combination
Finish: Blued; checkered walnut straight or pistol grip stock and forearm
Approximate wt.: 7 lbs.
Comments: Made from the mid-1940s to the 1990s.
Estimated Value: **Excellent:** **$1,000.00**
Very good: **$ 800.00**

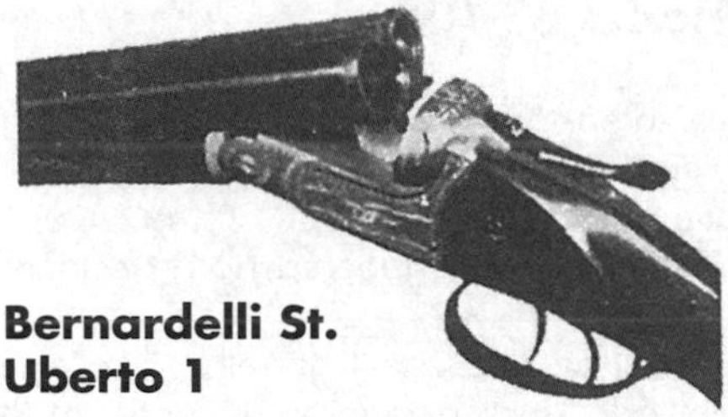

Bernardelli St. Uberto 1

BREDA

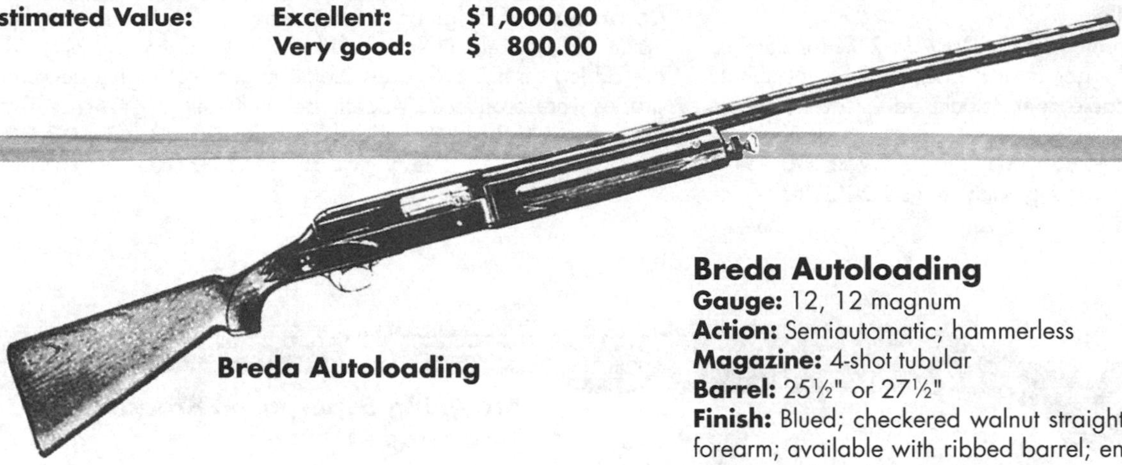

Breda Autoloading

Breda Autoloading

Gauge: 12, 12 magnum
Action: Semiautomatic; hammerless
Magazine: 4-shot tubular
Barrel: 25½" or 27½"
Finish: Blued; checkered walnut straight or pistol grip stock and forearm; available with ribbed barrel; engraving on grades 1, 2, and 3
Approximate wt.: 7¼ lbs.
Comments: Engraved models worth more, depending on grade and quality of engraving. Add 30% for magnum.
Estimated Value: **Excellent:** **$575.00**
Very good: **$460.00**

BROWNING

Browning BT-99

Browning Model BT-99 Plus

Gauge: 12
Action: Top lever break-open; automatic ejector; single shot
Magazine: None, single shot
Barrel: 32" or 34", choke tubes; high post, ventilated, tapered target rib with matted sight plane; front and center sight beads; ported barrel or stainless steel available
Finish: Blued; receiver engraved with rosette and scrolls; select walnut, checkered pistol grip stock and modified beavertail forearm; Monte Carlo style comb with recoil reducer system; adjustable for drop, cant, cast and length of pull; recoil pad
Approximate wt.: 8¾ lbs.
Comments: A trap shotgun with adjustable stock and patented recoil reduction system. Produced from 1989 to the mid-1990s. Add 1% for ported barrel; 30% for stainless steel; 13% for Pigeon Grade; 75% for Golden Clay.
Estimated Value: **Excellent:** **$1,340.00**
Very good: **$1,075.00**

Browning BT-99

Gauge: 12
Action: Top lever break-open; automatic ejector; hammerless; single shot
Magazine: None
Barrel: 32" or 34" full, modified, or improved modified choke; high post ventilated rib; later models have choke tubes (30" or 32" on Micro)
Finish: Blued; wide rib; checkered walnut pistol grip stock and forearm, or Monte Carlo stock; recoil pad; Pigeon Grade is satin gray steel with deep relief hand engraving
Approximate wt.: 8 to 8¼ lbs. (7¾ lbs. for Micro)
Comments: Made from the early 1970s to the 1990s. Add 17% for Pigeon Grade (discontinued); 35% for stainless; 160% for Golden Clay. BT-99 Trap was reintroduced in 2001 with conventional or adjustable comb stock (add 73% for adjustable stock model). BT-99 Micro was introduced in 2003 with compact dimensions for smaller shooters.
Estimated Value: **New (retail):** **$1,339.00**
Excellent: **$1,000.00**
Very good: **$ 800.00**

Browning Model BT-100

Gauge: 12
Action: Top lever break-open; hammerless; single shot; adjustable trigger pull; ejector-selector
Magazine: None, single shot
Barrel: 32" or 34", high ramp tapered rib; Invector-plus choke tubes
Finish: Stainless steel or blued steel barrel and receiver; checkered walnut pistol grip stock and forearm; optional thumbhole stock; adjustable or Monte Carlo-style stock
Approximate wt.: 8¾ lbs.
Comments: Introduced in the mid-1990s. Add 21% for stainless steel barrel receiver and trigger guard; add 14% for thumbhole stock; add 10% for adjustable comb stock; add 25% for Monte Carlo stock.

Estimated Value:	**Excellent:**	**$1,725.00**
	Very good:	**$1,375.00**

Browning Superposed

Gauge: 12; 20 added following World War II; 28 and 410 added in early 1960s
Action: Non-selective trigger; twin single triggers; selective trigger
Magazine: None
Barrel: Browning over and under double barrel; 26½", 28", 30", 32" choice of chokes; ventilated or matted rib
Finish: Blued; hand-checkered European walnut pistol grip stock and forearm; fluted comb; recoil pad; engraving
Approximate wt.: 6 to 8 lbs.
Comments: This gun first appeared in 1931 and has been made in a dozen different grades. More inlays and engraving are added on higher grades. Some expensive, highly decorative grades were produced. Made in Belgium until 1973.

Estimated Value:	**Excellent:**	**$2,000.00 – 7,500.00**
	Very good:	**$1,500.00 – 6,000.00**

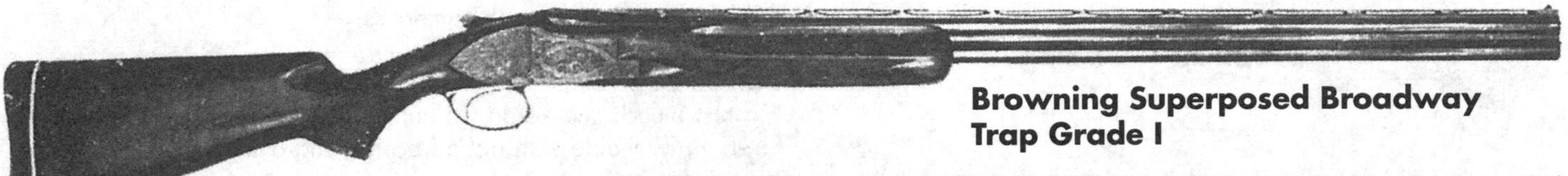

Browning Superposed Broadway Trap Grade I

Browning Super Light

Browning Superposed

Browning Super Light

Similar to Superposed except: lightweight; 26½" barrel; straight grip stock. Introduced in the late 1960s in many grades.

Estimated Value:	**Excellent:**	**$1,500.00 – 7,000.00**
	Very good:	**$1,200.00 – 5,500.00**

Browning Superposed Broadway Trap Grade I

Similar to Superposed but with wide ventilated rib. Introduced in 1960 in many grades.

Estimated Value:	**Excellent:**	**$1,500.00 – 7,000.00**
	Very good:	**$1,200.00 – 5,500.00**

Browning Superposed Magnum Grade I

Same gun as the Superposed except chambered for 3" magnum 12 gauge and with recoil pad.

Estimated Value:	**Excellent:**	**$1,500.00 – 7,000.00**
	Very good:	**$1,200.00 – 5,500.00**

Browning Citori Grade I

Gauge: 12, 20, 28, 410; regular and magnum
Action: Top lever break-open; hammerless; single selective trigger; automatic ejector
Magazine: None
Barrel: Over and under double barrel; 26" or 28", variety of choke combinations in 410, 28, or 20 gauge; 26", 28", or 30" variety of choke combinations in 12 gauge; ventilated rib; some models have choke tubes
Finish: Blued; checkered walnut stock and forearm; Hunting Model has pistol grip stock and beavertail forearm; Sporter has straight stock and lipped forearm; engraved receiver; high-polish finish on Hunting Model, oil finish on Sporter; Upland Special has straight stock; Lightning Model has rounded pistol grip; Satin Hunter has satin finish walnut and matte barrel and receiver
Approximate wt.: 6½ to 7¾ lbs.
Comments: Produced from the early 1970s to 2001. In 1982 a Superlight Model was added with straight stock and scaled-down, lipped forearm. Add 3% for 410 or 28 gauge; 4% for Superlight or Upland Special. Add 6% for 3½" chamber; deduct 5% for Satin Hunter.

Estimated Value:	**Excellent:**	**$1,100.00**
	Very good:	**$ 880.00**

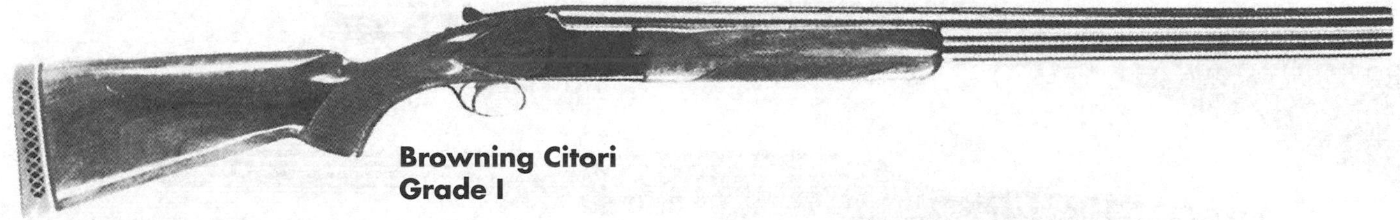

Browning Citori Grade I

Browning Citori Grade II

Similar to the Citori Grade I except: select walnut stock, satin gray receiver engraved with Canadian goose and ringneck pheasant scenes. Add 5% for 410 or 28 gauge.

Estimated Value:	**Excellent:**	**$1,145.00**
	Very good:	**$ 915.00**

Browning Citori Grade III

Similar to the Grade II except: gray receiver, scroll engraving and mallards and ringneck pheasants decoration; 20 gauge, 28 gauge and 410 bore have quail and grouse. Add 12% for 28 or 410 gauge.

Estimated Value:	**Excellent:**	**$2,000.00**
	Very good:	**$1,600.00**

Browning Citori Grade V

Similar to the Citori Grade III except: hand-checkered wood, hand-engraved receiver with mallard duck and ringneck pheasant scenes. Add 5% for 410 or 28 gauge; 3% for "Invector" choke tubes.

Estimated Value:	**Excellent:**	**$2,250.00**
	Very good:	**$1,800.00**

Browning Citori Grade VI

Similar to the Grade V Citori with grayed or blued receiver, deep relief engraving, gold plating and engraving of ringneck pheasants, mallard drakes, and English Setter. Add 7% for 28 gauge or 410 bore.

Estimated Value:	**Excellent:**	**$2,500.00**
	Very good:	**$2,000.00**

Browning Citori Sideplate

Similar to the Citori Grade V in 20 gauge Sporter style only; 26" improved cylinder and modified or modified and full choke; sideplates and receiver are decorated with etched upland game scenes of doves, ruffed grouse, quail, pointing dog; trigger guard tang is decorated and engraved. Introduced in 1981. Discontinued in 1984.

Estimated Value:	**Excellent:**	**$2,400.00**
	Very good:	**$1,900.00**

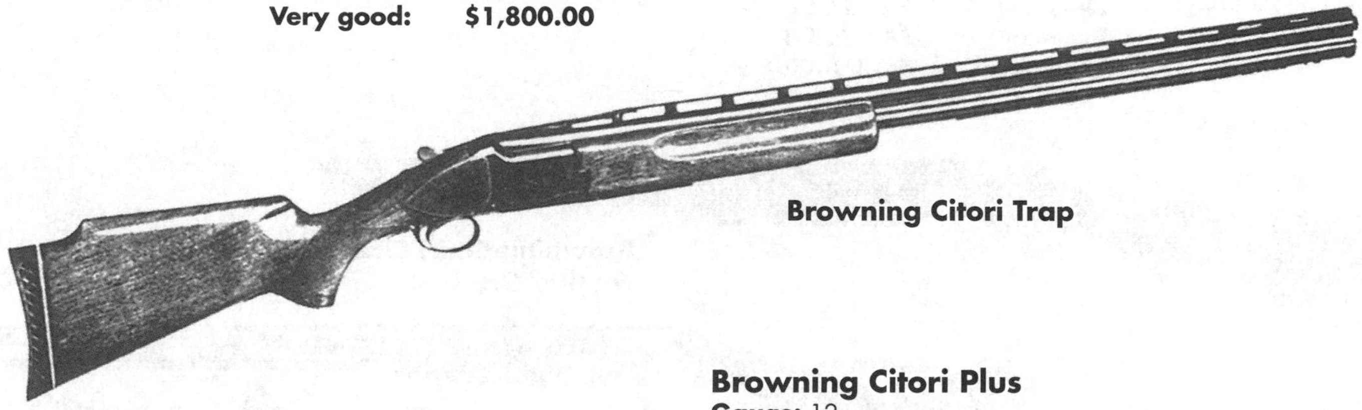

Browning Citori Trap

Browning Citori Trap

A trap version of the Citori in 12 gauge only; high post target rib; 30", 32" or 34" barrel; Monte Carlo stock. Add 15% for Grade II, 36% for Grade III, 75% for Grade VI, 105% for Golden Clay. Add 13% for adjustable comb.

Estimated Value:	**Excellent:**	**$1,290.00**
	Very good:	**$1,040.00**

Browning Citori Skeet

Similar to the Citori except: 26" or 28" skeet choke barrels; high post target rib. Add 15% for Grade II; 36% for Grade III; 75% for Grade VI; 117% for Golden Clay; 13% for adjustable comb.

Estimated Value:	**Excellent:**	**$1,400.00**
	Very good:	**$1,120.00**

Browning Citori Plus

Gauge: 12
Action: Top lever break-open; hammerless; automatic ejectors
Magazine: None
Barrel: 30" or 32" over and under double barrel with high post, ventilated, tapered target rib; matted sight plane; choke tubes; front and center sight beads; ported barrel available
Finish: Blued; receiver engraving; select walnut checkered pistol grip stock and modified beavertail forearm; Monte Carlo-style comb with recoil reduction system adjustable for drop, recoil pad cant, cast and length of pull
Approximate wt.: 9¼ to 9½ lbs.
Comments: A trap shotgun with adjustable stock and patented recoil reduction system. Introduced in 1990. Add $30.00 for ported barrel; 10% for Pigeon.

Estimated Value:	**Excellent:**	**$1,760.00**
	Very good:	**$1,410.00**

Browning Citori Superlite Feather

Browning Citori Super Lightning Grade I

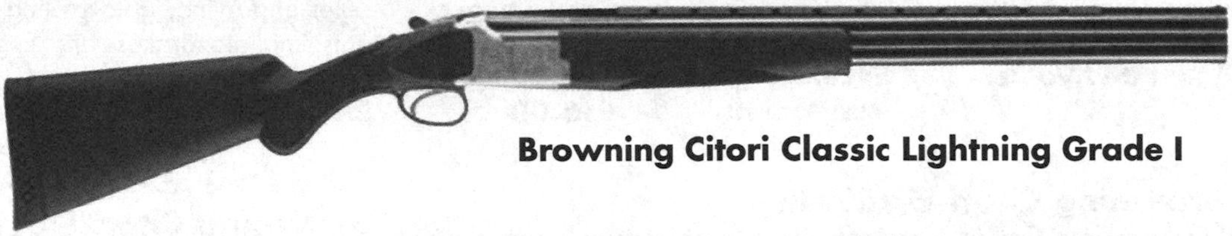

Browning Citori Classic Lightning Grade I

Browning Citori Superlite Feather

Gauge: 12, 20
Action: Top lever break-open; hammerless
Magazine: None
Barrel: 26" over and under double barrel; ventilated rib; choke tubes
Finish: Blued barrels; alloy receiver; gloss-finish checkered walnut straight-grip stock and Schnabel forearm; recoil pad on 12 gauge
Approximate wt.: 5¾ to 6¼ lbs.
Comments: Introduced in 2005.

Estimated Value:	**New (retail):**	**$2,116.00**
	Excellent:	**$1,585.00**
	Very good:	**$1,270.00**

Browning Citori Super Lightning Grade I

Similar to the Citori Lightning (see page 23) with gold accent engraved border receiver.

Estimated Value:	**Excellent:**	**$1,425.00**
	Very good:	**$1,140.00**

Browning Citori Classic Lightning Grade I

Similar to the Citori Gran Lightning (see page 23) with Grade I Superposed engraving; recoil pad on 12 gauge.

Estimated Value:	**Excellent:**	**$1,445.00**
	Very good:	**$1,150.00**

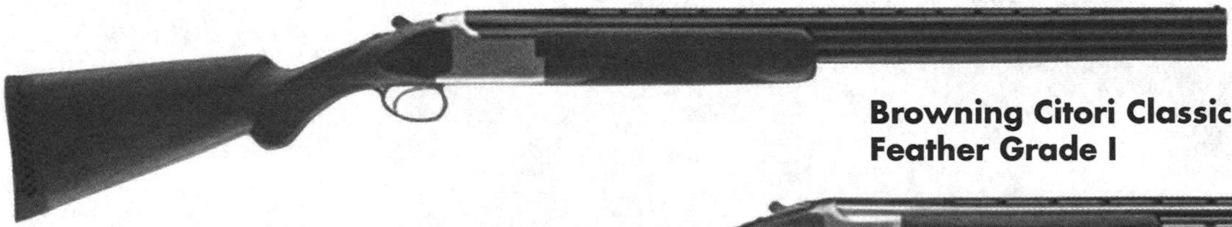

Browning Citori Classic Lightning Feather Grade I

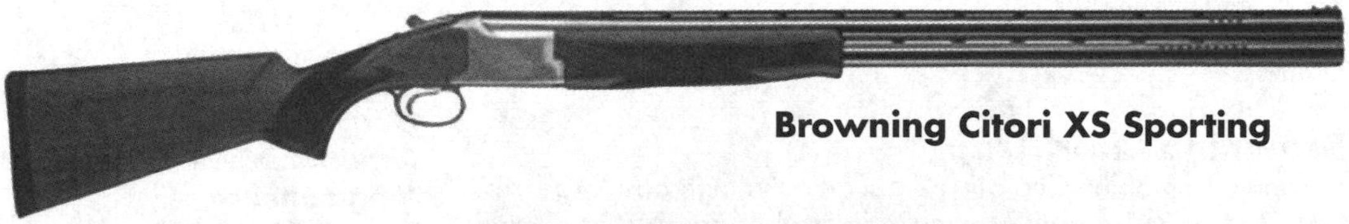

Browning Citori XS Sporting

Browning Citori Classic Lightning Feather Grade I

Similar to the Citori Classic Lightning Grade I with lightweight alloy receiver; 26" or 28" barrels.

Estimated Value:	**Excellent:**	**$1,500.00**
	Very good:	**$1,200.00**

Browning Citori XS Sporting

Gauge: 12, 20
Action: Top lever break-open; hammerless
Magazine: None
Barrel: 28", 30", or 32" over and under double barrel; ventilated rib and ventilated rib between barrels; ported barrels
Finish: Blued barrels; silver-nitride, gold-accented receiver; satin finish Grade II and III checkered walnut stock and palm-swell forearm
Approximate wt.: 7¼ to 8 lbs.
Comments: Introduced in 2005.

Estimated Value:	**Excellent:**	**$1,910.00**
	Very good:	**$1,525.00**

Browning Citori XS Special

Browning Citori XT Trap

Browning Citori XT Trap Gold

Browning Citori XS Special

Similar to the Citori XS Sporting with adjustable comb stock; 30" or 32" barrels; weighs 8¾ lbs. A high post rib model is also available.

Estimated Value:	**New (retail):**	**$3,349.00**
	Excellent:	**$2,500.00**
	Very good:	**$2,000.00**

Browning Citori XT Trap

Similar to the Citori XS Skeet; 30" or 32" barrels; 12 gauge only. Add 12% for adjustable comb.

Estimated Value:	**New (retail):**	**$2,789.00**
	Excellent:	**$2,100.00**
	Very good:	**$1,675.00**

Browning Citori XT Trap Gold

Similar to the Citori XT Trap with gold accent receiver and engraving of a game bird transforming into a clay target.

Estimated Value:	**New (retail):**	**$5,179.00**
	Excellent:	**$3,885.00**
	Very good:	**$3,100.00**

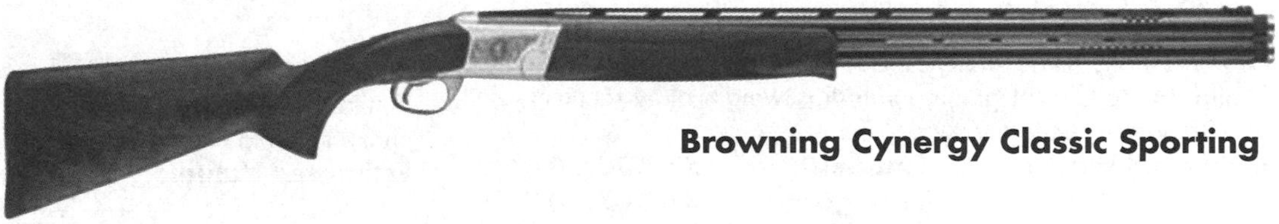

Browning Cynergy Classic Sporting

Browning Cynergy Classic Field

Browning Cynergy Classic Sporting

Similar to the Cynergy Classic Field; 28", 30", or 32" barrels; 2¾" chamber.

Approximate wt.: 7¾ to 8 lbs.
Comments: Introduced in 2006.

Estimated Value:	**New (retail):**	**$3,469.00**
	Excellent:	**$2,600.00**
	Very good:	**$2,100.00**

Browning Cynergy Classic Field

Gauge: 12; 3" chamber
Action: Top lever break-open hammerless
Magazine: None
Barrel: 26" or 28" over and under double barrel; ventilated rib and ventilated rib between barrels; choke tubes
Finish: Blued barrels; low profile silver nitride receiver; satin finish checkered walnut pistol grip stock and forearm; recoil pad
Approximate wt.: 7¾ lbs.
Comments: Introduced in 2006.

Estimated Value:	**New (retail):**	**$2,399.00**
	Excellent:	**$1,800.00**
	Very good:	**$1,450.00**

Browning Citori Sporting Hunter
Similar to the Citori Grade I with a forearm design similar to the Browning Superposed. Sporting pad on stock. Add 6% for 3½" chamber.

Estimated Value: **Excellent:** **$1,200.00**
Very good: **$ 960.00**

Browning Citori Lightning
Similar to the Citori Grade I with a rounded pistol grip stock; add 4% for 20 gauge scaled down Micro Lightning; add 4% for 28 gauge or 410 bore. Add 45% for Grade III, 110% for Grade VI (discontinued).

Estimated Value: **New (retail):** **$1,869.00**
Excellent: **$1,400.00**
Very good: **$1,125.00**

Browning Citori Gran Lightning
Similar to the Citori Lightning with select walnut stock and forearm. Add 4% for 28 gauge or 410 bore.

Estimated Value: **Excellent:** **$2,000.00**
Very good: **$1,600.00**

Browning Citori White Lightning
Similar to the Citori Lightning with a silver nitride receiver and engraved scroll and rosette design. 12 gauge only; 28 gauge, 20 gauge, and 410 bore added in 2000; add 4% for 28 gauge or 410 bore; 26" or 28" barrel. Introduced in 1998.

Estimated Value: **New (retail):** **$1,939.00**
Excellent: **$1,450.00**
Very good: **$1,150.00**

Browning Citori Lightning Feather

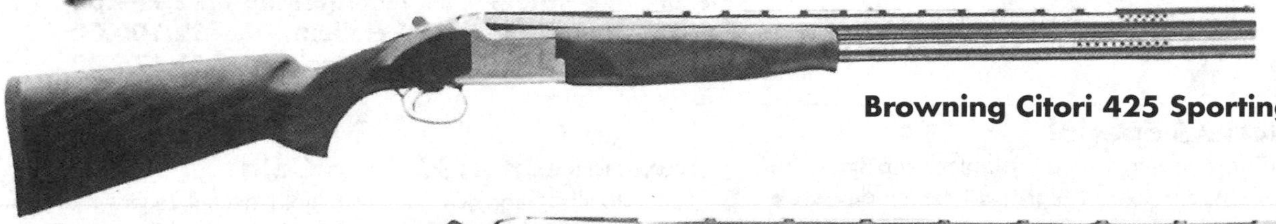

Browning Citori 425 Sporting Clays

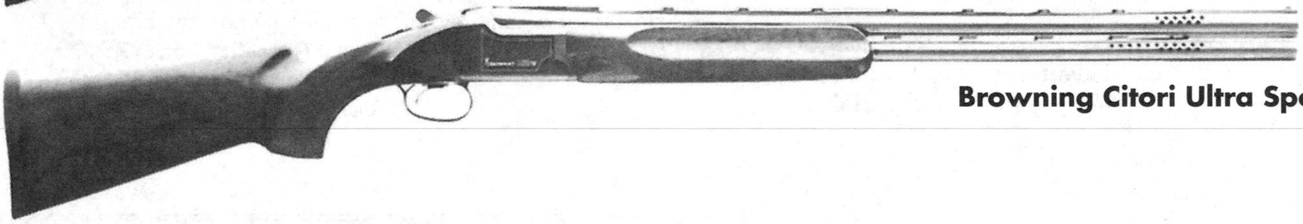

Browning Citori Ultra Sporter

Browning Citori Lightning Feather
Similar to the Citori Lightning with lightweight alloy receiver; 26" or 28" barrels; weighs 6¼ to 7 lbs.

Estimated Value: **Excellent:** **$1,430.00**
Very good: **$1,145.00**

Browning Citori 425 Sporting Clays
Similar to the Citori with a wide ribbed, ported barrel; 12 or 20 gauge; engraved grayed receiver; satin walnut finish; add 12% for adjustable comb; add 100% for Golden Clays model. WSSF (Women's Shooting Sports Foundation) model is available with turquoise-colored stock and forearm or natural walnut.

Estimated Value: **Excellent:** **$1,460.00**
Very good: **$1,170.00**

Browning Citori Ultra Sporter
Similar to the Citori 425 with ventilated side ribs; wide tapered rib; satin finish select walnut; blued or grayed receiver. Add 12% for adjustable comb; 85% for Golden Clays model. Made from 1989 to 2001.

Estimated Value: **Excellent:** **$1,350.00**
Very good: **$1,080.00**

Browning Citori 802 ES
Similar to the Citori Ultra Sporter with extended stainless invector choke tubes to extend barrel to 30" or 32".

Estimated Value: **Excellent:** **$1,530.00**
Very good: **$1,230.00**

Browning Citori 525 Sporting
Similar to the Citori 525 Field with higher quality finish; 28", 30", or 32" barrels; adjustable comb available on 12 and 20 gauge models. Add 10% for adjustable comb.

Estimated Value: **Excellent:** **$2,275.00**
Very good: **$1,820.00**

Browning Citori 525 Golden Clays
Similar to the Citori 525 Sporting with higher quality finish; engraving on receiver is highlighted in 24 karat gold. Add 4% for 28 gauge or 410 bore.

Estimated Value: **Excellent:** **$3,435.00**
Very good: **$2,750.00**

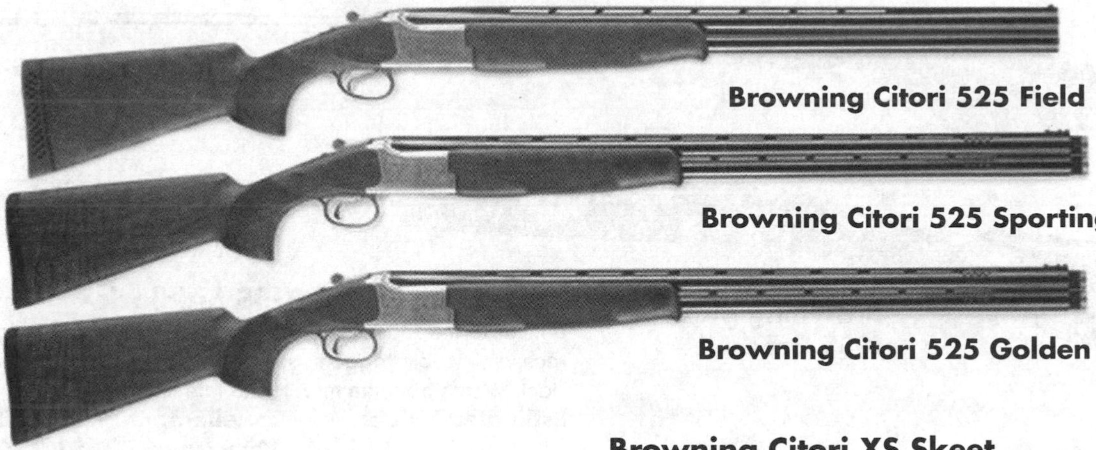

Browning Citori 525 Field

Browning Citori 525 Sporting

Browning Citori 525 Golden Clays

Browning Citori 525 Field

Gauge: 410 bore, 28, 20, 12
Action: Top lever break-open; hammerless
Magazine: None
Barrel: Over and under double barrel; 26" or 28" ventilated rib; invector choke tubes
Finish: Blued; silver nitride receiver; checkered walnut pistol grip stock and lipped forearm; ventilated recoil pad
Approximate wt.: 6½ to 7¾ lbs.
Comments: Introduced in 2003. Add 1% for 28 gauge or 410 bore.

Estimated Value:	**Excellent:**	**$1,610.00**
	Very good:	**$1,285.00**

Browning Citori XS Skeet

Gauge: 20, 12
Action: Top lever break-open; hammerless
Magazine: None
Barrel: 28" or 30", over and under double barrel; ventilated rib with ventilated rib between barrels; ported barrels
Finish: Blued barrels; silver nitride receiver with gold accents; checkered walnut pistol grip stock and forearm; adjustable comb available; recoil pad
Approximate wt.: 7 to 7½ lbs.
Comments: Introduced in 2003. Add 11% for adjustable comb.

Estimated Value:	**New (retail):**	**$2,989.00**
	Excellent:	**$2,250.00**
	Very good:	**$1,800.00**

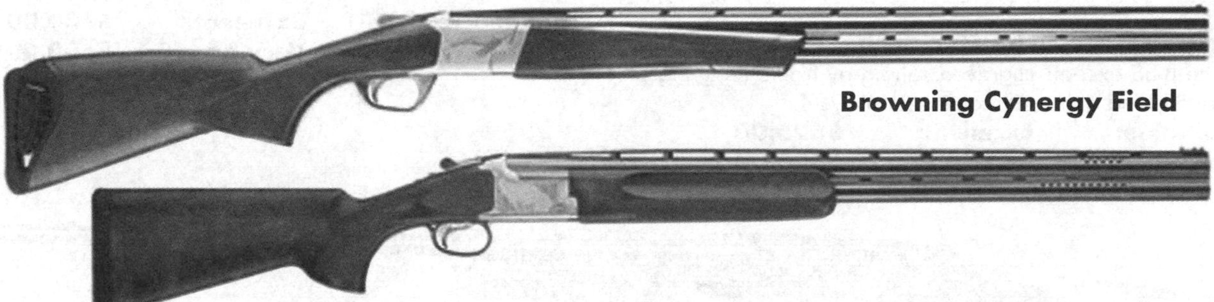

Browning Cynergy Field

Browning Citori XS Skeet

Browning Cynergy Field

Gauge: 12
Action: Top lever break-open; hammerless
Magazine: None
Barrel: 26" or 28" over and under double barrel; ventilated rib and ventilated rib between barrels; choke tubes; white bead front sight and mid bead sight
Finish: Blued barrels; low profile silver nitride receiver with engraving; checkered walnut pistol grip stock and tapered forearm; interchangable Inflex recoil pad system
Approximate wt.: 7¾ lbs.
Comments: Introduced in 2004.

Estimated Value:	**Excellent:**	**$1,535.00**
	Very good:	**$1,225.00**

Browning Cynergy Field Composite

Similar to the Cynergy Field with weather-resistant, lightweight composite stock and forearm with rubber overmoldings.

Estimated Value:	**Excellent:**	**$1,490.00**
	Very good:	**$1,190.00**

Browning Cynergy Sporting

Similar to the Cynergy Field with high-quality Grade III and IV walnut stock and forearm; 28", 30" or 32" ported barrels. Add 10% for adjustable comb model.

Estimated Value:	**Excellent:**	**$2,285.00**
	Very good:	**$1,825.00**

Browning Cynergy Sporting Composite

Similar to the Cynergy Sporting with weather-resistant, lightweight composite stock and forearm with rubber overmoldings. 28", 30" or 32" ported barrels. Available with "wood grain" coating.

Estimated Value:	**Excellent:**	**$2,135.00**
	Very good:	**$1,705.00**

Browning Model B-SS

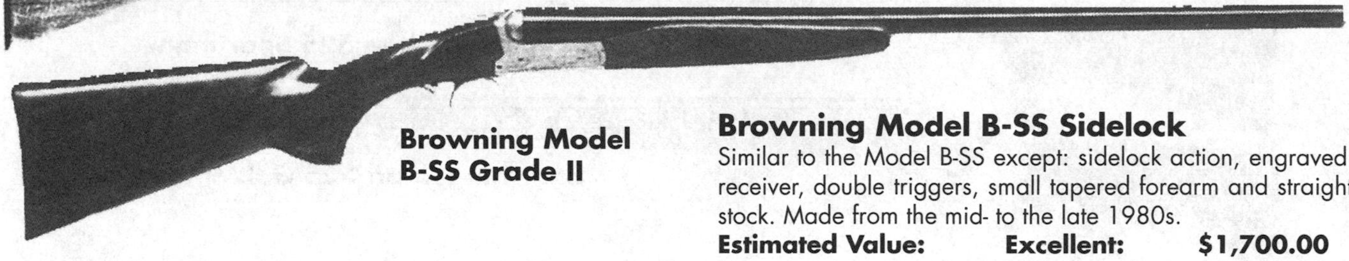

Browning Model B-SS Grade II

Browning Model B-SS

Gauge: 12, 20
Action: Top lever break-open; hammerless; automatic ejector
Magazine: None
Barrel: Side-by-side double barrel; in 12 gauge, 30" full and full or modified and full chokes; in 12 and 20 gauge, 28" modified and full chokes; 26" modified and full or improved cylinder and modified chokes
Finish: Blued; checkered walnut pistol grip stock and forearm
Approximate wt.: 7 to 7½ lbs.
Comments: Made from the early 1970s to 1988. Add 5% for barrel selector.

Estimated Value:	**Excellent:**	**$1,100.00**
	Very good:	**$ 880.00**

Browning Model B-SS Grade II

Similar to the B-SS except: engraved satin gray frame featuring a pheasant, quail, and ducks. Discontinued in 1984.

Estimated Value:	**Excellent:**	**$625.00**
	Very good:	**$500.00**

Browning Model B-SS Sidelock

Similar to the Model B-SS except: sidelock action, engraved gray receiver, double triggers, small tapered forearm and straight grip stock. Made from the mid- to the late 1980s.

Estimated Value:	**Excellent:**	**$1,700.00**
	Very good:	**$1,350.00**

Browning A-Bolt

Gauge: 12 (slugs), 3" chambers
Action: Bolt action, repeating
Magazine: 2-shot detachable box with hinged floor plate
Barrel: 22" rifled, 23" invector with rifled tube; adjustable rifle sights for rifled barrel
Finish: Checkered walnut, one-piece pistol grip stock and forearm on Hunter model; no glare graphite-fiberglass stock on Stalker model
Approximate wt.: 7 lbs.
Comments: Produced in the 1990s. Add 11% for sights; add 12% for walnut stock (Hunter model); add 8% for rifled barrel.

Estimated Value:	**Excellent:**	**$700.00**
	Very good:	**$560.00**

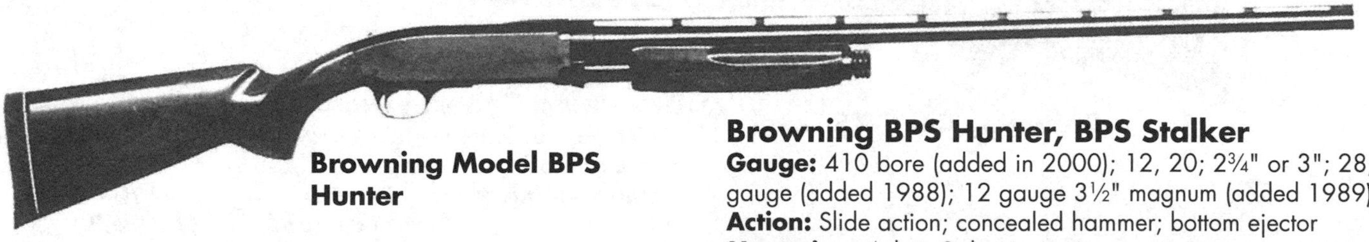

Browning Model BPS Hunter

Browning BPS Rifled Deer Hunter

Similar to the BPS Buck Special except: 22" rifled barrel; cantilever scope mount. Add 2% for 20 gauge; 3% for camouflage finish.

Estimated Value:	**New (retail):**	**$739.00**
	Excellent:	**$555.00**
	Very good:	**$445.00**

Browning BPS Waterfowl

Similar to the BPS except: 12 gauge only; camouflage finish. Add 15% for 3½" magnum.

Estimated Value:	**Excellent:**	**$475.00**
	Very good:	**$380.00**

Browning BPS Hunter, BPS Stalker

Gauge: 410 bore (added in 2000); 12, 20; 2¾" or 3"; 28, 10 gauge (added 1988); 12 gauge 3½" magnum (added 1989)
Action: Slide action; concealed hammer; bottom ejector
Magazine: 4-shot; 3-shot in magnum
Barrel: 26" improved cylinder bore, 28" modified choke, 30" or 32" full choke; ventilated rib; 20 gauge added in 1982 with variety of chokes; choke tubes on later models.
Finish: Blued; checkered walnut pistol grip stock and slide handle; Trap Model has Monte Carlo stock; Stalker Model has graphite-fiberglass composite stock, matte finish. Some special camouflage finishes available.
Approximate wt.: 7½ lbs., 9 lbs. magnum
Comments: Produced since the late 1970s. Add 6% for 410 bore and 28 gauge; add 20% for 3½" magnum; add 5% for Trap Model (discontinued). Add 20% – 30% for camouflage models.

Estimated Value:	**New (retail):**	**$599.00**
	Excellent:	**$450.00**
	Very good:	**$360.00**

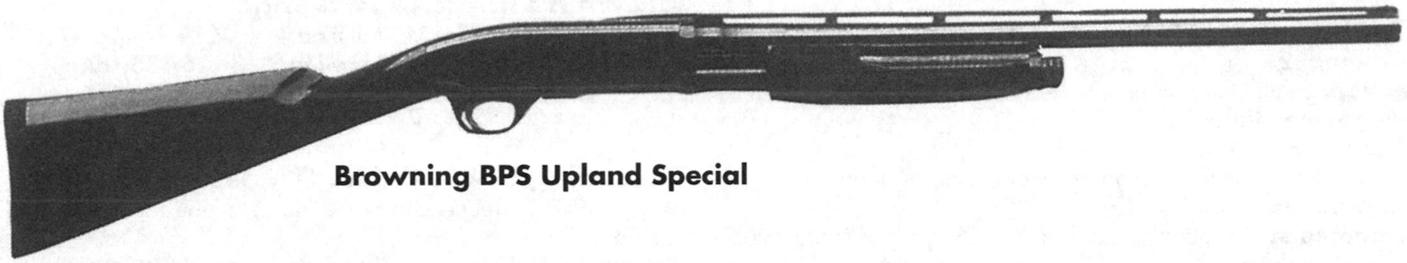

Browning BPS Upland Special

Browning BPS Upland Special
Similar to the BPS Hunter except: straight grip stock, 22", 24", or 26" barrel and invector choke tubes. Introduced in 1984. Add 7% for 24" or 26" barrel.

Estimated Value:	**New (retail):**	**$599.00**
	Excellent:	**$450.00**
	Very good:	**$360.00**

Browning BPS Youth and Ladies or BPS Micro
Similar to the Model BPS Hunter in 20 gauge only with 22" barrel, compact stock and recoil pad. Introduced in 1986.

Estimated Value:	**New (retail):**	**$599.00**
	Excellent:	**$450.00**
	Very good:	**$360.00**

Browning BPS Pigeon Grade Hunting
Same as the BPS Hunter except: 12 gauge only; select, high-grade stock and gold trim receiver; made in the early 1990s; invector chokes.

Estimated Value:	**Excellent:**	**$525.00**
	Very good:	**$420.00**

Browning BPS Deer Special
Similar to the BPS Hunter except: 12 gauge only; 20" barrel with 5" rifled slug choke tube; screw-adjustable rear sight; scope mount base; made in the 1990s.

Estimated Value:	**Excellent:**	**$455.00**
	Very good:	**$365.00**

Browning BPS Turkey Special
Similar to the BPS Hunter except: 12 gauge only; 20" barrel with newly designed extra full choke tube; receiver drilled and tapped for scope base; introduced in 1992.

Estimated Value:	**Excellent:**	**$395.00**
	Very good:	**$315.00**

Browning BPS Buck Special
Similar to the BPS Hunter except: 24" barrel for slugs, rifle sights. Add 5% for strap and swivels, 30% for 10 gauge; made in the 1990s.

Estimated Value:	**Excellent:**	**$435.00**
	Very good:	**$350.00**

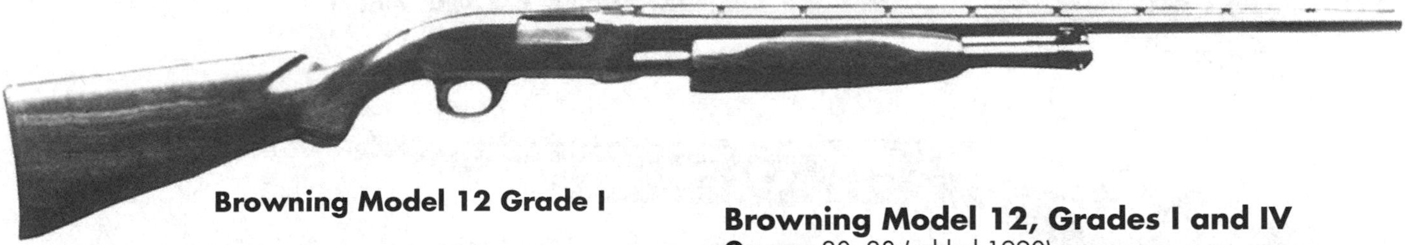

Browning Model 12 Grade I

Browning Model 42, Grades I and V
Same as Browning Model 12, Grades I and V except: 410 gauge with 3" chamber; produced in the early 1990s; add 70% for Grade V.

Estimated Value:	**Excellent:**	**$625.00**
	Very good:	**$500.00**

Browning Model 12, Grades I and IV
Gauge: 20, 28 (added 1990)
Action: Slide action, repeating; concealed hammer
Magazine: 5-shot tubular; 2-shot with plug
Barrel: 26" modified, high ventilated rib
Finish: Blued; checkered walnut pistol grip stock and slide handle; steel grip cap. Grade IV has engraved receiver with gold plated scenes.
Approximate wt.: 7 lbs.
Comments: A reintroduction of the popular Winchester Model 12 designed by John Browning. Produced from 1988 to the early 1990s. Add 60% for Grade IV.

Estimated Value:	**Excellent:**	**$675.00**
	Very good:	**$540.00**

Browning B.A.A.C. No. 1 Regular

Gauge: 12
Action: Semiautomatic, hammerless
Magazine: 4-shot
Barrel: 28"
Finish: Blued; walnut straight stock and grooved forearm
Approximate wt.: 7¾ lbs.
Comments: This gun was sold in the U.S. from 1902 to 1905. Made in Belgium.

Estimated Value:	**Excellent:**	**$575.00**
	Very good:	**$460.00**

Browning B.A.A.C. No. 2 Trap

Trap Grade version of the No. 1 with some checkering.

Estimated Value:	**Excellent:**	**$595.00**
	Very good:	**$475.00**

Browning B.A.A.C. Two Shot

Similar to the No. 1 in two-shot model.

Estimated Value:	**Excellent:**	**$435.00**
	Very good:	**$345.00**

Browning B.A.A.C. No. 0 Messenger

A short, 20" barrel version of the No. 1, made for bank guards, etc.

Estimated Value:	**Excellent:**	**$525.00**
	Very good:	**$420.00**

F.N. Browning Automatic

Similar to the B.A.A.C. No. 1 sold only overseas. Some models carried swivels for sling. Produced until Browning's American sales began in 1931.

Estimated Value:	**Excellent:**	**$500.00**
	Very good:	**$400.00**

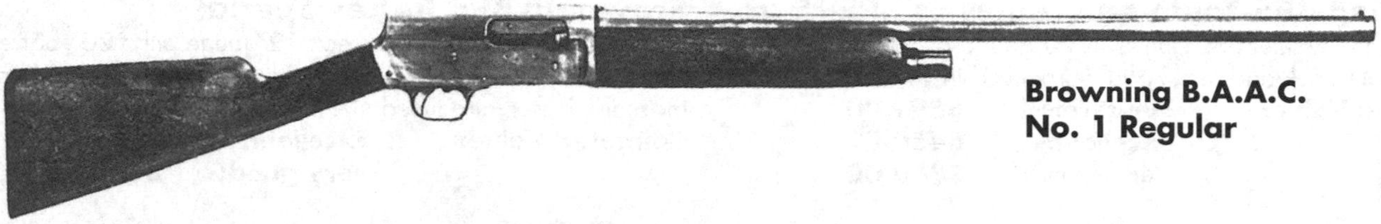

Browning B.A.A.C. No. 1 Regular

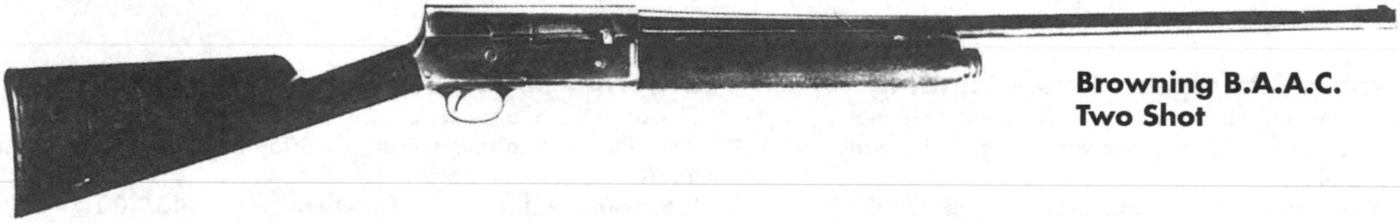

Browning B.A.A.C. Two Shot

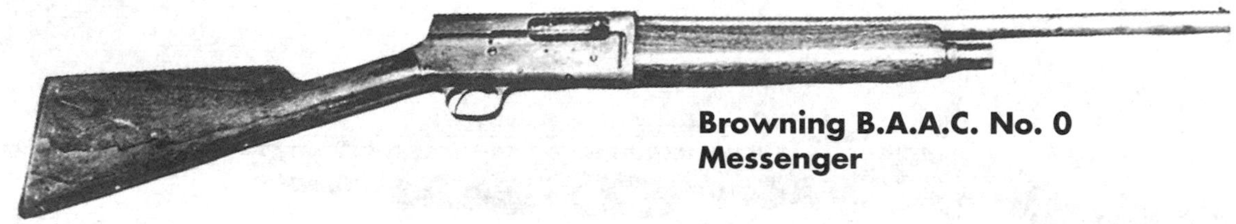

Browning B.A.A.C. No. 0 Messenger

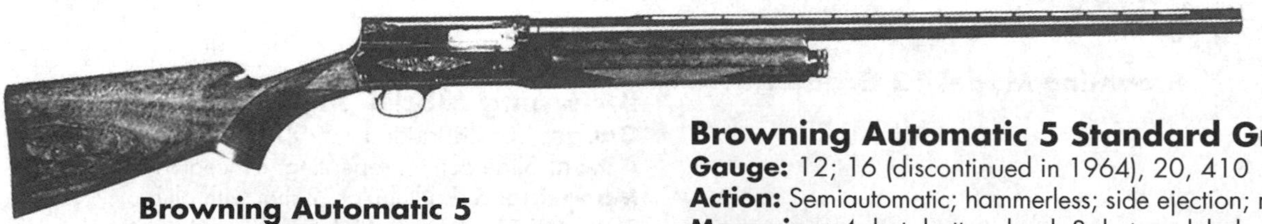

Browning Automatic 5 Standard Grade

Browning Automatic 5 Grades II, III, IV

Basically the same shotgun as the Standard Grade with engraving and improved quality on higher grades. Discontinued in the early 1940s. Add $50.00 for rib.

Estimated Value:	**Excellent:**	**$1,100.00 – 2,700.00**
	Very good:	**$ 885.00 – 2,150.00**

Browning Automatic 5 Standard Grade

Gauge: 12; 16 (discontinued in 1964), 20, 410
Action: Semiautomatic; hammerless; side ejection; recoiling barrel
Magazine: 4-shot, bottom load; 3-shot model also available
Barrel: 26" – 32" full choke, modified or cylinder bore; plain, raised matted rib or ventilated rib
Finish: Blued; checkered walnut, pistol grip stock and forearm
Approximate wt.: 7 to 8 lbs.
Comments: Made from about 1931 to 1973 in Belgium. Add 13% for ventilated rib.

Estimated Value:	**Excellent:**	**$650.00**
	Very good:	**$520.00**

Browning Auto-5 Light 12

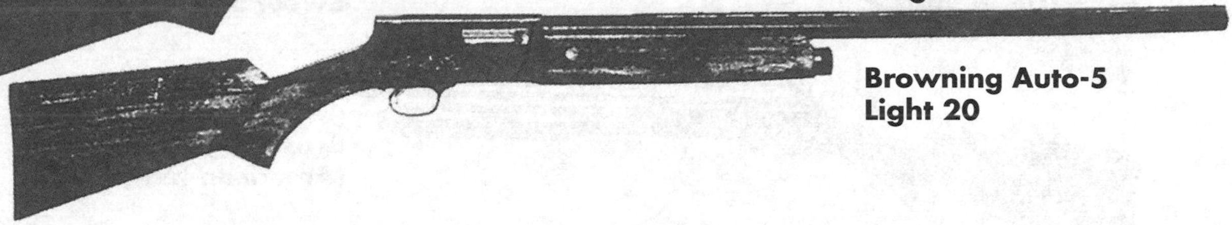

Browning Auto-5 Light 20

Browning Auto-5 Light 20
Basically the same as the Standard Grade except: 20 gauge only; a lightweight 26" or 28" barrel. Made from the late 1950s to the late 1990s. Add 25% for Belgian-made; rounded pistol grip reintroduced in 1987. Add 10% for ventilated rib.

Estimated Value: **Excellent:** **$625.00**
Very good: **$500.00**

Browning Auto-5 Trap
Basically the same as the Standard Grade except 12 gauge only; trap stock; 30" full choke; ventilated rib; made in Belgium until 1971. Add 25% for Belgian-made.

Estimated Value: **Excellent:** **$600.00**
Very good: **$480.00**

Browning Auto-5 Light 12
Basically the same as the Standard Grade except 12 gauge only and lightweight. Made from about 1948 to present. Add 25% for Belgian-made; rounded pistol grip reintroduced in 1987. Stalker model has graphite composite stock and non-glare finish.

Estimated Value: **Excellent:** **$625.00**
Very good: **$500.00**

Browning Auto-5 Light Skeet
Similar to the Light 12 and Light 20 except: 26" or 28" skeet choke barrel. Add 25% for Belgian-made.

Estimated Value: **Excellent:** **$600.00**
Very good: **$480.00**

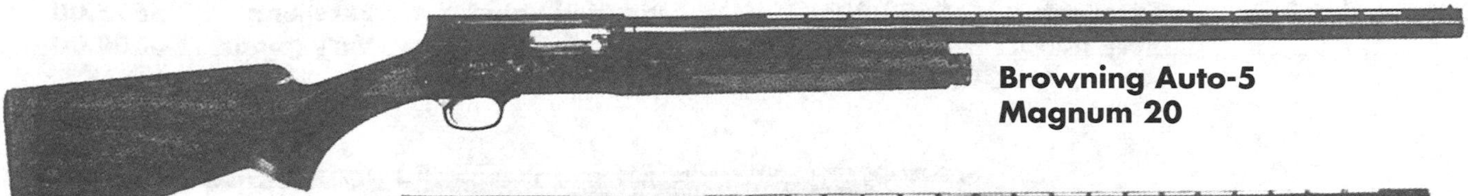

Browning Auto-5 Magnum 20

Browning Auto-5 Magnum 12

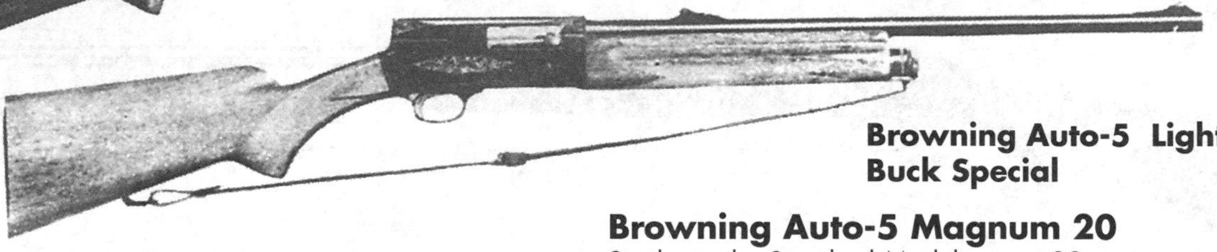

Browning Auto-5 Light Buck Special

Browning Auto-5 Light Buck Special
Similar to the Standard Model, 12 or 20 gauge; special 24" barrel choked and bored for slug. Made from the early 1960s to the late 1990s. Add 4% for strap and swivels; add 25% for Belgian-made.

Estimated Value: **Excellent:** **$550.00**
Very good: **$440.00**

Browning Auto-5 Buck Special Magnum
Same as the Buck Special, for 3" magnum shells, in 12 and 20 gauge. Add 4% for strap and swivels; add 25% for Belgian-made.

Estimated Value: **Excellent:** **$615.00**
Very good: **$495.00**

Browning Auto-5 Magnum 20
Similar to the Standard Model except 20 gauge magnum; 26" or 28" barrel. Made from the late 1960s to the present. Add 25% for Belgian-made; rounded pistol grip reintroduced in 1987. Add 10% for ventilated rib.

Estimated Value: **Excellent:** **$650.00**
Very good: **$520.00**

Browning Auto-5 Magnum 12
Similar to the Standard Model except 12 gauge magnum, equipped with recoil pad. Made from the late 1950s to the present. Also equipped with a 32" full choke barrel. Add 25% for Belgian-made; rounded pistol grip reintroduced in 1987 to the late 1990s. Stalker model has graphite composite stock and non-glare finish. Add 10% for ventilated rib.

Estimated Value: **Excellent:** **$675.00**
Very good: **$540.00**

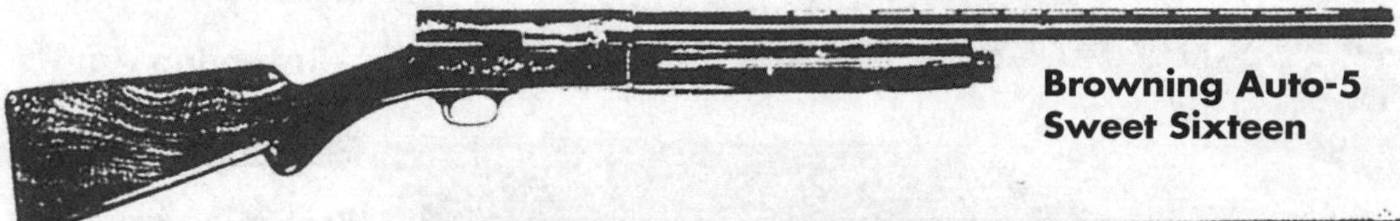

Browning Auto-5 Sweet Sixteen

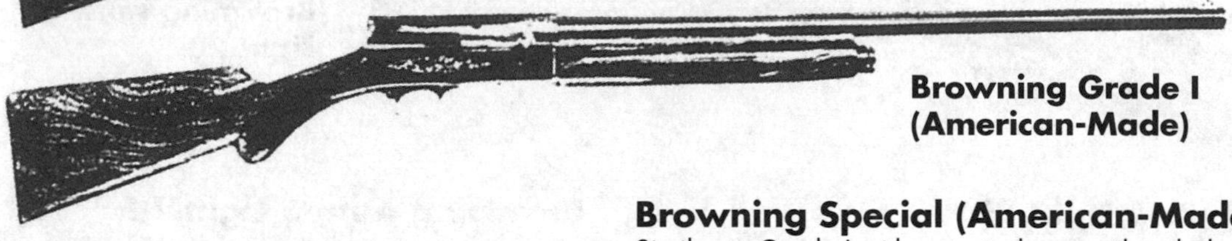

Browning Grade I (American-Made)

Browning Auto-5 Sweet Sixteen

A lightweight 16-gauge version of the Standard Model with a gold-plated trigger. Made from about 1936 to 1975 in Belgium. Reintroduced from 1987 to the early 1990s; add 30% for Belgium-made. Add 10% for ventilated rib.

Estimated Value:	**Excellent:**	**$1,000.00**
	Very good:	**$ 800.00**

Browning Grade I (American-Made)

Similar to Browning Standard Grade. Made by Remington from 1940 until about 1948. World War II forced the closing of the Fabrique Nationale plant in Belgium.

Estimated Value:	**Excellent:**	**$650.00**
	Very good:	**$520.00**

Browning Special (American-Made)

Similar to Grade I with a matted or ventilated rib.

Estimated Value:	**Excellent:**	**$650.00**
	Very good:	**$520.00**

Browning Special Skeet (American-Made)

Same as the Grade I with a Cutts Compensator.

Estimated Value:	**Excellent:**	**$650.00**
	Very good:	**$520.00**

Browning Utility (American-Made)

Similar to Grade I with Poly-Choke.

Estimated Value:	**Excellent:**	**$625.00**
	Very good:	**$500.00**

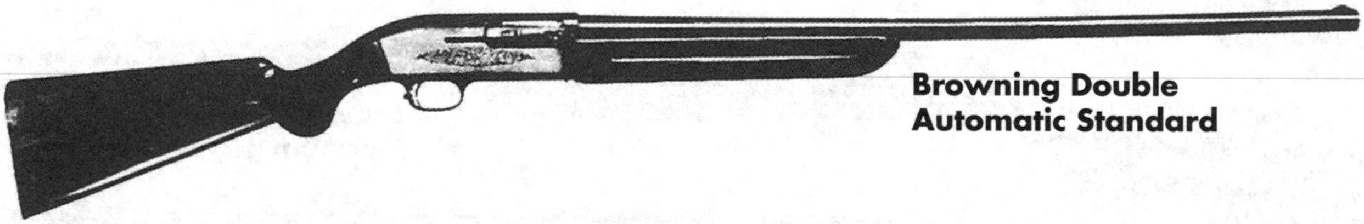

Browning Double Automatic Standard

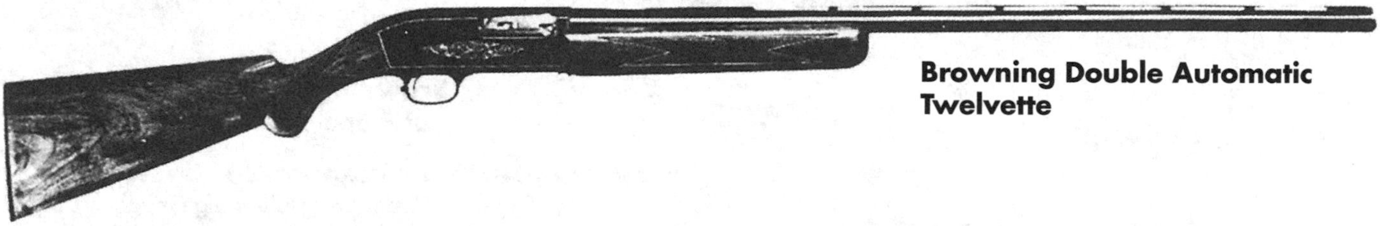

Browning Double Automatic Twelvette

Browning Double Automatic Twelvette

Basically the same as the Standard except: lightweight aluminum receiver. Made until the early 1970s.

Estimated Value:	**Excellent:**	**$600.00**
	Very good:	**$475.00**

Browning Double Automatic Twentyweight

A still lighter version of the Standard with 26½" barrel. Made until the early 1970s. Add 10% for ventilated rib.

Estimated Value:	**Excellent:**	**$625.00**
	Very good:	**$500.00**

Browning Double Automatic Standard

Gauge: 12
Action: Semiautomatic; short recoil, side ejection; hammerless; 2-shot
Magazine: 1-shot
Barrel: 30" or 28" full choke; 28" or 26" modified choke; 28" or 26" skeet; 26" cylinder bore or improved cylinder
Finish: Blued; checkered walnut pistol grip stock and forearm
Approximate wt.: 7¾ lbs.
Comments: Made from the mid-1950s to the early 1960s. Add 10% for ventilated rib.

Estimated Value:	**Excellent:**	**$525.00**
	Very good:	**$420.00**

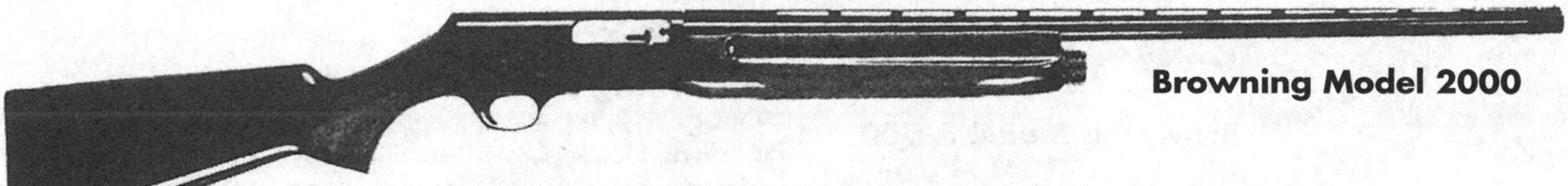

Browning Model 2000

Browning Model B-2000 Trap and Skeet

Browning Models 2000 or B-2000
Similar to the Automatic 5 shotgun except gas-operated. Introduced in the early 1970s in 12 and 20 gauge regular or magnum. Discontinued about 1981.

Estimated Value: **Excellent:** **$500.00**
Very good: **$400.00**

Browning Model B-2000 Trap and Skeet
Similar to the B-2000 with options of high-post ventilated rib and recoil pad on Trap Model.

Estimated Value: **Excellent:** **$475.00**
Very good: **$380.00**

Browning Model 2000 Buck Special
Similar to the 2000 except: 24" barrel; adjustable rifle sights; swivels.

Estimated Value: **Excellent:** **$475.00**
Very good: **$380.00**

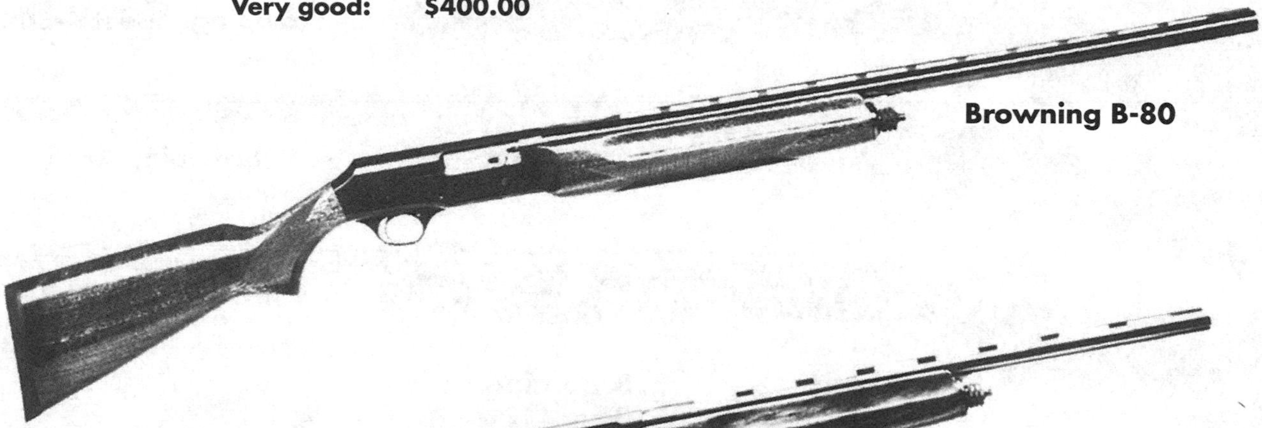

Browning B-80

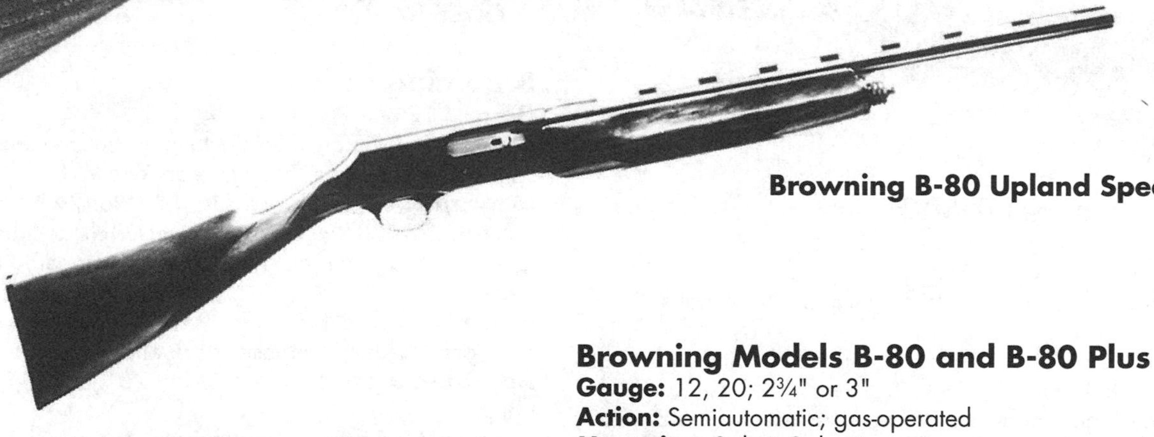

Browning B-80 Upland Special

Browning Model B-80 Buck Special
Similar to the B-80 with 24" slug barrel, rifle sights. Add $20.00 for strap and swivels.

Estimated Value: **Excellent:** **$550.00**
Very good: **$440.00**

Browning Model B-80 Upland Special
Similar to the Model B-80 with a straight grip stock and 22" barrel. Introduced in 1986. Discontinued in 1991.

Estimated Value: **Excellent:** **$475.00**
Very good: **$380.00**

Browning Models B-80 and B-80 Plus
Gauge: 12, 20; 2¾" or 3"
Action: Semiautomatic; gas-operated
Magazine: 3-shot, 2-shot in magnum
Barrel: 26", 28", 30", or 32" in a variety of chokes; internally chrome plated; ventilated rib; choke tubes available
Finish: Blued; checkered walnut semi-pistol grip stock and fluted, checkered forearm; alloy receiver on Superlight Model
Approximate wt.: 6 to 8 lbs.
Comments: Introduced in 1981. Superlight Model (B-80 Plus) added in 1982. Discontinued in 1991.

Estimated Value: **Excellent:** **$500.00**
Very good: **$400.00**

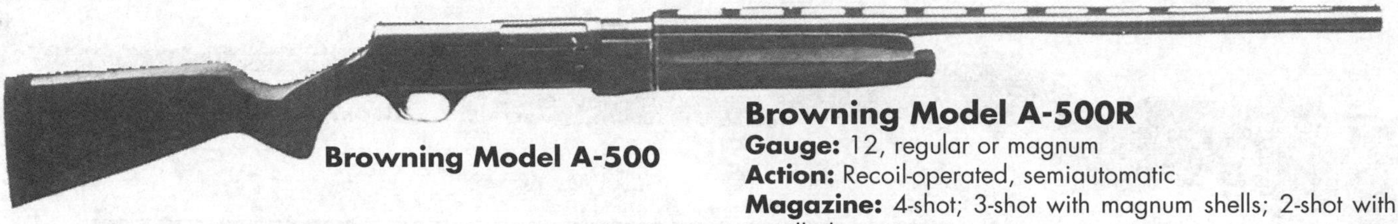

Browning Model A-500

Browning Model A-500

Gauge: 12, regular or magnum
Action: Short, recoil-operated, semiautomatic
Magazine: 4-shot tubular; 3-shot in magnum; plug included; magazine cut-off allows chambering of shell independent of magazine
Barrel: 26", 28", 30" choke tubes; ventilated rib; 24" Buck Special barrel available
Finish: Blued; checkered walnut pistol grip stock and forearm; recoil pad
Approximate wt.: 7¼ lbs.
Comments: Made from 1987 to 1991.

Estimated Value:	**Excellent:**	**$475.00**
	Very good:	**$380.00**

Browning Model A-500R

Gauge: 12, regular or magnum
Action: Recoil-operated, semiautomatic
Magazine: 4-shot; 3-shot with magnum shells; 2-shot with plug installed
Barrel: 26", 28", or 30" with choke tubes; ventilated rib with matted sighting surface
Finish: Blued; red accents on receiver; select checkered walnut pistol grip stock and forearm; gold trigger
Approximate wt.: 7¾ to 8 lbs.
Comments: Produced from 1990 to 1994.

Estimated Value:	**Excellent:**	**$500.00**
	Very good:	**$400.00**

Browning Model A-500R Buck Special

Similar to the Model A-500R with a 24" slug barrel, adjustable rear, and ramp front sights. Discontinued in the mid-1990s.

Estimated Value:	**Excellent:**	**$475.00**
	Very good:	**$380.00**

Browning Model A-500G

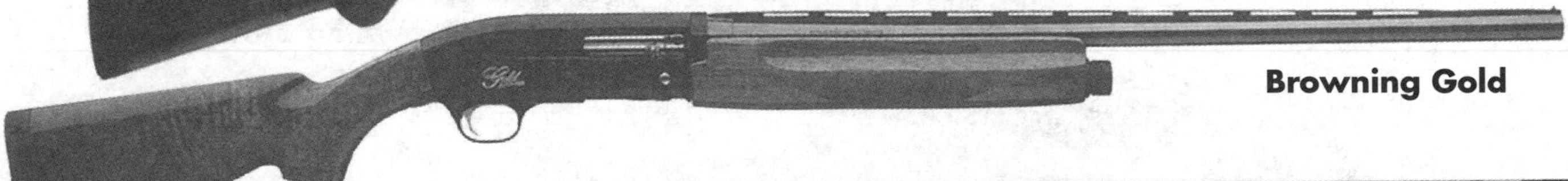

Browning Gold

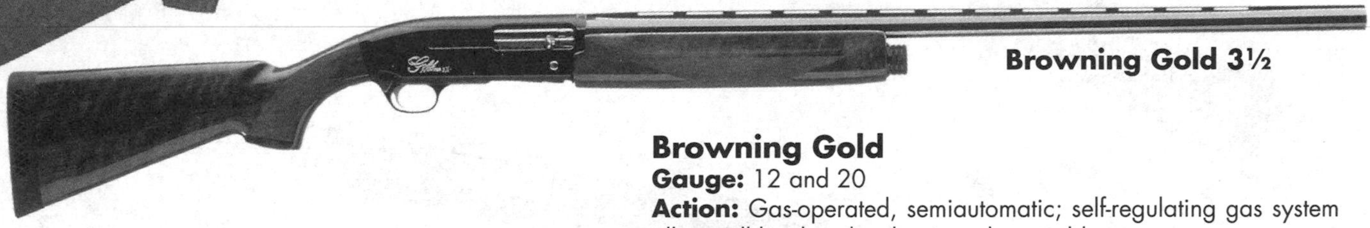

Browning Gold 3½

Browning Model A-500G

Gauge: 12, regular or magnum
Action: Gas-operated, semiautomatic
Magazine: 4-shot; 3-shot with magnum shells; 2-shot with plug installed
Barrel: 26", 28", or 30" barrel; ventilated rib with matted sighting surface; choke tubes
Finish: Blued; gold accents on receiver; select checkered walnut, pistol grip and forearm; recoil pad; gold trigger
Approximate wt.: 7¾ to 8½ lbs.
Comments: Produced from 1990 to 1994.

Estimated Value:	**Excellent:**	**$500.00**
	Very good:	**$400.00**

Browning Model A-500G Buck Special

Similar to the Model A-500G with a 24" slug barrel and adjustable rear, ramp front sights.

Estimated Value:	**Excellent:**	**$475.00**
	Very good:	**$380.00**

Browning Gold

Gauge: 12 and 20
Action: Gas-operated, semiautomatic; self-regulating gas system allows all loads to be shot interchangeably
Magazine: 3-shot for 3" shells; 4-shot for 2¾" shells; tubular
Barrel: 26", 28", or 30" with invector choke tube system; ventilated rib; the Sporting Clays models have tapered ribs and barrel ports
Finish: Non-glare black receiver; checkered walnut, pistol grip stock and forearm; composite stock and forearm on Stalker model
Approximate wt.: 6¾ lbs. for 20 gauge; 7½ lbs. for 12 gauge
Comments: Produced from the mid- to the late 1990s. Add 4% for Sporting Clays model.

Estimated Value:	**Excellent:**	**$550.00**
	Very good:	**$440.00**

Browning Gold 3½

Similar to the Gold model, designed for 3½" magnum shells; 12 gauge only; 26", 28", or 30" barrel; available with checkered walnut finish (Hunter Model) or composite stock and forearm (Stalker). Produced in the late 1990s.

Estimated Value:	**Excellent:**	**$600.00**
	Very good:	**$475.00**

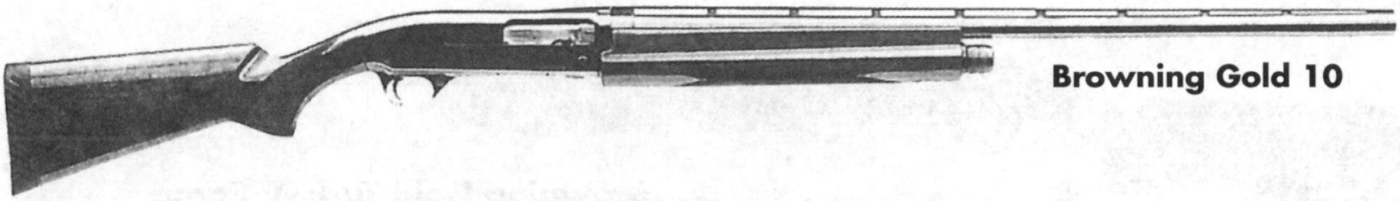

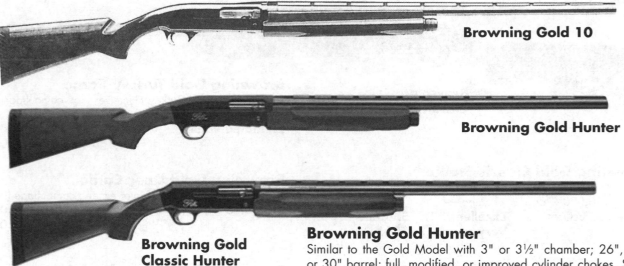

Browning Gold 10

Browning Gold Hunter

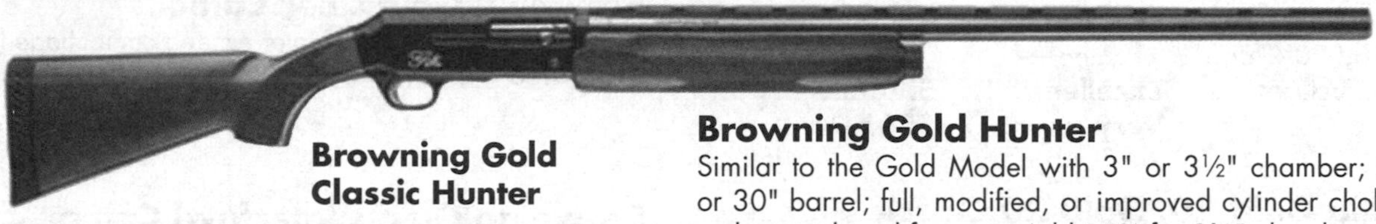

Browning Gold Classic Hunter

Browning Gold 10

Similar to the Gold Model except: 10 gauge; 3½" chamber; approximate weight is 10¾ lbs.; extra full choke turkey tube; the Stalker has a composite stock with a dull matte finish. Produced in the late 1990s.

Estimated Value: **Excellent:** **$800.00**
Very good: **$640.00**

Browning Gold Hunter

Similar to the Gold Model with 3" or 3½" chamber; 26", 28", or 30" barrel; full, modified, or improved cylinder chokes. Select walnut stock and forearm. Add 15% for 3½" chamber.

Estimated Value: **Excellent:** **$700.00**
Very good: **$560.00**

Browning Gold Classic Hunter

Similar to the Gold Hunter except: satin finish; semi-hump back magazine cut off.

Estimated Value: **Excellent:** **$700.00**
Very good: **$560.00**

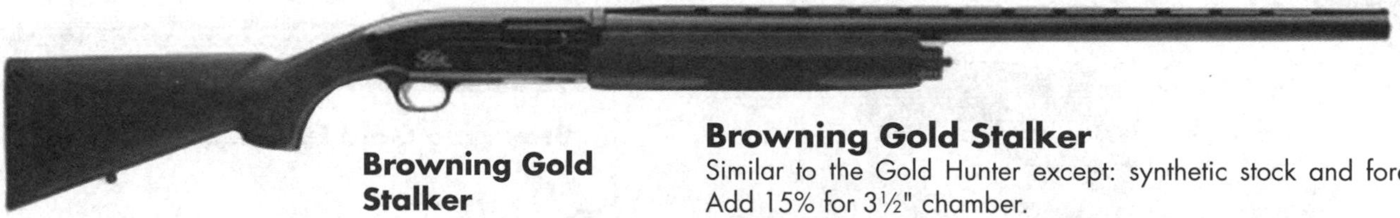

Browning Gold Stalker

Browning Gold Stalker

Similar to the Gold Hunter except: synthetic stock and forearm. Add 15% for 3½" chamber.

Estimated Value: **Excellent:** **$750.00**
Very good: **$600.00**

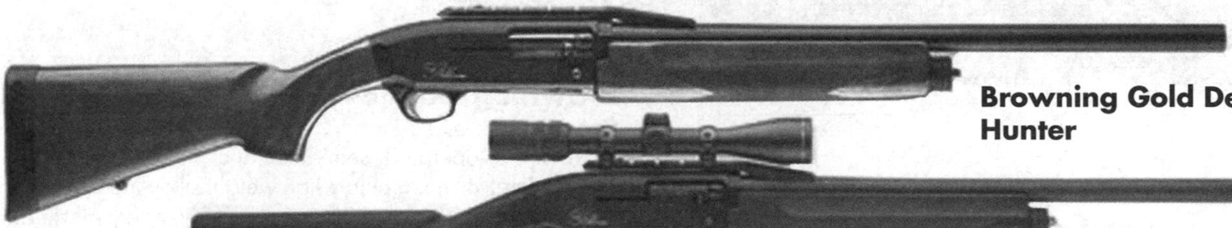

Browning Gold Deer Hunter

Browning Gold Deer Stalker

Browning Gold Turkey Hunter

Similar to the Gold Hunter except: 24" barrel. Add 20% for 3½" chamber.

Estimated Value: **Excellent:** **$650.00**
Very good: **$525.00**

Browning Gold Turkey Stalker

Similar to the Gold Turkey Hunter except: synthetic stock and forearm. Add 18% for 3½" chamber.

Estimated Value: **Excellent:** **$650.00**
Very good: **$525.00**

Browning Gold Deer Hunter

Similar to the Gold Hunter except: 22" fully rifled barrel and cantilever scope mount; 2¾" or 3" chamber.

Estimated Value: **Excellent:** **$750.00**
Very good: **$600.00**

Browning Gold Deer Stalker

Similar to the Gold Deer Hunter except: synthetic stock and forearm.

Estimated Value: **Excellent:** **$725.00**
Very good: **$580.00**

**Browning Gold
Classic Stalker**

Browning Gold Classic Stalker

Similar to the Gold Classic Hunter except: synthetic stock and forearm. Add 20% for 3½" chamber.

| Estimated Value: | Excellent: | $700.00 |
| | Very good: | $565.00 |

Browning Gold 20, Gold 20 Classic

Similar to the Gold except: 20 gauge only, 26" or 28" barrel. Classic has satin finish and semi-humpback magazine cut-off.

| Estimated Value: | Excellent: | $675.00 |
| | Very good: | $535.00 |

Browning Gold Turkey Camo

Similar to the Gold Turkey Hunter except: camouflage finish. Add 20% for 3½" chamber.

| Estimated Value: | Excellent: | $700.00 |
| | Very good: | $560.00 |

Browning Gold Deer Camo

Similar to the Gold Deer Hunter except: camouflage finish.

| Estimated Value: | Excellent: | $750.00 |
| | Very good: | $600.00 |

Browning Gold Waterfowl Camo

Similar to the Gold Hunter except: 26" barrel; camouflage finish. Add 18% for 3½" chamber.

| Estimated Value: | Excellent: | $725.00 |
| | Very good: | $580.00 |

Browning Gold Evolve

Browning Gold Evolve Sporting

Browning Gold FLD Stalker

Browning Gold NRA Sporting

Similar to the Gold Evolve with commemorative NRA engraving on the left side of the receiver. Introduced in 2006.

| Estimated Value: | Excellent: | $850.00 |
| | Very good: | $680.00 |

Browning Gold FLD Stalker

Similar to the Gold Classic Stalker except: aluminum alloy receiver.

| Estimated Value: | Excellent: | $735.00 |
| | Very good: | $585.00 |

Browning Gold Evolve

Gauge: 12
Action: Gas-operated, semiautomatic
Magazine: 4 shot tubular; lightweight alloy magazine tube
Barrel: 26", 28" or 30" improved cylinder, modified or full choke; ventilated rib
Finish: Blued; satin finish checkered walnut pistol grip stock and forearm; recoil pad
Approximate wt.: 6¾ to 7¼ lbs.
Comments: Introduced in 2004.

| Estimated Value: | Excellent: | $895.00 |
| | Very good: | $715.00 |

Browning Gold Evolve Sporting

Similar to the Gold Evolve. Comes with plastic hard case. Introduced in 2006.

| Estimated Value: | Excellent: | $945.00 |
| | Very good: | $755.00 |

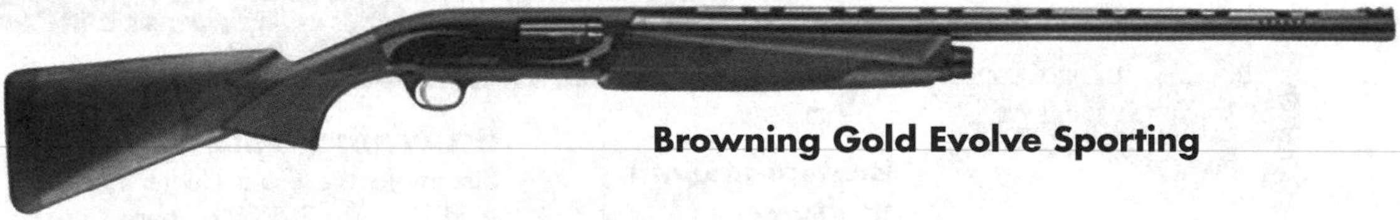

Browning Gold Upland Special

Browning Gold Fusion

Browning Gold Micro

Browning Gold Upland Special
Similar to the Gold Hunter except: straight-grip stock; 24" or 26" barrel.

Estimated Value:	**Excellent:**	**$725.00**
	Very good:	**$580.00**

Browning Gold Fusion
A high-grade version of the Gold Hunter with Turkish Walnut stock and forearm; adjustable comb system and five interchangeable choke tubes.

Estimated Value:	**Excellent:**	**$845.00**
	Very good:	**$675.00**

Browning Gold Micro
Similar to the Gold Hunter except: 24" or 26" barrel; shorter stock for young shooters.

Estimated Value:	**Excellent:**	**$725.00**
	Very good:	**$580.00**

Browning Gold Classic High Grade
Similar to the Gold 20 Classic except: nickel-plated satin finish; receiver engraved with doves and quail. Introduced in 2002.

Estimated Value:	**Excellent:**	**$1,425.00**
	Very good:	**$1,140.00**

Browning Gold Light 10
Similar to the Gold 10 except: lightweight aluminum receiver; 5-shot tubular magazine; synthetic stock and forearm in black or with camouflage finish. After 2003 only camo models were available.

Estimated Value:	**Excellent:**	**$975.00**
	Very good:	**$775.00**

Browning Gold Sporting Clays
Similar to the Gold Hunter except: 28" or 30" ported barrel; gloss wood finish; tapered ventilated rib; adjustable stock. Lady's model has 28" barrel and smaller overall dimensions (deduct 6%). Golden Clays model has engraved nickel receiver (add 50%).

Estimated Value:	**Excellent:**	**$890.00**
	Very good:	**$710.00**

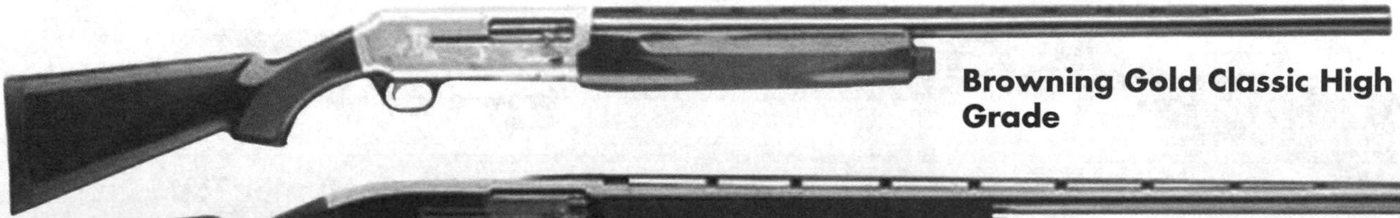

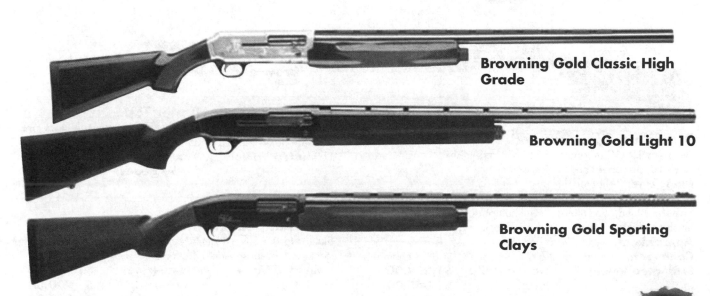

Browning Gold Classic High Grade

Browning Gold Light 10

Browning Gold Sporting Clays

Browning Gold Superlite FLD Hunter

Browning Gold Superlite Micro

Browning Gold Superlite Hunter

Browning Gold Superlite Hunter

Gauge: 12, 20, 12 magnum
Action: Gas-operated, semiautomatic
Magazine: 3-shot for 3½" shells; 4-shot for 3" shells; tubular
Barrel: 26" or 28" with invector choke tube system; ventilated rib
Finish: Blued; checkered, gloss-finish walnut pistol grip stock and forearm; alloy receiver and magazine tube
Approximate wt.: 6½ to 7½ lbs.
Comments: Introduced in 2006. Add 15% for 3½" chamber.

Estimated Value:	Excellent:	$870.00
	Very good:	$695.00

Browning Gold Superlite FLD Hunter

Similar to the Gold Superlite Hunter with semi-humpback receiver design. Not available in magnum. Introduced in 2006.

Estimated Value:	Excellent:	$810.00
	Very good:	$650.00

Browning Gold Superlite Micro

Similar to the Gold Superlite Hunter except: compact dimensions for smaller shooters; 20 gauge only; 26" barrel.

Estimated Value:	Excellent:	$810.00
	Very good:	$650.00

Browning Silver Hunter Topcote

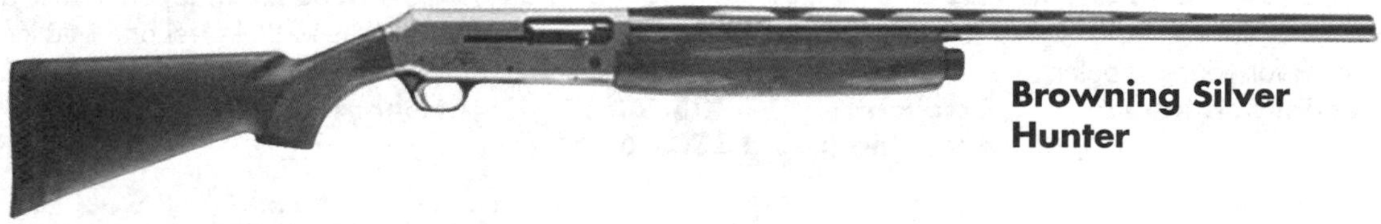

Browning Silver Hunter

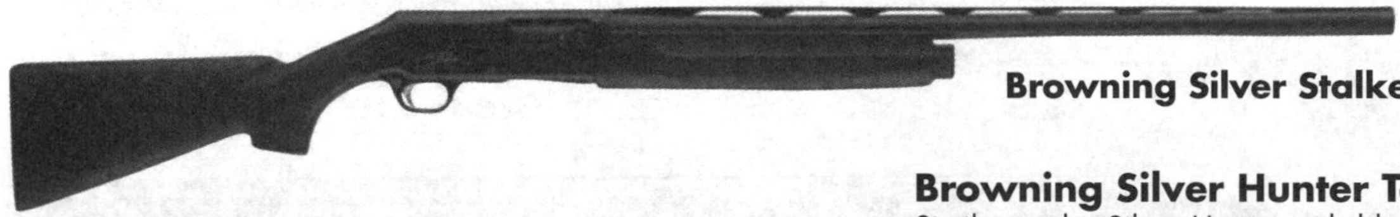

Browning Silver Stalker

Browning Silver Hunter

Gauge: 12, 12 magnum, 3" or 3½" chamber
Action: Gas-operated, semiautomatic
Magazine: 3-shot tubular
Barrel: 26", 28", 30", invector choke tubes; ventilated rib
Finish: Blued; silver-finish, semi-humpback alloy receiver; satin-finish checkered walnut, pistol grip stock and forearm; recoil pad
Approximate wt.: 7¼ to 7½ lbs.
Comments: Introduced in 2006. Add 16% for 3½" chamber.

Estimated Value:	New (retail):	$1,259.00
	Excellent:	$ 945.00
	Very good:	$ 750.00

Browning Silver Hunter Topcote

Similar to the Silver Hunter with black composite stock and forearm that has a dipped finish resembling wood. 3" chamber only.

Estimated Value:	Excellent:	$710.00
	Very good:	$565.00

Browning Silver Stalker

Similar to the Silver Hunter except: black matte finish; composite stock and forearm. Add 14% for 3½" chamber.

Estimated Value:	New (retail):	$1,199.00
	Excellent:	$ 900.00
	Very good:	$ 720.00

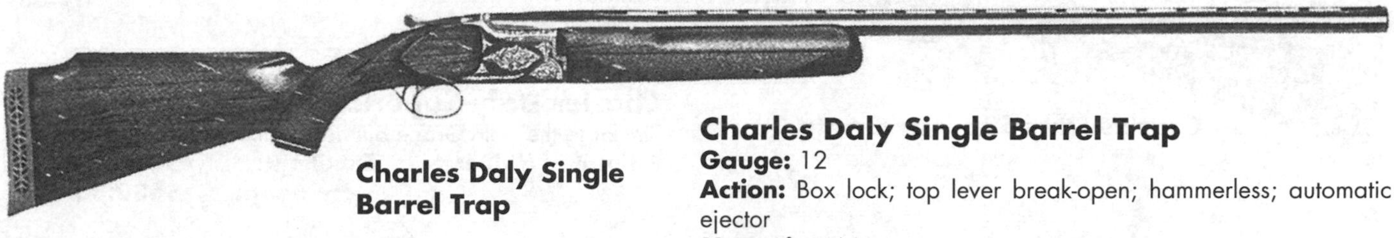

Charles Daly Single Barrel Trap

Charles Daly Commander 100

Gauge: 12, 16, 20, 28, 410
Action: Box lock; top lever break-open; hammerless; automatic ejector
Magazine: None
Barrel: Over and under double barrel; 26", 28", 30" improved cylinder and modified or modified and full chokes
Finish: Blued; checkered walnut straight or pistol grip stock and forearm; engraved
Approximate wt.: 5 to 7½ lbs.
Comments: Made from the mid-1930s to about 1939.
Estimated Value: **Excellent:** **$995.00**
Very good: **$795.00**

Charles Daly Commander 200

This is a fancier version of the Commander 100 with select wood, more engraving, and a higher quality finish.
Estimated Value: **Excellent:** **$1,000.00**
Very good: **$ 800.00**

Charles Daly Single Barrel Trap

Gauge: 12
Action: Box lock; top lever break-open; hammerless; automatic ejector
Magazine: None
Barrel: 32" or 34" full choke; ventilated rib
Finish: Blued; checkered walnut Monte Carlo pistol grip stock and beavertail forearm; recoil pad
Approximate wt.: 8 lbs.
Comments: Made from the late 1960s to the mid-1970s. This model should not be confused with the Single Barrel Trap Model made in the 1930s that is worth several times more.
Estimated Value: **Excellent:** **$1,200.00**
Very good: **$ 950.00**

Charles Daly Hammerless Double

Gauge: 10, 12, 16, 20, 28, 410
Action: Box lock; top lever break-open; hammerless; automatic ejector (except Superior)
Magazine: None
Barrel: Side-by-side double barrel; 26", 28", 30", 32"; choice of choke combinations
Finish: Blued; checkered walnut pistol grip stock and short tapered forearm; engraving
Approximate wt.: 4 to 8 lbs.
Comments: Manufactured in different grades, alike except for quality of finish and amount of engraving. Made from 1920 to 1935.
Estimated Value: **Excellent:** **$2,000.00 – 8,500.00**
Very good: **$1,600.00 – 6,750.00**

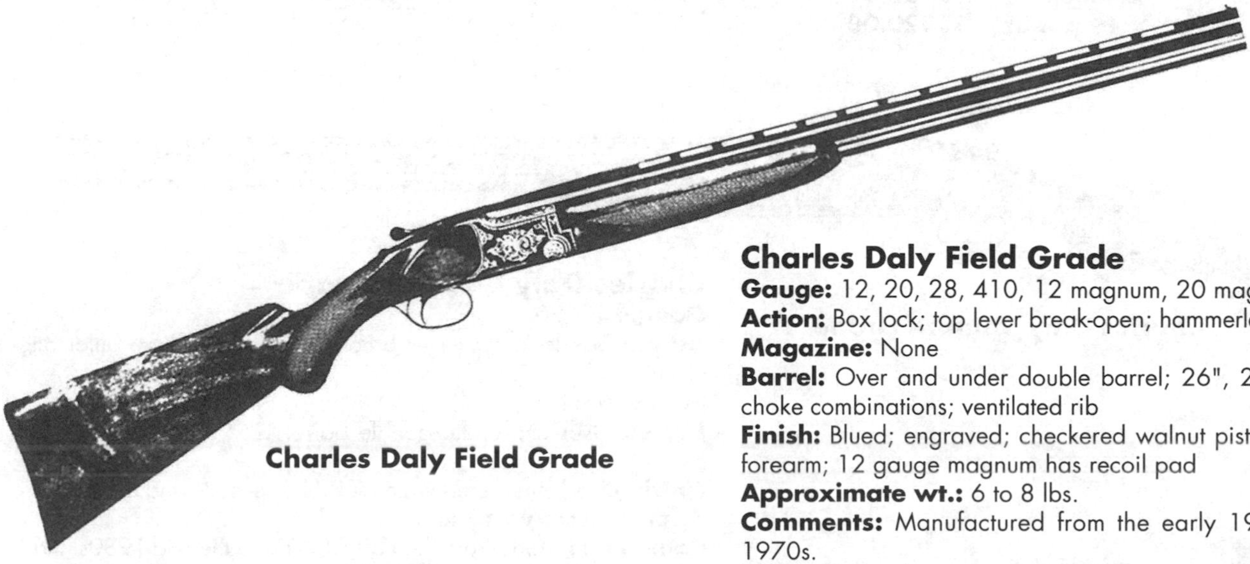

Charles Daly Field Grade

Charles Daly Field Grade

Gauge: 12, 20, 28, 410, 12 magnum, 20 magnum
Action: Box lock; top lever break-open; hammerless; single trigger
Magazine: None
Barrel: Over and under double barrel; 26", 28", 30", various choke combinations; ventilated rib
Finish: Blued; engraved; checkered walnut pistol grip stock and forearm; 12 gauge magnum has recoil pad
Approximate wt.: 6 to 8 lbs.
Comments: Manufactured from the early 1960s to the mid-1970s.
Estimated Value: **Excellent:** **$700.00**
Very good: **$560.00**

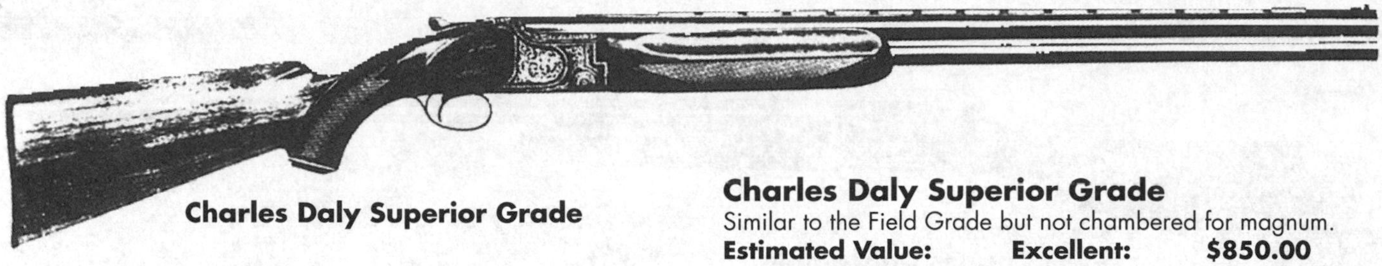

Charles Daly Superior Grade

Charles Daly Superior Grade

Similar to the Field Grade but not chambered for magnum.

Estimated Value:	**Excellent:**	**$850.00**
	Very good:	**$680.00**

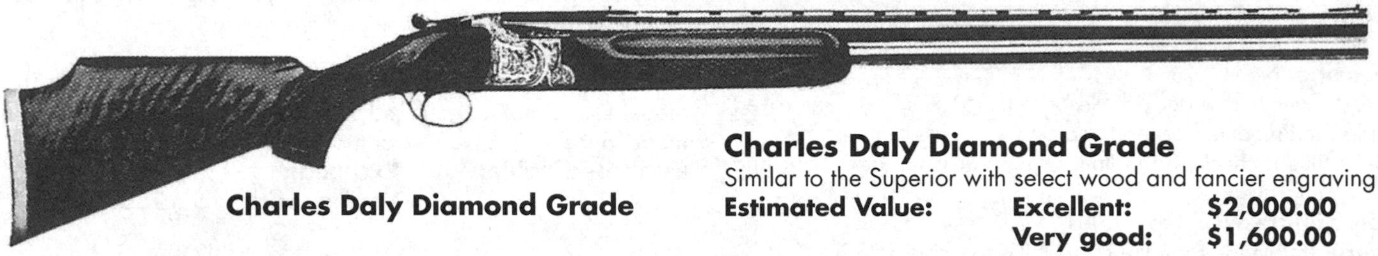

Charles Daly Diamond Grade

Charles Daly Diamond Grade

Similar to the Superior with select wood and fancier engraving.

Estimated Value:	**Excellent:**	**$2,000.00**
	Very good:	**$1,600.00**

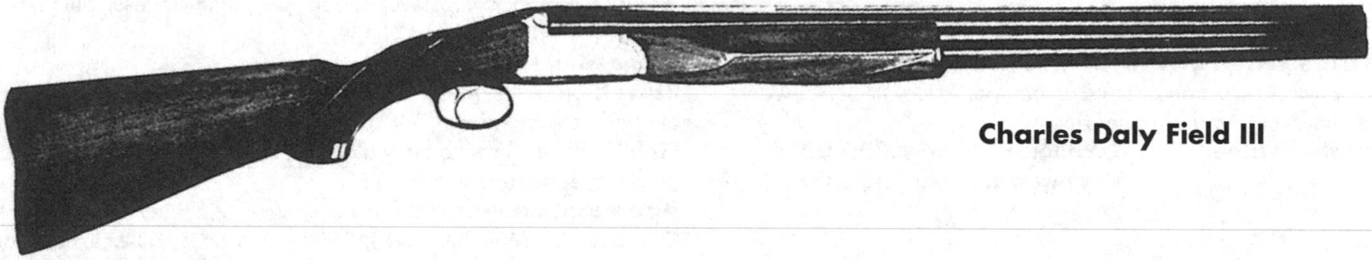

Charles Daly Field III

Charles Daly Field III

Similar to the Field Grade with some minor changes; double trigger.

Estimated Value:	**Excellent:**	**$650.00**
	Very good:	**$520.00**

Charles Daly Superior II

Similar to the Field III but higher quality.

Estimated Value:	**Excellent:**	**$700.00**
	Very good:	**$560.00**

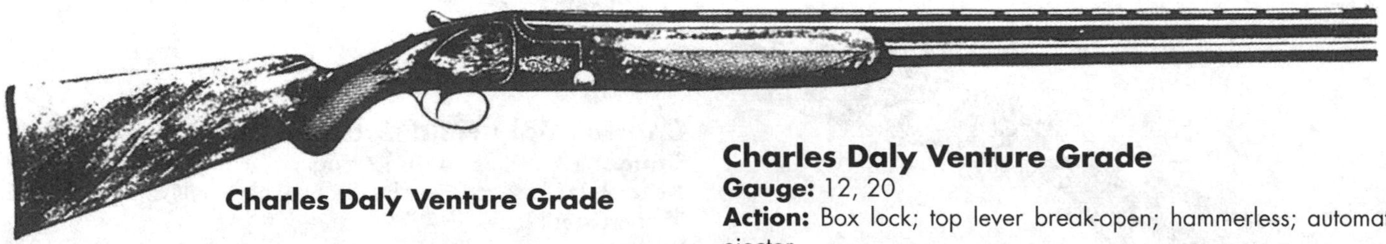

Charles Daly Venture Grade

Charles Daly Venture Grade

Gauge: 12, 20
Action: Box lock; top lever break-open; hammerless; automatic ejector
Magazine: None
Barrel: Over and under double barrel; 26", 28", 30", various chokes; ventilated rib
Finish: Blued; checkered walnut pistol grip stock and forearm
Approximate wt.: 7 to 8 lbs.
Comments: Made from the early 1970s to the mid-1980s. Add $25.00 for Skeet Model; $35.00 for Trap Model.

Estimated Value:	**Excellent:**	**$600.00**
	Very good:	**$480.00**

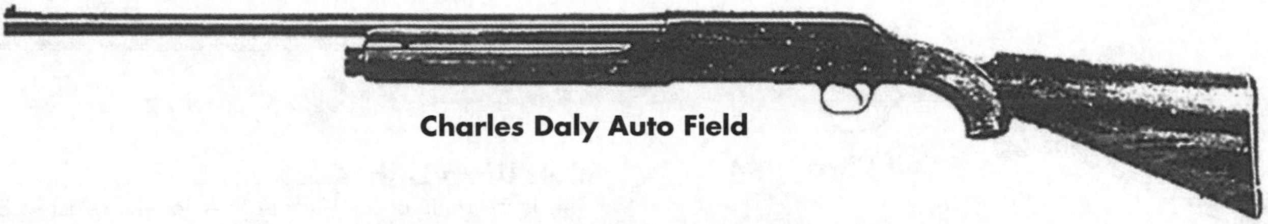

Charles Daly Auto Field

Charles Daly Auto Superior

Charles Daly Auto Field

Gauge: 12, 12 magnum
Action: Semiautomatic, recoil operated
Magazine: 5-shot tubular
Barrel: 26" improved cylinder or skeet, 28" modified or full, 30" full, chokes; ventilated rib
Finish: Blued; checkered walnut pistol grip stock and forearm
Approximate wt.: 7½ lbs.
Comments: Made from the mid-1970s to the 1990s.

Estimated Value:	**Excellent:**	**$400.00**
	Very good:	**$320.00**

Charles Daly Auto Superior

Similar to the Auto Field but higher quality.

Estimated Value:	**Excellent:**	**$415.00**
	Very good:	**$335.00**

COLT

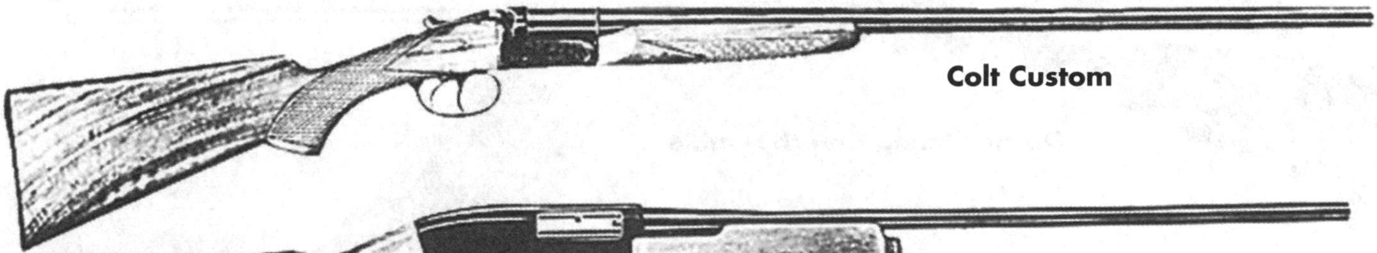

Colt Custom

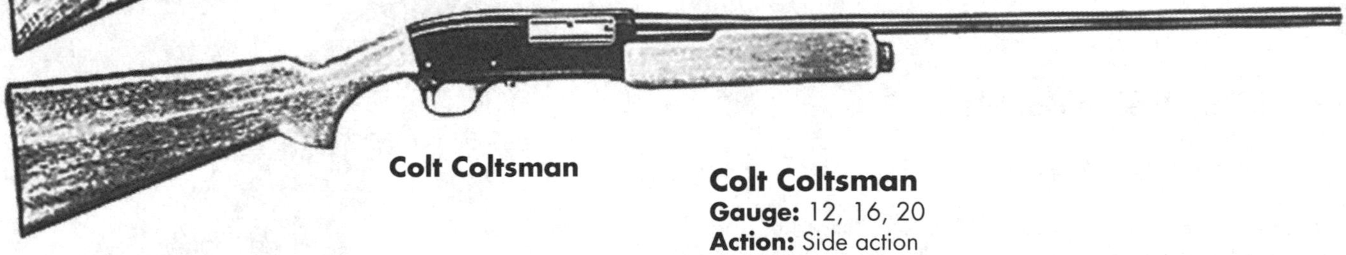

Colt Coltsman

Colt Custom

Gauge: 12, 16
Action: Box lock; top lever break-open; hammerless; double trigger; automatic ejector
Magazine: None
Barrel: Side-by-side double barrel; 26" improved and modified, 28" modified and full, or 30" full chokes
Finish: Blued; checkered walnut pistol grip stock and tapered forearm
Approximate wt.: 7 to 8 lbs.
Comments: Produced in the early 1960s.

Estimated Value:	**Excellent:**	**$750.00**
	Very good:	**$600.00**

Colt Coltsman

Gauge: 12, 16, 20
Action: Side action
Magazine: 4-shot
Barrel: 26" improved, 28" modified, 30" full chokes
Finish: Blued; plain walnut pistol grip stock and slide handle
Approximate wt.: 6½ to 7 lbs.
Comments: Made from the early to mid-1960s in takedown models.

Estimated Value:	**Excellent:**	**$325.00**
	Very good:	**$260.00**

Colt Coltsman Custom

A fancier version of the Coltsman with checkering and a ventilated rib.

Estimated Value:	**Excellent:**	**$375.00**
	Very good:	**$300.00**

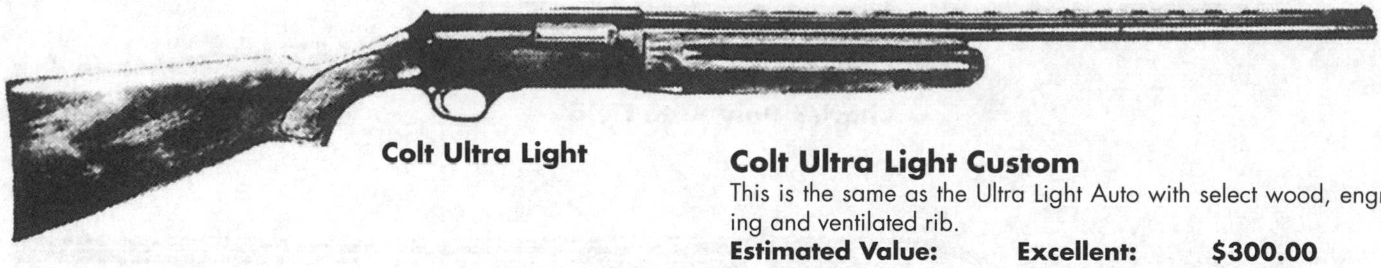

Colt Ultra Light

Colt Ultra Light

Gauge: 12, 20
Action: Semiautomatic
Magazine: 4-shot
Barrel: Chrome lined, 26" improved or modified, 28" modified or full, 30", 32" full chokes; rib available
Finish: Blued; checkered walnut pistol grip stock and forearm; alloy receiver
Approximate wt.: 6½ lbs.
Comments: A takedown shotgun produced during the mid-1960s. Add $15.00 for solid rib; $25.00 for ventilated rib.

Estimated Value:	**Excellent:**	**$325.00**
	Very good:	**$260.00**

Colt Ultra Light Custom

This is the same as the Ultra Light Auto with select wood, engraving and ventilated rib.

Estimated Value:	**Excellent:**	**$300.00**
	Very good:	**$240.00**

Colt Magnum Auto

Same as the Ultra Light Auto in magnum gauges and of heavier weight. Add $15.00 for solid rib; $25.00 for ventilated rib. Made in the mid-1960s.

Estimated Value:	**Excellent:**	**$340.00**
	Very good:	**$275.00**

Colt Magnum Auto Custom

Same as Magnum Auto with select wood, engraving, and ventilated rib. Produced in the mid-1960s.

Estimated Value:	**Excellent:**	**$400.00**
	Very good:	**$320.00**

DARNE

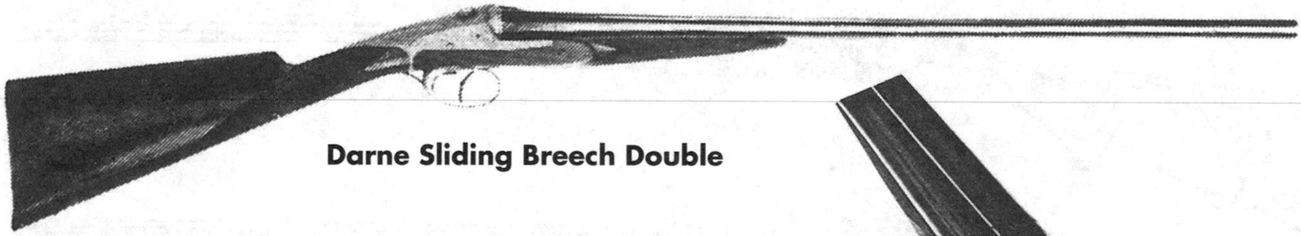

Darne Sliding Breech Double

Darne Sliding Breech Double

Gauge: 12, 16, 20, 28
Action: Sliding breech; selective ejectors; double trigger
Magazine: None
Barrel: Side-by-side double barrel; 25½" or 27½" modified and improved cylinder, raised rib
Finish: Blued; checkered walnut straight or pistol grip stock and forearm
Approximate wt.: 5¾ to 6¼ lbs.
Comments: A French shotgun.

Estimated Value:	**Excellent:**	**$1,000.00**
	Very good:	**$ 800.00**

Darne Deluxe

Same as the Sliding Breech Double with engraving and 28" modified and full choke barrels. 20 or 28 gauge.

Estimated Value:	**Excellent:**	**$2,000.00**
	Very good:	**$1,600.00**

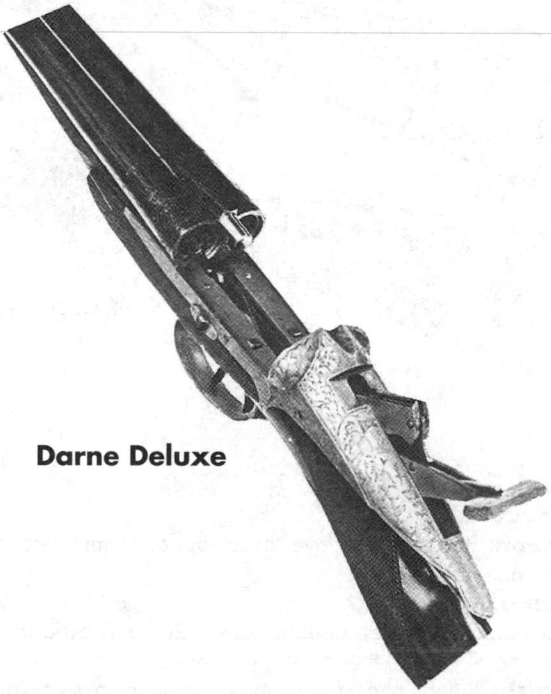

Darne Deluxe

Darne Supreme

Same as the Darne Deluxe except in 20 or 28 gauge; 25½" barrels; elaborate engraving and swivels.

Estimated Value:	**Excellent:**	**$2,750.00**
	Very good:	**$2,200.00**

Davidson Model 69SL

Davidson Model 73 Stagecoach

Gauge: 12, 20 magnum
Action: Box lock; top lever break-open; exposed hammers
Magazine: None
Barrel: Side-by-side double barrel; 20" improved cylinder and modified or modified and full chokes; matted rib
Finish: Blued; checkered walnut pistol grip stock and forearm; sights; engraved receiver
Approximate wt.: 7 lbs.
Comments: Made from the early to the late 1970s.

Estimated Value:	**Excellent:**	**$310.00**
	Very good:	**$250.00**

Davidson Model 69SL

Gauge: 12, 20
Action: Side lock, hammerless
Magazine: None
Barrel: Double barrel; 26" – 30", variety of chokes
Finish: Blued or nickel; checkered walnut pistol grip stock and forearm; gold trigger; bead sights; engraved
Approximate wt.: 6 to 7 lbs.
Comments: Made from the early 1960s to the late 1970s.

Estimated Value:	**Excellent:**	**$500.00**
	Very good:	**$400.00**

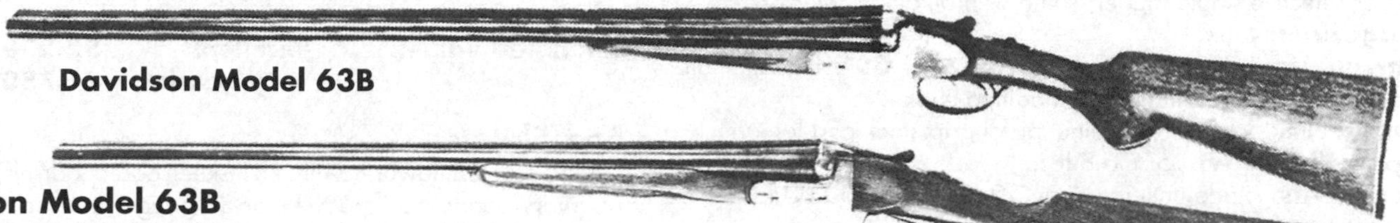

Davidson Model 63B

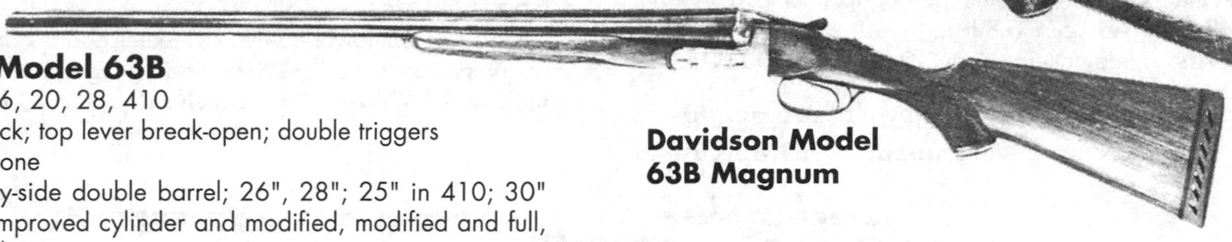

Davidson Model 63B Magnum

Davidson Model 63B

Gauge: 12, 16, 20, 28, 410
Action: Box lock; top lever break-open; double triggers
Magazine: None
Barrel: Side-by-side double barrel; 26", 28"; 25" in 410; 30" in 12 gauge; improved cylinder and modified, modified and full, full and full chokes
Finish: Blued or nickel; checkered walnut pistol grip stock and forearm; bead sights; some engraving
Approximate wt.: 6 to 7 lbs.
Comments: Produced in Spain.

Estimated Value:	**Excellent:**	**$335.00**
	Very good:	**$270.00**

Davidson Model 63B Magnum

Same as Model 63B in 10, 12, or 20 gauge magnum. Available with 32" barrel in 10 gauge. Add 20% for 10 gauge magnum.

Estimated Value:	**Excellent:**	**$395.00**
	Very good:	**$315.00**

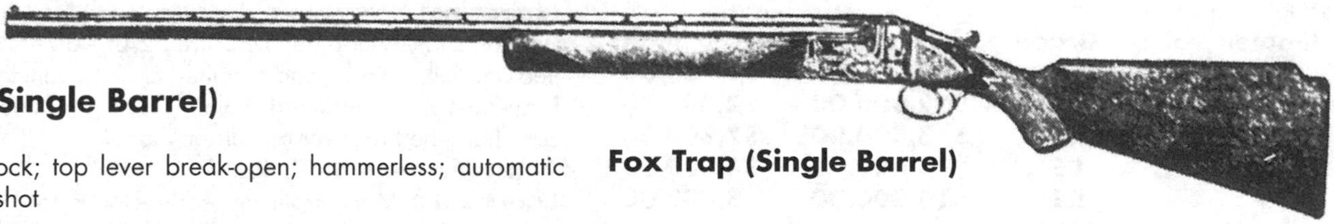

Fox Trap (Single Barrel)

Fox Trap (Single Barrel)

Gauge: 12
Action: Box lock; top lever break-open; hammerless; automatic ejector; single shot
Magazine: None
Barrel: 30", 32" trap bore; ventilated rib
Finish: Blued; checkered walnut half or full pistol grip stock and large forearm; some with recoil pad; decorated receiver; after 1931 Monte Carlo stock. Grades differ in quality of craftsmanship and decoration. ME Grade was made to order with inlaid gold and finest walnut wood.
Approximate wt.: 7 to 8 lbs.
Comments: Made until the early 1940s. Prices for grades made before 1932 are about 20% less.

Estimated Value:	**Grade**	**Excellent**	**Very good**
	JE	**$ 3,750.00**	**$3,000.00**
	KE	**$ 4,500.00**	**$3,600.00**
	LE	**$ 5,775.00**	**$4,620.00**
	ME	**$11,000.00**	**$8,800.00**

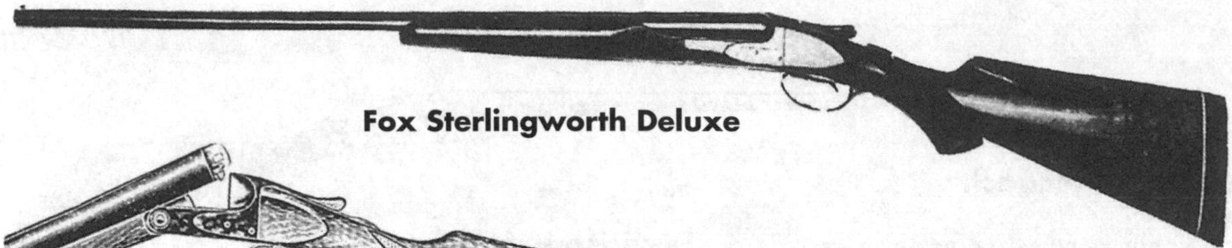

Fox Sterlingworth Deluxe

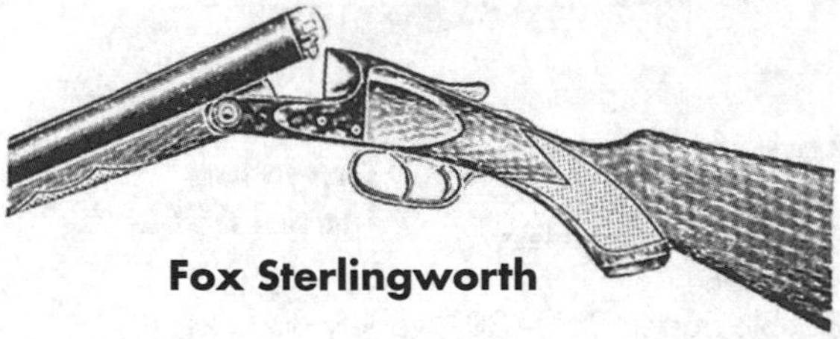

Fox Sterlingworth

Fox Sterlingworth

Gauge: 12, 16, 20
Action: Box lock; top lever break-open; hammerless; double trigger or selective single trigger; some with automatic ejector
Magazine: None
Barrel: Side-by-side double barrel; 26" – 30"; full and full, modified and full, cylinder and modified chokes
Finish: Blued; checkered walnut pistol grip stock and forearm
Approximate wt.: 5¾ to 8 lbs.
Comments: Made until the early 1940s. Add $50.00 for selective trigger; $75.00 for automatic ejector.

Estimated Value:	**Excellent:**	**$1,750.00**
	Very good:	**$1,400.00**

Fox Sterlingworth Deluxe

This is a fancy model Sterlingworth with ivory bead; recoil pad; 32" barrels; selective single trigger. Add $75.00 for automatic ejector.

Estimated Value:	**Excellent:**	**$2,000.00**
	Very good:	**$1,600.00**

Fox Sterlingworth Skeet

Basically the same as the Sterlingworth with skeet bore; 26" or 28" barrels; straight grip stock. Add $75.00 for automatic ejector.

Estimated Value:	**Excellent:**	**$2,200.00**
	Very good:	**$1,750.00**

Fox Skeeter

Similar to Sterlingworth with 28" skeet bored barrels; ventilated rib; ivory bead; recoil pad, 12 or 20 gauge; automatic ejector.

Estimated Value:	**Excellent:**	**$3,000.00**
	Very good:	**$2,400.00**

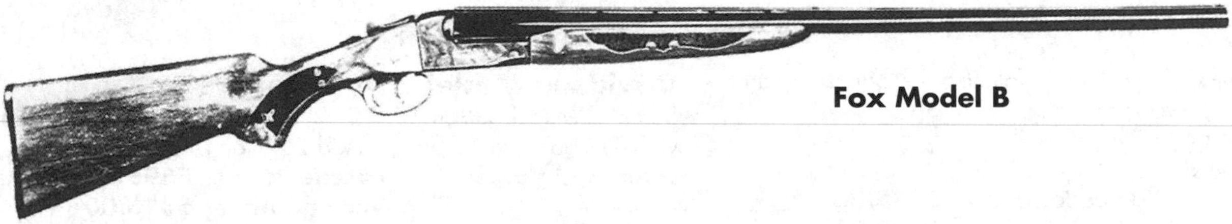

Fox Model B

Fox Hammerless Doubles

These are very similar to the Sterlingworth models, in varying degrees of increased quality. All have automatic ejectors except Grade A. Add $50.00 for selective single trigger; $125.00 for ventilated rib.

Estimated Value:	**Grade**	**Excellent**	**Very good**
	A	**$ 2,200.00**	**$1,750.00**
	AE	**$ 2,500.00**	**$2,000.00**
	BE	**$ 3,500.00**	**$2,800.00**
	CE	**$ 5,000.00**	**$4,000.00**
	DE	**$10,000.00**	**$8,000.00**

Fox Super Fox

Gauge: 12
Action: Box lock; top lever break-open; hammerless; double trigger; automatic ejector
Magazine: None
Barrel: Double barrel; 30" or 32" full choke
Finish: Blued; checkered walnut pistol grip stock and forearm
Approximate wt.: 7¾ to 9¾ lbs.
Comments: This is a long-range gun produced from the mid-1920s to the early 1940s.

Estimated Value:	**Excellent:**	**$1,700.00**
	Very good:	**$1,350.00**

Fox Models B and BE

Gauge: 12, 16, 20, 410
Action: Box lock; top lever break-open; hammerless; double triggers; plain ejector
Magazine: None
Barrel: Side-by-side double barrel; 24" – 30" full and full, modified and full, cylinder and modified chokes; ventilated rib
Finish: Blued; checkered walnut pistol grip stock and forearm; case hardened receiver on current model
Approximate wt.: 7½ lbs.
Comments: Made from the early 1940s to 1988. 16 gauge discontinued in the late 1970s. Model BE has automatic ejector.

Estimated Value:	**Excellent:**	**$350.00**
	Very good:	**$280.00**

Fox Model B Lightweight

Same as the Model B with 24" cylinder bore and modified choke barrels in 12 and 20 gauge.

Estimated Value:	**Excellent:**	**$360.00**
	Very good:	**$285.00**

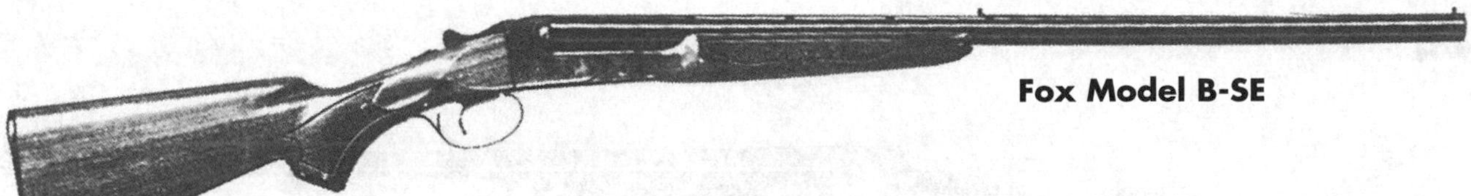

Fox Model B-SE

Fox Model B-ST

Fox Model B-DL

Fox Model B-SE

Basically the same as the Model B with automatic ejectors and a single trigger. In production from 1968 to 1988.

Estimated Value: **Excellent:** **$625.00**
Very good: **$500.00**

Fox Model B-ST

This is the same as Model B with gold-plated nonselective single trigger. Made from the mid-1950s to the mid-1960s.

Estimated Value: **Excellent:** **$425.00**
Very good: **$340.00**

Fox Models B-DL and B-DE

Both similar to the B-ST with chrome frame and beavertail forearm. Made from the early 1960s to the early 1970s.

Estimated Value: **Excellent:** **$450.00**
Very good: **$360.00**

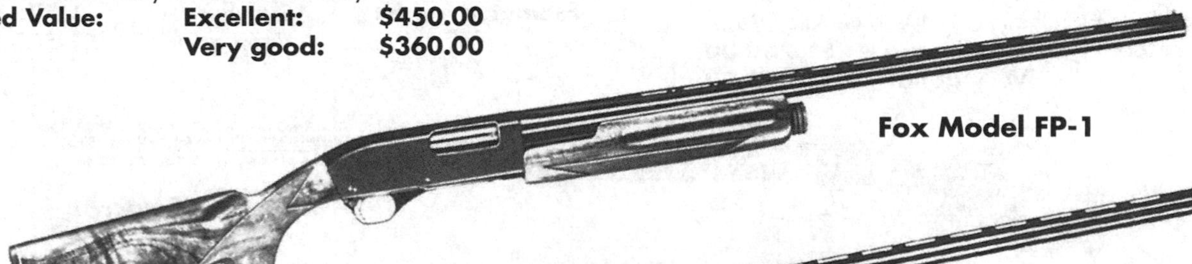

Fox Model FP-1

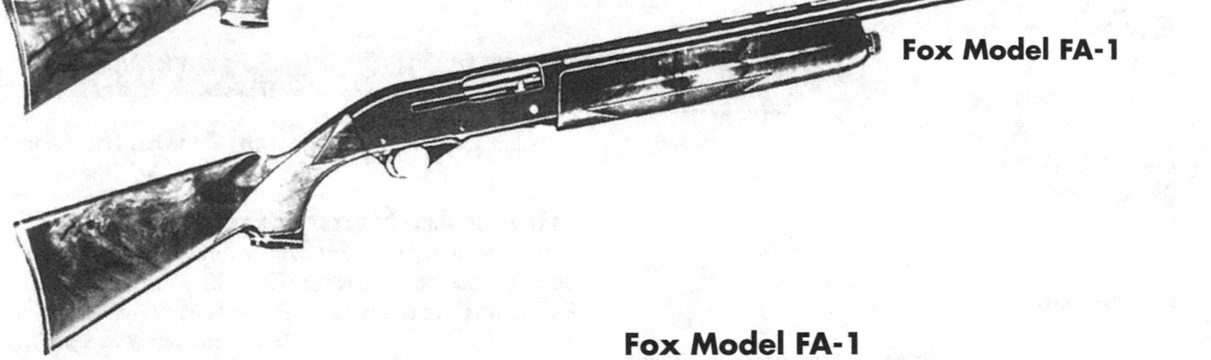

Fox Model FA-1

Fox Model FP-1

Gauge: 12; $2\frac{3}{4}$" or 3"
Action: Slide action, hammerless
Magazine: 4-shot tubular; 3-shot with 3" shells
Barrel: 28" modified, 30" full choke; ventilated rib
Finish: Blued; checkered walnut pistol grip stock and slide handle; rosewood cap with inlay
Approximate wt.: $7\frac{1}{4}$ lbs.
Comments: Produced from 1981 to 1983.
Estimated Value: **Excellent:** **$330.00**
Very good: **$265.00**

Fox Model FA-1

Gauge: 12; $2\frac{3}{4}$"
Action: Semiautomatic; gas-operated
Magazine: 3-shot tubular
Barrel: 28" modified; 30" full choke; ventilated rib
Finish: Blued; checkered walnut pistol grip stock and forearm; rosewood cap with inlay
Approximate wt.: $7\frac{1}{2}$ lbs.
Comments: Produced from 1981 to 1983.
Estimated Value: **Excellent:** **$300.00**
Very good: **$240.00**

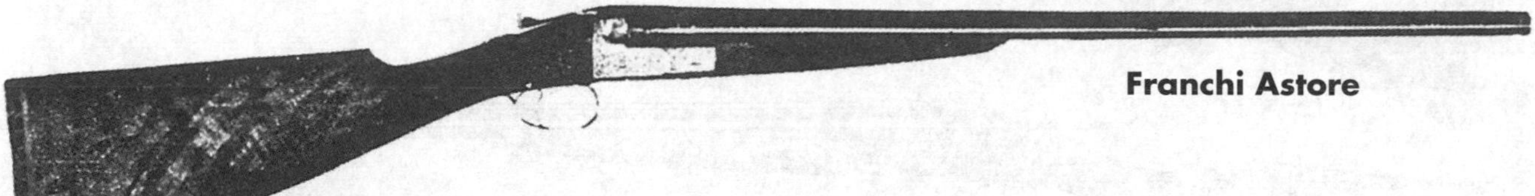

Franchi Astore

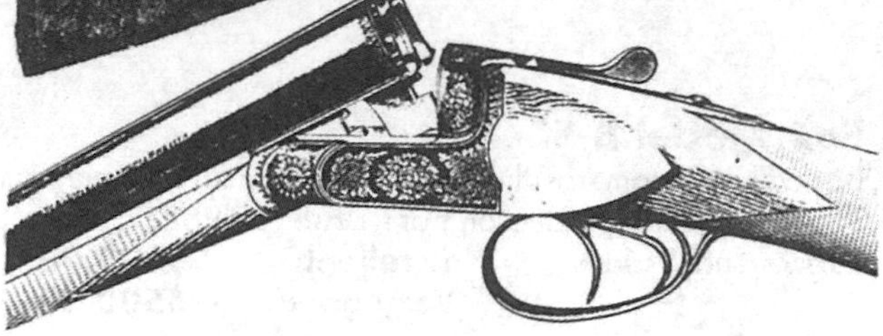

Franchi Airone

Franchi Airone

Gauge: 12
Action: Box lock; top lever break-open; hammerless; automatic ejector
Magazine: None
Barrel: Side-by-side double barrel; several lengths and choke combinations available
Finish: Blued; checkered walnut straight grip stock and short tapered forearm; engraved
Approximate wt.: 7 lbs.
Comments: Made from the mid-1940s to the late 1950s.

Estimated Value:	**Excellent:**	**$1,250.00**
	Very good:	**$1,000.00**

Franchi Astore

Gauge: 12
Action: Box lock; top lever break-open; hammerless; double triggers
Magazine: None
Barrel: Side-by-side double barrel; several lengths and choke combinations available
Finish: Blued; checkered walnut straight grip stock and short tapered forearm
Approximate wt.: 7 lbs.
Comments: Made from the mid-1950s to the late 1960s.

Estimated Value:	**Excellent:**	**$1,000.00**
	Very good:	**$ 800.00**

Franchi Astore 5

Same as the Astore with higher quality wood and engraving.

Estimated Value:	**Excellent:**	**$1,875.00**
	Very good:	**$1,500.00**

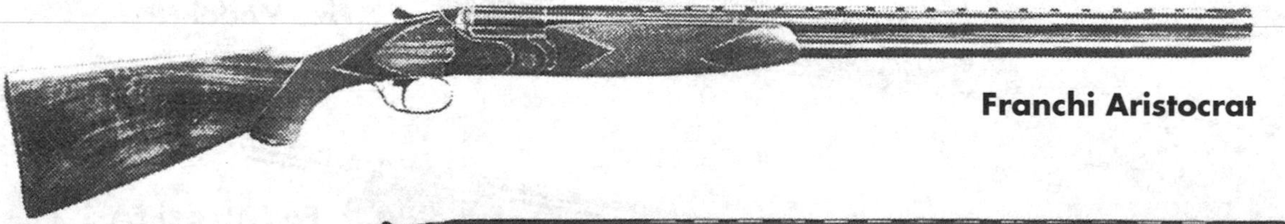

Franchi Aristocrat

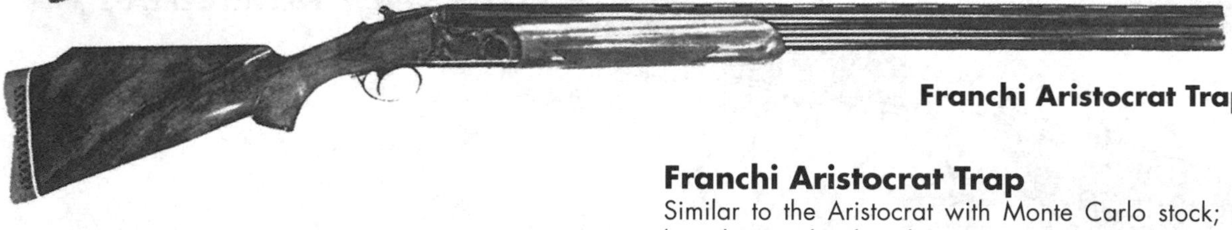

Franchi Aristocrat Trap

Franchi Aristocrat

Gauge: 12
Action: Box lock; top lever break-open; hammerless; automatic ejector; single trigger
Magazine: None
Barrel: Over and under double barrel; 24" cylinder bore and improved cylinder; 26" improved cylinder and modified, 28", 30" modified and full chokes; ventilated rib
Finish: Blued; checkered walnut pistol grip stock and forearm; engraved
Approximate wt.: 7 lbs.
Comments: Made from the early to the late 1960s.

Estimated Value:	**Excellent:**	**$700.00**
	Very good:	**$560.00**

Franchi Aristocrat Trap

Similar to the Aristocrat with Monte Carlo stock; chrome lined barrels; case hardened receiver; 30" barrels only.

Estimated Value:	**Excellent:**	**$725.00**
	Very good:	**$580.00**

Franchi Aristocrat Skeet

Same as the Aristocrat Trap with 26" skeet barrels.

Estimated Value:	**Excellent:**	**$675.00**
	Very good:	**$540.00**

Franchi Aristocrat Silver King

Similar to the Aristocrat with higher quality finish; select wood; engraving.

Estimated Value:	**Excellent:**	**$700.00**
	Very good:	**$560.00**

Franchi Falconet Buckskin

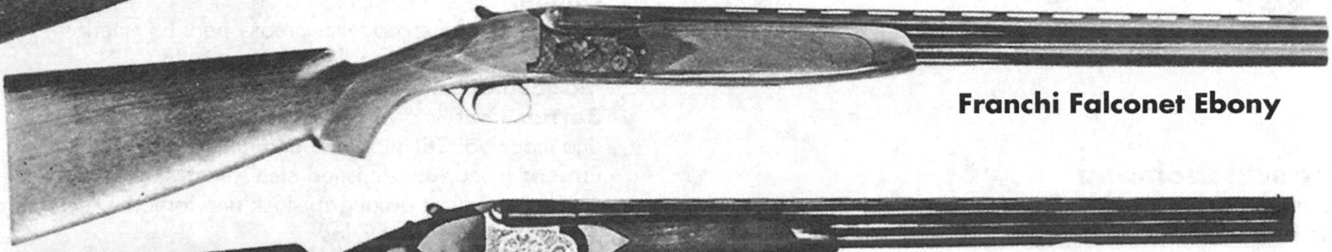

Franchi Falconet Ebony

Franchi Falconet Silver

Franchi Falconet Buckskin and Ebony

Gauge: 12, 20
Action: Box lock; top lever break-open; hammerless
Magazine: None
Barrel: Over and under double barrel; 24" – 30" barrels in several choke combinations; ventilated rib; chrome lined
Finish: Blued; colored frame with engraving; epoxy finished checkered walnut pistol grip stock and forearm
Approximate wt.: 6 to 7 lbs.
Comments: Made from about 1970 to the late 1970s. Buckskin and Ebony differ only in color of receiver and engraving.

Estimated Value:	**Excellent:**	**$600.00**
	Very good:	**$480.00**

Franchi Falconet Silver

Same as the Buckskin and Ebony except: 12 gauge only; pickled silver receiver.

Estimated Value:	**Excellent:**	**$650.00**
	Very good:	**$520.00**

Franchi Falconet Super

Similar to the Falconet Silver except: slightly different forearm; 12 gauge only; 27" or 28" barrels.

Estimated Value:	**Excellent:**	**$700.00**
	Very good:	**$560.00**

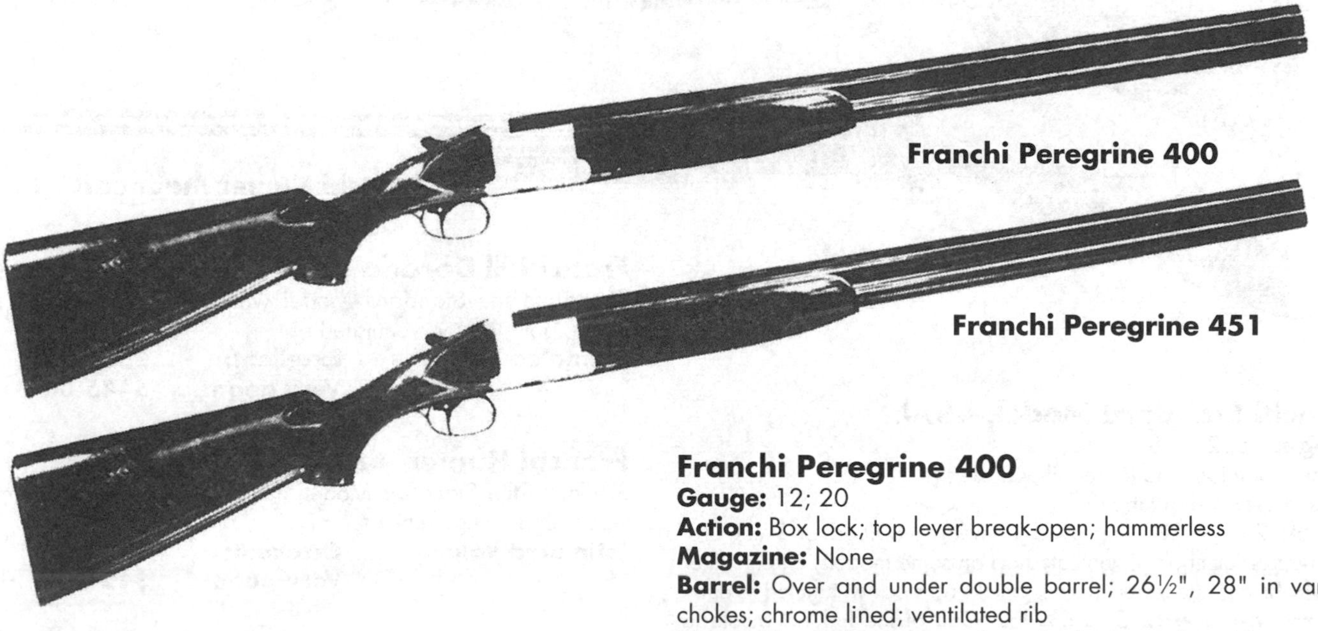

Franchi Peregrine 400

Franchi Peregrine 451

Franchi Peregrine 451

Similar to the 400 except: alloy receiver; lightweight.

Estimated Value:	**Excellent:**	**$650.00**
	Very good:	**$520.00**

Franchi Peregrine 400

Gauge: 12; 20
Action: Box lock; top lever break-open; hammerless
Magazine: None
Barrel: Over and under double barrel; 26½", 28" in various chokes; chrome lined; ventilated rib
Finish: Blued; checkered walnut pistol grip stock and forearm
Approximate wt.: 7 lbs.
Comments: Made from the mid- to the late 1970s.

Estimated Value:	**Excellent:**	**$700.00**
	Very good:	**$560.00**

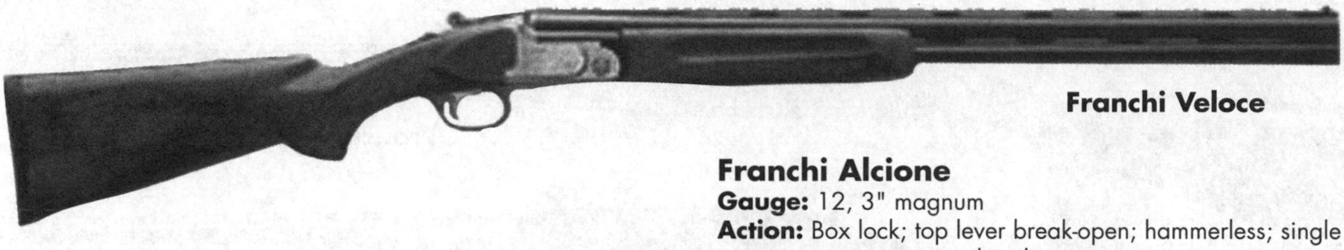

Franchi Veloce

Franchi Alcione

Gauge: 12, 3" magnum
Action: Box lock; top lever break-open; hammerless; single selective trigger; automatic split selective ejectors
Magazine: None
Barrel: Over and under double barrel; 26" improved cylinder and modified; 28" modified and full choke; ventilated rib
Finish: Blued; coin-finished steel receiver with scroll engraving; checkered walnut pistol grip stock and forearm; recoil pad
Approximate wt.: 7 lbs.
Comments: Produced in Italy. Deluxe models available, add 10% to 25%.

Estimated Value:	**Excellent:**	**$1,270.00**
	Very good:	**$1,025.00**

Franchi Veloce

Similar to the Alcione except: 20 or 28 gauge only; chrome-lined barrels; etching on receiver.

Estimated Value:	**Excellent:**	**$1,235.00**
	Very good:	**$ 985.00**

Franchi Diamond

Gauge: 12
Action: Box lock; top lever break-open; hammerless; single selective trigger; automatic extractors
Magazine: None
Barrel: Over and under double barrel; 28" modified and full choke; ventilated rib
Finish: Blued; checkered walnut pistol grip stock and forearm; silver-plated receiver
Approximate wt.: 6¾ lbs.
Comments: Produced in Italy. Made from 1954 to 1975.

Estimated Value:	**Excellent:**	**$1,200.00**
	Very good:	**$ 960.00**

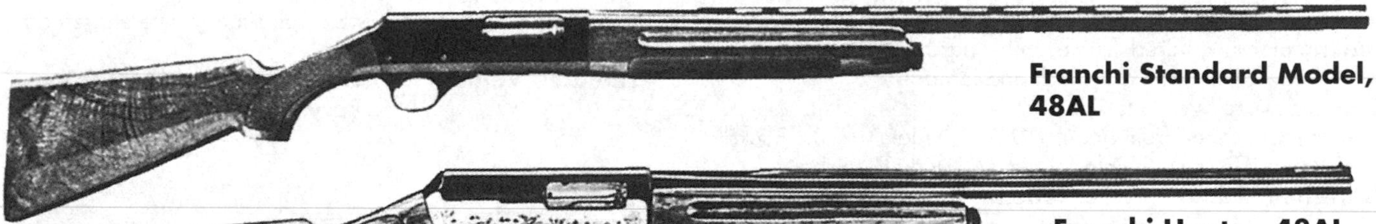

Franchi Standard Model, 48AL

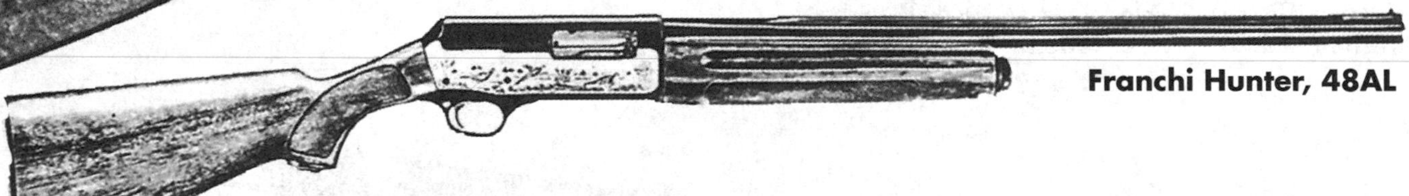

Franchi Hunter, 48AL

Franchi Hunter Magnum

Franchi Standard Model, 48AL

Gauge: 12, 20, 28
Action: Semiautomatic; recoil-operated
Magazine: 5-shot tubular
Barrel: 24" or 26" improved cylinder, modified or skeet, 28" modified or full chokes; ventilated rib on some models; chrome lined
Finish: Blued; checkered walnut pistol grip stock with fluted forearm
Approximate wt.: 5 to 6¼ lbs. One of the lightest autoloaders available.
Comments: Manufactured in Italy. Add 15% for deluxe models.

Estimated Value:	**New (retail):**	**$779.00**
	Excellent:	**$585.00**
	Very good:	**$465.00**

Franchi El Dorado

Similar to the Standard Model with heavy engraving; select wood; gold trigger; ventilated rib.

Estimated Value:	**Excellent:**	**$560.00**
	Very good:	**$445.00**

Franchi Hunter, 48AL

Similar to the Standard Model; 12 or 20 gauge; higher quality wood; engraving; ventilated rib.

Estimated Value:	**Excellent:**	**$525.00**
	Very good:	**$420.00**

Franchi Hunter Magnum

Same as the Hunter with recoil pad and chambered for magnum shells.

Estimated Value:	**Excellent:**	**$525.00**
	Very good:	**$420.00**

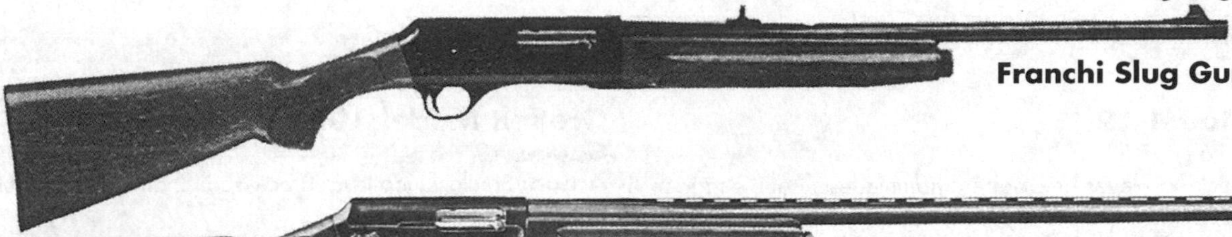

Franchi Slug Gun, 48AL

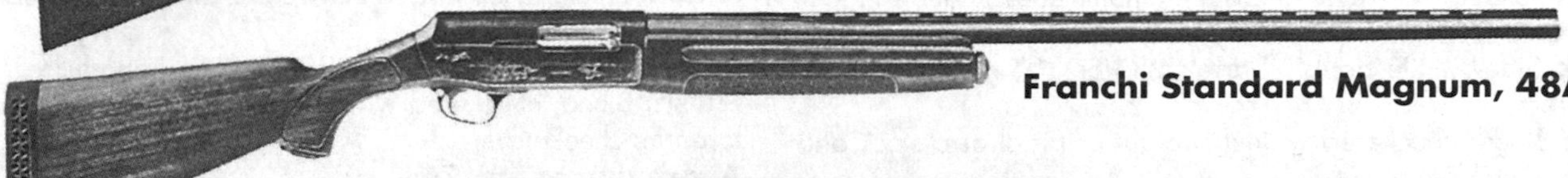

Franchi Standard Magnum, 48AL

Franchi Model 520

Franchi Standard Magnum, 48AL

Similar to the Standard with recoil pad; chambered for magnum shells; 12 or 20 gauge.

Estimated Value: **Excellent:** **$500.00**
Very good: **$400.00**

Franchi Slug Gun, 48AL

Similar to the Standard Model with a 22" cylinder bore barrel; sight; swivels; alloy receiver. Made from the mid-1950s to the early 1980s; 12 or 20 gauge.

Estimated Value: **Excellent:** **$425.00**
Very good: **$340.00**

Franchi Model 500

Similar to the Standard except: gas-operated; 12 gauge only; made for fast takedown.

Estimated Value: **Excellent:** **$450.00**
Very good: **$360.00**

Franchi Model 520

Similar to the Model 500 with deluxe features.

Estimated Value: **Excellent:** **$465.00**
Very good: **$375.00**

Franchi Model 530 Trap

Similar to the Model 520 except: Monte Carlo stock; high ventilated rib; three interchangeable choke tubes.

Estimated Value: **Excellent:** **$600.00**
Very good: **$480.00**

Franchi Variopress 612 and 620

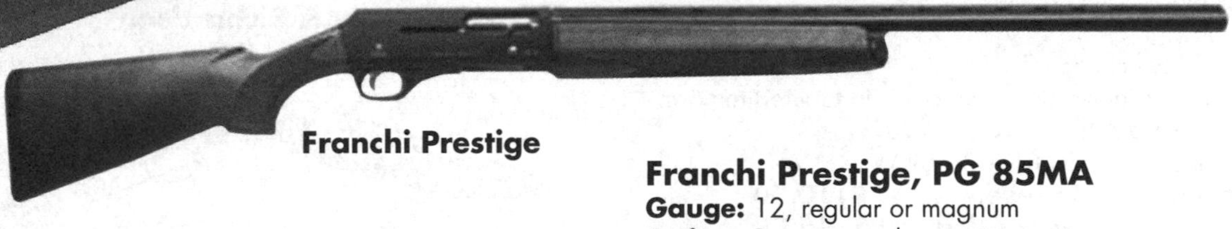

Franchi Prestige

Franchi Variopress 612 and 620

Gauge: 12 (612) or 20 (620)
Action: Gas-operated, repeating semiautomatic
Magazine: 5-shot tubular
Barrel: 24", 26", or 28"; three choke tubes. Defense model has 18½" barrel
Finish: Blued; checkered walnut pistol grip stock and forearm; synthetic or camouflage finish available
Approximate wt.: 6½ or 7½ lbs.
Comments: Introduced in 2001. Add 60% for Sporting model. Deduct 10% for Defense model.
Estimated Value: **Excellent:** **$550.00**
Very good: **$435.00**

Franchi Prestige, PG 85MA

Gauge: 12, regular or magnum
Action: Gas-operated, semiautomatic
Magazine: 5-shot tubular (2¾" shells)
Barrel: 24" slug, 26" improved cylinder or modified, 28" modified or full, 30" full; chrome lined; ventilated rib
Finish: Blued; checkered walnut pistol grip stock and fluted forearm; sights on slug barrel
Approximate wt.: 7½ lbs.
Comments: Produced from the mid-1980s to the early 1990s.
Estimated Value: **Excellent:** **$445.00**
Very good: **$355.00**

Franchi Elite

Similar to the Prestige with higher quality finish. Receiver has acid-etched wildlife scenes.

Estimated Value: **Excellent:** **$485.00**
Very good: **$385.00**

GREIFELT

Greifelt Model 22
Gauge: 12, 16
Action: Box lock; top lever break-open; hammerless; double trigger
Magazine: None
Barrel: Side-by-side double barrel; 28" or 30" modified or full choke
Finish: Blued; checkered walnut straight or pistol grip stock and forearm; cheekpiece
Approximate wt.: 7 lbs.
Comments: Made in the late 1940s.

Estimated Value:	**Excellent:**	**$2,000.00**
	Very good:	**$1,600.00**

Greifelt Model 22E
Same as Model 22 with automatic ejector.

Estimated Value:	**Excellent:**	**$2,250.00**
	Very good:	**$1,800.00**

Greifelt Model 103
Gauge: 12, 16
Action: Box lock; top lever break-open; hammerless; double triggers
Magazine: None
Barrel: Double barrel; 28" or 30" modified and full
Finish: Blued; checkered walnut straight or pistol grip stock and forearm; cheekpiece
Approximate wt.: 7 lbs.
Comments: Made in the late 1940s.

Estimated Value:	**Excellent:**	**$2,000.00**
	Very good:	**$1,600.00**

Greifelt Model 103E
Same as the Model 103 with automatic ejector.

Estimated Value:	**Excellent:**	**$2,200.00**
	Very good:	**$1,760.00**

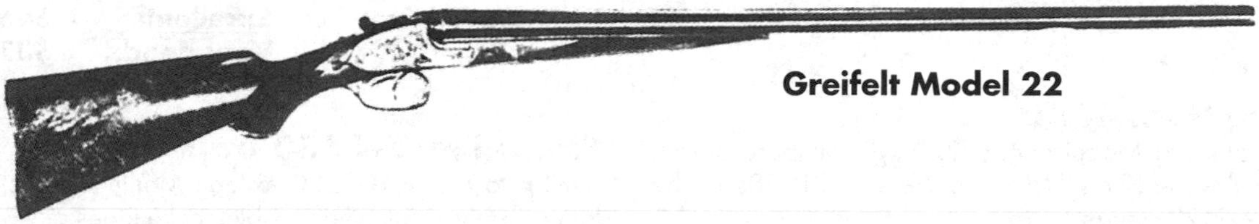

Greifelt Model 22

HARRINGTON + RICHARDSON

Harrington & Richardson No. 3
Gauge: 12, 16, 20, 410
Action: Box lock; top lever break-open; hammerless; single shot; automatic extractors
Magazine: None
Barrel: 26" – 32" full choke
Finish: Blued; walnut semi-pistol grip stock and tapered forearm
Approximate wt.: 5½ to 6½ lbs.
Comments: Made from about 1908 until World War II.

Estimated Value:	**Excellent:**	**$110.00**
	Very good:	**$ 85.00**

Harrington & Richardson No. 3

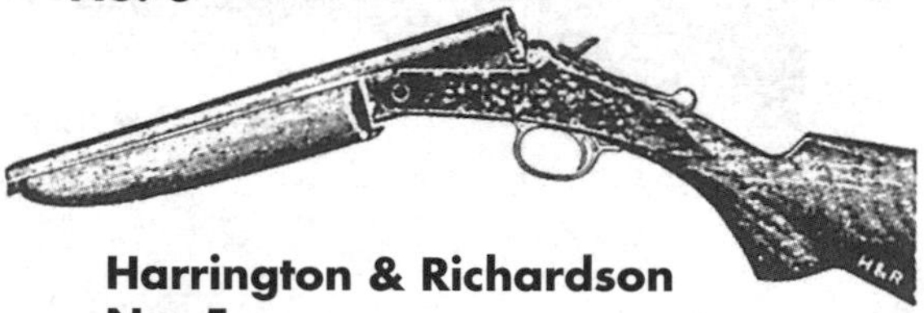

Harrington & Richardson No. 5

Harrington & Richardson No. 6

Harrington & Richardson No. 5
Gauge: 20, 28, 410
Action: Box lock; top lever break-open; exposed hammer; single shot; automatic extractors
Magazine: None
Barrel: 26", 28" full choke
Finish: Blued; walnut semi-pistol grip stock and tapered forearm
Approximate wt.: 4½ lbs.
Comments: Made from about 1908 until World War II.

Estimated Value:	**Excellent:**	**$125.00**
	Very good:	**$100.00**

Harrington & Richardson No. 6
Similar to the No. 5 in 10, 12, 16, and 20 gauge; heavier design and barrel lengths of 28" – 36". Weighs 5 to 8 lbs.

Estimated Value:	**Excellent:**	**$130.00**
	Very good:	**$105.00**

Harrington & Richardson No. 8

Similar to the No. 6 with different style forearm and in 12, 16, 20, 24, 28 and 410 gauges.

Estimated Value: **Excellent:** **$130.00**
Very good: **$105.00**

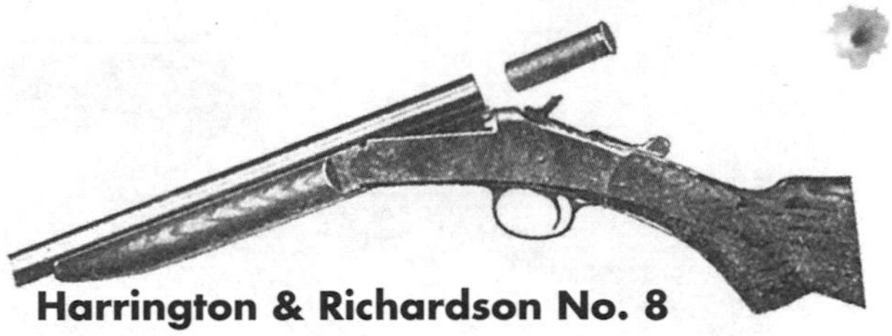

Harrington & Richardson No. 8

Harrington & Richardson No. 7 and No. 9

Similar to the No. 8 with smaller forearm and more rounded pistol grip. Not available in 24 gauge.

Estimated Value: **Excellent:** **$120.00**
Very good: **$ 95.00**

Harrington & Richardson No. 7

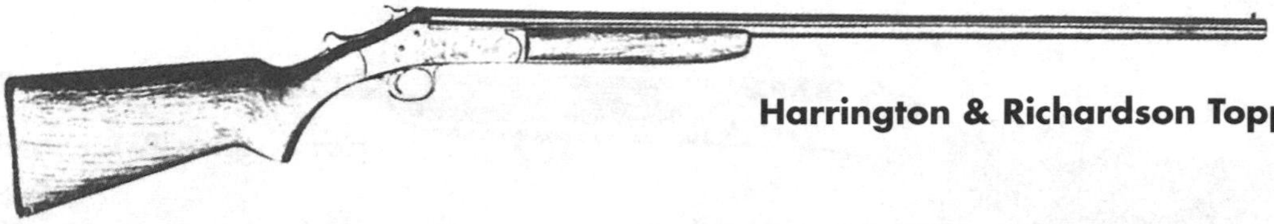

Harrington & Richardson Topper No. 48

Harrington & Richardson Topper No. 48

Similar to the No. 8. Made from the mid-1940s to the late 1950s.

Estimated Value: **Excellent:** **$150.00**
Very good: **$120.00**

Harrington & Richardson Topper No. 488 Deluxe

Similar to the No. 48 with chrome frame; recoil pad; black lacquered stock and forearm.

Estimated Value: **Excellent:** **$150.00**
Very good: **$120.00**

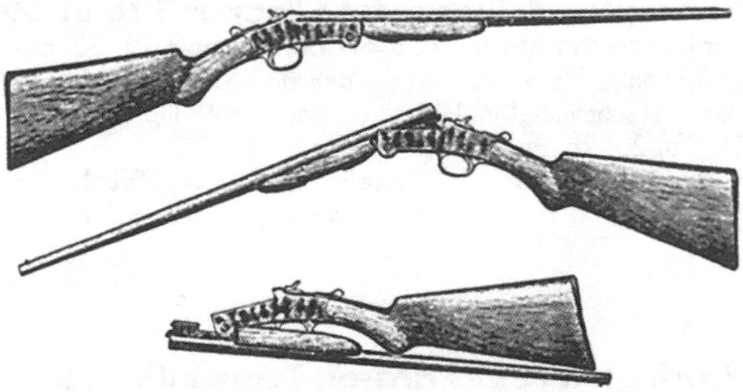

Harrington & Richardson Folding Model

Harrington & Richardson No. 148

Gauge: 12, 16, 20, 410
Action: Box lock; top lever break-open; hammerless; single shot; automatic extractor
Magazine: None
Barrel: 28" – 36" full choke
Finish: Blued; walnut semi-pistol grip stock and forearm; recoil pad
Approximate wt.: 5 to 6½ lbs.
Comments: Made from the late 1950s to the early 1960s.

Estimated Value: **Excellent:** **$130.00**
Very good: **$105.00**

Harrington & Richardson Topper Jr. 480

Youth version of the No. 48; 410 gauge; 26" barrel; smaller stock. Made from 1959 to 1962.

Estimated Value: **Excellent:** **$125.00**
Very good: **$100.00**

Harrington & Richardson Topper Jr. 580

Similar to the Topper Jr. 480 with color finish similar to 188 Deluxe. Made from 1958 to 1962.

Estimated Value: **Excellent:** **$140.00**
Very good: **$110.00**

Harrington & Richardson Folding Model

Gauge: 28, 410 with light frame; 12, 16, 20, 28, 410 with heavy frame
Action: Box lock; top lever break-open; exposed hammer; single shot
Magazine: None
Barrel: 22" in light frame; 26" in heavy frame; full choke
Finish: Blued; walnut semi-pistol grip stock and tapered forearm; sight
Approximate wt.: 5½ to 6¾ lbs.
Comments: This shotgun has a hinged frame; barrel folds against stock for storage. Made from about 1910 until World War II.

Estimated Value: **Excellent:** **$165.00**
Very good: **$130.00**

Harrington & Richardson Topper 188 Deluxe

Similar to the No. 148 with black, red, blue, green, pink, yellow, or purple lacquered finish; chrome-plated frame; 410 gauge only. Made from the late 1950s to the early 1960s.

Estimated Value: **Excellent:** **$140.00**
Very good: **$110.00**

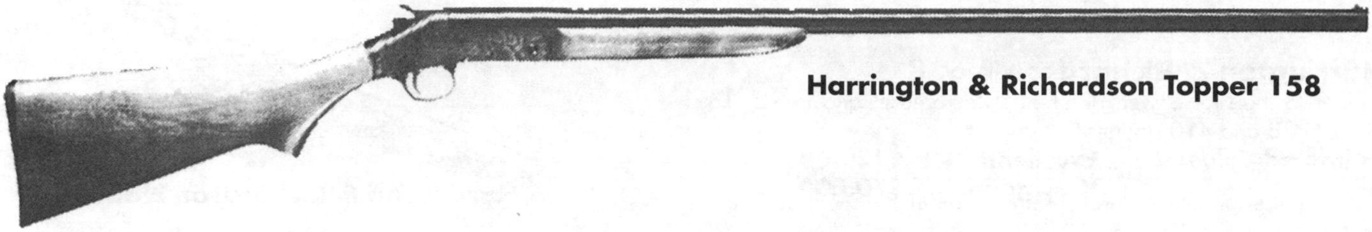

Harrington & Richardson Topper 158

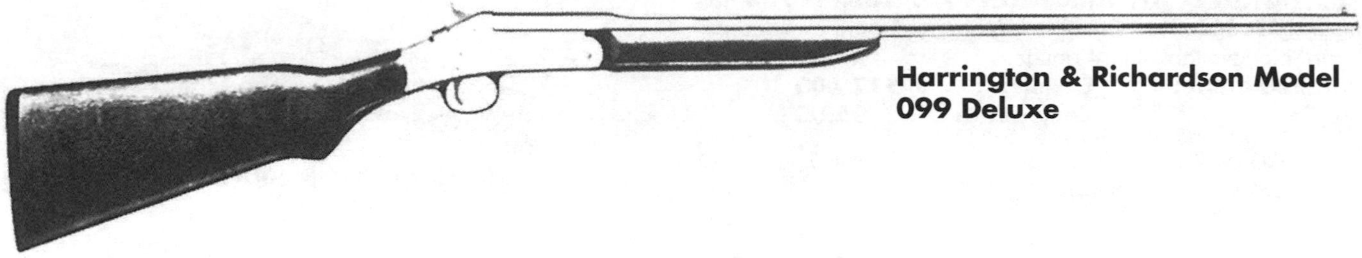

Harrington & Richardson Model 099 Deluxe

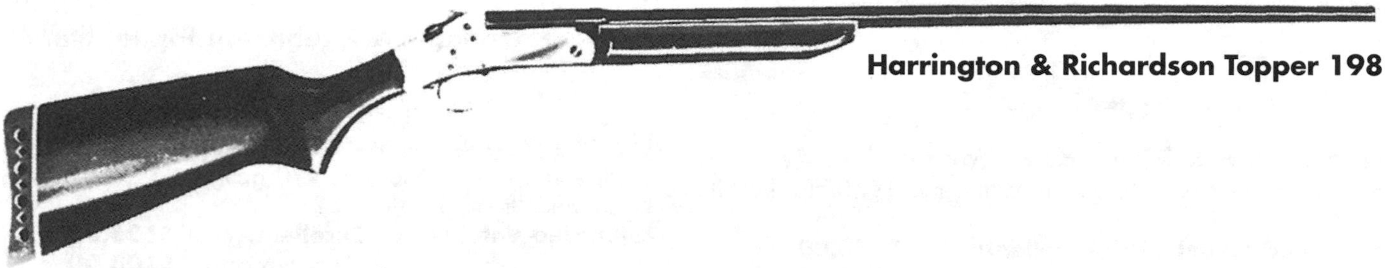

Harrington & Richardson Topper 198

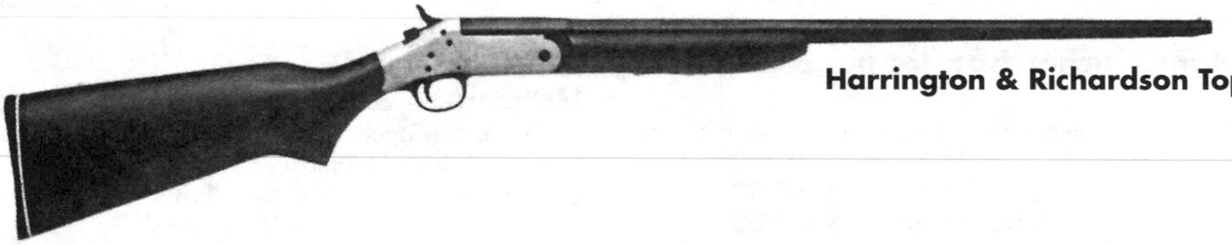

Harrington & Richardson Topper 098

Harrington & Richardson Topper 158 or 058

Gauge: 12, 16, 20, 28, 410
Action: Box lock; side lever, break-open; exposed hammer; single shot
Magazine: None
Barrel: 28" – 36", variety of chokes
Finish: Blued; plain wood, straight or semi-pistol grip stock and tapered forearm; recoil pad on early models
Approximate wt.: 5½ to 6½ lbs.
Comments: Made from the early 1960s to the mid-1970s as Model 158, mid-1970s to 1985 as 058. Also available in 058 combination with 22" rifle barrel in 22 Hornet or 30-30 Win. (Add 20%.)

Estimated Value:	**Excellent:**	**$125.00**
	Very good:	**$100.00**

Harrington & Richardson Model 099 Deluxe

Similar to the Model 158 with electro-less matte nickel finish. Introduced in 1982, discontinued in 1984.

Estimated Value:	**Excellent:**	**$130.00**
	Very good:	**$105.00**

Harrington & Richardson Topper 198 or 098

Similar to the Model 158 or 058 except: 12, 20, or 410 gauge only; black lacquered stock and forearm; nickel-plated frame. Discontinued in 1982, re-introduced in the late 1990s in 12, 16, 20, 28, and 410 gauges.

Estimated Value:	**Excellent:**	**$130.00**
	Very good:	**$105.00**

Harrington & Richardson Topper Jr. 098

Similar to the Topper 098 except has a 22" barrel and is designed for young shooters. Available in 20 gauge and 410 bore only.

Estimated Value:	**Excellent:**	**$130.00**
	Very good:	**$105.00**

Harrington & Richardson Topper Deluxe 098

Similar to the Topper 098 with screw-in choke system; 3½" chamber; add 25% for slug model with rifled barrel and sights.

Estimated Value:	**Excellent:**	**$140.00**
	Very good:	**$110.00**

Harrington & Richardson Topper Jr. Classic

Similar to the Topper Jr. 098 except with blued barrel and frame and checkered American black walnut stock and forearm.

Estimated Value:	**New (retail):**	**$169.95**
	Excellent:	**$120.00**
	Very good:	**$ 95.00**

Harrington & Richardson Model 258 Handy Gun

Similar to the Model 058 combination shotgun/rifle with nickel finish, 22" barrel; 20 gauge with 22 Hornet, 30-30, 44 magnum, 357 magnum, or 357 maximum rifle barrel; includes case. Produced in the mid-1980s.

Estimated Value:	**Excellent:**	**$200.00**
	Very good:	**$160.00**

Harrington & Richardson Topper Buck 162

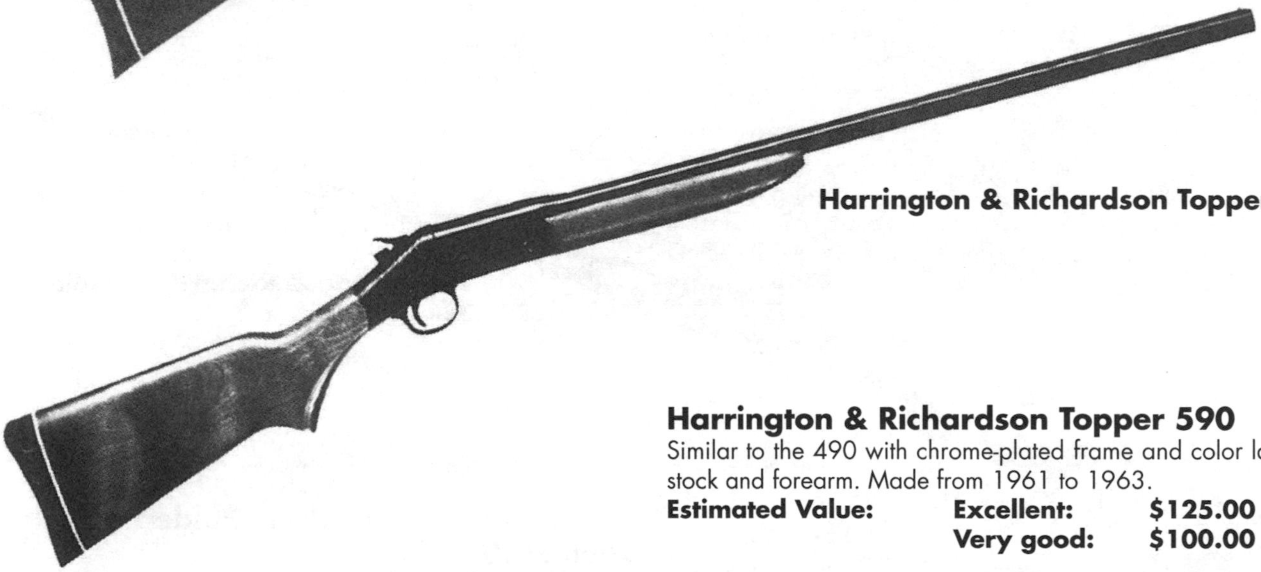

Harrington & Richardson Topper 490

Harrington & Richardson Topper 590

Similar to the 490 with chrome-plated frame and color lacquered stock and forearm. Made from 1961 to 1963.

Estimated Value:	**Excellent:**	**$125.00**
	Very good:	**$100.00**

Harrington & Richardson Topper 490 and 490 Greenwing

A youth version of the Model 158 and 058 with 26" barrel; shorter stock; 20, 28 and 410 gauges only. Greenwing has higher quality finish (1980 – 1986). Made from the early 1960s to 1986.

Estimated Value:	**Excellent:**	**$135.00**
	Very good:	**$110.00**

Harrington & Richardson Topper Buck162

Similar to the Model 158 and 058 with a 24" cylinder bore barrel for slugs; equipped with sights.

Estimated Value:	**Excellent:**	**$150.00**
	Very good:	**$120.00**

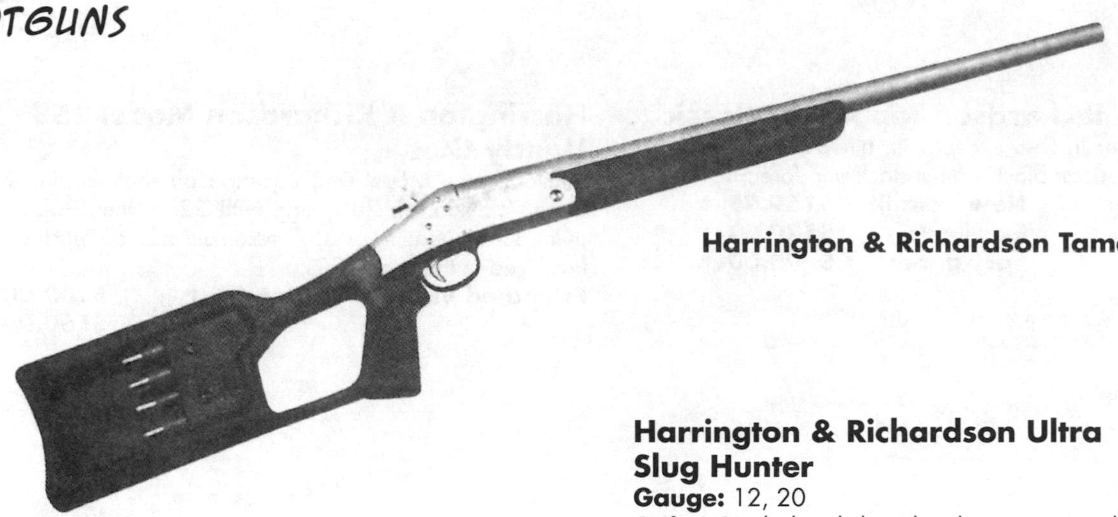

Harrington & Richardson Tamer

Harrington & Richardson Tamer

Gauge: 410, 3" chamber
Action: Box lock; side lever break-open, exposed hammer, single shot
Magazine: None, single shot
Barrel: 19" matte nickel
Finish: Matte nickel; black synthetic thumbhole pistol grip stock and forearm; shell storage in stock
Approximate wt.: 6 lbs.
Comments: Designed for harsh climates.

Estimated Value:	**New (retail):**	**$182.99**
	Excellent:	**$135.00**
	Very good:	**$110.00**

Harrington & Richardson Ultra Slug Hunter

Gauge: 12, 20
Action: Box lock; side lever break-open, exposed hammer, single shot
Magazine: None, single shot
Barrel: 22", or 24" heavy barrel
Finish: Blued; Monte Carlo walnut-stained checkered hardwood, semi-pistol grip stock and semi-beavertail forearm; swivels; deluxe model available with deluxe camouflage laminate finish and camouflage sling
Approximate wt.: 7 to 9 lbs.
Comments: Introduced in 12 gauge in 1995. In 1996, 20 gauge was added. Add 15% for Deluxe model; 20% for Whitetails Deluxe model.

Estimated Value:	**Excellent:**	**$195.00**
	Very good:	**$155.00**

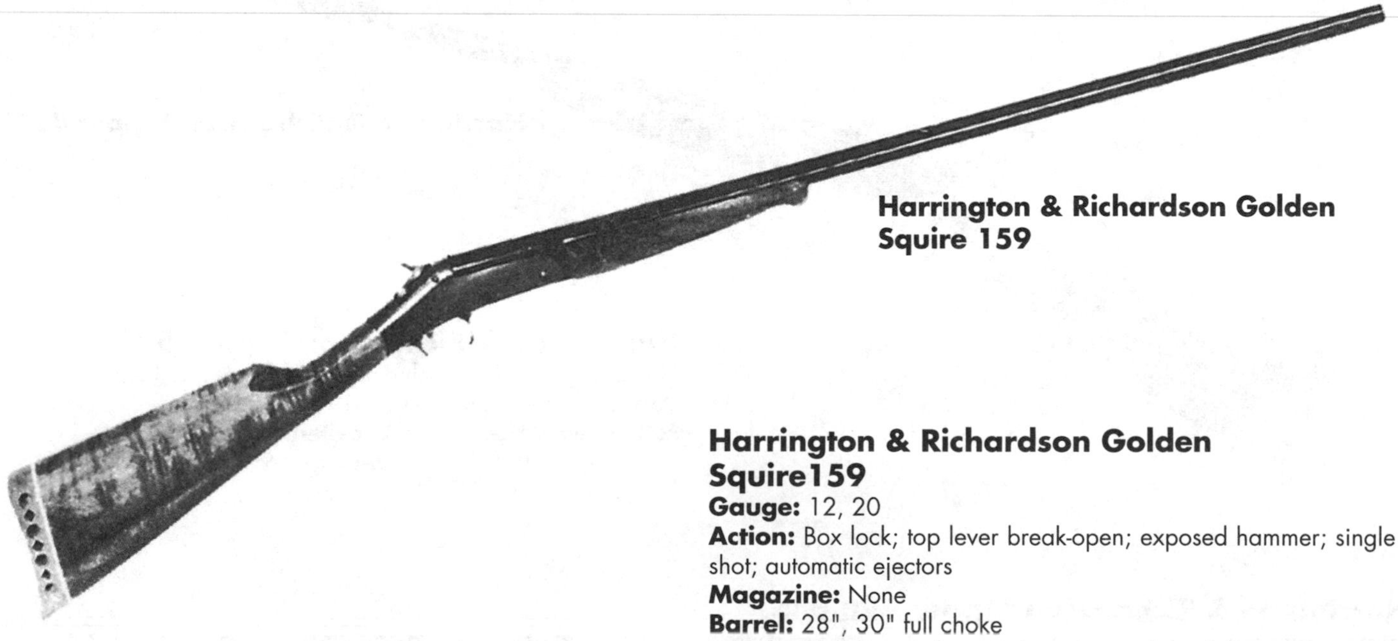

Harrington & Richardson Golden Squire 159

Harrington & Richardson Golden Squire Jr. 459

Similar to the 159 with a 26" barrel and shorter stock.

Estimated Value:	**Excellent:**	**$140.00**
	Very good:	**$110.00**

Harrington & Richardson Golden Squire159

Gauge: 12, 20
Action: Box lock; top lever break-open; exposed hammer; single shot; automatic ejectors
Magazine: None
Barrel: 28", 30" full choke
Finish: Blued; wood, straight grip stock and lipped forearm; recoil pad
Approximate wt.: 6½ lbs.
Comments: Made in the mid-1960s.

Estimated Value:	**Excellent:**	**$125.00**
	Very good:	**$100.00**

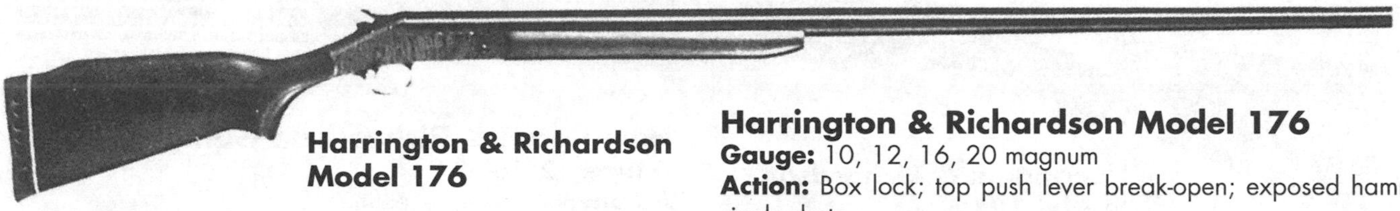

Harrington & Richardson Model 176

Harrington & Richardson Model 176

Gauge: 10, 12, 16, 20 magnum
Action: Box lock; top push lever break-open; exposed hammer; single shot
Magazine: None
Barrel: 32" or 36" full choke in 10 or 12 gauge; 32" full choke in 16 or 20 gauge
Finish: Blued; case hardened frame; plain hardwood Monte Carlo pistol grip stock and forearm; recoil pad
Approximate wt.: 8 to 10 lbs.
Comments: Produced from the late 1970s to the mid-1980s. All guns except 10 gauge discontinued in 1982.

Estimated Value:	**Excellent:**	**$150.00**
	Very good:	**$120.00**

Harrington & Richardson Model 176 Slug

Similar to the Model 176 with a 28" cylinder bore slug barrel; rifle sights; swivels. Produced from 1982 to 1985.

Estimated Value:	**Excellent:**	**$165.00**
	Very good:	**$135.00**

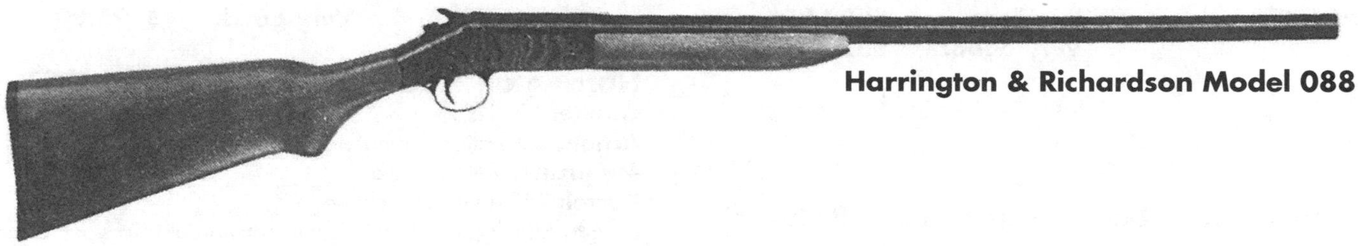

Harrington & Richardson Model 088

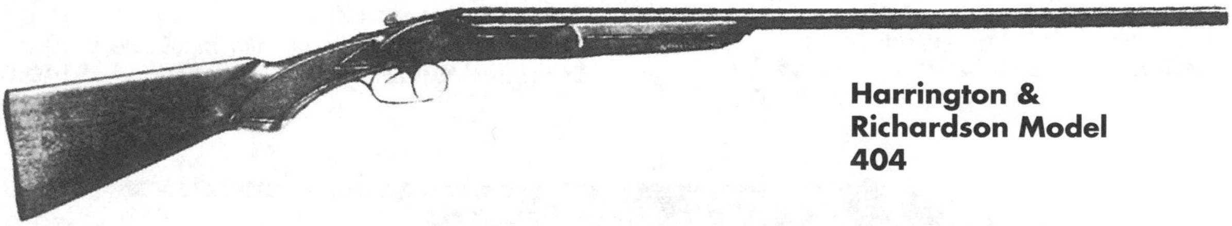

Harrington & Richardson Model 404

Harrington & Richardson Model 088

Gauge: 12, 16, 20, 410, regular or magnum
Action: Box lock; top lever break-open; exposed hammer; single shot
Magazine: None
Barrel: 28" modified or full in 12 gauge; 28" modified in 16 gauge; 26" modified or full in 20 gauge; 25" full in 410
Finish: Blued; case hardened frame; plain hardwood semi-pistol grip stock and forearm
Approximate wt.: 6 lbs.
Comments: An inexpensive line of all-purpose shotguns produced from the late 1970s to the mid-1980s.

Estimated Value:	**Excellent:**	**$125.00**
	Very good:	**$100.00**

Harrington & Richardson Model 088 Jr.

Similar to the Model 088 with a scaled-down stock and forearm; 25" barrel in 20 or 410 gauge.

Estimated Value:	**Excellent:**	**$135.00**
	Very good:	**$110.00**

Harrington & Richardson Model 404

Gauge: 12, 20, 410
Action: Box lock; side lever break-open
Magazine: None
Barrel: Side-by-side double barrel; 26", 28" variety of choke combinations
Finish: Blued; checkered wood semi-pistol grip stock and forearm
Approximate wt.: 5¾ to 7½ lbs.
Comments: Made from the late 1960s to the early 1970s.

Estimated Value:	**Excellent:**	**$225.00**
	Very good:	**$180.00**

Harrington & Richardson Model 404C

Similar to the 404 with Monte Carlo stock.

Estimated Value:	**Excellent:**	**$250.00**
	Very good:	**$200.00**

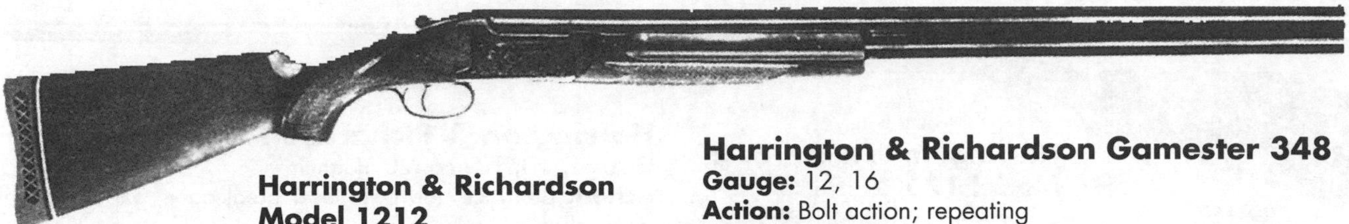

Harrington & Richardson Model 1212

Harrington & Richardson Model 1212

Gauge: 12
Action: Box lock; top lever break-open; single selective trigger
Magazine: None
Barrel: Over and under double barrel; 28" improved modified over improved cylinder; ventilated rib
Finish: Blued; decorated frame; checkered walnut pistol grip stock and forearm
Approximate wt.: 7 lbs.
Comments: Introduced in the mid-1970s. Manufactured in Spain for H&R. Discontinued in 1980.

Estimated Value:	**Excellent:**	**$400.00**
	Very good:	**$320.00**

Harrington & Richardson Model 1212 Waterfowl

Similar to the Model 1212 in 12 gauge magnum; 30" full choke over modified barrel; ventilated recoil pad.

Estimated Value:	**Excellent:**	**$365.00**
	Very good:	**$295.00**

Harrington & Richardson Gamester 348

Gauge: 12, 16
Action: Bolt action; repeating
Magazine: 2-shot
Barrel: 28" full choke
Finish: Blued; plain wood, semi-pistol grip stock and forearm
Approximate wt.: 7 lbs.
Comments: Made from about 1950 to 1954.

Estimated Value:	**Excellent:**	**$110.00**
	Very good:	**$ 90.00**

Harrington & Richardson Gamester 349 Deluxe

Similar to the 348 Model with adjustable choke; 26" barrel; recoil pad.

Estimated Value:	**Excellent:**	**$115.00**
	Very good:	**$ 95.00**

Harrington & Richardson Huntsman 351

Gauge: 12, 16
Action: Bolt action; repeating
Magazine: 2-shot tubular
Barrel: 26" adjustable choke
Finish: Blued; plain Monte Carlo semi-pistol grip stock and forearm; recoil pad
Approximate wt.: 7 lbs.
Comments: Made from the mid- to the late 1950s.

Estimated Value:	**Excellent:**	**$140.00**
	Very good:	**$110.00**

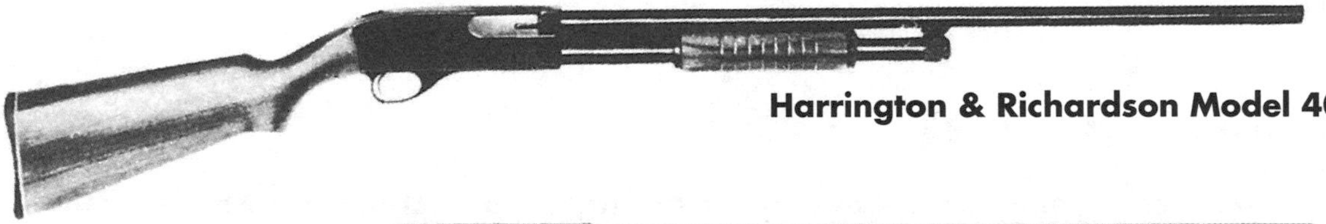

Harrington & Richardson Model 400

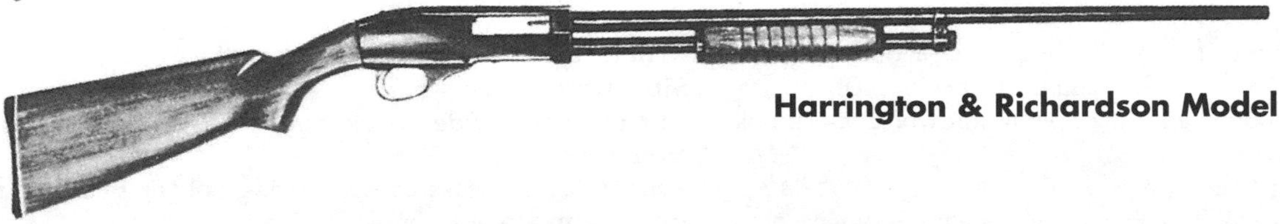

Harrington & Richardson Model 402

Harrington & Richardson Model 400

Gauge: 12, 16, 20
Action: Slide action; hammerless; repeating
Magazine: 5-shot tubular
Barrel: 28" full choke
Finish: Blued; semi-pistol grip stock and grooved slide handle; recoil pad on 12 and 16 gauges
Approximate wt.: 7½ lbs.
Comments: Made from the mid-1950s to the late 1960s.

Estimated Value:	**Excellent:**	**$175.00**
	Very good:	**$140.00**

Harrington & Richardson Model 401

Similar to the 400 with adjustable choke. Made in the early 1960s.

Estimated Value:	**Excellent:**	**$200.00**
	Very good:	**$160.00**

Harrington & Richardson Model 402

Similar to the 400 in 410 gauge only.

Estimated Value:	**Excellent:**	**$210.00**
	Very good:	**$165.00**

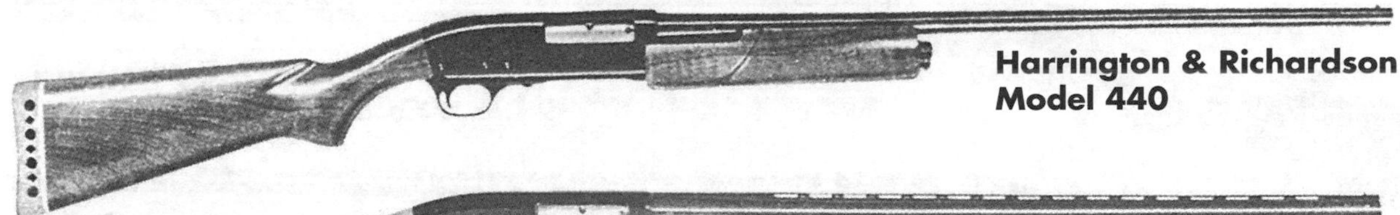

Harrington & Richardson Model 440

Harrington & Richardson Model 442

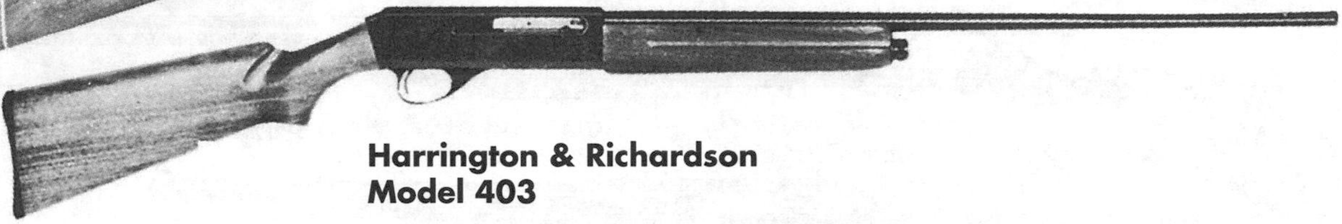

Harrington & Richardson Model 403

Harrington & Richardson Model 403

Gauge: 410
Action: Semiautomatic
Magazine: 4-shot tubular
Barrel: 26" full choke
Finish: Blued; wood semi-pistol grip stock and fluted forearm
Approximate wt.: 5¾ lbs.
Comments: Made in the mid-1960s.

Estimated Value:	**Excellent:**	**$300.00**
	Very good:	**$240.00**

Harrington & Richardson Model 440

Gauge: 12, 16, 20
Action: Slide action; hammerless; repeating
Magazine: 4-shot clip
Barrel: 24" – 28" variety of chokes
Finish: Blued; walnut semi-pistol grip stock and forearm; recoil pad
Approximate wt.: 7 lbs.
Comments: Made from the early to the mid-1970s.

Estimated Value:	**Excellent:**	**$180.00**
	Very good:	**$145.00**

Harrington & Richardson Model 442

Similar to the 440 with a ventilated rib and checkering.

Estimated Value:	**Excellent:**	**$210.00**
	Very good:	**$165.00**

HIGH STANDARD

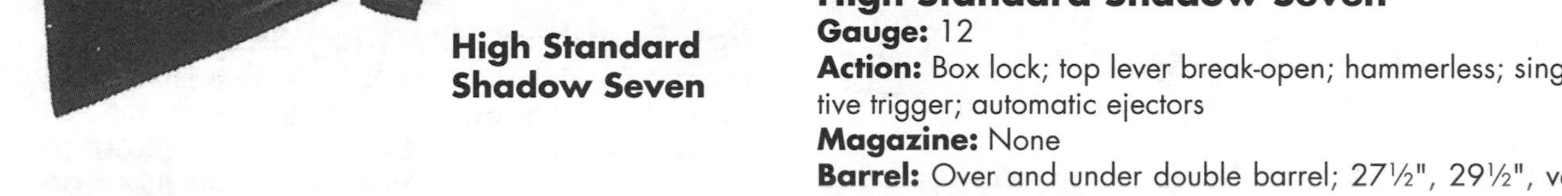

High Standard Shadow Indy

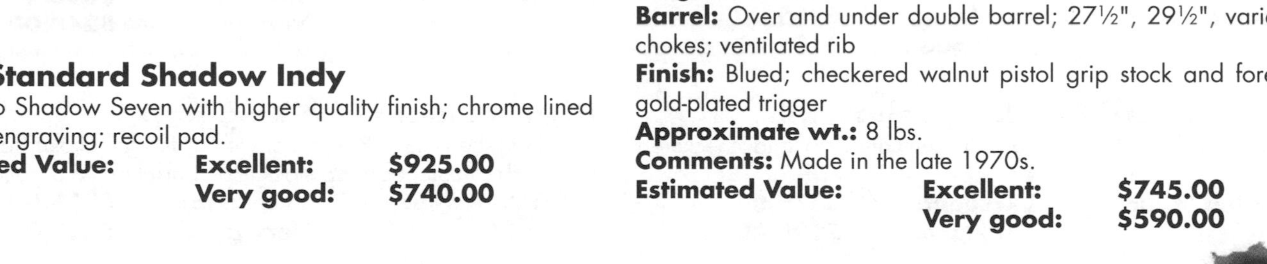

High Standard Shadow Seven

High Standard Shadow Indy

Similar to Shadow Seven with higher quality finish; chrome lined barrels; engraving; recoil pad.

Estimated Value:	**Excellent:**	**$925.00**
	Very good:	**$740.00**

High Standard Shadow Seven

Gauge: 12
Action: Box lock; top lever break-open; hammerless; single selective trigger; automatic ejectors
Magazine: None
Barrel: Over and under double barrel; 27½", 29½", variety of chokes; ventilated rib
Finish: Blued; checkered walnut pistol grip stock and forearm; gold-plated trigger
Approximate wt.: 8 lbs.
Comments: Made in the late 1970s.

Estimated Value:	**Excellent:**	**$745.00**
	Very good:	**$590.00**

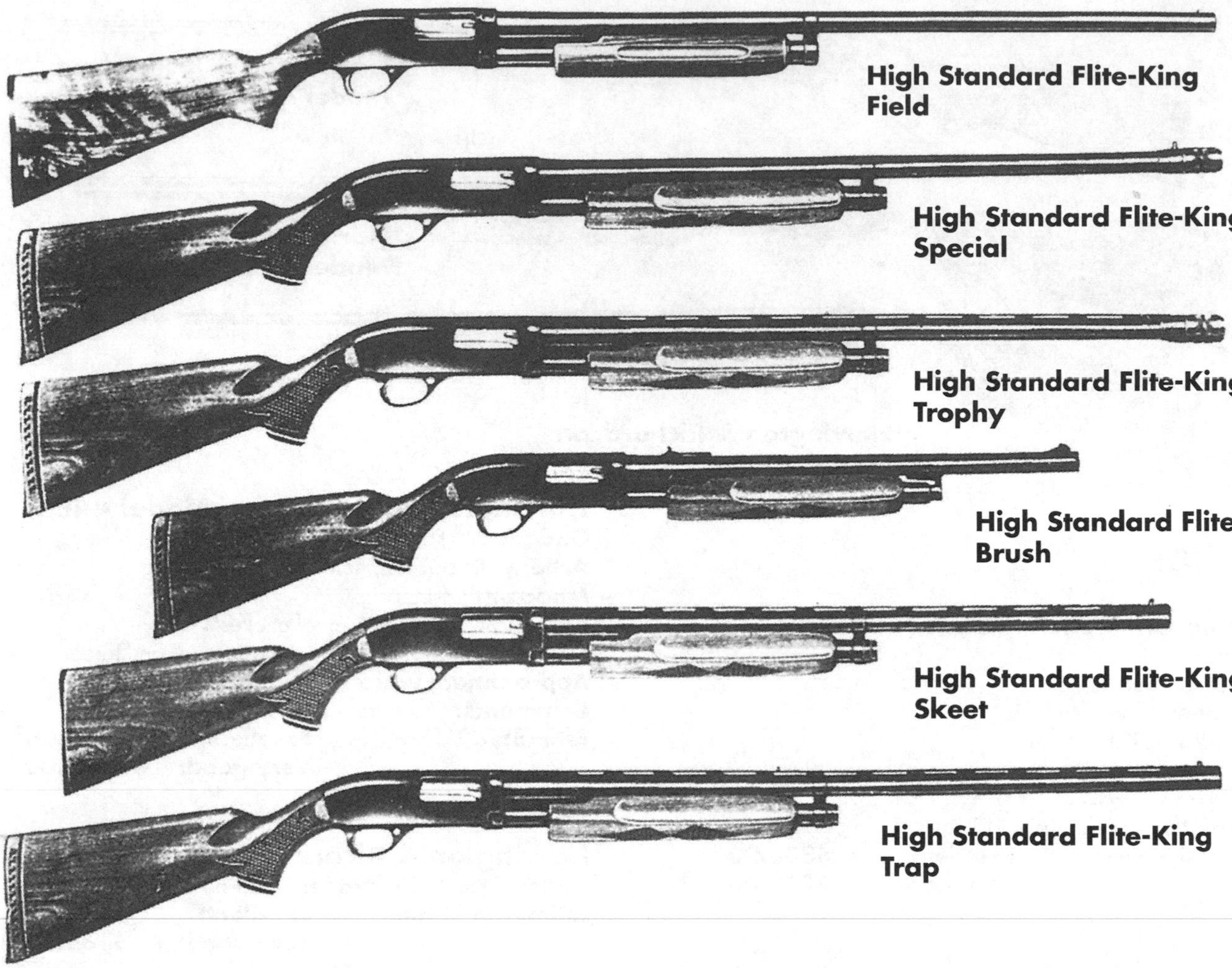

High Standard Flite-King Field

Gauge: 12, 16, 20, 410
Action: Slide action; hammerless; repeating
Magazine: 5-shot tubular; 4-shot tubular in 20 gauge
Barrel: 26" improved cylinder; 28" modified; 30" full chokes
Finish: Blued; plain walnut semi-pistol grip stock and grooved slide handle
Approximate wt.: 6 to 7¼ lbs.
Comments: Made from the early 1960s to the late 1970s.

Estimated Value:	**Excellent:**	**$250.00**
	Very good:	**$200.00**

High Standard Flite-King Special

Similar to Flite-King Field with an adjustable choke and 27" barrel. No. 410 gauge.

Estimated Value:	**Excellent:**	**$235.00**
	Very good:	**$185.00**

High Standard Flite-King Deluxe Rib

Similar to the Flite-King Field with ventilated rib and checkered wood.

Estimated Value:	**Excellent:**	**$275.00**
	Very good:	**$220.00**

High Standard Flite-King Trophy

Similar to the Deluxe Rib model with an adjustable choke and 27" barrel. No. 410 gauge.

Estimated Value:	**Excellent:**	**$300.00**
	Very good:	**$240.00**

High Standard Flite-King Brush

Similar to the Flite-King Field with an 18" or 20" cylinder bore barrel; rifle sights. 12 gauge only.

Estimated Value:	**Excellent:**	**$250.00**
	Very good:	**$200.00**

High Standard Flite-King Skeet

Similar to the Deluxe Rib model with a skeet choke; 26" ventilated rib barrel. Not available in 16 gauge.

Estimated Value:	**Excellent:**	**$300.00**
	Very good:	**$240.00**

High Standard Flite-King Trap

Similar to the Deluxe Rib model with a 30" full choke barrel; ventilated rib; recoil pad; trap stock. 26" barrel on 410 gauge.

Estimated Value:	**Excellent:**	**$275.00**
	Very good:	**$220.00**

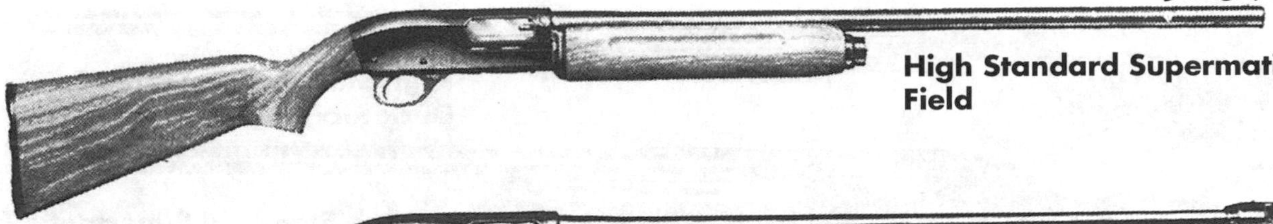

High Standard Supermatic Field

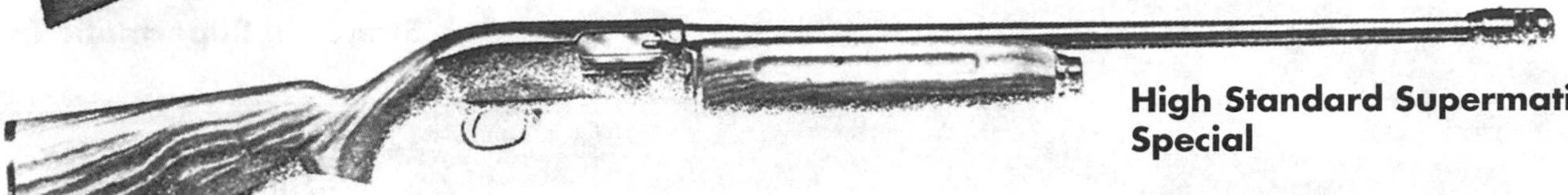

High Standard Supermatic Special

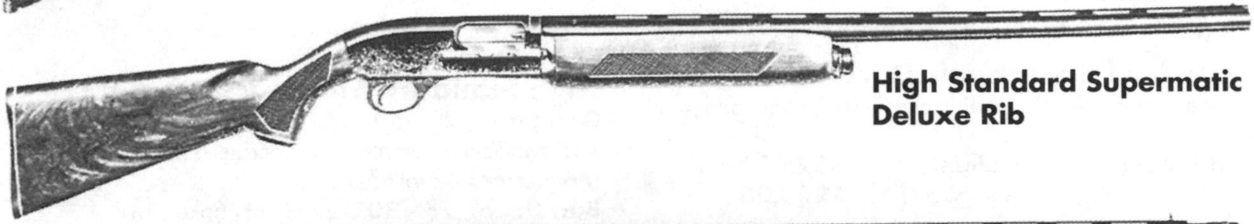

High Standard Supermatic Deluxe Rib

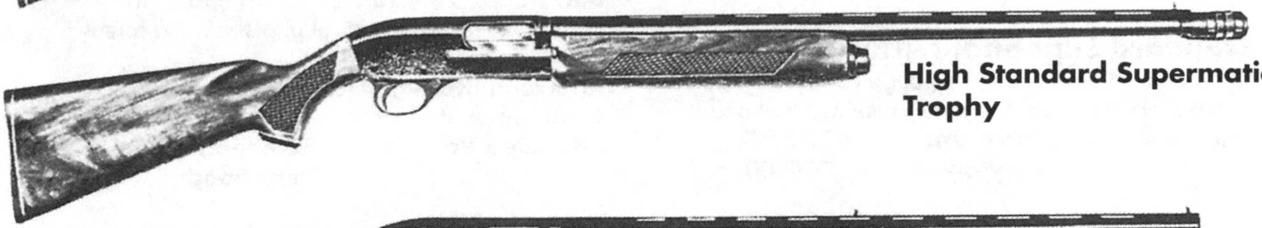

High Standard Supermatic Trophy

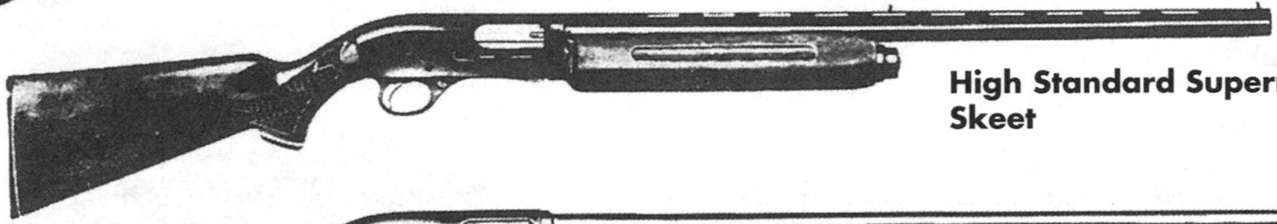

High Standard Supermatic Skeet

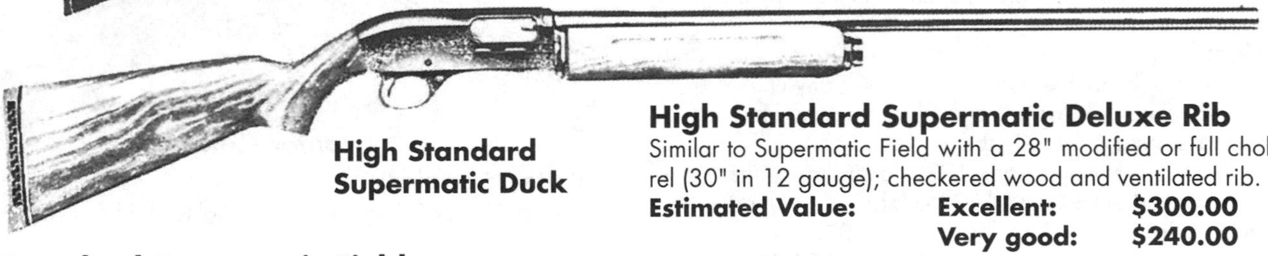

High Standard Supermatic Duck

High Standard Supermatic Field

Gauge: 12, 20, 20 magnum
Action: Semiautomatic, gas-operated; hammerless
Magazine: 4-shot tubular; 3-shot tubular in 20 magnum
Barrel: In 12 gauge: 26" improved; 28" modified or full, 30" full chokes. In 20 gauge: 26" improved; 28" modified or full chokes.
Finish: Blued; plain walnut semi-pistol grip stock and fluted forearm
Approximate wt.: 7 to 7½ lbs.
Comments: Available from about 1960 to the late 1970s; 20 gauge magnum from 1963 to the late 1970s.

Estimated Value:	**Excellent:**	**$315.00**
	Very good:	**$255.00**

High Standard Supermatic Special

Similar to the Supermatic Field with adjustable choke and 27" barrel.

Estimated Value:	**Excellent:**	**$275.00**
	Very good:	**$220.00**

High Standard Supermatic Deluxe Rib

Similar to Supermatic Field with a 28" modified or full choke barrel (30" in 12 gauge); checkered wood and ventilated rib.

Estimated Value:	**Excellent:**	**$300.00**
	Very good:	**$240.00**

High Standard Supermatic Trophy

Similar to the Supermatic Field with a 27" barrel; adjustable choke; ventilated rib; checkering.

Estimated Value:	**Excellent:**	**$325.00**
	Very good:	**$260.00**

High Standard Supermatic Skeet

Similar to Supermatic Field with a 26" ventilated rib barrel; skeet choke; checkered wood.

Estimated Value:	**Excellent:**	**$300.00**
	Very good:	**$240.00**

High Standard Supermatic Duck

Similar to the Supermatic Field in 12 gauge magnum with a 30" full choke barrel and recoil pad. Made from the early 1960s to the mid-1960s.

Estimated Value:	**Excellent:**	**$300.00**
	Very good:	**$240.00**

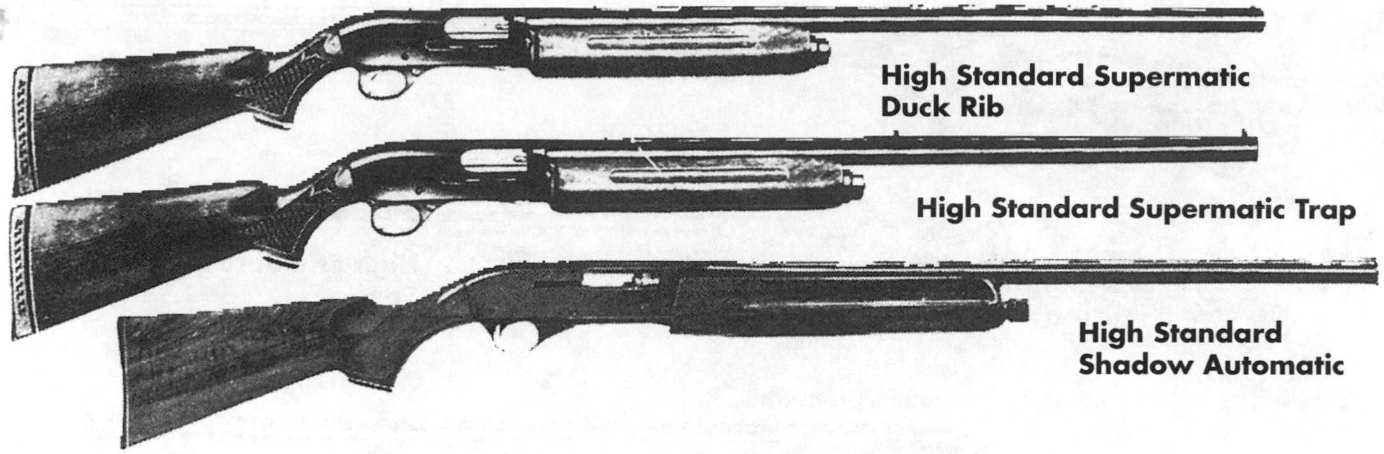

High Standard Supermatic Duck Rib

High Standard Supermatic Trap

High Standard Shadow Automatic

High Standard Supermatic Duck Rib

Similar to the Supermatic Duck with checkered wood and ventilated rib.

Estimated Value: **Excellent:** **$325.00**
Very good: **$260.00**

High Standard Supermatic Trap

Similar to the Supermatic Field in 12 gauge only; 30" full choke; ventilated rib; checkered trap stock and forearm; recoil pad.

Estimated Value: **Excellent:** **$325.00**
Very good: **$260.00**

High Standard Shadow Automatic

Gauge: 12, 20, regular or magnum
Action: Semiautomatic; gas-operated; hammerless
Magazine: 4-shot tubular
Barrel: 26", 28", 30"; variety of chokes; rib
Finish: Blued; walnut pistol grip stock and forearm; sights; recoil pad available
Approximate wt.: 7 lbs.
Comments: Made in the mid-1970s.
Estimated Value: **Excellent:** **$375.00**
Very good: **$300.00**

HUNTER

Hunter Fulton

Gauge: 12, 16, 20
Action: Box lock; top lever break-open; hammerless; double or single trigger
Magazine: None
Barrel: Side-by-side double barrel; 26" to 32" any choke
Finish: Blued; checkered walnut pistol grip stock and forearm
Approximate wt.: 6½ to 7½ lbs.
Comments: Made from the early 1920s until shortly after World War II in the United States. Add $50.00 for single trigger.
Estimated Value: **Excellent:** **$750.00**
Very good: **$600.00**

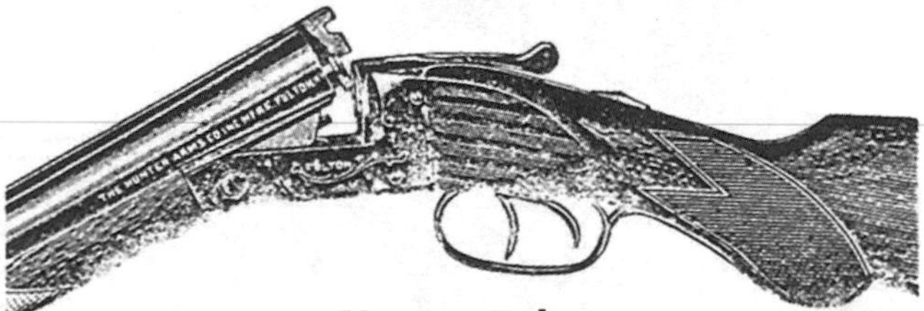

Hunter Fulton

Hunter Special

Similar to Hunter Fulton but higher quality. Add $50.00 for single trigger.

Estimated Value: **Excellent:** **$875.00**
Very good: **$700.00**

ITHACA

Ithaca Victory

Gauge: 12
Action: Box lock; top lever break-open; hammerless; single shot
Magazine: None
Barrel: 34" full choke; ventilated rib; trap grade
Finish: Blued; engraving; checkered pistol grip stock and forearm
Approximate wt.: 8 lbs.
Comments: Made from the early 1920s to World War II. Other grades in higher quality available, valued up to $6,000.00. Prices here are for standard grade. Made in five grades.
Estimated Value: **Excellent:** **$1,500.00**
Very good: **$1,200.00**

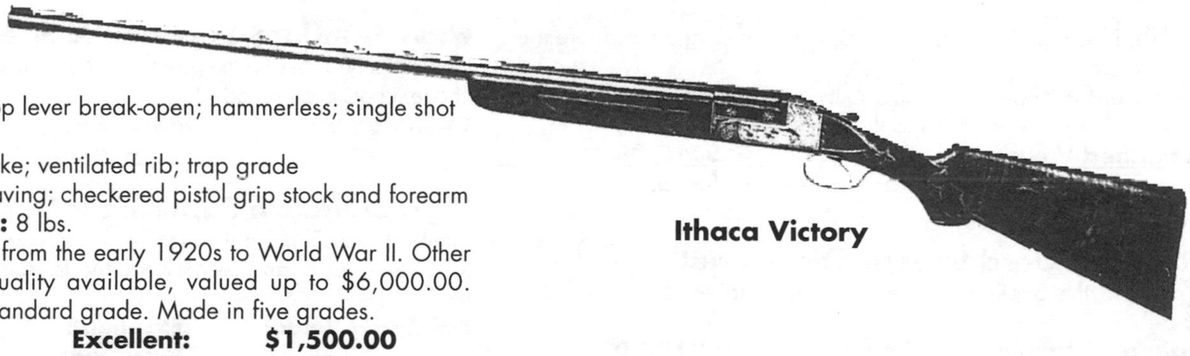

Ithaca Victory

Ithaca Hammerless Double Field Grade

Gauge: 12, 16, 20, 28, 410
Action: Box lock; top lever break-open; hammerless
Magazine: None
Barrel: Side-by-side double barrel; 26" – 32"; various chokes
Finish: Blued; checkered walnut pistol grip stock and short tapered forearm
Approximate wt.: 6 to 10 lbs.
Comments: Made in this style from the mid-1920s to the late 1940s. Add $50.00 for automatic ejector, magnum or ventilated rib. Made in eight various grades differing in quality, with values up to $8,000.00. Prices here for standard grade.

Estimated Value:	**Excellent:**	**$975.00**
	Very good:	**$780.00**

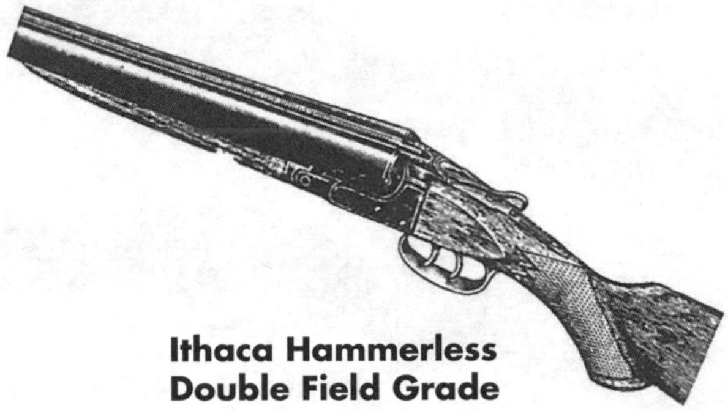

Ithaca Hammerless Double Field Grade

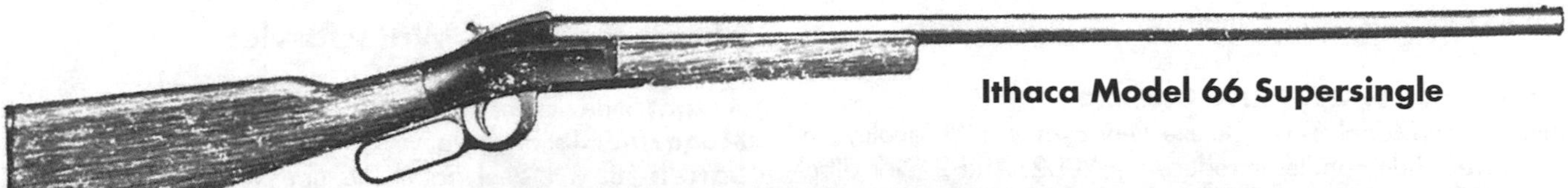

Ithaca Model 66 Supersingle

Ithaca Model 66 Supersingle Youth

Ithaca Model 66 Supersingle Youth

Similar to the 66 with shorter stock; 410 gauge; 25" barrel; recoil pad.

Estimated Value:	**Excellent:**	**$175.00**
	Very good:	**$140.00**

Ithaca Model 66 Supersingle

Gauge: 20, 410
Action: Lever action; exposed hammer; single shot
Magazine: None
Barrel: 26" full choke; 28" full or modified choke, 30" full choke
Finish: Blued; plain or checkered straight stock and forearm
Approximate wt.: 7 lbs.
Comments: Made from 1963 to the late 1970s. Add 20% for ventilated rib.

Estimated Value:	**Excellent:**	**$175.00**
	Very good:	**$140.00**

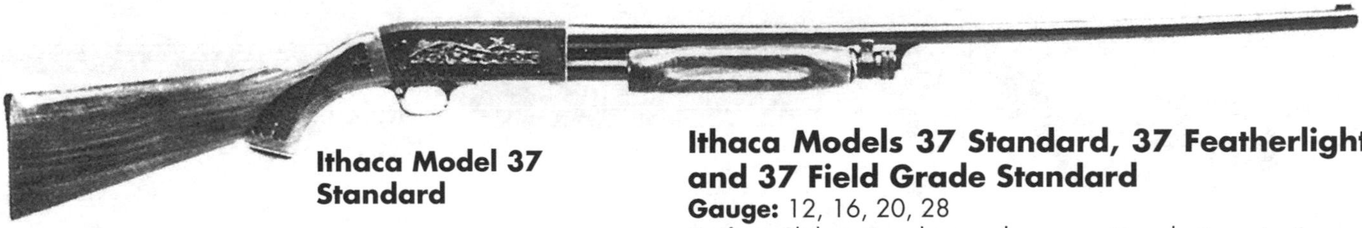

Ithaca Model 37 Standard

Ithaca Models 37V, 37 Featherlight Vent, and 37 Field Grade Vent

Similar to the Model 37 with ventilated rib. Manufactured with three interchangeable choke tubes; discontinued in the late 1980s.

Estimated Value:	**Excellent:**	**$300.00**
	Very good:	**$240.00**

Ithaca Model 37D Deluxe

Similar to the Model 37 with checkered stock and slide handle. Made from the mid-1950s to the 1970s.

Estimated Value:	**Excellent:**	**$400.00**
	Very good:	**$320.00**

Ithaca Models 37 Standard, 37 Featherlight, and 37 Field Grade Standard

Gauge: 12, 16, 20, 28
Action: Slide action; hammerless; repeating; bottom ejection
Magazine: 4-shot tubular
Barrel: 26" – 30" various chokes
Finish: Blued; walnut, semi-pistol grip stock and grooved slide handle; some with checkering
Approximate wt.: 6 to 7 lbs.
Comments: Made from 1937 to 1985; add 25% for magnum with interchangeable choke tubes.

Estimated Value:	**Excellent:**	**$350.00**
	Very good:	**$285.00**

Ithaca Model 37DV Deluxe Vent

Similar to the Model 37D Deluxe with ventilated rib. A youth model is available with a 24" barrel.

Estimated Value:	**Excellent:**	**$475.00**
	Very good:	**$380.00**

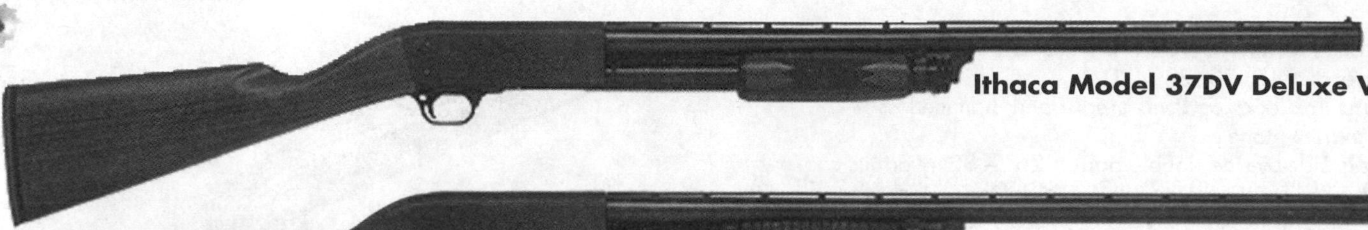

Ithaca Model 37DV Deluxe Vent

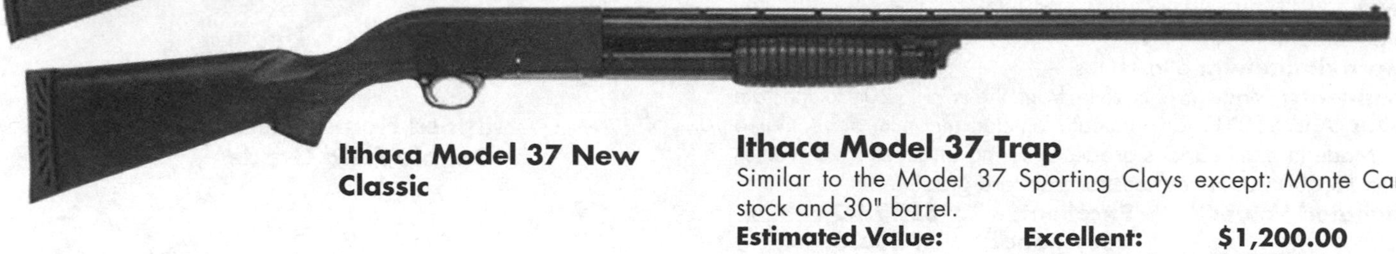

Ithaca Model 37 New Classic

Ithaca Model 37 New Classic

Similar to the Model 37DV Deluxe Vent except: high quality finish; grooved slide handle. Introduced in 2002. Add 2% for Ultralight model.

Estimated Value:	**Excellent:**	**$650.00**
	Very good:	**$520.00**

Ithaca Model 37 Sporting Clays

Similar to the Model 37DV Deluxe Vent except: configured for Sporting Clays; straight stock; 24", 26", or 28" barrel; antique-finished receiver with scrollwork engraving and gold inlay. Introduced in 2002.

Estimated Value:	**Excellent:**	**$1,100.00**
	Very good:	**$ 880.00**

Ithaca Model 37 Trap

Similar to the Model 37 Sporting Clays except: Monte Carlo stock and 30" barrel.

Estimated Value:	**Excellent:**	**$1,200.00**
	Very good:	**$ 950.00**

Ithaca Model 37 Waterfowler

Gauge: 12 (3" magnum)
Action: Slide action; hammerless; repeating
Magazine: 4-shot tubular
Barrel: 28" with steel-shot choke tube; ventilated rib
Finish: Camouflage with clear coating; recoil pad
Approximate wt.: 7 lbs.
Comments: Introduced in 2001.

Estimated Value:	**Excellent:**	**$500.00**
	Very good:	**$400.00**

Ithaca Model 37 Turkeyslayer

Gauge: 12, 20
Action: Slide action; hammerless; repeating
Magazine: 4-shot tubular
Barrel: 22"; extended full choke tube; sights
Finish: Blued; synthetic stock and slide handle
Approximate wt.: 6½ to 7 lbs.
Comments: Also available with a shortened youth stock.

Estimated Value:	**Excellent:**	**$475.00**
	Very good:	**$380.00**

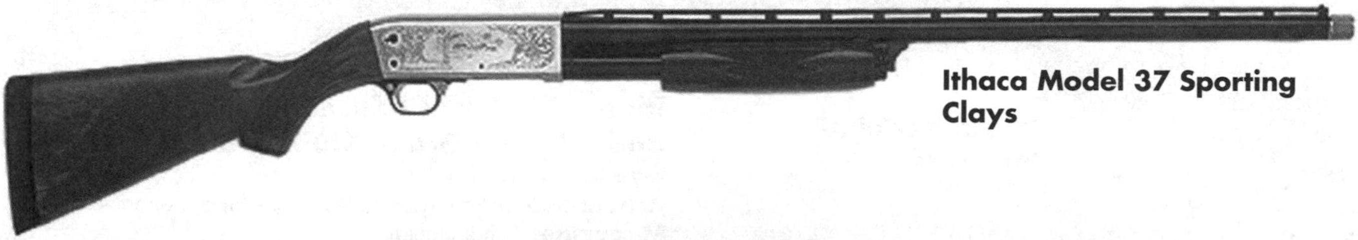

Ithaca Model 37 Sporting Clays

Ithaca Model 37 Trap

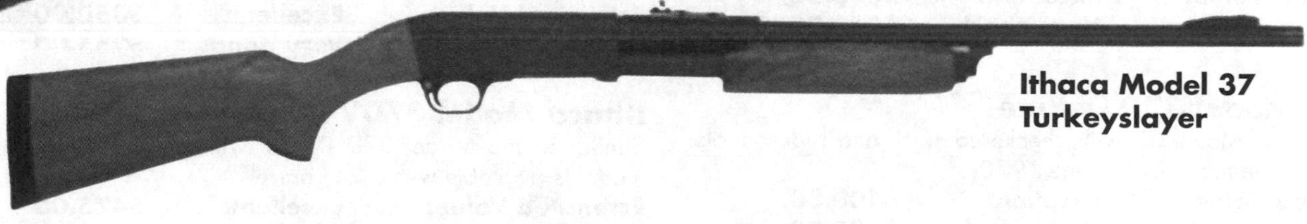

Ithaca Model 37 Turkeyslayer

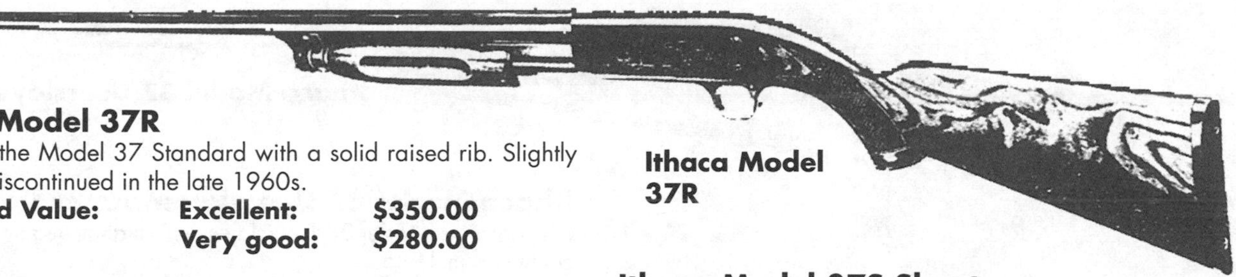

Ithaca Model 37R

Ithaca Model 37R

Similar to the Model 37 Standard with a solid raised rib. Slightly heavier. Discontinued in the late 1960s.

Estimated Value: **Excellent:** **$350.00**
Very good: **$280.00**

Ithaca Model 37R Deluxe

Similar to the Model 37D Deluxe with a raised solid rib. Made in the early 1960s. Checkered fancy walnut stock.

Estimated Value: **Excellent:** **$400.00**
Very good: **$320.00**

Ithaca Model 37T Trap

Similar to the Model 37S Skeet with trap stock; recoil pad; choice wood.

Estimated Value: **Excellent:** **$500.00**
Very good: **$400.00**

Ithaca Model 37 Supreme and 37 Featherlight Supreme

Similar to the Model 37T Target. Discontinued in 1987.

Estimated Value: **Excellent:** **$550.00**
Very good: **$440.00**

Ithaca Model 37S Skeet

Similar to the Model 37 Standard with extended slide handle and ventilated rib. Made in the mid-1950s.

Estimated Value: **Excellent:** **$500.00**
Very good: **$400.00**

Ithaca Model 37T Target

Available in skeet or trap version with high-quality finish and select wood. Replaced the 37S Skeet and 37T Trap. Made from the mid-1950s to about 1961.

Estimated Value: **Excellent:** **$500.00**
Very good: **$400.00**

Ithaca Model 37 Bear Stopper

A short barrel version of the Model 37; 18½" or 20" barrel; 12 gauge; one-hand grip and grooved slide handle; 5- or 8-shot magazine; blued or chrome finish. Add 5% for 8-shot; 10% for chrome. Produced in the early 1980s.

Estimated Value: **Excellent:** **$300.00**
Very good: **$240.00**

Ithaca Model 37 M&P

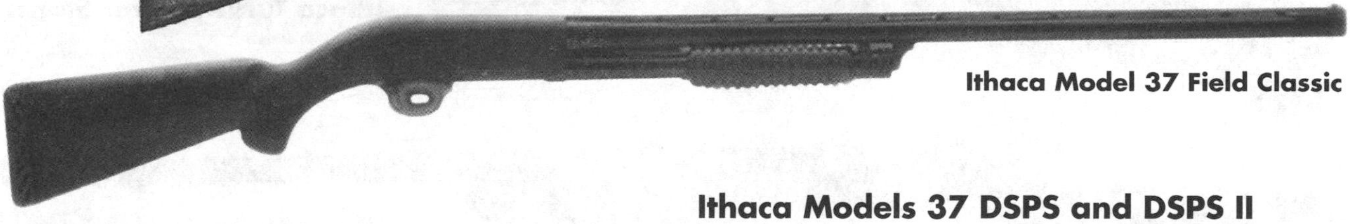

Ithaca Model 37 Field Classic

Ithaca Model 37 Field Classic

Similar to the Model 37 New Classic except: lesser quality finish. Introduced in 2001.

Estimated Value: **Excellent:** **$400.00**
Very good: **$320.00**

Ithaca Models 37 M&P and 87 M&P

Similar to the Model 37 for law enforcement use; 18" or 20" cylinder bore barrel; non-glare tung oil finish; parkerized or chrome finish metal; 5- or 8-shot magazine. Add 10% for chrome (discontinued in 1985); 7% for hand grip. Discontinued in 1987.

Estimated Value: **Excellent:** **$400.00**
Very good: **$320.00**

Ithaca Models 37 DSPS and DSPS II

A law enforcement version of the Model 37 Deerslayer; grooved slide handle; available in regular, parkerized, or chrome finished. Add 5% for 8-shot magazine; 15% for chrome finish (discontinued 1985); 5% less for Model DSPS II; discontinued in 1987.

Estimated Value: **Excellent:** **$400.00**
Very good: **$320.00**

Ithaca Model 37 Homeland Security

Similar to the Model 37 M&P except: available with synthetic or walnut stock and slide handle. Add 6% for ported barrel.

Estimated Value: **Excellent:** **$425.00**
Very good: **$340.00**

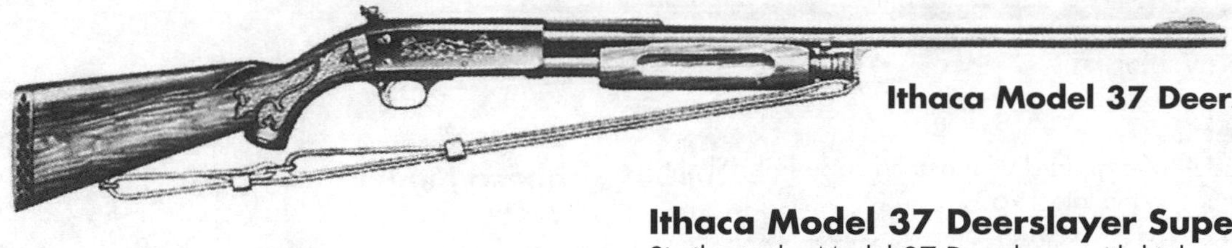

Ithaca Model 37 Deerslayer

Ithaca Model 37 Deerslayer and Deerslayer II

Similar to the Model 37 with a 20" or 25" barrel and rifle sights. Made from the 1960s to 1987; reintroduced in the late 1990s. 12 or 20 gauge. Add 9% for Deerslayer II.

Estimated Value:	**Excellent:**	**$435.00**
	Very good:	**$350.00**

Ithaca Model 37 Deerslayer Super Deluxe

Similar to the Model 37 Deerslayer with higher quality finish. Discontinued in 1985.

Estimated Value:	**Excellent:**	**$420.00**
	Very good:	**$335.00**

Ithaca Model 37 Deerslayer III

Similar to the Model 37 Deerslayer II except: 26" heavy barrel; 12 gauge only. Introduced in 2001.

Estimated Value:	**Excellent:**	**$600.00**
	Very good:	**$480.00**

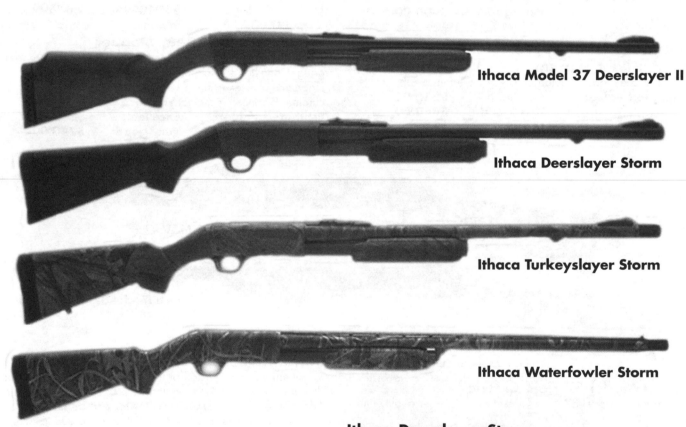

Ithaca Model 37 Deerslayer II

Ithaca Deerslayer Storm

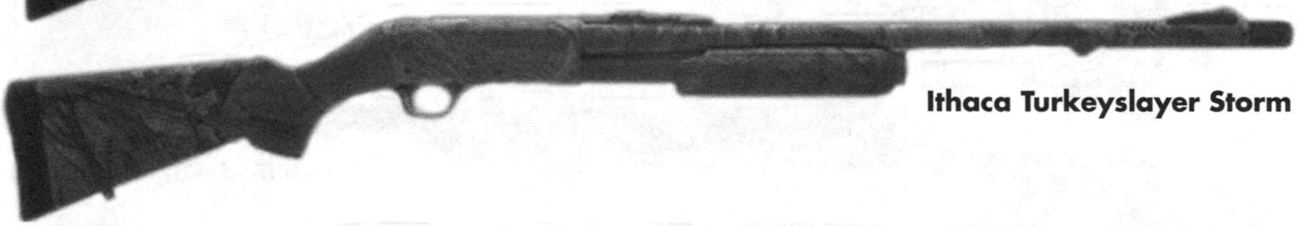

Ithaca Turkeyslayer Storm

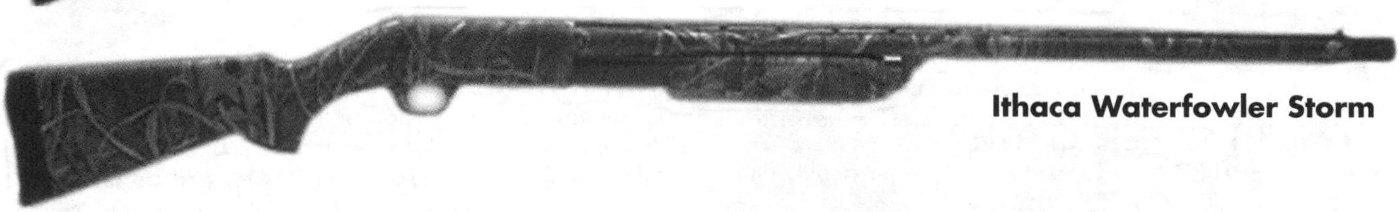

Ithaca Waterfowler Storm

Ithaca Waterfowler Storm

Similar to the Deerslayer Storm and Turkeyslayer Storm with 24", 26", 28", or 30" barrel with extended "Ithaca-choke" waterfowl full steel shot choke tube; camouflage finish.

Estimated Value:	**Excellent:**	**$375.00**
	Very good:	**$300.00**

Ithaca Deerslayer Storm

Similar to the Deerslayer II with parkerized finish and synthetic stock and forearm. Introduced in 2003.

Estimated Value:	**Excellent:**	**$300.00**
	Very good:	**$240.00**

Ithaca Turkeyslayer Storm

Similar to the Deerslayer Storm with a full turkey "Ithaca-choke" extended choke tube; ported barrel and a camouflage finish.

Estimated Value:	**Excellent:**	**$345.00**
	Very good:	**$275.00**

Ithaca Model 37 Camouflage Vent
Similar to the Model 37 Field Grade Vent with a rust-resistant camouflage finish in spring (green) or fall (brown); sling and swivels; 12 gauge, 26" or 28" full choke barrel. Introduced in 1986. Discontinued in 1987.

Estimated Value:	**Excellent:**	**$300.00**
	Very good:	**$240.00**

Ithaca Model 37 Ultra Deerslayer
Similar to the Ultra Featherlight with a 20" barrel for slugs; sights; recoil pad; swivels. Discontinued in 1987.

Estimated Value:	**Excellent:**	**$340.00**
	Very good:	**$270.00**

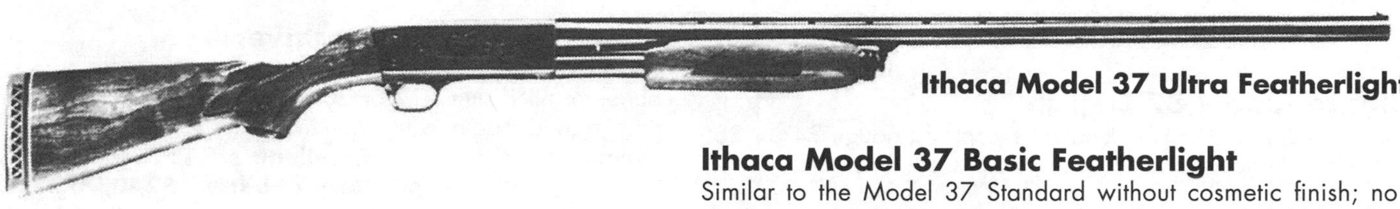

Ithaca Model 37 Ultra Featherlight

Ithaca English-Ultra Featherlight
Gauge: 12, 20
Action: Slide action; hammerless; repeating; aluminum receiver
Magazine: 3-shot tubular
Barrel: 25" full, modified or improved cylinder bore; ventilated rib
Finish: Blued; checkered walnut straight grip stock and slide handle; waterfowl scene on receiver
Approximate wt.: 4¾ lbs.
Comments: A lightweight English stock version of the Model 37 series. Made from 1982 to 1987.

Estimated Value:	**Excellent:**	**$400.00**
	Very good:	**$320.00**

Ithaca Model 37 Basic Featherlight
Similar to the Model 37 Standard without cosmetic finish; no checkering; finished in non-glare tung oil; grooved slide handle; "vapor blasted" metal surfaces with a non-glare finish; add 2% for ventilated rib, 30% for magnum. Introduced in 1979, discontinued in the mid-1980s.

Estimated Value:	**Excellent:**	**$200.00**
	Very good:	**$160.00**

Ithaca Model 37 Ultra Featherlight
A 20 gauge lightweight version of the Model 37; 25" ventilated rib barrel; recoil pad, gold trigger; special grip cap. Introduced in 1979. Currently available with interchangeable choke tubes. Renamed Model 87 in 1987.

Estimated Value:	**Excellent:**	**$300.00**
	Very good:	**$240.00**

Ithaca Model 87 Field

Ithaca Model 87 Field
Gauge: 12, 20
Action: Slide action; hammerless; repeating
Magazine: 3-shot tubular
Barrel: 26", 28", or 30"; 3 choke tubes; 3" chamber; ventilated rib
Finish: Blued; pressed checkered American walnut stock and side handle
Approximate wt.: 6¾ lbs. (20 gauge); 7 lbs. (12 gauge)
Comments: Introduced in 1987 to replace Model 37.

Estimated Value:	**Excellent:**	**$300.00**
	Very good:	**$240.00**

Ithaca Model 87 Deluxe
Same as Model 87 Field except: cut checkered stock and slide handle with a high gloss finish and gold trigger.

Estimated Value:	**Excellent:**	**$325.00**
	Very good:	**$265.00**

Ithaca Model 87 Ultra Field
Same as Model 87 Field except: aluminum receiver; discontinued in 1991.

Estimated Value:	**Excellent:**	**$350.00**
	Very good:	**$280.00**

Ithaca Models 87 M&P and 87DSPS
Same as Model 87 Field except: 12 gauge with 20" plain barrel; dull oil finished wood; parkerized or nickel finish; 5- or 8-shot magazine; fixed cylinder choke; add 25% for nickel finish.

Estimated Value:	**Excellent:**	**$375.00**
	Very good:	**$300.00**

Ithaca Model 87 Supreme
Same as Model 87 Field except: high grade finish and checkering; gold trigger; Raybar iridescent orange sight.

Estimated Value:	**Excellent:**	**$575.00**
	Very good:	**$460.00**

Ithaca Model 87 Turkey

Same as Model 87 Field except: 12 gauge with 24" or 22" barrel; smooth stock and slide handle; fixed full choke barrel or full choke tube; matte blue barrel with oil finished wood or camouflaged finish; add 9% for choke tube or camouflaged finish.

Estimated Value: **Excellent:** **$300.00**
Very good: **$240.00**

Ithaca Model 87 English

Same as English Ultra Featherlight except: 20 gauge 24" or 26" barrel; 3 changeable choke tubes; weighs 6¾ lbs.; steel receiver; introduced in 1987.

Estimated Value: **Excellent:** **$400.00**
Very good: **$320.00**

Ithaca Model 87 Camouflage Field

Same as Model 87 Field except: 12 gauge with 24", 26", or 28" barrel; smooth American walnut stock and grooved slide handle; camouflaged finish.

Estimated Value: **Excellent:** **$325.00**
Very good: **$260.00**

Ithaca Model 87 Deerslayer

Same as Model 87 Field except: 20" or 25" special bore plain barrel for rifled slugs; 12 or 20 gauge; smooth oil finished stock and grooved slide handle; plain matte finished barrel.

Estimated Value: **Excellent:** **$300.00**
Very good: **$240.00**

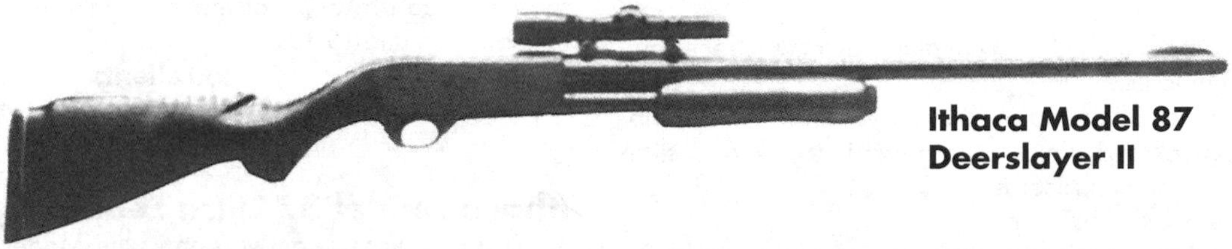

Ithaca Model 87 Deerslayer II

Ithaca Model 87 Deluxe Deerslayer

Same as Model 87 Field except: 20" and 25" barrel length; cut checkering with high gloss finish; plain barrel with Raybar front sight and adjustable rear; gold trigger; special bore slug barrel or rifled barrel; add 8% for rifled barrel.

Estimated Value: **Excellent:** **$325.00**
Very good: **$260.00**

Ithaca Model 87 Deerslayer II

Same as Model 87 Deluxe Deerslayer except: Monte Carlo stock; rifled barrel is permanently screwed into the receiver.

Estimated Value: **Excellent:** **$375.00**
Very good: **$300.00**

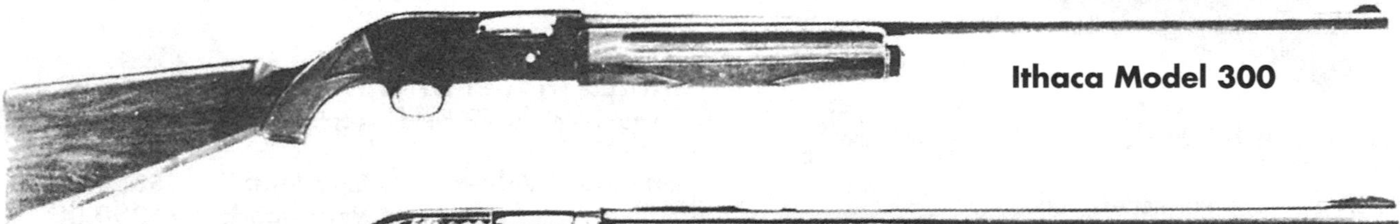

Ithaca Model 300

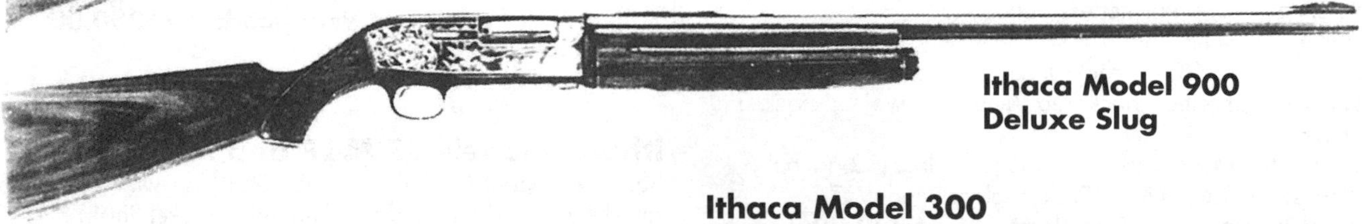

Ithaca Model 900 Deluxe Slug

Ithaca Model 900 Deluxe

Similar to the 300 except: ventilated rib; gold filled engraving; nameplate in stock; gold trigger.

Estimated Value: **Excellent:** **$290.00**
Very good: **$230.00**

Ithaca Model 900 Deluxe Slug

Similar to the 900 Deluxe with a 24" barrel for slugs; rifle sights.

Estimated Value: **Excellent:** **$300.00**
Very good: **$240.00**

Ithaca Model 300

Gauge: 12, 20
Action: Semiautomatic; recoil-operated; hammerless
Magazine: 3-shot tubular
Barrel: 26" improved cylinder; 28" modified or full, 30" full chokes
Finish: Blued; checkered walnut pistol grip stock and forearm
Approximate wt.: 6½ to 7 lbs.
Comments: Made from 1970 to 1973. Add $10.00 for ventilated rib.

Estimated Value: **Excellent:** **$250.00**
Very good: **$200.00**

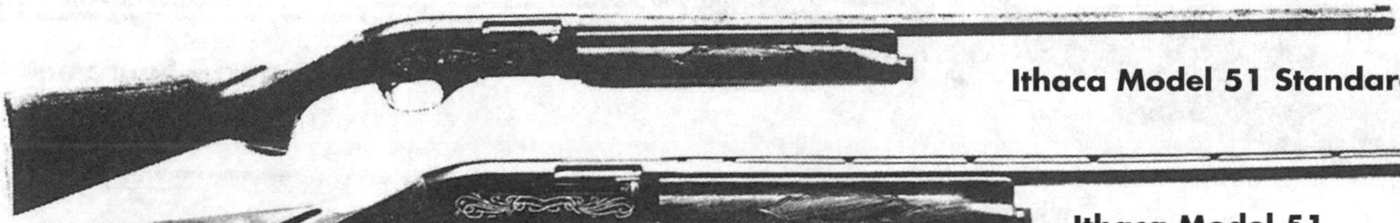

Ithaca Model 51 Standard

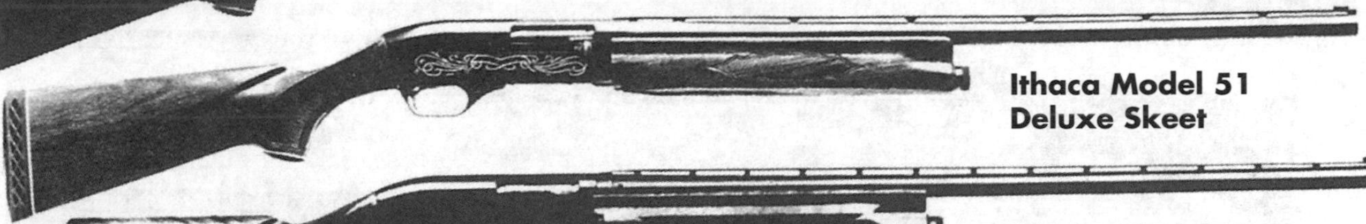

Ithaca Model 51 Deluxe Skeet

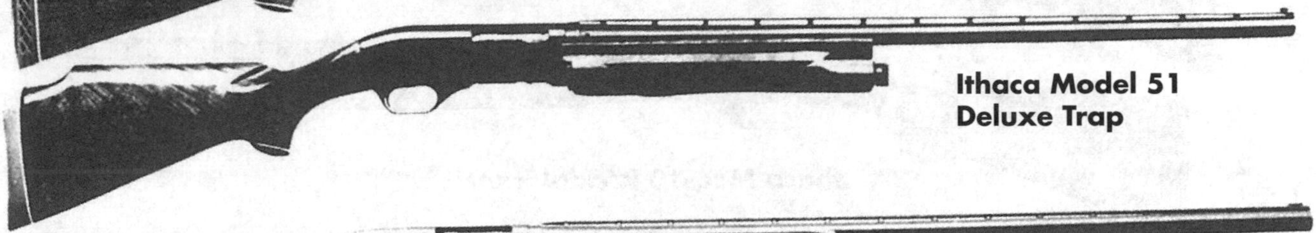

Ithaca Model 51 Deluxe Trap

Ithaca Model 51 Magnum

Ithaca Model 51 Deerslayer

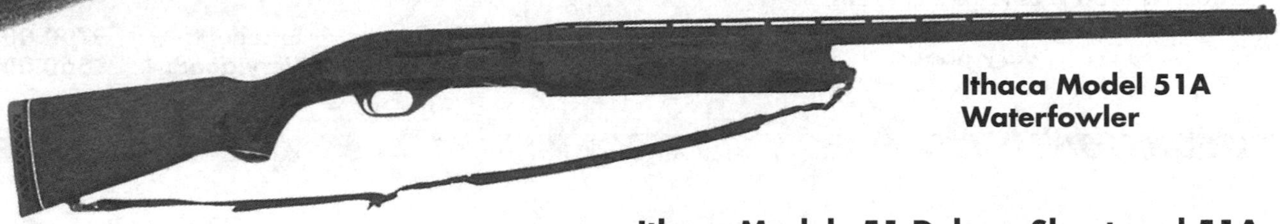

Ithaca Model 51A Waterfowler

Ithaca Models 51 Standard, 51 Featherlight, and 51A

Gauge: 12, 20
Action: Gas-operated, semiautomatic
Magazine: 3-shot tubular
Barrel: 26" – 30", various chokes; some with ventilated rib
Finish: Blued; checkered walnut pistol grip stock and forearm; decorated receiver
Approximate wt.: 7½ lbs.
Comments: Manufactured from 1970 to 1986. Add 12% for ventilated rib.

Estimated Value:	**Excellent:**	**$350.00**
	Very good:	**$280.00**

Ithaca Model 51 Magnum

Similar to the 51 but chambered for magnum shells; ventilated rib.

Estimated Value:	**Excellent:**	**$400.00**
	Very good:	**$320.00**

Ithaca Model 51 Deerslayer

Similar to the Model 51 with 24" barrel for slugs; sights; recoil pad; 12 gauge only.

Estimated Value:	**Excellent:**	**$325.00**
	Very good:	**$260.00**

Ithaca Models 51 Deluxe Skeet and 51A Supreme Skeet

Similar to the 51 with recoil pad; ventilated rib; 28" or 29" skeet choke barrel, 26" after 1985. Discontinued in the late 1980s.

Estimated Value:	**Excellent:**	**$425.00**
	Very good:	**$340.00**

Ithaca Models 51 Deluxe Trap and 51A Supreme Trap

Similar to the Model 51 except: 12 gauge only; select wood; 28" or 30" barrel; recoil pad. Add 5% for Monte Carlo stock. Discontinued in the late 1980s.

Estimated Value:	**Excellent:**	**$400.00**
	Very good:	**$320.00**

Ithaca Models 51A Waterfowler and 51A Turkey Gun

Similar to the Model 51A with matte-finish metal and flat-finish walnut. The Turkey model has a 26" ventilated rib barrel, the Waterfowler has a 30" ventilated rib barrel. Introduced in 1984. Add 10% for camouflage finish. Discontinued in the late 1980s.

Estimated Value:	**Excellent:**	**$400.00**
	Very good:	**$320.00**

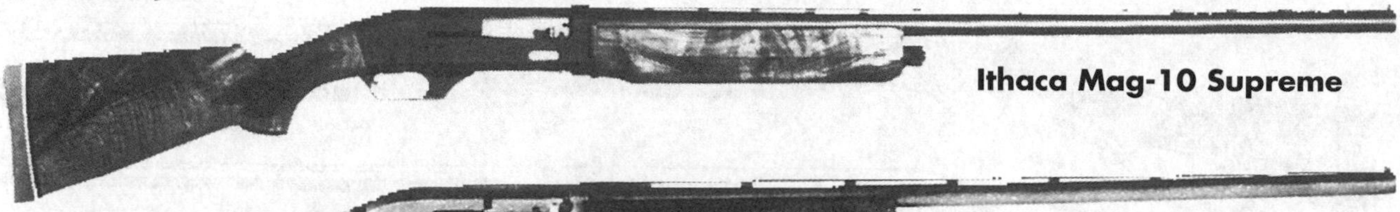

Ithaca Mag-10 Supreme

Ithaca Mag-10 Deluxe

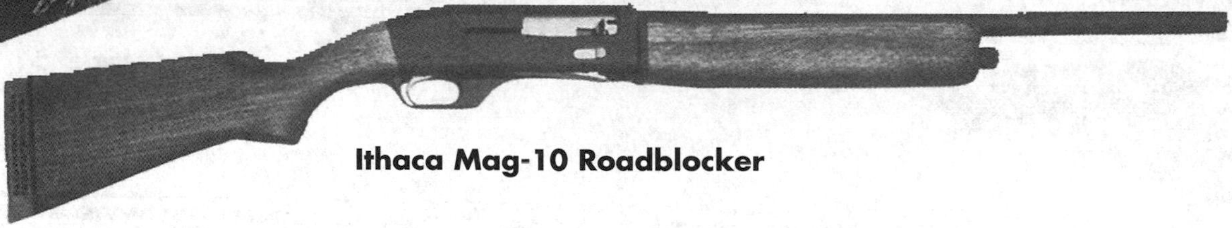

Ithaca Mag-10 Roadblocker

Ithaca Mag-10 Deluxe

Gauge: 10 magnum
Action: Semiautomatic; gas-operated
Magazine: 3-shot tubular
Barrel: 32" full choke; ventilated rib
Finish: Blued; checkered walnut pistol grip stock and forearm; recoil pad; swivels
Approximate wt.: 11½ lbs.
Comments: Deduct 15% to 20% for Ithaca Mag-10 Standard. Produced from the mid-1970s to the mid-1980s.

Estimated Value:	**Excellent:**	**$850.00**
	Very good:	**$680.00**

Ithaca Mag-10 Supreme

Similar to the Mag-10 Deluxe with higher quality finish and select wood.

Estimated Value:	**Excellent:**	**$975.00**
	Very good:	**$785.00**

Ithaca Mag-10 Roadblocker

A law enforcement version of the Mag-10 with a 20" barrel; plain stock; "vapor blasted" metal finish. Add 5% for ventilated rib.

Estimated Value:	**Excellent:**	**$700.00**
	Very good:	**$560.00**

IVER JOHNSON

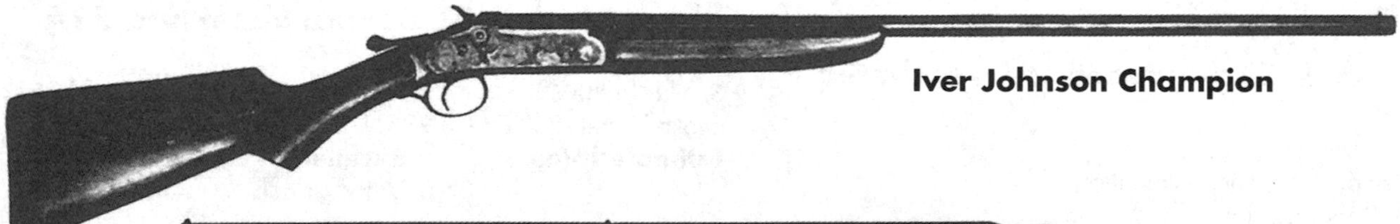

Iver Johnson Champion

Iver Johnson Special Trap

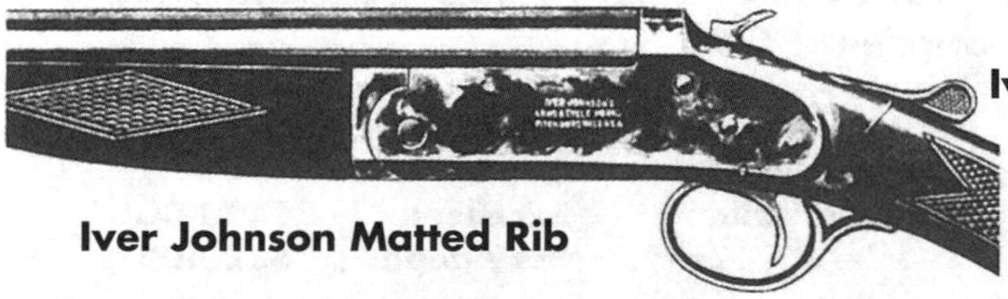

Iver Johnson Matted Rib

Iver Johnson Matted Rib

Similar to the Champion with a matted rib and checkering. Discontinued in the late 1940s.

Estimated Value:	**Excellent:**	**$250.00**
	Very good:	**$200.00**

Iver Johnson Special Trap

Similar to the Champion with a 32" ribbed barrel; checkered stock; 12 gauge only. Manufactured until the early 1940s.

Estimated Value:	**Excellent:**	**$400.00**
	Very good:	**$320.00**

Iver Johnson Champion

Gauge: 10, 12, 16, 20, 410
Action: Box lock; top lever break-open; hammerless; single shot; automatic ejectors
Magazine: None
Barrel: 26" – 30", full choke
Finish: Blued; hardwood semi-pistol grip stock and short tapered forearm
Approximate wt.: 7 lbs.
Comments: Made from about 1910 to the late 1950s.

Estimated Value:	**Excellent:**	**$200.00**
	Very good:	**$160.00**

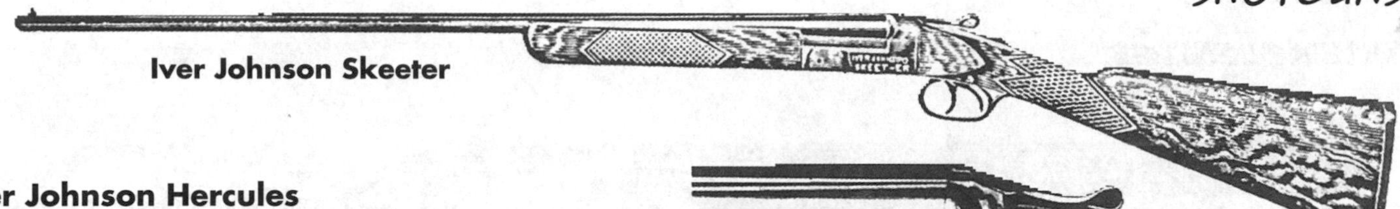

Iver Johnson Skeeter

Iver Johnson Hercules

Gauge: 12, 16, 20, 410
Action: Box lock; top lever break-open; hammerless
Magazine: None
Barrel: Side-by-side double barrel, 26" – 32" modified and full or full and full chokes
Finish: Blued; checkered walnut pistol grip stock and tapered forearm
Approximate wt.: 6 to 8 lbs.
Comments: Made from about 1920 to 1949. Available with some extras. Prices are for standard grade. Add $75.00 for single trigger or automatic ejectors.

Estimated Value:	**Excellent:**	**$1,000.00**
	Very good:	**$ 800.00**

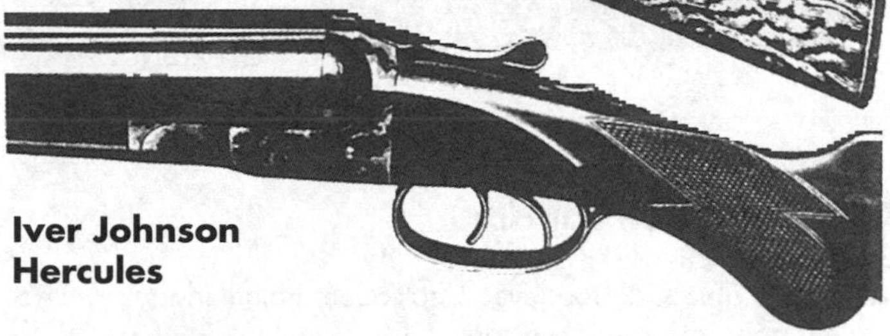

Iver Johnson Hercules

Iver Johnson Skeeter

Similar to the Hercules with addition of 28 gauge; 26" – 28" barrels; wide forearm. Add $100.00 for automatic ejectors; $100.00 for single selective trigger.

Estimated Value:	**Excellent:**	**$1,500.00**
	Very good:	**$1,200.00**

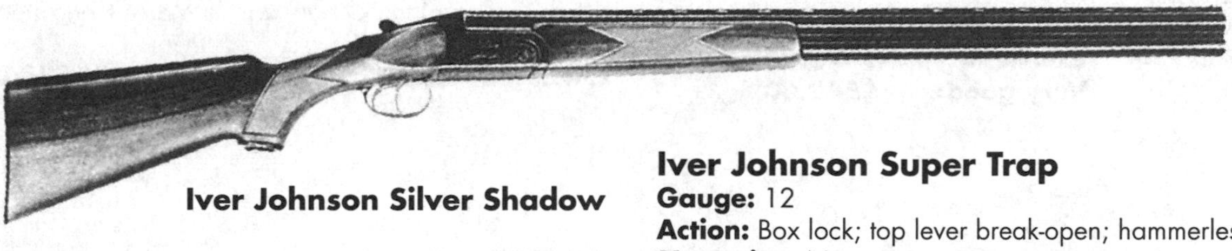

Iver Johnson Silver Shadow

Iver Johnson Silver Shadow

Gauge: 12
Action: Box lock; top lever break-open; hammerless
Magazine: None
Barrel: Over and under double barrel; 28" modified and full choke; ventilated rib
Finish: Blued; checkered walnut pistol grip stock and forearm
Approximate wt.: 8¼ lbs.
Comments: Manufactured in Italy for Iver Johnson. Add $75.00 for single trigger. Made in the 1970s.

Estimated Value:	**Excellent:**	**$500.00**
	Very good:	**$400.00**

Iver Johnson Super Trap

Gauge: 12
Action: Box lock; top lever break-open; hammerless
Magazine: None
Barrel: Side-by-side double barrel; 32" full choke; ventilated rib
Finish: Blued; checkered walnut pistol grip stock and forearm; recoil pad
Approximate wt.: 8½ lbs.
Comments: Production stopped during World War II. Available with some extras. Prices for standard grade; add $50.00 for non-selective single trigger; $100.00 for selective single trigger or automatic ejectors.

Estimated Value:	**Excellent:**	**$1,750.00**
	Very good:	**$1,400.00**

Iver Johnson Super Trap

KESSLER

Kessler 3-Shot

Gauge: 12, 16, 20
Action: Bolt action; hammerless; repeating
Magazine: 2-shot detachable box
Barrel: 26", 28", full choke
Finish: Blued; plain pistol grip stock and forearm; recoil pad
Approximate wt.: 6 to 7 lbs.
Comments: Made for a few years only in the early 1950s.

Estimated Value:	**Excellent:**	**$150.00**
	Very good:	**$120.00**

Kessler Lever Matic

Gauge: 12, 16, 20
Action: Lever action
Magazine: 3-shot
Barrel: 26", 28", 30", full choke
Finish: Blued; checkered walnut straight stock and forearm; recoil pad
Approximate wt.: 7 lbs.
Comments: Produced for only a few years in the early 1950s.

Estimated Value:	**Excellent:**	**$175.00**
	Very good:	**$140.00**

KLEINGUENTHER

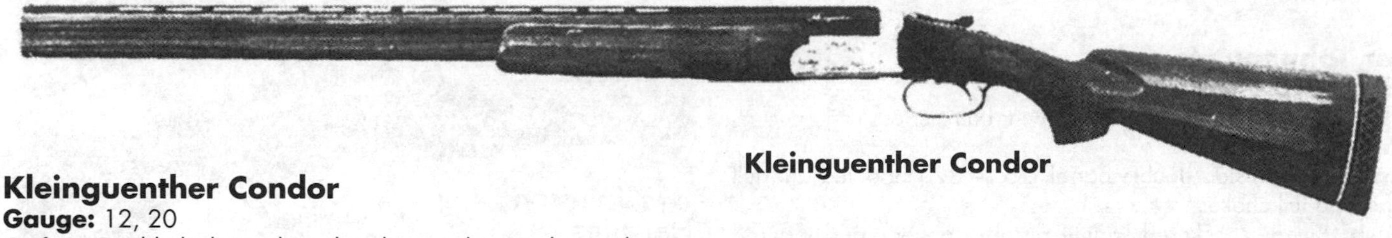

Kleinguenther Condor

Kleinguenther Condor

Gauge: 12, 20
Action: Double lock; top lever break-open; hammerless; selective single trigger; automatic ejectors
Magazine: None
Barrel: Over and under double barrel; ventilated rib; 26" improved and modified or skeet; 28" modified or modified and full; 30" modified and full or full in 12 gauge
Finish: Blued; checkered walnut pistol grip stock and forearm; recoil pad
Approximate wt.: 7½ lbs.
Comments: An Italian shotgun produced in the 1970s.

Estimated Value:	**Excellent:**	**$675.00**
	Very good:	**$540.00**

Kleinguenther Condor Skeet

A skeet version of the Condor with a wide rib.

Estimated Value:	**Excellent:**	**$700.00**
	Very good:	**$560.00**

Kleinguenther Condor Trap

A trap version of the Condor with a Monte Carlo stock, wide rib; available in 32" barrel.

Estimated Value:	**Excellent:**	**$725.00**
	Very good:	**$580.00**

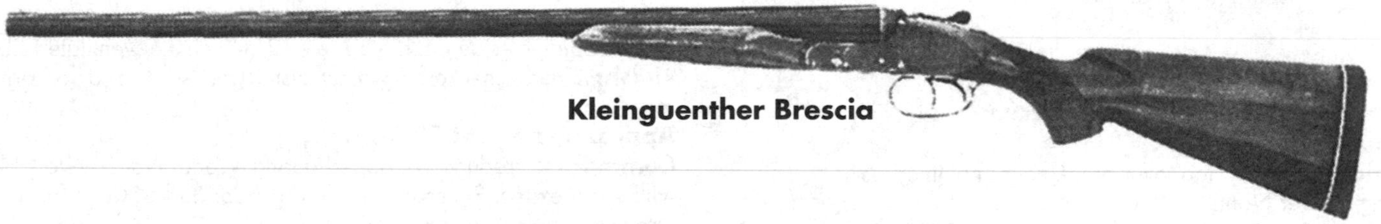

Kleinguenther Brescia

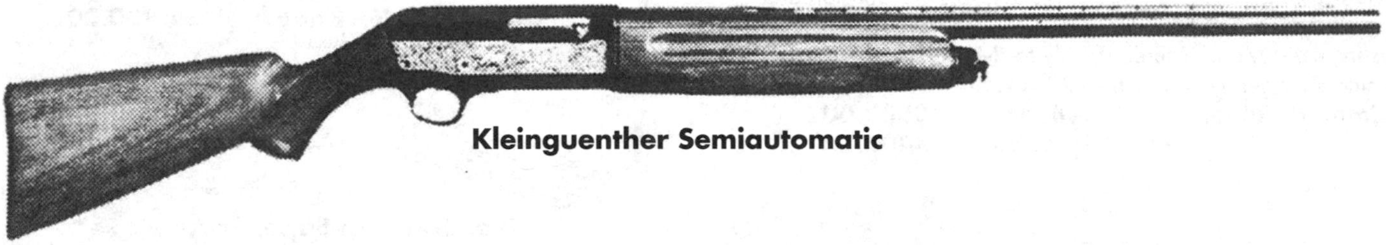

Kleinguenther Semiautomatic

Kleinguenther Brescia

Gauge: 12, 20
Action: Box lock; top lever break-open; hammerless; double trigger
Magazine: None
Barrel: Side-by-side double barrel; chrome lined, 28" improved or modified or modified and full chokes
Finish: Blued; checkered walnut pistol grip stock and tapered forearm
Approximate wt.: 7½ lbs.
Comments: Manufactured in Italy.

Estimated Value:	**Excellent:**	**$375.00**
	Very good:	**$300.00**

Kleinguenther Semiautomatic

Gauge: 12
Action: Semiautomatic; hammerless; side ejection
Magazine: 3-shot tubular
Barrel: Chrome lined; 25" skeet, 26" improved cylinder, 28" and 30" full chokes; ventilated rib
Finish: Blued; smooth walnut pistol grip stock and grooved forearm; engraved
Approximate wt.: 7½ lbs.
Comments: Made from the early to the mid-1970s.

Estimated Value:	**Excellent:**	**$300.00**
	Very good:	**$240.00**

L.C. Smith Single Barrel

Gauge: 12
Action: Box lock; top lever break-open; automatic ejectors, hammerless
Magazine: None, single shot
Barrel: 32", 34" choice of bore; ventilated rib
Finish: Blued; checkered walnut pistol grip stock and forearm; recoil pad
Approximate wt.: 8 lbs.
Comments: Produced by Hunter Arms from about 1917 to 1945 and Marlin from about 1946 to 1951. Priced for Hunter made.
Estimated Value:

	Olympic	Specialty	Crown
Excellent:	**$2,000.00**	**$2,500.00**	**$3,500.00**
Very good:	**$1,600.00**	**$2,000.00**	**$2,800.00**

L.C. Smith Single Barrel

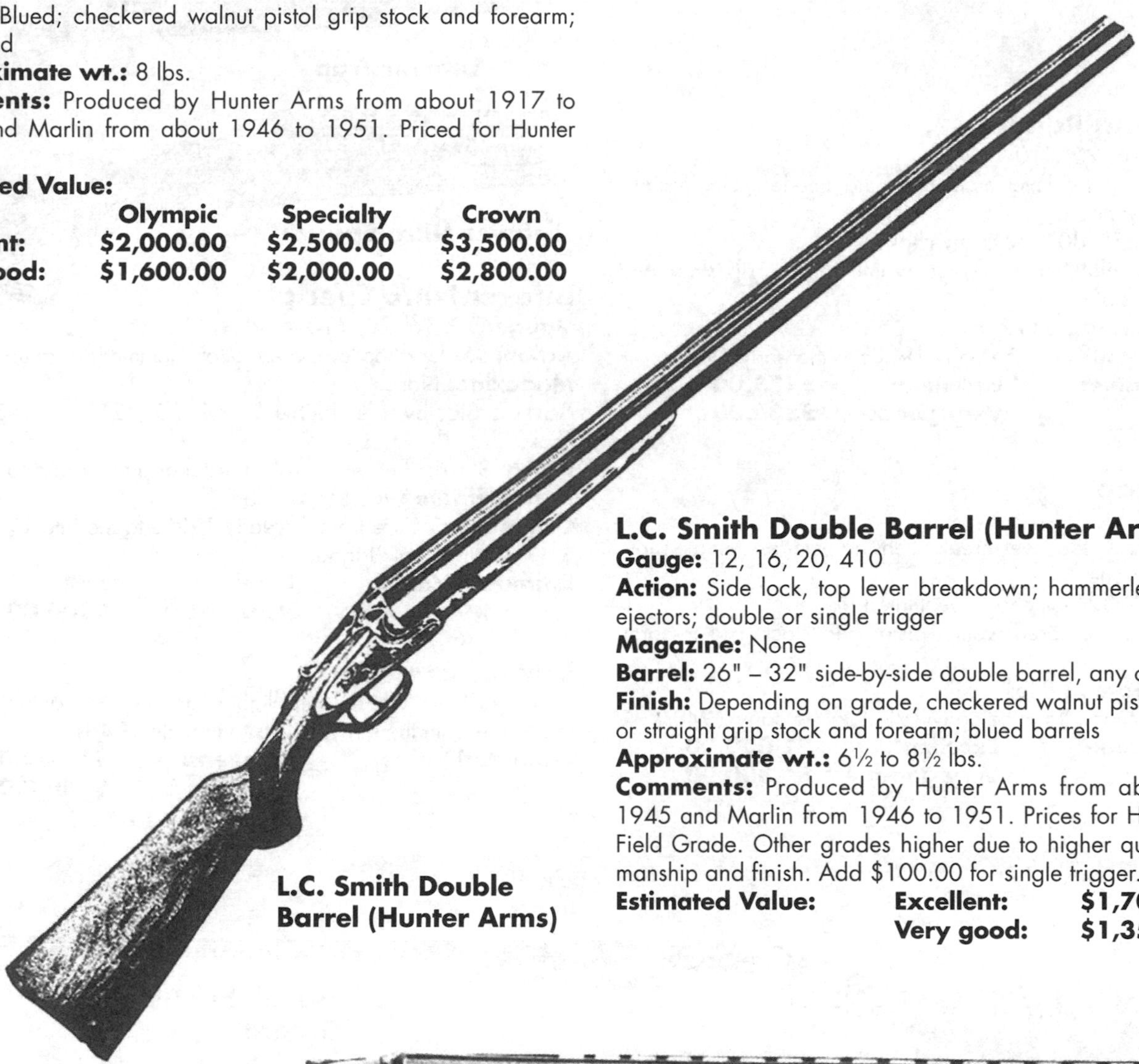

L.C. Smith Double Barrel (Hunter Arms)

L.C. Smith Double Barrel (Hunter Arms)

Gauge: 12, 16, 20, 410
Action: Side lock, top lever breakdown; hammerless; automatic ejectors; double or single trigger
Magazine: None
Barrel: 26" – 32" side-by-side double barrel, any choke
Finish: Depending on grade, checkered walnut pistol, semi-pistol or straight grip stock and forearm; blued barrels
Approximate wt.: 6½ to 8½ lbs.
Comments: Produced by Hunter Arms from about 1890 to 1945 and Marlin from 1946 to 1951. Prices for Hunter Arms in Field Grade. Other grades higher due to higher quality of workmanship and finish. Add $100.00 for single trigger.

Estimated Value:	**Excellent:**	**$1,700.00**
	Very good:	**$1,350.00**

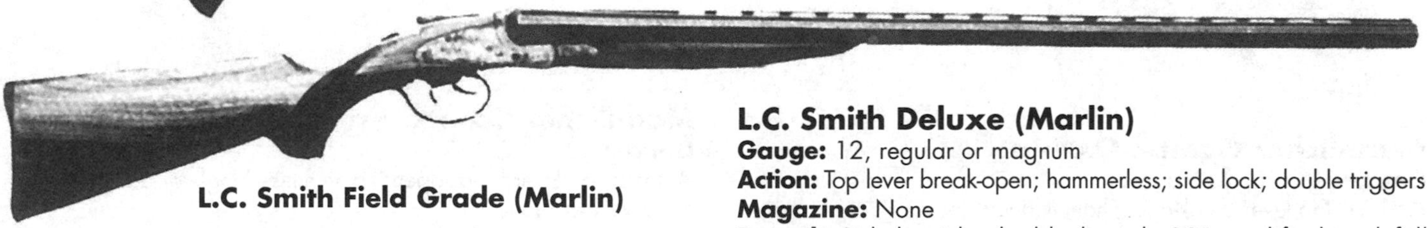

L.C. Smith Field Grade (Marlin)

L.C. Smith Deluxe (Marlin)

Gauge: 12, regular or magnum
Action: Top lever break-open; hammerless; side lock; double triggers
Magazine: None
Barrel: Side-by-side double barrel; 28" modified and full chokes; floating steel ventilated rib
Finish: Top quality, hand-fitted, hand-checkered walnut pistol grip stock and beavertail forearm; blued; case hardened side plates
Approximate wt.: 6¾ lbs.
Comments: Made from about 1968 to the mid-1970s.

Estimated Value:	**Excellent:**	**$875.00**
	Very good:	**$700.00**

L.C. Smith Field Grade (Marlin)

Same as the Deluxe Model with standard checkered walnut pistol grip stock and forearm and extruded ventilated rib. Made from about 1951 to 1968.

Estimated Value:	**Excellent:**	**$700.00**
	Very good:	**$560.00**

LEFEVER

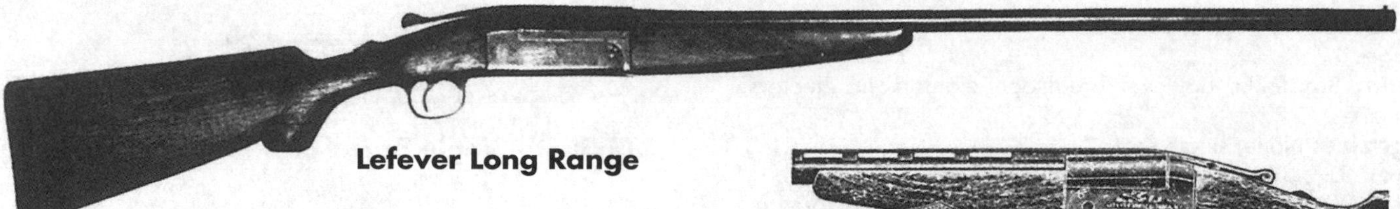

Lefever Long Range

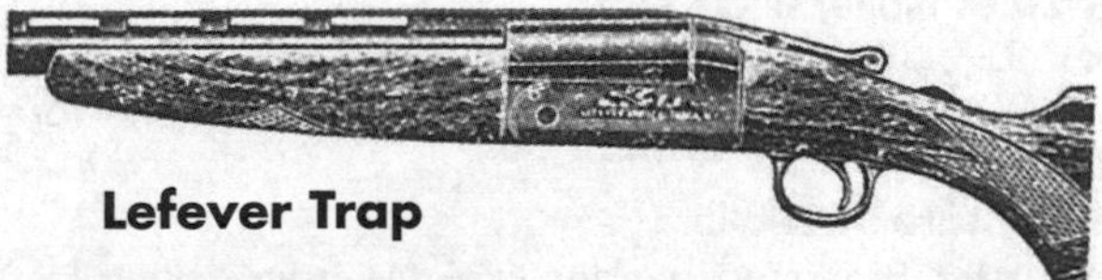

Lefever Trap

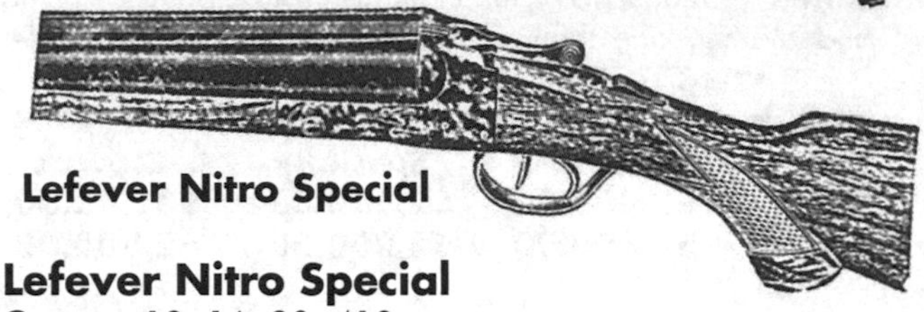

Lefever Nitro Special

Lefever Long Range

Gauge: 12, 16, 20, 410
Action: Box lock, top lever break-open; hammerless; single shot
Magazine: None
Barrel: 26", 28", 30", 32"; any choke
Finish: Blued; plain or checkered walnut pistol grip stock and forearm; bead sight
Approximate wt.: 5 to 7 lbs.
Comments: Made from the early 1920s to the early 1940s.
Estimated Value: **Excellent:** **$475.00**
Very good: **$380.00**

Lefever Trap

Gauge: 12
Action: Box lock; top lever break-open; hammerless; single shot
Magazine: None
Barrel: 30" or 32" full choke; ventilated rib
Finish: Blued; checkered walnut pistol grip stock and forearm; recoil pad
Approximate wt.: 8 lbs.
Comments: Made from the early 1920s to the early 1940s.
Estimated Value: **Excellent:** **$1,000.00**
Very good: **$ 800.00**

Lefever Nitro Special

Gauge: 12, 16, 20, 410
Action: Box lock; top lever break-open; hammerless; double triggers
Magazine: None
Barrel: Side-by-side double barrel; 26", 28", 30", 32"; any choke
Finish: Blued; checkered walnut pistol grip stock and forearm
Approximate wt.: 5½ to 7 lbs.
Comments: Made from the early 1920s to the late 1940s. Add $100.00 for single trigger.
Estimated Value: **Excellent:** **$625.00**
Very good: **$500.00**

Lefever Excelsior

Similar to Nitro Special with light engraving and automatic ejector. Made from the early 1920s to the late 1940s.
Estimated Value: **Excellent:** **$1,100.00**
Very good: **$ 880.00**

MANNLICHER

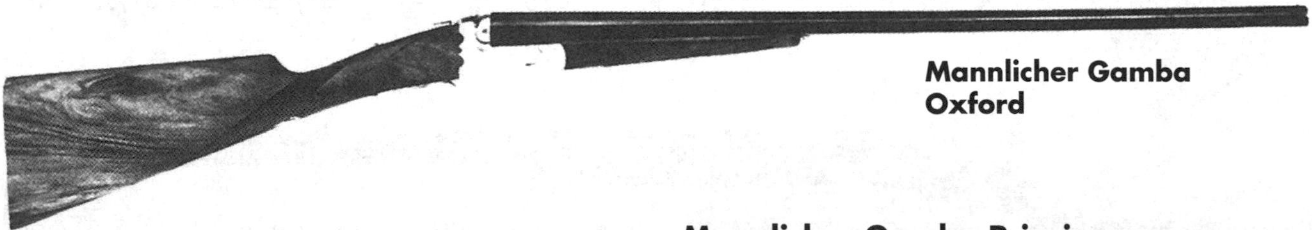

Mannlicher Gamba Oxford

Mannlicher Gamba Oxford

Gauge: 12, 20, 20 magnum
Action: Top lever break-open; hammerless; single or double trigger
Magazine: None
Barrel: Side-by-side double barrel; 26½" improved cylinder and modified or 27½" modified and full
Finish: Blued; engraved receiver; checkered walnut straight grip stock and tapered forearm
Approximate wt.: 5½ to 6½ lbs.
Comments: Add $140.00 for single trigger.
Estimated Value: **Excellent:** **$1,540.00**
Very good: **$1,230.00**

Mannlicher Gamba Principessa

Gauge: 28
Action: Top lever break-open; hammerless; single or double trigger
Magazine: None
Barrel: Side-by-side double barrel; 26" improved cylinder and modified or 28" modified and full
Finish: Blued; case hardened receiver with engraved scrollwork; checkered walnut straight grip stock and tapered forearm; beavertail forearm available; recoil pad
Approximate wt.: 5½ lbs.
Comments: Add $130.00 for single trigger.
Estimated Value: **Excellent:** **$1,400.00**
Very good: **$1,120.00**

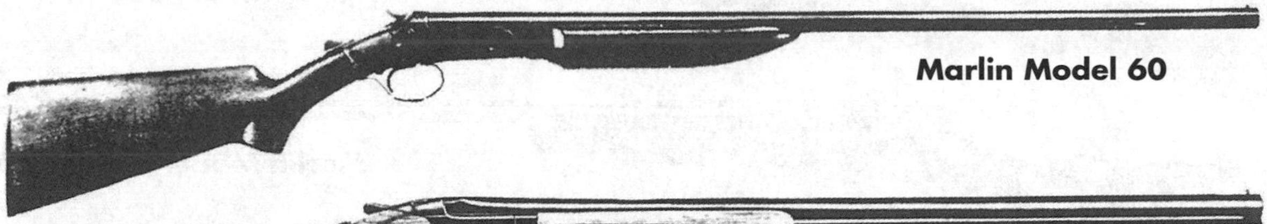

Marlin Model 60

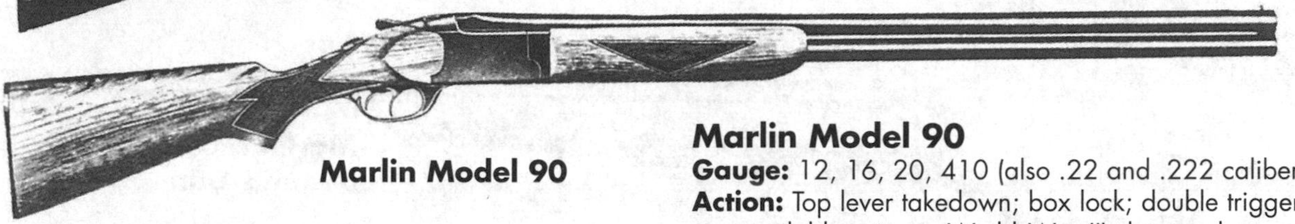

Marlin Model 90

Marlin Model 60
Gauge: 12
Action: Box lock; takedown breechloading; exposed hammer; single shot
Magazine: None
Barrel: 30" or 32" full choke; matted top; 2¾" chamber
Finish: Blued; walnut pistol grip stock and beavertail forearm
Approximate wt.: 6½ lbs.
Comments: This shotgun was made in 1923, a combination of Marlin and Hopkins and Allen parts. Less than 1,000 were manufactured.

Estimated Value:　　Excellent:　　$300.00
　　　　　　　　　　　　Very good:　　$240.00

Marlin Model 90
Gauge: 12, 16, 20, 410 (also .22 and .222 caliber)
Action: Top lever takedown; box lock; double trigger (single trigger available prior to World War II); hammerless; non-automatic extractors
Magazine: None
Barrel: Over and under double barrel, 26", 28", or 30" rifle; shotgun barrels available in 26"; 2¾" chamber, 3" chamber in 410; full, modified, skeet, or improved cylinder bore
Finish: Blued; plain or checkered walnut pistol grip stock and forearm; recoil pad
Approximate wt.: 6 to 7½ lbs.
Comments: This shotgun or combination was manufactured from about 1937 to 1958. Add $100.00 for 410 gauge; $75.00 for single trigger.

Estimated Value:　　Excellent:　　$525.00
　　　　　　　　　　　　Very good:　　$420.00

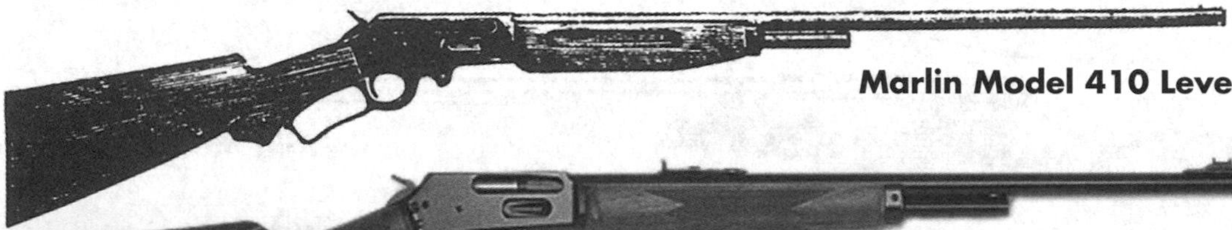

Marlin Model 410 Lever Action

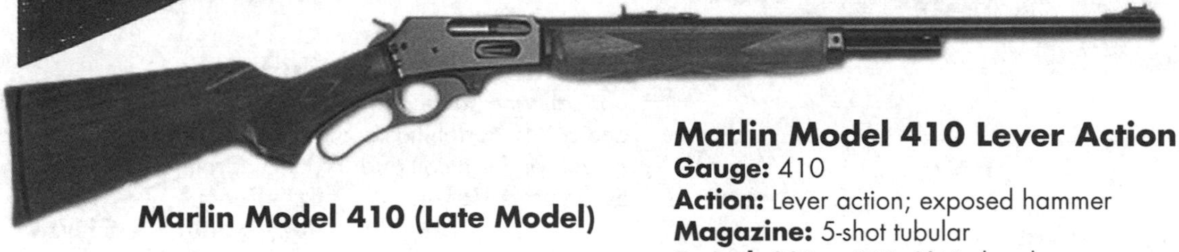

Marlin Model 410 (Late Model)

Marlin Model 50 DL
Gauge: 12, regular or magnum interchangeably (3" chamber)
Action: Bolt action, repeating
Magazine: 2-shot detachable box
Barrel: 28" modified choke with burnished bore for lead or steel shot; brass bead front sight with u-groove rear
Finish: Black fiberglass-filled synthetic, one-piece stock and forearm with molded-in checkering and swivels; rubber recoil pad
Approximate wt.: 7½ lbs.
Comments: Made from the mid- to the late 1990s.

Estimated Value:　　Excellent:　　$250.00
　　　　　　　　　　　　Very good:　　$200.00

Marlin Model 410 Lever Action
Gauge: 410
Action: Lever action; exposed hammer
Magazine: 5-shot tubular
Barrel: 22" or 26", 2½" chamber
Finish: Blued; walnut pistol grip stock and beavertail forearm
Approximate wt.: 6 lbs.
Comments: A solid frame lightweight shotgun produced from about 1929 to 1932.

Estimated Value:　　Excellent:　　$1,500.00
　　　　　　　　　　　　Very good:　　$1,200.00

Marlin Model 410 (Late Model)
Gauge: 410
Action: Lever action, repeating; exposed hammer
Magazine: 4-shot tubular
Barrel: 22" cylinder bore; bead fiber-optic front sight, adjustable rear
Finish: Blued; checkered walnut pistol grip stock and forearm
Approximate wt.: 7¾ lbs.
Comments: A reintroduction of Marlin's lever action 410 shotgun of the late 1920s and the early 1930s.

Estimated Value:　　Excellent:　　$500.00
　　　　　　　　　　　　Very good:　　$400.00

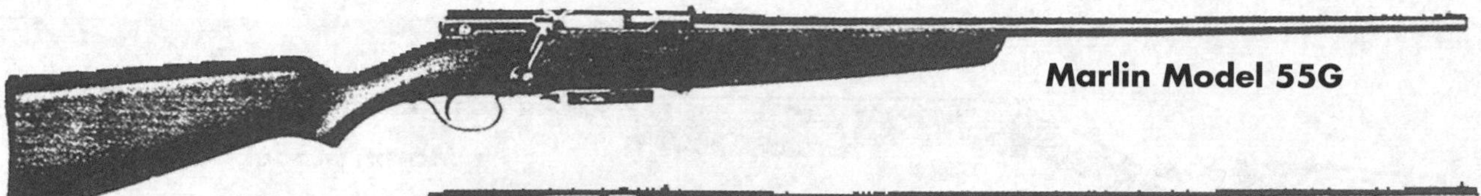

Marlin Model 55G

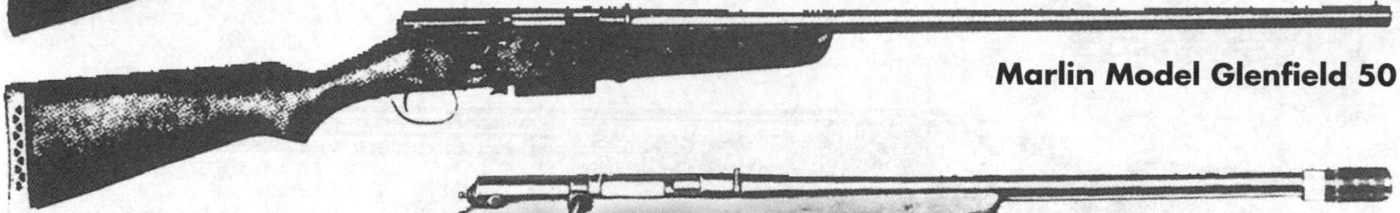

Marlin Model Glenfield 50

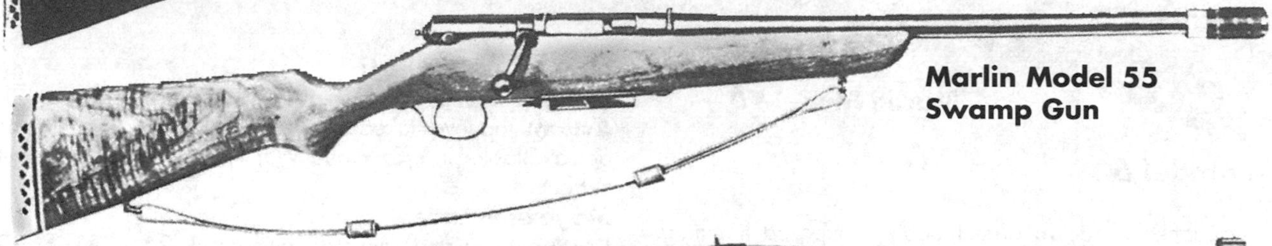

Marlin Model 55 Swamp Gun

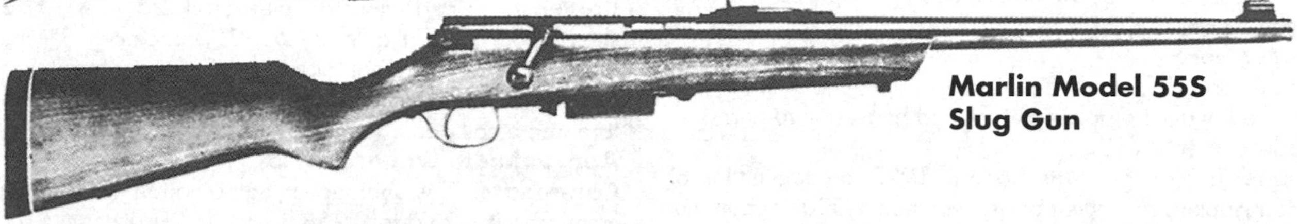

Marlin Model 55S Slug Gun

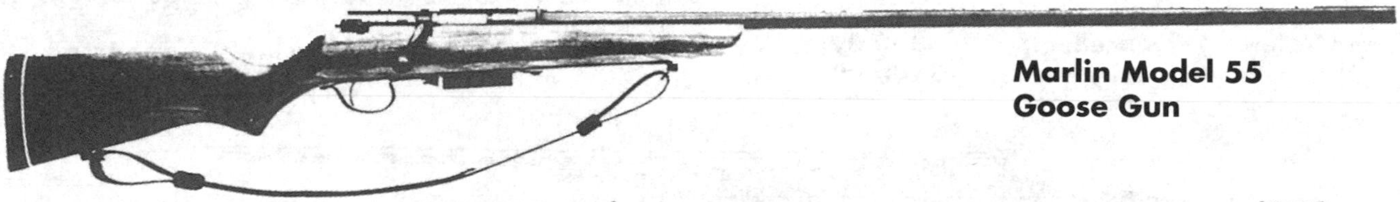

Marlin Model 55 Goose Gun

Marlin Model 55 Hunter

Marlin Model 55 Hunter

Gauge: 12, 16, 20
Action: Bolt action; repeating
Magazine: 2-shot detachable box
Barrel: 26" or 28" full choke; "Micro Choke" available; 2¾" or 3" chamber
Finish: Blued; walnut pistol grip stock and forearm; recoil pad optional
Approximate wt.: 7¼ lbs.
Comments: Made from about 1950 to 1965.
Estimated Value: **Excellent:** **$200.00**
Very good: **$160.00**

Marlin Models 55 Goose Gun and 55G DL

Same as the Model 55 Hunter except: swivels; recoil pad; extra long 36" full choke barrel; 12 gauge magnum only; weighs 8 lbs.; made from 1966 to the mid-1990s. 55G DL, introduced in the mid-1990s, has black synthetic stock.
Estimated Value: **Excellent:** **$325.00**
Very good: **$260.00**

Marlin Model 55S Slug Gun

Basically the same as Model 55 Hunter, this gun has rifle sights and a 24" barrel that is chambered for 2¾" and 3" shells. It has swivels and a recoil pad. Produced from 1973 to the late 1980s.
Estimated Value: **Excellent:** **$225.00**
Very good: **$180.00**

Marlin Models 55G, Glenfield 55G, and Glenfield 50

The same basic shotgun as the Marlin Model 55 Hunter. It was produced from about 1961 to 1966 as the 55G and Glenfield 55G. In 1966 it became the Glenfield 50.
Estimated Value: **Excellent:** **$200.00**
Very good: **$160.00**

Marlin Model 55 Swamp Gun

Same as the Model 55 Hunter except barrel is shortened with "Micro Choke," recoil pad is standard and it has swivels. It weighs about 6½ lbs. and is chambered for 3", 12 gauge magnum shells. Produced for two years beginning in 1963.
Estimated Value: **Excellent:** **$275.00**
Very good: **$225.00**

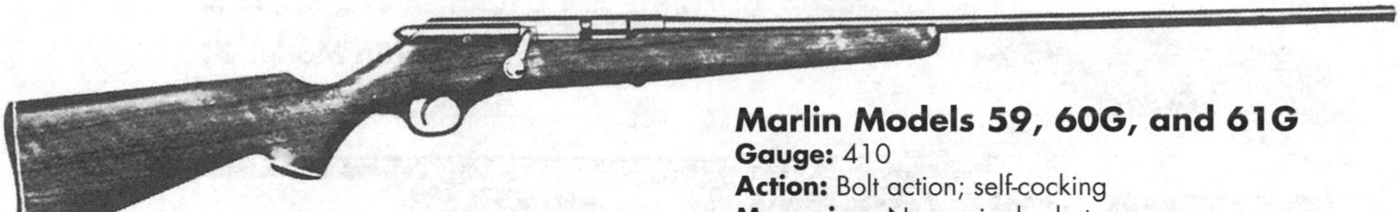

Marlin Model 59

Marlin Models 59, 60G, and 61G

Gauge: 410
Action: Bolt action; self-cocking
Magazine: None; single shot
Barrel: 24" full coke; chambered for 2½" or 3" shells
Finish: Blued; walnut pistol grip or semi-pistol grip stock and forearm
Approximate wt.: 5 lbs.
Comments: This takedown model was produced from about 1959 to 1961. It was replaced by Model 61G in 1962 which was replaced by the Model 60G in 1963 and discontinued in 1970.

Estimated Value:	**Excellent:**	**$175.00**
	Very good:	**$140.00**

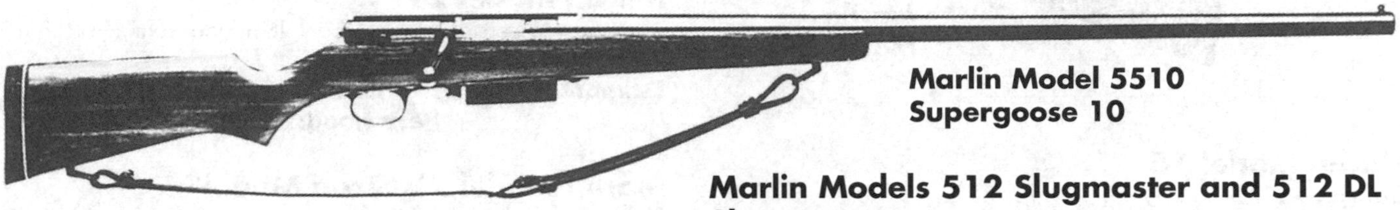

Marlin Model 5510 Supergoose 10

Marlin Model 5510 Supergoose 10

Gauge: 10 magnum
Action: Bolt action
Magazine: 2-shot detachable box (2⅞" shells must be loaded singly)
Barrel: 34" full choke; chambered for 2⅞" or 3½" shells
Finish: Blued; black walnut semi-pistol grip stock and forearm; swivels; recoil pad
Approximate wt.: 10½ lbs.
Comments: This is a more powerful version of the Marlin Goose Gun. Produced from 1976 to 1986.

Estimated Value:	**Excellent:**	**$375.00**
	Very good:	**$300.00**

Marlin Models 512 Slugmaster and 512 DL Slugmaster

Gauge: 12 (3" chamber), slug only
Action: Bolt action; repeating
Magazine: 2-shot detachable box
Barrel: 21" rifled (one turn in 28" for Sabot slugs or Foster-type rifled slugs); rifled barrel not designed for bird or buck shot; adjustable folding semi-buckhorn rear and ramp front sight with removable hood
Finish: Blued; checkered walnut finish, birch one-piece pistol grip stock and forearm with recoil pad and swivel studs; also black fiberglass-filled synthetic stock after 1997 (512 DL)
Approximate wt.: 8 lbs.
Comments: Introduced in 1994. Add 5% for 512 DL.

Estimated Value:	**Excellent:**	**$290.00**
	Very good:	**$235.00**

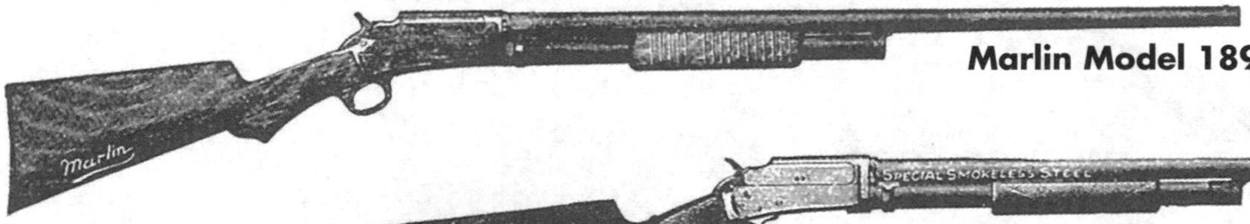

Marlin Model 1898

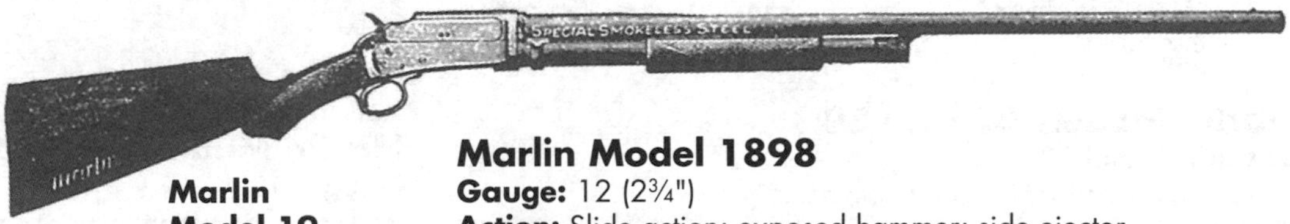

Marlin Model 19

Marlin Models 19 and 19G

Similar to the Model 1898 with improvements. Made from 1906 to 1907 in four grades; 19G produced until 1915.

Estimated Value:	**Excellent:**	**$500.00 – 1,500.00**
	Very good:	**$400.00 – 1,200.00**

Marlin Model 1898

Gauge: 12 (2¾")
Action: Slide action; exposed hammer; side ejector
Magazine: 5-shot tubular
Barrel: 26", 28", 30", or 32"
Finish: Blued; walnut pistol grip stock and grooved slide handle
Approximate wt.: 7¼ lbs.
Comments: This shotgun was produced in many grades from 1898 to 1905. Price for grade A (Field Grade).

Estimated Value:	**Excellent:**	**$500.00**
	Very good:	**$400.00**

Marlin Model 24

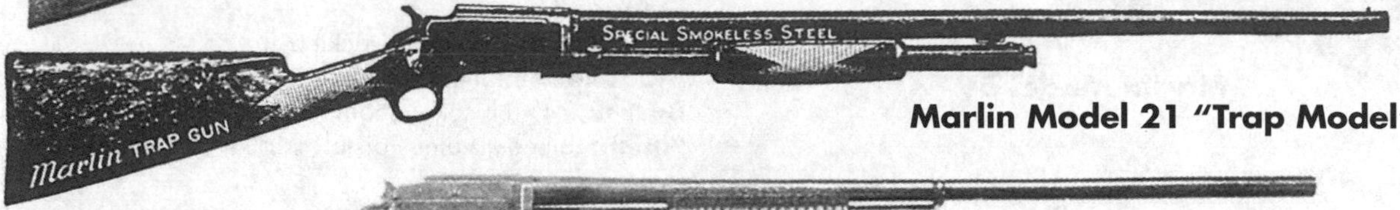

Marlin Model 21 "Trap Model"

Marlin Model 26

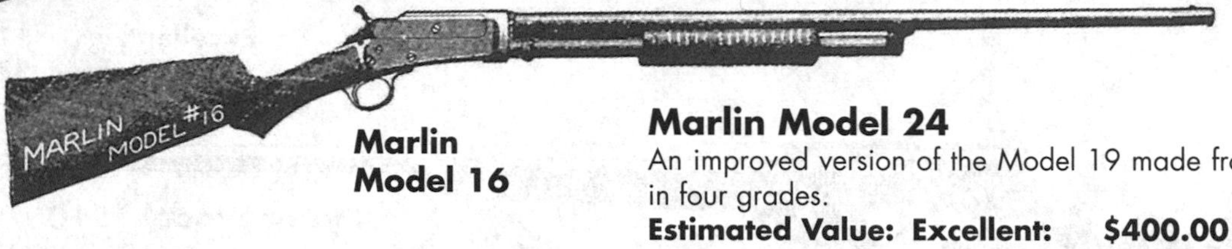

Marlin Model 16

Marlin Model 24

An improved version of the Model 19 made from 1908 to 1915 in four grades.

Estimated Value: Excellent: $400.00 – 1,500.00
Very good: $320.00 – 1,100.00

Marlin Model 21 "Trap Model"

Similar to the Model 19 with trap specifications. Made from 1907 to 1909 in four grades.

Estimated Value: Excellent: $400.00 – 1,400.00
Very good: $320.00 – 1,125.00

Marlin Model 26

Very similar to the Model 24 except: stock is straight grip; solid frame. Made from about 1909 to 1915.

Estimated Value: Excellent: $450.00
Very good: $360.00

Marlin Model 16

Gauge: 16 (2¾")
Action: Slide action; exposed hammer
Magazine: 5-shot tubular
Barrel: 26" or 28"
Finish: Blued; walnut pistol grip stock and forearm; some checkered, some with grooved slide handle
Approximate wt.: 6¼ lbs.
Comments: Takedown model made from about 1904 to 1910 in four grades.

Estimated Value: Excellent: $500.00 – 1,500.00
Very good: $400.00 – 1,200.00

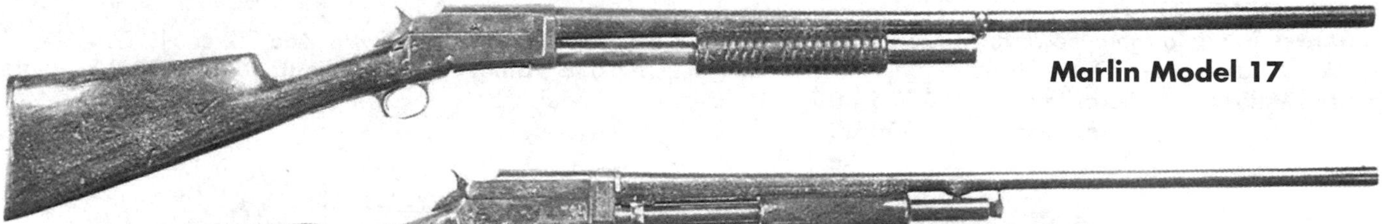

Marlin Model 17

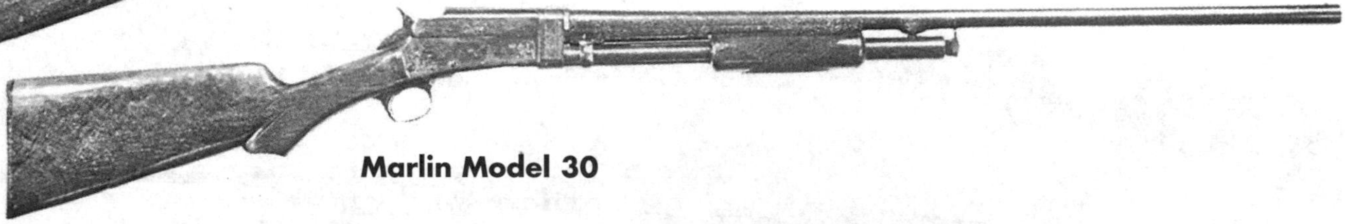

Marlin Model 30

Marlin Models 30 and 30G

Gauge: 16 and 20
Action: Slide action; exposed hammer
Magazine: 5-shot tubular
Barrel: 25", 26", 28" modified choke, 2¾" chamber
Finish: Blued; checkered walnut straight or pistol grip stock, grooved or checkered slide handle
Approximate wt.: 6¾ lbs.
Comments: Made from about 1910 to 1915. In 1915 it was called the Model 30G. Made in four grades.

Estimated Value: Excellent: $400.00 – 1,400.00
Very good: $320.00 – 1,125.00

Marlin Models 17 and 17G

Gauge: 12
Action: Slide action; exposed hammer
Magazine: 5-shot tubular
Barrel: 30" or 32" full choke; others available by special order
Finish: Blued; walnut pistol grip stock and grooved slide handle
Approximate wt.: 7½ lbs.
Comments: This solid frame shotgun was made from about 1906 to 1908; from 1908 to 1915 as Model 17G.

Estimated Value: Excellent: $500.00
Very good: $400.00

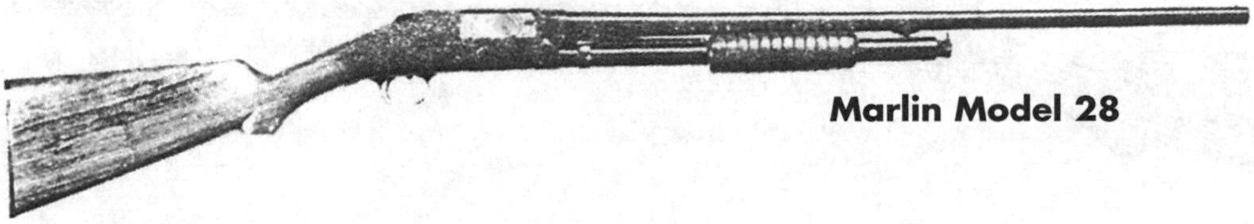

Marlin Model 28

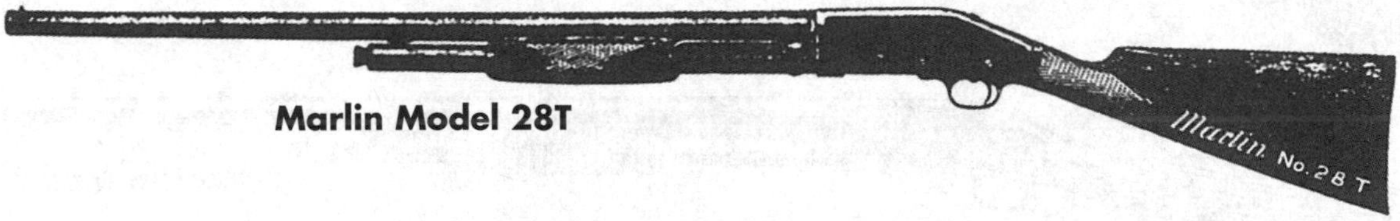

Marlin Model 28T

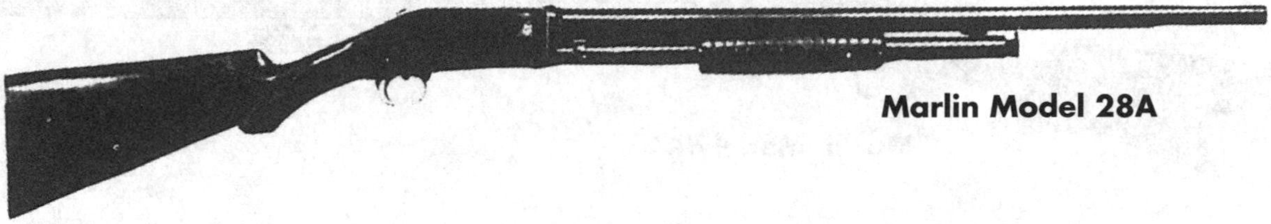

Marlin Model 28A

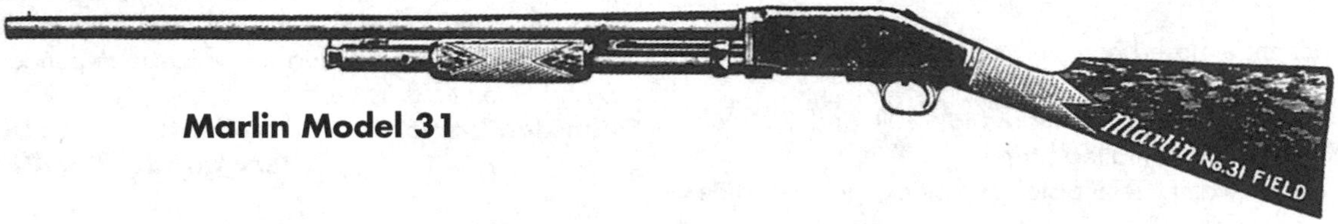

Marlin Model 31

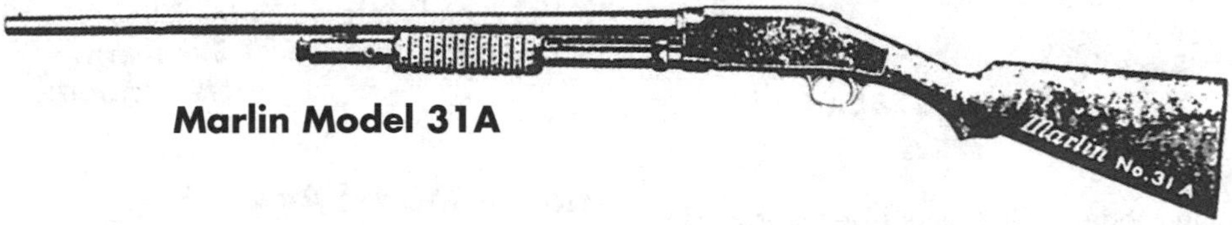

Marlin Model 31A

Marlin Models 28, 28T, and 28TS

Gauge: 12
Action: Slide action; hammerless; side ejector
Magazine: 5-shot tubular
Barrel: 26" or 28" cylinder bore or modified choke; 30" or 32" full choke
Finish: Blued; checkered walnut pistol grip stock and slide handle
Approximate wt.: 8 lbs.
Comments: This takedown shotgun was produced from about 1913 to just before World War I. The Model 28T and 28TS were Trap Grade guns with an available straight stock. Add $100.00 for Model 28T or 28TS.

Estimated Value:	**Excellent:**	**$425.00**
	Very good:	**$340.00**

Marlin Model 28A

Basically the same as the Model 28. Made from about 1920 to 1922 in four grades; replaced by the Model 43A.

Estimated Value:	**Excellent:**	**$300.00 – 1,000.00**
	Very good:	**$250.00 – 800.00**

Marlin Model 31

This shotgun is much like the Model 28 except: 20 or 16 gauge. Made from about 1915 to 1917. Four grades.

Estimated Value:	**Excellent:**	**$500.00 – 1,500.00**
	Very good:	**$400.00 – 1,200.00**

Marlin Model 31A

Very similar to the Model 28A in 20 gauge only. Replaced by the Model 44A.

Estimated Value:	**Excellent:**	**$450.00**
	Very good:	**$360.00**

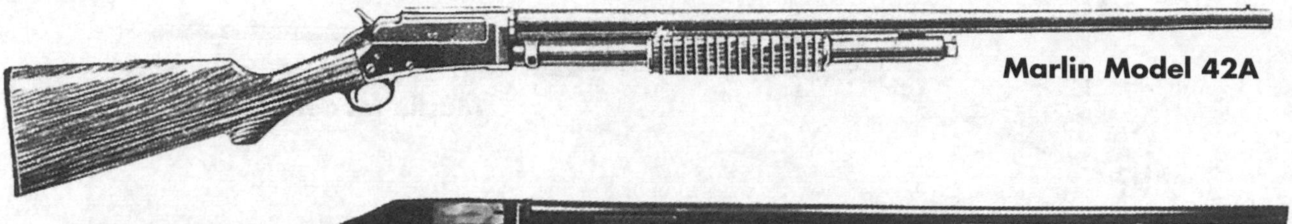

Marlin Model 42A

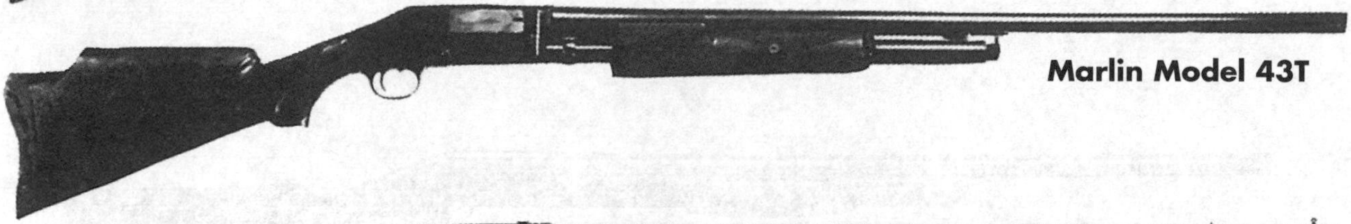

Marlin Model 43T

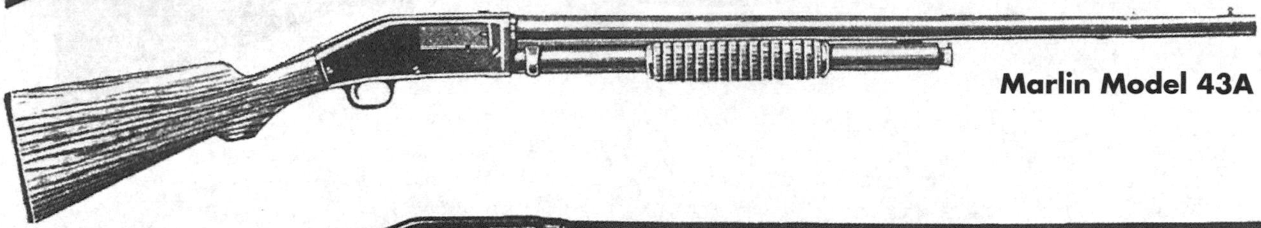

Marlin Model 43A

Marlin Model 44A

Marlin Model 42A

Gauge: 12
Action: Slide action; exposed hammer; side ejector
Magazine: 5-shot tubular; bottom load
Barrel: 26" cylinder bore, 28" modified, 30" and 32" full choke; 2¾" chamber; round matted barrel
Finish: Blued; black walnut semi-pistol grip stock, grooved slide handle
Approximate wt.: 7½ lbs.
Comments: A takedown shotgun manufactured from about 1922 to 1934.

Estimated Value:	**Excellent:**	**$350.00**
	Very good:	**$280.00**

Marlin Model 49

This shotgun is similar to the Model 42A. It was given away with stock in the corporation. It was produced from about 1925 to 1928.

Estimated Value:	**Excellent:**	**$575.00**
	Very good:	**$460.00**

Marlin Model 43A

Gauge: 12
Action: Slide action; hammerless; side ejection
Magazine: 5-shot tubular
Barrel: 26" cylinder bore, 28" modified, 30" and 32" full choke; 2¾" chamber
Finish: Blued; walnut pistol grip stock and grooved slide handle
Approximate wt.: 8 lbs.
Comments: Made from about 1923 to 1930. It was a new style takedown. Replaced by Model 53.

Estimated Value:	**Excellent:**	**$375.00**
	Very good:	**$300.00**

Marlin Models 43T and 43TS

Same basic shotgun as the Model 43A except: checkered Monte Carlo stock and forearm with recoil pad. The Model 43TS had a choice of many options and the value is dependent on the number and type of extras.

Estimated Value:	**Excellent:**	**$500.00**
	Very good:	**$400.00**

Marlin Model 53

Similar to Model 43A. Made in standard grade only, from 1929 to 1931, and replaced by Model 63A.

Estimated Value:	**Excellent:**	**$425.00**
	Very good:	**$340.00**

Marlin Model 44A

Gauge: 20
Action: Slide action; hammerless; side ejector
Magazine: 4-shot tubular; bottom load
Barrel: 25" or 28" cylinder bore, modified or full choke; 2¾" chamber
Finish: Blued; walnut pistol grip stock and grooved slide handle
Approximate wt.: 6 lbs.
Comments: A takedown model produced from about 1923 to 1935.

Estimated Value:	**Excellent:**	**$425.00**
	Very good:	**$340.00**

Marlin Model 44S

Same basic shotgun as the Model 44A except: either straight or pistol grip checkered stock and forearm.

Estimated Value:	**Excellent:**	**$475.00**
	Very good:	**$380.00**

Marlin Model 63A

Gauge: 12
Action: Slide action; hammerless; side ejector
Magazine: 5-shot tubular
Barrel: 26" cylinder bore, 28" modified choke, 30" or 32" full choke
Finish: Blued; plain walnut pistol grip stock and grooved slide handle
Approximate wt.: 8 lbs.
Comments: An improved version of the Model 43A. Made from about 1931 to 1935.

Estimated Value:	**Excellent:**	**$400.00**
	Very good:	**$320.00**

Marlin Models 63T and 63TS

The Model 63T was basically the same shotgun as the Model 63A except it was only produced in 30" or 32" barrel and had a checkered straight stock. The Model 63TS could be ordered to the buyer's specifications. Prices are for Standard Trap gun.

Estimated Value:	**Excellent:**	**$500.00**
	Very good:	**$400.00**

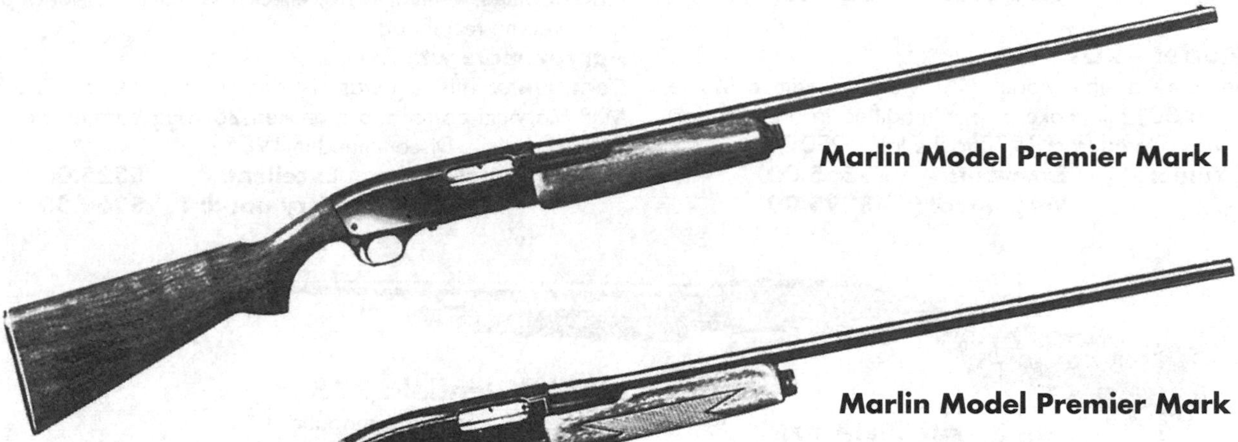

Marlin Model Premier Mark I

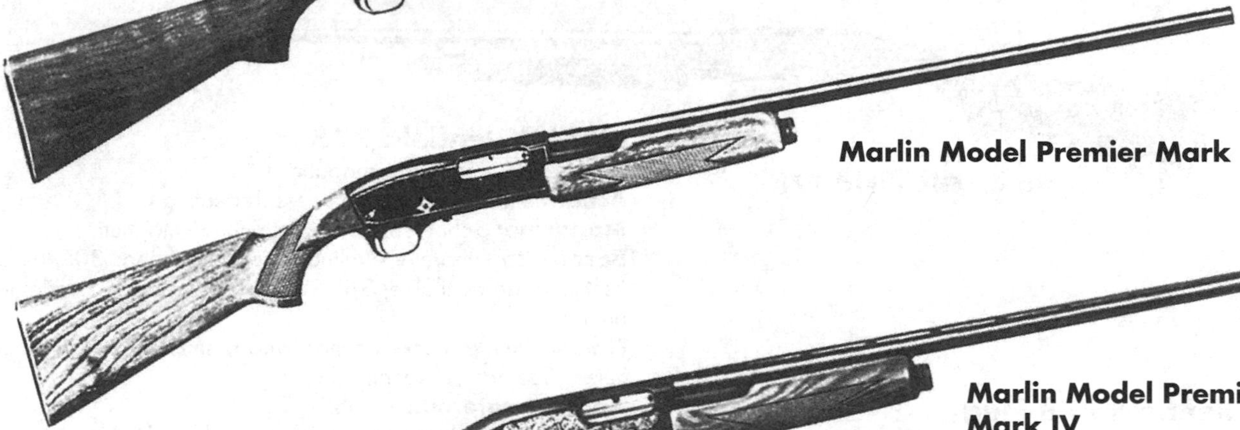

Marlin Model Premier Mark II

Marlin Model Premier Mark IV

Marlin Model Premier Mark I

Gauge: 12
Action: Slide action; hammerless; side ejector
Magazine: 3-shot tubular
Barrel: 26" cylinder bore, 28" modified, 30" full choke; ventilated rib available; 28" slug barrel with rifle sights available; $2\frac{3}{4}$" chamber
Finish: Blued; walnut pistol grip stock and forearm; recoil pad optional
Approximate wt.: 7 lbs.
Comments: Made from about 1960 to 1963.

Estimated Value:	**Excellent:**	**$300.00**
	Very good:	**$240.00**

Marlin Model Premier Mark II

This is basically the same shotgun as the Premier Mark I except the stock and forearm are checkered and the receiver is engraved.

Estimated Value:	**Excellent:**	**$325.00**
	Very good:	**$260.00**

Marlin Model Premier Mark IV

This is basically the same shotgun as the Mark II except the wood is more elaborate and the engraving heavier.

Estimated Value:	**Excellent:**	**$340.00**
	Very good:	**$272.00**

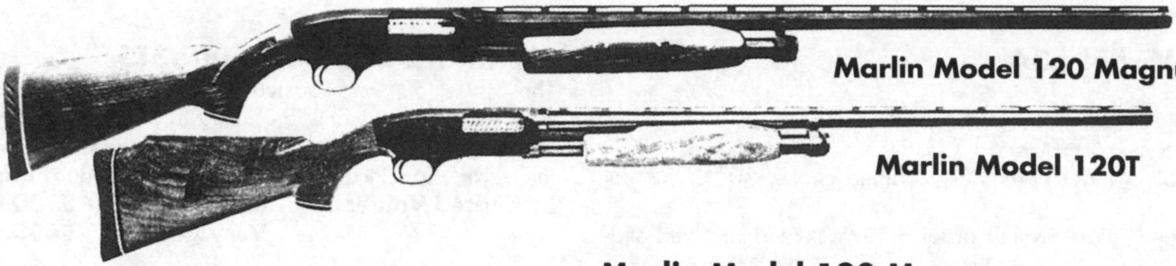

Marlin Model 120 Magnum

Marlin Model 120T

Marlin Deluxe 120 Slug Gun

Similar to the Marlin 120 with a 20" slug barrel and rifle sights. Produced from the late 1970s to 1986.

Estimated Value: **Excellent:** **$350.00**
Very good: **$280.00**

Marlin Model 120T

Basically the same as the Model 120 Magnum with a Monte Carlo stock and 30" full choke or 30" modified trap choke barrel. This gun was offered from 1973 to the late 1970s.

Estimated Value: **Excellent:** **$365.00**
Very good: **$295.00**

Marlin Model 120 Magnum

Gauge: 12 gauge magnum
Action: Slide action; hammerless
Magazine: 5-shot tubular (4-shot with 3" shells)
Barrel: 26" cylinder bore, 28" modified or 30" full choke
Finish: Blued; ventilated rib; checkered walnut, pistol grip stock and forearm; recoil pad
Approximate wt.: 7¾ lbs.
Comments: This gun was first offered in 1971. In 1973 a 40" MXR Magnum barrel and a choked 26" slug barrel were offered for the first time. Discontinued in 1986.

Estimated Value: **Excellent:** **$325.00**
Very good: **$260.00**

Marlin Glenfield 778

Marlin Glenfield 778

Gauge: 12, regular or magnum
Action: Slide action; hammerless; repeating
Magazine: 5-shot tubular; 4-shot with 3" magnum
Barrel: 26" improved cylinder; 28" modified; 30" full choke; ventilated rib available; 38" MXR full choke barrel available without rib
Finish: Blued; checkered hardwood, semi-pistol grip stock and fluted slide handle; recoil pad
Approximate wt.: 7¾ lbs.
Comments: Made from about the late 1970s to the early 1980s. Add $50.00 for ventilated rib or MXR barrel.

Estimated Value: **Excellent:** **$250.00**
Very good: **$200.00**

Marlin Glenfield 778 Slug

Similar to the Glenfield 778 with a 20" slug barrel and rifle sights.

Estimated Value: **Excellent:** **$250.00**
Very good: **$200.00**

MAUSER

Mauser Model 496 Trap

Mauser Model 496 Competition

Mauser Model 496 Trap

Gauge: 12
Action: Box lock; top lever break-open; hammerless; single shot
Magazine: None
Barrel: 32" modified or 34" full chokes; ventilated rib
Finish: Blued; checkered walnut Monte Carlo pistol grip stock and tapered forearm; engraved; recoil pad
Approximate wt.: 8½ lbs.
Comments: Imported in the 1970s.

Estimated Value: **Excellent:** **$475.00**
Very good: **$380.00**

Mauser Model 496 Competition

Similar to the Model 496 with select wood; higher ventilated rib.

Estimated Value: **Excellent:** **$455.00**
Very good: **$365.00**

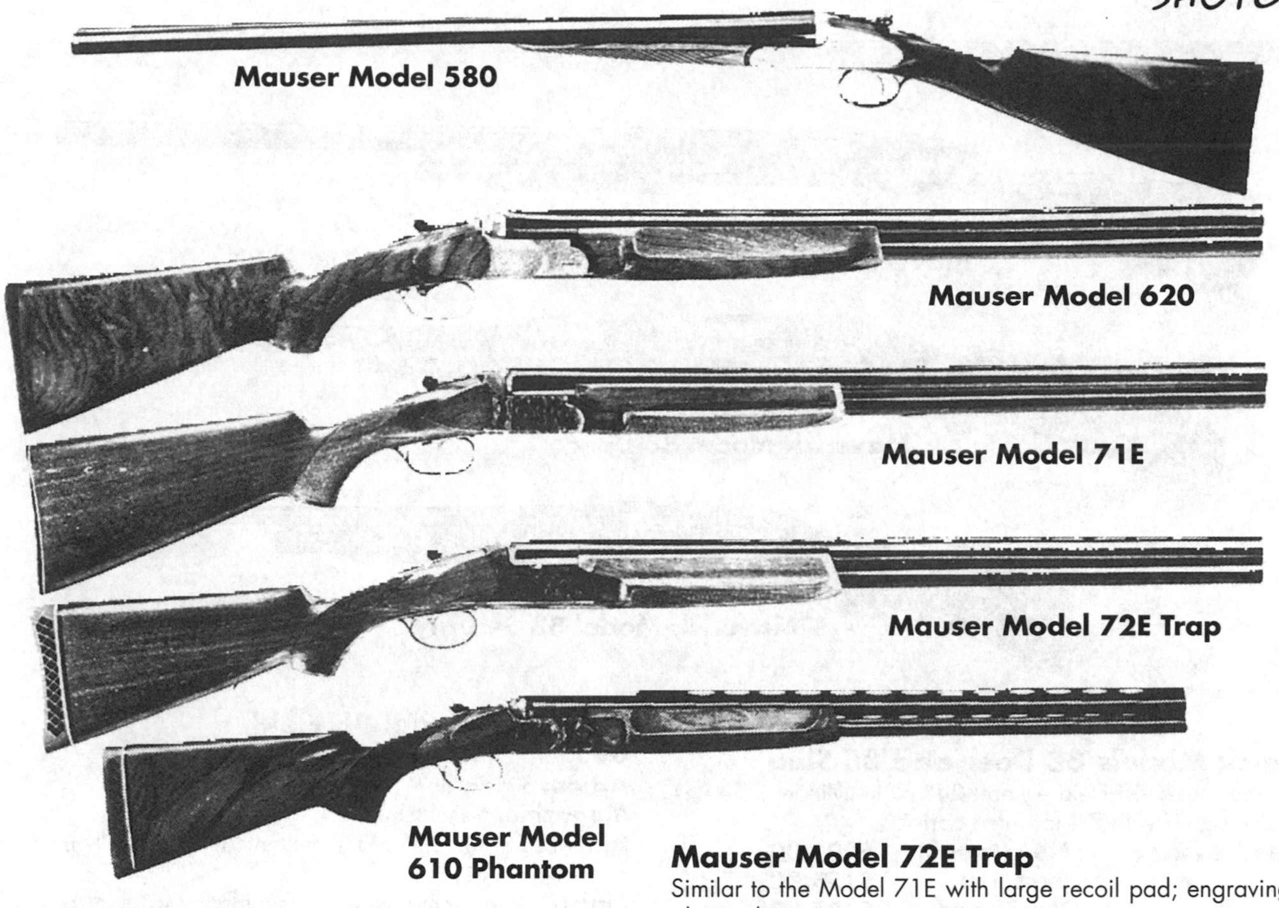

Mauser Model 580

Mauser Model 620

Mauser Model 71E

Mauser Model 72E Trap

Mauser Model 610 Phantom

Mauser Model 580

Gauge: 12
Action: Side lock; top lever break-open; hammerless
Magazine: None
Barrel: Side-by-side double barrel; 28" – 30", various chokes
Finish: Blued; checkered walnut straight stock and tapered forearm; engraved
Approximate wt.: 7¾ lbs.
Comments: Imported in the 1970s.

Estimated Value:	**Excellent:**	**$1,000.00**
	Very good:	**$ 800.00**

Mauser Model 620

Gauge: 12
Action: Box lock; top lever break-open; hammerless; automatic ejectors; single trigger
Magazine: None
Barrel: Over and under double barrel; 28", 30" improved cylinder and modified or modified and full or skeet chokes; ribbed
Finish: Blued; plain walnut pistol grip stock and forearm; recoil pad
Approximate wt.: 7½ lbs.
Comments: Imported from the early to the mid-1970s.

Estimated Value:	**Excellent:**	**$775.00**
	Very good:	**$625.00**

Mauser Model 71E

Similar to the Model 620 with double triggers and no recoil pad; 28" barrel.

Estimated Value:	**Excellent:**	**$400.00**
	Very good:	**$320.00**

Mauser Model 72E Trap

Similar to the Model 71E with large recoil pad; engraving; wide rib; single trigger.

Estimated Value:	**Excellent:**	**$425.00**
	Very good:	**$340.00**

Mauser Model 610 Phantom

Gauge: 12
Action: Box lock; top lever break-open; hammerless
Magazine: None
Barrel: Over and under double barrel; ventilated rib between barrels and on top barrel; 30", 32" various chokes
Finish: Blued; case hardened frame; checkered walnut pistol grip stock and forearm; recoil pad
Approximate wt.: 8 lbs.
Comments: Made in the mid-1970s.

Estimated Value:	**Excellent:**	**$650.00**
	Very good:	**$520.00**

Mauser Contest

Gauge: 12
Action: Top lever break-open; automatic ejectors; single selective trigger
Magazine: None
Barrel: Over and under double barrel; 27½" improved cylinder and improved modified
Finish: Blued; engraved gray side plates; checkered walnut pistol grip stock and lipped forearm
Approximate wt.: 7½ lbs.
Comments: Add $200.00 for Trap or Skeet model.

Estimated Value:	**Excellent:**	**$1,200.00**
	Very good:	**$ 975.00**

Maverick Model 88 Field

Maverick Model 88 Deer

Maverick Model 88 Security

Maverick Models 88 Deer and 88 Slug

Same as the Model 88 Field except: 24" plain cylinder bore barrel with rifle sights. Add 7% for rifled barrel.

Estimated Value:	**New (retail):**	**$206.00**
	Excellent:	**$155.00**
	Very good:	**$125.00**

Maverick Model 88 Security

Same as the Model 88 Field except: 18½" or 20" cylinder bore barrel; 5- or 7-shot magazine; available with pistol grip kit and/or heat shield; add 6% for 7 shot; add 6% for pistol grip kit or heat shield.

Estimated Value:	**New (retail):**	**$199.00**
	Excellent:	**$150.00**
	Very good:	**$120.00**

Maverick Model 88 Field

Gauge: 12 (3" chamber)
Action: Slide action; hammerless; repeating
Magazine: 5-shot tubular
Barrel: 28" or 30" plain or ventilated rib; full, modified, or accu-choke tubes
Finish: Blued; smooth black synthetic pistol grip stock and grooved slide handle
Approximate wt.: 7¼ lbs.
Comments: Introduced in the mid-1990s; add 8% for ventilated rib; add 5% for accu-choke tubes; add 10% for accu-choke tube set (full, modified, and improved cylinder).

Estimated Value:	**New (retail):**	**$249.00**
	Excellent:	**$185.00**
	Very good:	**$150.00**

Maverick Model 91

Maverick Model 91

Gauge: 12 (3½" chamber)
Action: Slide action; hammerless; repeating
Magazine: 4-shot tubular
Barrel: 18½" or 20" with plain or ventilated rib barrel and accu-mag choke tube or cylinder bore
Finish: Blued; black synthetic pistol grip stock and grooved slide handle
Approximate wt.: 7¾ lbs.
Comments: Introduced in the mid-1990s. Add 10% for ventilated rib barrel.

Estimated Value:	**Excellent:**	**$175.00**
	Very good:	**$140.00**

Maverick Model 88 Bullpup

Gauge: 12 regular or magnum
Action: Slide action; hammerless; repeating, using the basic Mossberg 500 action
Magazine: 5-shot or 7-shot tubular
Barrel: 18½" or 20" cylinder bore with top carrying handle and heat shield; rifle sights
Finish: Blued; black synthetic housing stock and pistol grips (2); pistol grip at trigger with grip safety and pistol grip slide handle
Approximate wt.: 9½ lbs.
Comments: Same as the Mossberg Model 500 Bullpup except: introduced in 1994 as Maverick. Discontinued in the late 1990s. Add 15% for ventilated rib.

Estimated Value:	**Excellent:**	**$200.00**
	Very good:	**$160.00**

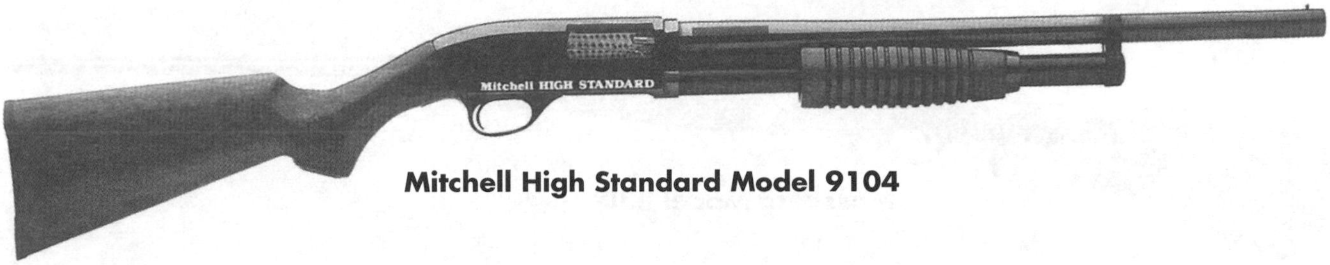

Mitchell High Standard Model 9104

Mitchell High Standard Model 9108

Mitchell High Standard Models 9104 and 9105

Gauge: 12
Action: Slide action; hammerless; repeating
Magazine: 5-shot tubular
Barrel: 20" plain barrel; bead sight (Model 9104)
Finish: Blued; plain smooth walnut semi-pistol grip stock and grooved slide handle
Approximate wt.: 6½ lbs.
Comments: Produced in the mid-1990s; add 7% for rifle sights (Model 9105).

Estimated Value:	**Excellent:**	**$200.00**
	Very good:	**$160.00**

Mitchell High Standard Models 9108, 9109, 9111, and 9113

Same as Models 9104 and 9105 except: 7-shot magazines (9108, 9109); 6-shot magazine and 18½" barrel on Model 9111 and 9113; military green or brown stock and slide handle. Add 7% for rifle sights.

Estimated Value:	**Excellent:**	**$220.00**
	Very good:	**$175.00**

Mitchell High Standard Model 9114

Mitchell High Standard Model 9115

Mitchell High Standard Model 9115

Same as Model 9104 except: 7-shot magazine; 18½" barrel; ventilated steel heat shield on barrel; parkerized finish; stealth gray synthetic stock and slide handle; buttstock has 4-shot storage capacity.

Estimated Value:	**Excellent:**	**$250.00**
	Very good:	**$200.00**

Mitchell High Standard Models 9114 and 9114FS

Same as Model 9104 except: 7-shot magazine; removable synthetic buttstock, "one hand" pistol grip and slide handle (Model 9114); Model 9114FS has a special folding steel buttstock which can be used folded or extended and a "one hand" pistol grip.

Estimated Value:	**Excellent:**	**$240.00**
	Very good:	**$195.00**

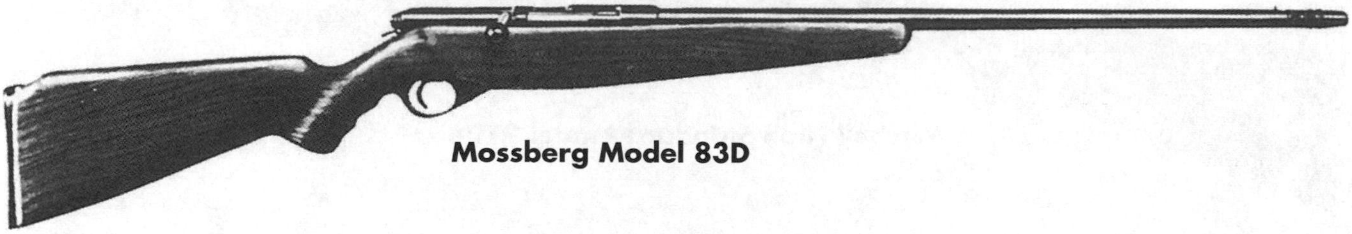

Mossberg Model 83D

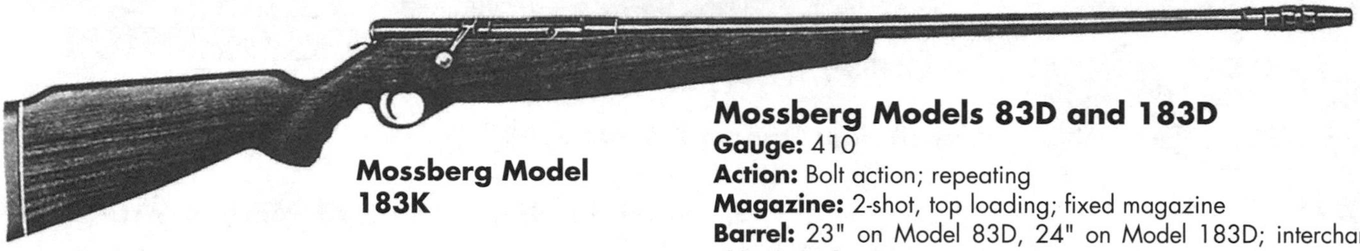

Mossberg Model 183K

Mossberg Models 83D and 183D

Gauge: 410
Action: Bolt action; repeating
Magazine: 2-shot, top loading; fixed magazine
Barrel: 23" on Model 83D, 24" on Model 183D; interchangeable choke fittings
Finish: Blued; hardwood Monte Carlo semi-pistol grip; one-piece stock and forearm
Approximate wt.: 5½ lbs.
Comments: Made as the Model 83D from about 1940 to 1947 and as the Model 183D from 1948 until the early 1970s.

Estimated-Value:	**Excellent:**	**$160.00**
	Very good:	**$125.00**

Mossberg Model 183K

Similar to the Model 183D with adjustable choke and recoil pad. Made from the early 1950s to the mid-1980s.

Estimated Value:	**Excellent:**	**$175.00**
	Very good:	**$140.00**

Mossberg Model 185K

Mossberg Model 190K

Mossberg Model 190K

Similar to the Model 183K in 16 gauge. Made from the mid-1950s to the early 1960s.

Estimated Value:	**Excellent:**	**$160.00**
	Very good:	**$125.00**

Mossberg Model 185K

Similar to the Model 183K in 20 gauge. Made from about 1950 to the early 1960s.

Estimated Value:	**Excellent:**	**$175.00**
	Very good:	**$140.00**

Mossberg Model 195K

Similar to the Model 183K in 12 gauge. Made from the mid-1950s to the early 1960s.

Estimated Value:	**Excellent:**	**$175.00**
	Very good:	**$140.00**

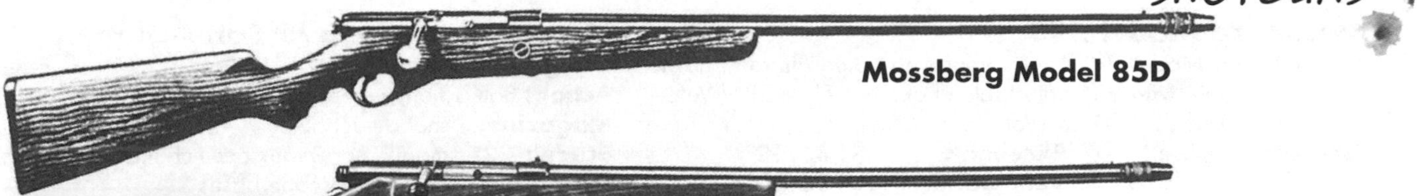
Mossberg Model 85D

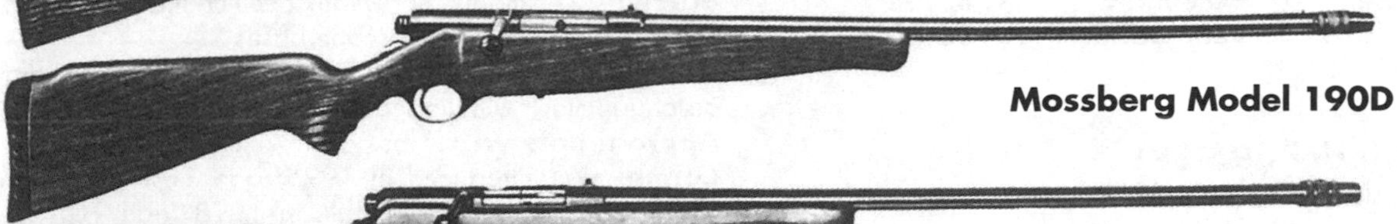
Mossberg Model 190D

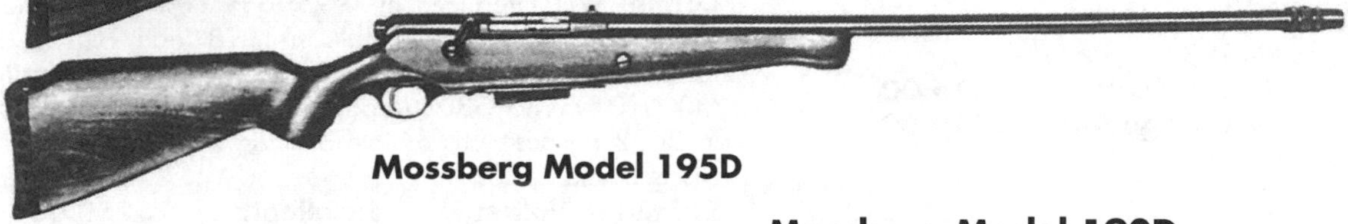
Mossberg Model 195D

Mossberg Models 85D and 185D

Gauge: 20
Action: Bolt action; repeating
Magazine: 2-shot detachable box
Barrel: 25" on Model 85D, 26" on Model 185D; interchangeable choke fittings
Finish: Blued; hardwood pistol grip, one-piece stock and forearm
Approximate wt.: 6½ lbs.
Comments: Made as the Model 85D from about 1940 to 1948, and as the Model 185D from 1948 to the early 1970s.

Estimated Value:	**Excellent:**	**$150.00**
	Very good:	**$120.00**

Mossberg Model 190D

Similar to the Model 185D in 16 gauge. Made from the mid-1950s to the early 1960s.

Estimated Value:	**Excellent:**	**$160.00**
	Very good:	**$125.00**

Mossberg Model 195D

Similar to the Model 185D in 12 gauge. Made from the mid-1950s to the early 1970s.

Estimated Value:	**Excellent:**	**$135.00**
	Very good:	**$110.00**

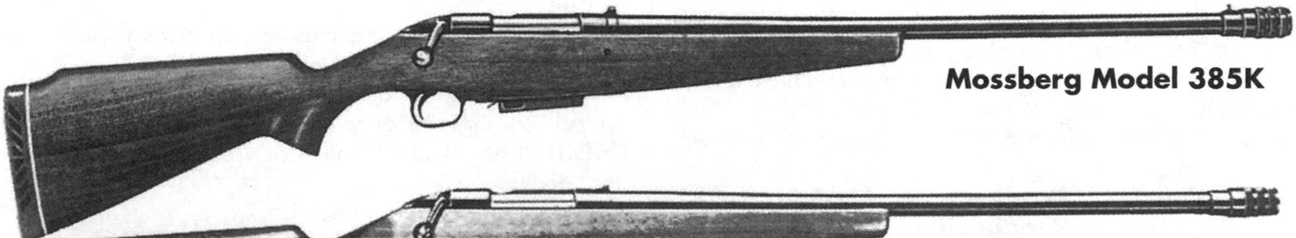
Mossberg Model 385K

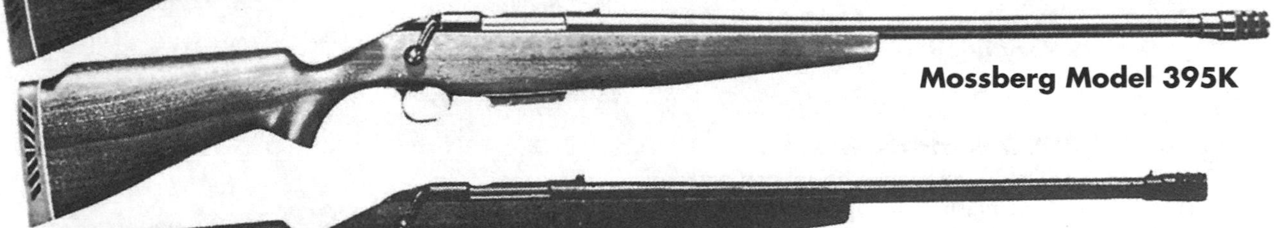
Mossberg Model 395K

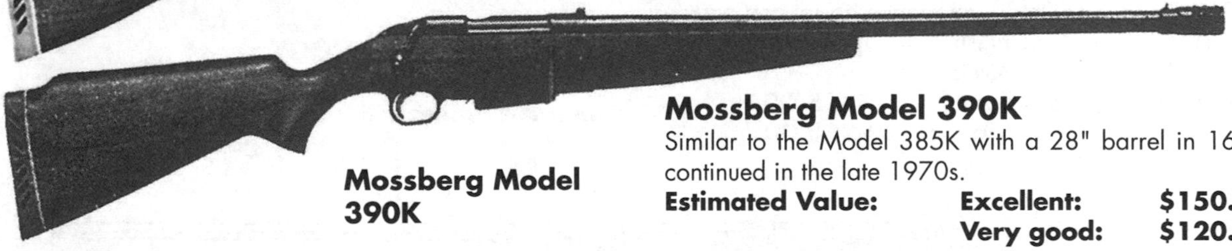
Mossberg Model 390K

Mossberg Model 385K

Gauge: 20
Action: Bolt action; repeating
Magazine: 2-shot detachable box
Barrel: 26" adjustable choke
Finish: Blued; wood Monte Carlo semi-pistol grip, one-piece stock and tapered forearm; recoil pad
Approximate wt.: 6½ lbs.
Comments: Made from the early 1960s to the early 1980s.

Estimated Value:	**Excellent:**	**$160.00**
	Very good:	**$125.00**

Mossberg Model 390K

Similar to the Model 385K with a 28" barrel in 16 gauge. Discontinued in the late 1970s.

Estimated Value:	**Excellent:**	**$150.00**
	Very good:	**$120.00**

Mossberg Model 395K

Similar to the Model 385K in 12 gauge. Weighs 7½ lbs.

Estimated Value:	**Excellent:**	**$135.00**
	Very good:	**$110.00**

Mossberg Model 585

Similar to the Model 385K with improved safety. Produced in the mid-1980s.

Estimated Value:	**Excellent:**	**$175.00**
	Very good:	**$140.00**

Mossberg Model 595

Similar to the Model 395K with improved safety. Introduced in 1984. Available with 28" adjustable choke barrel or 38" Waterfowl barrel. Add $20.00 for Waterfowl Model.

Estimated Value: **Excellent:** **$185.00**
Very good: **$150.00**

Mossberg Model 395 SPL

Similar to the Model 395K with a 38" full choke barrel for Waterfowl; swivels. Introduced in 1982.

Estimated Value: **Excellent:** **$175.00**
Very good: **$140.00**

Mossberg Model 695 Bolt Action

Gauge: 12, 3" chambers
Action: Bolt action, repeating
Magazine: 2-shot detachable
Barrel: 22" smooth bore with accu-choke or rifled bore; rifle sights and "Weaver-style" scope bases
Finish: Synthetic stock and forearm in matte or woodland finish; pistol grip stock with lipped fore-end
Approximate wt.: 7 lbs.
Comments: Introduced in 1995; add 10% for woodlands finish; fiber optic sights available in 1998 (add 10%). Add 11% for rifle sights. Model 695 with serial numbers ranging from M000101 to M015304 (produced 1995 – 1996) were recalled in 2002 because of possible discharge when closing the bolt. Discontinued 2003.

Estimated Value: **Excellent:** **$250.00**
Very good: **$200.00**

Mossberg Model 695 Bolt Action

Mossberg Model 3000 Field

Gauge: 12, 20; regular or magnum
Action: Slide action; hammerless; repeating
Magazine: 4-shot tubular, 3-shot in magnum
Barrel: 26" improved cylinder, 28" modified or full, 30" full; ventilated rib; "Multi-choke" available
Finish: Checkered walnut pistol grip stock and slide handle
Approximate wt.: 6¼ to 7½ lbs.
Comments: Produced in the mid-1980s. Add $25.00 for "Multi-choke."

Estimated Value: **Excellent:** **$300.00**
Very good: **$240.00**

Mossberg Model 3000 Waterfowler

Similar to the Model 3000 with 30" full choke barrel and parkerized, oiled finish or camouflage finish with "Speedfeed" storage stock (add 10%). Add 10% for "Multi-choke."

Estimated Value: **Excellent:** **$345.00**
Very good: **$280.00**

Mossberg Model 3000 Slug

Similar to the Model 3000 with a 22" slug barrel and rifle sights. Add $35.00 for black finish with "Speedfeed" storage stock.

Estimated Value: **Excellent:** **$305.00**
Very good: **$245.00**

Mossberg Model 200D

Gauge: 12
Action: Slide action; hammerless; repeating; slide handle is metal cover over wood forearm
Magazine: 3-shot detachable box
Barrel: 28" interchangeable choke fittings
Finish: Blued; wood Monte Carlo semi-pistol grip, one-piece stock and forearm
Approximate wt.: 7½ lbs.
Comments: Made from the mid- to the late 1950s.

Estimated Value: **Excellent:** **$160.00**
Very good: **$125.00**

Mossberg Model 200K

Similar to the Model 200D with adjustable choke.

Estimated Value: **Excellent:** **$175.00**
Very good: **$140.00**

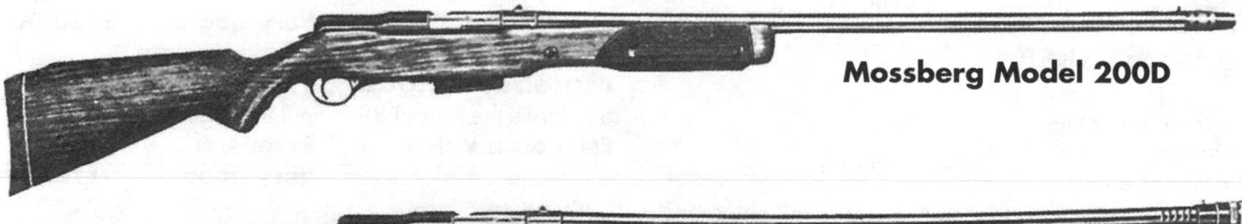

Mossberg Model 200D

Mossberg Model 200K

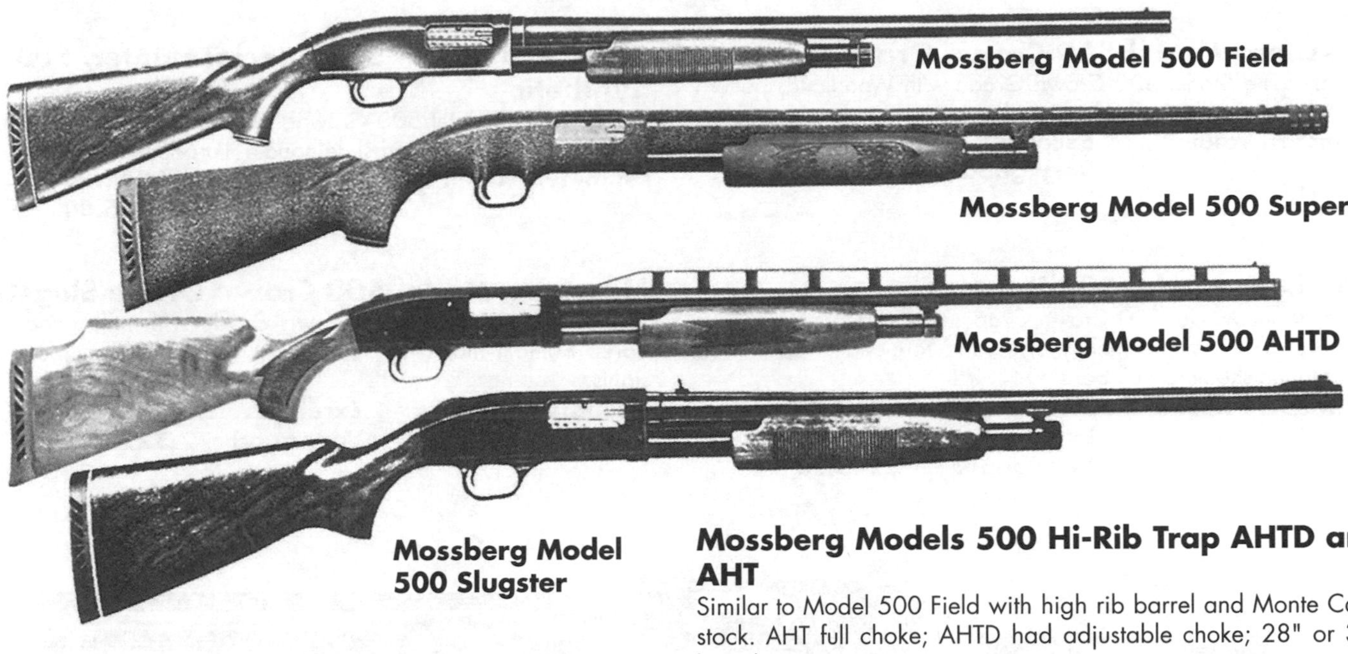

Mossberg Model 500 Field

Mossberg Model 500 Super

Mossberg Model 500 AHTD

Mossberg Model 500 Slugster

Mossberg Model 500 Field

Gauge: 12, 16, 20, 410
Action: Slide action; hammerless; repeating
Magazine: 5-shot tubular
Barrel: 24" cylinder or rifle bore; 26" adjustable choke or improved cylinder; 28" modified or full; 30" full choke in 12 gauge only; available with accu-choke after 1984; ventilated rib available
Finish: Blued; walnut finish stock and grooved slide handle; recoil pad
Approximate wt.: 6 to 8 lbs.
Comments: Manufactured from about 1960 to late 1990s. Add 15% for rifled barrel; add 8% for rifle sights.

Estimated Value:	**Excellent:**	**$245.00**
	Very good:	**$195.00**

Mossberg Model 500 Super

Similar to the Model 500 Field with checkered stock and slide handle and ventilated rib. 12 gauge magnum.

Estimated Value:	**Excellent:**	**$250.00**
	Very good:	**$200.00**

Mossberg Model 500 Crown Grade

Mossberg Model 500 Crown Grade

Similar to the Model 500 Field with checkered walnut pistol grip stock and slide handle.

Estimated Value:	**Excellent:**	**$265.00**
	Very good:	**$210.00**

Mossberg Models 500 Hi-Rib Trap AHTD and AHT

Similar to Model 500 Field with high rib barrel and Monte Carlo stock. AHT full choke; AHTD had adjustable choke; 28" or 30" barrel.

Estimated Value:	**Excellent:**	**$300.00**
	Very good:	**$240.00**

Mossberg Model 500 Slugster

Similar to Model 500 Field with 18" or 24" slug barrel and rifle sights. Add 20% for removable choke; add 15% for Trophy Model; add 12% for rifled barrel.

Estimated Value:	**Excellent:**	**$225.00**
	Very good:	**$180.00**

Mossberg Models 500 ALDR, CLDR, and ALDRX

Similar to Model 500 in 12 gauge (ALDR) and 20 gauge (CLDR) with removable choke. Add $50.00 for additional slugster barrel (ALDRX).

Estimated Value:	**Excellent:**	**$245.00**
	Very good:	**$195.00**

Mossberg Model 500 ALMR Duck Gun

Similar to 500 in 12 gauge with 30" or 32" ventilated rib barrel for 3" magnum. Discontinued in the early 1980s.

Estimated Value:	**Excellent:**	**$265.00**
	Very good:	**$210.00**

Mossberg Model 500 Viking

Same as the Mossberg Model 500 Field except: 12 and 20 gauge only; matte blue finish with green synthetic stock and slide handle; add 5% for 24" rifled barrel with rifle sights. Introduced in 1996.

Estimated Value:	**Excellent:**	**$225.00**
	Very good:	**$180.00**

Mossberg Model 500 Crown Grade Camo
Similar to the Model 500 Crown Grade with Woodlands pattern camouflage. Bantam model available.

Estimated Value: **Excellent:** **$275.00**
Very good: **$220.00**

Mossberg Model 500 Special Hunter, 500 Synthetic
Similar to the Model 500 Crown Grade except with parkerized finish, synthetic stock, and slide handle. Introduced in 1998.

Estimated Value: **Excellent:** **$245.00**
Very good: **$195.00**

Mossberg Model 500 Bantam
Similar to the Model 500 Crown Grade, scaled down for smaller shooters. Stock is one inch shorter and fore-end is positioned closer to the shooter; 410 bore.

Estimated Value: **New (retail):** **$413.00**
Excellent: **$310.00**
Very good: **$245.00**

Mossberg Model 500 Crown Grade Slugster
Similar to the Model 500 Crown Grade with fully rifled bore barel. Bantam model also available; add 10% for fiber optic sights.

Estimated Value: **Excellent:** **$280.00**
Very good: **$225.00**

Mossberg Model 500 Security and Persuader ATP8

Mossberg Model 500 Security and Persuader ATP8
Similar to the Model 500 ATP6 series with a 20" barrel, 8-shot capacity. Add 8% for rifle sights; 16% for parkerized finish; 24% for nickel finish; 12% for "Speedfeed" stock; 20% for camouflage finish. Discontinued in the mid-1990s.

Estimated Value: **Excellent:** **$200.00**
Very good: **$160.00**

Mossberg Model 500 Security and Persuader ATP6
Similar to the Model 500, built in several models for law enforcement use. 12 gauge, 6-shot, 18½" barrel. Add 17% for parkerized finish; 9% for rifle sights; 26% for nickel finish; 13% for "Speedfeed" stock; 22% for camouflage finish.

Estimated Value: **Excellent:** **$220.00**
Very good: **$175.00**

Mossberg 500 Security and Persuader CTP6, ETP6
Similar to the other 500 series law enforcement shotguns in 20 gauge (CTP6) or 410 bore (ETP6); 18½" barrel; 6-shot.

Estimated Value: **Excellent:** **$220.00**
Very good: **$175.00**

Mossberg Model 500 Mariner

Mossberg Model 500 Mariner
Similar to the Persuader series except it has a special Teflon and metal coating that is resistant to saltwater spray. Stock and slide handle are synthetic. Available in 6- or 9-shot version. Add 3% for 9-shot model, 10% for "Speedfeed" stock, 15% for ghost ring sight. Introduced in 1987.

Estimated Value: **New (retail):** **$609.00**
Excellent: **$455.00**
Very good: **$365.00**

Mossberg Model 500 Persuader Cruiser
Similar to the Model 500 ATP6 and ATP8 series law enforcement shotguns with "one-hand" grip. Add 30% for parkerized finish.

Estimated Value: **New (retail):** **$406.00**
Excellent: **$305.00**
Very good: **$245.00**

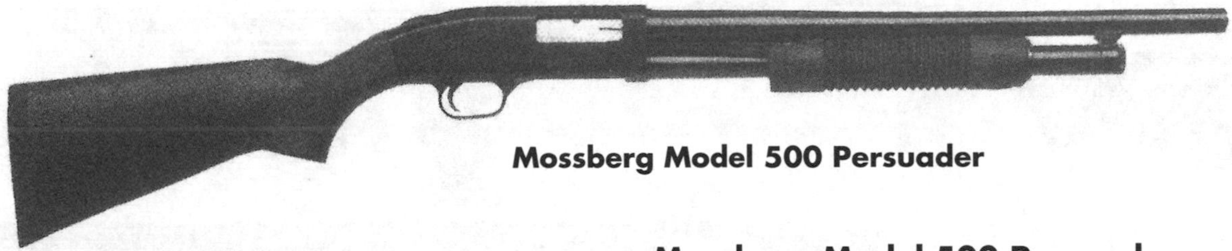

Mossberg Model 500 Persuader

Mossberg Model 500 Camper

Similar to the Model 500 Cruiser in 12 gauge, 20 gauge, or 410 bore; 18½" barrel; synthetic grip and slide handle; camouflage carrying case. Introduced in the late 1980s.

Estimated Value: **Excellent:** **$250.00**
Very good: **$200.00**

Mossberg Model 500 Persuader

Similar to the Model 500 Security and Persuader. Walnut stock and slide handle or synthetic stock and slide handle. Add 36% for parkerized finish with ghost ring sights.

Estimated Value: **New (retail):** **$420.00**
Excellent: **$315.00**
Very good: **$250.00**

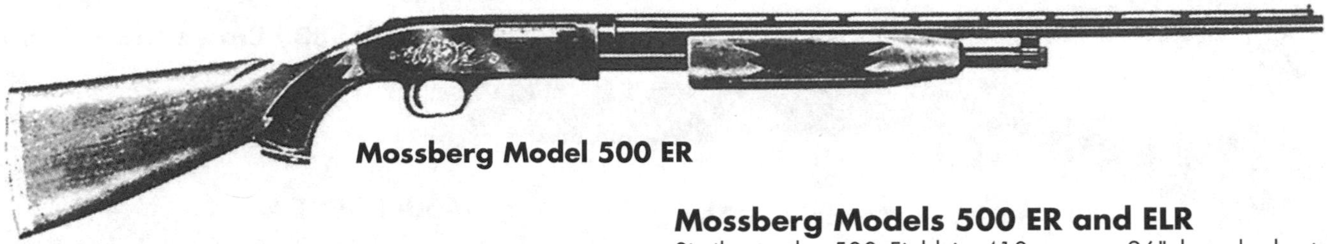

Mossberg Model 500 ER

Mossberg Model 500 APR Pigeon

Similar to the 500 Field except: engraving; ventilated rib. Made from the late 1960s to the late 1970s.

Estimated Value: **Excellent:** **$325.00**
Very good: **$260.00**

Mossberg Model 500 ARTR Trap

Similar to the 500 APR with a 30" full choke barrel; Monte Carlo stock. Discontinued in the late 1970s.

Estimated Value: **Excellent:** **$360.00**
Very good: **$285.00**

Mossberg Models 500 ER and ELR

Similar to the 500 Field in 410 gauge; 26" barrel; skeet version has checkering and ventilated rib. Discontinued in the early 1980s.

Estimated Value: **Excellent:** **$245.00**
Very good: **$195.00**

Mossberg Model 500 Regal

Similar to the Model 500 with deluxe finish, crown design on receiver. Produced in the mid-1980s. Add $20.00 for accu-choke.

Estimated Value: **Excellent:** **$245.00**
Very good: **$195.00**

Mossberg Model 500 Sporting

Mossberg Model 500 Bullpup

Gauge: 12 regular or magnum
Action: Slide action, hammerless; repeating, using the basic Mossberg 500 action
Magazine: 5-shot or 7-shot
Barrel: 18½" or 20" cylinder bore with top carrying handle and heat shield; rifle sights
Finish: Blued; black synthetic housing stock and pistol grips (2); pistol grip at trigger with grip safety and pistol grip slide handle
Approximate wt.: 9½ lbs.
Comments: Made from the mid-1980s to the early 1990s.
Estimated Value: **Excellent:** **$400.00**
Very good: **$320.00**

Mossberg Model 500 Sporting

Gauge: 12, 20, 410; regular or magnum
Action: Slide action, hammerless; repeating; double slide bars
Magazine: 5-shot tubular with 3-round field plug
Barrel: 20", 24", 26", 28" accu-choke tubes or fixed choke; plain or ventilated rib
Finish: Blued or camouflage with checkered walnut finish stock and slide handle or synthetic stock and slide handle
Approximate wt.: 6⅘ to 7⅕ lbs.
Comments: Introduced in 1990; add 18% for ghost ring sights; add 8% for camouflage finish.
Estimated Value: **New (retail):** **$364.00**
Excellent: **$275.00**
Very good: **$220.00**

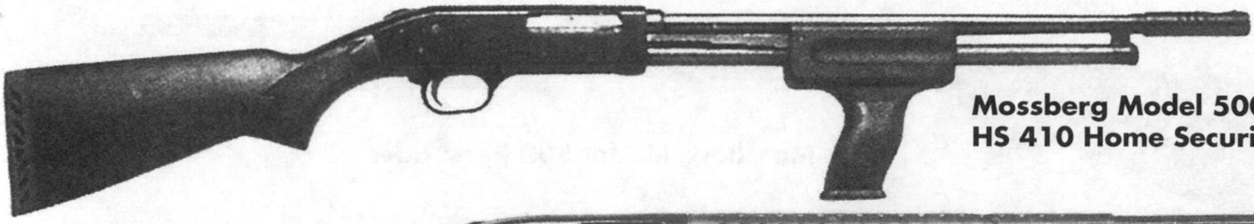

Mossberg Model 500
HS 410 Home Security

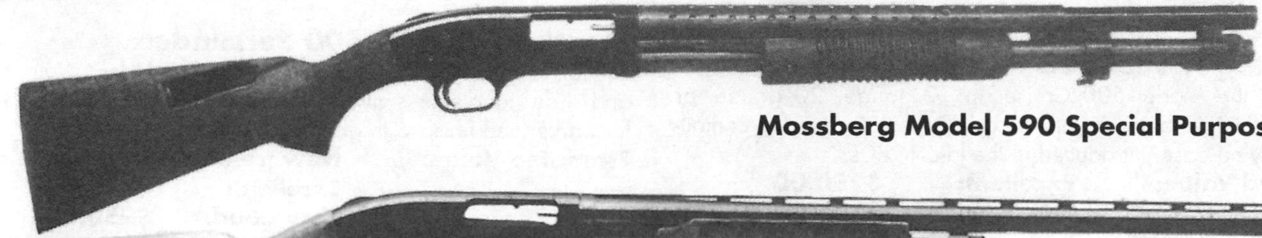

Mossberg Model 590 Special Purpose

Mossberg Model 835 Crown Grade Ulti-Mag

Mossberg Model 590DA

Mossberg Model 500 HS 410 Home Security

Gauge: 410; 3" chamber; 20 gauge after 1995
Action: Slide action, hammerless; repeating
Magazine: 4-shot tubular
Barrel: 18½" with muzzle brake and spreader choke (the spreader choke delivers almost twice the size circle of a regular shotgun pattern)
Finish: Blued; synthetic stock and slide handle, also vertical slide kit available; the laser sight model has a vertical hand grip slide which contains the light and battery
Approximate wt.: 6¼ lbs.
Comments: Introduced in 1990; add 82% for laser light model.

Estimated Value:	**New (retail):**	**$416.00**
	Excellent:	**$310.00**
	Very good:	**$250.00**

Mossberg Model 590 Special Purpose

Gauge: 12 regular
Action: Slide action, hammerless; repeating; double slide bars
Magazine: 9-shot tubular
Barrel: 20" cylinder bore metal heat shield, bayonet lug, and sling swivels; optional ghost ring sight
Finish: Blued or parkerized with synthetic stock and slide handle. "Speedfeed" stock available. Also, laser sight built into forearm is available. Heavy barrel available in 2002.
Approximate wt.: 7 lbs.
Comments: Introduced in 1990; add 15% for parkerized finish; add 10% for "speedfeed" stock; add 13% for ghost ring sight. Add 6% for heavy barrel.

Estimated Value:	**New (retail):**	**$485.00**
	Excellent:	**$365.00**
	Very good:	**$290.00**

Mossberg Model 590DA

Similar to the Model 590 Special Purpose with parkerized finish except: double action style trigger. Available with 18½" or 20" barrel (6- or 9- shot). Add 9% for ghost ring sight; 6% for 20" barrel; 17% for "speedfeed" model.

Estimated Value:	**Excellent:**	**$420.00**
	Very good:	**$335.00**

Mossberg 835 Field Grade Ulti-Mag

Gauge: 12 (3½" chamber); regular or magnum
Action: Slide action, hammerless; repeating; double slide bars
Magazine: 4- or 5-shot tubular
Barrel: 24" or 28" with ventilated rib and accu-mag choke tube or 24" with rifle sights and fixed cylinder bore choke; 26" added 2004.
Finish: Blued, walnut finish, checkered stock and slide handle
Approximate wt.: 7.3 to 7.7 lbs.
Comments: Made in the 1990s; add 4% for 24" fixed cylinder bore choke barrel with rifle sights.

Estimated Value:	**Excellent:**	**$300.00**
	Very good:	**$240.00**

Mossberg 835 Regal or Crown Grade Ulti-Mag

Same as 835 Field Grade Ulti-Mag except: walnut stock and slide handle; dual-comb stock (stock comb height can be changed by removing one bolt); 24" rifle bore barrel with scope base available; add 5% for 24" rifle bore barrel. Add 2% for matte finish.

Estimated Value:	**Excellent:**	**$300.00**
	Very good:	**$240.00**

Mossberg Model 835 Special Hunter

Similar to the Model 835 except with parkerized finish, 26" or 28" barrel, black synthetic stock and forearm, swivels. Introduced in 1998.

Estimated Value:	**Excellent:**	**$300.00**
	Very good:	**$240.00**

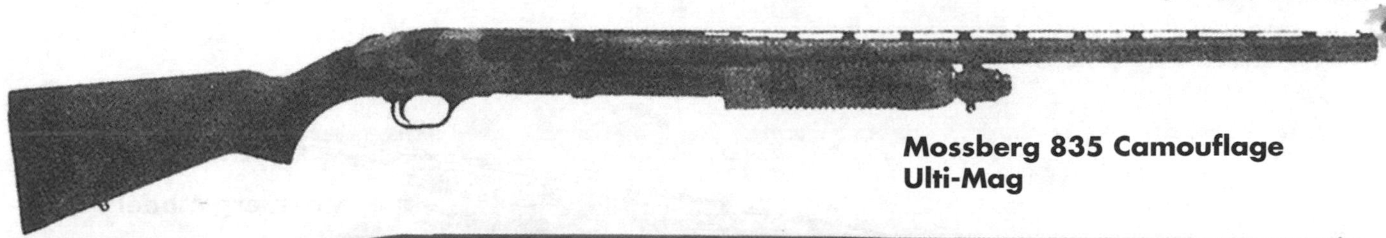

Mossberg 835 Camouflage Ulti-Mag

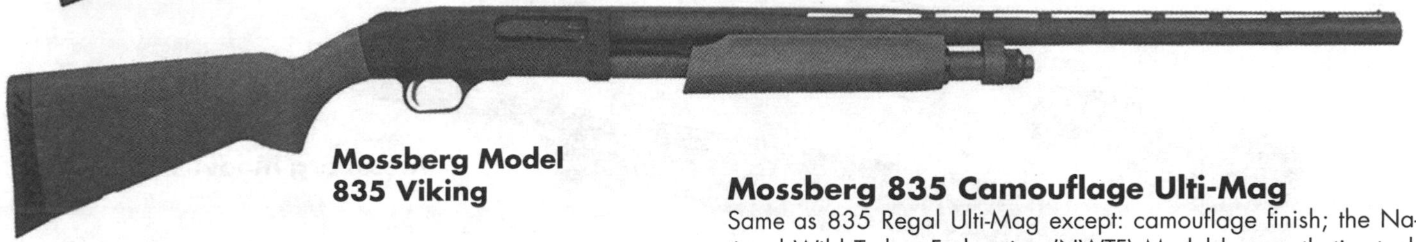

Mossberg Model 835 Viking

Mossberg Model 835 Viking

Similar to the Model 835 Field Grade except: matte blue finish with Viking green synthetic stock and slide handle; 28" ventilated rib barrel with modified choke tube. Produced in 1996 and 1997.

Estimated Value: **Excellent:** **$275.00**
Very good: **$220.00**

Mossberg 835 Camouflage Ulti-Mag

Same as 835 Regal Ulti-Mag except: camouflage finish; the National Wild Turkey Federation (NWTF) Model has synthetic stock (without dual comb feature) and slide handle with Realtree camouflage pattern and 24" barrel with x-full tube accu-mag choke; add 7% for the NWTF Model. Priced for Woodlands camo; add 40% for Mossy Oak or Realtree camo.

Estimated Value: **New (retail):** **$450.00**
Excellent: **$335.00**
Very good: **$270.00**

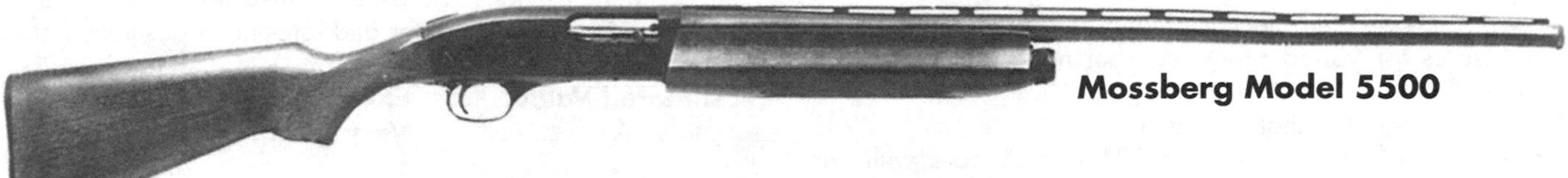

Mossberg Model 5500

Mossberg Model 5500 Slugster

Mossberg Model 935 Magnum

Mossberg Model 5500

Gauge: 12, regular or magnum
Action: Gas-operated, semiautomatic
Magazine: 4-shot tubular
Barrel: 26" improved cylinder, 28" modified, 30" full; 28" accu-choke with interchangeable tubes; ventilated rib available; 25" on youth model
Finish: Blued; checkered hardwood or synthetic semi-pistol grip stock and forearm; aluminum alloy receiver; small stock on youth model
Approximate wt.: 7½ lbs.
Comments: Produced from the early 1980s to the early 1990s. Deduct 20% for synthetic stock; add 5% for magnum.
Estimated Value: **Excellent:** **$225.00**
Very good: **$180.00**

Mossberg Model 5500 Slugster

Similar to the Model 5500 with 18½" or 24" slug barrel, rifle sights and swivels.

Estimated Value: **Excellent:** **$250.00**
Very good: **$200.00**

Mossberg Model 935 Magnum

Gauge: 12 magnum
Action: Gas-operated, semiautomatic
Magazine: tubular, 5-shot with 3" shells, 4-shot with 3½" shells
Barrel: 24", 26", or 28"; with interchangeable choke tubes; ventilated rib
Finish: Matte black or camouflage; synthetic stock and forearm
Approximate wt.: 7¾ lbs.
Comments: Introduced in 2003. Add 12% for camouflage finish.
Estimated Value: **New (retail):** **$631.00**
Excellent: **$475.00**
Very good: **$380.00**

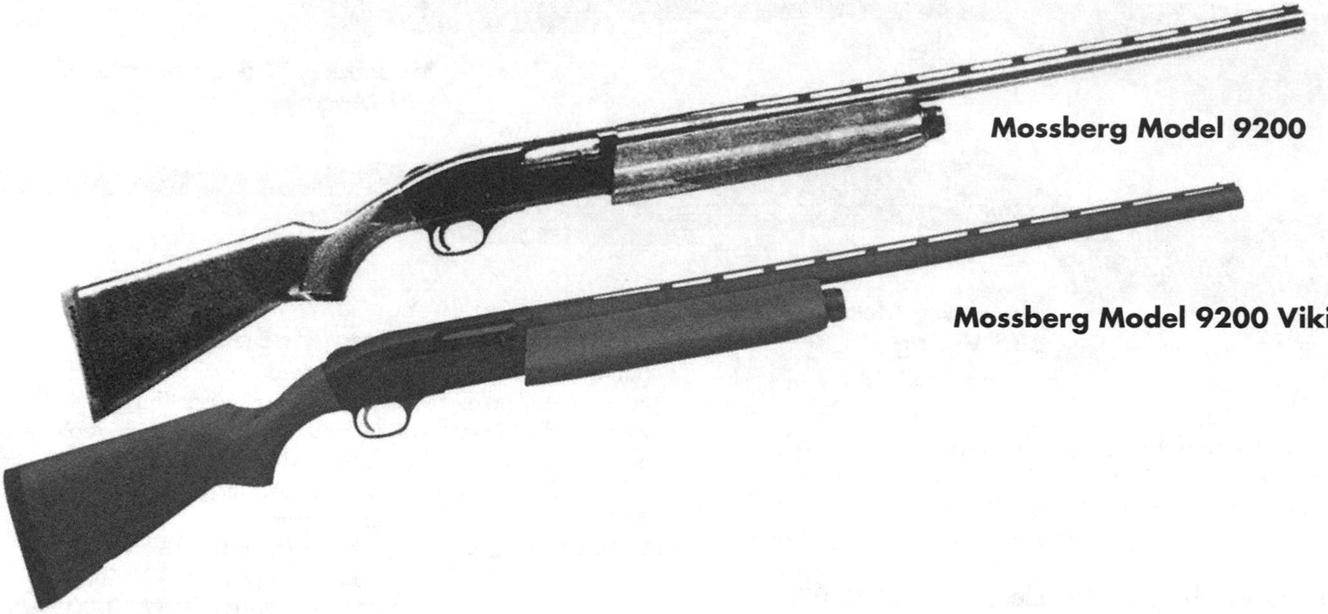

Mossberg Model 9200

Gauge: 12 regular and magnum, interchangeably
Action: Gas-operated, semiautomatic; a gas regulating system compensates for varied pressures from normal to 3" magnum loads.
Magazine: 4-shot; 3-shot in magnum
Barrel: 24" rifled bore; 24" or 28" smooth bore with accu-choke tubes; wide ventilated rib, white front bead and brass mid-point bead
Finish: Blued; checkered pistol grip, walnut stock and forearm; the 24" rifled bore has walnut finish dual-comb stock in blued finish; scope base or rifle sights are available
Approximate wt.: 7½ lbs.
Comments: Introduced in 1992; add 3% for scope base, 5% for fiber optic sights; add 5% for 24" rifled bore with dual-comb stock.

Estimated Value:	**Excellent:**	**$425.00**
	Very good:	**$340.00**

Mossberg Model 9200 Viking

Same as the Mossberg Model 9200 except: 28" ventilated rib barrel with modified choke tube; matte blue finish; green synthetic stock and forearm. Produced in 1996 and 1997.

Estimated Value:	**Excellent:**	**$325.00**
	Very good:	**$260.00**

Mossberg Model 9200 USST

Similar to the Model 9200 with a 26" ventilated rib barrel and extra skeet tube; has "U.S. Shooting Team" engraving; made in the late 1990s.

Estimated Value:	**Excellent:**	**$430.00**
	Very good:	**$345.00**

Mossberg Model 9200 Bantam

Similar to the Model 9200 except scaled down for smaller shooters. Stock is one inch shorter and fore-end is positioned closer to the shooter; 22" ventilated rib barrel.

Estimated Value:	**Excellent:**	**$430.00**
	Very good:	**$345.00**

Mossberg Model 9200 Camo

Similar to the Model 9200 except with a camouflage finish; 24" or 28" ventilated rib barrel; available in Woodlands camo, Mossy Oak, or Realtree; add 7% for a 28" barrel.

Estimated Value:	**Excellent:**	**$405.00**
	Very good:	**$325.00**

Mossberg Model 9200 Special Hunter

Similar to the Model 9200 except with a parkerized finish, 28" barrel, black synthetic stock and forearm, and swivels. Introduced in 1998.

Estimated Value:	**Excellent:**	**$370.00**
	Very good:	**$295.00**

Mossberg Model 9200 Jungle Gun

Similar to the Model 9200 Special Hunter except designed for military and security use; 18½" cylinder bore barrel. Introduced in 1998.

Estimated Value:	**Excellent:**	**$530.00**
	Very good:	**$425.00**

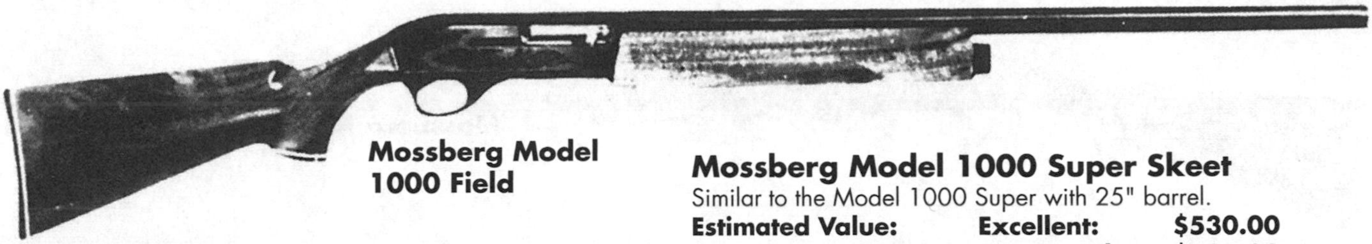

Mossberg Model 1000 Field

Mossberg Model 1000 Super

Gauge: 12 or 20, regular or magnum
Action: Gas-operated, semiautomatic
Magazine: 3-shot tubular
Barrel: 26", 28", 30" multi-choke; ventilated rib
Finish: Blued; checkered walnut pistol grip stock and forearm; recoil pad; scrolling on receiver
Approximate wt.: 6¾ to 7¾ lbs.
Comments: Produced in the mid-1980s in Japan.

Estimated Value:	**Excellent:**	**$450.00**
	Very good:	**$360.00**

Mossberg Model 1000 Super Waterfowler

Similar to the Model 1000 Super with dull wood and parkerized finish; 12 gauge only. Made in Japan.

Estimated Value:	**Excellent:**	**$460.00**
	Very good:	**$370.00**

Mossberg Model 1000 Super Slug

Similar to the Model 1000 Super with 22" slug barrel.

Estimated Value:	**Excellent:**	**$425.00**
	Very good:	**$340.00**

Mossberg Model 1000 Super Skeet

Similar to the Model 1000 Super with 25" barrel.

Estimated Value:	**Excellent:**	**$530.00**
	Very good:	**$425.00**

Mossberg Model 1000 Field

Similar to the Model 1000 Super with alloy receiver; various chokes available including a 26" skeet barrel; add $30.00 for multi-choke; Junior model has 22" barrel with multi-choke (add $25.00). Made in Japan.

Estimated Value:	**Excellent:**	**$375.00**
	Very good:	**$300.00**

Mossberg Model 1000 Slug

Similar to the Model 1000 Field with 22" slug barrel, rifle sights. Made in Japan.

Estimated Value:	**Excellent:**	**$350.00**
	Very good:	**$285.00**

Mossberg Model 1000 Trap

Similar to the Model 1000 Field with a 30" multi-choke barrel, recoil pad, Monte Carlo stock and high-rib barrel. Made in Japan.

Estimated Value:	**Excellent:**	**$490.00**
	Very good:	**$390.00**

Mossberg Model 712 Camouflage Slug

Mossberg Model 712 Camouflage Slug

Similar to the Model 712 with camouflage finish and "Speedfeed" storage stock. Add $20.00 for accu-choke. Produced in the mid-1980s. Made in Japan.

Estimated Value:	**Excellent:**	**$345.00**
	Very good:	**$280.00**

Mossberg Model 712 Regal

Similar to the Model 712 with deluxe finish, crown design on receiver. Produced in the mid-1980s. Add $20.00 for accu-choke. Made in Japan.

Estimated Value:	**Excellent:**	**$350.00**
	Very good:	**$280.00**

Mossberg Model 712

Gauge: 12, regular or magnum
Action: Gas-operated, semiautomatic
Magazine: 4-shot tubular, 3-shot in magnum
Barrel: 30" full, 28" modified, 24" accu-choke, 24" slug; ventilated rib available
Finish: Alloy receiver with anodized finish; checkered walnut finish semi-pistol grip stock and forearm; recoil pad; Junior Model has 13" stock
Approximate wt.: 7½ lbs.
Comments: This shotgun was designed to handle any 12 gauge shell interchangeably. Produced from 1986 to the late 1980s; add $15.00 for slug model with rifle sights; $15.00 for ventilated rib; $40.00 for accu-choke. Made in Japan.

Estimated Value:	**Excellent:**	**$325.00**
	Very good:	**$260.00**

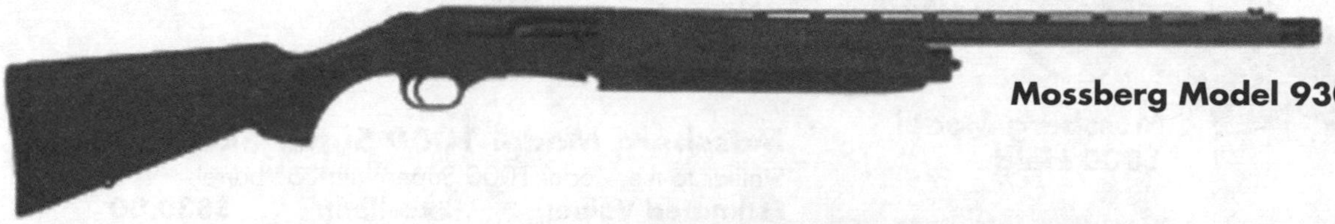

Mossberg Model 930 Turkey

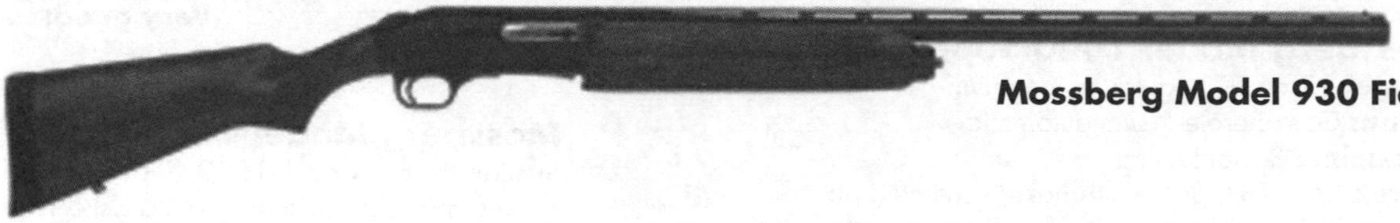

Mossberg Model 930 Field

Mossberg Model 930 Turkey

Similar to the Model 930 Field except: matte finish synthetic stock and forearm; accu-choke turkey tube; 24" barrel. Add 18% for camouflage finish.

Estimated Value: **New (retail): $561.00**
Excellent: $420.00
Very good: $335.00

Mossberg Model 930 Field

Gauge: 12; 2¾" or 3" chamber
Action: Gas-operated, semiautomatic
Magazine: 4-shot; 3-shot with 3" shells; tubular
Barrel: 26" or 28"; choke tubes; ventilated rib
Finish: Blued; checkered walnut pistol grip stock and forearm; recoil pad
Approximate wt.: 6½ to 7½ lbs.
Comments: Introduced in 2005.

Estimated Value: **New (retail): $561.00**
Excellent: $420.00
Very good: $335.00

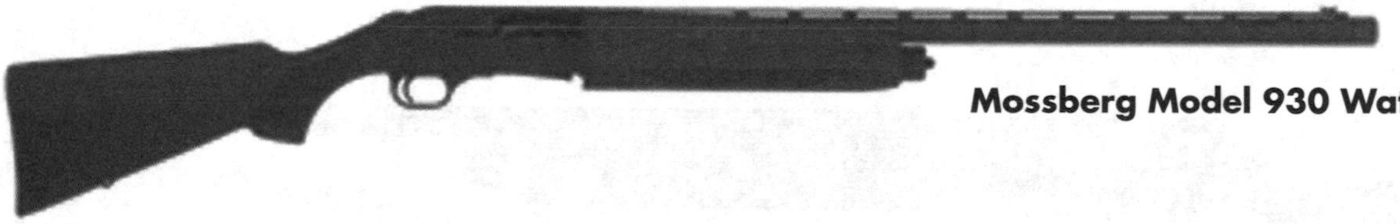

Mossberg Model 930 Waterfowl

Mossberg Model 930 Slugster

Mossberg Model 930 Waterfowl

Similar to the Model 930 Turkey except: 28" barrel with choke tubes. Add 3% for walnut stock and forearm, 21% for camouflage finish.

Estimated Value: **New (retail): $561.00**
Excellent: $420.00
Very good: $335.00

Mossberg Model 930 Slugster

Similar to the Model 930 Field except: 24" rifled barrel; rifle sights; black synthetic or walnut stock and forearm; Trophy model has Monte Carlo stock. Camouflage available. Add 8% for walnut.

Estimated Value: **New (retail): $561.00**
Excellent: $420.00
Very good: $335.00

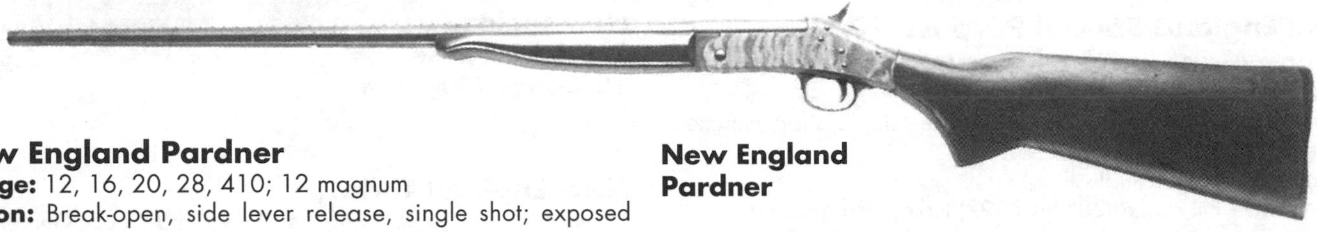

New England Pardner

New England Pardner

Gauge: 12, 16, 20, 28, 410; 12 magnum
Action: Break-open, side lever release, single shot; exposed hammer
Magazine: None, single shot
Barrel: 24", 26", 28", or 32"; full, modified or cylinder bore
Finish: Blued with color case hardened frame; hardwood walnut finish pistol grip, smooth stock and lipped forearm
Approximate wt.: 5 to 6 lbs.
Comments: Introduced in 1989. Add 5% for 32" barrel.

Estimated Value:	**New (retail):**	**$147.95**
	Excellent:	**$110.00**
	Very good:	**$ 90.00**

New England Tracker

Similar to the Pardner except has 24" cylinder bore slug barrel and rifle sights; swivels; 12 or 20 gauge.

Estimated Value:	**Excellent:**	**$125.00**
	Very good:	**$100.00**

New England Tracker II

Similar to the Tracker except 24" barrel is fully rifled for greater accuracy.

Estimated Value:	**Excellent:**	**$135.00**
	Very good:	**$110.00**

New England Mini-Pardner

Same as the Pardner except: 20 or 410 gauge only, 18½" barrel with short butt stock; weighs 4¾ lbs.; equipped with swivel studs. Introduced in 1989 and discontinued in 1992.

Estimated Value:	**Excellent:**	**$125.00**
	Very good:	**$100.00**

New England Deluxe Pardner

Same as the Pardner except: 12 or 20 gauge only with special double back-up buttstock (holds two spare shells) and recoil pad. Introduced in 1989 and discontinued in 1992.

Estimated Value:	**Excellent:**	**$135.00**
	Very good:	**$110.00**

New England Youth Pardner, Compact

Same as the Pardner except: 20, 28, or 410 gauge only with 22" barrel and straight grip, shorter stock with recoil pad. Introduced in 1989.

Estimated Value:	**New (retail):**	**$158.75**
	Excellent:	**$125.00**
	Very good:	**$100.00**

New England Survivor

New England Protector

Gauge: 12
Action: Break-open, side release, single shot exposed; hammer
Magazine: None, single shot
Barrel: 18½"
Finish: Blued or nickel; smooth hardwood walnut finish; pistol grip stock and lipped forearm; recoil pad; special double back-up buttstock holds two spare shells; swivels
Approximate wt.: 5¾ lbs.
Comments: Made from 1990 to 1992. Add 8% for nickel finish.

Estimated Value:	**Excellent:**	**$135.00**
	Very good:	**$110.00**

New England Survivor

Gauge: 12, 20, 410/45 Colt
Action: Box lock; side lever break-open, exposed hammer, single shot
Magazine: None, single shot
Barrel: 22" modified, matte blue or electroless nickel; 20" rifled barrel on 410/45 Colt with screw-in choke tube
Finish: Matte blue or electroless nickel; black synthetic thumbhole pistol grip stock and forearm; swivels, sling
Approximate wt.: 6 lbs.
Comments: Designed for harsh climates.

Estimated Value:	**Excellent:**	**$135.00**
	Very good:	**$110.00**

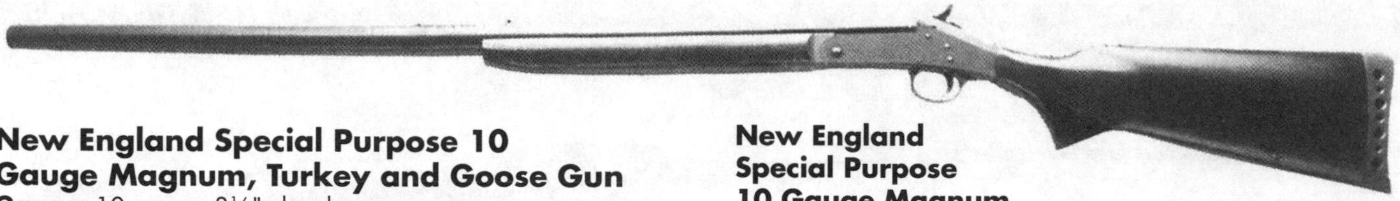

New England
Special Purpose
10 Gauge Magnum

New England Special Purpose 10 Gauge Magnum, Turkey and Goose Gun

Gauge: 10 gauge, 3½" chamber
Action: Break-open, side lever release, single shot; exposed hammer
Magazine: None, single shot
Barrel: 32" full choke; 28" (in 1992) turkey and goose gun
Finish: Blued; hardwood walnut finish, smooth, pistol grip stock and forearm; recoil pad; also camouflage matte finish stock and forearm
Approximate wt.: 10 lbs.
Comments: Introduced in 1989; discontinued in the late 1990s. Add 6% for camouflage finish; 20% for 32" barrel, 23% for 24" barrel with screw-in turkey full choke.

Estimated Value:	**Excellent:**	**$160.00**
	Very good:	**$125.00**

New England Turkey

Similar to the 10 gauge magnum Turkey and Goose Gun except: 24" barrel; mossy oak or bottom land camouflage finish.

Estimated Value:	**Excellent:**	**$125.00**
	Very good:	**$100.00**

New England Handi-Gun Combination

See New England Handi-Gun Combination in Rifle section.

NEW HAVEN (MOSSBERG)

New Haven Model 273

Gauge: 20
Action: Bolt action; hammerless; single shot
Magazine: None
Barrel: 24" full choke
Finish: Blued; plain walnut Monte Carlo semi-pistol grip one-piece stock and forearm
Approximate wt.: 6¼ lbs.
Comments: Made in the early 1960s.

Estimated Value:	**Excellent:**	**$100.00**
	Very good:	**$ 80.00**

New Haven Model 290

Gauge: 16
Action: Bolt action; hammerless; repeating
Magazine: 2-shot detachable box
Barrel: 28" removable full choke
Finish: Blued; walnut Monte Carlo pistol grip one-piece stock and tapered forearm
Approximate wt.: 6½ lbs.
Comments: Made in the early 1960s.

Estimated Value:	**Excellent:**	**$115.00**
	Very good:	**$ 95.00**

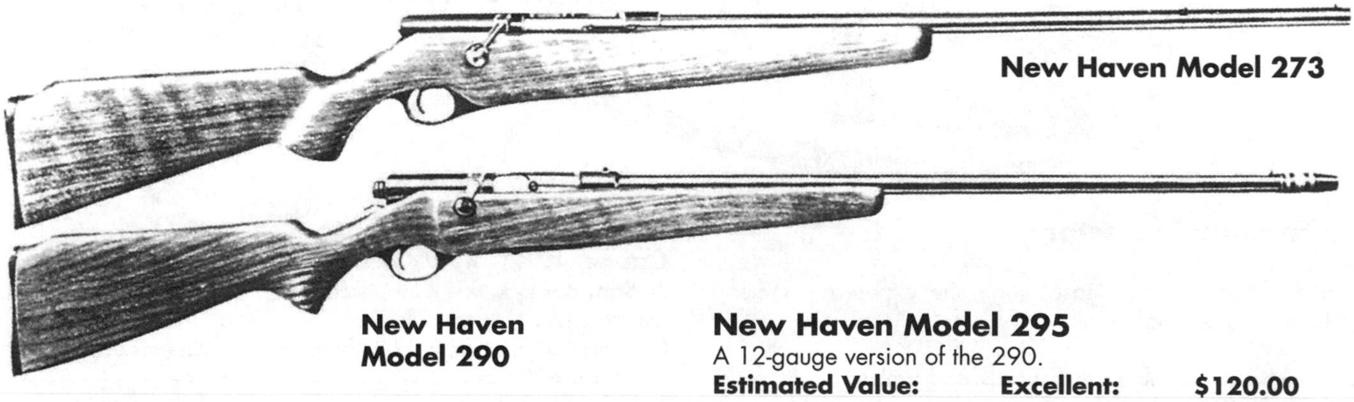

New Haven Model 273

New Haven Model 290

New Haven Model 295

A 12-gauge version of the 290.

Estimated Value:	**Excellent:**	**$120.00**
	Very good:	**$ 95.00**

New Haven Models 283 and 283T

A 410-gauge version of the 290 with a 24" barrel. Currently called 283T. Discontinued in the early 1980s.

Estimated Value:	**Excellent:**	**$125.00**
	Very good:	**$100.00**

New Haven Model 285

A 20-gauge version of the 290 with 24" barrel.

Estimated Value:	**Excellent:**	**$125.00**
	Very good:	**$100.00**

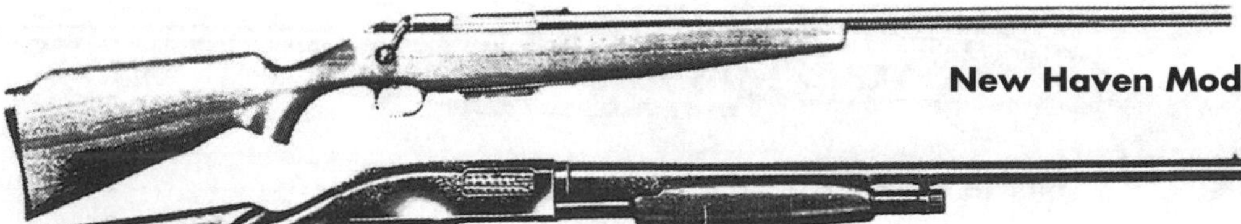

New Haven Model 495

New Haven Model 600

New Haven Models 495 and 495T

Gauge: 12
Action: Bolt action; hammerless; repeating
Magazine: 2-shot detachable box
Barrel: 28" full choke
Finish: Blued; walnut Monte Carlo semi-pistol grip stock and tapered forearm
Approximate wt.: 7½ lbs.
Comments: Made from the mid-1960s to the early 1980s.

Estimated Value:	**Excellent:**	**$130.00**
	Very good:	**$105.00**

New Haven Model 485T

A 20-gauge version of the Model 495; 26" barrel.

Estimated Value:	**Excellent:**	**$135.00**
	Very good:	**$110.00**

New Haven Model 600

Gauge: 12, 20, 410
Action: Slide action; hammerless; repeating
Magazine: 6-shot tubular
Barrel: 26" improved cylinder, 28" modified or full, 30" full chokes; ventilated rib, adjustable choke and interchangeable choke available
Finish: Blued; walnut semi-pistol grip stock and slide handle
Approximate wt.: 7½ lbs.
Comments: Made from the early 1960s to the early 1980s. Add $30.00 for ventilated rib; $20.00 for adjustable choke; $10.00 for interchangeable choke.

Estimated Value:	**Excellent:**	**$175.00**
	Very good:	**$140.00**

New Haven Model 600 AST

Similar to the Model 600 except: 24" barrel and rifle sights.

Estimated Value:	**Excellent:**	**$190.00**
	Very good:	**$150.00**

NOBLE

Noble Model 420

Noble Model 420

Gauge: 12, 16, 20
Action: Box lock; top lever break-open; hammerless; double triggers
Magazine: None
Barrel: Side-by-side double barrel, 28" modified and full
Finish: Blued; checkered walnut pistol grip stock and forearm
Approximate wt.: 6¾ lbs.
Comments: Made from the late 1950s to the early 1970s.

Estimated Value:	**Excellent:**	**$325.00**
	Very good:	**$260.00**

Noble Model 420EK

A fancy version of the Model 420 with automatic ejectors; select walnut; recoil pad; engraving; sights; gold inlay. Made in the late 1960s.

Estimated Value:	**Excellent:**	**$330.00**
	Very good:	**$265.00**

Noble Model 450E

Similar to the Model 420EK. Made from the late 1960s to the early 1970s.

Estimated Value:	**Excellent:**	**$340.00**
	Very good:	**$275.00**

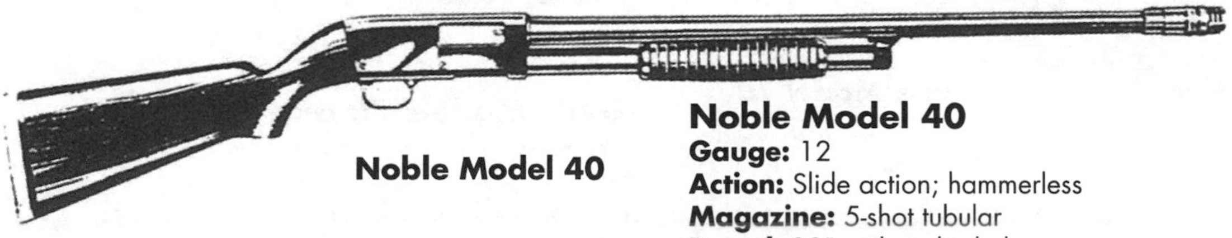

Noble Model 40

Noble Model 50

Basically the same gun as the Model 40 without recoil pad or "Multi-Choke."

Estimated Value:	**Excellent:**	**$165.00**
	Very good:	**$132.00**

Noble Model 40

Gauge: 12
Action: Slide action; hammerless
Magazine: 5-shot tubular
Barrel: 28" with multi-choke
Finish: Blued; plain walnut pistol grip stock and grooved slide handle; recoil pad
Approximate wt.: 7½ lbs.
Comments: Made from the early to the mid-1950s.

Estimated Value:	**Excellent:**	**$175.00**
	Very good:	**$140.00**

Noble Model 60

Noble Model 60

Gauge: 12, 16
Action: Slide action; hammerless
Magazine: 5-shot tubular
Barrel: 28" with variable choke
Finish: Blued; plain walnut pistol grip stock and grooved slide handle; recoil pad
Approximate wt.: 7½ lbs.
Comments: Manufactured in takedown version from the mid-1950s to the late 1960s.
Estimated Value: **Excellent:** **$185.00**
Very good: **$150.00**

Noble Model 60ACP

Very similar to Model 60 with a ventilated rib. Made from the late 1960s to the early 1970s.
Estimated Value: **Excellent:** **$190.00**
Very good: **$155.00**

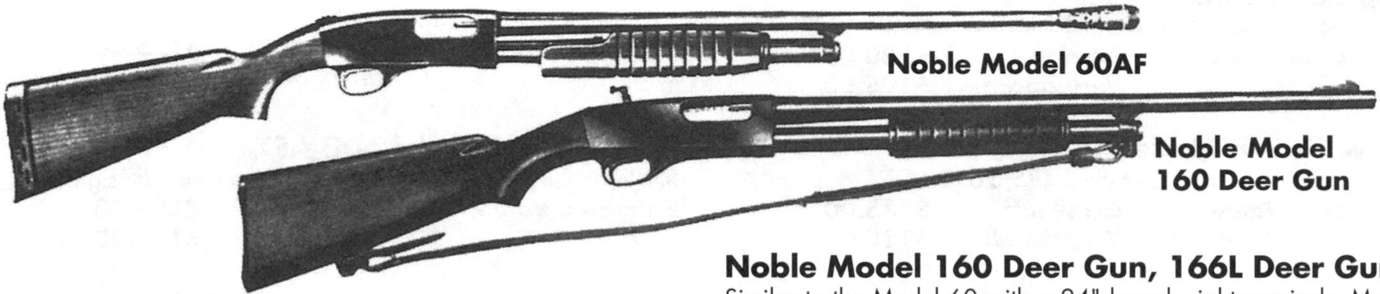

Noble Model 60AF

Noble Model 160 Deer Gun

Noble Model 60AF

A fancier version of the Model 60 with special steel barrel; select wood; fluted comb. Made only during the mid-1960s.
Estimated Value: **Excellent:** **$190.00**
Very good: **$155.00**

Noble Model 160 Deer Gun, 166L Deer Gun

Similar to the Model 60 with a 24" barrel; sights; swivels. Made in the mid-1960s as 160 and from the late 1960s to the early 1970s as 166L.
Estimated Value: **Excellent:** **$210.00**
Very good: **$165.00**

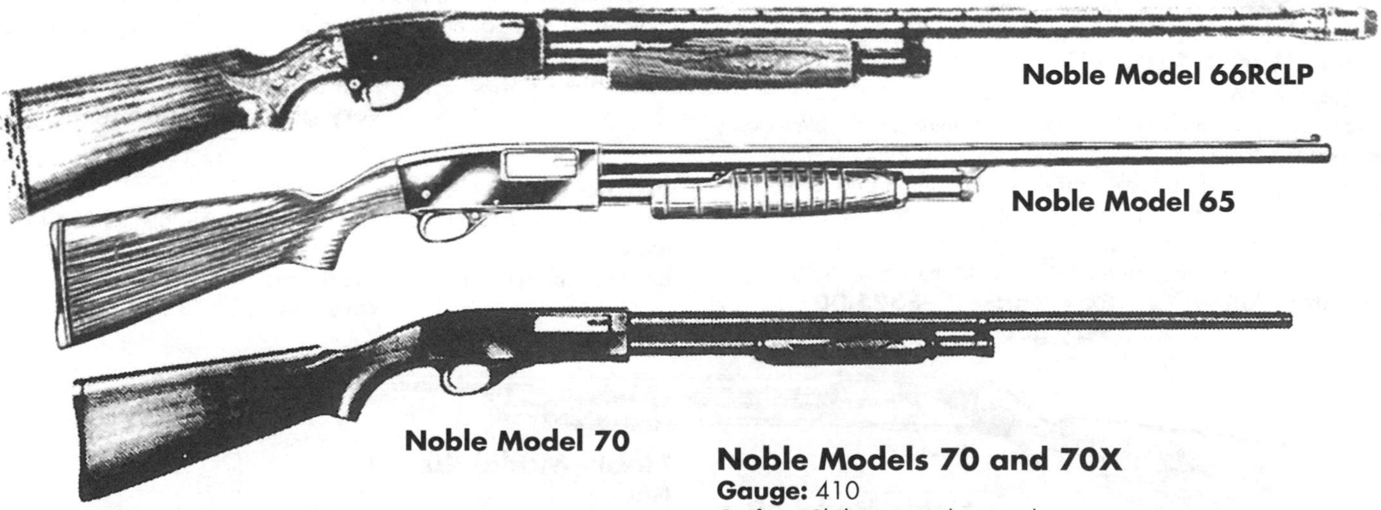

Noble Model 66RCLP

Noble Model 65

Noble Model 70

Noble Model 65

Basically the same as the Model 60 without the recoil pad or adjustable choke.
Estimated Value: **Excellent:** **$165.00**
Very good: **$132.00**

Noble Model 66RCLP

Similar to the Model 60ACP with a fancier checkered stock.
Estimated Value: **Excellent:** **$190.00**
Very good: **$155.00**

Noble Models 70 and 70X

Gauge: 410
Action: Slide action; hammerless
Magazine: 5-shot tubular
Barrel: 26" modified or full choke
Finish: Blued; checkered walnut pistol grip stock and slide handle
Approximate wt.: 6 lbs.
Comments: Made from the late 1950s to the late 1960s as Model 70 and from the late 1960s to the early 1970s as 70X.
Estimated Value: **Excellent:** **$180.00**
Very good: **$145.00**

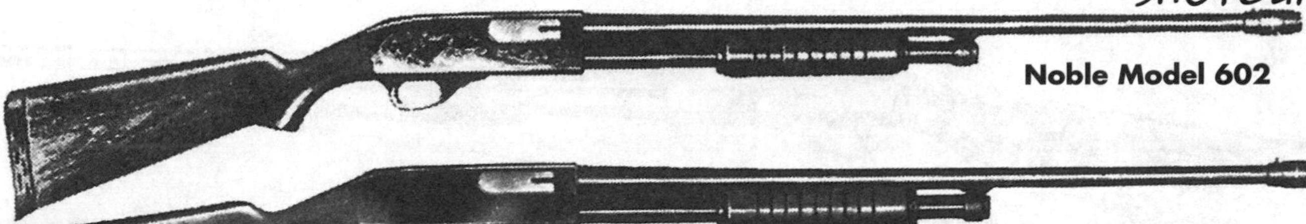

Noble Model 602

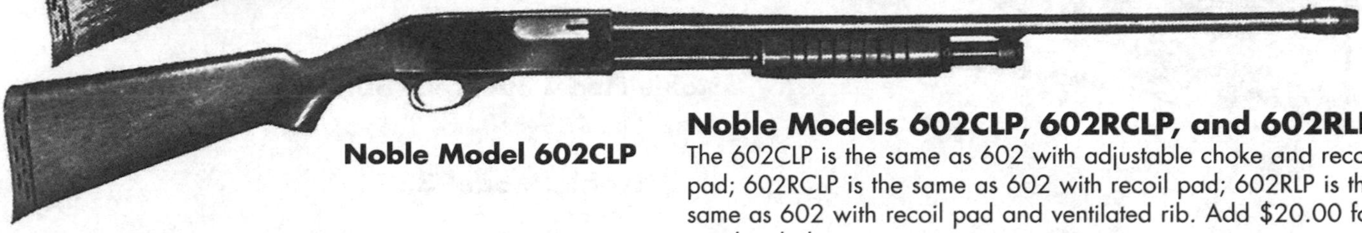

Noble Model 602CLP

Noble Model 602

Similar to the Model 70 in 20 gauge and 28" barrel; weighs 6½ lbs. Grooved slide handle.

Estimated Value: **Excellent:** **$175.00**
Very good: **$140.00**

Noble Models 602CLP, 602RCLP, and 602RLP

The 602CLP is the same as 602 with adjustable choke and recoil pad; 602RCLP is the same as 602 with recoil pad; 602RLP is the same as 602 with recoil pad and ventilated rib. Add $20.00 for ventilated rib.

Estimated Value: **Excellent:** **$200.00**
Very good: **$160.00**

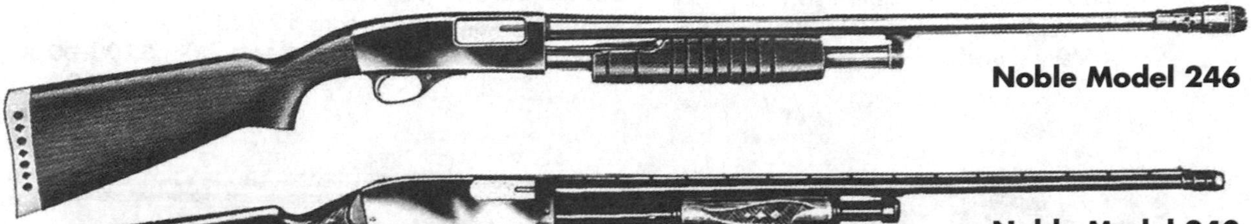

Noble Model 246

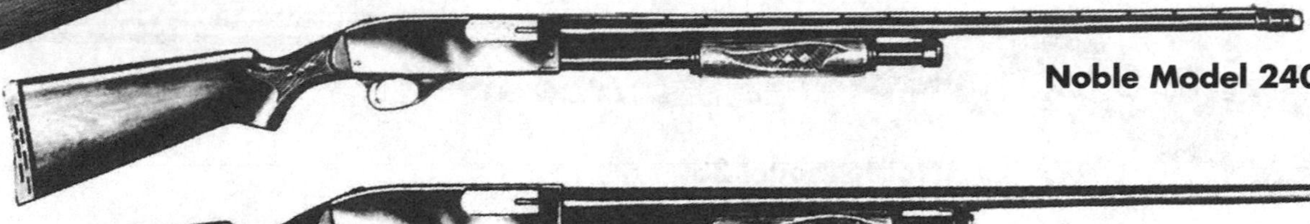

Noble Model 240

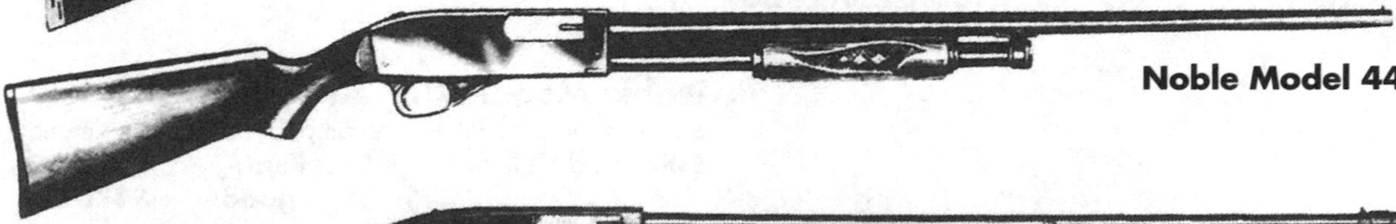

Noble Model 449

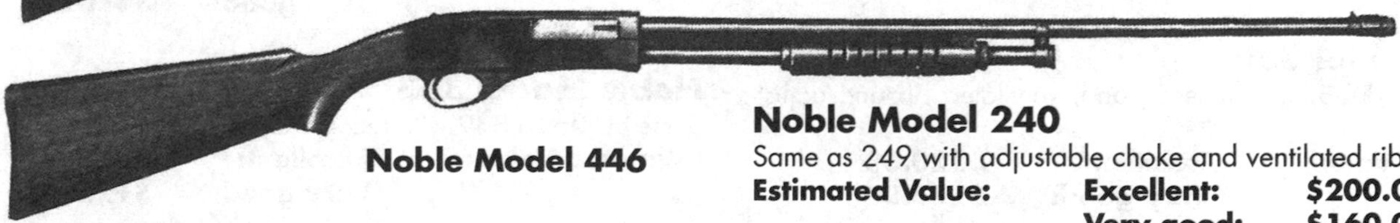

Noble Model 446

Noble Model 249

Gauge: 20
Action: Slide action; hammerless
Magazine: 5-shot tubular
Barrel: 28" modified or full choke
Finish: Blued; checkered walnut pistol grip stock and slide handle; recoil pad
Approximate wt.: 6½ lbs.
Comments: Produced in the early 1970s.
Estimated Value: **Excellent:** **$160.00**
Very good: **$130.00**

Noble Model 246

Same as 249 with adjustable choke.

Estimated Value: **Excellent:** **$175.00**
Very good: **$140.00**

Noble Model 243

Same as 249 with ventilated rib.

Estimated Value: **Excellent:** **$180.00**
Very good: **$145.00**

Noble Model 240

Same as 249 with adjustable choke and ventilated rib.

Estimated Value: **Excellent:** **$200.00**
Very good: **$160.00**

Noble Model 449

Similar to Model 249 without recoil pad and in 410 bore.

Estimated Value: **Excellent:** **$180.00**
Very good: **$145.00**

Noble Model 446

Similar to Model 246 without recoil pad and in 410 bore.

Estimated Value: **Excellent:** **$170.00**
Very good: **$135.00**

Noble Model 443

Similar to Model 243 without recoil pad and in 410 bore.

Estimated Value: **Excellent:** **$200.00**
Very good: **$160.00**

Noble Model 440

Similar to Model 240 without recoil pad and in 410 bore.

Estimated Value: **Excellent:** **$210.00**
Very good: **$170.00**

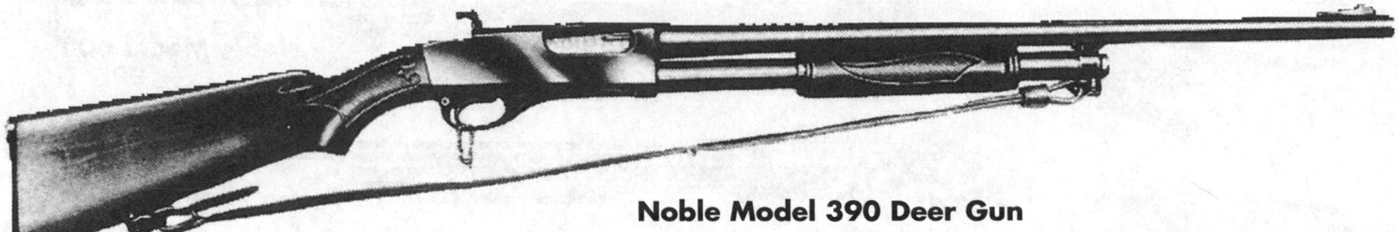

Noble Model 390 Deer Gun

Noble Model 339

Gauge: 12, 16
Action: Slide action; hammerless
Magazine: 6-shot tubular
Barrel: 28" modified or full choke
Finish: Blued; checkered walnut pistol grip stock and slide handle
Approximate wt.: 7½ lbs.
Comments: Made in the early 1970s.

Estimated Value:	**Excellent:**	**$200.00**
	Very good:	**$160.00**

Noble Model 390 Deer Gun

Similar to Model 339 with a 24" slug barrel; sights; swivels.

Estimated Value:	**Excellent:**	**$210.00**
	Very good:	**$170.00**

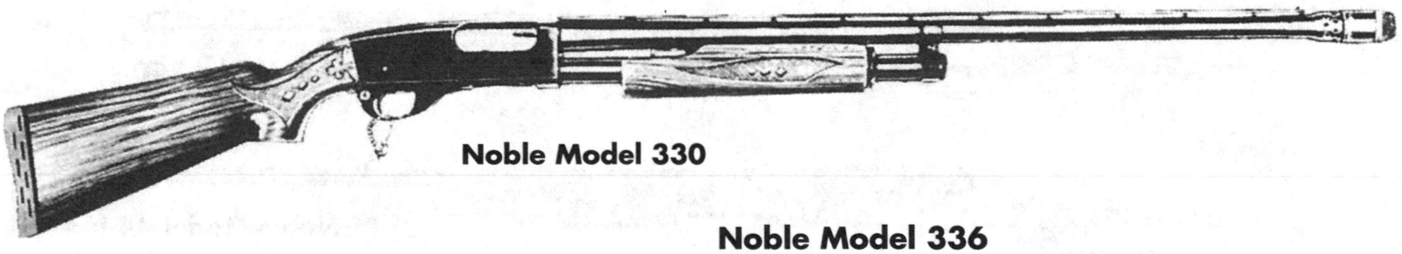

Noble Model 330

Noble Model 336

Same as Model 339 with recoil pad and adjustable choke.

Estimated Value:	**Excellent:**	**$210.00**
	Very good:	**$170.00**

Noble Model 330

Same as Model 339 with recoil pad, ventilated rib and adjustable choke.

Estimated Value:	**Excellent:**	**$220.00**
	Very good:	**$176.00**

Noble Model 333

Same as Model 339 with recoil pad and ventilated rib.

Estimated Value:	**Excellent:**	**$215.00**
	Very good:	**$175.00**

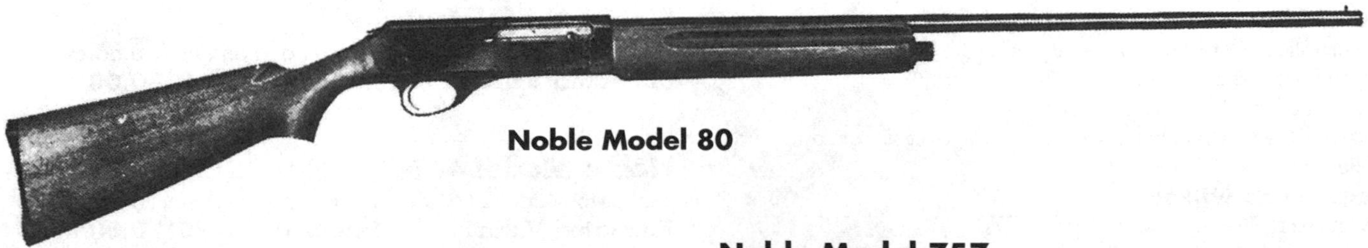

Noble Model 80

Noble Model 80

Gauge: 410
Action: Semiautomatic; hammerless
Magazine: 5-shot tubular
Barrel: 26" full choke
Finish: Blued; plain walnut pistol grip stock and forearm
Approximate wt.: 6 lbs.
Comments: Made in the mid-1960s.

Estimated Value:	**Excellent:**	**$225.00**
	Very good:	**$180.00**

Noble Model 757

Gauge: 20
Action: Slide action; hammerless
Magazine: 5-shot tubular
Barrel: 28" aluminum; adjustable choke
Finish: Black anodized aluminum; decorated receiver; checkered walnut pistol grip stock and slide handle; recoil pad
Approximate wt.: 4½ lbs.
Comments: A very light gun made in the early 1970s.

Estimated Value:	**Excellent:**	**$185.00**
	Very good:	**$150.00**

Parker Trojan

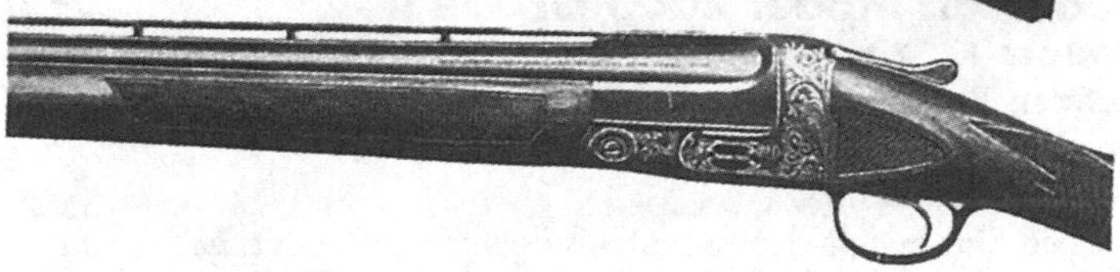

Parker Single Barrel Trap

Parker Single Barrel Trap

Gauge: 12
Action: Slide action; hammerless; top lever break-open; box lock
Magazine: None
Barrel: 30", 32", 34", any choke; ventilated rib
Finish: Blued; checkered walnut straight, full or semi-pistol grip stock
Approximate wt.: 6½ to 7½ lbs.
Comments: Grades differ according to workmanship, checkering, and engraving. Made from about 1917 to 1941. Manufacture of Parker guns was taken over by Remington in 1934 and this gun was called Remington Parker Model 930. There is a wide range of values for this gun. Prices for pre-1934 models.
Estimated Value: Excellent: $5,000.00 – 20,000.00
Very good: $3,500.00 – 16,000.00

Parker Trojan

Gauge: 12, 16, 20
Action: Top lever break-open; hammerless; box lock
Magazine: None
Barrel: Side-by-side double barrel; 26", 28", 30", full and full or modified and full chokes
Finish: Blued; checkered walnut pistol grip stock and forearm
Approximate wt.: 6½ to 8 lbs.
Comments: Made from about 1915 to 1939.
Estimated Value: Excellent: $2,000.00 – 3,500.00
Very good: $1,600.00 – 2,750.00

Parker Hammerless Double

Gauge: 10, 12, 16, 20, 28, 410
Action: Box lock; top lever break-open; hammerless; selective trigger and automatic ejectors after 1934
Magazine: None
Barrel: Side-by-side double barrel; 26", 28", 30", 32"; any choke combination
Finish: Blued; checkered walnut straight, full or semi-pistol grip stock and forearm
Approximate wt.: 6½ to 8½ lbs.
Comments: Grades vary according to workmanship, checkering, and engraving, with grades designated by letters (A.H.E., G.H.E., etc.). Manufacture of Parker guns was taken over by Remington in 1934 and this gun was called Remington Parker Model 920 until it was discontinued in 1941. There is a wide range of values for these guns. Prices for pre-1934 models.
Estimated Value: Excellent: $5,000.00 – 55,000.00
Very good: $3,500.00 – 42,000.00

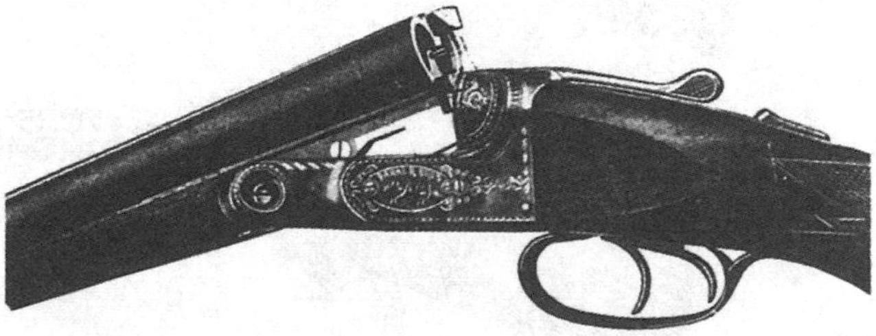

Parker Hammerless Double G.H.E.

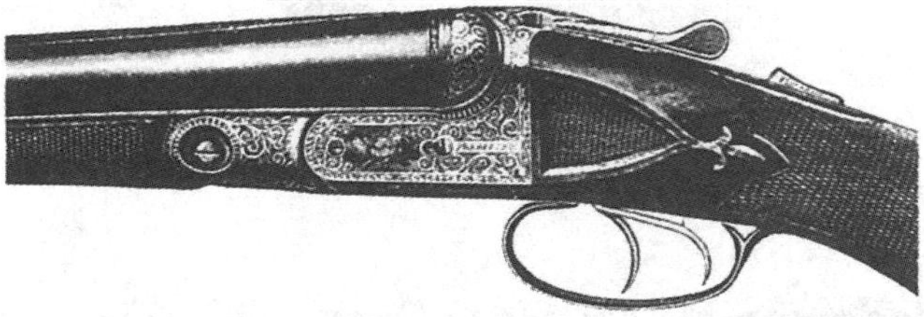

Parker Hammerless Double A.H.E.

Parker Hammerless Double

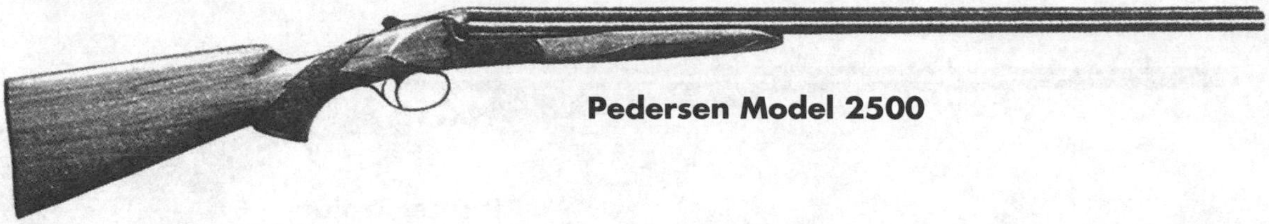

Pedersen Model 2500

Pedersen Model 2000 Grade II

Gauge: 12, 20
Action: Box lock; top lever break-open; hammerless; automatic ejectors; single selective trigger
Magazine: None
Barrel: Side-by-side double barrel; length to customer's specifications
Finish: Blued; checkered walnut pistol grip stock and tapered forearm; engraved
Approximate wt.: 7½ lbs.
Comments: Made in the mid-1970s.

Estimated Value:	**Excellent:**	**$2,100.00**
	Very good:	**$1,680.00**

Pedersen Model 2000 Grade I

Similar to Grade II with fancier engraving, gold filling on receiver, select walnut.

Estimated Value:	**Excellent:**	**$2,400.00**
	Very good:	**$1,925.00**

Pedersen Model 2500

A field version of the Model 2000; no engraving.

Estimated Value:	**Excellent:**	**$450.00**
	Very good:	**$360.00**

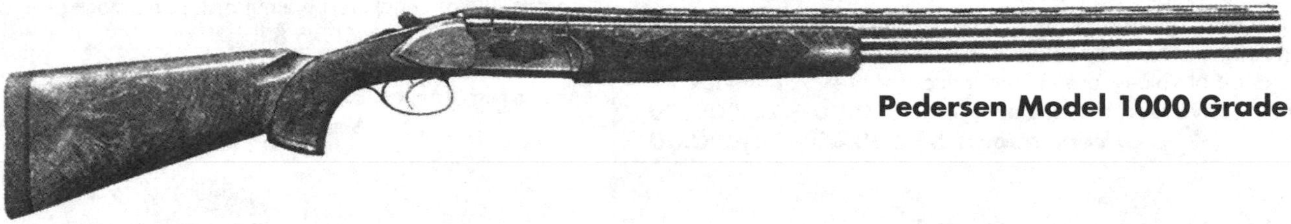

Pedersen Model 1000 Grade II

Pedersen Model 1000 Grade I

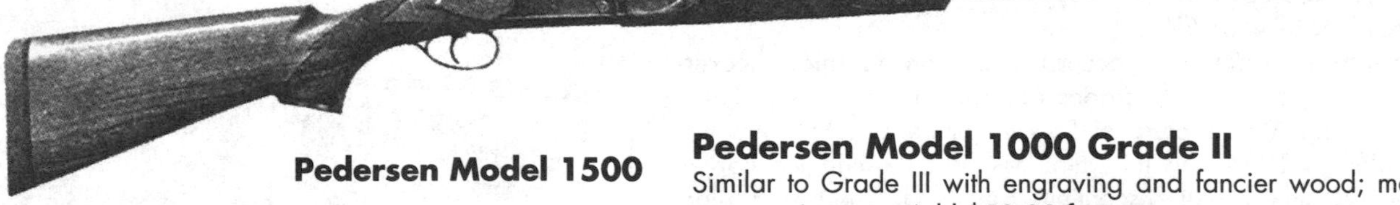

Pedersen Model 1500

Pedersen Model 1000 Grade III

Gauge: 12, 20
Action: Box lock; top lever break-open; hammerless; automatic ejectors; single selective trigger
Magazine: None
Barrel: Over and under double barrel; length made to customer's specifications; ventilated rib
Finish: Blued; checkered walnut pistol grip stock and forearm; recoil pad
Approximate wt.: 7½ lbs.
Comments: Produced in the mid-1970s.

Estimated Value:	**Excellent:**	**$1,000.00**
	Very good:	**$ 800.00**

Pedersen Model 1000 Grade II

Similar to Grade III with engraving and fancier wood; made to customer's specs. Add $50.00 for magnum.

Estimated Value:	**Excellent:**	**$1,500.00**
	Very good:	**$1,200.00**

Pedersen Model 1000 Grade I

Similar to Grade II with extensive engraving, select wood, gold filling on receiver; made to customer's specifications; in hunting, skeet, or trap models.

Estimated Value:	**Excellent:**	**$2,000.00**
	Very good:	**$1,600.00**

Pedersen Model 1500

A field version of the 1000 with standard barrel lengths only (26", 28", 30", or 32").

Estimated Value:	**Excellent:**	**$800.00**
	Very good:	**$650.00**

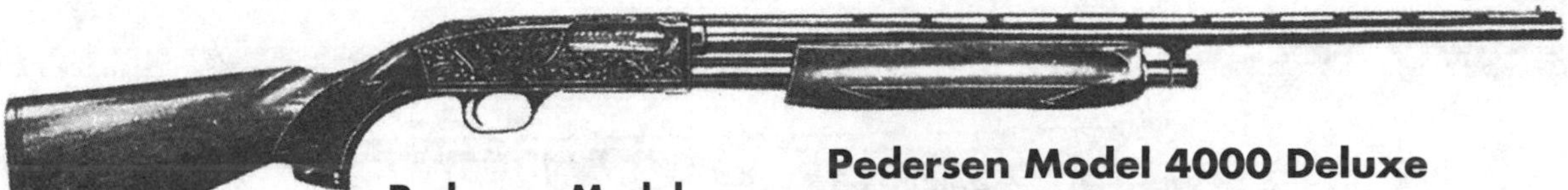

Pedersen Model 4000 Deluxe

Pedersen Model 4000 Deluxe

Gauge: 10, 12, 410
Action: Slide action; hammerless; side ejector
Magazine: Tubular
Barrel: 26", 28", 30", variety of chokes; ventilated rib
Finish: Blued; checkered walnut pistol grip stock and slide handle; recoil pad; floral engraving on receiver
Approximate wt.: 6¾ lbs.
Comments: Made in the mid-1970s.

Estimated Value:	**Excellent:**	**$475.00**
	Very good:	**$380.00**

PREMIER

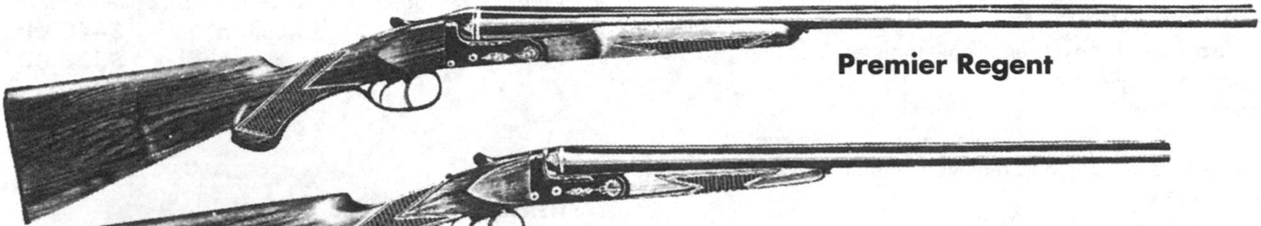

Premier Regent

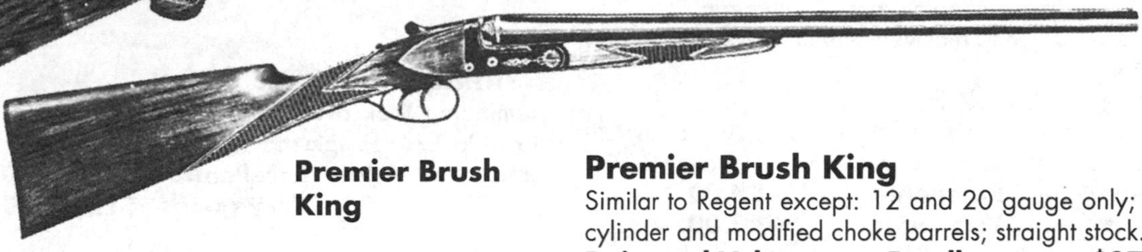

Premier Brush King

Premier Regent

Gauge: 12, 16, 20, 28, 410
Action: Box lock; top lever break-open; hammerless; double triggers
Magazine: None
Barrel: Side-by-side double barrel; 26", 28" modified and full chokes; matte rib
Finish: Blued; checkered walnut pistol grip stock and tapered forearm
Approximate wt.: 7 lbs.
Comments: Produced from the 1950s to the 1970s.

Estimated Value:	**Excellent:**	**$375.00**
	Very good:	**$300.00**

Premier Brush King

Similar to Regent except: 12 and 20 gauge only; 22" improved cylinder and modified choke barrels; straight stock.

Estimated Value:	**Excellent:**	**$375.00**
	Very good:	**$300.00**

Premier Magnum

Similar to Regent except: 10 gauge magnum with 32" barrels or 12 gauge magnum with 30" barrels; both gauges in full and full choke; recoil pad; beavertail forearm. Add $25.00 for 10 gauge magnum.

Estimated Value:	**Excellent:**	**$425.00**
	Very good:	**$340.00**

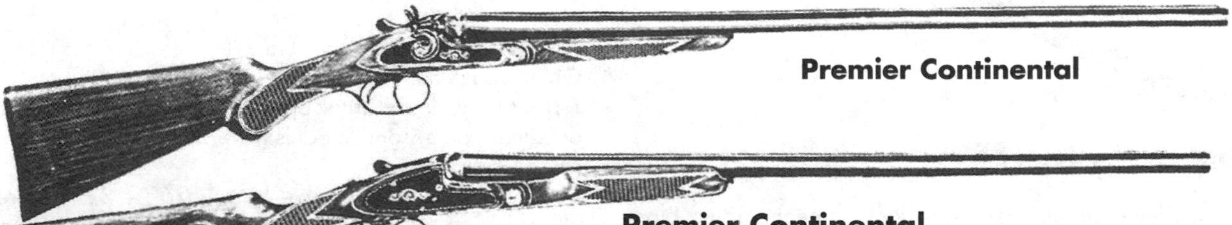

Premier Continental

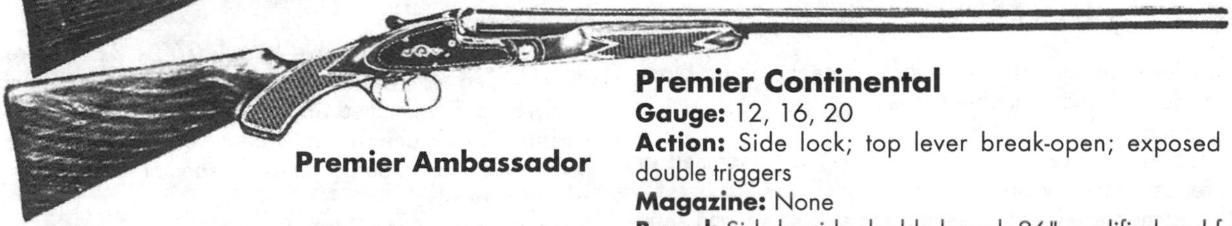

Premier Ambassador

Premier Ambassador

A hammerless version of the Continental. Also available in 410 gauge.

Estimated Value:	**Excellent:**	**$500.00**
	Very good:	**$400.00**

Premier Continental

Gauge: 12, 16, 20
Action: Side lock; top lever break-open; exposed hammer; double triggers
Magazine: None
Barrel: Side-by-side double barrel; 26" modified and full choke
Finish: Blued; checkered walnut pistol grip stock and tapered forearm
Approximate wt.: 7 lbs.
Comments: Produced from the 1950s to the 1970s.

Estimated Value:	**Excellent:**	**$300.00**
	Very good:	**$240.00**

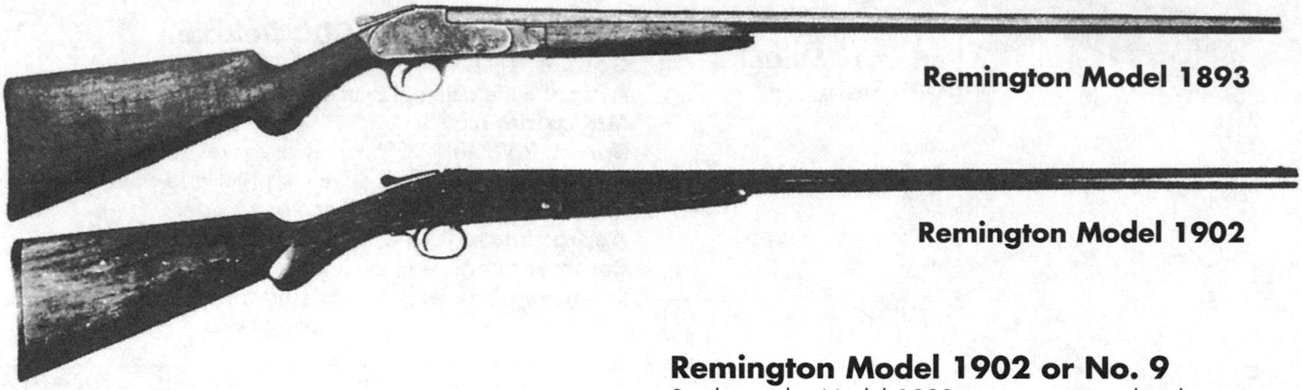

Remington Model 1893

Remington Model 1902

Remington Model 1893

Gauge: 10, 12, 16, 20
Action: Top lever break-open; semi-hammer (cocking lever on left), takedown; single shot
Magazine: None
Barrel: 28", 30", 32", or 34"; plain barrel with bead sight
Finish: Blued; case hardened receiver; smooth walnut, pistol grip stock and forearm
Approximate wt.: 5½ to 6½ lbs.
Comments: Made from about 1893 to 1906. Approximately 25,000 were produced. Also known as the Model No. 3 and the '93.

Estimated Value:	**Excellent:**	**$550.00**
	Very good:	**$440.00**

Remington Model 1902 or No. 9

Similar to the Model 1893 except improved with automatic ejector. Made from about 1902 to 1912. Also called Model No. 9.

Estimated Value:	**Excellent:**	**$440.00**
	Very good:	**$350.00**

Remington Parker 930

Remington took over production of the Parker shotguns from 1934 to 1941; single-shot hammerless.

Estimated Value:	**Excellent:**	**$2,200.00 – 5,500.00**
	Very good:	**$1,750.00 – 4,400.00**

Remington Model 1889

Remington Model 1894

Remington Model 1889

Gauge: 10, 12, 16
Action: Top lever break-open; side lock; breechloading black powder; exposed hammers; double trigger
Magazine: None
Barrel: Side-by-side double barrel; 28" – 32" full, modified or cylinder bore; Damascus or steel
Finish: Blued; checkered walnut semi-pistol grip stock and short forearm
Approximate wt.: 7½ to 9 lbs.
Comments: Made from about 1889 to 1909 in seven grades. Approximately 30,000 produced. Prices are for standard grade.

Estimated Value:	**Excellent:**	**$2,000.00**
	Very good:	**$1,600.00**

Remington Model 1894

Gauge: 10, 12, 16
Action: Top lever break-open; concealed hammers; triple lock; double triggers; some models have automatic ejectors
Magazine: None
Barrel: Side-by-side double barrel; 26" – 32" tapered barrels; full, modified, or cylinder bore; ordnance steel or Damascus barrels with concave matted rib
Finish: Blued; checkered walnut, straight or semi-pistol grip stock, and short tapered forearm; special engraving and inlays on higher grades
Approximate wt.: 7½ to 8½ lbs.
Comments: Made from about 1894 to 1910 in seven grades. Receivers marked "Remington Arms Co." on left side. Prices for standard grade. Deduct $125.00 for Damascus barrels.

Estimated Value:	**Excellent:**	**$1,375.00**
	Very good:	**$1,100.00**

Remington Model 1900

Remington Model 1900

Gauge: 12, 16
Action: Top lever break-open; concealed hammer; double triggers; automatic ejectors optional
Magazine: None
Barrel: Side-by-side double barrel; 28" or 32" steel or Damascus in standard chokes; matted rib
Finish: Checkered walnut pistol grip stock and short tapered forearm with gap at front for disassembly
Approximate wt.: 8 to 9 lbs.
Comments: Similar to Model 1894 except: lower grade; takedown model; internal forearm release. Made from about 1900 to 1910. Deduct $100.00 for Damascus barrels.

Estimated Value:	**Excellent:**	**$1,500.00**
	Very good:	**$1,200.00**

Remington Parker 920

Remington took over production of Parker shotguns from 1934 to 1941; double barrel hammerless; double triggers; 12 gauge.

Estimated Value:	**Excellent:**	**$2,200.00**
	Very good:	**$1,750.00**

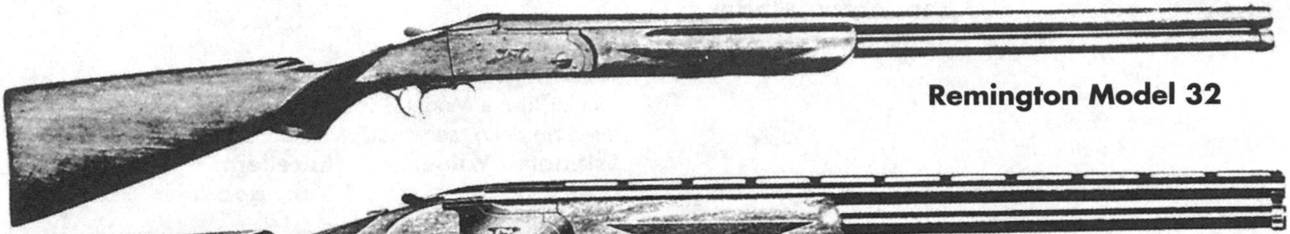

Remington Model 32

Remington Model 3200 Field Grade

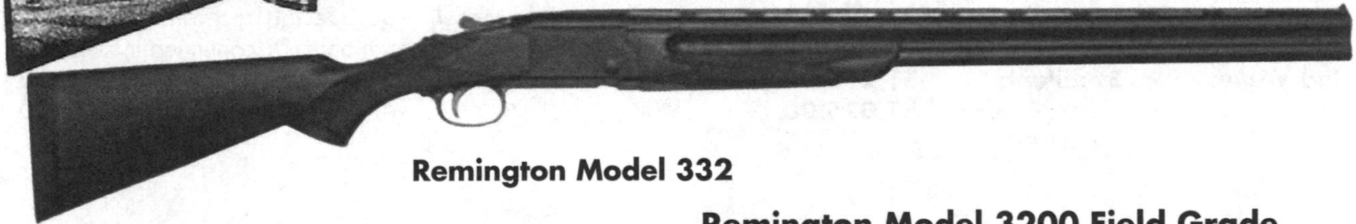

Remington Model 332

Remington Model 32

Gauge: 12
Action: Top lever break-open; concealed hammers; single selective trigger; automatic ejectors
Magazine: None
Barrel: Over and under double barrel; 26" – 32" plain, solid or ventilated rib; full and modified choke standard, but any combination available
Finish: Blued; engraved receiver; checkered walnut pistol grip stock and forearm
Approximate wt.: 7¾ to 8½ lbs.
Comments: One of the first modern American over and under double barrel shotguns produced. Made from about 1932 to 1942. Made in about six grades, high grades with fancier wood and engravings. Add $100.00 for solid rib; $200.00 for ventilated rib. Prices for standard grade.

Estimated Value:	**Excellent:**	**$2,250.00**
	Very good:	**$1,800.00**

Remington Model 332

Similar to the Model 32 except: improved lock design and produced with modern manufacturing technology. Introduced in 2002.

Estimated Value:	**Excellent:**	**$1,725.00**
	Very good:	**$1,380.00**

Remington Model 3200 Field Grade

Gauge: 12
Action: Top lever break-open; concealed hammer; selective single trigger; automatic ejectors
Magazine: None
Barrel: 26" – 30" over and under double barrel; ventilated rib; modified and full or improved cylinder and modified chokes
Finish: Blued; pointing dogs engraved on receiver; checkered walnut pistol grip stock and matching forearm
Approximate wt.: 7¾ to 8¾ lbs.
Comments: A modern version of the Model 32 started back in production in the early 1970s. Other models valued higher than Field Grade.

Estimated Value:	**Excellent:**	**$1,250.00**
	Very good:	**$1,000.00**

Remington Model 3200 Magnum

Similar to the Model 3200 Field Grade except: chambered for 12 gauge magnum; 30" barrels in full and full or modified and full chokes; receiver decorated with engraved scrollwork.

Estimated Value:	**Excellent:**	**$1,400.00**
	Very good:	**$1,120.00**

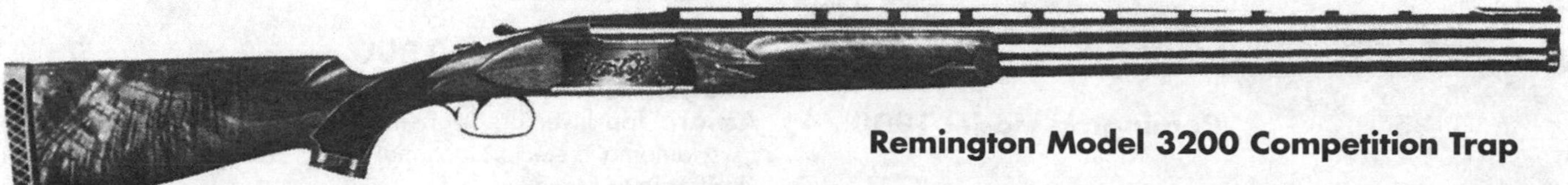

Remington Model 3200 Competition Trap

Remington Model 3200 Skeet

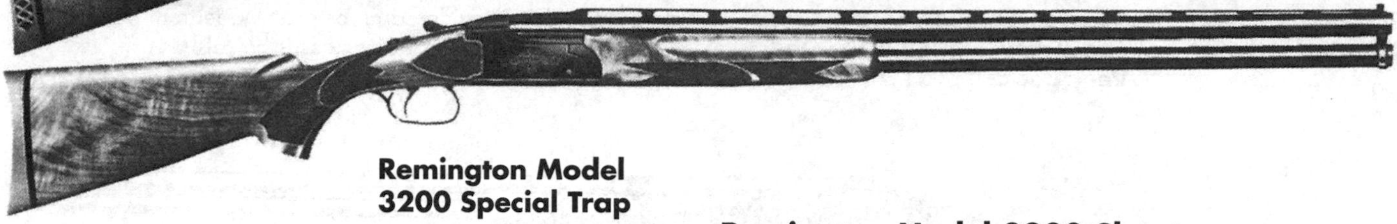

Remington Model 3200 Special Trap

Remington Model 3200 Skeet

Similar to the Model 3200 with a 26" or 28" skeet barrel; ventilated rib only; recoil pad; Monte Carlo stock.

Estimated Value: **Excellent: $1,350.00**
Very good: $1,080.00

Remington Model 3200 Special Trap

Similar to the Model 3200 with a 32" barrel; ventilated rib only; Monte Carlo stock available; recoil pad.

Estimated Value: **Excellent: $1,275.00**
Very good: $1,025.00

Remington Model 3200 Competition Trap

Similar to the Model 3200 Special Trap with a higher quality finish. Monte Carlo stock available. Discontinued in 1983.

Estimated Value: **Excellent: $2,000.00**
Very good: $1,600.00

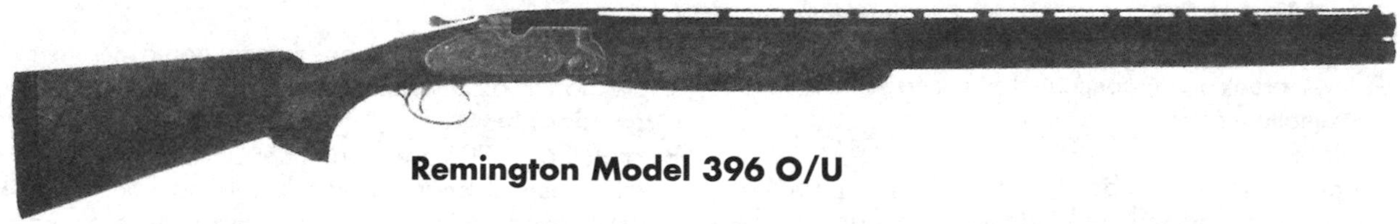

Remington Model 396 O/U

Remington Model 3200 Pigeon

Similar to the Model 3200 Competition Skeet with 28" improved modified and full choke barrels for live birds. Discontinued in 1983.

Estimated Value: **Excellent: $1,325.00**
Very good: $1,050.00

Remington Model 3200 Competition Skeet

Similar to the Model 3200 Skeet with a higher quality finish. Discontinued in 1983.

Estimated Value: **Excellent: $1,500.00**
Very good: $1,200.00

Remington Model 396 O/U

Gauge: 12
Action: Top lever break open, concealed hammer, single selective trigger; automatic ejectors, auto-safety on tang
Magazine: None
Barrel: Over and under double barrel, blued, 28" or 30" chrome-moly steel; ventilated rib; Remchoke tubes
Finish: Blued; checkered wood pistol grip stock and forearm with palm swell; engraved silver-colored receiver
Approximate wt.: 7½ lbs.
Comments: Produced in the mid- to the late 1990s. Prices shown are for Skeet model; add 7% for Sporting (Trap) model.

Estimated Value: **Excellent: $1,675.00**
Very good: $1,340.00

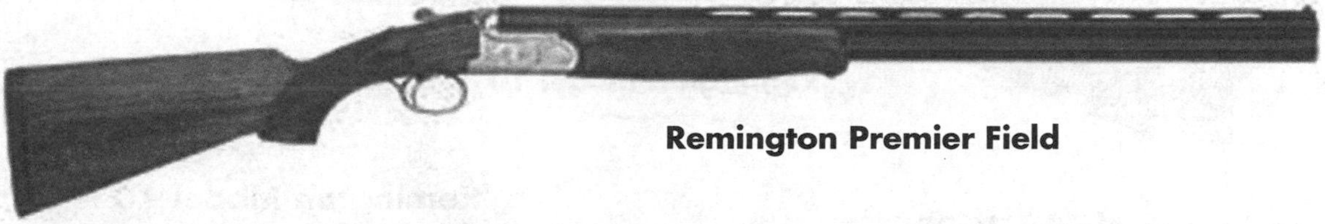

Remington Premier Field

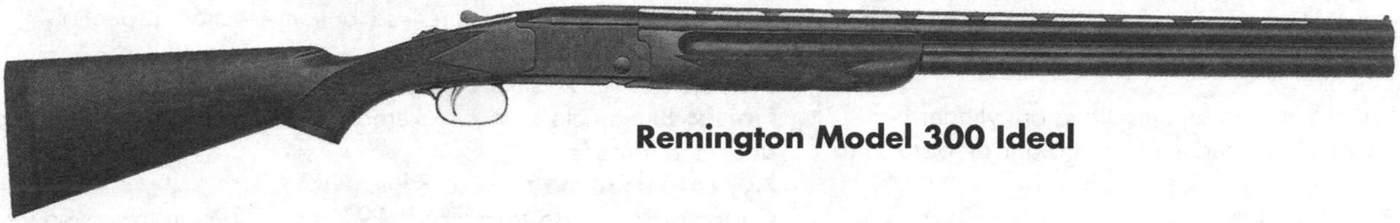

Remington Model 300 Ideal

Remington Model 300 Ideal

Gauge: 12
Action: Top lever, break-open; concealed hammer
Magazine: None
Barrel: 26", 28", or 30" over and under double barrel with ventilated rib
Finish: High polish blued; checkered walnut pistol grip stock and forearm; recoil pad
Approximate wt.: 7 to 8 lbs.
Comments: Made from 2000 to 2001.

Estimated Value:		
	Excellent:	**$1,500.00**
	Very good:	**$1,200.00**

Remington Premier Field

Gauge: 12, 20, 28
Action: Thumb lever, break-open; hammerless
Magazine: None
Barrel: 26" or 28" over and under double barrel; choke tubes; ventilated rib
Finish: Blued; nickel finish, engraved receiver; satin finish, checkered walnut pistol grip stock and lipped forearm
Approximate wt.: 7½ lbs.
Comments: Introduced in 2006.

Estimated Value:		
	New (retail):	**$2,100.00**
	Excellent:	**$1,575.00**
	Very good:	**$1,250.00**

Remington Premier Upland

Remington Premier Competition STS

Remington Premier Upland

Similar to the Premier Field except: oil finished stock and forearm; case-colored receiver with gold accents.

Estimated Value:		
	New (retail):	**$2,650.00**
	Excellent:	**$1,985.00**
	Very good:	**$1,590.00**

Remington Premier Competition STS

Similar to the Premier Field except: 12 gauge only; Titanium PVD-finished receiver; 28" or 30" barrel; gloss finish.

Estimated Value:		
	New (retail):	**$2,895.00**
	Excellent:	**$2,175.00**
	Very good:	**$1,735.00**

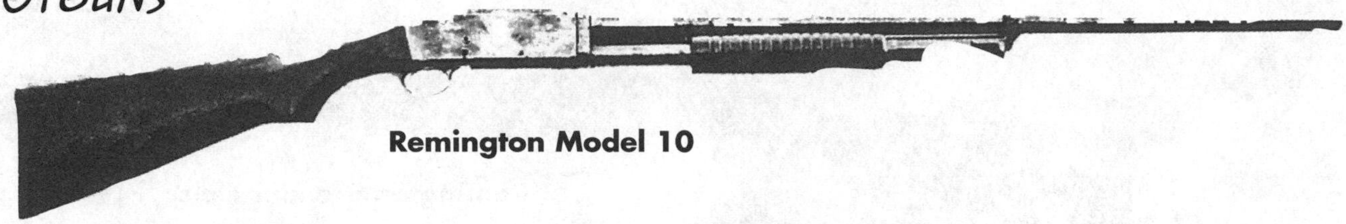

Remington Model 10

Remington Model 1908

Gauge: 12
Action: Slide action; hammerless; bottom ejection; repeating
Magazine: 5-shot tubular
Barrel: 26" – 32" steel barrel in full, modified or cylinder bore
Finish: Blued; plain or checkered walnut straight or pistol grip stock and forearm
Approximate wt.: 7½ to 8 lbs.
Comments: Made from about 1908 to 1910 in six grades with fancy checkering and engraving on higher grades. Marking on top of barrel "Remington Arms Co." and patent date. About 10,000 made. Prices for standard grade.

Estimated Value:	**Excellent:**	**$325.00**
	Very good:	**$260.00**

Remington Model 10

Gauge: 12
Action: Slide action; hammerless; bottom ejection; repeating
Magazine: 5-shot tubular
Barrel: 26" – 32" steel barrel in full, modified, or cylinder bore
Finish: Blued; plain or checkered walnut straight or pistol grip stock and forearm
Approximate wt.: 7½ to 8 lbs.
Comments: Made from about 1910 to 1929, an improved version of the Model 1908. Made in seven grades with fancy checkering and engraving on higher grades. Also produced in 20" barrel riot gun. Solid rib optional from 1910 to 1922; ventilated rib optional from 1922 to 1928. Prices for standard grade.

Estimated Value:	**Excellent:**	**$400.00**
	Very good:	**$320.00**

Remington Model 29

Remington Model 17

Gauge: 20
Action: Slide action; hammerless; bottom ejection; repeating
Magazine: 3-shot tubular
Barrel: 26" – 32" steel in full, modified, or cylinder bore; matted sighting groove on receiver or optional solid rib; 20" barrel on riot gun
Finish: Blued; plain or checkered walnut pistol grip stock and forearm
Approximate wt.: 7½ to 8 lbs.
Comments: Made from about 1917 to 1933 in seven grades. Higher grades have higher quality finish. Prices for standard grade.

Estimated Value:	**Excellent:**	**$375.00**
	Very good:	**$300.00**

Remington Model 29

Gauge: 12
Action: Slide action; hammerless; bottom ejection; repeating
Magazine: 5-shot tubular
Barrel: 26" – 32" steel in full, modified or cylinder bore; optional solid or ventilated rib; 20" barrel on riot gun
Finish: Blued; plain or checkered walnut pistol grip stock and forearm
Approximate wt.: 7½ to 8 lbs.
Comments: Made from about 1929 to 1933 in nine grades. Higher grades have higher quality finish. Prices for standard grade.

Estimated Value:	**Excellent:**	**$420.00**
	Very good:	**$335.00**

Remington Model 31

Gauge: 12, 16, 20
Action: Slide action; hammerless; side ejection; repeating
Magazine: 3-shot or 5-shot tubular
Barrel: 26", 32" steel; full, modified, cylinder, or skeet chokes; optional solid or ventilated rib
Finish: Blued; slightly grooved on receiver; plain or checkered pistol grip stock and forearm; forearm checkered or grooved
Approximate wt.: 6½ to 8 lbs.
Comments: Made from about 1931 to 1949 in eight grades. Higher grades differ in quality of finish. Prices for standard grades. Add $20.00 for solid rib; $25.00 for ventilated rib.

Estimated Value:	**Excellent:**	**$500.00**
	Very good:	**$400.00**

Remington Model 31 Skeet

Similar to the Model 31 except: 12 gauge only; 26" barrel; solid or ventilated rib; skeet choke. Add $20.00 for ventilated rib.

Estimated Value:	**Excellent:**	**$550.00**
	Very good:	**$450.00**

Remington Model 31R Riot Gun

Similar to the Model 31 in 12 gauge only with 20" plain barrel.

Estimated Value:	**Excellent:**	**$325.00**
	Very good:	**$260.00**

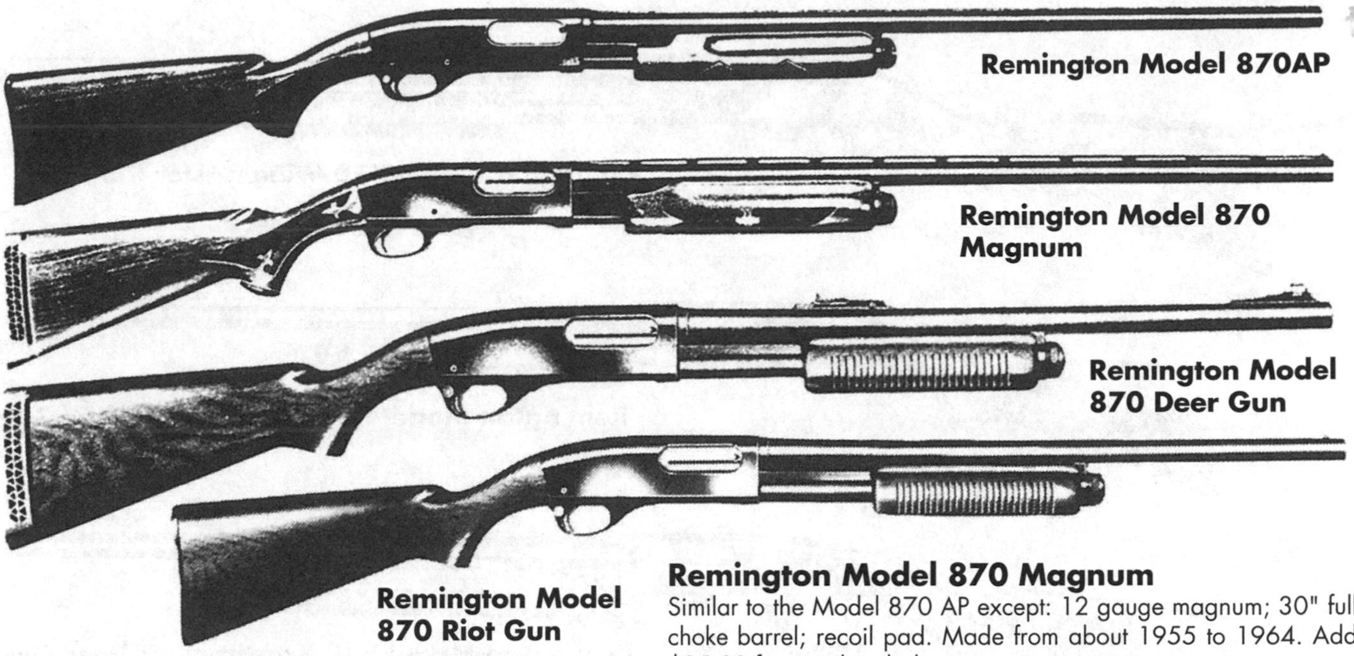

Remington Model 870AP

Remington Model 870 Magnum

Remington Model 870 Deer Gun

Remington Model 870 Riot Gun

Remington Model 870AP

Gauge: 12, 16, 20
Action: Slide action; hammerless; side ejector; repeating
Magazine: 4-shot tubular
Barrel: 26", 28", 30" in 12 gauge; 26" or 28" in 16 and 20 gauge; full, modified, or improved cylinder bore; plain or ventilated rib
Finish: Blued; plain or fancy; fluted comb, pistol grip stock, and grooved slide handle
Approximate wt.: 6½ to 8 lbs.
Comments: Made in many styles, grades, and variations from about 1950 to 1964. Higher grades have higher quality finish. Prices for standard grade. Add $25.00 for ventilated rib.

Estimated Value:	Excellent:	$350.00
	Very good:	$285.00

Remington Model 870 Magnum

Similar to the Model 870 AP except: 12 gauge magnum; 30" full choke barrel; recoil pad. Made from about 1955 to 1964. Add $25.00 for ventilated rib.

Estimated Value:	Excellent:	$375.00
	Very good:	$300.00

Remington Model 870 Riot Gun

Same as the Model 870 AP except: 12 gauge only; 20" plain barrel; improved cylinder bore.

Estimated Value:	Excellent:	$300.00
	Very good:	$240.00

Remington Model 870 Deer Gun

Similar to the Model 870 AP except: 12 gauge only; 26" barrel for slugs; rifle type adjustable sights. Made from about 1959 to 1964.

Estimated Value:	Excellent:	$300.00
	Very good:	$240.00

Remington Model 870 Wingmaster Field Gun

Remington Model 870 Special Purpose

Similar to the Model 870 with oil-finish wood and parkerized metal; recoil pad and nylon camo strap; 12 gauge; ventilated rib, 26" or 30" barrel. Introduced in 1985; discontinued in 1990s. "Rem Choke." Deduct 20% for synthetic stock.

Estimated Value:	Excellent:	$325.00
	Very good:	$260.00

Remington Model 870SP Deer Gun

Similar to the 870 Special Purpose with cantilever scope mount and 20" improved cylinder or rifled barrel and rifle sights. Introduced in 1986.

Estimated Value:	Excellent:	$420.00
	Very good:	$335.00

Remington Model 870 Wingmaster Field Gun

Gauge: 12, 16, 20, 28, 410 added in 1969; 16 gauge discontinued in the late 1980s and reintroduced 2002.
Action: Slide action; hammerless; side ejector; repeating
Magazine: 4-shot tubular
Barrel: 26" – 30" in 12 gauge; 26" or 28" in 16 and 20 gauge; 25" in 28 and 410 bore; full, modified, or improved cylinder bore; plain barrel or ventilated rib; "Rem Choke"
Finish: Blued; checkered walnut pistol grip stock with matching slide handle; recoil pad
Approximate wt.: 6½ to 7¼ lbs.
Comments: Improved version of the Model 870AP. Made in many grades and styles from about 1964 to present. Left-hand models and lightweight models also available. Prices for standard grades. Add 10% for left-hand model. Add 8% for gauges 28 or 410.

Estimated Value:	New (retail):	$699.00
	Excellent:	$525.00
	Very good:	$420.00

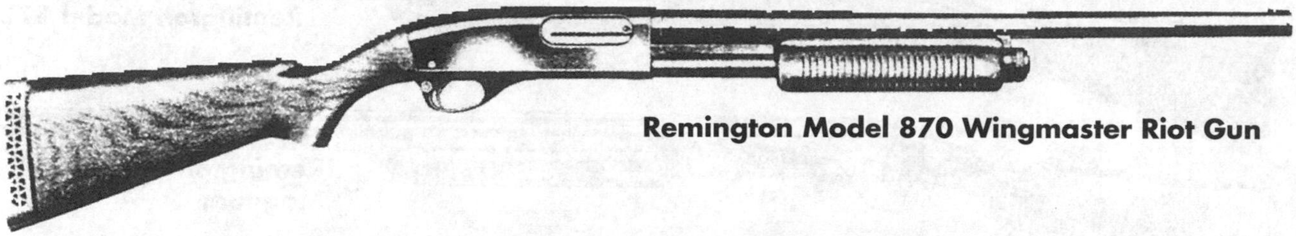

Remington Model 870 Wingmaster Riot Gun

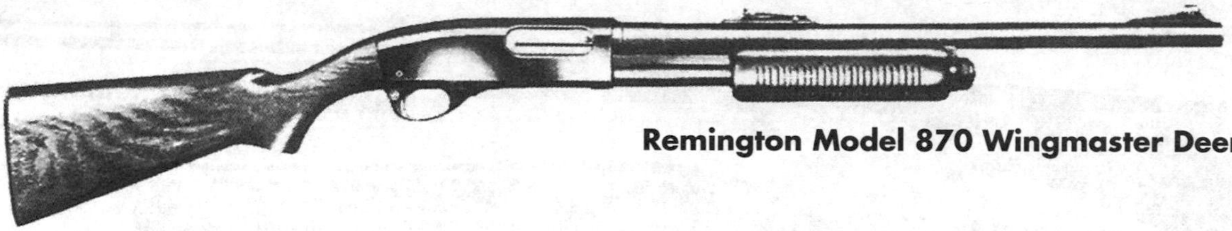

Remington Model 870 Wingmaster Deer Gun

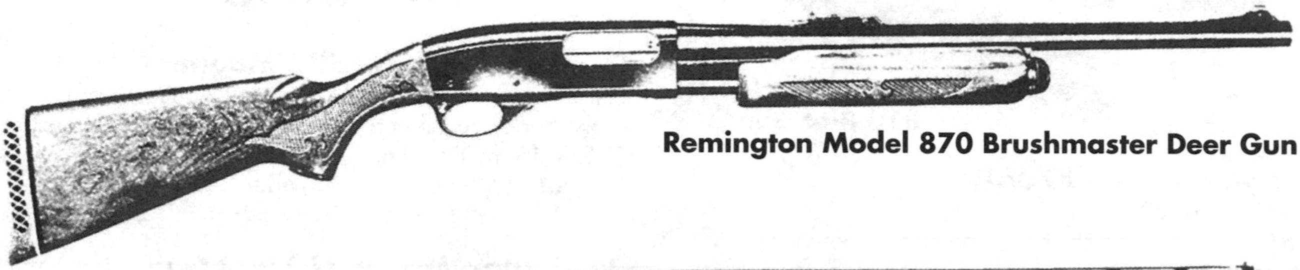

Remington Model 870 Brushmaster Deer Gun

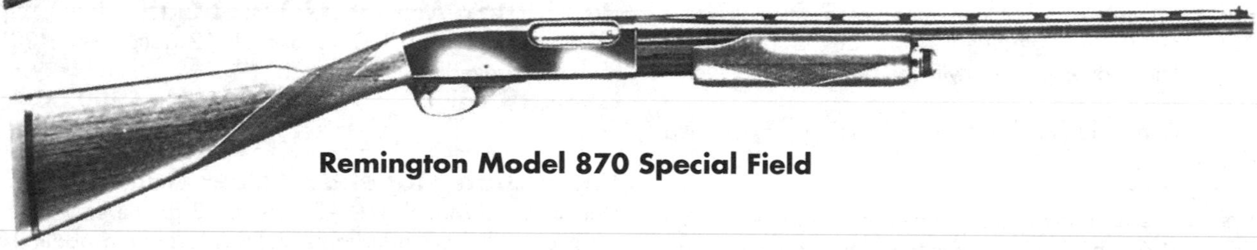

Remington Model 870 Special Field

Remington Model 870 Wingmaster Riot Gun, Police

Similar to the Model 870 Wingmaster except: 12 gauge only; 18" or 20" improved cylinder barrel; plain stock and grooved slide handle; designed for law enforcement use. Add 8% for rifle sights. Blued or parkerized finish.

Estimated Value: **Excellent:** **$400.00**
Very good: **$320.00**

Remington Model 870 Wingmaster Magnum

Same as the Model 870 Field Gun except: 12 or 20 magnum gauge only; full or modified choke. Add $30.00 for left-hand model; add 10% for "Rem Choke." Add 10% for ventilated rib.

Estimated Value: **Excellent:** **$325.00**
Very good: **$260.00**

Remington Model 870 SA Skeet

Similar to the Model 870 except: skeet choke; ventilated rib only; recoil pad. Made from the late 1970s to the early 1980s; 25" or 26" barrel.

Estimated Value: **Excellent:** **$350.00**
Very good: **$280.00**

Remington Model 870 Wingmaster Deer Gun

Same as Model 870 Wingmaster except: 12 gauge only; 20" barrel; rifle sights. Produced from 1964 to the mid-1980s.

Estimated Value: **Excellent:** **$400.00**
Very good: **$320.00**

Remington Model 870 Brushmaster Deer Gun

Same as the Model 870 Wingmaster Deer Gun except: 12 and 20 gauge; checkered stock and slide; recoil pad. Left-hand version introduced in 1983; discontinued in the mid-1990s. Add 8% for 12 gauge.

Estimated Value: **Excellent:** **$325.00**
Very good: **$260.00**

Remington Model 870 Special Field

Similar to the Model 870 with a straight grip stock, 21" or 23" ventilated rib barrel; 12 or 20 gauge; 3" chamber. Introduced in 1984; discontinued in the mid-1990s. Some models have "Rem Choke."

Estimated Value: **Excellent:** **$360.00**
Very good: **$285.00**

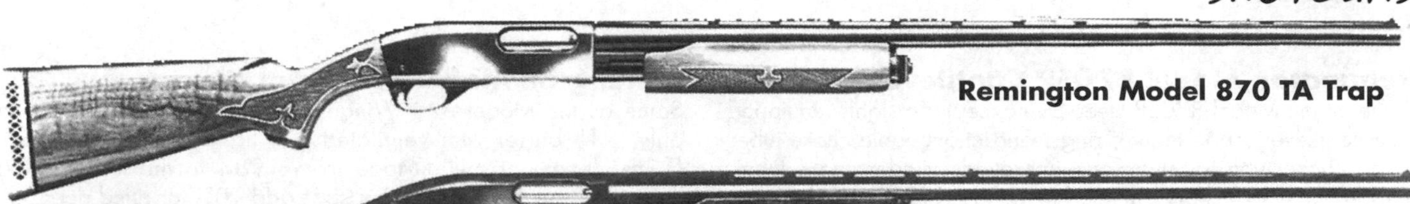

Remington Model 870 TA Trap

Remington Model 870 TB Trap

Remington Models 870 TA Trap, TB Trap, and TC Trap

Similar to the Model 870 with a 30" full choke barrel; ventilated rib; recoil pad; choice of Monte Carlo stock.

Estimated Value:	**Excellent:**	**$400.00**
	Very good:	**$320.00**

Remington Model 870 Wingmaster Super Magnum

Similar to the Model Wingmaster 870 Field Gun except: 12 gauge magnum only with 3½" chamber; 28" ventilated rib barrel. Introduced in 2000.

Estimated Value:	**New (retail):**	**$875.00**
	Excellent:	**$650.00**
	Very good:	**$525.00**

Remington Model 870 Express Super Magnum

Similar to the Model 870 Express except: 12 gauge magnum only with 3½" chamber. Available with walnut or synthetic stock and slide handle.

Estimated Value:	**New (retail):**	**$376.00**
	Excellent:	**$285.00**
	Very good:	**$225.00**

Remington Model 870 Express Super Magnum Turkey

Similar to the Model 870 Express Super Magnum except: 23" barrel. Available with black synthetic or camouflage finish. Add 28% for camouflage finish.

Estimated Value:	**New (retail):**	**$425.00**
	Excellent:	**$320.00**
	Very good:	**$255.00**

Remington Model 870 Express Deer Gun

Similar to the Model 870 Express except: 20" improved cylinder or fully rifled barrel; walnut or synthetic stock and slide handle. Add 10% for rifled barrel.

Estimated Value:	**New (retail):**	**$425.00**
	Excellent:	**$320.00**
	Very good:	**$255.00**

Remington Model 870 Competition Trap

Similar to the Model 870; single shot; 30" full choke; ventilated rib barrel; recoil pad; non-glare matte finish receiver. Introduced in 1982.

Estimated Value:	**Excellent:**	**$450.00**
	Very good:	**$360.00**

Remington Model 870 Wingmaster Classic Trap

Remington Model 870 Express

Gauge: 12, 20, 28, or 410 (magnum)
Action: Slide action; hammerless; side ejection repeating
Magazine: 4-shot tubular
Barrel: 25", 26", or 28" ventilated rib; "Rem-choke" or rifled deer barrel with sights
Finish: Blued; checkered hardwood or synthetic pistol grip stock and forearm
Approximate wt.: 6 to 7¼ lbs.
Comments: Introduced in 1987. Add 10% for left-hand. Add 10% for magnum.

Estimated Value:	**New (retail):**	**$359.00**
	Excellent:	**$270.00**
	Very good:	**$215.00**

Remington Model 870 Ltd. 20

Same as the Model 870 Wingmaster Field except: 20 gauge only; 23" barrel with ventilated rib; lightweight. Made from 1980 to 1984.

Estimated Value:	**Excellent:**	**$425.00**
	Very good:	**$340.00**

Remington Model 870 Wingmaster Classic Trap

Similar to the Model 870 Wingmaster Field Gun except: 30" "Rem-choke" barrel; American Walnut, Monte Carlo stock, and slide handle; recoil pad; engraved receiver.

Estimated Value:	**New (retail):**	**$839.00**
	Excellent:	**$630.00**
	Very good:	**$500.00**

Remington Model 870SP Cantilever

Same as the Model 870SP Deer Gun except: no sights; equipped with cantilever scope mount, rings, and changeable choke tubes (rifled choke tube for slugs and improved cylinder choke tube). Introduced in 1989; discontinued in the late 1990s.

Estimated Value: **Excellent:** **$300.00**
Very good: **$240.00**

Remington Model 870 Youth Gun

Same as the Model 870 Wingmaster Field except: 20 gauge only; 21" barrel with ventilated rib; lightweight; short stock (12½" length of pull). Made from 1984 to the late 1990s; changeable choke tubes after 1985; add 10% for rifled deer barrel with sights.

Estimated Value: **Excellent:** **$295.00**
Very good: **$235.00**

Remington Autoloading Riot Gun

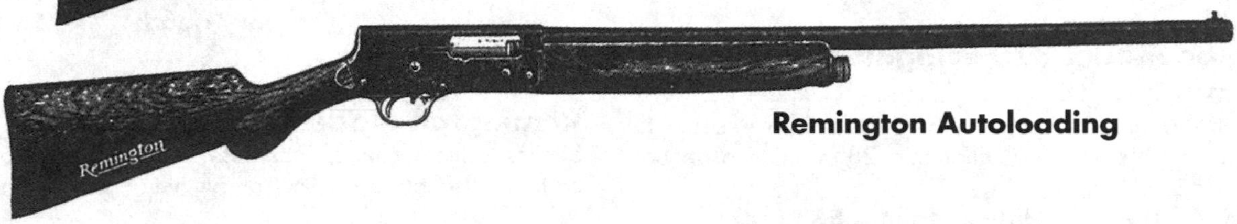

Remington Autoloading

Remington Autoloading Riot Gun

Similar to Autoloading except: 20" barrel; weighs 6¾ lbs.

Estimated Value: **Excellent:** **$375.00**
Very good: **$300.00**

Remington Autoloading

Gauge: 12
Action: Semiautomatic; concealed hammer
Magazine: 5-shot tubular
Barrel: 26", 28" steel; full, modified or cylinder bore
Finish: Blued; matted sight groove; plain or checkered straight or pistol grip stock and forearm
Approximate wt.: 7¾ lbs.
Comments: Made from about 1905 to 1910 in six grades. Prices for standard grade.
Estimated Value: **Excellent:** **$375.00**
Very good: **$300.00**

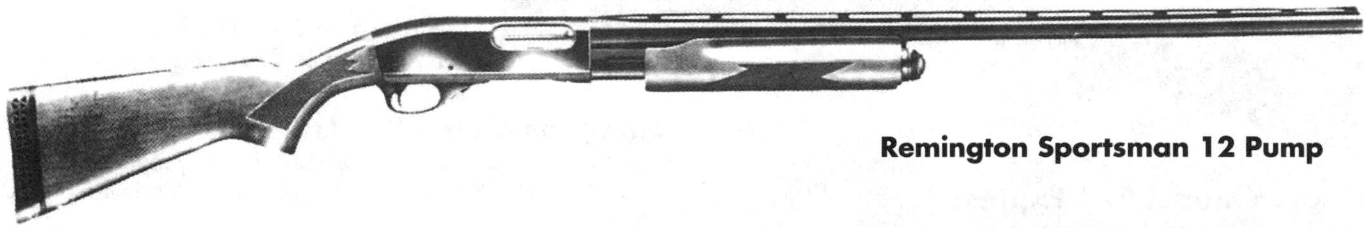

Remington Sportsman 12 Pump

Remington Sportsman 12 Pump

Gauge: 12, regular or magnum
Action: Slide action; hammerless; side ejector; repeating
Magazine: 4-shot tubular
Barrel: 28" modified, 30" full; ventilated rib
Finish: Blued; checkered walnut semi-pistol grip stock and slide handle; steel receiver; recoil pad
Approximate wt.: 6½ to 7½ lbs.
Comments: Introduced in 1984; discontinued in the late 1980s. Add $25.00 for "Rem-Choke."
Estimated Value: **Excellent:** **$300.00**
Very good: **$240.00**

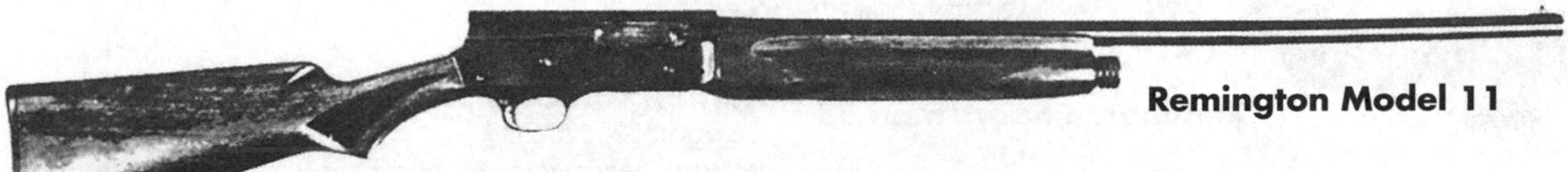

Remington Model 11

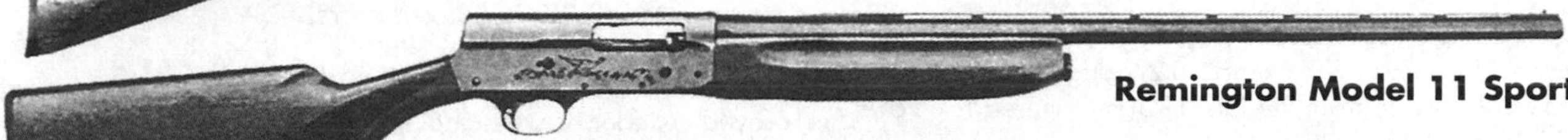

Remington Model 11 Sportsman

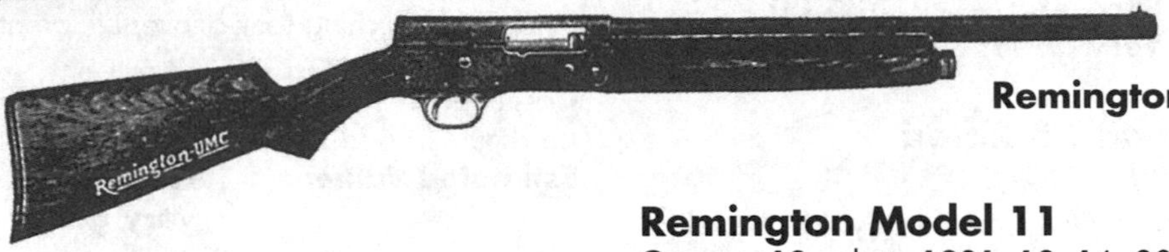

Remington Model 11 Riot Gun

Remington Model 11 Sportsman

Same as the Model 11 with a 2-shot magazine. Made from about 1931 to 1948 in six grades. Prices for standard grade. Add $15.00 for solid rib; $25.00 for ventilated rib.

Estimated Value:	**Excellent:**	**$575.00**
	Very good:	**$460.00**

Remington Model 11 Riot Gun

Same as the Model 11 except with a 20" plain barrel.

Estimated Value:	**Excellent:**	**$500.00**
	Very good:	**$400.00**

Remington Model 11

Gauge: 12 only to 1931; 12, 16, 20 from 1931 – 1948
Action: Semiautomatic; concealed hammer; side ejector; repeating
Magazine: 4-shot, bottom load
Barrel: 26" or 28" to 1931; 26", 28", 30", 32" from 1931 – 1948; full, modified, or cylinder
Finish: Blued; wood semi-pistol grip stock; straight grip on Trap grades; checkering and fancy wood on higher grades
Approximate wt.: 7½ to 8½ lbs.
Comments: Made from about 1911 to 1948 in six grades. Optional solid or ventilated rib available; rounded grip ends on stock from 1911 to 1916. Prices are for standard grade. Add $15.00 for ribbed barrel.

Estimated Value:	**Excellent:**	**$500.00**
	Very good:	**$400.00**

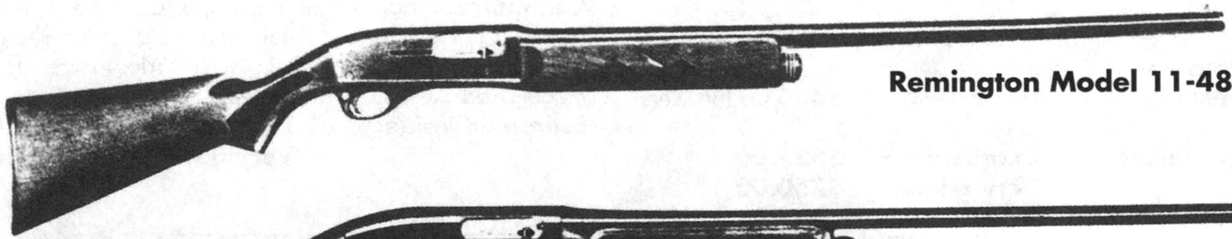

Remington Model 11-48

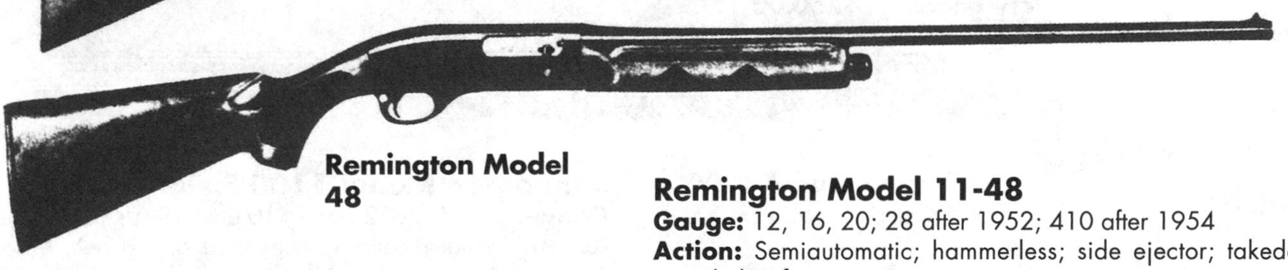

Remington Model 48

Remington Model 11-48 Riot Gun

Same general specifications as the Model 11-48 except: 12 gauge only; 20" plain barrel. Made from about 1954 to 1968.

Estimated Value:	**Excellent:**	**$325.00**
	Very good:	**$260.00**

Remington Model 48

Similar to the Model 11-48 except: 2-shot magazine; 12, 16, 20 gauge. Made from about 1948 to 1959 in several grades to replace the Model 11 Sportsman. Prices for standard model. Add $30.00 for ventilated rib.

Estimated Value:	**Excellent:**	**$350.00**
	Very good:	**$275.00**

Remington Model 11-48

Gauge: 12, 16, 20; 28 after 1952; 410 after 1954
Action: Semiautomatic; hammerless; side ejector; takedown; cross bolt safety
Magazine: 4-shot tubular; 3-shot in 28 and 410 gauge
Barrel: 26", 28", 30" in 12, 16 and 20 gauge; 25" in 28 and 410 bore; full, modified, or improved cylinder
Finish: Checkered walnut pistol grip stock with fluted comb, matching semi-beavertail forearm; higher grades are fancier
Approximate wt.: 6½ to 7½ lbs.
Comments: Made from about 1949 to 1968 in about seven grades. Replacing the Model 11, it had an improved action and the rear of the receiver was rounded off flush with the stock. Prices are for standard model. Add $30.00 for ventilated rib.

Estimated Value:	**Excellent:**	**$350.00**
	Very good:	**$275.00**

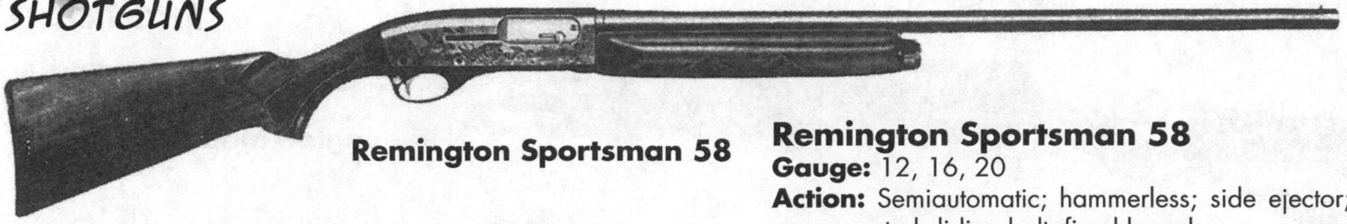

Remington Sportsman 58

Remington Sportsman 58 Magnum

Similar to the Sportsman 58 except: 12 gauge magnum; 30" barrel; recoil pad. Made from the late 1950s to the early 1960s. Add $30.00 for ventilated rib.

Estimated Value:	**Excellent:**	**$335.00**
	Very good:	**$265.00**

Remington Sportsman 58 Rifled Slug Special

Same as the Sportsman 58 except: 12 gauge only; 26" barrel for slugs; equipped with rifle sights.

Estimated Value:	**Excellent:**	**$350.00**
	Very good:	**$280.00**

Remington Sportsman 58

Gauge: 12, 16, 20
Action: Semiautomatic; hammerless; side ejector; solid breech; gas-operated sliding bolt; fixed barrel
Magazine: 2-shot tubular
Barrel: 26", 28", 30"; plain or ventilated rib; full, modified, improved cylinder or skeet chokes
Finish: Blued; checkered walnut pistol grip stock with fluted comb and matching semi-beavertail forearm
Approximate wt.: 6½ to 7½ lbs.
Comments: Made from about 1956 to 1963. Prices for standard model. Add $30.00 for ventilated rib.

Estimated Value:	**Excellent:**	**$325.00**
	Very good:	**$260.00**

Remington Sportsman 878 Automaster

Remington Sportsman 12 Auto

Gauge: 12
Action: Gas-operated, semiautomatic
Magazine: 4-shot tubular
Barrel: 28" modified, 30" full; ventilated rib; "Rem-Choke" available
Finish: Checkered hardwood semi-pistol grip stock and forearm
Approximate wt.: 7¾ lbs.
Comments: Produced in the mid-1980s. Add $30.00 for "Rem-Choke."

Estimated Value:	**Excellent:**	**$325.00**
	Very good:	**$260.00**

Remington Model 878 Automaster

Gauge: 12
Action: Semiautomatic; gas-operated; hammerless
Magazine: 2-shot tubular
Barrel: 26" – 30"; full, modified, improved cylinder or skeet chokes
Finish: Blued; plain or checkered walnut pistol grip stock and forearm
Approximate wt.: 7 lbs.
Comments: Made similar to the Sportsman 58 to fill in the sales line with a lower priced, plain, standard grade shotgun. Made from about 1959 to 1962 in two grades. Prices for standard model. Add $30.00 for ventilated rib.

Estimated Value:	**Excellent:**	**$300.00**
	Very good:	**$240.00**

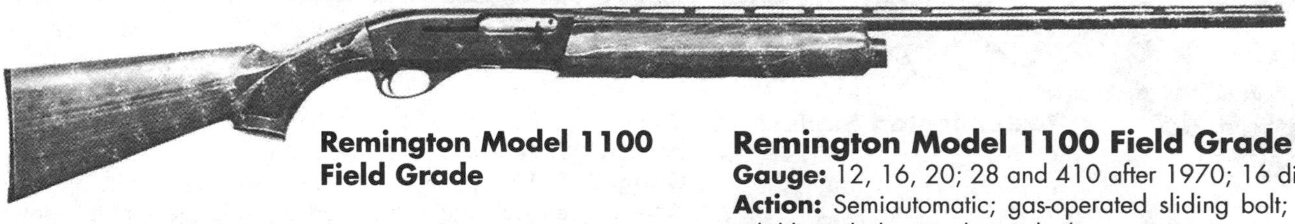

Remington Model 1100 Field Grade

Remington Model 1100 Ltd. 20

Same as the Model 1100 Field except: 20 gauge only; 23" ventilated rib barrel; lightweight; made from 1980 to 1984.

Estimated Value:	**Excellent:**	**$450.00**
	Very good:	**$360.00**

Remington Model 1100 Youth Gun

Same as the Model 1100 Field except: 20 gauge only; 21" ventilated rib barrel; lightweight; short stock (12½" length of pull). Made from 1984 to present. Changeable choke tubes after 1985; add $13.00 for "Rem-Choke."

Estimated Value:	**Excellent:**	**$375.00**
	Very good:	**$300.00**

Remington Model 1100 Field Grade

Gauge: 12, 16, 20; 28 and 410 after 1970; 16 discontinued
Action: Semiautomatic; gas-operated sliding bolt; fixed barrel; solid breech; hammerless; takedown
Magazine: 4-shot tubular
Barrel: 26", 28" in 16 and 20 gauge; 26", 28", 30" in 12 gauge; 25" in 28 and 410; full, modified, improved cylinder and skeet chokes; ventilated rib available
Finish: Blued; checkered wood pistol grip stock with fluted comb and matching forearm; engraved receiver
Approximate wt.: 6½ to 7½ lbs.
Comments: An improved, low-recoil shotgun to replace the 58, 11-48 and 878. Made from about 1963 to the present in several grades. Add $13.00 for "Rem-Choke." Add 15% for gauges 28 or 410. Add 20% for ventilated rib.

Estimated Value:	**Excellent:**	**$425.00**
	Very good:	**$340.00**

Remington Model 1100 Magnum

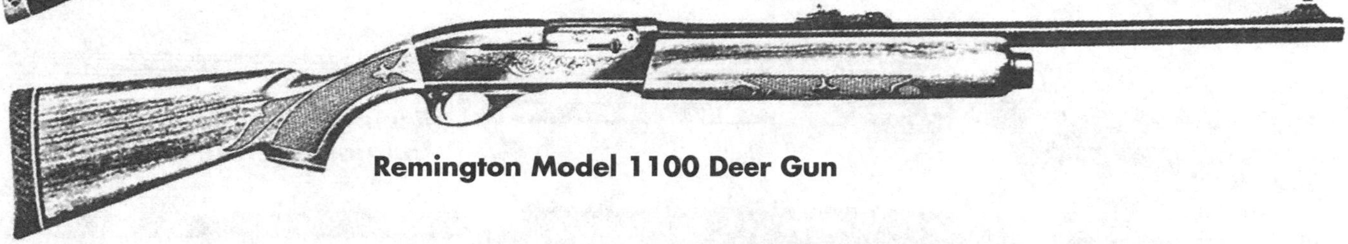

Remington Model 1100 Deer Gun

Remington Model 1100 Magnum

Similar to the Model 1100 except: 12 or 20 gauge magnum; 28" or 30" barrel; full or modified chokes; recoil pad. Add $30.00 for left-hand model.

Estimated Value:	**Excellent:**	**$450.00**
	Very good:	**$360.00**

Remington Model 1100 Deer Gun

Similar to the Model 1100 with a 22" plain barrel and adjustable rifle sights; bored for rifle slugs; 12 or 20 gauge lightweight. Left-hand version introduced in 1983.

Estimated Value:	**Excellent:**	**$450.00**
	Very good:	**$360.00**

Remington Model 1100 Special Purpose

Similar to the Model 1100 with oil-finished wood and parkerized metal; recoil pad and nylon camouflage strap; 12 gauge only; ventilated rib barrel. Introduced in 1985. Discontinued in 1987.

Estimated Value:	**Excellent:**	**$450.00**
	Very good:	**$360.00**

Remington Model 1100 SP Deer Gun

Similar to the Model 1100 Special Purpose with a 21" improved cylinder barrel and rifle sights. Produced in the mid-1980s.

Estimated Value:	**Excellent:**	**$400.00**
	Very good:	**$320.00**

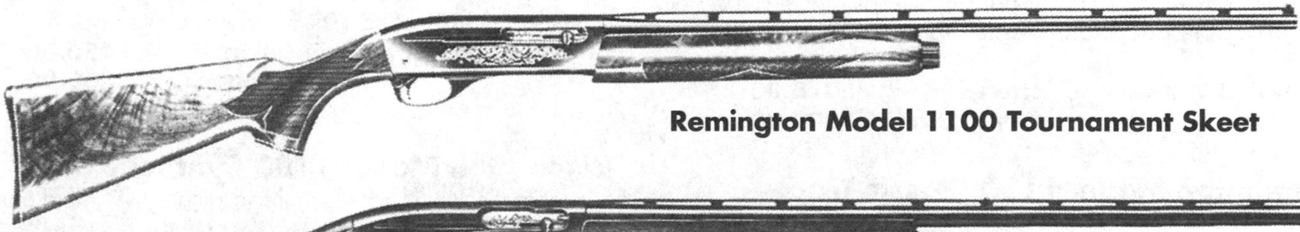

Remington Model 1100 Tournament Skeet

Remington Model 1100SA Skeet

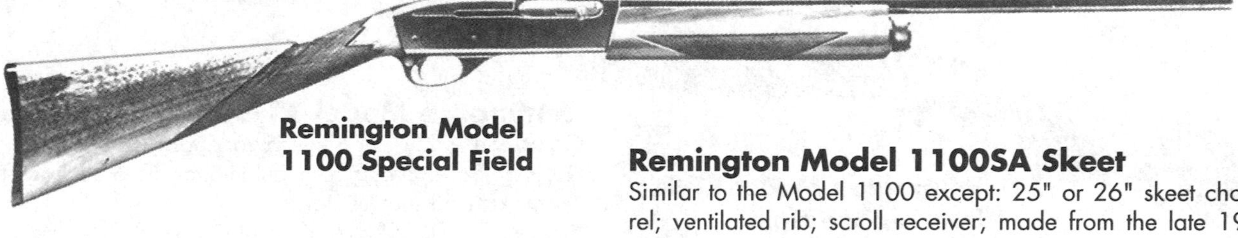

Remington Model 1100 Special Field

Remington Model 1100 Special Field

Similar to the Model 1100 except: straight grip stock and 21" or 23" ventilated rib barrel; 12 gauge or LT 20 Model, 2¾" chamber. Introduced in 1983; discontinued in the late 1990s.

Estimated Value:	**Excellent:**	**$425.00**
	Very good:	**$340.00**

Remington Model 1100SA Skeet

Similar to the Model 1100 except: 25" or 26" skeet choke barrel; ventilated rib; scroll receiver; made from the late 1970s to 1987.

Estimated Value:	**Excellent:**	**$450.00**
	Very good:	**$360.00**

Remington Model 1100 Tournament Skeet

Similar to the Model 1100SA Skeet with higher quality finish.

Estimated Value:	**Excellent:**	**$475.00**
	Very good:	**$380.00**

Remington Model 1100TA Trap, Monte Carlo Stock

Remington Model 1100 Tournament Trap

Remington Model 1100 Classic Trap

Remington Model 1100 Sporting

Similar to the Model 1100 Field Grade except: 12, 20, or 28 gauge; 25" (28 gauge) or 28" barrel; high quality walnut and high polish blued finish. Add 4% for 410 or 28 gauge.

Estimated Value: **New (retail):** **$868.00**
Excellent: **$650.00**
Very good: **$520.00**

Remington Model 1100TA Trap

Similar to the Model 1100 with a 30" full or modified trap barrel; ventilated rib only; recoil pad; choice of Monte Carlo stock (add $10.00). Add $30.00 for left-hand model. Discontinued in 1987.

Estimated Value: **Excellent:** **$375.00**
Very good: **$300.00**

Remington Model 1100 Classic Trap

Similar to the Model 1100 Sporting except: 30" light target "Rem-Choke" barrel; high gloss finish.

Estimated Value: **New (retail):** **$901.00**
Excellent: **$675.00**
Very good: **$540.00**

Remington Model 1100 Synthetic

Similar to the Model 1100 Field Grade except: matte black finish and synthetic stock and forearm; 12 or 20 gauge; 26" or 2" barrel.

Estimated Value: **New (retail):** **$839.00**
Excellent: **$630.00**
Very good: **$500.00**

Remington Model 1100 Tournament Trap

Similar to the Model 1100TA Trap with higher quality finish. Discontinued in 1987. Add 10% for Monte Carlo stock.

Estimated Value: **Excellent:** **$450.00**
Very good: **$360.00**

Remington Model 1100 Synthetic Deer

Similar to the Model 1100 Synthetic except: 21" rifled barrel and rifle sights. Add 7% for Cantilever Scope Mount model.

Estimated Value: **New (retail):** **$819.00**
Excellent: **$615.00**
Very good: **$490.00**

Remington Model 11-96 Euro Lightweight

Remington Model 1100 Synthetic Youth

Similar to the Model 1100 Synthetic except: 20 gauge only; 21" barrel. Add 10% for camouflage finish (Youth Turkey).

Estimated Value: **New (retail):** **$549.00**
Excellent: **$410.00**
Very good: **$330.00**

Remington Model 11-96 Euro Lightweight

Gauge: 12, 2¾", or 3" interchangeably
Action: Gas-operated, semiautomatic with pressure control valve
Magazine: 3-shot tubular
Barrel: Blued, 26" or 28" chrome-moly steel with chrome-plated bore and ventilated rib
Finish: Blued; checkered Claro-walnut pistol grip stock and forearm; receiver has fine line engraving
Approximate wt.: 7 lbs.
Comments: Made in the late 1990s. Voted 1997 Shotgun of the Year by *Shooting Industry* magazine.

Estimated Value: **Excellent:** **$700.00**
Very good: **$560.00**

Remington Model SP-10 Magnum

Gauge: 10
Action: Gas-operated (non-corrosive stainless steel gas system) semiautomatic; safety in rear of trigger guard
Magazine: 3-shot tubular
Barrel: 26" or 30" matte, non-reflective blued finish with ventilated rib; full and modified choke tubes
Finish: Checkered walnut pistol grip stock and forearm with low gloss satin finish to reduce glare; also synthetic stock and forearm available.
Approximate wt.: 11 lbs. (26" barrel); 11¼ lbs. (30" barrel)
Comments: Introduced in 1989. Some critical components of the Model SP-10 and other Remington 10 gauge shotguns are not interchangeable. Add 9% for Mossy Oak camouflage finish; 12% for Turkey camouflage.

Estimated Value:	**Excellent:**	**$1,100.00**
	Very good:	**$ 880.00**

Remington Model 11-87 Premier

Gauge: 12 or 20 gauge, regular or magnum, interchangeably
Action: Gas-operated, semiautomatic
Magazine: 3-shot tubular
Barrel: 26", 28", or 30" with "Rem-Choke"; light contour barrel available.
Finish: Blued; checkered walnut pistol grip stock and forearm
Approximate wt.: 8¼ lbs.
Comments: Right- and left-hand models available. Introduced in 1987. Add 10% for left-hand model.

Estimated Value:	**New (retail):**	**$793.00**
	Excellent:	**$595.00**
	Very good:	**$475.00**

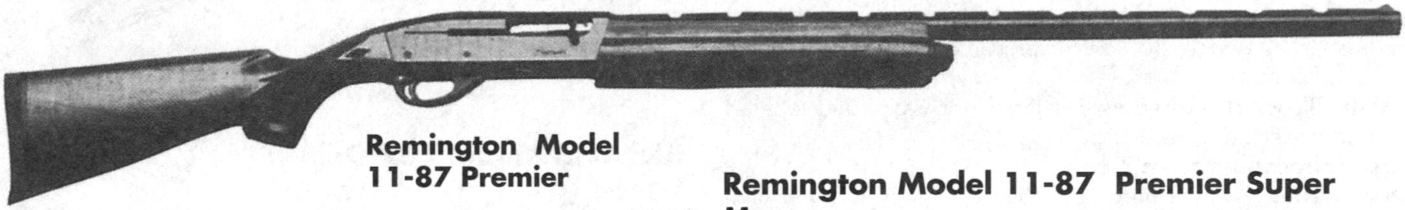

Remington Model 11-87 Premier

Remington Model 11-87 Premier Super Magnum

Similar to the Model 11-87 Premier except: walnut or synthetic stock and forearm; chambered for 3" or 3½" shells. Introduced in 2000. Add 10% for camouflage finish.

Estimated Value:	**New (retail):**	**$865.00**
	Excellent:	**$650.00**
	Very good:	**$520.00**

Remington Model 11-87 Premier Trap

Similar to the Model 11-87 Premier except: 30" barrel; full choke or with "Rem-Choke." Monte Carlo or regular stock. Add $13.00 for "Rem-Choke" or Monte Carlo stock. Add 4% for Sporting Clay; Premier Trap discontinued in the late 1990s.

Estimated Value:	**Excellent:**	**$525.00**
	Very good:	**$420.00**

Remington Model 11-87 Upland Special

Similar to the Model 11-87 Premier except: straight grip stock and 23" barrel. Introduced in 2000.

Estimated Value:	**New (retail):**	**$793.00**
	Excellent:	**$595.00**
	Very good:	**$475.00**

Remington Model 11-87 Special Purpose Camo

Similar to the Model 11-87 Premier except: camouflage finish. Introduced in 2000.

Estimated Value:	**New (retail):**	**$892.00**
	Excellent:	**$670.00**
	Very good:	**$535.00**

Remington Model 11-87 Special Purpose

Similar to the Model 11-87 Premier except: "Rem-Choke" barrel, non-glare finish, recoil pad, ventilated rib, and camouflage strap. Introduced in 1987.

Estimated Value:	**Excellent:**	**$500.00**
	Very good:	**$400.00**

Remington Model 11-87 Premier Skeet

Similar to the Model 11-87 Premier except: 26" skeet or "Rem-Choke" barrel. Weight, 7¾ lbs. Add $13.00 for "Rem-Choke."

Estimated Value:	**Excellent:**	**$500.00**
	Very good:	**$400.00**

Remington Model 11-87 Special Purpose Cantilever Deer Gun

Similar to the Model 11-87 Special Purpose Deer Gun except: matte black, non-reflective finish; cantilever deer scope mount. Introduced in the late 1990s.

Estimated Value:	**New (retail):**	**$875.00**
	Excellent:	**$650.00**
	Very good:	**$525.00**

Remington Model 11-87 Premier Cantilever

Same as the Model 11-87 Special Purpose Deer Gun except: no sights; equipped with cantilever scope mount, rings and changeable choke tubes (rifled choke tube for slugs and improved cylinder tube). Introduced in 1989.

Estimated Value:	**Excellent:**	**$625.00**
	Very good:	**$500.00**

Remington Model 11-87 Special Purpose Deer Gun

Similar to the Model 11-87 Special Purpose except: 21" improved cylinder barrel and rifle sights.

Estimated Value:	**New (retail):**	**$824.00**
	Excellent:	**$620.00**
	Very good:	**$495.00**

RICHLAND

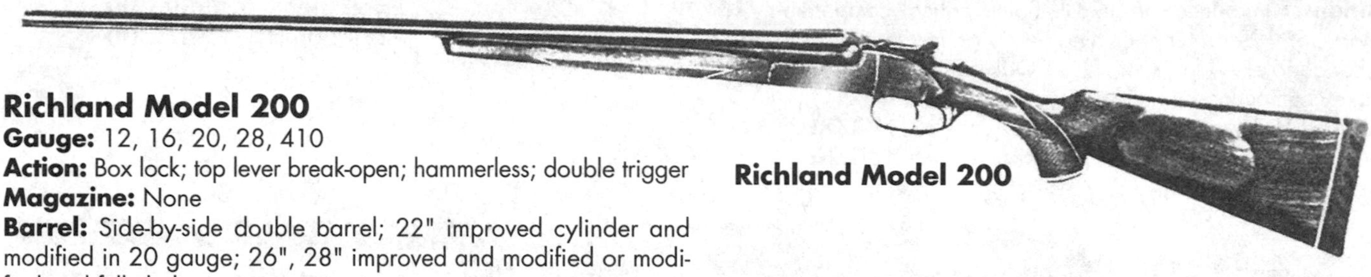

Richland Model 200

Richland Model 200

Gauge: 12, 16, 20, 28, 410
Action: Box lock; top lever break-open; hammerless; double trigger
Magazine: None
Barrel: Side-by-side double barrel; 22" improved cylinder and modified in 20 gauge; 26", 28" improved and modified or modified and full chokes
Finish: Blued; checkered walnut pistol grip stock and tapered forearm; cheekpiece; recoil pad
Approximate wt.: 6 to 7 lbs.
Comments: Manufactured from the early 1960s to the mid-1980s. Imported from Spain.

Estimated Value:	**Excellent:**	**$325.00**
	Very good:	**$260.00**

Richland Model 202

Same as the Model 200 with an extra set of barrels. Produced until the mid-1970s.

Estimated Value:	**Excellent:**	**$400.00**
	Very good:	**$320.00**

Richland Model 707 Deluxe

Gauge: 12, 20
Action: Box lock; top lever break-open; hammerless; double trigger
Magazine: None
Barrel: Side-by-side double barrel; 26", 28", 30" variety of chokes
Finish: Blued; checkered walnut pistol grip stock and tapered forearm; recoil pad
Approximate wt.: 7 lbs.
Comments: Made from the mid-1960s to the mid-1970s.

Estimated Value:	**Excellent:**	**$350.00**
	Very good:	**$280.00**

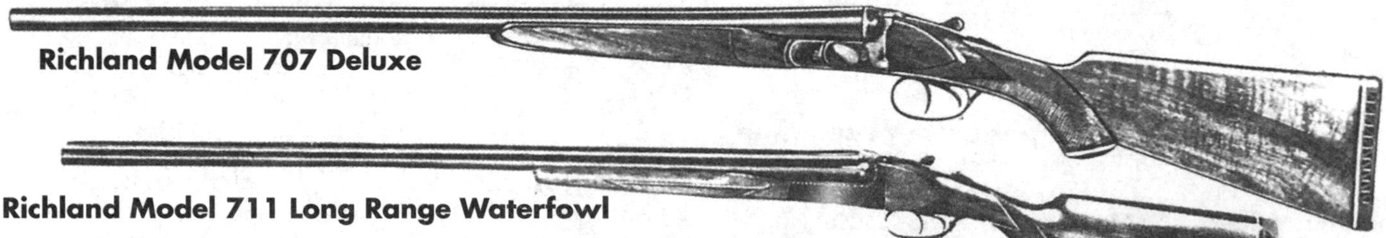

Richland Model 707 Deluxe

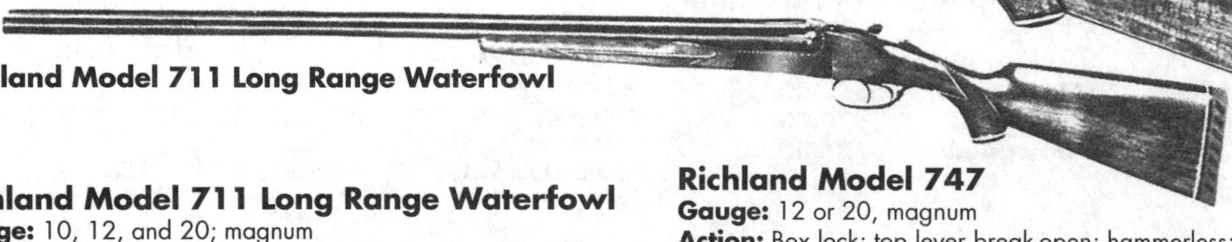

Richland Model 711 Long Range Waterfowl

Richland Model 711 Long Range Waterfowl

Gauge: 10, 12, and 20; magnum
Action: Box lock; top lever break-open; hammerless; double trigger
Magazine: None
Barrel: Side-by-side double barrel; 30", 32" full choke
Finish: Blued; checkered walnut pistol grip stock and tapered forearm
Approximate wt.: 8 to 10 lbs.
Comments: Made from the early 1960s until the 1980s; 10 gauge magnum only from 1981 to 1985.

Estimated Value:	**Excellent:**	**$350.00**
	Very good:	**$280.00**

Richland Model 747

Gauge: 12 or 20, magnum
Action: Box lock; top lever break-open; hammerless; single selective trigger
Magazine: None
Barrel: Over and under double barrel; 22" or 26" improved cylinder and modified, 28" modified and full
Finish: Blued; gray receiver; checkered walnut pistol grip stock and forearm; ventilated rib
Approximate wt.: 7 lbs.
Comments: Introduced in the mid-1980s.

Estimated Value:	**Excellent:**	**$400.00**
	Very good:	**$320.00**

Richland Model 808

Gauge: 12
Action: Box lock; top lever break-open; hammerless; non-selective single trigger
Magazine: None
Barrel: Over and under double barrel; 26" improved cylinder and modified; 28" modified and full; 30" full and full
Finish: Blued; checkered walnut pistol grip stock and forearm; ribbed barrel
Approximate wt.: 7 lbs.
Comments: Made from the early to the late 1960s.
Estimated Value: **Excellent:** **$400.00**
Very good: **$320.00**

Richland Model 844

Gauge: 12 magnum
Action: Box lock; top lever break-open; hammerless; non-selective single trigger
Magazine: None
Barrel: Over and under double barrel; 26" improved cylinder and modified; 28" modified and full; 30" full and full
Finish: Blued; checkered walnut pistol grip stock and forearm; ribbed barrel
Approximate wt.: 7 lbs.
Comments: Made in the early 1970s.
Estimated Value: **Excellent:** **$350.00**
Very good: **$280.00**

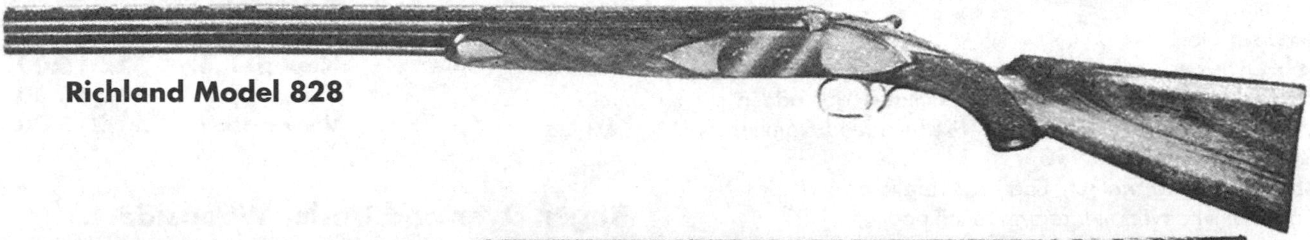
Richland Model 828

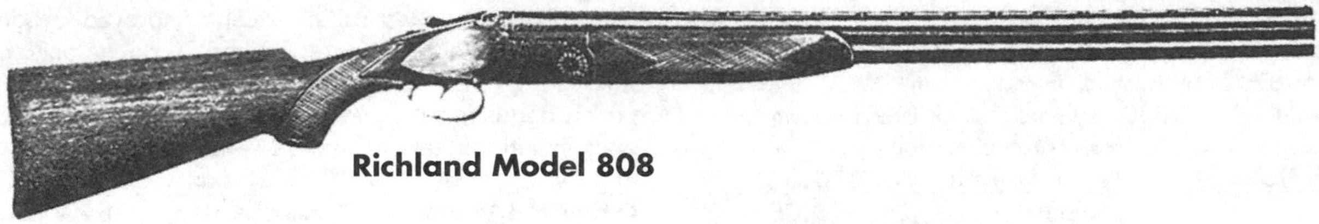
Richland Model 808

Richland Model 828

Gauge: 28
Action: Box lock; top lever break-open; hammerless
Magazine: None
Barrel: Over and under double barrel; 26" improved and modified; 28" modified and full chokes
Finish: Blued; case hardened receiver; checkered walnut pistol grip stock and forearm; ribbed barrel
Approximate wt.: 7 lbs.
Comments: Made in the early 1970s.
Estimated Value: **Excellent:** **$425.00**
Very good: **$345.00**

Richland Model 410 Ultra

Gauge: 410
Action: Box lock; top lever break-open; hammerless; single non-selective trigger
Magazine: None
Barrel: Over and under double barrel; 26" chrome lined, modified and full; ventilated rib
Finish: Blued; gray engraved receiver; checkered walnut pistol grip stock and forearm
Approximate wt.: 6 lbs.
Comments: A lightweight 410 shotgun introduced in 1985.
Estimated Value: **Excellent:** **$300.00**
Very good: **$240.00**

RUGER

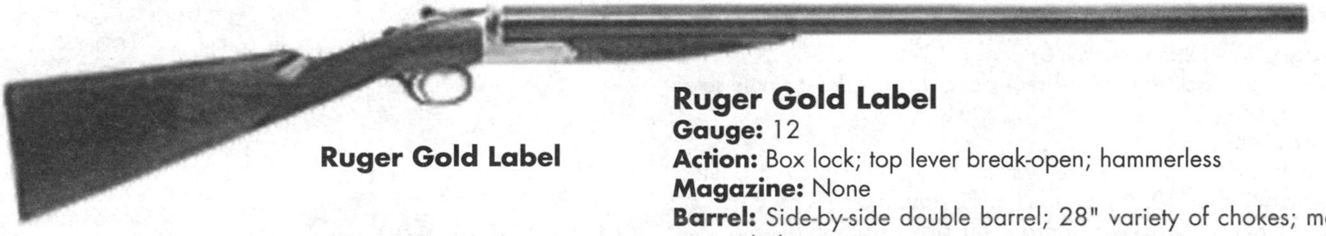
Ruger Gold Label

Ruger Gold Label

Gauge: 12
Action: Box lock; top lever break-open; hammerless
Magazine: None
Barrel: Side-by-side double barrel; 28" variety of chokes; matte serrated rib
Finish: Checkered walnut straight or pistol grip stock and tapered forearm; deeply blued steel barrels
Approximate wt.: 6⅓ lbs.
Comments: Introduced in 2001.
Estimated Value: **Excellent:** **$2,420.00**
Very good: **$1,935.00**

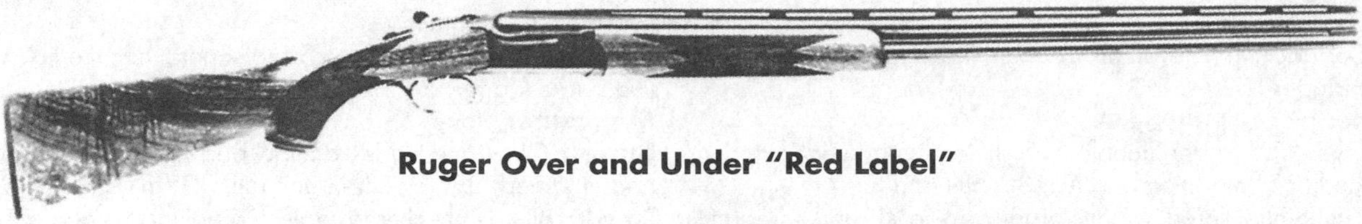

Ruger Over and Under "Red Label"

Ruger Over and Under "Red Label"

Gauge: 28, 20, 12 (3" chambers)
Action: Box lock; top lever break-open; hammerless; single selective trigger
Magazine: None
Barrel: Over and under double barrel; 26" or 28" with a variety of screw-in choke combinations; ventilated rib; added stainless steel receiver on 12 gauge in 1986; added stainless steel receiver on 20 gauge in 1990
Finish: Checkered walnut, English straight grip or pistol grip stock and semi-beavertail forearm; recoil pad
Approximate wt.: 7 to 8 lbs.
Comments: Introduced in the late 1970s; 12 gauge model added in 1982. English stock introduced in 1992; all-weather model introduced in 2000. Synthetic stock and forearm on all-weather models. Add 10% for engraved model.

Estimated Value:	**New (retail):**	**$2,015.00**
	Excellent:	**$1,510.00**
	Very good:	**$1,210.00**

Ruger "Red Label" Sporting Clay

Similar to Ruger Over and Under "Red Label" except: 12 and 20 gauge only (3" chambers); 30" barrels; checkered walnut pistol grip stock and forearm; four screw-in chokes with each gun (modified, improved cylinder, and two skeet chokes); two bead sighting system; introduced in 1992. All-weather model introduced in 2000.

Estimated Value:	**New (retail):**	**$2,015.00**
	Excellent:	**$1,510.00**
	Very good:	**$1,210.00**

Ruger Over and Under Woodside

Similar to Ruger "Red Label" except: improved cocking mechanism enhances opening ease; 12 and 20 gauge only; has unique stock design in which the buttstock extends forward as two side panels and is inletted into cutouts in the sides of the receiver; the stock material is select Circassian walnut in pistol grip or straight grip styles. Introduced in 1995; 20 gauge dropped in 2000.

Estimated Value:	**Excellent:**	**$1,415.00**
	Very good:	**$1,135.00**

SKB

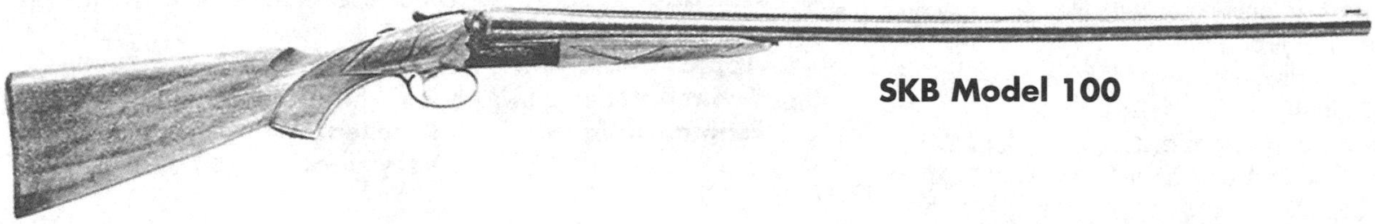

SKB Model 100

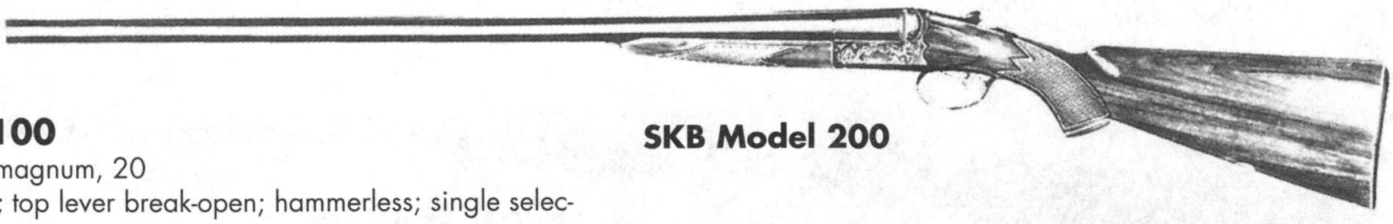

SKB Model 200

SKB Model 100

Gauge: 12, 12 magnum, 20
Action: Box lock; top lever break-open; hammerless; single selective trigger
Magazine: None
Barrel: Side-by-side double barrel; 26", 28" improved cylinder and modified or 30" full and full in 12 gauge
Finish: Blued; checkered hardwood pistol grip stock and short tapered forearm
Approximate wt.: 6 to 7 lbs.
Comments: Made from the mid-1960s to the mid-1970s.

Estimated Value:	**Excellent:**	**$700.00**
	Very good:	**$560.00**

SKB Models 200 and 200E

Similar to the Model SKB 100 with engraved silver-plated frame; wide forearm; select walnut; automatic selective ejectors; Model 200E has straight grip stock.

Estimated Value:	**Excellent:**	**$800.00**
	Very good:	**$640.00**

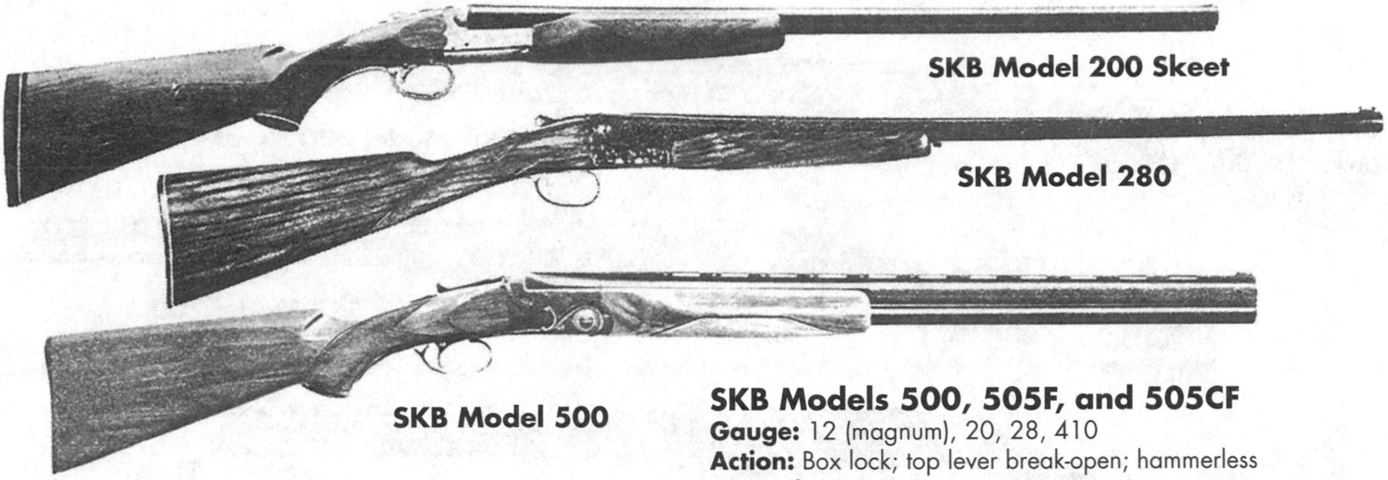

SKB Model 200 Skeet

SKB Model 280

SKB Model 500

SKB Model 200 Skeet

Similar to the Model 200 with 25" skeet choke barrels and recoil pad.

Estimated Value:	**Excellent:**	**$800.00**
	Very good:	**$640.00**

SKB Model 280

Similar to the Model 200 without silver frame. Has straight grip stock. Engraved game scene. Made from the early to the mid-1970s.

Estimated Value:	**Excellent:**	**$850.00**
	Very good:	**$680.00**

SKB Model 400

Similar to the Model 200 with side plate receiver; straight stock available.

Estimated Value:	**Excellent:**	**$1,000.00**
	Very good:	**$ 800.00**

SKB Models 500, 505F, and 505CF

Gauge: 12 (magnum), 20, 28, 410
Action: Box lock; top lever break-open; hammerless
Magazine: None
Barrel: Over and under double barrel; 26" improved cylinder and modified; 28", 30" modified and full; ventilated rib; chrome lined. Model 505CF has "inter" choke system
Finish: Blued; checkered walnut pistol grip stock and forearm; recoil pad on magnum; front sight; engraved receiver on Model 500
Approximate wt.: 6½ to 8 lbs.
Comments: Made from the mid-1960s to the mid-1980s as Model 500; as 505 to present. Add 9% for Sporting Clays model, 20% for Sportings Clays model with ported barrel.

Estimated Value:	**Excellent:**	**$750.00**
	Very good:	**$600.00**

SKB Models 500 Skeet and 505CSK

Similar to the Model 500 with 26" or 28" skeet choke barrels. Model 500 discontinued in the mid-1980s and replaced by Model 505CSK. Discontinued in the early 1990s.

Estimated Value:	**Excellent:**	**$600.00**
	Very good:	**$480.00**

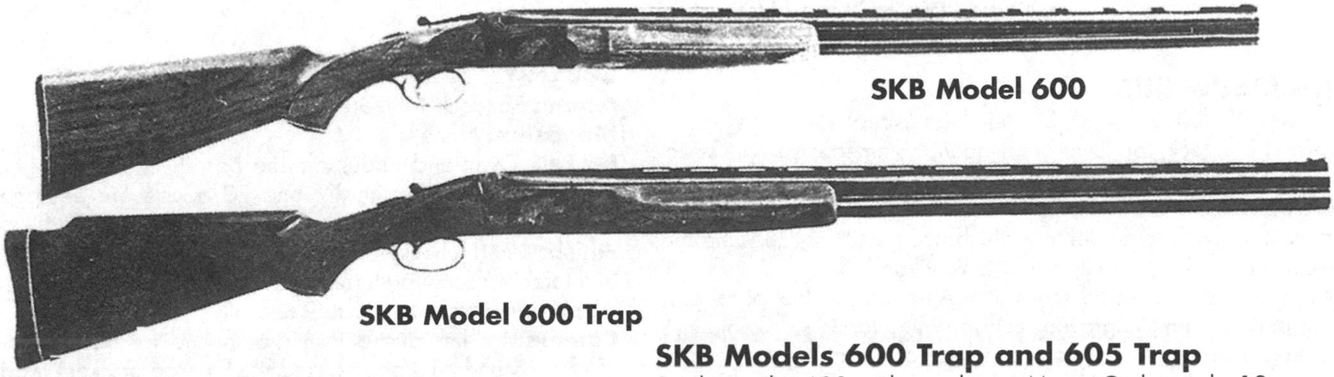

SKB Model 600

SKB Model 600 Trap

SKB Models 600 and 605F

Similar to the 500 with select wood; trigger-mounted barrel selector; silverplate receiver; middle sight.

Estimated Value:	**Excellent:**	**$800.00**
	Very good:	**$640.00**

SKB Models 600 Trap and 605 Trap

Similar to the 600 with regular or Monte Carlo stock; 12 gauge only; recoil pad, 30" or 32" full choke barrels on Model 600; "inter" choke system on Model 605 Trap (late 1980s). Discontinued in the early 1990s.

Estimated Value:	**Excellent:**	**$850.00**
	Very good:	**$680.00**

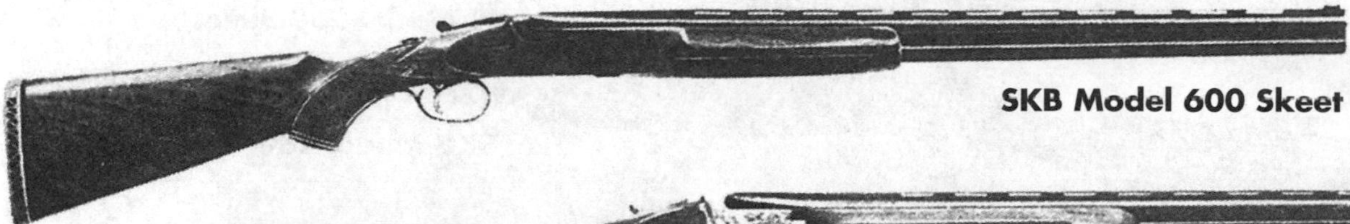

SKB Model 600 Skeet

SKB Model 700

SKB Model 785

SKB Models 600 Skeet and 605CSK

Similar to the Model 600 with 26" or 28" skeet choke barrels (Model 600) and recoil pad; "inter" choke system on Model 605CSK (late 1980s). Discontinued in early 1990s.

Estimated Value: **Excellent:** **$825.00**
Very good: **$660.00**

SKB Model 680

Similar to the Model 600 with a straight grip stock.

Estimated Value: **Excellent:** **$825.00**
Very good: **$660.00**

SKB Model 700

Similar to the Model 600 with higher quality finish and more extensive engraving. Made in the mid-1970s.

Estimated Value: **Excellent:** **$800.00**
Very good: **$640.00**

SKB Model 885

Gauge: 12, 20, 28, 410; 3" chambers except 28 gauge
Action: Box lock; top lever break-open; hammerless, single selective trigger; automatic ejectors
Magazine: None
Barrel: Over and under double barrel; 26" or 28" chrome bores with "inter" choke system and ventilated rib
Finish: Blued; checkered semi-fancy American walnut pistol grip stock and forearm; engraved receiver with classic side plate styling; engraved trigger guard tang, safety, and top lever
Approximate wt.: 6 to 8 lbs.
Comments: Available in the 1980s and 1990s. Add 2% for 28 gauge or 410; 8% for Sporting Clays.

Estimated Value: **Excellent:** **$1,600.00**
Very good: **$1,280.00**

SKB Model 685

Similar to the Model 885 except: different engraving with gold-plated scenes; regular box lock without classic side plates; add 3% for 28 gauge or 410; 8% for Sporting Clays model.

Estimated Value: **Excellent:** **$1,200.00**
Very good: **$ 960.00**

SKB Model 585 Field

Similar to the Model 685 except: standard American walnut stock and forearm; less engraving; add 4% for 28 gauge or 410; 12% for Sporting Clays model; 20% for Sporting Clays model with ported barrel.

Estimated Value: **Excellent:** **$1,000.00**
Very good: **$ 800.00**

SKB Model 785

Gauge: 12, 20, 28, 410
Action: Box lock with Greener-style cross bolt
Magazine: None
Barrel: Over and under double barrel; choke tubes; chrome lined; ventilated rib; the 12 and 20 gauge are equipped with ventilated side ribs (between barrels) to improve heat dissipation
Finish: Blued, checkered American Black walnut pistol grip stock and forearm; scroll pattern engraved receiver
Approximate wt.: 7½ to 9 lbs.
Comments: Introduced in 1996; priced for Field grade. Add 4% for 28 and 410 gauge; add 4% for Trap or Skeet grade; add 7% for Sporting Clays model; 13% for Sporting Clays model with ported barrel.

Estimated Value: **Excellent:** **$1,500.00**
Very good: **$1,200.00**

SKB Model 1300

Gauge: 12, 20, regular or magnum
Action: Semiautomatic
Magazine: 5-shot; 3-shot with plug
Barrel: 26" or 28" "inter" choke system; ventilated rib; slug barrel with rifle sights available
Finish: Blued, black receiver; checkered walnut pistol grip stock and forearm
Approximate wt.: 6½ to 7¼ lbs.
Comments: Add 1% for slug barrel with rifle sights.

Estimated Value:	**Excellent:**	**$375.00**
	Very good:	**$300.00**

SKB Model 1900

Similar to the Model 1300 with light receiver featuring engraved hunting scene, gold trigger. Add 5% for 30" barrel Trap Model.

Estimated Value:	**Excellent:**	**$415.00**
	Very good:	**$335.00**

SKB Model 3000

A presentation deluxe version of the Model 1900. Highback receiver. A trap version is available (add 2%).

Estimated Value:	**Excellent:**	**$550.00**
	Very good:	**$450.00**

SKB Model XL 300

SKB Model XL 300 Vent Rib

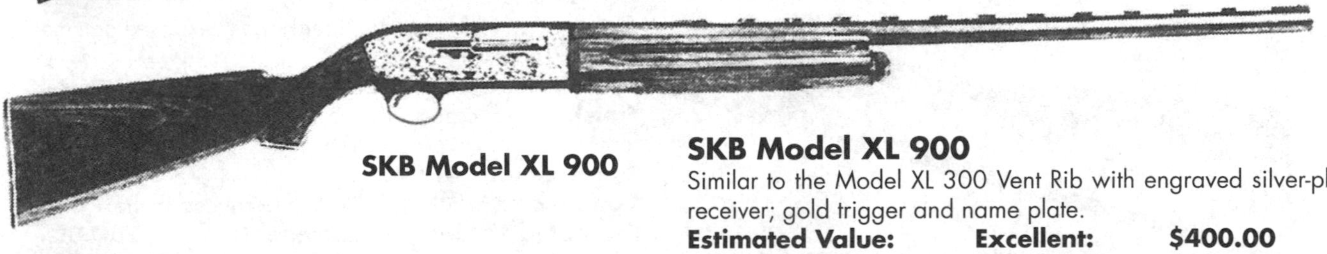
SKB Model XL 900

SKB Model XL 300

Gauge: 12, 20
Action: Gas-operated; semiautomatic; hammerless
Magazine: 5-shot tubular
Barrel: 26" improved cylinder or skeet; 28" modified or full; 30" modified or full chokes
Finish: Blued; decorated receiver; checkered walnut pistol grip stock and forearm
Approximate wt.: 6 to 7 lbs.
Comments: Made from the early to the late 1970s.

Estimated Value:	**Excellent:**	**$375.00**
	Very good:	**$300.00**

SKB XL 300 Vent Rib

Similar to the XL 300 with front sights and ventilated rib.

Estimated Value:	**Excellent:**	**$400.00**
	Very good:	**$320.00**

SKB Model XL 100 Slug

A no-frills slug gun with 20" barrel; rifle sights; swivels; similar to the Model XL 300.

Estimated Value:	**Excellent:**	**$375.00**
	Very good:	**$300.00**

SKB Model XL 900

Similar to the Model XL 300 Vent Rib with engraved silver-plated receiver; gold trigger and name plate.

Estimated Value:	**Excellent:**	**$400.00**
	Very good:	**$320.00**

SKB Model XL 900 Slug

Similar to the Model XL 900 with a 24" barrel for slugs; rifle sights; swivels.

Estimated Value:	**Excellent:**	**$375.00**
	Very good:	**$300.00**

SKB Model XL 900 Trap

Similar to the Model XL 900 with middle sight; no silver receiver; recoil pad; choice of regular or Monte Carlo stock.

Estimated Value:	**Excellent:**	**$400.00**
	Very good:	**$320.00**

SKB Model XL 900 Skeet

Similar to the Model XL 900 Trap with skeet stock and skeet choke barrel.

Estimated Value:	**Excellent:**	**$420.00**
	Very good:	**$335.00**

SKB Model XL 900 MR

Similar to the Model XL 900 except: 3" magnum; recoil pad.

Estimated Value:	**Excellent:**	**$435.00**
	Very good:	**$345.00**

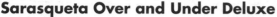

SARASQUETA

Sarasqueta Models 2 and 3

Gauge: 12, 16, 20, 28
Action: Box lock; top lever break-open; hammerless; double triggers
Magazine: None
Barrel: Side-by-side double barrel; standard barrel lengths and chokes made to customer's specifications
Finish: Blued; checkered walnut straight grip stock and forearm
Approximate wt.: Varies
Comments: Grades differ only in engraving style.
Estimated Value: Excellent: $400.00 – 650.00
Very good: $325.00 – 520.00

Sarasqueta Over and Under Deluxe

Gauge: 12
Action: Side lock; top lever break-open; hammerless; double triggers; automatic ejectors
Magazine: None
Barrel: Over and under double barrel; lengths and chokes made to customer's specifications
Finish: Blued; checkered walnut pistol grip stock and forearm
Approximate wt.: Varies
Comments: Made in the mid-1930s.
Estimated Value: Excellent: $1,200.00
Very good: $ 960.00

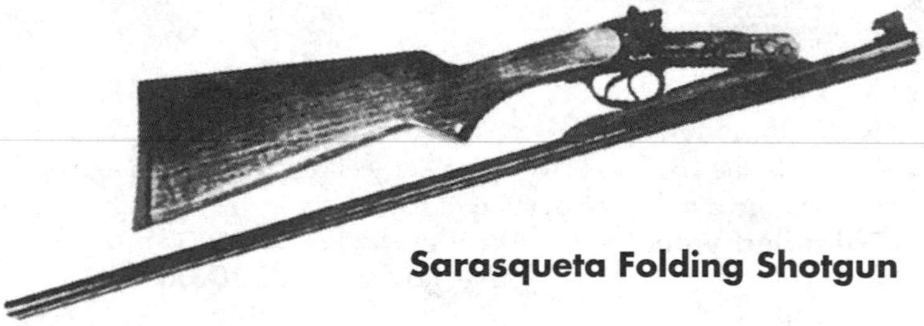

Sarasqueta Folding Shotgun

Sarasqueta Sidelock

Sarasqueta Sidelock, Grades 4 to 12

Gauge: 12, 16, 20, 28
Action: Side lock; top lever break-open; hammerless; double triggers
Magazine: None
Barrel: Side-by-side double barrel; standard barrel lengths and chokes available to customer's specifications
Finish: Blued; checkered walnut straight or pistol grip stock and forearm
Approximate wt.: Varies
Comments: A Spanish shotgun. Grades differ as to quality and extent of engraving.
Estimated Value: Excellent: $650.00 – 2,500.00
Very good: $550.00 – 2,000.00

Sarasqueta Folding Shotgun

Gauge: 410
Action: Box lock; top lever break-open; exposed hammer
Magazine: None
Barrel: Side-by-side double barrel; 26" choice of chokes
Finish: Blued; case-hardened frame; walnut pistol grip stock and forearm
Approximate wt.: Varies
Comments: A "folding" shotgun produced in the 1970s.
Estimated Value: Excellent: $200.00
Very good: $160.00

SAUER

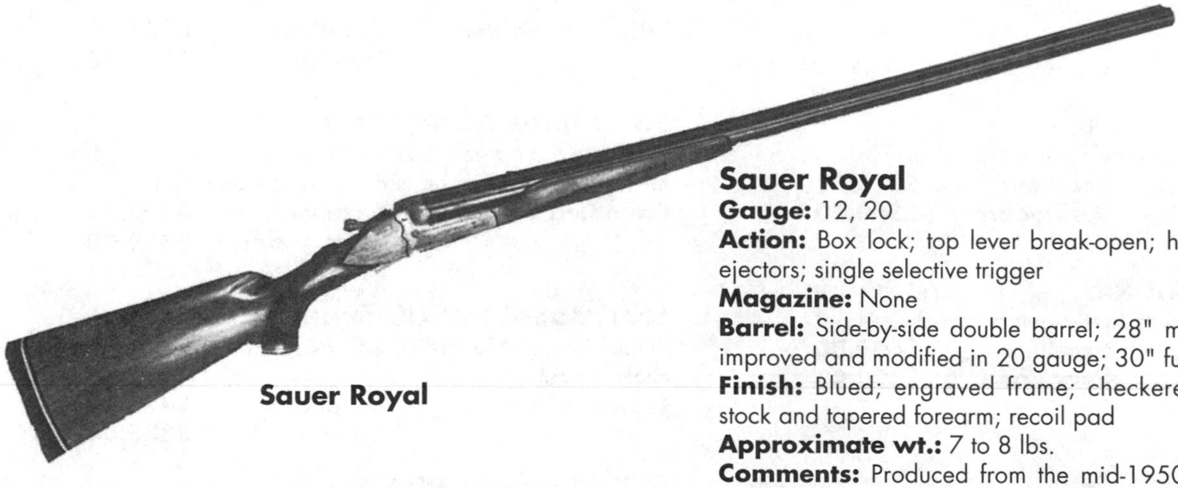

Sauer Royal

Sauer Royal

Gauge: 12, 20
Action: Box lock; top lever break-open; hammerless; automatic ejectors; single selective trigger
Magazine: None
Barrel: Side-by-side double barrel; 28" modified and full, 26" improved and modified in 20 gauge; 30" full in 12 gauge
Finish: Blued; engraved frame; checkered walnut pistol grip stock and tapered forearm; recoil pad
Approximate wt.: 7 to 8 lbs.
Comments: Produced from the mid-1950s to the late 1970s. Add 20% for 20 gauge.
Estimated Value: Excellent: $1,750.00
Very good: $1,400.00

Sauer Model 66 Field Grade

Sauer Model 66 Trap Grade

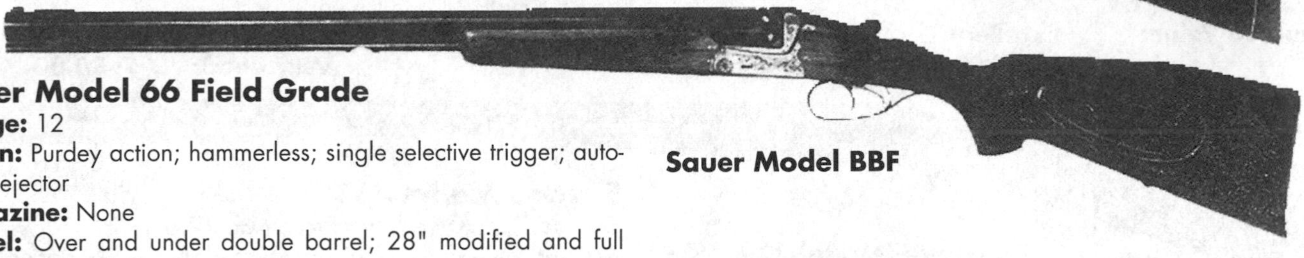

Sauer Model BBF

Sauer Model 66 Field Grade

Gauge: 12
Action: Purdey action; hammerless; single selective trigger; automatic ejector
Magazine: None
Barrel: Over and under double barrel; 28" modified and full choke; ventilated rib
Finish: Blued; checkered walnut pistol grip stock and forearm; recoil pad; engraving
Approximate wt.: 7 lbs.
Comments: Made from the mid-1960s to the mid-1970s. Prices are for Grade I. Fancier Grades II and III differ in quality and extent of engraving.

Estimated Value:	**Excellent:**	**$2,000.00**
	Very good:	**$1,600.00**

Sauer Model 66 Trap Grade

Basically the same as the Field Grade with 30" barrels and a trap stock. Produced in three grades. Prices for Grade I.

Estimated Value:	**Excellent:**	**$2,100.00**
	Very good:	**$1,675.00**

Sauer Model 66 Skeet

Basically the same as the Trap Model with 25" barrel in skeet choke. Prices are for Grade I. Made from the mid-1960s to the mid-1970s.

Estimated Value:	**Excellent:**	**$2,100.00**
	Very good:	**$1,675.00**

Sauer Model BBF

Gauge: 16
Caliber: 30-30, 30-06, 7 x 65
Action: Kersten lock; Blitz action; top lever break-open; hammerless; double trigger
Magazine: None
Barrel: Over and under rifle-shotgun combination; 25" Krupp barrels; rifle barrel and full choke shotgun barrel
Finish: Blued; checkered walnut Monte Carlo pistol grip stock and forearm; engraved; sights; swivels
Approximate wt.: 6 lbs.
Comments: Made from the mid-1960s to the 1970s; also available in deluxe model with extensive engraving (add 16%).

Estimated Value:	**Excellent:**	**$2,100.00**
	Very good:	**$1,675.00**

SAVAGE

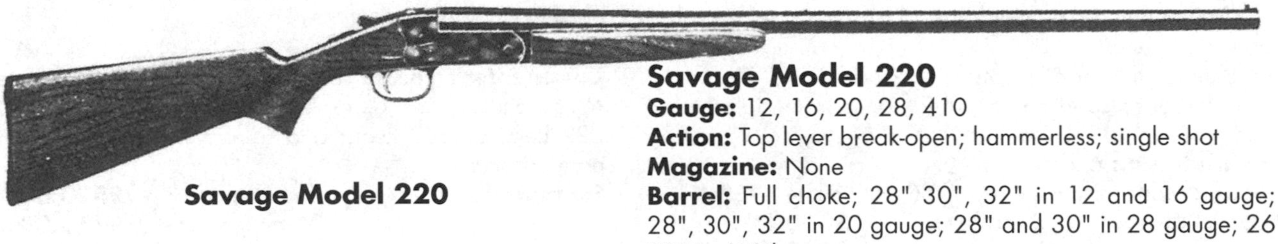

Savage Model 220

Savage Model 220

Gauge: 12, 16, 20, 28, 410
Action: Top lever break-open; hammerless; single shot
Magazine: None
Barrel: Full choke; 28" 30", 32" in 12 and 16 gauge; 26", 28", 30", 32" in 20 gauge; 28" and 30" in 28 gauge; 26" and 28" in 410 bore
Finish: Blued; plain wood, pistol grip stock and forearm
Approximate wt.: 6 lbs.
Comments: Made from the 1930s until the late 1940s. Reintroduced in the mid-1950s with 36" barrel. Replaced by Model 220L in the mid-1960s.

Estimated Value:	**Excellent:**	**$125.00**
	Very good:	**$100.00**

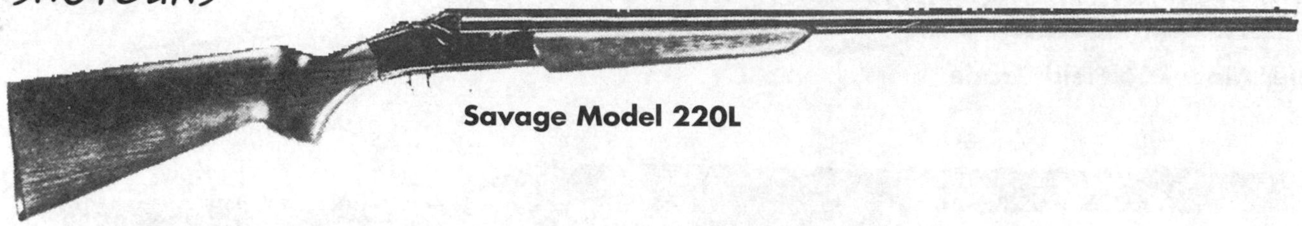

Savage Model 220L

Savage Model 220P

Basically the same as 220 except: no 410 gauge, has "Poly-Choke" and recoil pad.

Estimated Value: **Excellent:** **$125.00**
Very good: **$100.00**

Savage Model 220L

Similar to Model 220 except: has side lever break-open. Made from the mid-1960s to the early 1970s.

Estimated Value: **Excellent:** **$100.00**
Very good: **$ 80.00**

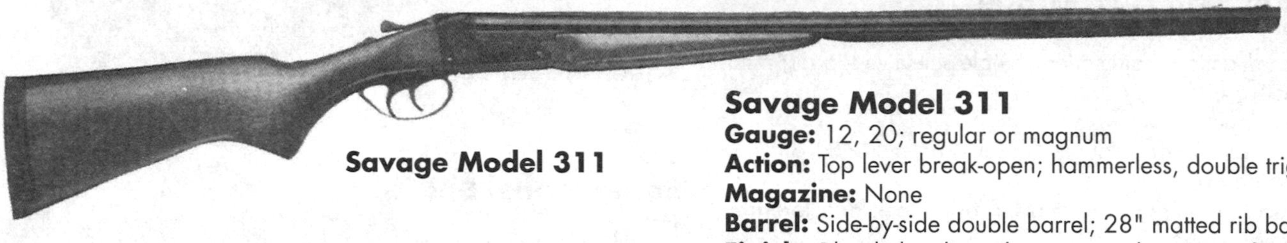

Savage Model 311

Savage Model 311

Gauge: 12, 20; regular or magnum
Action: Top lever break-open; hammerless, double trigger
Magazine: None
Barrel: Side-by-side double barrel; 28" matted rib barrels
Finish: Blued; hardwood, semi-pistol grip stock and tapered forearm
Approximate wt.: 7 lbs.
Comments: The Model 311 was originally a Stevens shotgun. In 1988 Savage dropped the Stevens designation; discontinued in the late 1980s.

Estimated Value: **Excellent:** **$275.00**
Very good: **$220.00**

Savage Model 311 Waterfowler

Similar to the Model 311 with parkerized finish.

Estimated Value: **Excellent:** **$300.00**
Very good: **$240.00**

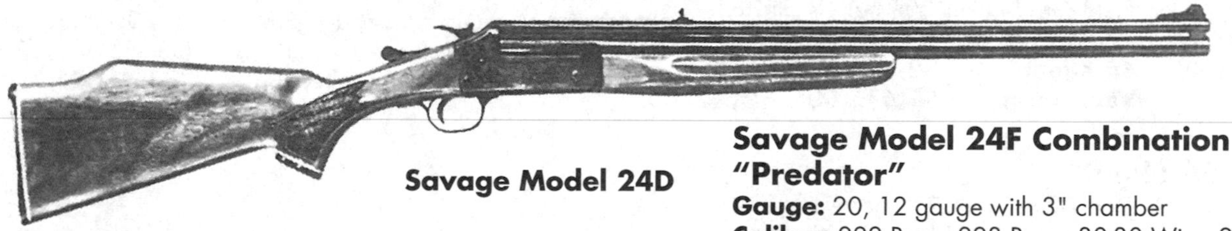

Savage Model 24D

Savage Model 24

Gauge: 20, 410
Caliber: 22 short, long, long rifle; 22 magnum
Action: Top lever break-open; exposed hammer; single trigger; bottom opening lever in the mid-1980s
Magazine: None
Barrel: Over and under double barrel; 24" rifle barrel over shotgun barrel
Finish: Blued; checkered walnut finish hardwood pistol grip stock and forearm; sporting rear and ramp front sights; case hardened receiver
Approximate wt.: 6 lbs.
Comments: Made from the early 1950s to the late 1980s.

Estimated Value: **Excellent:** **$350.00**
Very good: **$280.00**

Savage Model 24D

Deluxe version of the Model 24. Discontinued in the mid-1980s.

Estimated Value: **Excellent:** **$375.00**
Very good: **$300.00**

Savage Model 24F Combination and "Predator"

Gauge: 20, 12 gauge with 3" chamber
Caliber: 222 Rem., 223 Rem., 30-30 Win., 22 Hornet, 22 LR
Action: Top lever break-open; exposed hammer with barrel selector; hammer block safety
Magazine: None
Barrel: 24" rifle barrel over 24" shotgun barrel; any combination of rifle caliber and shotgun gauge; shotgun barrel in modified choke; modified and full choke tubes available
Finish: DuPont Rynite® two-piece stock and forearm. Some models with recoil pad.
Approximate wt.: 8 lbs.
Comments: Produced from the late 1980s to the present; add 4% for choke tube; 4% for CamoRynite® stock on 12 gauge with 222 Rem. or 223 Rem.; add 5% for 12 gauge, 15% for 410 bore adapter.

Estimated Value: **Excellent:** **$520.00**
Very good: **$415.00**

Savage Model 24V Combination

Same as the Model 24F Combination except: walnut finish hardwood stock and forearm; 20 gauge, 3" chamber under 222 Rem., 223 Rem., or 30-30 Win. rifle barrel. Made from the late 1980s to the early 1990s.

Estimated Value: **Excellent:** **$450.00**
Very good: **$360.00**

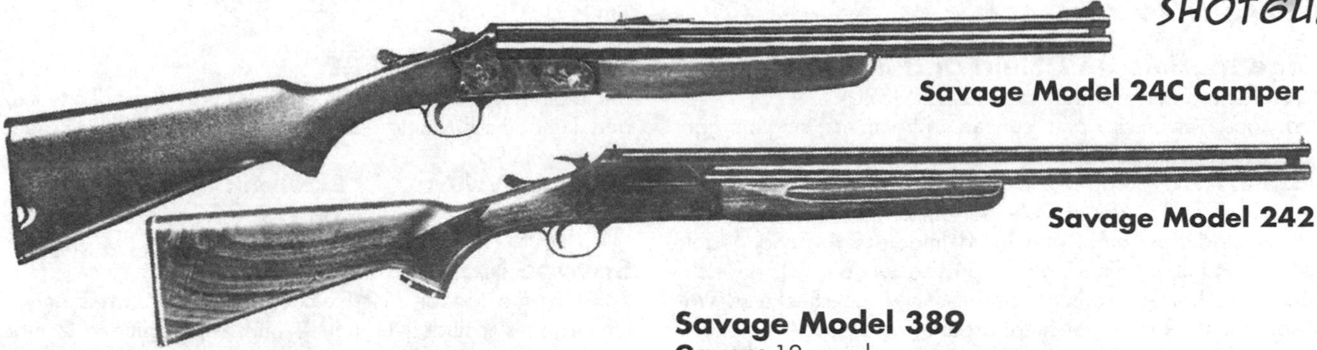

Savage Model 24C Camper

Savage Model 242

Savage Models 24C Camper and 24CS

A shorter version of the Model 24; 20" barrel; 5¾" lbs.; 22LR over 20 gauge barrel; butt plate opens for ammo storage area. Add $45.00 for satin nickel finish (Model 24CS) and extra pistol grip stock; discontinued in the late 1980s.

Estimated Value: **Excellent:** **$400.00**
Very good: **$320.00**

Savage Model 242

Similar to the Model 24 with 410 gauge over and under shotgun barrels; full choke; bead sights; made only in the late 1970s.

Estimated Value: **Excellent:** **$450.00**
Very good: **$360.00**

Savage Model 389

Gauge: 12, regular or magnum
Caliber: 222 or 308
Action: Top lever break-open; hammerless; double trigger; shotgun barrel over rifle barrel; tang safety
Magazine: None
Barrel: 25¾" over and under double barrel; changeable choke tubes
Finish: Blued; checkered walnut pistol grip stock and matching forearm; sling studs
Approximate wt.: 8 lbs.
Comments: Produced from the late 1980s to the early 1990s.

Estimated Value: **Excellent:** **$545.00**
Very good: **$435.00**

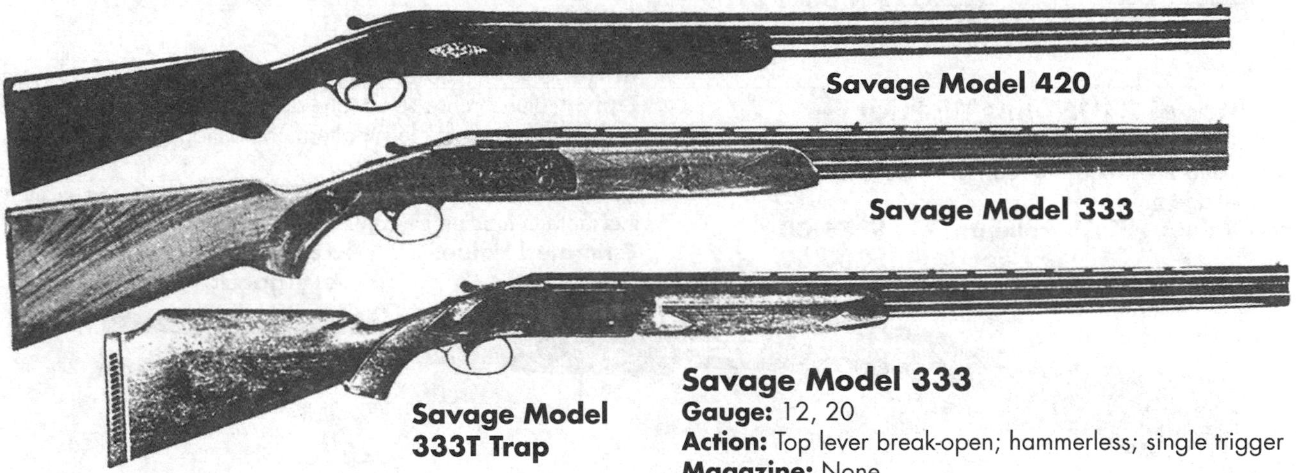

Savage Model 420

Savage Model 333

Savage Model 333T Trap

Savage Model 420

Gauge: 12, 16, 20
Action: Box lock; top lever break-open; hammerless; double triggers or non-selective single trigger
Magazine: None
Barrel: Over and under double barrel; 26" to 30" modified and full or cylinder bore and modified chokes
Finish: Blued; plain walnut pistol grip stock and forearm
Approximate wt.: 6¾ to 7¾ lbs.
Comments: Made from the mid-1930s until World War II. Add **$25.00** for single trigger.

Estimated Value: **Excellent:** **$475.00**
Very good: **$380.00**

Savage Model 430

Similar to Model 420 with special checkered walnut stock and forearm; matted upper barrel; recoil pad. Add $25.00 for single trigger.

Estimated Value: **Excellent:** **$525.00**
Very good: **$420.00**

Savage Model 333

Gauge: 12, 20
Action: Top lever break-open; hammerless; single trigger
Magazine: None
Barrel: Over and under double barrel; 26" to 30"; variety of chokes; ventilated rib
Finish: Blued; checkered walnut pistol grip stock and forearm
Approximate wt.: 6¼ to 7¼ lbs.
Comments: Made from the early to the late 1970s.

Estimated Value: **Excellent:** **$675.00**
Very good: **$540.00**

Savage Model 333T Trap

Similar to Model 333 with Monte Carlo stock and recoil pad in 12 gauge, 30" barrel.

Estimated Value: **Excellent:** **$725.00**
Very good: **$580.00**

Savage Model 330

Similar to Model 333 without ventilated rib.

Estimated Value: **Excellent:** **$650.00**
Very good: **$520.00**

Savage Models 312 Field and 320 Field

Gauge: 12, regular or magnum (312); 20 (320)
Action: Top lever break-open; concealed hammers; single trigger with safety acting as barrel selector
Magazine: None
Barrel: Over and under double barrel; 26" or 28"; ventilated rib; ivory bead front sight and bead middle sight; changeable choke tubes in full, modified, and improved cylinder with wrench
Finish: Blued barrels; satin chrome receiver; cut-checkered walnut pistol grip stock and matching forearm; recoil pad
Approximate wt.: 7 lbs.
Comments: Produced from 1990 to 1993.

Estimated Value:	**Excellent:**	**$700.00**
	Very good:	**$560.00**

Savage Model 312T

Same as Model 312 Field except: 30" barrels; choke tubes, 2 full and 1 modified; Monte Carlo stock; weighs 7¼ lbs. Produced in the early 1990s.

Estimated Value:	**Excellent:**	**$675.00**
	Very good:	**$540.00**

Savage Model 312SC

Same as the Model 312 Field except: 28" barrels only; seven choke tubes included (1 full, 2 improved cylinder, 2 modified, 1 #1 skeet, and 1 #2 skeet); "Sporting Clays" engraved on receiver. Produced in the early 1990s.

Estimated Value:	**Excellent:**	**$725.00**
	Very good:	**$580.00**

Savage Model 210FT Master Shot

Savage Model 210F Slug Warrior

Savage Model 210F Slug Warrior

Similar to the 210FT Master Shot except with black synthetic stock and forearm, and 24" rifled slug barrel. Introduced in 1997. Add 8% for camouflage finish.

Estimated Value:	**Excellent:**	**$375.00**
	Very good:	**$300.00**

Savage Model 210FT Master Shot

Gauge: 12, 3" chamber
Action: Bolt action, repeating
Magazine: 2-shot box
Barrel: 24" full choke, threaded for interchangeable choke tubes
Finish: Blued; checkered one-piece, pistol grip synthetic stock and forearm with fall leaf pattern camouflage; swivels; recoil pad
Approximate wt.: 7½ lbs.
Comments: Introduced in 1997 as Savage's re-entrance into the shotgun market. Discontinued in 2001.

Estimated Value:	**Excellent:**	**$400.00**
	Very good:	**$320.00**

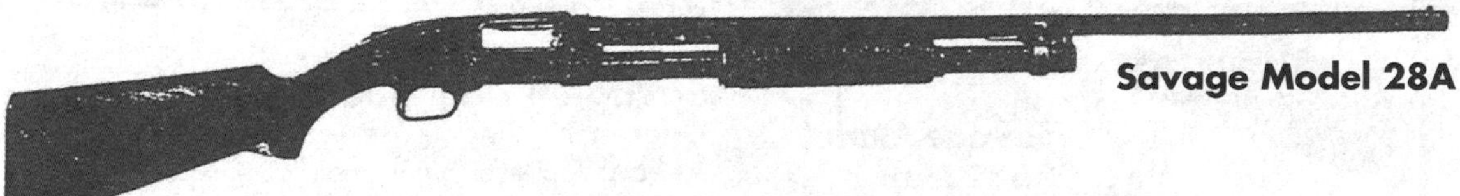

Savage Model 28A

Savage Model 28D Trap

Savage Models 28A and 28B Standard

Gauge: 12
Action: Slide action; hammerless; solid breech; side ejector
Magazine: 5-shot tubular
Barrel: 26", 28", 30", or 32" cylinder, modified or full choke; raised rib on Model 28B
Finish: Blued; checkered wood pistol grip stock and grooved slide handle
Approximate wt.: 7½ lbs.
Comments: Made from the late 1920s until the mid-1930s. Add $10.00 for matted rib.

Estimated Value:	**Excellent:**	**$350.00**
	Very good:	**$280.00**

Savage Model 28C Riot

Basically the same as Model 28A except with a 20" cylinder bore barrel. This was for use by police, bank guards, etc., for protection.

Estimated Value:	**Excellent:**	**$350.00**
	Very good:	**$280.00**

Savage Model 28D Trap

Basically the same as Model 28B except: special straight checkered walnut stock and checkered slide handle; 30" full choke barrel.

Estimated Value:	**Excellent:**	**$375.00**
	Very good:	**$300.00**

Savage Model 28S Special

Basically the same as Model 28B except: ivory bead front sight; checkered pistol grip stock; checkered forearm.

Estimated Value:	**Excellent:**	**$350.00**
	Very good:	**$280.00**

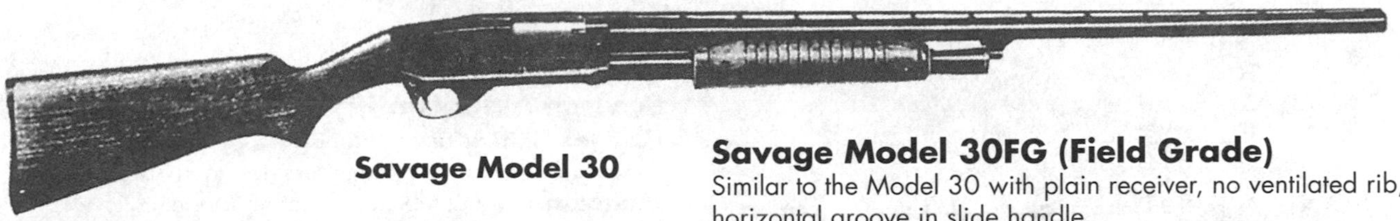

Savage Model 30

Savage Model 30

Gauge: 12, 20, 410
Action: Slide action; hammerless
Magazine: 4-shot tubular
Barrel: 26", 28", 30"; cylinder bore, modified or full choke; ventilated rib
Finish: Blued; decorated receiver; walnut pistol grip stock and grooved slide handle
Approximate wt.: 6½ lbs.
Comments: Made from the late 1950s to the late 1960s.
Estimated Value: **Excellent:** **$250.00**
Very good: **$200.00**

Savage Model 30T Trap

Fancy version of the Model 30 in 12 gauge; 30" full choke barrel; Monte Carlo stock; grooved slide handle; recoil pad. Introduced in the mid-1960s.
Estimated Value: **Excellent:** **$225.00**
Very good: **$180.00**

Savage Model 30FG (Field Grade)

Similar to the Model 30 with plain receiver, no ventilated rib, and horizontal groove in slide handle.
Estimated Value: **Excellent:** **$225.00**
Very good: **$180.00**

Savage Model 30FG Slug Gun

Same as the Model 30FG with 22" barrel and rifle sights, 12 gauge. Introduced in 1971, discontinued in the late 1970s.
Estimated Value: **Excellent:** **$225.00**
Very good: **$180.00**

Savage Model 30AC

Same as the Model 30FG with adjustable choke.
Estimated Value: **Excellent:** **$235.00**
Very good: **$185.00**

Savage Model 30D (Deluxe)

1970s version of the Model 30FG with recoil pad and horizontal groove in slide handle. Discontinued in the late 1970s.
Estimated Value: **Excellent:** **$245.00**
Very good: **$195.00**

Savage Model 30FG (Field Grade)

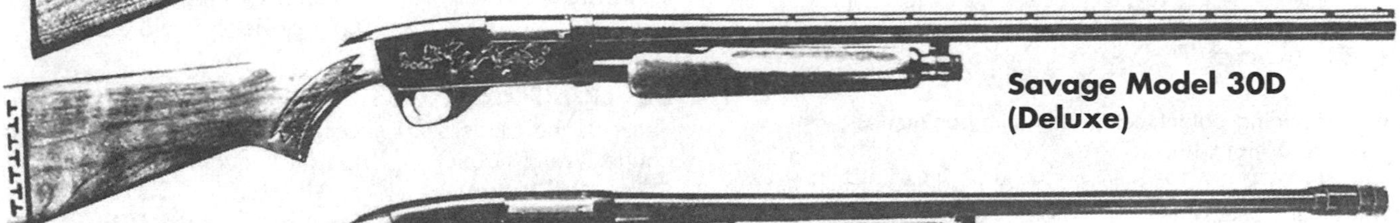

Savage Model 30D (Deluxe)

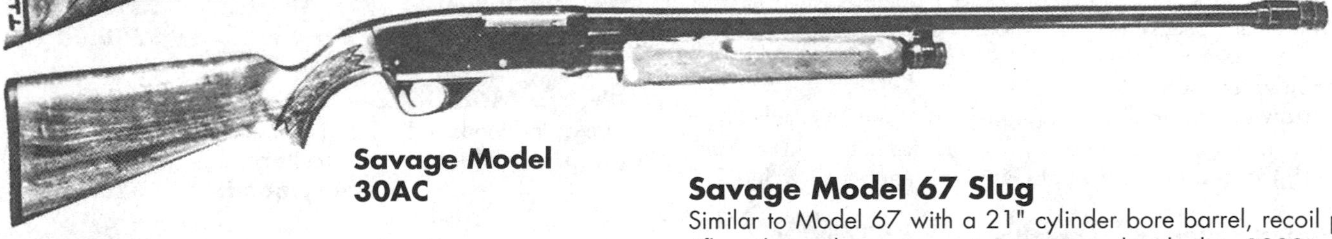

Savage Model 30AC

Savage Model 67

Gauge: 12, 20, regular or magnum
Action: Slide action; hammerless; side ejector; repeating
Magazine: 4-shot tubular, 3-shot in magnum
Barrel: 28" modified
Finish: Blued; hardwood, semi-pistol grip stock and grooved slide handle
Approximate wt.: 6¼ to 7½ lbs.
Comments: The Model 67 was originally a Stevens shotgun. In 1988 Savage dropped the Stevens designation; discontinued in the late 1980s.
Estimated Value: **Excellent:** **$175.00**
Very good: **$140.00**

Savage Model 67 Slug

Similar to Model 67 with a 21" cylinder bore barrel, recoil pad, rifle sights and scope mount. Discontinued in the late 1980s.
Estimated Value: **Excellent:** **$175.00**
Very good: **$140.00**

Savage Model 67VRT

Similar to the Model 67 with a ventilated rib barrel, interchangeable choke tubes and recoil pad. Discontinued in the late 1980s.
Estimated Value: **Excellent:** **$200.00**
Very good: **$160.00**

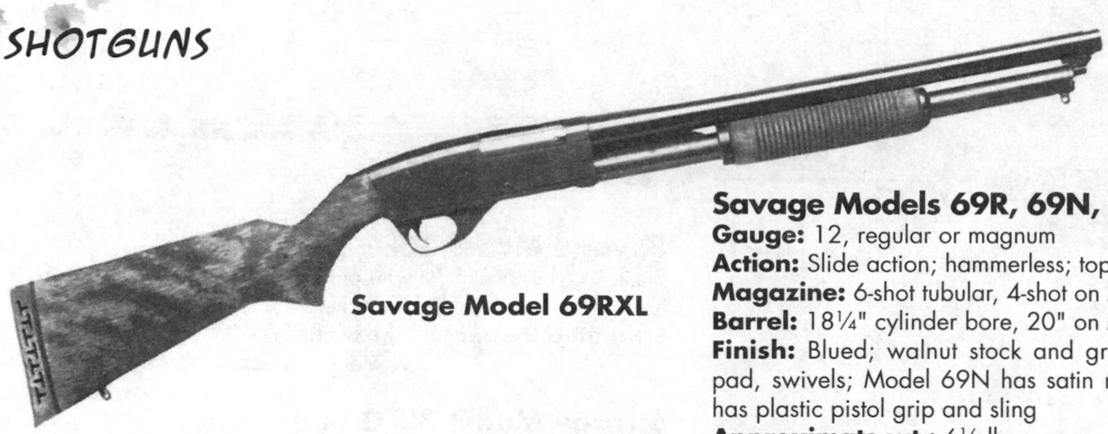

Savage Model 69RXL

Savage Models 69R, 69N, 69RXL, and 69RXG

Gauge: 12, regular or magnum
Action: Slide action; hammerless; top tang safety
Magazine: 6-shot tubular, 4-shot on Model 69R
Barrel: 18¼" cylinder bore, 20" on Model 69R
Finish: Blued; walnut stock and grooved slide handle; recoil pad, swivels; Model 69N has satin nickel finish; Model 69RXG has plastic pistol grip and sling
Approximate wt.: 6½ lbs.
Comments: A law enforcement shotgun introduced in 1982. Add 30% for Model 69N. (Models 69R and 69N discontinued in the mid-1980s.) Discontinued in the late 1980s.

Estimated Value:	**Excellent:**	**$200.00**
	Very good:	**$160.00**

Savage Model 720

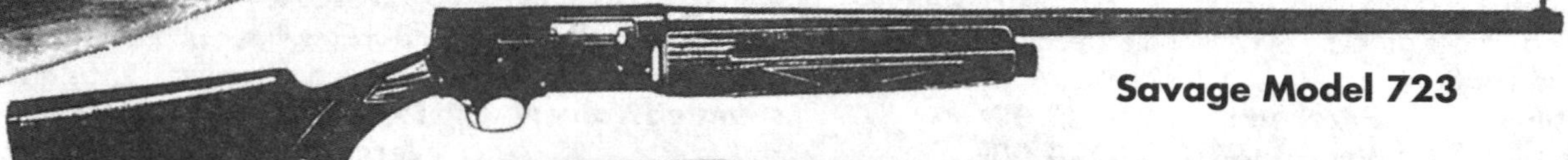

Savage Model 723

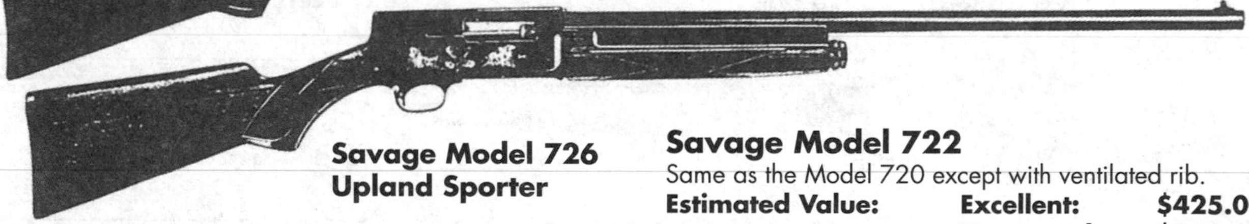

Savage Model 726 Upland Sporter

Savage Model 720

Gauge: 12
Action: Browning patent; semiautomatic; hammerless
Magazine: 4-shot tubular
Barrel: 28", 30", or 32" cylinder bore, modified or full choke
Finish: Blued; checkered walnut pistol grip stock and forearm; after 1940, engraved receiver
Approximate wt.: 8½ lbs.
Comments: Originally a Springfield shotgun, this takedown model was made from about 1930 until the late 1940s. In the early 1940s, Model 720R (Riot Gun) was introduced with a 20" barrel.

Estimated Value:	**Excellent:**	**$375.00**
	Very good:	**$300.00**

Savage Model 720-P

Basically the same as the Model 720 with "Poly-Choke," produced from the late 1930s to the 1940s; 3- or 5-shot; 12 gauge only.

Estimated Value:	**Excellent:**	**$400.00**
	Very good:	**$320.00**

Savage Model 721

Same as the Model 720 with matted rib.

Estimated Value:	**Excellent:**	**$400.00**
	Very good:	**$320.00**

Savage Model 722

Same as the Model 720 except with ventilated rib.

Estimated Value:	**Excellent:**	**$425.00**
	Very good:	**$340.00**

Savage Model 723

Same as the Model 720 except no 32" barrel; available in 16 gauge. Weighs about 7½ lbs.

Estimated Value:	**Excellent:**	**$375.00**
	Very good:	**$300.00**

Savage Model 724

Same as the Model 723 except with matted rib.

Estimated Value:	**Excellent:**	**$400.00**
	Very good:	**$320.00**

Savage Model 725

Same as the Model 723 except with ventilated rib.

Estimated Value:	**Excellent:**	**$425.00**
	Very good:	**$340.00**

Savage Model 726 Upland Sporter

Basically the same as the Model 720 except no 32" barrel; 2-shot tubular magazine; available in 16 gauge; decorated receiver.

Estimated Value:	**Excellent:**	**$400.00**
	Very good:	**$320.00**

Savage Model 727 Upland Sporter
Same as the Model 726 except with matted rib.
Estimated Value: **Excellent:** **$415.00**
Very good: **$335.00**

Savage Model 728 Upland Sporter
Same as the Model 726 except with ventilated rib.
Estimated Value: **Excellent:** **$425.00**
Very good: **$340.00**

Savage Model 740C Skeet Gun
Basically the same as the Model 726 with a skeet stock and "Cutts Compensator." Discontinued in the late 1940s.
Estimated Value: **Excellent:** **$425.00**
Very good: **$340.00**

Savage Model 745 Lightweight
Similar to the Model 720 with light alloy receiver. Made from the late 1930s to the 1940s; 3- or 5-shot; 12 gauge only.
Estimated Value: **Excellent:** **$375.00**
Very good: **$300.00**

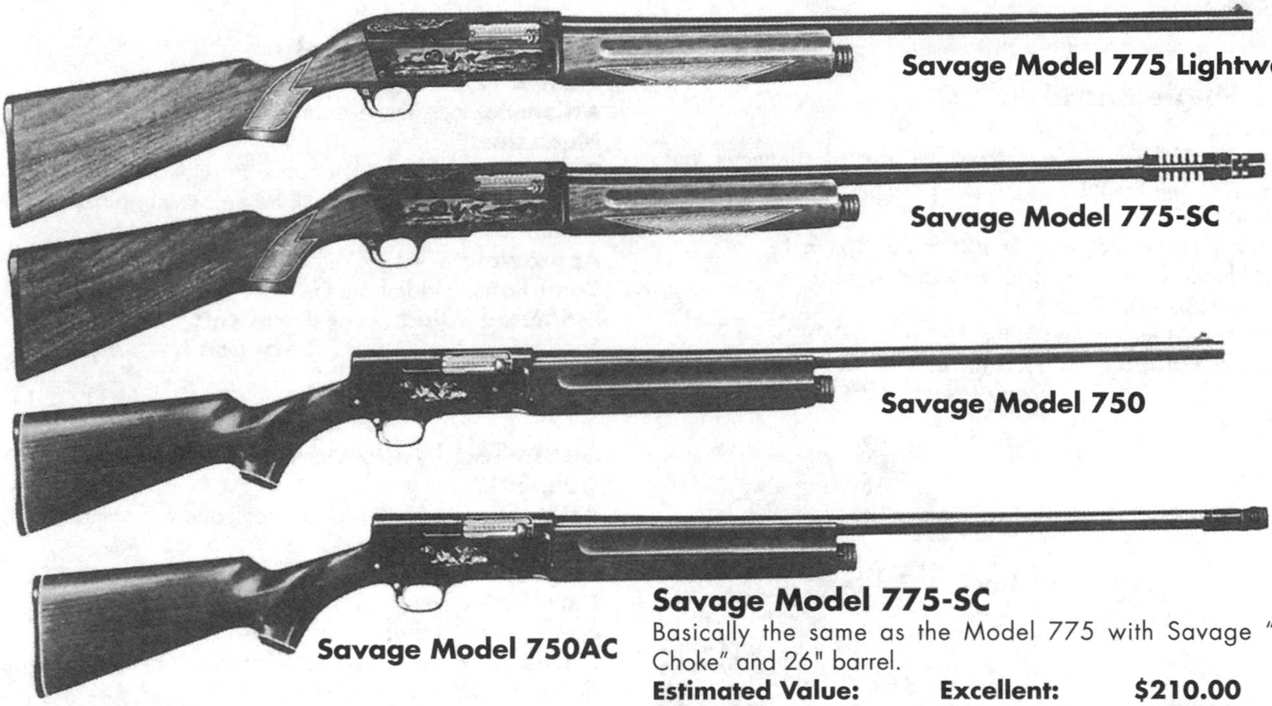

Savage Model 775 Lightweight

Savage Model 775-SC

Savage Model 750

Savage Model 750AC

Savage Model 755
Gauge: 12, 16
Action: Semiautomatic; hammerless
Magazine: 4-shot tubular; 3-shot tubular
Barrel: 26" cylinder bore; 28" full or modified; 30" full choke
Finish: Blued; checkered walnut pistol grip stock and forearm
Approximate wt.: 8 lbs.
Comments: Made from the late 1940s until the late 1950s; top of receiver flush with stock.
Estimated Value: **Excellent:** **$250.00**
Very good: **$200.00**

Savage Model 755-SC
Similar to the Model 755 with Savage "Super Choke."
Estimated Value: **Excellent:** **$240.00**
Very good: **$195.00**

Savage Model 775 Lightweight
Similar to the Model 755 with alloy receiver. Produced until the mid-1960s.
Estimated Value: **Excellent:** **$200.00**
Very good: **$160.00**

Savage Model 775-SC
Basically the same as the Model 775 with Savage "Super Choke" and 26" barrel.
Estimated Value: **Excellent:** **$210.00**
Very good: **$165.00**

Savage Model 750
Gauge: 12
Action: Browning patent; semiautomatic; hammerless
Magazine: 4-shot tubular
Barrel: 26" cylinder bore; 28" full or modified
Finish: Blued; checkered walnut pistol grip stock and forearm; decorated receiver
Approximate wt.: 7¼ lbs.
Comments: Made during the late 1960s.
Estimated Value: **Excellent:** **$260.00**
Very good: **$210.00**

Savage Model 750SC
Similar to the Model 750 with Savage "Super Choke." Made in 1962 for two years.
Estimated Value: **Excellent:** **$265.00**
Very good: **$215.00**

Savage Model 750AC
Same as the Model 750 except: adjustable choke. Made during the mid-1960s.
Estimated Value: **Excellent:** **$260.00**
Very good: **$210.00**

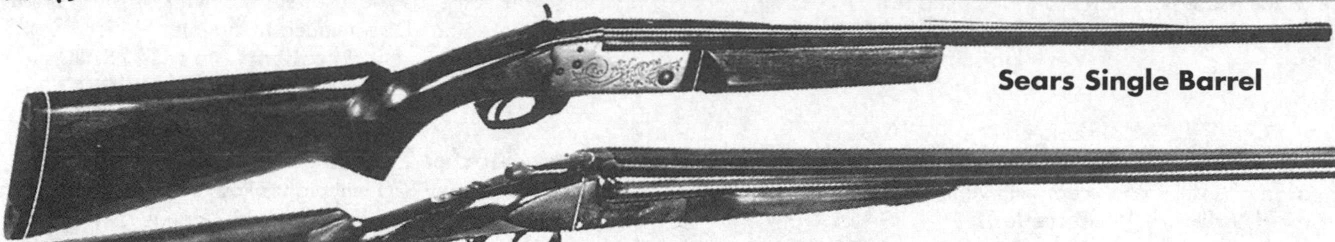

Sears Single Barrel

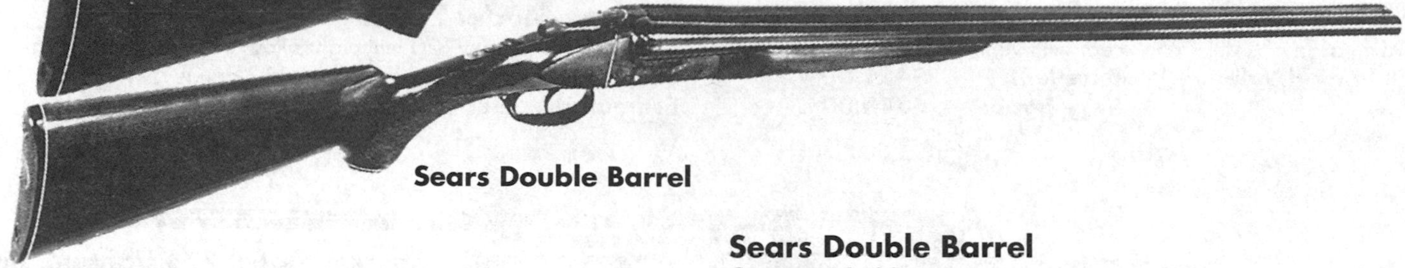

Sears Double Barrel

Sears Single Barrel
Gauge: 12, 20, 410
Action: Box lock; top lever break-open; exposed hammer; automatic ejector, single-shot
Magazine: None
Barrel: Full choke; 26" in 410; 28" in 20; 30" in 12
Finish: Blued; wood pistol grip stock and forearm
Approximate wt.: 7 lbs.
Comments: Manufactured in the 1970s and 1980s.

Estimated Value:	**Excellent:**	**$100.00**
	Very good:	**$ 80.00**

Sears Double Barrel
Gauge: 12, 20
Action: Box lock; top lever break-open; hammerless; double triggers
Magazine: None
Barrel: 28" side-by-side double barrel; variety of chokes
Finish: Blued; epoxied black frame; walnut pistol grip stock and forearm
Approximate wt.: 7½ lbs.
Comments: Made from the 1970s to the late 1980s.

Estimated Value:	**Excellent:**	**$150.00**
	Very good:	**$120.00**

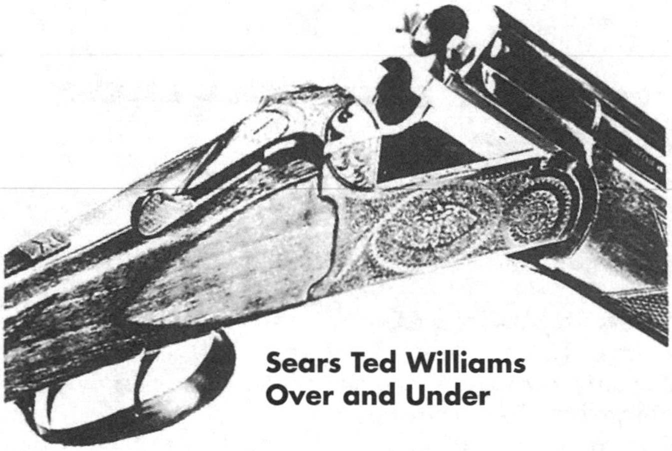

Sears Ted Williams Over and Under

Sears Ted Williams Over and Under
Gauge: 12, 20
Action: Box lock; top lever break-open; hammerless; automatic ejectors, selective trigger
Magazine: None
Barrel: Over and under double barrel; 26", 28" in standard chokes; ventilated rib; chrome lined
Finish: Blued; engraved steel receivers; checkered walnut pistol grip stock and forearm; recoil pad
Approximate wt.: 6¾ lbs.
Comments: Produced from the 1960s to the late 1970s.

Estimated Value:	**Excellent:**	**$200.00**
	Very good:	**$160.00**

Sears Bolt Action
Gauge: 410
Action: Bolt action; repeating
Magazine: 3-shot detachable clip
Barrel: 24" full choke
Finish: Blued; wood pistol grip stock and forearm
Approximate wt.: 5½ lbs.
Comments: Made from the 1960s to the late 1970s.

Estimated Value:	**Excellent:**	**$120.00**
	Very good:	**$ 95.00**

Sears Model 140
Gauge: 12, 20
Action: Bolt action; repeating
Magazine: 2-shot detachable clip
Barrel: 25" adjustable choke
Finish: Blued; wood pistol grip stock and forearm
Approximate wt.: 7 lbs.
Comments: Made from the 1960s to the late 1970s.

Estimated Value:	**Excellent:**	**$115.00**
	Very good:	**$100.00**

Sears Model 140

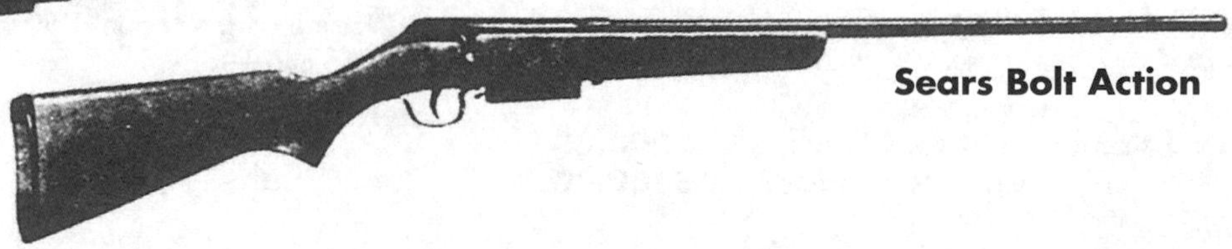

Sears Bolt Action

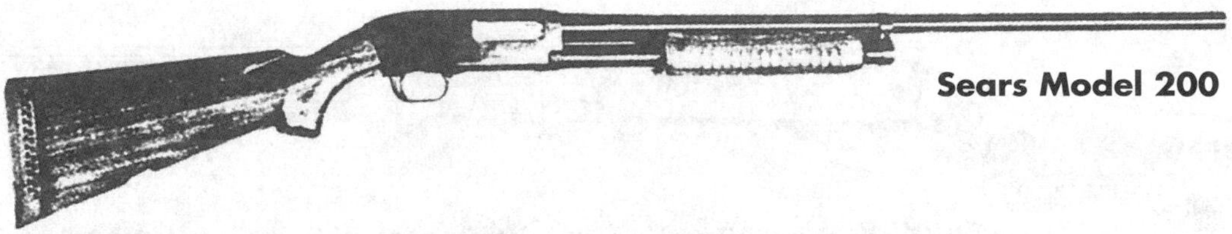

Sears Model 200

Sears Ted Williams 200

Sears Ted Williams 300

Gauge: 12, 20
Action: Semiautomatic, gas-operated; hammerless
Magazine: 3-shot tubular
Barrel: 27" adjustable choke; 28" modified or full chokes; ventilated rib
Finish: Blued; checkered walnut pistol grip stock and forearm; recoil pad
Approximate wt.: 7 lbs.
Comments: Add $10.00 for variable choke.

Estimated Value:	**Excellent:**	**$175.00**
	Very good:	**$140.00**

Sears Model 200

Gauge: 12, 20
Action: Slide action; hammerless; repeating
Magazine: 4-shot tubular
Barrel: 28" full or modified chokes
Finish: Blued; alloy receiver; wood pistol grip stock and forearm; recoil pad
Approximate wt.: 6½ lbs.
Comments: Add $20.00 for variable choke.

Estimated Value:	**Excellent:**	**$160.00**
	Very good:	**$130.00**

Sears Ted Williams 200

A fancier version of the 200 with checkered wood.

Estimated Value:	**Excellent:**	**$200.00**
	Very good:	**$160.00**

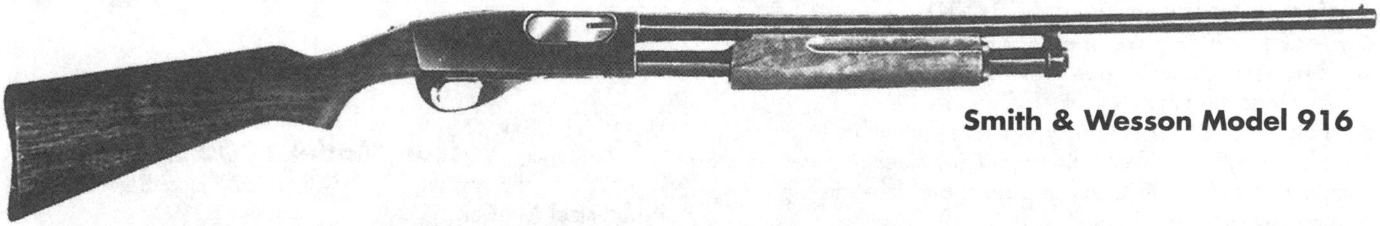

Smith & Wesson Model 916

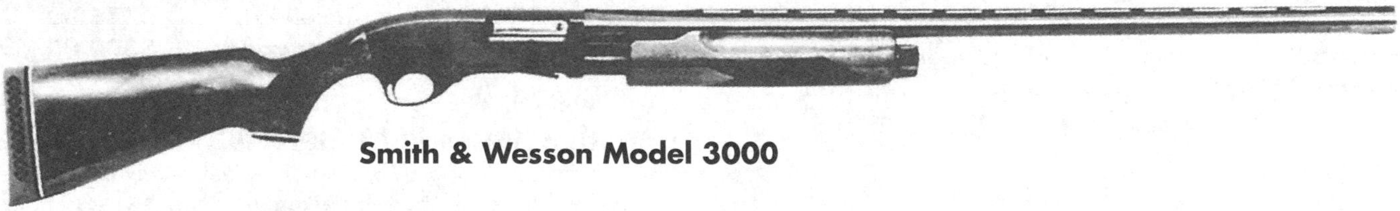

Smith & Wesson Model 3000

Smith & Wesson Model 916

Gauge: 12
Action: Slide action; hammerless; side ejector
Magazine: 5-shot tubular
Barrel: 20" cylinder bore; 26" improved cylinder, 28" modified, full or cylinder bore; ventilated rib on some models
Finish: Blued; satin finish receiver; walnut semi-pistol grip stock and grooved slide handle; recoil pad available
Approximate wt.: 7 lbs.
Comments: Made from the early 1970s to about 1980. Add $20.00 for Deer Model or ventilated rib.

Estimated Value:	**Excellent:**	**$200.00**
	Very good:	**$160.00**

Smith & Wesson Model 3000

Gauge: 12, 20, regular or magnum
Action: Slide action; repeating; hammerless
Magazine: 3-shot tubular
Barrel: 26" improved cylinder; 28" modified or full, 30" full; ventilated rib
Finish: Blued; checkered walnut pistol grip stock and fluted slide handle; recoil pad
Approximate wt.: 7 lbs.
Comments: Made from 1982 to 1985. Add $25.00 for "multi-choke" system.

Estimated Value:	**Excellent:**	**$350.00**
	Very good:	**$280.00**

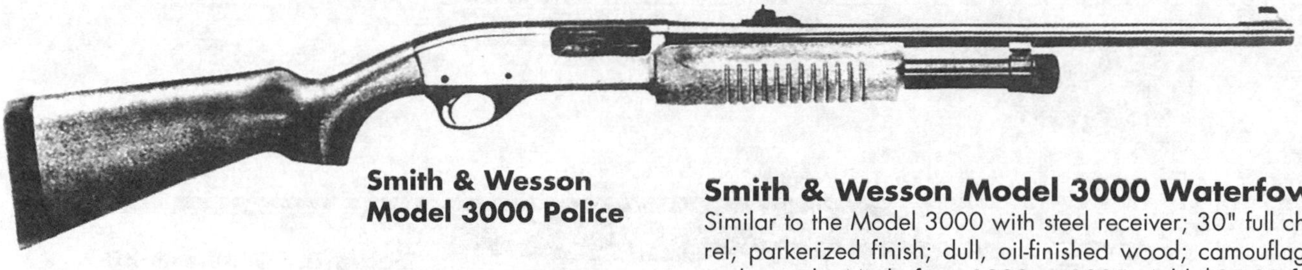

Smith & Wesson Model 3000 Police

Smith & Wesson Model 3000 Police

Similar to the Model 3000 with 18" or 20" slug or police cylinder barrel; blued or parkerized finish; bead or rifle sights; walnut finish, hardwood stock and grooved slide handle or plastic pistol grip and slide handle or folding stock. Add $25.00 for rifle sights; $10.00 for plastic pistol grip; $70.00 for folding stock.

Estimated Value: **Excellent:** **$375.00**
Very good: **$300.00**

Smith & Wesson Model 3000 Waterfowler

Similar to the Model 3000 with steel receiver; 30" full choke barrel; parkerized finish; dull, oil-finished wood; camouflaged sling and swivels. Made from 1982 to 1985. Add $25.00 for "multi-choke" system.

Estimated Value: **Excellent:** **$350.00**
Very good: **$280.00**

Smith & Wesson Model 3000 Slug

Similar to the Model 3000 with a 22" slug barrel; rifle sights; swivels.

Estimated Value: **Excellent:** **$325.00**
Very good: **$260.00**

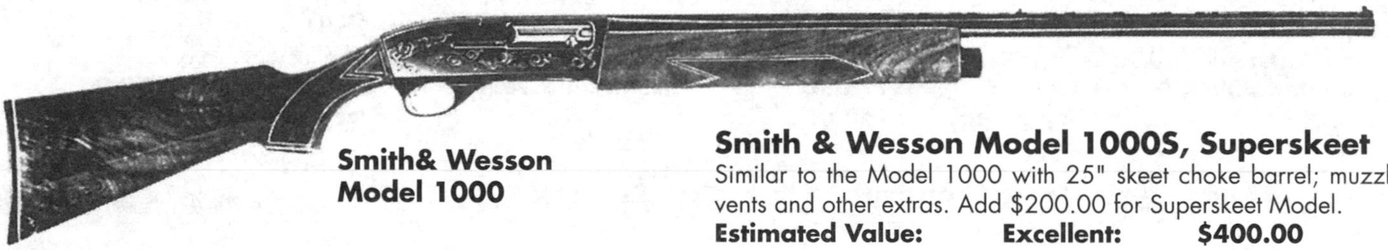

Smith& Wesson Model 1000

Smith & Wesson Model 1000

Gauge: 12, 20, regular or magnum
Action: Semiautomatic, gas-operated; hammerless; side ejection
Magazine: 4-shot tubular
Barrel: 26", 28", 30"; variety of chokes; ventilated rib
Finish: Blued; engraved alloy receiver; steel receiver on magnum; checkered walnut pistol grip stock and forearm; sights
Approximate wt.: 7½ lbs.
Comments: Manufactured from the early 1970s to mid-1980s. Add **$46.00** for magnum; $30.00 for "multi-choke" system.

Estimated Value: **Excellent:** **$325.00**
Very good: **$260.00**

Smith & Wesson Model 1000 Super 12

Similar to the Model 1000 except: "multi-choke" system; designed to use magnum shells. Made in 1984 and 1985.

Estimated Value: **Excellent:** **$350.00**
Very good: **$280.00**

Smith & Wesson Model 1000 Trap

Similar to the Model 1000 with Monte Carlo stock; steel receiver; 30" multi-choke barrel; other trap features.

Estimated Value: **Excellent:** **$475.00**
Very good: **$380.00**

Smith & Wesson Model 1000S, Superskeet

Similar to the Model 1000 with 25" skeet choke barrel; muzzle vents and other extras. Add $200.00 for Superskeet Model.

Estimated Value: **Excellent:** **$400.00**
Very good: **$320.00**

Smith & Wesson Model 1000 Slug

Similar to the Model 1000 with a 22" slug barrel, rifle sights, and steel receiver.

Estimated Value: **Excellent:** **$375.00**
Very good: **$300.00**

Smith & Wesson Model 1000 Waterfowler

Similar to the Model 1000 with a steel receiver; dull oil-finish stock; 30" full choke barrel; parkerized finish; swivels; recoil pad; camouflage sling. Introduced in 1982. Discontinued in 1985.

Estimated Value: **Excellent:** **$390.00**
Very good: **$310.00**

Smith & Wesson Model 1000 Super 12 Waterfowler

Similar to the Model 1000 Waterfowler with the "multi-choke" system. Introduced in 1984. Discontinued in 1985.

Estimated Value: **Excellent:** **$400.00**
Very good: **$320.00**

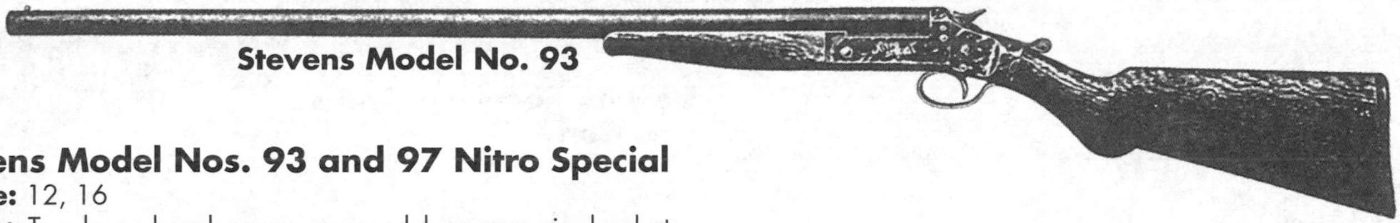

Stevens Model No. 93

Stevens Model Nos. 93 and 97 Nitro Special

Gauge: 12, 16
Action: Top lever break-open; exposed hammer; single shot; Model 97 has automatic ejector
Magazine: None
Barrel: Special steel; 28", 30", 32"
Finish: Blued; nickel-plated, case-hardened frame; plain walnut pistol grip stock and lipped forearm
Approximate wt.: 7 to 7½ lbs.
Comments: Made from 1907 to 1918.
Estimated Value: **Excellent:** **$125.00**
Very good: **$100.00**

Stevens Model No. 97 Nitro Special

Stevens Model Nos. 100, 110, and 120

Gauge: 12, 16, 20
Action: Top lever break-open; automatic ejector; exposed hammer; single shot
Magazine: None
Barrel: 28", 30", 32"
Finish: Blued; case hardened frame; walnut pistol grip stock and forearm; No. 100, no checkering; 110 and 120, checkered walnut
Approximate wt.: 6 to 7 lbs.
Comments: Produced from 1902 to 1904.
Estimated Value: **Excellent:** **$130.00**
Very good: **$105.00**

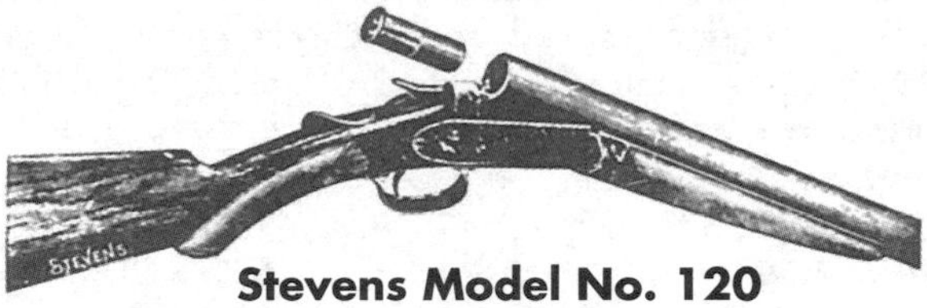

Stevens Model No. 120

Stevens Model No. 140

Similar to the Model 120 except it is hammerless and has an automatic safety. Made from 1902 to 1904.
Estimated Value: **Excellent:** **$135.00**
Very good: **$110.00**

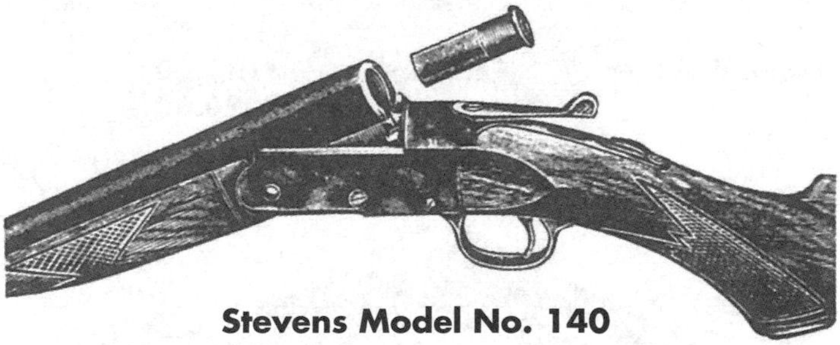

Stevens Model No. 140

Stevens Model Nos. 160, 165, and 170

Gauge: 12, 16, 20
Action: Break-open; exposed hammer; single shot; automatic ejector except on 160
Magazine: None
Barrel: 26", 28", 30", 32"
Finish: Blued; case-hardened frame; checkered walnut pistol grip stock and forearm except 160 which is plain
Approximate wt.: 6 to 7 lbs.
Comments: Made from 1903 to 1908.
Estimated Value: **Excellent:** **$120.00**
Very good: **$ 95.00**

Stevens Model No. 170

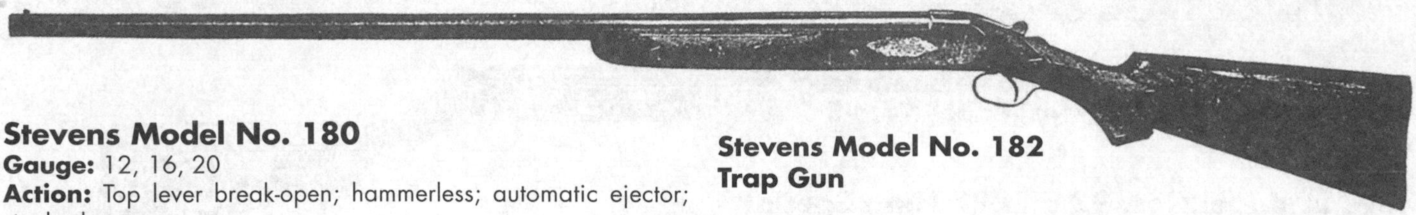

Stevens Model No. 182
Trap Gun

Stevens Model No. 180

Gauge: 12, 16, 20
Action: Top lever break-open; hammerless; automatic ejector; single shot
Magazine: None
Barrel: 26", 28", 30" modified; 32" or 36" full choke
Finish: Blued; case hardened frame; checkered walnut pistol grip stock and forearm
Approximate wt.: 6½ lbs.
Comments: Produced from 1903 to 1918.

Estimated Value:	**Excellent:**	**$125.00**
	Very good:	**$100.00**

Stevens Model Nos. 185, 190, and 195

Gauge: 12
Action: Top lever break-open; hammerless; automatic shell ejector; single shot
Magazine: None
Barrel: Round with octagon breech; 30" or 32"
Finish: Blued; case hardened frame; checkered walnut pistol grip stock and forearm; frame engraved on Nos. 190 and 195
Approximate wt.: 7 to 8 lbs.
Comments: These guns differ in quality of finish and engraving. Produced from 1903 to 1906.

Estimated Value:	**Excellent:**	**$150.00**
	Very good:	**$120.00**

Stevens Model No. 970

Similar to Model No. 185, this 12 gauge was made from around 1912 to 1918.

Estimated Value:	**Excellent:**	**$110.00**
	Very good:	**$ 90.00**

Stevens Model No. 85
Dreadnaught

Stevens Model No. 89
Dreadnaught

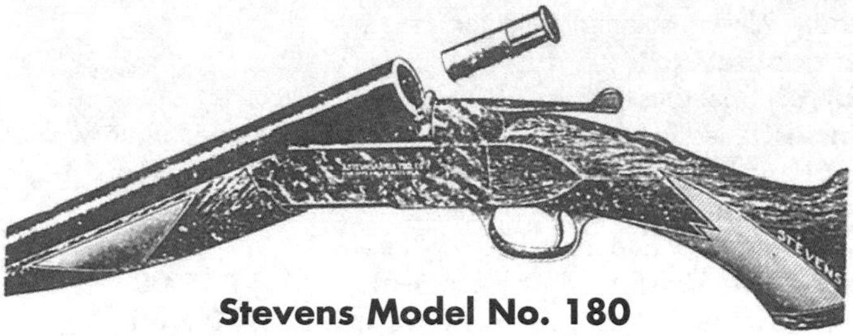

Stevens Model No. 180

Stevens Model No. 182 Trap Gun

Similar to Model No. 180 except: Trap Grade; 12 gauge only; matted top of barrel; scrollwork on frame. Made from around 1912 to 1920.

Estimated Value:	**Excellent:**	**$175.00**
	Very good:	**$145.00**

Stevens Model No. 195

Stevens Model No. 970

Stevens Model No. 85 Dreadnaught

Gauge: 12
Action: Top lever break-open; exposed hammer
Magazine: None, single shot
Barrel: 28", 30", 32" full choke
Finish: Blued; case-hardened frame; plain walnut pistol grip stock and lipped forearm
Approximate wt.: 7½ lbs.
Comments: Made from around 1910 to the mid-1920s.

Estimated Value:	**Excellent:**	**$110.00**
	Very good:	**$ 90.00**

Stevens Model No. 89 Dreadnaught

Same as the No. 85 with automatic ejector. Made until 1938.

Estimated Value:	**Excellent:**	**$115.00**
	Very good:	**$ 95.00**

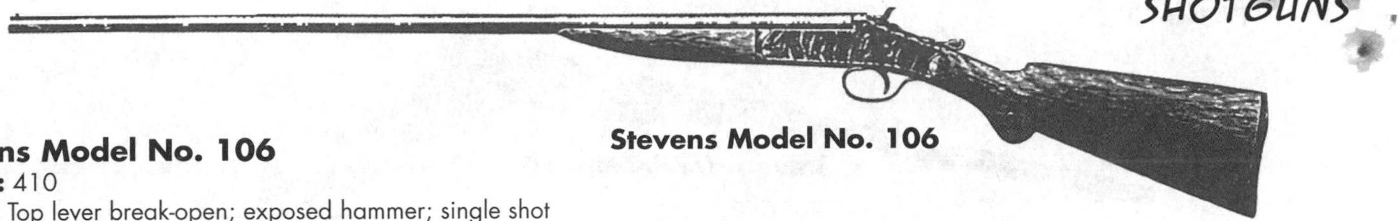

Stevens Model No. 106

Stevens Model No. 106

Gauge: 410
Action: Top lever break-open; exposed hammer; single shot
Magazine: None
Barrel: 26" or 30"
Finish: Blued; case-hardened frame; plain walnut pistol grip stock and forearm
Approximate wt.: 4½ lbs.
Comments: This lightweight, light-gauge gun was made from around 1912 to 1935.
Estimated Value: **Excellent:** **$110.00**
Very good: **$ 90.00**

Stevens Model No. 108

Same as the No. 106 with automatic ejector.
Estimated Value: **Excellent:** **$110.00**
Very good: **$ 90.00**

Stevens Springfield Model No. 958

Similar to the Model No. 108. Made from the mid-1920s to the early 1930s.
Estimated Value: **Excellent:** **$115.00**
Very good: **$ 95.00**

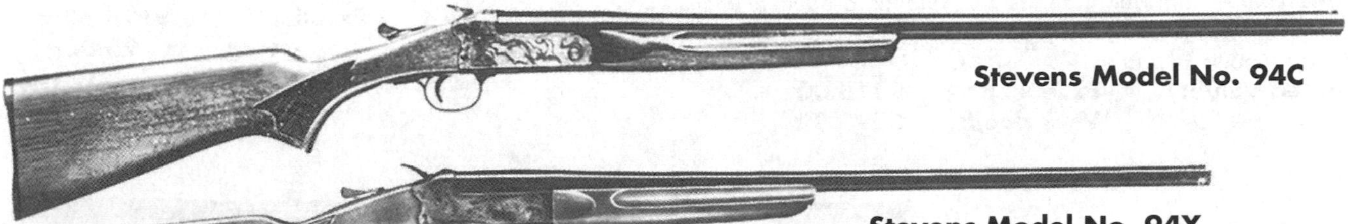

Stevens Model No. 94C

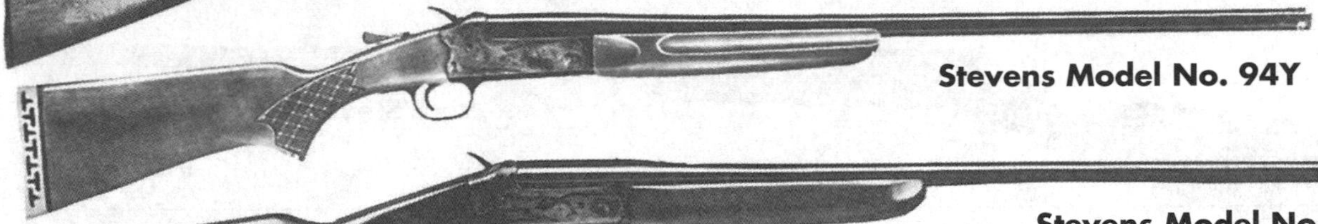

Stevens Model No. 94Y

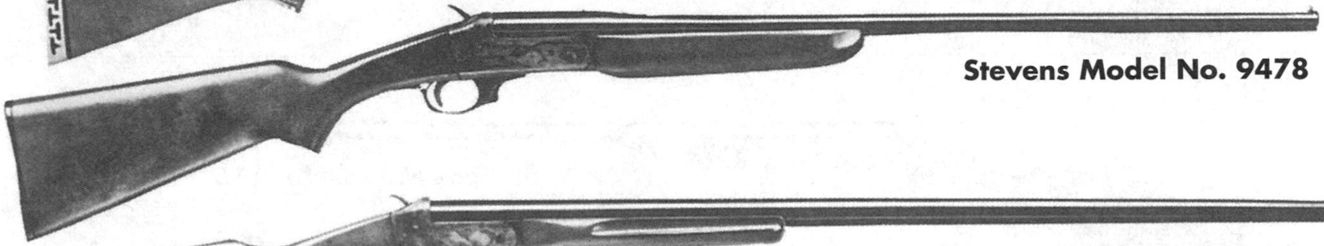

Stevens Model No. 9478

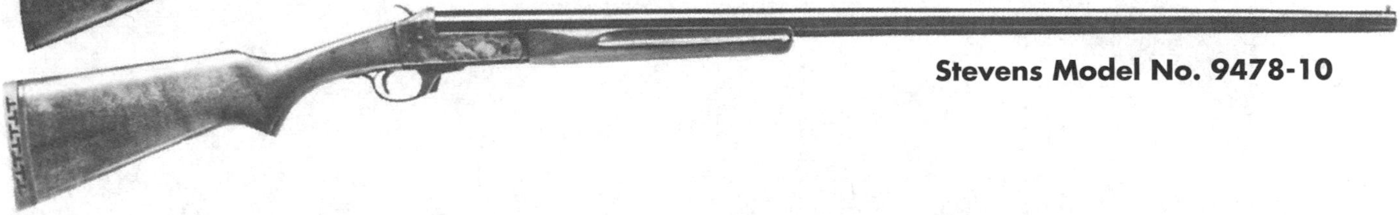

Stevens Model No. 9478-10

Stevens Model Nos. 94 and 94C

Gauge: 12, 16, 20, 410
Action: Top lever break-open; exposed hammer
Magazine: None
Barrel: 26", 28", 30", 32", 36" full choke
Finish: Blued; case hardened frame; checkered or plain walnut semi-pistol grip stock and grooved forearm
Approximate wt.: 6 to 8 lbs.
Comments: Model 94 made from 1939 to 1960. Model No. 94C made from 1960 to the mid-1980s.
Estimated Value: **Excellent:** **$125.00**
Very good: **$100.00**

Stevens Model No. 94Y

Similar to the Model 94C in youth version. Shorter stock; recoil pad, 26" barrel; 20 gauge modified or 410 full choke. Made from 1960 to 1963.
Estimated Value: **Excellent:** **$130.00**
Very good: **$105.00**

Stevens Model No. 9478

Similar to the Model 94C with lever release on the trigger guard; no checkering. Add $8.00 for 36" barrel.
Estimated Value: **Excellent:** **$100.00**
Very good: **$ 80.00**

Stevens Model No. 9478-10, Waterfowl

Similar to the Model 9478 with a 36" full choke barrel; 10 gauge only; recoil pad.
Estimated Value: **Excellent:** **$120.00**
Very good: **$ 95.00**

Stevens Model No. 9478-Y

Similar to the Model 9478 in 410 full or 20 modified gauges; 26" barrel; short stock with rubber butt plate.
Estimated Value: **Excellent:** **$100.00**
Very good: **$ 90.00**

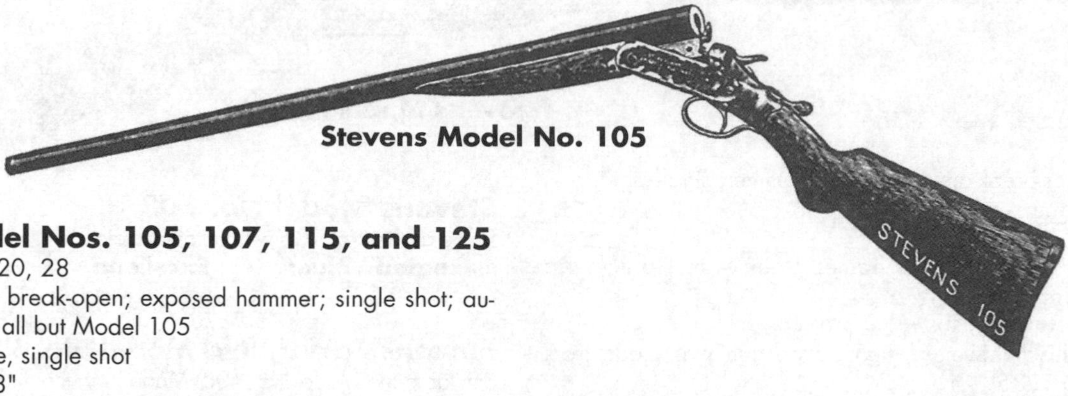

Stevens Model No. 105

Stevens Model Nos. 105, 107, 115, and 125

Gauge: 12, 16, 20, 28
Action: Top lever break-open; exposed hammer; single shot; automatic ejector on all but Model 105
Magazine: None, single shot
Barrel: 26" or 28"
Finish: Blued; case-hardened frame; checkered walnut straight grip stock and forearm except No. 107 (plain)
Approximate wt.: 5½ lbs.
Comments: A lightweight series of shotguns produced until about World War II for Model 105; 1950s for Model 107 and 1920s for Models 115 and 125.

Estimated Value:	**Excellent:**	**$115.00**
	Very good:	**$ 95.00**

Stevens Springfield Model No. 95

Similar to the Model 107. Made from the mid-1920s until the mid-1930s.

Estimated Value:	**Excellent:**	**$115.00**
	Very good:	**$ 95.00**

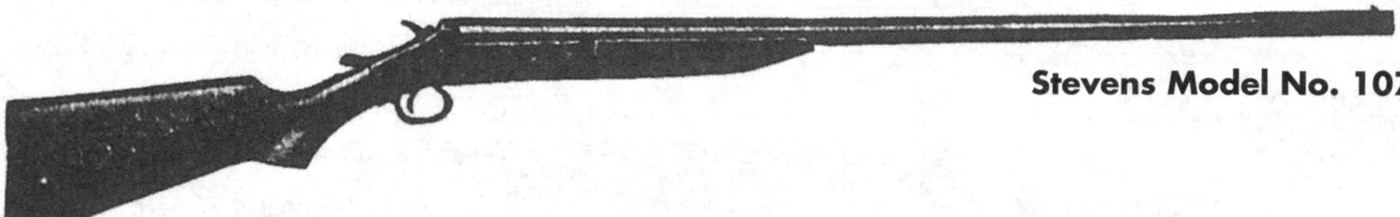

Stevens Model No. 107

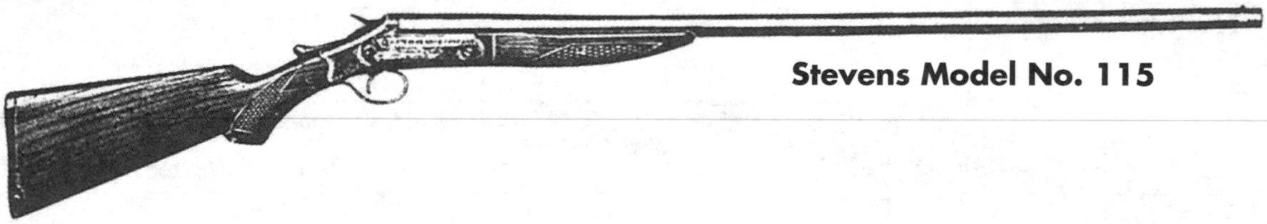

Stevens Model No. 115

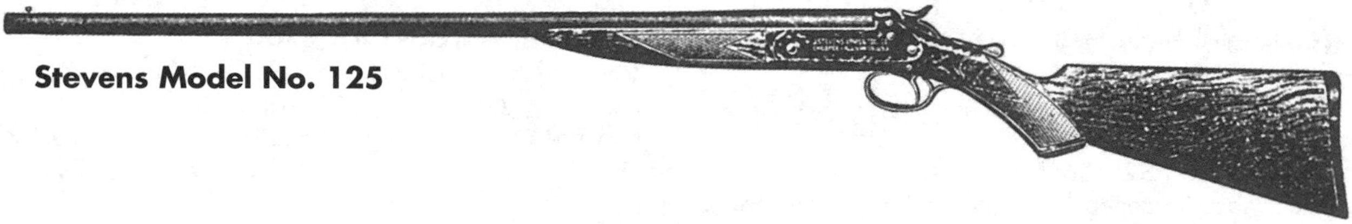

Stevens Model No. 125

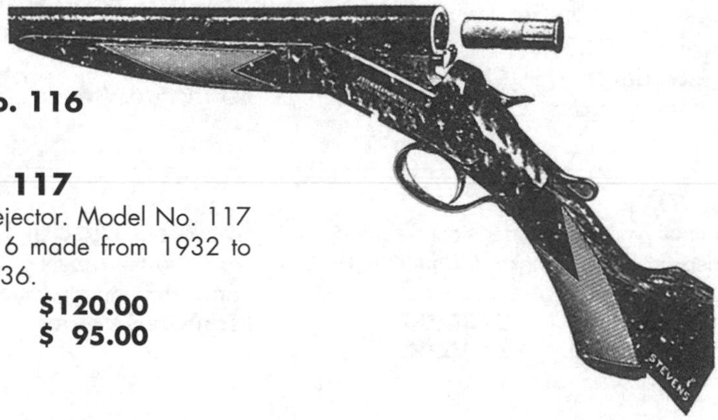

Stevens Model No. 116

Stevens Models No. 116 and 117

Similar to the Model 115 with automatic ejector. Model No. 117 is equipped with Lyman sights. Model 116 made from 1932 to 1942; Model 117 made from 1932 to 1936.

Estimated Value:	**Excellent:**	**$120.00**
	Very good:	**$ 95.00**

Stevens Model No. 250

Stevens Model No. 350

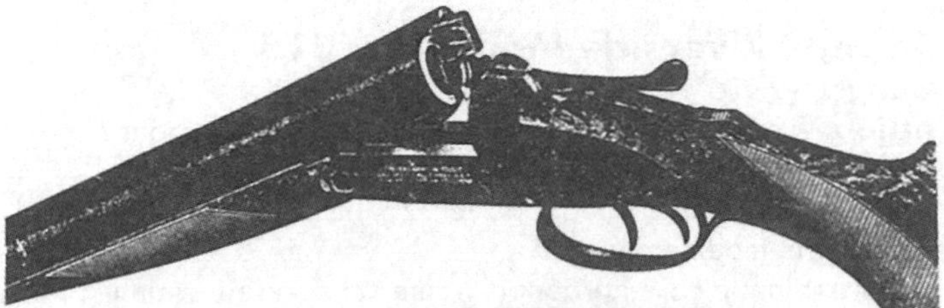

Stevens Model No. 355

Stevens Model No. 385

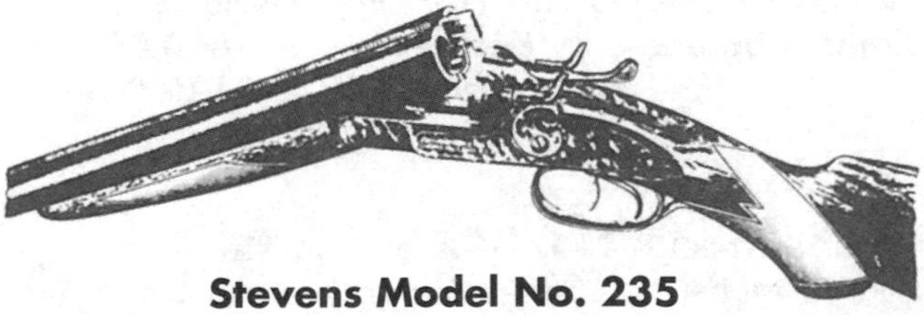

Stevens Model No. 235

Stevens Model No. 250

Gauge: 12
Action: Top lever break-open; exposed hammers; double trigger.
Magazine: None
Barrel: 28", 30", 32" side-by-side double barrel
Finish: Blued; checkered walnut pistol grip stock and forearm
Approximate wt.: 8 lbs.
Comments: Made from 1903 to 1908.

Estimated Value:	**Excellent:**	**$500.00**
	Very good:	**$400.00**

Stevens Model Nos. 260 and 270

Similar to Model 250 with special Damascus or twist barrels; available in 16 gauge. Manufactured from 1903 to 1906.

Estimated Value:	**Excellent:**	**$500.00**
	Very good:	**$400.00**

Stevens Model Nos. 350, 360, and 370

Gauge: 12, 16
Action: Top lever break-open; hammerless; double trigger
Magazine: None
Barrel: Side-by-side double barrel, matted rib, 28", 30", 32"
Finish: Blued; checkered walnut pistol grip stock and forearm
Approximate wt.: 7½ to 8½ lbs.
Comments: Produced from 1903 to 1908.

Estimated Value:	**Excellent:**	**$425.00**
	Very good:	**$340.00**

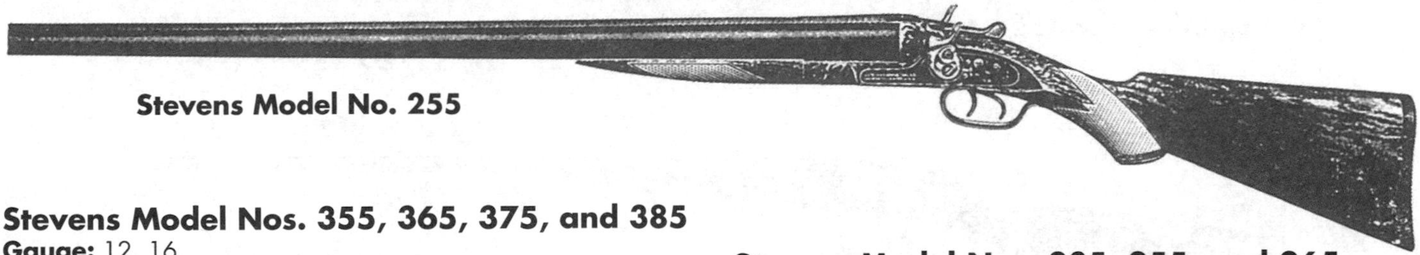

Stevens Model No. 255

Stevens Model Nos. 355, 365, 375, and 385

Gauge: 12, 16
Action: Top lever break-open; hammerless; double trigger
Magazine: None
Barrel: Side-by-side double barrel; Krupp steel; matted rib; 28", 30", 32"
Finish: Blued; checkered walnut straight or pistol grip stock and forearm; 355 and 365 plain; 375 some engraving; 385 engraved frame
Approximate wt.: 7 to 8½ lbs.
Comments: Made from 1907. Model No. 355 discontinued in World War I; all others in 1913.

Estimated Value:	**Excellent:**	**$700.00**
	Very good:	**$560.00**

Stevens Model Nos. 235, 255, and 265

Gauge: 12, 16
Action: Top lever break-open; exposed hammers; double triggers; box lock
Magazine: None
Barrel: Side-by-side double barrel; matted rib; 28", 30", 32"
Finish: Blued; checkered walnut pistol grip stock and forearm; case-hardened frame; No. 255 has checkered butt plate
Approximate wt.: 7 to 8½ lbs.
Comments: Made from around 1907 until 1928 (No. 235); Models 255 and 265 stopped around World War I.

Estimated Value:	**Excellent:**	**$425.00**
	Very good:	**$340.00**

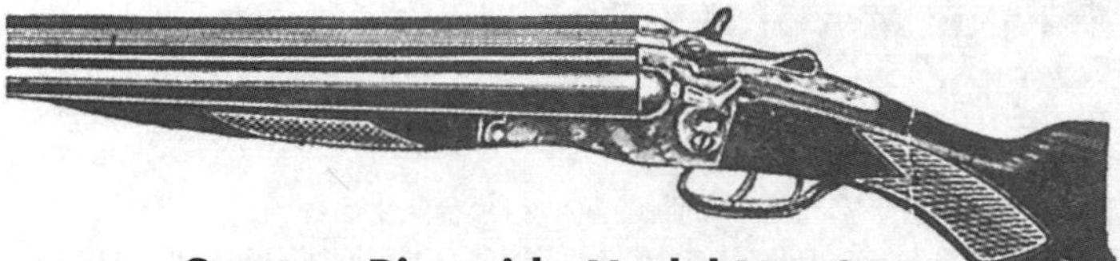

Stevens Riverside Model No. 215

Stevens Riverside Model No. 215

Gauge: 12, 16
Action: Top lever break-open; exposed hammer; double trigger
Magazine: None
Barrel: Side-by-side double barrel; 26", 28", 30", 32"; matted rib; full and modified chokes
Finish: Blued; case-hardened frame; checkered walnut pistol grip stock and forearm
Approximate wt.: 7½ to 8½ lbs.
Comments: Made from around 1912 to 1942.
Estimated Value: **Excellent:** **$425.00**
Very good: **$340.00**

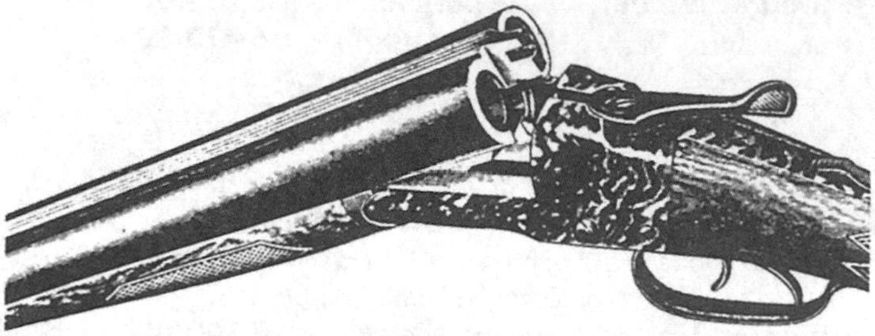

Stevens Riverside Model No. 315

Stevens Riverside Model No. 315

Gauge: 12, 16
Action: Top lever break-open; hammerless; double trigger
Magazine: None
Barrel: Side-by-side double barrel; 26", 28", 30", 32"; matted rib; full and modified chokes
Finish: Blued; case-hardened frame; checkered walnut semi-pistol grip stock and forearm
Approximate wt.: 7 to 7½ lbs.
Comments: Made from around 1912 until 1936.
Estimated Value: **Excellent:** **$400.00**
Very good: **$320.00**

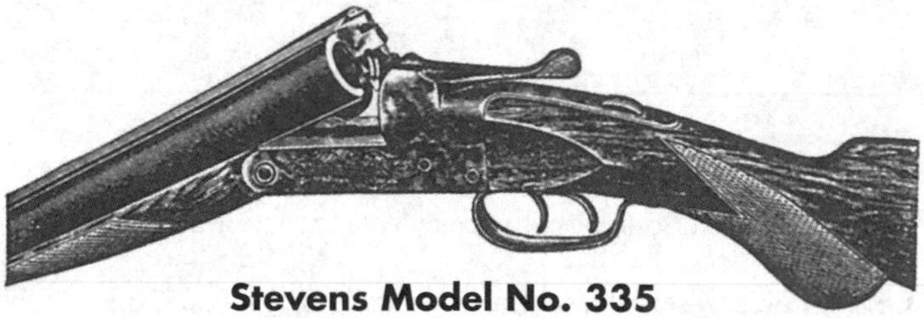

Stevens Model No. 335

Stevens Model No. 335

Similar to the Model No. 315. Made from around 1912 to 1930.
Estimated Value: **Excellent:** **$400.00**
Very good: **$320.00**

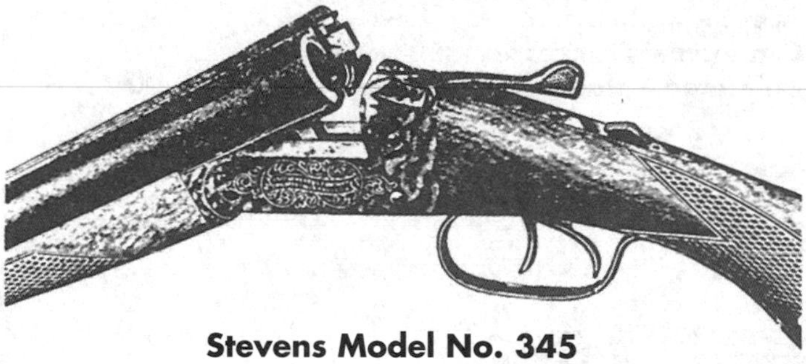

Stevens Model No. 345

Stevens Model No. 345

Similar to Model No. 335 in 20 gauge. Made from around 1912 to 1926.
Estimated Value: **Excellent:** **$400.00**
Very good: **$320.00**

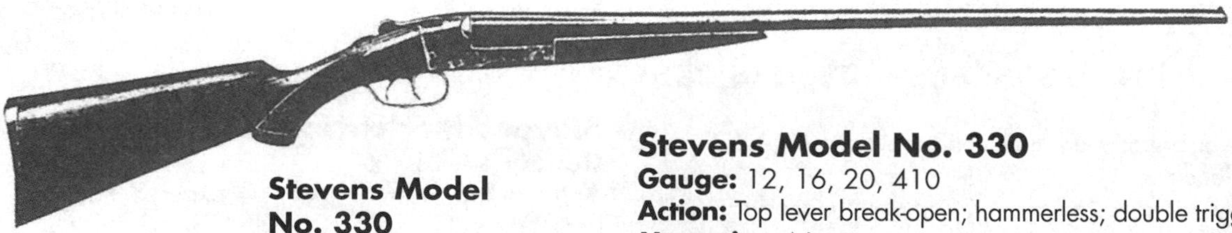

Stevens Model No. 330

Stevens Model No. 330

Gauge: 12, 16, 20, 410
Action: Top lever break-open; hammerless; double trigger; takedown
Magazine: None
Barrel: Side-by-side double barrel; 26" – 32"; right modified, left full choke; both full choke in 410
Finish: Blued; case-hardened frame; checkered black walnut pistol grip stock and forearm
Approximate wt.: 5¾ to 7¾ lbs.
Comments: Made from the mid-1920s until the mid-1930s.
Estimated Value: **Excellent:** **$375.00**
Very good: **$300.00**

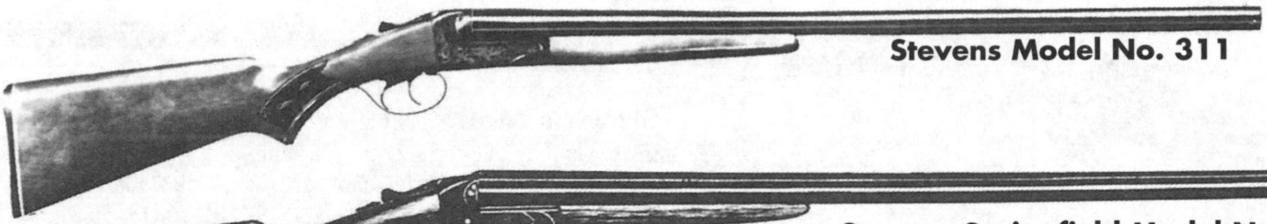

Stevens Model No. 311

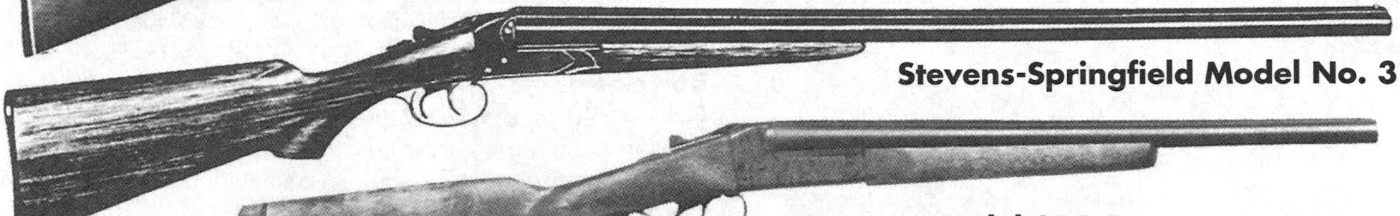

Stevens-Springfield Model No. 315

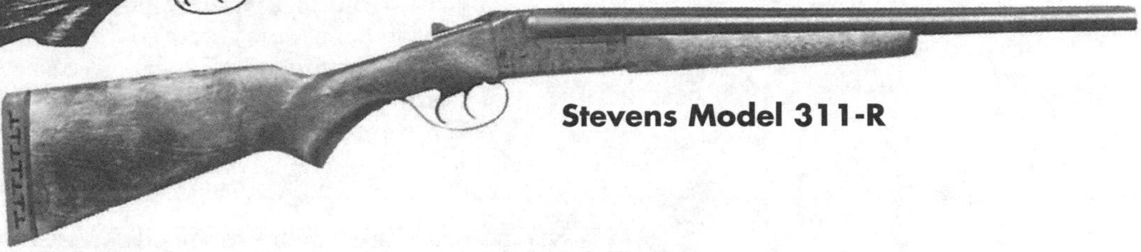

Stevens Model 311-R

Stevens Model No. 311 and Stevens-Springfield Model No. 311, Springfield Hammerless

Gauge: 12, 16, 20, 410
Action: Top lever break-open; hammerless; double trigger; takedown
Magazine: None
Barrel: Side-by-side double barrel; 24" – 32"; modified and full chokes; both full choke in 32" 12 gauge; matted rib
Finish: Blued; case-hardened frame; smooth walnut semi-pistol grip stock and forearm
Approximate wt.: 5½ to 7¾ lbs.
Comments: Made from about 1931 to the late 1980s. Add $30.00 for selective single trigger. 16 gauge discontinued in the late 1970s. See Savage Model No. 311.

Estimated Value:	**Excellent:**	**$400.00**
	Very good:	**$320.00**

Stevens-Springfield Model No. 315

A higher quality version of the Model 311.

Estimated Value:	**Excellent:**	**$450.00**
	Very good:	**$360.00**

Stevens Model 311-R

A law enforcement version of the Model 311 with 18¼" cylinder bore barrel; recoil pad; 12 gauge only. Produced from 1982 to 1988. See Savage Model 311-R.

Estimated Value:	**Excellent:**	**$300.00**
	Very good:	**$240.00**

Stevens Model No. 530

Gauge: 12, 16, 20, 410
Action: Top lever break-open; hammerless; box lock; double trigger
Magazine: None
Barrel: Side-by-side double barrel; 26" – 32"; modified choke and full chokes; both full choke in 32" 12 gauge and 410.
Finish: Blued; case-hardened frame; checkered walnut pistol grip stock and forearm
Approximate wt.: 6 to 7½ lbs.
Comments: Made from about 1935 to 1952.

Estimated Value:	**Excellent:**	**$400.00**
	Very good:	**$320.00**

Stevens Model No. 530ST

Same as the Model No. 530 with non-selective single trigger.

Estimated Value:	**Excellent:**	**$375.00**
	Very good:	**$300.00**

Stevens Model No. 530M

Same as the Model No. 530 except: plastic stock. Discontinued in the late 1940s.

Estimated Value:	**Excellent:**	**$375.00**
	Very good:	**$300.00**

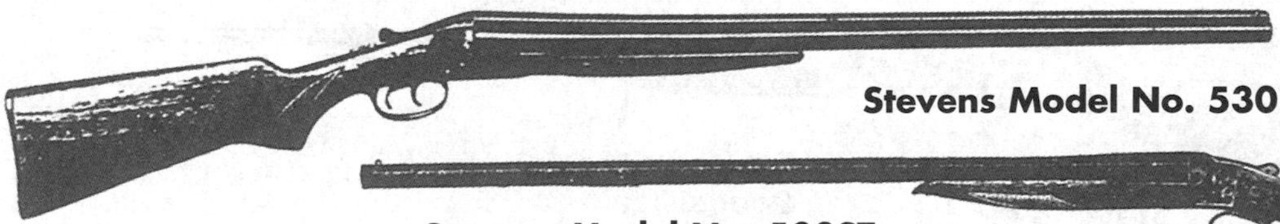

Stevens Model No. 530

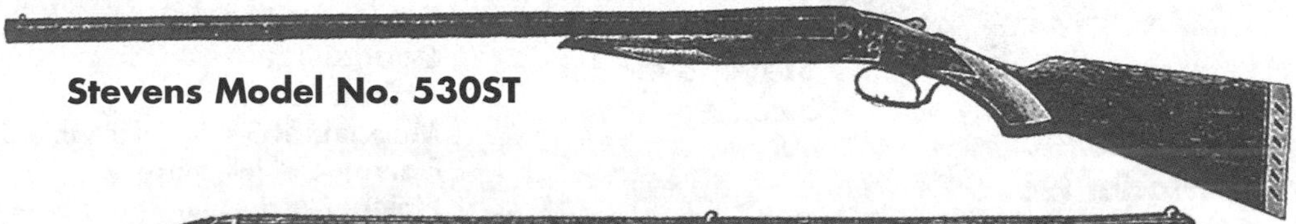

Stevens Model No. 530ST

Stevens Model No. 530M

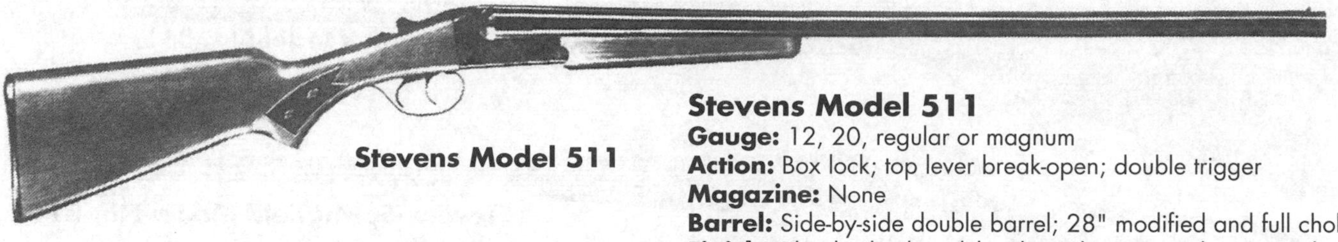

Stevens Model 511

Stevens Model 511

Gauge: 12, 20, regular or magnum
Action: Box lock; top lever break-open; double trigger
Magazine: None
Barrel: Side-by-side double barrel; 28" modified and full choke
Finish: Blued; checkered hardwood semi-pistol grip stock and small forearm; case-hardened frame
Approximate wt.: 7¾ lbs.
Comments: Produced in the late 1970s.

Estimated Value:	**Excellent:**	**$400.00**
	Very good:	**$320.00**

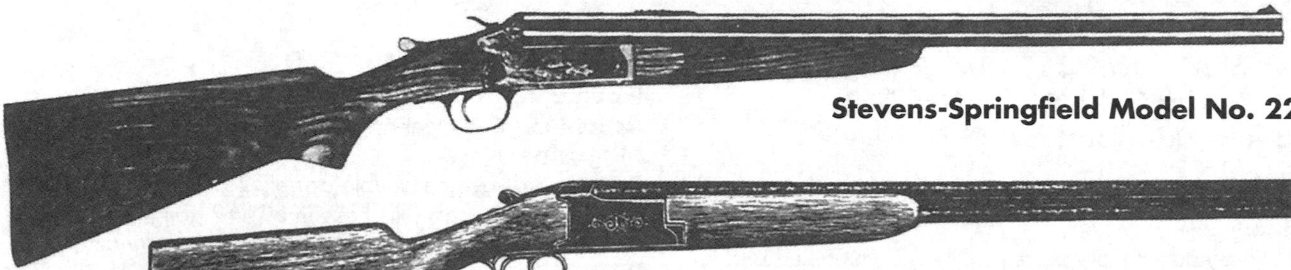

Stevens-Springfield Model No. 22-410

Stevens Model No. 240

Stevens Model No. 240

Gauge: 410
Action: Top lever break-open; hammerless; double trigger; takedown
Magazine: None
Barrel: 26" over and under double barrel; both barrels full choke
Finish: Blued; checkered plastic or wood pistol grip stock and forearm
Approximate wt.: 6½ lbs.
Comments: Made from about 1940 to 1948.

Estimated Value:	**Excellent:**	**$400.00**
	Very good:	**$320.00**

Stevens-Springfield Model No. 22-410

Gauge: 410 and 22 caliber rifle
Action: Top lever break-open; exposed hammer; single trigger; separate extractors
Magazine: None
Barrel: 24" over and under double barrel; 22 rifle over 410 shotgun
Finish: Blued; case-hardened frame; plastic semi-pistol grip stock and forearm; open rear, ramp front sights
Approximate wt.: 6 lbs.
Comments: Made from about 1940 to 1948. Later produced as Savage.

Estimated Value:	**Excellent:**	**$250.00**
	Very good:	**$200.00**

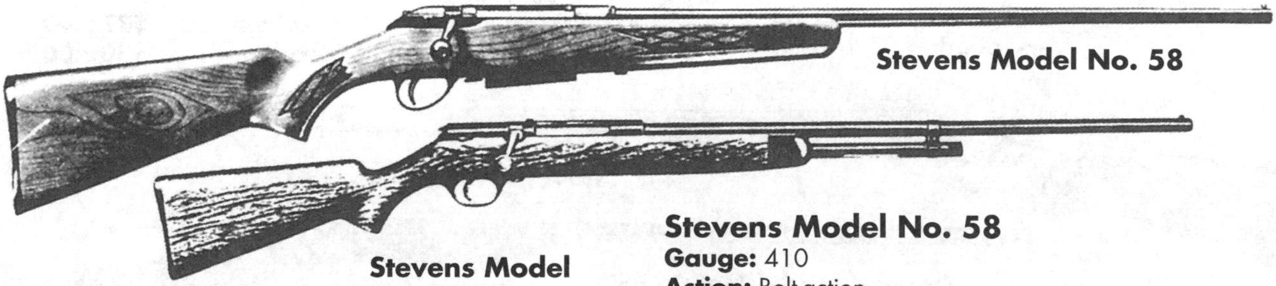

Stevens Model No. 58

Stevens Model No. 59

Stevens Model No. 59

Similar to Model No. 58 except: 5-shot tubular magazine. Made from about 1939 to the early 1970s.

Estimated Value:	**Excellent:**	**$140.00**
	Very good:	**$115.00**

Stevens Model No. 58

Gauge: 410
Action: Bolt-action
Magazine: 3-shot detachable box
Barrel: 24" full choke
Finish: Blued; plain walnut one-piece pistol grip stock and forearm
Approximate wt.: 5½ lbs.
Comments: Made from about 1935 to the late 1970s. Later versions have checkering.

Estimated Value:	**Excellent:**	**$135.00**
	Very good:	**$110.00**

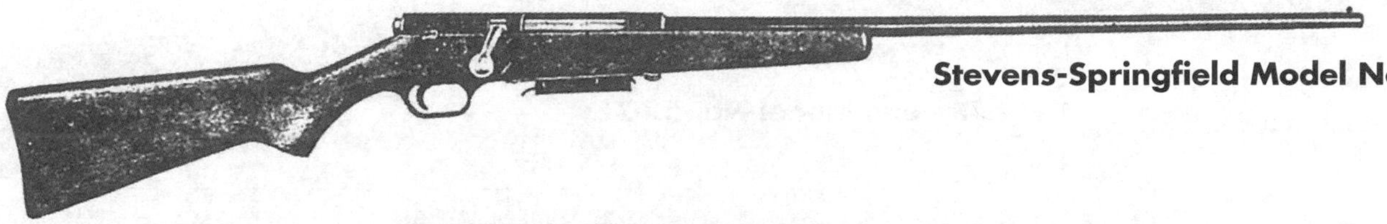

Stevens-Springfield Model No. 38

Stevens-Springfield Model No. 39

Stevens-Springfield Model No. 38

Similar to Stevens Model No. 58. Made from 1939 to 1947.

Estimated Value: **Excellent:** **$110.00**
Very good: **$ 90.00**

Stevens-Springfield Model No. 39

Similar to Stevens Model No. 59. Made from 1939 to 1947.

Estimated Value: **Excellent:** **$125.00**
Very good: **$100.00**

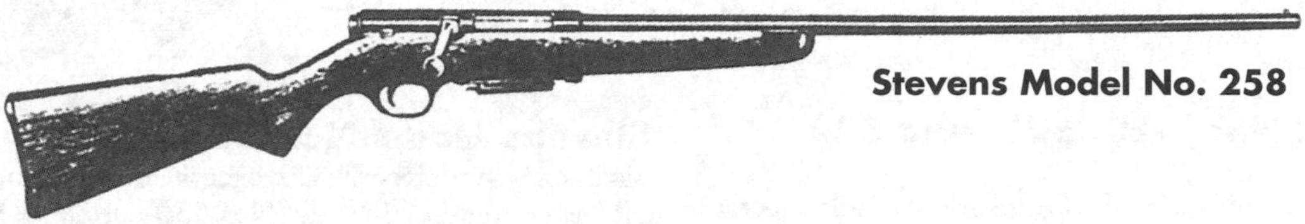

Stevens Model No. 258

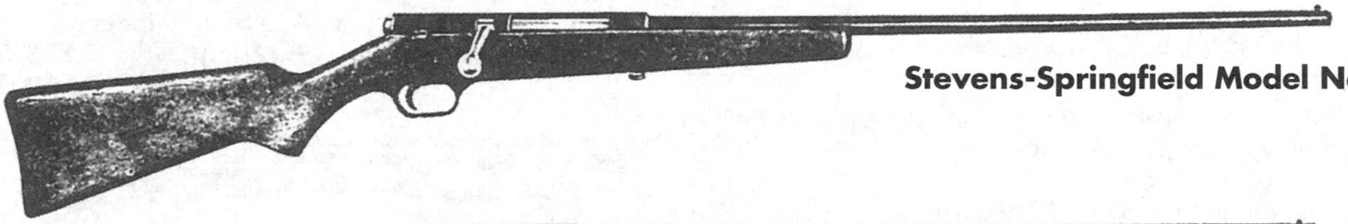

Stevens-Springfield Model No. 37

Stevens Model No. 124

Stevens Model No. 258

Gauge: 20
Action: Bolt action; repeating
Magazine: 2-shot detachable box
Barrel: 26" full choke
Finish: Blued; plain walnut one-piece pistol grip stock and forearm
Approximate wt.: 6¼ lbs.
Comments: This takedown shotgun was produced from 1939 until 1942.
Estimated Value: **Excellent:** **$125.00**
Very good: **$100.00**

Stevens Model No. 254

A single-shot version of the Model 258.

Estimated Value: **Excellent:** **$95.00**
Very good: **$75.00**

Stevens-Springfield Model No. 238

Similar to Stevens Model No. 258. Made from 1939 to 1947.

Estimated Value: **Excellent:** **$100.00**
Very good: **$ 80.00**

Stevens-Springfield Model No. 237

Similar to Stevens Model No. 254. Single-shot. Made from 1939 to 1942.

Estimated Value: **Excellent:** **$100.00**
Very good: **$ 80.00**

Stevens-Springfield Model No. 37

Similar to Stevens-Springfield Model No. 237 except 410 bore. Made from 1939 to 1942.

Estimated Value: **Excellent:** **$125.00**
Very good: **$100.00**

Stevens Model No. 124

Gauge: 12
Action: Bolt action repeating; cross bolt is pulled out and back to open, pushed forward and in to close; opening stroke of bolt ejects fired shell
Magazine: 2-shot
Barrel: 28" improved cylinder, modified or full choke
Finish: Blued; checkered plastic pistol grip stock and forearm
Approximate wt.: 7 lbs.
Comments: Made from about 1950 to 1956. Has the appearance of a semiautomatic but is a bolt action repeater.
Estimated Value: **Excellent:** **$200.00**
Very good: **$160.00**

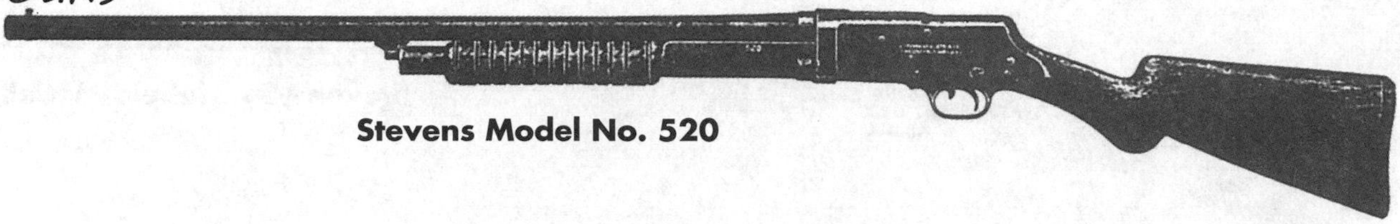

Stevens Model No. 520

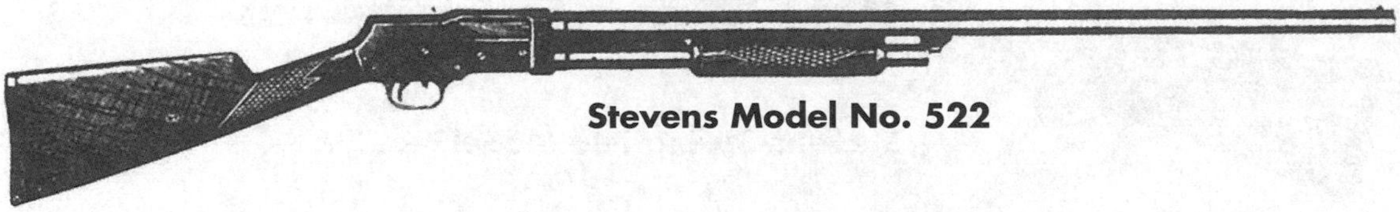

Stevens Model No. 522

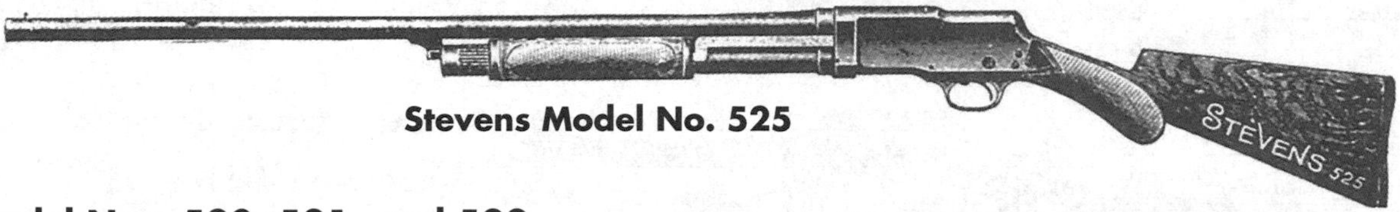

Stevens Model No. 525

Stevens Model Nos. 520, 521, and 522

Gauge: 12
Action: Browning patent; slide action; takedown; side ejector; hammerless
Magazine: 5-shot tubular
Barrel: 26" – 32"; full choke, modified or cylinder; matted rib on Model No. 521
Finish: Blued; walnut pistol grip stock and grooved slide handle; checkered straight grip and slide handle on Model No. 522
Approximate wt.: 8 lbs.
Comments: Made from about 1907 until World War II; Model No. 522 discontinued in 1928.

Estimated Value:	**Excellent:**	**$175.00**
	Very good:	**$140.00**

Stevens Model Nos. 525, 530, and 535

Similar to Model No. 520 except fancier grades; Model No. 525 is custom built; Model No. 530 custom built with engraved receiver and rib; Model No. 535 custom built, heavily engraved. Made from 1912 to 1918. Add $75.00 for engraving.

Estimated Value:	**Excellent:**	**$225.00**
	Very good:	**$180.00**

Stevens Model No. 535

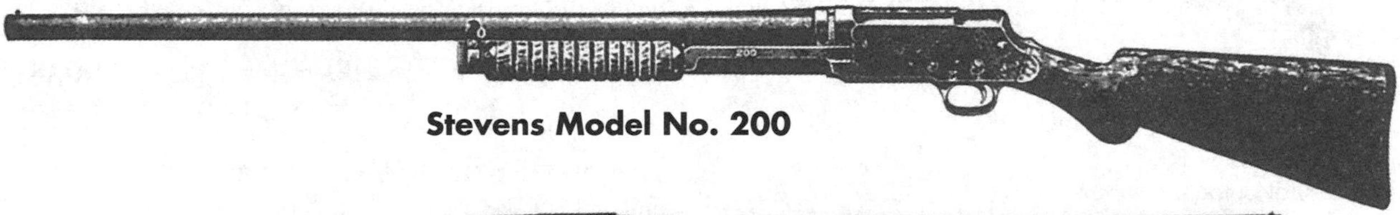

Stevens Model No. 200

Stevens Model No. 620

Stevens Model No. 200

Gauge: 20
Action: Pedersen patent slide action; hammerless; side ejector; takedown
Magazine: 5-shot tubular
Barrel: 26" – 32"; full choke, modified or cylinder bore
Finish: Blued; walnut pistol grip stock and grooved slide handle
Approximate wt.: 6½ lbs.
Comments: Made from about 1912 to 1918.

Estimated Value:	**Excellent:**	**$220.00**
	Very good:	**$175.00**

Stevens Model No. 620

Gauge: 12, 16, 20
Action: Slide action; hammerless; side ejector
Magazine: 5-shot tubular
Barrel: 26" – 32"; full choke, modified or cylinder bore
Finish: Blued; checkered walnut pistol grip stock and slide handle
Approximate wt.: 6 to 7¾ lbs.
Comments: A takedown shotgun made from about 1932 to 1958.

Estimated Value:	**Excellent:**	**$275.00**
	Very good:	**$220.00**

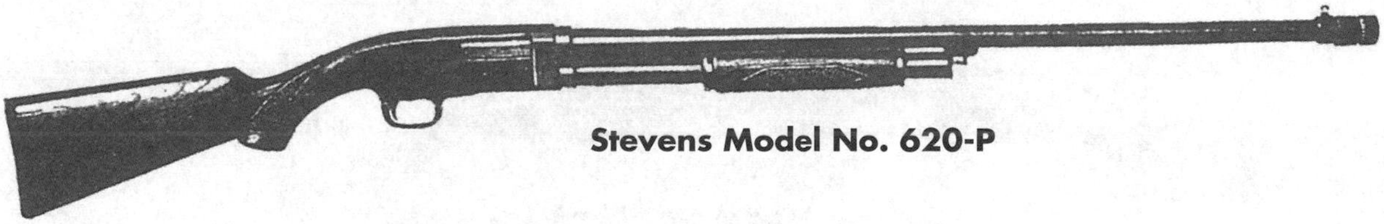

Stevens Model No. 620-P

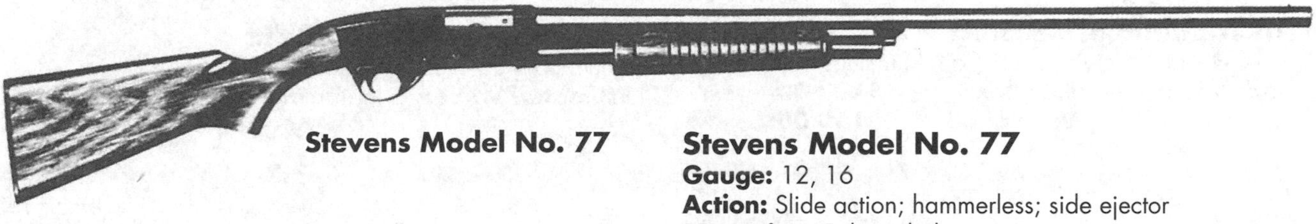

Stevens Model No. 77

Stevens Model No. 620-P

Same as Model No. 620 with "Poly-Choke."

Estimated Value: **Excellent:** **$280.00**
Very good: **$225.00**

Stevens Model No. 621

Same as Model No. 620 with matted rib. Made from 1932 to 1937.

Estimated Value: **Excellent:** **$285.00**
Very good: **$225.00**

Stevens Model No. 77

Gauge: 12, 16
Action: Slide action; hammerless; side ejector
Magazine: 5-shot tubular
Barrel: 26" or 28" improved cylinder, modified or full choke
Finish: Blued; plain walnut pistol grip stock and grooved slide handle
Approximate wt.: 7 lbs.
Comments: Made from the mid-1950s to the early 1970s.
Estimated Value: **Excellent:** **$175.00**
Very good: **$140.00**

Stevens Model No. 77-SC

Same as Model No. 77 with Savage "Super Choke" and recoil pad.

Estimated Value: **Excellent:** **$180.00**
Very good: **$140.00**

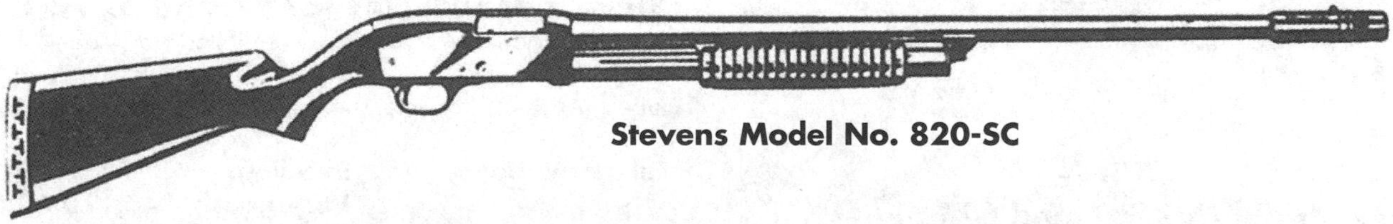

Stevens Model No. 820-SC

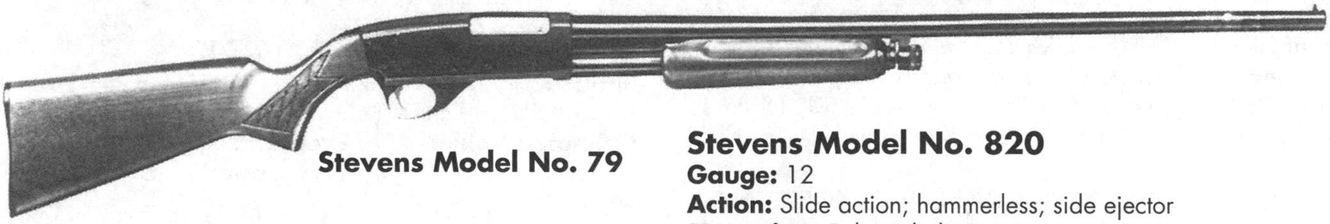

Stevens Model No. 79

Stevens Model No. 79

Gauge: 12, 20, 410, regular or magnum
Action: Slide action; hammerless; side ejector, repeating
Magazine: 4-shot tubular; 3-shot in magnum
Barrel: 28" modified or 30" full in 12 gauge; 28" modified or full in 20 gauge; 26" full in 410
Finish: Blued; checkered hardwood semi-pistol grip stock and fluted slide handle
Approximate wt.: 7 lbs.
Comments: Produced in the late 1970s.
Estimated Value: **Excellent:** **$185.00**
Very good: **$145.00**

Stevens Model No. 820

Gauge: 12
Action: Slide action; hammerless; side ejector
Magazine: 5-shot tubular
Barrel: 28" improved cylinder, modified or full choke
Finish: Blued; plain walnut semi-pistol grip stock and grooved slide handle
Approximate wt.: 7½ lbs.
Comments: Produced from about 1950 to 1956.
Estimated Value: **Excellent:** **$225.00**
Very good: **$175.00**

Stevens Model No. 820-SC

Same as Model No. 820 with Savage "Super Choke."

Estimated Value: **Excellent:** **$235.00**
Very good: **$185.00**

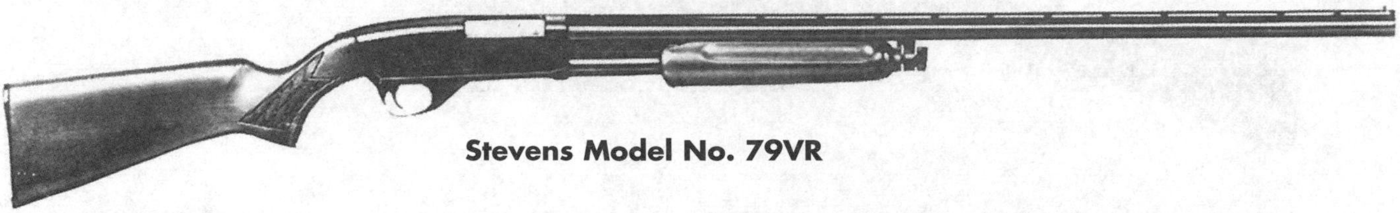

Stevens Model No. 79VR

Stevens Model No. 79 Slug

Similar to Model No. 79 with a 21" barrel for slugs; rifle sights.

Estimated Value: **Excellent:** **$190.00**
Very good: **$150.00**

Stevens Model No. 79VR

Similar to Model No. 79 with a ventilated rib.

Estimated Value: **Excellent:** **$200.00**
Very good: **$160.00**

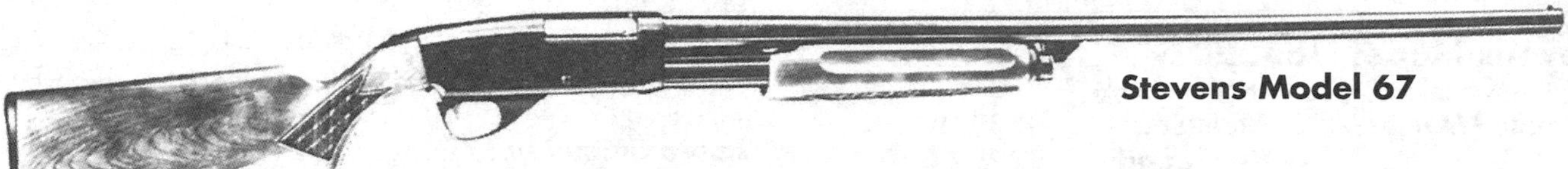

Stevens Model 67

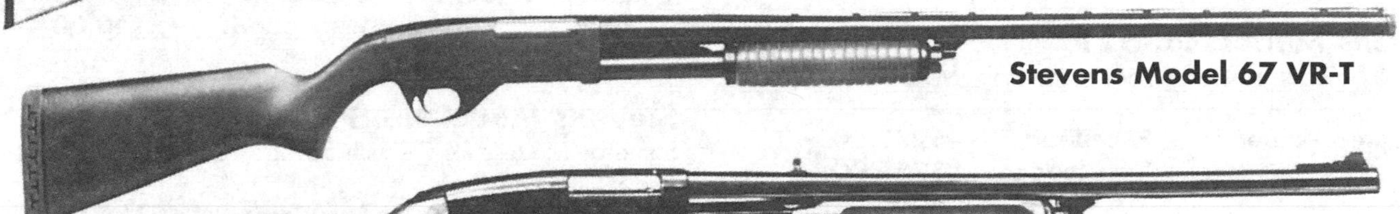

Stevens Model 67 VR-T

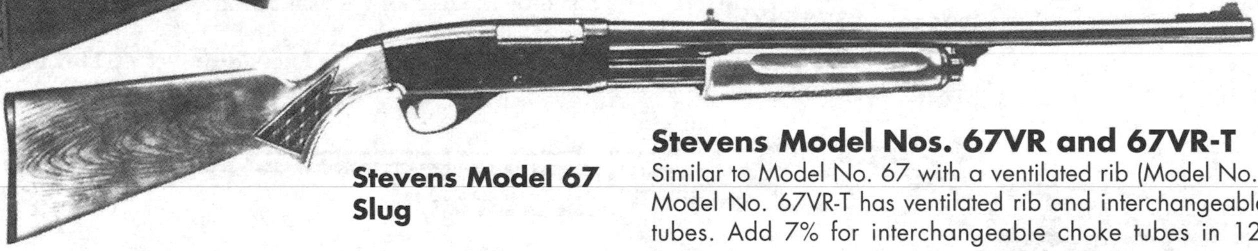

Stevens Model 67 Slug

Stevens Model Nos. 67 and 67T

Gauge: 12, 20, or 410, regular or magnum
Action: Slide action; hammerless; side ejector; repeating
Magazine: 4-shot tubular; 3-shot in magnum
Barrel: 28" modified or full; 26" full in 410; 30" full in 12 gauge; Model No. 67T has interchangeable choke tubes in 12 and 20 gauge only
Finish: Blued; hardwood, semi-pistol grip stock and fluted or grooved slide handle; some with recoil pad
Approximate wt.: 6¾ lbs.
Comments: Produced from the late 1970s to the late 1980s. Add $16.00 for Model No. 67T.

Estimated Value: **Excellent:** **$200.00**
Very good: **$160.00**

Stevens Model No. 67 Slug

Similar to Model No. 67 with a 21" barrel for slugs and rifle sights; 12 gauge only.

Estimated Value: **Excellent:** **$210.00**
Very good: **$165.00**

Stevens Model Nos. 67VR and 67VR-T

Similar to Model No. 67 with a ventilated rib (Model No. 67VR). Model No. 67VR-T has ventilated rib and interchangeable choke tubes. Add 7% for interchangeable choke tubes in 12 or 20 gauge.

Estimated Value: **Excellent:** **$210.00**
Very good: **$170.00**

Stevens Model Nos. 67VRT-K

Similar to Model No. 67VRT-T except: laminated camouflage stock. Produced from 1986 to 1988.

Estimated Value: **Excellent:** **$220.00**
Very good: **$175.00**

Stevens Model Nos. 67T-Y and 67VRT-Y

Gauge: 20
Action: Slide action; hammerless; repeating
Magazine: 4-shot
Barrel: 22" with three interchangeable choke tubes; ventilated rib on Model No. 67VRT-Y
Finish: Blued; hardwood, semi-pistol grip stock and grooved slide handle
Approximate wt.: 6 lbs.
Comments: Designed for the young shooter with a shorter 12" pull stock. Deduct $16.00 for plain barrel (Model No. 67T-Y). Made from 1985 to 1988.

Estimated Value: **Excellent:** **$210.00**
Very good: **$165.00**

Universal Model 101

Universal Model 101

Gauge: 12
Action: Box lock; top lever break-open; exposed hammer; single shot
Magazine: None
Barrel: 28", 30" full choke
Finish: Blued; plain wood pistol grip stock and tapered forearm
Approximate wt.: 7½ lbs.
Comments: Manufactured in the late 1960s.

Estimated Value:	**Excellent:**	**$100.00**
	Very good:	**$ 80.00**

Universal Single Wing

Similar to the Model 101. Made from the early to the mid-1970s.

Estimated Value:	**Excellent:**	**$100.00**
	Very good:	**$ 80.00**

Universal Model 202

Universal Double Wing

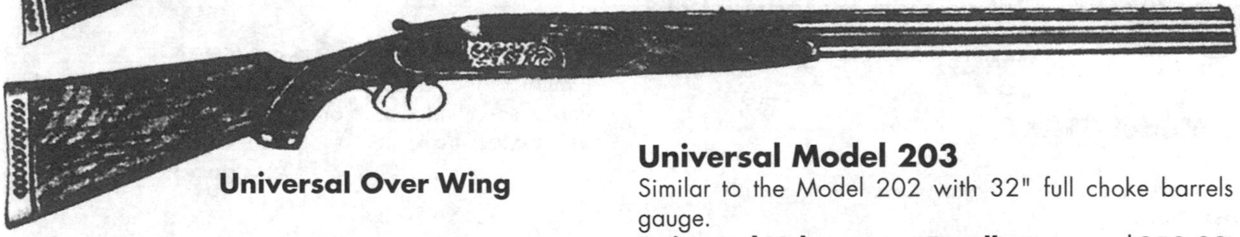

Universal Over Wing

Universal Model 202

Gauge: 12, 20, 410
Action: Box lock; top lever break-open; hammerless; double triggers
Magazine: None
Barrel: Side-by-side double barrel; 26" improved cylinder and modified; 28" modified and full chokes
Finish: Blued; checkered walnut pistol grip stock and forearm
Approximate wt.: 7 lbs.
Comments: Made in the late 1960s. Add 5% for 410.

Estimated Value:	**Excellent:**	**$250.00**
	Very good:	**$200.00**

Universal Double Wing

Similar to the Model 202 with recoil pad. Made from 1970 to 1975; 12 or 20 gauge magnum.

Estimated Value:	**Excellent:**	**$350.00**
	Very good:	**$280.00**

Universal Model 203

Similar to the Model 202 with 32" full choke barrels and 10 gauge.

Estimated Value:	**Excellent:**	**$250.00**
	Very good:	**$200.00**

Universal Model 2030

Similar to the Double Wing with 32" full choke barrels and 10 gauge.

Estimated Value:	**Excellent:**	**$350.00**
	Very good:	**$280.00**

Universal Over Wing

Gauge: 12, 20
Action: Box lock; top lever break-open; hammerless
Magazine: None
Barrel: Over and under double barrel; 26", 28", 30"; ventilated rib
Finish: Blued; checkered walnut pistol grip stock and forearm; sights; recoil pad; engraving available
Approximate wt.: 8 lbs.
Comments: Made from about 1970 to 1975. Add 10% for single trigger.

Estimated Value:	**Excellent:**	**$400.00**
	Very good:	**$320.00**

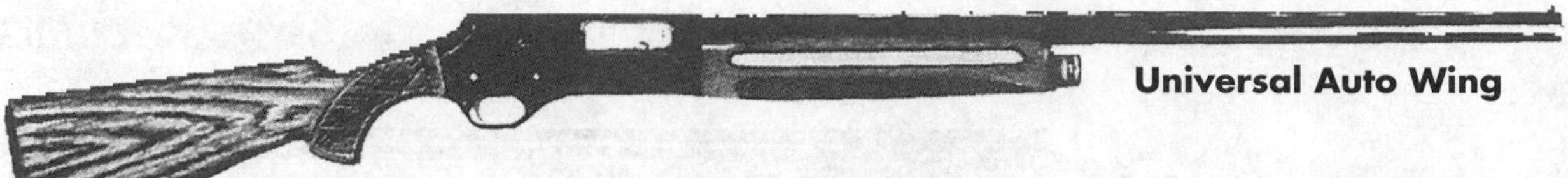

Universal Auto Wing

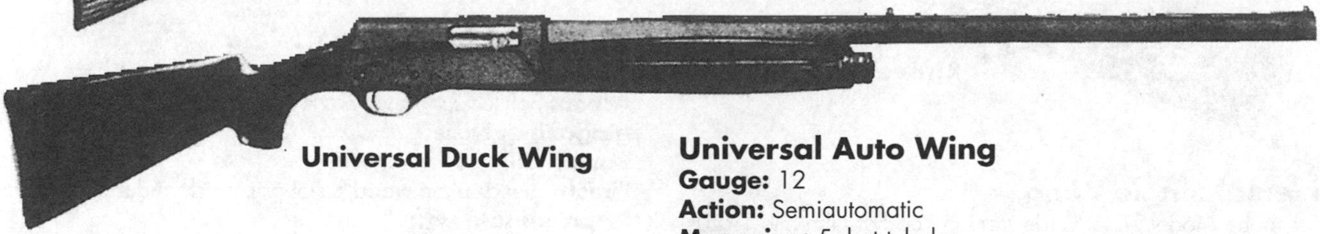

Universal Duck Wing

Universal Duck Wing

Similar to the Auto Wing with 28" or 30" full choke barrel. Teflon coated. Discontinued in the early 1970s.

Estimated Value: **Excellent:** **$225.00**
Very good: **$180.00**

Universal Auto Wing

Gauge: 12
Action: Semiautomatic
Magazine: 5-shot tubular
Barrel: 26", 28", 30"; variety of chokes; ventilated rib
Finish: Blued; checkered walnut pistol grip stock and forearm; sights
Approximate wt.: 8 lbs.
Comments: Made from about 1970 to 1975.
Estimated Value: **Excellent:** **$200.00**
Very good: **$160.00**

VALMET

Valmet Model 412KE

Valmet Model 412KE

Gauge: 12
Action: Top lever break-open; hammerless; automatic ejector
Magazine: None
Barrel: Over and under double barrel; 26" improved cylinder and modified; 28" modified and full; 30" modified and full in 12 gauge; ventilated rib
Finish: Blued; checkered walnut pistol grip stock and forearm; Monte Carlo stock with recoil pad; swivels
Approximate wt.: 7 lbs.
Comments: Made in Finland with interchangeable barrels available that make the shotgun a combination shotgun/rifle or a double rifle. Produced from the early 1980s to the mid-1980s.
Estimated Value: **Excellent:** **$700.00**
Very good: **$560.00**

Valmet Model 412K

Similar to the Model 412KE with 36" barrels. Made from the early to the late 1980s.

Estimated Value: **Excellent:** **$650.00**
Very good: **$520.00**

Valmet Model 412KE Trap

Similar to the Model 412KE except: 30" full choke barrels.

Estimated Value: **Excellent:** **$750.00**
Very good: **$600.00**

Valmet Model 412KE Skeet

Similar to the Model 412KE with 26" or 28" cylinder bore and improved cylinder bore or skeet choke barrels.

Estimated Value: **Excellent:** **$800.00**
Very good: **$640.00**

Valmet Model 412K Combination

Similar to the Model 412K with a 12 gauge improved modified barrel over a rifle barrel in caliber 222, 223, 243, 30-06, 308; 24" barrels. Introduced in 1982.

Estimated Value: **Excellent:** **$1,000.00**
Very good: **$ 800.00**

Valmet 12 Gauge

Gauge: 12
Action: Box lock; top lever break-open; single selective trigger
Magazine: None
Barrel: Over and under double barrel; 26" improved cylinder and modified; 28" modified and full; 30" modified and full or full and full chokes
Finish: Blued; checkered walnut pistol grip stock and wide forearm
Approximate wt.: 8 lbs.
Comments: Made from the late 1940s to the late 1960s in Finland.
Estimated Value: **Excellent:** **$500.00**
Very good: **$400.00**

Valmet Model 412S

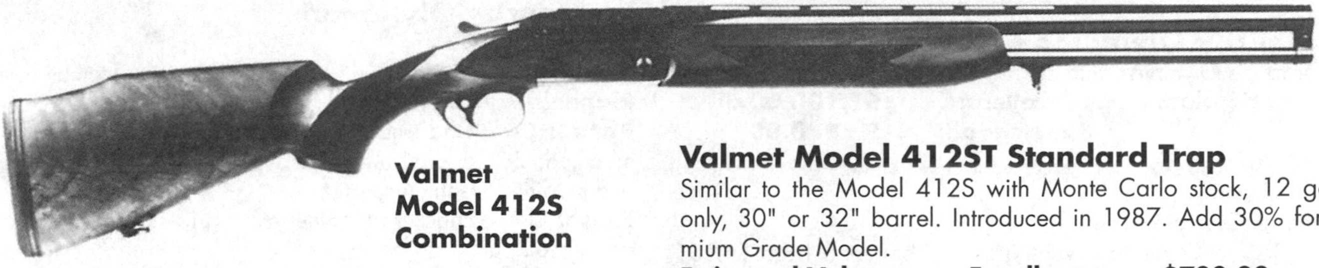

Valmet Model 412S Combination

Valmet Model 412S

Gauge: 12, 20; regular or magnum
Action: Top lever break-open; hammerless; automatic ejectors
Magazine: None
Barrel: Over and under double barrel; 26" cylinder bore and improved cylinder, improved cylinder or modified; 28" cylinder bore and modified or modified and full; 30" improved modified and full, modified and full; 36" full; ventilated rib
Finish: Blued; checkered walnut pistol grip stock and forearm, adjustable for barrel differences; butt plate adjusts to fit shooter
Approximate wt.: 7 lbs.
Comments: A shooting system with interchangeable barrels and adjustable butt plate; produced in Finland. Introduced in 1984.

Estimated Value:	**Excellent:**	**$800.00**
	Very good:	**$640.00**

Valmet Model 412ST Standard Trap

Similar to the Model 412S with Monte Carlo stock, 12 gauge only, 30" or 32" barrel. Introduced in 1987. Add 30% for Premium Grade Model.

Estimated Value:	**Excellent:**	**$700.00**
	Very good:	**$560.00**

Valmet Model 412ST Standard Skeet

Similar to the Model 412S with 28" skeet choke barrel. Introduced in 1987. Add 30% for Premium Grade Model.

Estimated Value:	**Excellent:**	**$725.00**
	Very good:	**$580.00**

Valmet Model 412S Combination

Similar to the Model 412S with 24" 12 gauge improved/modified barrel over a 222, 223, 243, 30-06, or 308 caliber rifle barrel.

Estimated Value:	**Excellent:**	**$850.00**
	Very good:	**$680.00**

WEATHERBY

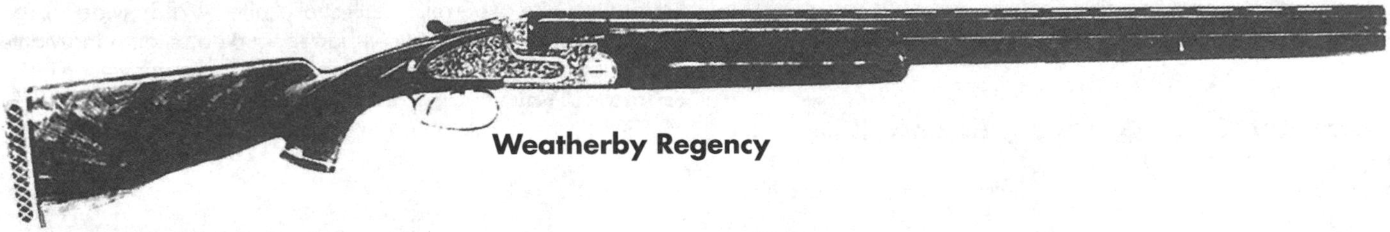

Weatherby Regency

Weatherby Regency Skeet

Similar to the Regency in skeet chokes with a 26" or 28" barrel.

Estimated Value:	**Excellent:**	**$1,500.00**
	Very good:	**$1,200.00**

Weatherby Regency Trap

Similar to the Regency with a wide ventilated rib barrel; 30" or 32" full and full, full and improved modified, or full and modified chokes; choice of regular or Monte Carlo stock; 12 gauge only.

Estimated Value:	**Excellent:**	**$1,500.00**
	Very good:	**$1,200.00**

Weatherby Regency

Gauge: 12, 20
Action: Box lock; top lever break-open; hammerless; automatic ejectors; single selective trigger
Magazine: None
Barrel: Over and under double barrel; 26", 28", 30"; variety of chokes; ventilated rib
Finish: Blued; checkered walnut pistol grip stock and fluted forearm; recoil pad
Approximate wt.: 7 to 7½ lbs.
Comments: Made from the early 1970s to the early 1980s.

Estimated Value:	**Excellent:**	**$1,200.00**
	Very good:	**$ 960.00**

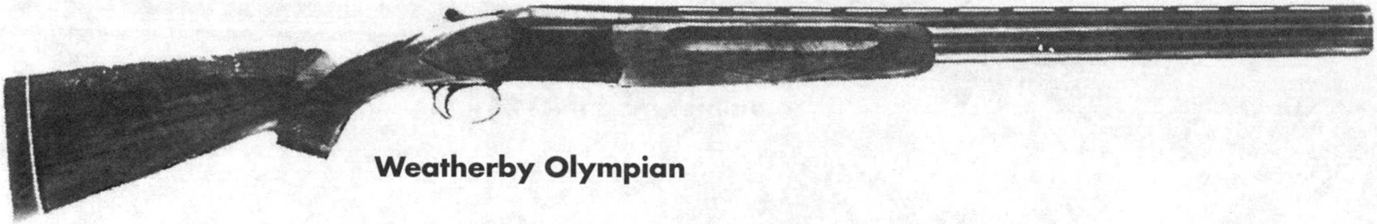

Weatherby Olympian

Weatherby Olympian

Gauge: 12, 20
Action: Box lock; top lever break-open; selective automatic ejectors
Magazine: None
Barrel: Over and under double barrel; 26" or 28" full and modified; 26" or 28" modified and improved cylinder; 30" full and modified; ventilated rib
Finish: Blued; checkered walnut pistol grip stock and fluted forearm; recoil pad
Approximate wt.: 7 to 8 lbs.
Comments: Made from the 1970s to the early 1980s.

Estimated Value:	**Excellent:**	**$1,000.00**
	Very good:	**$ 800.00**

Weatherby Olympian Skeet

Similar to the Olympian with 26" or 28" skeet choke barrel.

Estimated Value:	**Excellent:**	**$1,100.00**
	Very good:	**$ 880.00**

Weatherby Olympian Trap

Similar to the Olympian; ventilated rib between barrels; 30" or 32" full and modified or full and improved modified chokes; Monte Carlo or regular stock.

Estimated Value:	**Excellent:**	**$1,100.00**
	Very good:	**$ 880.00**

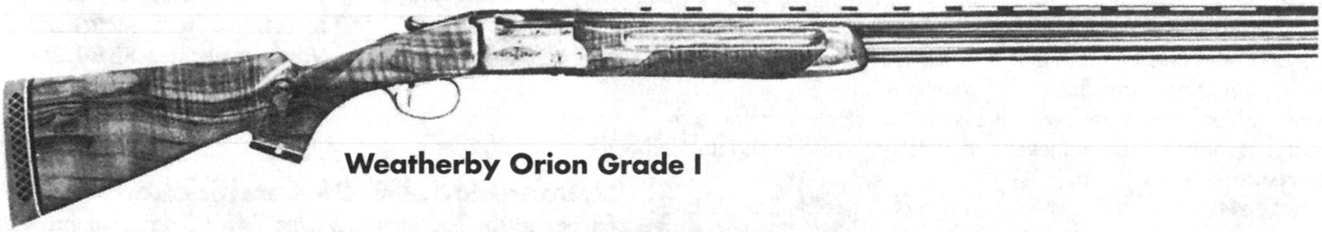

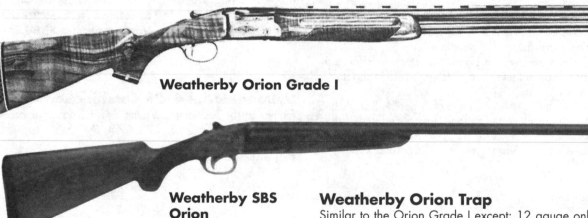

Weatherby Orion Grade I

Weatherby SBS Orion

Weatherby Orion Grades I, II, and III

Gauge: 12, 20, 28, 410
Action: Box lock; top lever break-open; selective automatic ejectors; single selective trigger
Magazine: None
Barrel: Over and under double barrel; 26" or 28" modified and improved cylinder; 28" or 30" full and modified; ventilated rib. Multi-choke after 1983.
Finish: Blued; checkered walnut pistol grip stock and fluted forearm; recoil pad; engraved receiver; rounded pistol grip available on Grade II (classic) or Grade III (classic). Straight stock was available on Grade III English, for a short time.
Approximate wt.: 6½ to 7½ lbs.
Comments: Introduced in 1982. 28 gauge and 410 added in 1988 and discontinued in the mid-1990s. Grade I discontinued 2005; add 20% for Grade III; add 59% for Sporting Clays.

Estimated Value:	**Excellent:**	**$1,275.00**
	Very good:	**$1,020.00**

Weatherby Orion Trap

Similar to the Orion Grade I except: 12 gauge only; 30" or 32" full and modified barrels; multi-choke after 1983; wide rib on top and ventilated rib between barrels; curved recoil pad; Monte Carlo or regular stock. Made in the 1980s to the early 1990s.

Estimated Value:	**Excellent:**	**$1,025.00**
	Very good:	**$ 820.00**

Weatherby Orion Skeet

Similar to the Orion Grade I except: 26" skeet choke barrels or multi-choke after 1983; 12 or 20 gauge.

Estimated Value:	**Excellent:**	**$980.00**
	Very good:	**$785.00**

Weatherby SBS Orion

Similar to the Orion except: side-by-side 26", 28", or 30" double barrel; 410, 28, 20, and 12 gauge; Turkish walnut, rounded pistol grip stock and semi-beavertail forearm.

Estimated Value:	**Excellent:**	**$900.00**
	Very good:	**$725.00**

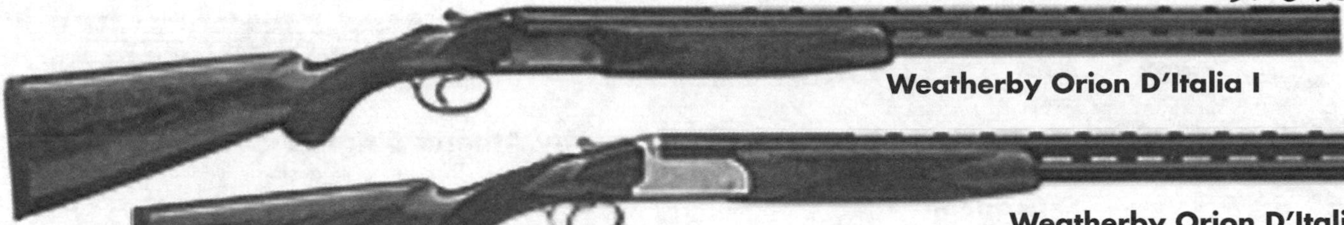

Weatherby Orion D'Italia I

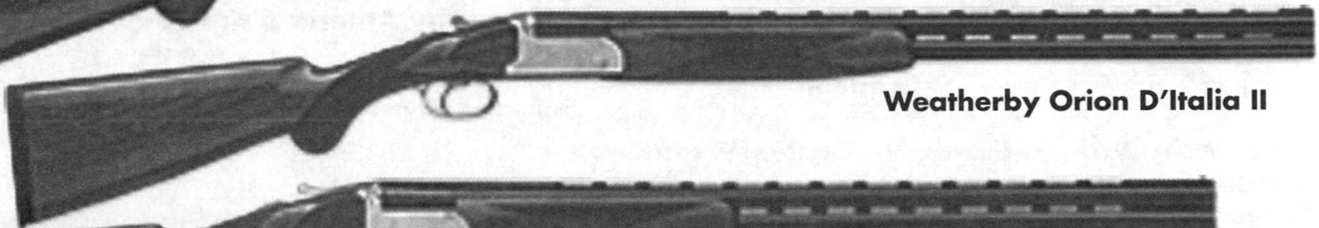

Weatherby Orion D'Italia II

Weatherby Orion D'Italia III

Weatherby Orion D'Italia I

Gauge: 12 or 20, 3" chambers
Action: Over and under double barrel
Magazine: None
Barrel: 26" or 28", ventilated rib above and between barrels, variety of chokes
Finish: Blued, high gloss checkered walnut pistol grip stock and forearm; engraved receiver with gold fill
Approximate wt.: 7 to 8 lbs.
Comments: A high-quality, lightweight hunting rifle.

Estimated Value:	**New (retail):**	**$1,699.00**
	Excellent:	**$1,275.00**
	Very good:	**$1,020.00**

Weatherby Orion D'Italia II

Similar to the Orion D'Italia I with rounded pistol grip, improved finish, and more extensive engraving.

Estimated Value:	**New (retail):**	**$1,899.00**
	Excellent:	**$1,425.00**
	Very good:	**$1,140.00**

Weatherby Orion D'Italia III

Similar to the Orion D'Italia II with hand-selected, oil-finished walnut stock, deluxe checkering, extensive engraving, and gold-plated game scene overlay.

Estimated Value:	**New (retail):**	**$2,199.00**
	Excellent:	**$1,650.00**
	Very good:	**$1,320.00**

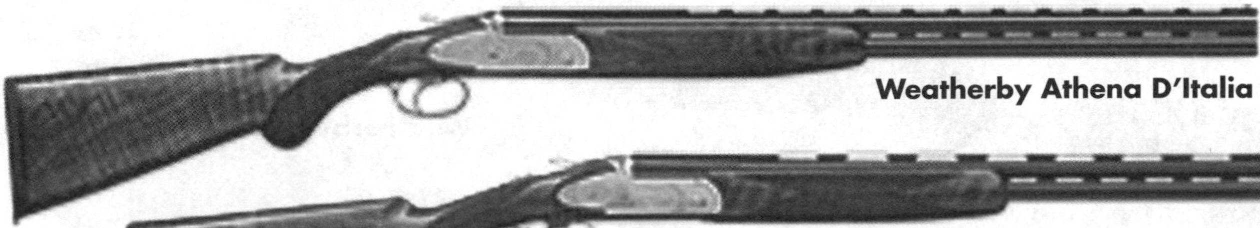

Weatherby Athena D'Italia III

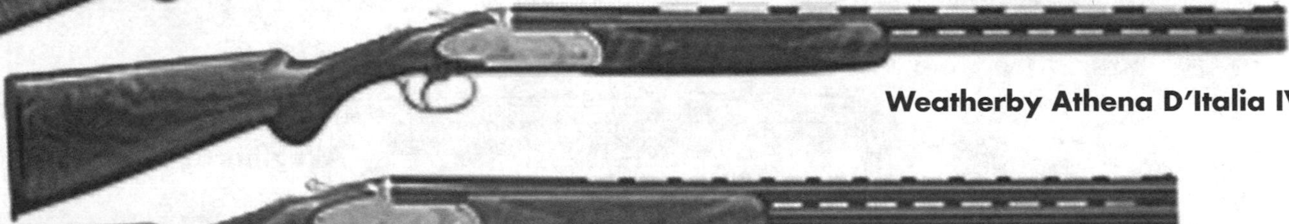

Weatherby Athena D'Italia IV

Weatherby Athena D'Italia V

Weatherby Athena D'Italia III

Gauge: 12 or 20, 3" chambers
Action: Over and under double barrel
Magazine: None
Barrel: 26" or 28" ventilated rib above and between barrels, variety of chokes
Finish: Blued, high gloss checkered deluxe walnut pistol grip stock and forearm; chrome-plated false side plates with a game bird scene in gold plate overlay
Approximately wt.: 6½ to 8 lbs.
Comments: A high-quality, lightweight hunting rifle.

Estimated Value:	**New (retail):**	**$2,599.00**
	Excellent:	**$1,950.00**
	Very good:	**$1,560.00**

Weatherby Athena D'Italia IV

Similar to the Athena D'Italia III with higher quality walnut and finish.

Estimated Value:	**New (retail):**	**$2,799.00**
	Excellent:	**$2,100.00**
	Very good:	**$1,680.00**

Weatherby Athena D'Italia V

Similar to the Athena D'Italia IV with top-of-the-line oil finished walnut stock and forearm, more intricate rose and scroll engraving.

Estimated Value:	**New (retail):**	**$3,999.00**
	Excellent:	**$3,000.00**
	Very good:	**$2,400.00**

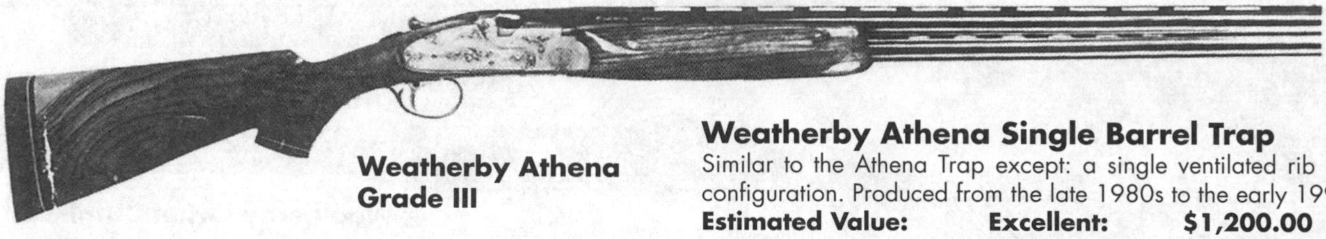

Weatherby Athena Grade III

Weatherby Athena Grade III, Grade IV, and Grade V

Gauge: 12, 20, 28, 410
Action: Box lock; top lever break-open; selective automatic ejectors; single selective trigger
Magazine: None
Barrel: Over and under double barrel; 26" or 28" modified and improved cylinder; 28" modified and full choke; ventilated rib on top and between barrels. Multi-choke after 1983.
Finish: Blued; special selected checkered walnut pistol grip stock and fluted forearm; high-luster finish; rosewood grip cap; recoil pad; silver-gray engraved receiver; rounded pistol grip available on Grade V Classic.
Approximate wt.: 7 to 8 lbs.
Comments: A high-quality superposed shotgun introduced in 1982. 28 gauge and 410 added in 1988 and discontinued in the mid-1990s. Add 10% for Grade V.
Estimated Value: **Excellent:** **$1,725.00**
Very good: **$1,375.00**

Weatherby Athena Single Barrel Trap

Similar to the Athena Trap except: a single ventilated rib barrel configuration. Produced from the late 1980s to the early 1990s.
Estimated Value: **Excellent:** **$1,200.00**
Very good: **$ 960.00**

Weatherby Athena Trap

Similar to the Athena in 12 gauge only in 30" or 32" full and improved modified or full and modified barrels; wide rib with center bead sight; curved recoil pad; Monte Carlo stock. Multi-choke after 1983.
Estimated Value: **Excellent:** **$1,200.00**
Very good: **$ 960.00**

Weatherby Athena Skeet

Similar to the Athena with 26" skeet choke barrels.
Estimated Value: **Excellent:** **$1,200.00**
Very good: **$ 960.00**

Weatherby SBS Athena

Similar to the Athena except: side-by-side 26", 28", or 30" double barrel. Turkish walnut stock and forearm.
Estimated Value: **Excellent:** **$1,200.00**
Very good: **$ 960.00**

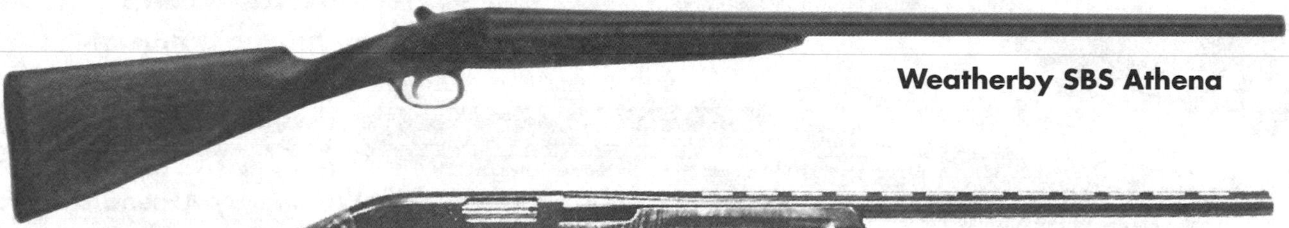

Weatherby SBS Athena

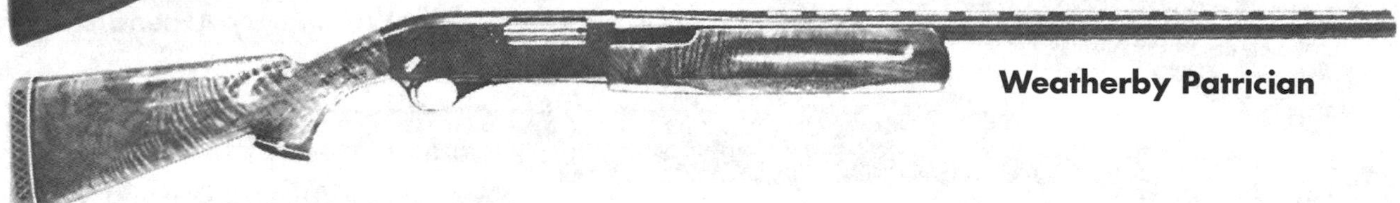

Weatherby Patrician

Weatherby Patrician Deluxe

Weatherby Patrician and Patrician II

Gauge: 12 reg. (Patrician); 12 magnum (Patrician II)
Action: Slide action; hammerless; side ejector
Magazine: Tubular
Barrel: 26", 28", 30"; variety of chokes; ventilated rib
Finish: Blued; checkered walnut pistol grip stock and grooved slide handle; recoil pad
Approximate wt.: 7½ lbs.
Comments: Made from the early 1970s to the early 1980s. Add 7% for Trap.
Estimated Value: **Excellent:** **$500.00**
Very good: **$400.00**

Weatherby Patrician Deluxe

Similar to the Patrician with decorated satin silver receiver and higher quality wood.
Estimated Value: **Excellent:** **$550.00**
Very good: **$440.00**

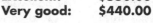

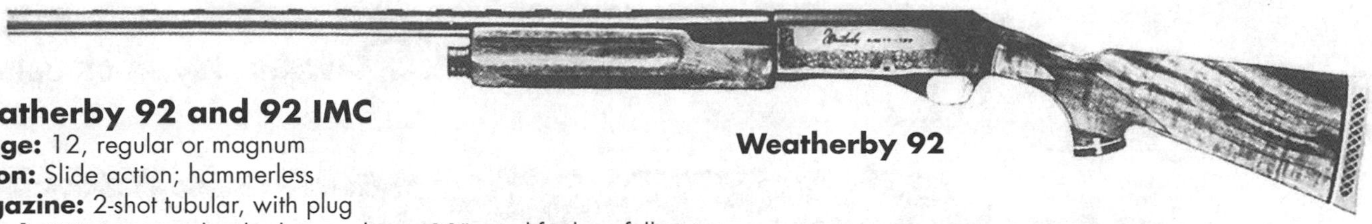

Weatherby 92

Weatherby 92 and 92 IMC

Gauge: 12, regular or magnum
Action: Slide action; hammerless
Magazine: 2-shot tubular, with plug
Barrel: 26" improved cylinder or skeet, 28" modified or full, 30" full; ventilated rib. Multi-choke barrel on all after 1983.
Finish: Blued; checkered walnut pistol grip stock and slide handle; high-gloss finish; rosewood grip cap; etched receiver; recoil pad
Approximate wt.: 7½ lbs.
Comments: Introduced in 1982. Trap Model discontinued in 1983; regular model discontinued in 1988.
Estimated Value: **Excellent:** **$350.00**
Very good: **$280.00**

Weatherby 92 Buckmaster

Similar to the Weatherby 92 with a 22" slug barrel and rifle sights.
Estimated Value: **Excellent:** **$300.00**
Very good: **$240.00**

Weatherby Centurion

Weatherby Centurion and Centurion II

Gauge: 12 reg. (Centurion); 12 mag. (Centurion II)
Action: Semiautomatic, gas-operated; hammerless
Magazine: Tubular
Barrel: 26", 28", 30"; variety of chokes; ventilated rib
Finish: Blued; checkered walnut pistol grip stock and grooved forearm; recoil pad
Approximate wt.: 7½ lbs.
Comments: Made from the early 1970s to the early 1980s. Add 7% for Trap.
Estimated Value: **Excellent:** **$500.00**
Very good: **$400.00**

Weatherby Centurion Deluxe

Similar to the Centurion with a decorated satin silver receiver and higher quality wood.
Estimated Value: **Excellent:** **$550.00**
Very good: **$440.00**

Weatherby 82

Weatherby 82 and 82 IMC

Gauge: 12, regular or magnum
Action: Gas-operated, semiautomatic; hammerless
Magazine: 2-shot tubular with plug
Barrel: 26" improved cylinder or skeet, 28" modified or full, 30" full; ventilated rib. Multi-choke barrel after 1983.
Finish: Blued; checkered walnut pistol grip stock and forearm; high gloss finish; rosewood grip cap; etched receiver; recoil pad
Approximate wt.: 7½ lbs.
Comments: Made from 1982 to 1991. Add 7% for Trap.
Estimated Value: **Excellent:** **$450.00**
Very good: **$360.00**

Weatherby 82 Buckmaster

Similar to the 82 except: 22" slug barrel and rifle sights.
Estimated Value: **Excellent:** **$475.00**
Very good: **$380.00**

Weatherby SAS

Gauge: 12, 20
Action: Gas-operated, semiautomatic
Magazine: 4-shot tubular
Barrel: 24", 26", 28", or 30" with choke tubes; ventilated rib. Slug model has 22" barrel.
Finish: Blued; checkered walnut pistol grip stock and forearm; synthetic finish or camouflage finish available
Approximate wt.: 7½ lbs.
Comments: Introduced in the late 1990s. Add 5% for camouflage; add 5% for Slug model.
Estimated Value: **Excellent:** **$600.00**
Very good: **$480.00**

Weatherby SA-08 Upland

Weatherby SA-08 Deluxe

Weatherby SA-08 Synthetic

Weatherby SA-08 Waterfowler 3.0

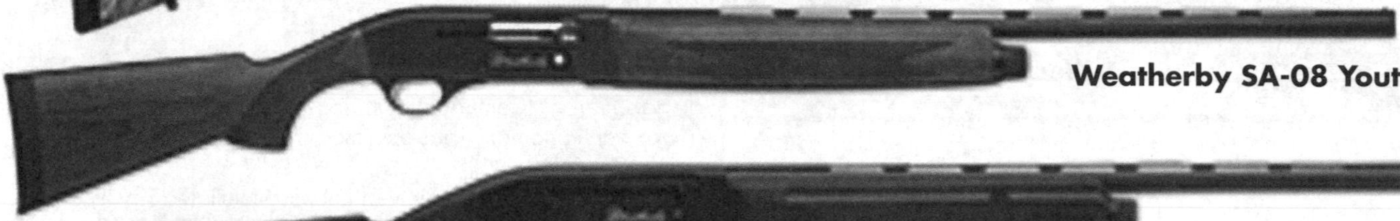

Weatherby SA-08 Youth

Weatherby SA-08 Synthetic Youth

Weatherby SA-08 Upland

Gauge: 12 or 20, 3" chambers
Action: Gas-operated, semiautomatic
Magazine: 4-shot tubular
Barrel: 26" or 28", ventilated rib, variety of chokes
Finish: Matte black; satin finish, checkered walnut pistol grip stock and forearm; recoil pad
Approximate wt.: 6 to 6¾ lbs.
Comments: A high-quality, lightweight hunting rifle.

Estimated Value:	**New (retail):**	**$719.00**
	Excellent:	**$540.00**
	Very good:	**$430.00**

Weatherby SA-08 Deluxe

Similar to the SA-08 Upland except: high gloss finish with high gloss walnut stock and forearm.

Estimated Value:	**New (retail):**	**$739.00**
	Excellent:	**$555.00**
	Very good:	**$445.00**

Weatherby SA-08 Synthetic

Similar to the SA-08 Upland except: lightweight injection-molded black synthetic stock and forearm.

Estimated Value:	**New (retail):**	**$449.00**
	Excellent:	**$335.00**
	Very good:	**$270.00**

Weatherby SA-08 Waterfowler 3.0

Similar to the SA-08 Synthetic except: camouflage finish; 12 gauge only.

Estimated Value:	**New (retail):**	**$699.00**
	Excellent:	**$500.00**
	Very good:	**$400.00**

Weatherby SA-08 Youth

A scaled-down version of the SA-08 Upland for smaller shooters. Available in 20 gauge only, with 26" barrel.

Estimated Value:	**New (retail):**	**$719.00**
	Excellent:	**$540.00**
	Very good:	**$430.00**

Weatherby SA-08 Synthetic Youth

Similar to the SA-08 Youth except lightweight injection-molded black synthetic stock and forearm.

Estimated Value:	**New (retail):**	**$569.00**
	Excellent:	**$425.00**
	Very good:	**$340.00**

Western Long Range

Western Long Range

Gauge: 12, 16, 20, 410
Action: Box lock; top lever break-open; hammerless; double or single trigger
Magazine: None
Barrel: Side-by-side double barrel; 26" – 32"; modified and full choke
Finish: Blued; plain walnut pistol grip stock and forearm
Approximate wt.: 7 lbs.
Comments: Made from the mid-1920s until the early 1940s by Western Arms Corp., which was later bought by Ithaca Arms Company. Add $25.00 for single trigger.

Estimated Value:	**Excellent:**	**$475.00**
	Very good:	**$380.00**

Western Field Model 100

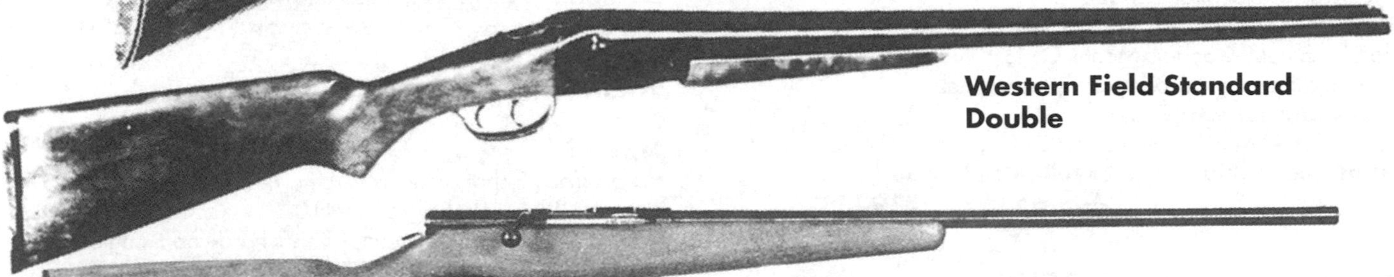
Western Field Standard Double

Western Field Model 150C

Western Field Model 100

Gauge: 12, 16, 20, 410
Action: Box lock; top lever break-open; hammerless; single shot
Magazine: None
Barrel: 26" – 30", full choke
Finish: Blued; wood semi-pistol grip stock and tapered forearm
Approximate wt.: 6¼ to 7 lbs.
Comments: Manufactured from the 1960s to the mid-1970s.

Estimated Value:	**Excellent:**	**$100.00**
	Very good:	**$ 80.00**

Western Field Standard Double

Gauge: 12, 16, 20, 410
Action: Box lock; top lever break-open; hammerless
Magazine: None
Barrel: Side-by-side double barrel; 26" – 30"; modified and full or full and full chokes; ribbed barrels
Finish: Blued; wood semi-pistol grip stock and short tapered forearm
Approximate wt.: 6½ to 7 lbs.
Comments: Made from the 1960s to the mid-1970s.

Estimated Value:	**Excellent:**	**$250.00**
	Very good:	**$200.00**

Western Field Model 150C

Gauge: 410
Action: Bolt action; repeating
Magazine: 3-shot; top loading
Barrel: 25"; full choke; 3" chamber
Finish: Blued; wood Monte Carlo pistol grip one-piece stock and forearm
Approximate wt.: 5½ lbs.
Comments: Manufactured in the early 1980s.

Estimated Value:	**Excellent:**	**$110.00**
	Very good:	**$ 90.00**

Western Field Model 170

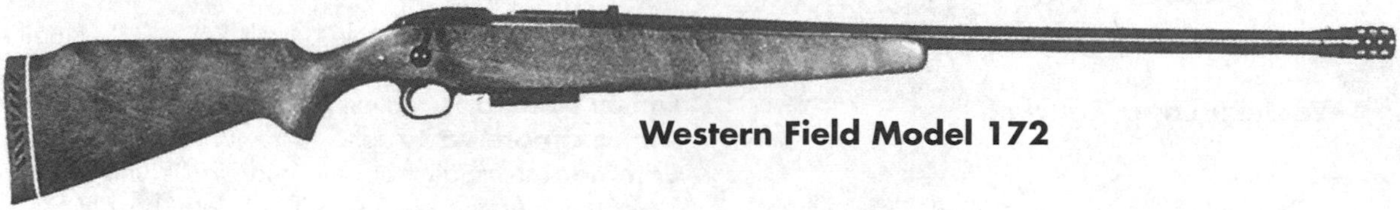

Western Field Model 172

Western Field Model 175

Western Field Model 170

Gauge: 12
Action: Bolt action; repeating
Magazine: 3-shot detachable clip
Barrel: 28"
Finish: Blued; wooden Monte Carlo semi-pistol grip, one-piece stock and forearm; recoil pad; sights; swivels
Approximate wt.: 7 lbs.
Comments: Made from the 1960s to the late 1970s.

Estimated Value:	**Excellent:**	**$115.00**
	Very good:	**$100.00**

Western Field Model 172

Similar to the Model 170 without sights or swivels; adjustable choke.

Estimated Value:	**Excellent:**	**$110.00**
	Very good:	**$ 85.00**

Western Field Model 175

Similar to the Model 172 in 20 gauge with a 26" barrel; without adjustable choke.

Estimated Value:	**Excellent:**	**$115.00**
	Very good:	**$ 95.00**

Western Field Bolt Action

Gauge: 12, 20, regular or magnum, 410
Action: Bolt action; repeating
Magazine: 3-shot detachable box; 410 top loading
Barrel: 28" full choke; 25" in 410
Finish: Blued; smooth walnut finish hardwood one-piece pistol grip stock and forearm
Approximate wt.: 6½ lbs.
Comments: Add $10.00 for 12 gauge.

Estimated Value:	**Excellent:**	**$120.00**
	Very good:	**$100.00**

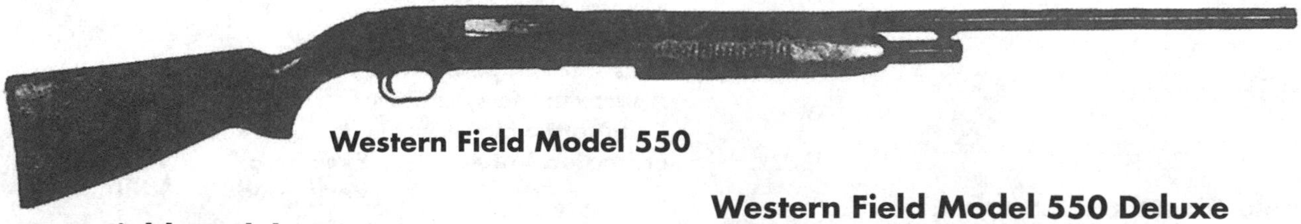

Western Field Model 550

Western Field Model 550

Gauge: 12, 20, 410, regular or magnum
Action: Slide action; hammerless; repeating
Magazine: 4-shot magnum, 5-shot regular, tubular
Barrel: 26" 410; 30" 12 gauge; full or modified choke
Finish: Blued; smooth hardwood pistol grip stock with fluted comb, grooved slide handle
Approximate wt.: 6½ lbs.
Comments: Add $20.00 for ventilated rib and variable choke.

Estimated Value:	**Excellent:**	**$175.00**
	Very good:	**$140.00**

Western Field Model 550 Deluxe

Gauge: 12, 20, regular or magnum
Action: Slide action; hammerless; repeating
Magazine: 5-shot tubular; 4-shot magnum
Barrel: 28" with 3 interchangeable "accu-choke" tubes; ventilated rib
Finish: Blued; checkered hardwood pistol grip stock and slide handle; recoil pad; engraved receiver
Approximate wt.: 7¼ lbs.
Comments: Made in the 1980s.

Estimated Value:	**Excellent:**	**$180.00**
	Very good:	**$145.00**

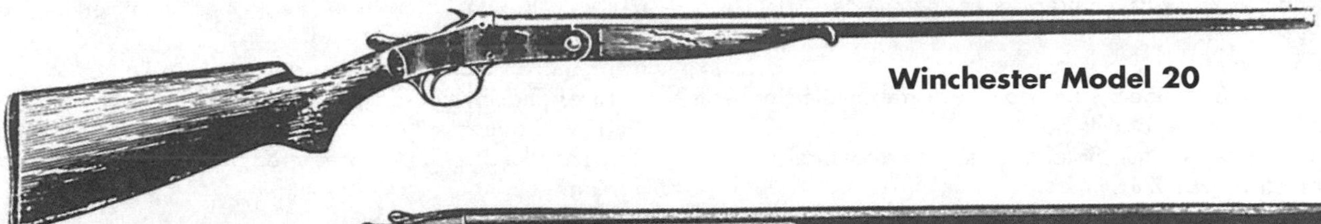

Winchester Model 20

Winchester Model 37

Winchester Model 20

Gauge: 410
Action: Top lever break-open; box lock; exposed hammer; single shot
Magazine: None
Barrel: 26" full choke
Finish: Blued; plain or checkered wood pistol grip stock and lipped forearm
Approximate wt.: 6 lbs.
Comments: Made from about 1920 to 1925.

Estimated Value:	**Excellent:**	**$675.00**
	Very good:	**$540.00**

Winchester Model 37

Gauge: 12, 16, 20, 28, 410
Action: Top lever break-open; partial visible hammer; automatic ejector
Magazine: None
Barrel: 26" – 32"; full choke, modified or cylinder bore
Finish: Blued; plain walnut semi-pistol grip stock and forearm
Approximate wt.: 6 lbs.
Comments: Made from the late 1930s to the mid-1960s. Add $1,000.00 for 28 gauge and $500.00 for 410 gauge.

Estimated Value:	**Excellent:**	**$325.00**
	Very good:	**$260.00**

Winchester Model 370

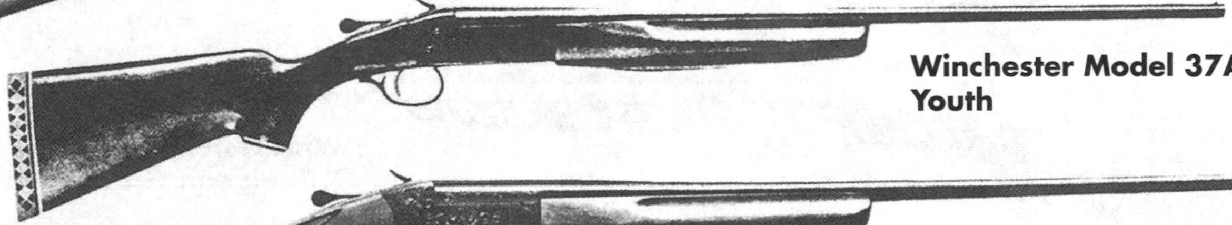

Winchester Model 37A Youth

Winchester Model 37A

Winchester Model 370

Gauge: 12, 16, 20, 28, 410
Action: Top lever break-open; box lock; exposed hammer; single shot; automatic ejector
Magazine: None
Barrel: 26" – 32" or 36" full choke; modified in 20 gauge
Finish: Blued; plain wood semi-pistol grip stock and forearm
Approximate wt.: 5¼ to 6¼ lbs.
Comments: Made from the late 1960s to the mid-1970s. Add $50.00 for 28 gauge or 410 bore.

Estimated Value:	**Excellent:**	**$200.00**
	Very good:	**$160.00**

Winchester Model 37A

Similar to the Model 370 but also available in 36" Waterfowl barrel; has checkered stock, fluted forearm; engraved receiver; gold-plated trigger. Manufactured from the late 1960s to the late 1970s. Add 6% for 36" barrel. Add $50.00 for 28 gauge or 410 bore.

Estimated Value:	**Excellent:**	**$300.00**
	Very good:	**$240.00**

Winchester Model 37A Youth

Similar to the Model 37A with 26" barrel.

Estimated Value:	**Excellent:**	**$325.00**
	Very good:	**$260.00**

Winchester Model 21

Gauge: 12, 16, 20
Action: Box lock; top lever break-open; hammerless, double or single trigger
Magazine: None
Barrel: 26" – 32" side-by-side double barrel; matted or ventilated rib; full, modified or cylinder bore
Finish: Checkered walnut, pistol grip stock and forearm
Approximate wt.: 7 lbs.
Comments: Made in this grade from 1930 to the late 1950s. Fancier grades were produced. Prices are for Field Grade. Add 18% for ventilated rib.
Estimated Value: **Excellent: $4,000.00 – 20,000.00**
Very good: $3,200.00 – 16,000.00

Winchester Model 24

Gauge: 12, 16, 20
Action: Box lock; top lever break-open; hammerless, automatic ejectors; double triggers
Magazine: None
Barrel: Side-by-side double barrel, 28" cylinder bore and modified in 12 gauge; other modified and full choke; raised matted rib
Finish: Blued; plain or checkered walnut pistol grip stock and forearm
Approximate wt.: 7½ lbs.
Comments: Made from the late 1930s to the late 1950s. Add $100.00 for 20 gauge or 16 gauge.
Estimated Value: **Excellent: $625.00**
Very good: $500.00

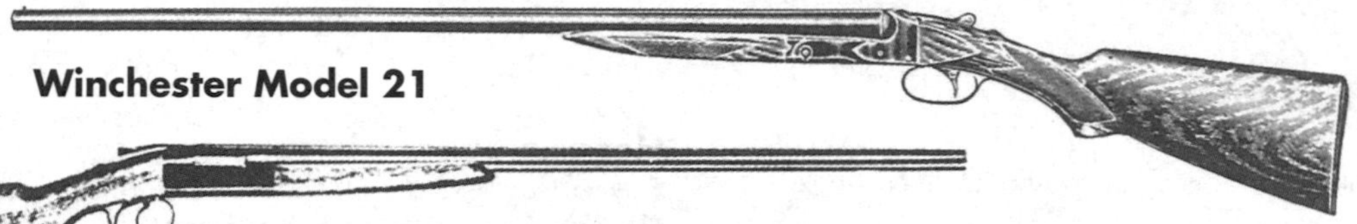

Winchester Model 21

Winchester Model 24

Winchester Model 23 Custom

Gauge: 12
Action: Box lock; top lever break-open; hammerless, single selective trigger
Magazine: None
Barrel: Side-by-side double barrel, 25½" "Winchoke"
Finish: Blued; checkered walnut, pistol grip stock and forearm
Approximate wt.: 6¾ lbs.
Comments: Made in the late 1980s and the early 1990s.
Estimated Value: **Excellent: $2,200.00**
Very good: $1,750.00

Winchester Model 23 Classic

Similar to the Model 23 Custom with 26" barrels; 12, 20, or 28 gauge improved cylinder and modified; 410 modified and full choke; engraving on receiver. Add 20% for 28 gauge or 410 bore.
Estimated Value: **Excellent: $2,000.00**
Very good: $1,600.00

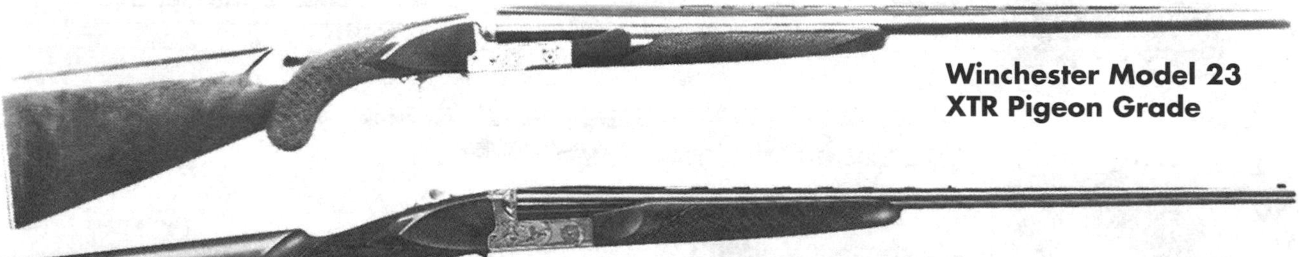

Winchester Model 23 XTR Pigeon Grade

Winchester Model 23 Pigeon Grade Lightweight

Winchester Model 23 Pigeon Grade Lightweight

Similar to the Model 23 XTR Pigeon Grade with a straight grip stock; rubber butt pad; 25½" ventilated rib barrels. Introduced in 1981. Discontinued in 1987. Add 3% for Winchoke.
Estimated Value: **Excellent: $2,200.00**
Very good: $1,750.00

Winchester Model 23 XTR Pigeon Grade

Gauge: 12, 20, regular or magnum
Action: Box lock; top lever break-open; hammerless; selective automatic ejector
Magazine: None
Barrel: Side-by-side double barrel; 26" improved cylinder and modified; 28" modified and full choke; tapered ventilated rib; Winchoke after 1980
Finish: Blued; checkered walnut semi-pistol grip stock and forearm; silver-gray engraved receiver
Approximate wt.: 6½ to 7 lbs.
Comments: Made from the late 1970s to the late 1980s.
Estimated Value: **Excellent: $2,000.00**
Very good: $1,600.00

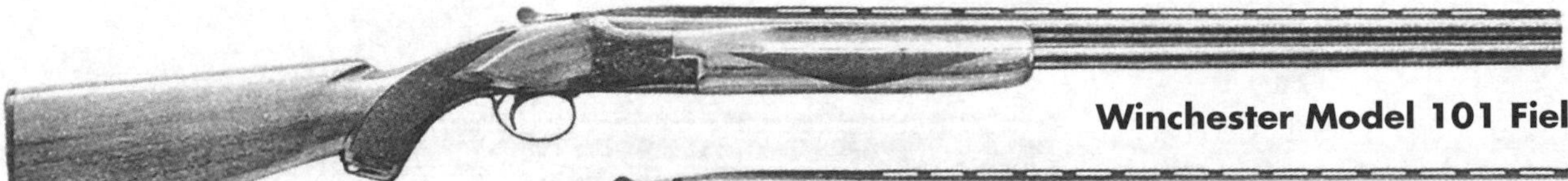

Winchester Model 101 Field

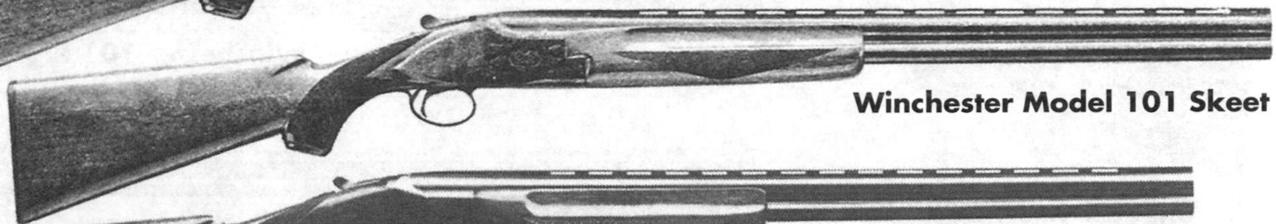

Winchester Model 101 Skeet

Winchester Xpert Model 96

Winchester Model 101 Field

Gauge: 12, 20, 28, 410, regular or magnum, 28, 410 discontinued in the late 1970s
Action: Box lock; top lever break-open; hammerless; single trigger; automatic ejector
Magazine: None
Barrel: Over and under double barrel; 26" – 30", various chokes; ventilated rib
Finish: Blued; checkered walnut pistol grip stock and wide forearm; recoil pad on magnum; engraved receiver
Approximate wt.: 6½ to 7½ lbs.
Comments: Made from the mid-1960s to about 1980. Add $150.00 for 410 or 28 gauge; $10.00 for magnum.

Estimated Value:	**Excellent:**	**$1,200.00**
	Very good:	**$ 960.00**

Winchester Model 101 Skeet

Similar to the Model 101 with skeet stock and choke. Add $150.00 for 410 or 28 gauge.

Estimated Value:	**Excellent:**	**$1,100.00**
	Very good:	**$ 880.00**

Winchester Model 101 Trap

Similar to the Model 101 with regular or Monte Carlo stock; recoil pad; 30" – 32" barrels; 12 gauge only.

Estimated Value:	**Excellent:**	**$1,250.00**
	Very good:	**$1,000.00**

Winchester Xpert Model 96

A lower cost version of the Model 101, lacking engraving as well as some of the internal and external extras. Produced in the late 1970s.

Estimated Value:	**Excellent:**	**$900.00**
	Very good:	**$720.00**

Winchester Xpert Model 96 Trap

Similar to the Xpert Model 96 with Monte Carlo stock and 30" barrel.

Estimated Value:	**Excellent:**	**$875.00**
	Very good:	**$700.00**

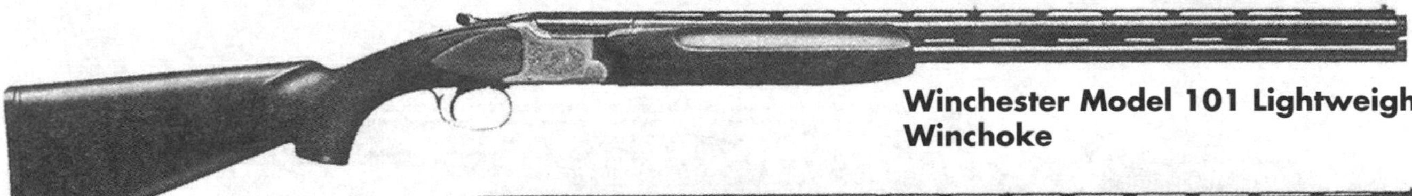

Winchester Model 101 Lightweight Winchoke

Winchester Model 101 Waterfowl Winchoke

Winchester Model 101 Lightweight Winchoke

Similar to the Model 101 Field with interchangeable choke tube system; lighter weight; ventilated rib between barrel. Introduced in 1981. 12 or 20 gauge.

Estimated Value:	**Excellent:**	**$1,400.00**
	Very good:	**$1,120.00**

Winchester Model 101 Waterfowl Winchoke

Similar to the Model 101 Lightweight Winchoke in 12 gauge only; 32" ventilated rib barrels; interchangeable choke tube system; recoil pad. Produced from 1981 to 1987.

Estimated Value:	**Excellent:**	**$1,700.00**
	Very good:	**$1,350.00**

Winchester Model 101 Waterfowler

Similar to the Model 101 Waterfowl Winchoke with sandblasted blued finish and low-luster finish. Introduced in 1987.

Estimated Value:	**Excellent:**	**$1,500.00**
	Very good:	**$1,200.00**

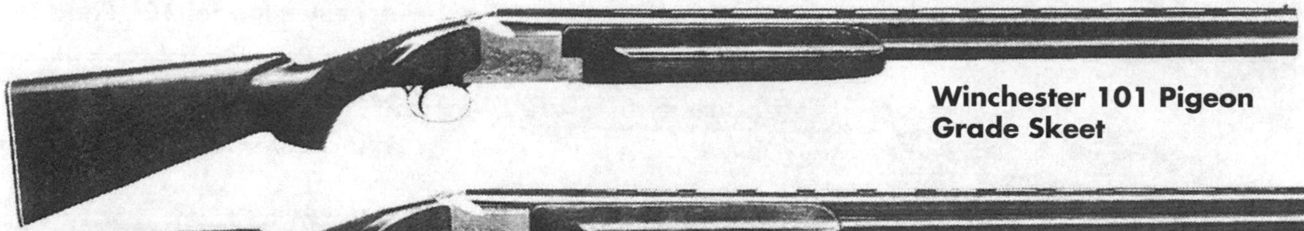

Winchester 101 Pigeon Grade Skeet

Winchester 101 Pigeon Grade Trap

Winchester 101 Pigeon Grade

Gauge: 12, 20, regular or magnum
Action: Box lock; top lever break-open; selective automatic ejector; single selective trigger
Magazine: None
Barrel: Over and under double barrel; 26" improved cylinder and modified; 28" modified and full; ventilated rib
Finish: Blued; checkered walnut pistol grip stock and fluted forearm; silver-gray engraved receiver; recoil pad on magnum
Approximate wt.: 7¼ lbs.
Comments: Made from the late 1970s to the early 1980s.

Estimated Value:	**Excellent:**	**$2,200.00**
	Very good:	**$1,750.00**

Winchester 101 Pigeon Grade Skeet

Similar to the Pigeon Grade with 27" or 28" skeet choke barrels; front and center sighting beads; 410 or 28 gauge available; add 10%.

Estimated Value:	**Excellent:**	**$1,650.00**
	Very good:	**$1,320.00**

Winchester 101 Pigeon Grade Trap

Similar to the Pigeon Grade with a 30" or 32" barrel; recoil pad; regular or Monte Carlo stock. Add 20% for Monte Carlo stock.

Estimated Value:	**Excellent:**	**$1,575.00**
	Very good:	**$1,260.00**

Winchester Supreme Field

Winchester Supreme Sporting

Winchester Supreme Sporting

Similar to the Supreme Field except: 28" or 30" barrel; 2¾" chamber; higher quality walnut; silver nitride receiver; recoil pad.

Estimated Value:	**Excellent:**	**$1,200.00**
	Very good:	**$ 960.00**

Winchester Supreme Field

Gauge: 12 (3" magnum)
Action: Top lever break-open
Magazine: None
Barrel: Over and under double barrel; 26" or 28"; ventilated rib
Finish: Blued; checkered walnut, pistol grip stock and forearm
Approximate wt: 7¼ lbs.
Comments: Introduced in 2001.

Estimated Value:	**Excellent:**	**$1,000.00**
	Very good:	**$ 800.00**

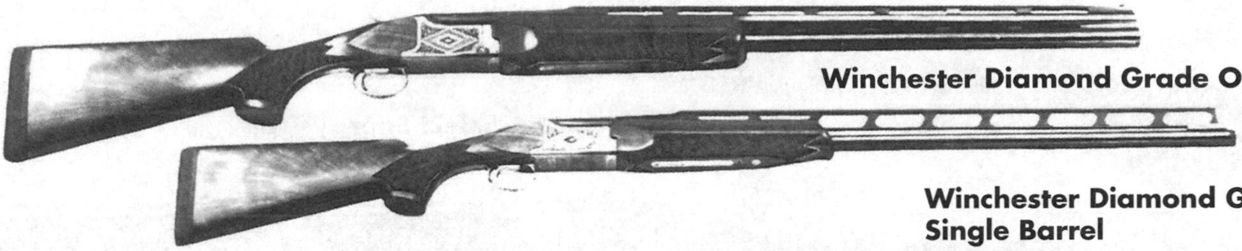

Winchester Diamond Grade O/U Skeet

Winchester Diamond Grade Single Barrel

Winchester Diamond Grade O/U Trap

Gauge: 12
Action: Top lever break-open
Magazine: None
Barrel: Over and under double barrel; 30" or 32" full choke top, interchangeable choke tube system bottom; ventilated rib on top and between barrels
Finish: Blued, silver-gray satin finish on receiver with engraving; checkered walnut pistol grip stock and lipped forearm; ebony inlay in pistol grip; regular or Monte Carlo stock; recoil pad
Approximate wt.: 8¾ to 9 lbs.
Comments: Made from 1982 to 1987.

Estimated Value:	**Excellent:**	**$1,700.00**
	Very good:	**$1,350.00**

Winchester Diamond Grade Single Barrel

Similar to the Diamond Grade O/U Trap but with only one 32" or 34" barrel; interchangeable choke tube system; high-ventilated rib. Introduced in 1982.

Estimated Value:	**Excellent:**	**$2,000.00**
	Very good:	**$1,600.00**

Winchester Diamond Grade O/U Skeet

Similar to the Diamond Grade O/U Trap in 12, 20, 28 gauges and 410 bore; 27" barrels. Introduced in 1982. Add $75.00 for Winchoke.

Estimated Value:	**Excellent:**	**$1,800.00**
	Very good:	**$1,450.00**

Winchester Diamond Grade Combination

Similar to the Diamond Grade O/U Trap with a set of 30" or 32" barrels and a 34" high-rib single barrel; lower barrel and single barrel use interchangeable choke tube system. Made from the early to the late 1980s.

Estimated Value:	**Excellent:**	**$2,500.00**
	Very good:	**$2,000.00**

Winchester Model 501 Grand European Skeet

Winchester Super Grade

Winchester Super Grade, Shotgun Rifle

Gauge: 12, 3" chamber
Caliber: 30-06, 300 Win. mag; 243 Win.
Action: Top lever break-open
Magazine: None
Barrel: Over and under combination; 12 gauge shotgun barrel with interchangeable choke tube system over rifle barrel
Sights: Folding leaf rear, blade front
Finish: Blued; silver-gray satin finish engraved receiver; checkered walnut Monte Carlo pistol grip stock and fluted forearm; recoil pad; swivels
Approximate wt.: 8½ lbs.
Comments: A limited production shotgun/rifle combination available in the early 1980s.

Estimated Value:	**Excellent:**	**$2,000.00**
	Very good:	**$1,600.00**

Winchester Model 501 Grand European Trap

Gauge: 12
Action: Top lever break-open
Magazine: None
Barrel: Over and under double barrel; 30" or 32" improved modified and full choke; ventilated rib on top and between barrels
Finish: Blued; silver-gray satin finish engraved receiver; checkered walnut pistol grip stock and fluted lipped forearm; regular or Monte Carlo stock; recoil pad
Approximate wt.: 8¼ to 8½ lbs.
Comments: A trap shotgun produced during the 1980s.

Estimated Value:	**Excellent:**	**$2,000.00**
	Very good:	**$1,600.00**

Winchester Model 501 Grand European Skeet

Similar to the Model 501 Grand European Trap with 27" skeet choke barrels; weighs 6½ to 7½ lbs. Produced from 1981 to 1987. 12 or 20 gauge.

Estimated Value:	**Excellent:**	**$2,000.00**
	Very good:	**$1,600.00**

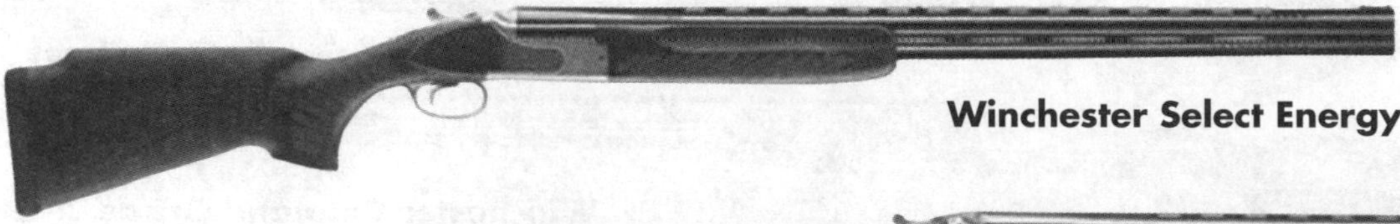

Winchester Select Energy Trap

Winchester Select Extreme Elegance

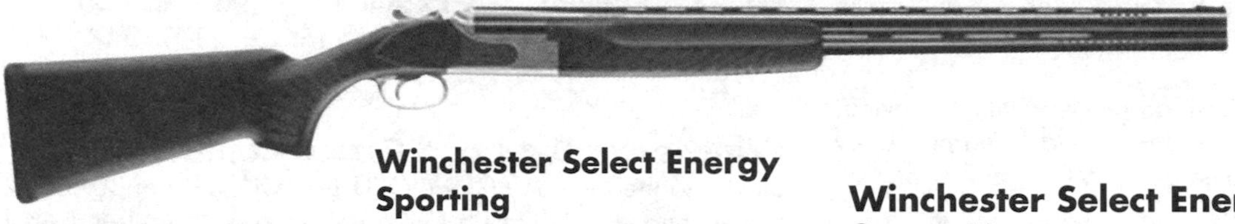

Winchester Select Energy Sporting

Winchester Select Energy Trap

Similar to the Select Energy Sporting except: 30" or 32" barrel; Monte Carlo stock. Add 8% for adjustable comb stock.

Estimated Value: **Excellent:** **$1,460.00**
Very good: **$1,170.00**

Winchester Select Extreme Elegance

Similar to the Select Energy Sporting except: 26" or 28" barrel; low profile, engraved receiver.

Estimated Value: **Excellent:** **$1,740.00**
Very good: **$1,390.00**

Winchester Select Energy Sporting

Gauge: 12
Action: Top lever break-open, hammerless
Magazine: None
Barrel: 28", 30", 32", over and under double barrel; ventilated rib above and between barrels; ported
Finish: Blued; checkered walnut pistol grip stock and forearm; recoil pad; adjustable comb available
Approximate wt.: 7¼ to 7¾ lbs.
Comments: Introduced in 2005. Add 8% for adjustable comb stock.

Estimated Value: **Excellent:** **$1,460.00**
Very good: **$1,170.00**

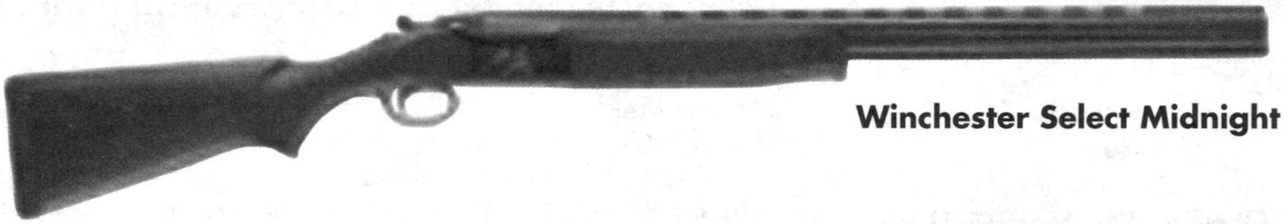

Winchester Select Midnight

Winchester Select Traditional Elegance

Winchester Select Traditional Elegance

Similar to the Select Energy Sporting except: 26" or 28" barrel; engraved gray receiver.

Estimated Value: **Excellent:** **$1,740.00**
Very good: **$1,390.00**

Winchester Select Midnight

Similar to the Select Energy Sporting except: 26" or 28" barrel; high gloss bluing; engraved receiver; satin-finish Grade II/III walnut stock and forearm.

Estimated Value: **Excellent:** **$1,785.00**
Very good: **$1,425.00**

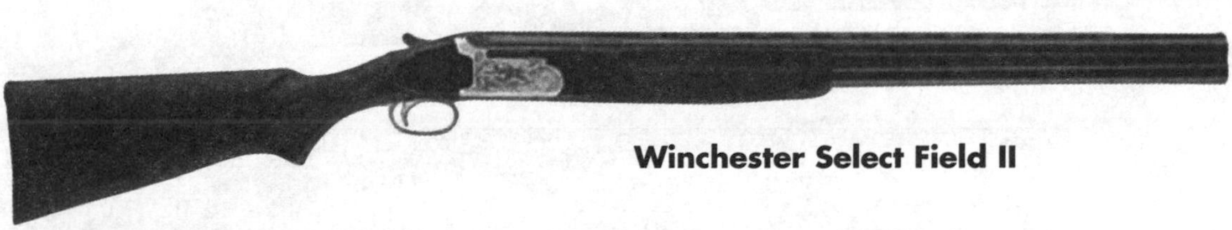

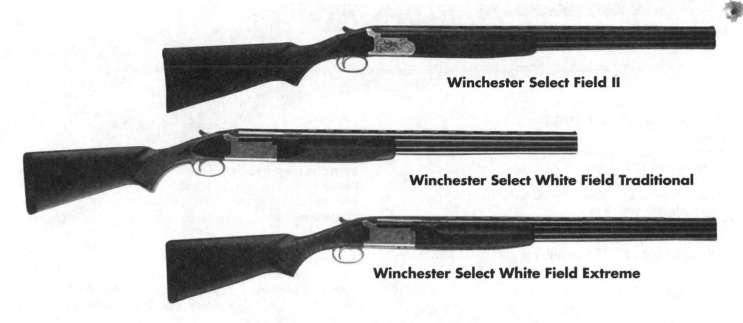

Winchester Select Field II

Winchester Select White Field Traditional

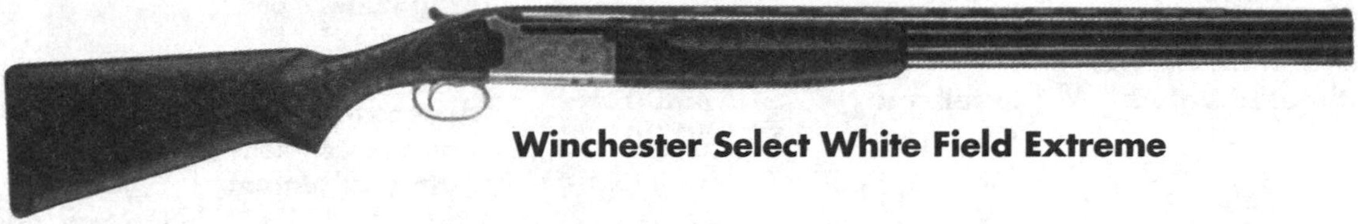

Winchester Select White Field Extreme

Winchester Select Field II

Similar to the Select Energy Sporting except: 26" or 28" barrel; gray nitride engraved receiver; Grade II walnut stock and forearm.

Estimated Value:	**New (retail):**	**$1,607.00**
	Excellent:	**$1,205.00**
	Very good:	**$ 965.00**

Winchester Select White Field Traditional

Similar to Select Field II except: lightweight barrels and low profile receiver.

Estimated Value:	**Excellent:**	**$1,150.00**
	Very good:	**$ 920.00**

Winchester Select White Field Extreme

Similar to the Select White Field Traditional.

Estimated Value:	**Excellent:**	**$1,150.00**
	Very good:	**$ 920.00**

Winchester Select Platinum

Winchester Select Model 101

Winchester Select Platinum

Similar to the Select Traditional Elegance except: fine-detailed engraving; lipped forearm; introduced in 2006.

Estimated Value:	**Excellent:**	**$1,665.00**
	Very good:	**$1,330.00**

Winchester Select Model 101

An improved version of Winchester's Model 101; high gloss, Grade II walnut stock and forearm. Introduced in 2006.

Estimated Value:	**New (retail):**	**$1,921.00**
	Excellent:	**$1,440.00**
	Very good:	**$1,150.00**

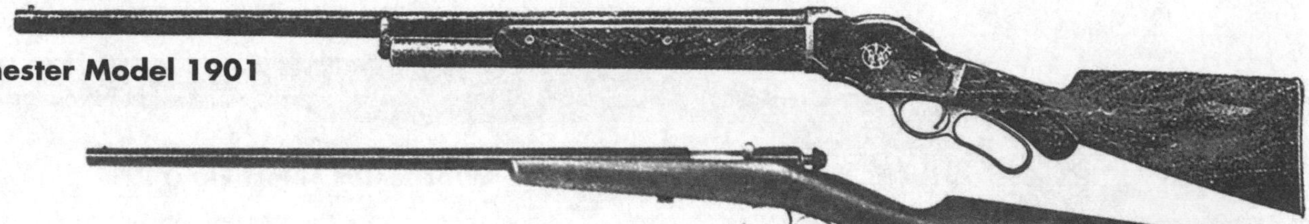

Winchester Model 1901

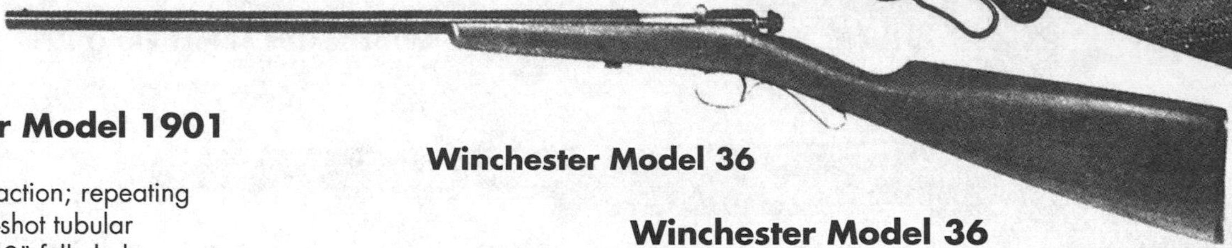

Winchester Model 36

Winchester Model 1901

Gauge: 10
Action: Lever action; repeating
Magazine: 4-shot tubular
Barrel: 30", 32" full choke
Finish: Blued; walnut, pistol grip stock and forearm
Approximate wt.: 8 to 9 lbs.
Comments: Made from 1901 to about 1920, an improved version of the Model 1887.
Estimated Value: **Excellent:** **$1,575.00**
Very good: **$1,250.00**

Winchester Model 36

Gauge: 9mm shot or ball cartridges
Action: Bolt action; single shot; rear cocking piece
Magazine: None
Barrel: 18"
Finish: Blued; straight grip one-piece stock and forearm
Approximate wt.: 3 lbs.
Comments: Made during the late 1920s.
Estimated Value: **Excellent:** **$800.00**
Very good: **$640.00**

Winchester Model 41

Gauge: 410
Action: Bolt action; single shot, rear cocking piece
Magazine: None
Barrel: 24" full choke
Finish: Blued; plain or checkered straight or pistol grip one-piece stock and forearm
Approximate wt.: 5 lbs.
Comments: Made from about 1920 to around 1935.
Estimated Value: **Excellent:** **$575.00**
Very good: **$460.00**

Winchester Model 9410

Gauge: 410
Action: Lever action; repeating
Magazine: 9-shot tubular
Barrel: 24"; rifle sights
Finish: Blued; checkered walnut, straight-grip stock and forearm; barrel band
Approximate wt.: 6¾ lbs.
Comments: Introduced in 2001. Add 11% for "invector" choke tubes.
Estimated Value: **Excellent:** **$800.00**
Very good: **$640.00**

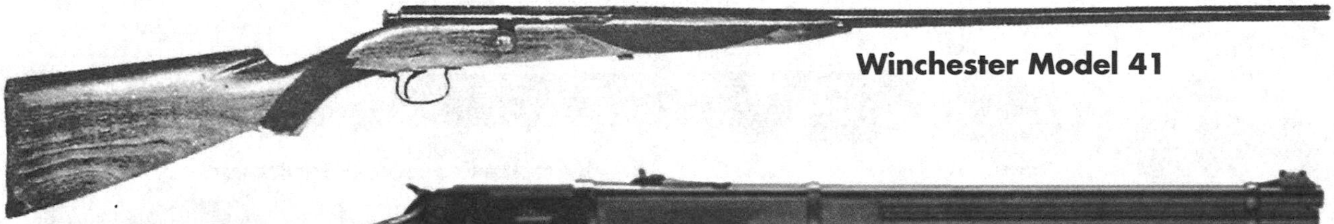

Winchester Model 41

Winchester Model 9410

Winchester Model 9410 Packer

Similar to the Model 9410 except: 20" barrel; ¾ tubular magazine holds 4 shots. Add 11% for "invector" choke tubes.
Estimated Value: **Excellent:** **$550.00**
Very good: **$440.00**

Winchester Model 9410 Semi-Fancy Traditional

Similar to the Model 9410 with higher quality checkered stock and forearm.
Estimated Value: **Excellent:** **$625.00**
Very good: **$500.00**

Winchester Model 9410 Packer Compact

Similar to the Model 9410 Packer with reduced stock dimensions for young shooters; weighs about 6 lbs.
Estimated Value: **Excellent:** **$550.00**
Very good: **$440.00**

Winchester Model 9410 Ranger

A value-priced version of the Model 9410 with smooth stock and forearm.
Estimated Value: **Excellent:** **$450.00**
Very good: **$360.00**

Winchester Model 12, Pre-'65

Winchester Model 12 Skeet, Pre-'65

Winchester Model 12 Trap, Pre-'65

Winchester Model 12 Duck, Pre-'65

Winchester Model 12 Field, After '72

Winchester Model 12 Super Pigeon, After '72

Winchester Model 12 Trap, After '72

Winchester Model 97

Winchester Model 97 Riot

Similar to the Model 97 with a 20" cylinder bore barrel.

Estimated Value:	**Excellent:**	**$1,400.00**
	Very good:	**$1,120.00**

Winchester Model 97 Trench

Similar to the Model 97 Riot with handguard and bayonet. Used in World War I.

Estimated Value:	**Excellent:**	**$4,000.00**
	Very good:	**$3,200.00**

Winchester Model 12

Gauge: 12, 16, 20, 28
Action: Slide action; hammerless; repeating
Magazine: 5-shot tubular
Barrel: 26" – 32", standard chokes available
Finish: Blued; plain or checkered walnut pistol grip stock and slide handle; some slide handles grooved
Approximate wt.: 6½ to 7½ lbs.
Comments: Made in various grades: Standard, Featherweight, Rib Barrel, Riot Gun, Duck, Skeet, Trap, Pigeon, and Super Pigeon from 1912 to about 1964. In 1972 Field Gun, Skeet and Trap were reissued. Deduct 50% for guns made after 1971. In 1963, Model 12 was offered with Hydro-coil recoil reducing system. Price for Standard Grade made before 1964. Add $50.00 for ventilated rib; $40.00 for raised matted rib; approximately 50% for Pigeon and approximately 120% for Super Pigeon grades. Deduct approximately 25% for Riot Gun.

Estimated Value:	**Excellent:**	**$1,200.00**
	Very good:	**$ 960.00**

Winchester Model 97

Gauge: 12, 16
Action: Slide action; exposed hammer; repeating
Magazine: 5-shot tubular
Barrel: 26", 28", 30", 32" modified, full choke or cylinder bore
Finish: Blued; plain wood, semi-pistol grip stock and grooved slide handle
Approximate wt.: 7¾ lbs.
Comments: Made from 1897 to the late 1950s. Made in Field Grade, Pigeon Grade, and Tournament Grade. Prices are for Field Grade. Add $2,000.00 for Pigeon Grade and $600.00 for Tournament Grade.

Estimated Value:	**Excellent:**	**$1,000.00**
	Very good:	**$ 800.00**

Winchester Model 12 Limited Edition

Gauge: 20
Action: Slide action; hammerless; repeating
Magazine: 5-shot tubular
Barrel: 26" improved cylinder choke, ventilated rib; metal or white bead front sight
Finish: Blued; checkered walnut pistol grip stock and slide handle; Grade I plain blued receiver, Grade IV has engraving and gold-plated dog and bird scenes
Approximate wt.: 6½ lbs.
Comments: Introduced in 1993; limited edition of 4,000 guns in Grade I and 1,000 guns in Grade IV; add 63% for Grade IV.

Estimated Value:	**Excellent:**	**$750.00**
	Very good:	**$600.00**

Winchester Model 42 Skeet

Winchester Model 42

Winchester Model 42 Skeet

Similar to the Model 42 available in straight stock; has matted rib and skeet choke barrel.

Estimated Value: **Excellent:** **$2,750.00**
Very good: **$2,200.00**

Winchester Model 42 Deluxe

Similar to the Model 42 with higher quality finish; ventilated rib; select wood; checkering.

Estimated Value: **Excellent:** **$5,000.00**
Very good: **$4,000.00**

Winchester Model 42

Gauge: 410
Action: Slide action; hammerless; repeating
Magazine: 5-shot tubular and 6-shot tubular
Barrel: 26", 28" modified, full choke or cylinder bore
Finish: Blued; plain walnut pistol grip stock and grooved slide handle
Approximate wt.: 6 lbs.
Comments: Made from the mid-1930s to the mid-1960s. Add $100.00 for matted rib and $150.00 for ventilated rib.
Estimated Value: **Excellent:** **$1,500.00**
Very good: **$1,200.00**

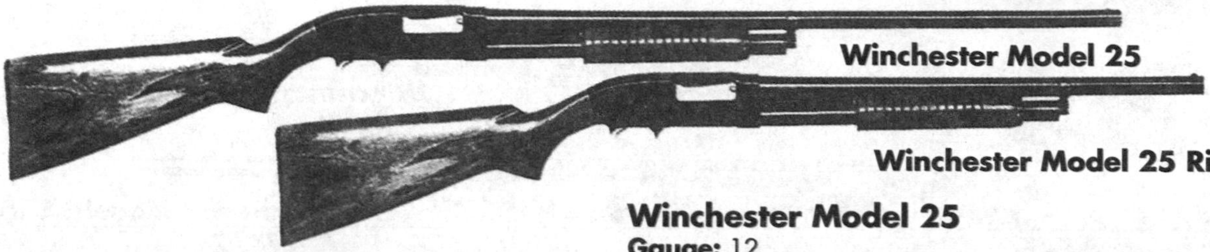

Winchester Model 25

Winchester Model 25 Riot Gun

Winchester Model 1200 Field

Gauge: 12, 16, 20, regular or magnum; 16 gauge dropped in the mid-1970s
Action: Front lock; rotary bolt; slide action; repeating
Magazine: 4-shot tubular
Barrel: 26" – 30"; various chokes or adjustable choke (Win-choke)
Finish: Blued; checkered walnut pistol grip stock and slide handle; recoil pad; alloy receiver
Approximate wt.: 6½ to 7½ lbs.
Comments: Made from the late 1960s to the late 1970s. Add $15.00 for magnum; $5.00 for adjustable choke; $25.00 for ventilated rib.
Estimated Value: **Excellent:** **$350.00**
Very good: **$280.00**

Winchester Model 25

Gauge: 12
Action: Slide action; hammerless; repeating
Magazine: 4-shot tubular
Barrel: 26", 28"; improved cylinder, modified or full chokes
Finish: Blued; plain walnut semi-pistol grip stock and grooved slide handle; sights
Approximate wt.: 7½ lbs.
Comments: Made from the late 1940s to the mid-1950s.
Estimated Value: **Excellent:** **$400.00**
Very good: **$320.00**

Winchester Model 25 Riot Gun

Similar to the Model 25 with a 25" cylinder bore barrel.

Estimated Value: **Excellent:** **$475.00**
Very good: **$380.00**

Winchester Model 1200 Field

Winchester Model 1200 Skeet

Winchester Model 1200 Trap

Winchester Model 1200 Skeet

Similar to the Model 1200 Field except: 12 and 20 gauge only; 26" skeet choke; ventilated rib barrel. Made to the mid-1970s.

Estimated Value: **Excellent:** **$375.00**
Very good: **$300.00**

Winchester Model 1200 Deer

Similar to the Model 1200 Field with 22" barrel, rifle sights. Made from the mid-1960s to the mid-1970s.

Estimated Value: **Excellent:** **$350.00**
Very good: **$280.00**

Winchester Model 1200 Trap

Similar to the Model 1200 Field with a 30" full choke barrel; ventilated rib; regular or Monte Carlo stock. Made from the late 1960s to the mid-1970s. Add 20% for Monte Carlo stock.

Estimated Value: **Excellent:** **$375.00**
Very good: **$300.00**

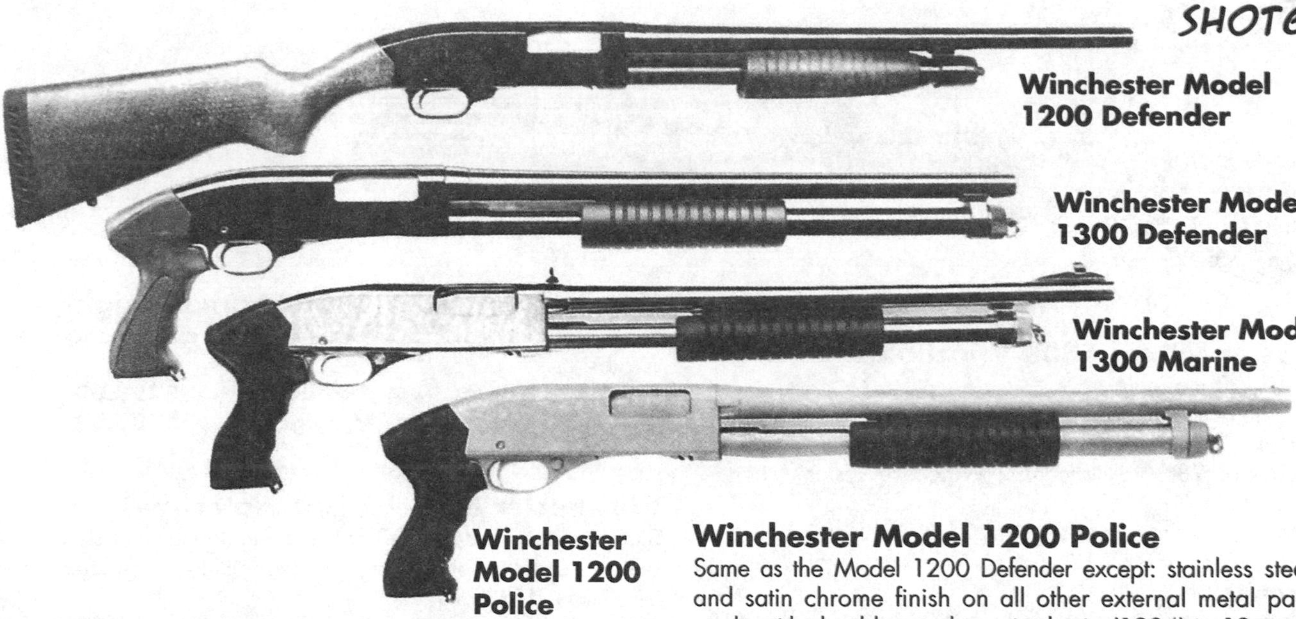

Winchester Model 1200 Defender

Winchester Model 1300 Defender

Winchester Model 1300 Marine

Winchester Model 1200 Police

Winchester Models 1200 and 1300 Defender

Gauge: 12, regular and magnum, 20
Action: Slide action front lock rotary bolt
Magazine: 6-shot tubular; 5-shot in magnum; or 8-shot
Barrel: 18" blue steel cylinder bore
Finish: Blued; plain wood or synthetic semi-pistol grip stock and grooved slide handle; full one-hand type pistol grip model made beginning in 1984
Approximate wt.: 6¾ lbs.; pistol grip model 5½ lbs.
Comments: Made from 1982 to the present. Also available with rifle sights (add 7%). Add 35% for combo model (field barrel plus 18" barrel).

Estimated Value:	**Excellent:**	**$350.00**
	Very good:	**$280.00**

Winchester Model 1200 Police

Same as the Model 1200 Defender except: stainless steel barrel and satin chrome finish on all other external metal parts. Also made with shoulder stock or pistol grip (1984) in 12 gauge only. Introduced in 1982.

Estimated Value:	**Excellent:**	**$400.00**
	Very good:	**$320.00**

Winchester Models 1200 and 1300 Marine

Same as the Model 1200 Police except: rifle sights standard. Introduced in 1982.

Estimated Value:	**Excellent:**	**$425.00**
	Very good:	**$340.00**

Winchester Model 1300 Camp Defender

Similar to the Model 1300 Defender except: 12 gauge only; 22" barrel, satin hardwood stock and slide handle; adjustable open sights. Introduced in 1999.

Estimated Value:	**Excellent:**	**$350.00**
	Very good:	**$280.00**

Winchester Model 1300XTR

Winchester Model 1300XTR Deer Gun

Winchester Model 1300XTR Deer Gun

Similar to the Model 1300XTR with a 22" barrel, rifle sights; sling; recoil pad. 12 gauge only. Made from about 1980 to the mid-1980s.

Estimated Value:	**Excellent:**	**$315.00**
	Very good:	**$250.00**

Winchester Model 1300 Upland Special

Similar to the Model 1300 except: straight stock and cylinder style forearm; 24" barrel. Introduced in the late 1990s.

Estimated Value:	**Excellent:**	**$325.00**
	Very good:	**$260.00**

Winchester Model 1300XTR

Gauge: 12, 20, regular or magnum
Action: Slide action; hammerless; repeating
Magazine: 3-shot tubular
Barrel: 26", 28", 30"; improved cylinder, modified or full choke; ventilated rib available
Finish: Blued; checkered walnut pistol grip stock and slide handle
Approximate wt.: 6½ lbs.
Comments: Made from the late 1970s to the early 1980s. Add $15.00 for ventilated rib.

Estimated Value:	**Excellent:**	**$300.00**
	Very good:	**$240.00**

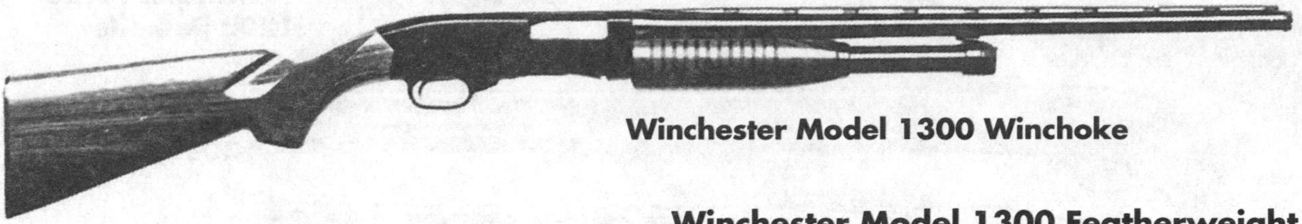

Winchester Model 1300 Winchoke

Winchester Model 1300 Winchoke

Gauge: 12, 20 magnum
Action: Slide action; hammerless; repeating
Magazine: 4-shot tubular
Barrel: 26" or 28"; ventilated rib; Winchoke system (changeable choke tubes)
Finish: Blued; checkered walnut straight or pistol grip stock and slide handle; recoil pad on 12 gauge
Approximate wt.: 7¼ lbs.
Comments: Made from the early 1980s to the mid-1990s. Lady's and youth model added in 1990.

Estimated Value:	**Excellent:**	**$270.00**
	Very good:	**$215.00**

Winchester Model 1300 Win-Tuff Deer Gun

Similar to the Model 1300XTR Deer Gun with rifled barrel. Black finish; laminated or walnut stock and forearm.

Estimated Value:	**Excellent:**	**$315.00**
	Very good:	**$250.00**

Winchester Model 1300 Featherweight

Similar to the Model 1300 Winchoke with a 22" barrel; weighs 6½ lbs.

Estimated Value:	**Excellent:**	**$290.00**
	Very good:	**$230.00**

Winchester Model 1300 Waterfowl

Similar to the Model 1300 Featherweight with sling swivels, 30" barrel; 12 gauge only; weighs 7 lbs.; dull finish on later models. Discontinued in 1991.

Estimated Value:	**Excellent:**	**$320.00**
	Very good:	**$255.00**

Winchester Model 1300 Turkey

Similar to the Model 1300 Waterfowl with a 22" barrel. Camouflage or Black Shadow finish. Add 5% for National Wild Turkey Federation model or Lady's model. Prices are for Black Shadow; add 25% for Realtree camouflage; Add 45% for Realtree full camouflage, Realtree gray, or Advantage camouflage.

Estimated Value:	**Excellent:**	**$250.00**
	Very good:	**$200.00**

Winchester Ranger

Winchester Ranger Deer Gun

Winchester Ranger, 1300 Ranger, and 1300 Black Shadow

Gauge: 12, 20, regular or magnum interchangeably
Action: Slide action; hammerless; side ejector
Magazine: 4-shot tubular; factory installed removable plug
Barrel: 26" or 28"; ventilated rib; interchangeable choke tubes
Finish: Blued; walnut-finished or synthetic, semi-pistol grip stock and grooved or checkered slide handle; recoil pad
Approximate wt.: 7¼ lbs.
Comments: Introduced in 1982. Add 13% for 1300 Walnut Field model, deduct 5% for Black Shadow Field model.

Estimated Value:	**Excellent:**	**$275.00**
	Very good:	**$220.00**

Winchester Ranger Deer Gun, 1300 Ranger Deer Gun, and Ranger Deer Combo

Similar to the Ranger with 22" or 24" cylinder bore deer barrel, rifle sights and recoil pad. Introduced in 1983. Available as Deer Combo only (field barrel and cylinder bore or rifled barrel) in the late 1990s (add 35%).

Estimated Value:	**Excellent:**	**$295.00**
	Very good:	**$235.00**

Winchester Ranger Youth, 1300 Ranger Youth, and 1300 Ranger Compact

Similar to the Ranger in 20 gauge; stock and forearm are modified for young shooters. Stock can be replaced with regular size stock; 22" modified or Winchoke barrel. Introduced in 1983.

Estimated Value:	**Excellent:**	**$275.00**
	Very good:	**$220.00**

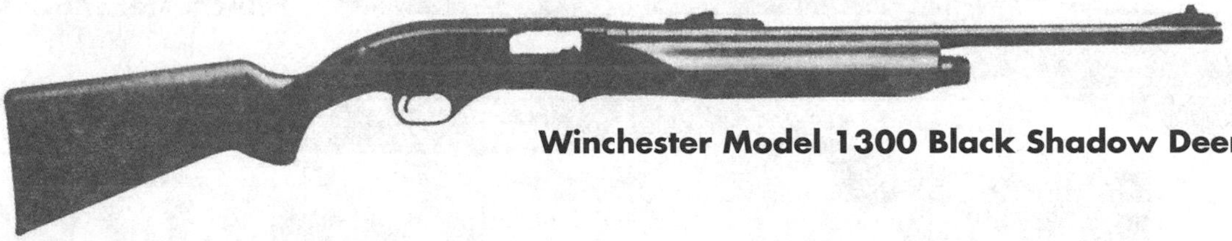

Winchester Model 1300 Black Shadow Deer

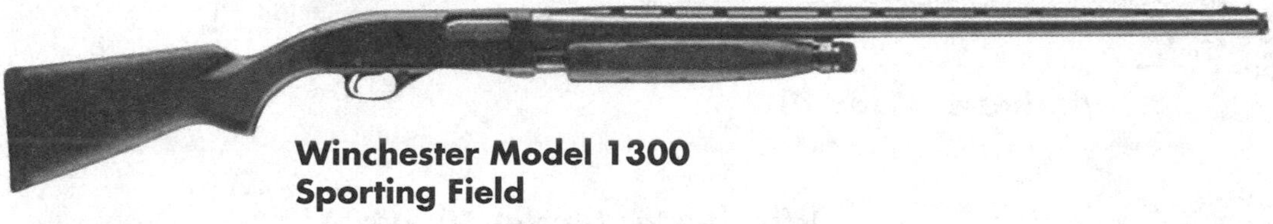

Winchester Model 1300 Sporting Field

Winchester Model 1300 Sporting Field

Gauge: 12, 3" chamber
Action: Slide action; hammerless; side ejector
Magazine: 4-shot tubular, removable plug
Barrel: 28"; choke tubes; ventilated rib
Finish: Blued; checkered walnut pistol grip stock and slide handle; recoil pad
Approximate wt.: 7½ lbs.
Comments: This is Winchester's 1300 shotgun with additional features.

Estimated Value:	**Excellent:**	**$335.00**
	Very good:	**$265.00**

Winchester Model 1300 Deer, Black Shadow Deer

Gauge: 12, 20, regular or magnum
Action: Slide action, hammerless, side ejector
Magazine: 4-shot tubular
Barrel: 22" plain or ventilated rib; smooth bore or rifled with rifle sights
Finish: Matte black, camouflaged, or black shadow; walnut or synthetic semi-pistol grip stock and checkered or grooved slide handle
Approximate wt.: 7 lbs.
Comments: Prices are for Black Shadow; add 36% for walnut stock; add 50% for camouflage finish; add 8% for rifled barrel; add 25% for 2 barrel Deer Combo; add 23% for cantilever scope mount.

Estimated Value:	**Excellent:**	**$285.00**
	Very good:	**$230.00**

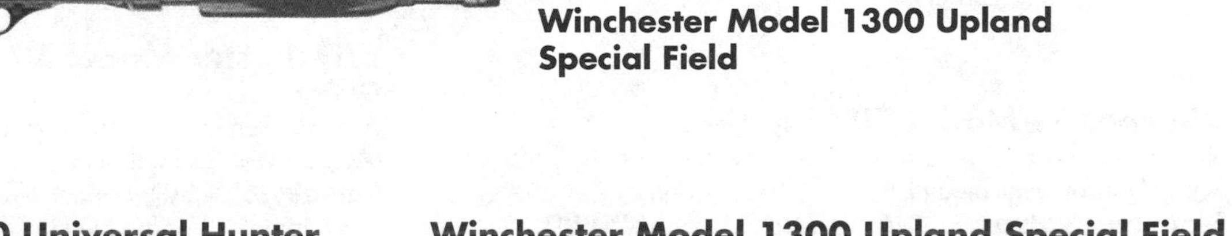

Winchester Model 1300 Universal Hunter

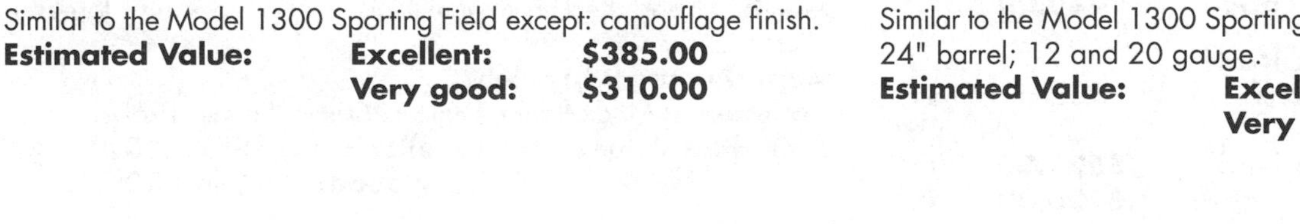

Winchester Model 1300 Upland Special Field

Winchester Model 1300 Universal Hunter

Similar to the Model 1300 Sporting Field except: camouflage finish.

Estimated Value:	**Excellent:**	**$385.00**
	Very good:	**$310.00**

Winchester Model 1300 Upland Special Field

Similar to the Model 1300 Sporting Field except: straight-grip stock; 24" barrel; 12 and 20 gauge.

Estimated Value:	**Excellent:**	**$335.00**
	Very good:	**$265.00**

Winchester Model 1911

Winchester Model 40 Skeet

Winchester Model 40

Winchester Model 1911

Gauge: 12
Action: Semiautomatic; hammerless
Magazine: 4-shot tubular
Barrel: 26" – 32"; various chokes
Finish: Blued; plain or checkered semi-pistol grip stock and forearm
Approximate wt.: 8 lbs.
Comments: Made from 1911 to the mid-1920s.

Estimated Value:	**Excellent:**	**$575.00**
	Very good:	**$460.00**

Winchester Model 40

Gauge: 12
Action: Semiautomatic; hammerless
Magazine: 4-shot tubular
Barrel: 28", 30"; modified or full choke
Finish: Blued; plain walnut pistol grip stock and forearm
Approximate wt.: 8 lbs.
Comments: Made in the early 1940s.

Estimated Value:	**Excellent:**	**$600.00**
	Very good:	**$480.00**

Winchester Model 40 Skeet

Similar to the Model 40 with a 24" skeet barrel; checkering; "Cutts Compensator."

Estimated Value:	**Excellent:**	**$775.00**
	Very good:	**$620.00**

Winchester Model 50

Gauge: 12, 20
Action: Semiautomatic; non-recoiling barrel; hammerless
Magazine: 2-shot tubular
Barrel: 26" – 30"; variety of chokes
Finish: Blued; checkered walnut pistol grip stock and forearm
Approximate wt.: 7¾ lbs.
Comments: Made from the mid-1950s to the early 1960s. Add $25.00 for ventilated rib.

Estimated Value:	**Excellent:**	**$500.00**
	Very good:	**$400.00**

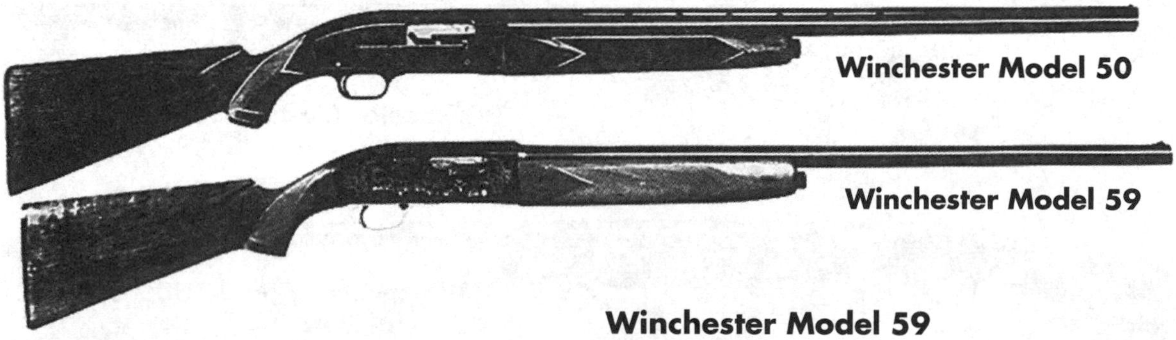

Winchester Model 50

Winchester Model 59

Winchester Model 50 Trap

Similar to the Model 50 except 12 gauge only; Monte Carlo stock; 30" full choke; ventilated rib.

Estimated Value:	**Excellent:**	**$600.00**
	Very good:	**$480.00**

Winchester Model 50 Skeet

Similar to the Model 50 with a skeet stock; 26" skeet choke barrel; ventilated rib.

Estimated Value:	**Excellent:**	**$525.00**
	Very good:	**$420.00**

Winchester Model 59

Gauge: 12
Action: Semiautomatic; hammerless; non-recoiling barrel
Magazine: 2-shot tubular
Barrel: 26" – 30"; variety of chokes; steel and glass fiber composition; interchangeable choke tubes available
Finish: Blued; checkered walnut pistol grip stock and forearm; alloy receiver
Approximate wt.: 6½ lbs.
Comments: Made from the late 1950s to the mid-1960s.

Estimated Value:	**Excellent:**	**$575.00**
	Very good:	**$460.00**

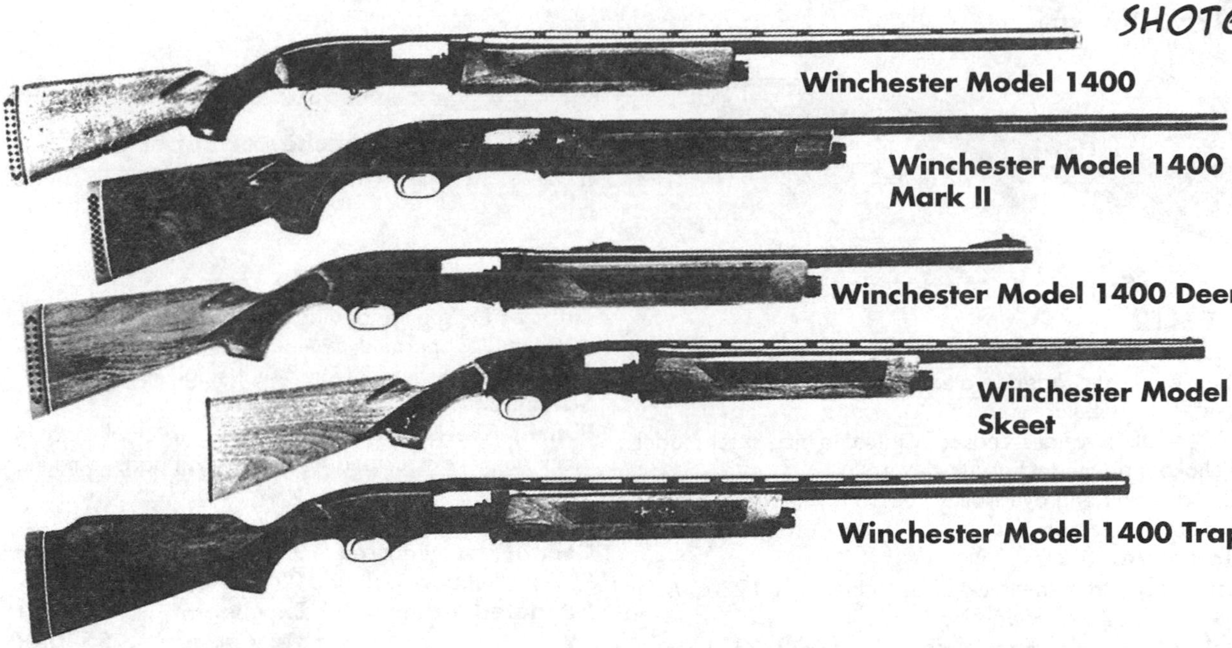

Winchester Model 1400

Winchester Model 1400 Mark II

Winchester Model 1400 Deer Gun

Winchester Model 1400 Skeet

Winchester Model 1400 Trap

Winchester Model 1400 or 1400 Winchoke

Gauge: 12, 16, 20
Action: Semiautomatic, gas-operated
Magazine: 2-shot tubular
Barrel: 26", 28", 30"; variety of chokes or adjustable choke; all 1979 models have adjustable choke
Finish: Blued; checkered walnut pistol grip stock and forearm; recoil pad available; Cycolak stock available with recoil reduction system until the late 1970s
Approximate wt.: 7½ lbs.
Comments: Made from the mid-1960s to the late 1970s. Add $25.00 for ventilated rib or Cycolak stock and recoil reduction system.

Estimated Value:	**Excellent:**	**$295.00**
	Very good:	**$235.00**

Winchester Model 1400 Mark II

Similar to the 1400 except: lighter weight and with minor improvements. Produced from the late 1960s to the late 1970s.

Estimated Value:	**Excellent:**	**$315.00**
	Very good:	**$250.00**

Winchester Model 1400 Deer Gun

Similar to the 1400 with a 22" barrel for slugs and sights.

Estimated Value:	**Excellent:**	**$300.00**
	Very good:	**$240.00**

Winchester Model 1400 Skeet

Similar to the 1400 in 12 or 20 gauge; 26" barrel with ventilated rib. Add $25.00 for recoil reduction system.

Estimated Value:	**Excellent:**	**$325.00**
	Very good:	**$265.00**

Winchester Model 1400 Trap

Similar to the 1400 in 12 gauge with a 30" full choke, ventilated rib barrel. Available with Monte Carlo stock. Add $25.00 for recoil reduction system.

Estimated Value:	**Excellent:**	**$330.00**
	Very good:	**$270.00**

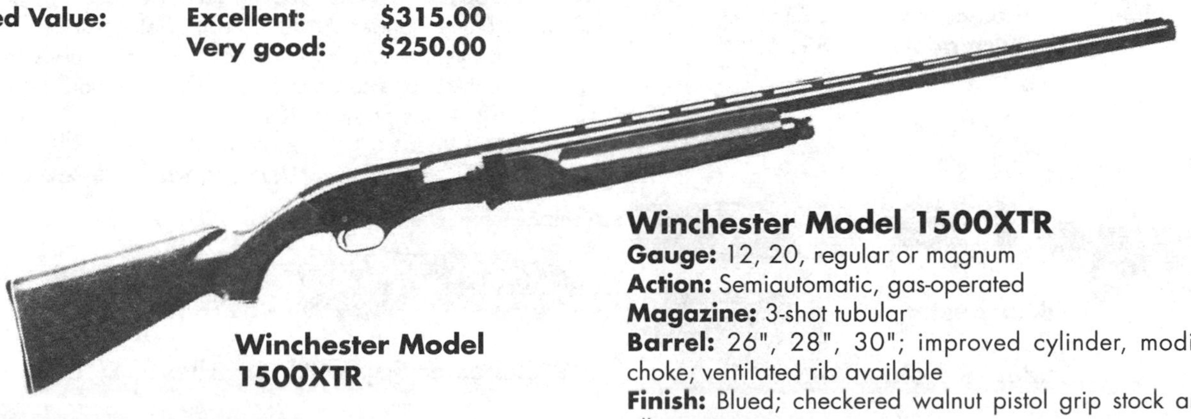

Winchester Model 1500XTR

Winchester Model 1500XTR Winchoke

Similar to the 1500XTR with removable choke tube system; 28" barrel only; add $35.00 for ventilated rib. Made in the early 1980s.

Estimated Value:	**Excellent:**	**$375.00**
	Very good:	**$300.00**

Winchester Model 1500XTR

Gauge: 12, 20, regular or magnum
Action: Semiautomatic, gas-operated
Magazine: 3-shot tubular
Barrel: 26", 28", 30"; improved cylinder, modified or full choke; ventilated rib available
Finish: Blued; checkered walnut pistol grip stock and forearm; alloy receiver
Approximate wt.: 6½ to 7 lbs.
Comments: Made from the late 1970s to the early 1980s. Add $25.00 for ventilated rib.

Estimated Value:	**Excellent:**	**$375.00**
	Very good:	**$300.00**

Winchester Super X Model 1

Winchester Super X Model 1 and Super X Model 1 XTR

Gauge: 12
Action: Semiautomatic, gas-operated
Magazine: 4-shot tubular
Barrel: 26" – 30"; various chokes; ventilated rib; skeet model has sheet choke; trap model has full choke
Finish: Blued; scroll engraved alloy receiver; checkered walnut pistol grip stock and forearm
Approximate wt.: 8¼ lbs.
Comments: Made from the mid-1970s to the early 1980s. Add 8% for skeet model; 11% for trap model.

Estimated Value:	**Excellent:**	**$600.00**
	Very good:	**$480.00**

Winchester Super X2

Gauge: 12, regular or magnum
Action: Gas-operated, semiautomatic
Magazine: 4-shot regular, 3-shot magnum
Barrel: 24", 26", or 28" ventilated rib
Finish: Checkered walnut, pistol grip stock and forearm, or black synthetic stock and forearm; recoil pad; camouflage version available.
Approximate wt.: 7¼ to 7¾ lbs.
Comments: Introduced in 1999. Add 14% for 3½" model; add 20% for Turkey model; add 22% for camouflage.

Estimated Value:	**Excellent:**	**$800.00**
	Very good:	**$640.00**

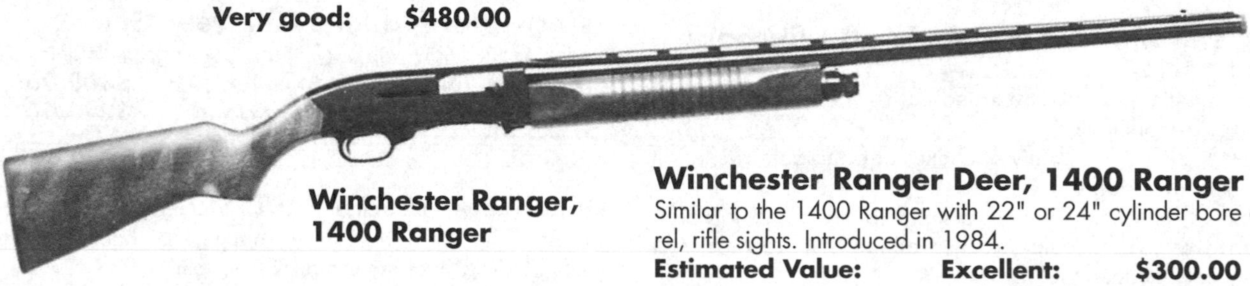

Winchester Ranger, 1400 Ranger

Winchester Ranger, 1400 Ranger

Gauge: 12, 20 regular or magnum
Action: Gas-operated semiautomatic
Magazine: 2-shot
Barrel: 26" or 28"; Winchoke interchangeable tubes and ventilated rib
Finish: Blued; hardwood semi-pistol grip stock and forearm
Approximate wt.: 7 lbs.
Comments: Introduced in 1983. Add 10% for walnut stock. Discontinued in the mid-1990s.

Estimated Value:	**Excellent:**	**$275.00**
	Very good:	**$225.00**

Winchester Ranger Deer, 1400 Ranger Deer

Similar to the 1400 Ranger with 22" or 24" cylinder bore deer barrel, rifle sights. Introduced in 1984.

Estimated Value:	**Excellent:**	**$300.00**
	Very good:	**$240.00**

Winchester Ranger Deer Combo

Similar to the Ranger 1400 Deer with extra 28" ventilated rib Winchoke barrel, hardwood stock.

Estimated Value:	**Excellent:**	**$360.00**
	Very good:	**$285.00**

Winchester 1400 Slug Hunter

Similar to the Ranger 1400 except: walnut stock; 22" barrel, improved cylinder and rifled sabot Winchoke tubes; drilled and tapped with scope base and rings; rifle sights; produced from the late 1980s to the early 1990s.

Estimated Value:	**Excellent:**	**$320.00**
	Very good:	**$260.00**

Winchester Super X2 Special Field

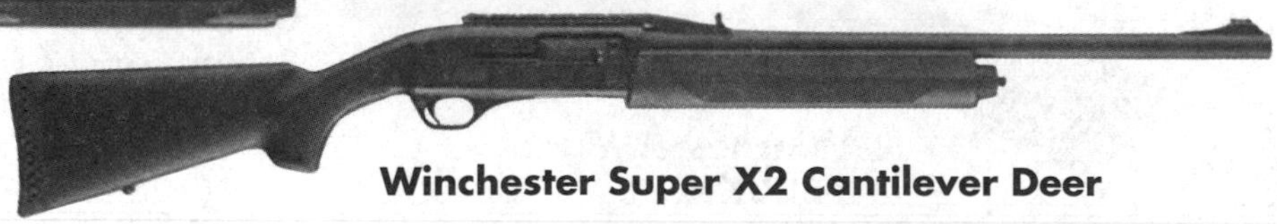

Winchester Super X2 Cantilever Deer

Winchester Super X2 Special Field

Similar to the Super X2 except: 26" or 28" barrel; light ventilated rib; weighs 6¾ lbs.

Estimated Value:	**Excellent:**	**$750.00**
	Very good:	**$600.00**

Winchester Super X2 Cantilever Deer

Similar to the Super X2 except: 22" rifled barrel; cantilever scope mount system; composite, matte black finish.

Estimated Value:	**Excellent:**	**$800.00**
	Very good:	**$640.00**

Winchester Super X2 Practical MK I

Winchester Super X2 Practical MK II

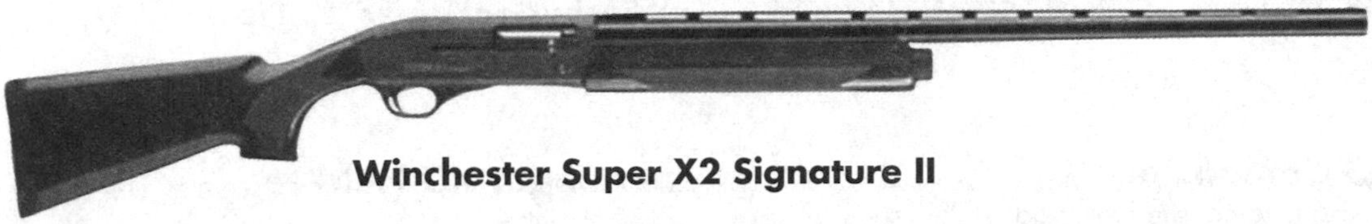

Winchester Super X2 Signature II

Winchester Super X2 Practical MK I

Similar to the Super X2 except: 8-shot extended magazine; 22" barrel; composite stock and forearm; recoil pad; weighs 8 lbs.

Estimated Value: **Excellent:** **$835.00**
Very good: **$670.00**

Winchester Super X2 Practical MK II

Similar to the Super X2 Practical MK I except: removable ghost-ring sight which mounts on the cantilever rail.

Estimated Value: **Excellent:** **$965.00**
Very good: **$775.00**

Winchester Super X2 Signature II

Similar to the Super X2 except: 28" or 30" barrel; spacer-adjustable stock for custom fit; red anodized receiver; black stock and forearm.

Estimated Value: **Excellent:** **$760.00**
Very good: **$610.00**

Winchester Super X2 Signature Red

Winchester Super X2 Sporting Clays

Winchester Super X2 Signature Red

Similar to the Super X2 Signature II except: black receiver; red finish hardwood stock and forearm with DuraTouch coating.

Estimated Value: **Excellent:** **$760.00**
Very good: **$610.00**

Winchester Super X2 Sporting Clays

Similar to the Super X2 except: 28" or 30" barrel; spacer-adjustable stock; low luster finish with satin finish on stock and forearm.

Estimated Value: **Excellent:** **$745.00**
Very good: **$600.00**

Winchester Super X3 Composite

Winchester Super X3 Cantilever Deer

Winchester Super X3 Field

Winchester Super X3 Composite

Similar to the Super X3 Field except: composite finish; add 10% for 3½" chamber.

Estimated Value:	**New (retail):**	**$1,269.00**
	Excellent:	**$ 950.00**
	Very good:	**$ 760.00**

Winchester Super X3 Cantilever Deer

Similar to the Super X3 Field except: 22" rifled barrel; composite finish; cantilever sight rail design.

Estimated Value:	**New (retail):**	**$1,199.00**
	Excellent:	**$ 900.00**
	Very good:	**$ 720.00**

Winchester Super X3 Field

Gauge: 12, 3" chamber
Action: Gas-operated, semiautomatic
Magazine: 3-shot tubular
Barrel: 26" or 28", ventilated rib
Finish: Gunmetal gray, alloy receiver; checkered walnut stock and forearm; recoil pad; camouflage finish available
Approximate wt.: 7 lbs.
Comments: A lightweight shotgun introduced in 2006. Add 20% for camouflage finish.

Estimated Value:	**New (retail):**	**$1,199.00**
	Excellent:	**$ 900.00**
	Very good:	**$ 720.00**

ZOLI

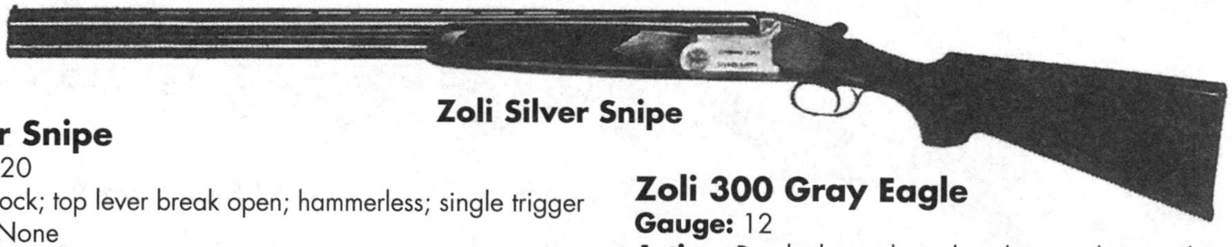

Zoli Silver Snipe

Zoli Silver Snipe

Gauge: 12, 20
Action: Box lock; top lever break open; hammerless; single trigger
Magazine: None
Barrel: Over and under double barrel; 26", 28", 30"; ventilated rib; chrome lined
Finish: Blued; checkered walnut pistol grip stock and forearm; engraved
Approximate wt.: 7 lbs.
Comments: Manufactured in Italy.

Estimated Value:	**Excellent:**	**$550.00**
	Very good:	**$440.00**

Zoli 300 Gray Eagle

Gauge: 12
Action: Box lock; top lever break-open; hammerless
Magazine: None
Barrel: Over and under double barrel; 26", 28"; ventilated rib; chrome lined; 3" chambers
Finish: Blued; checkered walnut pistol grip stock and forearm
Approximate wt.: 7 lbs.
Comments: Manufactured in Italy.

Estimated Value:	**Excellent:**	**$500.00**
	Very good:	**$400.00**

Zoli Golden Snipe

Similar to the Silver Snipe with automatic ejectors.

Estimated Value:	**Excellent:**	**$600.00**
	Very good:	**$480.00**

Zoli 302 Gray Eagle

Similar to the 300 in 20 gauge. Weighs about 6¼ lbs.

Estimated Value:	**Excellent:**	**$550.00**
	Very good:	**$440.00**

RIFLES

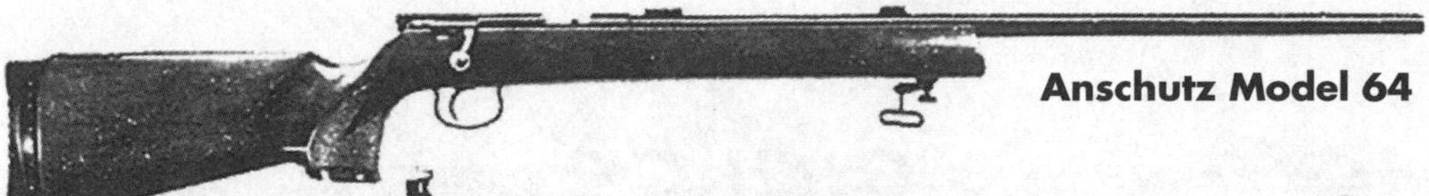
Anschutz Model 64

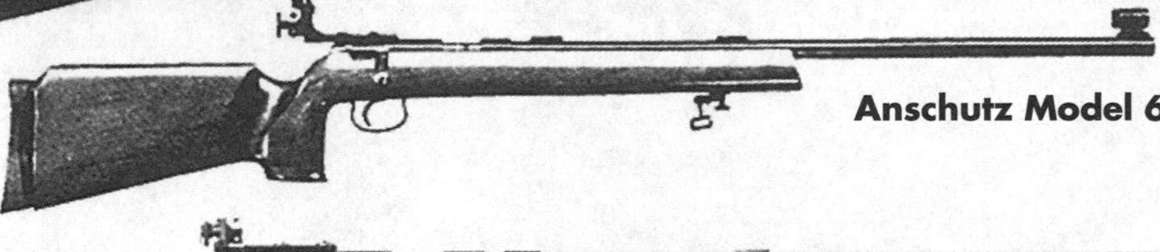
Anschutz Model 64S

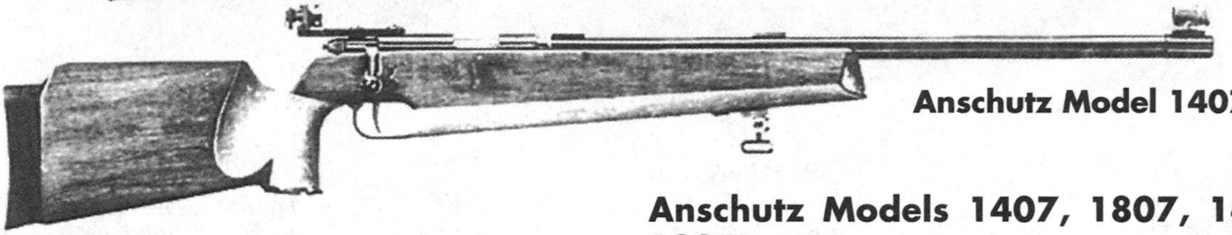
Anschutz Model 1407

Anschutz Model 64 and 64L Match

Caliber: 22 long rifle
Action: Bolt action; single shot
Magazine: None
Barrel: Blued; 26"
Sights: None
Stock and Forearm: Match style; checkered walnut one-piece pistol grip stock and forearm; thumbrest; cheekpiece; adjustable butt plate; forward swivel
Approximate wt.: 7¾ lbs.
Comments: A match rifle made from about 1967 to the early 1980s. Add $10.00 for left-hand action (Model 64L).

Estimated Value:	**Excellent:**	**$455.00**
	Very good:	**$365.00**

Anschutz Model 64S and 64SL Match

Similar to Models 64 and 64L with special match sights. Add $20.00 for left-hand version (Model 64SL).

Estimated Value:	**Excellent:**	**$450.00**
	Very good:	**$360.00**

Anschutz Mark 12 Target

Similar to the Model 64 with a heavy barrel; non-adjustable butt plate; handstop; tapered stock and forearm. Introduced in the late 1970s.

Estimated Value:	**Excellent:**	**$385.00**
	Very good:	**$310.00**

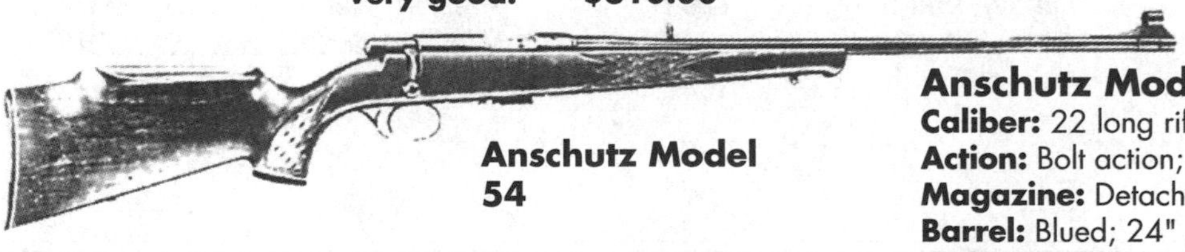
Anschutz Model 54

Anschutz Model 54M

Similar to the Model 54 in 22 Winchester magnum with a 4-shot clip.

Estimated Value:	**Excellent:**	**$525.00**
	Very good:	**$420.00**

Anschutz Models 1407, 1807, 1407L, and 1807L

Caliber: 22 long rifle
Action: Bolt action; single shot
Magazine: None
Barrel: Blued; 26"
Sights: None
Stock and Forearm: Walnut one-piece pistol grip stock and wide forearm; thumbrest; cheekpiece; adjustable butt plate; forward swivel
Approximate wt.: 10 lbs.
Comments: Match rifles made from about 1967 to the 1980s. Add $50.00 for left-hand action (Models 1407L and 1807L).

Estimated Value:	**Excellent:**	**$550.00**
	Very good:	**$440.00**

Anschutz Model 184

Caliber: 22 long rifle
Action: Bolt action; repeating
Magazine: 5-shot detachable clip
Barrel: Blued; 21½"
Sights: Folding leaf rear, hooded ramp front
Stock and Forearm: Checkered walnut Monte Carlo one-piece pistol grip stock and lipped forearm; swivels
Approximate wt.: 6 lbs.
Comments: Made from the mid-1960s to the mid-1970s.

Estimated Value:	**Excellent:**	**$340.00**
	Very good:	**$270.00**

Anschutz Model 54

Caliber: 22 long rifle
Action: Bolt action; repeating
Magazine: Detachable 5-shot clip or 10-shot clip
Barrel: Blued; 24"
Sights: Folding leaf rear, hooded ramp front
Stock and Forearm: Checkered walnut Monte Carlo one-piece pistol grip stock and lipped forearm
Approximate wt.: 6¾ lbs.
Comments: Made from the late 1960s to the early 1980s.

Estimated Value:	**Excellent:**	**$500.00**
	Very good:	**$400.00**

Anschutz Model 1432

Anschutz Model 153

Anschutz Model 1422D

Anschutz Model 141

Caliber: 22 long rifle, 22 magnum
Action: Bolt action; repeating
Magazine: Detachable 5-shot clip
Barrel: Blued; 24"
Sights: Folding leaf rear, hooded ramp front
Stock and Forearm: Checkered walnut Monte Carlo one-piece pistol grip stock and forearm
Approximate wt.: 6 lbs.
Comments: Made from the mid- to the late 1960s.

Estimated Value:	**Excellent:**	**$475.00**
	Very good:	**$380.00**

Anschutz Model 153

Similar to Model 141 with abruptly ended forearm trimmed in different wood. Made from the mid-1960s to the early 1980s.

Estimated Value:	**Excellent:**	**$500.00**
	Very good:	**$400.00**

Anschutz Bavarian 1700 and 1700D

Caliber: 22 long rifle, 22 Hornet, 222 Remington
Action: Bolt action; repeating; adjustable trigger
Magazine: 5-shot clip
Barrel: 24"; blued
Sights: Hooded ramp front; folding leaf rear
Stock and Forearm: Select checkered Monte Carlo walnut one-piece pistol grip stock and lipped forearm, cheekpiece; swivels; Classic has deep fluted comb; Custom has hand-carved cheekpiece and rosewood grip cap
Approximate wt.: 7¼ lbs.
Comments: Introduced in 1988. Add 10% for 22 Hornet or 222 Remington caliber.

Estimated Value:	**Excellent:**	**$1,120.00**
	Very good:	**$ 895.00**

Anschutz Models 1432 and 1432D Custom

Caliber: 22 Hornet
Action: Bolt action; repeating
Magazine: 5-shot clip
Barrel: Blued; 24"
Sights: Folding leaf rear, hooded ramp front
Stock and Forearm: Checkered walnut Monte Carlo one-piece pistol grip stock and lipped forearm; swivels
Approximate wt.: 6¾ lbs.
Comments: Discontinued in the late 1980s.

Estimated Value:	**Excellent:**	**$805.00**
	Very good:	**$645.00**

Anschutz Models 1422D, 1522D, 1532D, and Custom

Similar to the Model 1432D Custom except different calibers. Model 1422D is 22 long rifle; Model 1522D is 22 magnum; Model 1532D is 222 Remington. Discontinued in the late 1980s.
Estimated Value:

	1422D	**1522D**	**1532D**
Excellent:	**$825.00**	**$860.00**	**$770.00**
Very good:	**$825.00**	**$860.00**	**$770.00**

Anschutz Models 1422DCL,1522DCL,1532DCL, and Classic

Similar to the Custom models of this series except without deluxe features. Checkered walnut, one-piece pistol grip stock, and tapered forearm.
Estimated Value:

	1422DCL	**1522DCL**	**1532DCL**
Excellent:	**$770.00**	**$800.00**	**$715.00**
Very good:	**$615.00**	**$640.00**	**$570.00**

Anschutz Achiever

Caliber: 22 long rifle
Action: Bolt action; repeating
Magazine: 5- or 10-shot clip; single shot adapter
Barrel: 18½" or 19½"; blued
Sights: Hooded ramp, adjustable folding leaf rear
Stock and Forearm: Stippled European hardwood one-piece pistol grip stock and forearm; adjustable stock
Approximate wt.: 5 lbs.
Comments: Introduced in 1988.

Estimated Value:	**Excellent:**	**$400.00**
	Very good:	**$320.00**

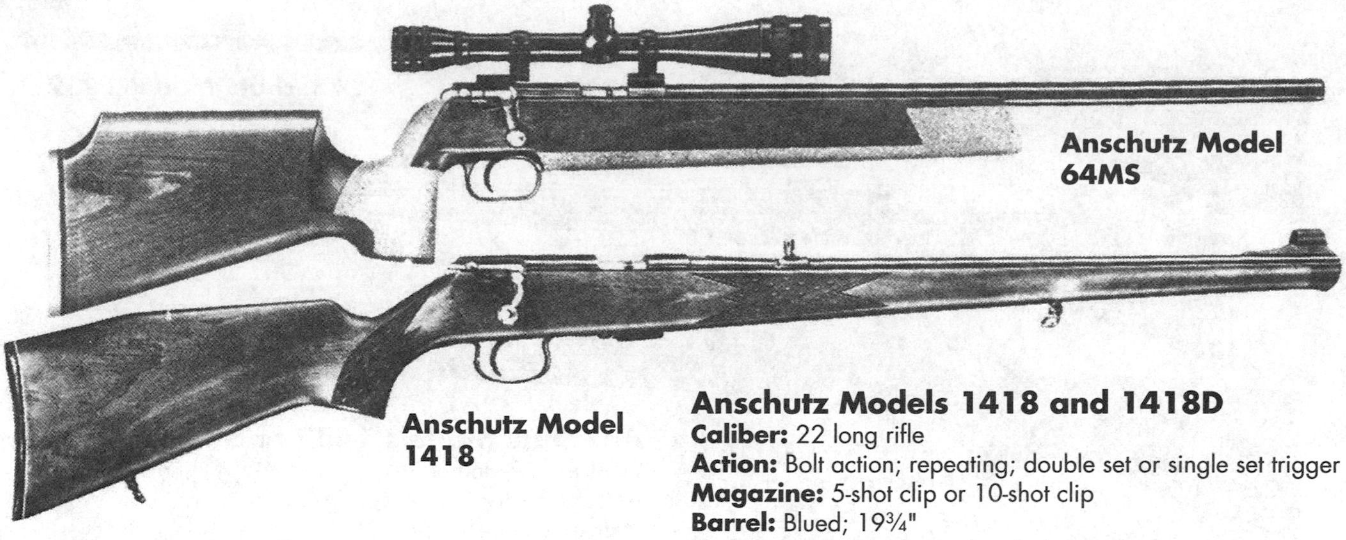

Anschutz Model 64MS

Anschutz Model 1418

Anschutz Model 64MS

Caliber: 22 long rifle
Action: Bolt action; single shot; adjustable two-stage trigger
Magazine: None
Barrel: 21¾" medium heavy
Sights: None; tapped for scope
Stock and Forearm: Silhouette-style, one-piece stippled pistol grip stock and forearm
Approximate wt.: 8 lbs.
Comments: A silhouette-style rifle made about 1982; add 6% for left-hand model.

Estimated Value:	**Excellent:**	**$810.00**
	Very good:	**$650.00**

Anschutz Model 54.18MS

Similar to the Model 64MS with a 22" barrel. Weighs 8½ lbs. Add 5% for left-hand model. Add 25% for Repeating Model; 50% for Repeating Deluxe (introduced in 1990).

Estimated Value:	**Excellent:**	**$1,290.00**
	Very good:	**$1,030.00**

Anschutz Model 164

Caliber: 22 long rifle
Action: Bolt action; repeating
Magazine: 5-shot clip or 10-shot clip
Barrel: Blued; 23"
Sights: Folding leaf rear, hooded ramp front
Stock and Forearm: Checkered walnut Monte Carlo one-piece pistol grip stock and lipped forearm
Approximate wt.: 6 lbs.
Comments: Made from the late 1960s to the early 1980s.

Estimated Value:	**Excellent:**	**$500.00**
	Very good:	**$400.00**

Anschutz Model 164M

Similar to the Model 164 in 22 Winchester magnum with a 4-shot clip.

Estimated Value:	**Excellent:**	**$525.00**
	Very good:	**$420.00**

Anschutz Models 1418 and 1418D

Caliber: 22 long rifle
Action: Bolt action; repeating; double set or single set trigger
Magazine: 5-shot clip or 10-shot clip
Barrel: Blued; 19¾"
Sights: Folding leaf rear, hooded ramp front
Stock and Forearm: Checkered European Monte Carlo stock and full-length forearm; cheekpiece; swivels
Approximate wt.: 5½ lbs.
Comments: Introduced in the late 1970s. Later called 1418D.

Estimated Value:	**Excellent:**	**$950.00**
	Very good:	**$760.00**

Anschutz Models 1416D, 1516D, and Classic

Similar to the Model 1418D and 1518D except: regular length forearm; different stock with more defined pistol grip; 23" barrel. Add $20.00 for magnum (Model 1516D).

Estimated Value:	**Excellent:**	**$610.00**
	Very good:	**$490.00**

Anschutz Models 1518 and 1518D

Similar to the Model 1418 except: 22 WMR only; 4-shot clip magazine. Currently called Model 1518D.

Estimated Value:	**Excellent:**	**$950.00**
	Very good:	**$760.00**

Anschutz Model 1433D

Similar to the Model 1418D except in 22 Hornet caliber. Discontinued in the late 1980s.

Estimated Value:	**Excellent:**	**$880.00**
	Very good:	**$720.00**

Anschutz Models 1411 and 1811

Caliber: 22 long rifle
Action: Bolt action; single shot
Magazine: None
Barrel: 27½"; heavy
Sights: None; tapped for scope
Stock and Forearm: Select walnut one-piece Monte Carlo pistol grip stock and forearm; adjustable cheekpiece; hand rest swivel; adjustable butt plate
Approximate wt.: 12 lbs.
Comments: A match-style rifle.

Estimated Value:	**Excellent:**	**$575.00**
	Very good:	**$460.00**

Anschutz Model 520 Sporter

Anschutz Mark 2000

Caliber: 22 long rifle
Action: Bolt action; hammerless; single shot
Magazine: None
Barrel: Blued; medium heavy; 26"
Sights: None; sights can be purchased separately to fit
Stock and Forearm: Smooth hardwood one-piece semi-pistol grip stock and forearm
Approximate wt.: 8½ lbs.
Comments: A match rifle designed for young shooters. Made during the 1980s.

Estimated Value:	**Excellent:**	**$575.00**
	Very good:	**$460.00**

Anschutz Model 520 Sporter and Mark 525 Sporter

Caliber: 22 long rifle
Action: Semiautomatic
Magazine: 10-shot clip
Barrel: Blued; 24"
Sights: Folding leaf rear, hooded ramp front
Stock and Forearm: Checkered walnut Monte Carlo semi-pistol stock and fluted forearm
Approximate wt.: 6½ lbs.
Comments: Introduced in the early 1980s; later called Mark 525 Sporter.

Estimated Value:	**Excellent:**	**$500.00**
	Very good:	**$400.00**

ARMALITE

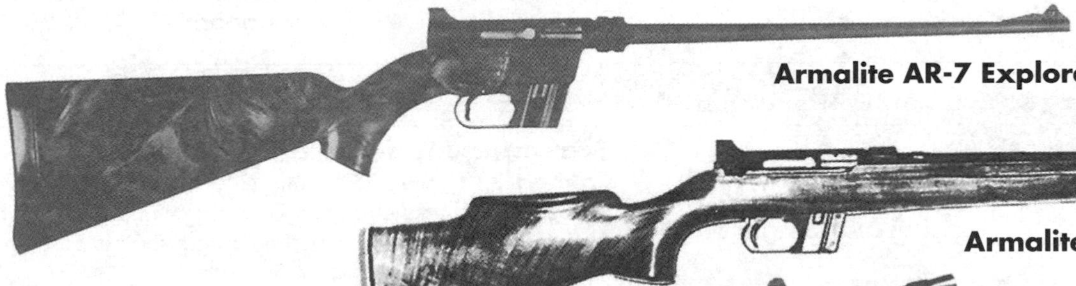

Armalite AR-7 Explorer

Armalite AR-7 Custom

Armalite AR-180 Sporter

Armalite AR-180 Sporter

Caliber: 223
Action: Semiautomatic, gas-operated
Magazine: 5-shot detachable box
Barrel: Blued; 18"
Sights: Adjustable rear and front; scope available
Stock and Forearm: Pistol grip; nylon folding stock; fiberglass forearm
Approximate wt.: 6½ lbs.
Comments: Made from the early 1970s to the 1980s.

Estimated Value:	**Excellent:**	**$900.00**
	Very good:	**$720.00**

Armalite AR-7 Explorer

Caliber: 22 long rifle
Action: Semiautomatic
Magazine: 8-shot clip
Barrel: 16"; aluminum and steel lined
Sights: Peep rear, blade front
Stock and Forearm: Fiberglass pistol grip stock (no forearm); stock acts as case for gun when dismantled
Approximate wt.: 2¾ lbs.
Comments: A lightweight alloy rifle designed to float; breaks down to fit into stock. Made from the early 1960s until the 1970s by Armalite. After about 1973 marketed as Charter Arms AR-7 Explorer until 1990.

Estimated Value:	**Excellent:**	**$150.00**
	Very good:	**$120.00**

Armalite AR-7 Custom

A sport version of the Explorer with a walnut Monte Carlo one-piece pistol grip stock and forearm. Slightly heavier.

Estimated Value:	**Excellent:**	**$175.00**
	Very good:	**$140.00**

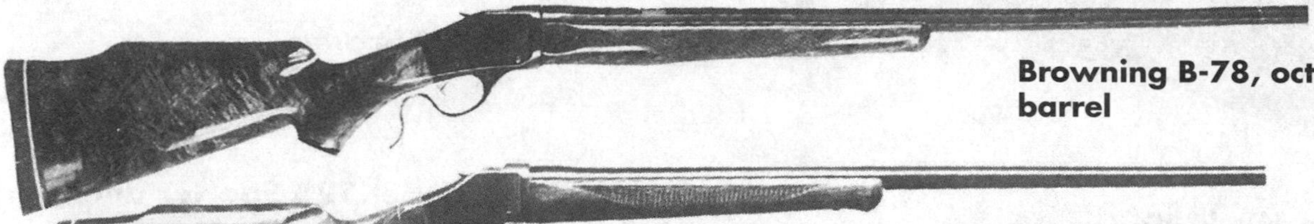

Browning B-78, octagon barrel

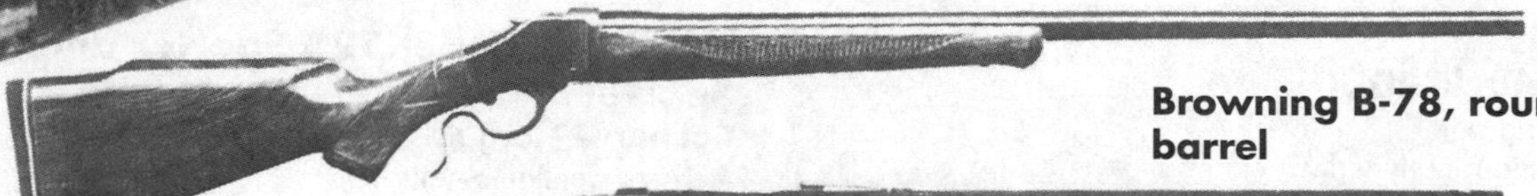

Browning B-78, round barrel

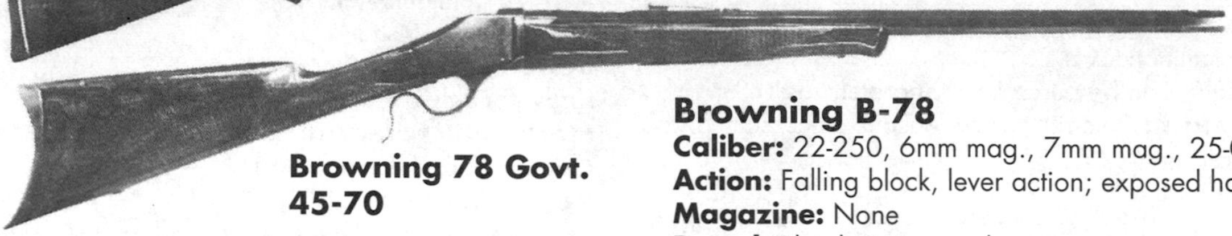

Browning 78 Govt. 45-70

Browning B-78

Caliber: 22-250, 6mm mag., 7mm mag., 25-06, 30-06
Action: Falling block, lever action; exposed hammer; single shot
Magazine: None
Barrel: Blued; 26"; round or octagon
Sights: None
Stock and Forearm: Checkered walnut Monte Carlo pistol grip stock and forearm
Approximate wt.: 7¾ to 8½ lbs.
Comments: A replica of John Browning's first patented rifle in 1878. Produced from the mid-1970s to the early 1980s.

Estimated Value:	**Excellent:**	**$725.00**
	Very good:	**$580.00**

Browning 78 Govt. 45-70

Similar to B-78 in Government 45-70 caliber with iron sights and straight grip stock, octagonal bull barrel. Made from the mid-1970s to the early 1980s.

Estimated Value:	**Excellent:**	**$725.00**
	Very good:	**$580.00**

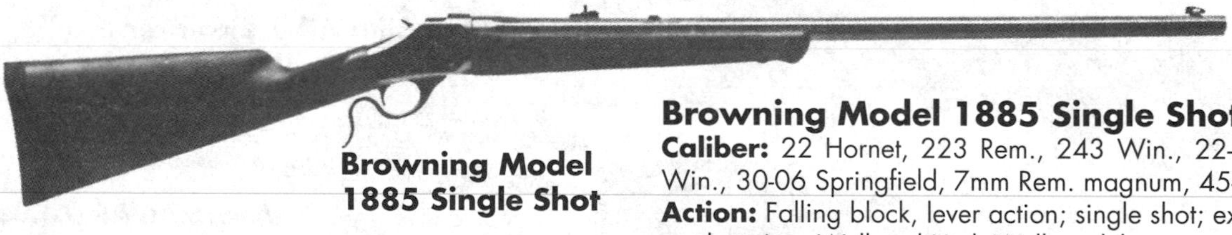

Browning Model 1885 Single Shot

Browning Model 1885 Single Shot

Caliber: 22 Hornet, 223 Rem., 243 Win., 22-250 Rem., 270 Win., 30-06 Springfield, 7mm Rem. magnum, 45-70 Govt.
Action: Falling block, lever action; single shot; exposed hammer; made in Low Wall and High Wall models
Magazine: None, single shot
Barrel: 24" Low Wall model and 28" High Wall model; octagon; blued
Sights: Drilled and tapped for scope; open sights on 45-70 model
Stock and Forearm: Checkered walnut straight grip or pistol grip stock and lipped forearm; recoil pad
Approximate wt.: 6½ lbs. Low Wall; 8¾ lbs. High Wall
Comments: Introduced in 1985. Based on John Browning's Winchester 1885.

Estimated Value:	**Excellent:**	**$800.00**
	Very good:	**$640.00**

Browning Model 1885 Single Shot Traditional Hunter

Same as the Model 1885 Single Shot except: caliber 30-30, 38-55, and 45-70 Govt. in High Wall model. Calibers 357 magnum, 44 magnum, and 45 Colt in Low Wall model; 24" barrel; Low Wall has half octagon and half round barrel.

Estimated Value:

	High Wall	**Low Wall**
Excellent:	**$925.00**	**$975.00**
Very good:	**$740.00**	**$780.00**

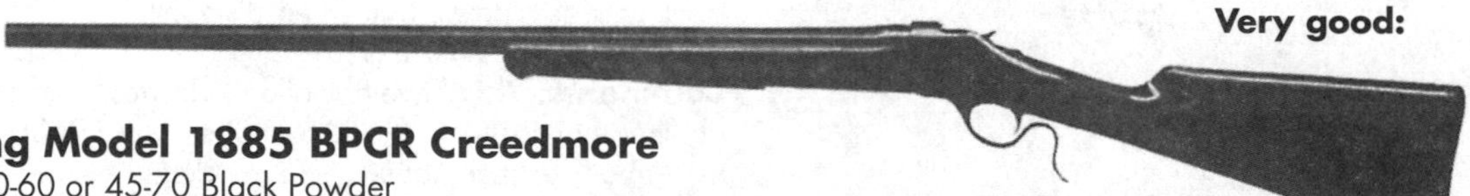

Browning Model 1885 BPCR

Browning Model 1885 BPCR Creedmore

Caliber: 40-60 or 45-70 Black Powder
Action: Falling block, lever action; single shot; exposed hammer
Magazine: None, single-shot
Barrel: 28" blued; round
Sights: Globe front; adjustable vernier rear
Stock and Forearm: Checkered walnut pistol grip stock with Schnabel forearm
Approximate wt.: 11 lbs.
Comments: Made in the 1990s.

Estimated Value:	**Excellent:**	**$1,350.00**
	Very good:	**$1,080.00**

Browning Model 1885 BPCR

Similar to the Model 1885 BPCR Creedmore except: calibers 40-65 (black powder only) and 45-70 Govt. (black powder or smokeless loads); 30" barrel.

Estimated Value:	**Excellent:**	**$1,325.00**
	Very good:	**$1,060.00**

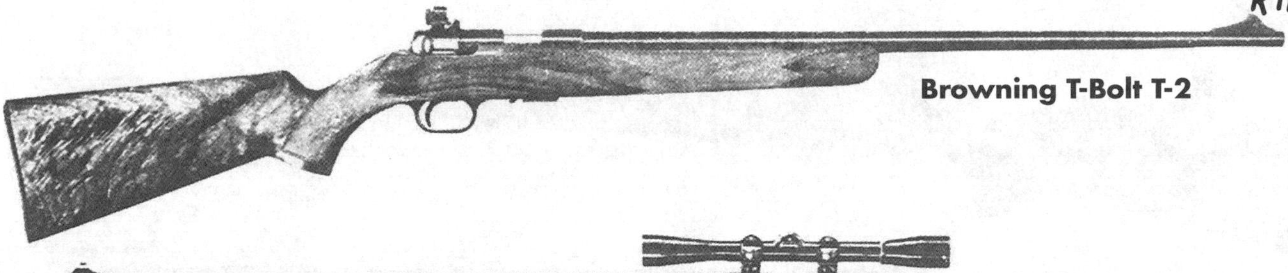

Browning T-Bolt T-2

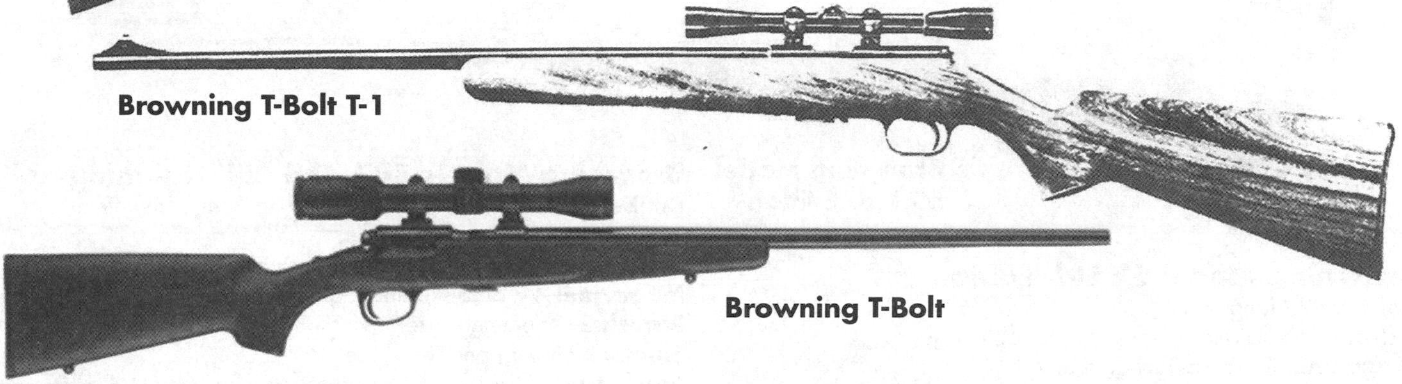

Browning T-Bolt T-1

Browning T-Bolt

Browning T-Bolt

A reintroduced version of Browning's T-Bolt. Drilled for scope mounts; satin finish walnut; swivels. Introduced in 2006. 22 magnum and 17 HMR caliber added 2008 (add 7%). A composite model is also available as well as a Target Varmint model. As with most Remington rifles, left-hand models are available.

Estimated Value:	**New (retail):**	**$709.00**
	Excellent:	**$530.00**
	Very good:	**$425.00**

Browning T Bolt, T-1 and T-2

Caliber: 22 short, long, long rifle
Action: Bolt action; hammerless; side ejector; repeating; single shot conversion
Magazine: Removable 5-shot box
Barrel: Blued; 22"
Sights: Peep rear, ramp front
Stock and Forearm: Walnut one-piece smooth (T-1) or checkered (T-2) pistol grip stock and forearm
Approximate wt.: 6 lbs.
Comments: Made from the mid-1960s to the mid-1970s in Belgium. Add 3% for T-2.

Estimated Value:	**Excellent:**	**$425.00**
	Very good:	**$340.00**

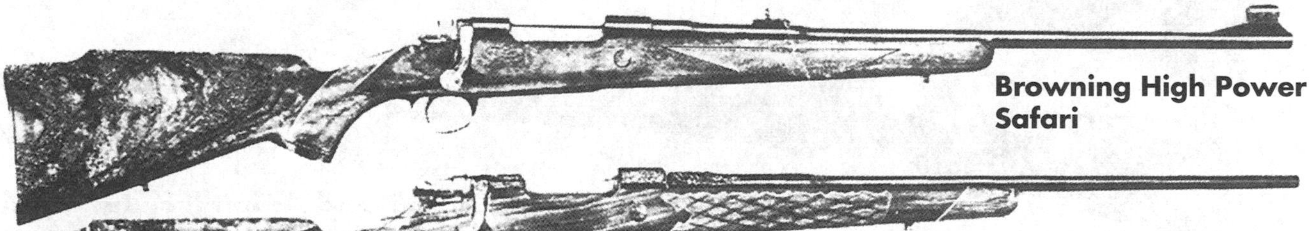

Browning High Power Safari

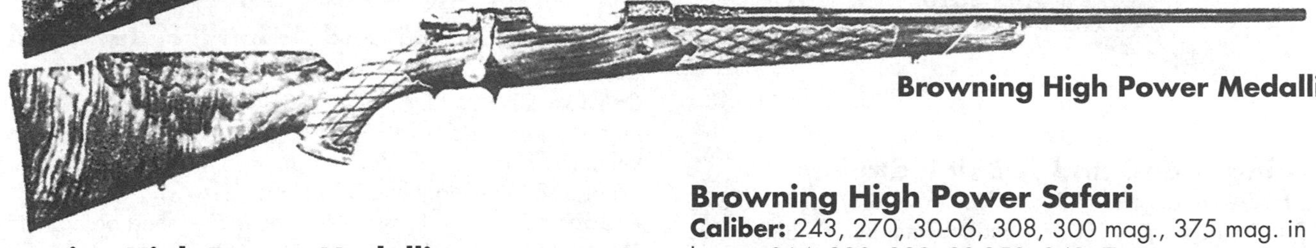

Browning High Power Medallion

Browning High Power Medallion

A higher grade version of the Safari with more engraving and higher quality wood. Made from the early 1960s to the mid-1970s.

Estimated Value:	**Excellent:**	**$2,000.00**
	Very good:	**$1,600.00**

Browning High Power Olympian

Highest grade of High Power models with complete engraving and some gold inlay. Made from the early 1960s to the mid-1970s.

Estimated Value:	**Excellent:**	**$3,500.00**
	Very good:	**$2,800.00**

Browning High Power Safari

Caliber: 243, 270, 30-06, 308, 300 mag., 375 mag. in 1960; later in 264, 338, 222, 22-250, 243, 7mm mag.
Action: Mauser-type bolt action; repeating
Magazine: 3- or 5-shot clip, depending on caliber
Barrel: Blued; 22" or 24"
Sights: Adjustable sporting rear, hooded ramp front
Stock and Forearm: Checkered walnut Monte Carlo one-piece pistol grip stock and forearm; magnum calibers have recoil pad; swivels
Approximate wt.: 6 to 8 lbs.
Comments: Made from about 1960 through the mid-1970s. Add 10% for long action.

Estimated Value:	**Excellent:**	**$975.00**
	Very good:	**$780.00**

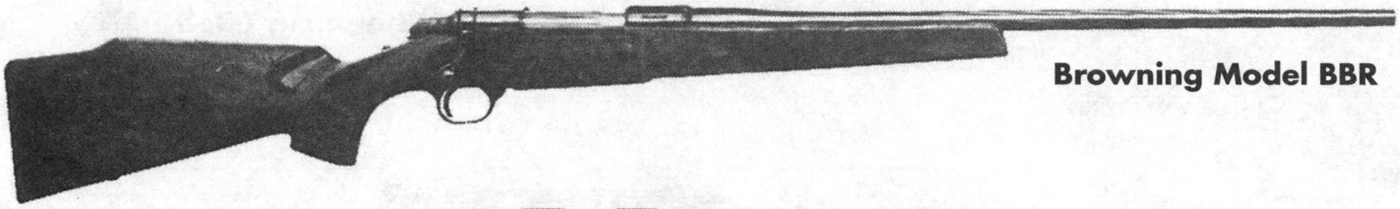

Browning Model BBR

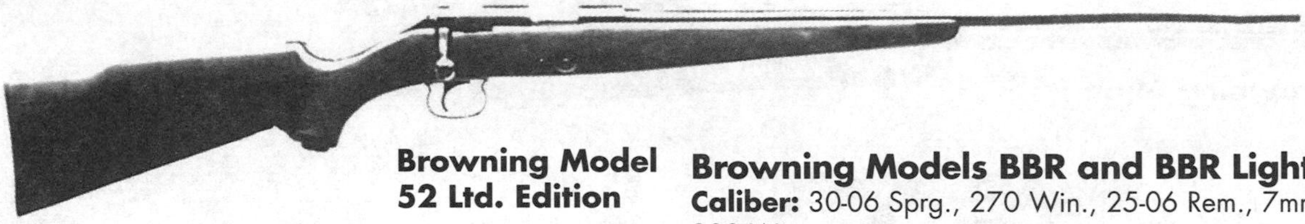

Browning Model 52 Ltd. Edition

Browning Model 52 Ltd. Edition

Caliber: 22 long rifle
Action: Bolt action; repeating; adjustable trigger
Magazine: 5-shot, detachable box
Barrel: 24"
Sights: None; tapped for scope
Stock and Forearm: Checkered high-grade walnut, pistol grip one-piece stock and forearm; rosewood fore-end
Approximate wt.: 7 lbs.
Comments: A limited edition reproduction of the Model 52 introduced in 1991. Only 5,000 of this model produced.

Estimated Value:	**Excellent:**	**$675.00**
	Very good:	**$540.00**

Browning Models BBR and BBR Lightning Bolt

Caliber: 30-06 Sprg., 270 Win., 25-06 Rem., 7mm Rem. mag., 300 Win. mag.
Action: Bolt action; short throw; repeating
Magazine: 4-shot; 3-shot in magnum; hinged floorplate
Barrel: 24" floating barrel; recessed muzzle
Sights: None; tapped for scope
Stock and Forearm: Checkered walnut Monte Carlo one-piece pistol grip stock and forearm; sling studs; recoil pad on mag.; stock and forearm changed slightly in 1982.
Approximate wt.: 8 lbs.
Comments: A high-powered hunting rifle made from late 1970s to 1985. A limited edition (1,000) with engraved elk scenes was introduced in 1984. Add 25% for limited edition.

Estimated Value:	**Excellent:**	**$500.00**
	Very good:	**$400.00**

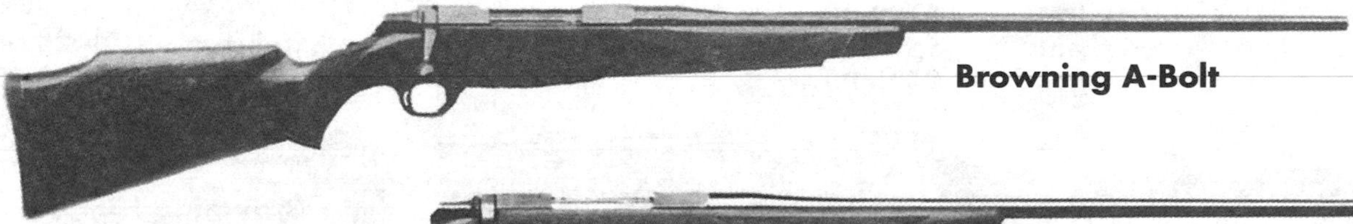

Browning A-Bolt

Browning A-Bolt Stalker

Browning A-Bolt and A-Bolt II Stalker

Similar to the A-Bolt and A-Bolt II Hunter except: calibers 375 H&H, 338 Win. mag., 300 Win. mag., 7mm Rem. mag., 25-06 Rem., 270 Rem., 280 Rem., 30-06 Sprg., 284 Win., and 257 Roberts. In three special finishes; Stainless Stalker has matte stainless steel with graphite fiberglass composite stock; Camo Stalker has multi-laminated wood stock with various shades of black and green, matte blue finish (discontinued 1991); Composite Stalker has graphite/fiberglass composite stock. Add 26% for stainless steel. Add 12% for BOSS System (Ballistic Optimizing Shooting System).

Estimated Value:	**New (retail):**	**$915.00**
	Excellent:	**$685.00**
	Very good:	**$549.00**

Browning A-Bolt and A-Bolt II Hunter and Classic

Caliber: 22-250 Rem., 223, 25 Win. magnum, 257 Roberts, 7mm-08 Rem., 25-06 Rem., 243 Win., 270 Win., 280, 7mm Rem. magnum, 300 Win. magnum, 30-06 Springfield, 308 Win., 338 Win. magnum, 375 H&H
Action: Bolt action; hammerless; repeating; short or long action
Magazine: 4-shot; 3-shot mag., 6-shot in 223; hinged floorplate
Barrel: 22" or 24"; blued
Sights: None, drilled and tapped for scope mounts. Hunter model available with open sights
Stock and Forearm: Checkered walnut, one-piece pistol grip stock and forearm; swivels; recoil pad on mag., classic satin finish
Approximate wt.: 6½ to 7¼ lbs.
Comments: Introduced in 1985; add 12% for sights. Add 14% for BOSS System; add 11% for Classic.

Estimated Value:	**New (retail):**	**$719.00**
	Excellent:	**$540.00**
	Very good:	**$430.00**

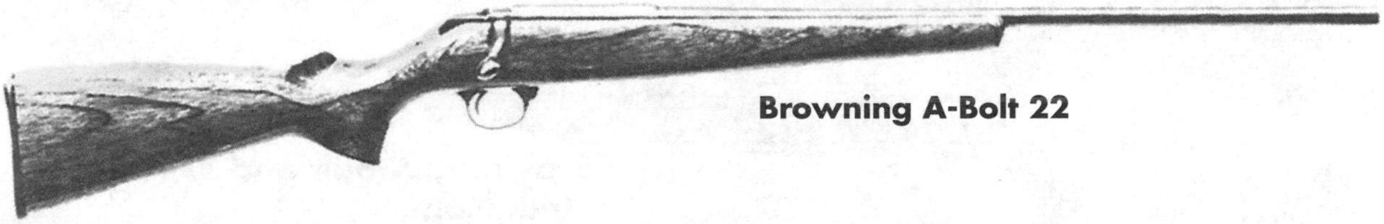

Browning A-Bolt 22

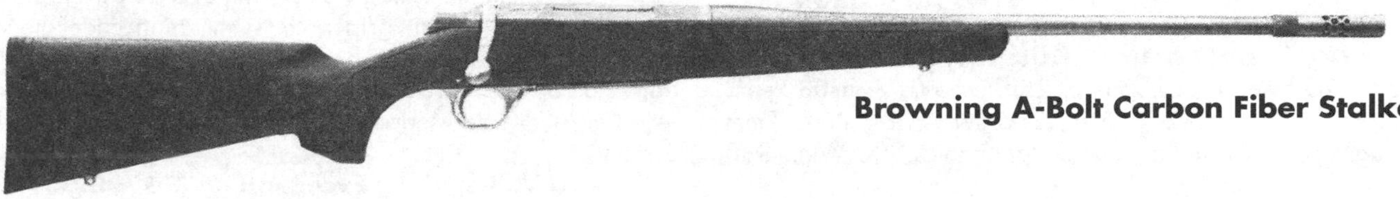

Browning A-Bolt Carbon Fiber Stalker

Browning A-Bolt Carbon Fiber Stalker

Similar to the A-Bolt II Stalker except: carbon fiber-wrapped, stainless steel-sleeve barrel; 22-250 Rem., and 300 Win. magnum calibers only; 22" or 26" barrel. Introduced in 2000.

Estimated Value:	**Excellent:**	**$1,250.00**
	Very good:	**$1,000.00**

Browning Euro-Bolt II

Similar to the A-Bolt and A-Bolt II Hunter except: calibers 7mm Rem. magnum, 270 Win., 30-06 Sprg., 243 Win., and 308 Win.; European Mannlicher-style bolt handle and lipped forearm; Monte Carlo stock. Add 11% for BOSS System (Ballistic Optimizing Shooting System).

Estimated Value:	**Excellent:**	**$550.00**
	Very good:	**$440.00**

Browning A-Bolt II Varmint

Similar to the A-Bolt II Hunter except: calibers 22-250, 308 Win., and 223 Rem.; heavier target barrel equipped with the BOSS System; black laminated wood stock; gloss or satin matte finish. Introduced in 1994.

Estimated Value:	**Excellent:**	**$660.00**
	Very good:	**$525.00**

Browning A-Bolt 22

Similar to the A-Bolt and A-Bolt II Hunter except: 22 long rifle or 22 mag. caliber; 5 or 15-shot clip; 22" barrel; wt. 5½ lbs.; add 3% for open sights; add 16% for mag.; add 32% for Gold Medallion model. Prices for Grade I.

Estimated Value:	**Excellent:**	**$325.00**
	Very good:	**$260.00**

Browning A-Bolt Micro Hunter

Similar to the A-Bolt II Hunter except: scaled down for smaller shooters; 20" or 22" barrel; available in 22 Hornet, 223 Rem., 22-250 Rem., 243 Win., 308 Win., 7mm-08 Rem. calibers; satin-finish walnut stock and forearm.

Estimated Value:	**New (retail):**	**$739.00**
	Excellent:	**$555.00**
	Very good:	**$445.00**

Browning A-Bolt Varmint Stalker

Similar to the A-Bolt II Varmint except: non-glare composite stock and forearm; 24" or 26" barrel; 22-250 Rem. or 223 Rem. calibers.

Estimated Value:	**Excellent:**	**$650.00**
	Very good:	**$525.00**

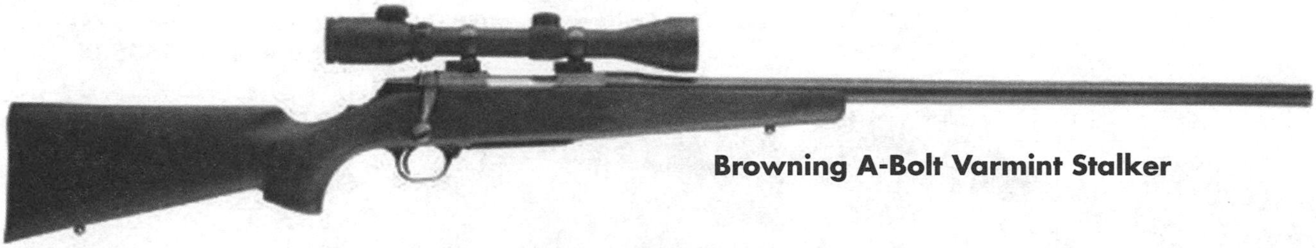

Browning A-Bolt Varmint Stalker

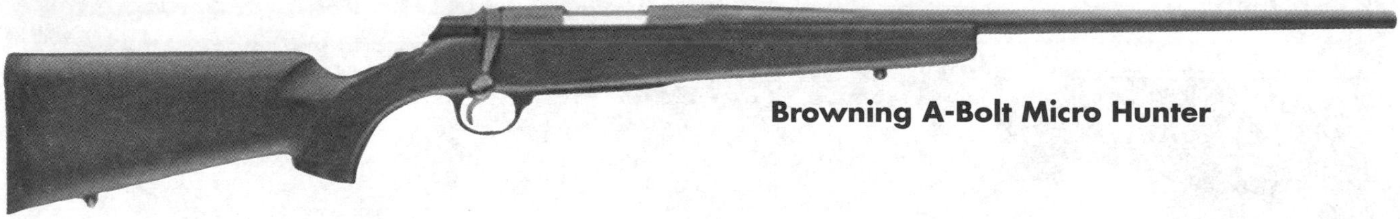

Browning A-Bolt Micro Hunter

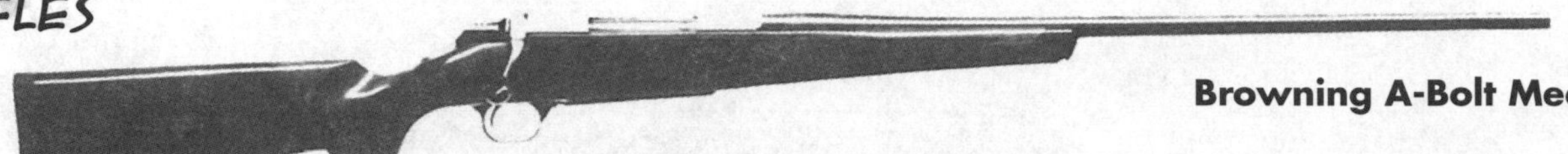

Browning A-Bolt Medallion

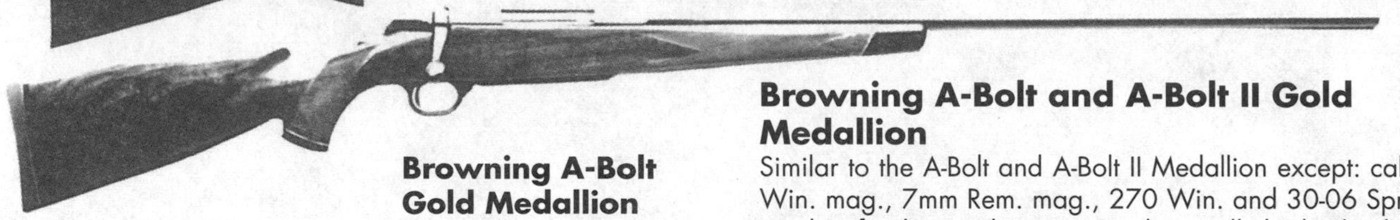

Browning A-Bolt Gold Medallion

Browning A-Bolt and A-Bolt II Medallion

Caliber: 22-250 Rem., 223 Rem., 257 Roberts, 7mm-08 Rem., 25-06 Rem., 243 Win., 270 Win., 280 Rem., 284 Win., 7mm Rem. mag., 300 Win. mag., 30-06 Springfield, 308 Win., 338 Win. mag., 375 H&H
Action: Bolt action; hammerless; repeating; short or long action
Magazine: 4-shot; 3-shot magnum; hinged floorplate
Barrel: 22" or 26"; blued, free-floating
Sights: None, drilled and tapped for scope mounts
Stock and Forearm: Checkered select high-gloss walnut, one-piece pistol grip stock and forearm; rosewood fore-end; swivels; recoil pad on mag.
Approximate wt.: 6½ to 7¼ lbs.
Comments: Add 12% for sights. Add 12% for BOSS System. Add 12% for 375 H&H caliber.

Estimated Value:	**New (retail):**	**$869.00**
	Excellent:	**$650.00**
	Very good:	**$520.00**

Browning A-Bolt II Custom Trophy

Caliber: 22 Hornet, 223 Rem., 22-250 Rem., 7mm-08 Rem., 243 Win., 308 Win.
Action: Bolt action; hammerless; repeating
Magazine: 4-shot; 6-shot in 223 Rem.; hinged floorplate
Barrel: 20"; octagon
Sights: None
Stock and Forearm: Checkered American walnut, one-piece pistol grip stock and forearm; swivels
Approximate wt.: 6¼ lbs.
Comments: Introduced in 1998.

Estimated Value:	**Excellent:**	**$1,070.00**
	Very good:	**$ 855.00**

Browning A-Bolt and A-Bolt II Gold Medallion

Similar to the A-Bolt and A-Bolt II Medallion except: calibers 300 Win. mag., 7mm Rem. mag., 270 Win. and 30-06 Sprg.; higher grade of select walnut, grip palm swell, high cheekpiece and fluted comb; brass spacers between stock and recoil pad, pistol grip and cap, and fore-end and tip; engraving covers flat sides of receiver and "Gold Medallion" is gold filled. Add 12% for BOSS System.

Estimated Value:	**Excellent:**	**$700.00**
	Very good:	**$560.00**

Browning A-Bolt and A-Bolt II Micro Medallion

A scaled-down version of the A-Bolt and A-Bolt II Medallion series. Shorter length of pull; 20" barrel; slimmer overall proportions. 4-shot magazine in calibers 22 Hornet, 243, 308, 7mm-08 Rem., 284 Win., 223 Rem. and 22-250.

Estimated Value:	**Excellent:**	**$525.00**
	Very good:	**$420.00**

Browning A-Bolt White Gold Medallion

Similar to the A-Bolt Gold Medallion except: stainless steel receiver and barrel.

Estimated Value:	**Excellent:**	**$750.00**
	Very good:	**$600.00**

Browning Acera

Caliber: 30-06 Sprg., 300 Win. magnum
Action: Straight-pull, two movement, bolt action, repeating
Magazine: 5-shot drop box; 4-shot with 300 Win. magnum
Barrel: Blued; 22" or 24"
Sights: None
Stock and Forearm: Smooth hardwood, pistol grip, one-piece stock and forearm
Approximate wt.: 7¼ and 7¾ lbs.
Comments: Introduced in 2000. Add 3% for magnum; 6% for the BOSS System.

Estimated Value:	**Excellent:**	**$675.00**
	Very good:	**$535.00**

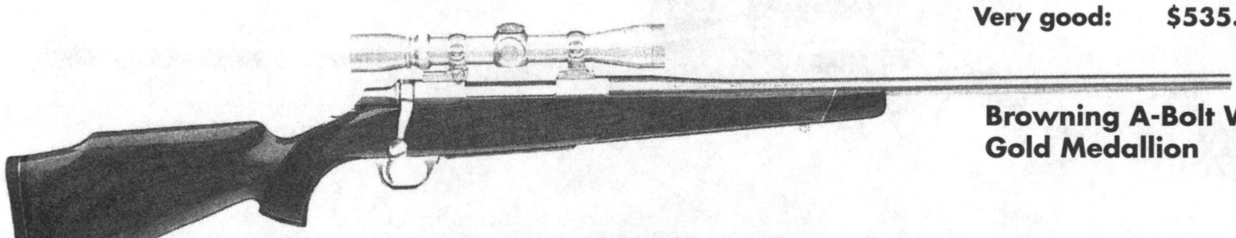

Browning A-Bolt White Gold Medallion

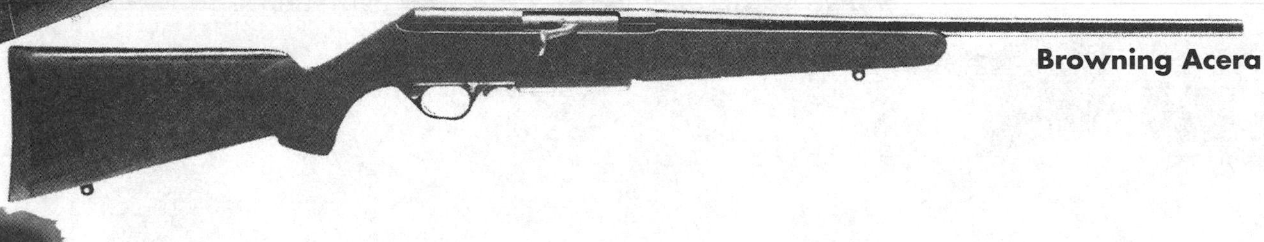

Browning Acera

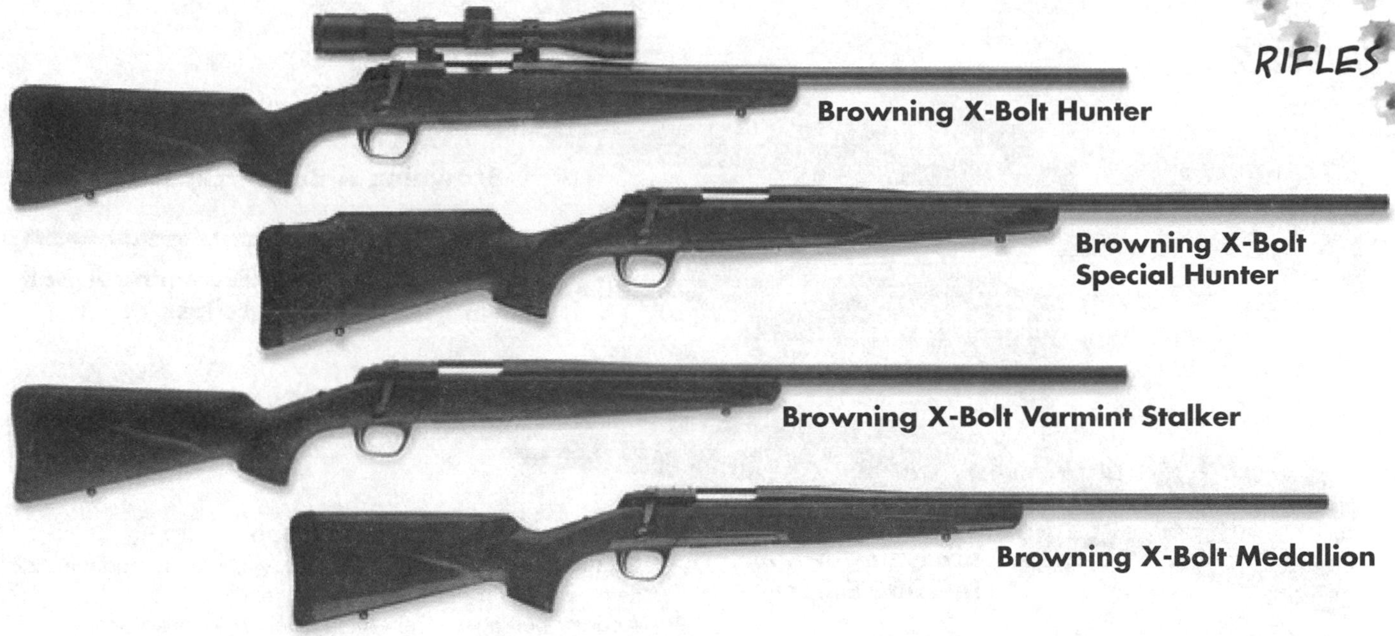

Browning X-Bolt Hunter

Caliber: 243 Win., 7mm-08 Rem., 308 Win., 25-06 Rem., 270 Win., 280 Rem., 30-06 Sprg., 7mm Rem. mag., 300 Win. mag., 338 Win. mag., 300 WSM, 270 WSM, 7mm WSM, 325 WSM, 223 Rem., 22-250 Rem.
Action: Bolt action, repeating; adjustable trigger; top-tang safety
Magazine: 4-, 5-, or 6-shot center-fed detachable rotary
Barrel: Low-luster blued, 22", 23", 24", or 26"
Sights: None
Stock and Forearm: One-piece checkered, satin-finish walnut pistol grip stock and forearm; swivels; recoil pad
Approximate wt.: 6½ to 7 lbs.
Comments: Browning's big game deer hunting rifle, available in a variety of calibers. Add 4% for magnum calibers.

Estimated Value:	**New (retail):**	**$899.00**
	Excellent:	**$675.00**
	Very good:	**$540.00**

Browning X-Bolt Micro Hunter

Similar to the X-Bolt Hunter except: stock and forearm scaled down for smaller shooters, 20" or 22" barrel and in 243 Win., 7mm-08 Rem., 308 Win., 300 WSM, 270 WSM, 7mm WSM, 325 WSM, 22-250 Rem. calibers; weighs 6 to 6½ lbs.

Estimated Value:	**New (retail):**	**$899.00**
	Excellent:	**$675.00**
	Very good:	**$540.00**

Browning X-Bolt Stainless Hunter

Similar to the X-Bolt Hunter except: low-luster stainless steel finish; weighs 6½ to 7 lbs.; add 3% for magnum calibers. Introduced in 2010.

Estimated Value:	**New (retail):**	**$1,059.00**
	Excellent:	**$ 795.00**
	Very good:	**$ 635.00**

Browning X-Bolt Special Hunter

Similar to the X-Bolt Hunter except: stock has raised cheekpiece, 325 WSM caliber only; 23" barrel; weighs 7 lbs., 3 oz.

Estimated Value:	**New (retail):**	**$979.00**
	Excellent:	**$735.00**
	Very good:	**$590.00**

Browning X-Bolt Stainless Hunter

Similar to the X-Bolt Hunter except: low-luster stainless steel finish; add 3% for magnum calibers.

Estimated Value:	**New (retail):**	**$1,059.00**
	Excellent:	**$ 795.00**
	Very good:	**$ 635.00**

Browning X-Bolt Composite Stalker

Similar to the X-Bolt Hunter except: stock and forearm are matte black composite with textured gripping surfaces. Add 4% for magnum calibers.

Estimated Value:	**New (retail):**	**$899.00**
	Excellent:	**$675.00**
	Very good:	**$540.00**

Browning X-Bolt Varmint Stalker

Similar to the X-Bolt Composite stalker except: 24" or 26" medium heavy barrel; 243 Win., 308 Win., 223 Rem., and 22-250 Rem. calibers only.

Estimated Value:	**New (retail):**	**$1,079.00**
	Excellent:	**$ 810.00**
	Very good:	**$ 645.00**

Browning X-Bolt Stainless Stalker

Similar to the X-Bolt Composite Stalker except: matte stainless steel finish. Add 3% for magnum calibers or for open sights.

Estimated Value:	**New (retail):**	**$1,119.00**
	Excellent:	**$ 840.00**
	Very good:	**$ 670.00**

Browning X-Bolt Medallion

Similar to the X-Bolt Hunter except: engraved receiver, glossy stock and forearm; rosewood fore-end grip and pistol grip cap. Add 2% for magnum calibers.

Estimated Value:	**New (retail):**	**$1,019.00**
	Excellent:	**$ 765.00**
	Very good:	**$ 610.00**

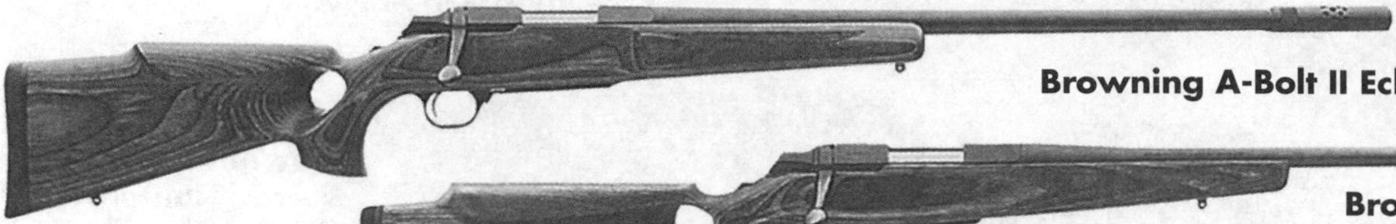

Browning A-Bolt II Eclipse Varmint

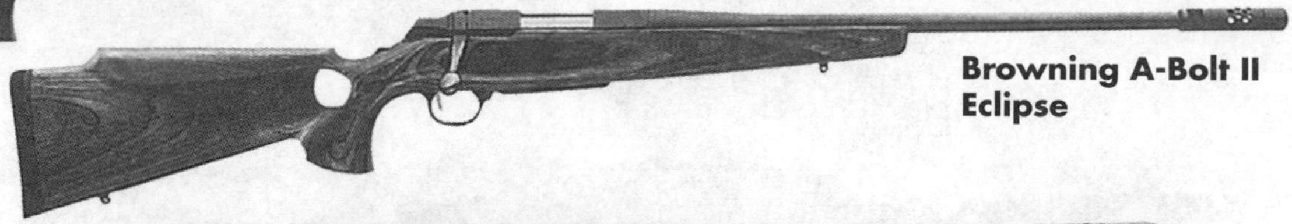

Browning A-Bolt II Eclipse

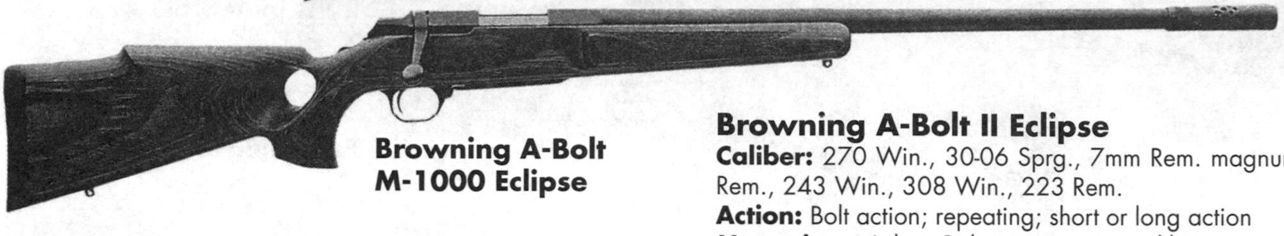

Browning A-Bolt M-1000 Eclipse

Browning A-Bolt II Eclipse Varmint

Similar to the A-Bolt II Eclipse except: calibers 22-250 Rem., 223 Rem., and 308 Win.; 26" heavy barrel.

Estimated Value: **Excellent:** **$800.00**
Very good: **$640.00**

Browning A-Bolt M-1000 Eclipse

Similar to the A-Bolt II Eclipse except: heavy barrel; available in 300 Win. magnum caliber only. Introduced in 2000. Additional calibers added 2004.

Estimated Value: **New (retail):** **$1,259.00**
Excellent: **$ 945.00**
Very good: **$ 755.00**

Browning A-Bolt II Eclipse

Caliber: 270 Win., 30-06 Sprg., 7mm Rem. magnum, 22/250 Rem., 243 Win., 308 Win., 223 Rem.
Action: Bolt action; repeating; short or long action
Magazine: 4-shot; 3-shot in magnum caliber
Barrel: 22"; 26" in magnum caliber; equipped with the Browning BOSS System located at the muzzle of the barrel; it reduces recoil by about 30% to 50% and has an adjustment which affects the barrel's vibration for best accuracy.
Sights: None
Stock and Forearm: Gray/black multi-laminated hardwood stock and forearm; custom thumbhole-style stock for maximum control
Approximate wt.: 7½ to 8 lbs.
Comments: Introduced in 1996.

Estimated Value: **Excellent:** **$800.00**
Very good: **$640.00**

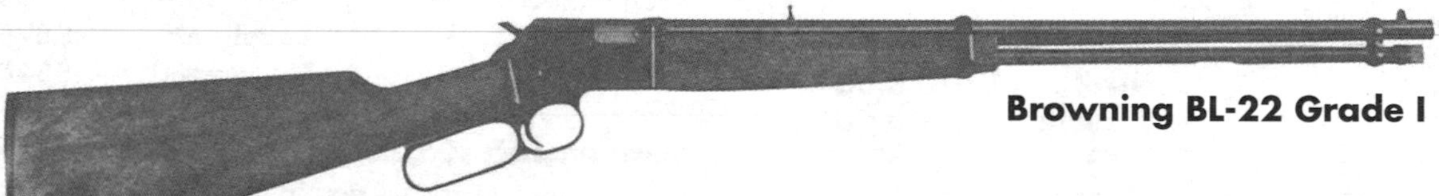

Browning BL-22 Grade I

Browning BL-22 Grade II

Browning BL-22 FLD

Browning BL-22 Grade I and Classic Grade I

Caliber: 22 short, long, long rifle (any combination)
Action: Lever action; short throw lever; exposed hammer
Magazine: Tubular; 15 long rifles; 17 longs; 22 shorts
Barrel: Blued; 20"
Sights: Folding adjustable rear, bead front
Stock and Forearm: Plain walnut straight grip stock and forearm; barrel band
Approximate wt.: 5 lbs.
Comments: A small, lightweight 22 caliber rifle produced from about 1959 to the present. Classic has satin finish; add 7% for NRA model.

Estimated Value: **New (retail):** **$559.00**
Excellent: **$420.00**
Very good: **$335.00**

Browning BL-22 Grade II and Classic Grade II

Similar to BL-22 with engraving; gold-plated trigger; checkered stock and forearm. Classic has satin finish.

Estimated Value: **New (retail):** **$639.00**
Excellent: **$480.00**
Very good: **$385.00**

Browning BL-22 FLD

Similar to the BL-22 Grade I except: satin nickel receiver; satin-finish walnut. Grade II has gold trigger (add 12%) and is available with octagon barrel (add 45%).

Estimated Value: **New (retail):** **$599.00**
Excellent: **$450.00**
Very good: **$360.00**

Browning BLR

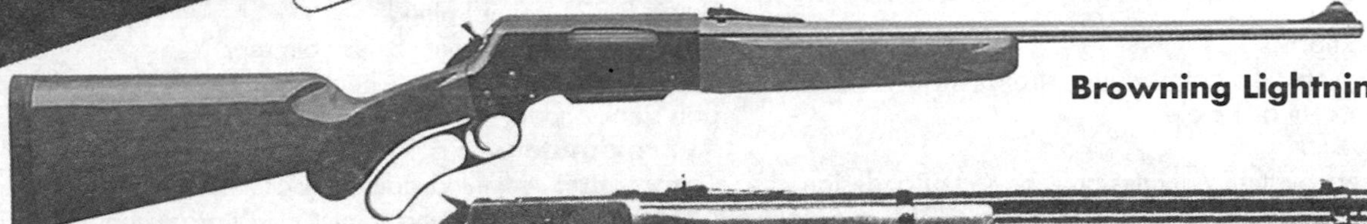

Browning Lightning BLR

Browning Model 92

Browning BLR Lightweight Pistol Grip

Browning BLR, '81 BLR

Caliber: 243, 270 Win., 30-06, 308, 358. 22-250 Rem. (added in 1982); calibers 222, 223 Rem., 257 Roberts, 284, and 7mm-08 Rem. added later
Action: Lever action; exposed hammer; repeating
Magazine: 4-shot removable box
Barrel: Blued; 20"
Sights: Adjustable rear, hooded ramp front
Stock and Forearm: Checkered walnut straight grip stock and forearm; recoil pad; barrel band
Approximate wt.: 6½ to 8½ lbs.
Comments: Made from the early 1970s to the mid-1990s. Add 6% for long action. Reintroduced in 2005.
Estimated Value: **Excellent:** **$575.00**
Very good: **$460.00**

Browning BLR Lightweight Pistol Grip

Similar to the Lightning BLR except: alloy receiver; lipped forearm. Add 20% for stainless steel finish.
Estimated Value: **New (retail):** **$919.00**
Excellent: **$690.00**
Very good: **$551.00**

Browning Lightning BLR

Caliber: 223 Rem., 22/250 Rem., 243 Win., 7mm-08 Rem., 308 Win., in short action; 270 Win., 30-06 Sprg., 7mm Rem. magnum, 300 Win. magnum, in long action
Action: Lever action; repeating; exposed hammer; short and long action
Magazine: 4-shot, 3-shot in magnum caliber; removable box magazine
Barrel: Blued; 20", 22", 24"; round
Sights: Adjustable rear with ramp front sight; drilled and tapped for scope mounts
Stock and Forearm: Checkered hardwood pistol grip stock and forearm
Approximate wt.: 6½ to 7½ lbs.
Comments: Introduced in 1996. Add 6% for long action model.
Estimated Value: **Excellent:** **$575.00**
Very good: **$460.00**

Browning Model 1895

Browning Model 92, B-92

Caliber: 44 magnum, 357 magnum (added 1982)
Action: Lever action; exposed three-position hammer; repeating
Magazine: 11-shot tubular
Barrel: 20"; round; blued
Sights: Adjustable cloverleaf rear, blade front
Stock and Forearm: Plain walnut straight grip stock and forearm; barrel band
Approximate wt.: 5½ lbs.
Comments: An authentic remake of the 1892 Winchester designed by John Browning. Introduced in the late 1970s. Discontinued in the late 1980s.
Estimated Value: **Excellent:** **$500.00**
Very good: **$400.00**

Browning Model 1895

Caliber: 30-06 Springfield
Action: Lever action; exposed hammer; repeating
Magazine: 5-shot non-detachable box
Barrel: 24"; blued
Sights: Buckhorn rear, beaded ramp front
Stock and Forearm: Walnut straight grip stock and lipped forearm; high grade has checkered stock with engraved steel gray receiver
Approximate wt.: 8 lbs.
Comments: Made in the mid-1980s, this is a newer version of John Browning's Model 1895 first produced by Winchester in 1896. Add 30% for high grade.
Estimated Value: **Excellent:** **$650.00**
Very good: **$520.00**

Browning Model 1886

Caliber: 45-70 Govt.
Action: Lever action; exposed hammer; repeating
Magazine: 8-shot tubular, side-port load
Barrel: 26"; octagon
Sights: Open buckhorn
Stock and Forearm: Smooth walnut straight-grip stock and forearm; metal, crescent butt plate
Approximate wt.: 9¼ lbs.
Comments: Based on the Winchester Model 1886 designed by John Browning. Made in the late 1980s. Add 35% for high grade.

Estimated Value:	**Excellent:**	**$950.00**
	Very good:	**$760.00**

Browning Model 53 Limited Edition

Caliber: 32-20 Win., round nose or hollow point only
Action: Lever action; exposed hammer; repeating
Magazine: 7-shot tubular, side-port load
Barrel: 22"; round; blued
Sights: Post bead front, adjustable rear
Stock and Forearm: Checkered, high-gloss walnut straight-grip stock and forearm
Approximate wt.: 6½ lbs.
Comments: A limited edition version of the Winchester Model 53 designed by Browning. Only 5,000 produced in 1991.

Estimated Value:	**Excellent:**	**$700.00**
	Very good:	**$560.00**

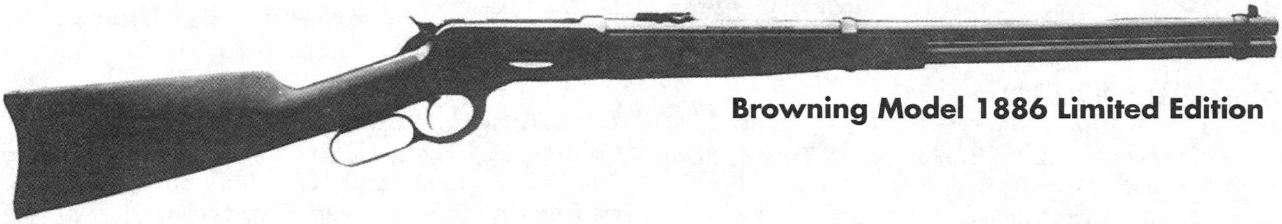

Browning Model 1886 Limited Edition

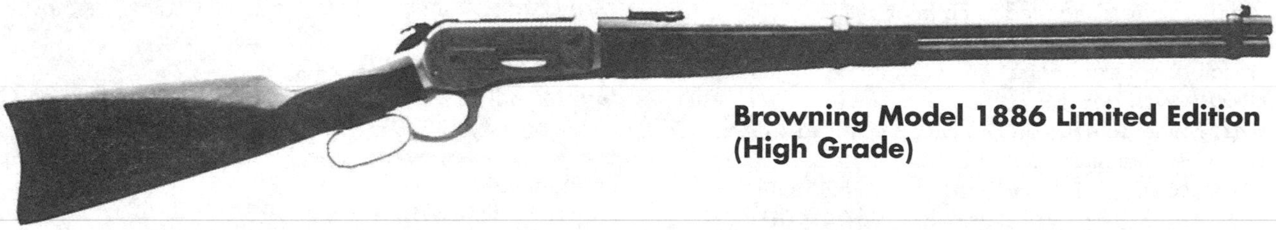

Browning Model 1886 Limited Edition (High Grade)

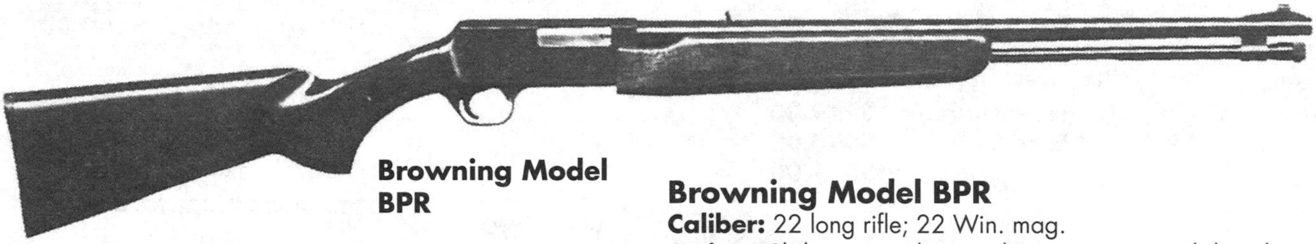

Browning Model BPR

Browning Model 1886 Limited Edition

Caliber: 45-70 Govt.
Action: Lever action; exposed hammer; repeating
Magazine: 8-shot tubular, side-port load
Barrel: 22"; blued; round
Sights: Open buckhorn
Stock and Forearm: Select walnut straight-grip stock and forearm; metal, crescent butt plate
Approximate wt.: 8 lbs.
Comments: A limited edition carbine based on the Winchester Model 1886 designed by John Browning. Produced in 1992. Add 35% for high grade.

Estimated Value:	**Excellent:**	**$1,000.00**
	Very good:	**$ 800.00**

Browning Model BPR

Caliber: 22 long rifle; 22 Win. mag.
Action: Slide action; hammerless; repeating; slide release on trigger guard
Magazine: 15-shot tubular; 11-shot on magnum
Barrel: Blued; 20¼"
Sights: Adjustable folding leaf rear, gold bead front
Stock and Forearm: Checkered walnut pistol grip stock and slide handle
Approximate wt.: 6¼ lbs.
Comments: Add 8% for magnum.

Estimated Value:	**Excellent:**	**$545.00**
	Very good:	**$435.00**

Browning Model BPR Grade II

Similar to the BPR in magnum only; engraved squirrels and rabbits on receiver.

Estimated Value:	**Excellent:**	**$425.00**
	Very good:	**$340.00**

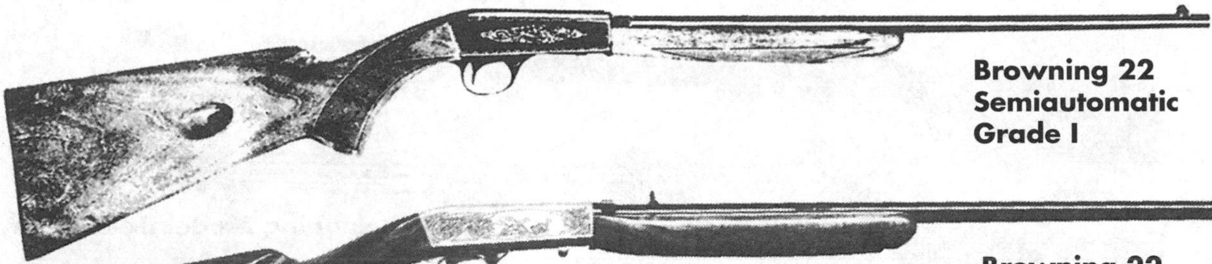

Browning 22 Semiautomatic Grade I

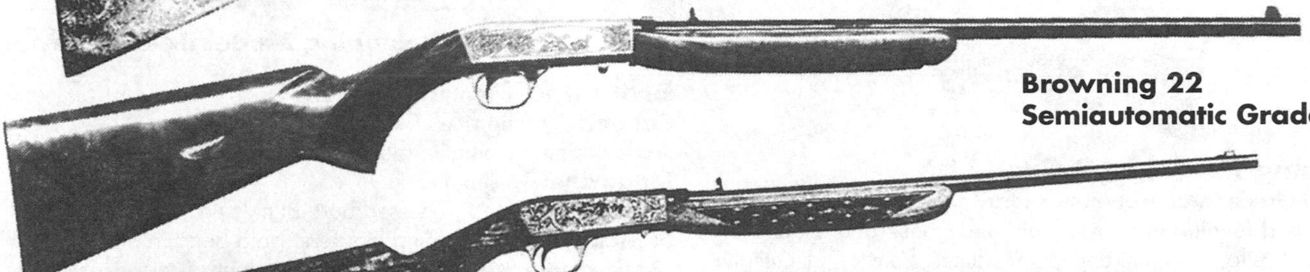

Browning 22 Semiautomatic Grade II

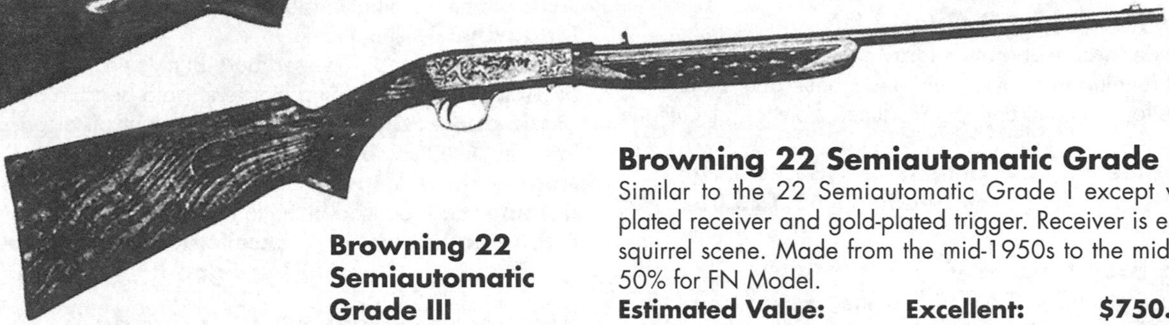

Browning 22 Semiautomatic Grade III

Browning 22 Semiautomatic Grade I

Caliber: 22 long rifle
Action: Browning semiautomatic; hammerless; bottom ejector
Magazine: 11-shot tubular in stock
Barrel: Blued; $22\frac{1}{4}$" or $19\frac{1}{4}$", satin stainless available
Sights: Adjustable rear, dovetail bead front
Stock and Forearm: Hand checkered walnut pistol grip stock and forearm; gray laminated wood available
Approximate wt.: $4\frac{1}{4}$ lbs.
Comments: This takedown model has been in production since the mid-1950s. Add 40% for FN or stainless steel.

Estimated Value:	**New (retail):**	**$659.00**
	Excellent:	**$495.00**
	Very good:	**$395.00**

Browning 22 Semiautomatic Grade II

Similar to the 22 Semiautomatic Grade I except with chrome-plated receiver and gold-plated trigger. Receiver is engraved with squirrel scene. Made from the mid-1950s to the mid-1980s. Add 50% for FN Model.

Estimated Value:	**Excellent:**	**$750.00**
	Very good:	**$600.00**

Browning 22 Semiautomatic Grade III

Same as the Grade II except engraving is of bird dog and birds, high-quality finish. Made from the mid-1950s to the mid-1980s. Add 75% for FN model.

Estimated Value:	**Excellent:**	**$1,200.00**
	Very good:	**$ 960.00**

Browning 22 Semiautomatic Grade VI

Same as the 22 Semiautomatic Grade I except: higher grade wood and finish; 24 karat gold-plated engraved blued or grayed receiver.

Estimated Value:	**New (retail):**	**$1,419.00**
	Excellent:	**$1,065.00**
	Very good:	**$ 850.00**

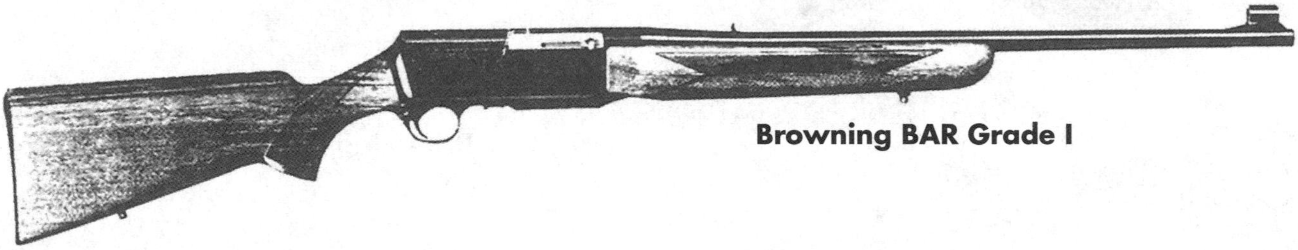

Browning BAR Grade I

Browning BAR Grade I

Caliber: 243 Win., 270 Win., 280 Rem., 308 Win., 30-06, 7mm Rem. mag., 300 Win. mag., 338 Win. mag.
Action: Semiautomatic, gas-operated; side ejector; hammerless
Magazine: 4-shot; 3-shot in mag.
Barrel: Blued; 22" or 24"
Sights: Optional folding rear and hooded ramp front
Stock and Forearm: Checkered walnut pistol grip stock and forearm; swivels; recoil pad on mag.
Approximate wt.: 7 to $8\frac{1}{4}$ lbs.
Comments: Made from the late 1960s to the early 1990s. Add 7% for magnum calibers. Add 3% for sights.

Estimated Value:	**Excellent:**	**$700.00**
	Very good:	**$560.00**

Browning BAR Grade II

Engraved version of BAR. Discontinued in the early 1970s. Add $50.00 for magnum.

Estimated Value:	**Excellent:**	**$875.00**
	Very good:	**$700.00**

Browning BAR Grade III

Similar to Grade I except: elaborate engraving featuring antelope head. Discontinued in the early 1970s. Reintroduced in 1979 with rams and elk engravings. Add 6% for magnum calibers. Discontinued in the mid-1980s.

Estimated Value:	**Excellent:**	**$1,100.00**
	Very good:	**$ 880.00**

Browning Model BAR Grade IV

Browning Model BAR-22 Grade II

Browning Model BAR Grade IV

Similar to Grade I with elaborate engraving featuring two running antelope and running deer. Magnum has moose and elk engravings. Add 5% for magnum caliber. Produced from 1971 until the mid-1980s.

Estimated Value: **Excellent:** **$1,400.00**
Very good: **$1,125.00**

Browning BAR Grade V

Similar to other grades of BAR. This is the fanciest model. Produced from 1971 to 1974.

Estimated Value: **Excellent:** **$2,800.00**
Very good: **$2,250.00**

Browning Model BAR-22

Caliber: 22 long rifle
Action: Semiautomatic; blow back; hammerless; repeating
Magazine: 15-shot tubular
Barrel: 20"; blued; recessed bore at muzzle
Sights: Adjustable folding leaf rear, gold bead front
Stock and Forearm: Checkered walnut pistol grip stock and forearm; fluted comb
Approximate wt.: 5¾ lbs.
Comments: Produced in the late 1970s to the mid-1980s.

Estimated Value: **Excellent:** **$475.00**
Very good: **$380.00**

Browning Model BAR-22 Grade II

Similar to the BAR-22 with engraved receiver, squirrels and rabbits.

Estimated Value: **Excellent:** **$525.00**
Very good: **$420.00**

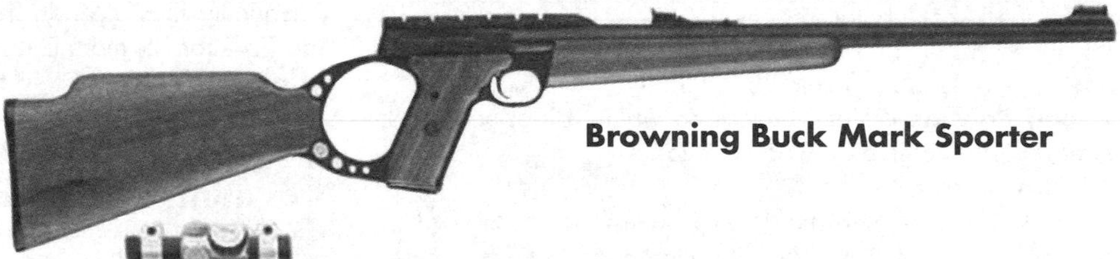

Browning Buck Mark Sporter

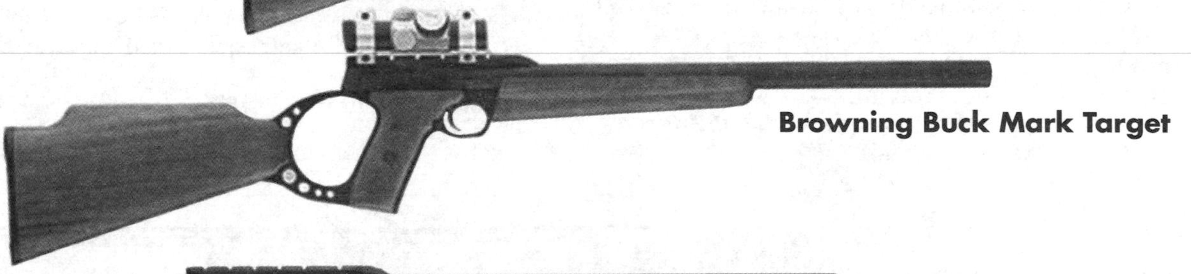

Browning Buck Mark Target

Browning Buck Mark Classic Target

Browning Buck Mark Target

Similar to the Buck Mark Sporter except: heavy bull barrel; integral rail scope mount.

Estimated Value: **New (retail):** **$659.00**
Excellent: **$495.00**
Very good: **$395.00**

Browning Buck Mark Classic Target, Buck Mark FLD

Similar to the Buck Mark Target except: gray laminated stock and forearm.

Estimated Value: **New (retail):** **$679.00**
Excellent: **$510.00**
Very good: **$405.00**

Browning Buck Mark Sporter

Calibre: 22 long rifle
Action: Straight blowback, single or double action; semiautomatic
Magazine: 10-shot clip; interchangeable with the Buck Mark handgun
Barrel: 18" tapered
Sights: Fiber optic sight system
Stock and forearm: Three-piece walnut Monte Carlo stock, pistol grip, and tapered forearm with open hand-rest between stock and pistol grip
Approximate wt: 4½ lbs.
Comments: Design based on Browning's Buck Mark pistol.

Estimated Value: **New (retail):** **$659.00**
Excellent: **$495.00**
Very good: **$395.00**

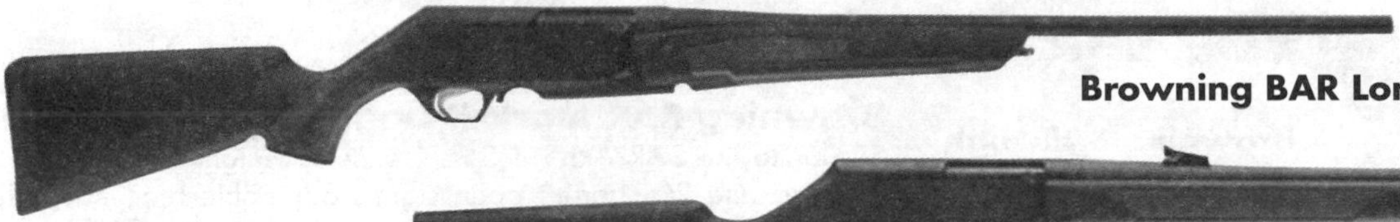

Browning BAR LongTrac Stalker

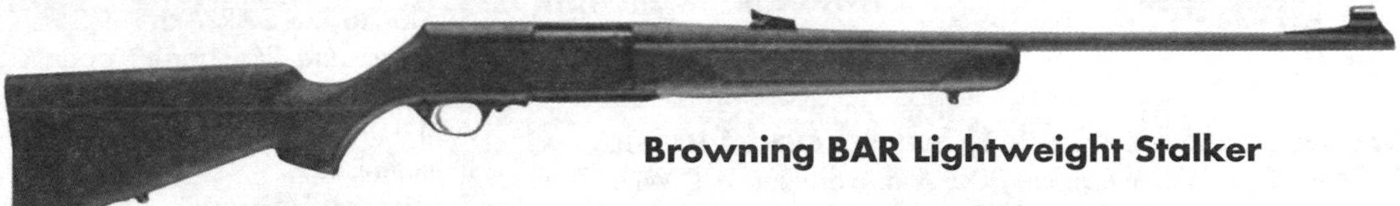

Browning BAR Lightweight Stalker

Browning BAR LongTrac

Browning BAR LongTrac Stalker

Similar to the BAR LongTrac except: matte blue finish; matte black composite stock and forearm. Add 9% for magnum calibers.

Estimated Value:	**New (retail):**	**$1,149.00**
	Excellent:	**$ 860.00**
	Very good:	**$ 645.00**

Browning BAR Lightweight Stalker

Similar to the BAR LongTrac Stalker except: 20", 22", or 24" barrel; additional calibers; weighs 7 to 7¾ lbs. Add 9% for magnum calibers.

Estimated Value:	**New (retail):**	**$1,119.00**
	Excellent:	**$ 840.00**
	Very good:	**$ 670.00**

Browning BAR LongTrac

Caliber: 270 Win., 30-06 Sprg., 7mm Rem. magnum, 300 Win. magnum
Action: Gas-operated, semiautomatic
Magazine: 4-shot detachable box; 3-shot magnum
Barrel: Blued; 22" or 24"
Sights: None; drilled and tapped for scope mount
Stock and Forearm: Satin finish checkered walnut, pistol grip stock and tapered forearm; alloy receiver; recoil pad
Approximate wt.: 6¾ to 7½ lbs.
Comments: Add 9% for magnum calibers. Add 4% for left-hand model.

Estimated Value:	**New (retail):**	**$1,119.00**
	Excellent:	**$ 840.00**
	Very good:	**$ 670.00**

Browning BAR ShortTrac Stalker

Browning BAR ShortTrac

Browning BAR ShortTrac Stalker

Similar to the BAR ShortTrac except: matte black composite stock and forearm.

Estimated Value:	**New (retail):**	**$1,149.00**
	Excellent:	**$ 860.00**
	Very good:	**$ 645.00**

Browning BAR ShortTrac

Caliber: 243 Win., 308 Win., 300 WSM, 270 WSM, 7mm WSM
Action: Gas-operated, semiautomatic
Magazine: 4-shot detachable box; 3-shot magnum
Barrel: Blued; 22" or 23"
Sights: None; drilled and tapped for scope mount
Stock and Forearm: Select checkered walnut pistol grip stock and tapered forearm; recoil pad; alloy receiver
Approximate wt.: 6¾ to 7¼ lbs.
Comments: Add 9% for magnum calibers. Add 4% for left-hand model.

Estimated Value:	**New (retail):**	**$1,179.00**
	Excellent:	**$ 885.00**
	Very good:	**$ 707.00**

Browning BAR High Grade Standard

Browning BAR Mark II Safari and Classic

Caliber: 338 Win. magnum, 300 Win. magnum, 270 Win., 7mm Rem. magnum, 30-06 Sprg., 270 Win., 308 Win., 243 Win.
Action: Gas-operated, semiautomatic; side ejector
Magazine: 4-shot; 3-shot magnum; hinged floor plate
Barrel: Blued; 22" or 24"
Sights: Optional adjustable rear, hooded ramp front
Stock and Forearm: Checkered walnut pistol grip stock and forearm; swivels
Approximate wt.: 7½ to 8½ lbs.
Comments: Introduced in the early 1990s. Add 8% for magnum calibers; 12% for BOSS System; 3% for open sights. Classic has satin finish (add 7%).

Estimated Value:	**New (retail):**	**$1,139.00**
	Excellent:	**$ 855.00**
	Very good:	**$ 685.00**

Browning BAR Mark II Lightweight

Similar to the BAR Mark II Safari except: weighs 7 lbs., alloy receiver, and 20" barrel; open sights; adjustable rear, hooded front; calibers: 243 Win., 270 Win., 30-06 Sprg., 308 Win. Add 10% for magnum caliber. Stalker model available with synthetic finish.

Estimated Value:	**Excellent:**	**$625.00**
	Very good:	**$500.00**

Browning BAR High Grade Standard

Similar to the BAR Mark II Safari except: 270 Win. or 30-06 Sprng. calibers; 22" barrel; select walnut stock and forearm; receiver engraved with scenes of white tail and mule deer with gold border.

Estimated Value:	**Excellent:**	**$1,375.00**
	Very good:	**$1,100.00**

Browning BAR High Grade Magnum

Similar to the BAR High Grade Standard except: 24" barrel; 7mm Rem. magnum or 300 Win. magnum calibers; engraving features moose and elk scenes.

Estimated Value:	**Excellent:**	**$1,425.00**
	Very good:	**$1,140.00**

BSA

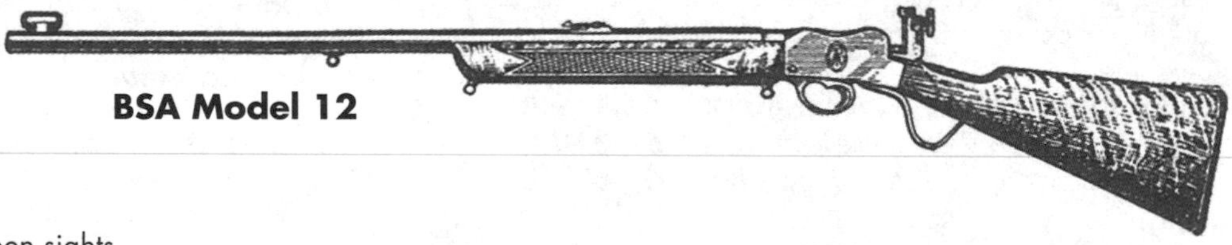

BSA Model 12

BSA Model 12

Caliber: 22 long rifle
Action: Martini-type; single shot
Magazine: None
Barrel: 29"; blued
Sights: Matched sights; some with open sights
Stock and Forearm: Checkered walnut straight grip stock and forearm; swivels
Approximate wt.: 9 lbs.
Comments: Made in England from about 1910 to 1930.

Estimated Value:	**Excellent:**	**$475.00**
	Very good:	**$380.00**

BSA Model 13

Similar to Model 12 with a 25" barrel. Weighs about 6 lbs.

Estimated Value:	**Excellent:**	**$425.00**
	Very good:	**$340.00**

BSA Model 15

Caliber: 22 long rifle
Action: Martini-type; single shot
Magazine: None
Barrel: Blued; 29"
Sights: Special BSA match sights
Stock and Forearm: Walnut stock and forearm; cheekpiece; swivels
Approximate wt.: 9½ lbs.
Comments: A match rifle made in England from about 1915 to the early 1930s.

Estimated Value:	**Excellent:**	**$450.00**
	Very good:	**$360.00**

BSA Model 13 Sporting

Similar to Model 13 in 22 Hornet caliber.

Estimated Value:	**Excellent:**	**$450.00**
	Very good:	**$360.00**

BSA Centurion

Similar to Model 15 with a special barrel guaranteed to produce accurate groups.

Estimated Value:	**Excellent:**	**$425.00**
	Very good:	**$340.00**

BSA Model 12/15

Similar to Model 12 and 15 in pre-war and post-war models. Made from the 1930s to about 1950.

Estimated Value:	**Excellent:**	**$400.00**
	Very good:	**$320.00**

BSA Model 12/15 Heavy Barrel

Similar to Model 12/15 with heavy barrel. Weighs about 11 lbs.

Estimated Value:	**Excellent:**	**$475.00**
	Very good:	**$380.00**

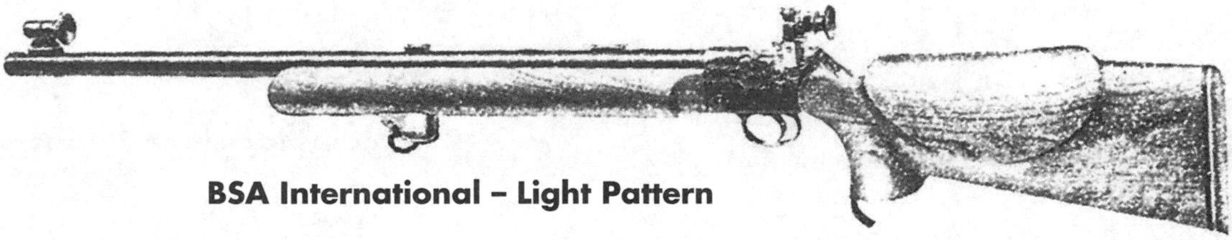

BSA International – Light Pattern

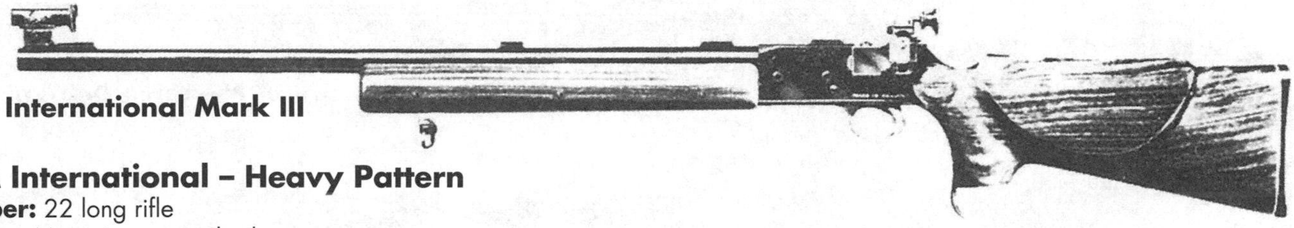

BSA International Mark III

BSA International – Heavy Pattern

Caliber: 22 long rifle
Action: Martini-type; single shot
Magazine: None
Barrel: Blued; 29"; heavy
Sights: Special Parker-Hale match sights
Stock and Forearm: Match style pistol grip stock with cheekpiece, wide forearm; hand stop; swivels
Approximate wt.: 13¾ lbs.
Comments: A target rifle made in England in the 1950s.

Estimated Value:	**Excellent:**	**$585.00**
	Very good:	**$465.00**

BSA International – Light Pattern

Similar to Heavy Pattern but lighter weight with a 26" barrel.

Estimated Value:	**Excellent:**	**$550.00**
	Very good:	**$440.00**

BSA International Mark II

Similar to Heavy and Light Patterns (choice of barrel). Stock and forearm changed slightly. Made from the early to the late 1950s.

Estimated Value:	**Excellent:**	**$550.00**
	Very good:	**$440.00**

BSA International Mark III

Similar to Heavy Pattern with different stock and forearm; alloy frame; floating barrel. Made from the late 1950s to the late 1960s.

Estimated Value:	**Excellent:**	**$750.00**
	Very good:	**$600.00**

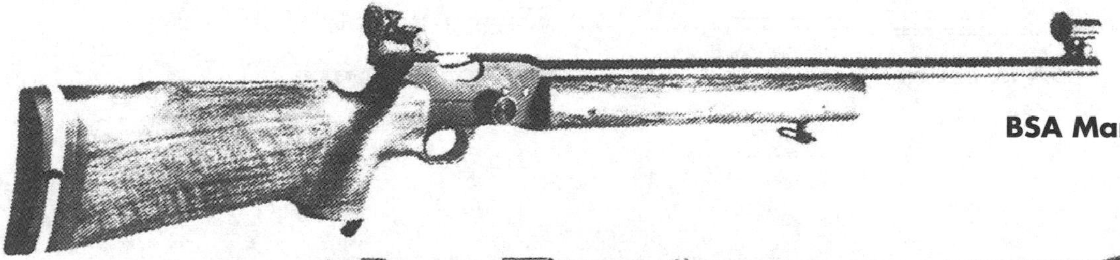

BSA Martini ISU

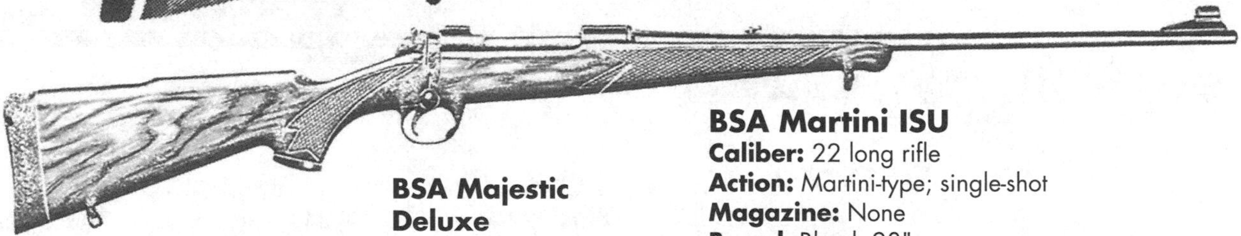

BSA Majestic Deluxe

BSA Majestic Deluxe

Caliber: 22 Hornet, 222, 243, 30-06, 308 Win., 7x57mm
Action: Mauser-type bolt action; repeating
Magazine: 4-shot box
Barrel: Blued; 22"
Sights: Folding leaf rear, hooded ramp front
Stock and Forearm: Checkered walnut Monte Carlo one-piece pistol grip stock and lipped forearm; swivels; cheekpiece; recoil pad
Approximate wt.: 7½ lbs.
Comments: Made in England from the early to the mid-1960s.

Estimated Value:	**Excellent:**	**$400.00**
	Very good:	**$320.00**

BSA Martini ISU

Caliber: 22 long rifle
Action: Martini-type; single-shot
Magazine: None
Barrel: Blued; 28"
Sights: Special Parker-Hale match sights
Stock and Forearm: Match-style walnut pistol grip; adjustable butt plate
Approximate wt.: 10½ lbs.
Comments: A match rifle, made in England.

Estimated Value:	**Excellent:**	**$750.00**
	Very good:	**$600.00**

BSA Mark V

Similar to ISU except; heavier barrel; weighs about 12½ lbs.

Estimated Value:	**Excellent:**	**$765.00**
	Very good:	**$610.00**

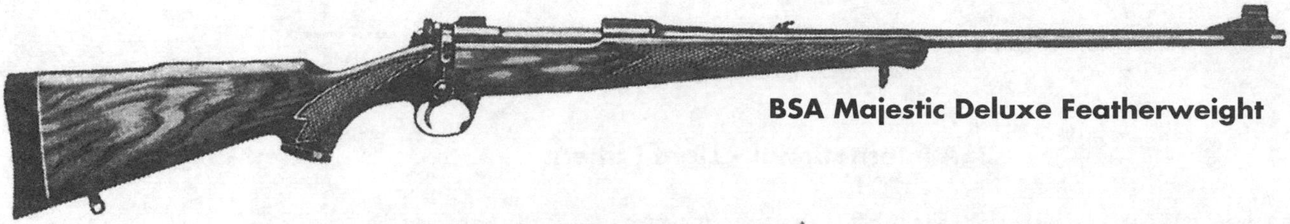

BSA Majestic Deluxe Featherweight

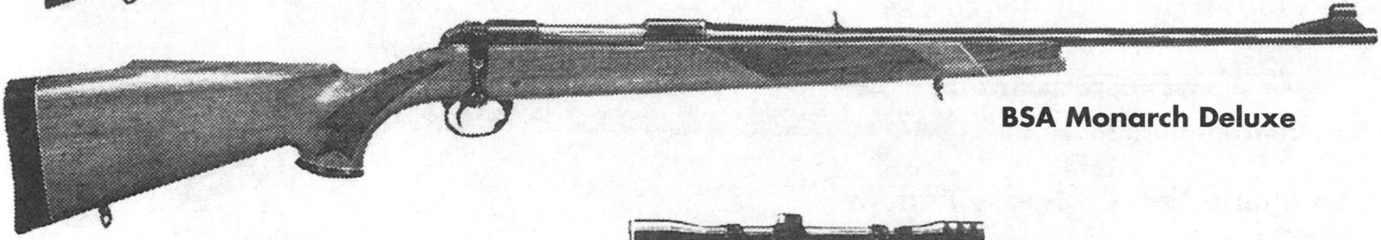

BSA Monarch Deluxe

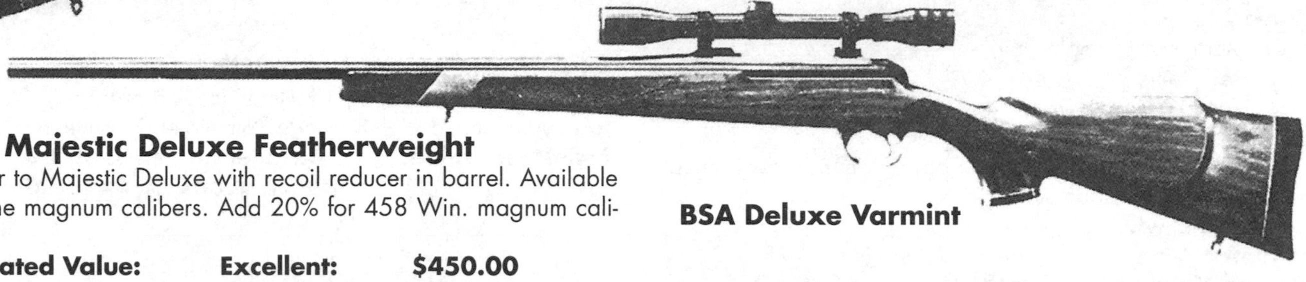

BSA Deluxe Varmint

BSA Majestic Deluxe Featherweight

Similar to Majestic Deluxe with recoil reducer in barrel. Available in some magnum calibers. Add 20% for 458 Win. magnum caliber.

Estimated Value:	**Excellent:**	**$450.00**
	Very good:	**$360.00**

BSA Monarch Deluxe

Similar to Majestic Deluxe with slight changes in stock and forearm and with a recoil pad. Made from the mid-1960s to the late 1970s.

Estimated Value:	**Excellent:**	**$400.00**
	Very good:	**$320.00**

BSA Deluxe Varmint

Similar to Monarch Deluxe with a heavier 24" barrel.

Estimated Value:	**Excellent:**	**$375.00**
	Very good:	**$300.00**

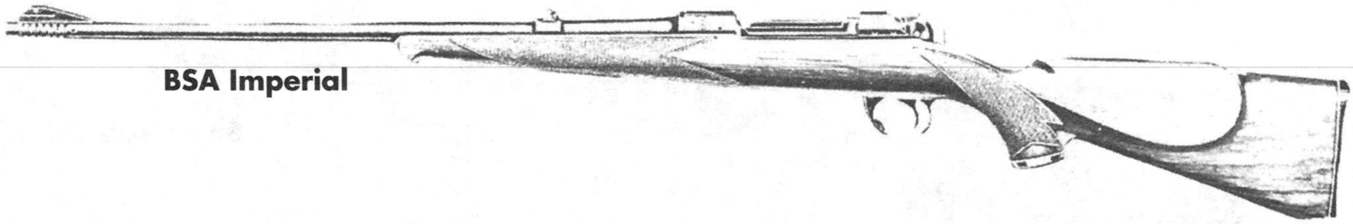

BSA Imperial

BSA CF-2

BSA Imperial

Caliber: 22 Hornet, 222, 243, 257 Roberts, 270 Win., 7x57mm, 300 Savage, 30-06, 308 Win.
Action: Bolt action; repeating
Magazine: 4-shot box
Barrel: Blued; 22"; recoil reducer
Sights: Open rear, ramp front
Stock and Forearm: Checkered walnut Monte Carlo one-piece pistol grip stock and lipped forearm; cheekpiece
Approximate wt.: 7 lbs.
Comments: Made in the early 1960s.

Estimated Value:	**Excellent:**	**$400.00**
	Very good:	**$320.00**

BSA CF-2

Caliber: 222 Rem., 22-250, 243 Win., 6.5x55, 7mm Mauser, 7x64, 270 Win., 308 Win., 30-06, 7mm Rem. mag., 300 Win. mag.
Action: Bolt action; repeating
Magazine: 4- or 5-shot box, 3-shot in magnum
Barrel: Blued; 23½"; 24" heavy barrel available in some calibers
Sights: Hooded ramp front, adjustable rear
Stock and Forearm: Checkered walnut Monte Carlo one-piece pistol grip stock and forearm; cheekpiece; contrasting fore-end tip and grip cap; swivels; recoil pad; European style has oil finish, American style has polyeurethane finish with white spacers.
Approximate wt.: 7½ to 8½ lbs.
Comments: Add 14% for European style; 8% for magnum calibers with heavy barrel.

Estimated Value:	**Excellent:**	**$500.00**
	Very good:	**$400.00**

Carl Gustaf Grade II

Carl Gustaf Grade II Magnum

Carl Gustaf Grade III

Carl Gustaf Swede

Carl Gustaf Grade II

Caliber: 22-250, 243, 25-06, 270, 6.5x55, 30-06, 308
Action: Bolt action; repeating
Magazine: 5-shot staggered column
Barrel: Blued; 23½"
Sights: Leaf rear, hooded ramp front
Stock and Forearm: Checkered walnut Monte Carlo one-piece pistol grip stock and forearm; swivels
Approximate wt.: 7 lbs.
Comments: Manufactured in Sweden.

Estimated Value:	**Excellent:**	**$625.00**
	Very good:	**$500.00**

Carl Gustaf Grade II Magnum

Similar to Grade II except magnum calibers; recoil pad; 3-shot magazine.

Estimated Value:	**Excellent:**	**$650.00**
	Very good:	**$520.00**

Carl Gustaf Grade III

Similar to Grade II with select wood; more checkering; high-quality finish; no sights.

Estimated Value:	**Excellent:**	**$800.00**
	Very good:	**$640.00**

Carl Gustaf Grade III Magnum

Similar to Grade II Magnum with select wood; more checkering; high-quality finish; no sights.

Estimated Value:	**Excellent:**	**$825.00**
	Very good:	**$660.00**

Carl Gustaf Swede

Similar to Grade II with lipped forearm but lacking the Monte Carlo comb.

Estimated Value:	**Excellent:**	**$625.00**
	Very good:	**$500.00**

Carl Gustaf Swede Deluxe

Similar to Grade III with lipped forearm.

Estimated Value:	**Excellent:**	**$775.00**
	Very good:	**$620.00**

Carl Gustaf Varmint Target

Carl Gustaf Varmint Target

Caliber: 22-250, 222, 243, 6.5x55
Action: Bolt action; repeating; large bolt knob
Magazine: 5-shot staggered column
Barrel: Blued; 27"
Sights: None
Stock and Forearm: Plain walnut Monte Carlo one-piece pistol grip stock and forearm
Approximate wt.: 9½ lbs.
Comments: Manufactured in Sweden.

Estimated Value:	**Excellent:**	**$675.00**
	Very good:	**$540.00**

CHARLES DALY

Charles Daly Hornet

Charles Daly Hornet

Caliber: 22 Hornet
Action: Bolt action; double triggers
Magazine: 5-shot box
Barrel: 24"
Sights: Leaf rear, hooded ramp front
Stock and Forearm: Checkered walnut one-piece stock and forearm
Approximate wt.: 7¾ lbs.
Comments: Made during the 1930s. Also marketed under the name Herold Rifle.

Estimated Value:	**Excellent:**	**$1,200.00**
	Very good:	**$ 960.00**

CHARTER ARMS

Charter Arms AR-7 Explorer

Charter Arms AR-7 Explorer

Caliber: 22 long rifle
Action: Semiautomatic
Magazine: 8-shot clip
Barrel: 16"; aluminum and steel lined, black, or silvertone
Sights: Peep rear, blade front
Stock and Forearm: Fiberglass, pistol grip stock (no forearm); stock acts as case for gun when dismantled. Also available in silvertone or camouflage.
Approximate wt.: 2¾ lbs.
Comments: A lightweight alloy rifle designed to float. Also dismantles to fit into stock. Made from about 1973 to 1990 by Charter Arms. Made by Armalite from about 1960 to 1973. Made by Survival Arms Inc. from 1990 to the mid-1990s.

Estimated Value:	**Excellent:**	**$130.00**
	Very good:	**$105.00**

COLT

Colt Colteer 1-22

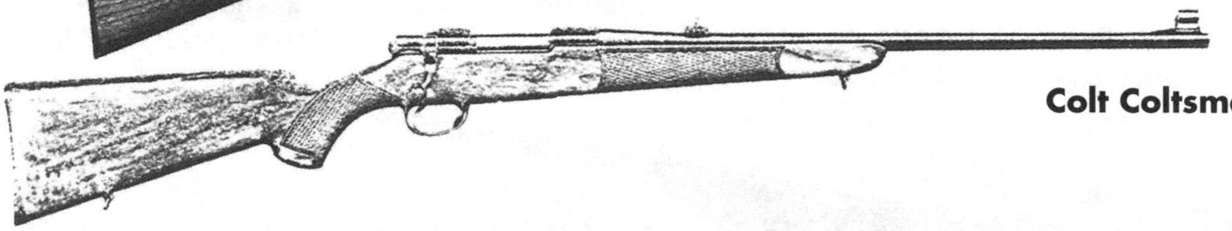

Colt Coltsman Standard

Colt Colteer 1-22

Caliber: 22 short, long, long rifle
Action: Bolt action; hammerless; single-shot
Magazine: None
Barrel: Blued; 20", 22"
Sights: Open rear, ramp front
Stock and Forearm: Plain walnut Monte Carlo pistol grip stock and forearm
Approximate wt.: 5 lbs.
Comments: Made for 10 years from about 1957.

Estimated Value:	**Excellent:**	**$315.00**
	Very good:	**$250.00**

Colt Coltsman Standard

Caliber: 223, 243, 264, 300 H&H magnum, 30-06
Action: Mauser-type, bolt action; repeating
Magazine: 5-shot box
Barrel: Blued; 22", 24"
Sights: No rear, ramp front
Stock and Forearm: Checkered walnut one-piece pistol grip stock and tapered forearm; swivels
Approximate wt.: 7 lbs.
Comments: Made from about 1957 to the early 1960s.

Estimated Value:	**Excellent:**	**$600.00**
	Very good:	**$300.00**

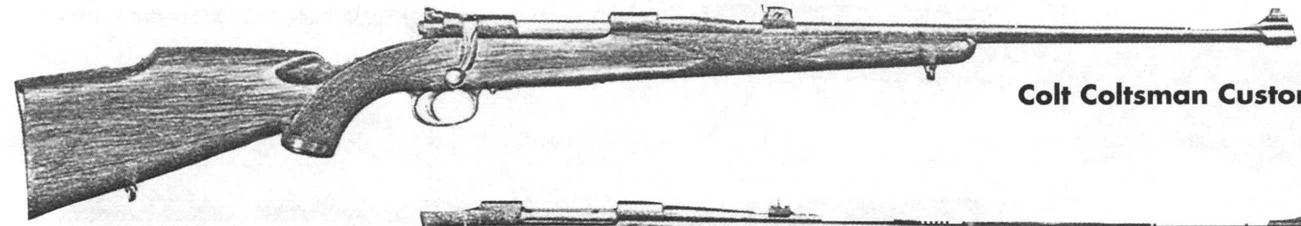

Colt Coltsman Custom

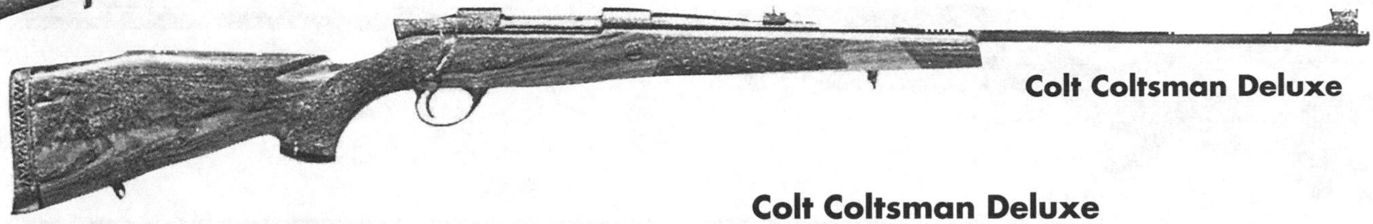

Colt Coltsman Deluxe

Colt Coltsman Custom
Similar to the deluxe with select wood; cheekpiece; engraving.
Estimated Value: **Excellent:** **$800.00**
Very good: **$640.00**

Colt Coltsman Deluxe
Similar to the standard model with higher quality wood and finish; adjustable rear sight; Monte Carlo stock.
Estimated Value: **Excellent:** **$800.00**
Very good: **$640.00**

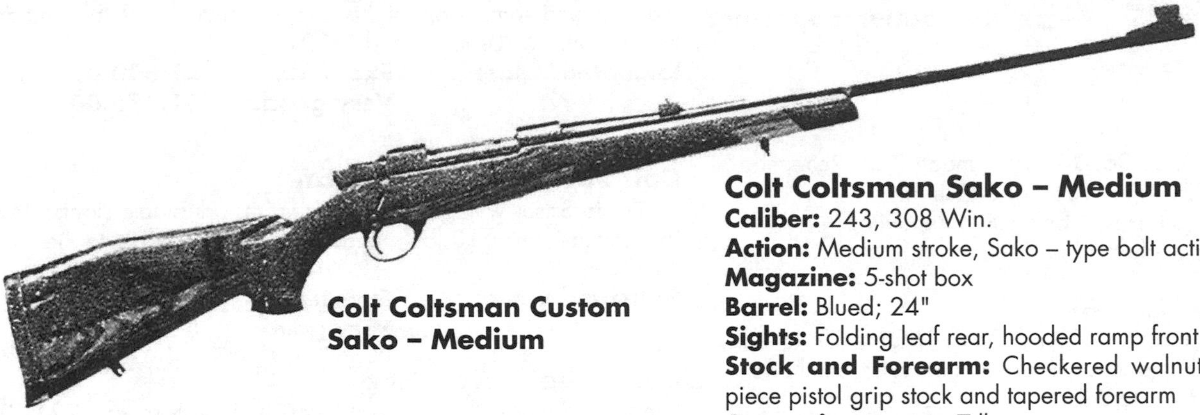

Colt Coltsman Custom Sako – Medium

Colt Coltsman Sako – Short
Caliber: 222, 222 magnum, 243, 308
Action: Short Sako – type bolt action; repeating
Magazine: 5-shot box
Barrel: Blued; 22"
Sights: Open rear, hooded ramp front
Stock and Forearm: Checkered walnut Monte Carlo pistol grip stock and tapered forearm; swivels
Approximate wt.: 7 lbs.
Comments: Made from the late 1950s to the mid-1960s.
Estimated Value: **Excellent:** **$500.00**
Very good: **$400.00**

Colt Coltsman Deluxe Sako – Short
Similar to Sako – Short with adjustable rear sight; higher quality finish; in calibers 243, 308. Discontinued in the early 1960s.
Estimated Value: **Excellent:** **$550.00**
Very good: **$440.00**

Colt Colstman Custom Sako – Short
Similar to Deluxe Sako – Short with select wood; cheekpiece; engraving. Made until the mid-1960s.
Estimated Value: **Excellent:** **$600.00**
Very good: **$480.00**

Colt Coltsman Sako – Medium
Caliber: 243, 308 Win.
Action: Medium stroke, Sako – type bolt action; repeating
Magazine: 5-shot box
Barrel: Blued; 24"
Sights: Folding leaf rear, hooded ramp front
Stock and Forearm: Checkered walnut Monte Carlo one-piece pistol grip stock and tapered forearm
Approximate wt.: 7 lbs.
Comments: Made from the early to the mid-1960s.
Estimated Value: **Excellent:** **$500.00**
Very good: **$400.00**

Colt Coltsman Custom Sako – Medium
Similar to standard Sako – Medium with higher quality finish and recoil pad.
Estimated Value: **Excellent:** **$600.00**
Very good: **$480.00**

Colt Coltsman Sako – Long
Caliber: 264, 270 Win., 300 H&H, 30-06, 375 H&H
Action: Long stroke, Sako-type bolt action; repeating
Magazine: 5-shot box
Barrel: Blued; 24"
Sights: Folding leaf rear, hooded ramp front
Stock and Forearm: Checkered walnut one-piece pistol grip stock and tapered forearm; swivels
Approximate wt.: 7 lbs.
Comments: Made from the early to the mid-1960s.
Estimated Value: **Excellent:** **$525.00**
Very good: **$420.00**

Colt Coltsman Custom Sako – Long
Similar to Sako – Long with higher quality finish; recoil pad; Monte Carlo stock.
Estimated Value: **Excellent:** **$575.00**
Very good: **$460.00**

Colt Sauer

Colt Sauer Grand African

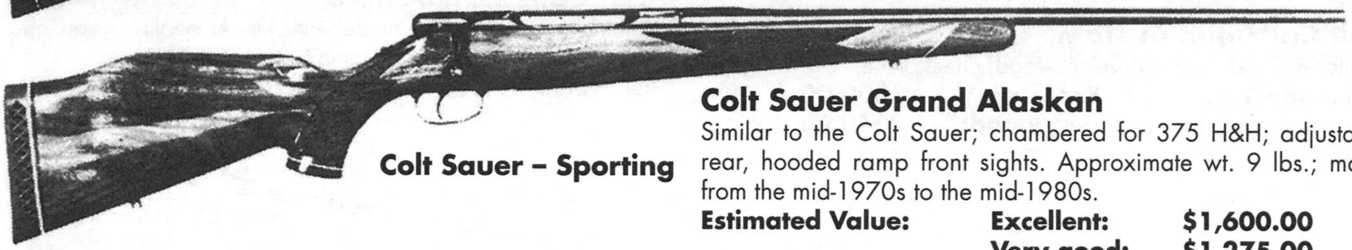

Colt Sauer – Sporting

Colt Sauer

Caliber: 25-06, 270, 30-06, 300 Win. mag., 7mm Rem. mag., 300 Weath. mag., 375 H&H mag., 458 Win. mag.
Action: Long stroke, Sauer-type bolt action; repeating
Magazine: 5-shot detachable box
Barrel: Blued; 24"
Sights: None; tapped for scope
Stock and Forearm: Checkered walnut Monte Carlo one-piece pistol grip stock and tapered forearm; swivels; recoil pad
Approximate wt.: 7½ to 8 lbs.
Comments: Made from the early 1970s to the mid-1980s. Add $50.00 for magnum.

Estimated Value:	**Excellent:**	**$1,500.00**
	Very good:	**$1,200.00**

Colt Sauer Grand Alaskan

Similar to the Colt Sauer; chambered for 375 H&H; adjustable rear, hooded ramp front sights. Approximate wt. 9 lbs.; made from the mid-1970s to the mid-1980s.

Estimated Value:	**Excellent:**	**$1,600.00**
	Very good:	**$1,275.00**

Colt Sauer Grand African

Similar to Sauer with higher quality finish; adjustable sights; 458 Win. caliber only; 10 lbs.; made from the mid-1970s to the mid-1980s.

Estimated Value:	**Excellent:**	**$1,700.00**
	Very good:	**$1,360.00**

Colt Sauer – Sporting

Similar to Sauer with short stroke action; chambered for 22-250, 243, 308 calibers. Made from the mid-1970s to the mid-1980s. Approximate wt.: 7½ to 8½ lbs.

Estimated Value:	**Excellent:**	**$1,500.00**
	Very good:	**$1,200.00**

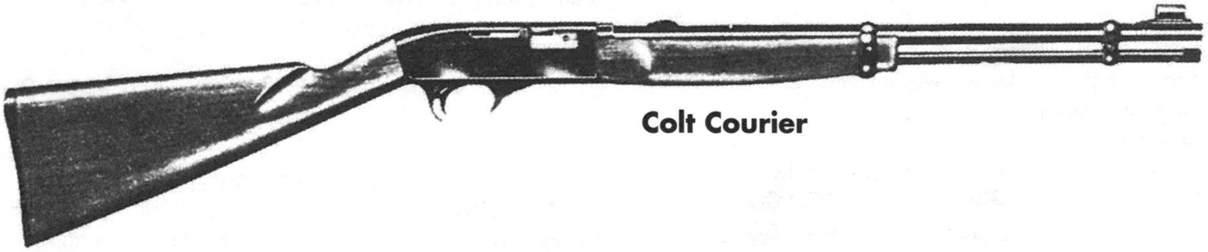

Colt Courier

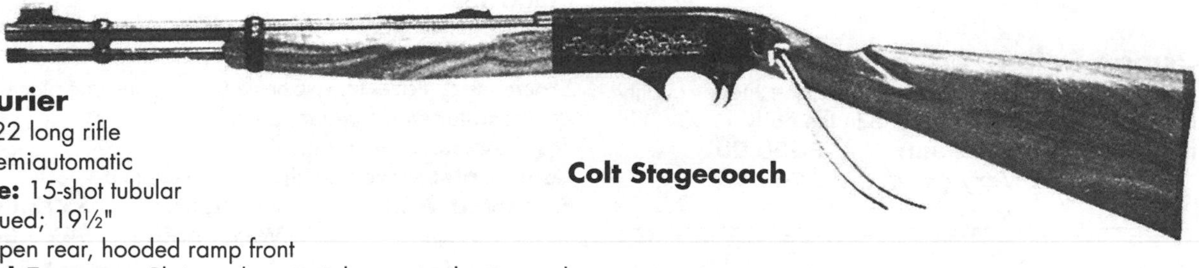

Colt Stagecoach

Colt Courier

Caliber: 22 long rifle
Action: Semiautomatic
Magazine: 15-shot tubular
Barrel: Blued; 19½"
Sights: Open rear, hooded ramp front
Stock and Forearm: Plain walnut straight or pistol grip stock and forearm; barrel band
Approximate wt.: 5 lbs.
Comments: Made from the mid-1960s to the late 1970s.

Estimated Value:	**Excellent:**	**$400.00**
	Very good:	**$320.00**

Colt Stagecoach

Similar to the Courier except: engraving, 16½" barrel; saddle ring with leather string. Made from the mid-1960s to 1976.

Estimated Value:	**Excellent:**	**$400.00**
	Very good:	**$320.00**

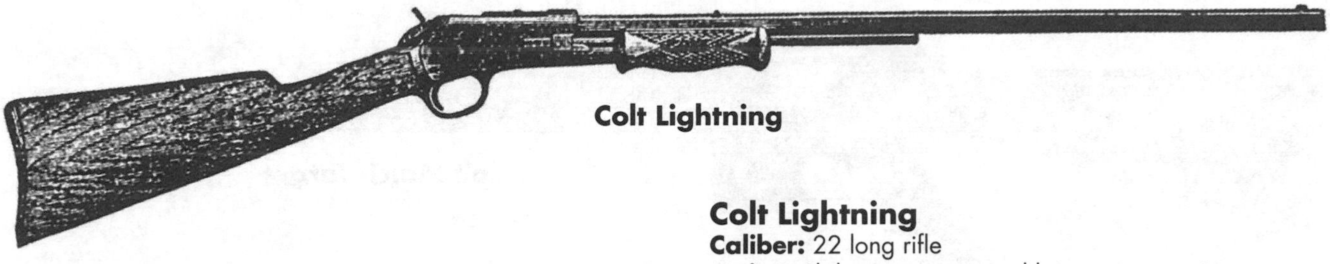

Colt Lightning

Colt Lightning

Caliber: 22 long rifle
Action: Slide action; exposed hammer; repeating
Magazine: Tubular: 15 longs, 16 shorts
Barrel: Blued; 24" round or octagon
Sights: Open rear, bead front
Stock and Forearm: Plain walnut straight pistol grip stock and checkered slide handle
Approximate wt.: 5¾ lbs.
Comments: Made from the 1880s to about 1905.

Estimated Value:	**Excellent:**	**$2,200.00**
	Very good:	**$1,750.00**

Colt AR-15

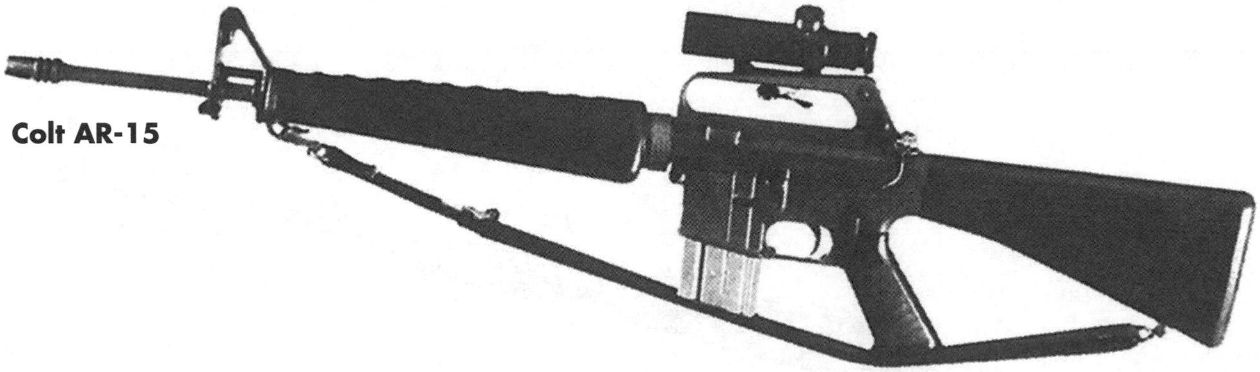

Colt AR-15, AR-15A2, and AR-15A2 Carbine

Caliber: 223; 9mm (1986 only)
Action: Gas-operated, semiautomatic
Magazine: 5-shot clip (223 cal.); 20-shot clip (9mm cal.)
Barrel: 20" with flash supressor; 16" with collapsible stock. Also heavy barrel available
Sights: Adjustable rear, post front adjustable for elevation; 3X and 4X scopes available
Stock and Forearm: Pistol grip; fiberglass shoulder stock and handguard; swivels; carrying handle; collapsible stock available in both calibers
Approximate wt.: 6 to 8 lbs.
Comments: Made from the mid-1960s to the early 1990s. Add 10% for collapsible stock (AR-15A2 Government model carbine); add 14% for target sight and heavy barrel (AR-15 A2H Bar).

Estimated Value:	**Excellent:**	**$1,275.00**
	Very good:	**$1,025.00**

Colt Target Lightweight

Similar to the AR-15 in 223 Rem., 9mm, or 7.62x39mm calibers, 16" barrel, introduced in the early 1990s.

Estimated Value:	**Excellent:**	**$900.00**
	Very good:	**$720.00**

Colt AR-15 A2 Delta H-Bar

Similar to the AR-15 A2 with 20" heavy barrel, 3x9 rubber armored variable power scope, removable cheekpiece, leather military-style sling and aluminum carrying case.

Estimated Value:	**Excellent:**	**$1,500.00**
	Very good:	**$1,200.00**

Colt Match Target

Colt Accurized Rifle

Caliber: 223 Rem.
Action: Gas-operated, semiautomatic
Magazine: 9-shot clip
Barrel: 24" heavy; matte black brushed stainless steel
Sights: None
Stock and Forearm: Synthetic pistol grip stock and handguard
Approximate wt.: 9¼ lbs.
Comments: Introduced in the late 1990s.

Estimated Value:	**Excellent:**	**$1,070.00**
	Very good:	**$ 855.00**

Colt Match Target

Similar to the AR-15 in 223 Rem. only with a 20" barrel. Introduced in the early 1990s. Add 5% for H-Bar.

Estimated Value:	**Excellent:**	**$890.00**
	Very good:	**$715.00**

Colt Target Competition H-Bar

Similar to the AR-15 in 223 Rem. only with a 20" or 16" heavy barrel. Introduced in the early 1990s, 8-shot clip in the mid-1990s.

Estimated Value:	**Excellent:**	**$955.00**
	Very good:	**$765.00**

FN (FABRIQUE NATIONALE)

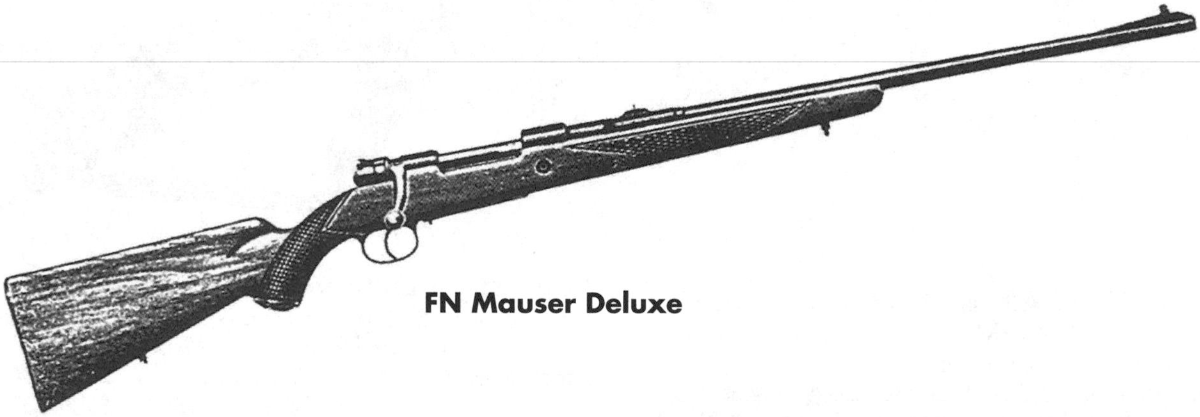

FN Mauser Deluxe

FN Mauser Deluxe Presentation

Similar to the Deluxe with Monte Carlo stock; engraving; select wood.

Estimated Value:	**Excellent:**	**$1,000.00**
	Very good:	**$ 800.00**

FN Mauser Deluxe

Caliber: 220, 243, 244, 250-3000, 270, 7mm, 300, 308, 30-06
Action: Mauser-type bolt action; repeating
Magazine: 5-shot box
Barrel: Blued; 24"
Sights: Adjustable rear, hooded ramp front
Stock and Forearm: Checkered one-piece pistol grip stock and forearm; swivels
Approximate wt.: 7½ to 8 lbs.
Comments: Made from World War II to the early 1960s.

Estimated Value:	**Excellent:**	**$650.00**
	Very good:	**$520.00**

FN Supreme

FN Supreme Magnum

Similar to the Supreme except in 264 magnum, 7mm magnum, and 300 Win. magnum calibers and 3-shot box magazine.

Estimated Value: **Excellent:** **$900.00**
Very good: **$725.00**

FN Supreme

Caliber: 243, 270, 7mm, 30-06, 308
Action: Mauser-type bolt action; repeating
Magazine: 5-shot box, 4-shot box in 308 or 243 calibers
Barrel: Blued; 22", 24"
Sights: Adjustable rear, hooded ramp front
Stock and Forearm: Checkered wood Monte Carlo one-piece pistol grip stock and tapered forearm; cheekpiece; swivels
Approximate wt.: 8 lbs.
Comments: Made from the late 1950s to the mid-1970s.
Estimated Value: **Excellent:** **$875.00**
Very good: **$700.00**

HARRINGTON + RICHARDSON

Harrington & Richardson 1873 Springfield Commemorative

Harrington & Richardson Little Big Horn Commemorative 174

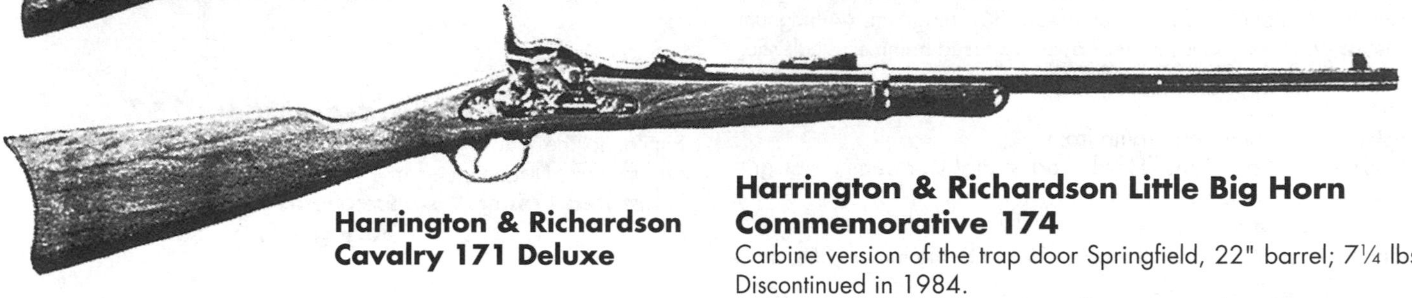

Harrington & Richardson Cavalry 171 Deluxe

Harrington & Richardson 1873 Springfield Commemorative

Caliber: 45-70 Govt.
Action: Trap door; single-shot
Magazine: None
Barrel: Blued; 32"
Sights: Adjustable rear, blade front
Stock and Forearm: One-piece straight grip stock and forearm; barrel band; swivels
Approximate wt.: $8\frac{3}{4}$ lbs.
Comments: Manufactured from the early 1970s to the mid-1980s; replica of the 1873 U.S. Springfield rifle.
Estimated Value: **Excellent:** **$425.00**
Very good: **$340.00**

Harrington & Richardson Little Big Horn Commemorative 174

Carbine version of the trap door Springfield, 22" barrel; $7\frac{1}{4}$ lbs. Discontinued in 1984.

Estimated Value: **Excellent:** **$700.00**
Very good: **$560.00**

Harrington & Richardson Cavalry Carbine 171

Similar to the Little Big Horn with saddle ring.

Estimated Value: **Excellent:** **$400.00**
Very good: **$320.00**

Harrington & Richardson Cavalry 171 Deluxe

Similar to the Cavalry Carbine 171, with engraving.

Estimated Value: **Excellent:** **$425.00**
Very good: **$340.00**

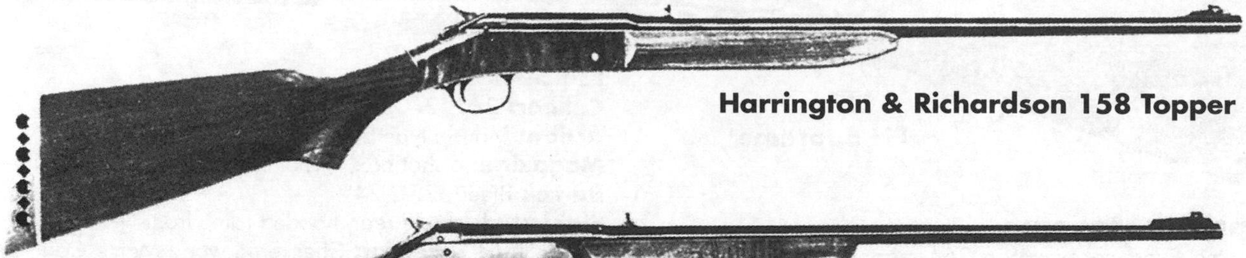

Harrington & Richardson 158 Topper

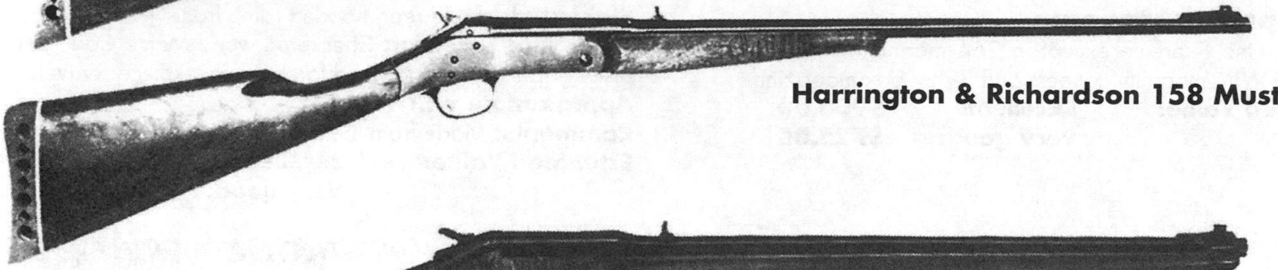

Harrington & Richardson 158 Mustang

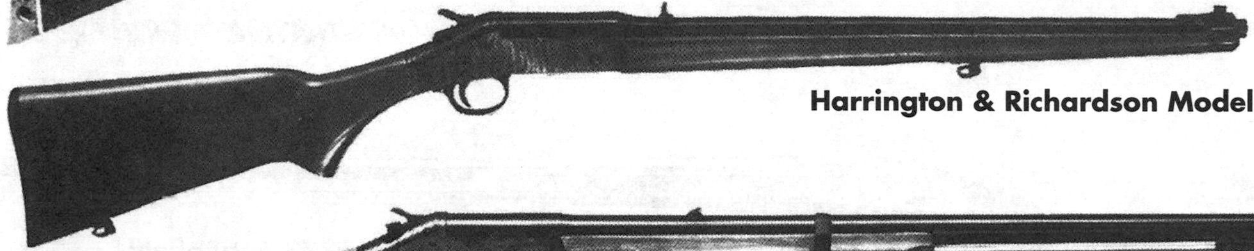

Harrington & Richardson Model 157

Harrington & Richardson Shikari 155

Harrington & Richardson 158 Topper

Caliber: 22 Rem. Jet, 22 Hornet, 30-30, 357 magnum, 44 magnum
Action: Box lock; top lever break-open; exposed hammer; single-shot
Magazine: None
Barrel: Blued; 22"
Sights: Adjustable rear, ramp front
Stock and Forearm: Hardwood straight or semi-pistol grip stock and forearm; recoil pad
Approximate wt.: 5 lbs.
Comments: Made from the early 1960s to the mid-1980s, magnum calibers added 1982.
Estimated Value: **Excellent:** **$225.00**
Very good: **$180.00**

Harrington & Richardson 158 C and 58 Topper

Similar to the 158 Topper with extra interchangeable 26" 410 or 20 gauge shotgun barrel. Add 18% for nickel finish.
Estimated Value: **Excellent:** **$225.00**
Very good: **$180.00**

Harrington & Richardson 158 Mustang

Similar to the 158 except 30-30 only, with gold-plated trigger and hammer; straight stock. Made from the mid- to the late 1960s.
Estimated Value: **Excellent:** **$225.00**
Very good: **$180.00**

Harrington & Richardson Model 157

Similar to the 158 with semi-pistol grip stock, full-length forearm and swivels. Discontinued in 1984.
Estimated Value: **Excellent:** **$200.00**
Very good: **$160.00**

Harrington & Richardson Shikari 155

Caliber: 44 magnum, 45-70 Govt.
Action: Single-shot; exposed hammer
Magazine: None
Barrel: Blued; 24", 28"
Sights: Folding leaf rear, blade front
Stock and Forearm: Wood straight grip stock and forearm; barrel band
Approximate wt.: 7 to 7¼ lbs.
Comments: Manufactured from the early 1970s to the early 1980s.
Estimated Value: **Excellent:** **$200.00**
Very good: **$160.00**

Harrington & Richardson Ultra

Harrington & Richardson Ultra

Caliber: 223 Rem., 243 Win. (Varmint); 25-06 Rem., 308 Win., 357 Rem. maximum (Hunter)
Action: Box lock, side lever release, break-open, exposed hammer, single-shot
Magazine: None, single-shot
Barrel: 24" blued, heavy barrel (Varmint); 22" blued or 26" blued in 25-06 (Hunter)
Sights: None, includes scope mount; 357 maximum Hunter has ramp front, fully adjustable rear
Stock and Forearm: Monte Carlo semi-pistol grip, checkered laminate stock and forearm with Natural finish (Varmint) or Cinnamon finish (Hunter); straight stock on 357 maximum Hunter
Approximate wt.: 5 to 8 lbs.
Comments: Prices for Hunter model. Add 2% for Varmint model. Add 16% for Whitetails Commemorative model with black walnut stock and forearm, Whitetails Unlimited logo, and 1998 edition date.

Estimated Value:	**Excellent:**	**$210.00**
	Very good:	**$165.00**

Harrington & Richardson Ultra Comp

Similar to the Ultra except with compensator barrel to reduce felt recoil; 24" barrel; 30-06 Sprg., or 270 Win. only.

Estimated Value:	**Excellent:**	**$240.00**
	Very good:	**$195.00**

Harrington & Richardson Pioneer 765

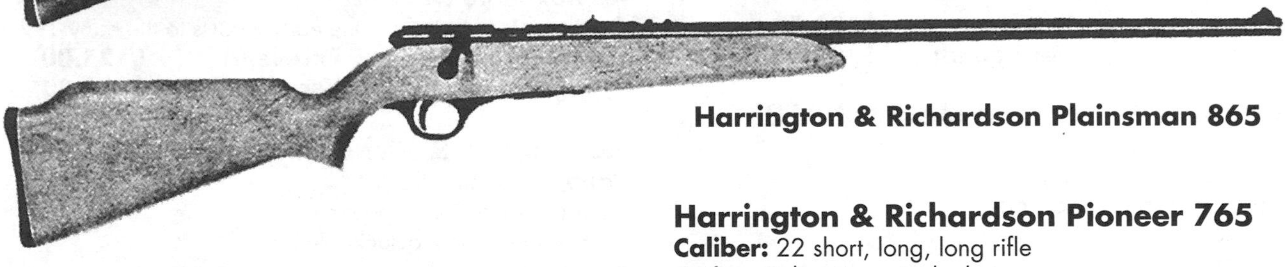

Harrington & Richardson Plainsman 865

Harrington & Richardson Pioneer 765

Caliber: 22 short, long, long rifle
Action: Bolt action; single-shot
Magazine: None
Barrel: Blued; 24"
Sights: Open rear, hooded bead front
Stock and Forearm: Wood Monte Carlo one-piece semi-pistol grip stock and forearm
Approximate wt.: 5 lbs.
Comments: Made from the late 1940s to the mid-1950s.

Estimated Value:	**Excellent:**	**$100.00**
	Very good:	**$ 80.00**

Harrington & Richardson Plainsman 865

Similar to the Pioneer 765 except repeating, with 5-shot clip; 22" barrel. Made from about 1950 to 1986.

Estimated Value:	**Excellent:**	**$125.00**
	Very good:	**$100.00**

Harrington & Richardson Pioneer 750

Harrington & Richardson Model 866
Similar to the Model 865 with full-length forearm. Made in the early 1970s.
Estimated Value: **Excellent:** **$150.00**
Very good: **$120.00**

Harrington & Richardson Pioneer 750
Similar to the Pioneer 765. Made from the mid-1950s to the mid-1980s.
Estimated Value: **Excellent:** **$100.00**
Very good: **$ 80.00**

Harrington & Richardson Model 751
Similar to the Pioneer 750 with full-length forearm. Made from the early to the mid-1970s.
Estimated Value: **Excellent:** **$125.00**
Very good: **$100.00**

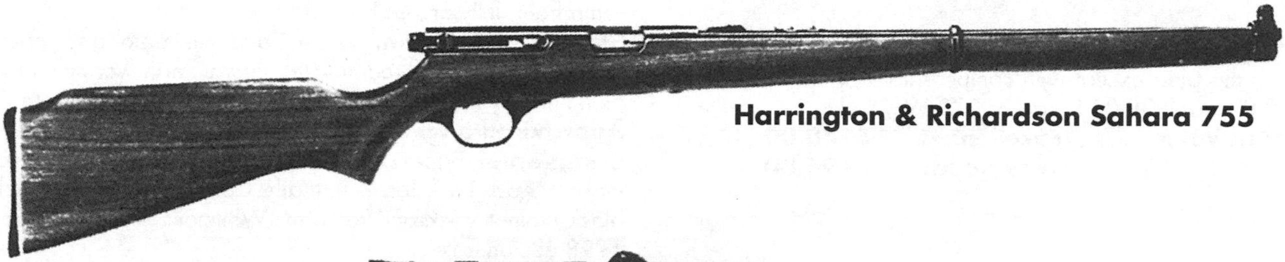

Harrington & Richardson Sahara 755

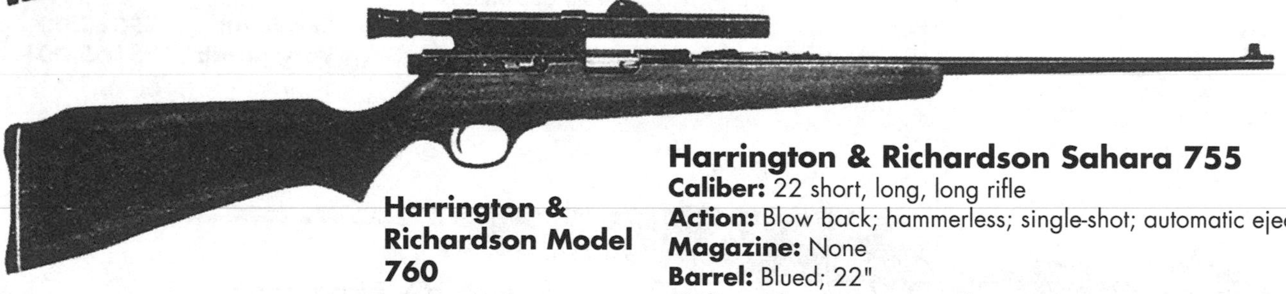

Harrington & Richardson Model 760

Harrington & Richardson Model 760
Similar to the Model 755 with short forearm. Discontinued in 1970.
Estimated Value: **Excellent:** **$100.00**
Very good: **$ 80.00**

Harrington & Richardson Medalist 450
Caliber: 22 long rifle
Action: Bolt action; repeating
Magazine: 5-shot detachable box
Barrel: Blued; 26"
Sights: None
Stock and Forearm: Target-style with pistol grip; swivels
Approximate wt.: 10½ lbs.
Comments: A target rifle made from the late 1940s to the early 1960s.
Estimated Value: **Excellent:** **$175.00**
Very good: **$140.00**

Harrington & Richardson Medalist 451
Similar to the Medalist 450 with extension rear sight and Lyman front sight.
Estimated Value: **Excellent:** **$200.00**
Very good: **$160.00**

Harrington & Richardson Sahara 755
Caliber: 22 short, long, long rifle
Action: Blow back; hammerless; single-shot; automatic ejector
Magazine: None
Barrel: Blued; 22"
Sights: Open rear, military front
Stock and Forearm: Monte Carlo one-piece semi-pistol grip stock and full-length forearm
Approximate wt.: 4 lbs.
Comments: Made from the early 1960s to the early 1970s.
Estimated Value: **Excellent:** **$125.00**
Very good: **$100.00**

Harrington & Richardson Sportster 250
Caliber: 22 long rifle
Action: Bolt action; repeating
Magazine: 5-shot detachable box
Barrel: Blued; 23"
Sights: Open rear, ramp front
Stock and Forearm: Wood one-piece semi-pistol grip stock and forearm
Approximate wt.: 6 lbs.
Comments: Made from the late 1940s to the early 1960s.
Estimated Value: **Excellent:** **$125.00**
Very good: **$100.00**

Harrington & Richardson 251
Similar to the 250 with a special Lyman rear sight.
Estimated Value: **Excellent:** **$125.00**
Very good: **$100.00**

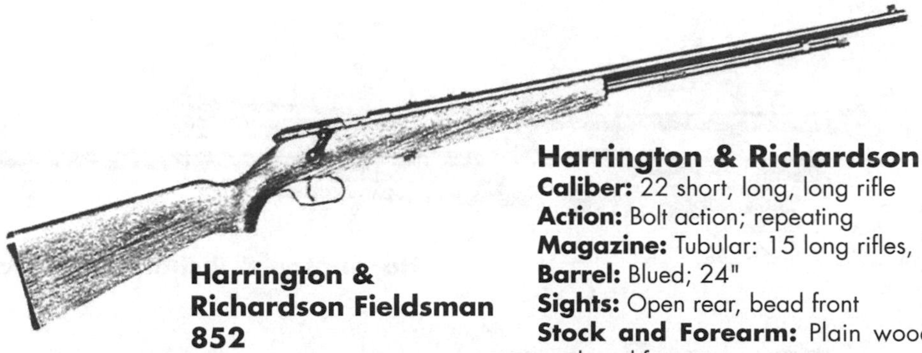

Harrington & Richardson Fieldsman 852

Harrington & Richardson Fieldsman 852

Caliber: 22 short, long, long rifle
Action: Bolt action; repeating
Magazine: Tubular: 15 long rifles, 17 longs, 21 shorts
Barrel: Blued; 24"
Sights: Open rear, bead front
Stock and Forearm: Plain wood one-piece semi-pistol grip stock and forearm
Approximate wt.: $5\frac{1}{2}$ lbs.
Comments: Made only in the early 1950s.
Estimated Value: **Excellent:** **$125.00**
Very good: **$100.00**

Harrington & Richardson Model 300

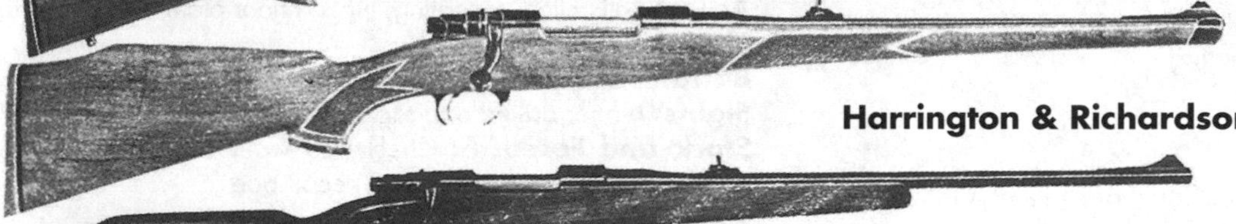

Harrington & Richardson Ultra 301

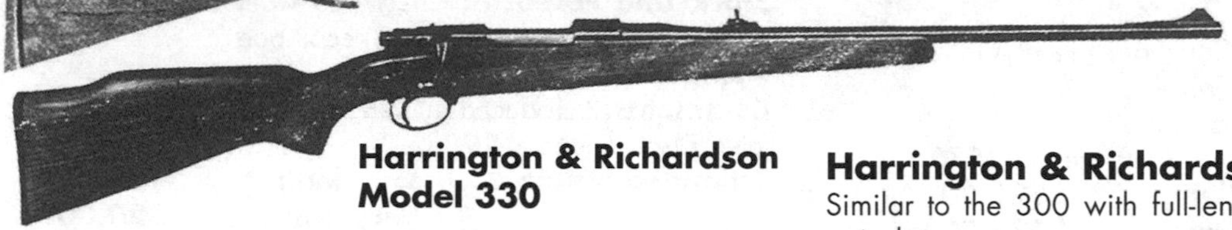

Harrington & Richardson Model 330

Harrington & Richardson Model 300

Caliber: 22-250 Rem., 243 Win., 270, 308, 30-06, 300 Win. mag., 7mm Rem. mag.
Action: Mauser-type bolt action; repeating
Magazine: 5-shot box, 3-shot in magnum
Barrel: Blued; 22" or 24"
Sights: Open rear, ramp front
Stock and Forearm: Checkered walnut Monte Carlo one-piece pistol grip stock and forearm; cheekpiece; recoil pad; swivels
Approximate wt.: $7\frac{3}{4}$ lbs.
Comments: Made from the mid-1960s to the early 1980s.
Estimated Value: **Excellent:** **$475.00**
Very good: **$375.00**

Harrington & Richardson Ultra 301

Similar to the 300 with full-length forearm and 18" barrel; no swivels.
Estimated Value: **Excellent:** **$495.00**
Very good: **$395.00**

Harrington & Richardson Model 330

Similar to the Model 300 with less fancy finish. Discontinued in the early 1970s.
Estimated Value: **Excellent:** **$375.00**
Very good: **$300.00**

Harrington & Richardson Model 333

Similar to the Model 330 with no checkering or sights.
Estimated Value: **Excellent:** **$285.00**
Very good: **$230.00**

Harrington & Richardson Ultra Wildcat 317

Harrington & Richardson 317 Presentation

Similar to the 317 with select wood, special basketweave checkering.
Estimated Value: **Excellent:** **$650.00**
Very good: **$520.00**

Harrington & Richardson Ultra Wildcat 317

Caliber: 17 Rem., 222, 223 or 17/223 (Handload)
Action: Bolt action, Sako-type; repeating
Magazine: 6-shot box
Barrel: Blued; 24"
Sights: None
Stock and Forearm: Wood Monte Carlo one-piece pistol grip stock and forearm; cheekpiece; recoil pad; swivels
Approximate wt.: $7\frac{3}{4}$ lbs.
Comments: Made from the late 1960s to the mid-1970s.
Estimated Value: **Excellent:** **$590.00**
Very good: **$475.00**

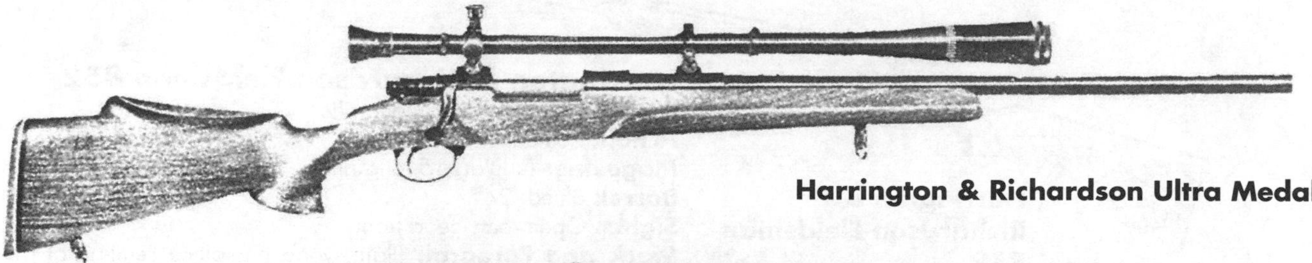

Harrington & Richardson Ultra Medalist 370

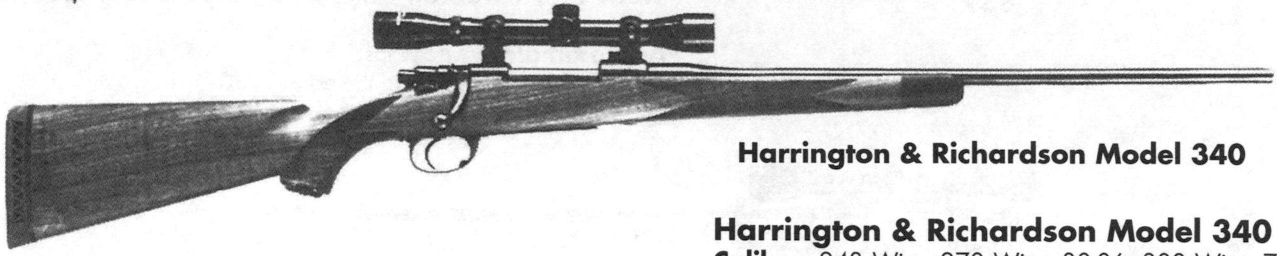

Harrington & Richardson Model 340

Harrington & Richardson Ultra Medalist 370

Caliber: 22-250, 243, 6mm Rem. Mag.
Action: Sako bolt action; repeating
Magazine: 4-shot box
Barrel: 24"; heavy
Sights: Open
Stock and Forearm: Monte Carlo one-piece grip stock and forearm; cheekpiece; recoil pad; swivels
Approximate wt.: 9 lbs.
Comments: Made from the late 1960s to the mid-1970s.

Estimated Value:	**Excellent:**	**$525.00**
	Very good:	**$420.00**

Harrington & Richardson Model 340

Caliber: 243 Win., 270 Win., 30-06, 308 Win., 7mm Mauser (7x57)
Action: Bolt action; repeating; hinged floor plate; adjustable trigger
Magazine: 5-shot
Barrel: Blued; 22"
Sights: None; drilled and tapped for sights or scope
Stock and Forearm: Checkered walnut one-piece pistol grip stock and forearm; cheekpiece; recoil pad
Approximate wt.: 7¼ lbs.
Comments: Introduced in 1981 in 30-06; other calibers added later. Discontinued in 1984.

Estimated Value:	**Excellent:**	**$400.00**
	Very good:	**$320.00**

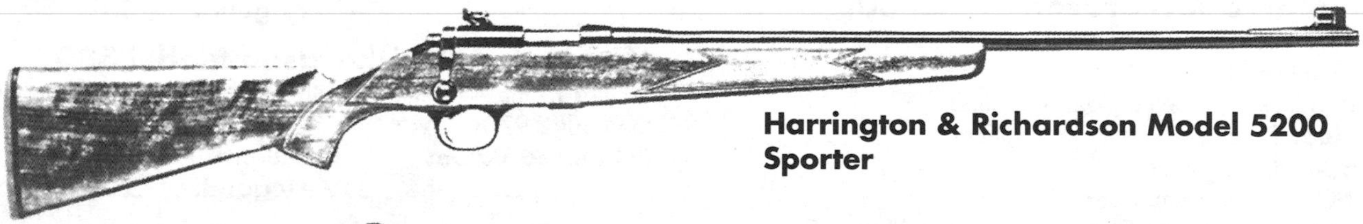

Harrington & Richardson Model 5200 Sporter

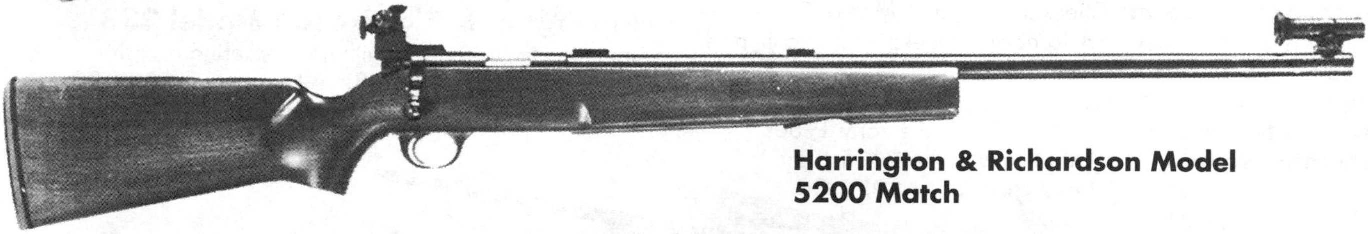

Harrington & Richardson Model 5200 Match

Harrington & Richardson Model 5200 Sporter

Caliber: 22 long rifle
Action: Bolt action; repeating
Magazine: 5-shot clip
Barrel: 24"; recessed muzzle
Sights: Adjustable receiver sight; hooded ramp front
Stock and Forearm: Checkered walnut one-piece semi-pistol grip stock and forearm; rubber recoil pad
Approximate wt.: 6½ lbs.
Comments: A sporting version of the Model 5200 introduced in 1982. Discontinued in 1983.

Estimated Value:	**Excellent:**	**$440.00**
	Very good:	**$350.00**

Harrington & Richardson Model 5200 Match

Caliber: 22 long rifle
Action: Bolt action, single-shot; adjustable trigger
Magazine: None
Barrel: 28"; heavy target weight, recessed muzzle
Sights: None; tapped for sights; scope bases included
Stock and Forearm: Smooth walnut one-piece match-style stock and forearm; swivels and hand stop; rubber recoil pad
Approximate wt.: 11 lbs.
Comments: A moderately-priced match rifle produced from 1981 to 1986.

Estimated Value:	**Excellent:**	**$460.00**
	Very good:	**$370.00**

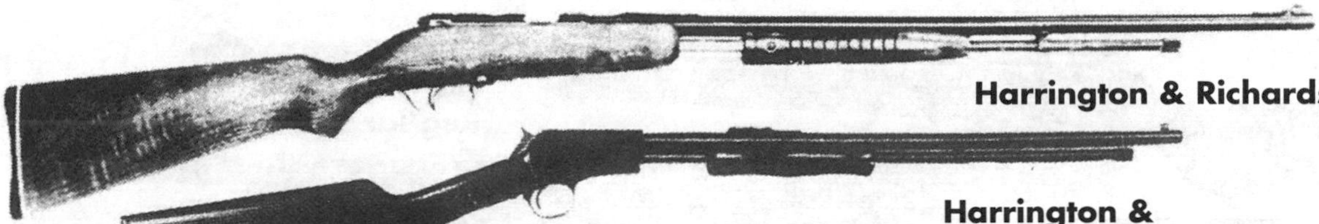

Harrington & Richardson Model 422

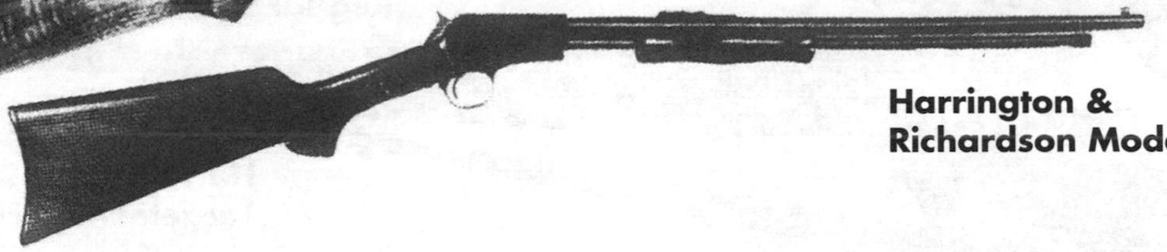

Harrington & Richardson Model 749

Harrington & Richardson Model 422

Caliber: 22 short, long, long rifle
Action: Slide action; hammerless; repeating
Magazine: Tubular: 15 long rifles, 17 longs, 21 shorts
Barrel: Blued; 24"
Sights: Open rear, ramp front
Stock and Forearm: Plain walnut semi-pistol grip stock and grooved slide handle
Approximate wt.: 6 lbs.
Comments: Made from the mid- to the late 1950s.

Estimated Value:	**Excellent:**	**$150.00**
	Very good:	**$120.00**

Harrington & Richardson Model 749

Caliber: 22 short, long, long rifle
Action: Slide action; hammerless; repeating
Magazine: Tubular: 18 shorts, 15 longs, 13 long rifles
Barrel: 19"; round, tapered
Sights: Open rear, blade front
Stock and Forearm: Plain hardwood pistol grip stock and tapered slide handle
Approximate wt.: 5 lbs.
Comments: Made in the early 1970s.

Estimated Value:	**Excellent:**	**$145.00**
	Very good:	**$115.00**

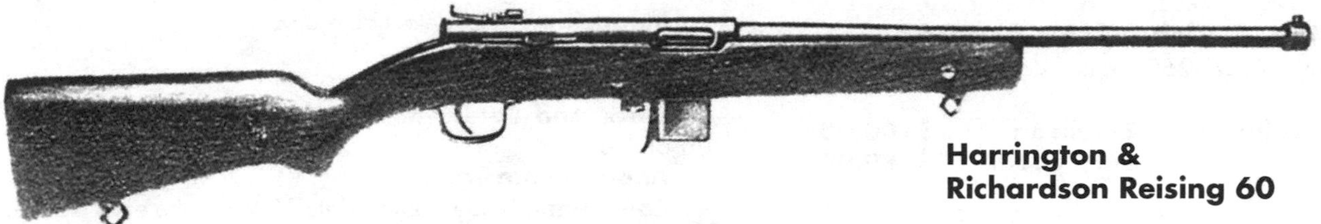

Harrington & Richardson Reising 60

Harrington & Richardson General 65

Harrington & Richardson Leatherneck 165

Harrington & Richardson Reising 60

Caliber: 45
Action: Semiautomatic
Magazine: 12- or 20-shot detachable box
Barrel: Blued; 18¼"
Sights: Open rear, blade front
Stock and Forearm: Plain wood one-piece semi-pistol grip stock and forearm
Approximate wt.: 7¼ lbs.
Comments: Manufactured during World War II.

Estimated Value:	**Excellent:**	**$1,000.00**
	Very good:	**$ 800.00**

Harrington & Richardson General 65

Caliber: 22 long rifle
Action: Semiautomatic
Magazine: 10-shot detachable box
Barrel: Blued; 23"
Sights: Peep rear, covered blade front
Stock and Forearm: Wood one-piece semi-pistol grip stock and forearm
Approximate wt.: 9 lbs.
Comments: Used as a Marine training rifle during World War II.

Estimated Value:	**Excellent:**	**$375.00**
	Very good:	**$300.00**

Harrington & Richardson Leatherneck 165

Lighter version of the 65 with ramp front sights. Made from World War II until the early 1960s.

Estimated Value:	**Excellent:**	**$200.00**
	Very good:	**$160.00**

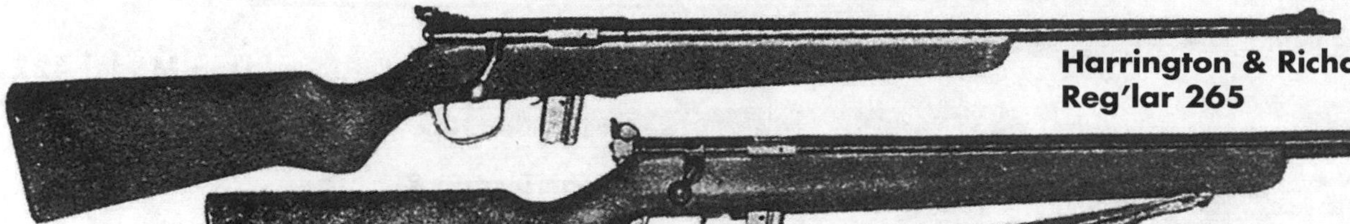

Harrington & Richardson Reg'lar 265

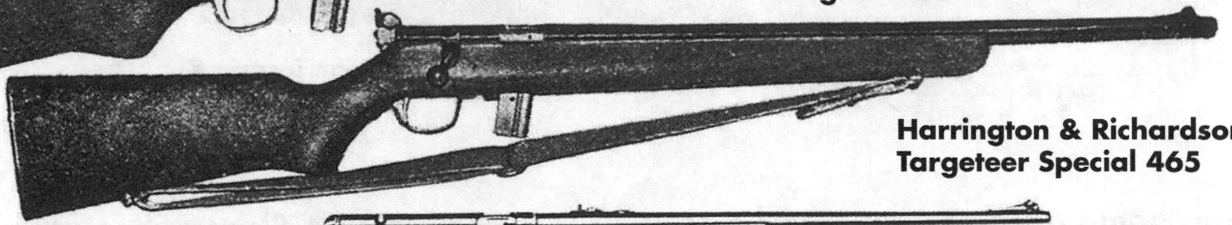

Harrington & Richardson Targeteer Special 465

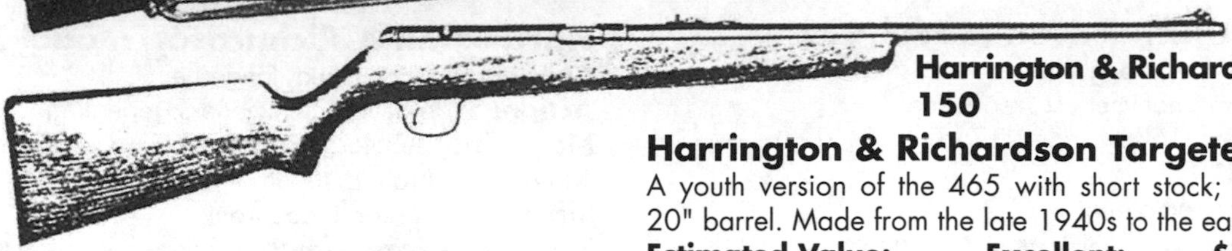

Harrington & Richardson Leatherneck 150

Harrington & Richardson Reg'lar 265

Similar to the 165 in bolt action with a 22" barrel. Made from World War II until about 1950.

Estimated Value: **Excellent:** **$125.00**
Very good: **$100.00**

Harrington & Richardson Ace 365

Similar to the Model 265 except single-shot. Made in the mid-1940s.

Estimated Value: **Excellent:** **$100.00**
Very good: **$ 80.00**

Harrington & Richardson Targeteer Special 465

Similar to the 265 with 25" barrel; swivels; slightly heavier. Made in the mid-1940s.

Estimated Value: **Excellent:** **$150.00**
Very good: **$120.00**

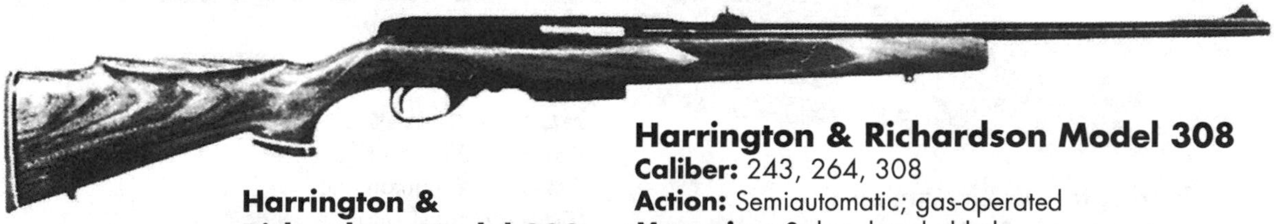

Harrington & Richardson Model 308

Harrington & Richardson Lynx 800

Caliber: 22 long rifle
Action: Semiautomatic; hammerless
Magazine: 10-shot clip
Barrel: Blued; 22"
Sights: Open rear, ramp front
Stock and Forearm: Walnut one-piece semi-pistol grip stock and forearm
Approximate wt.: 6 lbs.
Comments: Made from the late 1950s to about 1960.
Estimated Value: **Excellent:** **$130.00**
Very good: **$105.00**

Harrington & Richardson Targeteer Jr.

A youth version of the 465 with short stock; 5-shot magazine; 20" barrel. Made from the late 1940s to the early 1950s.

Estimated Value: **Excellent:** **$120.00**
Very good: **$ 95.00**

Harrington & Richardson Leatherneck 150

Caliber: 22 long rifle
Action: Semiautomatic; hammerless
Magazine: 5-shot detachable box
Barrel: Blued; 22"
Sights: Open rear, ramp front
Stock and Forearm: Wood one-piece semi-pistol grip stock and forearm
Approximate wt.: 7 lbs.
Comments: Made from the late 1940s to the early 1950s.
Estimated Value: **Excellent:** **$150.00**
Very good: **$120.00**

Harrington & Richardson Model 151

Similar to the 150 with a special peep rear sight.

Estimated Value: **Excellent:** **$160.00**
Very good: **$130.00**

Harrington & Richardson Model 308

Caliber: 243, 264, 308
Action: Semiautomatic; gas-operated
Magazine: 3-shot detachable box
Barrel: Blued; 22"
Sights: Adjustable rear, bead front
Stock and Forearm: Checkered walnut Monte Carlo one-piece pistol grip stock and forearm; cheekpiece; swivels
Approximate wt.: 7 lbs.
Comments: Made in the mid-1960s only; changed to the Model 360 in 1967.
Estimated Value: **Excellent:** **$350.00**
Very good: **$275.00**

Harrington & Richardson Model 360

Same as the Model 308. Made from 1967 to the early 1970s.

Estimated Value: **Excellent:** **$355.00**
Very good: **$280.00**

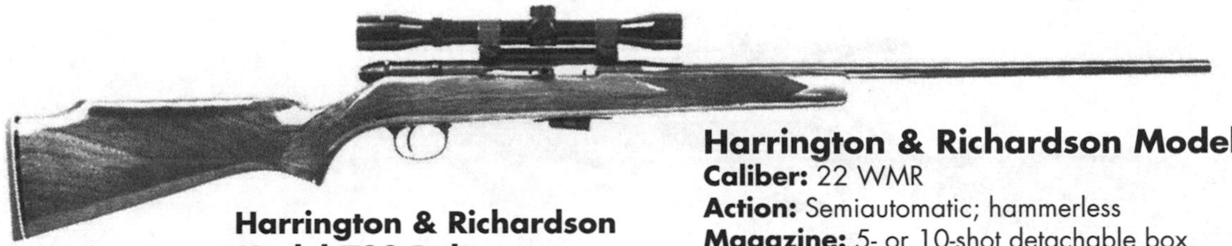

Harrington & Richardson Model 700 Deluxe

Harrington & Richardson Model 700

Caliber: 22 WMR
Action: Semiautomatic; hammerless
Magazine: 5- or 10-shot detachable box
Barrel: 22"
Sights: Adjustable folding rear; ramp blade front
Stock and Forearm: Plain walnut Monte Carlo one-piece pistol grip stock and forearm
Approximate wt.: 6½ lbs.
Comments: Produced from the late 1970s to the mid-1980s.
Estimated Value: **Excellent:** **$250.00**
Very good: **$200.00**

Harrington & Richardson Model 700 Deluxe

Similar to the Model 700 with select custom finish; checkering; cheekpiece; recoil pad; 4X scope.
Estimated Value: **Excellent:** **$350.00**
Very good: **$280.00**

HECKLER + KOCH

Heckler & Koch Model 300

Heckler & Koch Model 270

Heckler & Koch Model 270

Caliber: 22 long rifle
Action: Semiautomatic; blow back design
Magazine: 5- or 20-shot detachable box
Barrel: Blued; 20"
Sights: Diopter sights, adjustable for windage and elevation
Stock and Forearm: Plain walnut, one-piece semi-pistol grip stock and lipped forearm
Approximate wt.: 5½ lbs.
Comments: Discontinued in the mid-1980s.
Estimated Value: **Excellent:** **$625.00**
Very good: **$500.00**

Heckler & Koch Model 300

Caliber: 22 Win. mag.
Action: Semiautomatic; blow back design
Magazine: 5- or 15-shot detachable box
Barrel: Blued; 20"
Sights: Adjustable post front, adjustable V-notch rear
Stock and Forearm: Checkered walnut Monte Carlo one-piece pistol grip stock and lipped forearm; cheekpiece; swivels
Approximate wt.: 5¾ lbs.
Comments: Discontinued in 1992.
Estimated Value: **Excellent:** **$650.00**
Very good: **$520.00**

Heckler & Koch Models SL-6 and SL-7

Caliber: 223 (SL-6), 308 (SL-7)
Action: Semiautomatic
Magazine: 4-shot clip (SL-6); 3-shot clip (SL-7); 10-shot clip available for both rifles
Barrel: 17¾"; round black matte finish
Sights: Ring and post front; diopter adjustable rear
Stock and Forearm: Smooth European one-piece stock and forearm with ventilated wood handguard over barrel
Approximate wt.: 8½ lbs.
Comments: Produced in the mid-1980s.
Estimated Value: **Excellent:** **$1,000.00**
Very good: **$ 800.00**

Heckler & Koch Models 91 and 93

Caliber: 223 (Model 93); 308 (Model 91)
Action: Semiautomatic
Magazine: 25-shot clip (Model 93); 20-shot clip (Model 91); 5-shot clip available for both rifles
Barrel: 16¼" matte black (Model 93); 17¾" matte black (Model 91)
Sights: Ring and post front; diopter adjustable rear
Stock and Forearm: Matte black, fixed, high-impact plastic three-piece stock, forearm and pistol grip; a retractable metal stock is available
Approximate wt.: 8 lbs. (Model 93); 10 lbs. (Model 91)
Comments: Made from the 1970s to 1992. Add 12% for retractable metal stock.
Estimated Value: **Excellent:** **$2,500.00**
Very good: **$2,000.00**

Heckler & Koch Model 94 Carbine

Similar to the Model 91 and Model 93 in 9mm caliber; 30-shot clip; 16½" barrel; weighs 6½ lbs.; Add 12% for retractable metal stock.
Estimated Value: **Excellent:** **$3,000.00**
Very good: **$2,400.00**

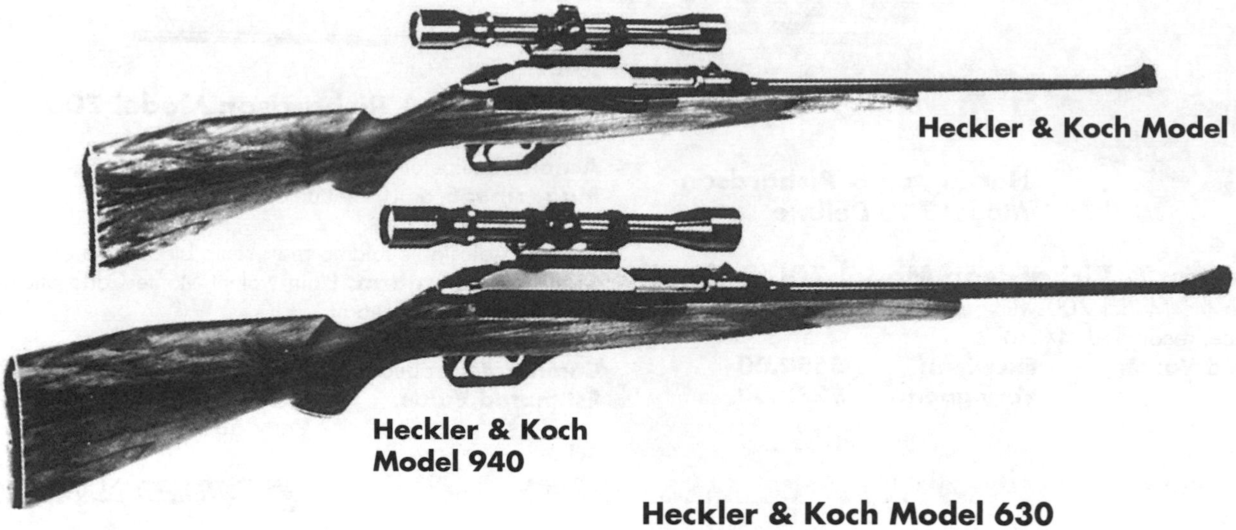

Heckler & Koch Model 770

Heckler & Koch Model 940

Heckler & Koch Model 770

Similar to the Model 630 in 243 or 308 Win. calibers; 20" barrel; weighs 8 lbs. 3-shot magazine.

Estimated Value: **Excellent:** **$1,250.00**
Very good: **$1,000.00**

Heckler & Koch Model 940

Similar to the Model 630 in 30-06 Springfield caliber; 22" barrel; weighs 8¾ lbs.; 3-shot magazine.

Estimated Value: **Excellent:** **$1,200.00**
Very good: **$ 960.00**

Heckler & Koch Model 630

Caliber: 221, 222, 223, Rem., 22 Hornet
Action: Semiautomatic
Magazine: 4-shot box; 10-shot available
Barrel: Blued; 18"
Sights: Adjustable post front, adjustable V-notch rear
Stock and Forearm: Checkered walnut Monte Carlo pistol grip, one-piece stock and lipped forearm; cheekpiece; swivels
Approximate wt.: 7 lbs.
Comments: Available in 223 Remington caliber only after the mid-1980s. Made from about 1982 to the late 1980s.
Estimated Value: **Excellent:** **$1,000.00**
Very good: **$ 800.00**

HENRY

Henry Acu-Bolt

Henry H001 Lever Action

Henry Acu-Bolt

Caliber: 17 HMR, 22 long rifle, 22 magnum
Action: Bolt action, single-shot
Magazine: none
Barrel: 20" stainless steel
Sights: Adjustable rear, ramp front; scope included
Stock and Forearm: Checkered synthetic one-piece pistol grip stock and forearm
Approximate wt.: 4¼ lbs.
Comments: A weather-resistant bolt action rifle.
Estimated Value: **New (retail):** **$399.95**
Excellent: **$300.00**
Very good: **$240.00**

Henry H001 Lever Action

Caliber: 22 short, long, or long rifle
Action: Lever action repeating; exposed hammer
Magazine: 21-shot (short), 17-shot (long), 15-shot (long rifle) tubular
Barrel: 18¼" blued
Sights: Adjustable rear, hooded ramp front
Stock and Forearm: American walnut straight stock and banded forearm
Approximate wt.: 5¼ lbs.
Comments: A classic western-style lever action rimfire rifle.
Estimated Value: **New (retail):** **$325.00**
Excellent: **$245.00**
Very good: **$200.00**

Henry H001 Youth Lever Action

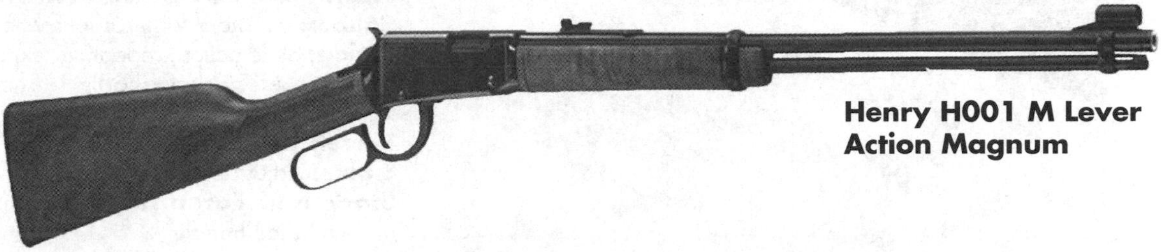

Henry H001 M Lever Action Magnum

Henry H001 Youth Lever Action

Caliber: 22 short, long, or long rifle
Action: Lever action repeating; exposed hammer
Magazine: 17-shot (short), 15-shot (long), 12-shot (long rifle) tubular
Barrel: 16⅛", blued
Sights: Adjustable rear, hooded ramp front
Stock and Forearm: American walnut straight stock and banded forearm
Approximate wt.: 4½ lbs.
Comments: A youth version of Henry's lever action.

Estimated Value:	**New (retail):**	**$325.00**
	Excellent:	**$245.00**
	Very good:	**$200.00**

Henry H001 M Lever Action Magnum

Caliber: 22 magnum
Action: Lever action repeating; exposed hammer
Magazine: 11-shot tubular
Barrel: 19¼", blued
Sights: Adjustable rear, hooded ramp front
Stock and Forearm: Checkered American walnut straight stock and banded forearm
Approximate wt.: 5½ lbs.
Comments: A classic western-style lever action magnum rimfire rifle.

Estimated Value:	**New (retail):**	**$475.00**
	Excellent:	**$355.00**
	Very good:	**$285.00**

Henry H001 L Lever Action Carbine

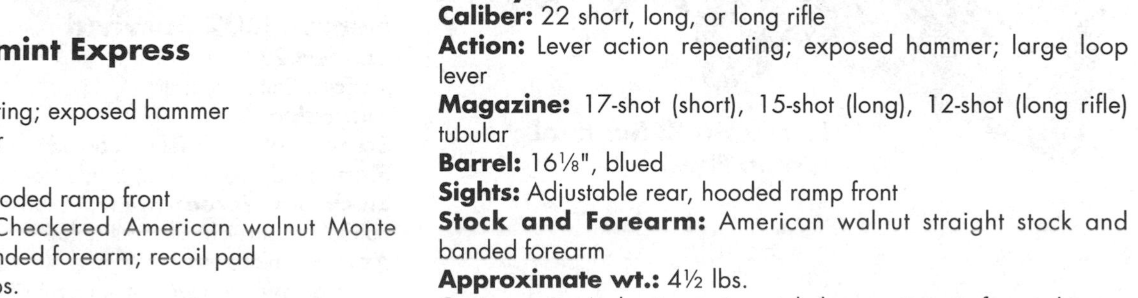

Henry H001 V Varmint Express

Henry H001 V Varmint Express

Caliber: 17 HMR
Action: Lever action repeating; exposed hammer
Magazine: 12-shot tubular
Barrel: 20", blued
Sights: Adjustable rear, hooded ramp front
Stock and Forearm: Checkered American walnut Monte Carlo straight stock and banded forearm; recoil pad
Approximate wt.: 5¾ lbs.
Comments: Designed for hunting small game.

Estimated Value:	**New (retail):**	**$549.95**
	Excellent:	**$410.00**
	Very good:	**$330.00**

Henry H001 L Lever Action Carbine

Caliber: 22 short, long, or long rifle
Action: Lever action repeating; exposed hammer; large loop lever
Magazine: 17-shot (short), 15-shot (long), 12-shot (long rifle) tubular
Barrel: 16⅛", blued
Sights: Adjustable rear, hooded ramp front
Stock and Forearm: American walnut straight stock and banded forearm
Approximate wt.: 4½ lbs.
Comments: A classic western-style lever action rimfire carbine.

Estimated Value:	**New (retail):**	**$340.00**
	Excellent:	**$255.00**
	Very good:	**$205.00**

Henry H003T Slide Action

Henry H003T Slide Action

Caliber: 22 short, long, or long rifle
Action: Slide action, repeating; exposed hammer
Magazine: 22-shot (short), 17-shot (long), 15-shot (long rifle) tubular
Barrel: 19¾" octagon, blued
Sights: Adjustable rear, bead front
Stock and Forearm: American walnut straight stock and grooved slide handle
Approximate wt.: 6 lbs.
Comments: Also available in 22 magnum (add 16%).

Estimated Value:	**New (retail):**	**$515.00**
	Excellent:	**$385.00**
	Very good:	**$310.00**

Henry H002 Survival
(Black Teflon Finish)

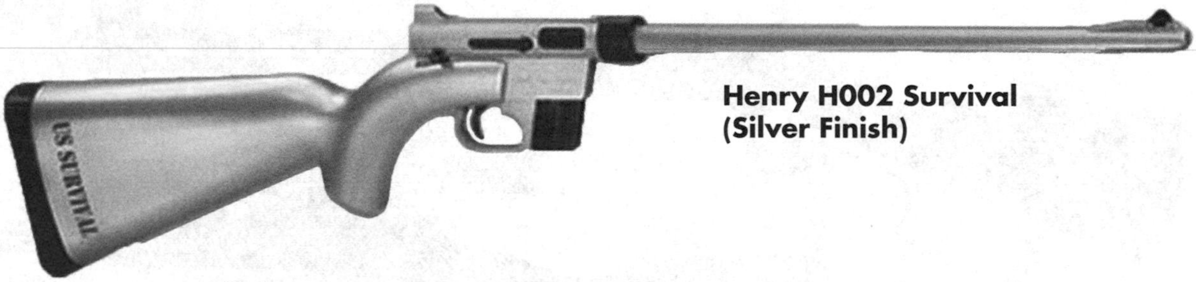

Henry H002 Survival
(Silver Finish)

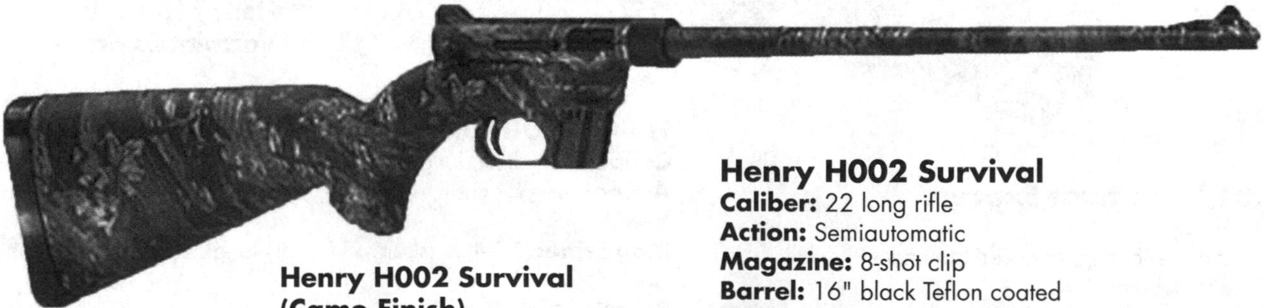

Henry H002 Survival
(Camo Finish)

Henry H002 Survival

Caliber: 22 long rifle
Action: Semiautomatic
Magazine: 8-shot clip
Barrel: 16" black Teflon coated
Sights: Adjustable rear, blade front
Stock and Forearm: Black ABS plastic pistol grip stock; camouflage or silver finish available
Approximate wt.: 2½ lbs.
Comments: Lightweight survival rifle that breaks down for stock storage. Add 20% for camouflage finish.

Estimated Value:	**New (retail):**	**$270.00**
	Excellent:	**$200.00**
	Very good:	**$160.00**

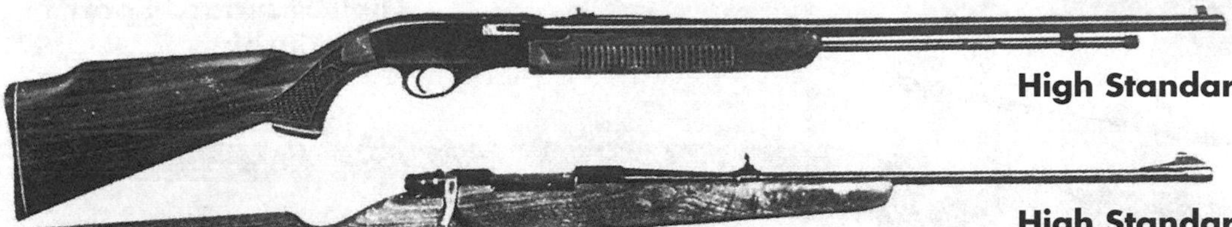

High Standard Flite King

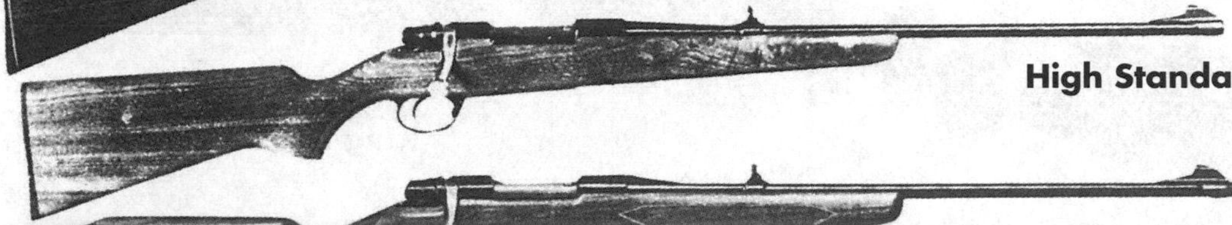

High Standard Hi Power

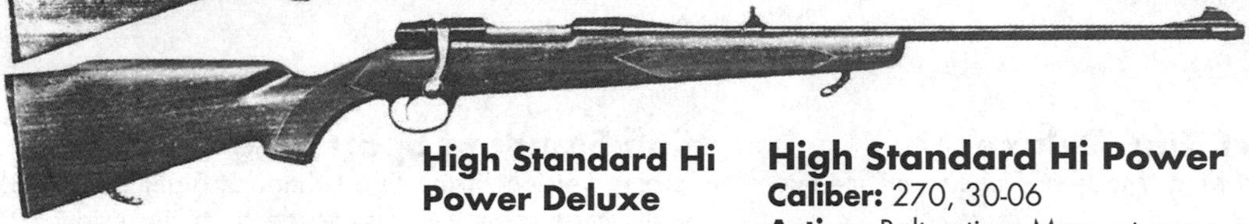

High Standard Hi Power Deluxe

High Standard Flite King

Caliber: 22 short, long, long rifle
Action: Slide action; hammerless; repeating
Magazine: Tubular: 17 long rifle, 19 long, 24 short
Barrel: Blued; 24"
Sights: Adjustable rear, post front
Stock and Forearm: Checkered walnut Monte Carlo pistol grip stock and grooved slide handle; early models have no checkering
Approximate wt.: 5½ lbs.
Comments: Made from about 1962 to the late 1970s.

Estimated Value:	**Excellent:**	**$150.00**
	Very good:	**$120.00**

High Standard Hi Power

Caliber: 270, 30-06
Action: Bolt action; Mauser-type; repeating
Magazine: 4-shot box
Barrel: Blued; 22"
Sights: Folding leaf rear, ramp front
Stock and Forearm: Walnut one-piece semi-pistol grip stock and tapered forearm
Approximate wt.: 7 lbs.
Comments: Made from the early to the mid-1960s.

Estimated Value:	**Excellent:**	**$330.00**
	Very good:	**$265.00**

High Standard Hi Power Deluxe

Similar to Hi Power with a checkered Monte Carlo stock and swivels.

Estimated Value:	**Excellent:**	**$350.00**
	Very good:	**$285.00**

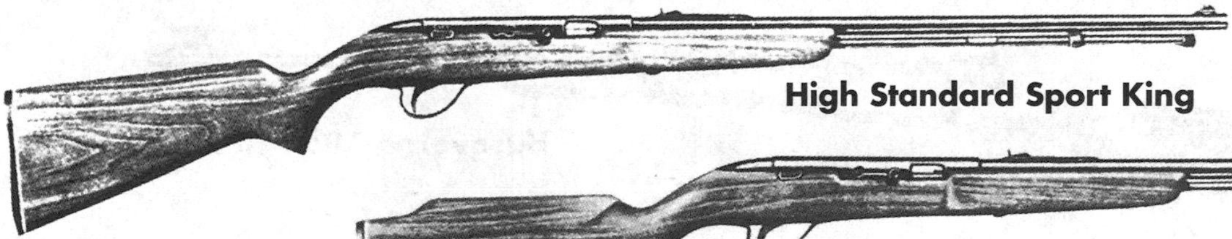

High Standard Sport King

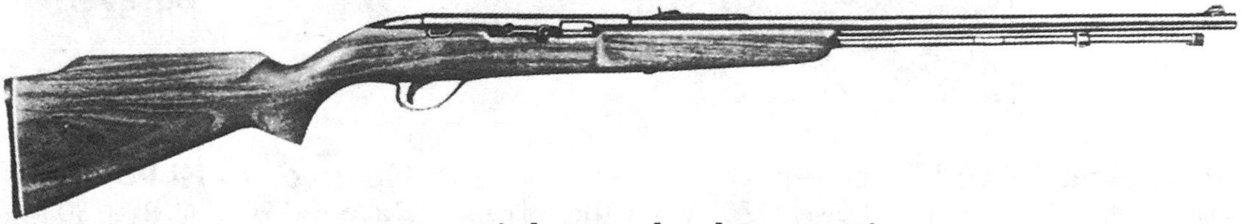

High Standard Sport King Special

High Standard Sport King Special

Similar to Sport King without checkering. Made from the early 1950s to the mid-1960s.

Estimated Value:	**Excellent:**	**$175.00**
	Very good:	**$140.00**

High Standard Sport King

Caliber: 22 short, long, long rifle
Action: Semiautomatic
Magazine: Tubular: 15 long rifles, 17 longs, 21 shorts
Barrel: Blued; 22¼"
Sights: Open rear, post front
Stock and Forearm: Checkered wood Monte Carlo one-piece pistol grip stock and forearm
Approximate wt.: 5½ lbs.
Comments: Sport King had no Monte Carlo stock before the mid-1970s; field model was made from about 1960 to the late 1970s.

Estimated Value:	**Excellent:**	**$150.00**
	Very good:	**$120.00**

High Standard Sport King Carbine

High Standard Sport King Deluxe

High Standard Sport King Deluxe

Same specifications as Sport King. Made as Deluxe until the mid-1970s.

Estimated Value: **Excellent:** **$200.00**
Very good: **$160.00**

High Standard Sport King Carbine

Carbine version of the Sport King. Straight stock; 18¼" barrel; smaller magazine; swivels. Made from the early 1960s to the early 1970s.

Estimated Value: **Excellent:** **$200.00**
Very good: **$160.00**

HUSQVARNA

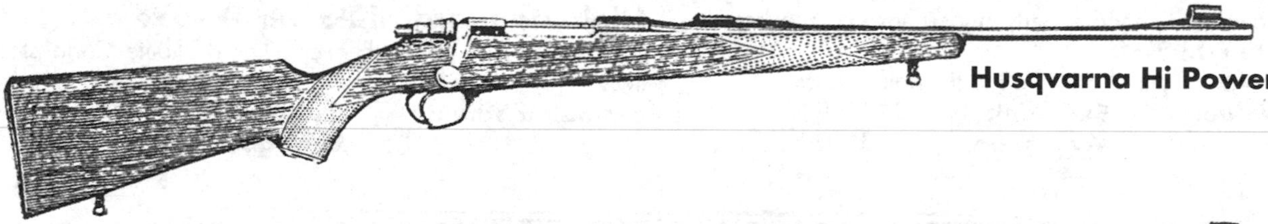

Husqvarna Hi Power

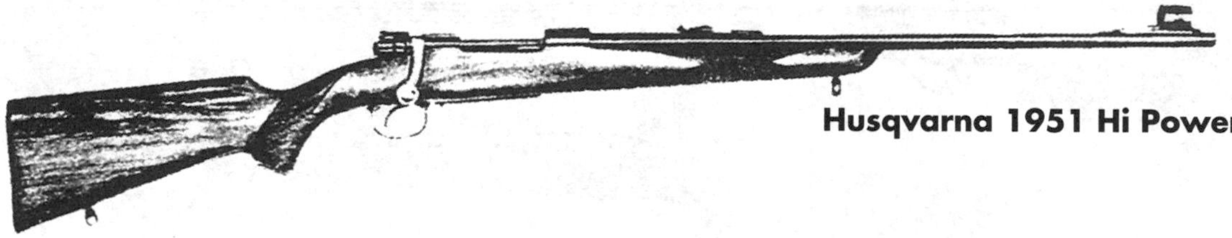

Husqvarna 1951 Hi Power

Husqvarna 1950 Hi Power

Similar to the Hi Power in 220 Swift, 270, and 30-06 calibers only. Made only in the early 1950s.

Estimated Value: **Excellent:** **$500.00**
Very good: **$400.00**

Husqvarna 1951 Hi Power

Similar to the 1950 Hi Power with a slightly higher comb stock. Made only in 1951.

Estimated Value: **Excellent:** **$500.00**
Very good: **$400.00**

Husqvarna Hi Power

Caliber: 220 Swift, 270, 30-06, 6.5x55, 8x57, 9.3x57
Action: Mauser-type bolt action; repeating
Magazine: 5-shot box
Barrel: Blued; 23¾"
Sights: Open rear, hooded ramp front
Stock and Forearm: Checkered beech one-piece pistol grip stock and tapered forearm; swivels
Approximate wt.: 7¾ lbs.
Comments: Made from World War II to the early 1950s.
Estimated Value: **Excellent:** **$475.00**
Very good: **$380.00**

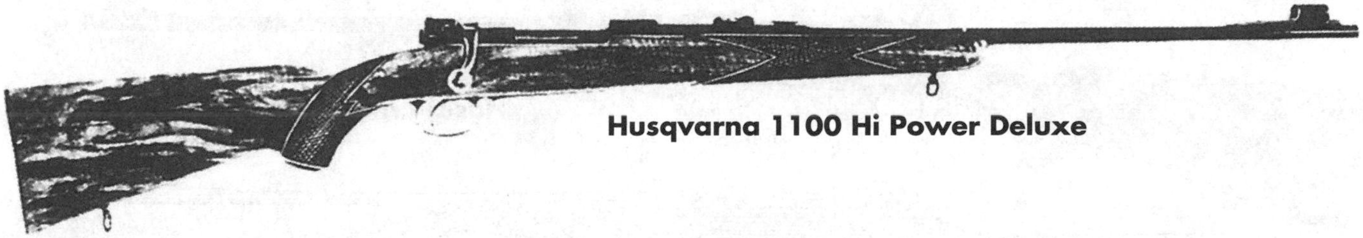

Husqvarna 1100 Hi Power Deluxe

Husqvarna 1000 Super Grade

Similar to the 1100 Hi Power Deluxe with a Monte Carlo stock.

Estimated Value:	**Excellent:**	**$550.00**
	Very good:	**$440.00**

Husqvarna 1100 Hi Power Deluxe

Similar to the 1951 Hi Power with walnut stock and forearm; made from the early to the mid-1950s.

Estimated Value:	**Excellent:**	**$525.00**
	Very good:	**$420.00**

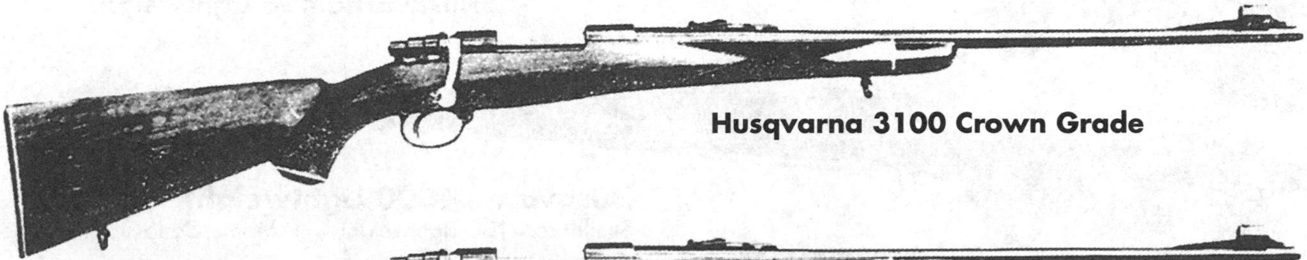

Husqvarna 3100 Crown Grade

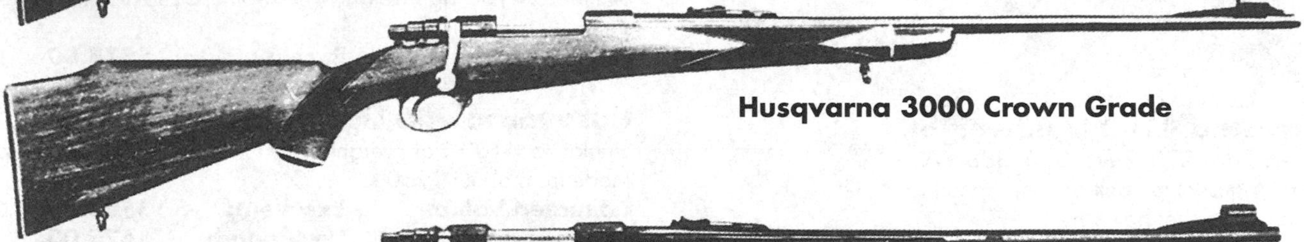

Husqvarna 3000 Crown Grade

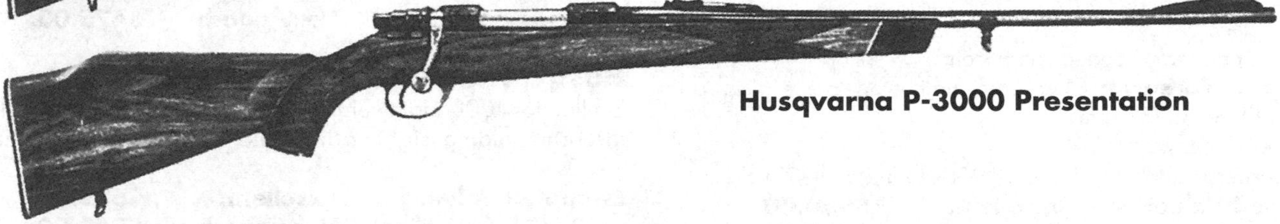

Husqvarna P-3000 Presentation

Husqvarna 6000 Imperial Custom

Husqvarna 3100 Crown Grade

Caliber: 243, 270, 7mm Rem., 30-06, 308 Win.
Action: Mauser-type bolt action; repeating
Magazine: 5-shot box
Barrel: Blued; 23¾"
Sights: Open rear, hooded ramp front
Stock and Forearm: Checkered walnut one-piece pistol grip stock and tapered forearm; swivels
Approximate wt.: 7 lbs.
Comments: Made from the mid-1950s to the mid-1970s.

Estimated Value:	**Excellent:**	**$550.00**
	Very good:	**$440.00**

Husqvarna 3000 Crown Grade

Similar to the 3100 Crown Grade with Monte Carlo stock.

Estimated Value:	**Excellent:**	**$575.00**
	Very good:	**$460.00**

Husqvarna P-3000 Presentation

A fancy version of the 3000 Crown Grade with engraving; select wood; adjustable trigger. Made in the late 1960s.

Estimated Value:	**Excellent:**	**$860.00**
	Very good:	**$685.00**

Husqvarna 6000 Imperial Custom

Similar to the 3100 Crown Grade with higher quality finish; folding sight; adjustable trigger. Made in the late 1960s.

Estimated Value:	**Excellent:**	**$600.00**
	Very good:	**$480.00**

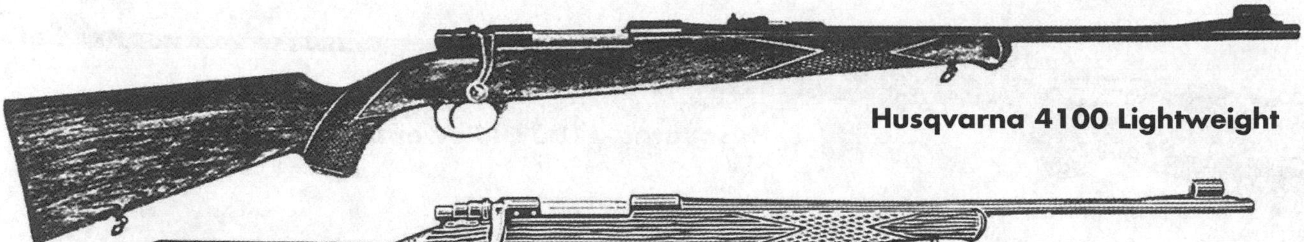

Husqvarna 4100 Lightweight

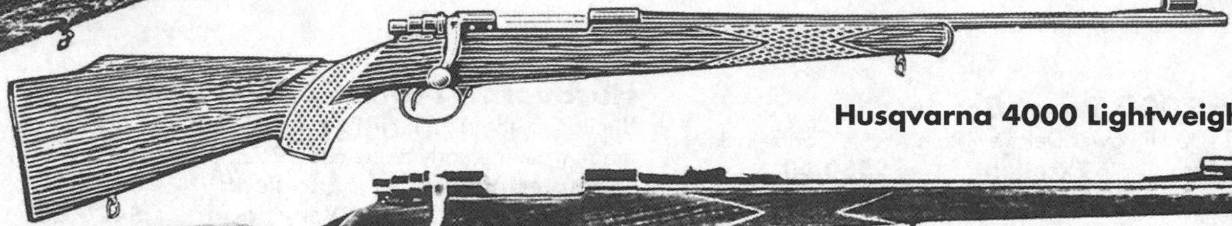

Husqvarna 4000 Lightweight

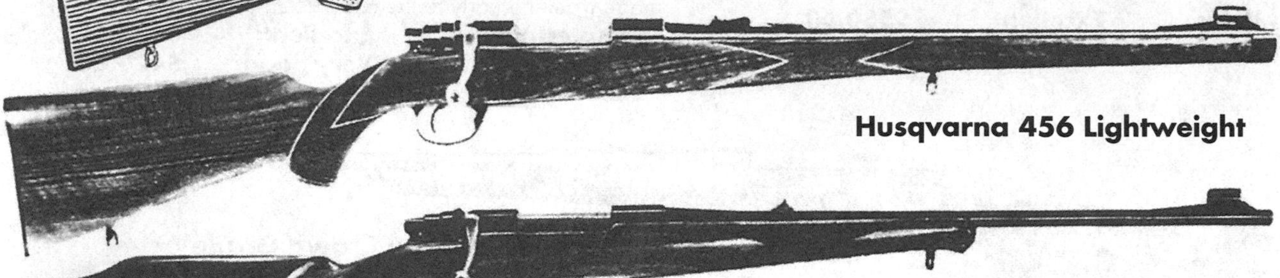

Husqvarna 456 Lightweight

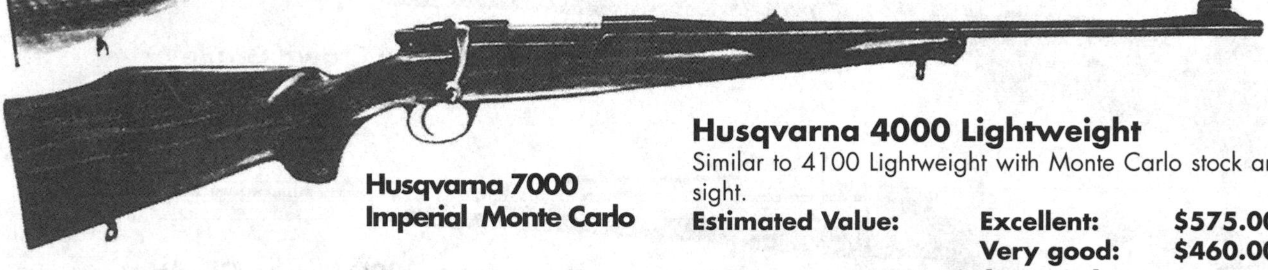

Husqvarna 7000 Imperial Monte Carlo

Husqvarna 4100 Lightweight

Caliber: 243, 270, 7mm, 306, 308 Win.
Action: Mauser-type bolt action; repeating
Magazine: 5-shot box
Barrel: Blued; 20½"
Sights: Open rear, hooded ramp front
Stock and Forearm: Checkered walnut one-piece pistol grip stock and tapered forearm
Approximate wt.: 6 lbs.
Comments: Made from the mid-1950s to the mid-1970s.

Estimated Value:	**Excellent:**	**$550.00**
	Very good:	**$440.00**

Husqvarna 4000 Lightweight

Similar to 4100 Lightweight with Monte Carlo stock and no rear sight.

Estimated Value:	**Excellent:**	**$575.00**
	Very good:	**$460.00**

Husqvarna 456 Lightweight

Similar to 4100 Lightweight with full-length stock and forearm. Made from about 1960 to 1970.

Estimated Value:	**Excellent:**	**$590.00**
	Very good:	**$475.00**

Husqvarna 7000 Imperial Monte Carlo

Similar to 4000 Lightweight with higher quality wood; lipped forearm; folding sight; adjustable trigger. Made in the late 1960s.

Estimated Value:	**Excellent:**	**$675.00**
	Very good:	**$540.00**

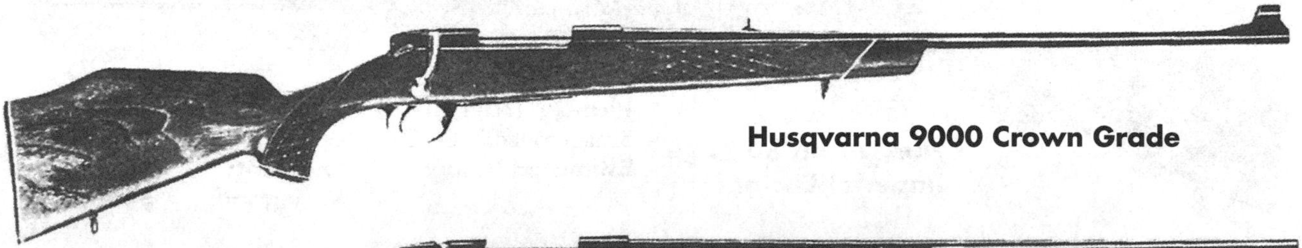

Husqvarna 9000 Crown Grade

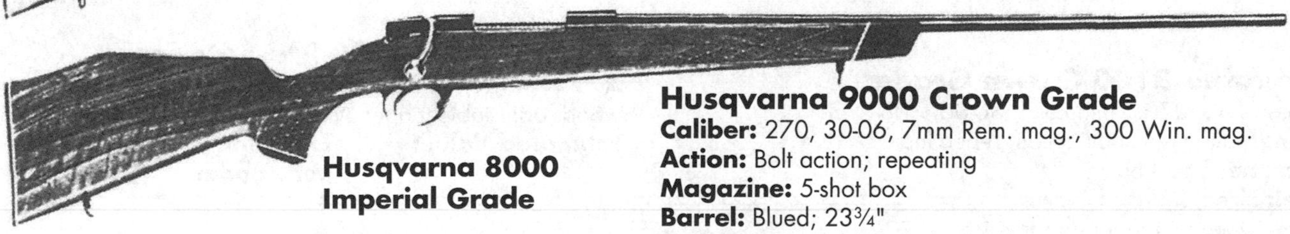

Husqvarna 8000 Imperial Grade

Husqvarna 8000 Imperial Grade

Similar to 9000 Crown Grade with select wood; engraving; no sights.

Estimated Value:	**Excellent:**	**$700.00**
	Very good:	**$560.00**

Husqvarna 9000 Crown Grade

Caliber: 270, 30-06, 7mm Rem. mag., 300 Win. mag.
Action: Bolt action; repeating
Magazine: 5-shot box
Barrel: Blued; 23¾"
Sights: Leaf rear, hooded ramp front
Stock and Forearm: Checkered walnut Monte Carlo one-piece pistol grip stock and forearm; swivels
Approximate wt.: 7¼ lbs.
Comments: Made in the early 1970s.

Estimated Value:	**Excellent:**	**$550.00**
	Very good:	**$440.00**

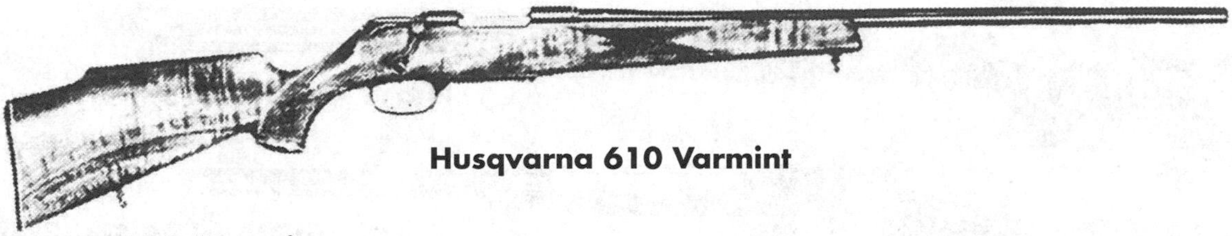

Husqvarna 610 Varmint

Husqvarna 610 Varmint

Caliber: 222
Action: Short stroke bolt action; repeating
Magazine: 4-shot detachable box
Barrel: Blued; 23¾"
Sights: None; tapped for scope
Stock and Forearm: Checkered walnut Monte Carlo one-piece pistol grip stock and forearm; cheekpiece
Approximate wt.: 6½ lbs.
Comments: Made in the late 1960s.

Estimated Value:	**Excellent:**	**$500.00**
	Very good:	**$400.00**

Husqvarna 358 Magnum

Caliber: 358 Norma mag.
Action: Bolt action; repeating
Magazine: 3-shot box
Barrel: Blued; 25½"
Sights: Folding leaf rear, hooded ramp front
Stock and Forearm: Checkered walnut Monte Carlo one-piece pistol grip stock and forearm; cheekpiece
Approximate wt.: 7¾ lbs.
Comments: Made in the late 1960s.

Estimated Value:	**Excellent:**	**$550.00**
	Very good:	**$440.00**

Ithaca Model LSA-55

Ithaca Model LSA-55 Deluxe

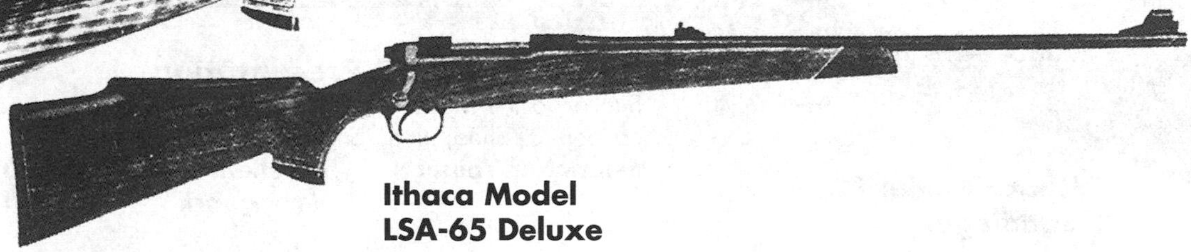

Ithaca Model LSA-65 Deluxe

Ithaca Model LSA-55

Caliber: 222, 22-250, 6mm, 243, 308
Action: Bolt action; repeating
Magazine: 3-shot detachable box
Barrel: Blued; 22"
Sights: Iron; adjustable rear, hooded ramp front
Stock and Forearm: Monte Carlo one-piece pistol grip stock and tapered forearm
Approximate wt.: 6½ lbs.
Comments: Made from the early 1970s to the late 1970s.

Estimated Value:	**Excellent:**	**$450.00**
	Very good:	**$360.00**

Ithaca Model LSA-55 Heavy Barrel

Similar to the Model LSA-55 except: cheekpiece; recoil pad; heavy barrel; weighs 8½ lbs.

Estimated Value:	**Excellent:**	**$550.00**
	Very good:	**$440.00**

Ithaca Model LSA-55 Deluxe

Similar to the Model LSA-55 except: checkering; recoil pad.

Estimated Value:	**Excellent:**	**$500.00**
	Very good:	**$400.00**

Ithaca Model LSA-65

Similar to the Model LSA-55 in 25-06, 270, 30-06, with a 4-shot magazine; weighs 7 lbs.

Estimated Value:	**Excellent:**	**$475.00**
	Very good:	**$380.00**

Ithaca Model LSA-65 Deluxe

Similar to the Model LSA-55 Deluxe in same calibers and weight as LSA-65.

Estimated Value:	**Excellent:**	**$500.00**
	Very good:	**$400.00**

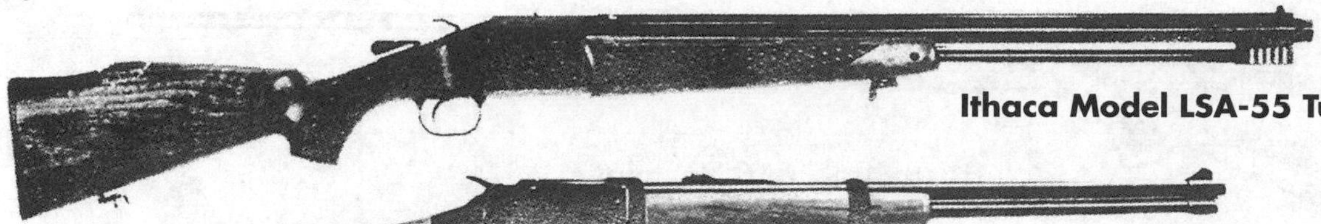

Ithaca Model LSA-55 Turkey Gun

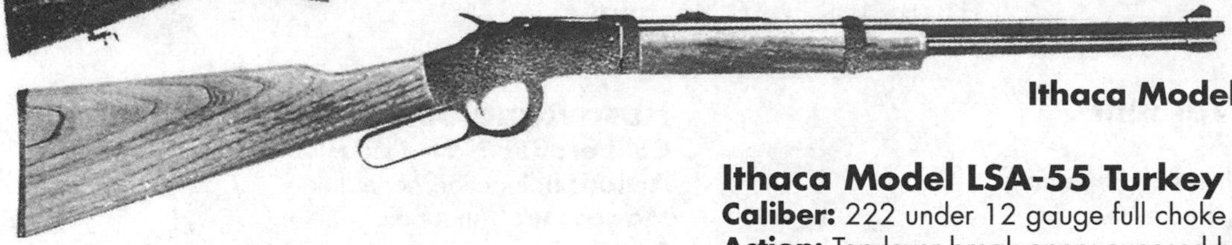

Ithaca Model 49 Saddlegun

Ithaca Model 49 Saddlegun

Caliber: 22 short, long, long rifle
Action: Lever action; exposed hammer; single-shot
Magazine: None
Barrel: Blued; 18"
Sights: Adjustable rear, bead front
Stock and Forearm: Plain wood straight grip stock and forearm; barrel band; recent model has checkering
Approximate wt.: 5½ lbs.
Comments: Made from about 1960 to the late 1970s.

Estimated Value:	**Excellent:**	**$225.00**
	Very good:	**$180.00**

Ithaca Model LSA-55 Turkey Gun

Caliber: 222 under 12 gauge full choke
Action: Top lever break open; exposed hammer
Magazine: None
Barrel: 24½" rifle under full choke shotgun with matted rib
Sights: Folding rear, dovetail front
Stock and Forearm: Checkered walnut Monte Carlo pistol grip stock and forearm; cheekpiece; recoil pad; swivels
Approximate wt.: 7 lbs.
Comments: An over and under combination manufactured in the 1970s.

Estimated Value:	**Excellent:**	**$700.00**
	Very good:	**$560.00**

Ithaca Model 49 Deluxe

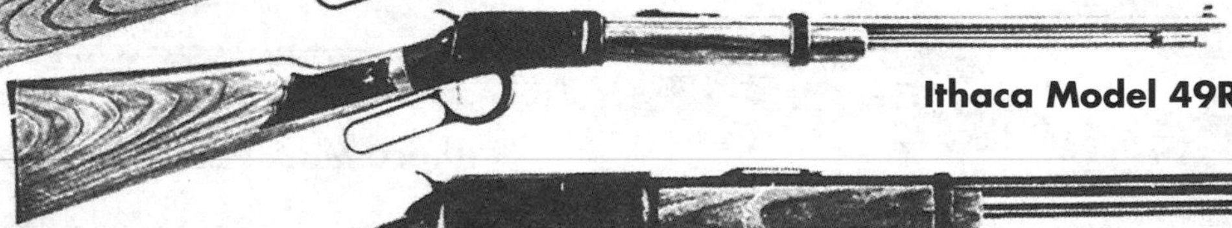

Ithaca Model 49R (Repeater)

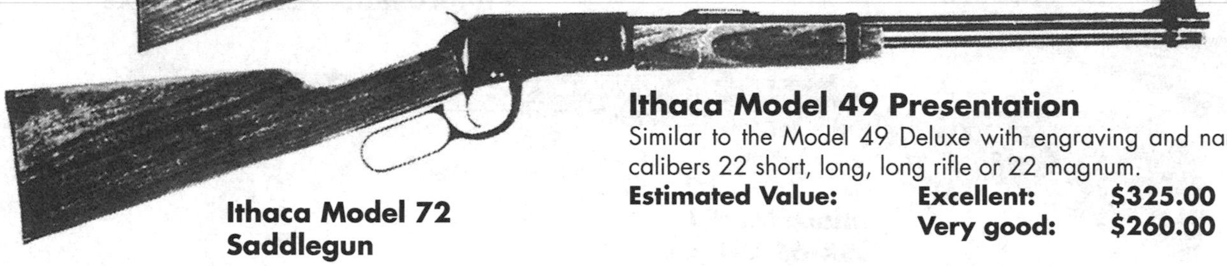

Ithaca Model 72 Saddlegun

Ithaca Model 49 Youth

Similar to the Model 49 with an abbreviated stock for young shooters.

Estimated Value:	**Excellent:**	**$150.00**
	Very good:	**$120.00**

Ithaca Model 49 Magnum

Similar to the Model 49 in 22 magnum rimfire.

Estimated Value:	**Excellent:**	**$225.00**
	Very good:	**$180.00**

Ithaca Model 49 Deluxe

Similar to the Model 49 with checkered stock, gold hammer and trigger and swivels. Discontinued in the mid-1970s.

Estimated Value:	**Excellent:**	**$225.00**
	Very good:	**$180.00**

Ithaca Model 49 Presentation

Similar to the Model 49 Deluxe with engraving and nameplate; calibers 22 short, long, long rifle or 22 magnum.

Estimated Value:	**Excellent:**	**$325.00**
	Very good:	**$260.00**

Ithaca Model 49R (Repeater)

Similar to the Model 49 with 20" barrel and 15-shot tubular magazine. Sold only in the late 1960s to the early 1970s.

Estimated Value:	**Excellent:**	**$250.00**
	Very good:	**$200.00**

Ithaca Model 72 Saddlegun

Caliber: 22 long rifle
Action: Lever action; exposed hammer; repeating
Magazine: 15-shot tubular
Barrel: Blued; 18½"
Sights: Adjustable rear, hooded ramp front
Stock and Forearm: Plain walnut straight grip stock and forearm; barrel band
Approximate wt.: 5½ lbs.
Comments: Made from the early to the late 1970s.

Estimated Value:	**Excellent:**	**$300.00**
	Very good:	**$240.00**

Ithaca Model 72 Deluxe

Ithaca Model 72 Magnum
Similar to the Model 72 in 22 magnum. Magazine holds 11 shots.
Estimated Value: **Excellent:** **$300.00**
Very good: **$240.00**

Ithaca Model 72 Deluxe
Similar to the Model 72 except: brushed silver receiver; engraving; octagon barrel; blade front sight.
Estimated Value: **Excellent:** **$325.00**
Very good: **$260.00**

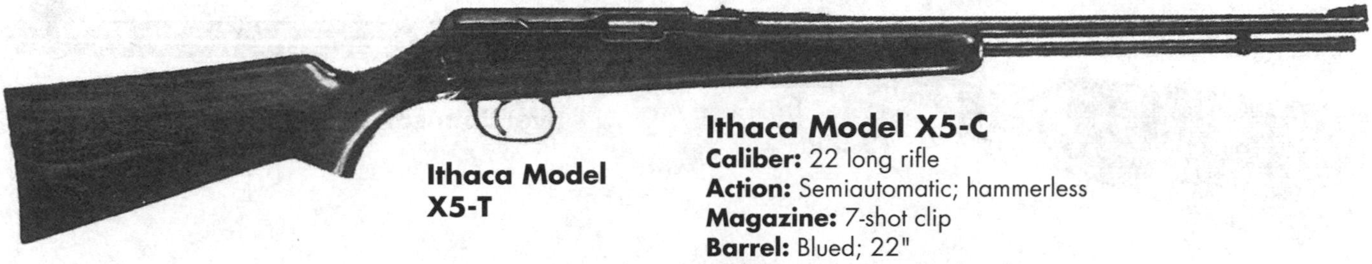

Ithaca Model X5-T

Ithaca Model X5-C
Caliber: 22 long rifle
Action: Semiautomatic; hammerless
Magazine: 7-shot clip
Barrel: Blued; 22"
Sights: Open rear, Raybar front
Stock and Forearm: Wood one-piece semi-pistol grip stock and forearm
Approximate wt.: 6¼ lbs.
Comments: Made from the late 1950s to about 1965.
Estimated Value: **Excellent:** **$175.00**
Very good: **$140.00**

Ithaca Model X5-T
Similar to the Model X5-C with a 16-shot tubular magazine.
Estimated Value: **Excellent:** **$185.00**
Very good: **$150.00**

IVER JOHNSON

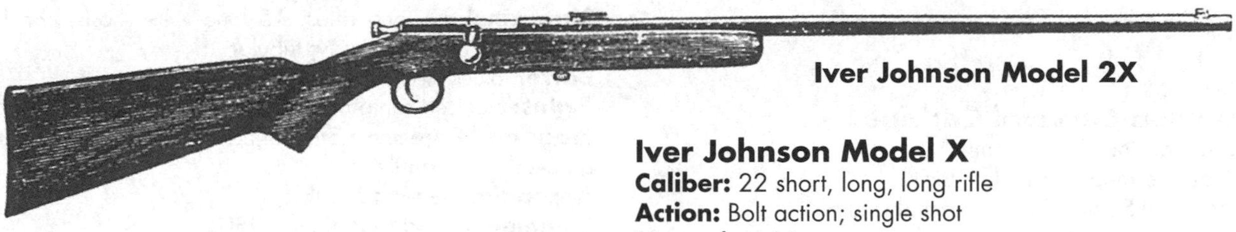

Iver Johnson Model 2X

Iver Johnson Lever Action
Caliber: 22 short, long, long rifle; 22 Win. magnum
Action: Lever action, side ejector; exposed hammer
Magazine: 21 shorts, 17 longs, 15 long rifles (mixed simultaneously); 12 magnum, tubular under barrel
Barrel: 18½"; round; blued
Sights: Hooded ramp front, adjustable rear
Stock and Forearm: Smooth hardwood stock and forearm, barrel band
Approximate wt.: 5¾ lbs.
Comments: Produced in the mid-1980s. Add 7% for magnum.
Estimated Value: **Excellent:** **$200.00**
Very good: **$160.00**

Iver Johnson Model X
Caliber: 22 short, long, long rifle
Action: Bolt action; single shot
Magazine: None
Barrel: Blued; 22"
Sights: Open rear, blade front
Stock and Forearm: Wood one-piece pistol grip stock and forearm
Approximate wt.: 4 lbs.
Comments: Made from the late 1920s to the early 1930s.
Estimated Value: **Excellent:** **$175.00**
Very good: **$140.00**

Iver Johnson Model 2X
Similar to the Model X with a 24" barrel and improved stock. Made from about 1932 to the mid-1950s.
Estimated Value: **Excellent:** **$200.00**
Very good: **$160.00**

Iver Johnson Li'l Champ

Caliber: 22 short, long or long rifle
Action: Bolt action; single shot
Magazine: None, single shot
Barrel: Blued; 16¼"
Sights: Blade front, adjustable rear
Stock and Forearm: Molded one-piece stock and forearm; nickel-plated bolt
Approximate wt.: 2¾ lbs.
Comments: A lightweight gun designed for young beginners.
Estimated Value: Excellent: $115.00
Very good: $ 95.00

Iver Johnson Wagonmaster

Caliber: 22 short, long or long rifle; 22 magnum
Action: Lever action; repeating
Magazine: 15 long rifles, 17 longs, 21 shorts, can be mixed and loaded simultaneously; tubular
Barrel: Blued; 18¼"
Sights: Hooded ramp front, adjustable leaf rear
Stock and Forearm: Smooth wood straight grip stock and forearm; barrel band
Approximate wt.: 5¾ lbs.
Comments: Currently available. Add 12% for magnum.
Estimated Value: Excellent: $200.00
Very good: $160.00

Iver Johnson Wagonmaster

Iver Johnson Li'l Champ

Iver Johnson Survival Carbine

Caliber: 30 carbine, 223 (5.7mm)
Action: Gas-operated, semiautomatic
Magazine: 5-, 15-, or 30-shot detachable clip
Barrel: 18"; blued or stainless steel
Sights: Aperture rear, blade front with protective ears
Stock and Forearm: Hard plastic, one-piece pistol grip stock and forearm; metal handguard; folding stock available
Approximate wt.: 5 lbs.
Comments: Produced from 1983 to 1986. Add 20% for folding stock; 25% for stainless steel finish.
Estimated Value: Excellent: $300.00
Very good: $240.00

Iver Johnson Targetmaster

Caliber: 22 short, long or long rifle
Action: Slide action, repeating
Magazine: 12 long rifles, 15 longs, 19 shorts, can be mixed and loaded simultaneously; tubular
Barrel: Blued; 18½"
Sights: Hooded ramp front, adjustable rear
Stock and Forearm: Smooth hardwood straight grip stock and grooved slide handle
Approximate wt.: 5¾ lbs.
Comments: Produced in the 1980s.
Estimated Value: Excellent: $200.00
Very good: $160.00

Iver Johnson Trailblazer

Caliber: 22 long rifle
Action: Semiautomatic, hammerless
Magazine: Clip
Barrel: Blued; 18½"
Sights: Open rear, blade front
Stock and Forearm: Checkered walnut, one-piece Monte Carlo semi-pistol grip stock and forearm
Approximate wt.: 5 lbs.
Comments: Produced from 1984 to 1986.
Estimated Value: Excellent: $155.00
Very good: $125.00

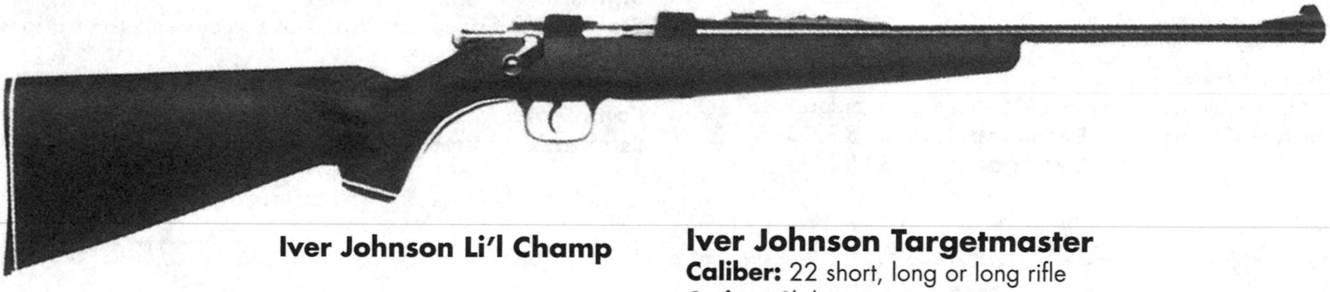

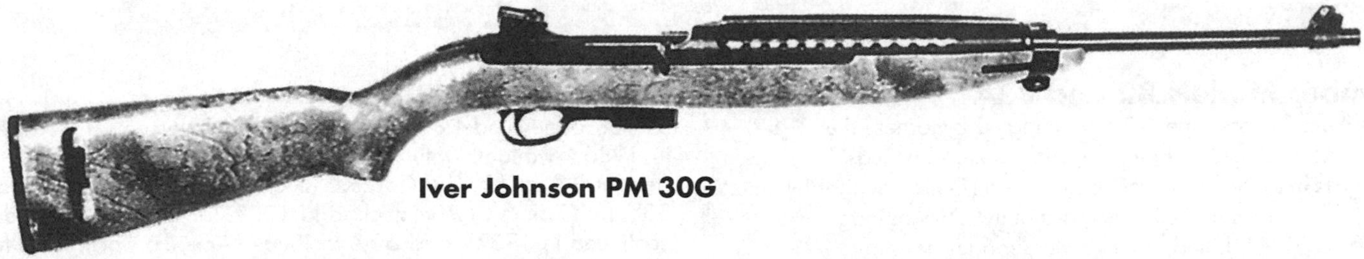

Iver Johnson PM 30G

Iver Johnson PM 30G, Model M1, PM30

Caliber: 30 M1, 223 (discontinued in 1985)
Action: Gas-operated, semiautomatic
Magazine: 15-shot detachable clip; 5- or 30-shot available
Barrel: 18"; blued or stainless steel
Sights: Aperture rear, blade front with protective ears
Stock and Forearm: Wood, semi-pistol grip one-piece stock and forearm; slot in stock; metal ventilated or wood handguard
Approximate wt.: 6 lbs.
Comments: Made from about 1960 to the late 1970s by Plainfield. Reintroduced in the late 1970s to the early 1990s by Iver Johnson. Add 20% for stainless steel (discontinued in 1985); add 7% for walnut stock.

Estimated Value:	**Excellent:**	**$400.00**
	Very good:	**$320.00**

Iver Johnson PM30S, Model M1 Sporter

Similar to the M1 Carbine with a wood handguard and no slot in the stock. Discontinued in the early 1980s.

Estimated Value:	**Excellent:**	**$325.00**
	Very good:	**$260.00**

Iver Johnson PM30P, Commando or Paratrooper

Similar to the M1 Carbine with pistol grip at rear and at forearm; telescoping wire shoulder stock. Add 20% for stainless steel.

Estimated Value:	**Excellent:**	**$425.00**
	Very good:	**$340.00**

Iver Johnson Models EW22 HBA and MHBA

Similar to the Model PM30 except: 22 long rifle or 22WRM; Add 15% for magnum; made in the early 1990s.

Estimated Value:	**Excellent:**	**$200.00**
	Very good:	**$160.00**

Iver Johnson Model 9MM

Similar to the Model PM30 in 9MM Parabellum with 16" barrel and 20-shot magazine; weighs 5½ lbs.

Estimated Value:	**Excellent:**	**$325.00**
	Very good:	**$260.00**

Johnson MMJ Spitfire

Johnson Custom Deluxe Sporter

Similar to the MMJ Spitfire with a Monte Carlo pistol grip stock and rear peep sight.

Estimated Value:	**Excellent:**	**$475.00**
	Very good:	**$380.00**

Johnson Folding Stock

Similar to the MMJ Spitfire with a special metal folding shoulder stock.

Estimated Value:	**Excellent:**	**$475.00**
	Very good:	**$380.00**

Johnson MMJ Spitfire

Caliber: 223
Action: Semiautomatic
Magazine: 5-, 15-, 30-shot clip
Barrel: Blued; 18"
Sights: Adjustable rear, ramp front
Stock and Forearm: Wood one-piece semi-pistol grip stock and forearm; wood handguard
Approximate wt.: 5 lbs.
Comments: A conversion of the M1 carbine. Made in the mid-1960s.

Estimated Value:	**Excellent:**	**$400.00**
	Very good:	**$320.00**

Kimber Models 82 and 82A

Caliber: 22 long rifle, 22 Win. mag., 22 Hornet (after 1982)
Action: Bolt action; repeating; rear locking bolt lugs
Magazine: 5-shot detachable box (10-shot available) in 22 long rifle; 3-shot in 22 Hornet; 4-shot in 22 Win. mag.
Barrel: 22½"; blued; light sporter; sporter; target
Sights: None, drilled for scope; beaded ramp front and folding leaf rear available
Stock and Forearm: Checkered walnut, one-piece pistol grip stock and forearm (Classic); available with optional Monte Carlo stock and cheekpiece; swivels
Approximate wt.: 6½ lbs.
Comments: Produced as Model 82 from 1980 to 1986 and as Model 82A after 1986. Add 6% for .22 WMR or .22 Hornet; add 10% for Cascade stock (discontinued in 1987); add 33% for Custom Classic stock; add 52% for Super America stock (discontinued in 1986). Discontinued in 1992.

Estimated Value:	**Excellent:**	**$895.00**
	Very good:	**$715.00**

Kimber Model 82B

Similar to the Model 82A with internal improvements. Introduced in 1986. Available with sporter or varmint barrel. Classic stock standard. Add 12% for Cascade stock (discontinued 1987); add 33% for Custom Classic stock; add 100% for Brownell stock (discontinued in 1987); add 50% for Super America stock; 14% for Continental stock; add 95% for Super Continental stock. Discontinued in 1992.

Estimated Value:	**Excellent:**	**$675.00**
	Very good:	**$540.00**

Kimber Models 84 and 84A

Similar to the Model 82 except Mini-Mauser-type action. Introduced in 1984 in 223 Rem. caliber; 221 Fireball, 222 Rem. mag., 17 Rem. 17 Match IV, 6x47 and 6x45 calibers added in 1986. Known as Model 84A in 1987. Add 12% for Cascade stock (discontinued in 1987); add 28% for Custom Classic stock.

Estimated Value:	**Excellent:**	**$825.00**
	Very good:	**$660.00**

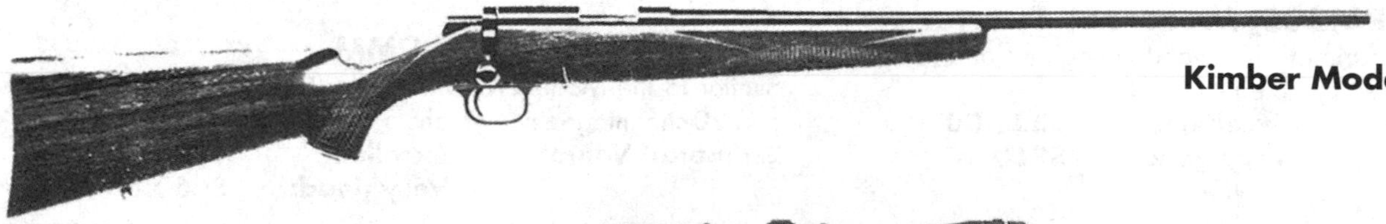

Kimber Model 82

Kimber Model 84C Single Shot

Kimber 82A Government

A single-shot, 22-bolt action target rifle designed for the Army; heavy target barrel and stock; built on the Kimber 82A action.

Estimated Value:	**Excellent:**	**$525.00**
	Very good:	**$420.00**

Kimber Model 82 M/S

Similar to the Model 82 except single-shot; 20½" heavy barrel, adjustable target trigger; competition stock; 22 long rifle caliber only; this gun is designed for metallic silhouette shooting. Produced from 1982 to 1992.

Estimated Value:	**Excellent:**	**$600.00**
	Very good:	**$448.00**

Kimber Mini-Classic

An adult 22-bolt action with an 18" barrel, lipped forearm; built on the Model 82A action. Introduced in 1988.

Estimated Value:	**Excellent:**	**$550.00**
	Very good:	**$445.00**

Kimber Model 84B

Similar to the Model 84 with internal improvements. Produced from 1987 to 1992. Add 12% for Continental stock; 90% for Super Continental; 50% for Super America.

Estimated Value:	**Excellent:**	**$825.00**
	Very good:	**$660.00**

Kimber Model 84C Single Shot

Caliber: 17 Rem., 223 Rem.
Action: Mauser-type bolt action single shot; adjustable trigger
Magazine: None, single-shot
Barrel: 25"; fluted stainless steel
Sights: None
Stock and Forearm: Checkered walnut, one-piece pistol grip stock and wide forearm; matte blue receiver
Approximate wt.: 7½ lbs.
Comments: Introduced in the mid-1990s.

Estimated Value:	**Excellent:**	**$1,000.00**
	Very good:	**$ 800.00**

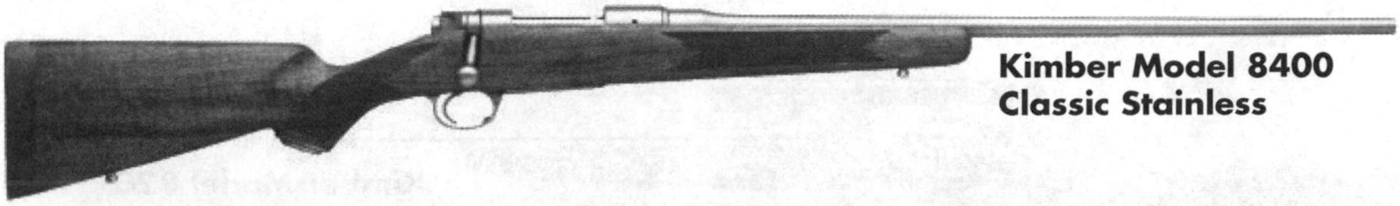

Kimber Model 8400 Classic Stainless

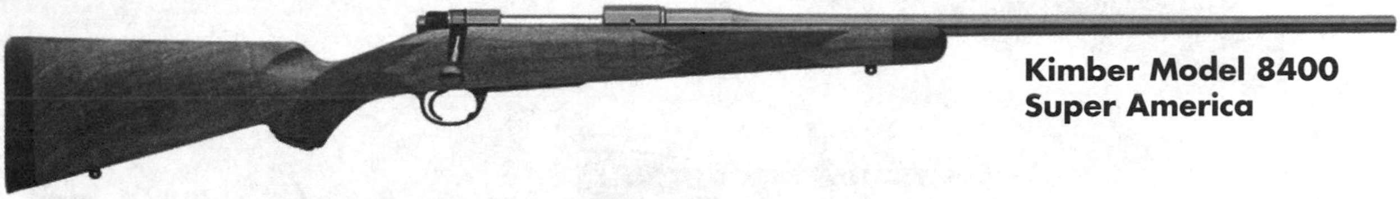

Kimber Model 8400 Super America

Kimber Model 8400 Montana

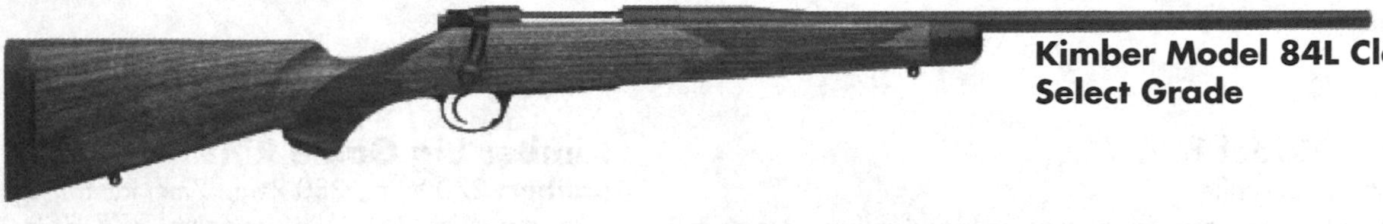

Kimber Model 84L Classic Select Grade

Kimber Model 8400 Classic

Caliber: 270 WSM, 300 WSM, 300 Win. mag., and 325 WSM
Action: Bolt action, repeating; short or standard length; claw extractor; 3-position safety
Magazine: 5-shot detachable box
Barrel: Blued, matte finish, 24"
Sights: None
Stock and Forearm: One-piece checkered, grade A walnut pistol grip stock and forearm; swivels; recoil pad and steel grip cap
Approximate wt.: 7 lbs.
Comments: A high-quality hunting rifle designed for Winchester Short Magnum cartridges, but expanded to include standard length actions.

Estimated Value:	**New (retail):**	**$1,172.00**
	Excellent:	**$ 875.00**
	Very good:	**$ 705.00**

Kimber Model 8400 Classic Stainless

Similar to the Model 8400 Classic except: satin stainless steel finish; weighs approximately 6 lbs., 10 oz., not available in 300 Win. mag. caliber.

Estimated Value:	**New (retail):**	**$1,223.00**
	Excellent:	**$ 915.00**
	Very good:	**$ 735.00**

Kimber Model 8400 Classic Select Grade

Similar to the Model 8400 Classic except: stock and forearm are made from grade A French walnut.

Estimated Value:	**New (retail):**	**$1,359.00**
	Excellent:	**$1,020.00**
	Very good:	**$ 815.00**

Kimber Model 8400 Super America

Similar to the Model 8400 Classic except: stock and forearm are made from grade AAA walnut. Finish is highly polished blue.

Estimated Value:	**New (retail):**	**$2,240.00**
	Excellent:	**$1,680.00**
	Very good:	**$1,345.00**

Kimber Model 8400 Montana

Caliber: 270 WSM, 300 WSM, 325 WSM, 300 Win. mag., 338 Win. mag.
Action: Bolt action, repeating; short or standard length; claw extractor, 3-position safety
Magazine: 5-shot detachable box
Barrel: Satin stainless steel, 24"
Sights: None
Stock and Forearm: One-piece, Kevlar-Carbon Fiber pistol grip stock and forearm; recoil pad; swivels
Approximate wt.: 6 lbs., 9 oz.
Comments: A stainless steel, synthetic stock addition to the 8400 line.

Estimated Value:	**New (retail):**	**$1,312.00**
	Excellent:	**$ 985.00**
	Very good:	**$ 785.00**

Kimber Model 84L Classic

Caliber: 270 Win., 30-06 Sprg.
Action: Bolt action, repeating; claw extractor; 3-position safety
Magazine: 5-shot detachable box
Barrel: Blued, matte finish, 24"
Sights: None
Stock and Forearm: One-piece checkered, grade A walnut pistol grip stock and forearm; swivels; recoil pad and steel grip cap
Approximate wt.: 6 lbs., 2 oz.
Comments: A high-quality, lightweight hunting rifle.

Estimated Value:	**New (retail):**	**$1,172.00**
	Excellent:	**$ 875.00**
	Very good:	**$ 705.00**

Kimber Model 84L Classic Select Grade

Similar to the Model 8400 Classic except: stock and forearm are made from grade A French walnut.

Estimated Value:	**New (retail):**	**$1,359.00**
	Excellent:	**$1,020.00**
	Very good:	**$ 815.00**

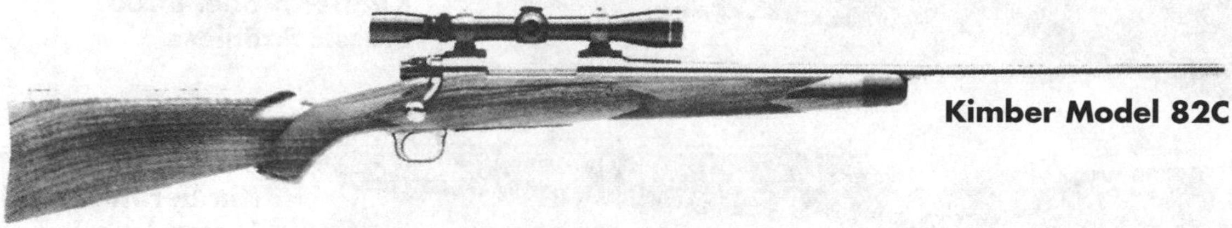

Kimber Model 82C

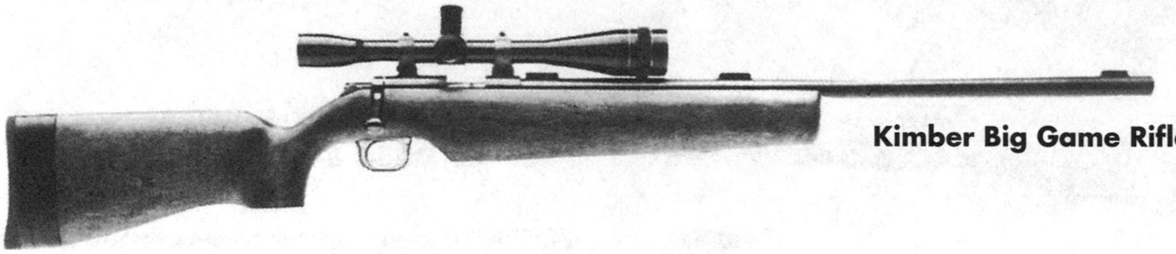

Kimber Big Game Rifle

Kimber Model 82C

Caliber: 22 long rifle
Action: Bolt action, repeating; rear bolt locking lugs, rocker-style safety
Magazine: 4-shot detachable box; optional 10-shot magazine available
Barrel: Blued; 22½"; 20", 18"; also stainless steel
Sights: None; drilled for scope mount
Stock and Forearm: Walnut or synthetic one-piece pistol grip stock and forearm; Monte Carlo on Super America Model; swivel studs
Approximate wt.: 6½ lbs.
Comments: Produced in the 1990s; add 69% for Super America Model. Add 15% for stainless steel barrel; add 14% for Varmint.

Estimated Value:	**Excellent:**	**$700.00**
	Very good:	**$560.00**

Kimber Model 84C Centerfire

Caliber: 17 Rem., 222 Rem., 223 Rem.
Action: Mauser-type bolt action, repeating; adjustable trigger
Magazine: 4-shot; hinged floor plate
Barrel: 22"; blued or stainless steel
Sights: None
Stock and Forearm: Checkered walnut, one-piece pistol grip stock and wide forearm; polished blued action
Approximate wt.: 6¾ lbs.
Comments: Produced in the 1990s. Add 39% for Super America Model.

Estimated Value:	**Excellent:**	**$925.00**
	Very good:	**$740.00**

Kimber Model 84M Longmaster

Similar to the Model 84M Varmint except: 24" barrel; 308 Win. caliber.

Estimated Value:	**New (retail):**	**$1,255.00**
	Excellent:	**$ 940.00**
	Very good:	**$ 750.00**

Kimber Big Game Rifle

Caliber: 270 Win., 280 Rem., 7mm Rem. magnum, 30-06, 300 Win. magnum, 338 Win. magnum, 375 H&H, 416 Rigby (African model) introduced in 1989
Action: Bolt action, repeating, combining features of the pre-'64 Winchester Model 70 and the Mauser 98
Magazine: 5-shot in calibers .270, 280 and 30-06, 3-shot in calibers 7mm mag., 300 mag., 338 mag. 375 H&H, or 416 Rigby
Barrel: 22½" featherweight barrel in 270, 280, 30-06; 24" medium barrel in 7mm, 300, 338; 24" heavy barrel in 375 H&H or 416 Rigby
Sights: None
Stock and Forearm: Checkered walnut one-piece pistol grip stock and forearm; black forearm tip; swivels
Approximate wt.: 7¾ to 8½ lbs.
Comments: Produced from 1988 to 1992; add 11% for 375 H&H; add 30% for Custom Classic; add 11% for Super America; add 100% for African.

Estimated Value:	**Excellent:**	**$1,700.00**
	Very good:	**$1,350.00**

Kimber K770

Caliber: 270 Win., 30-06 Sprg.
Action: Bolt action, repeating
Magazine: 4-shot box with hinged floor plate
Barrel: Blued; 22½"
Sights: None
Stock and Forearm: Checkered hardwood pistol grip stock and forearm
Approximate wt.: 7 lbs.
Comments: Produced in the 1990s; add 65% for Super America Model.

Estimated Value:	**Excellent:**	**$625.00**
	Very good:	**$500.00**

Kimber Model 84M Classic

Kimber Model 84M Varmint

Kimber Model 84M Longmaster VT

Kimber Model 84M Classic

Caliber: 22-250 Rem., 243 Win., 260 Rem., 7mm-08 Rem., 308 Win.
Action: Mauser-type, bolt action repeating
Magazine: 5-shot; hinged floor plate
Barrel: 22" blued; stainless steel available
Sights: None
Stock and forearm: Checkered walnut pistol grip, one-piece stock and forearm/hand-rubbed oil finish
Approximate wt.: 5¾"
Comments: Introduced in 2001. Add 10% for stainless steel barrel and action.

Estimated Value:	**New (retail):**	**$1,114.00**
	Excellent:	**$ 835.00**
	Very good:	**$ 665.00**

Kimber Model 84M Varmint

Similar to the 84M Classic except: 22-250 Rem. caliber; 26" stainless steel barrel; weighs 7 lbs.

Estimated Value:	**New (retail):**	**$1,255.00**
	Excellent:	**$ 940.00**
	Very good:	**$ 755.00**

Kimber Model 84M Longmaster VT

Similar to the 84M Varmint except: high-comb gray laminate stock and forearm.

Estimated Value:	**New (retail):**	**$1,391.00**
	Excellent:	**$1,045.00**
	Very good:	**$ 835.00**

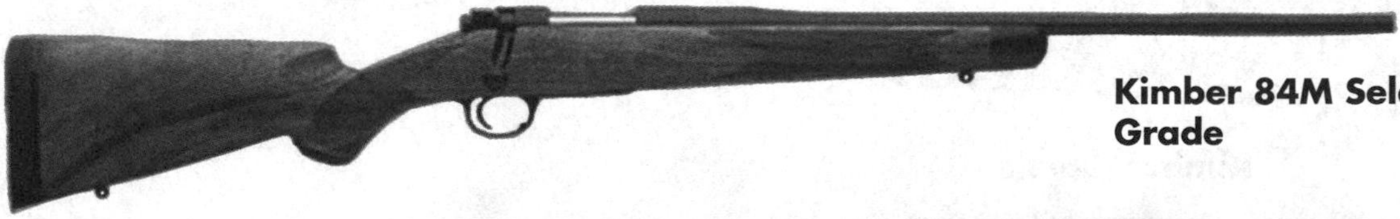

Kimber 84M Select Grade

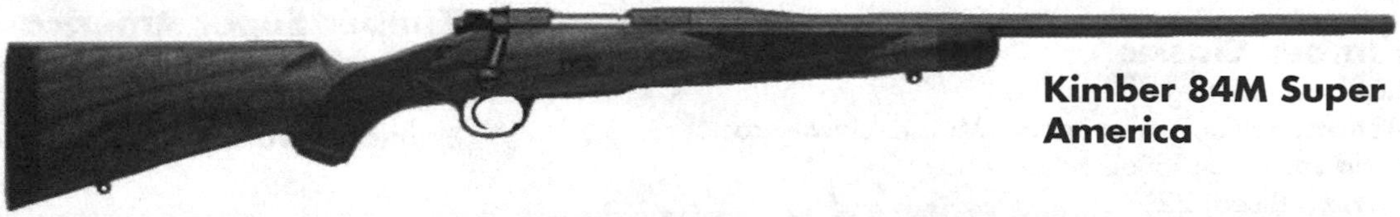

Kimber 84M Super America

Kimber 84M Select Grade

Similar to the 84M Classic except: high grade walnut stock and forearm with ebony tip.

Estimated Value:	**New (retail):**	**$1,359.00**
	Excellent:	**$1,020.00**
	Very good:	**$ 815.00**

Kimber 84M Super America

Similar the 84M Select Grade except: higher quality, hand rubbed oil finished walnut; cheekpiece.

Estimated Value:	**New (retail):**	**$2,124.00**
	Excellent:	**$1,595.00**
	Very good:	**$1,275.00**

Kimber 84M Pro Varmint

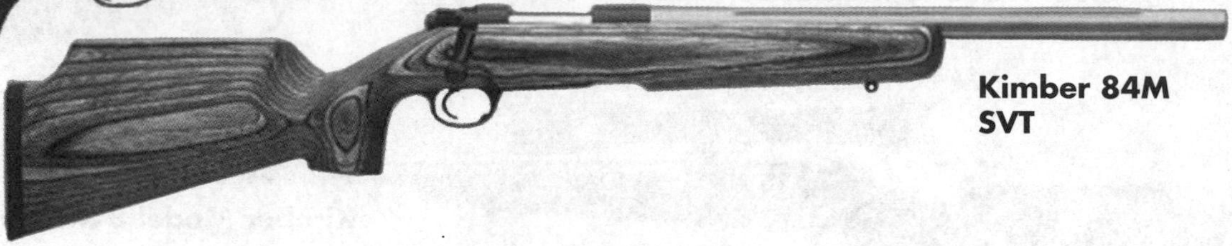

Kimber 84M SVT

Kimber 84M Pro Varmint

Similar to the 84M Varmint except: hand-rubbed oil finish; gray laminated stock and forearm; fluted barrel.

Estimated Value: **New (retail):** **$1,391.00**
Excellent: **$1,045.00**
Very good: **$ 835.00**

Kimber 84M SVT

Similar to the Longmaster VT except: 18½" barrel; 223 Rem. caliber.

Estimated Value: **New (retail):** **$1,391.00**
Excellent: **$1,045.00**
Very good: **$ 835.00**

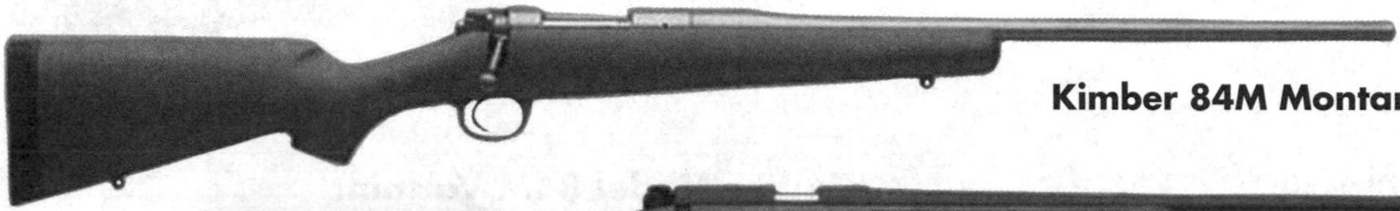

Kimber 84M Montana

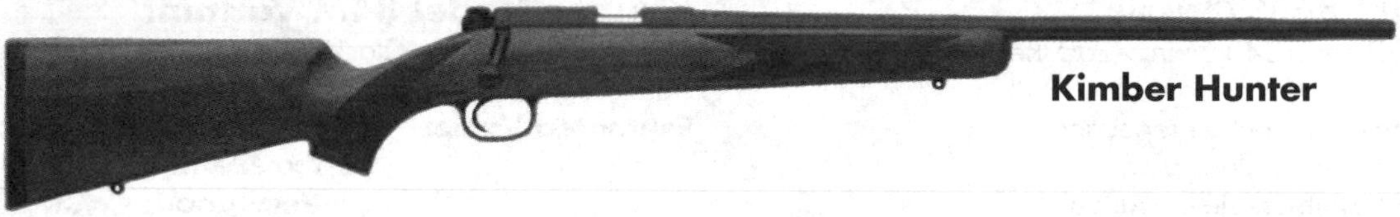

Kimber Hunter

Kimber 84M Montana

Similar to the 84M Classic except: Kevlar carbon fiber composite stock and forearm; stainless steel finish.

Estimated Value: **New (retail):** **$1,312.00**
Excellent: **$ 985.00**
Very good: **$ 785.00**

Kimber Hunter

Caliber: 17 Mach 2, 22 long rifle
Action: Bolt action, repeating; Mauser claw extractor
Magazine: 5-shot detachable box
Barrel: Blued; 22" contoured
Sights: None; drilled and tapped for scope mount
Stock and Forearm: Checkered walnut, one-piece stock and forearm; recoil pad; swivels
Approx. wt.: 6½ lbs.
Comments: Add 4% for 17 Mach 2 caliber.
Estimated Value: **Excellent:** **$645.00**
Very good: **$515.00**

Kimber Classic

Kimber Classic

Caliber: 22 long rifle
Action: Bolt action repeating; Mauser claw extractor
Magazine: 5-shot detachable box
Barrel: Blued; 22"
Sights: None
Stock and Forearm: Checkered walnut, one-piece pistol grip stock and forearm; steel grip cap
Approximate wt.: 6½ lbs.
Comments: Introduced in 2000.
Estimated Value: **Excellent:** **$915.00**
Very good: **$735.00**

Kimber Super America

Similar to the Classic except: higher quality walnut stock, beaded cheekpiece, ebony fore-end tip; black recoil pad.

Estimated Value: **Excellent:** **$1,490.00**
Very good: **$1,195.00**

Kimber SVT

Similar to the Classic except: 18" fluted, stainless steel bull barrel; gray laminated wood stock with high comb; recoil pad.

Estimated Value: **Excellent:** **$805.00**
Very good: **$645.00**

Kimber HS

Kimber Classic Varmint

Kimber Custom Classic

Kimber Classic Pro Varmint

Kimber HS

Similar to the Classic except: 24" medium barrel; high comb Monte Carlo stock.

Estimated Value: **Excellent:** **$730.00**
Very good: **$585.00**

Kimber Classic Varmint

Similar to the Classic except: 20" heavy sporter contour stainless steel barrel; hand-rubbed oil finish stock and forearm. Also available in 17 Mach 2 caliber.

Estimated Value: **Excellent:** **$845.00**
Very good: **$675.00**

Kimber Custom Classic

Similar to the Classic except: higher grade walnut stock and forearm with ebony tip.

Estimated Value: **Excellent:** **$1,205.00**
Very good: **$ 965.00**

Kimber Classic Pro Varmint

Similar to the Classic Varmint except: fluted barrel; gray laminated stock and forearm; add 5% for 17 Mach 2 Caliber.

Estimated Value: **Excellent:** **$885.00**
Very good: **$710.00**

KLEINGUENTHER

Kleinguenther K-14

Kleinguenther MV 2130

Caliber: 243, 270, 30-06, 300 mag., 308, 7mm Rem.
Action: Mauser-type bolt action, repeating
Magazine: 2-shot box
Barrel: Blued; 25"
Sights: None; drilled for scope
Stock and Forearm: Checkered walnut Monte Carlo one-piece pistol grip stock and tapered forearm; recoil pad
Approximate wt.: 7 lbs.
Comments: Made in the 1970s.
Estimated Value: **Excellent:** **$700.00**
Very good: **$560.00**

Kleinguenther K-14

Caliber: Same as MV 2130, also 25-06, 7x57, 375 H&H
Action: Bolt action
Magazine: Hidden clip, 3-shot
Barrel: Blued; 24", 26"
Sights: Open rear, ramp front
Stock and Forearm: Checkered walnut one-piece pistol grip stock and tapered forearm; recoil pad
Approximate wt.: 7¼ lbs.
Comments: Made in the 1970s.
Estimated Value: **Excellent:** **$1,000.00**
Very good: **$ 800.00**

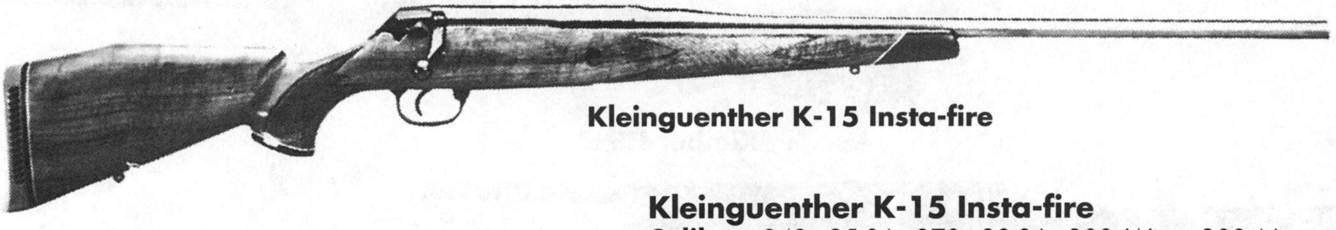

Kleinguenther K-15 Insta-fire

Kleinguenther Model K-22
Caliber: 22 long rifle, 22 WMR
Action: Bolt action; repeating; adjustable trigger
Magazine: 5-shot hidden clip
Barrel: 21½"; chrome-poly steel
Sights: None; tapped for scope
Stock and Forearm: Checkered beechwood, Monte Carlo pistol grip one-piece stock and forearm; swivels; cheekpiece
Approximate wt.: 6½ lbs.
Comments: A rimfire rifle designed to be as accurate as the K-15. Made from the mid-1980s to the early 1990s. Add 16% for magnum, 30% for deluxe, 110% for deluxe custom.
Estimated Value: **Excellent:** **$450.00**
Very good: **$360.00**

Kleinguenther K-15 Insta-fire
Caliber: 243, 25-06, 270, 30-06, 308 Win., 308 Norma mag., 300 Win. mag., 7mm Rem. mag., 375 H&H, 7x57, 270 mag., 300 Weath. mag., 257 Weath. mag.
Action: Bolt action; repeating; adjustable trigger
Magazine: 5-shot hidden clip; 3-shot in magnum
Barrel: 24"; 26" in magnum
Sights: None; tapped for scope
Stock and Forearm: Checkered walnut Monte Carlo one-piece pistol grip stock and forearm; rosewood fore-end and cap; swivels; left- or right-hand model
Approximate wt.: 7½ lbs.
Comments: A high-powered rifle advertised as "the world's most accurate hunting rifle." Engraving and select wood at additional cost. Add 5% for magnum or left-hand model. Made from the late 1970s to the early 1990s.
Estimated Value: **Excellent:** **$1,200.00**
Very good: **$ 960.00**

MANNLICHER

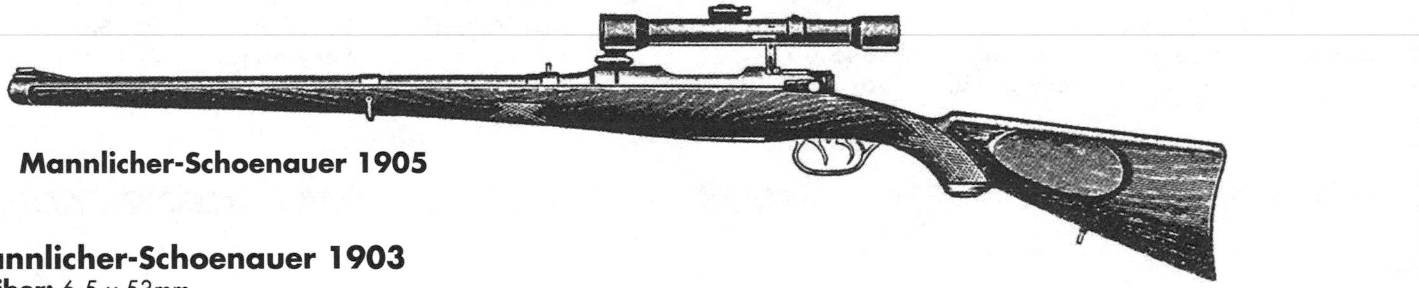

Mannlicher-Schoenauer 1905

Mannlicher-Schoenauer 1903
Caliber: 6.5 x 53mm
Action: Bolt action; repeating; double set trigger; "butter knife" style bolt handle
Magazine: 5-shot rotary
Barrel: Blued; 17¾"
Sights: Two leaf rear, ramp front
Stock and Forearm: Walnut semi-pistol grip stock and tapered, full-length forearm; swivels; cheekpiece
Approximate wt.: 6½ lbs.
Comments: Made from 1903 to World War II.
Estimated Value: **Excellent:** **$3,000.00**
Very good: **$2,400.00**

Mannlicher-Schoenauer 1905
Similar to the 1903 model with a 19¾" barrel and in 9x56mm caliber.
Estimated Value: **Excellent:** **$1,500.00**
Very good: **$1,200.00**

Mannlicher-Schoenauer 1908
Similar to the 1903 model with a 19¾" barrel and in 7x57 and 8x56mm calibers.
Estimated Value: **Excellent:** **$1,700.00**
Very good: **$1,350.00**

Mannlicher-Schoenauer 1910
Similar to the 1903 model with a 19¾" barrel and in 9.5x56mm caliber.
Estimated Value: **Excellent:** **$1,650.00**
Very good: **$1,325.00**

Mannlicher-Schoenauer 1924
Similar to the 1903 model with a 19¾" barrel and in 30-06. Made from 1924 to World War II.
Estimated Value: **Excellent:** **$2,250.00**
Very good: **$1,800.00**

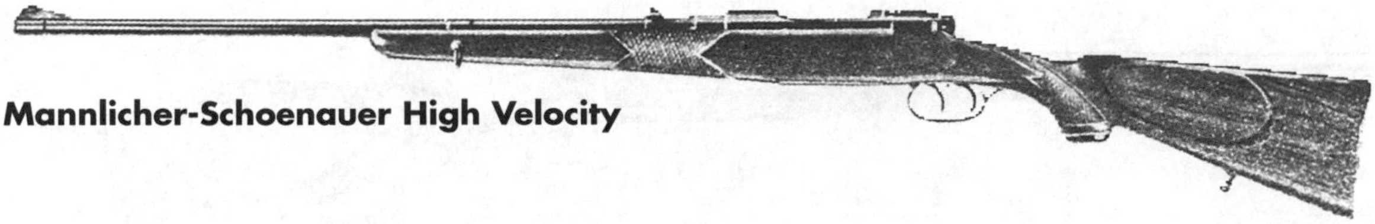

Mannlicher-Schoenauer High Velocity

Mannlicher-Schoenauer 1950 Sporter

Mannlicher-Schoenauer 1950 Carbine

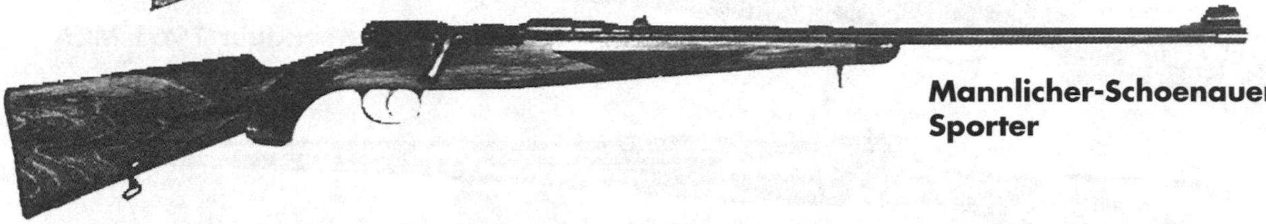

Mannlicher-Schoenauer 1952 Sporter

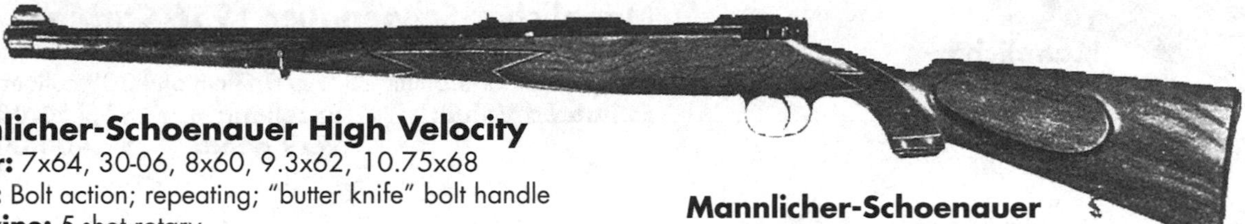

Mannlicher-Schoenauer 1952 Carbine

Mannlicher-Schoenauer High Velocity

Caliber: 7x64, 30-06, 8x60, 9.3x62, 10.75x68
Action: Bolt action; repeating; "butter knife" bolt handle
Magazine: 5-shot rotary
Barrel: Blued; 23¾"
Sights: Three-leaf rear, ramp front
Stock and Forearm: Checkered walnut one-piece pistol grip stock and tapered forearm; cheekpiece; swivels
Approximate wt.: 7½ lbs.
Comments: Made from the early 1920s to World War II.

Estimated Value:	**Excellent:**	**$2,250.00**
	Very good:	**$1,800.00**

Mannlicher-Schoenauer 1950 Sporter

Caliber: 257, 270 Win., 30-06
Action: Bolt action; repeating; "butter knife" bolt handle
Magazine: 5-shot rotary
Barrel: Blued; 24"
Sights: Folding leaf rear, hooded ramp front
Stock and Forearm: Checkered walnut one-piece pistol grip stock and tapered forearm; cheekpiece; swivels
Approximate wt.: 7¼ lbs.
Comments: Made in the early 1950s.

Estimated Value:	**Excellent:**	**$1,300.00**
	Very good:	**$1,050.00**

Mannlicher-Schoenauer 1950 Carbine

Similar to the Sporter with a 20" barrel and full-length forearm.

Estimated Value:	**Excellent:**	**$1,275.00**
	Very good:	**$1,025.00**

Mannlicher-Schoenauer 1950-6.5

Similar to the 1950 Carbine with 18" barrel and in 6.5x53mm caliber.

Estimated Value:	**Excellent:**	**$1,500.00**
	Very good:	**$1,200.00**

Mannlicher-Schoenauer 1952 Sporter

Similar to the 1950 Sporter with slight changes in stock and with slanted bolt handle. Made from about 1952 to 1956.

Estimated Value:	**Excellent:**	**$1,750.00**
	Very good:	**$1,400.00**

Mannlicher-Schoenauer 1952 Carbine

Similar to the 1952 Sporter with a 20" barrel and full-length forearm.

Estimated Value:	**Excellent:**	**$2,000.00**
	Very good:	**$1,600.00**

Mannlicher-Schoenauer 1952-6.5

Similar to the 1952 Carbine with 18" barrel and in 6.5x53mm caliber.

Estimated Value:	**Excellent:**	**$1,675.00**
	Very good:	**$1,350.00**

Mannlicher-Schoenauer 1956 Sporter

Mannlicher-Schoenauer 1956 Carbine

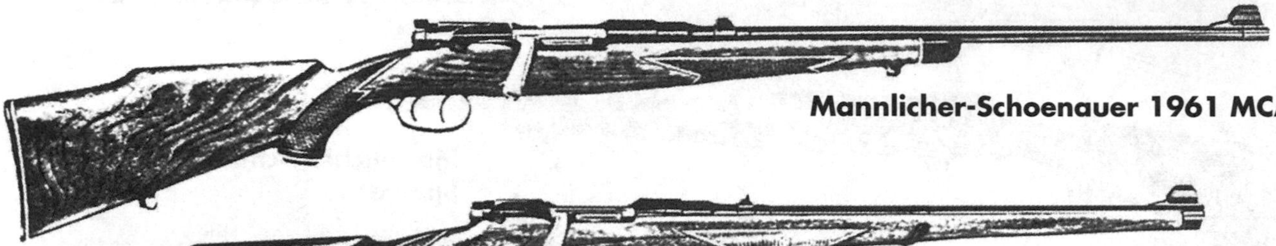

Mannlicher-Schoenauer 1961 MCA

Mannlicher-Schoenauer 1961 MCA Carbine

Mannlicher-Schoenauer 1956 Sporter

Caliber: 243, 30-06
Action: Bolt action; repeating; "butter knife" slanted bolt handle
Magazine: 5-shot rotary
Barrel: Blued; 22"
Sights: Folding leaf rear, hooded ramp front
Stock and Forearm: Checkered walnut pistol grip stock and forearm; high comb; cheekpiece; swivels
Approximate wt.: 7 lbs.
Comments: Made from the mid-1950s to about 1960.

Estimated Value:	**Excellent:**	**$1,675.00**
	Very good:	**$1,340.00**

Mannlicher-Schoenauer 1956 Carbine

Similar to the 1956 Sporter with 20" barrel, full-length forearm, and addition of 6.5mm, 257, 270, 7mm and 308 calibers.

Estimated Value:	**Excellent:**	**$1,750.00**
	Very good:	**$1,400.00**

Mannlicher-Schoenauer 1961 MCA

Similar to the 1956 Sporter with Monte Carlo stock. Made from the early 1960s to the early 1970s.

Estimated Value:	**Excellent:**	**$1,675.00**
	Very good:	**$1,340.00**

Mannlicher-Schoenauer 1961 MCA Carbine

Similar to the 1956 Carbine with Monte Carlo stock. Made from the early 1960s to the early 1970s.

Estimated Value:	**Excellent:**	**$1,750.00**
	Very good:	**$1,400.00**

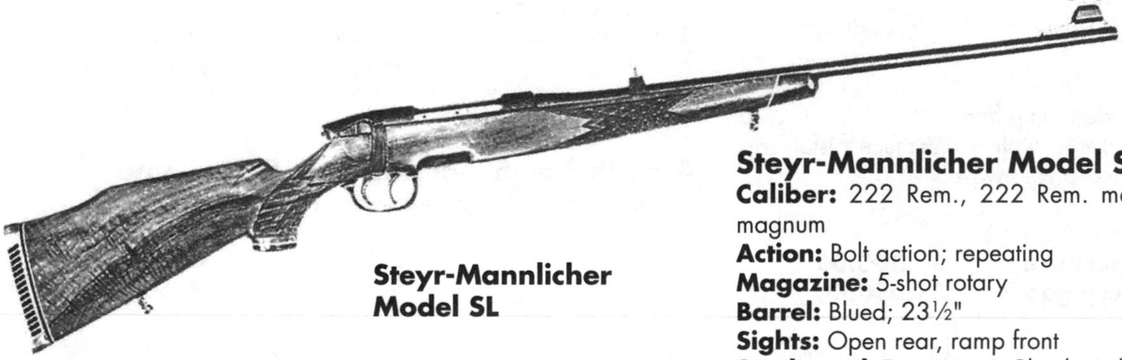

Steyr-Mannlicher Model SL

Steyr-Mannlicher SL Carbine

Similar to the Model SL with a 20" barrel and full-length forearm.

Estimated Value:	**Excellent:**	**$1,600.00**
	Very good:	**$1,280.00**

Steyr-Mannlicher Model SL

Caliber: 222 Rem., 222 Rem. magnum, 223 Rem., 5.6x50 magnum
Action: Bolt action; repeating
Magazine: 5-shot rotary
Barrel: Blued; 23½"
Sights: Open rear, ramp front
Stock and Forearm: Checkered walnut Monte Carlo pistol grip, one-piece stock and tapered forearm; recoil pad; cheekpiece; swivels
Approximate wt.: 5½ lbs.
Comments: Made from the mid-1960s to about 2000.

Estimated Value:	**Excellent:**	**$1,750.00**
	Very good:	**$1,400.00**

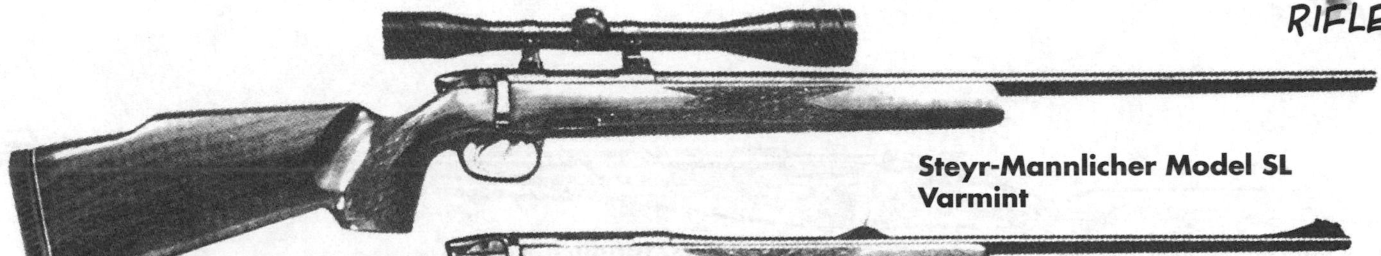

Steyr-Mannlicher Model SL Varmint

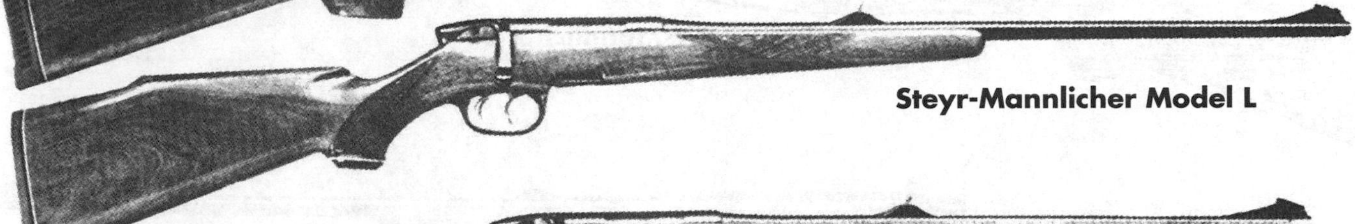

Steyr-Mannlicher Model L

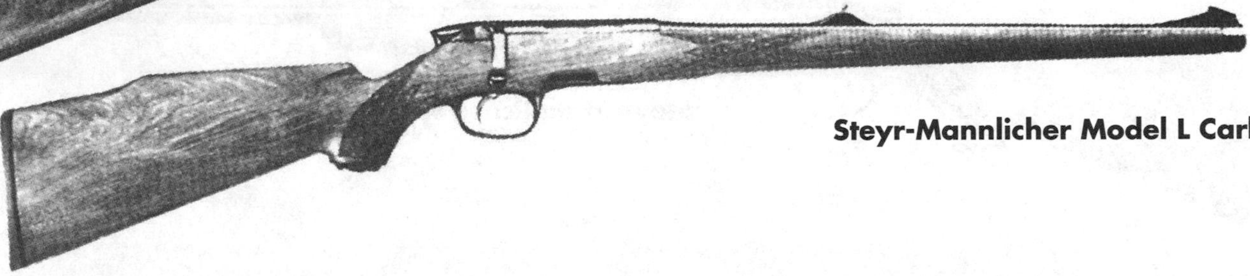

Steyr-Mannlicher Model L Carbine

Steyr-Mannlicher Model SL Varmint

Similar to the Model SL with a fiberglass or walnut half stock and 26" heavy barrel. 222 Rem. or 223 Rem. calibers.

Estimated Value: **Excellent:** **$1,840.00**
Very good: **$1,470.00**

Steyr-Mannlicher Model L Varmint

Similar to the Model L with a varmint stock and 26" heavy barrel. 22-250 Rem., 243 Win., or 308 Win.

Estimated Value: **Excellent:** **$1,840.00**
Very good: **$1,470.00**

Steyr-Mannlicher Model L

Similar to the SL in 22-250 Rem., 5.6x57, 6mm Rem., 7mm, 243 Win., 308 Win.

Estimated Value: **Excellent:** **$1,690.00**
Very good: **$1,350.00**

Steyr-Mannlicher Model L Carbine

Similar to the Model L with a 20" barrel and full-length forearms.

Estimated Value: **Excellent:** **$1,840.00**
Very good: **$1,470.00**

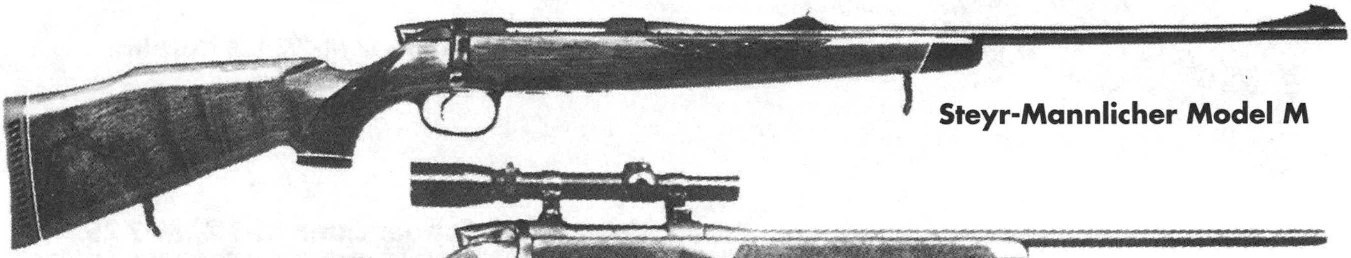

Steyr-Mannlicher Model M

Steyr-Mannlicher Model MIII Professional

Steyr-Mannlicher Model MIII Professional

Similar to the Model M with a parkerized metal finish and ABS Cycolac stock; 23½" barrel only.

Estimated Value: **Excellent:** **$750.00**
Very good: **$600.00**

Steyr-Mannlicher Model M

Caliber: 6.5x55, 7x64, 270 Win., 30-06, 25-06 Rem.; 7x57, 9.3x62
Action: Bolt action; repeating
Magazine: 5-shot rotary
Barrel: Blued; 20" on full stock; 23½" on half stock
Sights: Open rear, ramp front
Stock and Forearm: Checkered walnut Monte Carlo pistol grip stock; standard or full-length forearm; cheekpiece; swivels; left-hand model available
Approximate wt.: 6½ lbs.
Comments: Imported in the 1970s and 1980s. Add 8% for left-hand model; 8% for full stock.

Estimated Value: **Excellent:** **$1,775.00**
Very good: **$1,420.00**

Steyr-Mannlicher S

Steyr-Mannlicher S/T, Tropical

Steyr-Mannlicher S

Similar to the Model M with 26" barrel in magnum caliber, 7mm Rem., 257 Weath., 264 Win. 6.5x68, 300 H&H, 300 Win., 338 Win., 375 H&H and 458 Win. Half stock only; butt magazine optional. Add $50.00 for buttstock 4-shot magazine.

Estimated Value: **Excellent:** **$2,450.00**
Very good: **$1,985.00**

Steyr-Mannlicher S/T, Tropical

Similar to the Model S with a heavy barrel; 375 H&H mag. 9.3x64 and 458 Win. mag. calibers. Add $50.00 for buttstock magazine.

Estimated Value: **Excellent:** **$2,245.00**
Very good: **$1,795.00**

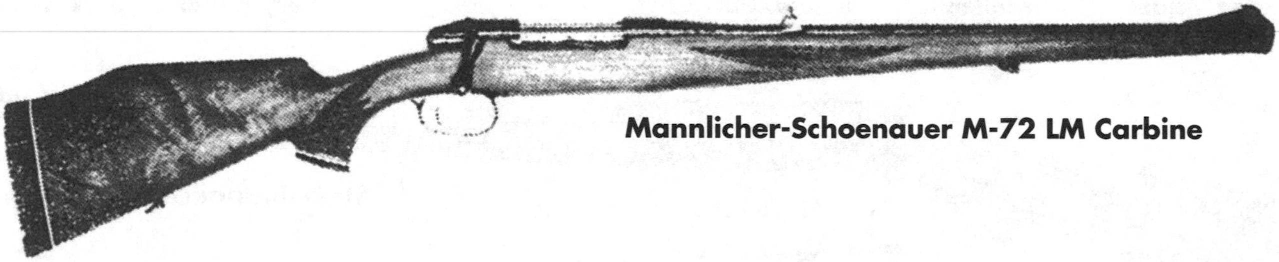

Mannlicher-Schoenauer M-72 LM Carbine

Steyr-Mannlicher ML 79, Luxus

Caliber: 7x57, 7x64, 270 Win., 30-06 Springfield; others available on request
Action: Bolt action; short stroke; repeating
Magazine: 3-shot detachable, 6-shot available
Barrel: 23½"; 20" on full stock model
Sights: Adjustable V-notch open rear, adjustable hooded ramp front
Stock and Forearm: Checkered European walnut Monte Carlo one-piece pistol grip stock and forearm; cheekpiece; swivels; full-length stock available
Approximate wt.: 7 lbs.
Comments: Currently produced. Add 7% for full-length stock or 6-shot magazine.

Estimated Value: **Excellent:** **$1,950.00**
Very good: **$1,560.00**

Mannlicher-Schoenauer M-72, M-72S

Caliber: 22-250, 5.6x57, 243, 6.5x57, 6mm, 7x57, 270
Action: Bolt action; repeating
Magazine: 5-shot rotary
Barrel: Blued; 23½"
Sights: Open rear, ramp front
Stock and Forearm: Checkered walnut one-piece pistol grip stock and tapered forearm; cheekpiece; recoil pad; swivels
Approximate wt.: 7½ lbs.
Comments: Made from the mid- to the late 1970s.

Estimated Value: **Excellent:** **$1,100.00**
Very good: **$ 880.00**

Mannlicher-Schoenauer M-72 LM Carbine

Similar to the M-72 with a 20" barrel and full-length forearm.

Estimated Value: **Excellent:** **$1,000.00**
Very good: **$ 800.00**

Steyr-Mannlicher Model SSG Marksman

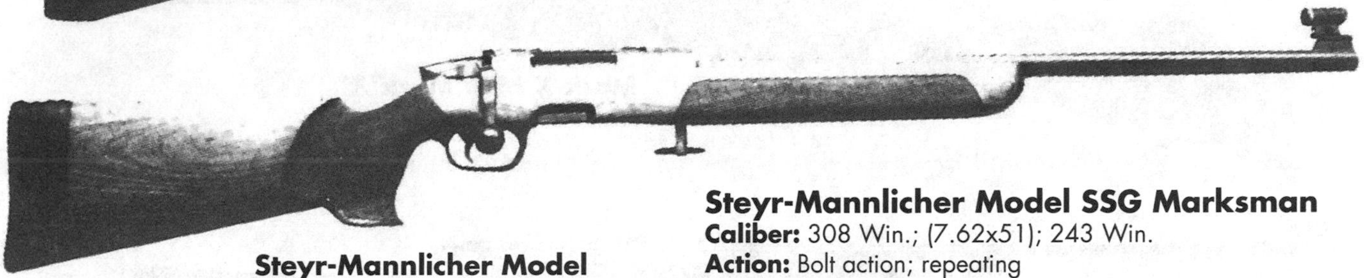

Steyr-Mannlicher Model SSG Match

Steyr-Mannlicher Model SSG Match

A match rifle similar to the SSG Marksman with a heavy barrel; peep sight; stippled checkering; hand stop; weighs 11 lbs.; deduct 12% for ABS Cycolac stock.

Estimated Value: **Excellent:** **$2,095.00**
Very good: **$1,675.00**

Steyr-Mannlicher Model SSG Marksman

Caliber: 308 Win.; (7.62x51); 243 Win.
Action: Bolt action; repeating
Magazine: 5-shot
Barrel: 26"; heavy barrel available
Sights: Folding leaf rear, hooded ramp front; match sights available
Stock and Forearm: Checkered European walnut or ABS Cycolac synthetic one-piece stock and forearm
Approximate wt.: 8½ lbs.
Comments: Deduct 20% for ABS Cycolac stock.
Estimated Value: **Excellent:** **$1,730.00**
Very good: **$1,385.00**

MARK X

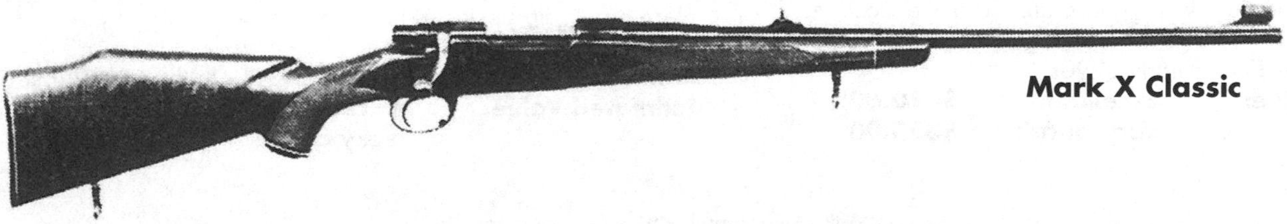

Mark X Classic

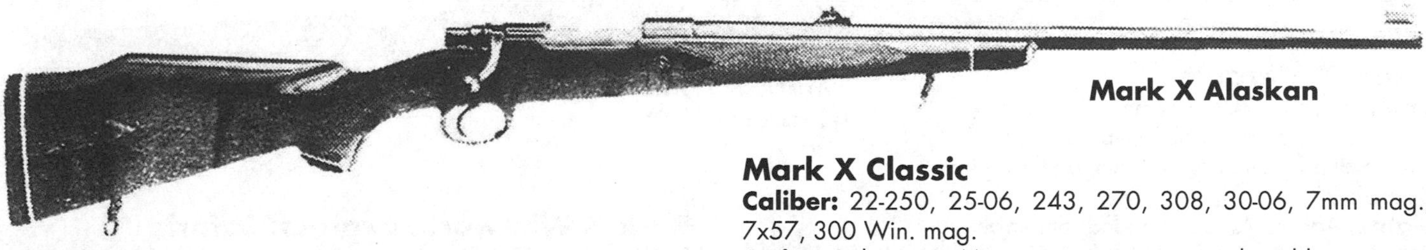

Mark X Alaskan

Mark X Alaskan

Caliber: 375 H&H, 458 Win. magnum
Action: Mauser-type bolt action; repeating; adjustable trigger
Magazine: 3-shot box with hinged floor plate
Barrel: Blued; 24"
Sights: Adjustable rear, hooded ramp front
Stock and Forearm: Checkered, select walnut, Monte Carlo pistol grip, one-piece stock and forearm; recoil pad; swivels
Approximate wt.: 6 lbs.
Comments: Distributed by Interarms.
Estimated Value: **Excellent:** **$485.00**
Very good: **$390.00**

Mark X Classic

Caliber: 22-250, 25-06, 243, 270, 308, 30-06, 7mm mag., 7x57, 300 Win. mag.
Action: Bolt action; Mauser-type; repeating; adjustable trigger
Magazine: 3-shot box with hinged floor plate
Barrel: 24"
Sights: None on some models; others adjustable rear, hooded ramp front
Stock and Forearm: Checkered walnut Monte Carlo one-piece pistol grip stock and forearm; swivels
Approximate wt.: 7½ lbs.
Comments: Add $15.00 for sights.
Estimated Value: **Excellent:** **$400.00**
Very good: **$320.00**

Mark X Viscount

Mark X Mini Mark X

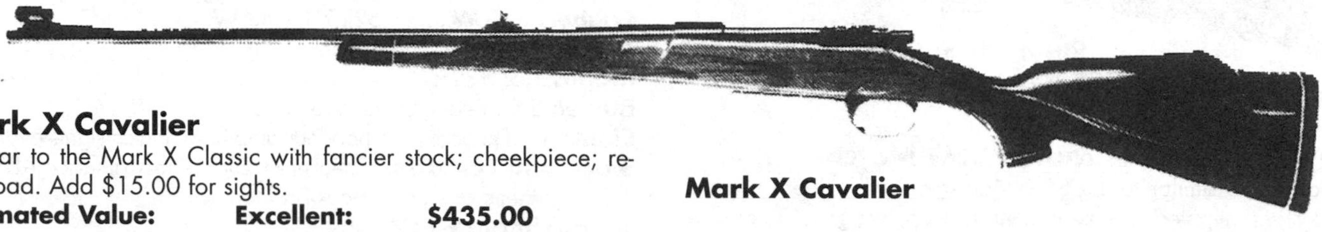

Mark X Cavalier

Mark X Cavalier

Similar to the Mark X Classic with fancier stock; cheekpiece; recoil pad. Add $15.00 for sights.

Estimated Value: **Excellent:** **$435.00**
Very good: **$345.00**

Mark X Viscount

Similar to the Mark X Classic except: special hammer-forged, chrome vanadium steel barrel; add 5% for mag.

Estimated Value: **Excellent:** **$400.00**
Very good: **$320.00**

Mark X LTW

Similar to the Viscount with lightweight Carbolite stock in 270, 30-06 or 7mm Rem. magnum. Introduced in 1988. Add 5% for mag. Discontinued in the early 1990s.

Estimated Value: **Excellent:** **$410.00**
Very good: **$335.00**

Mark X Mini Mark X

Caliber: 223, 7.62x39
Action: Bolt action; repeating; Mauser action scaled down for 223 caliber
Magazine: 5-shot
Barrel: Blued; 20"
Sights: Adjustable rear, hooded ramp front
Stock and Forearm: Checkered walnut, Monte Carlo one-piece pistol grip stock and forearm
Approximate wt.: 6¼ lbs.
Comments: Produced from the late 1980s to the mid-1990s.
Estimated Value: **Excellent:** **$395.00**
Very good: **$320.00**

Mark X Whitworth Express

Mark X Marquis

Caliber: 243, 270, 7x57mm, 308, 30-06
Action: Bolt action; Mauser-type; repeating
Magazine: 5-shot box with hinged floor plate
Barrel: 20"
Sights: Adjustable rear, hooded ramp front
Stock and Forearm: Checkered walnut Monte Carlo one-piece full-length pistol grip stock and forearm; swivels; cheekpiece
Approximate wt.: 7½ lbs.
Comments: Distributed by Interarms.
Estimated Value: **Excellent:** **$410.00**
Very good: **$325.00**

Mark X Continental

Similar to the Marquis with a "butter knife" bolt handle and double set triggers.

Estimated Value: **Excellent:** **$425.00**
Very good: **$340.00**

Mark X Whitworth Express, Safari

Caliber: 375 H&H mag., 458 Win. mag.
Action: Bolt action; Mauser style; repeating; adjustable trigger
Magazine: 3-shot box with hinged floor plate
Barrel: 24"
Sights: 3 leaf express rear sight; hooded ramp front
Stock and Forearm: Checkered European walnut, Monte Carlo one-piece stock and forearm; cheekpiece; swivels; recoil pad
Approximate wt.: 7½ lbs.
Comments: Produced from the late 1980s to the mid-1990s.
Estimated Value: **Excellent:** **$625.00**
Very good: **$500.00**

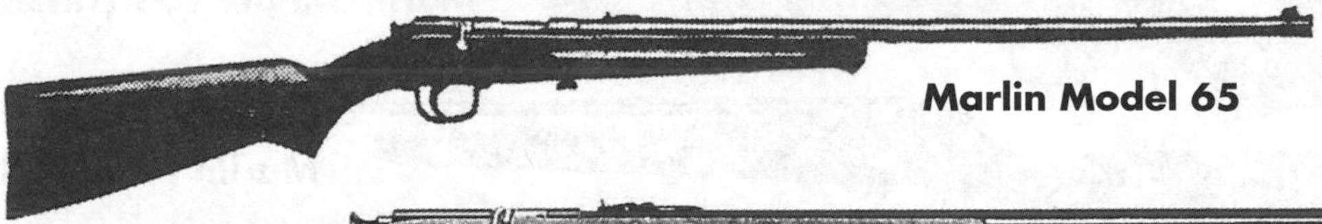

Marlin Model 65

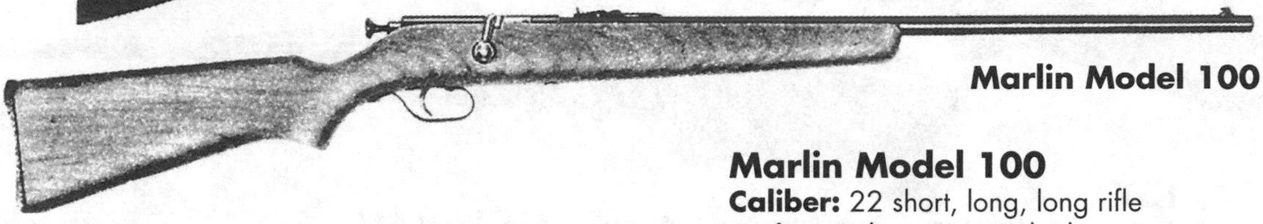

Marlin Model 100

Marlin Models 65 and 65E

Caliber: 22 short, long, long rifle
Action: Bolt action; single-shot
Magazine: None
Barrel: 24"; round
Sights: Open rear, bead front; peep rear, hooded front on 65E
Stock and Forearm: Pistol grip stock and grooved forearm
Approximate wt.: 5 lbs.
Comments: This was a takedown rifle that was made between 1932 and 1935.

Estimated Value:	**Excellent:**	**$110.00**
	Very good:	**$ 90.00**

Marlin Model 100S Tom Mix Special

Same as the Model 100 except hooded front sight, peep rear sight. Made from 1937 to 1942.

Estimated Value:	**Excellent:**	**$350.00**
	Very good:	**$280.00**

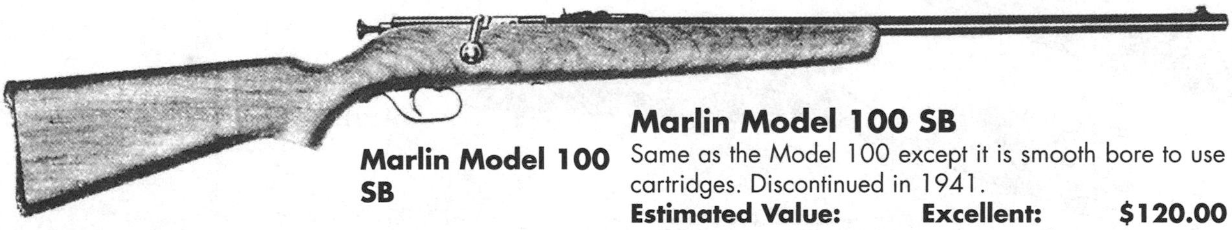

Marlin Model 100 SB

Marlin Models 2000 and 2000A Target

Caliber: 22 long rifle
Action: Bolt action; thumb safety; red cocking indicator
Magazine: None; single-shot
Barrel: Heavy, 22"; selected Micro-groove with match chamber and recessed muzzle
Sights: Adjustable target peep rear, hooded front with seven aperture inserts
Stock and Forearm: High-comb fiberglass/Kevlar stock with stipple-finish forearm; stock butt plate adjustable for length of pull, height and angle on 2000A
Approximate wt.: 8 lbs.
Comments: A target rifle produced from 1992 to 1996.

Estimated Value:	**Excellent:**	**$470.00**
	Very good:	**$380.00**

Marlin Model 2000L

Similar to the Model 2000A except has a one-piece laminated black/gray, ambidextrous pistol grip stock and forearm. Introduced in 1997.

Estimated Value:	**Excellent:**	**$560.00**
	Very good:	**$450.00**

Marlin Model 100

Caliber: 22 short, long, long rifle
Action: Bolt action; single-shot
Magazine: None
Barrel: 24"; round
Sights: Open rear, bead front
Stock and Forearm: Plain pistol grip stock and forearm
Approximate wt.: 4¾ lbs.
Comments: Takedown model was manufactured from 1936 to 1960. In 1960 it became the Model 100G or Glenfield, and was replaced in the mid-1960s by the Glenfield 10.

Estimated Value:	**Excellent:**	**$115.00**
	Very good:	**$ 90.00**

Marlin Model 100G; Glenfield 10

Basically the same as Marlin Model 100.

Estimated Value:	**Excellent:**	**$115.00**
	Very good:	**$ 90.00**

Marlin Model 100 SB

Same as the Model 100 except it is smooth bore to use with shot cartridges. Discontinued in 1941.

Estimated Value:	**Excellent:**	**$120.00**
	Very good:	**$ 95.00**

Marlin Models 101 and 101-DL

Basically the same as Model 100 except beavertail forearm. Peep rear, hooded front sights on 101-DL. Made from 1951 to the late 1970s.

Estimated Value:	**Excellent:**	**$110.00**
	Very good:	**$ 90.00**

Marlin Model 122 Target Rifle

Caliber: 22 short, long, long rifle
Action: Bolt action; single-shot
Magazine: None
Barrel: 22"; round
Sights: Open rear, hooded ramp front
Stock and Forearm: Wood Monte Carlo pistol grip stock and forearm; swivels
Approximate wt.: 5 lbs.
Comments: Made from about 1961 to 1965.

Estimated Value:	**Excellent:**	**$100.00**
	Very good:	**$ 80.00**

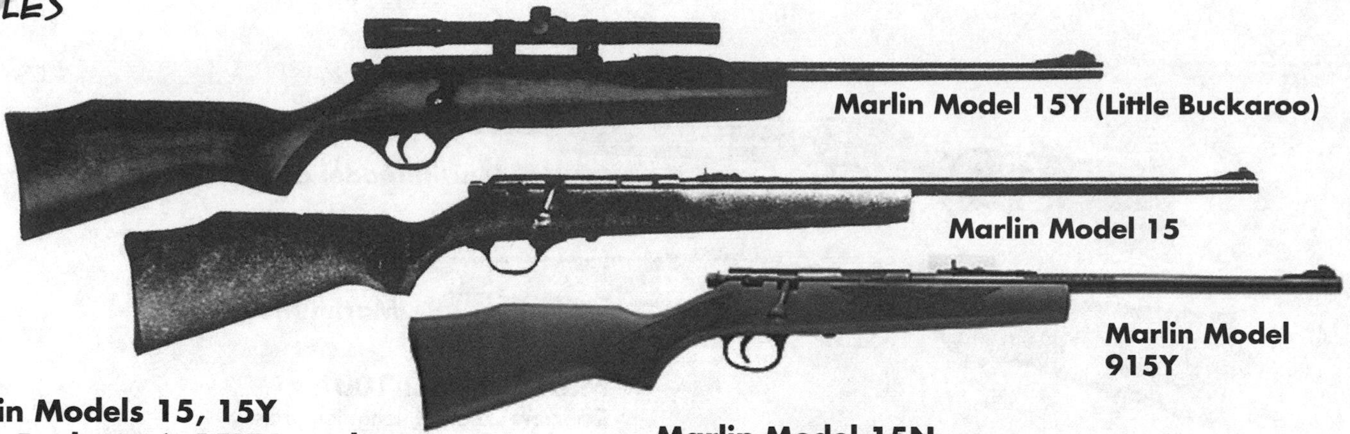

Marlin Model 15Y (Little Buckaroo)

Marlin Model 15

Marlin Model 915Y

Marlin Models 15, 15Y (Little Buckaroo), 15YN, and15YS
Caliber: 22 short, long or long rifle
Action: Bolt action; single-shot
Magazine: None
Barrel: 22"; round, 16¼" on 15Y and 15YN
Sights: Adjustable open rear, ramp front
Stock and Forearm: Checkered hardwood, Monte Carlo pistol grip one-piece stock and forearm
Approximate wt.: 5½ lbs., 4½ lbs. (15Y)
Comments: Model 15 made from the late 1970s to the mid-1980s. Models 15Y and 15YN are for young shooters; produced from the late 1980s to date. Model 15YS has stainless steel finish (add 11%).

Estimated Value:	Excellent:	$155.00
	Very good:	$125.00

Marlin Model 15N
Similar to the Model 15YN except with full-size Monte Carlo stock and forearm. Introduced in 1998.

Estimated Value:	Excellent:	$145.00
	Very good:	$115.00

Marlin Model 915Y
A youth rifle similar to the Model 15. Model 915YS has a stainless steel finish (add 10%).

Estimated Value:	New (retail):	$229.00
	Excellent:	$170.00
	Very good:	$135.00

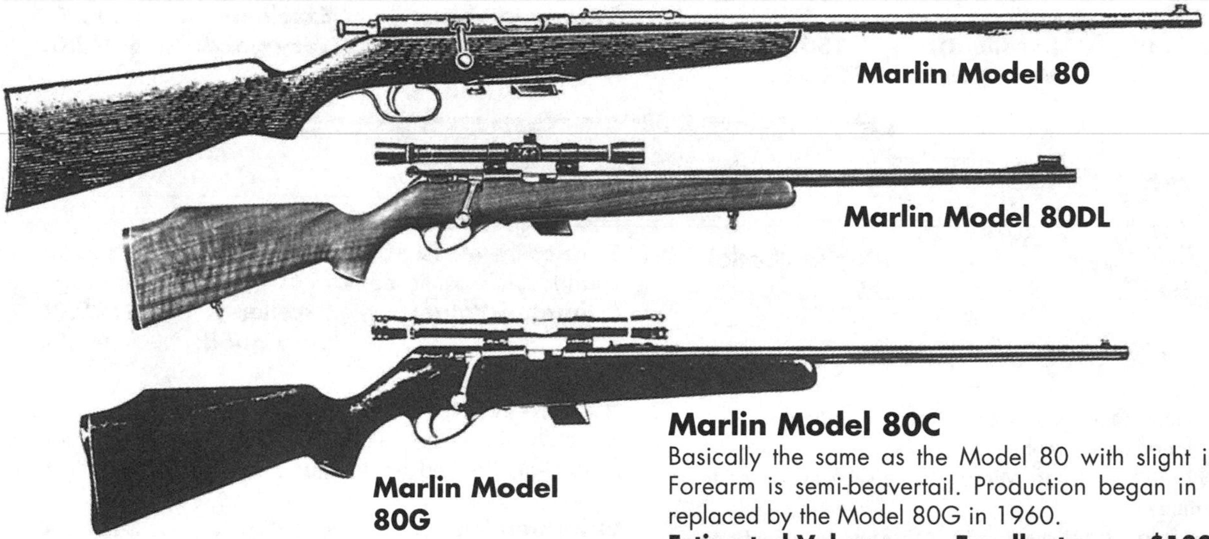

Marlin Model 80

Marlin Model 80DL

Marlin Model 80G

Marlin Model 80C

Marlin Models 80 and 80E
Caliber: 22 short, long, long rifle
Action: Bolt action; takedown type; repeating
Magazine: 8-shot detachable box
Barrel: 24"
Sights: Open rear, bead front; peep rear, hooded front on 80E
Stock and Forearm: Plain pistol grip stock and forearm
Approximate wt.: 6¼ lbs.
Comments: Production began about 1934 and continued until the mid-1940s.

Estimated Value:	Excellent:	$125.00
	Very good:	$100.00

Marlin Model 80C
Basically the same as the Model 80 with slight improvements. Forearm is semi-beavertail. Production began in 1946; it was replaced by the Model 80G in 1960.

Estimated Value:	Excellent:	$130.00
	Very good:	$105.00

Marlin Model 80DL
Same rifle as Model 80C except: swivels; hooded front sight; peep rear sight. Discontinued in 1965.

Estimated Value:	Excellent:	$135.00
	Very good:	$110.00

Marlin Model 80G
The same rifle as Marlin Model 80C. Made from about 1960 to 1966.

Estimated Value:	Excellent:	$130.00
	Very good:	$105.00

Marlin Model 81

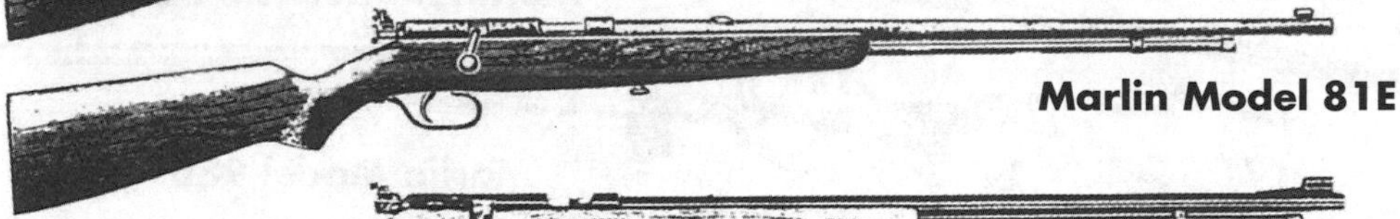
Marlin Model 81E

Marlin Model 81-DL

Marlin Glenfield Model 81G

Marlin Models 81 and 81E

Caliber: 22 short, long, long rifle
Action: Bolt action; repeating
Magazine: Tubular under barrel: 24 shorts, 20 longs, 18 long rifles
Barrel: 24"
Sights: Open rear, bead front; peep rear, hooded front on Model 81E
Stock and Forearm: Plain pistol grip stock and forearm
Approximate wt.: 6¼ lbs.
Comments: This takedown model was produced from about 1937 to the mid-1940s.

Estimated Value:	**Excellent:**	**$130.00**
	Very good:	**$105.00**

Marlin Model 81C

An improved Model 81; semi-beavertail forearm. It was produced from 1946 to 1970.

Estimated Value:	**Excellent:**	**$145.00**
	Very good:	**$115.00**

Marlin Model 81-DL

Same as the Model 81C except it has swivels; hooded front sight, peep rear sight. Made from about 1946 to 1965.

Estimated Value:	**Excellent:**	**$150.00**
	Very good:	**$120.00**

Marlin Glenfield Model 81G

Basically the same as the Marlin Model 81C. It was produced as the Model 81G from about 1960 to 1965.

Estimated Value:	**Excellent:**	**$125.00**
	Very good:	**$100.00**

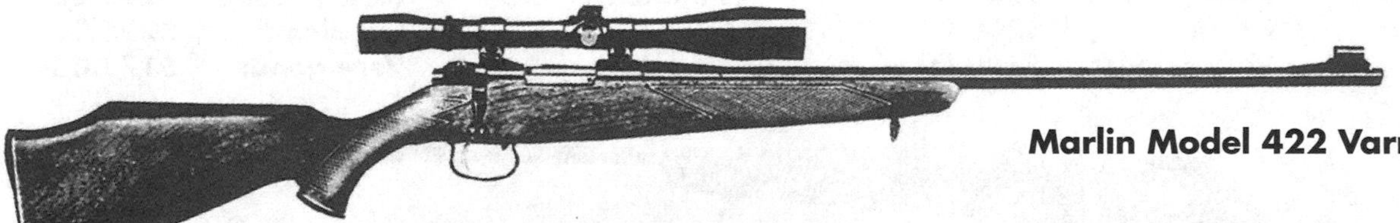
Marlin Model 422 Varmint King

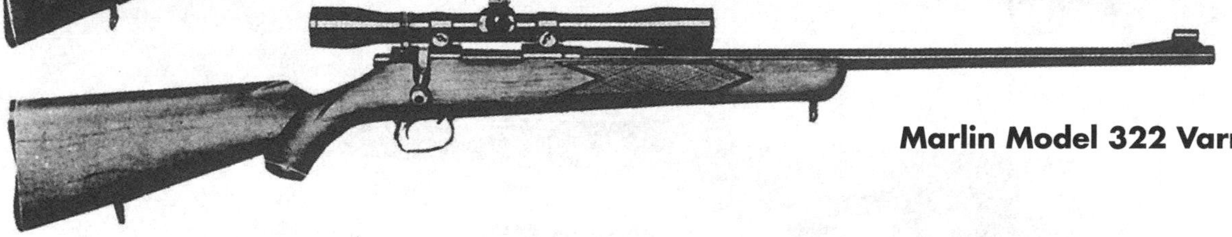
Marlin Model 322 Varmint

Marlin Model 322 Varmint

Caliber: 222 Rem.
Action: Bolt action (Sako Short, Mauser); repeating
Magazine: 3-shot clip
Barrel: 24"
Sights: Peep sight rear, hooded ramp front
Stock and Forearm: Checkered hardwood stock and forearm
Approximate wt.: 7½ lbs.
Comments: Made for only three years beginning about 1954.

Estimated Value:	**Excellent:**	**$700.00**
	Very good:	**$560.00**

Marlin Model 422 Varmint King

Caliber: 222 Rem.
Action: Bolt action; repeating
Magazine: 3-shot detachable clip
Barrel: 24"; round
Sights: Peep sight rear, hooded ramp front
Stock and Forearm: Checkered Monte Carlo pistol grip stock and forearm
Approximate wt.: 7 lbs.
Comments: Replaced Model 322 about 1958 but was discontinued after one year.

Estimated Value:	**Excellent:**	**$800.00**
	Very good:	**$640.00**

Marlin Model 455 Sporter

Marlin Model 980

Marlin Model 980S

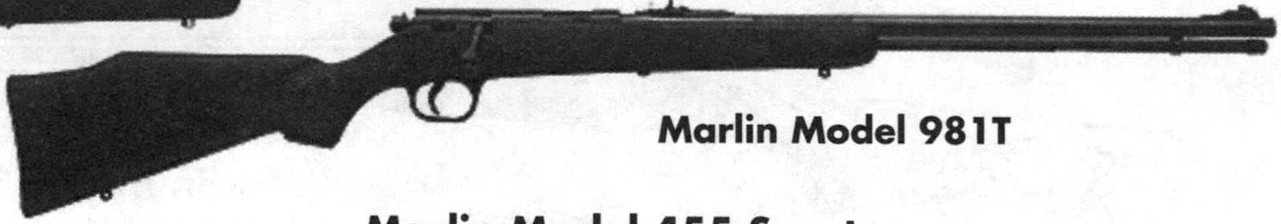

Marlin Model 981T

Marlin Model 980

Caliber: 22 Win. mag.
Action: Bolt action; repeating
Magazine: 8-shot clip
Barrel: Blued; 24"; round
Sights: Open rear, hooded ramp front
Stock and Forearm: Monte Carlo one-piece stock and forearm; swivels
Approximate wt.: 6 lbs.
Comments: Made from about 1962 until 1970.

Estimated Value:	**Excellent:**	**$125.00**
	Very good:	**$100.00**

Marlin Model 981T

Similar to the Model 980 except: 22 short, long, or long rifle caliber; tubular magazine.

Estimated Value:	**New (retail):**	**$269.00**
	Excellent:	**$200.00**
	Very good:	**$160.00**

Marlin Model 455 Sporter

Caliber: 270, 30-06, 308
Action: Bolt action; FN Mauser action with Sako trigger
Magazine: 5-shot box
Barrel: 24"; round, stainless steel
Sights: Receiver sight — Lyman 48, hooded ramp front
Stock and Forearm: Checkered wood Monte Carlo stock and forearm; cheekpiece
Approximate wt.: 8½ lbs.
Comments: Made from about 1957 to 1959.

Estimated Value:	**Excellent:**	**$725.00**
	Very good:	**$580.00**

Marlin Model 980S

Similar to the Model 980 except: 22 long rifle caliber; 7-shot nickel-plated clip; stainless steel barrel; fiberglass-filled synthetic stock and forearm.

Estimated Value:	**New (retail):**	**$298.00**
	Excellent:	**$225.00**
	Very good:	**$175.00**

Marlin Model MR-7B

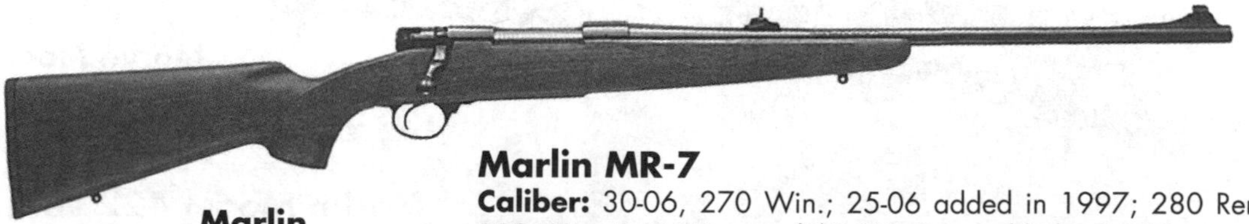

Marlin MR-7

Marlin Model MR-7B

Similar to the Model MR-7 except with walnut-finished Maine birch stock and forearm; internal magazine; 270 Win. or 30-06 Sprg. only. Produced in the late 1990s. Deduct 7% for no sights.

Estimated Value:	**Excellent:**	**$400.00**
	Very good:	**$320.00**

Marlin MR-7

Caliber: 30-06, 270 Win.; 25-06 added in 1997; 280 Rem., 308 Win., 243 Win., and 22-250 Rem. added in 1998
Action: Bolt action, repeating; adjustable trigger pull; 3-position safety
Magazine: 4-shot detachable box with hinged floor plate
Barrel: 22"; round, blued; 6-groove rifling and recessed muzzle
Sights: Brass bead ramp front, adjustable rear
Stock and Forearm: Cut checkered black walnut one-piece, pistol grip stock and forearm; swivel studs and rubber rifle butt pad
Approximate wt.: 7½ lbs.
Comments: Produced in the late 1990s. Add 7% for sights.

Estimated Value:	**Excellent:**	**$460.00**
	Very good:	**$375.00**

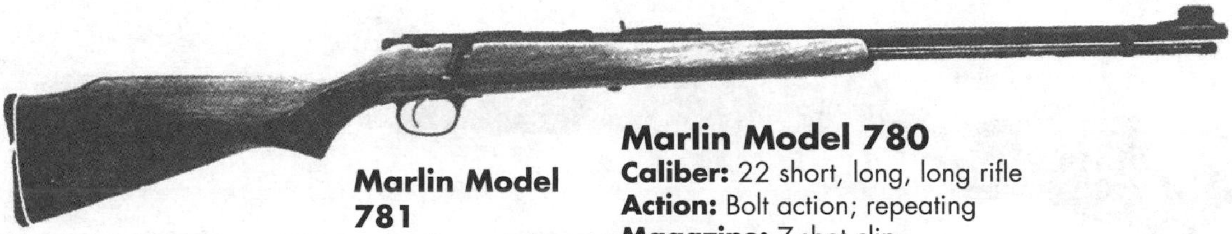

Marlin Model 781

Marlin Model 780

Caliber: 22 short, long, long rifle
Action: Bolt action; repeating
Magazine: 7-shot clip
Barrel: Blued; 22"
Sights: Adjustable rear, ramp front
Stock and Forearm: Checkered walnut Monte Carlo one-piece semi-pistol grip stock and forearm
Approximate wt.: 6 lbs.
Comments: Produced from about 1971 to the late 1980s.

Estimated Value:	**Excellent:**	**$100.00**
	Very good:	**$ 80.00**

Marlin Model 781

Same as the Model 780 except tubular magazine; 25 shorts, 19 longs, 17 long rifles. Weighs 5½ lbs.

Estimated Value:	**Excellent:**	**$120.00**
	Very good:	**$ 95.00**

Marlin Model 81TS

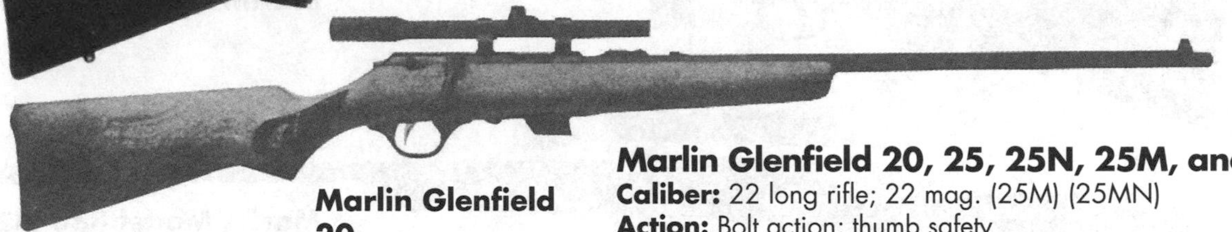

Marlin Glenfield 20

Marlin Glenfield 20, 25, 25N, 25M, and 25MN

Caliber: 22 long rifle; 22 mag. (25M) (25MN)
Action: Bolt action; thumb safety
Magazine: 7-shot clip
Barrel: 22"; round, blued; micro-groove barrel
Sights: Open rear, ramp front
Stock and Forearm: Checkered walnut finish, semi-pistol grip stock and plain forearm; Model 25N has no checkering
Approximate wt.: 5½ lbs.
Comments: Produced from about 1966 to the early 1980s as Model 20; currently sold as Model 25N. Add 15% for magnum (25M, 25MN).

Estimated Value:	**Excellent:**	**$155.00**
	Very good:	**$125.00**

Marlin Model 81TS

Similar to the Model 25N except has tubular under-barrel magazine that holds 25 shorts, 19 longs, or 17 long rifles; black fiberglass-filled synthetic stock and forearm; weighs 6 lbs. Introduced in 1998.

Estimated Value:	**Excellent:**	**$155.00**
	Very good:	**$125.00**

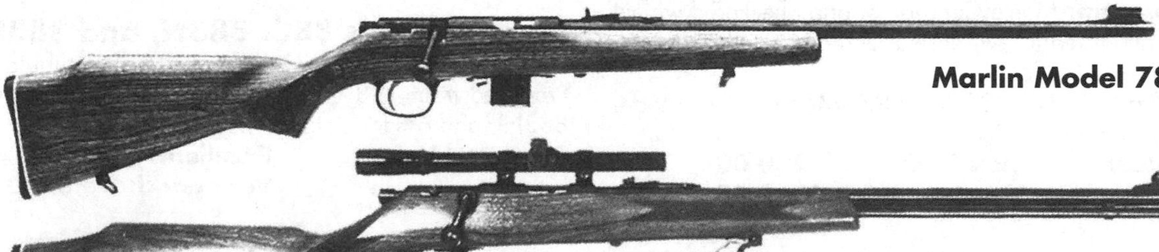

Marlin Model 782

Marlin Model 783

Marlin Model 782

Caliber: 22 Win. magnum
Action: Bolt action; repeating
Magazine: 7-shot clip
Barrel: 22"
Sights: Adjustable rear, ramp front
Stock and Forearm: Monte Carlo one-piece semi-pistol grip stock and forearm
Approximate wt.: 6 lbs.
Comments: Produced from 1971 to the late 1980s.

Estimated Value:	**Excellent:**	**$150.00**
	Very good:	**$115.00**

Marlin Model 783

Same as the Model 782 except 12-shot tubular magazine.

Estimated Value:	**Excellent:**	**$160.00**
	Very good:	**$120.00**

Marlin Model 880

Marlin Model 881

Marlin Model 882SS

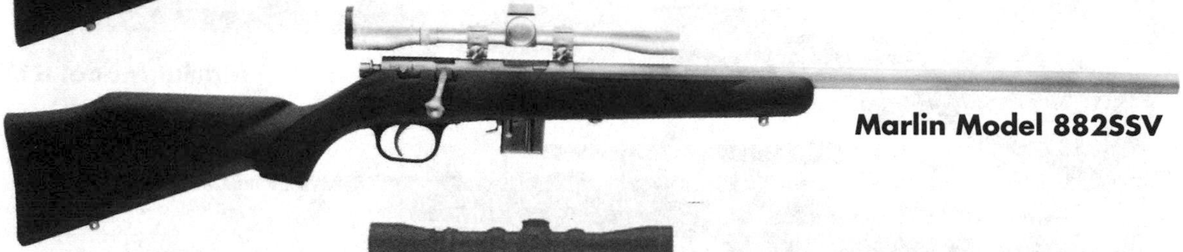
Marlin Model 882SSV

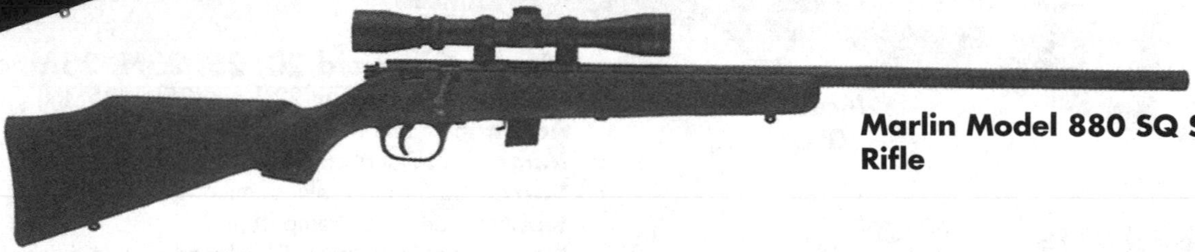
Marlin Model 880 SQ Squirrel Rifle

Marlin Models 880 and 880SS

Caliber: 22 long rifle
Action: Bolt action; thumb safety, red cocking indicator
Magazine: 7-shot clip
Barrel: 22"; blued or stainless steel (Model 880SS)
Sights: Ramp front, brass bead with wide scan hood; adjustable folding semi-buckhorn rear
Stock and Forearm: Monte Carlo pistol grip checkered walnut one-piece stock and forearm; swivel studs and rubber rifle butt pad
Approximate wt.: 5½ lbs.
Comments: Made from 1989 to 1997 (Model 880). Model 880SS in production until 2005.

Estimated Value:	**Excellent:**	**$200.00**
	Very good:	**$160.00**

Marlin Model 881

Same as the Model 880 except: tubular magazine; which holds 17 long rifles; Produced from 1989 to the mid-1990s.

Estimated Value:	**Excellent:**	**$190.00**
	Very good:	**$155.00**

Marlin Models 882, 882L, and 882SS

Same as the Model 880 except: 22 Win. mag. rim fire only. Produced from 1989 to date; walnut or laminated (Model 882L) stock; add 6% for laminated stock. Add 7% for stainless steel (Model 882SS).

Estimated Value:	**Excellent:**	**$200.00**
	Very good:	**$160.00**

Marlin Model 882SSV

Similar to the Model 882SS except with 22" heavy barrel and no sights.

Estimated Value:	**Excellent:**	**$225.00**
	Very good:	**$180.00**

Marlin Models 883, 883N, and 883SS

Same as the Model 882 except: 12-shot tubular magazine. Produced from 1989 to date. Add 10% for nickel plate (Model 883N); add 6% for stainless steel (Model 883SS).

Estimated Value:	**Excellent:**	**$250.00**
	Very good:	**$200.00**

Marlin Model 880 SQ Squirrel Rifle

Caliber: 22 long rifle
Action: Bolt action; repeating
Magazine: 7-shot clip
Barrel: 22"; heavy micro-groove with double bedding screws; drilled and tapped for sights
Sights: None; receiver is grooved for scope mount
Stock and Forearm: Black fiberglass-filled synthetic one-piece pistol grip stock and forearm
Approximate wt.: 6½ lbs.
Comments: Introduced in 1996.

Estimated Value:	**Excellent:**	**$225.00**
	Very good:	**$180.00**

Marlin Model 925M

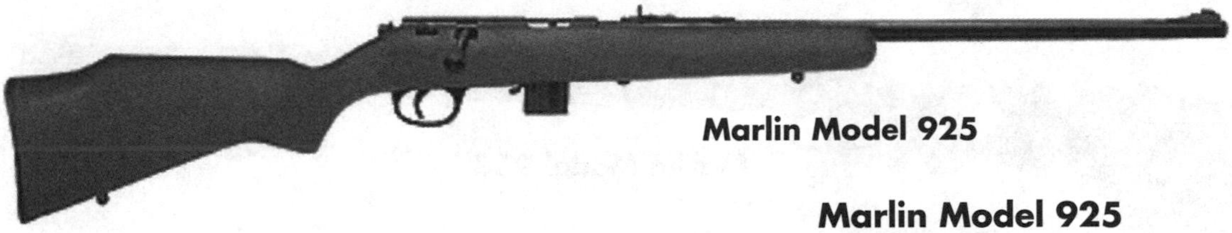

Marlin Model 925

Marlin Model 925

Caliber: 22 long rifle
Action: Bolt action, repeating
Magazine: 7-shot clip
Barrel: Blued; 22"
Sights: Adjustable open rear, ramp front
Stock and Forearm: Smooth hardwood, one-piece Monte Carlo stock and forearm; camouflage model (Model 925C); fiberglass-filled synthetic stock (Model 925R)
Approx. wt.: 5½ lbs.
Comments: Add 10% for Models 925C or 925R.

Estimated Value:	**New (retail):**	**$249.00**
	Excellent:	**$185.00**
	Very good:	**$150.00**

Marlin Model 925M

Similar to the Model 925 except: 22 Win. magnum. Model 925C has camouflage finish (add 10%).

Estimated Value:	**New (retail):**	**$249.00**
	Excellent:	**$185.00**
	Very good:	**$150.00**

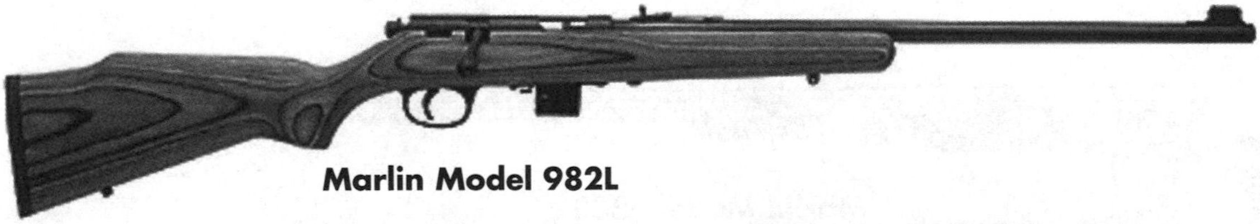

Marlin Model 982L

Marlin Model 982

Marlin Model 982

Caliber: 22 Win. magnum
Action: Bolt action, repeating
Magazine: 7-shot clip
Barrel: Blued; 22"
Sights: Adjustable rear, ramp front
Stock and Forearm: Checkered American black walnut, one-piece pistol grip stock and forearm; swivels
Approx. wt.: 6 lbs.
Comments: Introduced in 2004.

Estimated Value:	**Excellent:**	**$245.00**
	Very good:	**$195.00**

Marlin Model 982L

Similar to the Model 982 with laminated two-tone brown hardwood stock and forearm.

Estimated Value:	**Excellent:**	**$245.00**
	Very good:	**$195.00**

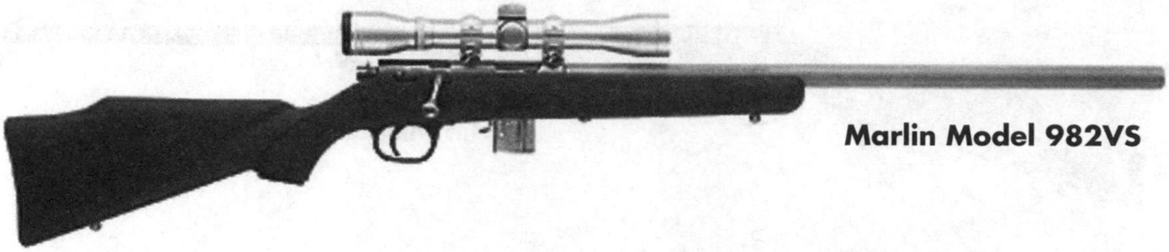

Marlin Model 982VS

Marlin Model 983

Marlin Model 982VS

Similar to the Model 982 except: heavy stainless steel barrel; nickel-plated clip; black fiberglass-filled synthetic stock and forearm.

Estimated Value:	**New (retail):**	**$349.00**
	Excellent:	**$260.00**
	Very good:	**$210.00**

Marlin Model 983

Similar to the Model 982 except: tubular magazine.

Estimated Value:	**New (retail):**	**$308.00**
	Excellent:	**$230.00**
	Very good:	**$185.00**

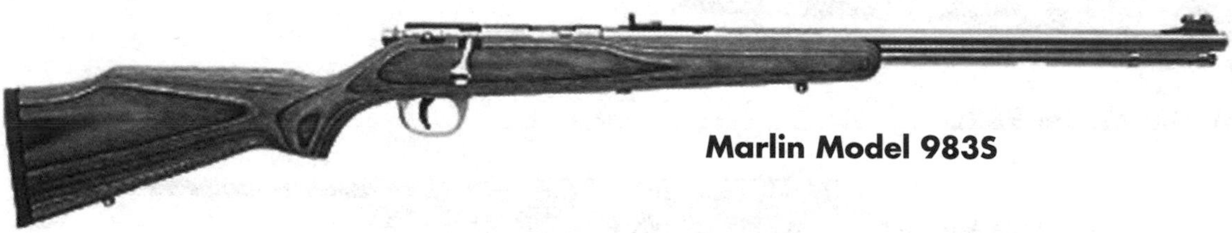

Marlin Model 983S

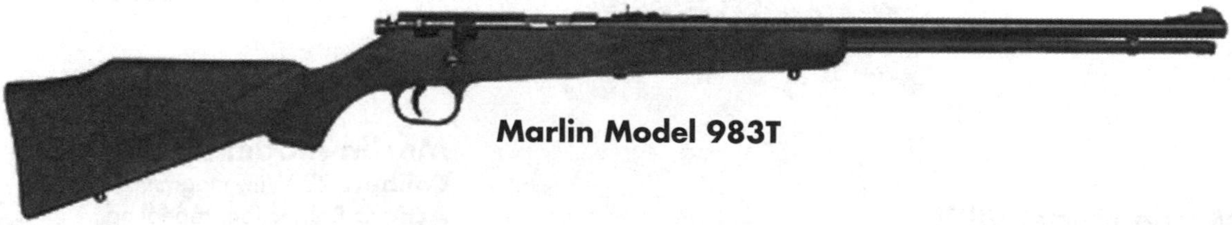

Marlin Model 983T

Marlin Model 983S

Similar to the Model 983 except: stainless steel barrel and laminated brown two-tone stock and forearm.

Estimated Value:	**New (retail):**	**$369.00**
	Excellent:	**$275.00**
	Very good:	**$220.00**

Marlin Model 983T

Similar to the Model 983 with black fiberglass-filled synthetic stock and forearm.

Estimated Value:	**New (retail):**	**$269.00**
	Excellent:	**$200.00**
	Very good:	**$160.00**

Marlin Model 917VS

Marlin Model 917V

Marlin Model 917V

Caliber: 17 Horn. magnum
Action: Bolt action, repeating
Magazine: 7-shot clip
Barrel: Blued; 22" heavy barrel
Sights: None; drilled and tapped for scope mount
Stock and Forearm: Smooth hardwood Monte Carlo one-piece stock and forearm; swivels
Approx. wt.: 6 lbs.
Comments: Introduced in 2004.

Estimated Value:	**New (retail):**	**$279.00**
	Excellent:	**$210.00**
	Very good:	**$165.00**

Marlin Model 917VS

Similar to the Model 917V except: laminated gray/black hardwood stock and forearm; 22" heavy stainless steel barrel; nickel-plated clip and swivels.

Estimated Value:	**New (retail):**	**$419.00**
	Excellent:	**$315.00**
	Very good:	**$250.00**

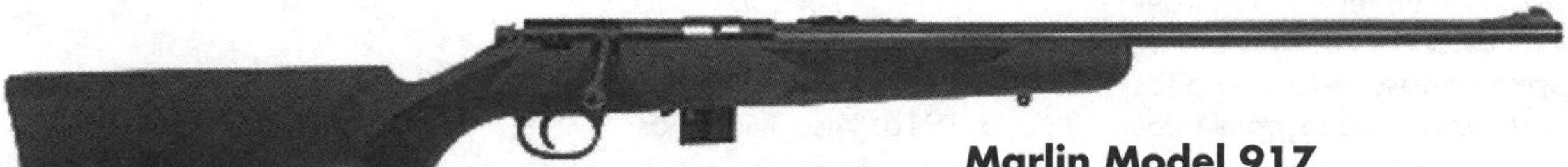

Marlin Model 917

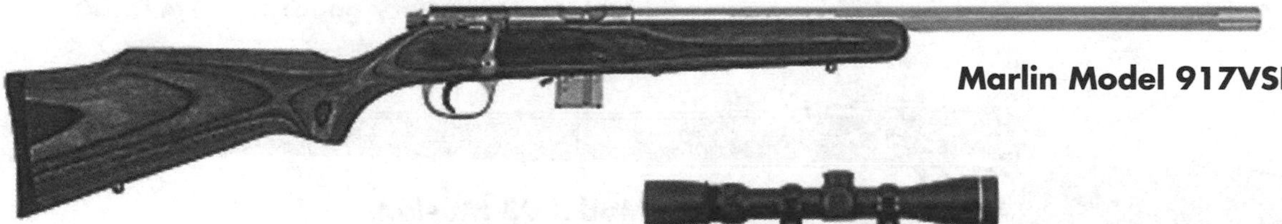

Marlin Model 917VSF

Marlin Model 917VR

Marlin Model 917

Similar to the Model 917V except: sporter barrel; checkered fiberglass-filled synthetic, matte black stock and forearm.

Estimated Value:	**New (retail):**	**$309.00**
	Excellent:	**$230.00**
	Very good:	**$185.00**

Marlin Model 917VSF

Similar to the Model 917VS except: fluted barrel.

Estimated Value:	**New (retail):**	**$449.00**
	Excellent:	**$335.00**
	Very good:	**$265.00**

Marlin Model 917VR

Similar to the 917V except: checkered fiberglass-filled synthetic matte black stock and forearm.

Estimated Value:	**New (retail):**	**$319.00**
	Excellent:	**$235.00**
	Very good:	**$190.00**

Marlin Model 92

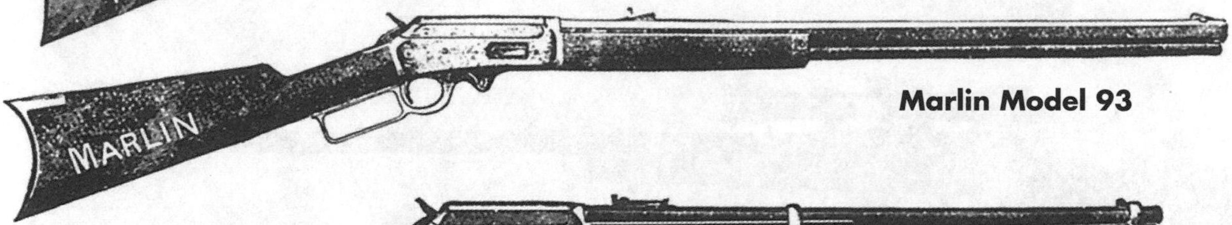

Marlin Model 93

Marlin Model 93 Carbine

Marlin Model 92

Caliber: 22 short, long, long rifle; 32 short or long, rim fire or center fire
Action: Lever action; exposed hammer
Magazine: 22 caliber: 25 shorts, 20 longs, 28 long rifles; 32 caliber: 17 shorts, 14 longs; tubular under barrel; 16" barrel: 15 shorts, 12 longs, 10 long rifles
Barrel: 16", 24", 26", 28"; round or octagon, blued
Sights: Open rear, blade front
Stock and Forearm: Plain walnut straight grip stock and forearm
Approximate wt.: 5 to 6 lbs.
Comments: Made from about 1892 to 1916. Also known as Model 1892.

Estimated Value:	**Excellent:**	**$1,700.00**
	Very good:	**$1,350.00**

Marlin Model 93

Caliber: 25-36, 30-30, 32 Spec., 32-40, 38-55, 44 Win.
Action: Lever action; exposed hammer; repeating
Magazine: 10-shot tubular; under barrel
Barrel: 26" – 32"; round or octagon
Sights: Open rear, bead front
Stock and Forearm: Plain walnut straight grip stock and forearm
Approximate wt.: 7 to 8 lbs.
Comments: Manufactured from about 1893 to 1915 and 1920 to 1933. Produced in both takedown and solid frame models. Also known as Model 1893.

Estimated Value:	**Excellent:**	**$1,850.00**
	Very good:	**$1,475.00**

Marlin Model 93 Carbine

Basically the same as the Model 93 except: produced in 30-30 and 32 special caliber only; standard carbine sights; 20" round barrel; 7-shot magazine. Weighs between 6 and 7 lbs.

Estimated Value:	**Excellent:**	**$1,850.00**
	Very good:	**$1,475.00**

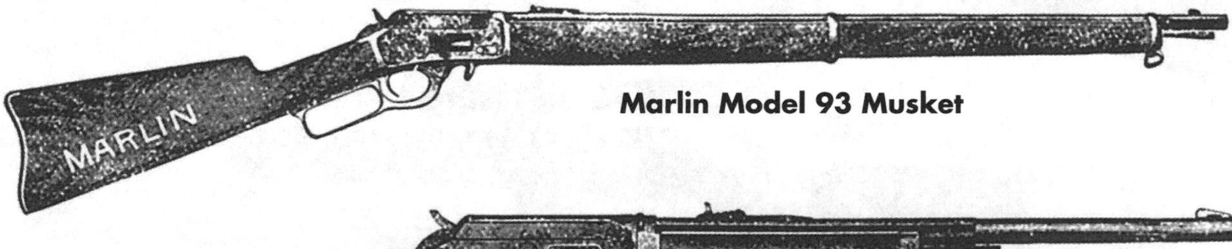

Marlin Model 93 Musket

Marlin Model 93 Sporting Carbine

Marlin Model 93 Sporting Carbine

Basically the same as Model 93 Carbine except the smaller magazine carries 5 shots.

Estimated Value:	**Excellent:**	**$2,000.00**
	Very good:	**$1,600.00**

Marlin Model 93 Musket

Same as the Model 93 except: 30" standard barrel; equipped with a musket stock; military forearm; ramrod; angular bayonet. Production stopped about 1915.

Estimated Value:	**Excellent:**	**$2,000.00**
	Very good:	**$1,600.00**

Marlin Model 1894 (Current)

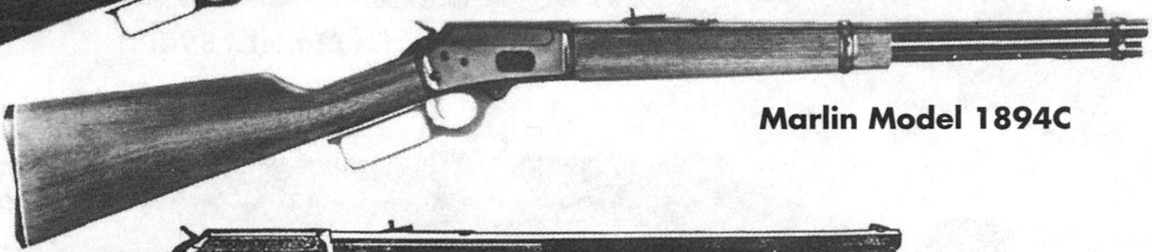

Marlin Model 1894C

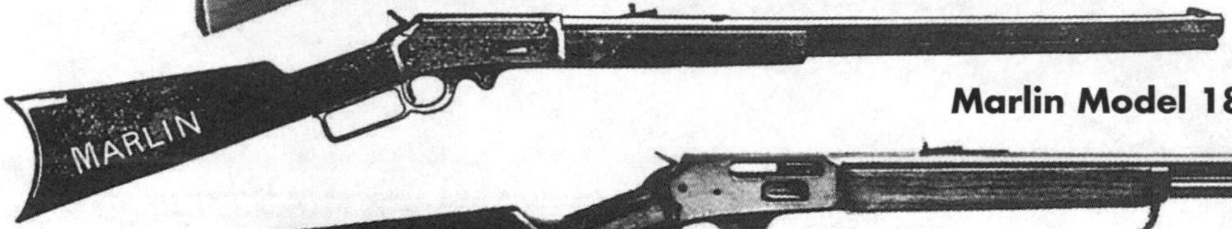

Marlin Model 1895

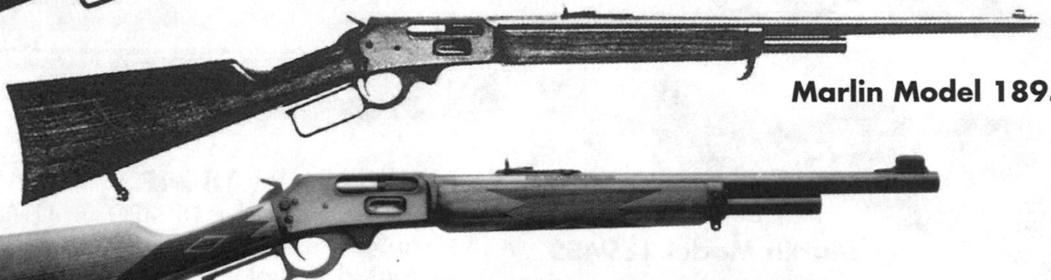

Marlin Model 1895S

Marlin Model 1895G Guide Gun

Marlin Model 1894CL

Similar to the current Model 1894S except: 25-20 or 32-30 caliber; 218 Bee added in 1990. 6-shot magazine; 22" barrel; weighs 6¼ lbs. Produced from 1988 to the mid-1990s.

Estimated Value:	**Excellent:**	**$425.00**
	Very good:	**$340.00**

Marlin Models 1894 and 1894S

Caliber: 25-20, 32-30, 38-40; (early models made from 1894 to 1935); current model is 44 mag. (1970s to the present); 41 mag. added 1984; 45 long Colt added 1988: 41 mag. and 45 long Colt dropped in 1990
Action: Lever action; exposed hammer; repeating
Magazine: 10-shot tubular
Barrel: Round or octagon; 20", 24" – 32"; 20" currently
Sights: Open rear, bead front
Stock and Forearm: Plain or checkered walnut straight or pistol grip stock and forearm
Approximate wt.: 7 lbs.
Comments: Made from about 1894 to 1935 in both takedown and solid frame models. Reintroduced in the late 1970s in 44 magnum with 20" barrel. Hammer block safety added 1986 (Model 1894S).

Estimated Value:		**Current**	**Early**
	New (retail):	**$576.00**	
	Excellent:	**$430.00**	**$1,600.00**
	Very good:	**$345.00**	**$1,280.00**

Marlin Models 1894C, 1894CS, and 1894M

Similar to the current Model 1894 except: 357 Mag. caliber; 18½" barrel; 9-shot magazine. Produced from 1979 to the present. Hammer block safety added in 1986.

Estimated Value:	**New (retail):**	**$576.00**
	Excellent:	**$430.00**
	Very good:	**$345.00**

Marlin Model 1895

Caliber: 33 WCF, 38-56, 40-65, 40-70, 40-82, 45-70
Action: Lever action; exposed hammer; repeating
Magazine: 9-shot tubular, under barrel
Barrel: 24"; octagon or round; blued
Sights: Open rear, bead front
Stock and Forearm: Walnut straight or pistol grip stock and forearm
Approximate wt.: 8 lbs.
Comments: Made in solid frame and takedown models from about 1895 to 1920.

Estimated Value:	**Excellent:**	**$1,600.00**
	Very good:	**$1,280.00**

Marlin Models 1895S and 1895SS

Similar to the Model 1895; introduced in the late 1970s; 45-70 Govt. caliber; 22" barrel; 4-shot magazine; swivels.

Estimated Value:	**New (retail):**	**$639.95**
	Excellent:	**$480.00**
	Very good:	**$385.00**

Marlin Models 1895G Guide Gun and 1895GS

Similar to the Model 1895SS except with straight grip stock, ventilated recoil pad, and 18½" ported barrel; weighs 6 to 7 lbs. Introduced in 1998. Model 1895GS has a stainless steel finish (add 16%).

Estimated Value:	**New (retail):**	**$639.95**
	Excellent:	**$480.00**
	Very good:	**$385.00**

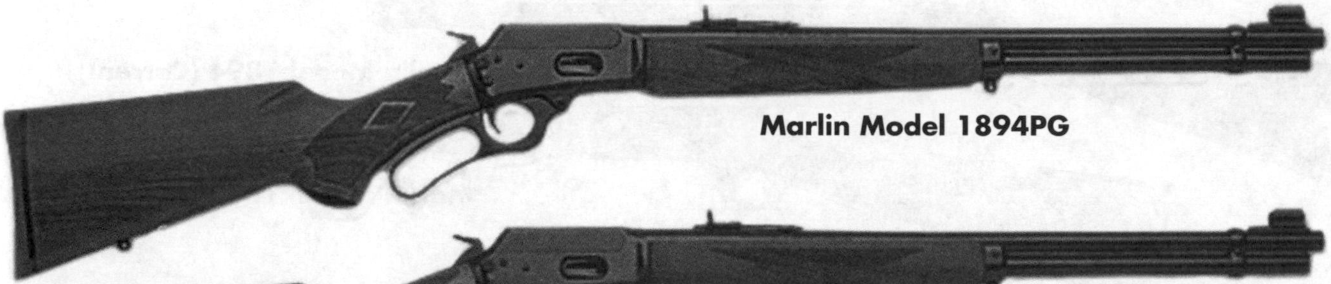

Marlin Model 1894PG

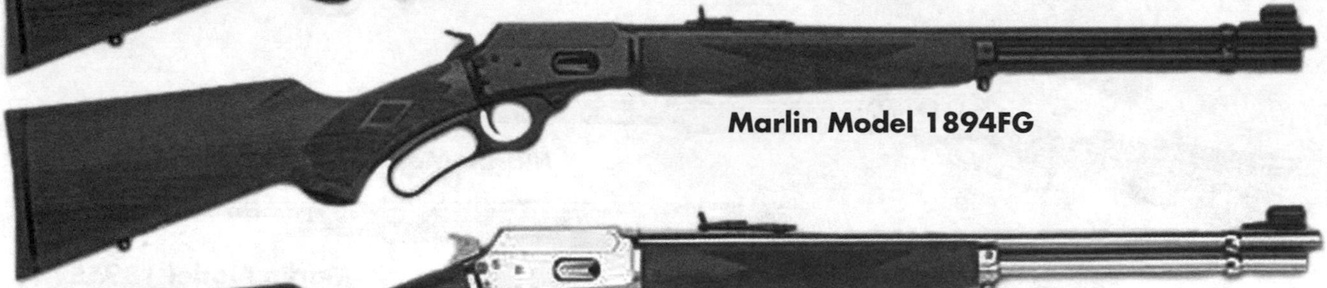

Marlin Model 1894FG

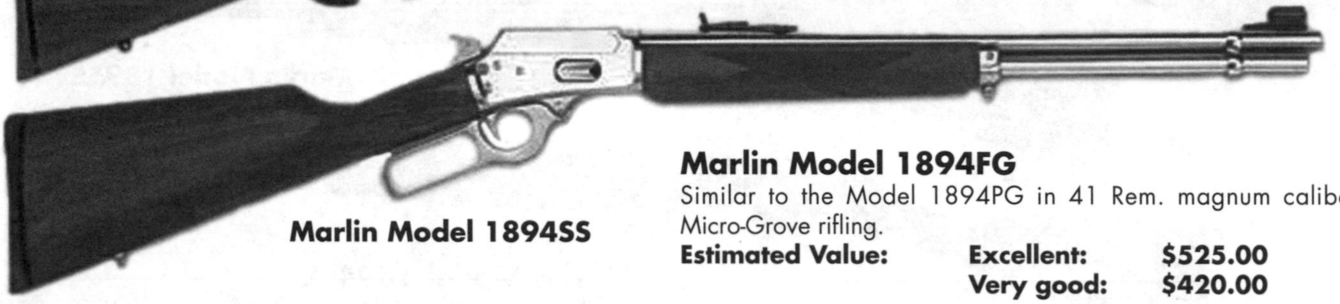

Marlin Model 1894SS

Marlin Model 1894PG

Similar to the current Model 1894 with a 20" barrel with Ballard-type rifling; checkered American black walnut stock and forearm.

Estimated Value: **Excellent:** **$525.00**
Very good: **$420.00**

Marlin Model 1894FG

Similar to the Model 1894PG in 41 Rem. magnum caliber; Micro-Grove rifling.

Estimated Value: **Excellent:** **$525.00**
Very good: **$420.00**

Marlin Model 1894SS

Similar to the Model 1894PG with stainless steel receiver and barrels; 44 Rem. magnum or 44 Special caliber.

Estimated Value: **Excellent:** **$525.00**
Very good: **$420.00**

Marlin Model 1894 Cowboy

Marlin Model 1894 Cowboy II

Marlin Model 1894 Cowboy II

Similar to the Model 1894 Cowboy except: in calibers 44-40, 357 magnum, and 44 magnum. Introduced in 1997.

Estimated Value: **New (retail):** **$822.00**
Excellent: **$615.00**
Very good: **$495.00**

Marlin Model 1894 Cowboy

Caliber: 45 long Colt
Action: Lever action, repeating; squared finger lever
Magazine: 10-shot tubular
Barrel: 24"; tapered, octagon; blued
Sights: Adjustable marble, semi-buckhorn rear, carbine type hooded front; receiver is tapped for scope mount
Stock and Forearm: Cut checkered black walnut, straight grip stock and forearm, with metal end
Approximate wt.: 7½ lbs.
Comments: Introduced in 1996.
Estimated Value: **New (retail):** **$822.00**
Excellent: **$615.00**
Very good: **$495.00**

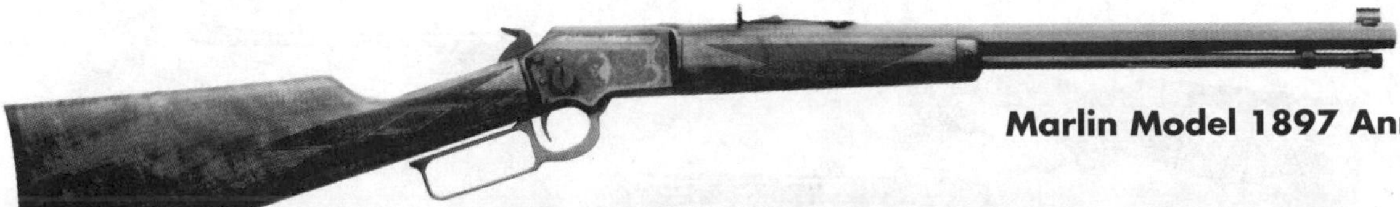

Marlin Model 1897 Annie Oakley

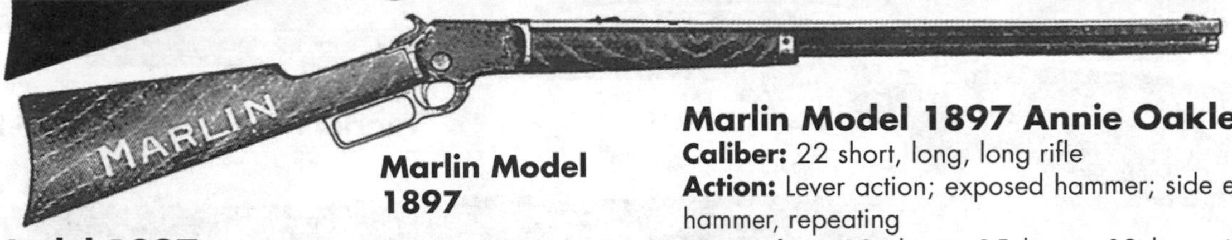

Marlin Model 1897

Marlin Model 1897

Caliber: 22 short, long, long rifle
Action: Lever action; exposed hammer; repeating
Magazine: 25 shorts, 20 longs, 18 long rifles in full length; 16 shorts, 12 longs, 10 long rifles in half length; tubular under barrel
Barrel: Blued; 16", 24", 26", 28"
Sights: Open rear, bead front
Stock and Forearm: Plain walnut straight or pistol grip stock and forearm
Approximate wt.: 6 lbs.
Comments: Made from about 1897 to 1914 and 1919 to 1921.

Estimated Value:	**Excellent:**	**$1,750.00**
	Very good:	**$1,400.00**

Marlin Model 1897 Annie Oakley

Caliber: 22 short, long, long rifle
Action: Lever action; exposed hammer; side ejector, rebounding hammer, repeating
Magazine: 19 shorts, 15 longs, 13 long rifles; tubular under barrel
Barrel: 18½"; tapered octagon; blued
Sights: Adjustable marble semi-buckhorn rear, marble carbine front with brass bead
Stock and Forearm: American black walnut straight-grip stock and forearm; steel fore-end cap, hard rubber butt plate
Approximate wt.: 5½ lbs.
Comments: Commemorates Annie Oakley, the famous target shooter. Receiver features roll engraving on both sides; gold Annie Oakley "signature" on bolt. Produced in the late 1990s.

Estimated Value:	**Excellent:**	**$800.00**
	Very good:	**$640.00**

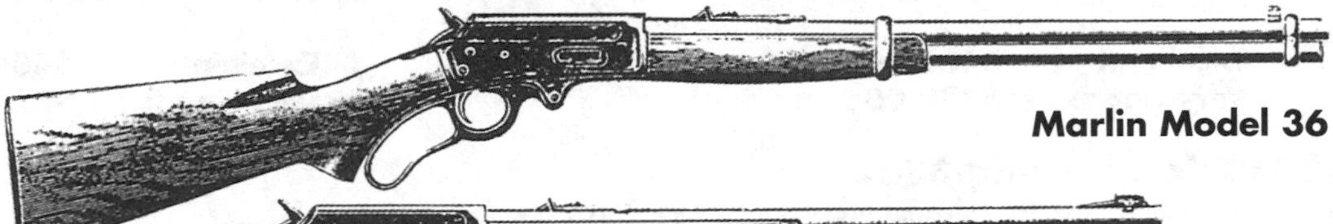

Marlin Model 36

Marlin Model 36 Sporting Carbine

Marlin Model 36 Sporting Carbine

Same as Model 36A except: lighter; 20" barrel.

Estimated Value:	**Excellent:**	**$1,000.00**
	Very good:	**$ 800.00**

Marlin Model 36

Caliber: 30-30, 32 Special
Action: Lever action; exposed hammer; repeating
Magazine: 6-shot tubular
Barrel: 20"; round; blued
Sights: Open rear, bead front
Stock and Forearm: Pistol grip stock and semi-beavertail forearm; carbine barrel band
Approximate wt.: 6½ lbs.
Comments: Made from about 1936 to 1942 and 1946 to 1948.

Estimated Value:	**Excellent:**	**$1,000.00**
	Very good:	**$ 800.00**

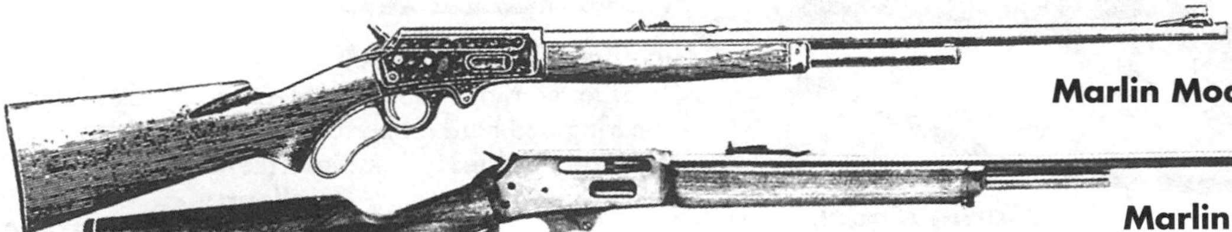

Marlin Model 36A

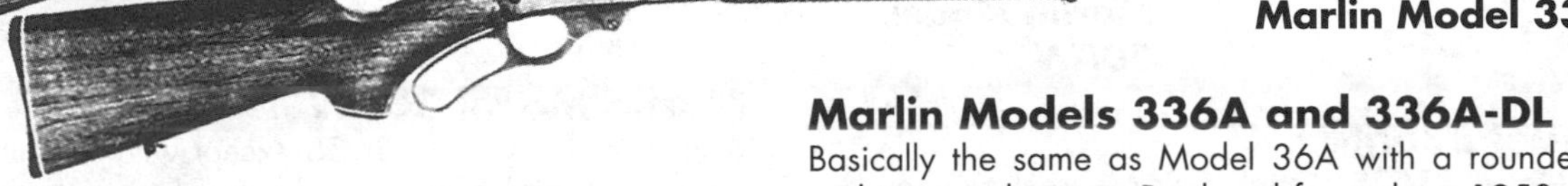

Marlin Model 336A

Marlin Model 36A

Same as Model 36 except: barrel is 24", ⅔ magazine; weighs slightly more; hooded front sight.

Estimated Value:	**Excellent:**	**$600.00**
	Very good:	**$480.00**

Marlin Models 336A and 336A-DL

Basically the same as Model 36A with a rounded breech bolt and improved action. Produced from about 1950 to 1963. Reintroduced in the 1970s. Checkered stock and forearm and swivels on Model 336A-DL.

Estimated Value:	**Excellent:**	**$375.00**
	Very good:	**$300.00**

Marlin Model 36H-DL

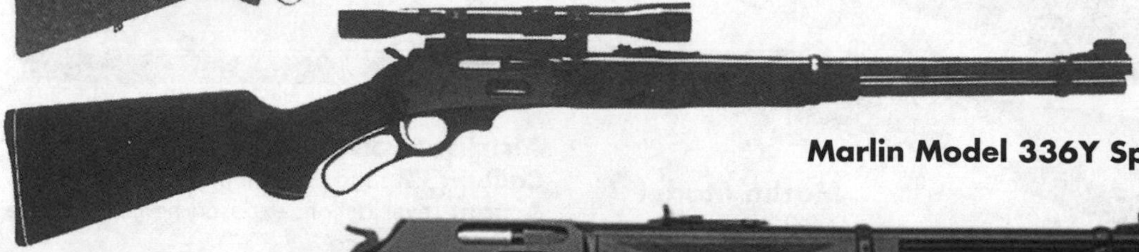

Marlin Model 336Y Spike Horn

Marlin Model 336C Carbine

Marlin Model 336 Cowboy

Marlin Model 36H-DL

Same as the Model 36A except stock and forearm are checkered and have swivels.

Estimated Value: **Excellent:** **$400.00**
Very good: **$320.00**

Marlin Models 336C Carbine and 336CS

Basically the same as the Model 36 except: checkered walnut stock; round breech bolt and improved action. 35 Rem. caliber was introduced and the 32 Special dropped in 1963; 375 Win. added in 1984. Produced from about 1948 to the present. Hammer block safety added in 1986.

Estimated Value: **New (retail):** **$530.00**
Excellent: **$400.00**
Very good: **$320.00**

Marlin Model 336Y Spike Horn

Similar to the Model 336CS in a compact format for young shooters; 16½" barrel.

Estimated Value: **Excellent:** **$400.00**
Very good: **$320.00**

Marlin Model 336 Cowboy

Similar to the Model 336CS except: straight stock; squared finger lever; 24" tapered octagon barrel; available in 30-30 Win. or 38-55 Win. calibers. Introduced in 1999.

Estimated Value: **Excellent:** **$545.00**
Very good: **$440.00**

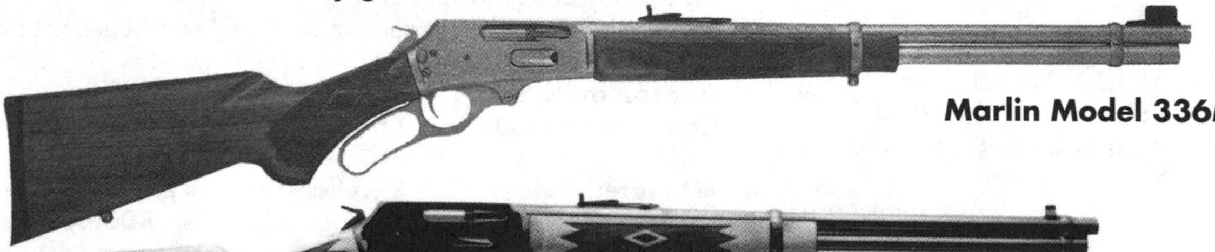

Marlin Model 336M

Marlin Model 30AW

Marlin Model 336M

Similar to the Model 336CS except: stainless steel receiver, barrel, lever, trigger guard plate, magazine tube, and loading gate. Introduced in 2000.

Estimated Value: **Excellent:** **$500.00**
Very good: **$400.00**

Marlin Model 336W

Similar to the Model 336CS except: gold-plated trigger; padded nylon sling and hard rubber butt plate.

Estimated Value: **New (retail):** **$452.00**
Excellent: **$340.00**
Very good: **$270.00**

Marlin Model 30AW

Similar to the Model 336CS except with walnut-finished Maine birch stock and forearm; gold-plated trigger; screw adjustable open rear sight; sling. Produced in the late 1990s.

Estimated Value: **Excellent:** **$300.00**
Very good: **$240.00**

Marlin Model 336T Texan Carbine

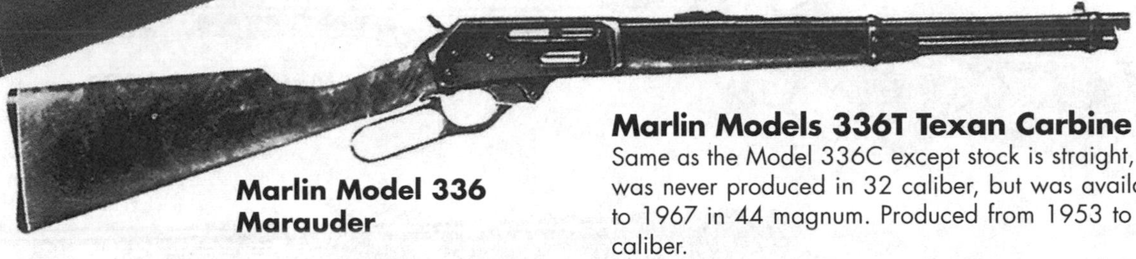

Marlin Model 336 Marauder

Marlin Models 336T Texan Carbine and 336TS

Same as the Model 336C except stock is straight, 18½" barrel. It was never produced in 32 caliber, but was available from 1963 to 1967 in 44 magnum. Produced from 1953 to 1987 in 30-30 caliber.

Estimated Value:	**Excellent:**	**$450.00**
	Very good:	**$360.00**

Marlin Model 336ER

Similar to the Model 336C in 356 Winchester or 308 Winchester calibers; recoil pad, swivels, and strap. Made from 1983 to 1988.

Estimated Value:	**Excellent:**	**$750.00**
	Very good:	**$600.00**

Marlin Model 336 Marauder

Same as the Model 336T except weight is slightly less and barrel is only 16¼". Made from about 1963 to 1964.

Estimated Value:	**Excellent:**	**$675.00**
	Very good:	**$540.00**

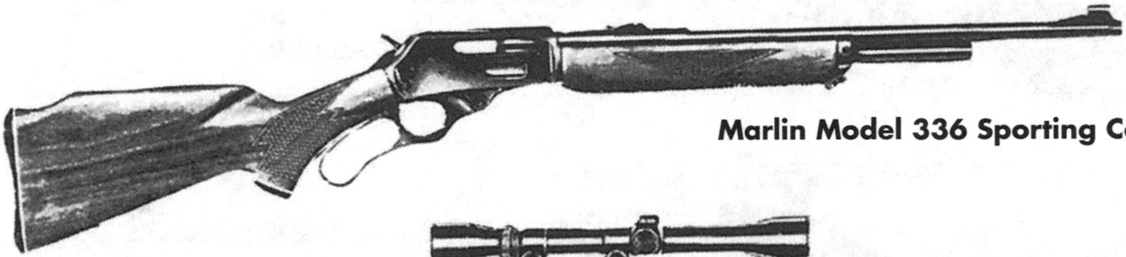

Marlin Model 336 Sporting Carbine

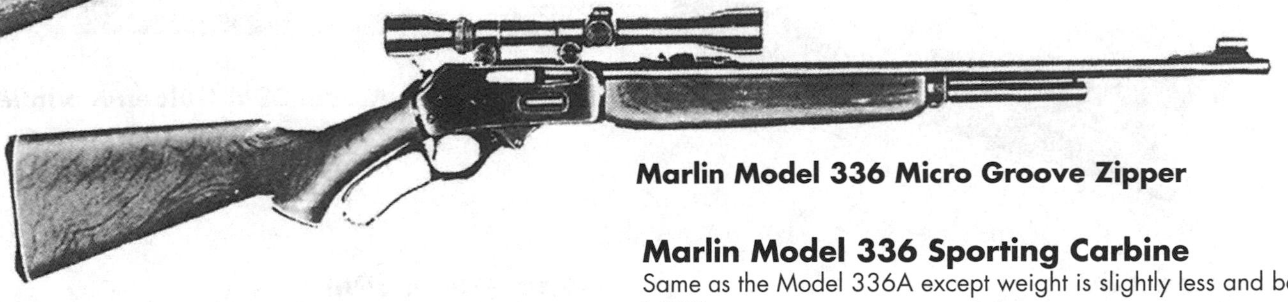

Marlin Model 336 Micro Groove Zipper

Marlin Model 336 Micro Groove Zipper

Same as the Model 336A except: Caliber 219 Zipper.

Estimated Value:	**Excellent:**	**$1,000.00**
	Very good:	**$ 800.00**

Marlin Model 336LTS

Similar to the Model 336TS except: 30-30 Win. caliber, 16¼" barrel, rubber butt pad; weighs 6½ lbs. Made from 1988 to the early 1990s.

Estimated Value:	**Excellent:**	**$325.00**
	Very good:	**$260.00**

Marlin Model 336 Sporting Carbine

Same as the Model 336A except weight is slightly less and barrel is 20".

Estimated Value:	**Excellent:**	**$400.00**
	Very good:	**$320.00**

Marlin Model 336 Zane Grey Century

Same basic rifle as the Model 336A except: 22" octagon barrel; brass fore-end cap; brass butt plate and medallion on receiver. Only 10,000 were produced in 1972.

Estimated Value:	**Excellent:**	**$425.00**
	Very good:	**$340.00**

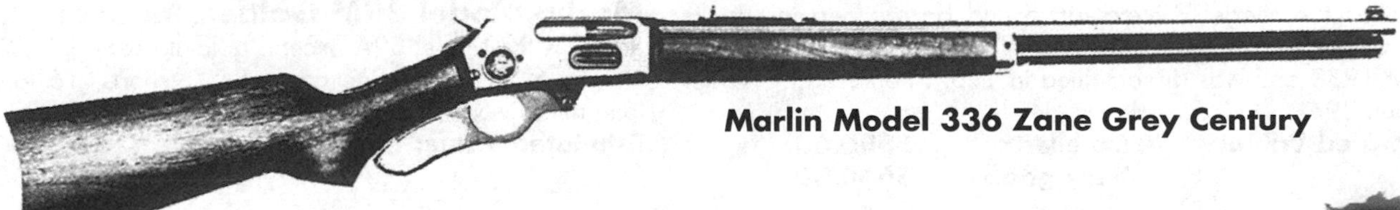

Marlin Model 336 Zane Grey Century

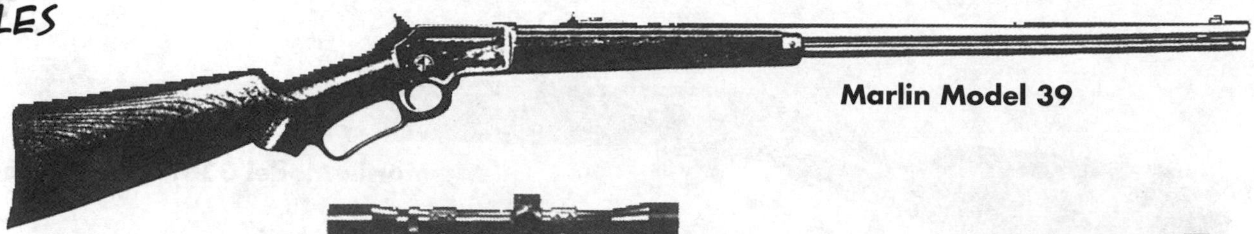

Marlin Model 39

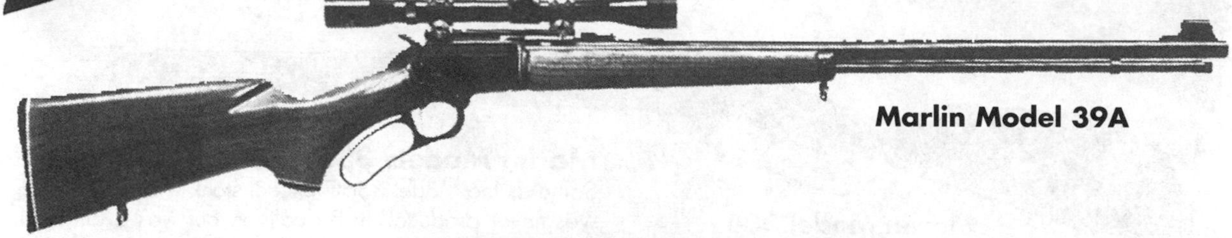

Marlin Model 39A

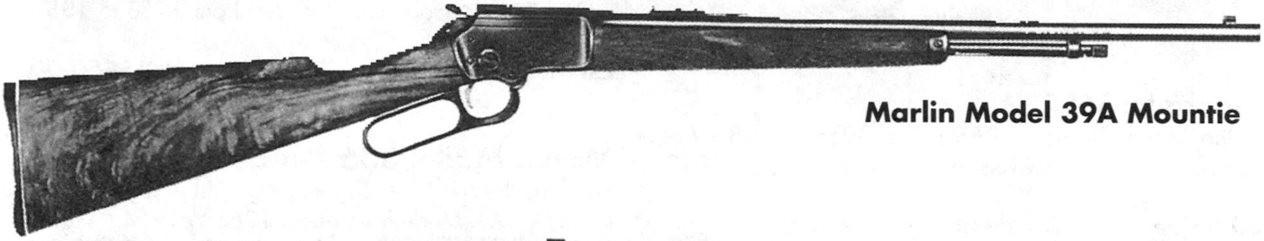

Marlin Model 39A Mountie

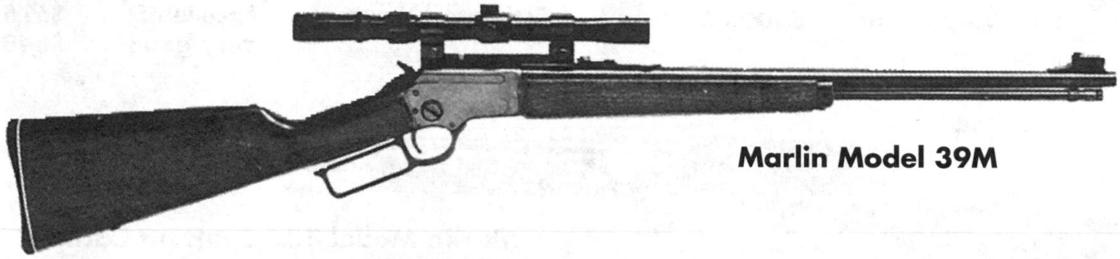

Marlin Model 39M

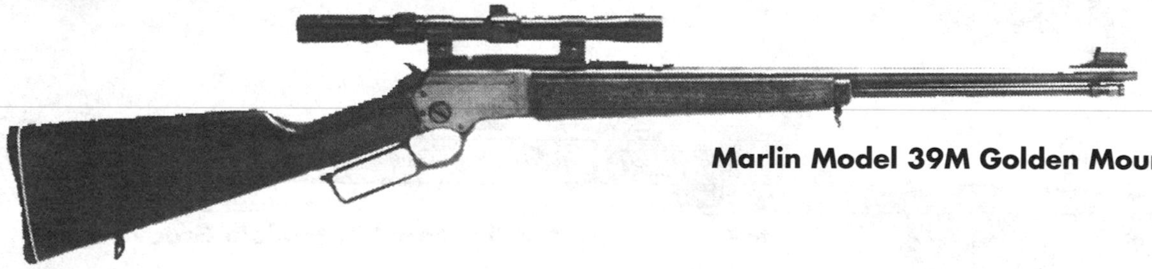

Marlin Model 39M Golden Mountie

Marlin Model 39

Caliber: 22 short, long, long rifle
Action: Lever action; exposed hammer; repeating; takedown-type
Magazine: 25 shorts, 20 longs, 18 long rifles; tubular under barrel
Barrel: 24"; octagon
Sights: Bead front, open adjustable rear
Stock and Forearm: Plain pistol grip stock and forearm
Approximate wt.: 6½ lbs.
Comments: Made from about 1921 to 1937.

Estimated Value:	**Excellent:**	**$1,500.00**
	Very good:	**$1,200.00**

Marlin Model 39A

Same as the Model 39 except: round barrel; heavier stock; semi-beavertail forearm; weighs 6½ lbs. Began production about 1938 and was discontinued in 1957. Replaced by Model Golden 39A.

Estimated Value:	**Excellent:**	**$800.00**
	Very good:	**$640.00**

Marlin Model 39M

Similar to the Model 39A except: 20" barrel; less capacity magazine; straight grip stock.

Estimated Value:	**Excellent:**	**$500.00**
	Very good:	**$400.00**

Marlin Model 39A Mountie

Same as the Model 39 except: straight grip, lighter stock with trim forearm; weighs 6 to 6½ lbs.; 20" barrel; made from the 1950s to 1960.

Estimated Value:	**Excellent:**	**$500.00**
	Very good:	**$400.00**

Marlin Model 39M Golden Mountie

Same as the Model 39A except: gold-plated trigger; 20" barrel; weighs 6 lbs.; magazine capacity 21 shorts, 16 longs, or 15 long rifles. Made from the 1950s to 1988.

Estimated Value:	**Excellent:**	**$600.00**
	Very good:	**$480.00**

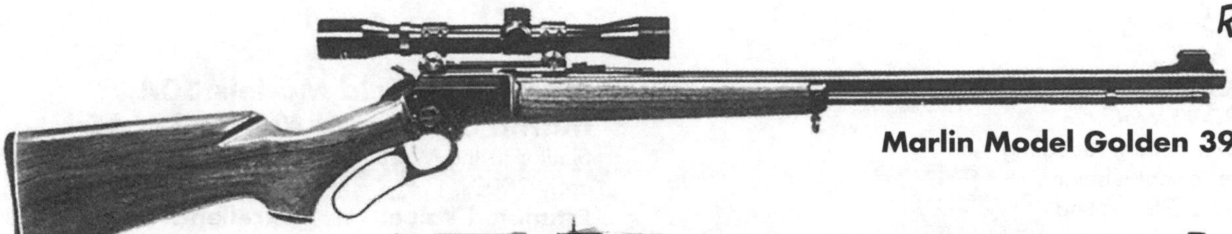

Marlin Model Golden 39A

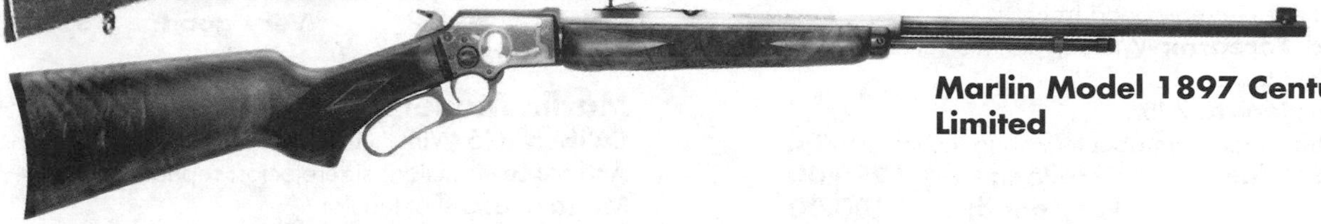

Marlin Model 1897 Century Limited

Marlin Models Golden 39A and 39AS

Caliber: 22 short, long, long rifle
Action: Lever action; exposed hammer; takedown-type; gold-plated trigger; Model 39AS has hammer block safety and rebounding hammer
Magazine: 26 shorts, 21 longs, 19 long rifle; tubular
Barrel: 24"; micro-groove round barrel
Sights: Bead front with removable hood; adjustable folding semi-buckhorn rear
Stock and Forearm: Walnut plain or checkered pistol grip stock and forearm; steel nose cap on forearm tip
Approximate wt.: 6 to 7 lbs.
Comments: Made from about 1958 to the present; sling swivels; hammer block safety added in 1988.

Estimated Value:	**New (retail):**	**$593.00**
	Excellent:	**$445.00**
	Very good:	**$355.00**

Marlin Model 39TDS

Similar to the Model 39AS except: smaller; tubular magazine holds 16 shorts, 12 longs, 11 long rifles; 16½" barrel; weighs 5¼ lbs. Made from 1988 to the mid-1990s. Comes with floatable zippered case; gun can be disassembled and assembled without tools.

Estimated Value:	**Excellent:**	**$375.00**
	Very good:	**$300.00**

Marlin Model 1897 Century Limited

Similar to the Model Golden 39AS except with higher grade of walnut, curved hard rubber butt plate; magazine holds 19 shorts, 15 longs, 13 long rifles; receiver is roll-engraved and selectively gold-plated. Produced in 1997 to commemorate 100 years of Marlin's first quality lever action takedown 22 rifle.

Estimated Value:	**Excellent:**	**$1,000.00**
	Very good:	**$ 800.00**

Marlin Model 1897 Cowboy

Marlin Model 444

Marlin Models 444, 444S, 444SS, and 444P

Caliber: 444 Marlin
Action: Lever action; repeating
Magazine: 5-shot tubular under barrel
Barrel: Blued; 24" or 22"; micro-groove; 18½" ported barrel (Model 444P)
Sights: Folding open rear, hooded ramp front
Stock and Forearm: Monte Carlo or plain, checkered or smooth, straight or pistol grip stock; barrel band; swivels
Approximate wt.: 7½ lbs.
Comments: Made from about 1965 to the present. Currently called Model 444SS and Model 444P; add 2% for Model 444P. Hammer block safety added in 1986.

Estimated Value:	**New (retail):**	**$639.95**
	Excellent:	**$480.00**
	Very good:	**$385.00**

Marlin Model 1897 Cowboy

Similar to the Model Golden 39AS except: tapered octagon barrel, straight grip stock. Introduced in 1999.

Estimated Value:	**Excellent:**	**$525.00**
	Very good:	**$425.00**

Marlin Glenfield Model 30

Caliber: 30-30 Win.
Action: Lever action; repeating
Magazine: 6-shot tubular
Barrel: Blued; 20"; round
Sights: Adjustable rear, bead front
Stock and Forearm: Walnut, plain or checkered; semi-pistol grip stock and forearm
Approximate wt.: 7 lbs.
Comments: Made from about 1966 to the late 1970s.

Estimated Value:	**Excellent:**	**$250.00**
	Very good:	**$200.00**

Marlin Glenfield Model 30GT

Similar to the Model Glenfield 30 with a straight grip stock and 18½" barrel. Made from the late 1970s to the early 1980s.

Estimated Value:	**Excellent:**	**$240.00**
	Very good:	**$195.00**

Marlin Glenfield Models 30A, Marlin 30AS, and Marlin 336AS

Similar to the Model Glenfield 30. Made from the late 1970s to early 2000s.

Estimated Value:	**Excellent:**	**$320.00**
	Very good:	**$255.00**

Marlin Model 375

Caliber: 375 Win.
Action: Lever action; side ejector; repeating
Magazine: 5-shot tubular
Barrel: 20"; round
Sights: Adjustable semi-buckhorn rear, ramp front with brass bead
Stock and Forearm: Plain walnut pistol grip stock and forearm with fluted comb; swivels
Approximate wt.: 6¾" lbs.
Comments: Produced from 1980 to the mid-1980s.

Estimated Value:	**Excellent:**	**$325.00**
	Very good:	**$260.00**

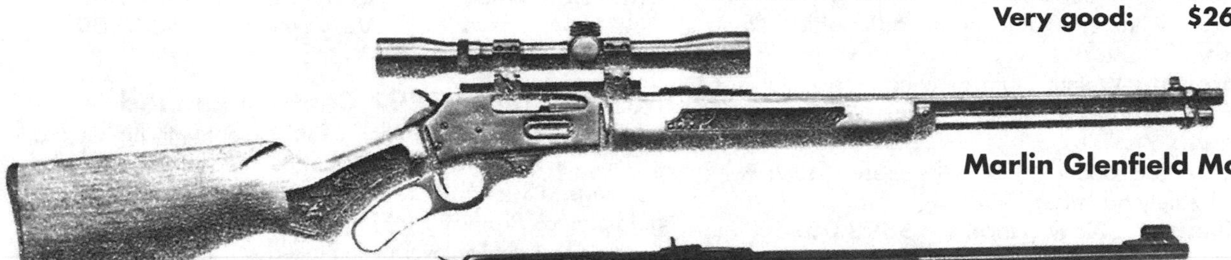

Marlin Glenfield Model 30

Marlin Model 375

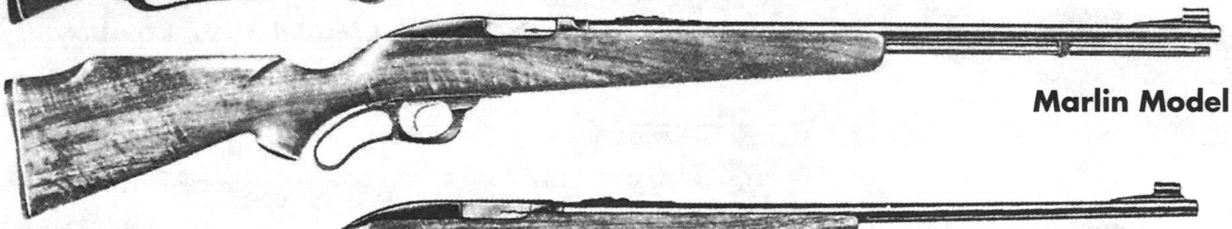

Marlin Model 57

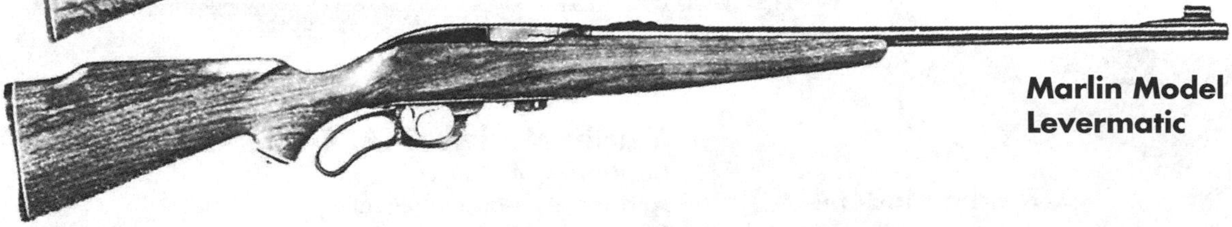

Marlin Model 56 Levermatic

Marlin Model 57

Caliber: 22 short, long, long rifle
Action: Lever action; repeating
Magazine: Tubular under barrel; 19 long rifles, 21 longs, 27 shorts
Barrel: Blued; 22"; round
Sights: Open rear, hooded ramp front
Stock and Forearm: Plain Monte Carlo pistol grip stock and forearm
Approximate wt.: 6¼ lbs.
Comments: Made from about 1959 to 1965.

Estimated Value:	**Excellent:**	**$300.00**
	Very good:	**$240.00**

Marlin Model 56 Levermatic

Caliber: 22 short, long, long rifle
Action: Lever action; repeating
Magazine: 8-shot clip
Barrel: Blued; 22"; round
Sights: Open rear, hooded ramp front
Stock and Forearm: Monte Carlo pistol grip stock and forearm
Approximate wt.: 5¾ lbs.
Comments: Similar to the Model 57, made from about 1955 to 1965.

Estimated Value:	**Excellent:**	**$275.00**
	Very good:	**$225.00**

Marlin Model 57M Levermatic

Caliber: 22 Win. mag.
Action: Lever action; repeating
Magazine: 15-shot tubular; under barrel
Barrel: 24"; round
Sights: Open rear, hooded ramp front
Stock and Forearm: Monte Carlo pistol grip stock and forearm
Approximate wt.: 6¼ lbs.
Comments: Similar to the Model 57; made from about 1960 to 1969.

Estimated Value:	**Excellent:**	**$325.00**
	Very good:	**$260.00**

Marlin Model 62 Levermatic

Caliber: 256 mag. (1963 to 1966); 30 carbine (1966 to 1969)
Action: Lever action; repeating
Magazine: 4-shot clip
Barrel: Blued; 23"; round
Sights: Open rear, hooded ramp front
Stock and Forearm: Monte Carlo pistol grip stock and forearm
Approximate wt.: 7 lbs.
Comments: Made from about 1963 to 1969. Add 10% for mag.

Estimated Value:	**Excellent:**	**$425.00**
	Very good:	**$340.00**

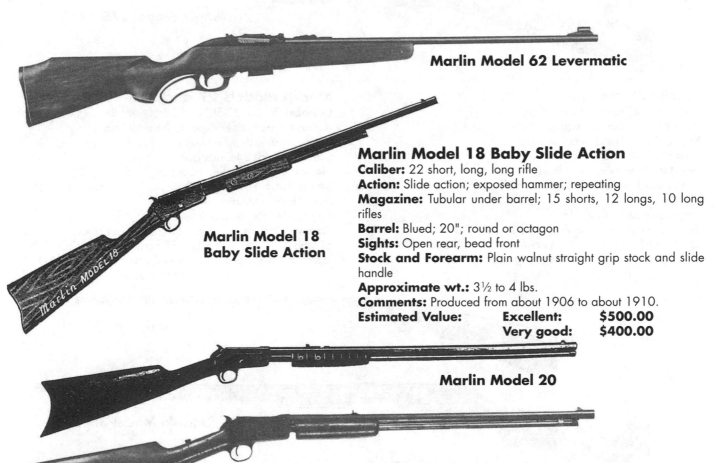

Marlin Model 62 Levermatic

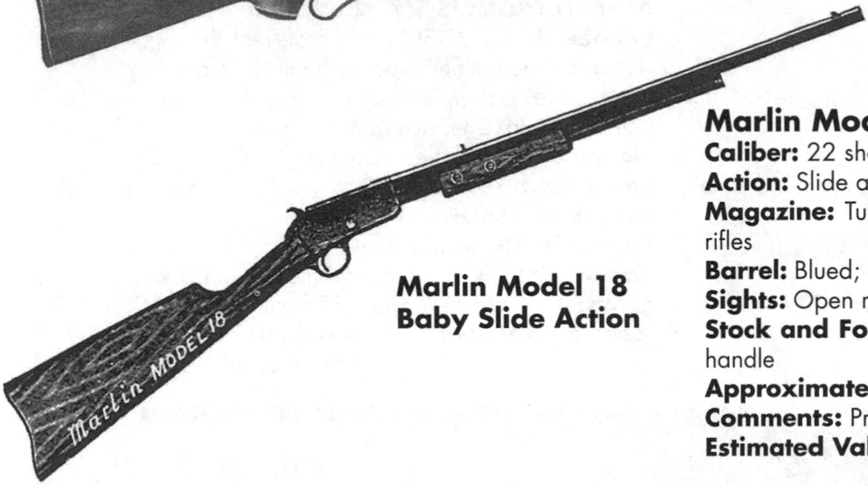

Marlin Model 18 Baby Slide Action

Marlin Model 18 Baby Slide Action

Caliber: 22 short, long, long rifle
Action: Slide action; exposed hammer; repeating
Magazine: Tubular under barrel; 15 shorts, 12 longs, 10 long rifles
Barrel: Blued; 20"; round or octagon
Sights: Open rear, bead front
Stock and Forearm: Plain walnut straight grip stock and slide handle
Approximate wt.: 3½ to 4 lbs.
Comments: Produced from about 1906 to about 1910.

Estimated Value:	**Excellent:**	**$500.00**
	Very good:	**$400.00**

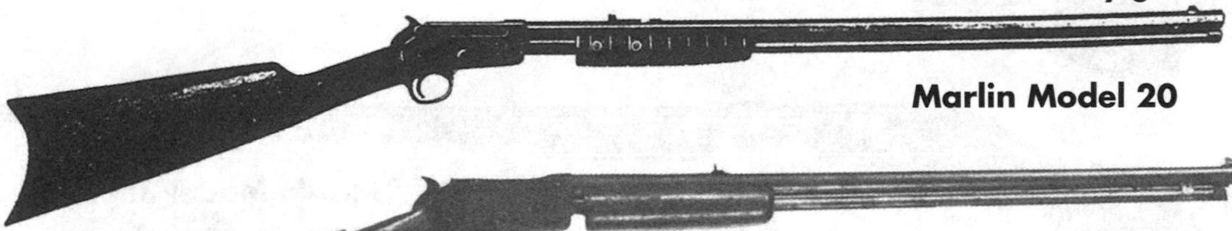

Marlin Model 20

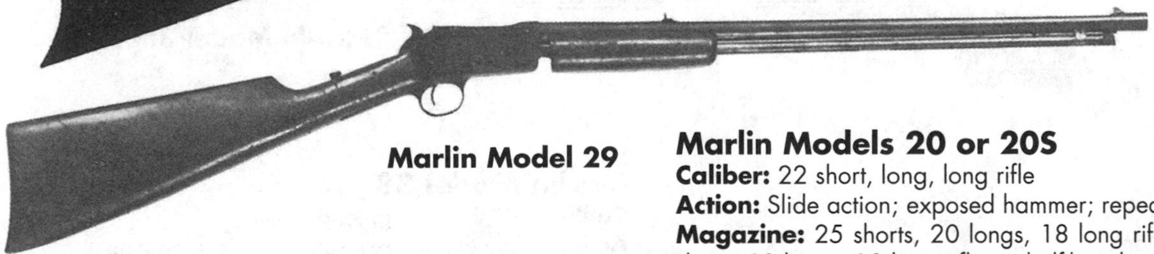

Marlin Model 29

Marlin Model 29

Similar to the Model 20 except: 23" round barrel and smooth slide handle. Made from about 1913 to 1916.

Estimated Value:	**Excellent:**	**$450.00**
	Very good:	**$360.00**

Marlin Models 20 or 20S

Caliber: 22 short, long, long rifle
Action: Slide action; exposed hammer; repeating
Magazine: 25 shorts, 20 longs, 18 long rifles in full length; 15 shorts, 12 longs, 10 long rifles in half-length; tubular, under barrel
Barrel: Blued; 24"; octagon
Sights: Open rear, bead front
Stock and Forearm: Plain walnut straight grip stock and grooved slide handle
Approximate wt.: 5 lbs.
Comments: Produced from about 1907 to 1920 as Model 20 and as Model 20S until discontinued about 1922.

Estimated Value:	**Excellent:**	**$475.00**
	Very good:	**$380.00**

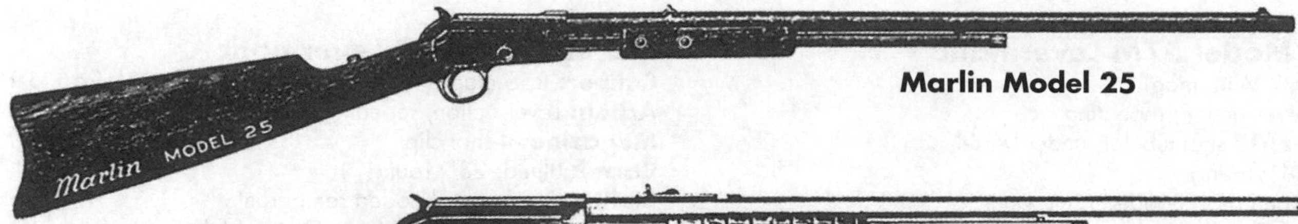

Marlin Model 25

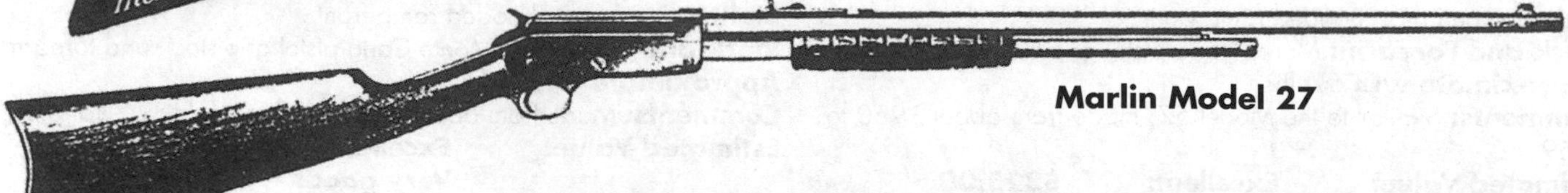

Marlin Model 27

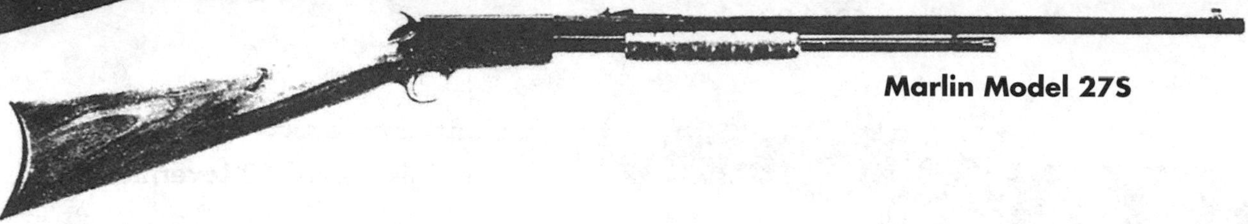

Marlin Model 27S

Marlin Model 25

Caliber: 22 short and 22 CB caps only
Action: Slide action; exposed hammer; repeating
Magazine: 15-shot tubular, under barrel
Barrel: Blued; 23"; octagon
Sights: Open rear, bead front
Stock and Forearm: Plain walnut straight grip stock and slide handle
Approximate wt.: 4 lbs.
Comments: Made for about one year in 1909.

Estimated Value:	**Excellent:**	**$650.00**
	Very good:	**$520.00**

Marlin Models 27 and 27S

Caliber: 25-20, 32-30, and 25 Stevens RF
Action: Slide action; exposed hammer; repeating
Magazine: 6-shot, 2/3 tubular
Barrel: Blued; 24"; octagon
Sights: Open rear, bead front
Stock and Forearm: Plain walnut straight grip stock and grooved slide handle
Approximate wt.: 5¾ lbs.
Comments: Takedown model made from about 1910 to 1915 as Model 27 and as Model 27S from 1920 to 1932.

Estimated Value:	**Excellent:**	**$650.00**
	Very good:	**$520.00**

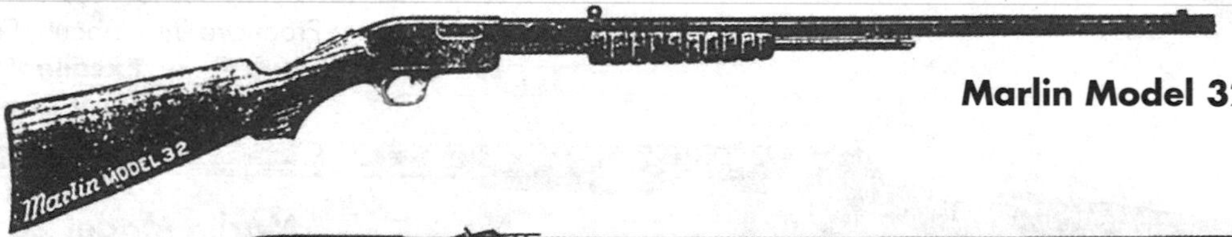

Marlin Model 32

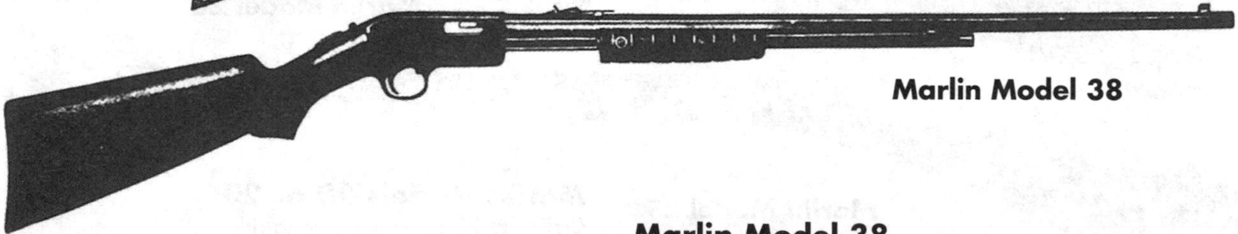

Marlin Model 38

Marlin Model 32

Caliber: 22 short, long, long rifle
Action: Slide action; concealed hammer; repeating
Magazine: 25 shorts, 20 longs, 18 long rifles in full length; 15 shorts, 12 longs, 10 long rifles in 2/3 length; tubular, under barrel
Barrel: Blued; 24"; octagon
Sights: Open rear, bead front
Stock and Forearm: Walnut pistol grip stock and grooved slide handle
Approximate wt.: 5½ lbs.
Comments: Takedown model made around 1914 for about one year.

Estimated Value:	**Excellent:**	**$600.00**
	Very good:	**$480.00**

Marlin Model 38

Caliber: 22 short, long, long rifle
Action: Slide action; exposed hammer; repeating
Magazine: 15 shorts, 12 longs, 10 long rifles, 2/3 tubular, under barrel
Barrel: Blued; 24"; octagon or round
Sights: Open rear, bead front
Stock and Forearm: Plain pistol grip stock and grooved slide handle
Approximate wt.: 5½ lbs.
Comments: Takedown model; made from about 1921 to about 1930.

Estimated Value:	**Excellent:**	**$450.00**
	Very good:	**$360.00**

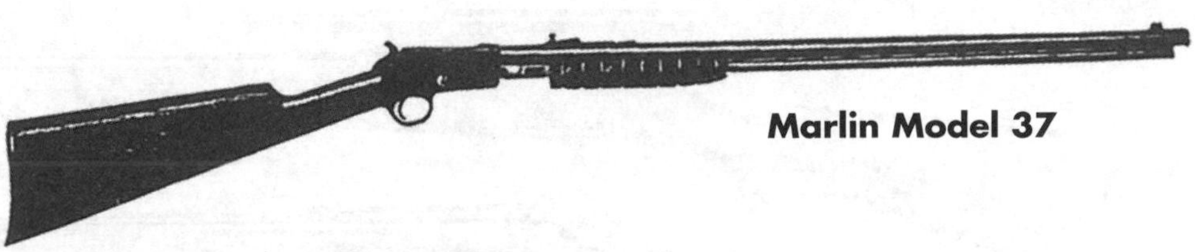

Marlin Model 37

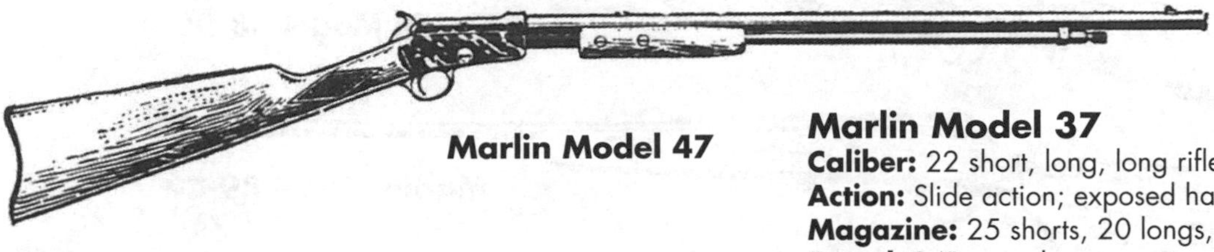

Marlin Model 47

Marlin Model 47

Basically the same as Model 37, used as a bonus giveaway with purchase of Marlin stocks. Discontinued in 1931 after six years of production.

Estimated Value: **Excellent:** **$700.00**
Very good: **$560.00**

Marlin Model 37

Caliber: 22 short, long, long rifle
Action: Slide action; exposed hammer; repeating
Magazine: 25 shorts, 20 longs, 18 long rifles; tubular
Barrel: 24"; round
Sights: Open rear, bead front
Stock and Forearm: Walnut pistol grip stock and forearm
Approximate wt.: 5 lbs.
Comments: Takedown model; made from about 1923 to 1933.
Estimated Value: **Excellent:** **$450.00**
Very good: **$360.00**

Marlin Model 50

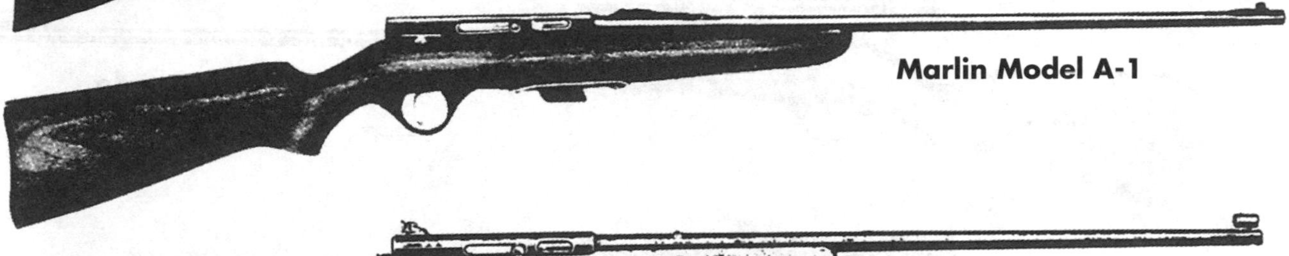

Marlin Model A-1

Marlin Model A-1E

Marlin Models 50 and 50E

Caliber: 22 long rifle
Action: Semiautomatic; takedown model; side ejector
Magazine: 6-shot detachable box
Barrel: Blued; 24"; round
Sights: Open rear, bead front; peep sights on Model 50E
Stock and Forearm: Plain one-piece pistol grip stock and finger grooved forearm
Approximate wt.: 6 lbs.
Comments: Production started about 1931 and stopped about three years later.
Estimated Value: **Excellent:** **$150.00**
Very good: **$120.00**

Marlin Models A-1 and A-1E

Caliber: 22 long rifle
Action: Semiautomatic; side ejector
Magazine: 6-shot detachable box
Barrel: Blued; 24"
Sights: Open rear, bead front; peep sights on Model A-1E
Stock and Forearm: Plain pistol grip stock and forearm
Approximate wt.: 6 lbs.
Comments: Takedown model made from about 1935 to 1946.
Estimated Value: **Excellent:** **$130.00**
Very good: **$105.00**

Marlin Model A-1C and A-1DL

An improved Model A-1; semi-beavertail forearm. Made from about 1940 for six years. Peep sights and swivels on A-1DL.
Estimated Value: **Excellent:** **$150.00**
Very good: **$120.00**

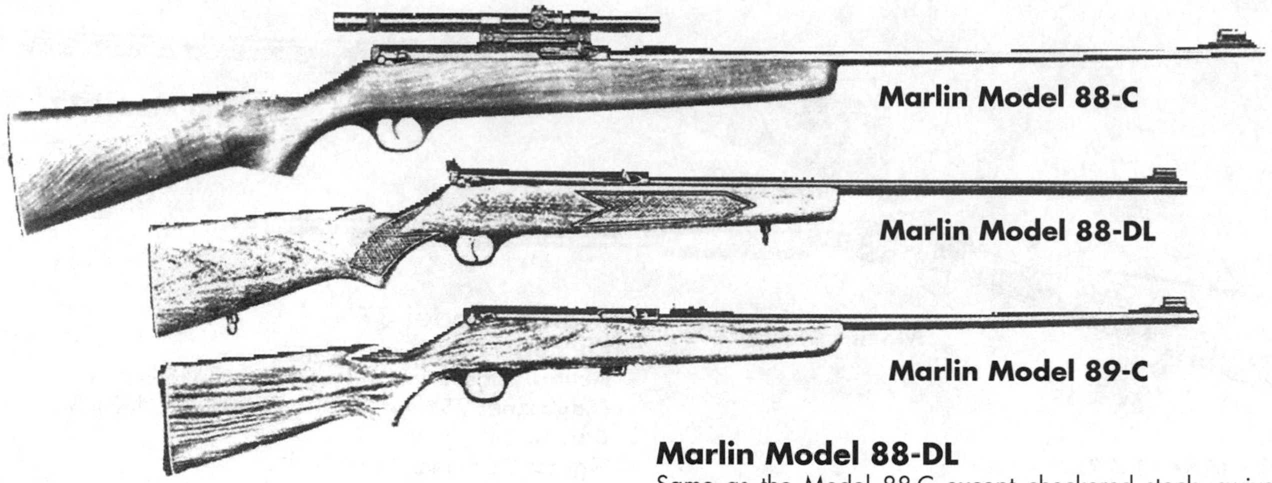

Marlin Model 88-C

Marlin Model 88-DL

Marlin Model 89-C

Marlin Model 88-C

Caliber: 22 long rifle
Action: Semiautomatic; side ejector
Magazine: 14-shot tubular, in stock
Barrel: Blued; 24"; round
Sights: Open rear, hooded front
Stock and Forearm: Pistol grip stock and forearm
Approximate wt.: 6¾ lbs.
Comments: A takedown model produced from about 1947 to 1956.

Estimated Value:	**Excellent:**	**$150.00**
	Very good:	**$120.00**

Marlin Model 88-DL

Same as the Model 88-C except checkered stock, swivels and peep sight on receiver. Produced for three years beginning about 1953.

Estimated Value:	**Excellent:**	**$165.00**
	Very good:	**$135.00**

Marlin Models 89-C and 89-DL

Same as the Model 88-C except magazine is 7- or 12-shot clip and it has a tapered forearm. Produced from about 1950 to 1961. Model 89-DL has swivels and peep sights.

Estimated Value:	**Excellent:**	**$140.00**
	Very good:	**$110.00**

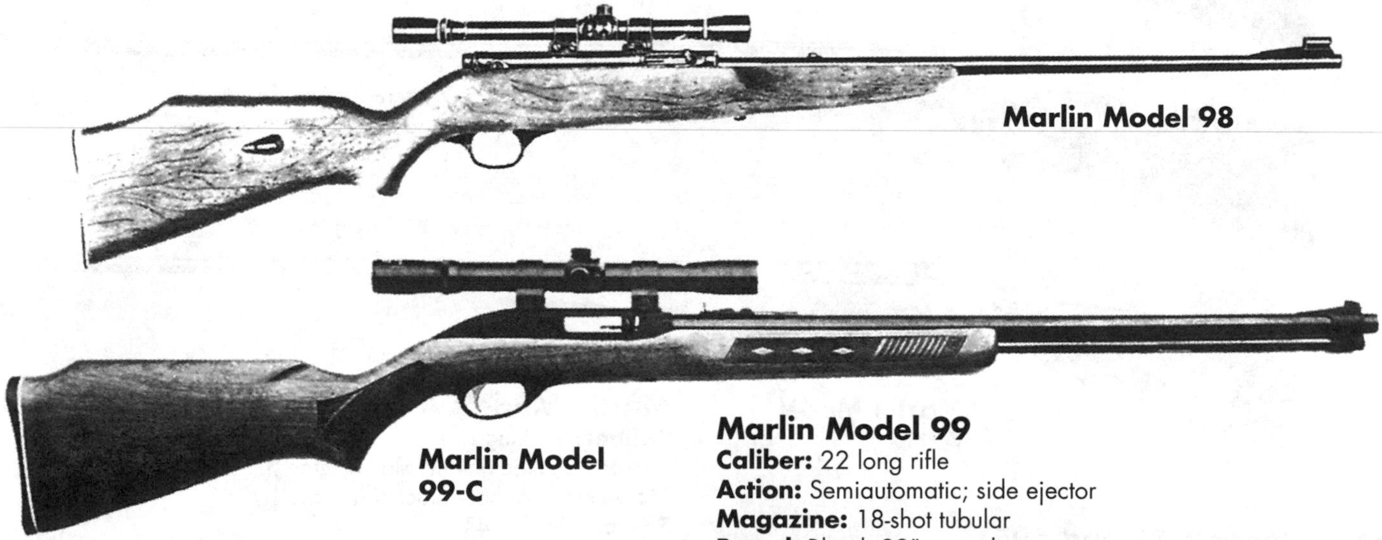

Marlin Model 98

Marlin Model 99-C

Marlin Model 98

Caliber: 22 long rifle
Action: Semiautomatic; side ejector
Magazine: 15-shot tubular
Barrel: Blued; 22"; round
Sights: Open rear, hooded ramp front
Stock and Forearm: Walnut Monte Carlo with cheekpiece
Approximate wt.: 6¾ lbs.
Comments: Produced from about 1957 to 1959. Replaced by Model 99.

Estimated Value:	**Excellent:**	**$135.00**
	Very good:	**$110.00**

Marlin Model 99

Caliber: 22 long rifle
Action: Semiautomatic; side ejector
Magazine: 18-shot tubular
Barrel: Blued; 22"; round
Sights: Open rear, hooded ramp front
Stock and Forearm: Plain pistol grip stock and forearm
Approximate wt.: 5½ lbs.
Comments: Made from about 1959 until 1961.

Estimated Value:	**Excellent:**	**$125.00**
	Very good:	**$100.00**

Marlin Model 99-C

Same as the Model 99 except Monte Carlo stock (some are checkered); gold-plated trigger; grooved receiver. Made from 1962 to the late 1970s.

Estimated Value:	**Excellent:**	**$130.00**
	Very good:	**$105.00**

Marlin Model 99DL

Marlin Model 99G

Marlin Model 99DL

Same as the Model 99C except: swivels and jeweled breech bolt. Made for five years beginning about 1960.

Estimated Value: **Excellent:** **$125.00**
Very good: **$100.00**

Marlin Glenfield Model 99G

Basically the same as the Model 99 with a plain stock. Made from about 1963 to 1965.

Estimated Value: **Excellent:** **$100.00**
Very good: **$ 80.00**

Marlin Model 989

Marlin Glenfield Model 989G

Marlin Glenfield Model 989G

Basically the same as the Marlin Model 989 except plain stock and bead front sight. Made from about 1962 to 1964.

Estimated Value: **Excellent:** **$130.00**
Very good: **$105.00**

Marlin Model 989

Caliber: 22 long rifle only
Action: Semiautomatic; side ejector
Magazine: 7-shot clip
Barrel: Blued; 22"; round
Sights: Open rear, hooded ramp front
Stock and Forearm: Monte Carlo pistol grip stock and forearm
Approximate wt.: 5½ lbs.
Comments: Produced for four years beginning in 1962.
Estimated Value: **Excellent:** **$140.00**
Very good: **$115.00**

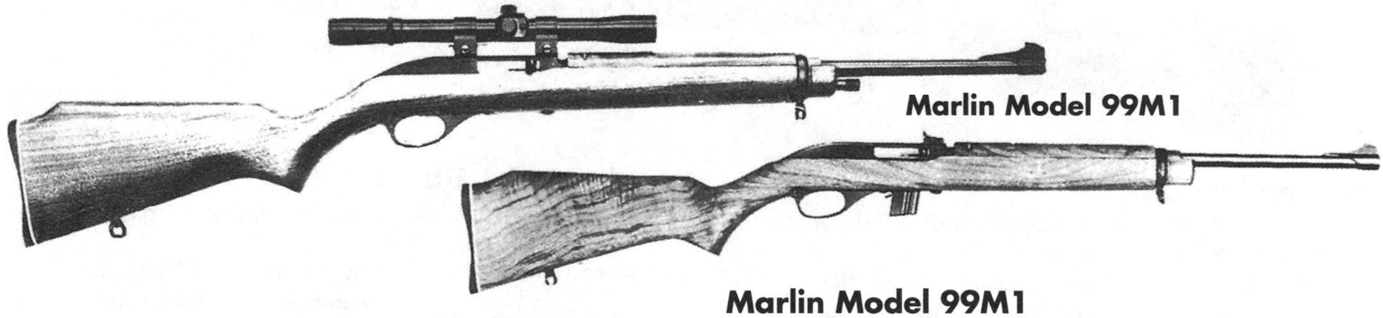

Marlin Model 99M1

Marlin Model 989M2

Marlin Model 922M

Caliber: 22 Win. magnum rim fire
Action: Semiautomatic; "last shot" bolt hold open; aluminum alloy receiver
Magazine: 7-shot clip
Barrel: Blued; 20½"; micro-groove rifling
Sights: Adjustable folding rear; ramp front with removable hood
Stock and Forearm: Checkered walnut Monte Carlo pistol grip stock and forearm; butt pad and swivel studs
Approximate wt.: 6½ lbs.
Comments: Introduced in 1993.
Estimated Value: **Excellent:** **$335.00**
Very good: **$265.00**

Marlin Model 99M1

Caliber: 22 long rifle
Action: Semiautomatic; side ejector
Magazine: 9-shot tubular
Barrel: Blued; 18"; micro-groove
Sights: Open rear, ramp front (military)
Stock and Forearm: Carbine stock, hand guard and barrel band; swivels
Approximate wt.: 4½ lbs.
Comments: Styled after the U.S. 30 M1 Carbine; in production from about 1966 to the late 1970s.
Estimated Value: **Excellent:** **$160.00**
Very good: **$130.00**

Marlin Model 989M2

Same as the Model 99M1 except: 7-shot clip magazine.

Estimated Value: **Excellent:** **$130.00**
Very good: **$105.00**

Marlin Model 60

Marlin Model 70P Papoose

Marlin Models 70P and 70PSS Papoose

Caliber: 22 long rifle
Action: Semiautomatic; side ejector
Magazine: 7-shot clip
Barrel: 16¼" quick takedown; 70PSS stainless steel
Sights: Adjustable rear, ramp front; 4X scope included
Stock and Forearm: Smooth walnut-finish hardwood, semi-pistol grip stock with abbreviated forearm; black fiberglass-filled synthetic stock on Model 70PSS
Approximate wt.: 3¼ lbs.
Comments: Made from 1986 to the mid-1990s as Model 70P, then changed to Model 70PSS with stainless steel barrel and bolt. A quick takedown rifle with built-in flotation case included. Prices are for Model 70PSS.

Estimated Value:	**New (retail):**	**$299.00**
	Excellent:	**$225.00**
	Very good:	**$180.00**

Marlin Models 60 and 60SS

Caliber: 22 long rifle
Action: Semiautomatic; side ejector
Magazine: 17-shot tubular; reduced to 14-shot in 1992
Barrel: Blued or stainless steel (60SS); 22"; round
Sights: Open rear, ramp front
Stock and Forearm: Checkered or smooth hardwood semi-pistol grip stock and forearm; or Monte Carlo stock; gray/black laminated stock on Model 60SS
Approximate wt.: 5½ lbs.
Comments: Made from about 1960 to the present. Add 50% for stainless steel (Model 60SS) barrel, bolt and outer magazine tube.

Estimated Value:	**New (retail):**	**$185.00**
	Excellent:	**$135.00**
	Very good:	**$110.00**

Marlin Model 75C

Same as the Model 60 except: 13-shot magazine, 18" barrel. Discontinued in 1990.

Estimated Value:	**Excellent:**	**$125.00**
	Very good:	**$100.00**

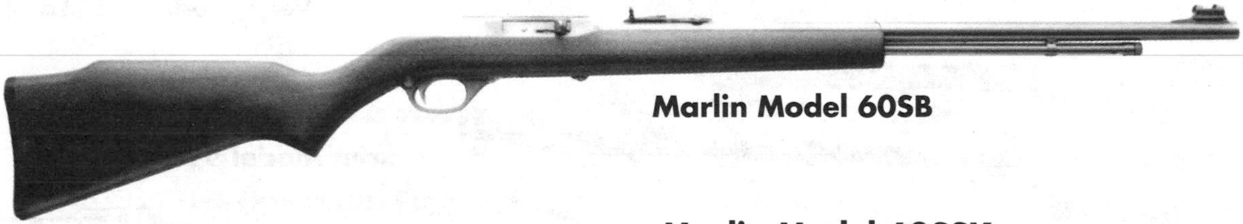

Marlin Model 60SB

Marlin Model 60SB

Similar to the Model 60SS except with walnut-finished Maine birch stock and forearm. Introduced in 1998.

Estimated Value:	**New (retail):**	**$235.00**
	Excellent:	**$175.00**
	Very good:	**$140.00**

Marlin Model 60SSK

Similar to the Model 60SS except with black fiberglass-filled synthetic Monte Carlo stock. Introduced in 1998.

Estimated Value:	**New (retail):**	**$250.00**
	Excellent:	**$185.00**
	Very good:	**$150.00**

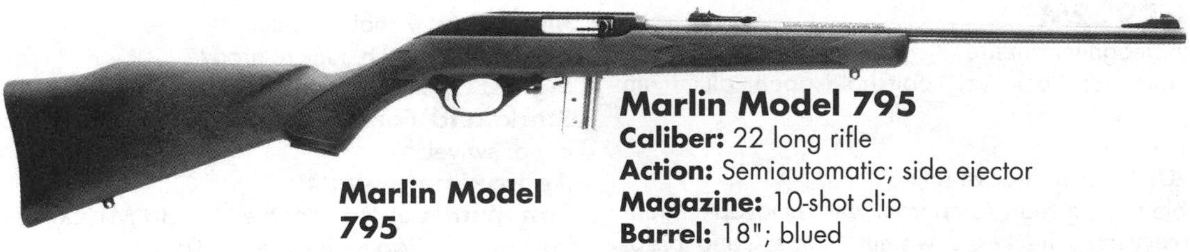

Marlin Model 795

Marlin Model 7000

Similar to the Model 795 except with 18" heavy target barrel, lipped forearm, and no sights. Introduced in 1997.

Estimated Value:	**Excellent:**	**$185.00**
	Very good:	**$145.00**

Marlin Model 795

Caliber: 22 long rifle
Action: Semiautomatic; side ejector
Magazine: 10-shot clip
Barrel: 18"; blued
Sights: Ramp front with brass bead, adjustable open rear
Stock and Forearm: Monte Carlo, one-piece checkered black fiberglass-filled synthetic stock and forearm; swivels
Approximate wt.: 5 lbs.
Comments: Introduced in 1997. Add 30% for stainless steel.

Estimated Value:	**New (retail):**	**$175.00**
	Excellent:	**$130.00**
	Very good:	**$105.00**

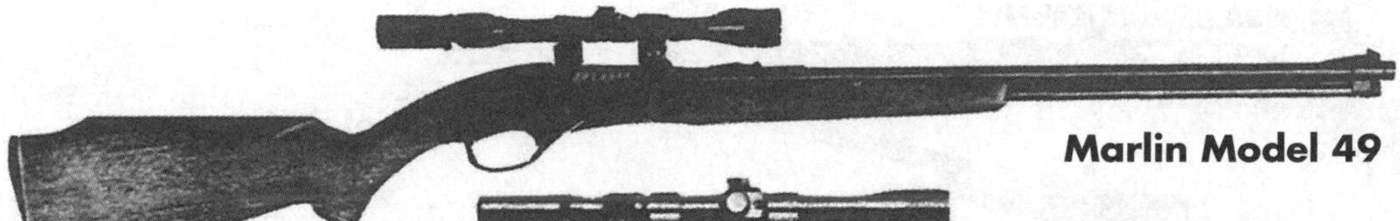

Marlin Model 49

Marlin Model 49DL

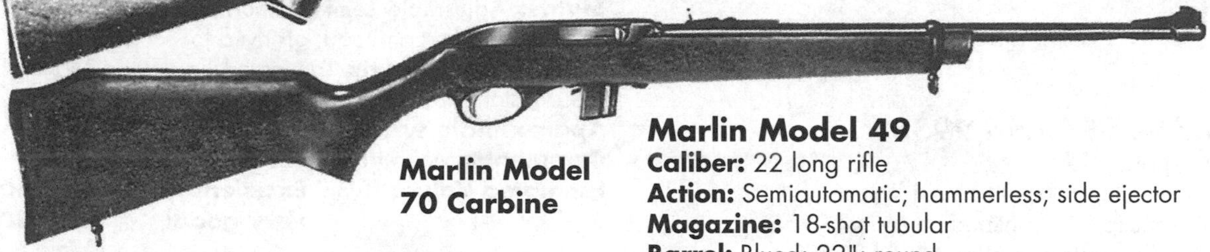

Marlin Model 70 Carbine

Marlin Models 70 Carbine and 70HC

Caliber: 22 long rifle
Action: Semiautomatic; hammerless; side ejector
Magazine: 7-shot clip; 70HC has 5-, 15-, or 25-shot clip
Barrel: Blued; 18"; round; micro-groove
Sights: Open rear, ramp front
Stock and Forearm: Walnut Monte Carlo one-piece stock and forearm; barrel band; swivels
Approximate wt.: 5½ lbs.
Comments: Model 70 was made from 1966 to 1990; Model 70HC was made from 1988 to the mid-1990s.

Estimated Value:	**Excellent:**	**$145.00**
	Very good:	**$115.00**

Marlin Model 49

Caliber: 22 long rifle
Action: Semiautomatic; hammerless; side ejector
Magazine: 18-shot tubular
Barrel: Blued; 22"; round
Sights: Adjustable open rear, ramp front
Stock and Forearm: Monte Carlo plain two-piece pistol grip stock and forearm
Approximate wt.: 5½ lbs.
Comments: Made from the late 1960s to the mid-1970s.

Estimated Value:	**Excellent:**	**$140.00**
	Very good:	**$110.00**

Marlin Model 49DL

Same as the Model 49 except: checkered stock and forearm; gold-plated trigger. Made from about 1971 to the late 1970s.

Estimated Value:	**Excellent:**	**$150.00**
	Very good:	**$120.00**

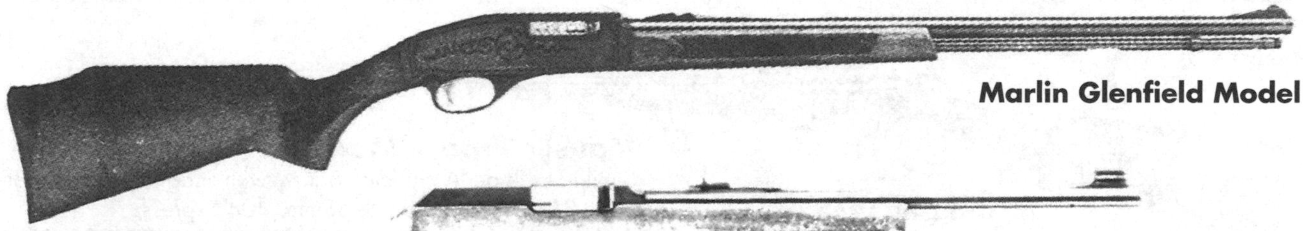

Marlin Glenfield Model 40

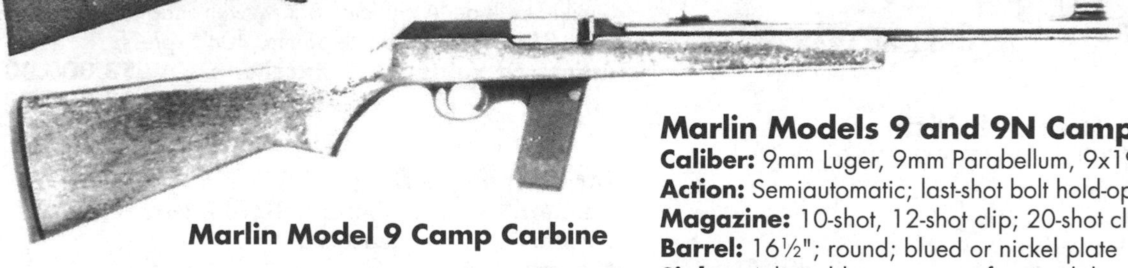

Marlin Model 9 Camp Carbine

Marlin Glenfield Model 40

Caliber: 22 long rifle
Action: Semiautomatic; hammerless; side ejector
Magazine: 18-shot tubular
Barrel: 22"
Sights: Adjustable open rear, ramp front
Stock and Forearm: Checkered hardwood Monte Carlo semi-pistol grip stock and forearm
Approximate wt.: 5½ lbs.
Comments: Made in the late 1970s.

Estimated Value:	**Excellent:**	**$130.00**
	Very good:	**$105.00**

Marlin Models 9 and 9N Camp Carbine

Caliber: 9mm Luger, 9mm Parabellum, 9x19
Action: Semiautomatic; last-shot bolt hold-open
Magazine: 10-shot, 12-shot clip; 20-shot clip available
Barrel: 16½"; round; blued or nickel plate
Sights: Adjustable rear, ramp front with brass bead
Stock and Forearm: Walnut finished hardwood pistol grip stock and forearm; rubber butt pad
Approximate wt.: 6¾ lbs.
Comments: Made from 1985 to the late 1990s. Nickel-plated (Model 9N) model discontinued in the mid-1990s.

Estimated Value:	**Excellent:**	**$300.00**
	Very good:	**$240.00**

Marlin Model 45

Similar to the Model 9 except: 45ACP caliber; 7-shot clip. Made from 1986 to the late 1990s.

Estimated Value:	**Excellent:**	**$300.00**
	Very good:	**$240.00**

Marlin Model 990

Marlin Model 995

Marlin Models 995 and 995SS

Caliber: 22 long rifle
Action: Semiautomatic; last shot bolt hold-open
Magazine: 7-shot clip; nickel plated on Model 995SS
Barrel: 18"; blued; stainless steel on Model 995SS
Sights: Ramp front sight with orange post and cut-away wide-scan hood; adjustable open rear
Stock and Forearm: Checkered walnut finish Monte Carlo, one-piece pistol grip stock and forearm (Model 995); black fiber-glass-filled synthetic Monte Carlo, one-piece pistol grip stock and forearm on Model 995SS with molded checkering
Approximate wt.: 5 lbs.
Comments: Model 995 discontinued in the mid-1990s and Model 995SS produced in the late 1990s. Prices are for Model 995SS; deduct 10% for blued model (Model 995).
Estimated Value: **Excellent:** **$185.00**
Very good: **$150.00**

Marlin Model 990L

Caliber: 22 long rifle
Action: Semiautomatic; last-shot bolt hold-open
Magazine: 14-shot tubular
Barrel: 22"; round with Micro-groove rifling
Sights: Adjustable semi-buckhorn rear, ramp front with brass bead and wide-scan hood; grooved for scope
Stock and Forearm: Laminated hardwood Monte Carlo one-piece pistol grip stock and forearm
Approximate wt.: 5½ lbs.
Comments: Made from 1992 to the mid-1990s.
Estimated Value: **Excellent:** **$175.00**
Very good: **$140.00**

Marlin Model 990

Caliber: 22 long rifle
Action: Semiautomatic; side ejector
Magazine: 18-shot tubular
Barrel: 22"; round
Sights: Adjustable folding semi-buckhorn rear, ramp front with brass bead
Stock and Forearm: Checkered walnut Monte Carlo one-piece pistol grip stock and forearm
Approximate wt.: 5½ lbs.
Comments: Made from the late 1970s to 1988.
Estimated Value: **Excellent:** **$160.00**
Very good: **$130.00**

MAUSER

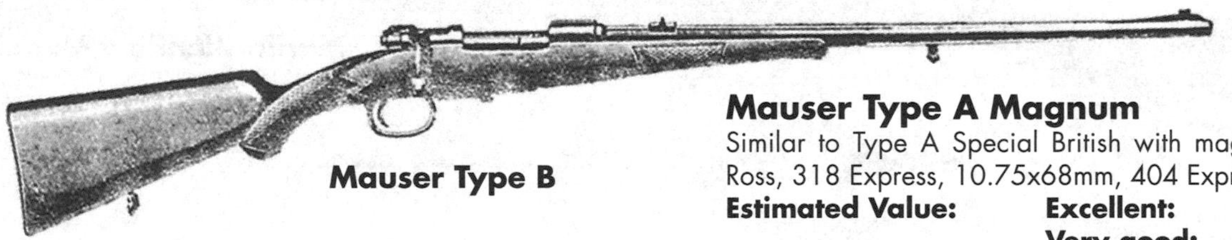

Mauser Type B

Mauser Type A Special British

Caliber: 30-06, 7x57, 8x60, 9x57, 9.3x62mm
Action: Bolt action; repeating
Magazine: 5-shot box
Barrel: Blued; 23½"; octagon or round
Sights: Express rear, hooded ramp front
Stock and Forearm: Checkered walnut one-piece pistol grip stock and tapered forearm; swivels
Approximate wt.: 7¼ lbs.
Comments: Made from about 1910 to 1938.
Estimated Value: **Excellent:** **$2,700.00**
Very good: **$2,160.00**

Mauser Type A Short Model

Similar to Type A Special British with 21½" barrel and a short action. 65x54, 8x51 and 250-3000 cal.
Estimated Value: **Excellent:** **$2,500.00**
Very good: **$2,000.00**

Mauser Type A Magnum

Similar to Type A Special British with magnum action for 280 Ross, 318 Express, 10.75x68mm, 404 Express.
Estimated Value: **Excellent:** **$3,000.00**
Very good: **$2,400.00**

Mauser Type B

Caliber: 30-06, 7x57, 8x57, 8x60, 9.3x62, 10.75x68
Action: Bolt action; repeating
Magazine: 5-shot box
Barrel: Blued; 23½"
Sights: Leaf rear, ramp front
Stock and Forearm: Checkered walnut one-piece pistol grip stock and lipped forearm; swivels
Approximate wt.: 7½ lbs.
Comments: Made from about 1910 to 1940.
Estimated Value: **Excellent:** **$2,200.00**
Very good: **$1,750.00**

Mauser Type K

Similar to Type B with 21½" barrel and short action.
Estimated Value: **Excellent:** **$3,500.00**
Very good: **$2,800.00**

Mauser Model 98

Mauser Type M

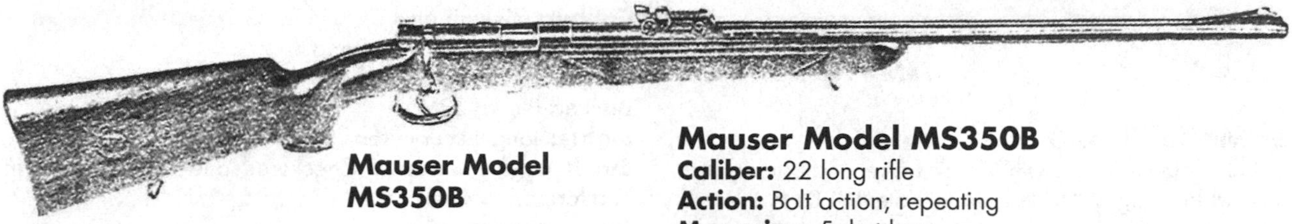

Mauser Model MS350B

Mauser Model 98

Caliber: 7mm, 7.9mm
Action: Bolt action; repeating
Magazine: 5-shot box
Barrel: Blued; 23½"
Sights: Adjustable rear, blade front
Stock and Forearm: Walnut one-piece semi-pistol grip stock and fluted forearm; barrel band
Approximate wt.: 7½ lbs.
Comments: Made from about 1920 to 1938.
Estimated Value: **Excellent:** **$750.00**
Very good: **$600.00**

Mauser Type M

Caliber: 30-06, 6.5x54, 7x57, 8x52, 8x60, 9x57
Action: Bolt action; repeating
Magazine: 5-shot box
Barrel: Blued; 19¾"
Sights: 3 leaf rear, ramp front
Stock and Forearm: Checkered walnut one-piece pistol grip stock and full-length forearm; swivels
Approximate wt.: 6½ lbs.
Comments: Made from about 1910 to 1940.
Estimated Value: **Excellent:** **$2,500.00**
Very good: **$2,000.00**

Mauser Type S

Caliber: 6.5x54, 7x57, 8x51, 8x60, 9x57
Action: Bolt action; repeating
Magazine: 5-shot box
Barrel: Blued; 19¾"
Sights: 3 leaf rear, ramp front
Stock and Forearm: Checkered walnut one-piece pistol grip stock and lipped full-length forearm; swivels
Approximate wt.: 6½ lbs.
Comments: Made from about 1910 to 1940.
Estimated Value: **Excellent:** **$2,500.00**
Very good: **$2,000.00**

Mauser Model MS350B

Caliber: 22 long rifle
Action: Bolt action; repeating
Magazine: 5-shot box
Barrel: Blued; 27½"
Sights: Micrometer rear, ramp front
Stock and Forearm: Match-type; checkered pistol grip; swivels
Approximate wt.: 8 lbs.
Comments: Made from the mid-1920s to the mid-1930s.
Estimated Value: **Excellent:** **$700.00**
Very good: **$560.00**

Mauser Model ES350

Similar to the Model MS350B with different sights and 26¾" barrel. Made from the mid- to the late 1930s. Single-shot.
Estimated Value: **Excellent:** **$550.00**
Very good: **$440.00**

Mauser Model ES350B

Similar to the Model MS350B in single-shot. Target sights.
Estimated Value: **Excellent:** **$475.00**
Very good: **$380.00**

Mauser Model ES340

Caliber: 22 long rifle
Action: Bolt action; single-shot
Magazine: None
Barrel: Blued; 25½"
Sights: Tangent curve rear, ramp front
Stock and Forearm: Checkered walnut one-piece pistol grip stock and forearm; swivels
Approximate wt.: 6½ lbs.
Comments: Made from the early 1920s to the mid-1930s.
Estimated Value: **Excellent:** **$400.00**
Very good: **$320.00**

Mauser Model ES340B

Similar to the Model ES340 with a 26¾" barrel. Made from the mid- to the late 1930s.
Estimated Value: **Excellent:** **$400.00**
Very good: **$320.00**

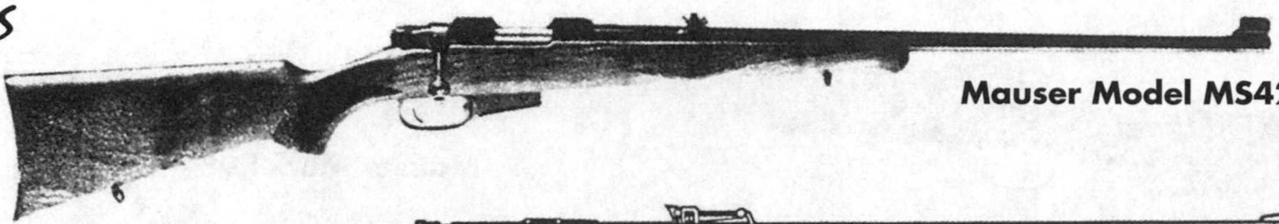

Mauser Model MS420

Mauser Model MS420B

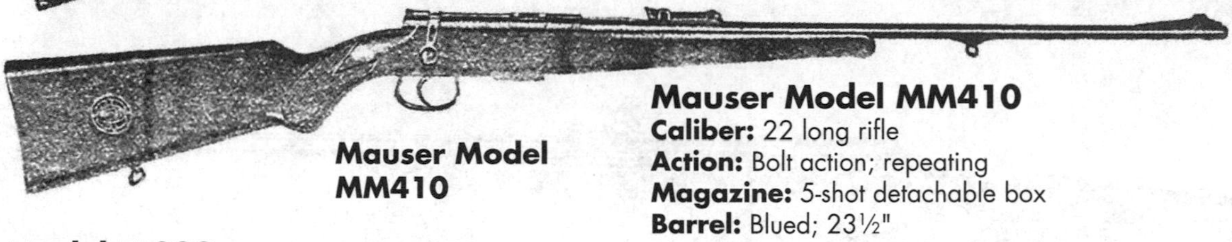

Mauser Model MM410

Mauser Model EL320

Similar to the Model ES340 with 23½" barrel, adjustable rear sight and bead front sight. Made from the late 1920s to the mid-1930s.

Estimated Value: **Excellent:** **$400.00**
Very good: **$320.00**

Mauser Model MS420

Caliber: 22 long rifle
Action: Bolt action; repeating
Magazine: 5-shot detachable box
Barrel: Blued; 25½"
Sights: Tangent curve rear, ramp front
Stock and Forearm: Checkered walnut one-piece pistol grip stock and forearm; swivels
Approximate wt.: 6½ lbs.
Comments: Made from the mid-1920s to the mid-1930s.
Estimated Value: **Excellent:** **$750.00**
Very good: **$600.00**

Mauser Model MS420B

Similar to the Model MS420 with better wood. Made from the mid- to the late 1930s.

Estimated Value: **Excellent:** **$650.00**
Very good: **$520.00**

Mauser Model MM410

Caliber: 22 long rifle
Action: Bolt action; repeating
Magazine: 5-shot detachable box
Barrel: Blued; 23½"
Sights: Tangent curve rear, ramp front
Stock and Forearm: Checkered one-piece pistol grip stock and forearm; swivels
Approximate wt.: 6½ lbs.
Comments: Made from the mid-1920s to the mid-1930s.
Estimated Value: **Excellent:** **$600.00**
Very good: **$480.00**

Mauser Model MM410B

Similar to the Model MM410 except lighter weight model. Made from the mid- to the late 1930s.

Estimated Value: **Excellent:** **$575.00**
Very good: **$460.00**

Mauser Model DSM34

Similar to the Model 98 in appearance, in 22 long rifle with a 26" barrel. Made from the mid-1930s to the late 1930s. Single-shot.

Estimated Value: **Excellent:** **$450.00**
Very good: **$360.00**

Mauser Model KKW

Similar to the Model DSM34. Made from the mid- to the late 1930s.

Estimated Value: **Excellent:** **$500.00**
Very good: **$400.00**

Mauser Model 2000

Mauser Model 2000

Caliber: 270 Win., 308 Win., 30-06
Action: Bolt action; repeating; adjustable trigger
Magazine: 5-shot box; hinged floor plate
Barrel: 24"; Krupp steel
Sights: Folding leaf rear, hooded ramp front
Stock and Forearm: Checkered walnut Monte Carlo one-piece pistol grip stock and forearm; swivels; cheekpiece
Approximate wt.: 7½ lbs.
Comments: Made from the late 1960s to the early 1970s.
Estimated Value: **Excellent:** **$500.00**
Very good: **$400.00**

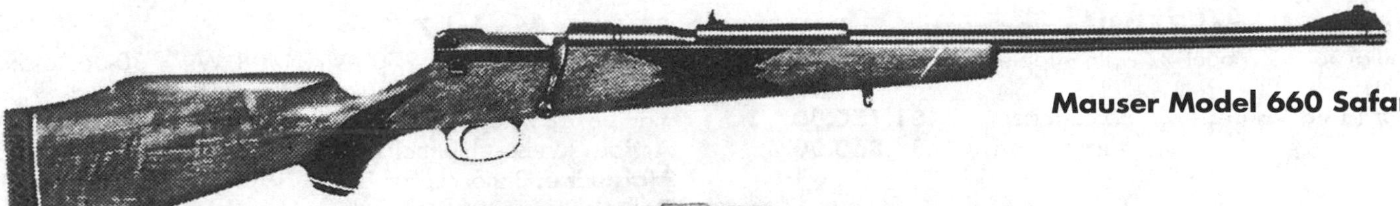

Mauser Model 660 Safari

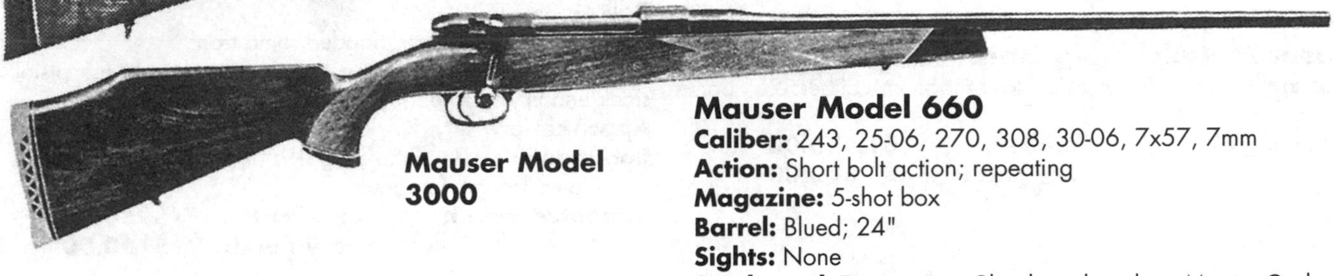

Mauser Model 3000

Mauser Model 3000

Caliber: 243, 270, 30-06, 308, 375 H&H mag., 7mm mag., 300 Win. mag.
Action: Bolt action; repeating
Magazine: 5-shot box
Barrel: 22", 26" magnum
Sights: None
Stock and Forearm: Checkered walnut Monte Carlo one-piece pistol grip stock and forearm; recoil pad
Approximate wt.: 7 lbs.
Comments: Made in the 1970s. Add $50.00 for mag.

Estimated Value:	**Excellent:**	**$520.00**
	Very good:	**$420.00**

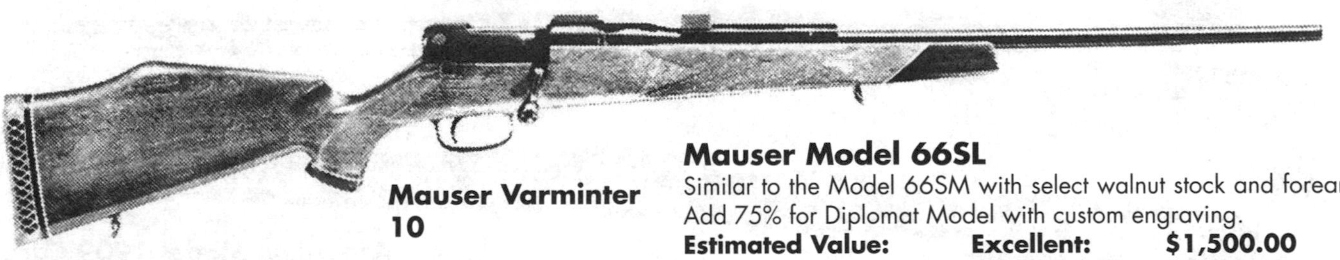

Mauser Varminter 10

Mauser Model 66S

Caliber: 243, 6.5x57, 270, 7x64, 30-06, 308, 5.6x61 V.H. mag., 6.5x68 mag., 7mm Rem. mag., 7mm V.H. mag., 8x68S mag., 300 Win. mag., 300 Weath. mag., 9.3x62 mag., 9.3x64 mag.
Action: Mauser telescopic short bolt action; repeating
Magazine: 5-shot box
Barrel: Blued; 21", 24", 26"; interchangeable barrels available
Sights: Adjustable rear, hooded ramp front
Stock and Forearm: European walnut, checkered Monte Carlo one-piece pistol grip stock and forearm; rosewood tip; recoil pad; full-length forearm available
Approximate wt.: 7 lbs.
Comments: Add 10% for full-length forearm.

Estimated Value:	**Excellent:**	**$2,000.00**
	Very good:	**$1,600.00**

Mauser Model 66SM

Similar to the Model 66S with lipped forearm (no rosewood tip) and internal alterations. Add 10% for full-length forearm.

Estimated Value:	**Excellent:**	**$1,350.00**
	Very good:	**$1,075.00**

Mauser Model 660

Caliber: 243, 25-06, 270, 308, 30-06, 7x57, 7mm
Action: Short bolt action; repeating
Magazine: 5-shot box
Barrel: Blued; 24"
Sights: None
Stock and Forearm: Checkered walnut Monte Carlo one-piece pistol grip stock and forearm; recoil pad
Approximate wt.: 7 lbs.
Comments: Made in the early 1970s.

Estimated Value:	**Excellent:**	**$750.00**
	Very good:	**$600.00**

Mauser Model 660 Safari

Similar to the Model 660 except: 28" barrel; express rear sight and ramp front sight; calibers 458 Win., 375 H&H, 338 Win., and 7mm Rem.; approximate weight 9 lbs.

Estimated Value:	**Excellent:**	**$800.00**
	Very good:	**$640.00**

Mauser Model 66SL

Similar to the Model 66SM with select walnut stock and forearm. Add 75% for Diplomat Model with custom engraving.

Estimated Value:	**Excellent:**	**$1,500.00**
	Very good:	**$1,200.00**

Mauser Model 66S Big Game

Similar to the Model 66S in 375 H&H or 458 Win. magnum caliber; 26" barrel; fold-down rear sight; weighs about 10 lbs.

Estimated Value:	**Excellent:**	**$1,950.00**
	Very good:	**$1,560.00**

Mauser Varminter 10

Caliber: 22-250
Action: Bolt action; repeating
Magazine: 5-shot box
Barrel: Blued; 24"; heavy
Sights: None
Stock and Forearm: Checkered walnut Monte Carlo one-piece pistol grip stock and forearm
Approximate wt.: 8 lbs.
Comments: Made in the 1970s.

Estimated Value:	**Excellent:**	**$450.00**
	Very good:	**$360.00**

Mauser Model 77DJV Sportsman

Similar to the Model 77 with stippled stock and forearm; no sights.

Estimated Value:	**Excellent:**	**$1,150.00**
	Very good:	**$ 860.00**

Mauser Model 77 Big Game

Similar to the Model 77 in 375 H&H magnum caliber; 26" barrel.

Estimated Value:	**Excellent:**	**$1,070.00**
	Very good:	**$ 800.00**

Mauser Model 77

Caliber: 243 Win., 270 Win., 308 Win., 30-06, 6.5x57, 7x64, 7mm Rem. mag., 6.5x68 mag., 300 Win. mag., 9.3x62 mag., 8x68S mag.
Action: Mauser short bolt action; repeating
Magazine: 3-shot clip
Barrel: Blued; 20", 24", 26"
Sights: Adjustable rear, hooded ramp front
Stock and Forearm: Checkered walnut one-piece pistol grip stock and lipped forearm; recoil pad; swivels
Approximate wt.: 7½ lbs.
Comments: Made in the early 1980s. Add 10% for 20" or 26" barrel or full-length forearm.

Estimated Value:	**Excellent:**	**$950.00**
	Very good:	**$760.00**

MILITARY, ARGENTINE

Argentine Model 1891 Mauser

Argentine Model 1891 Carbine

Argentine Model 1909 Mauser

Argentine Model 1909 Carbine

Argentine Model 1891 Mauser

Caliber: 7x65mm rimless
Action: Manually operated bolt action; straight bolt handle
Magazine: 5-shot single column box
Barrel: 29"; round barrel; cleaning rod in forearm
Sights: Barleycorn front; rear adjustable for elevation
Stock and Forearm: Military-type, one-piece straight grip stock and full forearm; bayonet lug; two barrel bands
Approximate wt.: 8½ lbs.
Comments: Similar to 7.65mm M1890 Turkish Mauser; obsolete.

Estimated Value:	**Very good:**	**$385.00**
	Good:	**$310.00**

Argentine Model 1909 Carbine

Similar to the Model 1909 Rifle except: 17½" barrel; approximate wt. 6½ lbs.; with and without bayonet lugs.

Estimated Value:	**Very good:**	**$550.00**
	Good:	**$440.00**

Argentine Model 1891 Carbine

Similar to the Model 1891 rifle except: 17½" barrel; approximate wt. 6½ lbs.; two versions, one with and one without bayonet lug; some still used as police weapons.

Estimated Value:	**Very good:**	**$445.00**
	Good:	**$355.00**

Argentine Model 1909 Mauser

Caliber: 7.65mm rimless
Action: Manually operated bolt with straight handle
Magazine: 5-shot staggered row box magazine
Barrel: 29"; round barrel
Sights: Barleycorn, tangent leaf rear
Stock and Forearm: Military-type, one-piece semi-pistol grip stock and full forearm; two barrel bands; cleaning rod in forearm
Approximate wt.: 9 lbs.
Comments: A slight modification of the German Gewehr 98; obsolete.

Estimated Value:	**Very good:**	**$465.00**
	Good:	**$375.00**

British Lee-Enfield Mark I

British Lee-Enfield Mark I Carbine

British Lee-Enfield Mark I

Caliber: 303
Action: Bolt action; repeating; curved bolt handle
Magazine: 10-shot detachable box with cut-off
Barrel: 30"
Sights: Barleycorn front, vertical leaf rear
Stock and Forearm: Plain military-type stock and forearm
Approximate wt.: 9¼ lbs.
Comments: Adopted by the British Army about 1899.
Estimated Value: **Very good:** **$785.00**
Good: **$630.00**

British Lee-Enfield Mark I Carbine

Similar to the Lee Enfield Mark I rifle except 21" barrel.
Estimated Value: **Very good:** **$900.00**
Good: **$725.00**

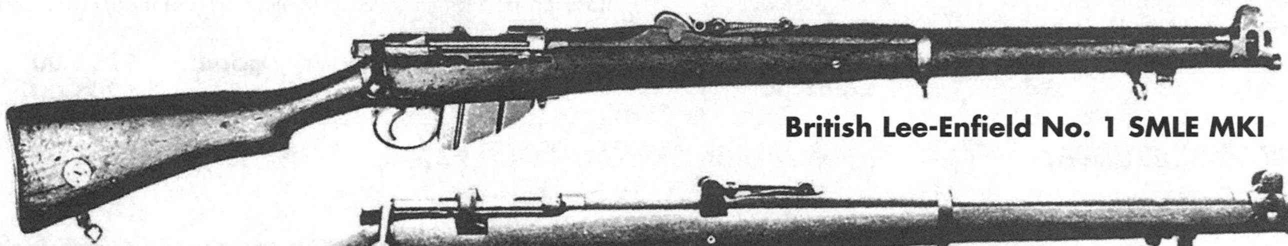

British Lee-Enfield No. 1 SMLE MKI

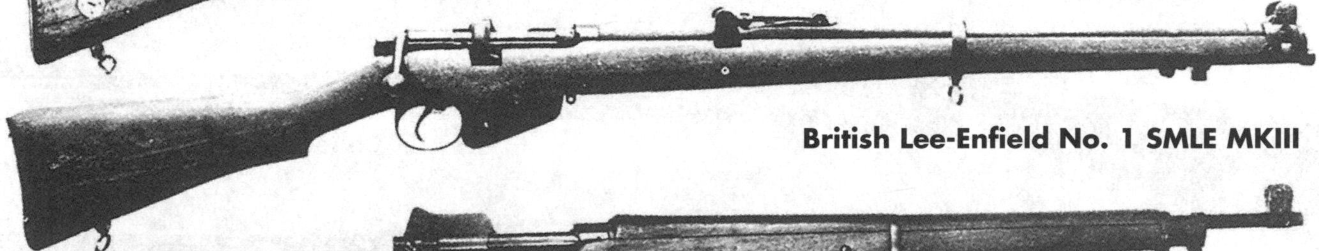

British Lee-Enfield No. 1 SMLE MKIII

British (Pattern 14) No. 3 MKI

British (Pattern 14) No. 3 MKI

Caliber: 303
Action: Bolt action; modified Mauser-type action; cocked as bolt is moved forward
Magazine: 5-shot non-removable box
Barrel: 26"
Sights: Blade front with protective ears, vertical leaf with aperture rear
Stock and Forearm: Plain military stock with wood handguard over barrel
Approximate wt.: 9 lbs.
Comments: Made in U.S.A. during World War I for the British Army.
Estimated Value: **Very good:** **$785.00**
Good: **$630.00**

British Lee-Enfield No. 1 SMLE MKI

Caliber: 303
Action: Bolt action; curved bolt handle
Magazine: 10-shot detachable box with cut-off
Barrel: 25¼"
Sights: Barleycorn front with protective ears; tangent leaf rear
Stock and Forearm: Plain wood military stock to the muzzle with full-length wood hand guard over barrel
Approximate wt.: 8 lbs.
Comments: Adopted about 1902 by the British Army.
Estimated Value: **Very good:** **$785.00**
Good: **$630.00**

British Lee-Enfield No. I SMLE MKIII

Similar to No. 1 SMLE MKI except: modified and simplified for mass production; adopted in 1907 and modified again in 1918.
Estimated Value: **Very good:** **$785.00**
Good: **$630.00**

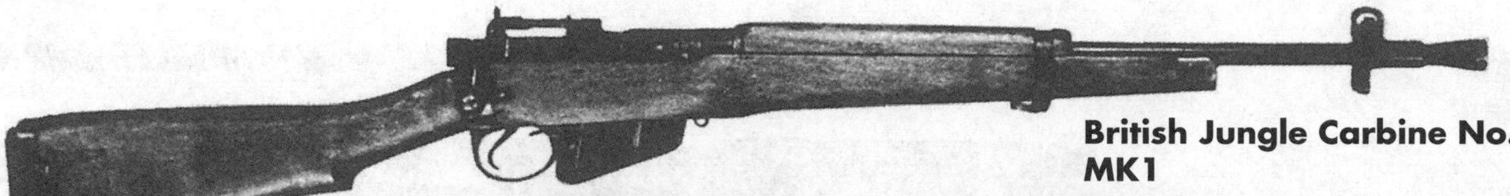

British Jungle Carbine No. 5 MK1

British Lee-Enfield No. 4 MK1

British Jungle Carbine No. 5 MK1
Caliber: 303
Action: Bolt action
Magazine: 10-shot detachable box
Barrel: 18¾"
Sights: Blade front with protective ears; vertical leaf rear with aperture
Stock and Forearm: Military-type, one-piece stock and forearm; wood handguard over barrel; one barrel band
Approximate wt.: 7 lbs.
Comments: Made during World War II for jungle fighting.
Estimated Value: Very good: $425.00
 Good: $335.00

British Lee-Enfield No. 4 MK1
Caliber: 303
Action: Bolt action
Magazine: 10-shot detachable box
Barrel: 25"
Sights: Blade front with protective ears; vertical leaf with aperture rear
Stock and Forearm: Plain military stock with wood hand guard over barrel
Approximate wt.: 8¾ lbs.
Comments: First made about 1931 and was redesigned for mass production in 1939 by utilizing stamped parts and other shortcuts.
Estimated Value: Very good: $255.00
 Good: $205.00

⊙**MILITARY, CHILEAN**

Chilean Model 1895

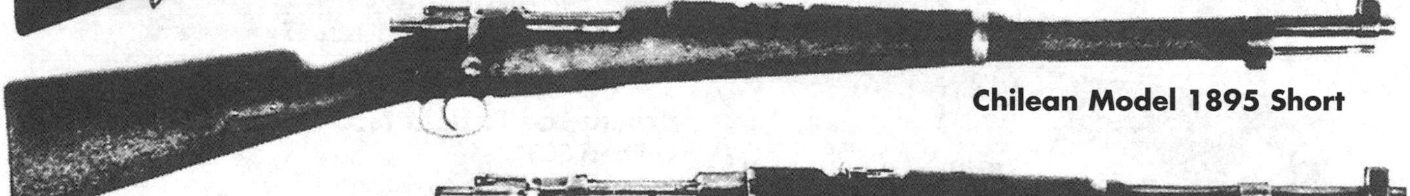

Chilean Model 1895 Short

Chilean Model 1895 Carbine

Chilean Model 1895 Short
Similar to Model 1895 rifle except: 22" barrel; approximate wt. 8½ lbs.
Estimated Value: Very good: $300.00
 Good: $240.00

Chilean Model 1895 Carbine
Similar to Model 1895 rifle except: 18¼" barrel; approximate wt. 7½ lbs.
Estimated Value: Very good: $275.00
 Good: $220.00

Chilean Model 1895
Caliber: 7mm
Action: Bolt action; straight or turned bolt handle; similar to the Spanish Model 1893 Mauser
Magazine: 5-shot staggered non-detachable box
Barrel: 29"
Sights: Barleycorn front; leaf rear
Stock and Forearm: Plain military-type stock with wood hand-guard over barrel
Approximate wt.: 9 lbs.
Comments: Since Chile's adoption of the FN rifle, quantities of the Chilean Mausers have been purchased by American arms dealers.
Estimated Value: Very good: $330.00
 Good: $265.00

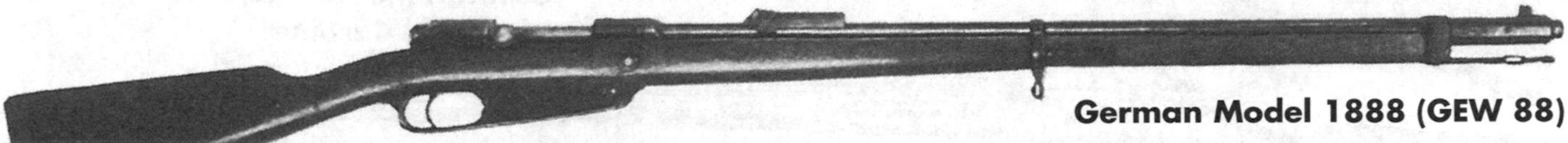

German Model 1888 (GEW 88)

German Model 1888 Carbine

German Model 1888 Carbine

Similar to the Model 1888 rifle except: 18" barrel; approximate wt. $6\frac{3}{4}$ lbs.; full-length stock to muzzle; curved flattened top bolt handle.

Estimated Value: **Very good:** **$315.00**
Good: **$255.00**

German Model 1891

Similar to the Model 1888 Carbine except: stacking hook under forearm and although it is called a rifle, it has an 18" barrel like the carbines.

Estimated Value: **Very good:** **$345.00**
Good: **$275.00**

German Model 1888 (GEW 88)

Caliber: 7.92 x 57mm
Action: Bolt action; straight bolt handle
Magazine: 5-shot in line non-detachable box
Barrel: 29"
Sights: Barleycorn front; leaves with "v" rear notches
Stock and Forearm: Plain straight grip military stock; no handguard but uses a metal barrel jacket that covers barrel to muzzle
Approximate wt.: $8\frac{3}{4}$ lbs.
Comments: This arm is sometimes called a Mauser or Mannlicher but actually it is neither; it combines the magazine of the Mannlicher with the bolt features of the Mauser 1871/84; it is unsafe to use with the modern 7.92mm cartridge.

Estimated Value: **Very good:** **$285.00**
Good: **$230.00**

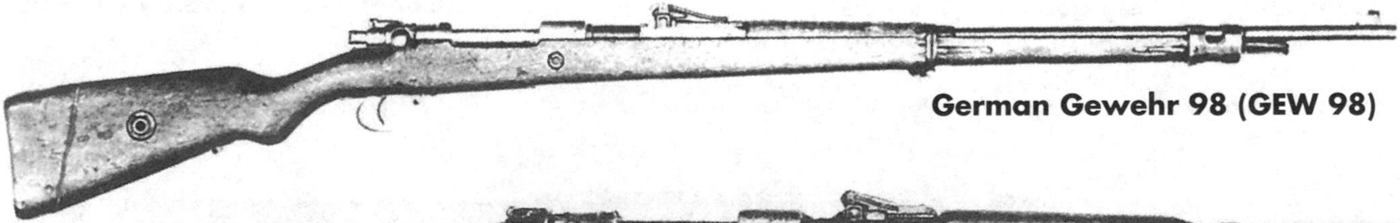

German Gewehr 98 (GEW 98)

German Model 98 (Kar 98) Carbine

German Model 98 (Kar 98) Carbine

Similar to the Model Gewehr 98 rifle except: 17" barrel; approximate wt. $7\frac{1}{2}$ lbs.; full stock to muzzle; section of forearm from barrel band to muzzle tapered to much smaller size than rest of forearm; curved bolt handle.

Estimated Value: **Very good:** **$540.00**
Good: **$435.00**

German Model Gewehr 98 (GEW 98)

Caliber: 7.92mm
Action: Bolt action; straight or curved bolt handle
Magazine: 5-shot staggered non-detachable box; also during World War II, 20- and 25-shot magazines
Barrel: 29"
Sights: Barleycorn front; tangent bridge-type or tangent leaf "v" rear
Stock and Forearm: Plain military semi-pistol grip stock and forearm; wood handguard
Approximate wt.: 9 lbs.
Comments: This was one of the principal rifles of the German Army in World War I; it also appeared in a caliber 22 training rifle in World War I by fitting a liner in the barrel.

Estimated Value: **Very good:** **$510.00**
Good: **$410.00**

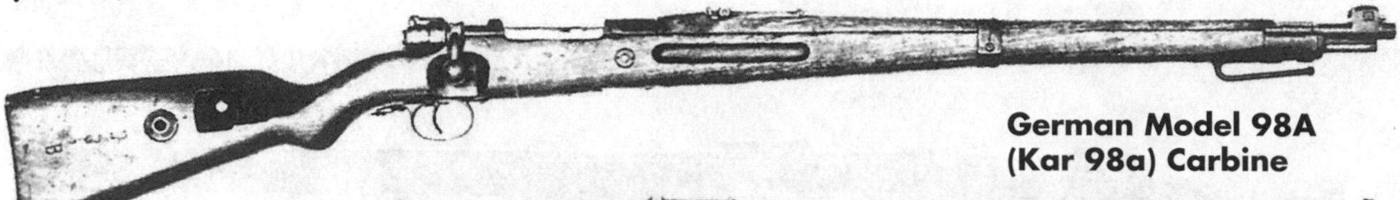

German Model 98A (Kar 98a) Carbine

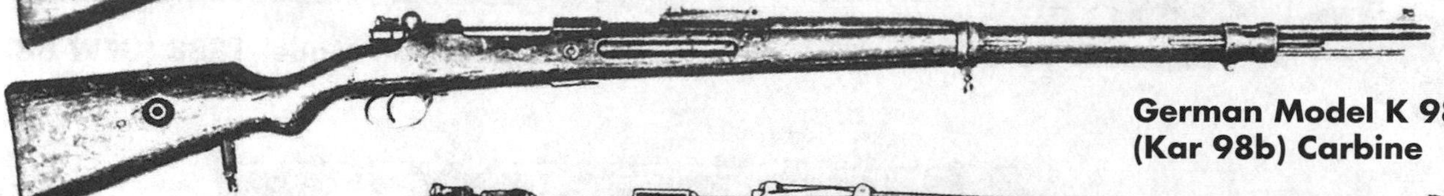

German Model K 98b (Kar 98b) Carbine

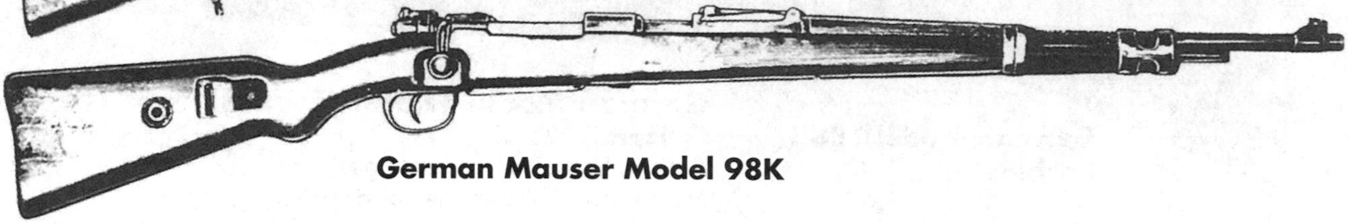

German Mauser Model 98K

German Model 98A (Kar 98a) Carbine

Similar to the Model Gewehr 98 rifle except: 24" barrel; appeared in 1904 and made in tremendous quantities until 1918; used in World War I and had limited use in World War II; cut out in stock below bolt handle; curved bolt handle; grip grooves on forearm; stacking hook.

Estimated Value: **Very good:** **$480.00**
Good: **$385.00**

German Model K 98b (Kar 98b) Carbine

Although designed as a carbine, it is the same length and is similar to the Model Gewehr 98 rifle except: turned-down bolt; grip grooved forearm; these were used in the 1920s and early in World War II.

Estimated Value: **Very good:** **$450.00**
Good: **$360.00**

German Mauser Model 98K

Caliber: 7.92mm
Action: Bolt action; turned-down bolt handle
Magazine: 5-shot staggered row non-detachable box
Barrel: 24"
Sights: Barleycorn open or hooded front, tangent rear with "v" notch
Stock and Forearm: Plain military semi-pistol grip stock and forearm; wood handguard; cut out in stock under bolt handle
Approximate wt.: 8¾ lbs.
Comments: The standard infantry rifle during World War II; widely fluctuating prices on these rifles because some have special unit markings which affect their values.
Estimated Value: **Very good:** **$240.00 – 900.00**
Good: **$195.00 – 725.00**

MILITARY, ITALIAN

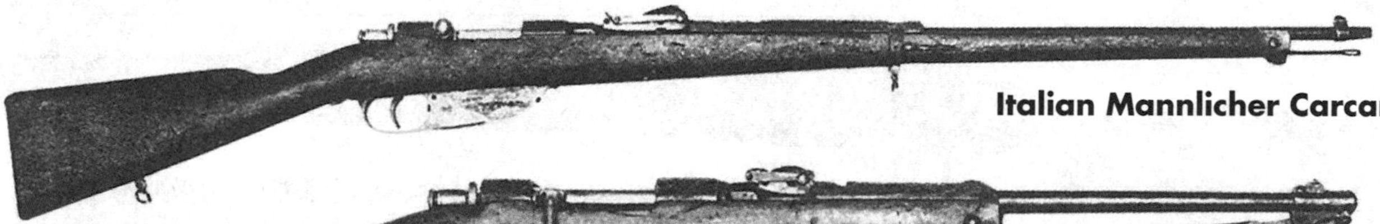

Italian Mannlicher Carcano M1891

Italian Mannlicher Carcano M1891 Carbine

Italian Mannlicher Carcano M1891

Caliber: 6.5mm
Action: Bolt action; straight bolt handle; a modified Mauser-type action
Magazine: 6-shot in line non-detachable box
Barrel: 30½"
Sights: Barleycorn front, tangent rear with "v" notch graduated from 500 to 2000 meters
Stock and Forearm: Plain straight grip military stock with wood handguard over barrel
Approximate wt.: 8¾ lbs.
Comments: Uses knife-type bayonet.
Estimated Value: **Very good:** **$225.00**
Good: **$180.00**

Italian Mannlicher Carcano M1891 Carbine

Generally the same specifications as the Carcano M1891 military rifle except: 18" barrel; bent bolt handle; folding bayonet permanently attached; approximate wt. 7 lbs.

Estimated Value: **Very good:** **$195.00**
Good: **$155.00**

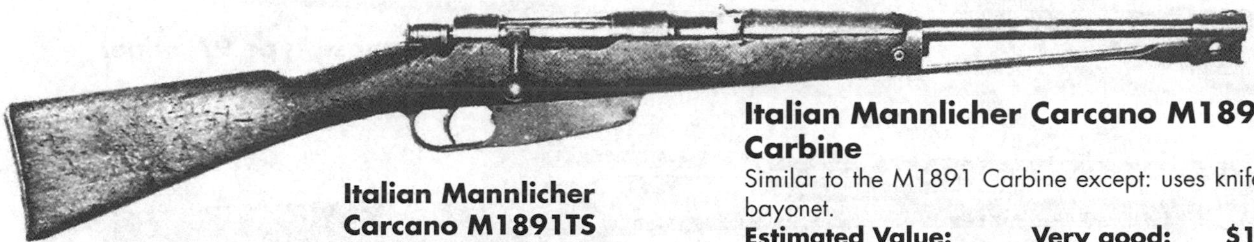

Italian Mannlicher Carcano M1891TS Carbine

Italian Mannlicher Carcano M1891TS Carbine

Similar to the M1891 Carbine except: uses knife-type removable bayonet.

Estimated Value: **Very good:** **$195.00**
Good: **$155.00**

Italian Mannlicher Carcano M1938

Italian Mannlicher Carcano M1938

Caliber: 7.35mm, 6.5mm
Action: Bolt action; bent bolt handle
Magazine: 6-shot in line, non-detachable box
Barrel: 21"
Sights: Barleycorn front, adjustable rear
Stock and Forearm: Plain straight grip military stock; wood handguard over barrel
Approximate wt.: 7½ lbs.
Comments: First of the Italian rifles chambered for the 7.35mm cartridge; in 1940 the 7.35mm caliber was dropped; this is the type rifle allegedly used to assassinate President John F. Kennedy in 1963; it was a 6.5mm made in 1940 and sold in U.S.A. as army surplus.
Estimated Value: **Very good:** **$250.00**
Good: **$200.00**

Italian Mannlicher Carcano M1938 Carbine

Similar to the Carcano M1938 military rifle except: 18" barrel; folding bayonet permanently attached.

Estimated Value: **Very good:** **$195.00**
Good: **$155.00**

Italian Mannlicher Carcano M1938 TS Carbine

Same as the M1938 Carbine except: detachable knife-type bayonet.

Estimated Value: **Very good:** **$170.00**
Good: **$135.00**

MILITARY, JAPANESE

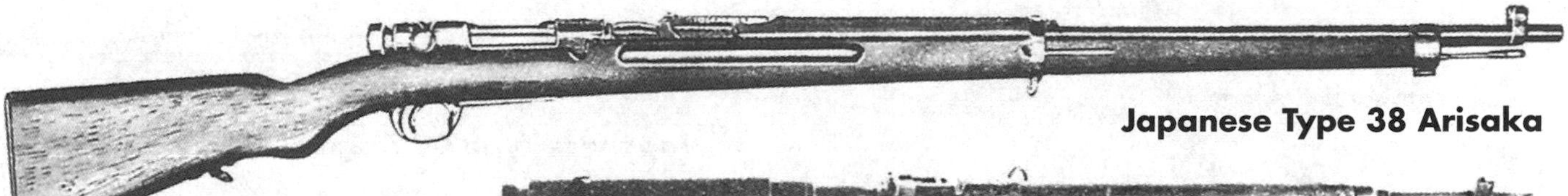

Japanese Type 38 Arisaka

Japanese Type 38 Arisaka Carbine

Japanese Type 38 Arisaka

Caliber: 6.5mm Japanese
Action: Bolt action; straight bolt handle
Magazine: 5-shot box magazine with floor plate
Barrel: 31½"; round
Sights: Barleycorn front with protecting ears, rear sight adjustable for elevation
Stock and Forearm: Military finish; plain wood one-piece full stock; semi-pistol grip; steel butt plate; cleaning rod under barrel; wood handguard on top of barrel; two steel barrel bands with bayonet lug on front band
Approximate wt.: 9¼ lbs.
Comments: Adopted by Japanese military in 1905, the 38th year of the Meiji reign.
Estimated Value: **Very good:** **$285.00**
Good: **$225.00**

Japanese Type 38 Arisaka Carbine

Similar to the Type 38 Arisaka rifle except: 20" barrel; folding bayonet; approximate wt. 7¼ lbs.; some were converted for paratrooper use by fitting of a hinged buttstock.

Estimated Value:

	Carbine	Paratrooper Carbine
Very good:	**$250.00**	**$310.00**
Good:	**$200.00**	**$250.00**

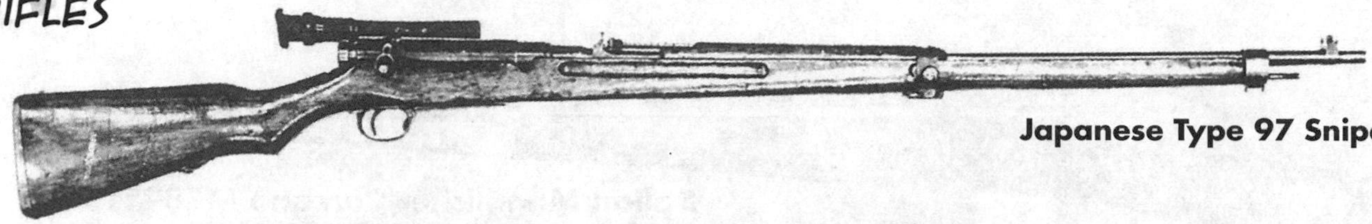

Japanese Type 97 Sniper

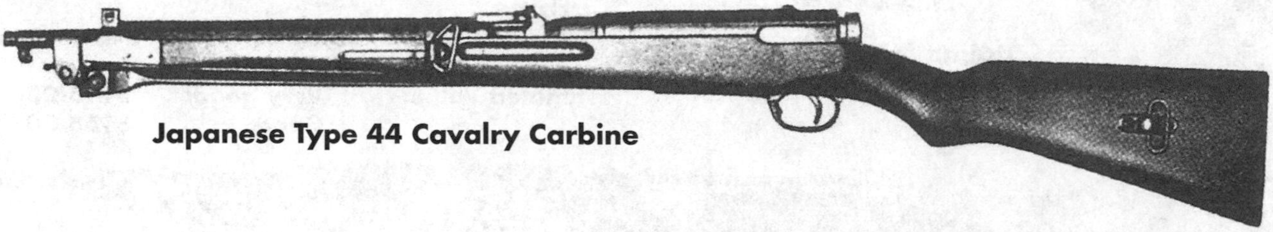

Japanese Type 44 Cavalry Carbine

Japanese Type 97 Sniper

Similar to the Type 38 Arisaka rifle except: a sniper's version was adopted in 1937 with a 2.5 power scope; approximate wt. with scope: 11 lbs. Prices are for rifle with scope.

Estimated Value: **Very good:** **$1,000.00**
Good: **$ 800.00**

Japanese Type 44 Cavalry Carbine

Similar to the Type 38 Arisaka Carbine except: heavier weight, about 9 lbs.; adopted by Japanese military in 1911, the 44th year of the Meiji reign; permanently attached folding bayonet.

Estimated Value: **Very good:** **$210.00**
Good: **$165.00**

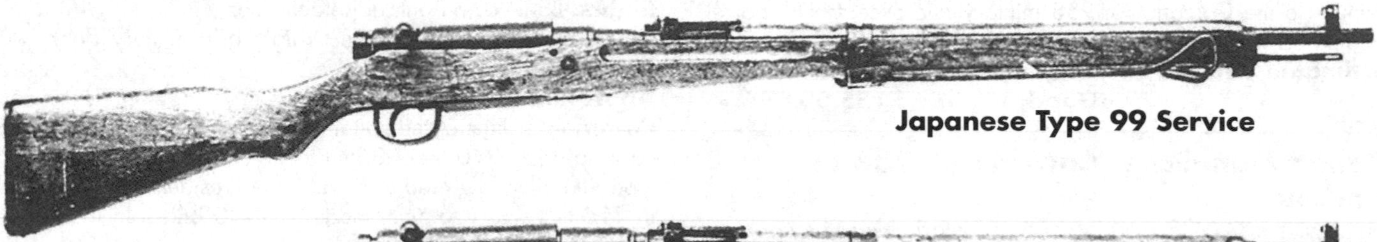

Japanese Type 99 Service

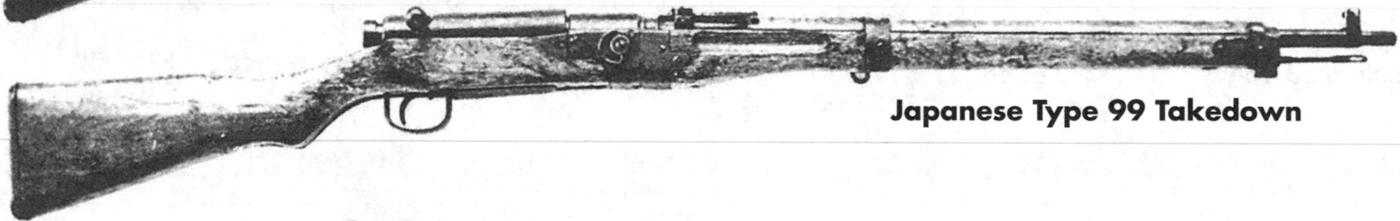

Japanese Type 99 Takedown

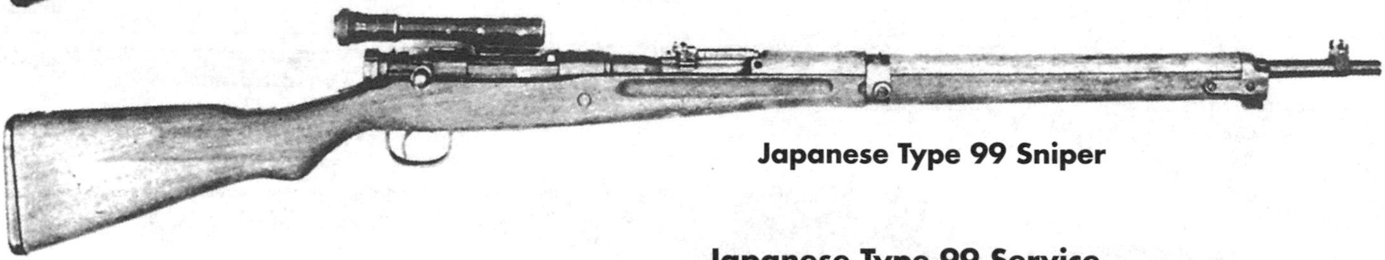

Japanese Type 99 Sniper

Japanese Type 99 Takedown

Similar to the Type 99 Service rifle except it has a 25" barrel only. A takedown model, it has a screw-in key that serves as a locking pin. When key is removed, the barrel can be unscrewed from the receiver; however, the takedown arrangement was unsatisfactory because it weakened the receiver and affected the accuracy.

Estimated Value: **Very good:** **$480.00**
Good: **$385.00**

Japanese Type 99 Sniper

Similar to the Type 99 Service rifle except: adopted in 1942 and equipped with a 4X scope; 25½" barrel only. Prices include matching number and scope mounted.

Estimated Value: **Very good:** **$1,050.00**
Good: **$ 840.00**

Japanese Type 99 Service

Caliber: 7.7mm Japanese
Action: Bolt action
Magazine: 5-shot magazine, non-detachable
Barrel: 25½" or 31½"; round
Sights: Fixed front, adjustable or fixed rear
Stock and Forearm: Military finish; plain wood, one-piece full stock; semi-pistol grip; steel butt plate; cleaning rod under barrel; some had bipod attached under forearm; wood handguard on top of barrel; two steel barrel bands with bayonet lug on front band
Approximate wt.: 8½ to 9 lbs.
Comments: Some of the last rifles made were of poor quality and unsafe to shoot with heavy load cartridges. Adopted by Japanese military in 1939, which was Japanese year of 2599.

Estimated Value: **Very good:** **$420.00**
Good: **$335.00**

Mexican Model 1895 Mauser

Mexican Model 1902

Mexican Arisaka (Japanese Type 38 Rifle)

Mexican Model 1936

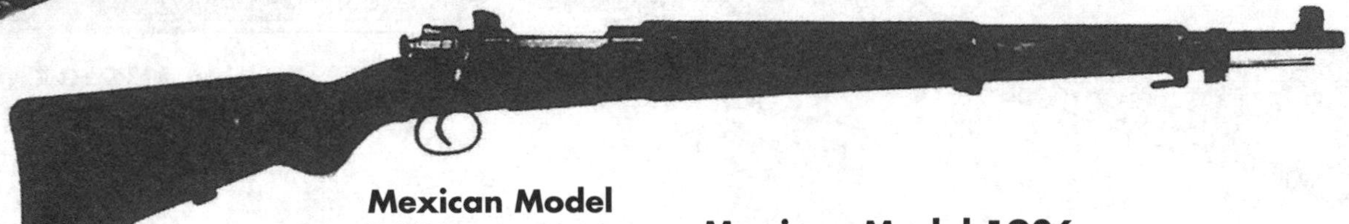

Mexican Model 1954

Mexican Model 1895 Mauser

Almost identical to the Spanish 1893 military rifle in caliber 7mm. See Spanish Model 1893 for description.

Estimated Value:	**Very good:**	**$165.00**
	Good:	**$135.00**

Mexican Models 1902 and 1912 Mauser

Almost identical to the Model 1895 Mauser military rifle except that the actions were more like the actions found in the Model 98 7.92 German rifle.

Estimated Value:	**Very good:**	**$220.00**
	Good:	**$175.00**

Mexican Arisaka (Japanese Type 38 Rifle)

Between 1910 and 1920, Mexico procured arms from many companies. The Arisaka rifle was purchased from Japan in caliber 7mm and had the Mexican escutcheon stamped on the receiver.

Estimated Value:	**Very good:**	**$440.00**
	Good:	**$355.00**

Mexican Model 1936

Caliber: 7mm
Action: Bolt action; curved bolt handle; Mauser short-type action
Magazine: 5-shot staggered row, non-detachable box
Barrel: 20"
Sights: Hooded barleycorn front; tangent rear with "v" notch
Stock and Forearm: Plain semi-pistol grip stock with grip grooves in forearm; wood handguard
Approximate wt.: 8½ lbs.
Comments: A very well-made gun of Mexican manufacture; resembles the U.S. M1903-A1 Springfield in appearance.

Estimated Value:	**Very good:**	**$330.00**
	Good:	**$265.00**

Mexican Model 1954

Caliber: 30-06
Action: Bolt action; curved bolt handle
Magazine: 5-shot staggered row, non-detachable box
Barrel: 24"
Sights: Hooded barleycorn front; ramp-type aperture rear
Stock and Forearm: Plain semi-pistol grip military stock and wood handguard; stock is made of laminated plywood
Approximate wt.: 9 lbs.
Comments: This rifle is patterned after the U.S. M1903-A3 Springfield military rifle.

Estimated Value:	**Very good:**	**$330.00**
	Good:	**$265.00**

Russian Moisin-Nagant M1891

Caliber: 7.62mm
Action: Bolt action; straight bolt; hexagonal receiver
Magazine: 5-shot box with hinged floor plate
Barrel: 31½"
Sights: Blade front, leaf rear
Stock and Forearm: Plain straight grip, military stock and gripped grooved forearm; early models had no handguard and used swivels for attaching sling; later models (beginning about 1908) used sling slots and had wooden handguard
Approximate wt.: 9¾ lbs.
Comments: Adopted in 1891 by Imperial Russia.

Estimated Value:	**Very good:**	**$165.00**
	Good:	**$135.00**

Russian M1910 Carbine

Caliber: 7.62mm
Action: Bolt action; straight bolt handle; hexagonal receiver
Magazine: 5-shot box with floor plate
Barrel: 20"
Sights: Blade front, leaf-type rear adjustable for elevation
Stock and Forearm: Plain straight grip military stock; sling slots in stock and forearm; wooden handguard and grip grooved forearm
Approximate wt.: 7½ lbs.
Comments: This carbine does not accept a bayonet.

Estimated Value:	**Very good:**	**$165.00**
	Good:	**$135.00**

Russian Moisin-Nagant M1891

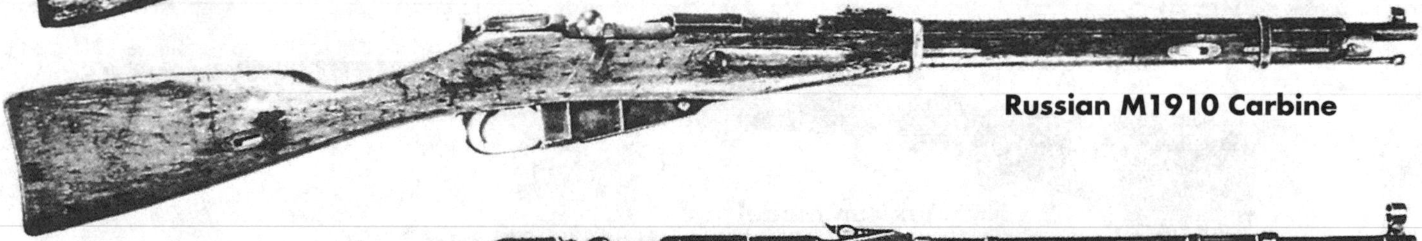
Russian M1910 Carbine

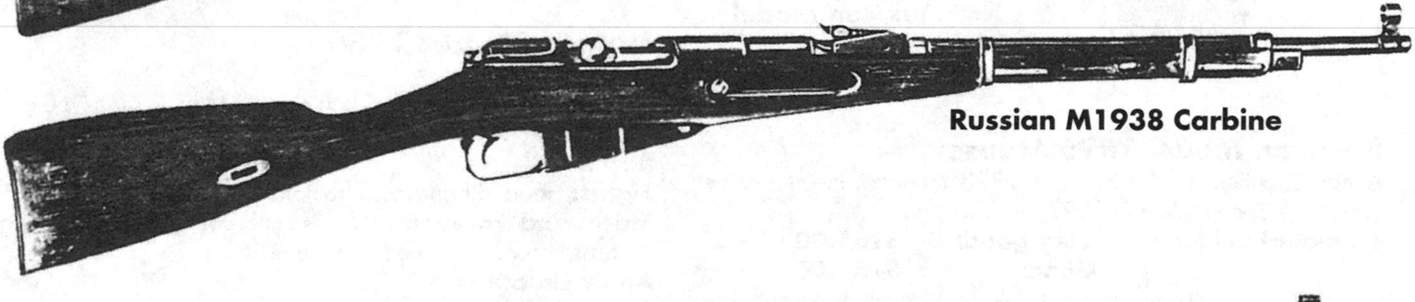
Russian M1938 Carbine

Russian Tokarev M1938

Russian M1938 Carbine

This carbine was replaced by M1910 and is very similar except: it has a round receiver; hooded front sight and tangent-type rear graduated from 100 to 1000 meters; no bayonet attachment.

Estimated Value:	**Very good:**	**$495.00**
	Good:	**$395.00**

Russian Tokarev M1938

Caliber: 7.62mm
Action: Semiautomatic; gas operated
Magazine: 10-shot removable box
Barrel: 25"
Sights: Hooded post front, tangent rear
Stock and Forearm: Plain semi-pistol grip two-piece stock and forearm; cleaning rod on right side of forearm; sling swivels
Approximate wt.: 8¾ lbs.
Comments: The first of the Tokarev series; wasn't very successful and was replaced by the Tokarev M1940.

Estimated Value:	**Very good:**	**$550.00**
	Good:	**$440.00**

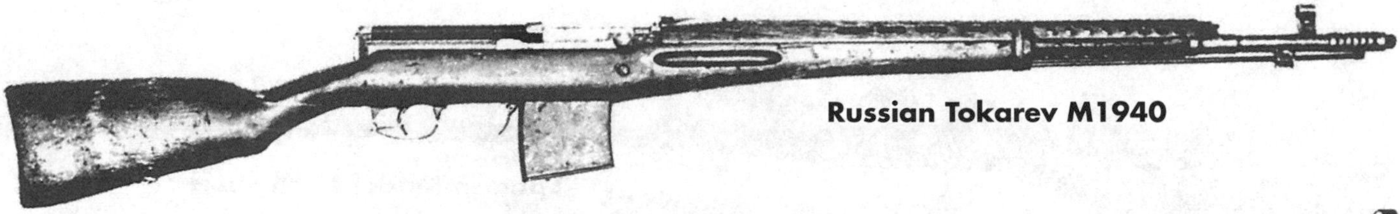

Russian Tokarev M1940

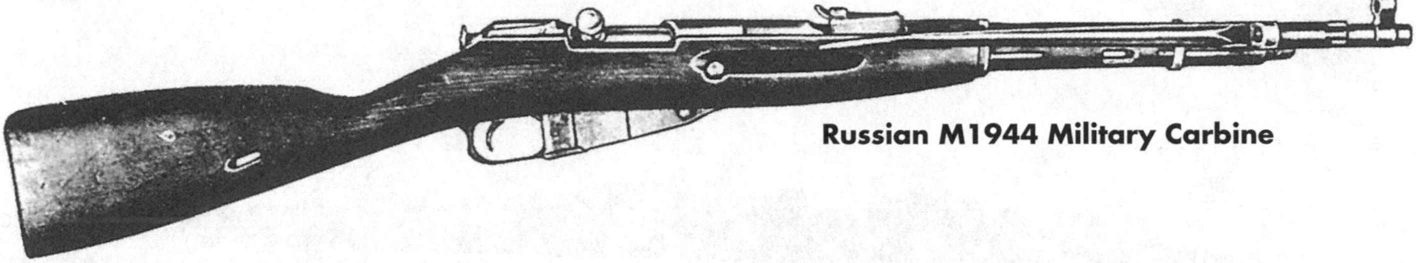

Russian M1944 Military Carbine

Russian Tokarev M1940

Similar to the Tokarev M1938 except: improved version; cleaning rod in forearm under barrel; 24½" barrel.

Estimated Value: **Very good:** **$575.00**
Good: **$465.00**

Russian M1944 Military Carbine

Similar to the M1938 Carbine except: introduced during World War II; permanently fixed bayonet which folds along the right side of the stock; barrel length 20½".

Estimated Value: **Very good:** **$550.00**
Good: **$440.00**

Spanish Model 1893

Spanish Model 1893 Short

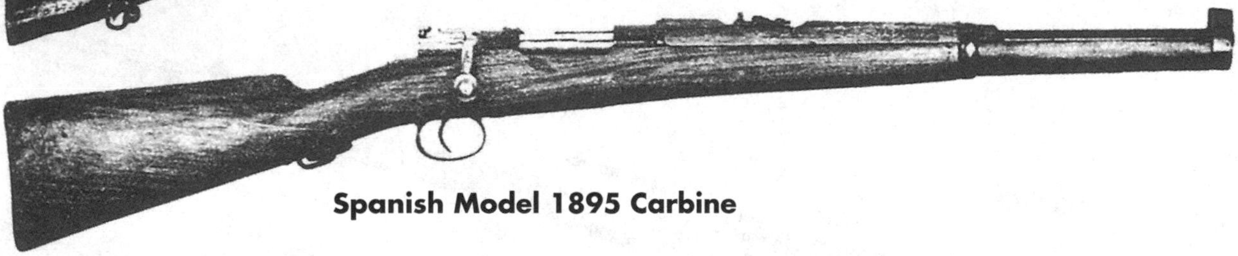

Spanish Model 1895 Carbine

Spanish Model 1893

Caliber: 7.57mm
Action: Bolt action; straight bolt handle
Magazine: 5-shot staggered row non-detachable
Barrel: 30"
Sights: Barleycorn front, leaf rear
Stock and Forearm: Plain straight grip military stock with wooden handguard over barrel
Approximate wt.: 9 lbs.
Comments: A number of variations in the Model 1893 were made; it was the principal rifle used in the Spanish-American War.

Estimated Value: **Very good:** **$165.00**
Good: **$135.00**

Spanish Model 1893 Short

Similar to the Model 1893 rifle except: 22" barrel; approximate wt. 8½ lbs.; curved bolt handle.

Estimated Value: **Very good:** **$220.00**
Good: **$175.00**

Spanish Model 1895 Carbine

Similar to the M1893 rifle except: 18" barrel; full stock to muzzle; barleycorn front sight with protective ears; approximate wt. 7½ lbs.

Estimated Value: **Very good:** **$195.00**
Good: **$155.00**

Spanish Model 1916 Short

Spanish Standard Model Mauser

Spanish Model 1916 Short

Caliber: 7.57mm
Action: Bolt action; bolt handle curved down
Magazine: 5-shot staggered row, non-detachable box
Barrel: 24"
Sights: Barleycorn front with ears, tangent rear
Stock and Forearm: Plain military stock and wooden handguard
Approximate wt.: 8½ lbs.
Comments: Made in large quantities during the Spanish Civil War; later many were converted to caliber 7.62mm NATO.

Estimated Value:	**Very good:**	**$135.00**
	Good:	**$110.00**

Spanish Standard Model Mauser

Caliber: 7.92mm
Action: Bolt action; straight bolt handle
Magazine: 5-shot staggered row, non-detachable box
Barrel: 24"
Sights: Barleycorn front, tangent rear
Stock and Forearm: Plain military semi-pistol grip stock and forearm grooved for finger grip; wooden handguard
Approximate wt.: 9 lbs.
Comments: Procured in large quantities from other countries during the Spanish Civil War.

Estimated Value:	**Very good:**	**$165.00**
	Good:	**$135.00**

Spanish Model 1943

Spanish Model 1943

Caliber: 7.92mm
Action: Bolt action; curved bolt handle
Magazine: 5-shot staggered row, non-detachable box
Barrel: 24"
Sights: Barleycorn front, tangent rear
Stock and Forearm: Plain military semi-pistol grip stock and forearm grooved for finger grip; wooden handguard
Approximate wt.: 9 lbs.
Comments: Adopted in 1943 and continued to mid-1950s; this is a modified copy of the German 7.92mm Kar 98K.

Estimated Value:	**Very good:**	**$175.00**
	Good:	**$140.00**

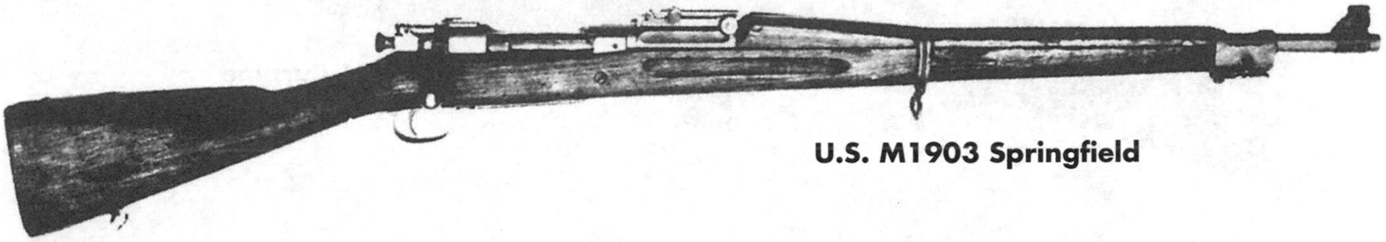

U.S. M1903 Springfield

U.S. M1903 Springfield

Caliber: 30-06
Action: Bolt action; repeating; manual thumb safety at rear of bolt; turned-down bolt handle; action is basically a modification of the Mauser Model 98
Magazine: 5-shot staggered row, non-detachable box magazine
Barrel: 24"
Sights: Blade front, leaf with aperture and notched battle rear
Stock and Forearm: Plain, straight one-piece stock and forearm; wooden handguard over barrel; a cleaning rod-type bayonet contained in the forearm under barrel
Approximate wt.: 8¾ lbs.
Comments: Adopted by U.S. in 1903; made by Springfield and Rock Island.

Estimated Value:	**Very good:**	**$960.00**
	Good:	**$765.00**

U.S. M1903-A1 Springfield

Basically the same as the M1903 military rifle except: pistol grip stock; checkered butt plate and serrated trigger; adopted in 1929 and made until 1939 by Springfield Armory — last serial number was about 1,532,878; in 1942 Remington Arms Co. made about 348,000 with a few minor modifications before the M1903-A3 was adopted; serial numbers from 3,000,001 to 3,348,085.

Estimated Value:	**Very good:**	**$1,020.00**
	Good:	**$ 815.00**

U.S. M1903-A3 Springfield

Generally the same as the U.S. M1903-A1 except: many parts are stamped sheet metal and other modifications to lower cost and increase production; straight or pistol grip stock; made during World War II under emergency conditions.

Estimated Value:	**Very good:**	**$930.00**
	Good:	**$745.00**

U.S. M1917 Enfield

Caliber: 30-06
Action: Bolt action; repeating; cocked as bolt is moved forward; bolt handle is crooked rearward; modified Mauser-type action
Magazine: 5-shot staggered row, non-detachable box-type
Barrel: 26"
Sights: Blade front with protecting ears, leaf with aperture rear
Stock and Forearm: Plain one-piece semi-pistol grip stock and forearm; wooden handguard over barrel
Approximate wt.: 8¼ lbs.
Comments: This gun was developed from the British P-13 and P-14 system as an emergency weapon for the U.S. in World War I. Made from about 1917 to 1918. Also manufactured in the U.S. for Great Britain in caliber 303 in 1917.

Estimated Value:	**Very good:**	**$1,020.00**
	Good:	**$ 815.00**

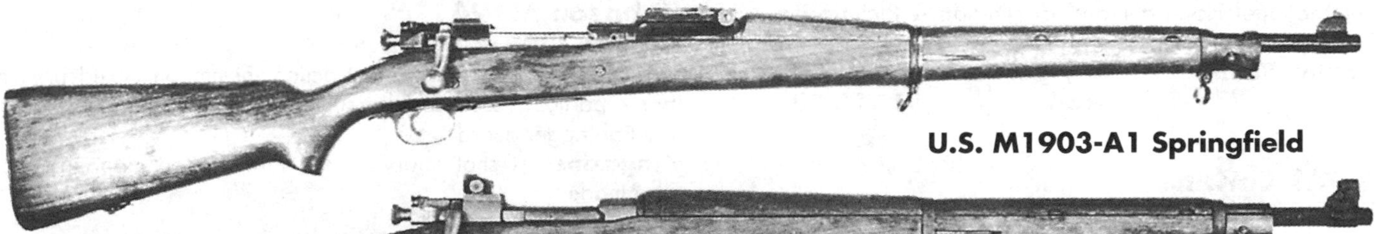

U.S. M1903-A1 Springfield

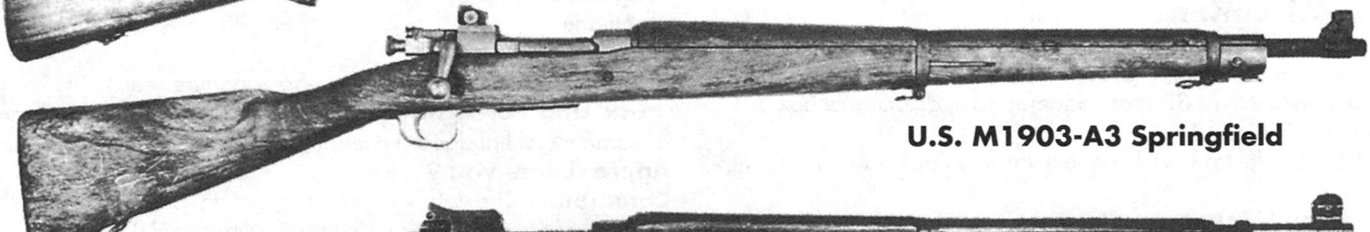

U.S. M1903-A3 Springfield

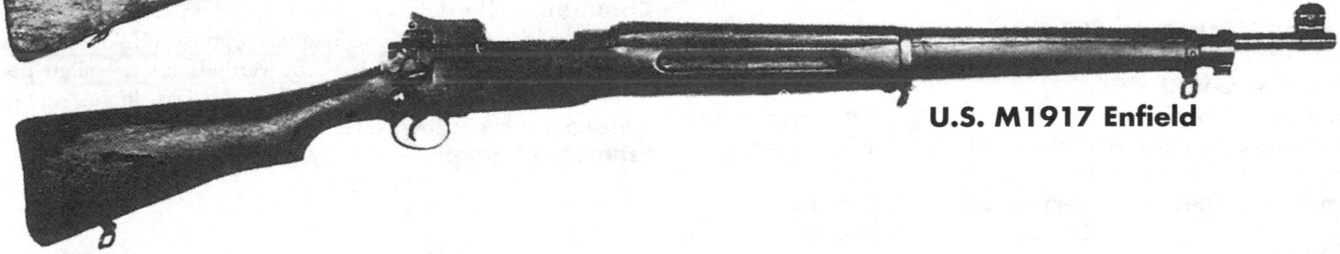

U.S. M1917 Enfield

U.S. M1 Carbine

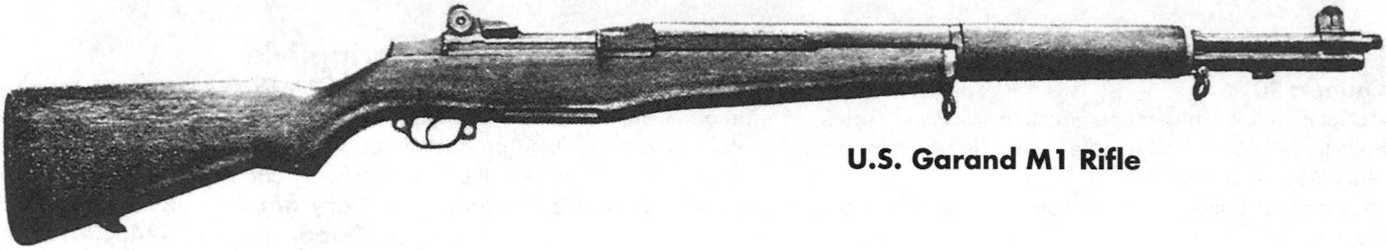

U.S. Garand M1 Rifle

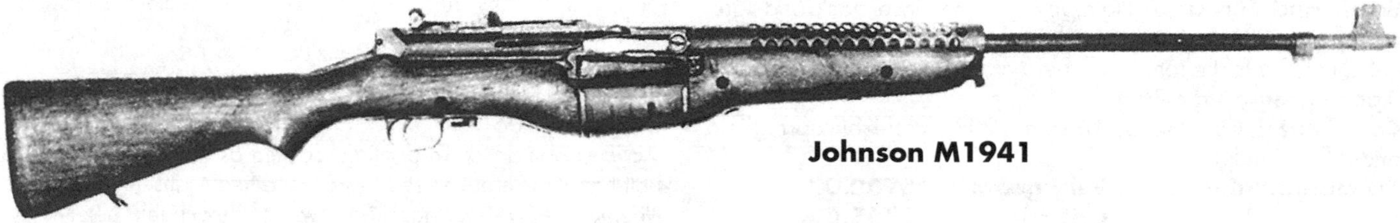

Johnson M1941

U.S. Garand M1 Rifle

Caliber: 30-06, 308 Win. (7.62 NATO)
Action: Semiautomatic; gas-operated
Magazine: 8-shot staggered row, non-detachable box
Barrel: 24"
Sights: Blade front with protective ears, aperture rear or flip-over type rear
Stock and Forearm: One-piece stock and forearm; wooden handguard over top of barrel
Approximate wt.: 9½ lbs.
Comments: Produced by Winchester and Springfield during World War II. Additional M1's produced after World War II by International Harvester and Harrington & Richardson. Add $150.00 for Winchester.

Estimated Value:	**Very good:**	**$1,500.00**
	Good:	**$1,200.00**

U.S. M1 Carbine

Caliber: 30 M1 Carbine
Action: Semiautomatic; gas-operated
Magazine: 15- or 30-shot staggered row, detachable box
Barrel: 18"
Sights: Blade front with protective ears, aperture rear or flip-down rear
Stock and Forearm: One-piece wood stock and forearm; wooden handguard on top of barrel
Approximate wt.: 5½ lbs.
Comments: Developed during World War II to replace the sidearms used by non-commissioned officers, special troops, and company grade officers.

Estimated Value:	**Very good:**	**$815.00**
	Good:	**$650.00**

U.S. M1 A1 Carbine

Same general specifications as U.S. M1 Carbine except: folding metal stock; 25" overall length when folded; approximate wt. 6¼ lbs.

Estimated Value:	**Very good:**	**$1,200.00**
	Good:	**$ 960.00**

Johnson M1941

Caliber: 30-06
Action: Semiautomatic; recoil action; hesitation-locked breech; barrel partially recoils to begin unlocking phase; manual safety in front of trigger guard
Magazine: 10-shot rotary-type; a vertical feed magazine was also made
Barrel: 22"
Sights: Post front with protective ears, aperture rear
Stock and Forearm: Plain wood semi-pistol grip stock and forearm; metal handguard over barrel above forearm
Approximate wt.: 9½ lbs.
Comments: The Johnson was thought to be superior to the M1 but a series of tests and demonstrations in 1939 and 1940 indicated otherwise; used by U.S. Marines for a limited period in World War II and by the Dutch in the East Indies; many re-barreled in other calibers after World War II.

Estimated Value:	**Very good:**	**$2,400.00**
	Good:	**$1,920.00**

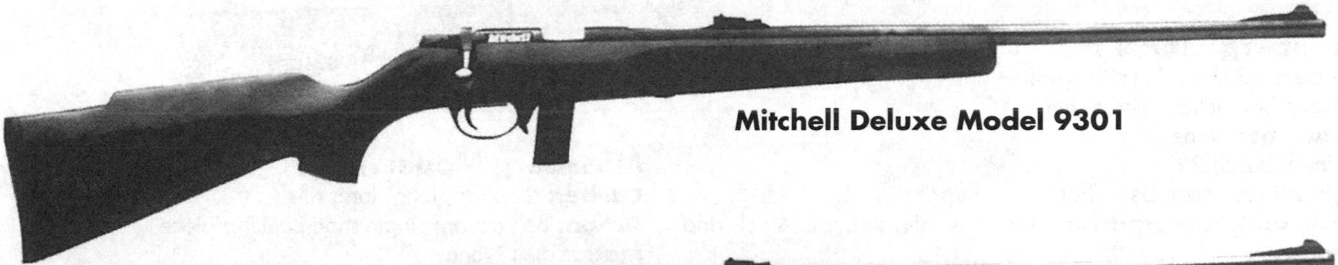

Mitchell Deluxe Model 9301

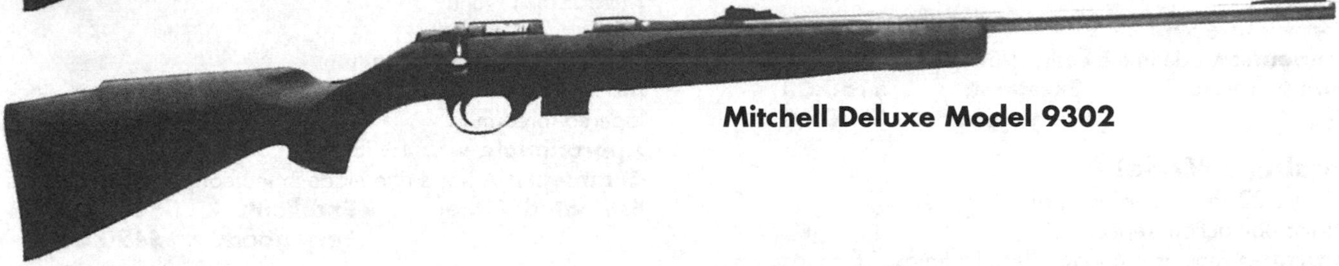

Mitchell Deluxe Model 9302

Mitchell Deluxe Models 9301 and 9302

Caliber: 22 long rifle (9301); 22 WRM (9302)
Action: Bolt action; repeating
Magazine: 10-shot clip (9301); 5-shot clip (9302)
Barrel: Blued; 22" or 24"
Sights: Adjustable rear, ramp front
Stock and Forearm: Checkered walnut one-piece Monte Carlo pistol grip stock and forearm
Approximate wt.: 6 lbs.
Comments: Made in the 1990s. Add 2% for 22WRM (9302).

Estimated Value:	**Excellent:**	**$225.00**
	Very good:	**$180.00**

Mitchell Standard Models 9303 and 9304

Same as Deluxe Models 9301 and 9302 except: plain, smooth, one-piece walnut stock and forearm; add 2% for WRM. Made in the 1990s.

Estimated Value:	**Excellent:**	**$215.00**
	Very good:	**$170.00**

Mitchell Model 15/22

Mitchell Models 15/22 and 15/22D Carbine

Caliber: 22 long rifle
Action: Semiautomatic
Magazine: 15-shot clip
Barrel: Blued; 20" or 22"
Sights: Open adjustable rear, ramp front
Stock and Forearm: Checkered walnut or rosewood one-piece semi-pistol grip stock and forearm on 1522D. Plain, smooth walnut one-piece semi-pistol grip stock and forearm on 15/22
Approximate wt.: 5½ lbs.
Comments: Made from the early 1990s to the mid-1990s. Model 15/22D is deluxe model, add 25%.

Estimated Value:	**Excellent:**	**$135.00**
	Very good:	**$105.00**

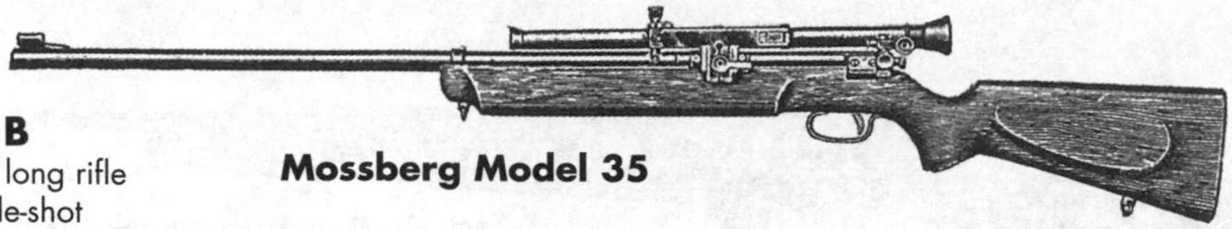

Mossberg Model 35

Mossberg Model B
Caliber: 22 short, long, long rifle
Action: Bolt action; single-shot
Magazine: None
Barrel: Blued; 22"
Sights: Open rear, bead front
Stock and Forearm: Plain wood semi-pistol grip stock and forearm
Approximate wt.: 5 lbs.
Comments: Made in the early 1930s.
Estimated Value: **Excellent:** **$150.00**
Very good: **$120.00**

Mossberg Model R
Caliber: 22 short, long, long rifle
Action: Bolt action; repeating
Magazine: Tubular; 14 long rifles, 16 longs, 20 shorts
Barrel: Blued; 24"
Sights: Open rear, bead front
Stock and Forearm: Walnut semi-pistol grip stock and forearm
Approximate wt.: 5 lbs.
Comments: Made in the early 1930s.
Estimated Value: **Excellent:** **$165.00**
Very good: **$135.00**

Mossberg Model 10
Caliber: 22 short, long, long rifle
Action: Bolt action; single-shot
Magazine: None
Barrel: Blued; 22"
Sights: Open rear, bead front
Stock and Forearm: Walnut semi-pistol grip stock and forearm; swivels
Approximate wt.: 4 lbs.
Comments: Made from the early to the mid-1930s. Takedown-type.
Estimated Value: **Excellent:** **$125.00**
Very good: **$105.00**

Mossberg Model 20
Similar to the Model 10 with a 24" barrel and grooved forearm. Made in the mid-1930s.
Estimated Value: **Excellent:** **$120.00**
Very good: **$100.00**

Mossberg Model 30
Similar to the Model 20 with peep rear sight and hooded ramp front sight. Made in the mid-1930s.
Estimated Value: **Excellent:** **$120.00**
Very good: **$100.00**

Mossberg Model 40
Similar to the Model 30 with tubular magazine that holds 16 long rifles, 18 longs, 22 shorts; bolt action; repeating. Made in the mid-1930s.
Estimated Value: **Excellent:** **$125.00**
Very good: **$105.00**

Mossberg Model M
Caliber: 22 short, long, long rifle
Action: Bolt action; single-shot; cocking piece
Magazine: None
Barrel: 20"; round
Sights: Open rear, blade front
Stock and Forearm: Plain one-piece semi-pistol grip stock and tapered forearm
Approximate wt.: 4¼ lbs.
Comments: A boy's rifle made in the early 1930s.
Estimated Value: **Excellent:** **$150.00**
Very good: **$120.00**

Mossberg Model 14
Caliber: 22 short, long, long rifle
Action: Bolt action; single-shot
Magazine: None
Barrel: Blued; 24"
Sights: Peep rear, hooded ramp front
Stock and Forearm: Plain one-piece semi-pistol grip stock and forearm; swivels
Approximate wt.: 5½ lbs.
Comments: Made in the mid-1930s.
Estimated Value: **Excellent:** **$115.00**
Very good: **$ 95.00**

Mossberg Model 34
Similar to the Model 14, made in the mid-1930s.
Estimated Value: **Excellent:** **$110.00**
Very good: **$ 85.00**

Mossberg Model 35
Caliber: 22 long rifle
Action: Bolt action; single-shot
Magazine: None
Barrel: Blued; 26" heavy
Sights: Micrometer rear, hooded ramp front
Stock and Forearm: Plain walnut one-piece semi-pistol grip stock and forearm; cheekpiece; swivels
Approximate wt.: 8¼ lbs.
Comments: Made in the mid-1930s.
Estimated Value: **Excellent:** **$200.00**
Very good: **$160.00**

Mossberg Model 35A
Similar to the Model 35; target stock and sights. Made in the late 1930s.
Estimated Value: **Excellent:** **$225.00**
Very good: **$180.00**

Mossberg Model 35A-LS
Similar to the Model 35A with special Lyman sights.
Estimated Value: **Excellent:** **$245.00**
Very good: **$195.00**

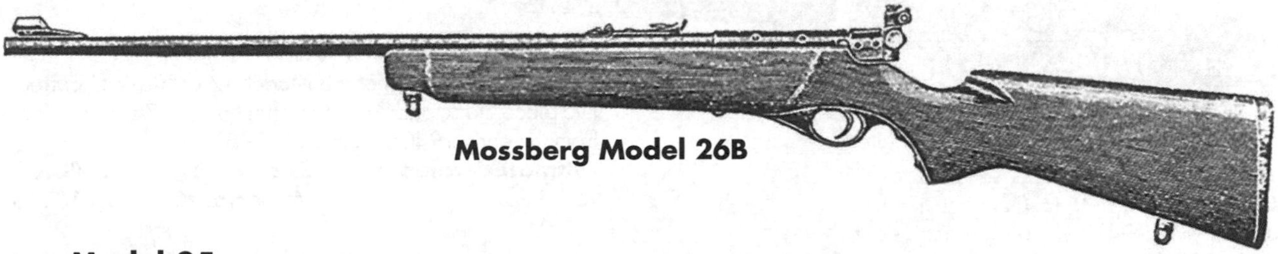

Mossberg Model 26B

Mossberg Model 25

Caliber: 22 short, long, long rifle
Action: Bolt action; single-shot
Magazine: None
Barrel: Blued; 24"
Sights: Peep rear, hooded ramp front
Stock and Forearm: Plain walnut one-piece pistol grip stock and forearm; swivels
Approximate wt.: 5 lbs.
Comments: Made in the mid-1930s.

Estimated Value:	**Excellent:**	**$120.00**
	Very good:	**$100.00**

Mossberg Model 25A

Similar to the Model 25 with higher quality finish and better wood. Made in the late 1930s.

Estimated Value:	**Excellent:**	**$130.00**
	Very good:	**$105.00**

Mossberg Model 26B

Caliber: 22 short, long, long rifle
Action: Bolt action; single-shot
Magazine: None
Barrel: Blued; 26"
Sights: Micrometer rear, hooded ramp front
Stock and Forearm: Plain one-piece semi-pistol grip stock and forearm; swivels
Approximate wt.: 5½ lbs.
Comments: Made in the late 1930s.

Estimated Value:	**Excellent:**	**$125.00**
	Very good:	**$100.00**

Mossberg Model 26C

Similar to the Model 26B without swivels or peep sight.

Estimated Value:	**Excellent:**	**$110.00**
	Very good:	**$ 85.00**

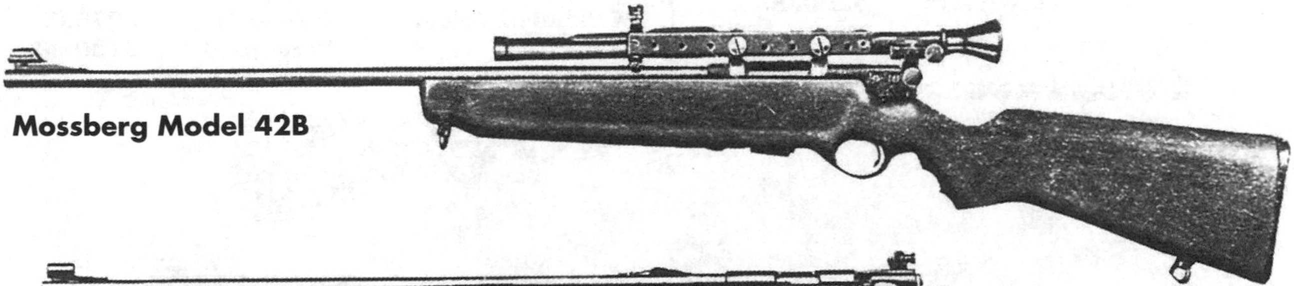

Mossberg Model 42B

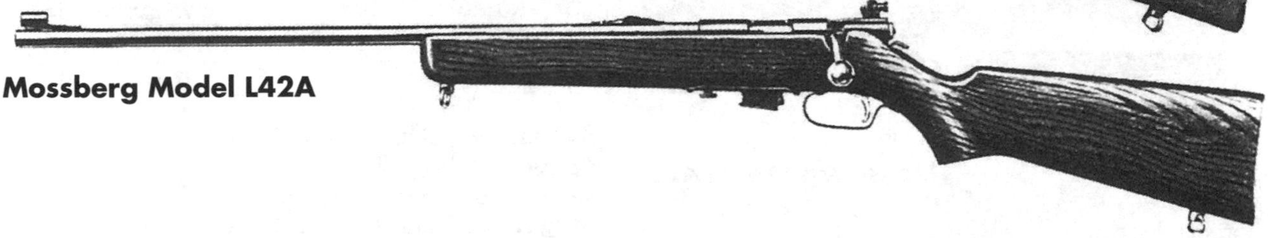

Mossberg Model L42A

Mossberg Model 42

Caliber: 22 short, long, long rifle
Action: Bolt action; repeating
Magazine: 7-shot detachable
Barrel: Blued; 24"
Sights: Open rear, receiver peep, hooded ramp front
Stock and Forearm: Plain walnut one-piece semi-pistol grip stock and forearm; swivels
Approximate wt.: 5 lbs.
Comments: Made in the mid-1930s; takedown model.

Estimated Value:	**Excellent:**	**$130.00**
	Very good:	**$105.00**

Mossberg Models 42A and L42A

Similar to the Model 42 but higher quality. Model L42A is left-hand action. Made in the late 1930s.

Estimated Value:	**Excellent:**	**$140.00**
	Very good:	**$115.00**

Mossberg Model 42B

An improved version of the Model 42A with micrometer peep sight and 5-shot magazine. Made from the late 1930s to the early 1940s.

Estimated Value:	**Excellent:**	**$150.00**
	Very good:	**$120.00**

Mossberg Model 42C

Mossberg Model 42C

Similar to the Model 42B without the peep sight.

Estimated Value: **Excellent:** **$130.00**
Very good: **$100.00**

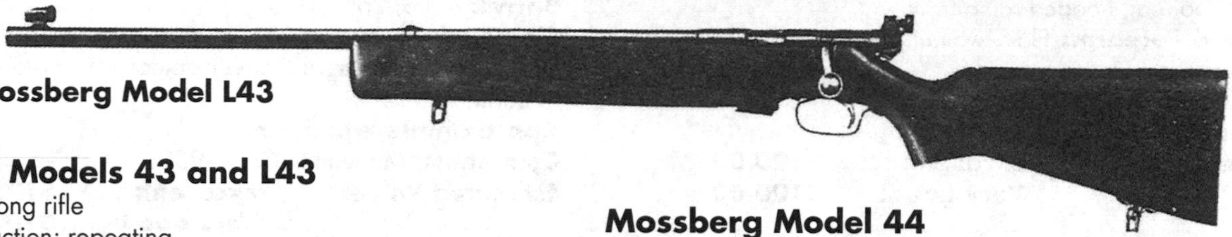

Mossberg Model L43

Mossberg Models 43 and L43

Caliber: 22 long rifle
Action: Bolt action; repeating
Magazine: 7-shot detachable box
Barrel: Blued; 26"
Sights: Special Lyman sights
Stock and Forearm: Walnut one-piece semi-pistol grip stock and forearm; cheekpiece; swivels
Approximate wt.: 8¼ lbs.
Comments: Made in the late 1930s. Model L43 is left-handed.
Estimated Value: **Excellent:** **$250.00**
Very good: **$200.00**

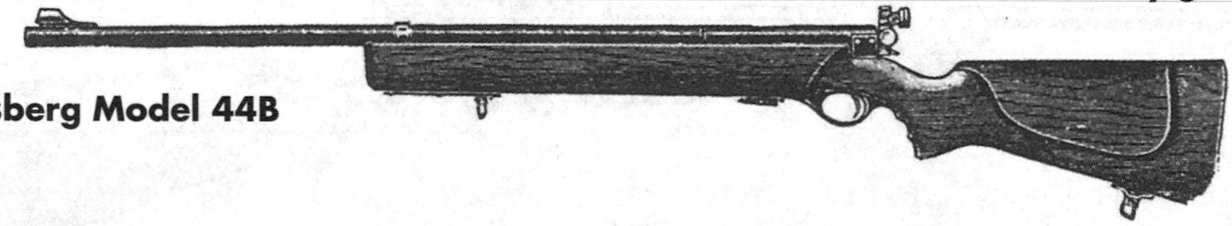

Mossberg Model 44B

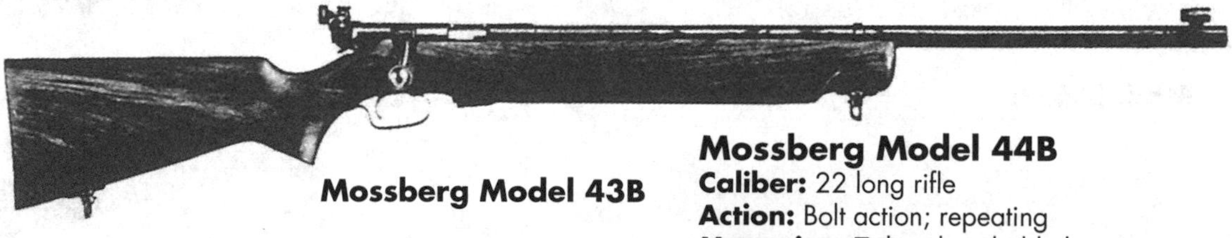

Mossberg Model 43B

Mossberg Model 43B

Similar to the Model 44B with special Lyman sights.

Estimated Value: **Excellent:** **$250.00**
Very good: **$200.00**

Mossberg Model 44 U.S.

Improved version of the Model 44B. Made from the early 1930s to the late 1940s; used as a training rifle for U.S. armed forces in World War II.

Estimated Value: **Excellent:** **$225.00**
Very good: **$165.00**

Mossberg Model 42M

More modern version of the Model 42 with a 23" barrel; full-length; two-piece stock and forearm; cheekpiece; 7-shot magazine. Made from the early 1940s to the early 1950s.

Estimated Value: **Excellent:** **$140.00**
Very good: **$115.00**

Mossberg Model 42MB

Similar to the Model 42. Used as a military training rifle in Great Britain in World War II; full stock.

Estimated Value: **Excellent:** **$210.00**
Very good: **$175.00**

Mossberg Model 44

Caliber: 22 short, long, long rifle
Action: Bolt action; repeating
Magazine: Tubular; 16 long rifles, 18 longs, 22 shorts
Barrel: Blued; 24"
Sights: Peep rear, hooded ramp front
Stock and Forearm: Plain walnut one-piece semi-pistol grip stock and forearm; swivels
Approximate wt.: 6 lbs.
Comments: Made in the mid-1930s.
Estimated Value: **Excellent:** **$225.00**
Very good: **$180.00**

Mossberg Model 44B

Caliber: 22 long rifle
Action: Bolt action; repeating
Magazine: 7-shot detachable box
Barrel: 26"; heavy barrel
Sights: Micrometer receiver, hooded front
Stock and Forearm: Plain one-piece semi-pistol grip stock and forearm; swivels; cheekpiece
Approximate wt.: 8 lbs.
Comments: Made from the late 1930s to the early 1940s.
Estimated Value: **Excellent:** **$200.00**
Very good: **$160.00**

Mossberg Model 35B

Single-shot version of the Model 44B. Made in the 1930s.

Estimated Value: **Excellent:** **$188.00**
Very good: **$150.00**

Mossberg Model 45

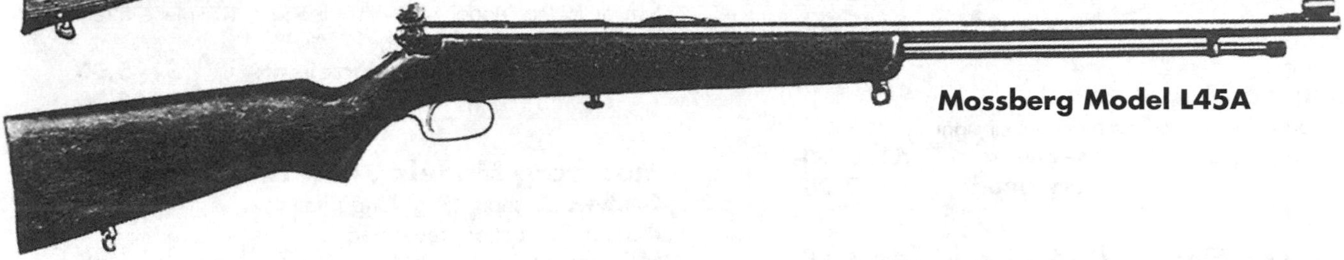

Mossberg Model L45A

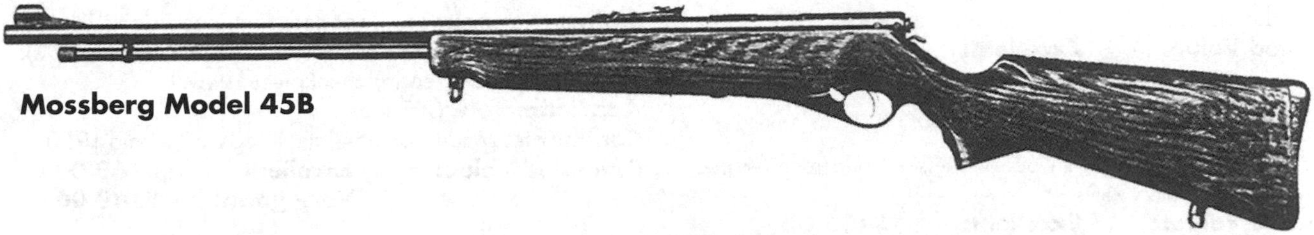

Mossberg Model 45B

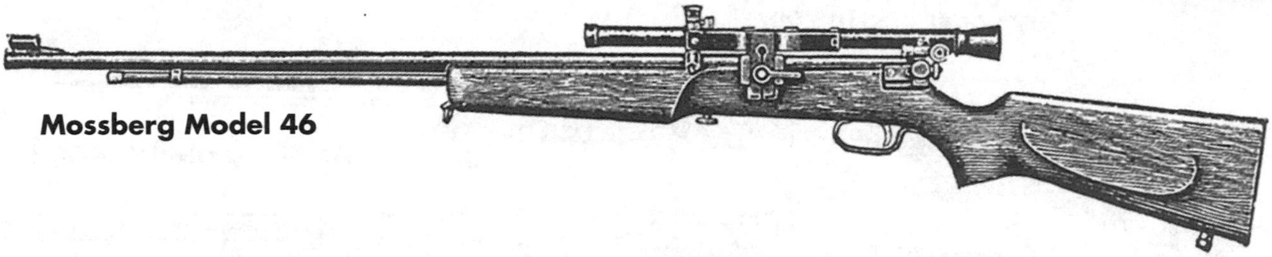

Mossberg Model 46

Mossberg Model 45

Caliber: 22 short, long, long rifle
Action: Bolt action; repeating
Magazine: Tubular; 15 long rifles, 18 longs, 22 shorts
Barrel: Blued; 24"
Sights: Peep rear, hooded ramp front
Stock and Forearm: Plain one-piece semi-pistol grip stock and forearm; swivels
Approximate wt.: 6¾ lbs.
Comments: Made in the mid-1930s.

Estimated Value: **Excellent:** **$175.00**
Very good: **$140.00**

Mossberg Model 45C

Similar to the Model 45 without sights.

Estimated Value: **Excellent:** **$130.00**
Very good: **$105.00**

Mossberg Models 45A and L45A

Improved version of the Model 45, made in the late 1930s. Model L45A is left-handed action.

Estimated Value: **Excellent:** **$165.00**
Very good: **$135.00**

Mossberg Model 45AC

Similar to the Model 45A without sights.

Estimated Value: **Excellent:** **$135.00**
Very good: **$110.00**

Mossberg Model 45B

Similar to the Model 45A with open rear sight. Made in the late 1930s.

Estimated Value: **Excellent:** **$150.00**
Very good: **$120.00**

Mossberg Model 46

Caliber: 22 short, long, long rifle
Action: Bolt action; repeating
Magazine: Tubular; 15 long rifles, 18 longs, 22 shorts
Barrel: Blued; 26"
Sights: Micrometer rear, hooded ramp front
Stock and Forearm: Plain one-piece semi-pistol grip stock and forearm; cheekpiece; swivels
Approximate wt.: 7½ lbs.
Comments: Made in the mid-1930s.

Estimated Value: **Excellent:** **$200.00**
Very good: **$160.00**

Mossberg Model 46C
A heavy barrel version of the Model 46.
Estimated Value: **Excellent:** **$175.00**
Very good: **$140.00**

Mossberg Model 46A
An improved version of the Model 46; made in the late 1930s.
Estimated Value: **Excellent:** **$175.00**
Very good: **$140.00**

Mossberg Model 46AC
Similar to the Model 46A with open rear sight.
Estimated Value: **Excellent:** **$150.00**
Very good: **$120.00**

Mossberg Models 46A-LS and L46A-LS
Similar to the Model 46A with special Lyman sights. Model L46A-LS is left-handed action.
Estimated Value: **Excellent:** **$160.00**
Very good: **$130.00**

Mossberg Model 46B
Similar to the Model 46A with open rear sight and receiver peep sight. Made in the late 1930s.
Estimated Value: **Excellent:** **$130.00**
Very good: **$105.00**

Mossberg Model 46BT
A heavy barrel version of the Model 46B. Made in the late 1930s.
Estimated Value: **Excellent:** **$185.00**
Very good: **$150.00**

Mossberg Model 46M
Similar to the Model 46 with full-length, two-piece forearm. Made from about 1940 to the early 1950s.
Estimated Value: **Excellent:** **$175.00**
Very good: **$145.00**

Mossberg Models 346K and 346B
Caliber: 22 short, long, long rifle
Action: Bolt action; repeating
Magazine: Tubular; 20 long rifles, 23 longs, 30 shorts
Barrel: Blued; 26"
Sights: Micrometer rear, hooded front; peep sights (346B)
Stock and Forearm: Plain Monte Carlo one-piece pistol grip stock and lipped forearm; cheekpiece; swivels
Approximate wt.: 7 lbs.
Comments: Made from the late 1940s to the mid-1950s.
Estimated Value: **Excellent:** **$160.00**
Very good: **$140.00**

Mossberg Model L46A-LS

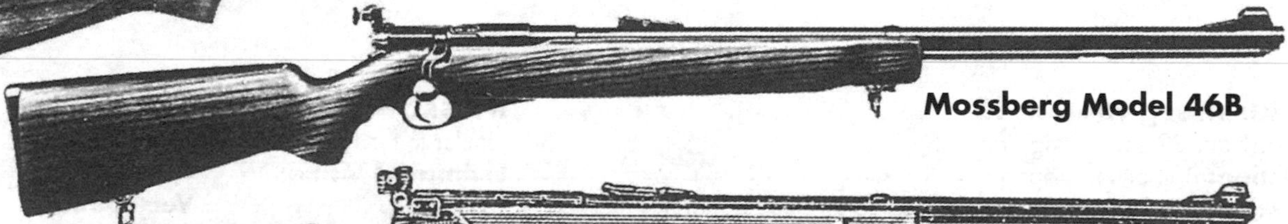
Mossberg Model 46B

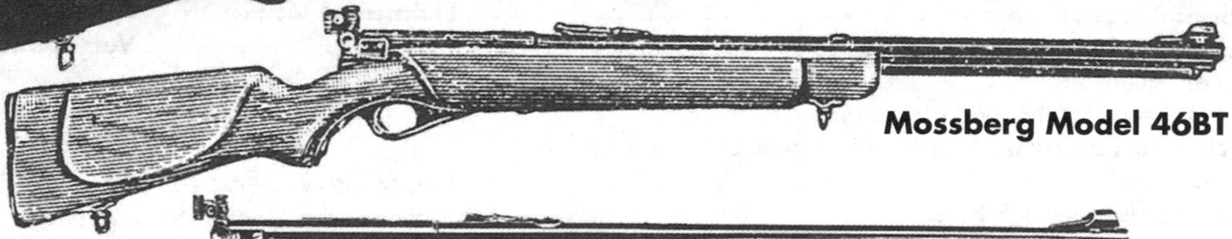
Mossberg Model 46BT

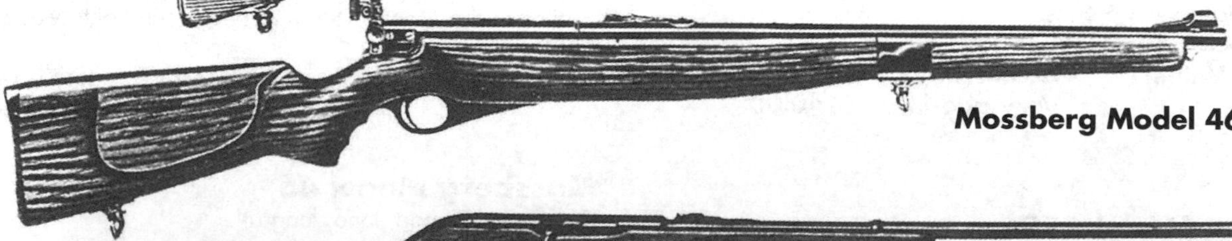
Mossberg Model 46M

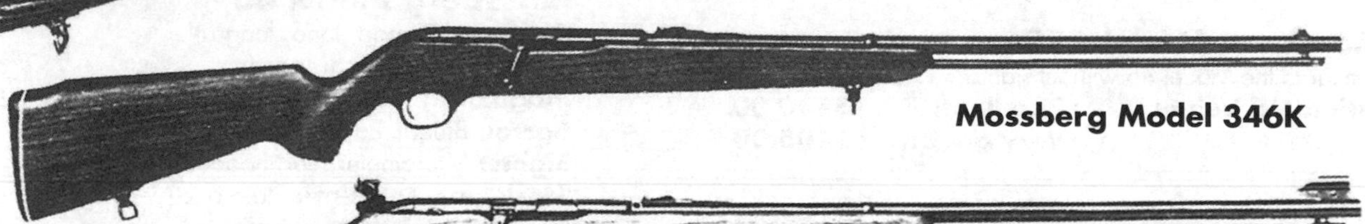
Mossberg Model 346K

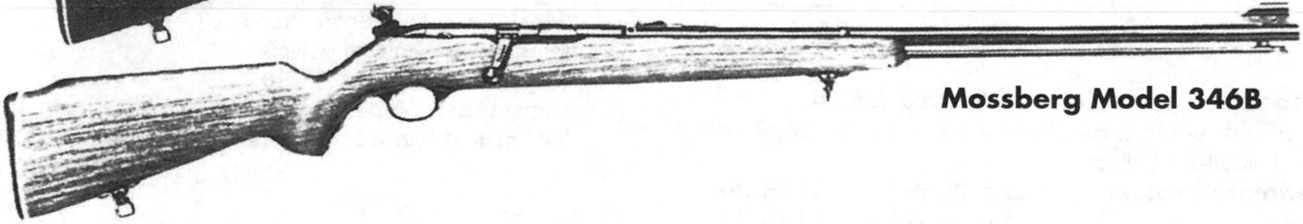
Mossberg Model 346B

Mossberg Model 320K

Mossberg Model 340K

Mossberg Model 340B

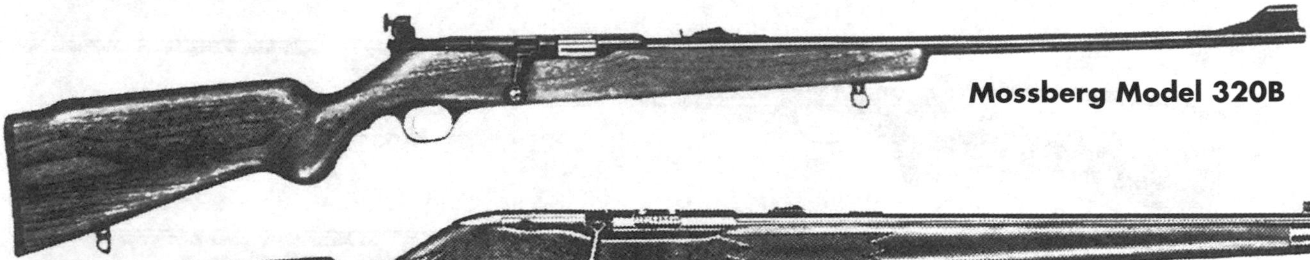

Mossberg Model 320B

Mossberg Model 340M Carbine

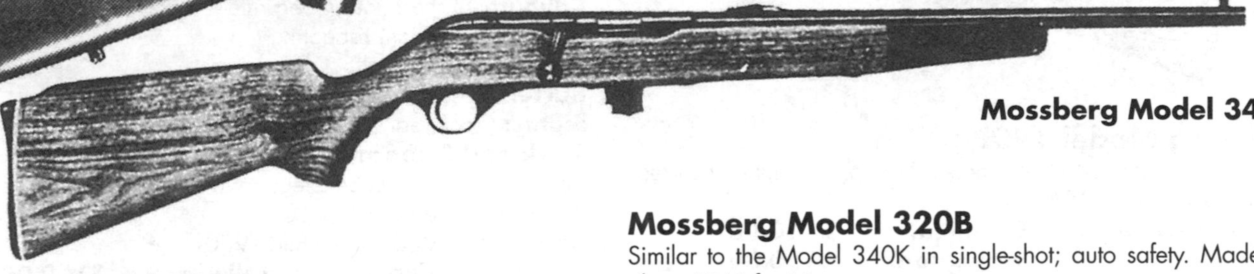

Mossberg Model 342K

Mossberg Model 320K

Single-shot version of the Model 346K. Weighs about 5¾ lbs. Discontinued about 1960.

Estimated Value: **Excellent:** **$115.00**
Very good: **$ 95.00**

Mossberg Model 340K

Similar to the Model 346K with 7-shot clip magazine.

Estimated Value: **Excellent:** **$150.00**
Very good: **$120.00**

Mossberg Model 340B

Similar to the Model 346B with 7-shot clip magazine.

Estimated Value: **Excellent:** **$170.00**
Very good: **$135.00**

Mossberg Model 320B

Similar to the Model 340K in single-shot; auto safety. Made from about 1960 for 11 years.

Estimated Value: **Excellent:** **$145.00**
Very good: **$115.00**

Mossberg Model 340M Carbine

Similar to the Model 340K with full-length forearm and 18" barrel. Made in the early 1970s.

Estimated Value: **Excellent:** **$250.00**
Very good: **$200.00**

Mossberg Model 342K

Similar to the Model 340K with 18" barrel; hinged forearm for forward grip; side-mounted swivels. Made from the late 1950s to the mid-1970s.

Estimated Value: **Excellent:** **$150.00**
Very good: **$120.00**

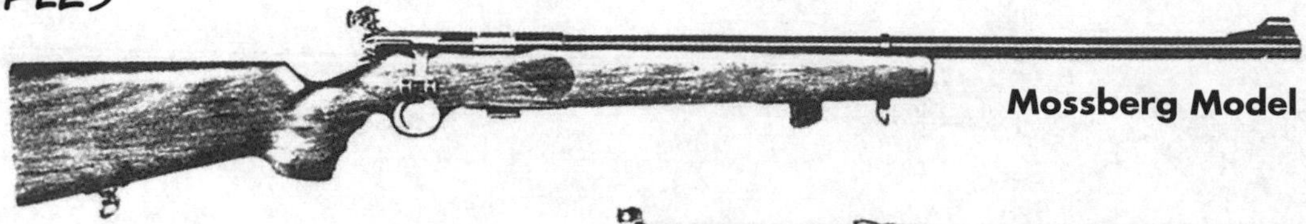

Mossberg Model 144

Mossberg Model 146B

Mossberg Model 144

Caliber: 22 long rifle
Action: Bolt action; repeating
Magazine: 7-shot clip
Barrel: Blued; 26"; heavy
Sights: Micrometer receiver, hooded front
Stock and Forearm: Walnut one-piece semi-pistol grip stock and forearm; hand rest; swivels
Approximate wt.: 8 lbs.
Comments: Made from the late 1940s to the mid-1980s.

Estimated Value:	**Excellent:**	**$250.00**
	Very good:	**$200.00**

Mossberg Model 146B

Caliber: 22 short, long, long rifle
Action: Bolt action; repeating
Magazine: Tubular; 20 long rifles, 23 longs, 30 shorts
Barrel: Blued; 26"
Sights: Micrometer receiver, hooded front
Stock and Forearm: Plain Monte Carlo one-piece pistol grip stock and lipped forearm; cheekpiece; swivels
Approximate wt.: 7 lbs.
Comments: Made from the late 1940s to the mid-1950s.

Estimated Value:	**Excellent:**	**$175.00**
	Very good:	**$140.00**

Mossberg Model 140K

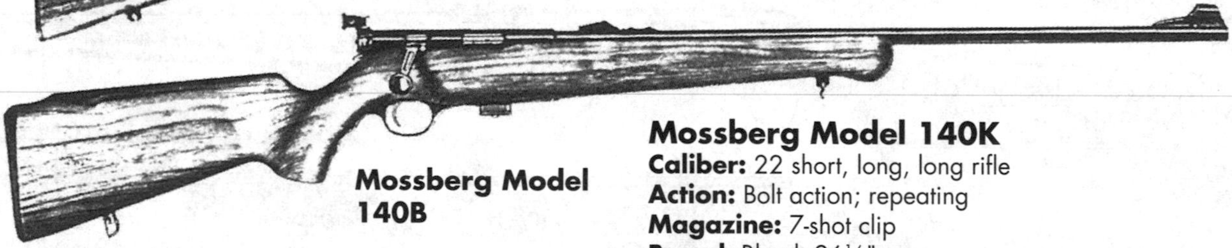

Mossberg Model 140B

Mossberg Model 140B

Similar to the Model 140K with hooded ramp front sight, peep rear sight. Made in the late 1950s.

Estimated Value:	**Excellent:**	**$150.00**
	Very good:	**$120.00**

Mossberg Model 140K

Caliber: 22 short, long, long rifle
Action: Bolt action; repeating
Magazine: 7-shot clip
Barrel: Blued; 26½"
Sights: Open rear, bead front
Stock and Forearm: Walnut Monte Carlo one-piece pistol grip stock and forearm; cheekpiece; swivels
Approximate wt.: 5¾ lbs.
Comments: Made in the mid-1950s.

Estimated Value:	**Excellent:**	**$150.00**
	Very good:	**$120.00**

Mossberg Model 640K

Mossberg Model 640K

Caliber: 22 magnum
Action: Bolt action; repeating
Magazine: 5-shot box
Barrel: Blued; 24"
Sights: Open rear, bead front; adjustable
Stock and Forearm: Checkered walnut Monte Carlo one-piece pistol grip stock and forearm; swivels
Approximate wt.: 6 lbs.
Comments: Made from about 1960 to the mid-1980s.

Estimated Value:	**Excellent:**	**$155.00**
	Very good:	**$125.00**

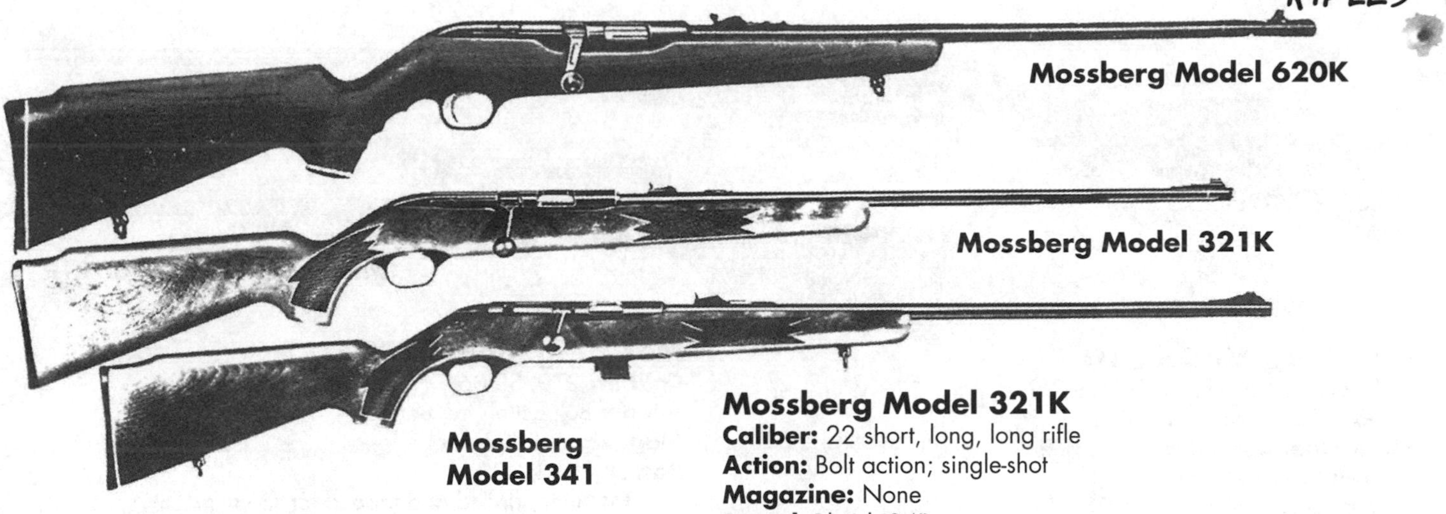

Mossberg Model 620K

Mossberg Model 321K

Mossberg Model 341

Mossberg Model 620K

Similar to the Model 640K in single-shot. Discontinued in the mid-1960s.

Estimated Value: **Excellent:** **$160.00**
Very good: **$125.00**

Mossberg Model 341

Similar to the Model 321K with 7-shot clip magazine; swivels; bolt action; repeating; adjustable sights.

Estimated Value: **Excellent:** **$120.00**
Very good: **$ 95.00**

Mossberg Model 321K

Caliber: 22 short, long, long rifle
Action: Bolt action; single-shot
Magazine: None
Barrel: Blued; 24"
Sights: Open rear, ramp front
Stock and Forearm: Checkered Monte Carlo one-piece pistol grip stock and forearm
Approximate wt.: 6½ lbs.
Comments: Made from the early 1970s to the early 1980s.
Estimated Value: **Excellent:** **$130.00**
Very good: **$105.00**

Mossberg Model 800A

Mossberg Model 800 Varmint

Mossberg Model 800A

Caliber: 308, 243, 22-250, 222 Rem.
Action: Bolt action; repeating
Magazine: 4-shot box
Barrel: Blued; 22"
Sights: Leaf rear, ramp front
Stock and Forearm: Checkered wood Monte Carlo one-piece pistol grip stock and forearm; swivels
Approximate wt.: 6½ lbs.
Comments: Made from the late 1960s to the late 1970s.
Estimated Value: **Excellent:** **$225.00**
Very good: **$180.00**

Mossberg Model 800 Varmint

Similar to the Model 800A with a 24" barrel and scope mounts. In 243 and 22-250 calibers.

Estimated Value: **Excellent:** **$230.00**
Very good: **$185.00**

Mossberg Model 800 Target

Similar to the Model 800A with scope mounts and scope in 308, 243, 22-250 calibers. Made from the late 1960s to the early 1970s.

Estimated Value: **Excellent:** **$250.00**
Very good: **$190.00**

Mossberg Model RM-7A

Caliber: 30-06
Action: Bolt action; repeating
Magazine: 4-shot rotary
Barrel: 22"; round
Sights: Adjustable folding leaf rear, ramp front
Stock and Forearm: Checkered walnut one-piece pistol grip stock and forearm; fluted comb; recoil pad
Approximate wt.: 7½ lbs.
Comments: Made in the late 1970s.
Estimated Value: **Excellent:** **$245.00**
Very good: **$195.00**

Mossberg Model RM-7B

Similar to the Model RM-7A except: 7mm Rem. magnum caliber, 3-shot magazine, 24" barrel.

Estimated Value: **Excellent:** **$260.00**
Very good: **$210.00**

Mossberg Model 810

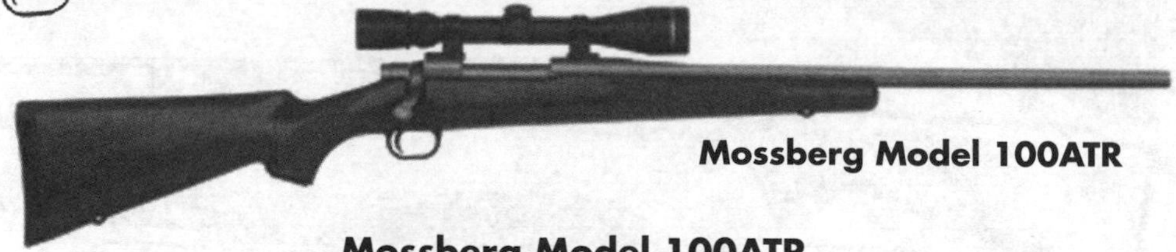

Mossberg Model 100ATR

Mossberg Model 810

Caliber: 30-06, 7mm Rem. mag., 270 Win., 338 Win. mag
Action: Bolt action; repeating
Magazine: 4-shot detachable box
Barrel: Blued; 22"
Sights: Leaf rear, ramp front
Stock and Forearm: Checkered Monte Carlo one-piece pistol grip stock and forearm; swivels; recoil pad
Approximate wt.: 7½ to 8 lbs.
Comments: Add 7% for 7mm Rem. mag. Made from the early to the late 1970s.

Estimated Value:	**Excellent:**	**$290.00**
	Very good:	**$230.00**

Mossberg Model 100ATR

Caliber: 270, 30-06
Action: Bolt action, repeating
Magazine: 4-shot box
Barrel: Blued; 22″
Sights: None; drilled and tapped for scope mount
Stock and Forearm: Checkered synthetic, one-piece pistol grip stock and forearm
Approximate wt.: 7 lbs.
Comments: Introduced in 2005.

Estimated Value:	**New (retail):**	**$424.00**
	Excellent:	**$320.00**
	Very good:	**$255.00**

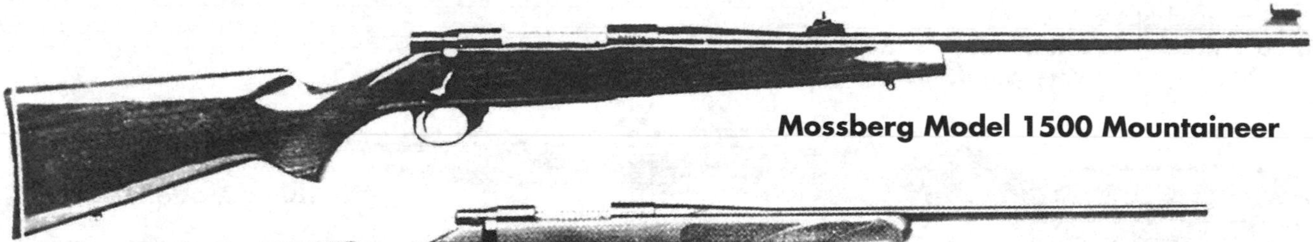

Mossberg Model 1500 Mountaineer

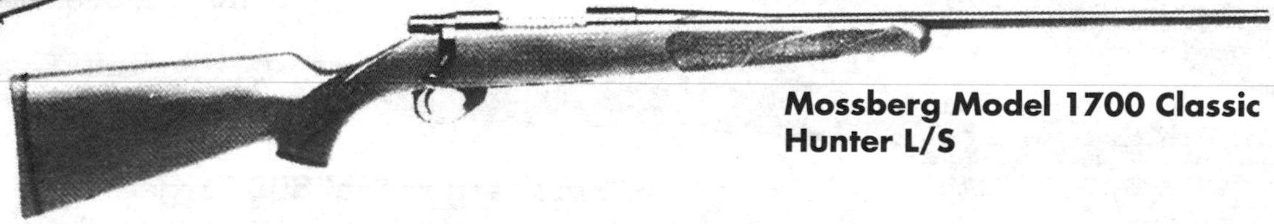

Mossberg Model 1700 Classic Hunter L/S

Mossberg Model 1500 Varmint

Mossberg Model 1500 Mountaineer

Caliber: 223, 22-250, 243, 270, 308, 30-06, 7mm magnum, 300 Win. magnum, 338 Win. magnum
Action: Bolt action, hammerless; repeating
Magazine: 5- or 6-shot box
Barrel: 22" or 24"
Sights: Available with or without adjustable rear, hooded ramp front
Stock and Forearm: Checkered walnut one-piece pistol grip stock and forearm; recoil pad on magnum
Approximate wt.: 7¾ lbs.
Comments: Produced from 1985 to 1988. Add 6% for magnum; Add 8% for sights.

Estimated Value:	**Excellent:**	**$325.00**
	Very good:	**$260.00**

Mossberg Model 1500 Varmint

Similar to the Model 1500 with a 24" heavy barrel in 223, 22-250, or 308 caliber; Monte Carlo stock; available in blued or parkerized finish. Discontinued in the late 1980s.

Estimated Value:	**Excellent:**	**$340.00**
	Very good:	**$275.00**

Mossberg Model 1550 Mountaineer

Similar to the Model 1500 with removable magazine, 22" and 24" barrel, in 243, 270, and 30-06 calibers; add 8% for sights. Discontinued in the late 1980s.

Estimated Value:	**Excellent:**	**$280.00**
	Very good:	**$220.00**

Mossberg Model 1700 Classic Hunter L/S

Similar to the Model 1500 with 22" barrel, removable magazine, lipped forearm, pistol grip cap and recoil pad, in calibers: 243, 270, and 30-06. Discontinued in the late 1980s.

Estimated Value:	**Excellent:**	**$375.00**
	Very good:	**$300.00**

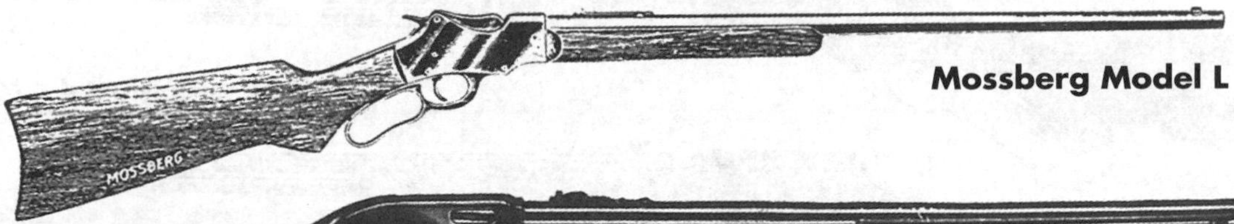
Mossberg Model L

Mossberg Model 400 Palomino

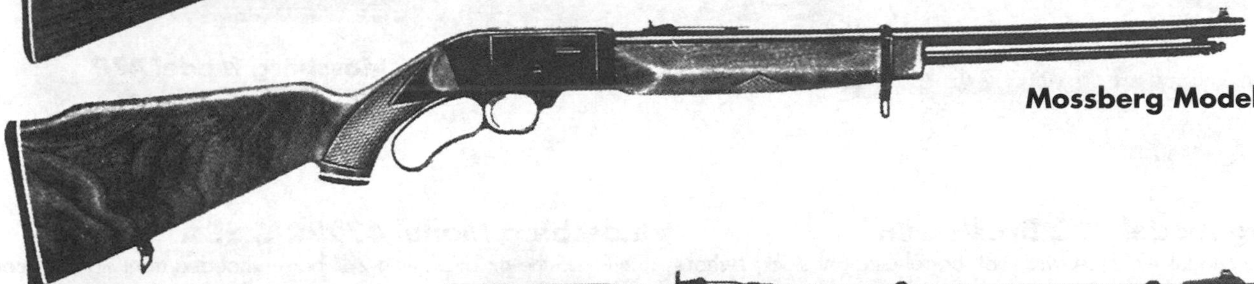
Mossberg Model 402

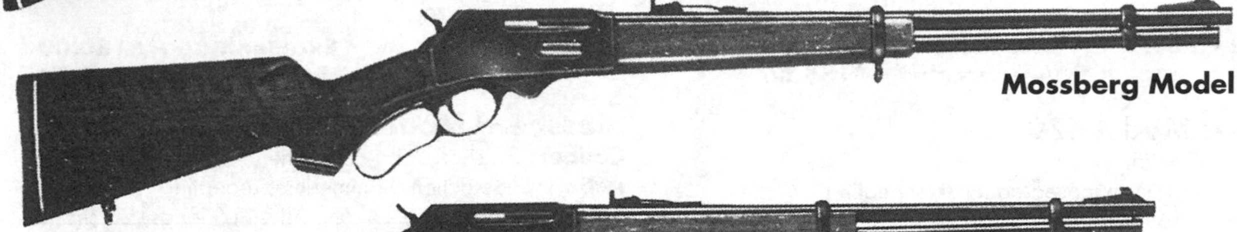
Mossberg Model 472PCA

Mossberg Model 472SCA

Mossberg Model L

Caliber: 22 short, long, long rifle
Action: Lever action, falling block; single-shot
Magazine: None
Barrel: Blued; 24"
Sights: Open rear, bead front
Stock and Forearm: Plain walnut semi-pistol grip stock and small forearm
Approximate wt.: 5 lbs.
Comments: Made from the late 1920s to the early 1930s.

Estimated Value:	**Excellent:**	**$400.00**
	Very good:	**$320.00**

Mossberg Model 400 Palomino

Caliber: 22 short, long, long rifle
Action: Lever action, hammerless; repeating
Magazine: Tubular; 15 long rifles, 17 longs, 20 shorts
Barrel: Blued; 24"
Sights: Adjustable open rear, bead front
Stock and Forearm: Checkered walnut Monte Carlo pistol grip stock and forearm; barrel bands; swivels
Approximate wt.: 4¾ lbs.
Comments: Made in the early 1960s.

Estimated Value:	**Excellent:**	**$200.00**
	Very good:	**$160.00**

Mossberg Model 402

Similar to the Model 400 except 18½" or 20" barrel, smaller capacity magazine. Discontinued in the early 1970s.

Estimated Value:	**Excellent:**	**$225.00**
	Very good:	**$180.00**

Mossberg Models 472PCA, SCA; and 479PCA, SCA

Caliber: 30-30, 35 Rem.
Action: Lever action; exposed hammer; repeating
Magazine: 6-shot tubular
Barrel: Blued; 20" or 24"
Sights: Adjustable rear, ramp front
Stock and Forearm: Plain pistol grip stock and forearm; barrel band; swivels; or straight grip stock (SCA)
Approximate wt.: 7½ lbs.
Comments: Sold first as the 472 Series, then 479 Series.

Estimated Value:	**Excellent:**	**$200.00**
	Very good:	**$160.00**

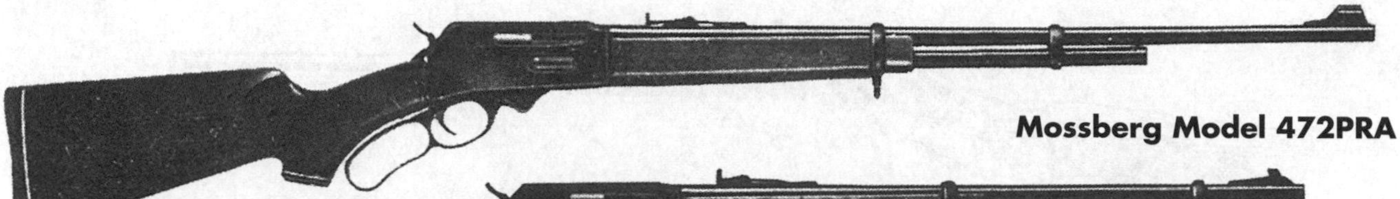

Mossberg Model 472PRA

Mossberg Model 472 Brush Gun

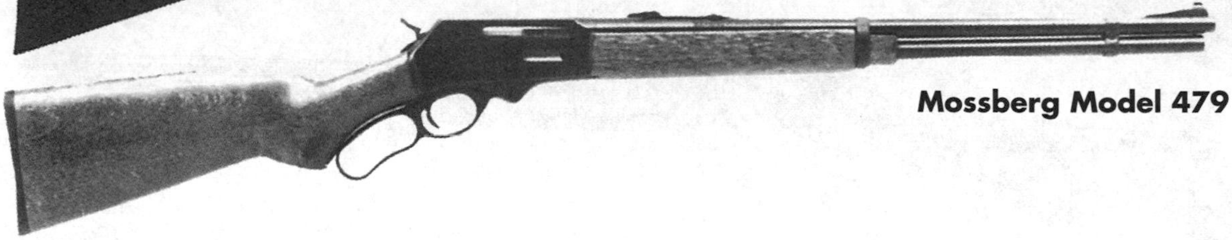

Mossberg Model 479

Mossberg Model 472 Brush Gun

Similar to the Model 472PCA with 18" barrel; straight stock; 5-shot magazine.

Estimated Value: **Excellent:** **$200.00**
Very good: **$155.00**

Mossberg Model 479

Caliber: 30-30 Win.
Action: Lever action, exposed hammer, repeating
Magazine: 5-shot tubular
Barrel: 20"
Sights: Adjustable open rear, beaded ramp front; drilled and tapped for scope
Stock and Forearm: Hardwood semi-pistol grip stock and forearm; barrel band
Approximate wt.: 6¾ lbs.
Comments: Produced from the early to the mid-1980s.
Estimated Value: **Excellent:** **$210.00**
Very good: **$160.00**

Mossberg Model 472PRA, SBA

Similar to the 472PCA with 24" barrel; hooded front sight. Discontinued in the late 1970s.

Estimated Value: **Excellent:** **$180.00**
Very good: **$145.00**

Mossberg Model K

Caliber: 22 short, long, long rifle
Action: Slide action; hammerless; repeating
Magazine: Tubular; 14 long rifles, 16 longs, 20 shorts
Barrel: Blued; 22"
Sights: Open rear, bead front
Stock and Forearm: Plain walnut straight grip stock and grooved slide handle
Approximate wt.: 5 lbs.
Comments: Made from the early 1920s to the early 1930s; takedown model.
Estimated Value: **Excellent:** **$215.00**
Very good: **$175.00**

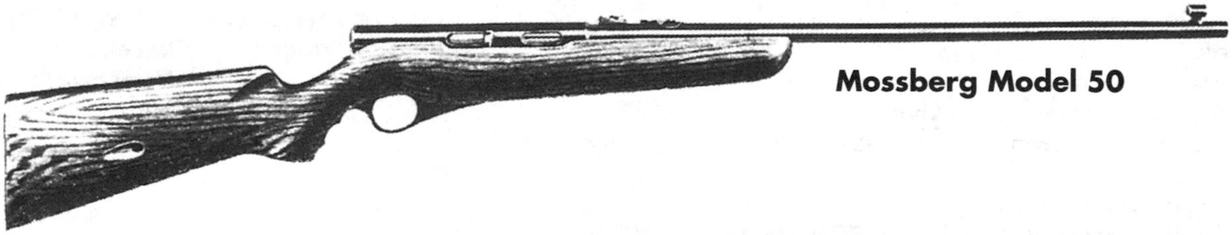

Mossberg Model 50

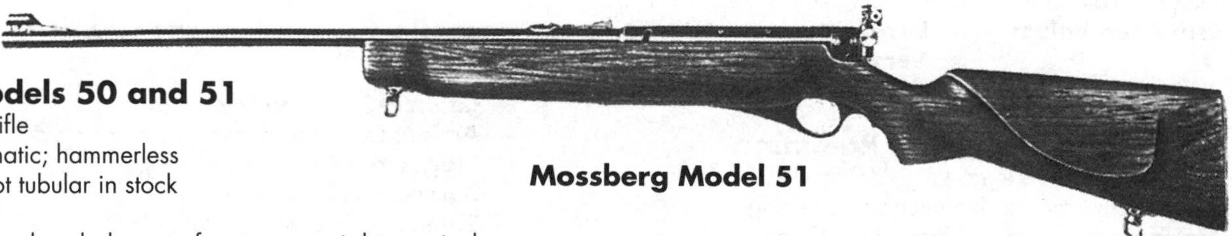

Mossberg Model 51

Mossberg Models 50 and 51

Caliber: 22 long rifle
Action: Semiautomatic; hammerless
Magazine: 15-shot tubular in stock
Barrel: Blued; 24"
Sights: Open rear, hooded ramp front; peep sights, swivels (Model 51)
Stock and Forearm: Walnut one-piece semi-pistol grip stock and forearm
Approximate wt.: 7 lbs.
Comments: Made from the late 1930s to the early 1940s.
Estimated Value: **Excellent:** **$150.00**
Very good: **$120.00**

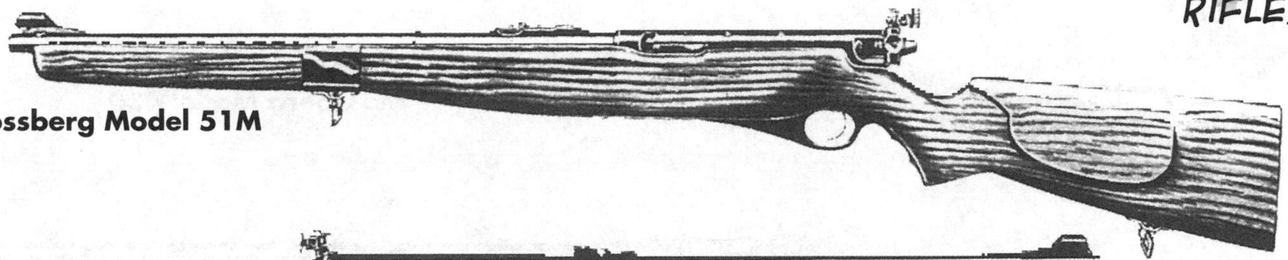

Mossberg Model 51M

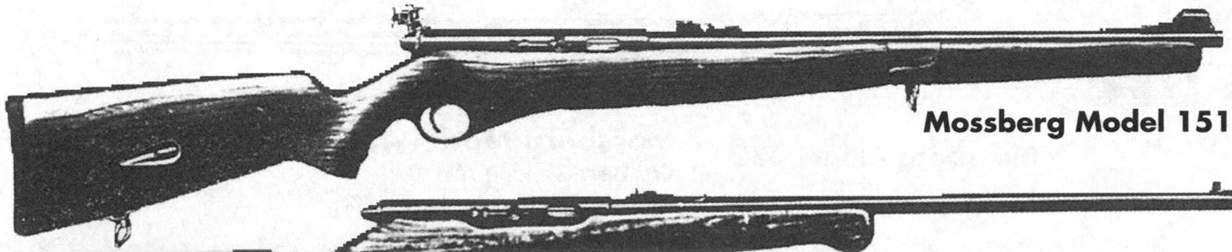

Mossberg Model 151M

Mossberg Model 151K

Mossberg Model 51M

Similar to the Model 51 with full-length, two-piece forearm and 20" barrel. Made from the late 1930s to the mid-1940s.

Estimated Value: **Excellent:** **$150.00**
Very good: **$125.00**

Mossberg Model 151M

Improved version of the Model 51M with easy takedown features. Made from the mid-1940s to the late 1950s.

Estimated Value: **Excellent:** **$155.00**
Very good: **$130.00**

Mossberg Model 151K

Similar to the Model 151M with Monte Carlo stock; standard length lipped forearm; 24" barrel; no peep sight or swivels. Made in the early 1950s.

Estimated Value: **Excellent:** **$150.00**
Very good: **$120.00**

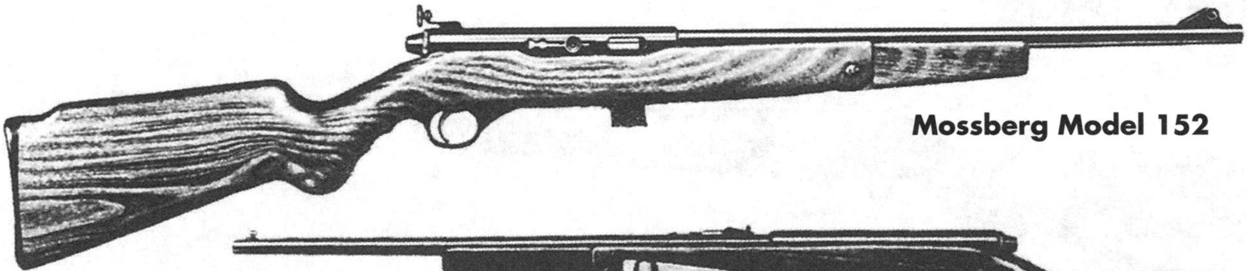

Mossberg Model 152

Mossberg Model 152K

Mossberg Model 142

Mossberg Model 152

Caliber: 22 long rifle
Action: Semiautomatic
Magazine: 7-shot detachable box
Barrel: Blued; 18"
Sights: Peep rear, military front
Stock and Forearm: Plain one-piece semi-pistol grip stock and hinged forearm for forward grip; side-mounted swivels
Approximate wt.: 5 lbs.
Comments: Made from the late 1940s to the late 1950s.
Estimated Value: **Excellent:** **$160.00**
Very good: **$125.00**

Mossberg Model 152K

Similar to the Model 152 with open rear sight; shorter barrel. Made in the 1950s.

Estimated Value: **Excellent:** **$140.00**
Very good: **$110.00**

Mossberg Model 142

Similar to the Model 152 except bolt action; available in short, long or long rifle; with peep sight.

Estimated Value: **Excellent:** **$125.00**
Very good: **$105.00**

Mossberg Model 142K

Similar to the Model 142 with open rear sight.

Estimated Value: **Excellent:** **$120.00**
Very good: **$100.00**

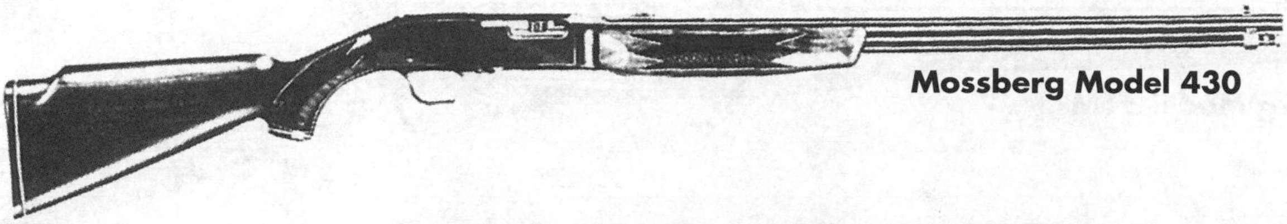

Mossberg Model 430

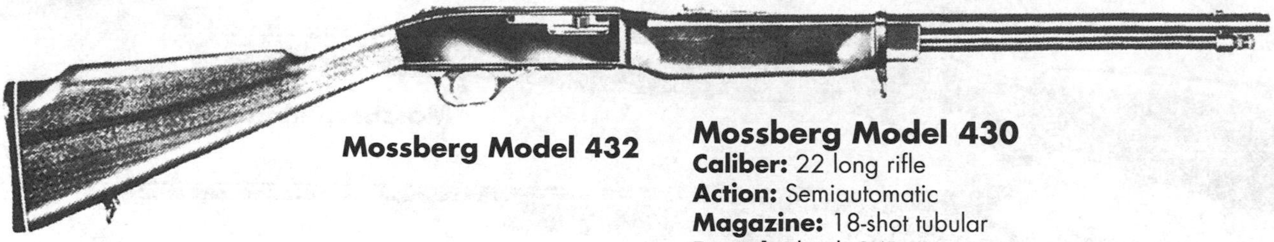

Mossberg Model 432

Mossberg Model 430

Caliber: 22 long rifle
Action: Semiautomatic
Magazine: 18-shot tubular
Barrel: Blued; 24"
Sights: Open rear, bead front
Stock and Forearm: Checkered walnut Monte Carlo pistol grip stock and forearm
Approximate wt.: 6¼ lbs.
Comments: Made in the early 1970s.

Estimated Value:	**Excellent:**	**$135.00**
	Very good:	**$110.00**

Mossberg Model 432

Similar to the Model 430 with straight grip stock; barrel band; smaller capacity magazine.

Estimated Value:	**Excellent:**	**$135.00**
	Very good:	**$110.00**

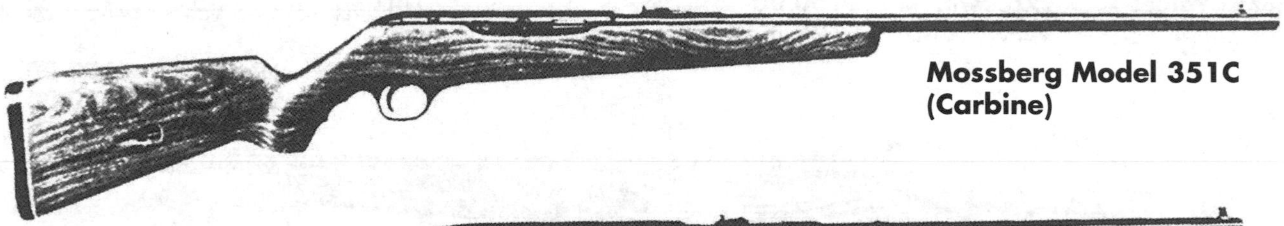

Mossberg Model 351C (Carbine)

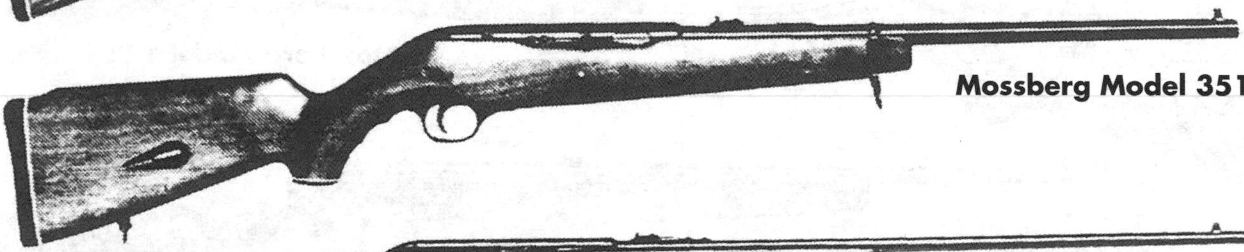

Mossberg Model 351K

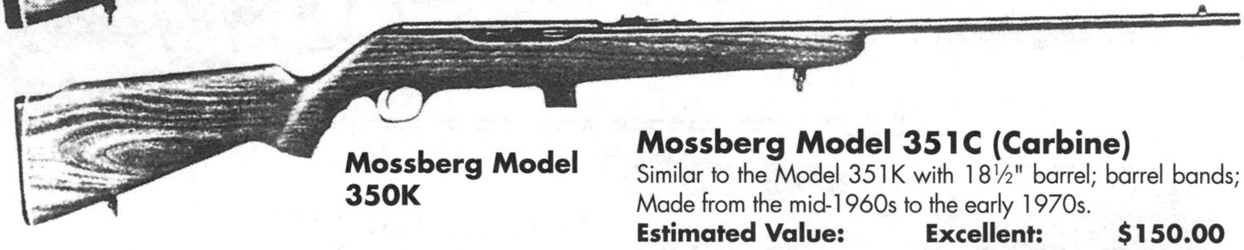

Mossberg Model 350K

Mossberg Model 351C (Carbine)

Similar to the Model 351K with 18½" barrel; barrel bands; swivels. Made from the mid-1960s to the early 1970s.

Estimated Value:	**Excellent:**	**$150.00**
	Very good:	**$120.00**

Mossberg Model 351K

Caliber: 22 long rifle
Action: Semiautomatic
Magazine: 15-shot tubular, in stock
Barrel: Blued; 24"
Sights: Open rear, bead front
Stock and Forearm: Walnut Monte Carlo one-piece semi-pistol grip stock and forearm
Approximate wt.: 6 lbs.
Comments: Made from about 1960 to 1970.

Estimated Value:	**Excellent:**	**$145.00**
	Very good:	**$115.00**

Mossberg Model 350K

Caliber: 22 long rifle
Action: Semiautomatic
Magazine: 7-shot clip
Barrel: Blued; 23½"
Sights: Open rear, bead front
Stock and Forearm: Walnut Monte Carlo one-piece semi-pistol grip stock and forearm
Approximate wt.: 6 lbs.
Comments: Made from the late 1950s to the early 1970s.

Estimated Value:	**Excellent:**	**$120.00**
	Very good:	**$100.00**

Mossberg Model 377 Plinkster

Mossberg Model 352K Carbine

Mossberg Model 377 Plinkster

Caliber: 22 long rifle
Action: Semiautomatic; hammerless
Magazine: 15-shot tubular; stock load
Barrel: 20"; round
Sights: None; 4X scope standard
Stock and Forearm: Structural foam; one-piece Monte Carlo pistol grip stock and forearm; thumbhole
Approximate wt.: 6¼ lbs.
Comments: Made from the late 1970s to the mid-1980s.

Estimated Value:	**Excellent:**	**$160.00**
	Very good:	**$125.00**

Mossberg Model 352K Carbine

Caliber: 22 long rifle
Action: Semiautomatic
Magazine: 7-shot clip
Barrel: Blued; 18½"
Sights: Open rear, bead front
Stock and Forearm: Walnut Monte Carlo one-piece pistol grip stock and forearm; swivels; hinged forearm
Approximate wt.: 5 lbs.
Comments: Made from the late 1950s to the early 1970s.

Estimated Value:	**Excellent:**	**$145.00**
	Very good:	**$115.00**

Mossberg Model 353

Similar to the Model 352K except: 18" barrel, adjustable sight. Made from the early 1970s to the mid-1980s.

Estimated Value:	**Excellent:**	**$150.00**
	Very good:	**$120.00**

MUSKETEER

Musketeer Mauser

Musketeer Mauser

Caliber: 243, 25-06, 270, 264 mag., 308, 30-06, 7mm mag., 300 mag.
Action: FN Mauser bolt action
Magazine: 5-shot, 3-shot magnum
Barrel: Blued; 24"
Sights: Leaf rear, hooded ramp front
Stock and Forearm: Checkered walnut Monte Carlo one-piece pistol grip stock and forearm
Approximate wt.: 7¼ lbs.
Comments: Made from the 1960s to the early 1970s.

Estimated Value:	**Excellent:**	**$425.00**
	Very good:	**$340.00**

Musketeer Carbine

Same as Musketeer Mauser except shorter barrel.

Estimated Value:	**Excellent:**	**$400.00**
	Very good:	**$320.00**

NEW ENGLAND

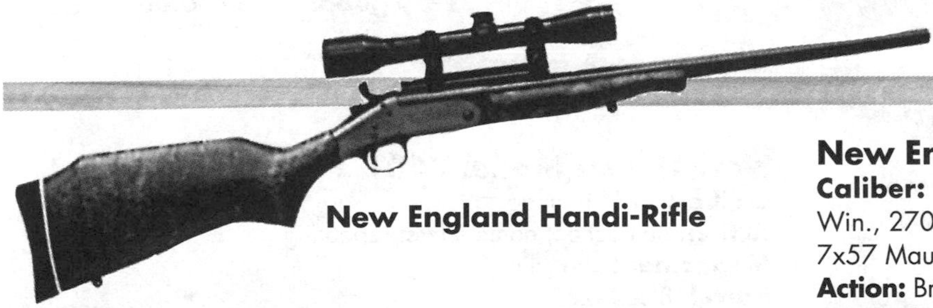

New England Handi-Rifle

New England Handi-Rifle

Caliber: 223 Rem., 22 Hornet, 22-250, 30-30 Win., 243 Win., 270 Win., 30-06, 308 Win., 45-70 Govt., 44 Rem. mag., 7x57 Maus., 7x64 Brenneke, 280 Rem.
Action: Break-open top release lever; exposed hammer single-shot
Magazine: None
Barrel: Blued; 22", 24", 22" bull barrel
Sights: Ramp front; adjustable folding rear, some models have no sights but are tapped for scope mounts
Stock and Forearm: Hardwood, walnut finish, pistol grip, Monte Carlo or plain smooth stock and lipped forearm
Approximate wt.: 7 lbs.
Comments: Made from the late 1980s to the late 1990s. Add 1% for 7x57 or 7x64 (24" barrel); add 2% for 280 Rem. (26" barrel).

Estimated Value:	**Excellent:**	**$200.00**
	Very good:	**$160.00**

New England Handi-Gun Combination

Same as the Handi-Rifle except any combination of rifle or shotgun barrels are available to be used interchangeably. Shotgun barrels have brass bead front sight with blued or nickel finish (add 10%); 22" barrel in 12 or 20 gauge. Prices are for rifle and shotgun barrel combinations. Made in the late 1980s to the mid-1990s.

Estimated Value:	**Excellent:**	**$225.00**
	Very good:	**$180.00**

New England Handi-Rifle Youth

Similar to the Handi-Rifle except with reduced stock dimensions for young shooters; 22" barrel; 223 Rem., 243 Win. calibers. Made in the late 1990s.

Estimated Value: **Excellent:** **$160.00**
Very good: **$125.00**

New England Synthetic Handi-Rifle

Similar to the Handi-Rifle except with stock and forearm made from high density black polymer. Not available in 7x57 or 7x64. Add 2% for 280 Rem. (26" barrel).

Estimated Value: **Excellent:** **$165.00**
Very good: **$130.00**

New England Super Light

Similar to the Synthetic Handi-Rifle with a 20" light-contour barrel, and lightweight polymer stock and forearm; weighs just over 5 lbs.; 22 Hornet, 223 Rem., or 243 Win. only.

Estimated Value: **Excellent:** **$170.00**
Very good: **$135.00**

New England Super Light Youth

Similar to the Super Light with reduced stock dimensions for young shooters.

Estimated Value: **Excellent:** **$165.00**
Very good: **$130.00**

New England Survivor

Caliber: 223 Rem., 357 magnum
Action: Break-open top release lever, exposed hammer, single-shot
Magazine: None
Barrel: 22"; matte blued or electroless nickel
Sights: Ramp front, fully adjustable rear on 357 magnum; no sights on 223 Rem.; both tapped for scope mounts
Stock and Forearm: Black matte polymer, full pistol grip stock with thumbhole and forearm; swivels; sling
Approximate wt.: 6 lbs.
Comments: Stock compartment for storage. Made in the late 1990s.

Estimated Value: **Excellent:** **$165.00**
Very good: **$130.00**

NEW HAVEN

New Haven Model 453T

New Haven Model 453T

Caliber: 22 short, long, long rifle
Action: Semiautomatic; hammerless
Magazine: 7-shot clip
Barrel: Blued; 18"
Sights: Open rear, bead front
Stock and Forearm: Plain one-piece Monte Carlo pistol grip stock and forearm
Approximate wt.: 5½ lbs.
Comments: Introduced in the late 1970s.

Estimated Value: **Excellent:** **$125.00**
Very good: **$100.00**

New Haven Model 453TS

Similar to the Model 453T with a 4X scope.

Estimated Value: **Excellent:** **$135.00**
Very good: **$110.00**

New Haven Model 740T

New Haven Model 740T

Caliber: 22 Win. mag.
Action: Bolt action; hammerless; repeating
Magazine: 5-shot clip
Barrel: Blued; 26"
Sights: Open rear, blade front
Stock and Forearm: Plain birch one-piece Monte Carlo pistol grip stock and forearm
Approximate wt.: 6½ lbs.
Comments: Introduced in the late 1970s.

Estimated Value: **Excellent:** **$130.00**
Very good: **$105.00**

New Haven Model 740TS

Similar to the Model 740T with 4X scope.

Estimated Value: **Excellent:** **$140.00**
Very good: **$115.00**

New Haven Model 679

Caliber: 30-30 Win.
Action: Lever-action; exposed hammer; repeating
Magazine: 5-shot tubular
Barrel: Blued; 20"
Sights: Open rear, ramp front
Stock and Forearm: Plain birch semi-pistol grip stock and fore-arm; barrel band
Approximate wt.: 6¾ lbs.
Comments: Made from the late 1970s to the early 1980s.

Estimated Value: **Excellent:** **$190.00**
Very good: **$150.00**

Newton Standard, 1st Model

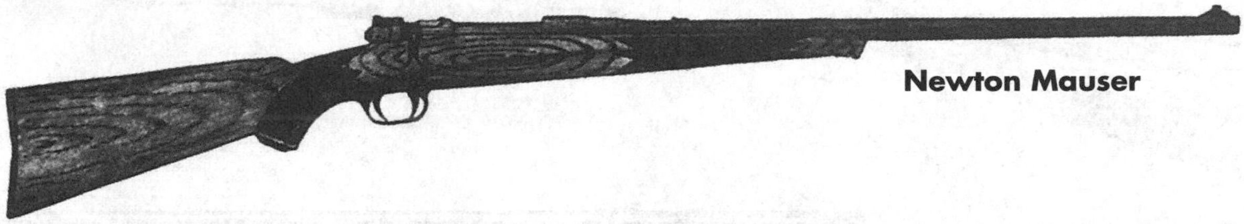
Newton Mauser

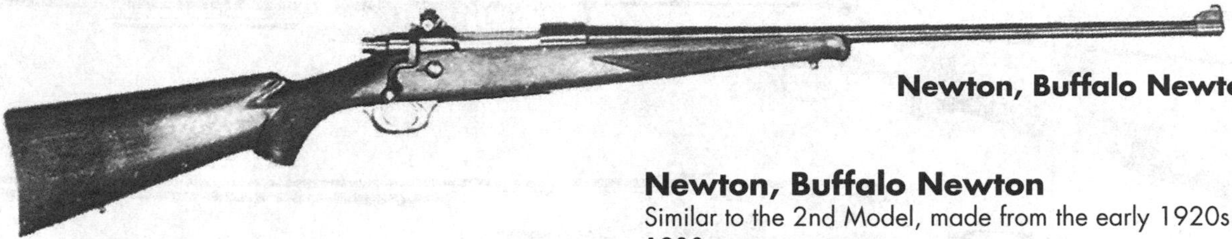
Newton, Buffalo Newton

Newton Standard, 1st Model

Caliber: 22, 256, 280, 30-06, 30 Newton, 35 Newton
Action: Bolt action; double set trigger
Magazine: 5-shot box
Barrel: Blued; 24"
Sights: Open rear, ramp front
Stock and Forearm: Checkered wood pistol grip stock and forearm
Approximate wt.: 7½ lbs.
Comments: Made for a short time before World War I.

Estimated Value:	**Excellent:**	**$1,750.00**
	Very good:	**$1,400.00**

Newton Standard, 2nd Model

Very similar to the 1st Model with improved action. Made in the 1920s.

Estimated Value:	**Excellent:**	**$1,750.00**
	Very good:	**$1,400.00**

Newton, Buffalo Newton

Similar to the 2nd Model, made from the early 1920s to the early 1930s.

Estimated Value:	**Excellent:**	**$2,000.00**
	Very good:	**$1,600.00**

Newton Mauser

Caliber: 256
Action: Mauser-type bolt action; reversed double set trigger
Magazine: 5-shot box
Barrel: Blued; 24"
Sights: Open rear, ramp front
Stock and Forearm: Checkered wood pistol grip stock and forearm
Approximate wt.: 7 lbs.
Comments: Made in the early 1920s.

Estimated Value:	**Excellent:**	**$1,750.00**
	Very good:	**$1,400.00**

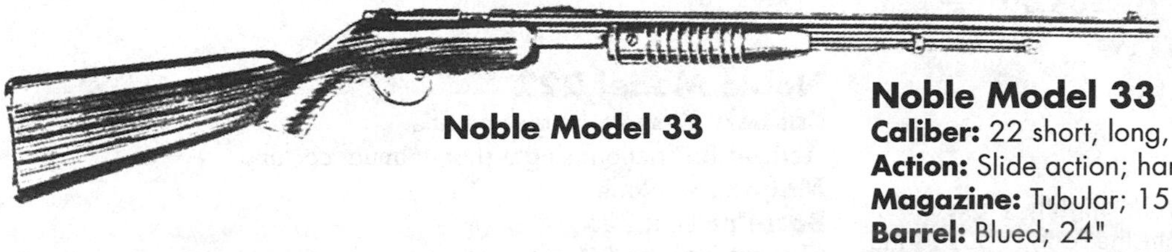
Noble Model 33

Noble Model 33A

Similar to the Model 33 with a wood stock and grooved slide handle. Made until the mid-1950s.

Estimated Value:	**Excellent:**	**$85.00**
	Very good:	**$70.00**

Noble Model 33

Caliber: 22 short, long, long rifle
Action: Slide action; hammerless; repeating
Magazine: Tubular; 15 long rifles, 17 longs, 21 shorts
Barrel: Blued; 24"
Sights: Open rear, blade front
Stock and Forearm: Semi-pistol grip tenite stock and slide handle
Approximate wt.: 6 lbs.
Comments: Made from the late 1940s to the early 1950s.

Estimated Value:	**Excellent:**	**$85.00**
	Very good:	**$70.00**

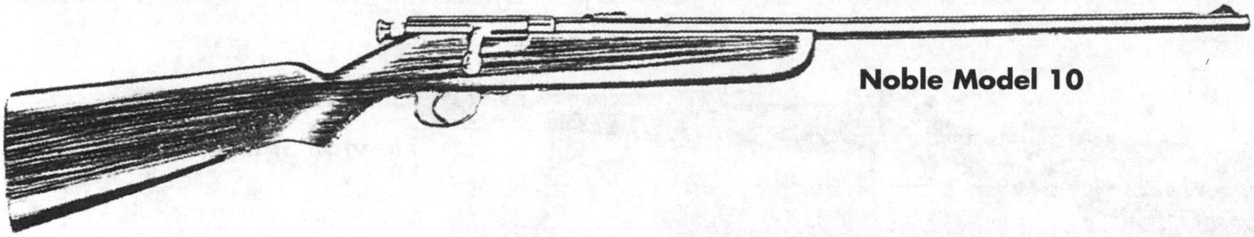

Noble Model 10

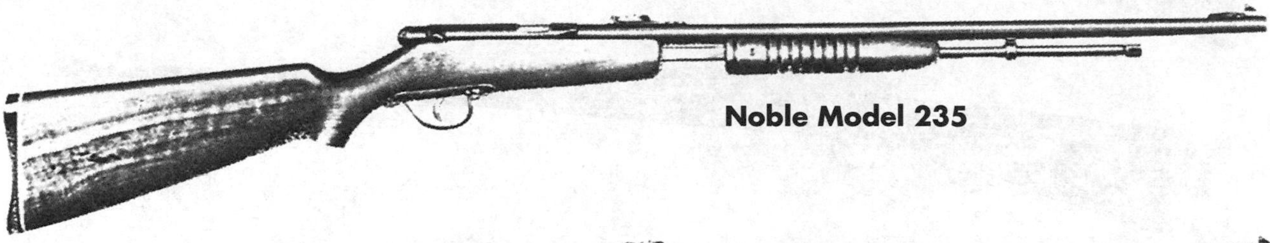

Noble Model 235

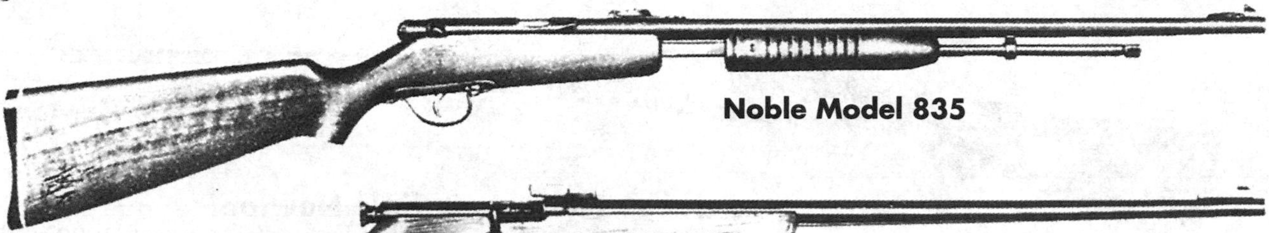

Noble Model 835

Noble Model 222

Noble Model 10

Caliber: 22 short, long, long rifle
Action: Bolt action; single shot
Magazine: None
Barrel: Blued; 24"
Sights: Open rear, bead front
Stock and Forearm: Walnut one-piece semi-pistol grip stock and forearm
Approximate wt.: 4 lbs.
Comments: Made from the mid- to the late 1950s.
Estimated Value: **Excellent:** **$85.00**
Very good: **$65.00**

Noble Model 20

Similar to the Model 10 with 22" barrel; slightly curved butt plate; manual cocking device. Made from the late 1950s to the early 1960s.
Estimated Value: **Excellent:** **$75.00**
Very good: **$60.00**

Noble Model 235

Caliber: 22 short, long, long rifle
Action: Slide action; hammerless; repeating
Magazine: Tubular; 15 long rifles, 17 longs, 21 shorts
Barrel: Blued; 24"
Sights: Open rear, ramp front
Stock and Forearm: Wood semi-pistol grip stock and grooved slide handle
Approximate wt.: 5½ lbs.
Comments: Made from the early 1950s to the early 1970s.
Estimated Value: **Excellent:** **$150.00**
Very good: **$120.00**

Noble Model 835

Similar to the Model 235. Made in the early 1970s.
Estimated Value: **Excellent:** **$80.00**
Very good: **$65.00**

Noble Model 222

Caliber: 22 short, long, long rifle
Action: Bolt action; single shot; manual cocking
Magazine: None
Barrel: Blued; 22"
Sights: Peep or "V" notch rear, ramp front
Stock and Forearm: Wood one-piece semi-pistol grip stock and forearm
Approximate wt.: 5 lbs.
Comments: Made from the late 1950s to the early 1970s.
Estimated Value: **Excellent:** **$90.00**
Very good: **$70.00**

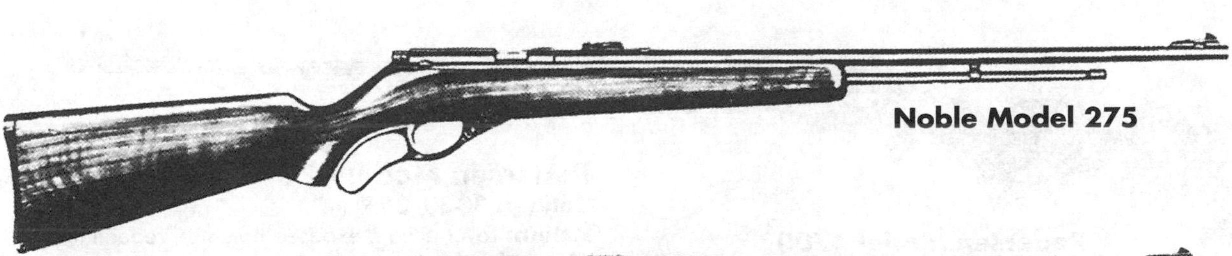

Noble Model 275

Noble Model 875

Noble Model 285

Noble Models 275 and 875

Caliber: 22 short, long, long rifle
Action: Lever action; hammerless; repeating
Magazine: Tubular; 15 long rifles, 17 longs, 21 shorts
Barrel: Blued; 24"
Sights: Open rear, ramp front
Stock and Forearm: Wood one-piece semi-pistol grip stock and forearm
Approximate wt.: 5½ lbs.
Comments: Model 275 made from the late 1950s to the early 1970s; Model 875 made from the early to the mid-1970s.

Estimated Value:	**Excellent:**	**$150.00**
	Very good:	**$120.00**

Noble Models 285 and 885

Caliber: 22 long rifle
Action: Semiautomatic
Magazine: 15-shot tubular
Barrel: Blued; 22"
Sights: Open adjustable rear, blade front
Stock and Forearm: Wood one-piece semi-pistol grip stock and forearm
Approximate wt.: 5½ lbs.
Comments: Made from the early to the mid-1970s.

Estimated Value:	**Excellent:**	**$125.00**
	Very good:	**$100.00**

PEDERSEN

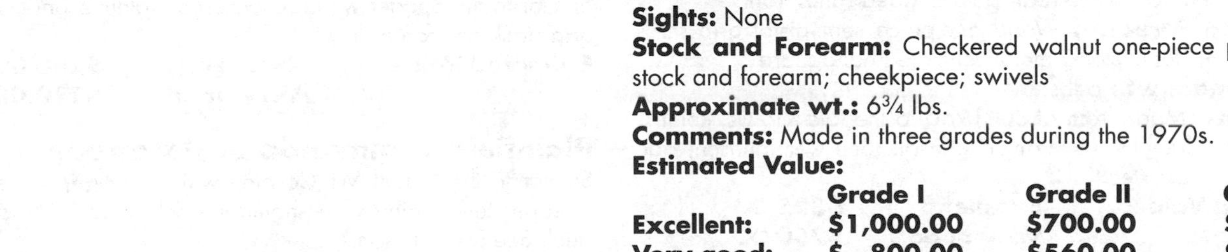

Pedersen Model 3000

Pedersen Model 3000

Caliber: 270, 30-06, 7mm mag., 338 Win mag.
Action: Bolt action; adjustable trigger
Magazine: 3-shot box
Barrel: Blued; 22", 24"
Sights: None
Stock and Forearm: Checkered walnut one-piece pistol grip stock and forearm; cheekpiece; swivels
Approximate wt.: 6¾ lbs.
Comments: Made in three grades during the 1970s.
Estimated Value:

	Grade I	**Grade II**	**Grade III**
Excellent:	**$1,000.00**	**$700.00**	**$560.00**
Very good:	**$ 800.00**	**$560.00**	**$450.00**

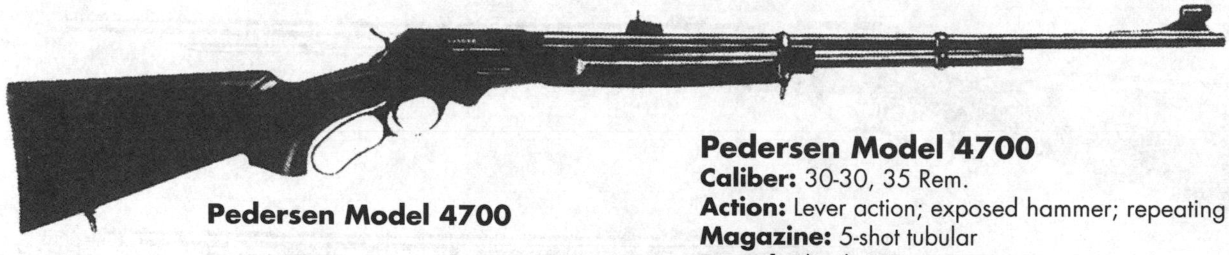

Pedersen Model 4700

Pedersen Model 4700
Caliber: 30-30, 35 Rem.
Action: Lever action; exposed hammer; repeating
Magazine: 5-shot tubular
Barrel: Blued; 24"
Sights: Open rear, hooded ramp front
Stock and Forearm: Walnut pistol grip stock and short forearm; barrel band; swivels
Approximate wt.: 7½ lbs.
Comments: Made during the 1970s.
Estimated Value: **Excellent:** **$320.00**
Very good: **$260.00**

PLAINFIELD

Plainfield Model M1

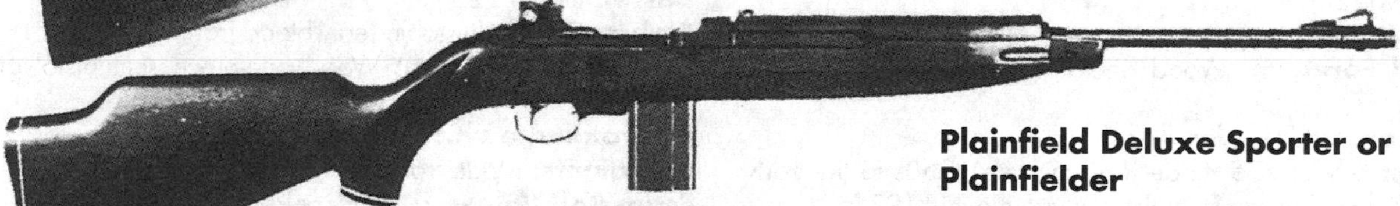

Plainfield Deluxe Sporter or Plainfielder

Plainfield Commando or Paratrooper

Plainfield Model M1
Caliber: 30 M1, 223 (5.7mm)
Action: Semiautomatic, gas-operated
Magazine: 15-shot detachable clip
Barrel: Blued or stainless steel; 18"
Sights: Open adjustable rear, gold beaded ramp front
Stock and Forearm: Wood one-piece semi-pistol grip stock and forearm; slot in stock; metal ventilated handguard
Approximate wt.: 6 lbs.
Comments: Made from about 1960 to the late 1970s. Reintroduced in the late 1970s by Iver Johnson. See Iver Johnson; add 30% for stainless steel.
Estimated Value: **Excellent:** **$325.00**
Very good: **$260.00**

Plainfield Model M1 Sporter
Similar to the Model M1 Carbine with a wooden handguard and no slot in the stock. See Iver Johnson.
Estimated Value: **Excellent:** **$250.00**
Very good: **$200.00**

Plainfield Deluxe Sporter or Plainfielder
Similar to the Sporter with a checkered walnut Monte Carlo pistol grip stock and forearm.
Estimated Value: **Excellent:** **$260.00**
Very good: **$210.00**

Plainfield Commando or Paratrooper
Similar to the Model M1 Carbine with pistol grip at rear and at forearm; telescoping wire shoulder stock. Add 30% for stainless steel. See Iver Johnson.
Estimated Value: **Excellent:** **$375.00**
Very good: **$300.00**

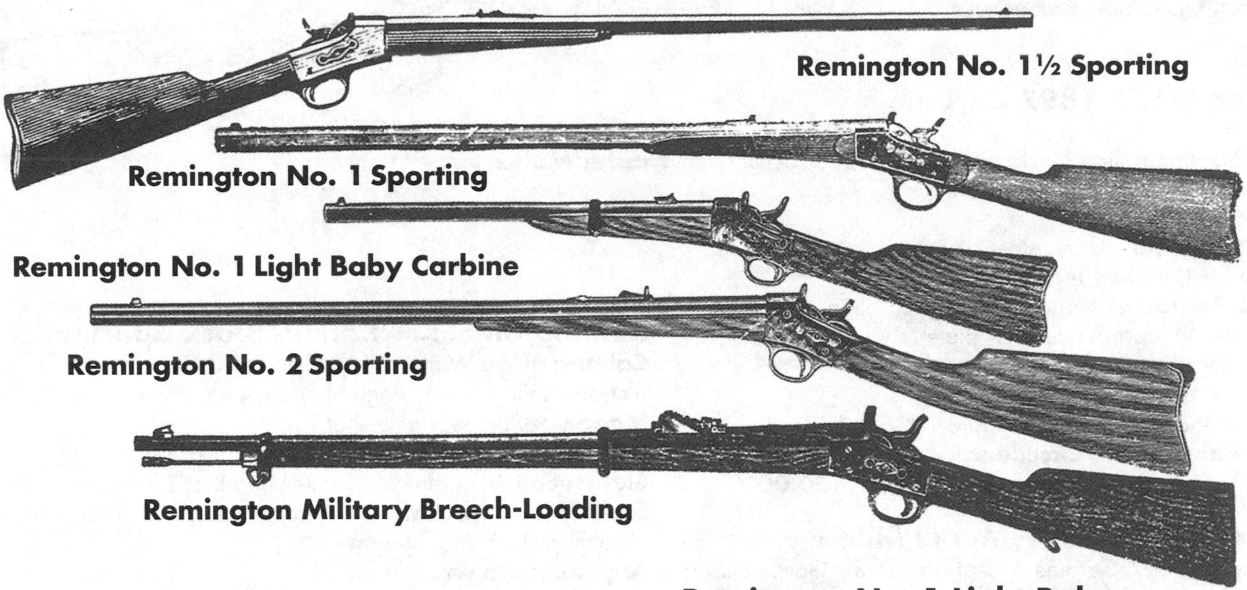

Remington Military Breech-Loading

Caliber: C.F. 43 Spanish, 43 Egyptian, 50-70 Government, 58 Berdan. Early models used rimfire cartridges. Models for center-fire cartridges produced after 1872.
Action: Single-shot; rolling block with single trigger; visible hammer
Magazine: None
Barrel: 30" to 36"; round
Sights: Military (post front and folding leaf rear)
Stock and Forearm: Plain walnut straight stock and forearm; long forearm with ram rod; steel butt plate on stock
Approximate wt.: 8 to 11 lbs.
Comments: Made from about 1867 to 1902 (large number sold to Egypt, France and Spain) and sold commercially in U.S. Some are unmarked; some have Arabic marked barrels, and some are marked Remington.

Estimated Value:	**Excellent:**	**$2,500.00**
	Very good:	**$2,000.00**

Remington No. 1 Sporting

Caliber: Early guns for rim fire 50-70, 44 long and extra long or 46 long and extra long. After 1872 made for centerfire 40-50, 40-70, 44-77, 45-70, or 45 sporting cartridge.
Action: Single-shot; rolling block with single trigger; visible hammer
Magazine: None
Barrel: 28" or 30"; tapered octagon
Sights: Sporting front, folding leaf rear
Stock and Forearm: Plain walnut straight grip stock with flanged-top steel butt plate and short plain walnut forearm with thin round front
Approximate wt.: 8½ to 12 lbs.
Comments: Made from about 1868 to 1902.

Estimated Value:	**Excellent:**	**$3,000.00**
	Very good:	**$2,400.00**

Remington No. 1 Light Baby Carbine

Caliber: 44-40
Action: Single-shot; rolling block with single trigger; visible hammer
Magazine: None
Barrel: 20"; light round
Sights: Pointed post front, military folding leaf rear
Stock and Forearm: Plain oiled walnut straight stock with metal butt plate and short forearm; barrel band
Approximate wt.: 5¾ lbs.
Comments: Made from about 1892 to 1902.

Estimated Value:	**Excellent:**	**$4,000.00**
	Very good:	**$3,200.00**

Remington No. 1½ Sporting

Similar to No. 1 Sporting rifle except: lighter action, stocks, and smaller caliber barrels; approximate wt. 5½ to 7 lbs.; made in the following pistol calibers: rimfire 22 short, long and extra long; 25 Stevens and 25 longs; 32 or 38 long and extra long; centerfire Winchester 32-20; 38-40; or 44-40; barrel lengths 24", 26", 28", or 30". Made from about 1869 to 1902.

Estimated Value:	**Excellent:**	**$2,750.00**
	Very good:	**$2,200.00**

Remington No. 2 Sporting

Caliber: Early models were for rimfire 22, 25, 32, or 38. Later models for centerfire 25-21, 25-25, 25-20, 32 long, 38 long, or 38-40
Action: Single-shot; rolling block
Magazine: None
Barrel: 24" to 30"; lightweight; octagon
Sights: Bead front sight; sporting adjustable rear
Stock and Forearm: Plain, oil finish, walnut, straight grip stock and lipped forearm
Approximate wt.: 5 to 6 lbs.
Comments: Made from about 1873 to 1910.

Estimated Value:	**Excellent:**	**$1,750.00**
	Very good:	**$1,400.00**

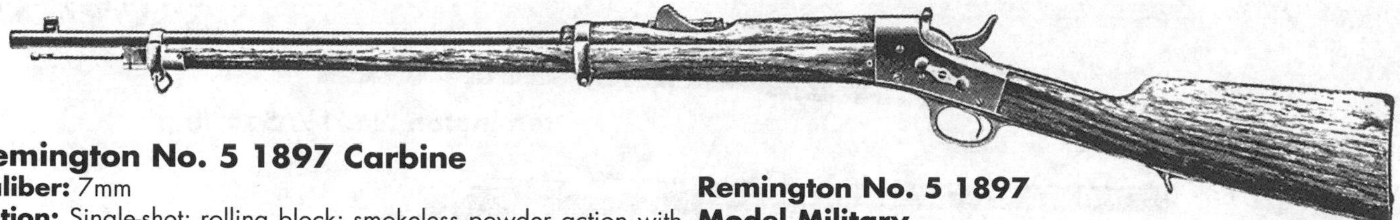

Remington No. 5 1897 Model Military

Remington No. 5 1897 Carbine

Caliber: 7mm
Action: Single-shot; rolling block; smokeless powder action with case-hardened steel frame; visible hammer
Magazine: None
Barrel: 20"; round; smokeless steel barrel
Sights: Post front, military rear
Stock and Forearm: Plain straight grip, oiled walnut, two-piece stock and forearm; steel butt plate; short forearm; barrel band; handguard on top of barrel
Approximate wt.: 5 lbs.
Comments: Made from about 1897 to 1906.

Estimated Value:	**Excellent:**	**$2,250.00**
	Very good:	**$1,800.00**

Remington No. 5 1897 Model Military

Similar to No. 5 1897 Carbine except also in 30 Govt. caliber; 30" light round tapered barrel; full stock with steel butt plate and capped forearm; two barrel bands; handguard on top of barrel; weighs 8½ lbs. Made from about 1897 to 1906.

Estimated Value:	**Excellent:**	**$2,500.00**
	Very good:	**$2,000.00**

Remington No. 1 Rolling Block Sporter

Caliber: 30-30 Win., 444 Marlin, 45-70 Govt.
Action: Rolling block, single-shot, exposed hammer
Magazine: None, single shot
Barrel: 30"; round or half-round and half-octagon
Sights: Buck horn rear with white-bead blade front
Stock and Forearm: Checkered American walnut, two-piece pistol grip stock and forearm
Approximate wt.: 8¼ lbs.
Comments: A re-introduction of the Remington No. 1 Sporting rolling block rifle for collectors and traditional-minded hunters. Made in the late 1990s.

Estimated Value:	**Excellent:**	**$3,500.00**
	Very good:	**$2,800.00**

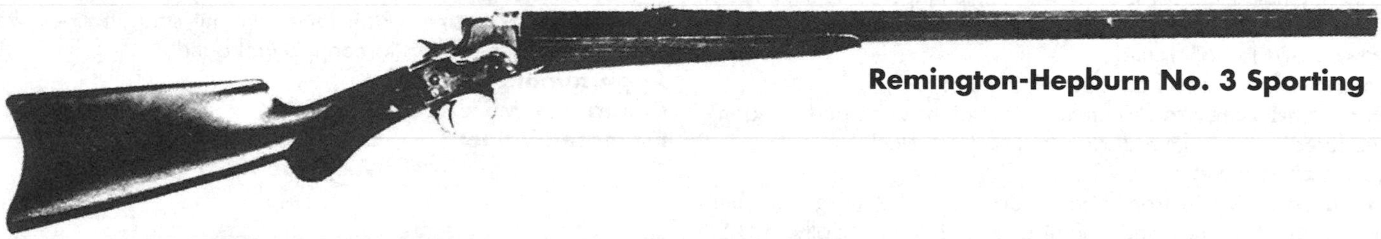

Remington-Hepburn No. 3 Sporting

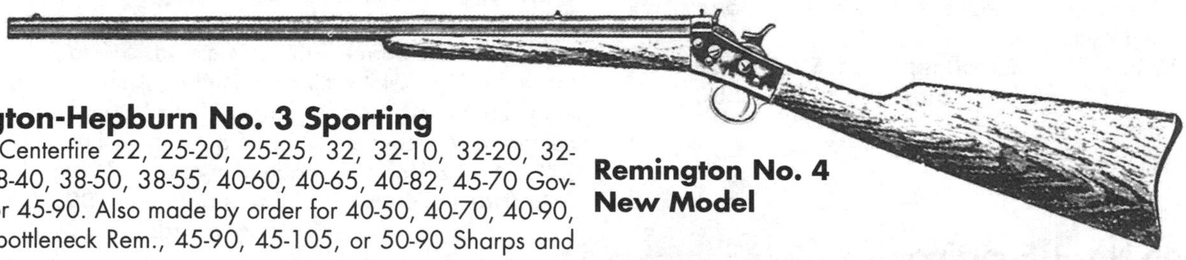

Remington No. 4 New Model

Remington-Hepburn No. 3 Sporting

Caliber: Centerfire 22, 25-20, 25-25, 32, 32-10, 32-20, 32-40, 38, 38-40, 38-50, 38-55, 40-60, 40-65, 40-82, 45-70 Government, or 45-90. Also made by order for 40-50, 40-70, 40-90, or 44-77 bottleneck Rem., 45-90, 45-105, or 50-90 Sharps and 50-70 Govt.
Action: Hepburn drop block; side lever opens and closes action; single-shot with low visible hammer; early models with single trigger; later models with single or double set triggers
Magazine: None
Barrel: 28" – 32"; round, octagon, or half octagon
Sights: Blade front; sporting rear adjustable for elevation
Stock and Forearm: Plain straight grip or checkered pistol grip, oiled wood stock with steel butt plate and matching short forearm
Approximate wt.: 8 to 12 lbs.
Comments: Made from about 1880 to 1906.

Estimated Value:	**Excellent:**	**$3,500.00**
	Very good:	**$2,800.00**

Remington No. 4 New Model

Caliber: Rimfire only in 22 short, long and long rifle, 25 Stevens or 32 long
Action: Single-shot; rolling block; light short action with automatic shell ejection; visible hammer
Magazine: None
Barrel: 22½" light octagon in 22 and 25 caliber; 24" in 32 caliber; round barrel after about 1931
Sights: Bead front, plain "V" notch rear
Stock and Forearm: Plain varnished, two-piece straight grip stock and forearm; short round front forearm
Approximate wt.: 4¼ lbs.
Comments: Made from about 1891 to 1934.

Estimated Value:	**Excellent:**	**$850.00**
	Very good:	**$680.00**

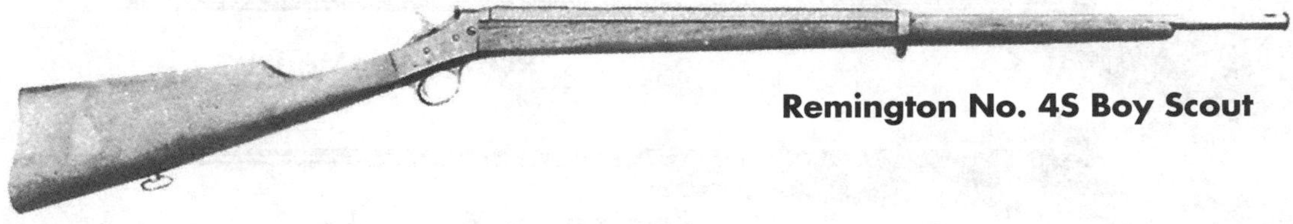

Remington No. 4S Boy Scout

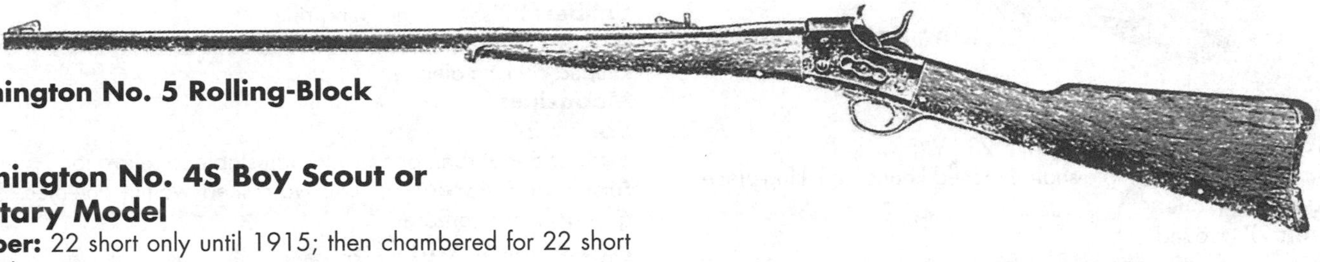

Remington No. 5 Rolling-Block

Remington No. 4S Boy Scout or Military Model

Caliber: 22 short only until 1915; then chambered for 22 short or 22 long
Action: Single-shot; case-hardened No. 4 rolling-block action; visible hammer
Magazine: None
Barrel: 28"; medium, round barrel
Sights: Blade front; open "V" notch rear adjustable for elevation
Stock and Forearm: Musket-style, oiled walnut, one-piece, full-length stock and forearm with steel butt plate and one barrel band; bayonet lug; handguard on barrel
Approximate wt.: 5 lbs.
Comments: Called Boy Scout model from 1913 to 1915; renamed Military Model about 1916. Made from about 1913 to 1932.

Estimated Value:	**Excellent:**	**$2,200.00**
	Very good:	**$1,760.00**

Remington No. 5 Rolling-Block

Caliber: 7mm Mauser, 30-30, 30-40 Krag, 303 British, 32-40, 32 SPL, 38-55
Action: New Ordnance steel, single-shot; rolling-block; smokeless powder action with case-hardened frame
Magazine: None
Barrel: 28" – 30"; light steel round barrel
Sights: Blade front, Rocky Mountain rear
Stock and Forearm: Plain walnut, two-piece straight grip stock and forearm; steel butt plate; lipped forearm
Approximate wt.: 7¼ lbs.
Comments: Made from about 1896 to 1906.

Estimated Value:	**Excellent:**	**$2,200.00**
	Very good:	**$1,760.00**

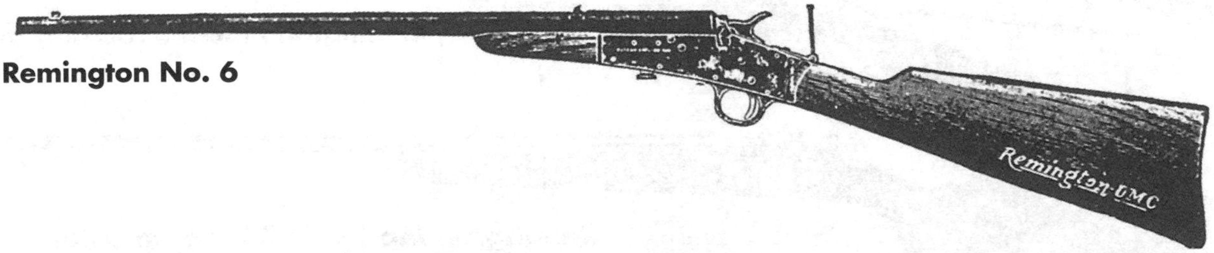

Remington No. 6

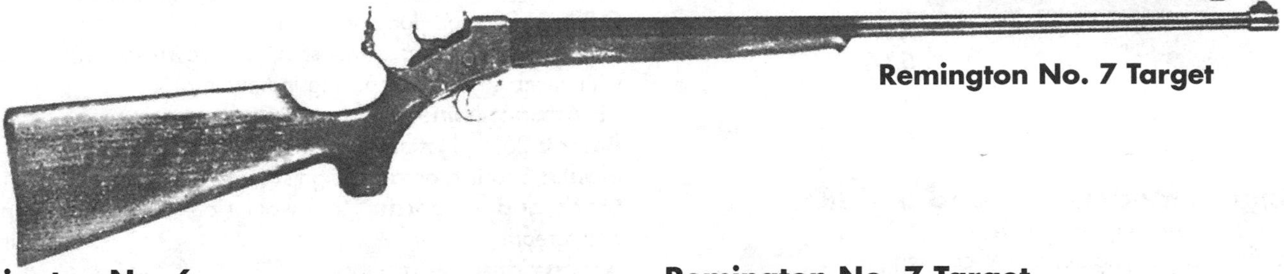

Remington No. 7 Target

Remington No. 6

Caliber: 22 short, long, long rifle, 32 short and long RF
Action: Single-shot; rolling-block; visible hammer
Magazine: None
Barrel: 20"; round tapered barrel
Sights: Bead front; open rear; also tang peep sight available
Stock and Forearm: Plain walnut straight grip stock and forearm; steel butt plate
Approximate wt.: 4 lbs.
Comments: Made from about 1902 to 1934.

Estimated Value:	**Excellent:**	**$725.00**
	Very good:	**$580.00**

Remington No. 7 Target

Caliber: 22 long rifle, 32 MRF or 25 Stevens RF
Action: Single-shot; rolling block; visible hammer
Magazine: None
Barrel: 24", 26", 28"; half-octagon barrel
Sights: Bead front, adjustable dovetail rear
Stock and Forearm: Checkered walnut pistol grip stock and forearm; rubber butt plate; lipped forearm
Approximate wt.: 7 lbs.
Comments: Made from about 1904 to 1910.

Estimated Value:	**Excellent:**	**$4.000.00**
	Very good:	**$3,200.00**

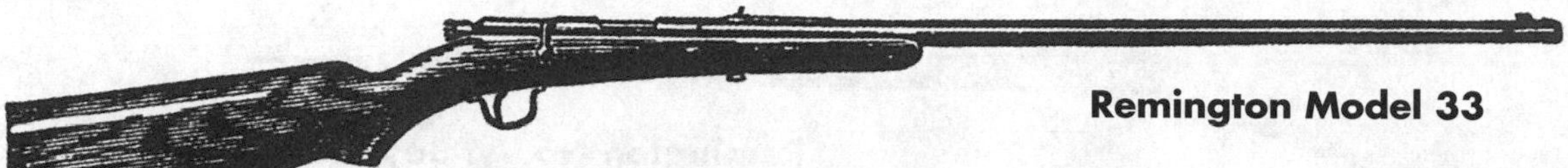

Remington Model 33

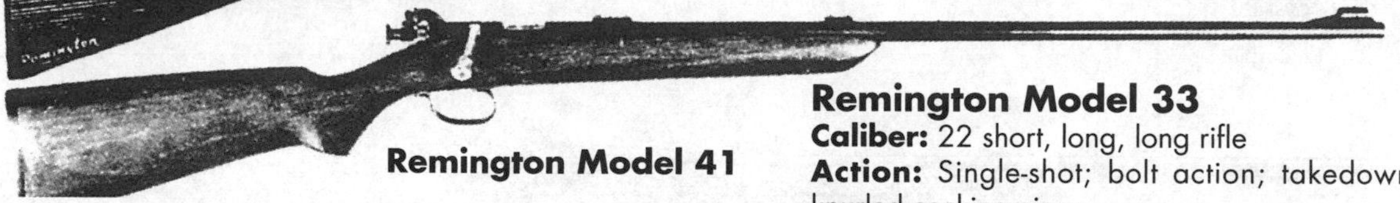

Remington Model 41

Remington Model 41

Caliber: 22 short, long, long rifle 22 WRF
Action: Bolt action; single-shot; exposed knurled cocking-piece
Magazine: None
Barrel: 27"; round
Sights: Bead or hooded ramp front sight, open rear adjustable for elevation or rear peep sight
Stock and Forearm: Plain, one-piece pistol grip stock and forearm; hard rubber butt plate
Approximate wt.: 5 lbs.
Comments: Made from about 1936 to 1940.

Estimated Value:	**Excellent:**	**$225.00**
	Very good:	**$180.00**

Remington Model 33

Caliber: 22 short, long, long rifle
Action: Single-shot; bolt action; takedown model; exposed knurled cocking-piece
Magazine: None
Barrel: 24"; round
Sights: Bead front, open rear, adjustable for elevation
Stock and Forearm: Plain varnished walnut one-piece pistol grip stock and forearm
Approximate wt.: 4 lbs.
Comments: Made from about 1931 to 1936; finger grooves added to forearm in 1934.

Estimated Value:	**Excellent:**	**$175.00**
	Very good:	**$140.00**

Remington Model 33 NRA Junior Target

Same as Model 33 except: post front sight; rear peep sight; equipped with 1" leather sling; swivels; approximate wt. 4½ lbs.

Estimated Value:	**Excellent:**	**$250.00**
	Very good:	**$200.00**

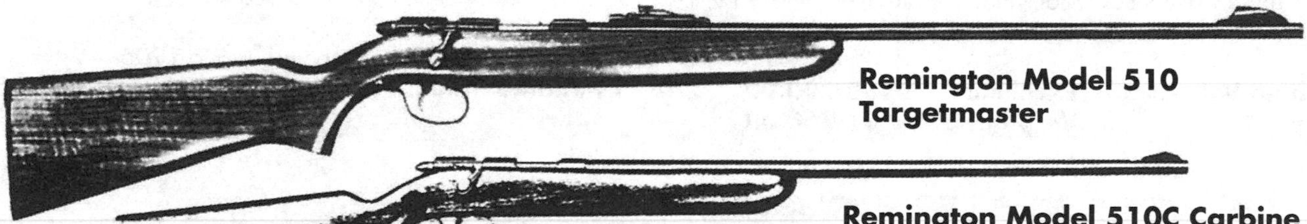

Remington Model 510 Targetmaster

Remington Model 510C Carbine

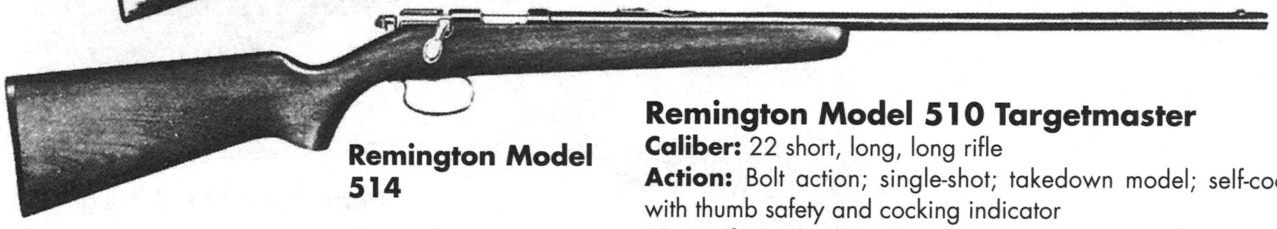

Remington Model 514

Remington Models 514 and 514BR

Caliber: 22 short, long, long rifle
Action: Bolt action; single-shot; self-cocking
Magazine: None
Barrel: 21" (514BR) or 24"; light round
Sights: Sporting or target sights
Stock and Forearm: Plain walnut one-piece pistol grip stock and forearm
Approximate wt.: 4¼ lbs.
Comments: Made from about 1948 to 1972 in three models; 514 Standard Model; 514P has target sights (rear peep sight); 514BR boy's rifle has 1" shorter stock and 21" barrel.

Estimated Value:	**Excellent:**	**$150.00**
	Very good:	**$120.00**

Remington Model 510 Targetmaster

Caliber: 22 short, long, long rifle
Action: Bolt action; single-shot; takedown model; self-cocking with thumb safety and cocking indicator
Magazine: None
Barrel: 25" light round
Sights: Sporting or target sights
Stock and Forearm: Plain walnut one-piece pistol grip stock and forearm
Approximate wt.: 5 lbs.
Comments: Made from about 1939 to 1962 in three models: 510A Standard model; 510P with peep sights, and 510SB, a smooth-bore chambered for 22 shot shells.

Estimated Value:	**Excellent:**	**$165.00**
	Very good:	**$130.00**

Remington Model 510C Carbine

Same as Model 510 single-shot rifle except: 21" barrel and approximate wt. of 5½ lbs. Made from about 1961 to 1962.

Estimated Value:	**Excellent:**	**$125.00**
	Very good:	**$100.00**

Remington Model 10 Nylon

Remington Model 10 Nylon
Caliber: 22 short, long, long rifle
Action: Bolt action; self-cocking; single-shot
Magazine: None
Barrel: 19½"; round
Sights: Ramp front; adjustable open rear
Stock and Forearm: Nylon checkered one-piece pistol grip stock and forearm; shotgun butt plate
Approximate wt.: 4 lbs.
Comments: Made from about 1963 to 1964.

Estimated Value:	**Excellent:**	**$300.00**
	Very good:	**$240.00**

Remington Model 10 SB
Same as Model 10 except: smooth bore; chambered for 22 shot shells.

Estimated Value:	**Excellent:**	**$300.00**
	Very good:	**$240.00**

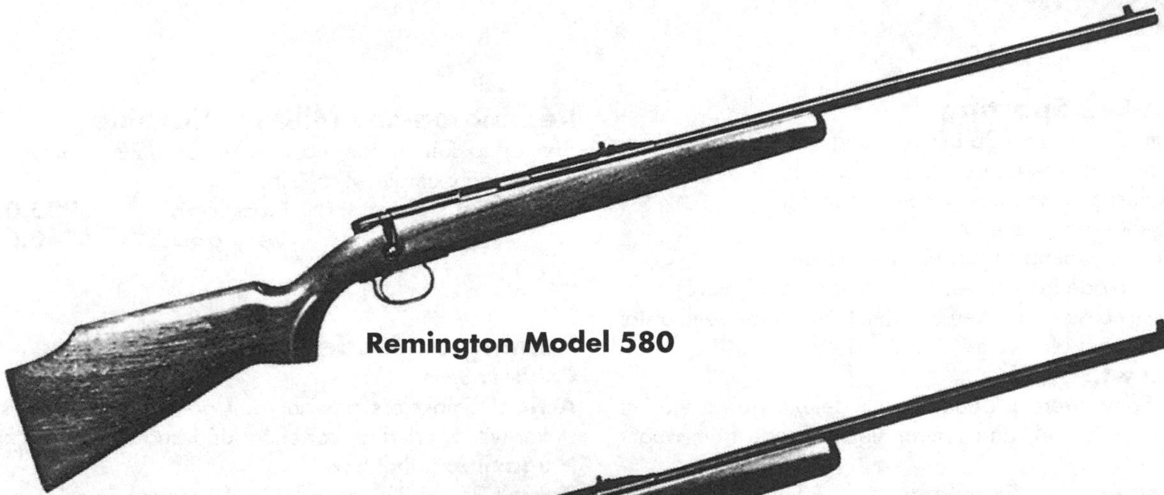

Remington Model 580

Remington Model 580SB

Remington Model 580
Caliber: 22 short, long, long rifle
Action: Bolt action; single-shot; self-cocking striker
Magazine: None
Barrel: 24"; round
Sights: Bead front; adjustable open rear
Stock and Forearm: Plain wood Monte Carlo one-piece pistol grip stock and forearm; plastic shotgun butt plate
Approximate wt.: 5 lbs.
Comments: Made from about 1967 to the late 1970s. Also available in boy's model with shorter stock for young shooters.

Estimated Value:	**Excellent:**	**$200.00**
	Very good:	**$160.00**

Remington Model 580SB
Same as Model 580 except: smooth bore for 22 long rifle shot shell only.

Estimated Value:	**Excellent:**	**$225.00**
	Very good:	**$180.00**

Remington-Lee Sporting

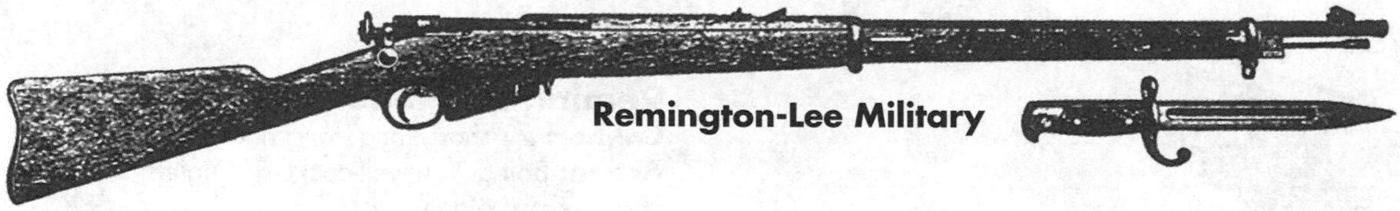

Remington-Lee Military

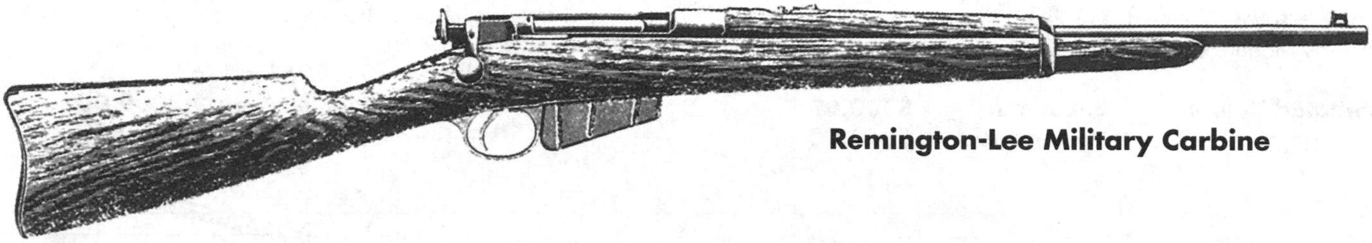

Remington-Lee Military Carbine

Remington-Lee Sporting

Caliber: 6mm U.S. Navy, 30-30 Sporting, 30-40 U.S. Govt. 7mm Mauser, or 7.65mm Mauser
Action: Smokeless powder, bolt action; repeating
Magazine: 5-shot removable box
Barrel: 24" to 28"; round smokeless steel barrel
Sights: Bead or blade front, open rear adjustable for elevation
Stock and Forearm: Checkered walnut one-piece semi-pistol grip stock and grooved forearm
Approximate wt.: 6¾ lbs.
Comments: Some were produced with deluxe grand walnut stock, half-octagon barrel, and Lyman sights. Made from about 1897 to 1906.

Estimated Value: **Excellent:** **$1,200.00**
Very good: **$ 960.00**

Remington-Lee Military

Caliber: 30-40 Krag, 303 British, 6mm Lee Navy, 7mm Mauser, or 7.65mm Mauser
Action: Smokeless powder, bolt action; repeating, rimless cartridges
Magazine: 5-shot removable box
Barrel: 29"; round smokeless steel barrel
Sights: Post front; folding leaf rear
Stock and Forearm: Plain walnut one-piece straight grip stock and long forearm; cleaning rod; barrel bands; wooden hanguard on top of barrel
Approximate wt.: 8½ lbs.
Comments: Made from about 1897 to 1902.

Estimated Value: **Excellent:** **$1,200.00**
Very good: **$ 960.00**

Remington-Lee Military Carbine

Similar to Remington-Lee rifle except: 20" barrel; one barrel band; approximate wt. 6½ lbs.

Estimated Value: **Excellent:** **$925.00**
Very good: **$740.00**

Remington Model 1907-15

Caliber: 8mm
Action: Smokeless powder bolt action; repeating; self-cocking striker with knurled top for uncocking and manual cocking
Magazine: 5-shot box
Barrel: 26" to 31"; round with 4 groove rifling
Sights: Ivory bead dovetail front, folding leaf rear
Stock and Forearm: Plain walnut one-piece stock and long forearm; barrel bands; cleaning rod
Approximate wt.: 8 to 9 lbs.
Comments: Made from about 1907 to 1915; left side of action marked "Remington MLE 1907-15"; right side of barrel near action marked "RAC 1907-15."

Estimated Value: **Excellent:** **$800.00**
Very good: **$640.00**

Remington Model 1907-15 Carbine

Same as Remington Model 1907-15 except: 22" barrel; no barrel bands; short forearm; approximate wt.: 6½ lbs.

Estimated Value: **Excellent:** **$725.00**
Very good: **$580.00**

Remington, Enfield Pattern, 1914 Military

Caliber: 303 British (rimmed)
Action: British smokeless powder bolt action; repeating; self-cocking on down stroke of bolt handle
Magazine: 5-shot box
Barrel: 26"; round tapered barrel
Sights: Protected post front; protected folding leaf rear
Stock and Forearm: Oil finished walnut, one-piece stock and forearm; wooden handguard on top of barrel; modified pistol grip stock; full-length forearm with two barrel bands
Approximate wt.: 10 lbs.
Comments: Made from about 1915 to 1916 for the British Army; Serial number on action and bolt, "R" preceding action serial number; approximately 600,000 produced.

Estimated Value:	**Excellent:**	**$1,000.00**
	Very good:	**$ 800.00**

Remington, Enfield U.S. Model 1917 Military

Caliber: 30-06 Govt., rimless
Action: Smokeless powder bolt action; repeating; self-cocking on down stroke of bolt handle; actions made with interchangeable parts
Magazine: 5-shot box
Barrel: 26"; round tapered
Sights: Protected post front, protected folding leaf rear
Stock and Forearm: Plain one-piece walnut stock and forearm; wooden handguard over barrel; modified pistol grip stock; full-length forearm with finger grooves and two barrel beads; sling loops and bayonet lug
Approximate wt.: 10 lbs.
Comments: Made from about 1917 to 1918. Marked "Model of 1917," Remington and serial no. on bridge.

Estimated Value:	**Excellent:**	**$1,200.00**
	Very good:	**$ 960.00**

Remington, Enfield Pattern, 1914 Military

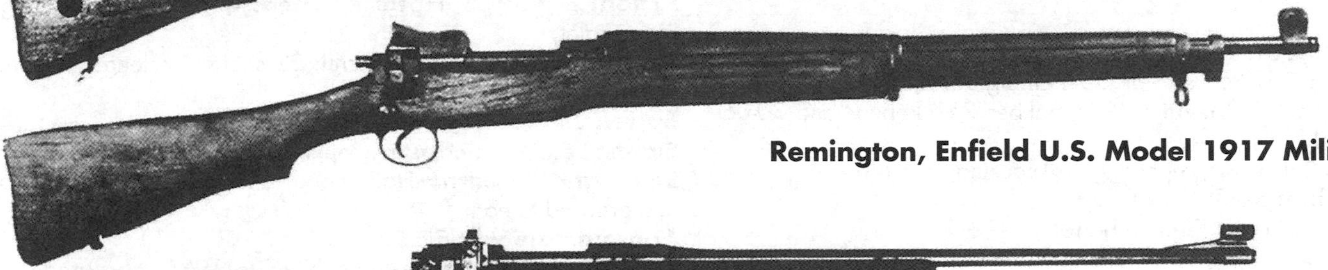

Remington, Enfield U.S. Model 1917 Military

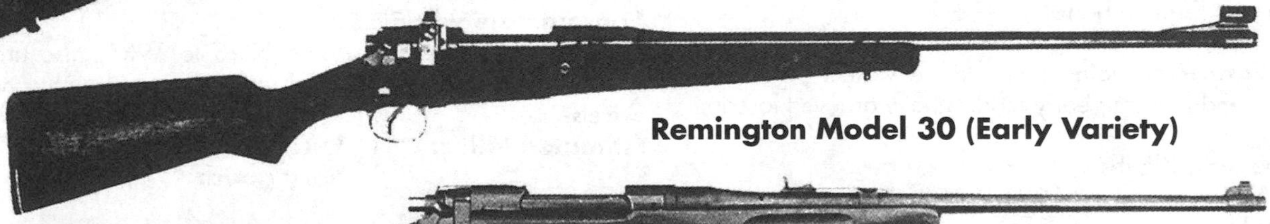

Remington Model 30 (Early Variety)

Remington Model 30 (Intermediate Variety)

Remington Model 30 (Early Variety)

Caliber: 30-06 Govt.
Action: Improved 1917 Enfield bolt action; repeating; self-cocking when bolt is closed; hinged floor plate
Magazine: 5-shot box
Barrel: 24"; light round
Sights: Slip-on band front sight, adjustable rear sight
Stock and Forearm: Plain walnut, one-piece pistol grip stock and grooved lipped forearm; steel butt plate
Approximate wt.: 8 lbs.
Comments: Made from about 1921 to 1926; approximately 8,500 produced; marked "Remington Arms Co. Inc., Remington Ilion Works, Ilion, N.Y. Made in U.S.A."

Estimated Value:	**Excellent:**	**$850.00**
	Very good:	**$680.00**

Remington Model 30 (Intermediate Variety)

Same as Model 30 (Early Variety) rifle except: calibers 30-06 Govt. 25, 30, 32, and 35 Remington and 7mm Mauser; 22" barrel length; also made in 20" barrel carbine. Made from about 1926 to 1930. Approximate wt. 7 lbs.

Estimated Value:	**Excellent:**	**$825.00**
	Very good:	**$660.00**

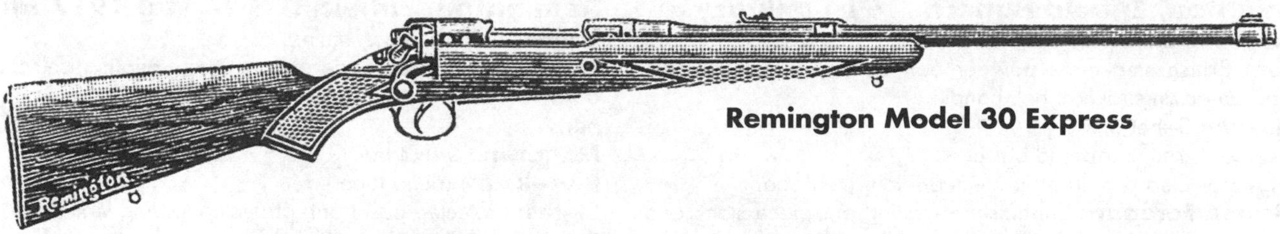

Remington Model 30 Express

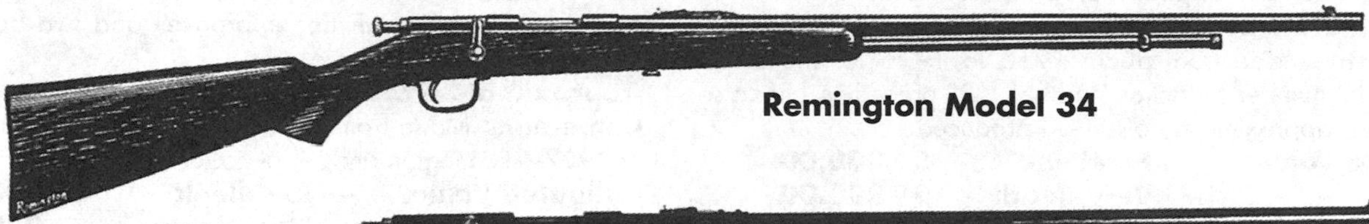

Remington Model 34

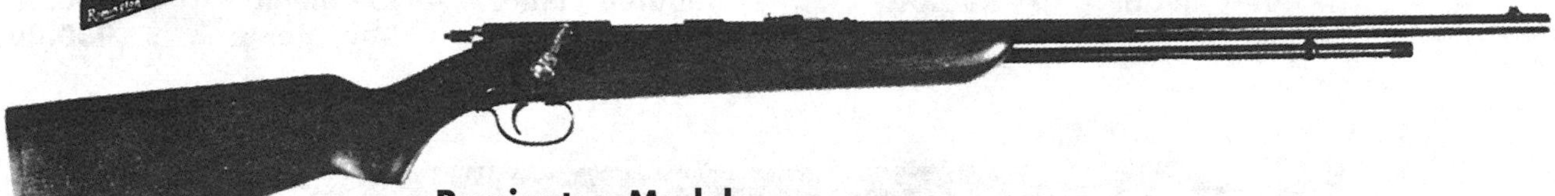

Remington Model 341 Sportsmaster

Remington Model 30 Express

Caliber: 25, 30, 32, or 35 Remington, 30-06 Govt., 7mm Mauser until 1936. After 1936 caliber 257 Roberts and 30-06 Govt. only
Action: Bolt action; repeating; self-cocking; thumb safety
Magazine: 5-shot box
Barrel: 22" or 24"; round barrel
Sights: Bead front, adjustable open rear
Stock and Forearm: Plain or checkered walnut pistol grip one-piece stock and forearm; early models have grooved forearm with lipped tip
Approximate wt.: 7½ lbs.
Comments: Made from about 1921 to 1940.
Estimated Value: **Excellent:** **$725.00**
Very good: **$580.00**

Remington Model 30R Carbine

Same as the Model 30 Express except: 20" barrel; plain walnut one-piece stock and forearm; approximate wt. 7 lbs.
Estimated Value: **Excellent:** **$530.00**
Very good: **$425.00**

Remington Model 30S Sporting

Similar to the Model 30 Express except: caliber 257 Roberts, 7mm Mauser, or 30-06; approximate wt. 8 lbs.; rear peep sight; special grade high-comb stock; produced from about 1930 to 1940; 24" barrel.
Estimated Value: **Excellent:** **$625.00**
Very good: **$500.00**

Remington Model 34

Caliber: 22 short, long, long rifle
Action: Bolt action; repeating; takedown model; self-cocking; thumb safety
Magazine: Tubular under barrel; 22 shorts, 17 longs, 15 long rifles
Barrel: 24"; round
Sights: Bead front, adjustable open rear
Stock and Forearm: Plain wood, one-piece pistol grip stock and grooved forearm
Approximate wt.: 5½ lbs.
Comments: Made from about 1933 to 1935; also produced in Model 34NRA Target model with rear peep sight and sling swivels.
Estimated Value: **Excellent:** **$190.00**
Very good: **$155.00**

Remington Model 341 Sportsmaster

Caliber: 22 short, long, long rifle
Action: Bolt action; repeating; takedown model; self-cocking; thumb safety
Magazine: Tubular under barrel; 22 shorts, 17 longs, 15 long rifles
Barrel: 27"; round
Sights: Bead front, open rear adjustable for elevation
Stock and Forearm: Plain wood one-piece pistol grip stock and forearm
Approximate wt.: 6 lbs.
Comments: Made from about 1935 to 1940.
Estimated Value: **Excellent:** **$165.00**
Very good: **$130.00**

Remington Model 341S Sportsmaster

Same as Model 341 except: smooth bore for 22 shot cartridges.
Estimated Value: **Excellent:** **$170.00**
Very good: **$140.00**

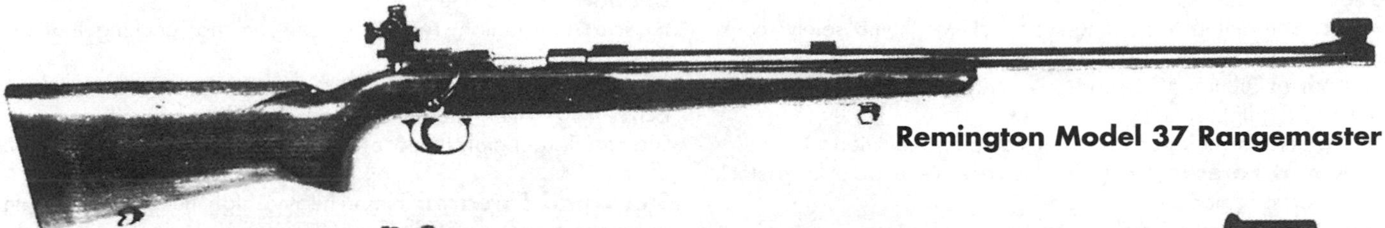

Remington Model 37 Rangemaster

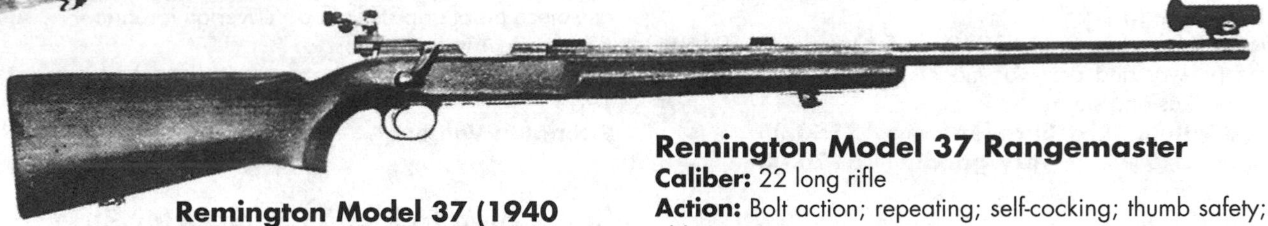

Remington Model 37 (1940 Model)

Remington Model 37 Rangemaster

Caliber: 22 long rifle
Action: Bolt action; repeating; self-cocking; thumb safety; adjustable trigger
Magazine: 5-shot clip and single-shot adapter
Barrel: 28"; heavy, semi-floating target barrel
Sights: Target sights; drilled for scope mount
Stock and Forearm: Heavy target, one-piece walnut stock and forearm; high flute comb stock with plain pistol grip and steel butt plate; early models had rounded beavertail forearm with one barrel band; barrel band dropped in 1938 and forearm modified.
Approximate wt.: 12 lbs.
Comments: Made from about 1937 to 1940.

Estimated Value:	**Excellent:**	**$600.00**
	Very good:	**$480.00**

Remington Model 37 (1940 Model)

Similar to the Model 37 rifle except: improved trigger mechanism; redesigned stock; wide beavertail forearm; produced from about 1940 to 1955.

Estimated Value:	**Excellent:**	**$650.00**
	Very good:	**$520.00**

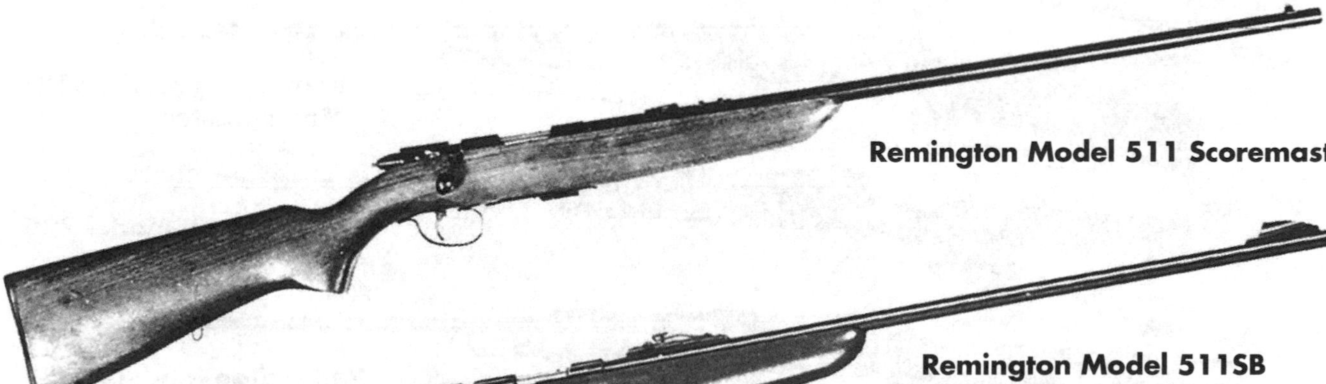

Remington Model 511 Scoremaster

Remington Model 511SB

Remington Model 511 Scoremaster

Caliber: 22 short, long, long rifle
Action: Bolt action; repeating; self-cocking; thumb safety and cocking indicator
Magazine: 6-shot clip; also 10-shot clip after 1952
Barrel: 25"; light round
Sights: Open sporting sights
Stock and Forearm: Plain walnut one-piece pistol grip stock and forearm
Approximate wt.: $5\frac{3}{4}$ lbs.
Comments: Made from about 1939 to 1962 with production stopped during World War II.

Estimated Value:	**Excellent:**	**$200.00**
	Very good:	**$160.00**

Remington Model 511SB

Same as the Model 511 Scoremaster rifle except: smooth bore for using 22 shot cartridges.

Estimated Value:	**Excellent:**	**$215.00**
	Very good:	**$175.00**

Remington Model 512 Sportmaster

Caliber: 22 short, long, long rifle
Action: Bolt action; repeating; self-cocking; thumb safety; cocking indicator
Magazine: Tubular ; 22 shorts, 17 longs, 15 long rifles
Barrel: 25"; light round
Sights: Bead front, open rear adjustable for elevation
Stock and Forearm: Plain walnut one-piece pistol grip stock and forearm; composition butt plate
Approximate wt.: 5½ lbs.
Comments: Made from about 1940 to 1942 and from 1946 to 1962; the pre-war and post-war models may have minor differences in markings and stocks.

Estimated Value:	**Excellent:**	**$150.00**
	Very good:	**$120.00**

Remington Model 512SB

Same as the Model 512 Sportmaster except: smooth bore for 22 shot cartridges.

Estimated Value:	**Excellent:**	**$140.00**
	Very good:	**$115.00**

Remington Model 513T Matchmaster

Caliber: 22 long rifle
Action: Bolt action; repeating; self-cocking; cocking indicator; adjustable trigger
Magazine: 6-shot clip
Barrel: 27"; medium round barrel; semi-floating type
Sights: Target sights; top of receiver grooved for scope mount after 1954
Stock and Forearm: Plain, heavy, high fluted comb; walnut one-piece pistol grip stock and beavertail forearm
Approximate wt.: 9 lbs.
Comments: Made from about 1940 to 1942 and 1945 to 1968.

Estimated Value:	**Excellent:**	**$375.00**
	Very good:	**$300.00**

Remington Model 513S Sporter Rifle

Similar to the Model 513T Matchmaster except: lighter sporting checkered walnut one-piece stock and forearm; approximate wt. 6¾ lbs.; ramp front sight and adjustable open rear sight; produced from about 1940 to 1958.

Estimated Value:	**Excellent:**	**$450.00**
	Very good:	**$360.00**

Remington Model 512 Sportmaster

Remington Model 512SB

Remington Model 513T Matchmaster

Remington Model 720

Remington Model 721

Remington Model 720

Caliber: 257 Roberts, 270 Win., 30-06 Govt.
Action: Bolt action; repeating; self-cocking; side safety
Magazine: 5-shot box; removable floor plate
Barrel: 20", 22", or 24"; round
Sights: Ramp front, adjustable open rear sights
Stock and Forearm: Checkered walnut one-piece pistol grip stock and forearm
Approximate wt.: 8 lbs.
Comments: Made from about 1941 to 1946. Add 20% for 257 Roberts.

Estimated Value:	**Excellent:**	**$1,600.00**
	Very good:	**$1,275.00**

Remington Model 721

Caliber: 270, 30-06 or 300 mag.; 280 Rem. (after 1959)
Action: Bolt action; repeating; self-cocking; adjustable trigger
Magazine: 3- or 4-shot box with fixed floor plate
Barrel: 24" or 26"; round
Sights: Ramp front, sporting rear with step elevator
Stock and Forearm: Checkered or plain walnut one-piece pistol grip stock and forearm
Approximate wt.: 8 lbs.
Comments: Made from about 1948 to 1958 in six grades; standard grade made from 1948 to 1961. Prices are for standard grade.

Estimated Value:	**Excellent:**	**$400.00**
	Very good:	**$320.00**

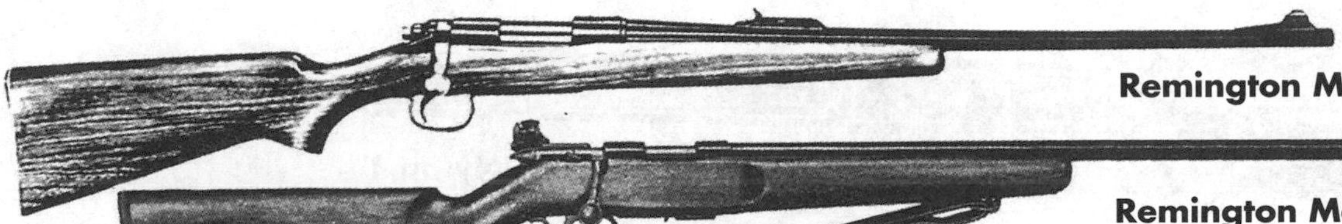

Remington Model 722

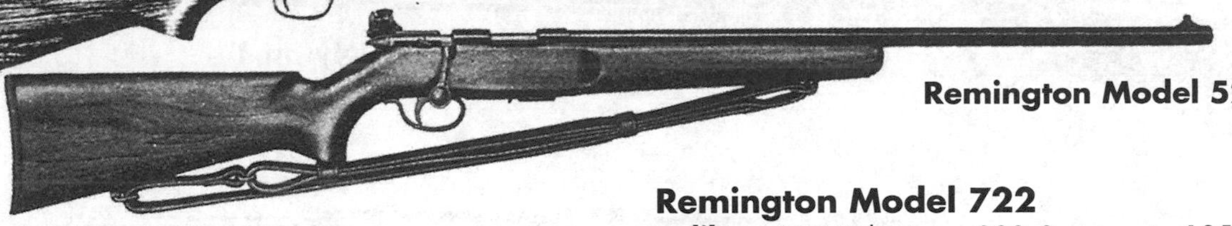

Remington Model 521TL Target

Remington Model 521TL Target

Caliber: 22 long rifle
Action: Bolt action; repeating; self-cocking; thumb safety; cocking indicator
Magazine: 5- or 10-shot clip
Barrel: 25"; medium weight round barrel
Sights: Post front, Lyman #57 receiver sight (peep sight)
Stock and Forearm: Heavy target one-piece pistol grip stock and beavertail forearm; varnished or oil finished; rubber butt plate
Approximate wt.: 6½ lbs.
Comments: Made from about 1948 to 1968; a low cost rifle intended for junior target shooters.

Estimated Value:	**Excellent:**	**$300.00**
	Very good:	**$240.00**

Remington Model 722

Caliber: 257 Roberts or 300 Savage; in 1950 222 Rem.; in 1956 308 Win. and 244 Rem.; in 1958 222 Rem. mag.; in 1960 243 Win.
Action: Bolt action; repeating; adjustable trigger
Magazine: 4- or 5-shot box; fixed floor plate
Barrel: 22" or 24"; round
Sights: Ramp bead front, open adjustable rear
Stock and Forearm: Checkered or plain varnished walnut one-piece pistol grip stock and forearm; after 1950 option of high-comb stock and tapered forearm
Approximate wt.: 7 to 8½ lbs.
Comments: Made from about 1948 to 1958 in seven grades; standard grade made from about 1948 to 1961. Prices are for standard grade.

Estimated Value:	**Excellent:**	**$400.00**
	Very good:	**$320.00**

Remington Model 725 (Early)

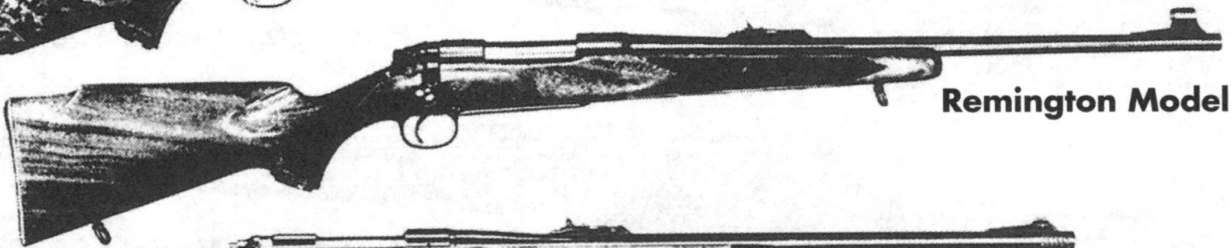

Remington Model 725 (Late)

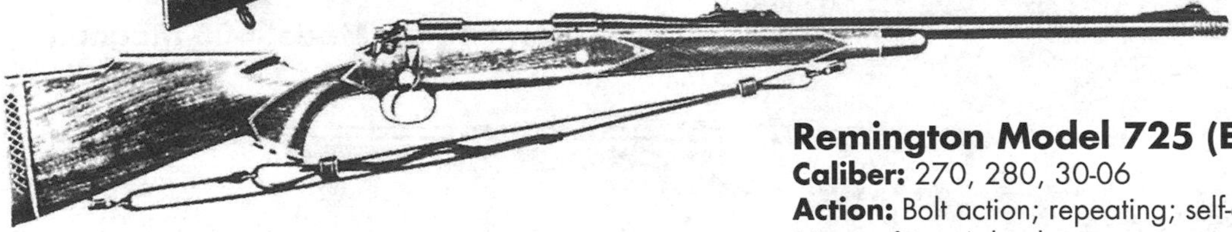

Remington Model 725 Magnum

Remington Model 725 Magnum

Caliber: 375 or 458 Win. magnum
Action: Bolt action; repeating; self-cocking; thumb safety
Magazine: 3-shot box
Barrel: 26"; heavy round barrel with muzzle brake
Sights: Ramp front, deluxe adjustable rear
Stock and Forearm: Fancy reinforced, checkered walnut Monte Carlo one-piece pistol grip stock and forearm; stock with cap and rubber recoil pad; black forearm tip; quick detachable leather sling
Approximate wt.: 9 lbs.
Comments: Made from about 1960 to 1961 in three grades. Priced for ADL grade.

Estimated Value:	**Excellent:**	**$1,250.00**
	Very good:	**$1,000.00**

Remington Model 725 (Early)

Caliber: 270, 280, 30-06
Action: Bolt action; repeating; self-cocking; thumb safety
Magazine: 4-shot box
Barrel: 22"; round
Sights: Adjustable open rear, hooded ramp front
Stock and Forearm: Checkered walnut Monte Carlo one-piece pistol grip stock and forearm; capped grip stock with shotgun butt plate and sling loops
Approximate wt.: 7½ lbs.
Comments: Made from about 1958 to 1959.

Estimated Value:	**Excellent:**	**$650.00**
	Very good:	**$520.00**

Remington Model 725 (Late)

Same as Model 725 (Early) except: in additional calibers 243 Win.; 244 Rem.; 222 Rem.; 24" barrel in 222 Rem. and aluminum butt plate on all calibers. Made from about 1960 to 1961 in three grades. Prices are for standard grade.

Estimated Value:	**Excellent:**	**$725.00**
	Very good:	**$580.00**

Remington Nylon 11

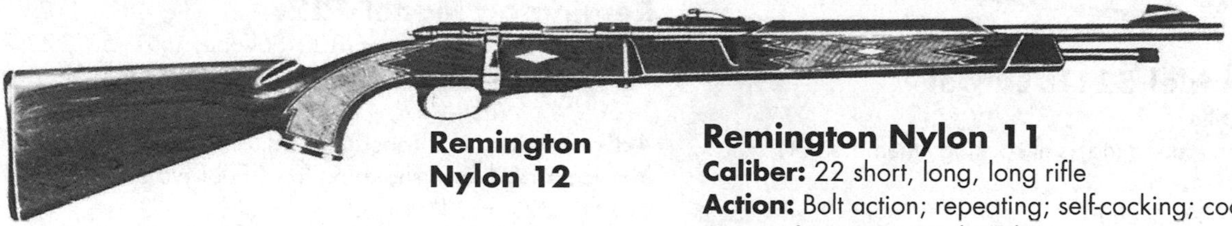

Remington Nylon 12

Remington Nylon 11

Caliber: 22 short, long, long rifle
Action: Bolt action; repeating; self-cocking; cocking indicator
Magazine: 6- or 10-shot clip
Barrel: 19½"; round
Sights: Ramp front, adjustable open rear
Stock and Forearm: Polished brown nylon one-piece stock, forearm and handguard over barrel; checkered, capped, pistol grip stock with shotgun butt plate; checkered forearm with blunt reversed cap; white liners and two white diamond inlays on each side
Approximate wt.: 4½ lbs.
Comments: Made from about 1962 to 1964.

Estimated Value:	**Excellent:**	**$300.00**
	Very good:	**$240.00**

Remington Nylon 12

Similar to Remington Nylon 11 Rifle except: 14- to 21-shot tubular magazine under barrel.

Estimated Value:	**Excellent:**	**$325.00**
	Very good:	**$260.00**

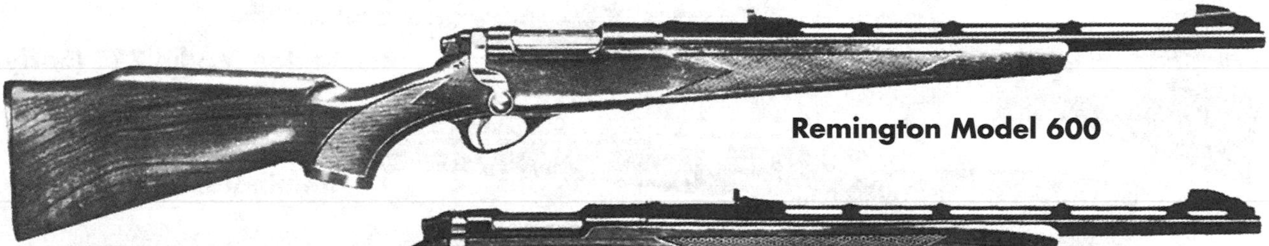

Remington Model 600

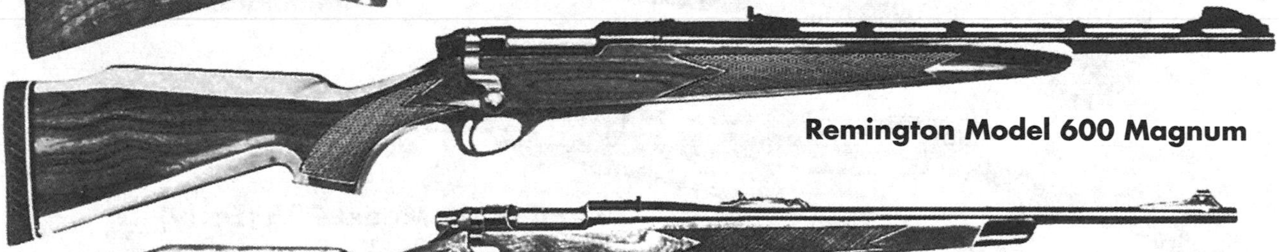

Remington Model 600 Magnum

Remington Model 660

Remington Model 600

Caliber: 6mm Rem., 222 Rem., 243 Win., 308 Win., 35 Rem.
Action: Bolt action; repeating
Magazine: 5-shot box
Barrel: 18½"; ventilated rib
Sights: Open rear, bead front
Stock and Forearm: Checkered walnut Monte Carlo one-piece pistol grip stock and forearm
Approximate wt.: 6 lbs.
Comments: A carbine-style rifle made in the mid-1960s. Add 50% for 223 Rem.

Estimated Value:	**Excellent:**	**$525.00**
	Very good:	**$420.00**

Remington Model 600 Magnum

Similar to the Model 600 except: magnum calibers; 4-shot magazine; walnut and beechwood stock; recoil pad.

Estimated Value:	**Excellent:**	**$850.00**
	Very good:	**$680.00**

Remington Model 660

Similar to the Model 600 except: 20" barrel without ventilated rib; beaded front sight; made in the late 1960s and the early 1970s.

Estimated Value:	**Excellent:**	**$525.00**
	Very good:	**$420.00**

Remington Model 660 Magnum

Similar to the Model 600 Magnum except: 20" barrel without ventilated rib; beaded front sight; made in the late 1960s to the early 1970s.

Estimated Value:	**Excellent:**	**$825.00**
	Very good:	**$665.00**

Remington Model 581

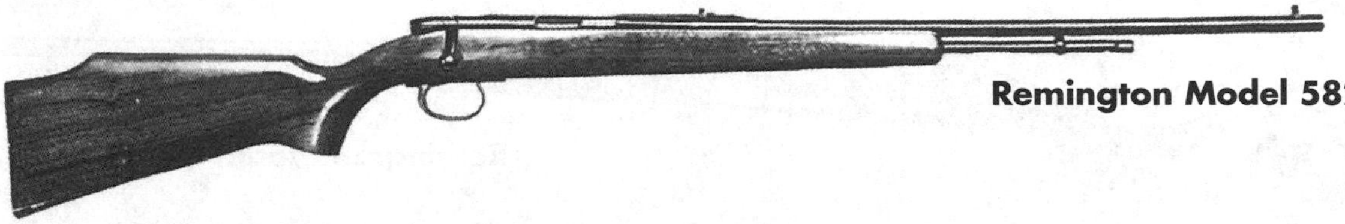

Remington Model 582

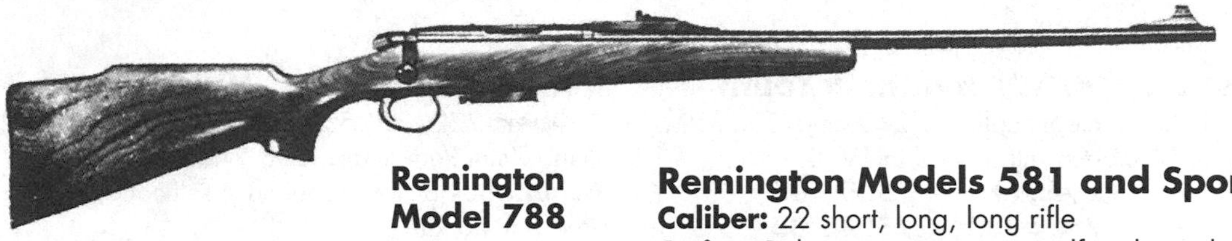

Remington Model 788

Remington Model 788

Caliber: 222, 22-250, 223 Rem., 6mm Rem., 243 Win., 308 Win.; 7mm-08 Rem. added in 1980
Action: Bolt action; repeating; self-cocking; thumb safety
Magazine: 5-shot clip in 222; 4-shot clip in other calibers
Barrel: 24" round tapered barrel in calibers 222, 22-250 and 223 Rem.; 22" barrel in other calibers; 18½" barrel available in 1980
Sights: Blade front, adjustable rear
Stock and Forearm: Monte Carlo one-piece pistol grip stock and forearm
Approximate wt.: 7½ lbs.
Comments: Made from about 1967 to 1983. Add 5% for left-handed action, $50.00 for scope.

Estimated Value:	**Excellent:**	**$525.00**
	Very good:	**$420.00**

Remington Models 581 and Sportsman 581S

Caliber: 22 short, long, long rifle
Action: Bolt action; repeating; self-cocking; thumb safety
Magazine: 5-shot clip; single shot adapter
Barrel: 24"; round
Sights: Bead front, adjustable open rear sight
Stock and Forearm: Plain hardwood Monte Carlo one-piece pistol grip stock and forearm
Approximate wt.: 5¼ lbs.
Comments: Made from about 1967 to 1983; reintroduced in 1986 to the late 1990s as Sportsman 581S.

Estimated Value:	**Excellent:**	**$225.00**
	Very good:	**$180.00**

Remington Model 582

Same as the Model 581 except: 15 to 20-shot tubular magazine. Add 8% for swivels and sling.

Estimated Value:	**Excellent:**	**$200.00**
	Very good:	**$160.00**

Remington Model 591

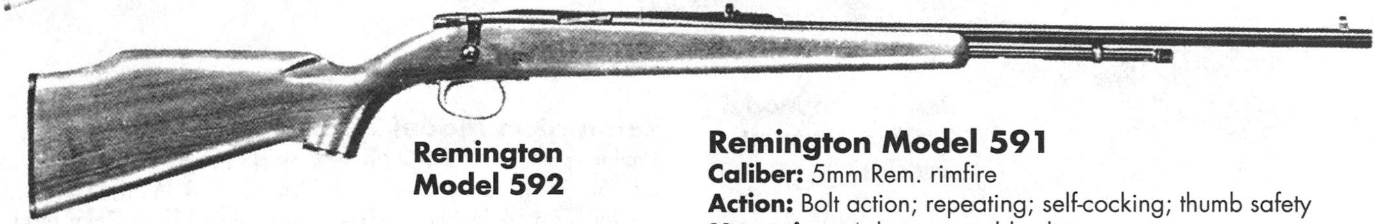

Remington Model 592

Remington Model 592

Same as the Model 591 except 10-shot tubular magazine under barrel.

Estimated Value:	**Excellent:**	**$275.00**
	Very good:	**$220.00**

Remington Model 591

Caliber: 5mm Rem. rimfire
Action: Bolt action; repeating; self-cocking; thumb safety
Magazine: 4-shot removable clip
Barrel: 24"; round
Sights: Bead post front; adjustable open rear
Stock and Forearm: Monte Carlo plain one-piece hardwood pistol grip stock and forearm
Approximate wt.: 5 lbs.
Comments: Made from about 1970 to 1974.

Estimated Value:	**Excellent:**	**$275.00**
	Very good:	**$220.00**

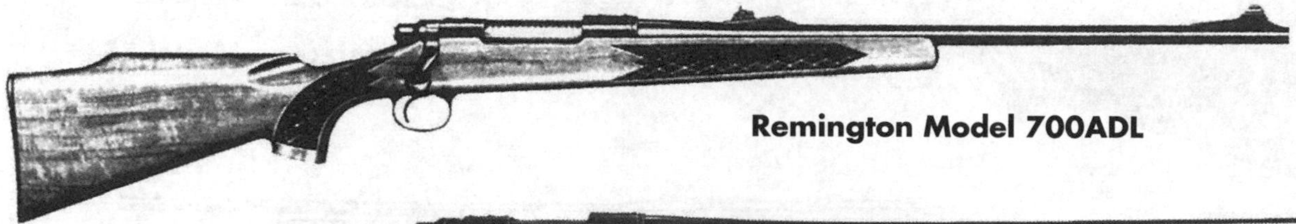

Remington Model 700ADL

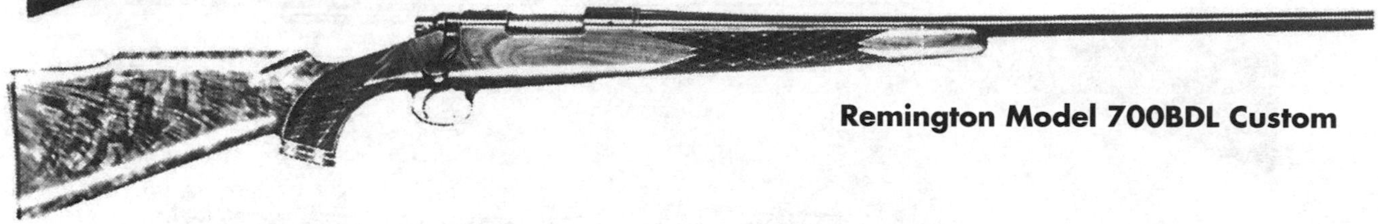

Remington Model 700BDL Custom

Remington Model 700ADL SyntheticYouth

Similar to Model 700ADL except: calibers 243 and 308 Win. only; synthetic stock is 1" shorter. Introduced in 1998.

Estimated Value: **Excellent:** **$390.00**
Very good: **$315.00**

Remington Model 700BDL Custom

Similar to Model 700ADL except: custom deluxe grade with black forearm end; additional calibers: 17 Rem., 223 Rem., 264 Win. mag., 280 Rem., 7mm-08 Rem., 300 Win. mag., 35 Whelen, 338 Win. mag.; Add 5% for mag. Models produced in late 1987 were recalled by Remington. These rifles may contain an improperly manufactured part in the trigger mechanism.

Estimated Value: **New (retail):** **$927.00**
Excellent: **$695.00**
Very good: **$555.00**

Remington Models 700ADL and 700ADL-LS

Caliber: 222, 22-250, 6mm Rem., 243 Win., 25-06 Rem., 270 Win., 7mm Rem. mag., 308 Win., 30-06
Action: Bolt action; repeating; self-cocking; thumb safety; checkered bolt handle
Magazine: 3- or 5-shot box magazine
Barrel: 22" or 24"; round tapered barrel
Sights: Ramp front; adjustable, notched, removable rear
Stock and Forearm: Checkered walnut Monte Carlo pistol grip, one-piece stock and forearm; synthetic stock; 700 ADL-LS has laminated stock
Approximate wt.: 7½ lbs.
Comments: Produced from about 1962 to the present. Add 5% for mag. Deduct 12% for synthetic stock; add 10% for laminated stock (LS). Models produced in late 1987 were recalled by Remington. These rifles may contain an improperly manufactured part in the trigger mechanism.

Estimated Value: **Excellent:** **$455.00**
Very good: **$365.00**

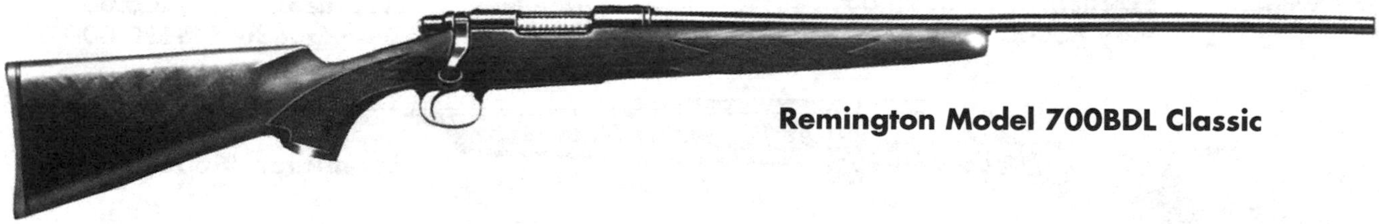

Remington Model 700BDL Classic

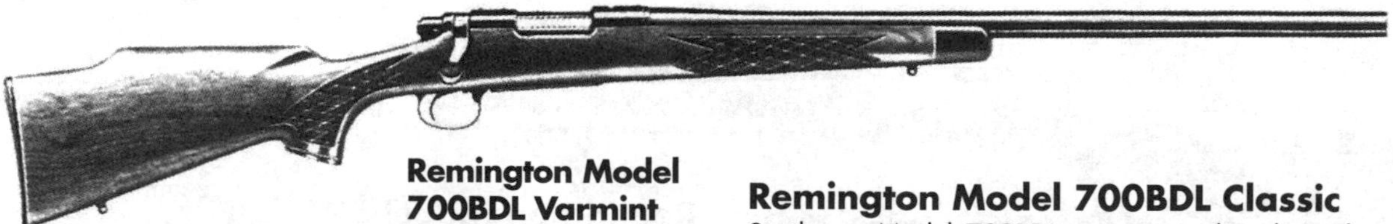

Remington Model 700BDL Varmint Special

Remington Model 700BDL Varmint Special

Similar to Model 700BDL except: heavy barrel without sights in 222 Rem., 22-250 Rem., 223 Rem., 6mm Rem., 243 Win., 25-06 Rem., 7mm-08, 308 Win. Models produced in late 1987 were recalled by Remington. These rifles may contain an improperly manufactured part in the trigger mechanism.

Estimated Value: **Excellent:** **$475.00**
Very good: **$380.00**

Remington Model 700BDL Classic

Similar to Model 700BDL except: stock styling changes; calibers 22-250 Rem., 6mm Rem., 243 Win., 270 Win., 30-06. Add 5% for mag. A limited number were available in 7mm mag. (in 1981); 257 Roberts (in 1982); 300 H&H magnum (in 1983); 250 Savage (in 1984); 350 Rem. magnum (in 1985); 264 Win. magnum (in 1986). Models produced in late 1987 were recalled by Remington. These rifles may contain an improperly manufactured part in the trigger mechanism. Produced in 220 Swift in 1992.

Estimated Value: **Excellent:** **$600.00**
Very good: **$480.00**

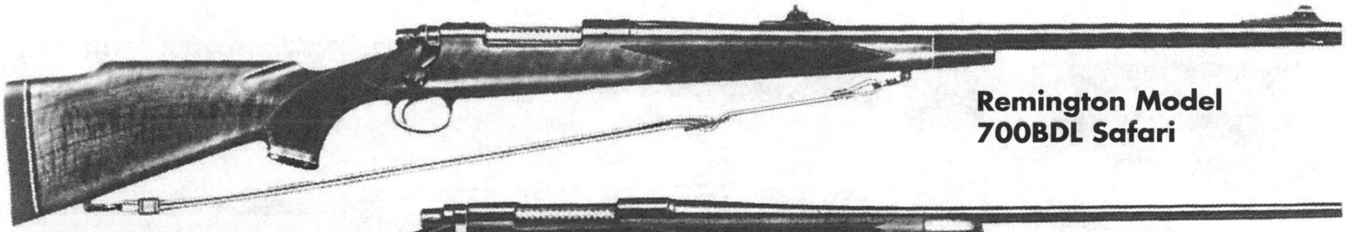

Remington Model 700BDL Safari

Remington Model 700 "Mountain Rifle" DM

Remington Model 700 "Mountain Rifle" DM

Similar to the Model 700BDL except: 270 Win., 280 Rem. and 30-06 caliber, 25-06 Rem. added 1992, 260 Rem. added 1998; approximate wt. 7 lbs.; 4-shot detachable magazine; no sights; introduced in 1986. Models produced in late 1987 were recalled by Remington. Some of these rifles may contain an improperly manufactured part in the trigger mechanism.

Estimated Value: **New (retail):** **$1,052.00**
Excellent: **$ 790.00**
Very good: **$ 630.00**

Remington Model 700BDL Safari

Similar to the Model 700BDL except: 375 H&H mag. and 458 Win. mag.; recoil pad. 8mm Rem. mag. caliber added in 1986. Models produced in late 1987 were recalled by Remington. These rifles may contain an improperly manufactured part in the trigger mechanism. Available after 1989 as a special-order model from the custom shop.

Estimated Value: **Excellent:** **$1,000.00**
Very good: **$ 800.00**

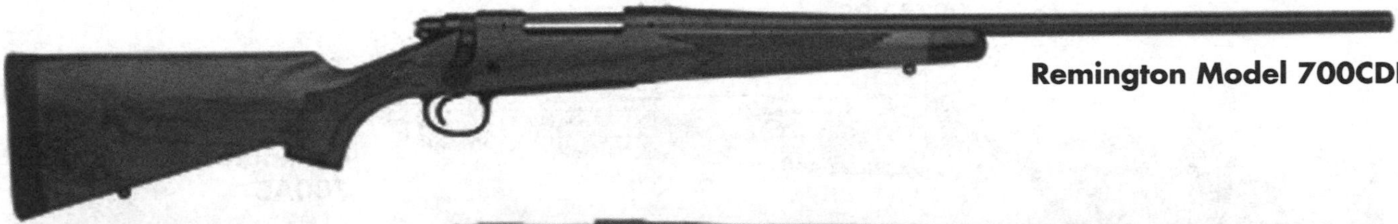

Remington Model 700CDL

Remington Model 700 Etron X

Remington Model 700FS

Similar to the Model 700ADL except it has a Kevlar® reinforced fiberglass stock (gray or gray camouflage); in calibers: 243 Win., 270 Win., 30-06, 308 Win., 7mm Rem. magnum. Produced from 1987 to 1990. Models produced in late 1987 were recalled by Remington. These rifles may contain an improperly manufactured part in the trigger mechanism.

Estimated Value: **Excellent:** **$550.00**
Very good: **$440.00**

Remington Model 700RS

Similar to the Model 700BDL except: DuPont Rynite® stock; textured finish; calibers: 270 Win., 280 Rem., 30-06. Introduced in 1987. Models produced in late 1987 were recalled by Remington. These rifles may contain an improperly manufactured part in the trigger mechanism.

Estimated Value: **Excellent:** **$475.00**
Very good: **$380.00**

Remington Model 700CDL

Similar to the Model 700BDL Classic; satin finish walnut stock and forearm; black grip cap and forearm tip. Introduced in 2004.

Estimated Value: **New (retail):** **$959.00**
Excellent: **$720.00**
Very good: **$575.00**

Remington Model 700 Etron X

Caliber: 220 Swift, 22-250 Rem., 243 Win.
Action: Bolt action, repeating; cased centerfire cartridges are fired by a completely non-mechanical system that ignites primers by means of an electrical impulse; key switch under pistol grip
Magazine: 4-shot box
Barrel: 26" fluted stainless steel
Sights: None
Stock and forearm: Black, one-piece pistol grip stock and forearm; swivels
Approximate wt.: 8¾ lbs.
Comments: Based on the Model 700 with a unique electronic ignition system. Introduced in 2002.

Estimated Value: **Excellent:** **$1,500.00**
Very good: **$1,200.00**

Remington Model 700 Titanium

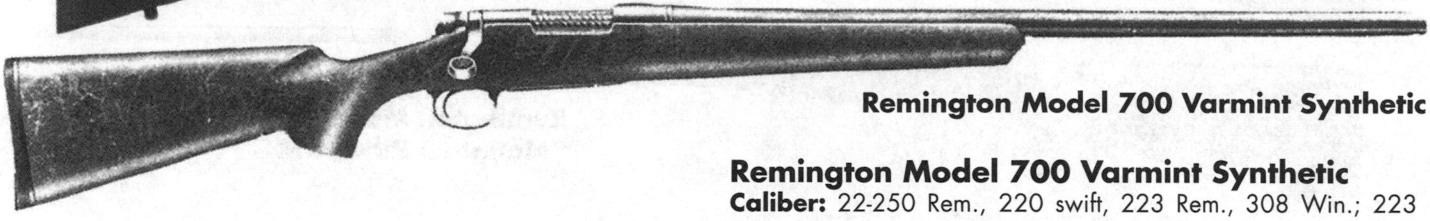

Remington Model 700 Varmint Synthetic

Remington Model 700 Titanium
Caliber: 260 Rem., 270 Win., 7mm-08 Rem., 30-06 Sprng., 308
Action: Bolt action, repeating; titanium receiver
Magazine: 4-shot box
Barrel: 22" contoured, stainless steel
Sights: None
Stock and forearm: Black, one-piece pistol grip carbon-fiber composite stock and forearm; swivels
Approximate wt: 5¼ to 5½ lbs.
Comments: An extremely lightweight rifle in the 700 line, introduced in 2002.

Estimated Value:	Excellent:	$975.00
	Very good:	$780.00

Remington Model 700 Varmint Synthetic
Caliber: 22-250 Rem., 220 swift, 223 Rem., 308 Win.; 223 Rem., 243 Win., 7mm-08 Rem. added in 1998
Action: Bolt action; repeating; thumb safety
Magazine: 4- or 5-shot box
Barrel: 24" black matte finish; 26" heavy or stainless steel fluted, ported barrel
Sights: None, drilled and tapped for scope mount
Stock and Forearm: Composite Kevlar®, fiberglass, and graphite; textured black and gray non-reflective finish; swivel studs; resin-impregnated laminated stock also available in 1998.
Approximate wt.: 8¾ lbs.
Comments: Introduced in 1992. Add 20% for stainless steel fluted barrel. Deduct 10% for laminated stock.

Estimated Value:	Excellent:	$550.00
	Very good:	$440.00

Remington Model 700AS

Remington Model 710

Remington Model 710
Caliber: 270 Win., 30-06 Sprng.
Action: Bolt action, repeating (short throw); thumb safety
Magazine: 4-shot removable dual-stack box
Barrel: 22"
Sights: None; pre-mounted 3-9x40 scope included
Stock and forearm: Dark-gray textured synthetic, one-piece stock and forearm
Approximate wt.: 7⅛" lbs.
Comments: Introduced in 2002.

Estimated Value:	Excellent:	$315.00
	Very good:	$255.00

Remington Model 700AS
Caliber: 22-250, 243 Win., 270 Win., 280 Rem., 30-06 Win., 7mm Rem. magnum, 300 Weatherby magnum
Action: Bolt action; repeating; thumb safety
Magazine: 3- or 4-shot box
Barrel: 22"; blued in all calibers except 22-250, 7mm Rem. mag. and 300 Weatherby mag. which have 24" blued barrel
Sights: Hooded ramp front; adjustable rear
Stock and Forearm: Synthetic resin, one-piece pistol grip stock and forearm; solid recoil pad
Approximate wt.: 6¾ lbs.
Comments: Made from 1990 to 1992. Add 4% for 7mm Remington mag. and 300 Weatherby mag.

Estimated Value:	Excellent:	$470.00
	Very good:	$375.00

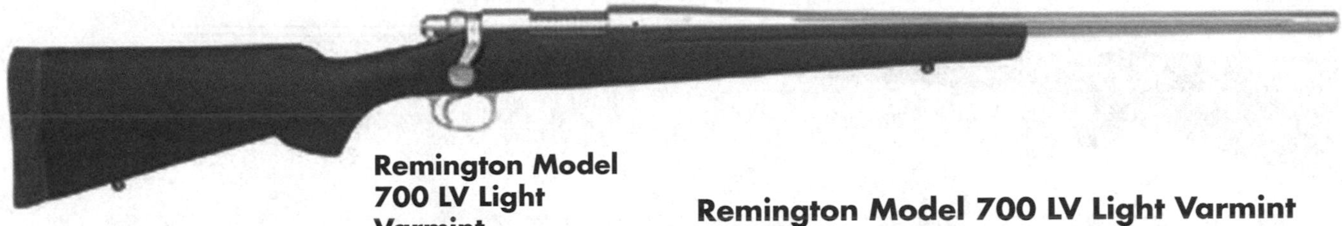

Remington Model 700 LV Light Varmint

Remington Model 700 LV Light Varmint

Similar to the Model 700 Variant Synthetic; 22" fluted, stainless steel barrel; black composite stock and forearm; recoil pad; 17 Rem., Fireball, 223 Rem., 22-250 Rem. calibers; weighs 6¾ lbs. Introduced in 2004.

Estimated Value:	**Excellent:**	**$750.00**
	Very good:	**$600.00**

Remington Model 700 Sendero

Caliber: 25-06 Rem., 270 Win., 7mm Rem. magnum, 300 Win. magnum
Action: Bolt action; repeating
Magazine: 3- or 4-shot box
Barrel: 26"; heavy, black matte finish or stainless steel fluted; free floating barrel
Sights: None, drilled and tapped for scope mount
Stock and Forearm: Smooth black Kevlar® fiberglass and graphite one-piece pistol grip stock and forearm
Approximate wt.: 7¼ lbs.
Comments: Introduced in 1994. Add 4% for magnum; add 21% for stainless steel fluted barrel.

Estimated Value:	**New (retail):**	**$1,359.00**
	Excellent:	**$1,020.00**
	Very good:	**$ 815.00**

Remington Model 700 Camo Synthetic

Caliber: 22-250 Rem., 243 Win., 270 Win., 280 Rem., 7mm-08 Rem., 7mm Rem. magnum, 30-06, 308 Win., 300 Weatherby magnum
Action: Bolt action; repeating; thumb safety
Magazine: 3- or 5-shot box
Barrel: 22" or 24"; camouflaged
Sights: Hooded ramp front, adjustable rear
Stock and Forearm: Camouflaged synthetic one-piece pistol grip stock and forearm; recoil pad; swivel studs
Approximate wt.: 7¾ lbs.
Comments: Produced from 1992 to the mid-1990s. Add 5% for mag.

Estimated Value:	**Excellent:**	**$495.00**
	Very good:	**$395.00**

Remington Model 504

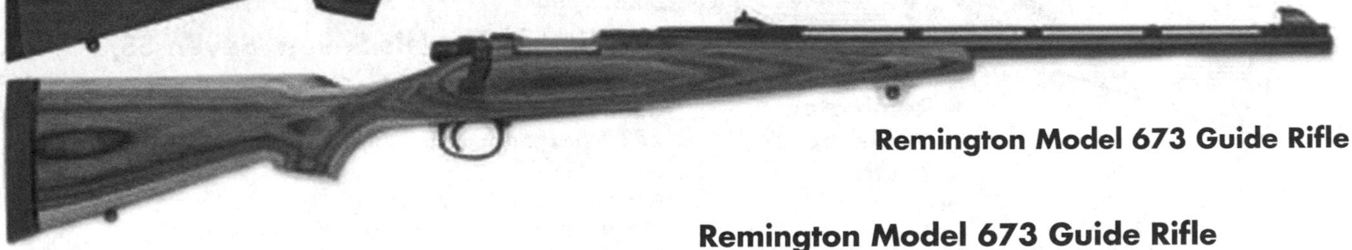

Remington Model 673 Guide Rifle

Remington Model 504

Caliber: 22 long rifle
Action: Bolt action; repeating
Magazine: 6-shot, flush-mount detachable metal box magazine
Barrel: 20" blued
Sights: None, drilled and tapped for scope mounts
Stock and Forearm: Checkered American walnut one-piece pistol grip stock and forearm; rubber butt pad; swivels
Approximate wt.: 6 lbs.
Comments: Introduced in 2004.

Estimated Value:	**Excellent:**	**$560.00**
	Very good:	**$445.00**

Remington Model 673 Guide Rifle

Caliber: 350 Rem. magnum, 300 Rem. SA Ultra Mag, 308 Win., 6.5mm Rem. magnum
Action: Bolt action; repeating
Magazine: 4 or 5-shot box with floor plate
Barrel: 22" blued; contour with ventilated rib
Sights: Ramp front, adjustable rear on incline ramp
Stock and Forearm: Weather-resistant laminated stock with alternating light and dark stripes; checkered one-piece pistol grip stock and forearm; swivels
Approximate wt.: 7½ lbs.
Comments: A centerfire rifle based on Model Seven design. Introduced in 2003, 308 Win. and 6.5mm Rem. magnum added in 2004.

Estimated Value:	**Excellent:**	**$560.00**
	Very good:	**$445.00**

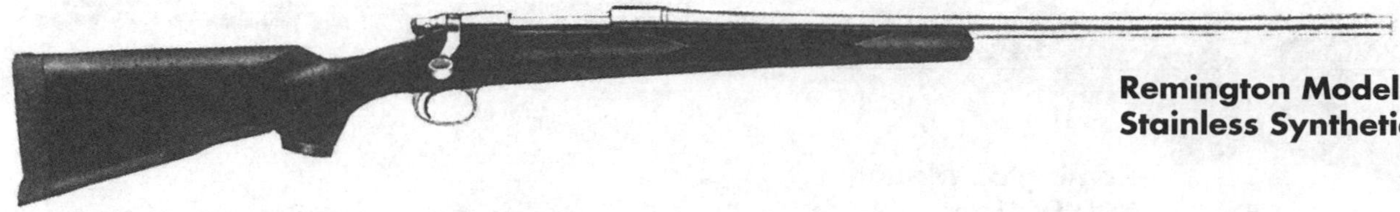

Remington Model 700BDL Stainless Synthetic SS

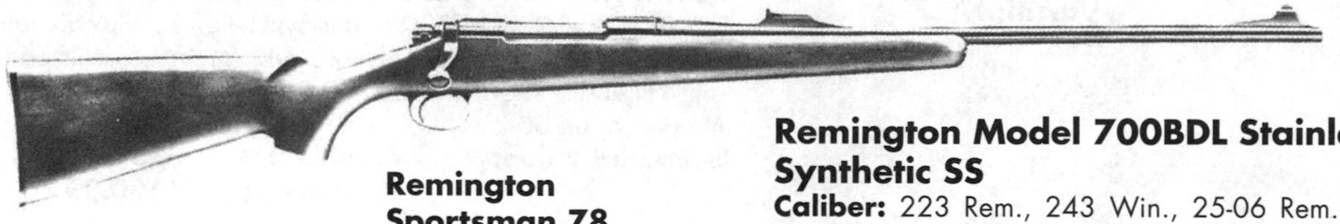

Remington Sportsman 78

Remington Sportsman 78

Similar to the Model 700 except: lesser quality finish; hardwood with no checkering; 22" barrel; 270 Win. and 30-06 calibers in 1984; 243 and 308 calibers added in 1985; 223 caliber added in 1986. Models produced in late 1987 were recalled by Remington. These rifles may contain an improperly manufactured part in the trigger mechanism; discontinued in 1990.

Estimated Value: **Excellent:** **$375.00**
Very good: **$300.00**

Remington Model 700BDL Stainless Synthetic SS

Caliber: 223 Rem., 243 Win., 25-06 Rem., 270 Win., 280 Rem., 6mm Rem., 7mm-08 Rem., 308 Win., 300 Wby. mag., 30-06 Sprg., 7mm Rem. mag., 7mm Wby. mag., 300 Win. mag., 338 Win. mag.
Action: Bolt action; repeating; thumb safety
Magazine: 4-shot box
Barrel: 24"; stainless steel, matte finish
Sights: None, drilled and tapped for scope mount
Stock and Forearm: Black textured checkered synthetic one-piece pistol grip stock and forearm; swivel studs
Approximate wt.: 8¾ lbs.
Comments: Introduced in 1992. Add 5% for mag.

Estimated Value: **Excellent:** **$675.00**
Very good: **$540.00**

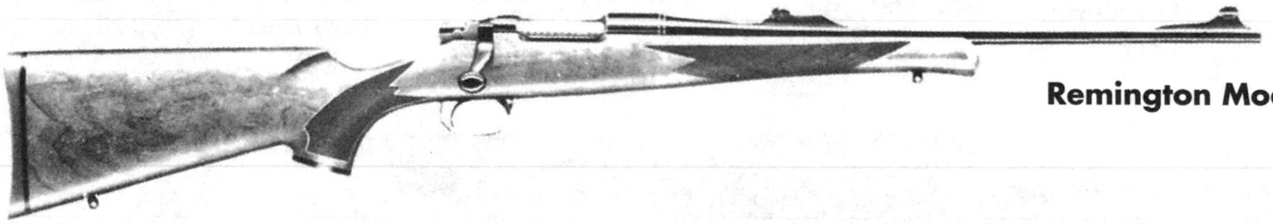

Remington Model Seven

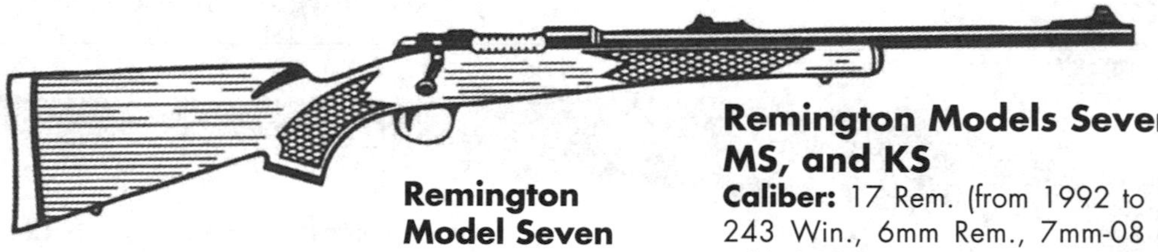

Remington Model Seven Youth

Remington Model Seven LS and Seven LSS

Similar to the Model Seven with laminated stock. Introduced in 2000. LSS has stainless steel barrel (add 15%).

Estimated Value: **Excellent:** **$550.00**
Very good: **$440.00**

Remington Model Seven Youth

Same as Model Seven except: shorter stock; calibers 243 Win., 7mm-08 Rem., 260 Rem. caliber added 1997; approximate wt. 6 lbs. Introduced in 1993.

Estimated Value: **Excellent:** **$430.00**
Very good: **$345.00**

Remington Models Seven, Seven SS, MS, and KS

Caliber: 17 Rem. (from 1992 to 1996), 222 Rem., 223 Rem., 243 Win., 6mm Rem., 7mm-08 Rem., 308 Win.; 260 Rem. added 1997
Action: Bolt action; repeating
Magazine: 4- or 5-shot box with floor plate
Barrel: 18½" or 20"; blued; stainless steel available after 1993
Sights: Adjustable rear on inclined ramp; ramp front
Stock and Forearm: Checkered walnut one-piece pistol grip stock and slightly lipped forearm; recoil pad; Mannlicher wood stock (MS) or synthetic stock and black matte finish (KS) after mid-1990s.
Approximate wt.: 6¼ lbs.
Comments: Introduced in 1983. 222 caliber discontinued in 1985. Models produced in late 1987 were recalled by Remington. These rifles may contain an improperly manufactured part in the trigger mechanism; add 5% for 17 Rem.; add 10% for stainless steel.

Estimated Value: **New (retail):** **$741.00**
Excellent: **$555.00**
Very good: **$445.00**

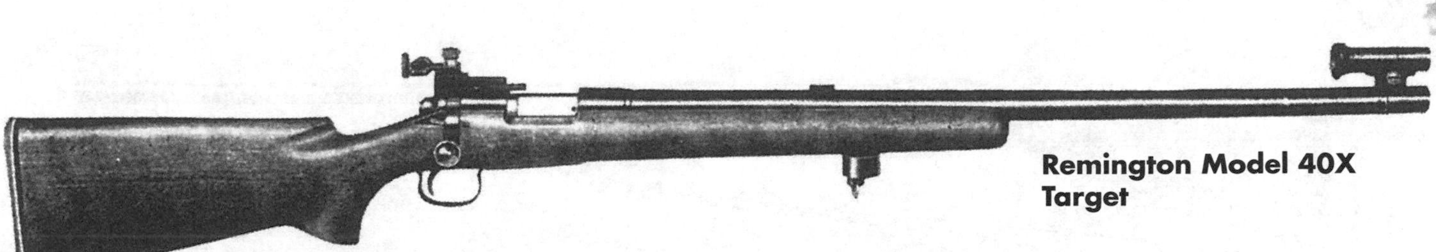

Remington Model 40X Target

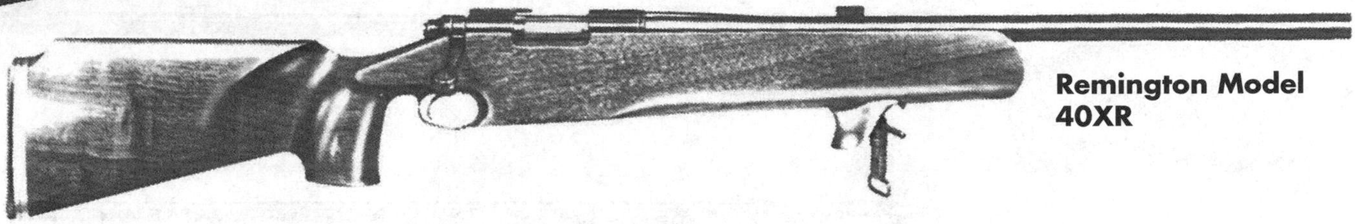

Remington Model 40XR

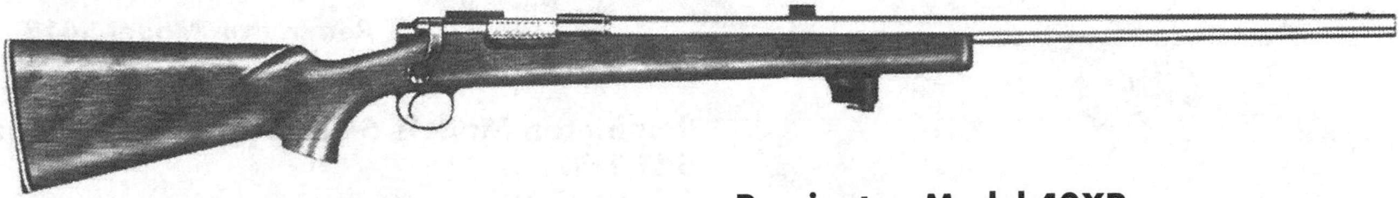

Remington Model 40XB Rangemaster

Remington Model 40X Target

Caliber: 22 long rifle in 1960; 222 Rem. in 1961; 308, 30-06; others on special order
Action: Bolt action; single shot; self-cocking; thumb safety; adjustable trigger
Magazine: None
Barrel: 28"; standard or heavy round barrel with bedding device in forearm
Sights: Removable target sights, scope block on barrel
Stock and Forearm: Oiled, plain, heavy target one-piece pistol grip stock and blade front; rubber shotgun butt plate; high fluted comb stock
Approximate wt.: 11 to 12 lbs.
Comments: Made from about 1956 to 1963. Replaced by Model 40XB match rifle in 1964 to 1975.

Estimated Value:	**Excellent:**	**$750.00**
	Very good:	**$600.00**

Remington Model 40XR

A target rifle similar to the Model 40X Target with widened stock and forearm; adjustable butt plate; hand stop; introduced in the late 1970s; 22 long rifle only; add 15% for Kevlar® stock. Models produced in late 1987 were recalled by Remington. These rifles may contain an improperly manufactured part in the trigger mechanism.

Estimated Value:	**Excellent:**	**$875.00**
	Very good:	**$700.00**

Remington Model 40XB Rangemaster

Similar to the Model 40X target except: stainless steel barrel. Available in calibers 222 Rem., 22-250 Rem., 243 Win., 6mm Rem., 25-06 Rem., 7mm Rem. mag. 7.62mm NATO, 30-06, 30-338, 300 Win. mag.; add 7% for repeating model. Models produced in late 1987 were recalled by Remington. These rifles may contain an improperly manufactured part in the trigger mechanism; discontinued in 1989.

Estimated Value:	**Excellent:**	**$865.00**
	Very good:	**$695.00**

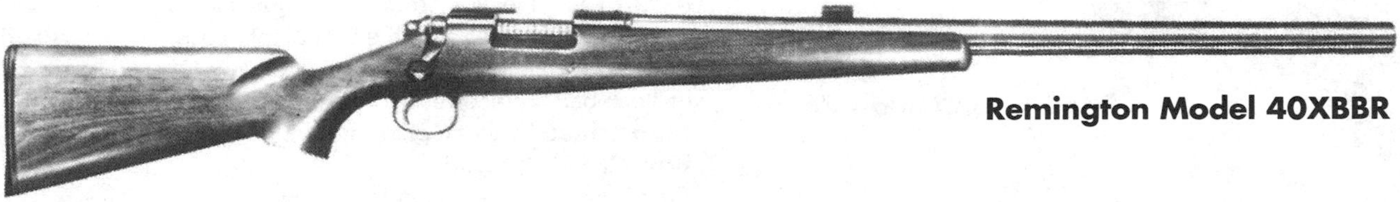

Remington Model 40XBBR

Remington Model 40XBKS

Similar to the Model 40XB Rangemaster except: DuPont Kevlar® reinforced stock, free-floating barrel and match-grade trigger. Available in left- or right-handed models, single-shot or repeating models. Available as a special-order item.

Estimated Value:	**Excellent:**	**$1,000.00**
	Very good:	**$ 800.00**

Remington Model 40XBBR

Similar to the Model 40XB Rangemaster with a 20" or 24" barrel. Models produced in late 1987 were recalled by Remington. These rifles may contain an improperly manufactured part in the trigger mechanism.

Estimated Value:	**Excellent:**	**$950.00**
	Very good:	**$760.00**

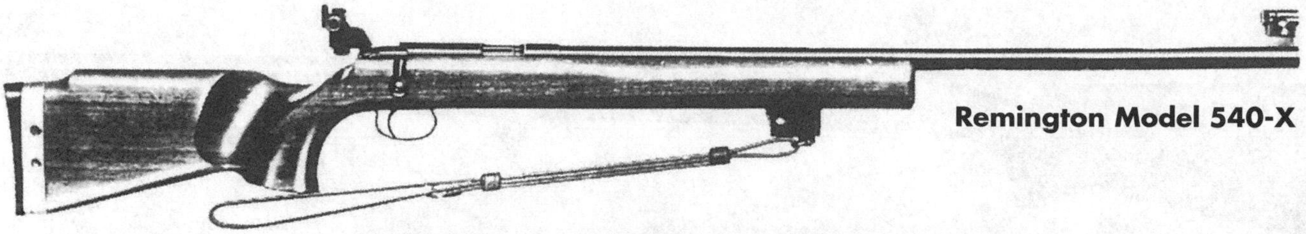

Remington Model 540-X

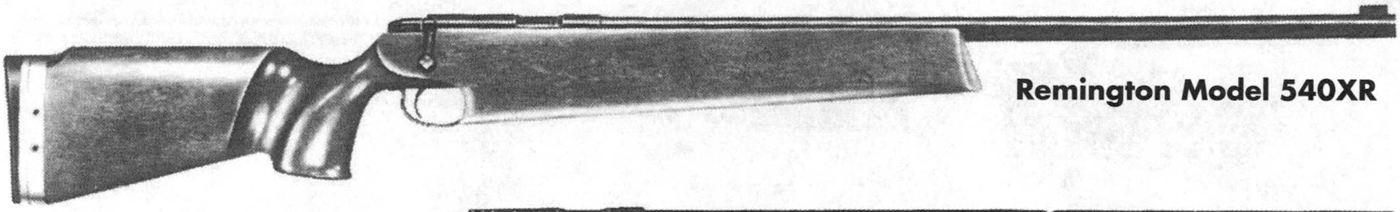

Remington Model 540XR

Remington Model 541S Custom

Remington Models 540-X and 540XR

Caliber: 22 long rifle
Action: Bolt action; single shot; self-cocking striker; slide safety; adjustable match trigger
Magazine: None
Barrel: 26"; heavy target barrel (540X)
Sights: Receiver drilled and tapped for scope mount; sights optional equipment
Stock and Forearm: Full pistol grip, heavy wood one-piece stock and forearm; thumb-grooved stock with 4-way adjustable butt plate rail
Approximate wt.: 8¾ lbs.
Comments: Made from about 1970 to 1983. A heavy rifle designed for bench shooting.

Estimated Value:	**Excellent:**	**$475.00**
	Very good:	**$380.00**

Remington Models 541S Custom, 541-T, and 541 THB

Caliber: 22 short, long, long rifle
Action: Bolt action; repeating; self-cocking; thumb safety
Magazine: 5-shot clip
Barrel: 24"; standard or heavy barrel (541-T HB)
Sights: None; drilled and tapped for scope
Stock and Forearm: One-piece checkered pistol grip stock and forearm
Approximate wt.: 5½ lbs.
Comments: Designed after the Remington Model 540X Target rifle; made from about 1972 to 1983 as Model 541S. Reintroduced in 1986 as Model 541-T. Add 7% for heavy barrel (HB). Discontinued in the late 1990s.

Estimated Value:	**Excellent:**	**$500.00**
	Very good:	**$400.00**

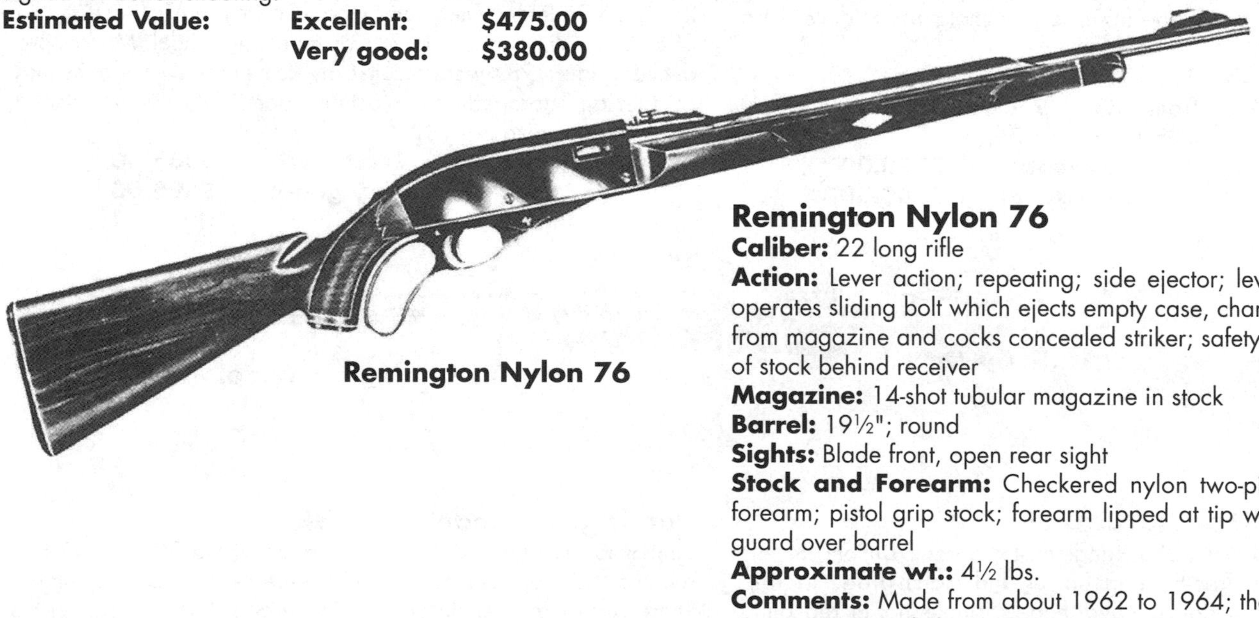

Remington Nylon 76

Remington Nylon 76

Caliber: 22 long rifle
Action: Lever action; repeating; side ejector; lever under stock operates sliding bolt which ejects empty case, chambers cartridge from magazine and cocks concealed striker; safety located on top of stock behind receiver
Magazine: 14-shot tubular magazine in stock
Barrel: 19½"; round
Sights: Blade front, open rear sight
Stock and Forearm: Checkered nylon two-piece stock and forearm; pistol grip stock; forearm lipped at tip with nylon handguard over barrel
Approximate wt.: 4½ lbs.
Comments: Made from about 1962 to 1964; the only lever action repeater made by Remington Arms Co.

Estimated Value:	**Excellent:**	**$800.00**
	Very good:	**$640.00**

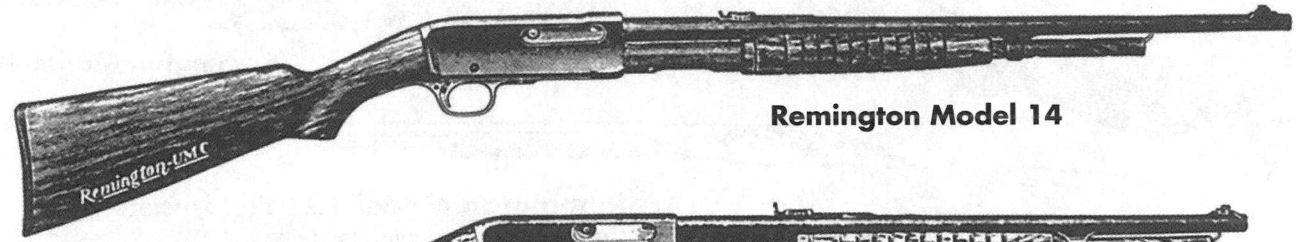

Remington Model 14

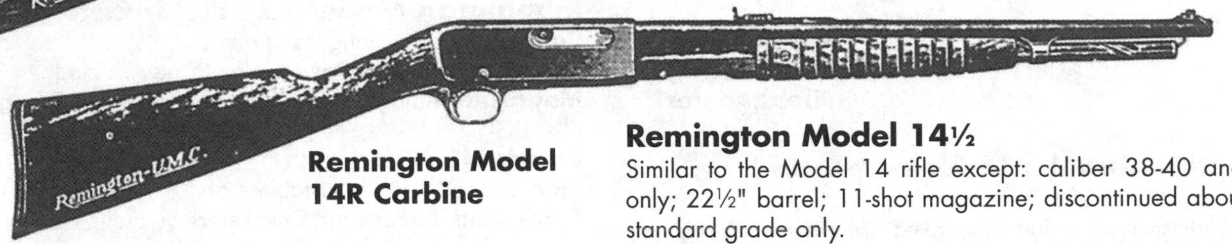

Remington Model 14R Carbine

Remington Model 14

Caliber: 25, 30, 32, 35 Rem.
Action: Slide action; hammerless; takedown model
Magazine: 5-shot tubular, under barrel
Barrel: 22"; round
Sights: Bead front, adjustable rear
Stock and Forearm: Plain or checkered walnut pistol grip stock and grooved or checkered forearm
Approximate wt.: 7 lbs.
Comments: Made from about 1912 to 1935 in four grades; higher grades had checkering and engraving. Prices are for standard grade.

Estimated Value:	**Excellent:**	**$425.00**
	Very good:	**$340.00**

Remington Model 14½

Similar to the Model 14 rifle except: caliber 38-40 and 44-40 only; 22½" barrel; 11-shot magazine; discontinued about 1925; standard grade only.

Estimated Value:	**Excellent:**	**$900.00**
	Very good:	**$720.00**

Remington Model 14½ Carbine

Same as the Model 14½ rifle except: 18½" barrel and 9-shot magazine.

Estimated Value:	**Excellent:**	**$1,000.00**
	Very good:	**$ 800.00**

Remington Model 14R Carbine

Same as the Model 14 rifle except: 18½" barrel; straight grip stock; approximate wt. 6 lbs.; standard grade only.

Estimated Value:	**Excellent:**	**$775.00**
	Very good:	**$620.00**

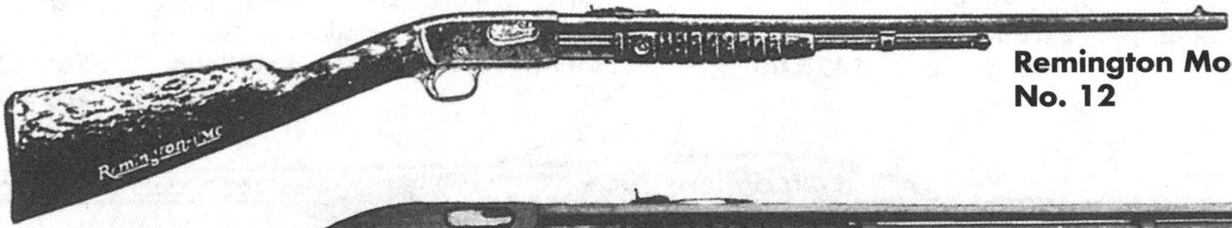

Remington Model No. 12

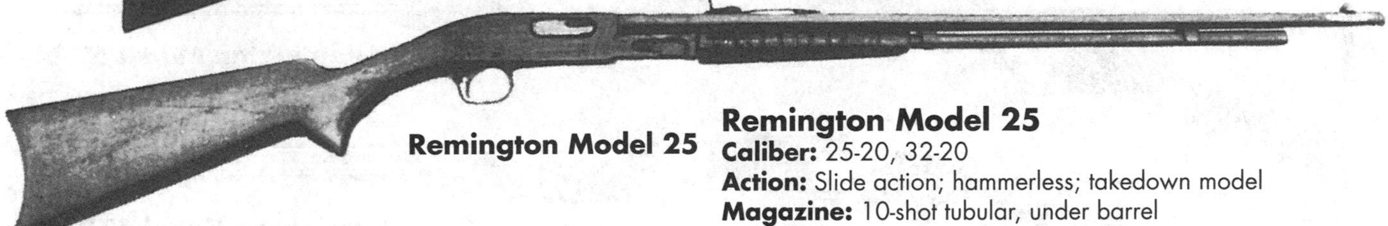

Remington Model 25

Remington Model No. 12

Caliber: 22 short, long, long rifle
Action: Slide action; hammerless; takedown model
Magazine: 10- to 15-shot tubular, under barrel
Barrel: 22" or 24"; round or octagon
Sights: Bead front, rear adjustable for elevation
Stock and Forearm: Plain or engraved; varnished plain or checkered, straight or pistol grip, walnut stock with rubber or steel butt plate; forearm grooved or checkered walnut
Approximate wt.: 5½ lbs.
Comments: Made from about 1909 to 1936 in four grades; higher grades have checkering and engraving. Prices are for standard (plain) grade.

Estimated Value:	**Excellent:**	**$500.00**
	Very good:	**$400.00**

Remington Model 25

Caliber: 25-20, 32-20
Action: Slide action; hammerless; takedown model
Magazine: 10-shot tubular, under barrel
Barrel: 24"
Sights: Bead front, open rear
Stock and Forearm: Checkered or plain walnut pistol grip stock and grooved or checkered slide handle
Approximate wt.: 6 lbs.
Comments: Made from about 1923 to 1936 in four grades; higher grades has checkering and engraving. Prices are for standard (plain) grade.

Estimated Value:	**Excellent:**	**$725.00**
	Very good:	**$580.00**

Remington Model 25R Carbine

Same as the Model 25 rifle except: 18½" barrel; straight grip stock; 6-shot magazine; approximate wt. 4½ lbs.; standard grade only.

Estimated Value:	**Excellent:**	**$975.00**
	Very good:	**$780.00**

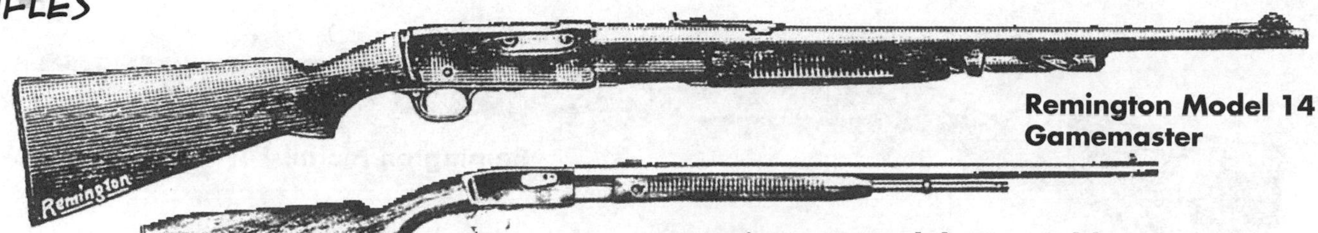

Remington Model 141 Gamemaster

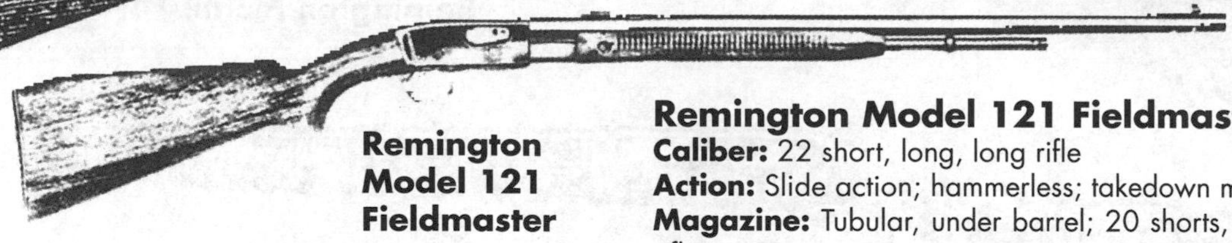

Remington Model 121 Fieldmaster

Remington Model 141 Gamemaster

Caliber: 30, 32, and 35 Rem.
Action: Slide action; hammerless; takedown model
Magazine: 5-shot tubular, under barrel
Barrel: 24"; round
Sights: Ramp front, adjustable rear
Stock and Forearm: Checkered or plain walnut pistol grip stock and grooved or checkered semi-beavertail slide handle
Approximate wt.: 7 lbs.
Comments: Made from about 1936 to 1942 and from 1946 to 1950 in four grades; higher grades have checkered pistol grip stock and forearm and engraving. Prices are for standard (plain) grade.

Estimated Value:	**Excellent:**	**$550.00**
	Very good:	**$440.00**

Remington 141R Carbine

Same as the Model 141 Gamemaster except: 18½" barrel; approximate wt. 5½ lbs.; standard grade only.

Estimated Value:	**Excellent:**	**$525.00**
	Very good:	**$420.00**

Remington Model 121 Fieldmaster

Caliber: 22 short, long, long rifle
Action: Slide action; hammerless; takedown model
Magazine: Tubular, under barrel; 20 shorts, 15 longs, 14 long rifles
Barrel: 24"; round
Sights: Bead front, adjustable rear
Stock and Forearm: Checkered or plain walnut pistol grip stock and grooved or checkered semi-beavertail slide handle
Approximate wt.: 6 lbs.
Comments: Made from about 1936 to 1942 and from 1946 to 1950 in four grades; higher grades are checkered and engraved. Prices are for standard grade.

Estimated Value:	**Excellent:**	**$475.00**
	Very good:	**$380.00**

Remington Model 121SB

Same as the Model 121 except smooth bore barrel for 22-shot cartridges.

Estimated Value:	**Excellent:**	**$550.00**
	Very good:	**$440.00**

Remington Model 121S

Similar to the Model 121 except: caliber 22 Rem. special only; 12-shot magazine; standard grade.

Estimated Value:	**Excellent:**	**$600.00**
	Very good:	**$480.00**

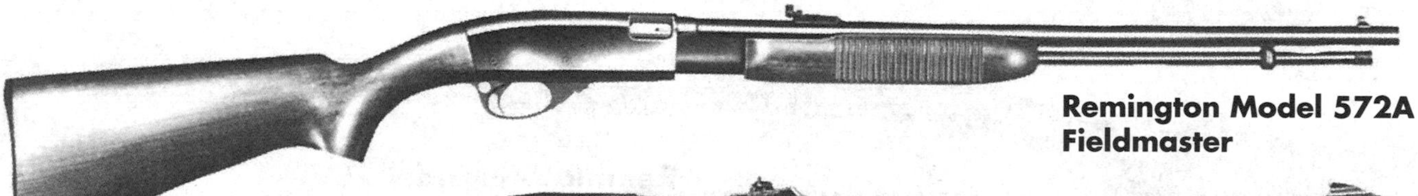

Remington Model 572A Fieldmaster

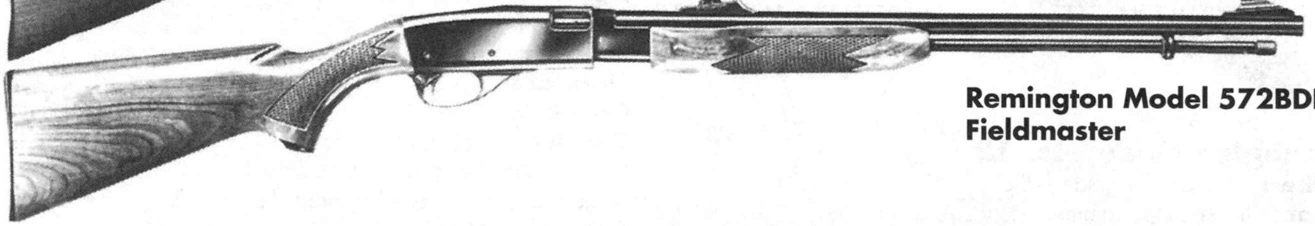

Remington Model 572BDL Fieldmaster

Remington Model 572SB

Same as the Model 572A Fieldmaster except: smooth bore for 22-shot cartridges; standard grade only.

Estimated Value:	**Excellent:**	**$300.00**
	Very good:	**$240.00**

Remington Model 572BDL Fieldmaster

Deluxe version of the 572A Fieldmaster with Monte Carlo stock. Currently produced.

Estimated Value:	**New (retail):**	**$607.00**
	Excellent:	**$455.00**
	Very good:	**$365.00**

Remington Model 572A Fieldmaster

Caliber: 22 short, long, long rifle
Action: Slide action; hammerless; solid frame; side ejector
Magazine: 14- to 20-shot tubular, under barrel
Barrel: 21" and 24"; round tapered
Sights: Bead front, adjustable open rear
Stock and Forearm: Checkered or plain walnut pistol grip stock and grooved or checkered slide handle
Approximate wt.: 5½ lbs.
Comments: Made from about 1955 to 1987.

Estimated Value:	**Excellent:**	**$275.00**
	Very good:	**$220.00**

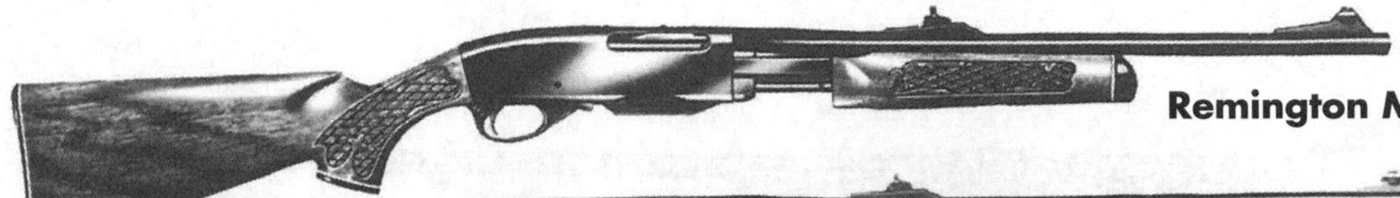

Remington Model 760 Carbine

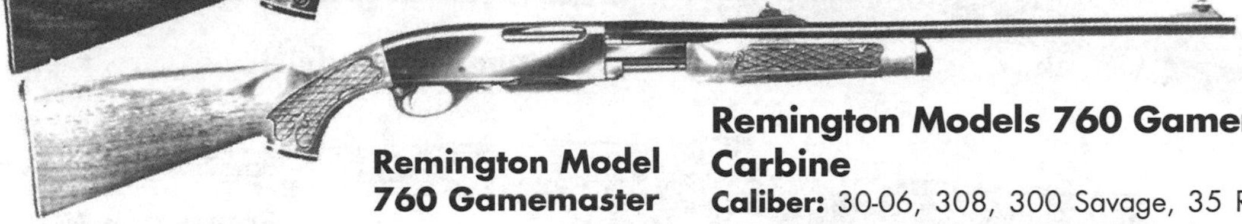

Remington Model 760 Gamemaster

Remington Models 760 Gamemaster and 760 Carbine

Caliber: 30-06, 308, 300 Savage, 35 Rem., 280, 270 Win., 257 Roberts, 244 Rem., 243 Win., 6mm Rem., 223 and 222; presently made in calibers 30-06, 308 Win., 270 Rem., 243 Win. and 6mm Rem.
Action: Slide action; hammerless; side ejector; solid frame; cross-bolt safety
Magazine: 4-shot box
Barrel: 22" round tapered; 18½" on carbine
Sights: Ramp bead front, adjustable open rear
Stock and Forearm: Checkered or plain walnut pistol grip stock and semi-beavertail slide handle
Approximate wt.: 7½ lbs.
Comments: Made from about 1952 to about 1980; carbine from 1960 to 1969 in 270 or 280 caliber; from 1962 to about 1980 in 30-06 and 308 Win.

Estimated Value:	**Excellent:**	**$600.00**
	Very good:	**$480.00**

Remington Model 760 BDL Gamemaster

Similar to the Model 760 with basketweave checkering, Monte Carlo stock; available in 30-06, 270, 308 calibers.

Estimated Value:	**Excellent:**	**$400.00**
	Very good:	**$320.00**

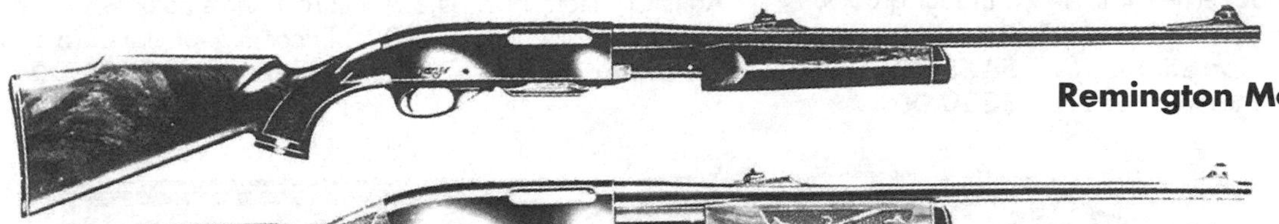

Remington Model Six

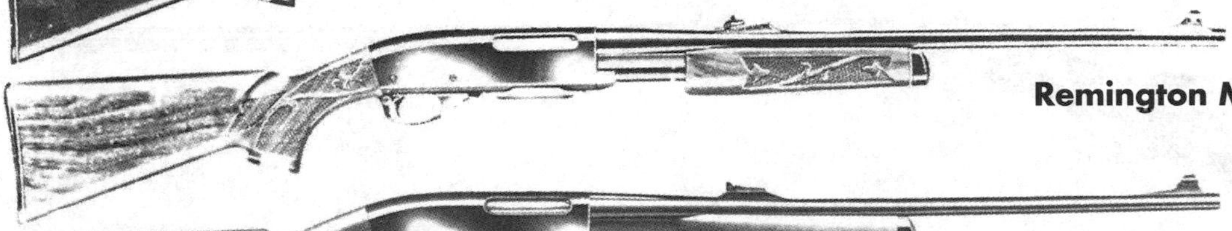

Remington Model 7600

Remington Sportsman 76

Remington Model Six

Caliber: 6mm Rem., 243 Win., 270 Win., 30-06, 308 Win.
Action: Slide action; hammerless; repeating
Magazine: 4-shot clip
Barrel: Blued; 22"
Sights: Blade ramp front, adjustable sliding ramp rear
Stock and Forearm: Checkered walnut Monte Carlo pistol grip stock and slide handle; black grip cap and fore-end tip; recessed finger groove in slide handle; cheekpiece; high-gloss finish
Approximate wt.: 7½ lbs.
Comments: Introduced in 1981 to replace the Model 760. Discontinued in 1987. Custom grades are available at increased prices. 6mm Rem. dropped in 1985.

Estimated Value:	**Excellent:**	**$440.00**
	Very good:	**$350.00**

Remington Models 7600 and 7600SP

Caliber: 243 Win., 270 Win., 280 Rem., 30-06, 308 Win., 35 Whelen (dropped in mid-1990s)
Action: Slide action; hammerless; repeating
Magazine: 4-shot clip
Barrel: Blued; 18½" or 22"
Sights: Blade ramp front, adjustable sliding ramp rear
Stock and Forearm: Satin or gloss finish; plain or Monte Carlo checkered walnut stock and slide handle; synthetic stock available in the 1990s
Approximate wt.: 7½ lbs.
Comments: Produced from the mid-1980s to the present. The Model 7600SP is a Special Purpose model with non-reflective finish on wood and metal. Deduct 18% for synthetic stock.

Estimated Value:	**New (retail):**	**$792.00**
	Excellent:	**$595.00**
	Very good:	**$475.00**

Remington Sportsman 76

Similar to the Model 7600 with lesser quality finish; hardwood with no checkering; 22" barrel; 30-06 caliber only. Produced from 1984 to 1987.

Estimated Value:	**Excellent:**	**$375.00**
	Very good:	**$300.00**

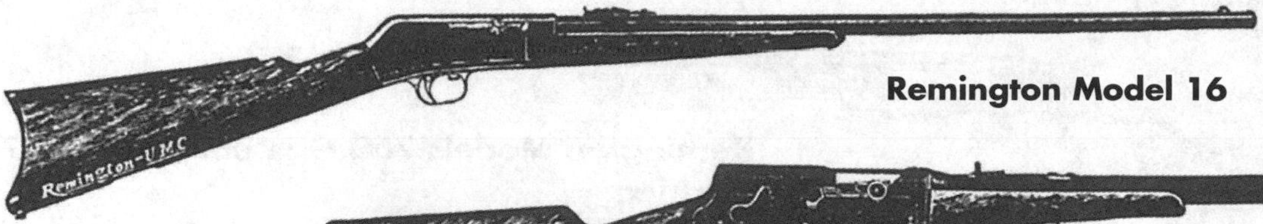

Remington Model 16

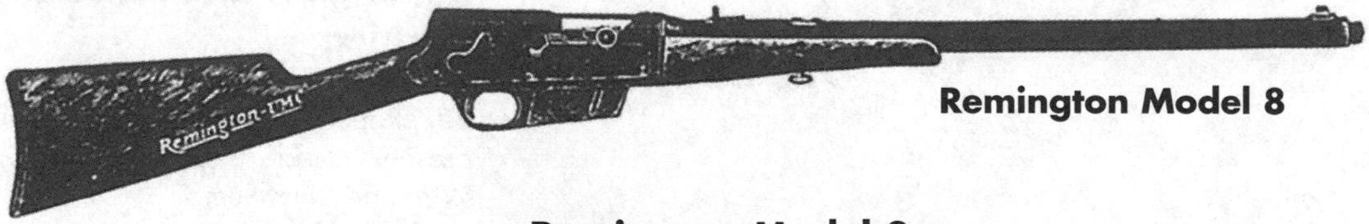

Remington Model 8

Remington Model 16

Caliber: 22 Rem. automatic
Action: Semiautomatic; hammerless; solid breech; sliding bolt; side ejector; takedown model
Magazine: 15-shot tubular, in stock
Barrel: 22"; round
Sights: Bead front, adjustable notch sporting rear
Stock and Forearm: Plain or engraved; varnished, plain or checkered, straight grip, two-piece walnut stock and forearm; steel butt plate and blunt lip on forearm
Approximate wt.: 5¾ lbs.
Comments: Made from about 1914 to 1928 in four grades: A, C, D, and F. Prices are for standard grade.

Estimated Value:	**Excellent:**	**$475.00**
	Very good:	**$380.00**

Remington Model 8

Caliber: 25, 30, 32, or 35 Rem.
Action: Semiautomatic; top ejector; for smokeless powder; takedown model; solid breech and sliding barrel type
Magazine: 5-shot detachable box
Barrel: 22"; round
Sights: Bead front, open rear
Stock and Forearm: Plain or engraved; varnished, plain or checkered, two-piece walnut straight grip stock and forearm; rubber or steel butt plate and lipped forearm
Approximate wt.: 7¾ lbs.
Comments: Made from about 1906 to 1936 in five grades: A, C, D, E, and F; jacket marked "Manufactured by the Remington Arms Co. Ilion, N.Y., U.S.A." "Browning's Patent's Oct. 8, 1900. Oct. 15, 1900. July 2, 1902." Prices are for standard grade.

Estimated Value:	**Excellent:**	**$625.00**
	Very good:	**$500.00**

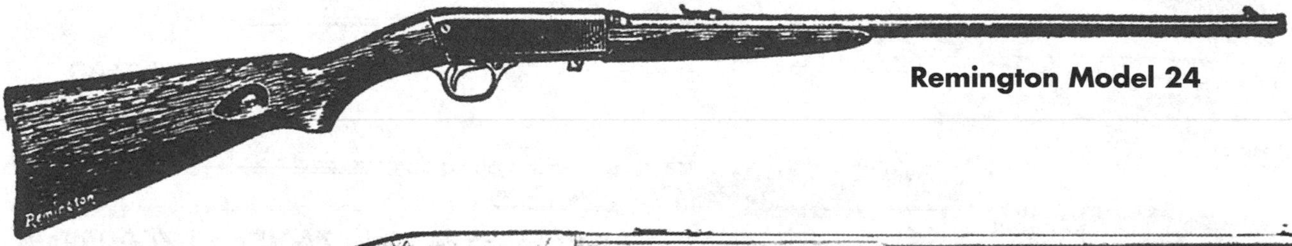

Remington Model 24

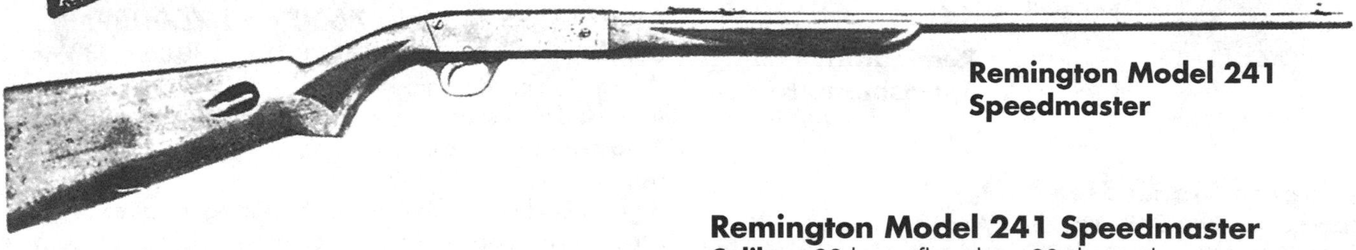

Remington Model 241 Speedmaster

Remington Model 24

Caliber: 22 long rifle only or 22 short only
Action: Semiautomatic; hammerless; solid breech; sliding bolt; bottom ejector
Magazine: 15-shot stock tube in 22 short and 10-shot in 22 long rifle
Barrel: 19"; round
Sights: Bead front, adjustable rear
Stock and Forearm: Plain or engraved; varnished, plain or checkered, two-piece walnut semi-pistol grip stock and forearm; steel butt plate with lipped forearm
Approximate wt.: 4¾ lbs.
Comments: Made from about 1922 to 1935 in five grades: A, C, D, E, and F. Prices are for standard grade.

Estimated Value:	**Excellent:**	**$525.00**
	Very good:	**$420.00**

Remington Model 241 Speedmaster

Caliber: 22 long rifle only or 22 short only
Action: Semiautomatic; hammerless; solid breech; bottom ejection; takedown type; sliding bolt action; thumb safety
Magazine: 15-shot in 22 short; 10-shot in 22 long rifle; tubular in stock
Barrel: 24"; round
Sights: Bead front, notched rear adjustable for elevation
Stock and Forearm: Plain or engraved; varnished walnut, plain or checkered, two-piece pistol grip stock and forearm; semi-beavertail
Approximate wt.: 6 lbs.
Comments: Improved version of Model 24; produced from about 1935 to 1951 in five grades: A, B, D, E, and F. Prices are for standard grade.

Estimated Value:	**Excellent:**	**$425.00**
	Very good:	**$340.00**

Remington Model 81 Woodsmaster

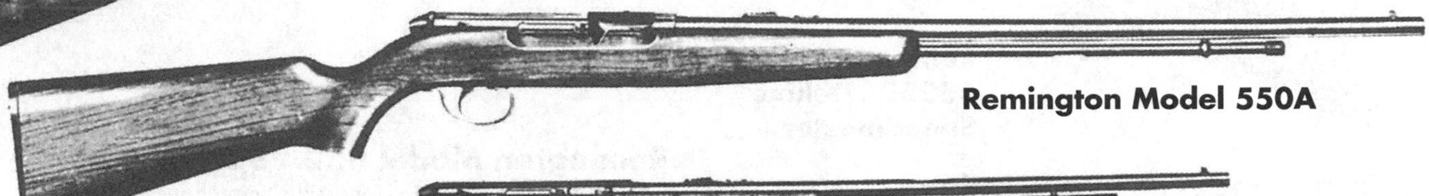

Remington Model 550A

Remington Model 550 Gallery

Remington Model 550A

Caliber: 22 short, long, long rifle
Action: Semiautomatic; hammerless; side ejector; solid breech; sliding bolt; floating power piston which permits using 22 short, long, or long rifle interchangeably and still functions as semiautomatic; takedown-type with thumb safety
Magazine: 20-shot tubular in 22 short; 15-shot in 22 long rifle
Barrel: 24"; round
Sights: Dovetail bead front, notched rear adjustable for elevation
Stock and Forearm: One-piece plain varnished pistol grip stock and forearm; hard rubber butt plate
Approximate wt.: 6½ lbs.
Comments: Replaced the Model 241 because it was less expensive to produce. Made from about 1941 to 1942 and from 1946 to 1970. Receiver grooved for telescope sight mounts.

Estimated Value:	**Excellent:**	**$275.00**
	Very good:	**$220.00**

Remington Model 550 Gallery

Similar to the Model 550A except chambered for 22 short caliber only.

Estimated Value:	**Excellent:**	**$300.00**
	Very good:	**$240.00**

Remington Model 81 Woodsmaster

Caliber: From 1936 to 1942, 25, 30, 32, 35 Rem.; from 1946 to 1950, 30, 32, 35, 300 Savage
Action: Semiautomatic; top ejector; takedown model; solid breech; sliding barrel type
Magazine: 5-shot detachable box
Barrel: 22"; round
Sights: Bead front, sporting rear with notched elevator
Stock and Forearm: Plain or engraved; varnished walnut, plain or checkered two-piece pistol grip stock and forearm; rubber butt plate and semi-beavertail forearm
Approximate wt.: 7¾ lbs.
Comments: Made from about 1936 to 1942 and from 1946 to 1950 in five grades: A, B, D, E, and F. An improved version of the Model 8. Prices are for standard grade.

Estimated Value:	**Excellent:**	**$575.00**
	Very good:	**$460.00**

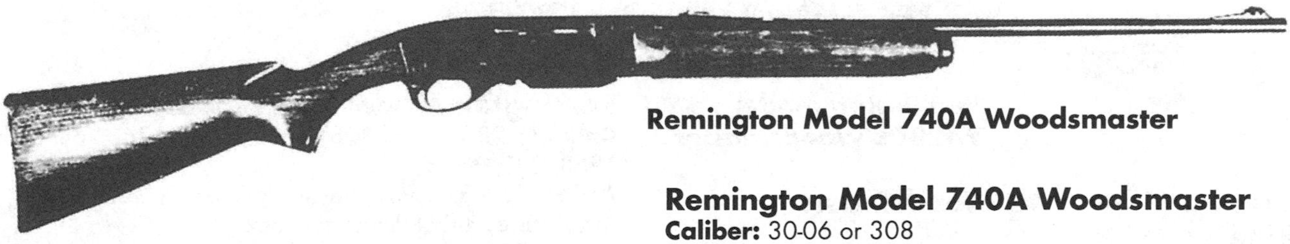

Remington Model 740A Woodsmaster

Remington Model 740A Woodsmaster

Caliber: 30-06 or 308
Action: Semiautomatic; gas-operated; side ejector; hammerless
Magazine: 4-shot detachable box
Barrel: 22"; round
Sights: Ramp front, open rear adjustable for elevation
Stock and Forearm: Plain pistol two-piece pistol grip stock and semi-beavertail forearm with finger grooves
Approximate wt.: 7½ lbs.
Comments: Made from about 1950 to 1960.

Estimated Value:	**Excellent:**	**$350.00**
	Very good:	**$280.00**

Remington Model 740ADL Deluxe Grade

Same as the Model 740A except: deluxe checkered stock and forearm; also grip cap and sling swivels.

Estimated Value:	**Excellent:**	**$425.00**
	Very good:	**$340.00**

Remington Model 740BDL Special Grade

Similar to the Model 740ADL Deluxe Grade except stock and forearm have deluxe finish on select wood.

Estimated Value:	**Excellent:**	**$450.00**
	Very good:	**$360.00**

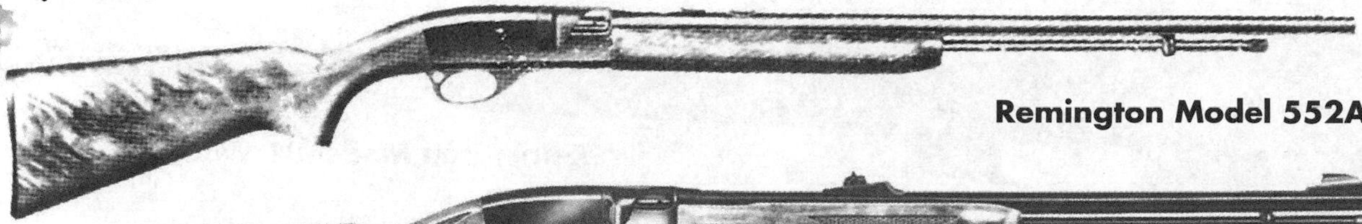

Remington Model 552A Speedmaster

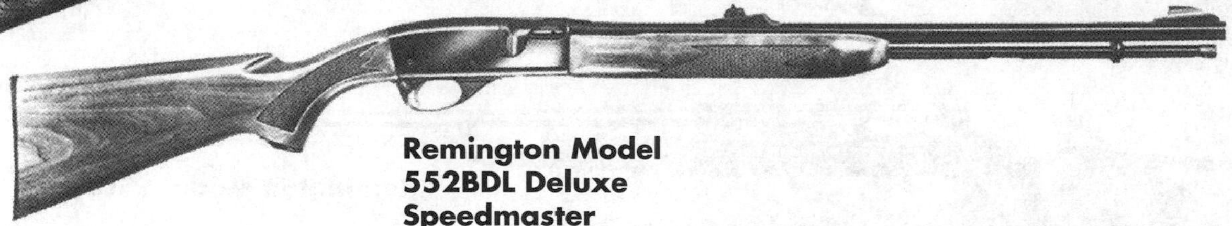

Remington Model 552BDL Deluxe Speedmaster

Remington Model 552BDL Deluxe Speedmaster

Same as the Model 552 Speedmaster except: higher quality finish, Monte Carlo or regular, checkered stock and forearm; ramp front sight; adjustable rear; made from about 1961 to the present.

Estimated Value:	**New (retail):**	**$593.00**
	Excellent:	**$445.00**
	Very good:	**$355.00**

Remington Model 552 GS Gallery Special

Same as the Model 552 Speedmaster except: 22 short only.

Estimated Value:	**Excellent:**	**$225.00**
	Very good:	**$175.00**

Remington Model 552A Speedmaster

Caliber: 22 short, long, long rifle, interchangeably
Action: Semiautomatic; hammerless; side ejector; solid breech; sliding bolt; floating power piston which permits using 22 short, long, long rifle cartridges interchangeably
Magazine: 20-shot tubular in 22 short, 15-shot in long rifle; under barrel
Barrel: 21" and 23"; round tapered
Sights: Bead front; notched adjustable rear
Stock and Forearm: Plain smooth two piece pistol grip stock and semi-beavertail forearm; butt plate
Approximate wt.: 5¾ lbs.
Comments: Made from about 1958 to 1987.

Estimated Value:	**Excellent:**	**$225.00**
	Very good:	**$180.00**

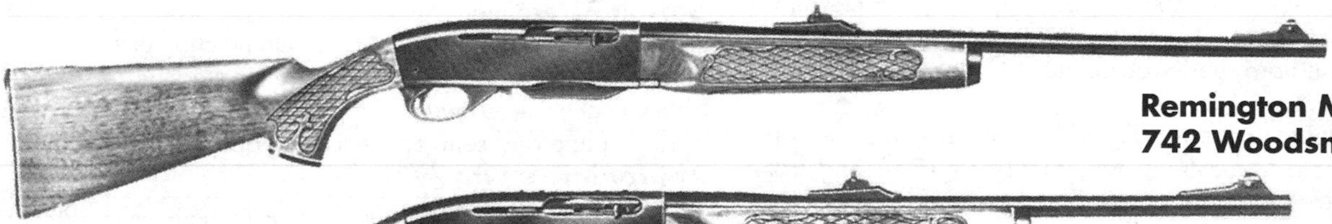

Remington Model 742 Woodsmaster

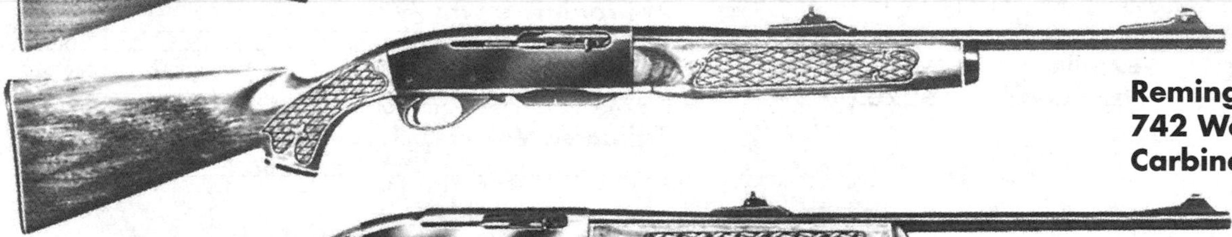

Remington Model 742 Woodsmaster Carbine

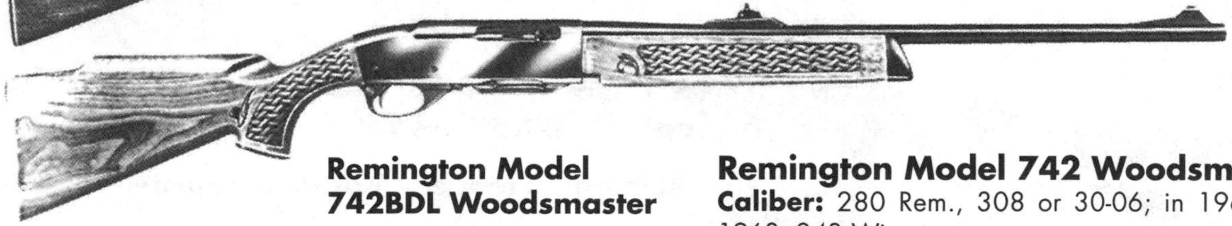

Remington Model 742BDL Woodsmaster

Remington Model 742 Woodsmaster Carbine

Same as the Model 742 Woodsmaster rifle except: 18½" barrel; approximate wt.: 6½ lbs.; calibers 280, 30-06, or 308.

Estimated Value:	**Excellent:**	**$400.00**
	Very good:	**$320.00**

Remington Model 742BDL Woodsmaster

Same as the Model 742 Woodsmaster rifle except: 30-06 or 308 caliber, checkered Monte Carlo stock; black tipped forearm.

Estimated Value:	**Excellent:**	**$450.00**
	Very good:	**$360.00**

Remington Model 742 Woodsmaster

Caliber: 280 Rem., 308 or 30-06; in 1963, 6mm Rem.; in 1968, 243 Win.
Action: Semiautomatic; hammerless; gas-operated
Magazine: 4-shot detachable box
Barrel: 22"; round tapered
Sights: Gold bead front, adjustable rear
Stock and Forearm: Plain or checkered and standard or deluxe finish two-piece walnut stock and semi-beavertail forearm; aluminum butt plate
Approximate wt.: 7½ lbs.
Comments: Manufactured from about 1960 to about 1980; in 1969 Remington advertised many fancy grades. Prices are for standard grade.

Estimated Value:	**Excellent:**	**$400.00**
	Very good:	**$320.00**

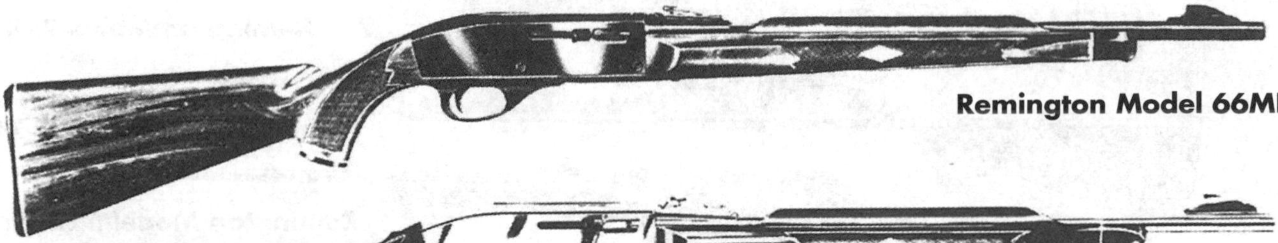
Remington Model 66MB

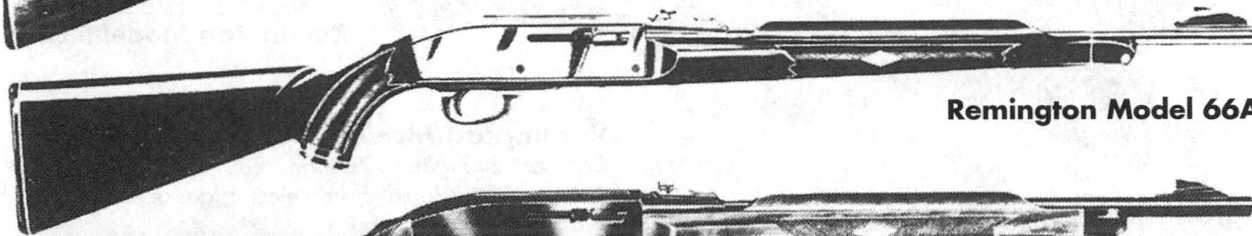
Remington Model 66AB

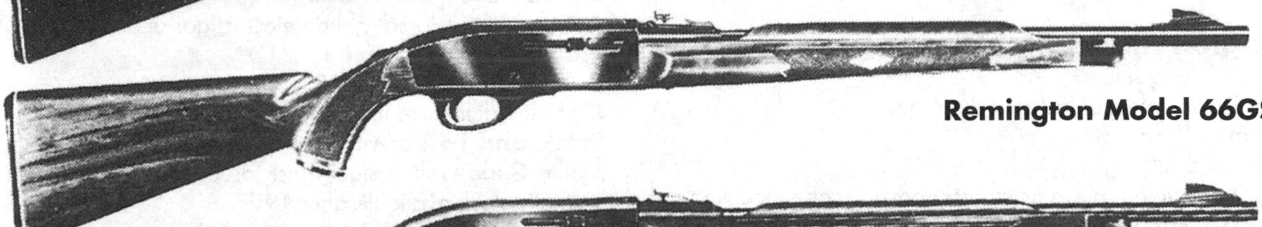
Remington Model 66GS

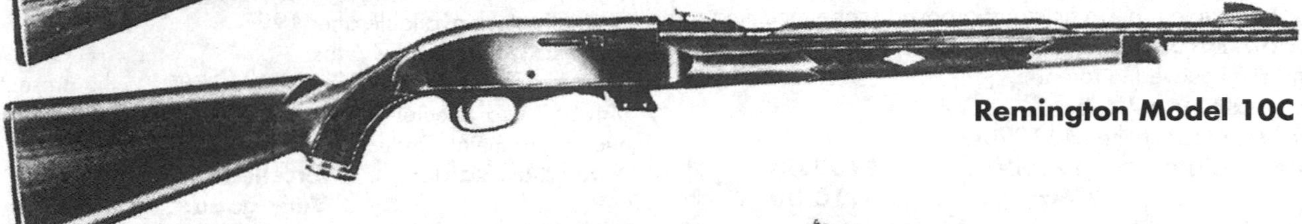
Remington Model 10C

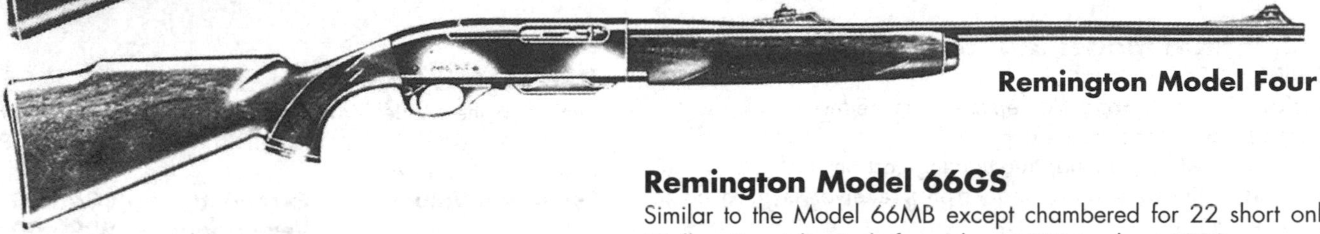
Remington Model Four

Remington Models 66MB and 66SG

Caliber: 22 long rifle
Action: Semiautomatic; side ejector; solid breech; sliding bolt
Magazine: 14-shot tubular in stock
Barrel: 20"; round
Sights: Blade front; rear sight adjustable for windage and elevation
Stock and Forearm: Du-Pont Zytel® nylon, brown or Seneca Green one-piece receiver, stock and forearm; checkered pistol grip stock and lipped forearm which covers top of barrel
Approximate wt.: 4 lbs.
Comments: Made from about 1959 to 1987; a design concept in which the stock, receiver, and forearm are made in one piece; Model 66SG is Seneca Green.

Estimated Value:	**Excellent:**	**$200.00**
	Very good:	**$160.00**

Remington Models 66AB and 66BD

Same as Remington Model 66MB except: black stock and forearm with chrome-plated barrel and receiver covers; made about 1962. Model 66AB was discontinued in 1984. Model 66BD has black receiver, discontinued in 1987.

Estimated Value:	**Excellent:**	**$225.00**
	Very good:	**$180.00**

Remington Model 66GS

Similar to the Model 66MB except chambered for 22 short only (Gallery Special). Made from about 1963 to about 1980.

Estimated Value:	**Excellent:**	**$190.00**
	Very good:	**$150.00**

Remington Model 10C

Same as Remington Model 66MB except: 10-shot removable box magazine. Made from about 1970 to the late 1970s.

Estimated Value:	**Excellent:**	**$175.00**
	Very good:	**$140.00**

Remington Model Four

Caliber: 6mm Rem., 243 Win., 270 Win., 280 Rem. (7mm Express Rem.); 30-06, 308 Win.
Action: Semiautomatic; side ejector; gas-operated
Magazine: 4-shot clip
Barrel: Blued; 22"
Sights: Blade front ramp, adjustable sliding ramp rear
Stock and Forearm: Checkered walnut Monte Carlo pistol grip stock and forearm; black grip cap and fore-end tip; recessed finger groove in forearm; cheekpiece; high-gloss finish
Approximate wt.: 7½ lbs.
Comments: Produced from 1981 to 1987. Replaced the Model 742. Custom grades are available at increased prices. 6mm dropped in 1985

Estimated Value:	**Excellent:**	**$575.00**
	Very good:	**$460.00**

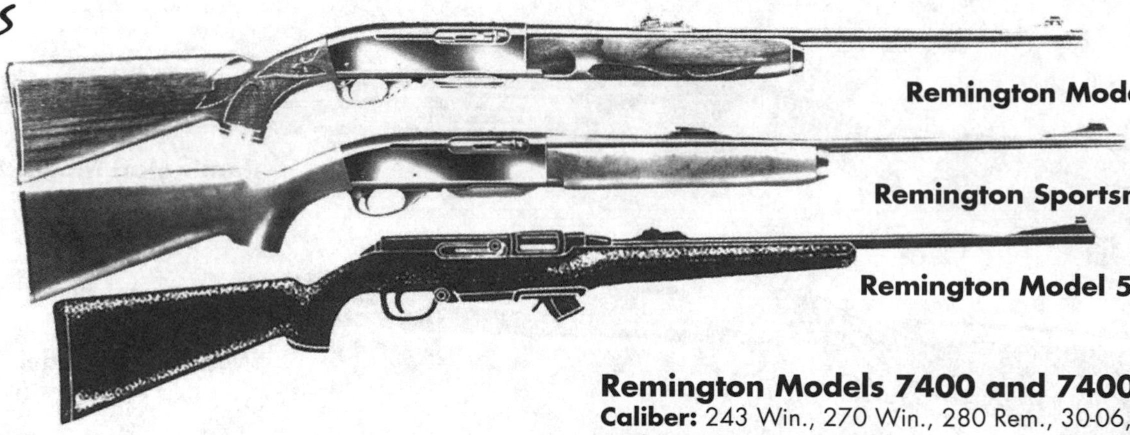

Remington Model 7400

Remington Sportsman 74

Remington Model 522 Viper

Remington Model 522 Viper

Caliber: 22 long rifle
Action: Semiautomatic; last shot open bolt
Magazine: 10-shot clip
Barrel: Blued; 20"
Sights: Adjustable rear, ramp front; grooved scope mounting rail
Stock and Forearm: Black, checkered synthetic pistol grip stock and semi-beavertail forearm
Approximate wt.: 4½ lbs.
Comments: Made in the mid-1990s.

Estimated Value:	**Excellent:**	**$135.00**
	Very good:	**$110.00**

Remington Model 597 Sporter

Caliber: 22 long rifle
Action: Semiautomatic; side ejector; hammerless
Magazine: 10-shot dual stack
Barrel: Blued; 20" round; free floating carbon steel
Sights: Adjustable rear, bead front; receiver is grooved for scope mount
Stock and Forearm: Walnut finish smooth hardwood, one-piece stock and forearm; swivels
Approximate wt.: 5½ lbs.
Comments: Introduced in 1998. Discontinued in 2001.

Estimated Value:	**Excellent:**	**$130.00**
	Very good:	**$105.00**

Remington Model 597 Magnum

Similar to the Model 597 Sporter except: caliber 22 Win. mag., 9-shot magazine; weighs 6 lbs.; black synthetic stock with beavertail-shaped forearm.

Estimated Value:	**New (retail):**	**$193.00**
	Excellent:	**$145.00**
	Very good:	**$115.00**

Remington Model 597 Magnum LS

Same as the Model 597 Magnum except: resin impregnated laminated wood stock and forearm.

Estimated Value:	**New (retail):**	**$587.00**
	Excellent:	**$440.00**
	Very good:	**$350.00**

Remington Model 597 LSS

Same as the Model 597 Sporter except: laminated light and dark wood stock and forearm; stainless steel barrel.

Estimated Value:	**Excellent:**	**$175.00**
	Very good:	**$140.00**

Remington Models 7400 and 7400SP

Caliber: 243 Win., 270 Win., 280 Rem., 30-06, 308 Win.
Action: Semiautomatic; side ejector; gas-operated
Magazine: 4-shot clip
Barrel: Blued; 18½" or 22"
Sights: Adjustable, inclined ramp rear, ramp front
Stock and Forearm: Satin or gloss finish; checkered plain or Monte Carlo walnut stock and forearm; black matte finish and synthetic stock available after 1997
Approximate wt.: 7½ lbs.
Comments: Produced from the mid-1980s to the present. Model 7400SP is a Special Purpose model with non-reflective finish on wood and metal. Deduct 17% for synthetic stock.

Estimated Value:	**Excellent:**	**$475.00**
	Very good:	**$380.00**

Remington Sportsman 74

Similar to the Model 7400 with lesser quality finish; hardwood with no checkering: 22" barrel; 30-06 caliber only. Produced from 1984 to 1987.

Estimated Value:	**Excellent:**	**$360.00**
	Very good:	**$290.00**

Remington Model 597SS

Same as the Model 597 Sporter except: stainless steel barrel; gray synthetic stock and forearm.

Estimated Value:	**New (retail):**	**$283.00**
	Excellent:	**$210.00**
	Very good:	**$170.00**

Remington Model 597

Same as the Model 597 Sporter except: dark gray synthetic stock and forearm.

Estimated Value:	**New (retail):**	**$193.00**
	Excellent:	**$145.00**
	Very good:	**$115.00**

Remington Model 597 Custom Target

Caliber: 22 long rifle, 22WMR
Action: Semiautomatic; side ejector; hammerless
Magazine: 10-shot box (22 long rifle); 9-shot box mag.
Barrel: 20"; satin-finish heavy stainless steel; round free-floating
Sights: None, receiver is grooved for scope mount
Stock and Forearm: Ergonomically-shaped green laminated wood with Monte Carlo profile and beavertail-style forearm
Approximate wt.: 6 lbs.
Comments: Made in the late 1990s.

Estimated Value:	**Excellent:**	**$450.00**
	Very good:	**$360.00**

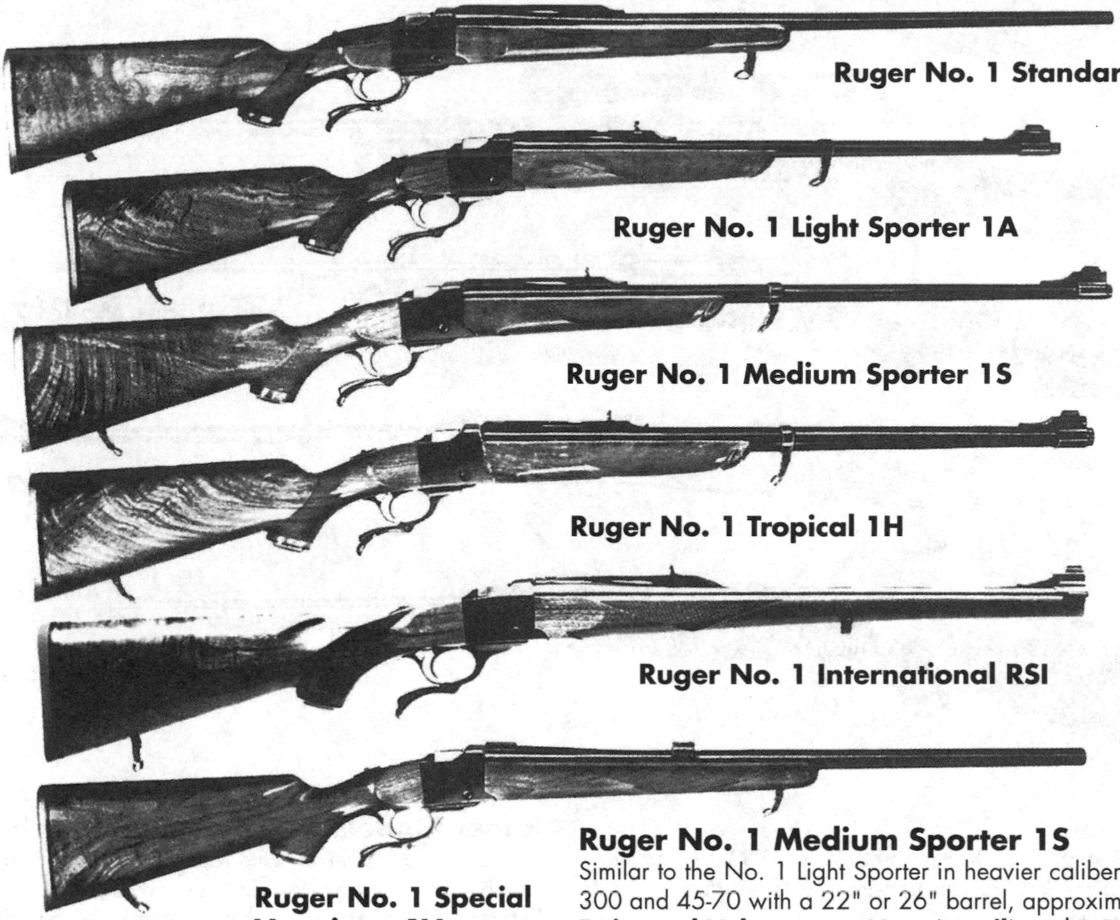

Ruger No. 1 Standard 1B

Caliber: 218 Bee, 22 Hornet, 22-250, 220 Swift, 223, 243, 25-06, 6mm Rem., 257 Roberts, 280, 270, 30-06, 7mm Rem. mag., 300 Win. Mag.; 338 Win. mag.
Action: Falling block; under lever; single shot; hammerless
Magazine: None
Barrel: 26"; tapered, stainless steel available
Sights: None
Stock and Forearm: Checkered walnut or black laminate pistol grip stock and forearm; swivels
Approximate wt.: 8 lbs.
Comments: Made from the late 1960s to the present; add 3% for stainless steel.

Estimated Value:	**New (retail):**	**$1,182.00**
	Excellent:	**$ 885.00**
	Very good:	**$ 710.00**

Ruger No. 1 Light Sporter 1A

Similar to the No. 1 Standard 1B in 243, 270, 30-06, or 7x57mm; 22" barrel; approximate wt.: 8 lbs., open sights. Add 4% for stainless steel model.

Estimated Value:	**New (retail):**	**$1,182.00**
	Excellent:	**$ 885.00**
	Very good:	**$ 710.00**

Ruger No. 1 Medium Sporter 1S

Similar to the No. 1 Light Sporter in heavier calibers, 7mm, 338, 300 and 45-70 with a 22" or 26" barrel, approximate wt. 8 lbs.

Estimated Value:	**New (retail):**	**$1,182.00**
	Excellent:	**$ 885.00**
	Very good:	**$ 710.00**

Ruger No. 1 Tropical 1H

A 24" barrel version of No. 1 in 375 H&H mag., 404 jeffery, 416 Rigby, 416 Rem. mag., 458 mag. only. Approximate wt. 9 lbs.; open sights. Add 4% for stainless steel model.

Estimated Value:	**New (retail):**	**$1,182.00**
	Excellent:	**$ 885.00**
	Very good:	**$ 710.00**

Ruger No. 1 International RSI

Similar to the No. 1 with a 20" barrel with full-length forearm; available in calibers 243 Win., 30-06, 270 Win. and 7x57mm; approximate wt. 7¼ lbs.

Estimated Value:	**New (retail):**	**$1,222.00**
	Excellent:	**$ 915.00**
	Very good:	**$ 735.00**

Ruger No. 1 Special Varminter 1V

Similar to the No. 1 in 22PPC, 22-250, 220 Swift, 223, 25-06, 6mm calibers; heavy 24" barrel. Approximate wt. 9 lbs. Add 4% for stainless steel model.

Estimated Value:	**New (retail):**	**$1,182.00**
	Excellent:	**$ 885.00**
	Very good:	**$ 710.00**

Ruger No. 3

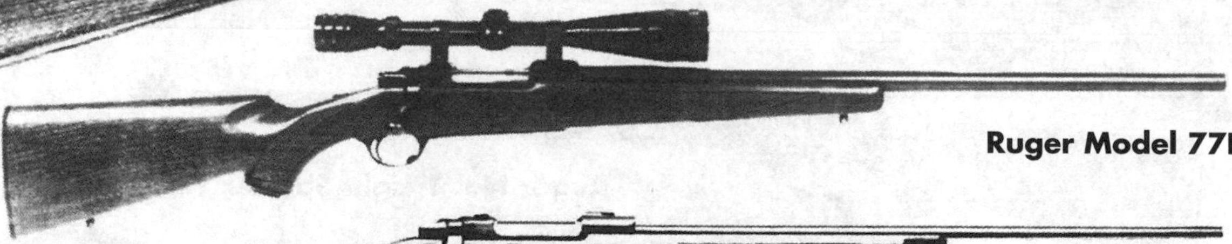

Ruger Model 77R

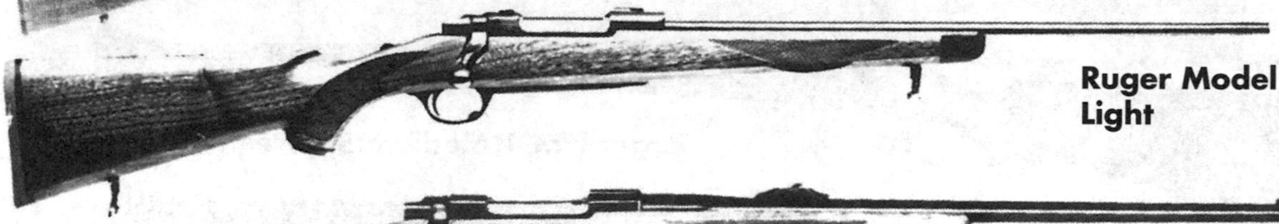

Ruger Model 77RL Ultra Light

Ruger Model 77 Round Top

Ruger Model 77 International

Ruger No. 3

Caliber: 22 Hornet, 30-40 Krag, 45-70, 223, 375 Win., 44 mag.
Action: Falling block, under lever; hammerless; single-shot
Magazine: None
Barrel: Blued; 22"
Sights: Folding leaf rear, bead front
Stock and Forearm: Plain walnut straight grip stock and forearm; barrel band
Approximate wt.: 6 lbs.
Comments: Made from the late 1960s to the mid-1980s.

Estimated Value:	**Excellent:**	**$550.00**
	Very good:	**$440.00**

Ruger Models 77R, 77RS, and 77RS Tropical

Caliber: 220 Swift, 22-250, 25-06, 243 Win., 257, 270 Win., 280 Rem., 7mm Rem. mag., 7x57mm, 300 mag., 30-06, 35 Whelen, 338 mag., 458 Win. mag. (Tropical)
Action: Bolt action; repeating; either short or magnum action
Magazine: 5-shot box with hinged floor plate; 4-shot in magnum calibers
Barrel: Blued; 22" or 24"
Sights: Adjustable leaf rear, beaded ramp front; or no sights, integral scope mounts
Stock and Forearm: Checkered walnut, pistol grip, one-piece stock and tapered forearm; recoil pad
Approximate wt.: 6¾ lbs., 7 lbs., 8¾ lbs.
Comments: Made from the late 1960s to the early 1990s. Add 16% for 458 mag. (Tropical); add 10% for sights.

Estimated Value:	**Excellent:**	**$450.00**
	Very good:	**$360.00**

Ruger Models 77 Round Top and M-77ST

Similar to the Model 77 with round top receiver and open sights. Made from the early 1970s to the early 1980s.

Estimated Value:	**Excellent:**	**$400.00**
	Very good:	**$320.00**

Ruger Models 77 International and M-77RSI

Similar to the Model 77RS with 18½" barrel and full-length Mannlicher-type forearm; 22-250, 250-3000, 243, 308, 270, and 30-06 calibers; no sights, integral scope mounts. Produced from 1982 to the late 1990s.

Estimated Value:	**Excellent:**	**$500.00**
	Very good:	**$400.00**

Ruger Model 77RL Ultra Light

Similar to the Model 77R with 20" barrel; approximate wt. 6 lbs. Produced from 1984 to 1991. Calibers 22-250, 243, 270, 250-3000, 257, 30-06, and 308.

Estimated Value:	**Excellent:**	**$460.00**
	Very good:	**$365.00**

Ruger Models 77V Varmint and M-77 Varmint

Similar to the Model 77RS in 22-250, 220 Swift, 243, 6mm, 308, or 25-06 calibers; 24" heavy barrel or 26" tapered barrel; no sights. Made from the early 1970s to the early 1990s. Approximate wt.: 9 lbs.

Estimated Value:	**Excellent:**	**$455.00**
	Very good:	**$360.00**

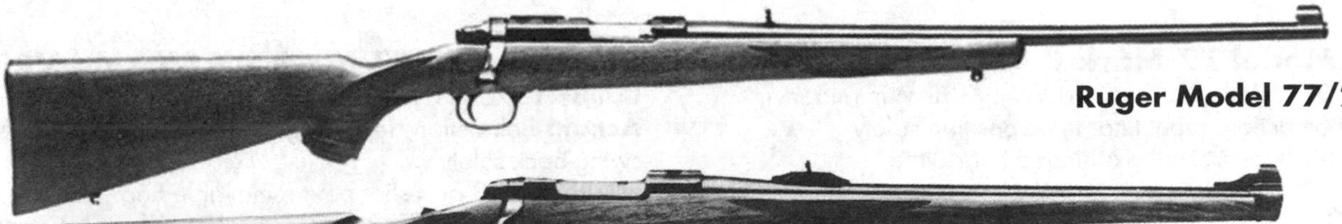

Ruger Model 77/22

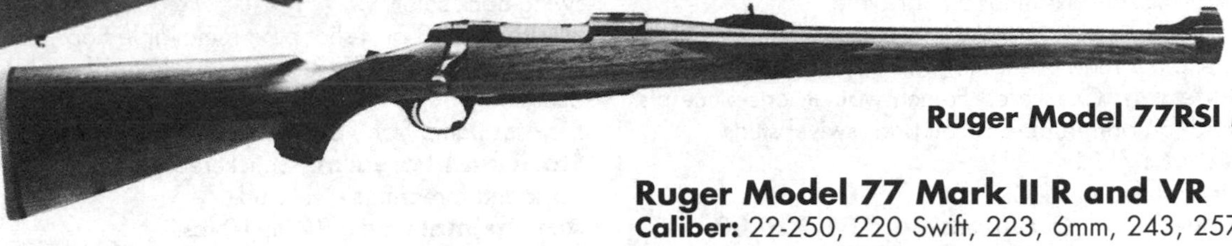

Ruger Model 77RSI Mark II

Ruger Model 77RLS

Caliber: 270, 30-06
Action: Bolt action; repeating; long action
Magazine: 5-shot box; hinged floor plates; 4-shot mag.
Barrel: 18½"
Sights: Beaded ramp front; adjustable leaf rear
Stock and Forearm: Checkered pistol grip, one-piece stock and tapered forearm; rubber recoil pad; swivel studs
Approximate wt.: 6 lbs.
Comments: Made from the late 1960s to the early 1990s.

Estimated Value:	**Excellent:**	**$460.00**
	Very good:	**$365.00**

Ruger Model 77/22

Caliber: 22 long rifle; 22 mag. (after 1989); 22 Hornet (in the early 1990s)
Action: Bolt action; repeating; three-position safety
Magazine: Detachable rotary magazine; 10-shot (22LR); 9-shot (22 mag.)
Barrel: 20" blued or 20" all stainless steel
Sights: Ramp front, folding leaf rear; or 1" scope rings
Stock and Forearm: Checkered walnut, one piece, pistol grip stock and forearm; stainless steel models have laminated wood or all-weather stocks (Zytel®)
Approximate wt.: 6¼ lbs.
Comments: Introduced in 1984. Add 6% for laminated stock and SS barrel; add 4½% for all-weather stock and SS barrel; add 5% for sights; add 5% for 22 Hornet.

Estimated Value:	**New (retail):**	**$777.00**
	Excellent:	**$575.00**
	Very good:	**$465.00**

Ruger Model 77 Mark II R and VR

Caliber: 22-250, 220 Swift, 223, 6mm, 243, 257 Roberts, 25-06, 6.5x55, 270, 30-06, 7mm, 308
Action: Bolt action; repeating; stainless steel bolt; three-position, swing-back safety (in rear position bolt is locked and gun won't fire; in the center position the bolt will operate but the gun won't fire; in the forward position the bolt will operate and the gun will fire); short action bolt
Magazine: 4-shot box with hinged floor plate
Barrel: Blued; 22" or 24"; stainless steel available
Sights: None; 1" scope rings
Stock and Forearm: Checkered walnut, one-piece pistol grip stock and tapered forearm
Approximate wt.: 7 lbs.
Comments: Produced from 1989 until 2007. Add 6% for stainless steel.

Estimated Value:	**Excellent:**	**$520.00**
	Very good:	**$415.00**

Ruger Models 77 Mark II RP, VRP, and RSP

Same as the Model 77 Mark II R except: all stainless steel; all-weather fiberglass stock (DuPont Zytel®); calibers 223, 243, 270 Win., 280 Rem., 7mm Rem. mag., 30-06, 300 Win. mag., 308, 338 Win. mag. Add 10% for open sights.

Estimated Value:	**Excellent:**	**$455.00**
	Very good:	**$360.00**

Ruger Model 77 Mark II VT

Similar to the Model Mark II R except: calibers: 22PPC, 22-250, 220 Swift, 25-06, 223, 243, 6mm, and 308; laminated wood stock; 26" stainless steel heavy barrel; weighs 10 lbs. Introduced in 1992.

Estimated Value:	**Excellent:**	**$600.00**
	Very good:	**$480.00**

Ruger Model 77/17

Ruger Model 77/17

Similar to the Model 77/22 but chambered for the 17 caliber Hornady Magnum Rimfire cartridge; available in blued with walnut or synthetic stock or stainless steel with black laminate stock; add 10% for stainless steel.

Estimated Value:	**New (retail):**	**$777.00**
	Excellent:	**$575.00**
	Very good:	**$465.00**

Ruger Model 77RSI Mark II

Similar to the Model 77 Mark II except: full-length, one-piece pistol grip stock and forearm.

Estimated Value:	**New (retail):**	**$967.00**
	Excellent:	**$725.00**
	Very good:	**$580.00**

Ruger Model 77 Mark II Express

Caliber: 270, 7mm, 30-06, 300 Win., 338 Win. magnum
Action: Bolt action; repeating; three-position safety
Magazine: 3- or 4-shot box; hinged floor plate
Barrel: 22"; blued
Sights: Open express rear, on sighting rib; ramp front
Stock and Forearm: Checkered French walnut, one-piece pistol grip stock and forearm; rubber recoil pad; swivel studs
Approximate wt.: 7½ lbs.
Comments: Introduced in 1992.

Estimated Value:	**Excellent:**	**$1,220.00**
	Very good:	**$ 975.00**

Ruger Model 77 Mark II RSM and VRSM

Caliber: 375 H&H, 404 Jeffery, 416 Rigby, 458 Win. mag.
Action: Bolt action; repeating; stainless steel bolt; three-position, swing-back safety
Magazine: 3 or 4-shot box; removable floor plate
Barrel: 24"; blued with sighting plane of cross serrations to reduce glare
Sights: Ramp front, open express rear
Stock and Forearm: Checkered walnut, one-piece pistol grip stock and forearm; swivel studs
Approximate wt.: 9¼ to 10 lbs.
Comments: Introduced in 1990.

Estimated Value:	**Excellent:**	**$1,750.00**
	Very good:	**$1,400.00**

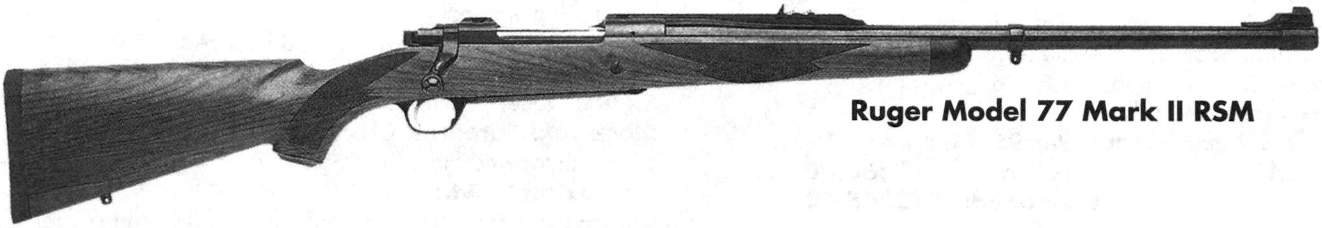

Ruger Model 77 Mark II RSM

Ruger Model 77 Mark II RL and VRL

Similar to the Model 77 Mark II R except: calibers 223, 243, 257 Roberts, 270 Win. and 308, 30-06; 20" barrel; approximate wt. 6 lbs.; black fore-end tip; introduced in 1990.

Estimated Value:	**New (retail):**	**$837.00**
	Excellent:	**$625.00**
	Very good:	**$500.00**

Ruger Model 77 Mark II RS and VRS

Same as the Model 77 Mark II R except: calibers 6mm, 243, 25-06, 7mm Rem. mag., 270 Win., 30-06, 300 Win. mag., 308, 338 Win. mag., 458 Win. mag.; open sights (ramp front and express rear). Introduced in 1990.

Estimated Value:	**Excellent:**	**$585.00**
	Very good:	**$465.00**

Ruger Model 96/22

Ruger Model 96/44

Caliber: 44 magnum
Action: Lever action, repeating; hammerless
Magazine: 4-shot detachable rotary
Barrel: 18½"; blued
Sights: Gold bead front; adjustable folding leaf rear
Stock and Forearm: Smooth hardwood, one-piece pistol grip stock and forearm; metal barrel band at end of forearm
Approximate wt.: 6 lbs.
Comments: Produced from 1996 to 2007.

Estimated Value:	**Excellent:**	**$450.00**
	Very good:	**$360.00**

Ruger Models 96/22 and 96/17m

Caliber: 22 long rifle, 22 WMR; 17 HMR
Action: Lever action, repeating; hammerless
Magazine: 10-shot (22 long rifle); 9-shot (22 WMR); detachable rotary
Barrel: 18½"; blued
Sights: Gold bead front; adjustable for elevation, folding leaf rear
Stock and Forearm: Smooth hardwood, one-piece pistol grip stock and forearm; metal barrel band at end of forearm
Approximate wt.: 5¼ lbs.
Comments: Introduced in 1996. Add 5% for 22 WMR.

Estimated Value:	**Excellent:**	**$325.00**
	Very good:	**$260.00**

Ruger Carbine PC

Ruger Carbine PC
Caliber: 9mm; 40 Auto
Action: Gas-operated, semiautomatic
Magazine: 9-shot clip
Barrel: 16¼"; blued
Sights: Post front, adjustable rear or ghost ring rear
Stock and Forearm: Synthetic polymer semi-pistol grip one-piece stock and forearm.
Approximate wt.: 6⅜ lbs.
Comments: Introduced in the late 1990s. Add 5% for ghost ring sight.

Estimated Value:	**Excellent:**	**$475.00**
	Very good:	**$380.00**

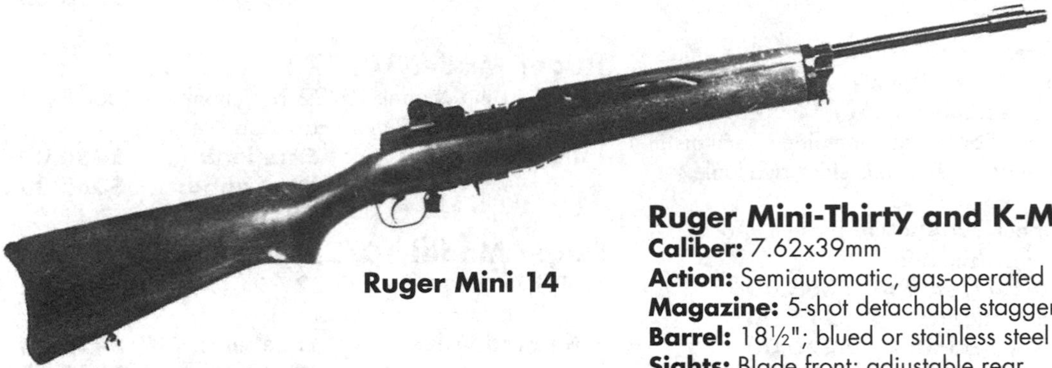

Ruger Mini 14

Ruger Mini 14 and K-Mini 14
Caliber: 223 commercial or military
Action: Semiautomatic, gas-operated
Magazine: 5-shot detachable box; 10- and 20-shot available
Barrel: Blued; 18½"; also stainless steel after 1979
Sights: Adjustable rear, blade front
Stock and Forearm: Plain walnut, semi-pistol grip, one-piece stock and forearm; handguard over barrel; folding stock and pistol grip available after the mid-1980s
Approximate wt.: 6½ lbs.
Comments: Made from 1974 to the present. Add 10% for stainless steel.

Estimated Value:	**New (retail):**	**$881.00**
	Excellent:	**$660.00**
	Very good:	**$530.00**

Ruger Mini-Thirty and K-Mini-Thirty
Caliber: 7.62x39mm
Action: Semiautomatic, gas-operated
Magazine: 5-shot detachable staggered box
Barrel: 18½"; blued or stainless steel
Sights: Blade front; adjustable rear
Stock and Forearm: Plain walnut, pistol grip one-piece stock and forearm with handguard over barrel; synthetic stock and forearm available.
Approximate wt.: 7 lbs.
Comments: Introduced in 1988. A modified version of the Mini-14 Ranch Rifle. Add 9½% for stainless steel (K-Mini-Thirty).

Estimated Value:	**Excellent:**	**$670.00**
	Very good:	**$535.00**

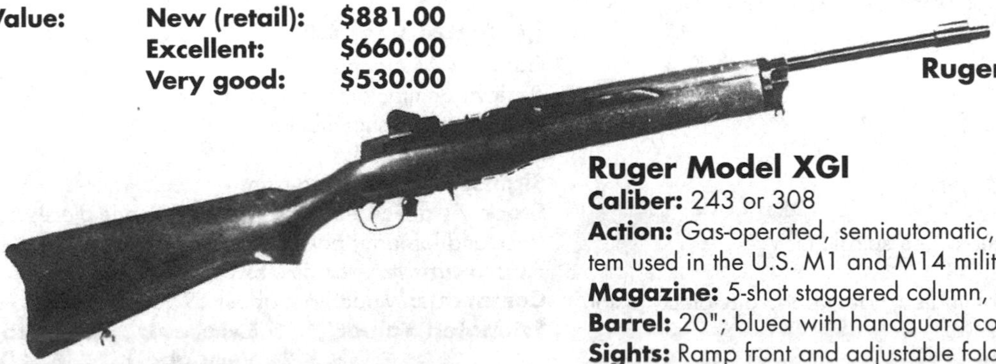

Ruger Model XGI

Ruger Mini 14/5R and K-Mini14/5R Rifle
Similar to the Mini 14 with internal improvements and integral scope mounts. Introduced in 1982; add 9½% for stainless steel (K-Mini 14/5R).

Estimated Value:	**Excellent:**	**$525.00**
	Very good:	**$420.00**

Ruger Model XGI
Caliber: 243 or 308
Action: Gas-operated, semiautomatic, based on the Garand system used in the U.S. M1 and M14 military rifles
Magazine: 5-shot staggered column, detachable box
Barrel: 20"; blued with handguard cover
Sights: Ramp front and adjustable folding peep rear
Stock and Forearm: Plain one-piece American hardwood, reinforced with steel liners
Approximate wt.: 8 lbs.
Comments: Produced from 1986 to 1988.

Estimated Value:	**Excellent:**	**$450.00**
	Very good:	**$360.00**

Ruger Model 10/22

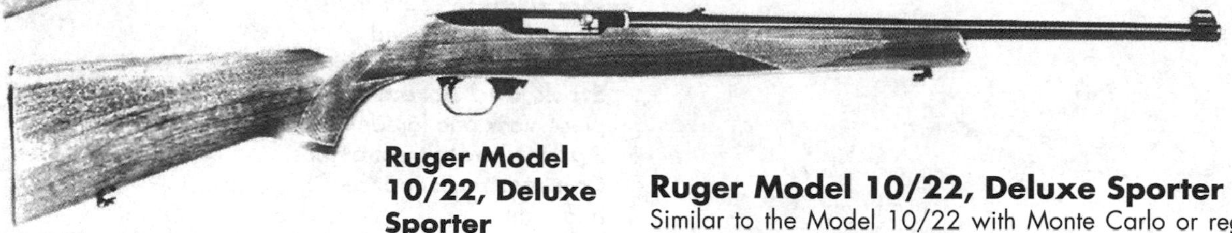

Ruger Model 10/22, Deluxe Sporter

Ruger Model 10/22

Caliber: 22 long rifle, 22 magnum
Action: Semiautomatic
Magazine: 10-shot detachable rotary
Barrel: Blued; 18½"; stainless steel available
Sights: Adjustable leaf rear, bead front
Stock and Forearm: Plain hardwood one-piece semi-pistol grip stock and forearm; barrel band; synthetic stock available
Approximate wt.: 5 lbs.
Comments: Made from about 1964 to the present. Add 20% for stainless steel model with synthetic stock.

Estimated Value:	**New (retail):**	**$366.00**
	Excellent:	**$275.00**
	Very good:	**$220.00**

Ruger Model 10/22, Deluxe Sporter

Similar to the Model 10/22 with Monte Carlo or regular checkered walnut stock; fluted bandless forearm.

Estimated Value:	**Excellent:**	**$265.00**
	Very good:	**$210.00**

Ruger Model 10/17

Similar to the Model 10/22 but chambered for the 17 caliber Hornady Magnum Rimfire cartridge.

Estimated Value:	**Excellent:**	**$450.00**
	Very good:	**$360.00**

Ruger Model 10/22, International

Similar to the Model 10/22 with full-length stock and swivels. Add 8% for stainless steel barrel.

Estimated Value:	**Excellent:**	**$425.00**
	Very good:	**$340.00**

Ruger Deerfield

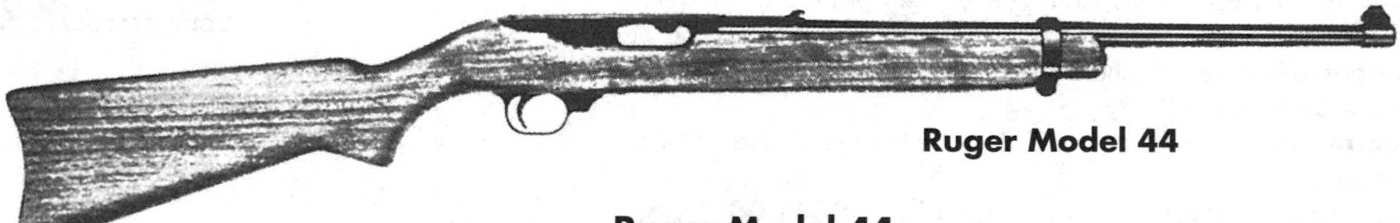

Ruger Model 44

Ruger Model 10/22T

Caliber: 22 long rifle
Action: Semiautomatic
Magazine: 10-shot rotary
Barrel: 20"; blued, hammer-forged spiral finish
Sights: None
Stock and Forearm: Laminated hardwood, one-piece pistol grip stock and forearm
Approximate wt.: 7¼ lbs.
Comments: Introduced in 1996. Add 10% for stainless steel.

Estimated Value:	**Excellent:**	**$375.00**
	Very good:	**$300.00**

Ruger Model 44

Caliber: 44 magnum
Action: Semiautomatic, gas-operated
Magazine: 4-shot tubular
Barrel: Blued; 18½"
Sights: Leaf rear, bead front
Stock and Forearm: Plain walnut one-piece, semi-pistol grip stock and forearm; barrel band
Approximate wt.: 5¾ lbs.
Comments: Made from about 1960 to the mid-1980s.

Estimated Value:	**Excellent:**	**$425.00**
	Very good:	**$340.00**

Ruger Deerfield

Similar to the Model 44 except: engineering and design refinements; rotary magazine; introduced in 2002.

Estimated Value:	**Excellent:**	**$550.00**
	Very good:	**$440.00**

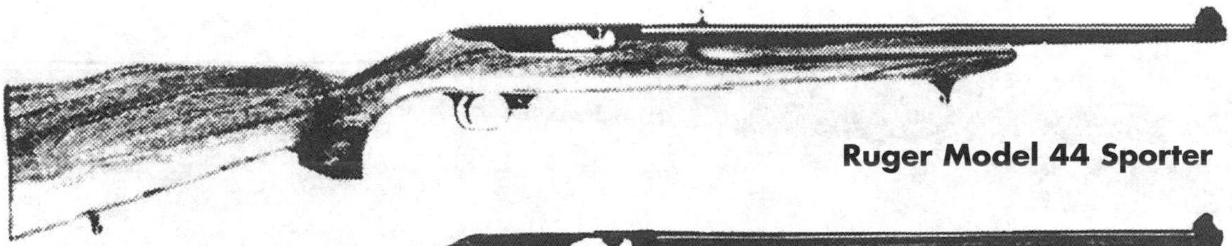

Ruger Model 44 Sporter

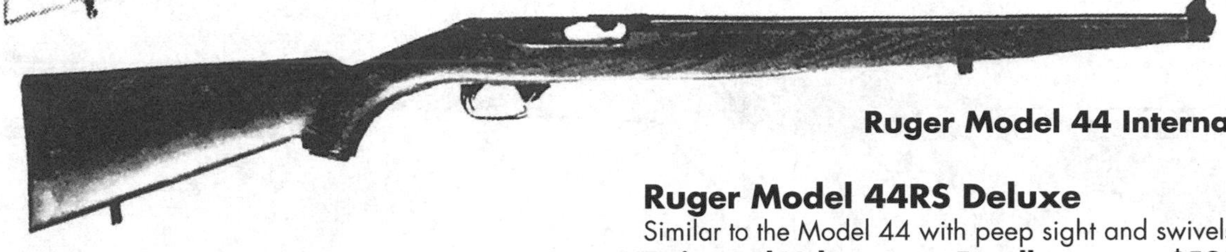

Ruger Model 44 International

Ruger Model 44 Sporter

Similar to the Model 44 with Monte Carlo stock, fluted forearm and swivels. Made from the 1960s to the early 1970s.

Estimated Value:	**Excellent:**	**$575.00**
	Very good:	**$460.00**

Ruger Model 44RS Deluxe

Similar to the Model 44 with peep sight and swivels.

Estimated Value:	**Excellent:**	**$525.00**
	Very good:	**$420.00**

Ruger Model 44 International

Similar to the Model 44 with a full-length stock and swivels. Made from the 1960s to the early 1970s.

Estimated Value:	**Excellent:**	**$575.00**
	Very good:	**$460.00**

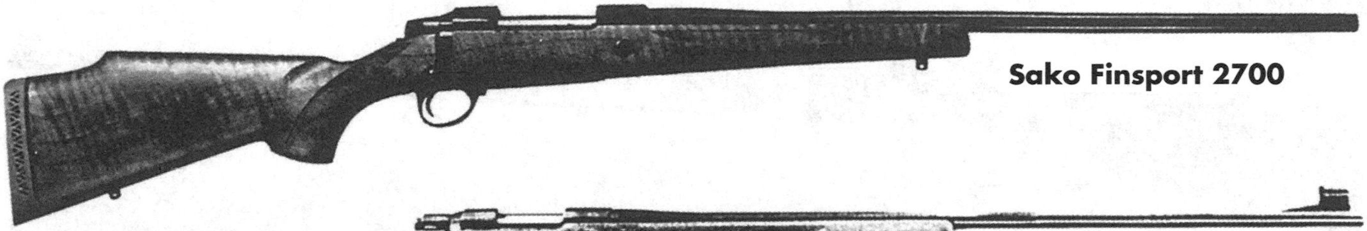

Sako Finsport 2700

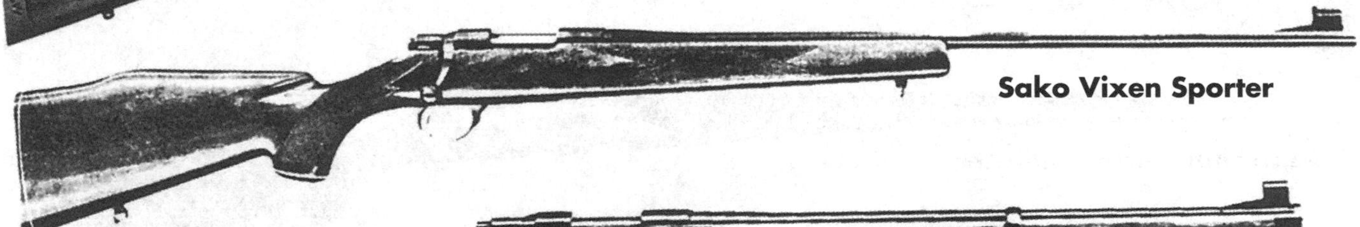

Sako Vixen Sporter

Sako Vixen Mannlicher

Sako Finsport 2700

Caliber: 270 Win., 30-06, 7mm Rem. mag., 338 Win. mag.
Action: Long throw bolt action; adjustable trigger
Magazine: 5-shot
Barrel: Blued; 23½"
Sights: None
Stock and Forearm: Checkered walnut, Monte Carlo pistol grip, one-piece stock and forearm; recoil pad; swivels
Approximate wt.: 6½ lbs.
Comments: Produced from 1983 to the late 1980s.

Estimated Value:	**Excellent:**	**$850.00**
	Very good:	**$680.00**

Sako Vixen Sporter

Caliber: 218 Bee, 22 Hornet, 222, 222 mag., 223
Action: Bolt action, short stroke, Mauser-type
Magazine: 5-shot
Barrel: Blued; 23½"
Sights: Open rear, hooded ramp front
Stock and Forearm: Checkered walnut, Monte Carlo pistol grip, one-piece stock and forearm; swivels
Approximate wt.: 6½ lbs.
Comments: Made from World War II to the early 1970s.

Estimated Value:	**Excellent:**	**$885.00**
	Very good:	**$710.00**

Sako Vixen Mannlicher

Similar to the Vixen Sporter with a full-length stock; 20" barrel; barrel band.

Estimated Value:	**Excellent:**	**$925.00**
	Very good:	**$740.00**

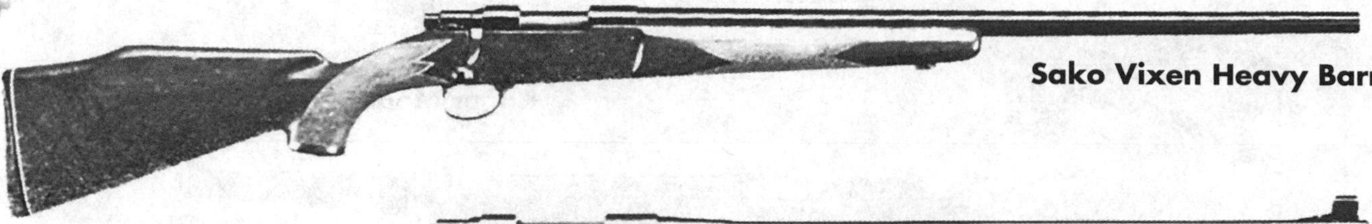

Sako Vixen Heavy Barrel

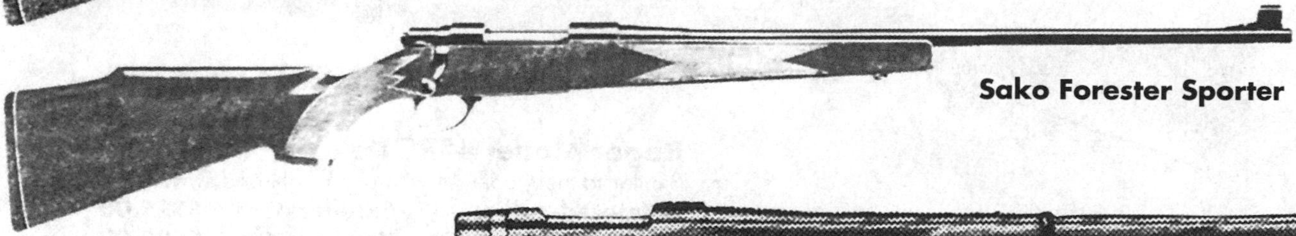

Sako Forester Sporter

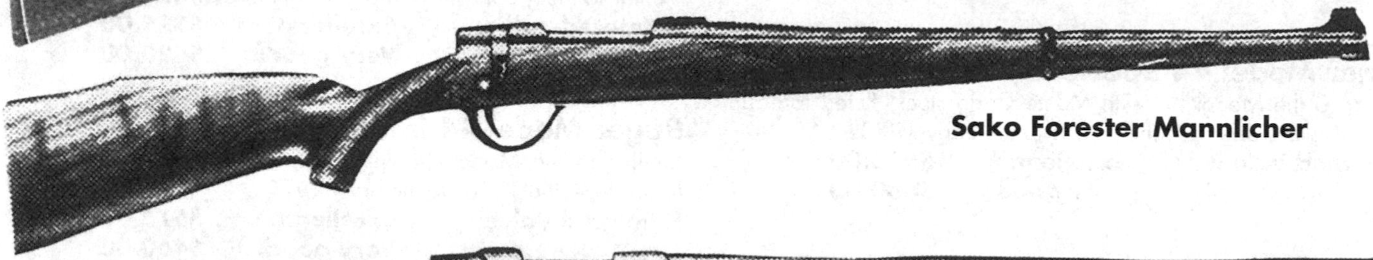

Sako Forester Mannlicher

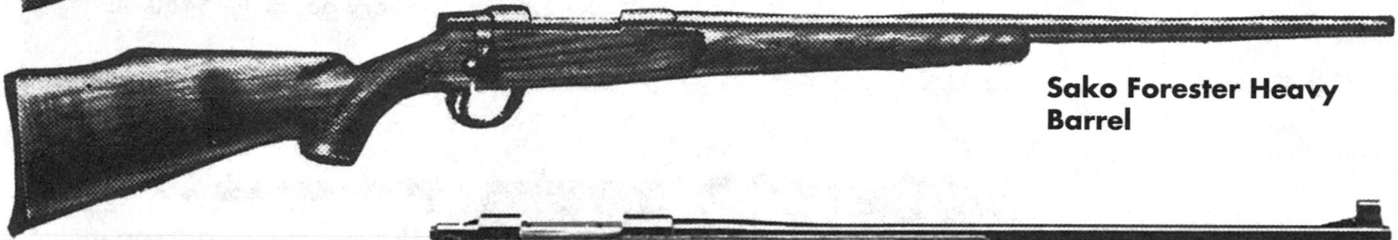

Sako Forester Heavy Barrel

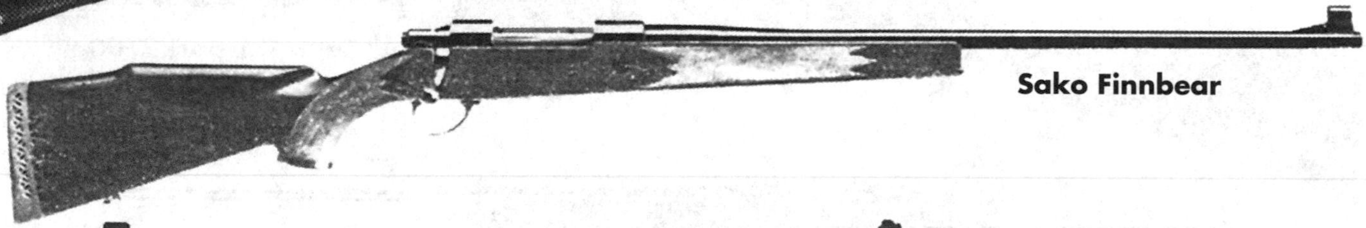

Sako Finnbear

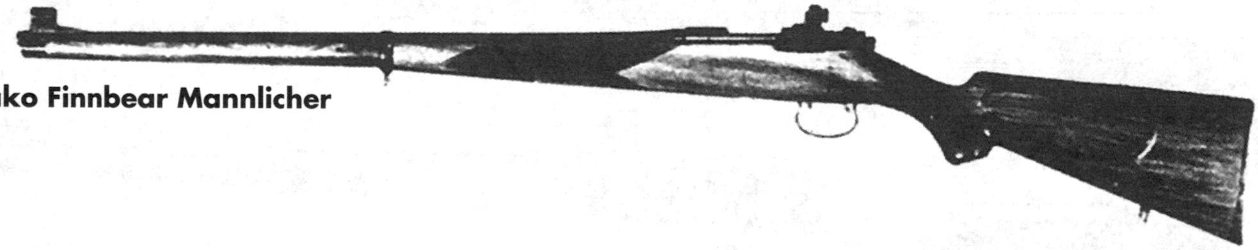

Sako Finnbear Mannlicher

Sako Vixen Heavy Barrel

Similar to the Vixen Sporter with heavy barrel and in larger calibers only.

Estimated Value: **Excellent:** **$875.00**
Very good: **$700.00**

Sako Forester Sporter

Similar to the Vixen Sporter with medium action and in 22-250, 243, and 308 calibers. Made from the late 1950s to the early 1970s.

Estimated Value: **Excellent:** **$850.00**
Very good: **$680.00**

Sako Forester Mannlicher

Similar to the Forester Sporter with full-length stock; 20" barrel; barrel band.

Estimated Value: **Excellent:** **$875.00**
Very good: **$700.00**

Sako Forester Heavy Barrel

Similar to the Forester Sporter with a heavy 24" barrel.

Estimated Value: **Excellent:** **$850.00**
Very good: **$680.00**

Sako Finnbear

Similar to the Vixen Sporter with long action; recoil pad; 25-06, 264 magnum, 270, 30-06, 300 magnum, 7mm magnum; 375 H&H. Made from the early 1960s to the early 1970s.

Estimated Value: **Excellent:** **$885.00**
Very good: **$710.00**

Sako Finnbear Mannlicher

Similar to the Finnbear with: full-length stock; 20" barrel; barrel band.

Estimated Value: **Excellent:** **$925.00**
Very good: **$740.00**

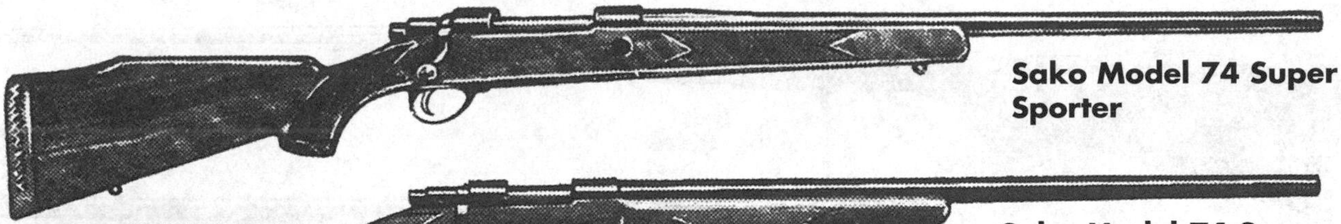

Sako Model 74 Super Sporter

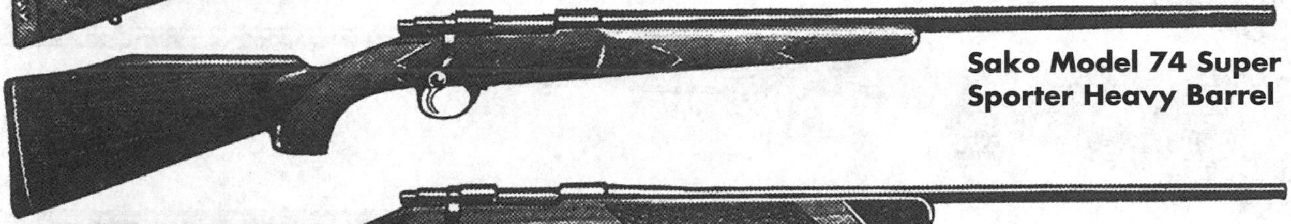

Sako Model 74 Super Sporter Heavy Barrel

Sako Model 74 Deluxe Sporter

Sako Model 74 Super Sporter

Similar to the Vixen, Forester, and Finnbear in short action, medium action, and long action; 23" or 24" barrel. Made in the 1970s.

Estimated Value: **Excellent:** **$725.00**
Very good: **$580.00**

Sako Model 74 Super Sporter Heavy Barrel

Similar to Model 74 Super Sporter in short, medium, or long action and heavy barrel.

Estimated Value: **Excellent:** **$750.00**
Very good: **$600.00**

Sako Model 74 Deluxe Sporter

Similar to Model 74 Super Sporter with recoil pad, select wood and high-quality finish. Add $25.00 for magnum.

Estimated Value: **Excellent:** **$775.00**
Very good: **$620.00**

Sako Mauser

Sako Model A11 Standard Hunter

Sako Mauser

Caliber: 270, 30-06
Action: FN Mauser bolt action; repeating
Magazine: 5-shot box
Barrel: Blued; 24"
Sights: Leaf rear, hooded ramp front
Stock and Forearm: Checkered walnut Monte Carlo one-piece pistol grip stock and tapered forearm; swivels
Approximate wt.: 7½ lbs.
Comments: Made from World War II to about 1960.

Estimated Value: **Excellent:** **$700.00**
Very good: **$560.00**

Sako Mauser Magnum

Similar to Sako Mauser in magnum calibers 300 H&H and 375 H&H; recoil pad.

Estimated Value: **Excellent:** **$775.00**
Very good: **$620.00**

Sako Model A1 Standard Hunter

Caliber: 17 Rem., 222 Rem., 223 Rem.
Action: Bolt action; repeating; short throw
Magazine: 5-shot
Barrel: 23½"
Sights: None
Stock and Forearm: Checkered walnut Monte Carlo one-piece pistol grip stock and forearm; lacquer or oil finish; laminated grain and fiberglass available in 1989; swivels
Approximate wt.: 6½ lbs.
Comments: Add 4% for 17 Rem. caliber; add 20% for laminated stock and 30% for fiberglass stock.

Estimated Value: **Excellent:** **$925.00**
Very good: **$740.00**

Sako Model A11 Standard Hunter

Similar to the A1 Standard Hunter except: medium throw action in 220 Swift, 22-250 Rem., 243 Win., 7mm-08, 308 Win. calibers. Add 12% for laminated stock and 30% for fiberglass stock.

Estimated Value: **Excellent:** **$925.00**
Very good: **$740.00**

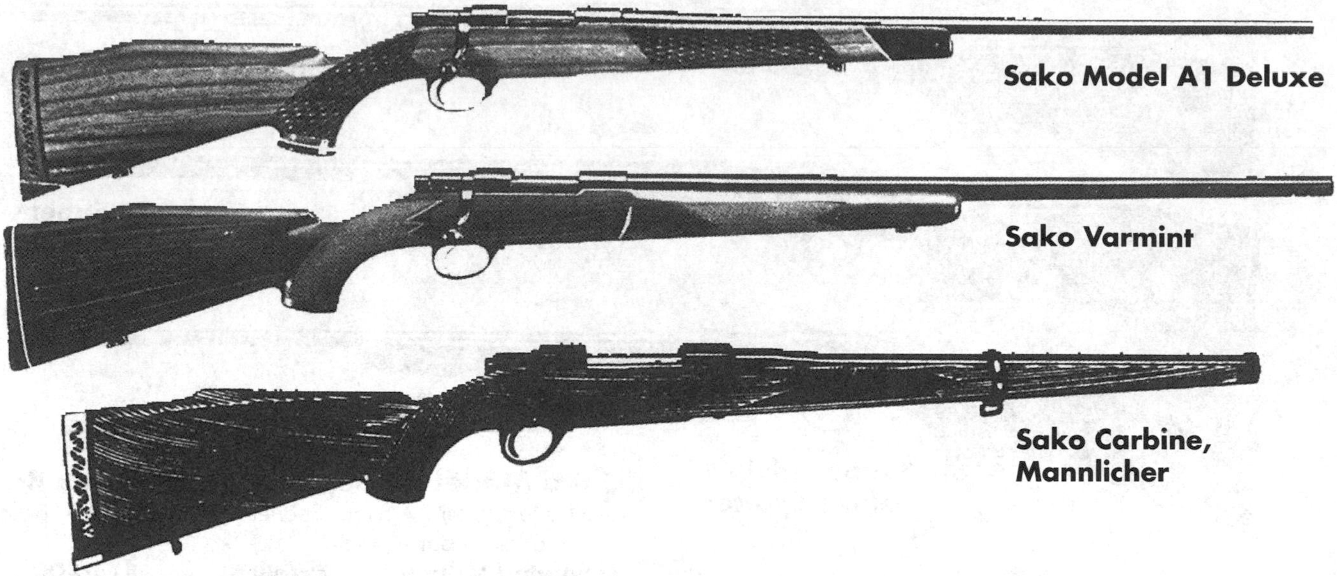

Sako Model A1 Deluxe

Sako Varmint

Sako Carbine, Mannlicher

Sako Model A111 Standard Hunter

Similar to the Model A1 Standard Hunter except: long throw action; 25-06 Rem., 6.5x55, 270 Win., 280 Rem., 7x64, 30-06, 7mm Rem. magnum, 300 Win. magnum, 338 Win. magnum, 9.3x62, 375 H&H mag, 416 Rigby; recoil pad. Add 4% for mag. Add 12% for laminated stock. Add 30% for fiberglass stock.

Estimated Value:	**Excellent:**	**$935.00**
	Very good:	**$750.00**

Sako Model A1 Deluxe

A deluxe version of the A1 Standard Hunter; recoil pad.

Estimated Value:	**Excellent:**	**$1,350.00**
	Very good:	**$1,100.00**

Sako Model A11 Deluxe

Similar to the Model A11 Standard Hunter with deluxe features; recoil pad.

Estimated Value:	**Excellent:**	**$1,350.00**
	Very good:	**$1,100.00**

Sako Model A111 Deluxe

Similar to the Model A111 Standard Hunter with deluxe features. Add 3% for magnum.

Estimated Value:	**Excellent:**	**$1,375.00**
	Very good:	**$1,115.00**

Sako Varmint

Similar to Models A1, A11, and A111 Standard Hunter except: heavy varmint barrel; calibers 17 Rem., 222 Rem., 223 Rem., 22-250 Rem., 243 Win., 308 Win., 7mm-08.

Estimated Value:	**Excellent:**	**$1,175.00**
	Very good:	**$ 940.00**

Sako Carbine, Mannlicher

Similar to Models A1, A11, and A111 Standard Hunter except: 20" barrel and full-length forearm; calibers 243 Win., 270 Win., 308 Win., 30-06, 338 Win. mag. Add 6% for 375 H&H and 3% for other magnums.

Estimated Value:	**Excellent:**	**$1,175.00**
	Very good:	**$ 940.00**

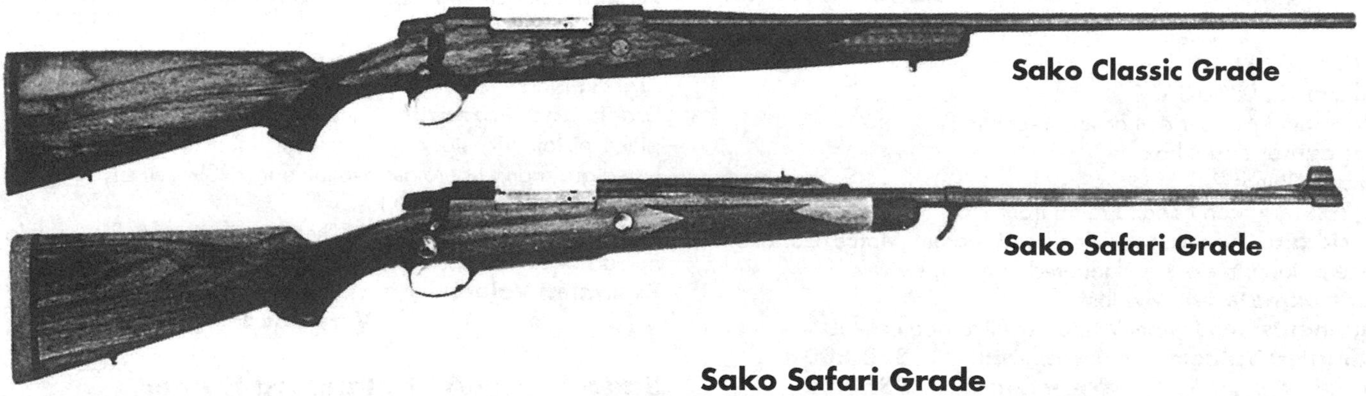

Sako Classic Grade

Sako Safari Grade

Sako Classic Grade

Similar to the A11 and A111 Standard Hunter except: styling changes; 243 Win., 270 Win., 30-06, 7mm Rem. mag.; select walnut stock. Add 5% for 7mm Rem. mag.

Estimated Value:	**Excellent:**	**$925.00**
	Very good:	**$740.00**

Sako Safari Grade

Similar to the A111 Deluxe with extended magazine, barrel band swivels, select French walnut stock; choice of satin or matte blue finish; calibers 300 Win. mag., 338 Win. mag., 375 H&H mag., 416 Rigby.

Estimated Value:	**Excellent:**	**$2,350.00**
	Very good:	**$1,880.00**

Sako Finnwolf Sporter

Sako Model 78

Caliber: 22 long rifle, 22 Win. magnum, 22 Hornet
Action: Bolt action; repeating
Magazine: 5-shot; 4-shot in magnum
Barrel: 22½"; heavy barrel available
Sights: Folding leaf rear, hooded ramp front
Stock and Forearm: One-piece checkered walnut Monte Carlo pistol grip stock and forearm; swivels
Approximate wt.: 6¾ lbs.
Comments: Made from the late 1970s to the late 1980s. Add 5% for 22 Hornet.

Estimated Value:	**Excellent:**	**$600.00**
	Very good:	**$480.00**

Sako Finnwolf Sporter

Caliber: 243, 308
Action: Lever action; hammerless; repeating
Magazine: 4-shot clip
Barrel: Blued; 23"
Sights: No rear, hooded ramp front
Stock and Forearm: Checkered walnut Monte Carlo one-piece pistol grip stock and tapered forearm; swivels
Approximate wt.: 7 lbs.
Comments: Made from the mid-1960s to the early 1970s.

Estimated Value:	**Excellent:**	**$875.00**
	Very good:	**$700.00**

Sako Finnwolf Deluxe Sporter

Same as Finnwolf Sporter with select wood.

Estimated Value:	**Excellent:**	**$900.00**
	Very good:	**$720.00**

Sako Model 78

Sako Finnfire

Caliber: 22 long rifle
Action: Bolt action; repeating
Magazine: 5-shot clip
Barrel: 22½"; standard or heavyweight; blued
Sights: Adjustable rear, hooded ramp front
Stock and Forearm: Checkered walnut one-piece pistol grip stock and tapered forearm; swivel studs
Approximate wt.: 5½ lbs.
Comments: Introduced in 1994. Add 11% for heavy barrel.

Estimated Value:	**Excellent:**	**$700.00**
	Very good:	**$560.00**

Sako Model TRG-S

Caliber: 25-06 Rem., 270 Win., 6.5 x 55SS 30-06, 7mm Rem. magnum, 300 Win. magnum, 338 Win. magnum, 300 Wby. magnum, 338 Lapua magnum, 375 H&H; 270 Wby. mag., 7mm Wby. mag., 340 Wby. mag. (added in 1996)
Action: Bolt action, repeating; three bolt locking lugs
Magazine: 5-shot; 4-shot in 375 H&H; detachable box
Barrel: Blued; 22", 24", 26" in magnum calibers; matte blue finish
Sights: None; scope mount rails
Stock and Forearm: Fiberglass, plain one-piece pistol grip stock and forearm; swivel studs
Approximate wt.: 7¾ lbs.
Comments: Introduced in 1994. Add 5% for magnum.

Estimated Value:	**Excellent:**	**$725.00**
	Very good:	**$580.00**

Sako Model 75 Hunter

Sako Model 75 Finnlight

Sako Model 75 Varmint

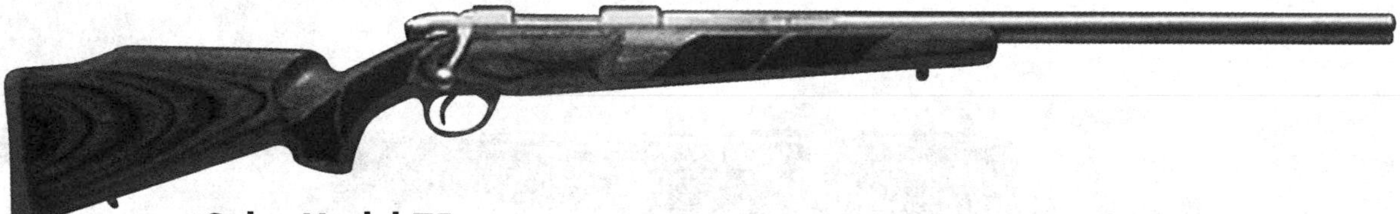

Sako Model 75
Varmint Stainless

Sako Model 75 Hunter

Caliber: 222 Rem., 22-250 Rem., 223 Rem., 243 Win., 25-06 Rem., 6.5x55, 270 Win., 7x64, 7mm Rem. magnum, 7mm Rem. Ultramag, 30-06, 300 Win. magnum, 300 Wby. magnum, 300 Rem. Ultramag, 338 Win. magnum, 375 H&H magnum, 9.3x62
Action: Bolt action, repeating; short, medium, or long throw actions
Magazine: 5-shot detachable
Barrel: 22", 22½", 22¾", 24¼", 26" blued or stainless
Sights: Leaf rear, hooded ramp front
Stock and forearm: Checkered, high-grade walnut Monte Carlo, one-piece pistol grip stock and forearm; oil finish or matte lacquered finish; recoil pad; swivels
Approximate wt.: 6¼ to 8¾ lbs.
Comments: Manufactured in Finland. Deluxe model available with higher quality finish.

Estimated Value:	**Excellent:**	**$1,000.00**
	Very good:	**$ 800.00**

Sako Model 75 Finnlight

Similar to the Model 75 Hunter except: 243 Win., 25-06 Rem., 6.5x55, 270 Win., 7mm-08 Rem., 7mm Rem. magnum, 300 Win. magnum, 308 Win., 30-06 calibers, 20¼", 20¾", or 22¾" lightweight barrel; composite stock and forearm.

Estimated Value:	**Excellent:**	**$1,000.00**
	Very good:	**$ 800.00**

Sako Model 75 Varmint

Similar to the Model 75 Hunter except: 17 Rem., 222 Rem., 22-250 Rem., 223 Rem., 243 Win., 270 Win., 7mm-08 Rem., 7mm Rem. magnum, 300 Win. magnum, 300 Wby. magnum, 308 Win., 30-06, 338 Win. magnum, 375 H&H magnum; 23½" or 26" barrel.

Estimated Value:	**Excellent:**	**$1,000.00**
	Very good:	**$ 800.00**

Sako Model 75 Varmint Stainless

Similar to the Model 75 Varmint except: 222 Rem., 22-250 Rem., 223 Rem., 243 Win., 7mm-08 Rem., 308 Win. calibers; 23½" stainless steel barrel; laminated stock and forearm.

Estimated Value:	**Excellent:**	**$1,000.00**
	Very good:	**$ 800.00**

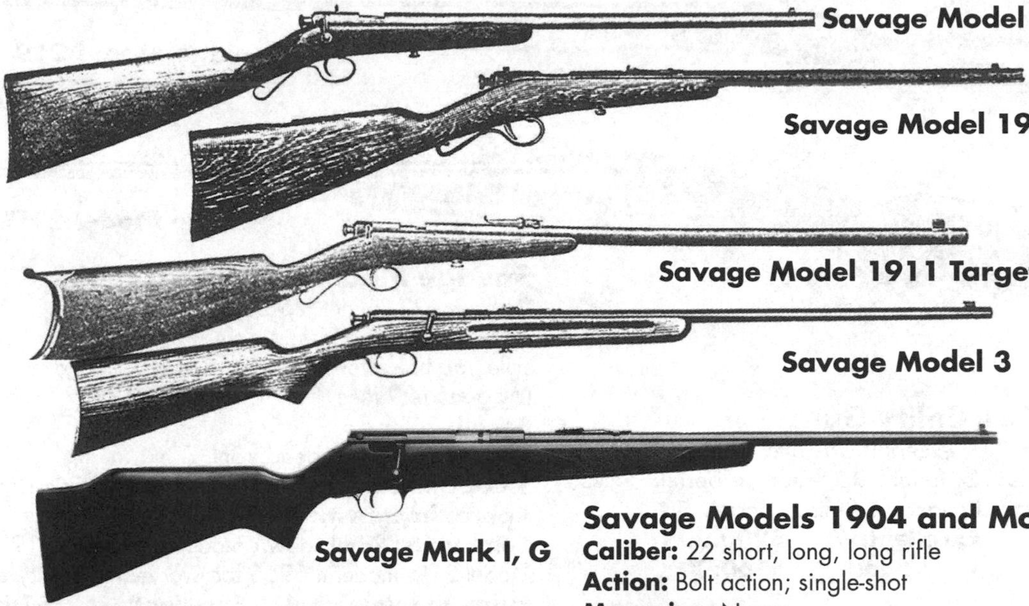
Savage Model 1904
Savage Model 1905
Savage Model 1911 Target
Savage Model 3
Savage Mark I, G

Savage Model 30G Stevens Favorite

A re-introduction of the famous Stevens Favorite boy's rifle, similar to the Stevens Model No. 72 Crackshot produced in the 1970s and 1980s except with a lipped forearm. Introduced in the 1990s. Add 18% for full octagon barrel.

Estimated Value:	**New (retail):**	**$291.00**
	Excellent:	**$220.00**
	Very good:	**$175.00**

Savage Model 1905

Caliber: 22 short, long, long rifle
Action: Bolt action; single shot
Magazine: None
Barrel: 22"
Sights: Open rear, bead front
Stock and Forearm: Plain one-piece straight grip stock and forearm
Approximate wt.: 5 lbs.
Comments: A lightweight takedown boy's rifle produced until about 1917.

Estimated Value:	**Excellent:**	**$185.00**
	Very good:	**$145.00**

Savage Mark I, G, GY, and SB

Caliber: 22 short, long, long rifle
Action: Bolt action; self-cocking, single-shot
Magazine: None
Barrel: Blued; 20¾"; 19" (Mark I GY) youth model
Sights: Bead front, adjustable open rear; receiver is dovetailed for scope mounting
Stock and Forearm: Walnut finished, checkered one-piece, Monte Carlo stock and forearm
Approximate wt.: 5½ lbs.
Comments: Introduced in the mid-1990s; also made in youth model (Mark I, GY) and "smooth bore" shot shell model (Mark I, SB).

Estimated Value:	**New (retail):**	**$233.00**
	Excellent:	**$175.00**
	Very good:	**$140.00**

Savage Models 1904 and Model 04

Caliber: 22 short, long, long rifle
Action: Bolt action; single-shot
Magazine: None
Barrel: 18"
Sights: Open rear, bead front
Stock and Forearm: Straight wood one-piece stock and forearm
Approximate wt.: 3 lbs.
Comments: This is a boy's lightweight takedown rifle produced from 1904 to 1917 as Model 1904 and from 1924 to 1930 as Model 04.

Estimated Value:	**Excellent:**	**$200.00**
	Very good:	**$160.00**

Savage Models 3, 3S, and 3ST

Caliber: 22 short, long, long rifle
Action: Bolt action; single-shot
Magazine: None
Barrel: 26" before World War II, 24" after
Sights: Open rear, bead front; Models 3S and 3ST have peep rear and hooded front
Stock and Forearm: One-piece walnut semi-pistol grip stock and forearm; Model 3ST has swivels
Approximate wt.: 4 to 5 lbs.
Comments: A takedown model produced from 1933 until the early 1950s. The Model 3ST was discontinued before World War II.

Estimated Value:	**Excellent:**	**$175.00**
	Very good:	**$140.00**

Savage Model 1911 Target

Caliber: 22 short
Action: Bolt action; single-shot
Magazine: None
Barrel: 20"
Sights: Adjustable rear, bead front
Stock and Forearm: Walnut one-piece straight grip stock and forearm
Approximate wt.: 4 lbs.
Comments: Made from 1911 to 1916.

Estimated Value:	**Excellent:**	**$350.00**
	Very good:	**$280.00**

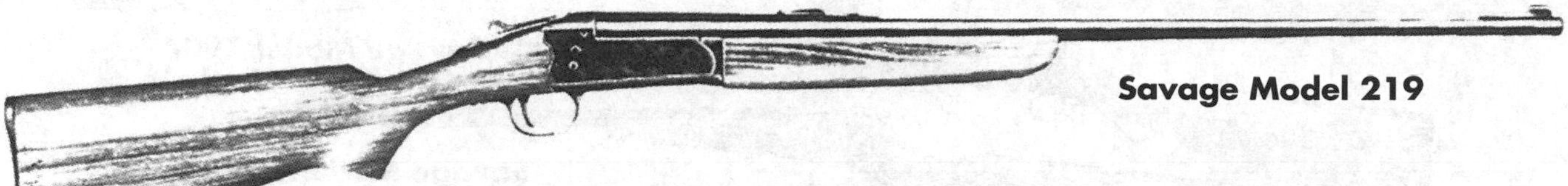

Savage Model 219

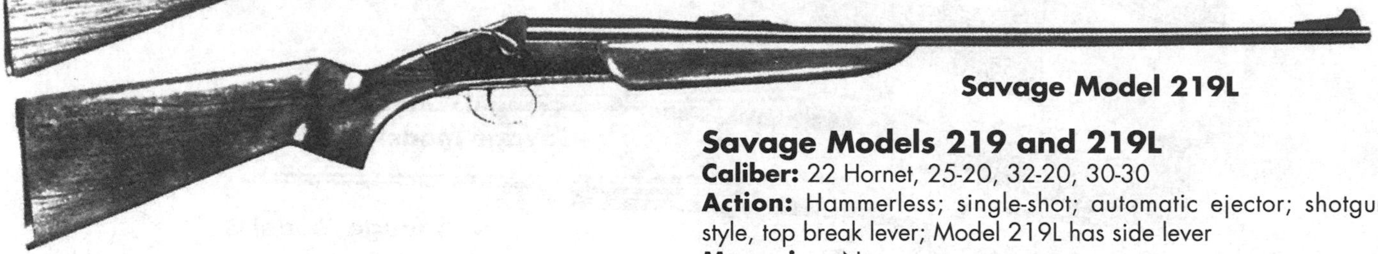

Savage Model 219L

Savage Models 219 and 219L

Caliber: 22 Hornet, 25-20, 32-20, 30-30
Action: Hammerless; single-shot; automatic ejector; shotgun style, top break lever; Model 219L has side lever
Magazine: None
Barrel: 26"
Sights: Open rear, bead front
Stock and Forearm: Plain walnut pistol grip stock and forearm
Approximate wt.: 6 lbs.
Comments: A takedown model made from 1938 to 1965 as Model 219; made in 1965 for two years as Model 219L.

Estimated Value:	**Excellent:**	**$200.00**
	Very good:	**$160.00**

Savage Model 221 Utility Gun

Same rifle as the Model 219 except it was offered in 30-30 only with an interchangeable 12 gauge, 30" shotgun barrel. Prices include the 12 gauge interchangeable shotgun barrel.

Estimated Value:	**Excellent:**	**$200.00**
	Very good:	**$160.00**

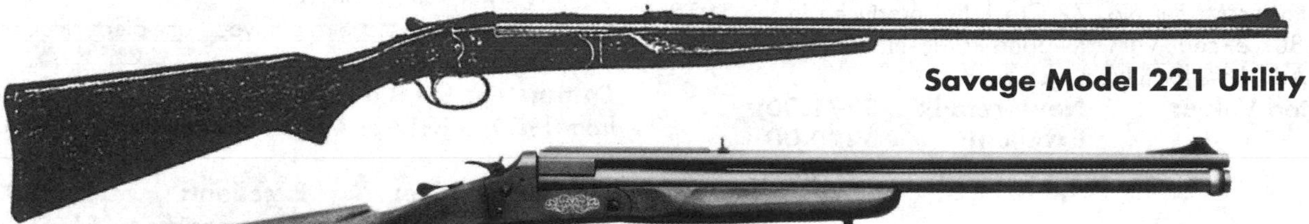

Savage Model 221 Utility Gun

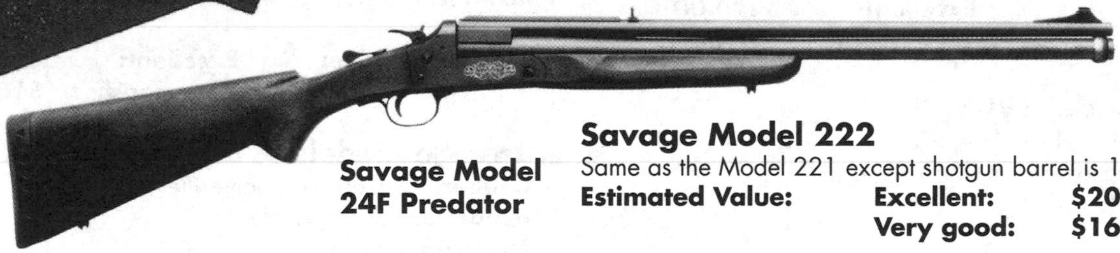

Savage Model 24F Predator

Savage Model 222

Same as the Model 221 except shotgun barrel is 16 gauge, 28".

Estimated Value:	**Excellent:**	**$200.00**
	Very good:	**$160.00**

Savage Model 223

Same as the Model 221 except shotgun barrel is 20 gauge, 28".

Estimated Value:	**Excellent:**	**$200.00**
	Very good:	**$160.00**

Savage Model 24F Predator

Gauge: 12, 20
Caliber: 22 Hornet, 223 Rem., 30-30 Win., rifle barrel over 12 gauge, 3" chamber shotgun barrel with changeable choke tubes; 22 long rifle, 22 Hornet, 223 Rem., 30-30 Win., rifle barrel over 20 gauge shotgun barrel with modified choke
Action: Breakdown rifle over shotgun barrel with a two-way opening lever; built-in, two-position barrel selector on the exposed hammer and a cross-bolt safety
Magazine: None
Barrel: 24" rifle over shotgun barrel
Sights: Rifle sight; drilled and tapped for scope mounts
Stock and Forearm: Black graphite fiberglass-filled composite material; pistol girp and recoil pad standard
Approximate wt.: 8 lbs.
Comments: A combination gun for predator and wild turkey hunting. Introduced in the mid-1990s. Add 5% for 12 gauge model.

Estimated Value:	**Excellent:**	**$500.00**
	Very good:	**$400.00**

Savage Model 227

Same as the Model 221 except it is 22 Hornet and the shotgun barrel is 12 gauge, 30".

Estimated Value:	**Excellent:**	**$225.00**
	Very good:	**$180.00**

Savage Model 228

Same as the Model 227 except shotgun barrel is 16 gauge, 28".

Estimated Value:	**Excellent:**	**$225.00**
	Very good:	**$180.00**

Savage Model 229

Same as the Model 227 except shotgun barrel is 20 gauge, 28".

Estimated Value:	**Excellent:**	**$225.00**
	Very good:	**$180.00**

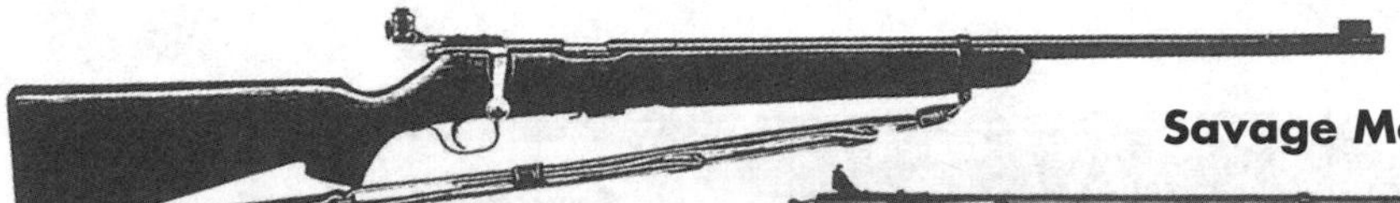

Savage Model 19

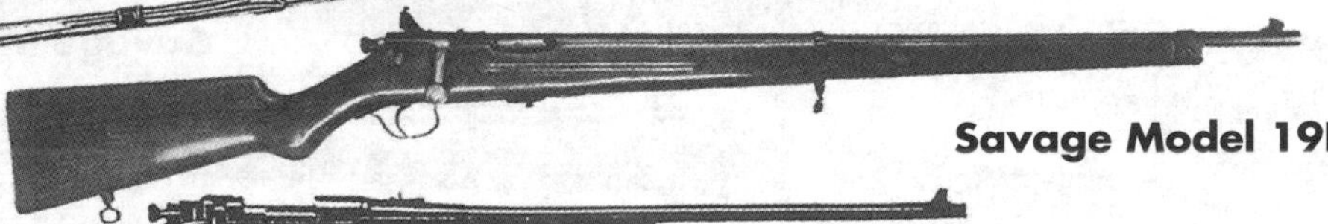

Savage Model 19NRA

Savage Model 20

Savage Model 19NRA Match Rifle

Caliber: 22 long rifle
Action: Bolt action; repeating
Magazine: 5-shot detachable box
Barrel: 25"
Sights: Adjustable peep rear, blade front
Stock and Forearm: Wood full military pistol grip stock and forearm
Approximate wt.: 7 lbs.
Comments: Made from 1919 until 1932.

Estimated Value:	**Excellent:**	**$450.00**
	Very good:	**$360.00**

Savage Model 20

Caliber: 300 Savage, 250-3000
Action: Bolt action; repeating
Magazine: 5-shot
Barrel: 22" in 250 caliber; 24" in 300 caliber
Sights: Open rear, bead front; in 1926, rear peep sight
Stock and Forearm: Checkered walnut pistol grip stock and forearm; in 1926 cut to semi-pistol grip
Approximate wt.: 5¾ to 7 lbs.
Comments: Made from 1920 through 1929.

Estimated Value:	**Excellent:**	**$750.00**
	Very good:	**$600.00**

Savage Models 19 and 19L Target

Caliber: 22 long rifle
Action: Bolt action; repeating; speed lock
Magazine: 5-shot detachable box
Barrel: 25"
Sights: Extension rear, hooded front
Stock and Forearm: Walnut pistol grip stock and beavertail forearm; swivels
Approximate wt.: 7½ lbs.
Comments: Made from 1933 to the mid-1940s. Model 19L has special Lyman receiver and front sights; add $10.00 to $15.00.

Estimated Value:	**Excellent:**	**$400.00**
	Very good:	**$320.00**

Savage Model 19M

Same as the Model 19 except: heavier 28" barrel. Approximate wt. is 9¼ lbs.

Estimated Value:	**Excellent:**	**$375.00**
	Very good:	**$300.00**

Savage Model 19H Hornet

Same as the Model 19 except loading port, bolt mechanism and magazine are like Model 23D; 22 Hornet caliber only.

Estimated Value:	**Excellent:**	**$550.00**
	Very good:	**$440.00**

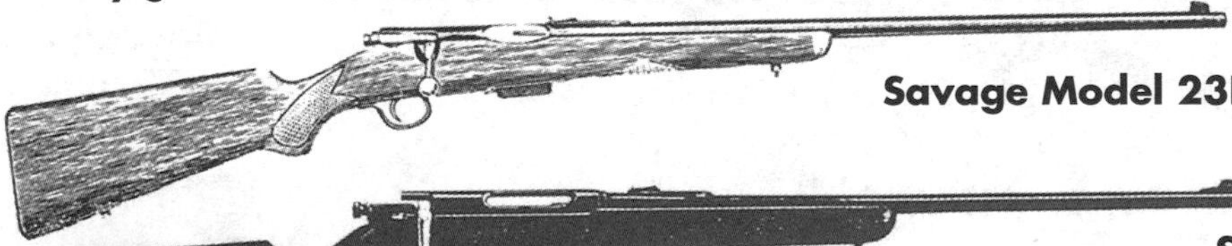

Savage Model 23B

Savage Model 40

Savage Models 23A Sporter, 23AA, 23B, 23C, and 23D

Caliber: 22 long rifle (Model 23A, 23AA); from 1933 to 1947 in 22 Hornet (Model 23D); 25-20 (Model 23B); 32-20 (Model 23C)
Action: Bolt action; from 1933 to 1942 (Model 23AA) speed lock
Magazine: 5-shot detachable box
Barrel: 23"; 25" from 1933 until 1942 on Model 23B
Sights: Open rear, bead or blade front
Stock and Forearm: Plain walnut semi-pistol grip stock and forearm
Approximate wt.: 6 to 6½ lbs.
Comments: Produced: Model 23A from 1923 to 1933; Model 23AA with improved lock, 1933 to 1942; Model 23B, 1933 to 1942; Models 23C and 23D, 1933 to 1947.

Estimated Value:	**Excellent:**	**$300.00**
	Very good:	**$240.00**

Savage Model 40

Caliber: 250-3000, 300 Savage, 30-30, 30-06
Action: Bolt action; repeating
Magazine: 4-shot detachable box
Barrel: 22" for caliber 250-3000 and 30-30; 24" for other models
Sights: Open rear, ramp front
Stock and Forearm: Plain walnut pistol grip stock and lipped forearm after 1936; checkered stock after 1940
Approximate wt.: 7½ lbs.
Comments: Made from 1928 until World War II.

Estimated Value:	**Excellent:**	**$400.00**
	Very good:	**$320.00**

Savage Model 45

This is a special grade version of Model 40. It has a checkered stock and forearm and a special receiver sight. Discontinued in 1940.

Estimated Value:	**Excellent:**	**$425.00**
	Very good:	**$340.00**

Savage Model 4

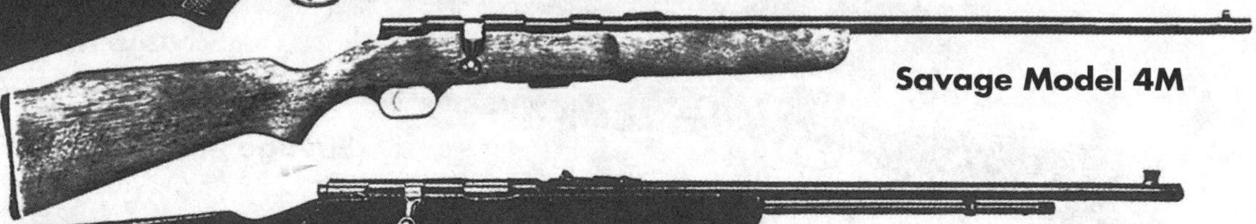

Savage Model 4M

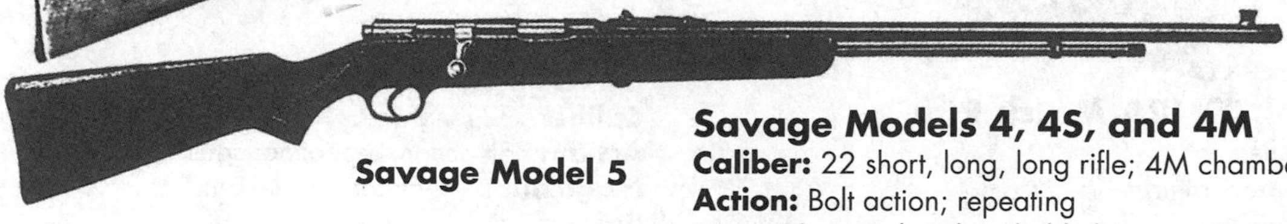

Savage Model 5

Savage Models 4, 4S, and 4M

Caliber: 22 short, long, long rifle; 4M chambered for 22 mag.
Action: Bolt action; repeating
Magazine: 5-shot detachable box
Barrel: 24"
Sights: Open rear, bead front; 4S has peep rear and hooded front
Stock and Forearm: Checkered walnut pistol grip stock and grooved forearm on pre-World War II models; plain on post-World War II models
Approximate wt.: 5½ lbs.
Comments: Models 4 and 4S were produced from 1933 until the mid-1960s. Model 4M was made during the early to the mid-1960s. Add $10.00 for Model 4M.

Estimated Value:	**Excellent:**	**$200.00**
	Very good:	**$160.00**

Savage Models 5 and 5S

Similar to Model 4 except the magazine is tubular and the gun weighs about 6 lbs. Model 5S has peep rear and hooded front sight. They were produced from the mid-1930s until 1961; caliber 22 short, long and long rifle. Add $10.00 for Model 5S.

Estimated Value:	**Excellent:**	**$225.00**
	Very good:	**$180.00**

Savage Mark II G

Savage Mark II LV

Savage Mark II G, II GY, and II GXP

Caliber: 22 long rifle, 17HM2
Action: Bolt action; repeating
Magazine: 10-shot detachable clip
Barrel: Blued; 20¾"; 19" (Mark II GY) youth model
Sights: Bead front, adjustable open rear
Stock and Forearm: Walnut finished, checkered one-piece, hardwood stock and forearm; camouflage finish avilable
Approximate wt.: 5½ lbs.
Comments: Introduced in the mid-1990s; also made in youth model (Mark II GY). Add 4% for factory mounted scope (Mark II GXP). Add 10% for camouflage finish.

Estimated Value:	**New (retail):**	**$233.00**
	Excellent:	**$175.00**
	Very good:	**$140.00**

Savage Mark II F, II FXP

Similar to Model II G except: black synthetic stock and forearm. Introduced in 1998. Add 5% for factory mounted scope (Mark II FXP); add 25% for 17HM2 caliber.

Estimated Value:	**New (retail):**	**$207.00**
	Excellent:	**$155.00**
	Very good:	**$125.00**

Savage Mark II FSS

Similar to Mark II F except: stainless steel action and barrel. Add 7% for 17HM2 caliber.

Estimated Value:	**New (retail):**	**$281.00**
	Excellent:	**$210.00**
	Very good:	**$170.00**

Savage Mark II FV

Similar to Mark II F except: 21" heavy barrel. Introduced in 1998.

Estimated Value:	**New (retail):**	**$280.00**
	Excellent:	**$210.00**
	Very good:	**$170.00**

Savage Mark II LV

Similar to Mark II FV except: gray laminated hardwood stock.

Estimated Value:	**Excellent:**	**$185.00**
	Very good:	**$150.00**

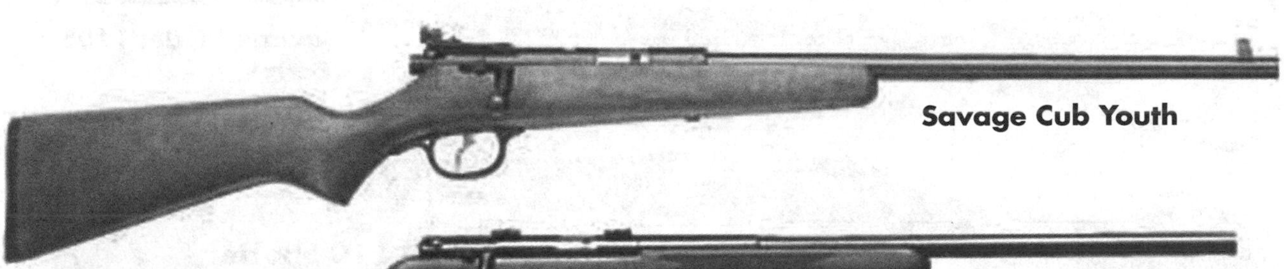

Savage Cub Youth

Savage Mark II FVSS

Savage Mark II BV

Savage Mark II FVSS

Similar to Mark II FV with stainless steel receiver and barrel.

Estimated Value:	**Excellent:**	**$225.00**
	Very good:	**$175.00**

Savage Mark II BV

Similar to the Mark II LV with a heavy target barrel; weighs 6¼ lbs.

Estimated Value:	**New (retail):**	**$352.00**
	Excellent:	**$265.00**
	Very good:	**$210.00**

Savage Cub Youth

Caliber: 22 short, long, long rifle
Action: Bolt action; single-shot
Magazine: none
Barrel: 16¼" blued
Sights: Bead post front, peep rear
Stock and Forearm: Smooth, one-piece pistol grip walnut finish hardwood stock and forearm
Approximate wt.: 3¼ lbs.
Comments: A compact 22 rifle for young shooters.

Estimated Value:	**New (retail):**	**$220.00**
	Excellent:	**$165.00**
	Very good:	**$132.00**

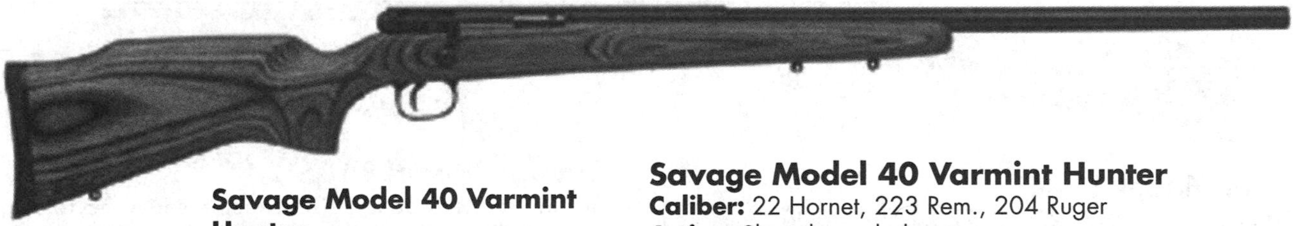

Savage Model 40 Varmint Hunter

Savage Mark II BVSS

Similar to the Mark II BV with stainless steel receiver and barrel.

Estimated Value:	**Excellent:**	**$235.00**
	Very good:	**$185.00**

Savage Model 40 Varmint Hunter

Caliber: 22 Hornet, 223 Rem., 204 Ruger
Action: Short throw, bolt action
Magazine: Single-shot
Barrel: 24" or 26" blued
Sights: None, drilled and tapped for scope mounts
Stock and Forearm: Smooth one-piece laminated pistol grip stock and extra wide beavertail forearm
Approximate wt.: 7¾ lbs.
Comments: Introduced in 2004. Add 9% for 223 Rem., or 204 Ruger caliber.

Estimated Value:	**New (retail):**	**$582.00**
	Excellent:	**$435.00**
	Very good:	**$350.00**

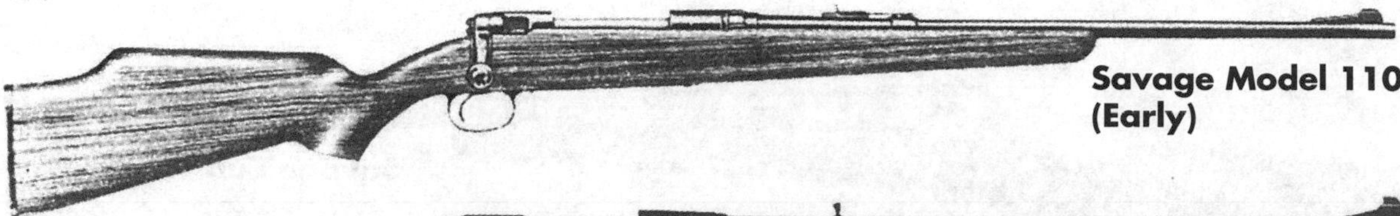

Savage Model 110E (Early)

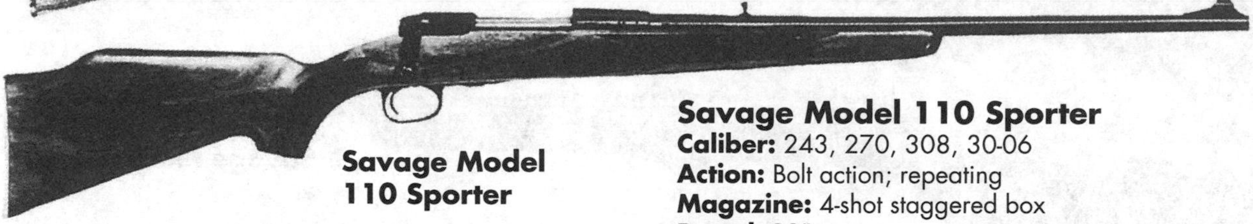

Savage Model 110 Sporter

Savage Model 110E (Early)

Caliber: 243 Win., 7mm Rem. mag., 30-06
Action: Bolt action; repeating
Magazine: 4-shot staggered box; 3-shot in magnum
Barrel: Blued; 20"; stainless steel in magnum
Sights: Open rear, ramp front
Stock and Forearm: One-piece checkered or plain walnut Monte Carlo stock and forearm; mag. has recoil pad
Approximate wt.: 6¾ to 7¾ lbs.
Comments: Made from 1963 to the late 1970s. A later model was also designated 110E.

Estimated Value:	**Excellent:**	**$300.00**
	Very good:	**$240.00**

Savage Model 110 Sporter

Caliber: 243, 270, 308, 30-06
Action: Bolt action; repeating
Magazine: 4-shot staggered box
Barrel: 22"
Sights: Open rear, ramp front
Stock and Forearm: Checkered walnut pistol grip stock and forearm
Approximate wt.: 6¾ lbs.
Comments: Made from 1958 until the early 1960s when it was replaced by Model 110E.

Estimated Value:	**Excellent:**	**$300.00**
	Very good:	**$240.00**

Savage Model 110MC

Same as the Model 110 Sporter except: 22-250 caliber added; 24" barrel; Monte Carlo stock. Made from the late 1950s to about 1969.

Estimated Value:	**Excellent:**	**$350.00**
	Very good:	**$280.00**

Savage Model 110S

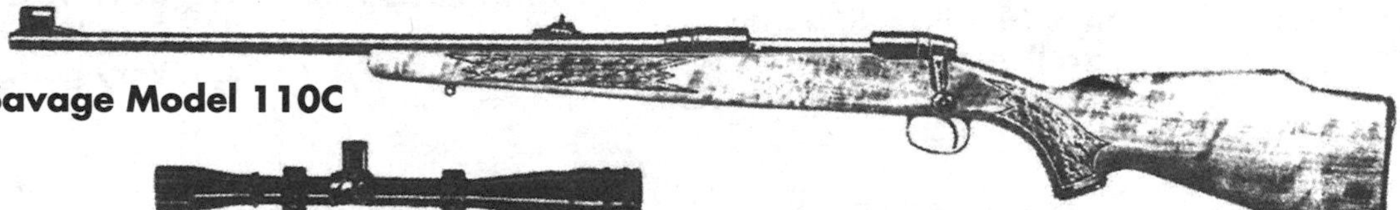

Savage Model 110C

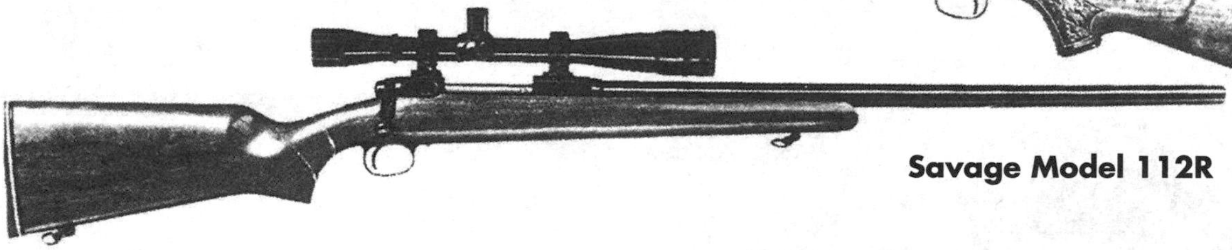

Savage Model 112R

Savage Model 110C

Caliber: 22-250, 243, 25-06, 270, 308, 30-06, 7mm Rem. mag., 300 Win. mag.
Action: Bolt action; repeating
Magazine: 4-shot clip, 3-shot clip in mag. calibers
Barrel: 22" and 24"; 24" in mag. calibers
Sights: Open rear, ramp front
Stock and Forearm: Checkered walnut Monte Carlo stock and forearm; mag. has recoil pad
Approximate wt.: 6¾ to 8 lbs.
Comments: This rifle was produced from 1966 to 1986. Add 10% for mag. calibers.

Estimated Value:	**Excellent:**	**$375.00**
	Very good:	**$300.00**

Savage Model 110S

Similar to the Model 110C except: heavy barrel; no sights; stippled checkering; recoil pad; 7mm/08 and 308 calibers; produced from the late 1970s to the mid-1980s.

Estimated Value:	**Excellent:**	**$375.00**
	Very good:	**$300.00**

Savage Model 112R

A varmint rifle similar to the Model 110C except: plain walnut one-piece semi-pistol grip stock and forearm; swivels; recoil pad; no sights; 22-250 and 25-06 calibers; made from about 1979 to the early 1980s.

Estimated Value:	**Excellent:**	**$350.00**
	Very good:	**$280.00**

Savage Model 110M

Savage Model 110M

Caliber: 7mm Rem. mag., 264, 300, 338 Win.
Action: Bolt action; repeating
Magazine: 4-shot box, staggered
Barrel: 24"
Sights: Open rear, ramp front
Stock and Forearm: Walnut Monte Carlo pistol grip stock and forearm; recoil pad
Approximate wt.: 7½ to 8 lbs.
Comments: Made from 1963 to 1969.
Estimated Value: **Excellent:** **$375.00**
Very good: **$300.00**

Savage Model 110D

Caliber: 223, 243, 270, 30-06, 7mm Rem. magnum, 338 Win. magnum
Action: Bolt action; repeating
Magazine: 4-shot internal box; 3-shot for magnums
Barrel: 22"; blue; 24" for magnums
Sights: Hooded ramp front, adjustable rear
Stock and Forearm: Select walnut, checkered semi-pistol grip, Monte Carlo, one-piece stock and forearm
Approximate wt.: 6¾ lbs; 7 lbs. in magnum
Comments: Produced from 1986 to 1988. Add 18% for mag. calibers.
Estimated Value: **Excellent:** **$375.00**
Very good: **$320.00**

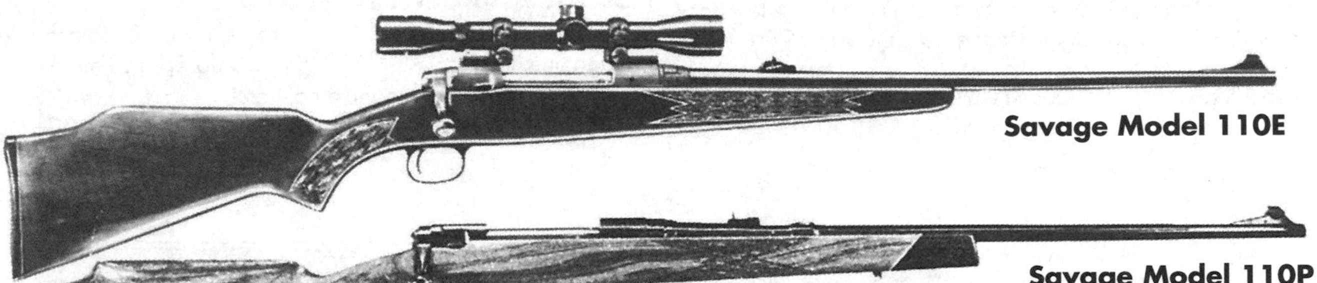

Savage Model 110E

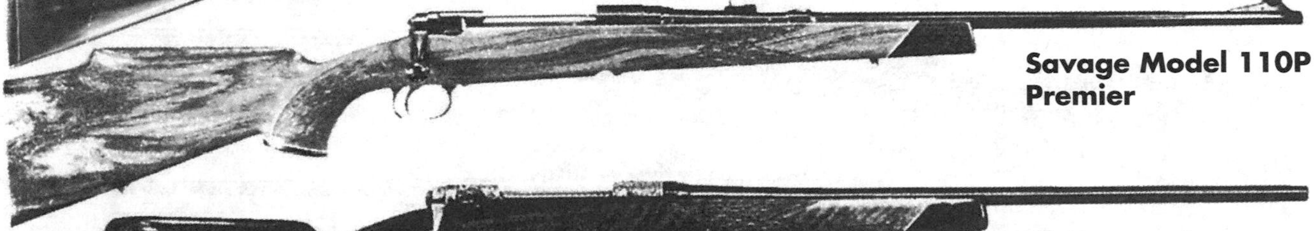

Savage Model 110P Premier

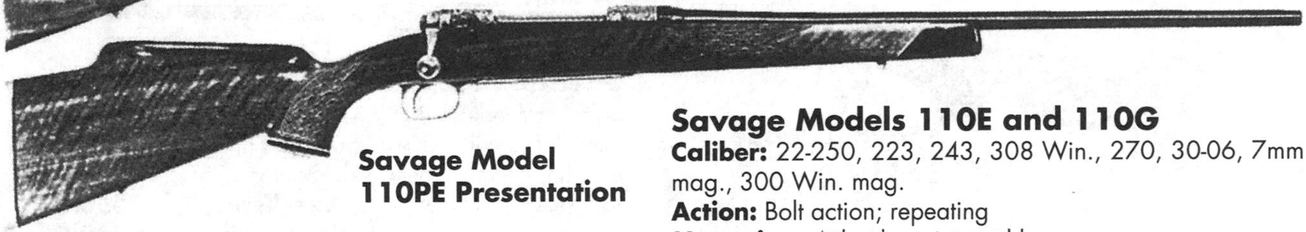

Savage Model 110PE Presentation

Savage Model 110P Premier

Caliber: 243 Win., 7mm Rem. mag., 30-06
Action: Bolt action; repeating
Magazine: 4-shot box, staggered; 3-shot in mag.
Barrel: Blued; 22"; 24" stainless steel in mag.
Sights: Open rear folding leaf, ramp front
Stock and Forearm: Walnut and rosewood Monte Carlo stock and forearm; swivels; mag. has recoil pad
Approximate wt.: 7 to 8 lbs.
Comments: Made from the mid-1960s until the 1970s; add 10% for mag. calibers.
Estimated Value: **Excellent:** **$500.00**
Very good: **$400.00**

Savage 110PE Presentation

Same as the Model 110P Premier except: receiver, floor plate, and trigger guard are engraved. Produced for two years beginning in 1968. Add 10% for mag.
Estimated Value: **Excellent:** **$700.00**
Very good: **$560.00**

Savage Models 110E and 110G

Caliber: 22-250, 223, 243, 308 Win., 270, 30-06, 7mm Rem. mag., 300 Win. mag.
Action: Bolt action; repeating
Magazine: 4-shot box, internal box
Barrel: Blued; 22"; 24" in 7mm mag. and 300 Win. mag.
Sights: None; removable ramp front and removable adj. rear optional
Stock and Forearm: Checkered hardwood, Monte Carlo walnut finish, one-piece pistol grip stock and forearm
Approximate wt.: 7 lbs.
Comments: Sold from the late 1970s to 1981 as Stevens, and from 1982 to the 1990s as Savage. Add 5% for sights.
Estimated Value: **Excellent:** **$325.00**
Very good: **$260.00**

Savage Models 110V and 110GV

Similar to Models 110E and 110G except: 22-250 or 223 caliber. No sights; a heavy 26" barrel. Recoil pad. Produced from the mid-1980s to the early 1990s. Approximate wt.: 9 lbs.
Estimated Value: **Excellent:** **$335.00**
Very good: **$265.00**

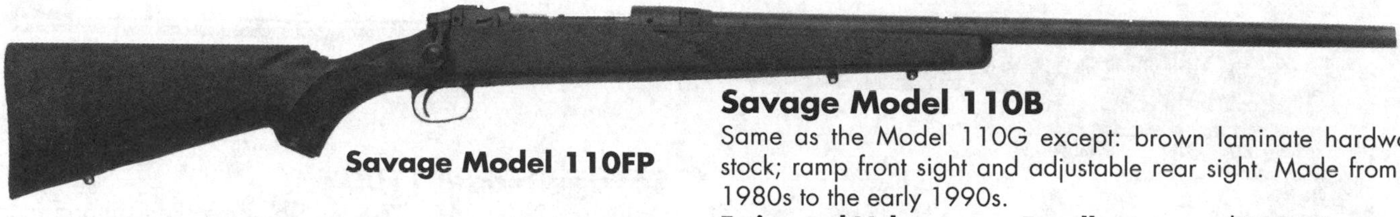

Savage Model 110FP

Savage Model 110FP, Police, Tactical

Similar to the Model 110G except: 223 Remington, 25-06 Rem., 30-06 Spfld., 308 Winchester, 7mm Rem. mag., and 300 Win. caliber; heavy 24" barrel; non-reflective black finish on metal parts; black all-weather DuPont Rynite® one-piece stock and forearm; sling studs and bi-pod mount; no sights; drilled and tapped for scope mounts. Pillar bedded stock. Introduced in 1990.

Estimated Value: **Excellent:** **$475.00**
Very good: **$380.00**

Savage Model 110F

Same as the Model 110G except: black DuPont Rynite® stock and forearm; add 4% for sights. Made from the late 1980s to the early 1990s.

Estimated Value: **Excellent:** **$375.00**
Very good: **$300.00**

Savage Model 110B

Same as the Model 110G except: brown laminate hardwood stock; ramp front sight and adjustable rear sight. Made from the 1980s to the early 1990s.

Estimated Value: **Excellent:** **$350.00**
Very good: **$280.00**

Savage Model 110GXP3

Similar to the Model 110G except with a factory-mounted and bore-sighted 3x9x32 scope and leather, military-style sling. Available in 223 Rem., 22-250 Rem., 243 Win., 25-06 Rem., 270 Win., 30-06 Sprg., 308 Win., 7mm Rem. magnum, and 300 Win. magnum calibers.

Estimated Value: **New (retail):** **$691.00**
Excellent: **$515.00**
Very good: **$415.00**

Savage Model 110GCXP3

Similar to the Model 110GXP3 except with a detachable box magazine. Available in 270 Win., 30-06 Sprg., 7mm Rem. magnum, and 300 Win. magnum calibers.

Estimated Value: **Excellent:** **$375.00**
Very good: **$300.00**

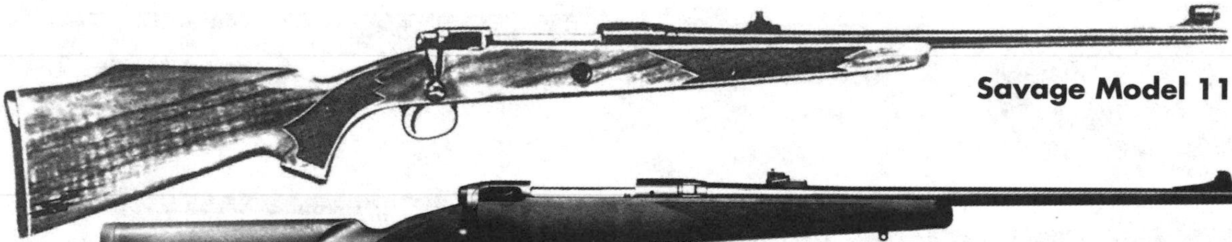

Savage Model 111

Savage Model 111G

Savage Models 111F and 111G

Caliber: 223 Rem., 22-250 Rem., 243 Win., 250 Sav., 25-06 Rem., 270 Win., 300 Sav., 30-06 Sprng., 308 Win., 7mm Rem. magnum, 7mm-08 Rem., 300 Win. magnum, 338 Win. magnum
Action: Bolt action; repeating; top loading
Magazine: 4-shot top loading; 3-shot in magnum
Barrel: 22" or 24"; blued
Sights: Open adjustable rear, ramp front; each receiver drilled and tapped for scope mounts
Stock and Forearm: Graphite/fiberglass filled (Model 111F) or walnut finish hardwood, one-piece checkered pistol grip stock and forearm with rubber recoil pad; swivel studs
Approximate wt.: 6¼ to 7 lbs.
Comments: Introduced in 1994. Add 10% for magnum or Model 111G.

Estimated Value: **Excellent:** **$425.00**
Very good: **$335.00**

Savage Models 111FC and 111GC

Same as Models 111F and 111G except: detachable box magazine; 270 Win., 30-06 Sprng., 7mm Rem. magnum, and 300 Win. magnum calibers. Add 2% for 111FC.

Estimated Value: **Excellent:** **$350.00**
Very good: **$280.00**

Savage Model 111

Caliber: 7mm (7x57), 243, 270, 30-06, 7mm magnum
Action: Bolt action; repeating
Magazine: 4-shot box; 3-shot box in magnum
Barrel: 24"
Sights: Adjustable removable rear, removable hooded ramp front
Stock and Forearm: Checkered walnut Monte Carlo one-piece pistol grip stock and forearm; swivels
Approximate wt.: 6¾ lbs.
Comments: A deluxe high-powered rifle made from the mid- to the late 1970s. Add $10.00 for magnum.

Estimated Value: **Excellent:** **$350.00**
Very good: **$280.00**

Savage Model 111GNS

Similar to the Model 111G with no sights.

Estimated Value: **Excellent:** **$395.00**
Very good: **$315.00**

Savage Model 111FAK Express

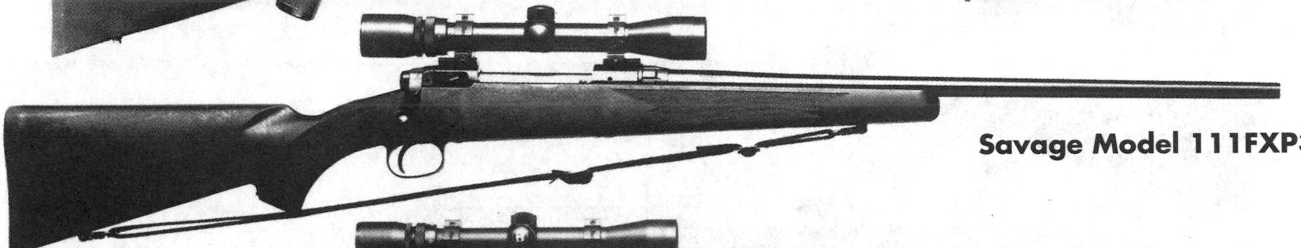

Savage Model 111FXP3

Savage Model 111FCXP3

Savage Model 110GY

Similar to the Model 111G except: slightly smaller; 22" barrel; available in 223 Rem., 243 Win., 270 Win., and 308 Win. calibers; weighs 6¼ lbs.

Estimated Value:	**Excellent:**	**$320.00**
	Very good:	**$255.00**

Savage Model 111FAK Express

Similar to the Model 111F except with blued alloy steel barrel, composite stock, and adjustable muzzle brake; available in 270 Win., 30-06 Sprg., 7mm Rem. magnum, 300 Win. magnum, and 338 Win magnum calibers.

Estimated Value:	**Excellent:**	**$375.00**
	Very good:	**$300.00**

Savage Model 111FXP3

Similar to the Model 111F except with a factory mounted and bore sighted scope and a black nylon sling. Available in 223 Rem., 22-250 Rem., 243 Win., 25-06 Rem., 270 Win., 30-06 Sprg., 308 Win., 7mm Win. magnum, 300 Win. magnum, 338 Win. magnum.

Estimated Value:	**New (retail):**	**$659.00**
	Excellent:	**$495.00**
	Very good:	**$395.00**

Savage Model 111FCXP3

Similar to the Model 111FXP3 except with a detachable box magazine. Available in 270 Win., 30-06 Sprg., 7mm Rem. magnum, 300 Win. magnum.

Estimated Value:	**New (retail):**	**$519.00**
	Excellent:	**$390.00**
	Very good:	**$310.00**

Savage Model 110FM Sierra

Savage Model 112V

Savage Model 112V

Caliber: 222, 223, 22-250, 220 Swift, 25-06, 243
Action: Bolt action; single-shot; hammerless
Magazine: None
Barrel: 26"; chrome-moly steel; tapered
Sights: None
Stock and Forearm: Checkered walnut one-piece pistol grip stock and forearm; fluted comb; swivels
Approximate wt.: 9¼ lbs.
Comments: A varmint rifle made in the mid- to the late 1970s.

Estimated Value:	**Excellent:**	**$320.00**
	Very good:	**$255.00**

Savage Model 110FM Sierra

Caliber: 243 Win., 270 Win., 308 Win., 30-06 Sprg
Action: Bolt action; repeating
Magazine: 4-shot top loading
Barrel: 20"; blued
Sights: None, drilled and tapped for scope mounts
Stock and Forearm: Checkered graphite/fiberglass-filled, one-piece pistol grip stock and forearm; rubber butt plate; swivels
Approximate wt.: 6¼ lbs.
Comments: A lightweight, compact hunting rifle introduced in the late 1990s.

Estimated Value:	**Excellent:**	**$350.00**
	Very good:	**$285.00**

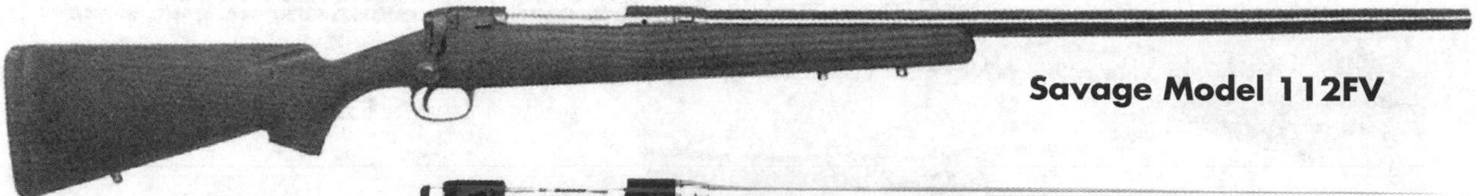

Savage Model 112FV

Savage Model 112FVSS-S

Savage Model 112BVSS

Savage Models 112FV and 112FVSS

Caliber: 22-250 Rem., or 223 Rem. (Model 112FV) Model 112FVSS also 25-06 Rem., 30-06 Sprg., 308 Win., 7mm Rem. mag., 300 Win. mag.
Action: Bolt action; repeating; top loading
Magazine: 5-shot top loading
Barrel: 26" blued (Model 112FV); 26" stainless steel (Model 112FVSS); recessed target style muzzle
Sights: None; drilled and tapped for scope mounts
Stock and Forearm: Graphite/fiberglass-filled, checkered one-piece stock and forearm; swivel studs
Approximate wt.: 9 to 10 lbs.
Comments: Introduced in 1994. Deduct 28% for Model 112FV.
Estimated Value: **Excellent:** **$425.00**
Very good: **$340.00**

Savage Model 112FVSS-S

Similar to Model FVSS except: single-shot; 22-250 Rem., 223 Rem., 220 Swift, and 300 Win. mag. calibers. Introduced in 1994.
Estimated Value: **Excellent:** **$425.00**
Very good: **$340.00**

Savage Model 112BVSS

Same as the Model 112FVSS except: calibers 223, 22-250 Rem., 25-06 Rem., 30-06, 308 Win., 7mm, and 300 Win.; heavy-prone laminated wood stock and forearm.
Estimated Value: **Excellent:** **$579.00**
Very good: **$460.00**

Savage Model 112BVSS-S

Same as the Model 112FVSS-S except: heavy-prone laminated wood stock and forearm.
Estimated Value: **Excellent:** **$465.00**
Very good: **$370.00**

Savage Model 112BT

A competition version of Model 112 available in 223 Rem., and 308 Win. calibers; 26" blackened stainless steel, heavy contour barrel; target style, laminated wood stock with ebony tipped vented forearm.
Estimated Value: **Excellent:** **$770.00**
Very good: **$615.00**

Savage Model 114U Ultra

Savage Models 114C and 114CE

Caliber: 270 Win., 30-06 Sprng., 7mm Rem. magnum, 300 Win. magnum
Action: Bolt action; repeating
Magazine: 4-shot or 5-shot removable box; 3-shot in mag.
Barrel: 22" blued; 24" in magnum calibers
Sights: Open adjustable rear, ramp front on Model 114CE; no sights on Model 114C; drilled and tapped for scope mount
Stock and Forearm: Select grade checkered walnut one-piece pistol grip stock and forearm; lipped forearm on Model 114CE; swivel studs
Approximate wt.: 7¼ lbs.
Comments: Introduced in 1994. Add 15% for Model 114CE.
Estimated Value: **Excellent:** **$405.00**
Very good: **$325.00**

Savage Model 114U Ultra

Similar to the Model 114CE except: high luster, high gloss finish; internal 4-shot box magazine; ebony fore-end cap. Introduced in 2000.
Estimated Value: **Excellent:** **$400.00**
Very good: **$320.00**

Savage Model 116US

Similar to the Model 114C except with select grade, high gloss American Walnut stock and forearm; alloy stainless steel barrel.
Estimated Value: **Excellent:** **$565.00**
Very good: **$450.00**

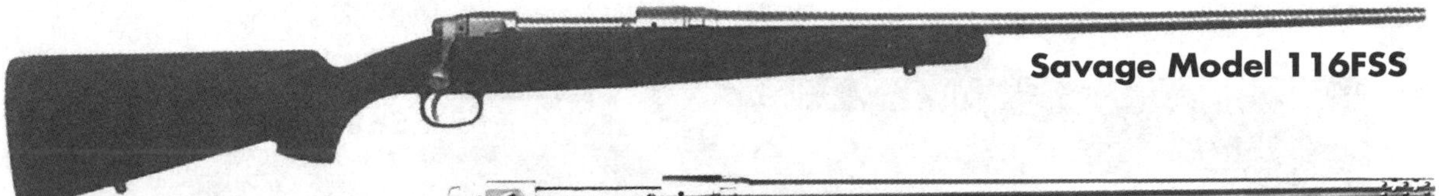

Savage Model 116FSS

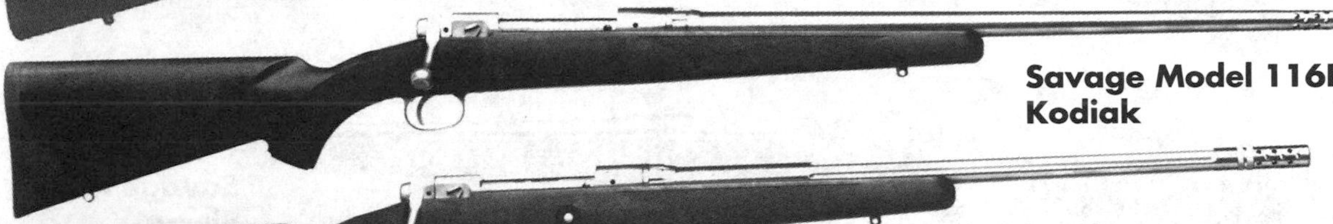

Savage Model 116FSK Kodiak

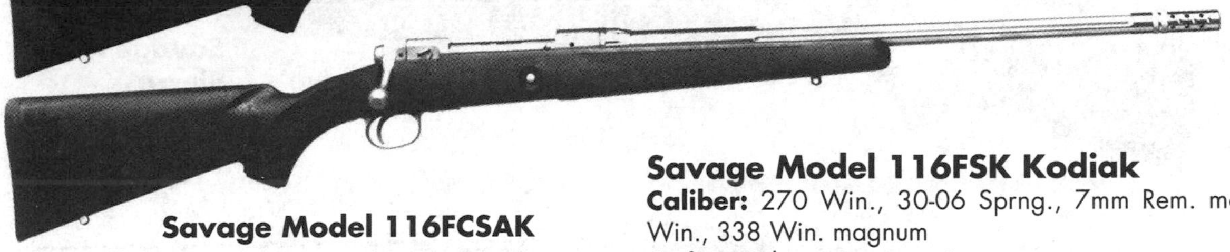

Savage Model 116FCSAK

Savage Model 116FSS

Caliber: 223 Rem., 243 Win., 270 Win., 30-06 Sprng., 308 Win., 7mm Rem. magnum, 300 Win. magnum, 338 Win. magnum
Action: Bolt action; repeating
Magazine: 4-shot top loading; 3-shot in magnum
Barrel: 22"; stainless steel; 24" in magnum
Sights: None; drilled and tapped for scope mounts
Stock and Forearm: Graphite/fiberglass filled, composite, one-piece, checkered pistol grip stock and forearm; swivel studs
Approximate wt.: 6¾ lbs.
Comments: Produced from the early 1990s to early 2000s.

Estimated Value:	**Excellent:**	**$445.00**
	Very good:	**$355.00**

Savage Model 116CS

Similar to the Model 116FSS except: 270 Win., 30-06 Sprng., 7mm Rem. magnum, and 300 Win. magnum only; stainless steel removable box-type magazine. Introduced in the early 1990s.

Estimated Value:	**Excellent:**	**$430.00**
	Very good:	**$345.00**

Savage Model 116FSK Kodiak

Caliber: 270 Win., 30-06 Sprng., 7mm Rem. magnum, 300 Win., 338 Win. magnum
Action: Bolt action; repeating
Magazine: 4-shot top loading; 3-shot in magnum calibers
Barrel: 22"; stainless steel; shock supressor muzzle
Sights: None, drilled and tapped for scope mounts
Stock and Forearm: Graphite/fiberglass-filled, one-piece stock and forearm
Approximate wt.: 6½ lbs.
Comments: Produced from the early 1990s to the early 2000s.

Estimated Value:	**Excellent:**	**$425.00**
	Very good:	**$340.00**

Savage Model 116FSAK

Same as the Model 116FSK except: it has an adjustable muzzle brake system with fluted barrel.

Estimated Value:	**Excellent:**	**$515.00**
	Very good:	**$410.00**

Savage Model 116FCSAK

Same as the Model 116FSAK except: no 338 Win. magnum caliber, stainless steel removable box magazine. Introduced in 1994; on-off choice in recoil reduction.

Estimated Value:	**Excellent:**	**$500.00**
	Very good:	**$400.00**

Savage Model 116SE Safari

Savage Model 116SE Safari

Caliber: 458 Win. magnum, 300 Win. magnum, 338 Win. magnum
Action: Bolt action; repeating
Magazine: 3-shot top loading
Barrel: 24"; stainless steel with adjustable muzzle brake (AMB); sling stud
Sights: Special 3-leaf classic express rear; ramp front
Stock and Forearm: Select grade figured walnut, one-piece checkered pistol grip stock and forearm with ebony tip and rubber butt plate
Approximate wt.: 8½ lbs.
Comments: Introduced in the mid-1990s.

Estimated Value:	**Excellent:**	**$730.00**
	Very good:	**$585.00**

Savage Model 12FV

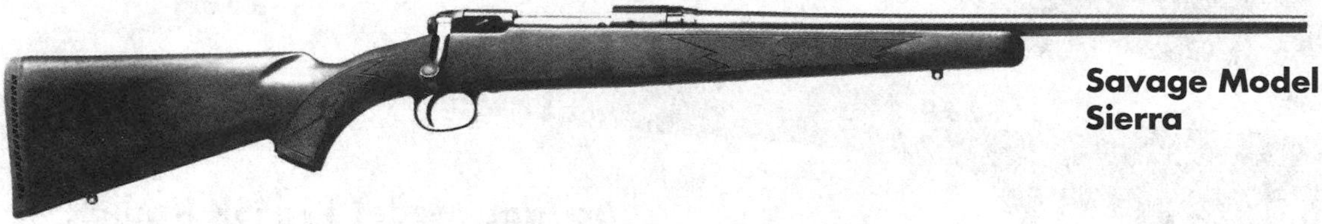

Savage Model 10FM Sierra

Savage Model 16FSS

Savage Model 12FV

Caliber: 223 Rem., 22-250 Rem.
Action: Short throw bolt action; repeating
Magazine: 4-shot top loading
Barrel: Blued; 26"
Sights: None, drilled and tapped for scope mounts
Stock and Forearm: Checkered one-piece, black synthetic pistol-grip stock and forearm; recoil pad
Approximate wt.: 9 lbs.
Comments: Introduced in 1998.

Estimated Value:	**New (retail):**	**$676.00**
	Excellent:	**$500.00**
	Very good:	**$400.00**

Savage Models 12FVSS and 12FVSS-S

Similar to the Model 12FV except with fluted stainless steel barrel; also available in 308 Win. caliber. Introduced in 1998. Single-shot version available (Model 12FVSS-S).

Estimated Value:	**New (retail):**	**$840.00**
	Excellent:	**$630.00**
	Very good:	**$500.00**

Savage Models 12BVSS and 12BVSS-S

Similar to the Model 12FVSS except it has brown laminated wood stock with flat beavertail forearm. Single-shot version available (Model 12BVSS-S).

Estimated Value:	**New (retail):**	**$925.00**
	Excellent:	**$695.00**
	Very good:	**$555.00**

Savage Model 10FP

Similar to the Model 12FV except for police, tactical, and military use; 24" barrel; 223 Rem., 308 Win. calibers; weighs 8 lbs. Introduced in 1998.

Estimated Value:	**Excellent:**	**$475.00**
	Very good:	**$380.00**

Savage Model 10FM Sierra

Similar to the Model 10FP except with 20" barrel, available in 223 Rem., 243 Win., 308 Win.; weighs 6 lbs. Introduced in 1998.

Estimated Value:	**Excellent:**	**$350.00**
	Very good:	**$285.00**

Savage Model 10FCM Scout

Similar to the Model 10FM except: detachable 4-shot box magazine, ghost ring rear sight. Introduced in the late 1990s.

Estimated Value:	**Excellent:**	**$420.00**
	Very good:	**$335.00**

Savage Model 10GY

Similar to the Model 10FM except: 22" barrel with open rear, ramp front sights; wood stock and forearm; designed for smaller shooters.

Estimated Value:	**Excellent:**	**$420.00**
	Very good:	**$335.00**

Savage Model 16FSS

Similar to the Model 10FM except: 22" stainless steel barrel. Introduced in 1998.

Estimated Value:	**New (retail):**	**$699.00**
	Excellent:	**$525.00**
	Very good:	**$420.00**

Savage Model 11G

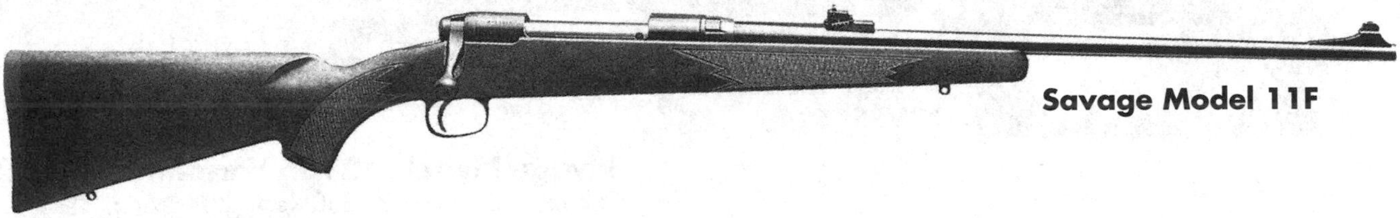

Savage Model 11F

Savage Model 11G

Similar to the Model 11F with wood stock and forearm.

Estimated Value:	**Excellent:**	**$435.00**
	Very good:	**$350.00**

Savage Model 11F

Similar to the Model 10FM except: 22" barrel with open rear, ramp front sights; 223 Rem., 22-250 Rem., 243 Win., 308 Win. calibers. Deduct 2% for no sights.

Estimated Value:	**Excellent:**	**$425.00**
	Very good:	**$335.00**

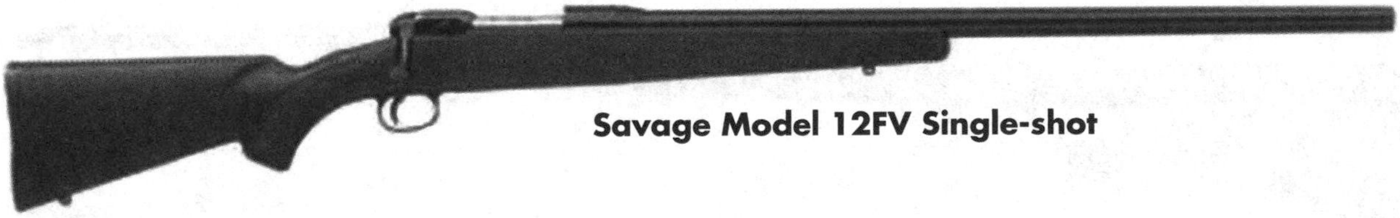

Savage Model 12FV Single-shot

Savage Model 12 Varminter Low Profile

Similar to the Model 12BVSS in 223 Rem., 22-250 Rem., or 204 Ruger calibers. 24" or 26" barrel. Low profile stock and extra-wide beavertail forearm.

Estimated Value:	**New (retail):**	**$1,021.00**
	Excellent:	**$ 765.00**
	Very good:	**$ 615.00**

Savage Model 12FV Single-shot

A single-shot version of the Model 12FV in 204 Ruger caliber.

Estimated Value:	**New (retail):**	**$676.00**
	Excellent:	**$510.00**
	Very good:	**$405.00**

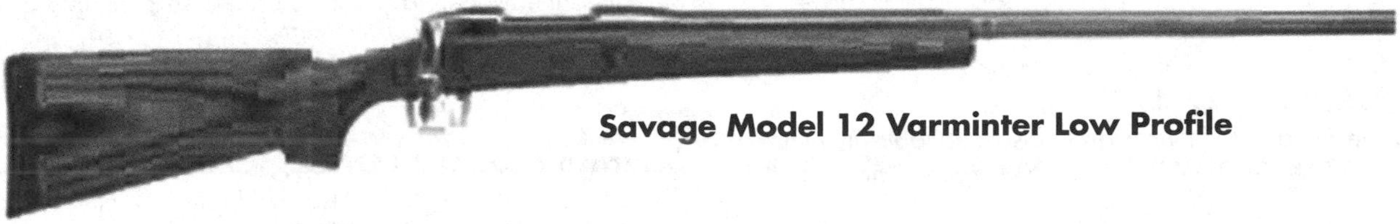

Savage Model 12 Varminter Low Profile

Savage Model 12FVY Youth

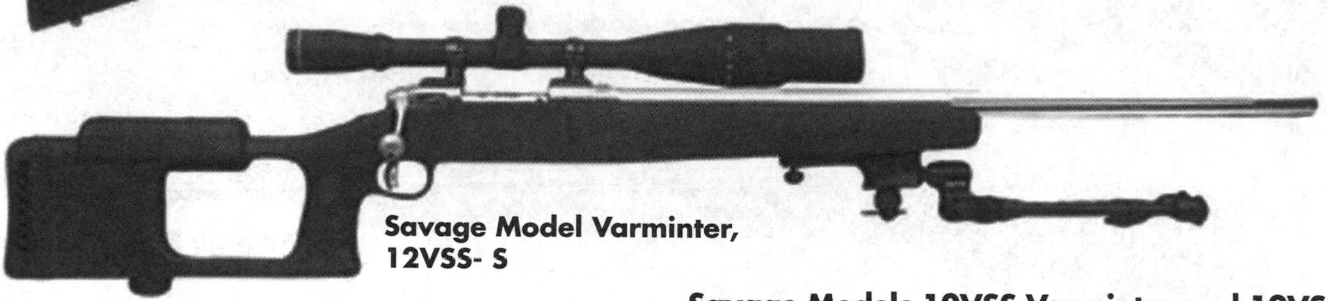

Savage Model Varminter, 12VSS- S

Savage Models 12VSS Varminter and 12VSS-S

Caliber: 223 Rem., 22-250 Rem., 308 Win.
Action: Short throw bolt action; repeating
Magazine: 4-shot box; Model 12VSS-S is single-shot version
Barrel: 26" fluted stainless steel
Sights: None, drilled and tapped for scope mounts
Stock and Forearm: Adjustable synthetic pistol grip stock with accessory rail; swivels
Approximate wt.: 11¼ lbs.
Comments: Introduced in 2003

Estimated Value:	**Excellent:**	**$700.00**
	Very good:	**$560.00**

Savage Model 12FVY Youth

A youth version of the Model 12FV in 223 Rem. or 22-250 Rem. calibers.

Estimated Value:	**Excellent:**	**$440.00**
	Very good:	**$350.00**

Savage Model 11FNS

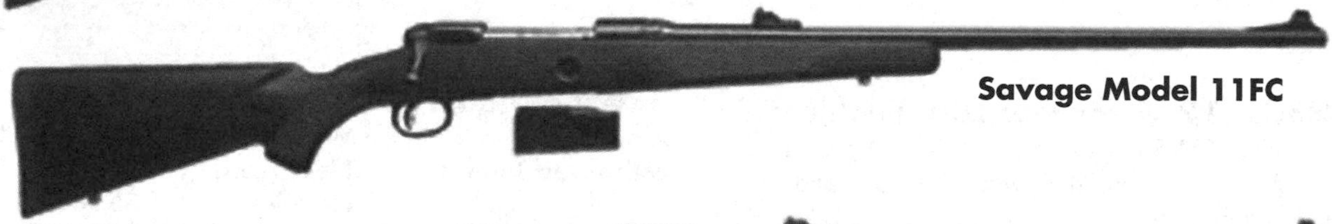

Savage Model 11FC

Savage Model 11GNS

Savage Model 11FNS

Similar to the Model 11F; no sights; also available in 7mm-08 Rem., 270 WSM, 300 WSM, and 204 Ruger. Introduced in 2004.

Estimated Value:	**New (retail):**	**$591.00**
	Excellent:	**$445.00**
	Very good:	**$355.00**

Savage Model 11FC

Similar to the Model 11F; 22" barrel; also available in 7mm-08 Rem. caliber.

Estimated Value:	**Excellent:**	**$405.00**
	Very good:	**$325.00**

Savage Model 11GNS

Similar to the Model 11G. Also available in 7mm-08 Rem., 270 WSM, 7mm WSM, and 300 WSM.

Estimated Value:	**New (retail):**	**$635.00**
	Excellent:	**$475.00**
	Very good:	**$380.00**

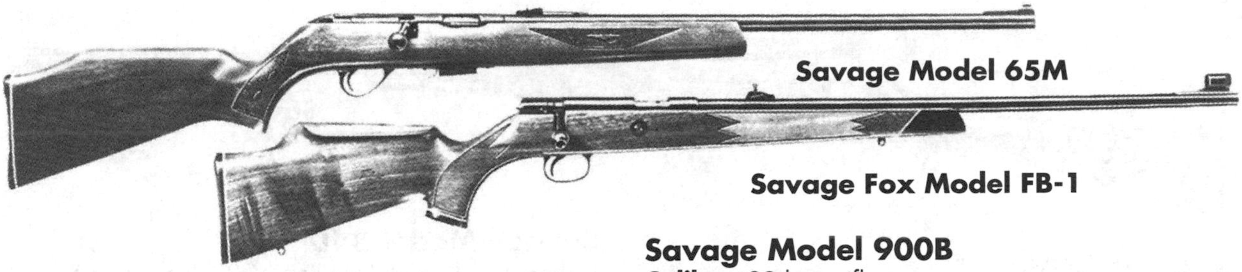

Savage Model 65M

Savage Fox Model FB-1

Savage Model 65M

Caliber: 22 magnum
Action: Bolt action; repeating
Magazine: 5-shot clip
Barrel: Blued; 22"
Sights: Open rear, ramp front
Stock and Forearm: Checkered walnut one-piece semi-pistol grip stock and forearm
Approximate wt.: 5¾ lbs.
Comments: Made in the late 1970s.

Estimated Value:	**Excellent:**	**$145.00**
	Very good:	**$115.00**

Savage Fox Model FB-1

Caliber: 22 short, long, long rifle
Action: Bolt action; repeating
Magazine: 5-shot detachable clip
Barrel: Blued; 24"
Sights: Adjustable leaf rear, hooded ramp front; drilled and tapped for scope
Stock and Forearm: Checkered walnut Monte Carlo one-piece, semi-pistol grip stock and forearm; cheekpiece swivels; rosewood fore-end tip and grip cap
Approximate wt.: 6½ lbs.
Comments: Introduced in 1981, discontinued in 1982.

Estimated Value:	**Excellent:**	**$250.00**
	Very good:	**$200.00**

Savage Model 900B

Caliber: 22 long rifle
Action: Bolt action; repeating
Magazine: 5-shot clip and clip holder
Barrel: Blued; 21", free floated heavy target barrel with a snow cover to prevent obstructions from entering the barrel
Sights: Receiver peep sights, target front with seven aperture inserts
Stock and Forearm: Natural finish hardwood target stock and forearm with butt hook and hand stop
Approximate wt.: 8¼ lbs.
Comments: Made from the mid-1990s to 1998.

Estimated Value:	**Excellent:**	**$425.00**
	Very good:	**$340.00**

Savage Model 900TR

Similar to the Model 900B except: no clip holders; no snow cover; walnut finish hardwood stock and forearm; 25" barrel; approximate wt. 8 lbs.

Estimated Value:	**Excellent:**	**$350.00**
	Very good:	**$280.00**

Savage Model 900S (Silhouette Rifle)

Similar to the Model 900TR except: 21" heavy contour barrel; no sight; silhouette-style high comb; satin walnut finish; scope bases installed.

Estimated Value:	**Excellent:**	**$340.00**
	Very good:	**$275.00**

Savage Model 982DL

Savage Model 982MDL

Savage Model 982DL

Caliber: 22 short, long, long rifle
Action: Bolt action; repeating
Magazine: 5-shot clip, push-button release
Barrel: Blued; 22"
Sights: Ramp front, folding leaf rear
Stock and Forearm: Checkered walnut one-piece Monte Carlo semi-pistol grip stock and forearm
Approximate wt.: 6 lbs.
Comments: Introduced in 1981, discontinued in 1982.

Estimated Value:	**Excellent:**	**$145.00**
	Very good:	**$115.00**

Savage Model 982MDL

Caliber: 22 mag.
Action: Bolt action; repeating
Magazine: 5-shot detachable clip
Barrel: Blued; 22"
Sights: Ramp front, folding leaf rear; grooved for scope
Stock and Forearm: Checkered walnut Monte Carlo one-piece semi-pistol grip stock and forearm
Approximate wt.: 6 lbs.
Comments: Produced from 1981 to 1982.

Estimated Value:	**Excellent:**	**$150.00**
	Very good:	**$120.00**

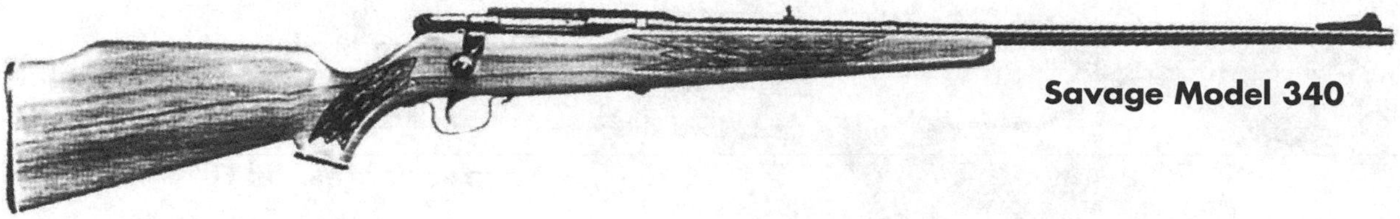

Savage Model 340

Savage Model 340S

Same as the Model 340 except: sights are peep rear, hooded front. Produced from about 1955 to 1960.

Estimated Value: **Excellent:** **$275.00**
Very good: **$220.00**

Savage Model 340C Carbine

Same as the Model 340 except: caliber 30-30; 18" barrel. Produced in the 1960s. Peep sight, checkered stock, and sling swivels.

Estimated Value: **Excellent:** **$250.00**
Very good: **$200.00**

Savage Model 340

Caliber: 22 Hornet, 222 Rem., 223 Rem., 30-30
Action: Bolt action; repeating
Magazine: 4-shot clip in 22 Hornet and 222 Rem.; 3-shot clip in 30-30
Barrel: 20", 22", 24"
Sights: Open rear, ramp front; hooded ramp after 1980
Stock and Forearm: Plain walnut pistol grip stock and forearm; checkered after 1965
Approximate wt.: 6 to 7 lbs.
Comments: Made from 1950 to 1986; before 1950 this model was manufactured as a Stevens.

Estimated Value: **Excellent:** **$300.00**
Very good: **$240.00**

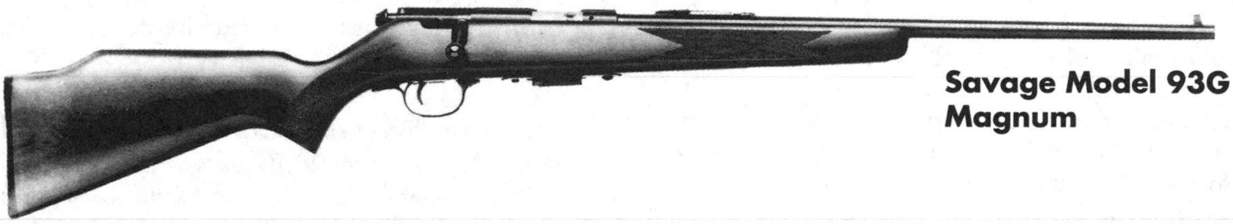

Savage Model 93G Magnum

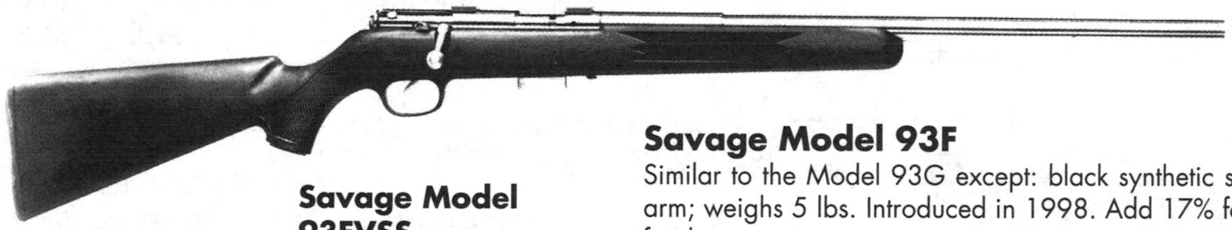

Savage Model 93FVSS

Savage Model 93G Magnum

Caliber: 22 WMR
Action: Bolt action; repeating
Magazine: 5-shot clip
Barrel: Blued; 20¾"
Sights: Bead front, sporting rear with height adjustment
Stock and Forearm: Walnut stained, cut checkered, hardwood one-piece Monte Carlo stock and forearm
Approximate wt.: 5¾ lbs.
Comments: Introduced in the mid-1990s.

Estimated Value: **New (retail):** **$268.00**
Excellent: **$200.00**
Very good: **$160.00**

Savage Model 93F

Similar to the Model 93G except: black synthetic stock and forearm; weighs 5 lbs. Introduced in 1998. Add 17% for camouflage finish.

Estimated Value: **New (retail):** **$248.00**
Excellent: **$185.00**
Very good: **$150.00**

Savage Model 93FSS

Similar to the Model 93F except: stainless steel action and barrel.

Estimated Value: **New (retail):** **$315.00**
Excellent: **$235.00**
Very good: **$190.00**

Savage Model 93FVSS

Similar to the Model 93FSS except has a 21" heavy barrel.

Estimated Value: **New (retail):** **$359.00**
Excellent: **$270.00**
Very good: **$215.00**

Savage Model 1899 (99)

Savage Model 1899 Military

Savage Model 1899 (99)

Caliber: 303 Savage, 25-35, 32-40, 38-55, 30-30
Action: Lever action; hammerless
Magazine: 5-shot rotary
Barrel: 20", 22", or 26"; round, half octagon, or octagon
Sights: Adjustable rear dovetail; open sporting front
Stock and Forearm: Walnut straight grip stock and tapered forearm
Approximate wt.: 7½ lbs.
Comments: The backbone of the Savage line which has been manufactured in many variations over the years. Produced from 1899 to 1922.

Estimated Value:	**Excellent:**	**$1,375.00**
	Very good:	**$1,100.00**

Savage Model 1899 Military

Same as the Model 99 except: barrel is 28"; bayonet; stock is musket style; sights are military. Produced from about 1899 to 1907; caliber 30-30 Win.

Estimated Value:	**Excellent:**	**$1,500.00**
	Very good:	**$1,200.00**

Savage Model 99A

Basically the same as the Model 1899 in solid frame and in calibers 300 Savage, 303 Savage, and 30-30. It was produced from 1922 to 1937. Later models in calibers 243, 308, 250 Savage, and 300 Savage from about 1970 to 1984. Add 30% for early models.

Estimated Value:	**Excellent:**	**$1,275.00**
	Very good:	**$1,025.00**

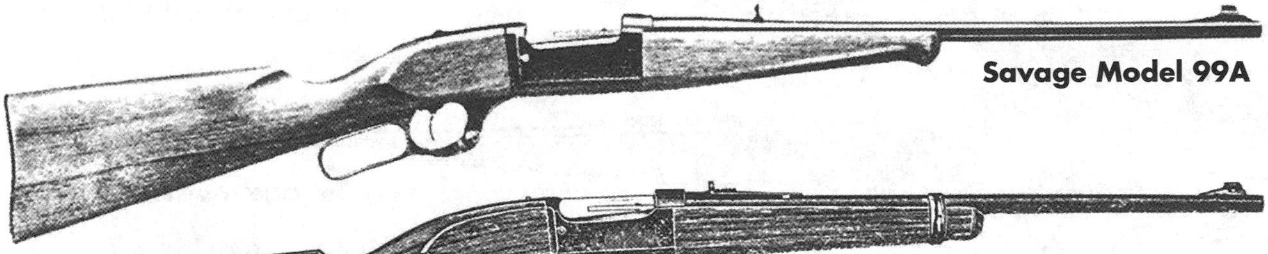

Savage Model 99A

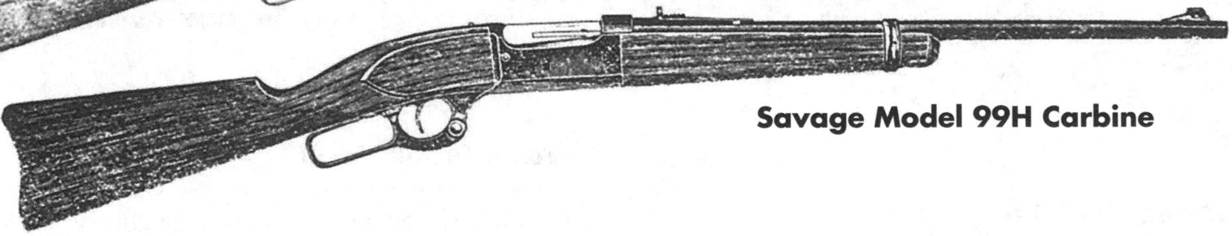

Savage Model 99H Carbine

Savage Model 99B

Takedown version of Model 99A; produced from about 1922 to 1937.

Estimated Value:	**Excellent:**	**$1,650.00**
	Very good:	**$1,325.00**

Savage Model 99H Carbine

Basically the same as the Model 99A with the addition of 250-3000 caliber; short barrel; carbine stock and forearm; barrel bands. Produced from 1932 to 1941.

Estimated Value:	**Excellent:**	**$1,650.00**
	Very good:	**$1,325.00**

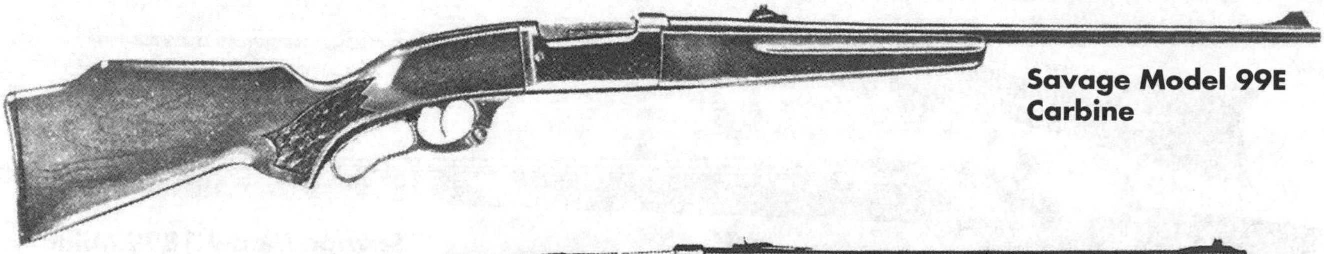

Savage Model 99E Carbine

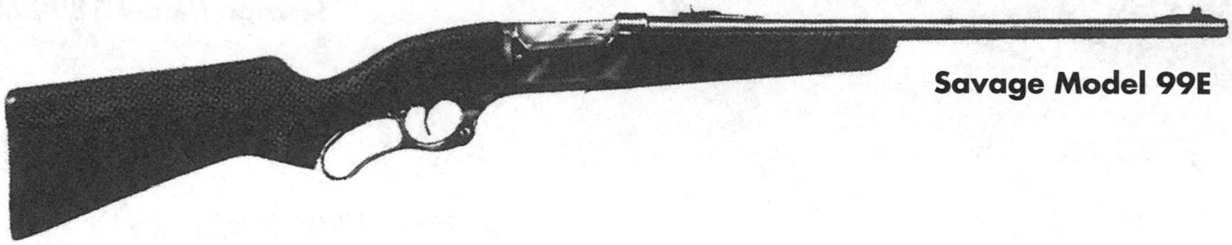

Savage Model 99E

Savage Model 99E

Similar to the Model 99A in 22 Hi Power, 250-3000, 30-30, 300 savage, 303 Savage; 22" or 24" barrel. Unlipped tapered forearm. Made from about 1922 to 1937.

Estimated Value:	**Excellent:**	**$1,400.00**
	Very good:	**$1,120.00**

Savage Model 99E Carbine

Similar to the Model 99H in 243 Win., 250 Savage, 300 Savage, 308 Win., calibers only. Checkered walnut stock and tapered forearm without barrel band. Production began in 1961. Monte Carlo stock after 1982. Discontinued in 1985.

Estimated Value:	**Excellent:**	**$1,275.00**
	Very good:	**$1,025.00**

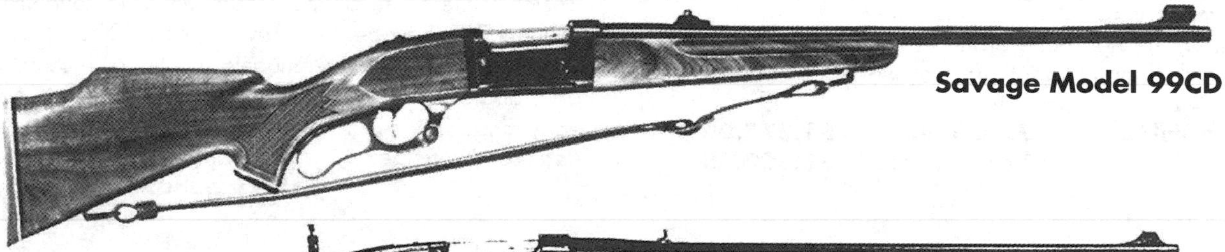

Savage Model 99CD

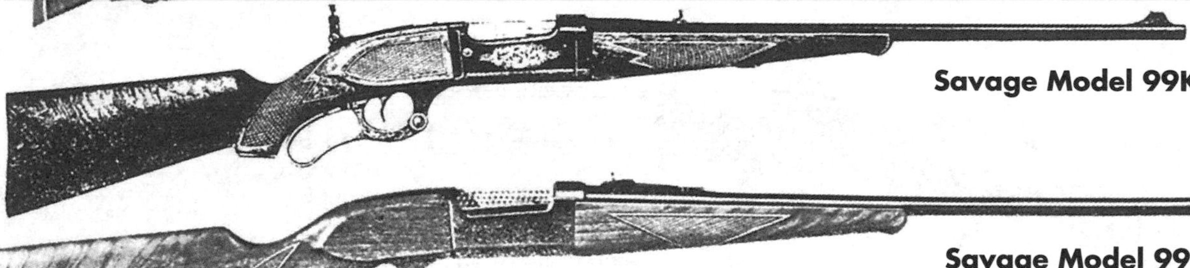

Savage Model 99K

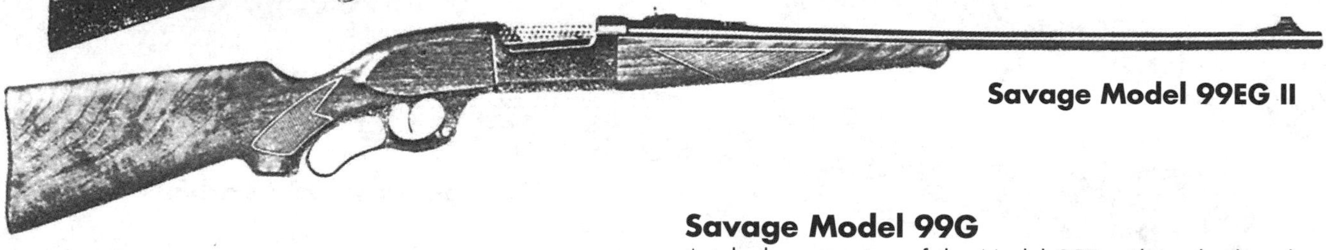

Savage Model 99EG II

Savage Model 99EG II

This is the Model G produced after World War II, from 1946 to 1961.

Estimated Value:	**Excellent:**	**$1,000.00**
	Very good:	**$ 800.00**

Savage Model 99CD

A solid-frame version of the Model 99F with a checkered pistol grip stock and forearm. In production from 1955 to about 1980; 4-shot detachable box magazine.

Estimated Value:	**Excellent:**	**$1,200.00**
	Very good:	**$ 960.00**

Savage Model 99G

A takedown version of the Model 99E with a checkered walnut pistol grip stock and forearm. Made from about 1921 to 1941.

Estimated Value:	**Excellent:**	**$1,100.00**
	Very good:	**$ 880.00**

Savage Model 99K

A fancy Model 99G with deluxe stock and light engraving. Rear peep sight; folding middle sight. Made from the early 1930s to the early 1940s.

Estimated Value:	**Excellent:**	**$1,500.00**
	Very good:	**$1,200.00**

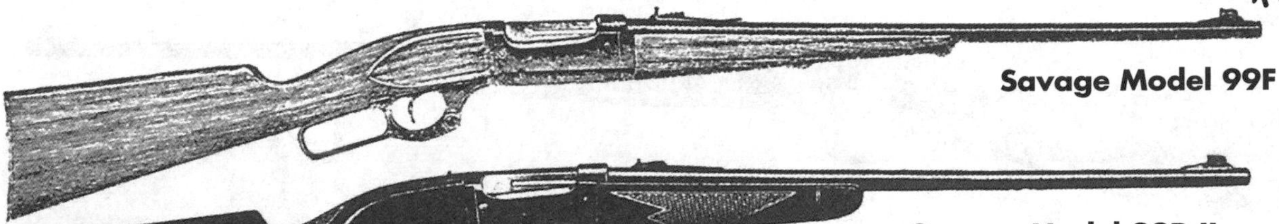

Savage Model 99F

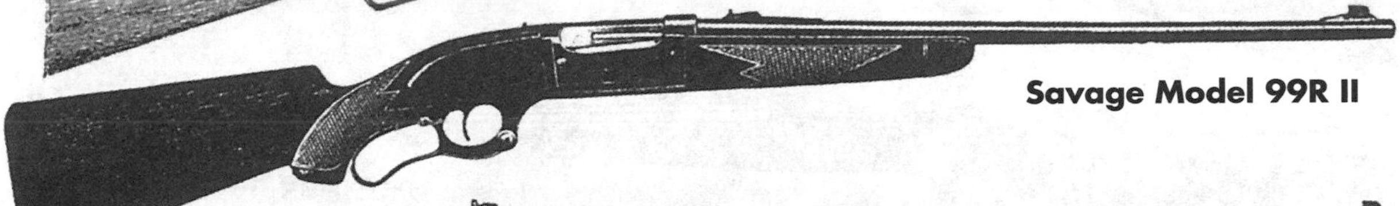

Savage Model 99R II

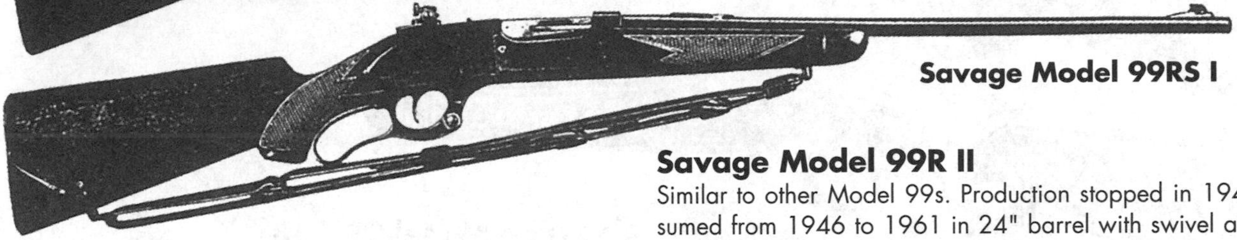

Savage Model 99RS I

Savage Model 99F

This is a lightweight takedown version of Model 99E, produced until about 1940. Production resumed about 1955 to 1972 in caliber 243, 300, and 308. Add $160.00 for pre-1940.

Estimated Value:	**Excellent:**	**$750.00**
	Very good:	**$600.00**

Savage Model 99R II

Similar to other Model 99s. Production stopped in 1940 and resumed from 1946 to 1961 in 24" barrel with swivel attachments in a variety of calibers. Add 50% for pre-World War II models.

Estimated Value:	**Excellent:**	**$800.00**
	Very good:	**$640.00**

Savage Models 99RS I and 99RS II

Same as the Model 99 except: those before World War II have rear peep sight and folding middle sight. Those made after the war have a special receiver sight. Discontinued in 1961; solid frame. Add 50% for pre-World War II models. Model 99RS I, pre-WWII model; Model 99RS II, after WWII.

Estimated Value:	**Excellent:**	**$850.00**
	Very good:	**$680.00**

Savage Model 99PE Presentation

Savage Model 99DE Citation

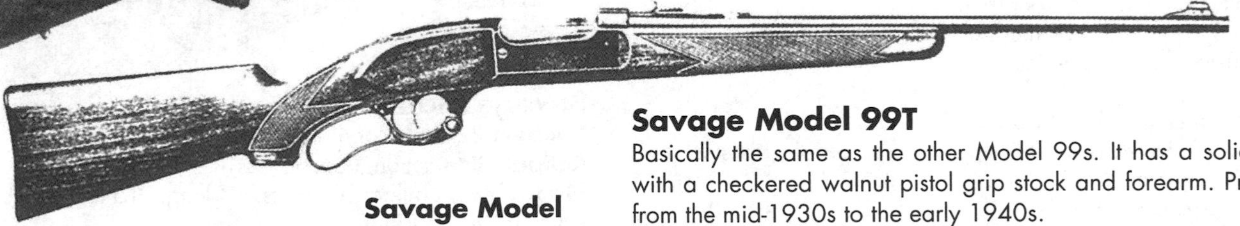

Savage Model 99T

Savage Model 99PE Presentation

Much like the Model 99DL except engraved receiver, hand checkered Monte Carlo stock and forearm. Produced from 1968 to 1970.

Estimated Value:	**Excellent:**	**$1,500.00**
	Very good:	**$1,200.00**

Savage Model 99T

Basically the same as the other Model 99s. It has a solid frame with a checkered walnut pistol grip stock and forearm. Produced from the mid-1930s to the early 1940s.

Estimated Value:	**Excellent:**	**$1,200.00**
	Very good:	**$ 960.00**

Savage Model 99DE Citation

A less elaborate example of the Model 99PE. Produced from 1968 to 1970.

Estimated Value:	**Excellent:**	**$1,000.00**
	Very good:	**$ 800.00**

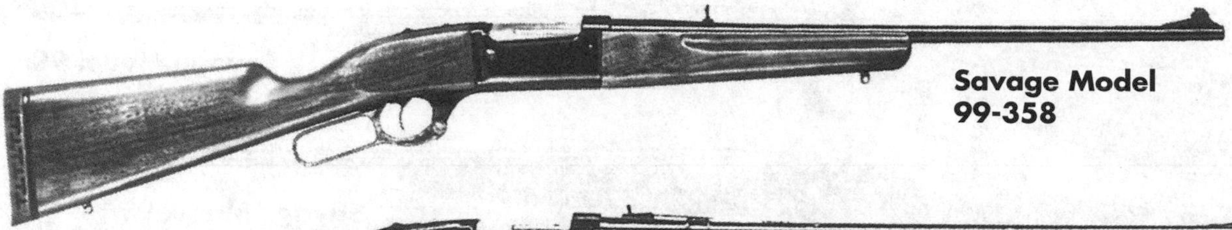

Savage Model 99-358

Savage Model 99DL

Savage Model 99C

Savage Model 99C

Caliber: 22-250, 243, 308, 7mm/08, (22-250 and 7mm/08 dropped in the 1980s)
Action: Hammerless lever action; cocking indicator
Magazine: 3- or 4-shot detachable clip
Barrel: 22"; chrome-moly steel
Sights: Detachable hooded ramp front; adjustable rear
Stock and Forearm: Checkered walnut semi-pistol grip, two-piece stock, and tapered forearm; Monte Carlo stock after 1982
Approximate wt.: 7½ lbs.
Comments: Made from 1965 to 1998.

Estimated Value:	**Excellent:**	**$750.00**
	Very good:	**$600.00**

Savage Model 99-358

Similar to the Model 99A in 358 caliber; forearm rounded; swivels; recoil pad. Made from the late 1970s to the early 1980s.

Estimated Value:	**Excellent:**	**$500.00**
	Very good:	**$400.00**

Savage Model 99-375

Similar to the Model 99-358 in 375 Win. caliber.

Estimated Value:	**Excellent:**	**$475.00**
	Very good:	**$380.00**

Savage Model 99DL

This is a late Model 99, in production from about 1960 to the mid-1970s. Basically the same as Model 99F with a Monte Carlo stock and swivels.

Estimated Value:	**Excellent:**	**$425.00**
	Very good:	**$340.00**

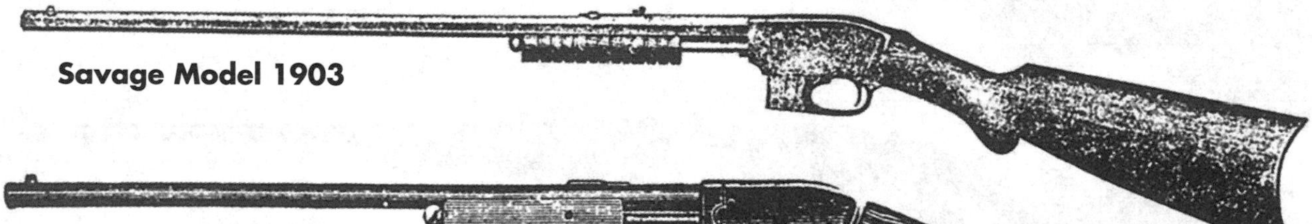

Savage Model 1903

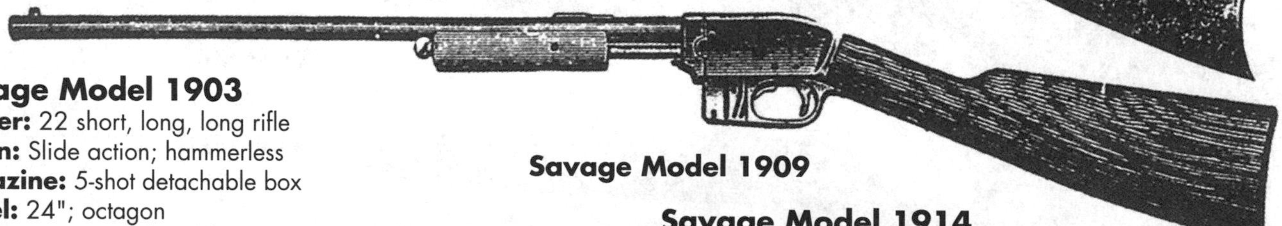

Savage Model 1909

Savage Model 1903

Caliber: 22 short, long, long rifle
Action: Slide action; hammerless
Magazine: 5-shot detachable box
Barrel: 24"; octagon
Sights: Open rear, bead front
Stock and Forearm: Checkered walnut pistol grip stock and grooved slide handle
Approximate wt.: 5 lbs.
Comments: This takedown model was produced from 1903 to 1922.

Estimated Value:	**Excellent:**	**$325.00**
	Very good:	**$260.00**

Savage Model 1909

A lighter version of the Model 1903 with a straight stock and forearm and a round 20" barrel. Discontinued about 1915.

Estimated Value:	**Excellent:**	**$300.00**
	Very good:	**$240.00**

Savage Model 1914

Caliber: 22 short, long, long rifle
Action: Slide action; hammerless
Magazine: Tubular; 20 shorts, 17 longs, 15 long rifles
Barrel: 24"; octagon or half octagon
Sights: Open rear, bead front
Stock and Forearm: Plain wood pistol grip stock and grooved slide handle
Approximate wt.: 5¾ lbs.
Comments: A takedown rifle produced from about 1915 until 1924.

Estimated Value:	**Excellent:**	**$325.00**
	Very good:	**$260.00**

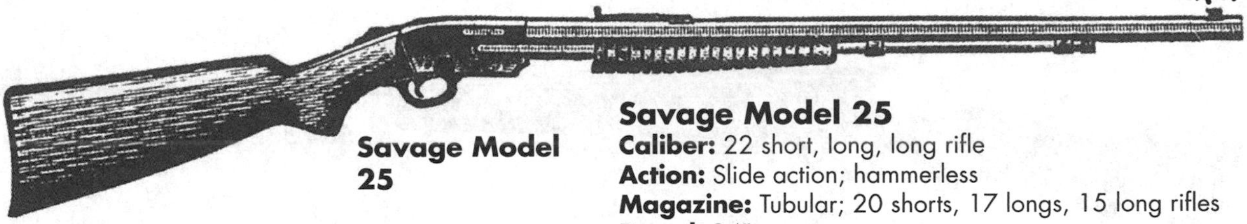

Savage Model 25

Savage Model 29

Similar to the Model 25 except pre-war models were checkered; barrel is round on post-war models. Made from 1929 until the late 1960s. Add $50.00 for pre-World War II models with octagon barrel.

Estimated Value: **Excellent:** **$375.00**
Very good: **$300.00**

Savage Model 25

Caliber: 22 short, long, long rifle
Action: Slide action; hammerless
Magazine: Tubular; 20 shorts, 17 longs, 15 long rifles
Barrel: 24"; octagon
Sights: Open rear, blade front
Stock and Forearm: Walnut pistol grip stock and grooved slide handle
Approximate wt.: 5¾ lbs.
Comments: A takedown model produced from the mid-1920s until 1929.

Estimated Value: **Excellent:** **$400.00**
Very good: **$320.00**

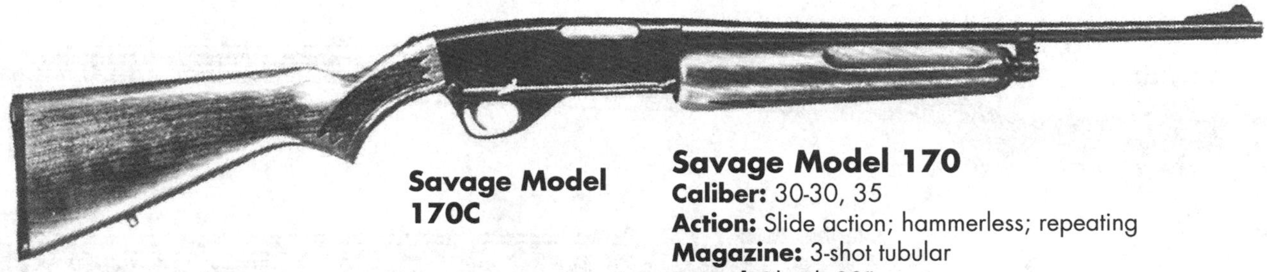

Savage Model 170C

Savage Model 170C

A carbine version of Model 170; not available with a Monte Carlo stock; 18½" barrel; not available in 35 caliber.

Estimated Value: **Excellent:** **$300.00**
Very good: **$240.00**

Savage Model 170

Caliber: 30-30, 35
Action: Slide action; hammerless; repeating
Magazine: 3-shot tubular
Barrel: Blued; 22"
Sights: Ramp front, folding leaf rear, hooded ramp after 1980
Stock and Forearm: Checkered walnut Monte Carlo semi-pistol grip stock and fluted slide handle; swivels
Approximate wt.: 6¾ lbs.
Comments: Made from the late 1970s to the early 1980s.

Estimated Value: **Excellent:** **$350.00**
Very good: **$280.00**

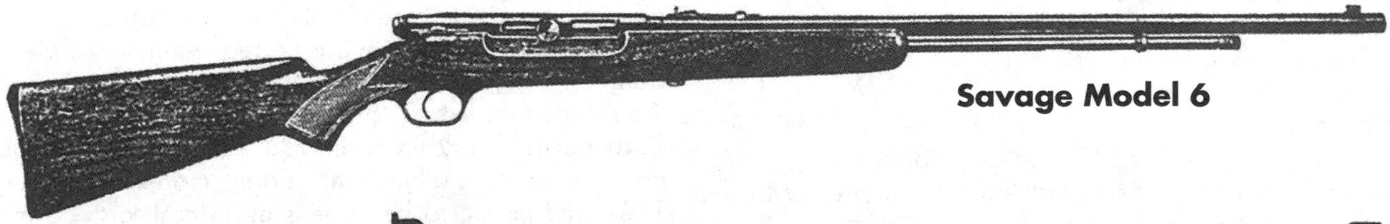

Savage Model 6

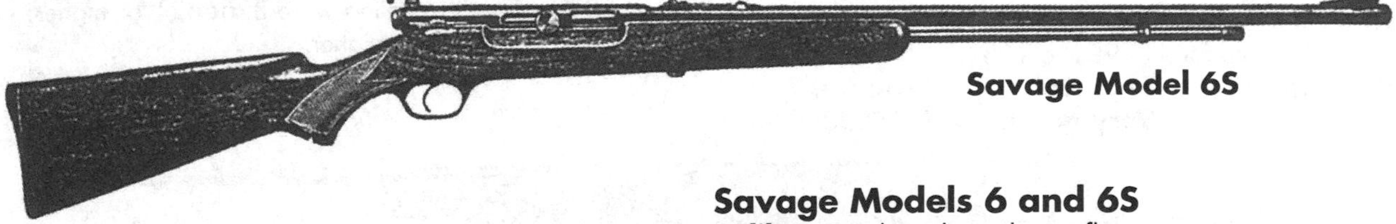

Savage Model 6S

Savage Model 1912

Caliber: 22 long rifle
Action: Semiautomatic; hammerless
Magazine: 7-shot detachable box
Barrel: 20" half octagon
Sights: Open rear, bead front
Stock and Forearm: Plain wood straight grip stock and forearm
Approximate wt.: 4½ lbs.
Comments: This takedown was Savage's first semiautomatic; discontinued in 1916.

Estimated Value: **Excellent:** **$425.00**
Very good: **$340.00**

Savage Models 6 and 6S

Caliber: 22 short, long, long rifle
Action: Semiautomatic
Magazine: Tubular; 21 shorts, 17 longs, 15 long rifles
Barrel: 24"
Sights: Open rear, bead front; Model 6S has peep rear, hooded front
Stock and Forearm: Checkered walnut pistol grip before World War II; plain walnut pistol grip after the war
Approximate wt.: 6 lbs.
Comments: A takedown model manufactured from 1938 until the late 1960s.

Estimated Value: **Excellent:** **$225.00**
Very good: **$180.00**

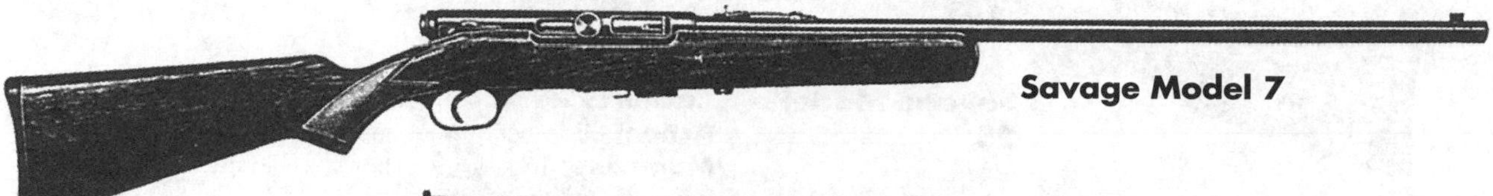
Savage Model 7

Savage Model 7S

Savage Models 7 and 7S

Basically the same as Models 6 and 6S except they are equipped with a 5-shot detachable box magazine. Produced from the late 1930s until the early 1950s.

Estimated Value: **Excellent:** **$170.00**
Very good: **$135.00**

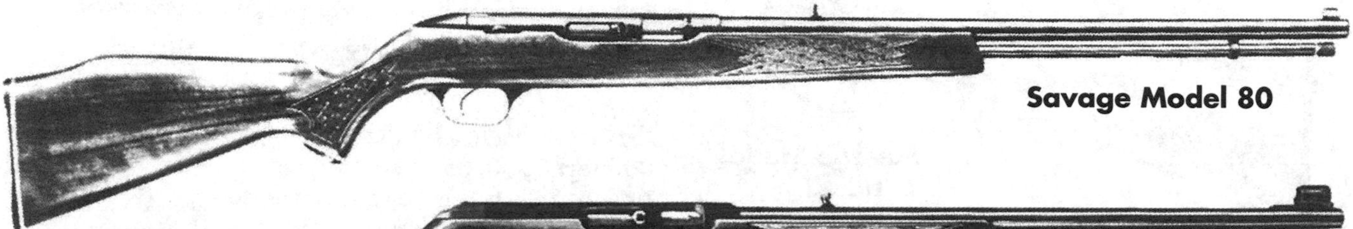
Savage Model 80

Savage Model 980DL

Savage Model 980DL

Caliber: 22 long rifle
Action: Semiautomatic
Magazine: 15-shot tubular
Barrel: Blued; 20"
Sights: Hooded ramp front, folding leaf adjustable rear
Stock and Forearm: Checkered walnut one-piece Monte Carlo semi-pistol grip stock and forearm
Approximate wt.: 6 lbs.
Comments: Produced from 1981 to 1984.
Estimated Value: **Excellent:** **$150.00**
Very good: **$120.00**

Savage Model 80

Caliber: 22 long rifle
Action: Semiautomatic
Magazine: 15-shot tubular
Barrel: Blued; 20"
Sights: Open rear, blade front
Stock and Forearm: Checkered walnut one-piece Monte Carlo pistol grip stock and forearm
Approximate wt.: 6 lbs.
Comments: Made from the mid- to the late 1970s. Due to a possible safety malfunction, certain models were recalled in 1982 and inspected by Stevens at no cost to the owner. Serial numbers that were recalled were B256621 or higher; C000001 or higher; D000001 or higher.
Estimated Value: **Excellent:** **$135.00**
Very good: **$110.00**

Savage Model 64G

Savage Model 64G

Caliber: 22 long rifle
Action: Semiautomatic, hammerless
Magazine: 10-shot detachable clip
Barrel: Blued; 20¼"
Sights: Bead front, adjustable rear
Stock and Forearm: Checkered wood, one-piece Monte Carlo stock and forearm
Approximate wt.: 5½ lbs.
Comments: Produced in the 1990s.
Estimated Value: **New (retail):** **$193.00**
Excellent: **$145.00**
Very good: **$115.00**

Savage Model 64F

Similar to the Model 64G with black synthetic stock and forearm. Add 23% for camouflage finish.

Estimated Value: **New (retail):** **$156.00**
Excellent: **$115.00**
Very good: **$ 95.00**

Savage Model 64FV

Savage Model 64GXP
Similar to the Model 64G with the addition of a 4x15mm factory-mounted scope.

Estimated Value:	**Excellent:**	**$135.00**
	Very good:	**$110.00**

Savage Model 64FXP
Similar to the Model 64F with the addition of a 4x15mm factory mounted scope.

Estimated Value:	**New (retail):**	**$167.00**
	Excellent:	**$125.00**
	Very good:	**$100.00**

Savage Model 64FV
Similar to the Model 64F except: has a 21" heavy barrel; no sights.

Estimated Value:	**Excellent:**	**$155.00**
	Very good:	**$125.00**

Savage Model 64FSS

Savage Model 64FVSS

Savage Model 64F

Savage Model 64FSS
Similar to the Model 64F with stainless steel receiver and barrel.

Estimated Value:	**Excellent:**	**$165.00**
	Very good:	**$130.00**

Savage Model 64F Camo
Similar to the Model 64F with camouflage finish.

Estimated Value:	**Excellent:**	**$140.00**
	Very good:	**$110.00**

Savage Model 64FVSS
Similar to the Model 64FV with stainless steel receiver and barrel.

Estimated Value:	**Excellent:**	**$200.00**
	Very good:	**$160.00**

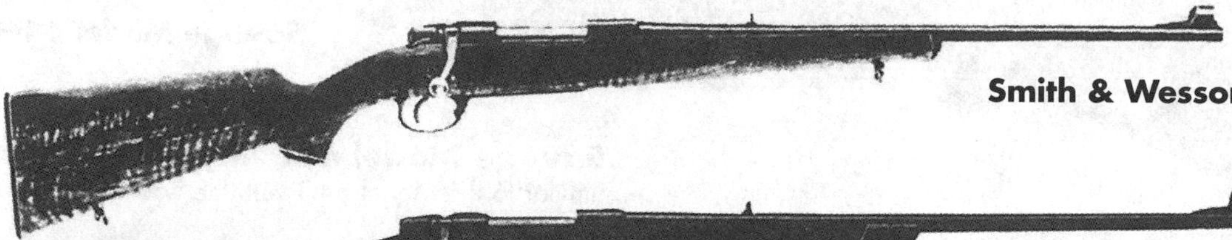

Smith & Wesson Model A

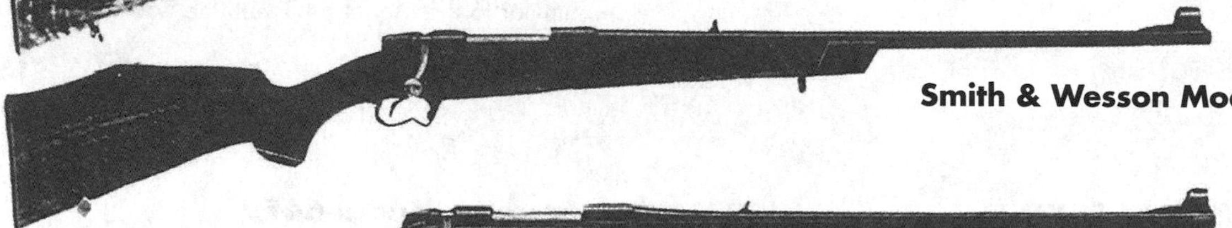

Smith & Wesson Model B

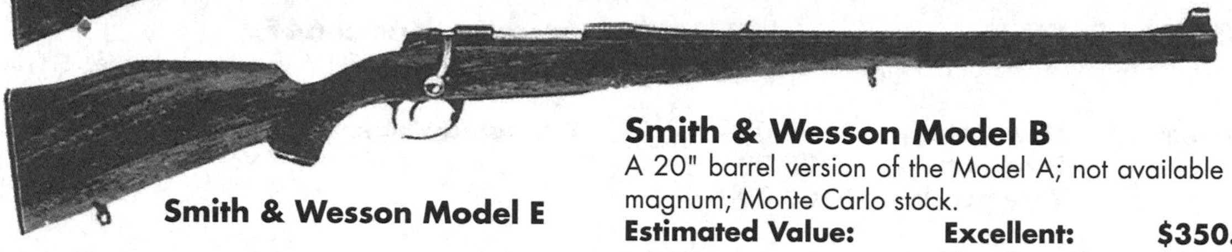

Smith & Wesson Model E

Smith & Wesson Model A

Caliber: 22-250, 243, 270, 308, 30-06, 7mm mag., 300 mag.
Action: Bolt action; repeating; adjustable trigger
Magazine: 5-shot box
Barrel: Blued; 23¾" tapered
Sights: Folding rear, hooded ramp front with silver bead
Stock and Forearm: Checkered walnut Monte Carlo one-piece pistol grip stock and tapered forearm
Approximate wt.: 7 lbs.
Comments: Made only in the early 1970s.

Estimated Value:	**Excellent:**	**$375.00**
	Very good:	**$300.00**

Smith & Wesson Model B

A 20" barrel version of the Model A; not available in 22-250 or magnum; Monte Carlo stock.

Estimated Value:	**Excellent:**	**$350.00**
	Very good:	**$280.00**

Smith & Wesson Model C

Same as the Model B except straight grip stock.

Estimated Value:	**Excellent:**	**$360.00**
	Very good:	**$285.00**

Smith & Wesson Model D

Same as the Model C with full-length forearm.

Estimated Value:	**Excellent:**	**$400.00**
	Very good:	**$320.00**

Smith & Wesson Model E

Same as the Model B with full-length forearm.

Estimated Value:	**Excellent:**	**$425.00**
	Very good:	**$340.00**

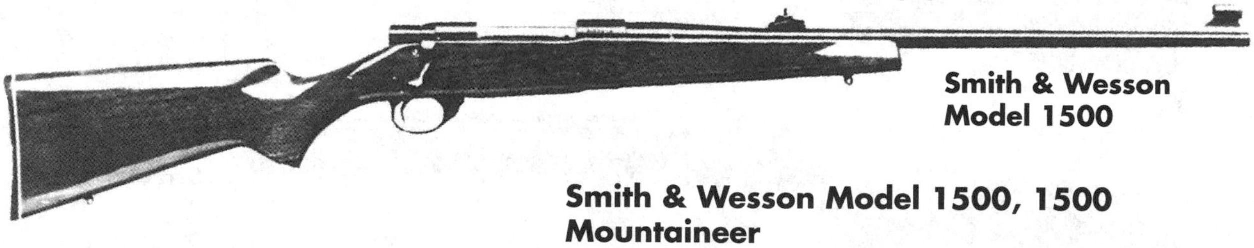

Smith & Wesson Model 1500

Smith & Wesson Model 1700LS Classic Hunter

Similar to the Model 1500 except: lightweight with lipped forearm; 5-shot magazine with removable floor plate; calibers 243 Win., 270 Win. and 30-06. Made in the mid-1980s.

Estimated Value:	**Excellent:**	**$425.00**
	Very good:	**$340.00**

Smith & Wesson Model 1500 Deluxe Varmint

Similar to the Model 1500 with a 22" heavy barrel, adjustable trigger; 222 Rem., 22-250 Rem. and 223 Rem. calibers. Produced from 1982 to 1985. Add 3% for parkerized finish.

Estimated Value:	**Excellent:**	**$400.00**
	Very good:	**$320.00**

Smith & Wesson Model 1500, 1500 Mountaineer

Caliber: 30-06, 270 Win., 243 Win., 25-06 Rem., 7mm Rem. mag., 300 Win. mag.; 222 Rem.; 223 Rem. and 308 Win. added in 1982
Action: Bolt action; hammerless; repeating
Magazine: 5-shot box
Barrel: 23½"
Sights: None; Optional folding rear, hooded ramp front
Stock and Forearm: Checkered walnut pistol grip, one-piece stock and forearm; swivels; recoil pad on mag.
Approximate wt.: 7 lbs.
Comments: Discontinued in 1985. Add 4% for magnum; 19% for Deluxe Model; 7% for sights.

Estimated Value:	**Excellent:**	**$375.00**
	Very good:	**$300.00**

Standard Model G

Caliber: 25-35, 30-30, 25 Rem., 30 Rem., 35 Rem.
Action: Semiautomatic; gas-operated; hammerless; can also be operated as slide action by closing gas port
Magazine: 4- or 5-shot tubular
Barrel: Blued; 22"
Sights: Bead front, open rear
Stock and Forearm: Wood straight grip stock and slide handle
Approximate wt.: 7¾ lbs.
Comments: Made in the early 1900s, the Standard Model G was one of the first gas-operated autoloaders available.
Estimated Value: **Excellent:** **$800.00**
Very good: **$640.00**

Standard Model M

A slide action version of the Standard Model G.
Estimated Value: **Excellent:** **$700.00**
Very good: **$560.00**

Stevens Model No. 14½ Little Scout

Stevens Model No. 14 Little Scout

Caliber: 22 long rifle
Action: Pivoted block; exposed hammer; single-shot
Magazine: None
Barrel: 18"; round
Sights: Blade front; open rear
Stock and Forearm: Plain walnut one-piece straight grip stock and forearm
Approximate wt.: 2½ lbs.
Comments: Made from 1904 to about 1912; then it was replaced by Model 14½.
Estimated Value: **Excellent:** **$425.00**
Very good: **$340.00**

Stevens Model No. 14½ Little Scout

Similar to the Model No. 14 Little Scout except: rolling block action; two-piece stock, and short forearm. Produced from 1912 to World War II.
Estimated Value: **Excellent:** **$400.00**
Very good: **$320.00**

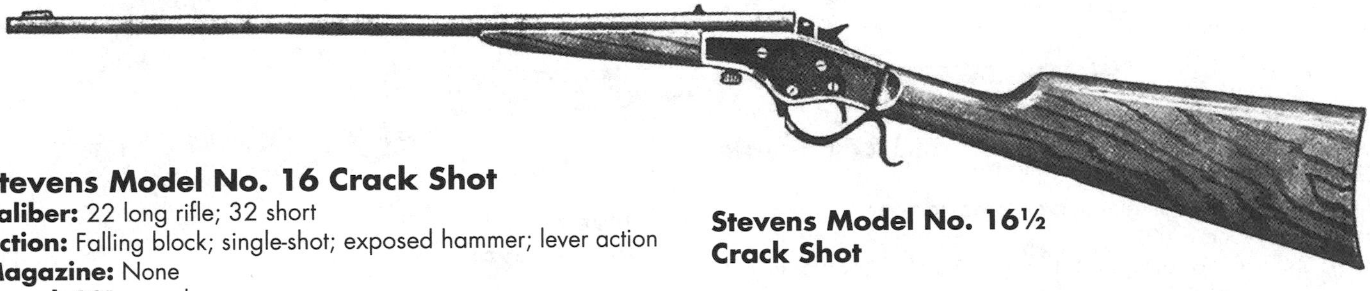

Stevens Model No. 16½ Crack Shot

Stevens Model No. 16 Crack Shot

Caliber: 22 long rifle; 32 short
Action: Falling block; single-shot; exposed hammer; lever action
Magazine: None
Barrel: 20"; round
Sights: Open rear, blade front
Stock and Forearm: Plain walnut straight grip stock with slightly lipped forearm
Approximate wt.: 3¾ lbs.
Comments: Produced until 1912 when it was replaced by Model No. 26.
Estimated Value: **Excellent:** **$475.00**
Very good: **$380.00**

Stevens Model No. 16½ Crack Shot

Same as the Model No. 16 except it is smooth bore for shot cartridges. Produced from 1907 to 1912.
Estimated Value: **Excellent:** **$450.00**
Very good: **$360.00**

Stevens Tip Up Model No. 2

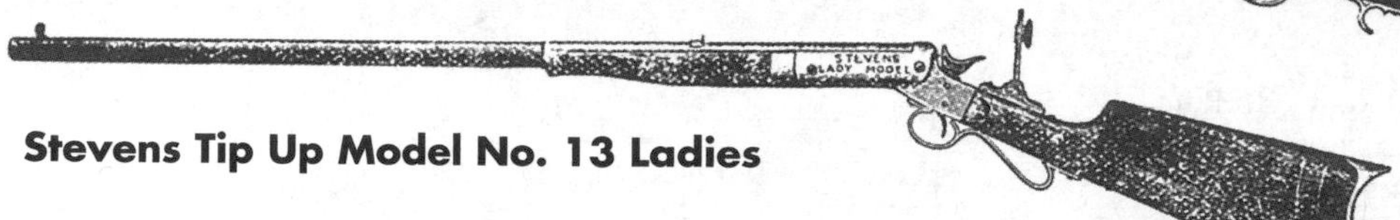

Stevens Tip Up Model No. 13 Ladies

Stevens Model No. 15 Maynard Jr.

Stevens Model No. 15 Maynard Jr.

Caliber: 22 long rifle or short
Action: Lever tip up; exposed hammer
Magazine: None
Barrel: 18"; part octagon
Sights: Open rear, blade front
Stock and Forearm: Plain walnut, straight stock and short forearm
Approximate wt.: 2¾ lbs.
Comments: Made to compete with cheap imports. Produced from 1901 to 1910.

Estimated Value:	**Excellent:**	**$500.00**
	Very good:	**$400.00**

Stevens Model No. 15½ Maynard Jr.

Same as the Model No. 15 except: smooth bore for 22 long rifle shot cartridges.

Estimated Value:	**Excellent:**	**$525.00**
	Very good:	**$420.00**

Stevens Tip Up Model Nos. 2, 5, 6, 7, 8, 9, 11 Ladies, and 13 Ladies

Caliber: RF 22 long rifles, 25 Stevens, 32 long (in Model No. 11)
Action: Single-shot, tip up; exposed hammer
Magazine: None
Barrel: 24" octagon for No. 2; 28" half octagon optional on No. 7; all others 24" half octagon
Sights: Beach combination front, open rear; peep on No. 5, No. 7 and No. 13; blade front, open rear on No. 2; open on No. 11
Stock and Forearm: Walnut straight stock and forearm; no forearm on No. 2 and No. 5
Approximate wt.: 5½ to 6½ lbs.
Comments: Produced until they were replaced in 1902 by a line of falling block rifles.

Estimated Value:	**Excellent:**	**$500.00**
	Very good:	**$400.00**

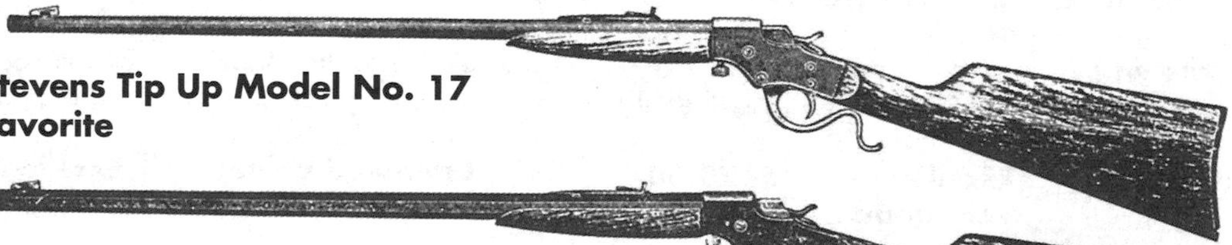

Stevens Tip Up Model No. 17 Favorite

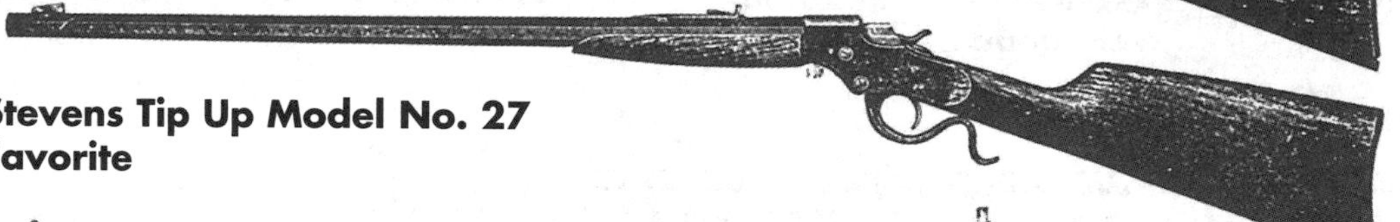

Stevens Tip Up Model No. 27 Favorite

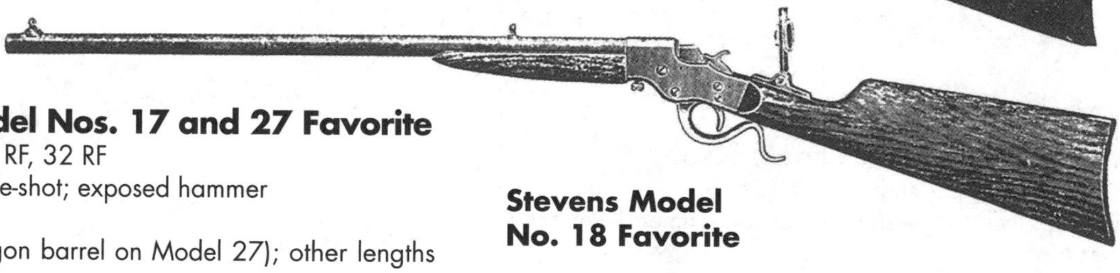

Stevens Model No. 18 Favorite

Stevens Tip Up Model Nos. 17 and 27 Favorite

Caliber: 22 long rifle, 25 RF, 32 RF
Action: Lever action; single-shot; exposed hammer
Magazine: None
Barrel: 24"; round (octagon barrel on Model 27); other lengths available as option
Sights: Open rear, Rocky Mountain front
Stock and Forearm: Plain walnut straight grip stock, short tapered forearm
Approximate wt.: 4 to 5 lbs.
Comments: Takedown model produced from the 1890s until the mid-1930s.

Estimated Value:	**Excellent:**	**$500.00**
	Very good:	**$400.00**

Stevens Model Nos. 18 and 28 Favorite

Same as Model No. 17 except it has a Beach combination front sight, Vernier peep rear sight, and leaf middle sight. Model 28 has octagon barrel.

Estimated Value:	**Excellent:**	**$525.00**
	Very good:	**$420.00**

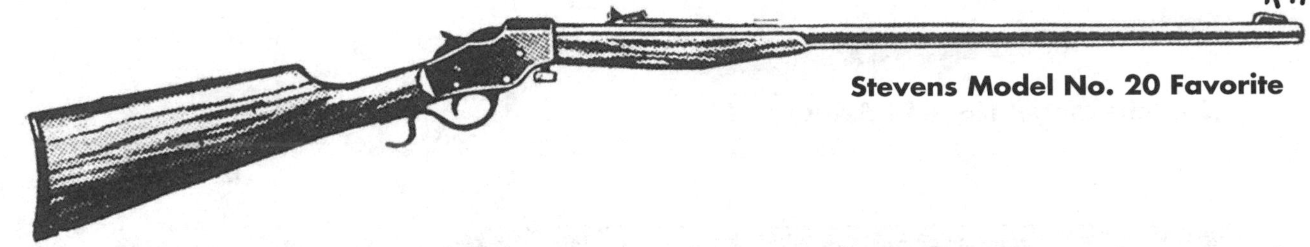

Stevens Model No. 20 Favorite

Same as the Model No. 17 except the barrel is smooth bore for 22 RF and 32 RF shot cartridges.

Estimated Value: **Excellent:** **$500.00**
Very good: **$400.00**

Stevens Model Nos. 19 and 29 Favorite

Same as the Model No. 17 except it has Lyman front sight, leaf middle sight, and Lyman combination rear sight. Model 29 has octagon barrel.

Estimated Value: **Excellent:** **$525.00**
Very good: **$420.00**

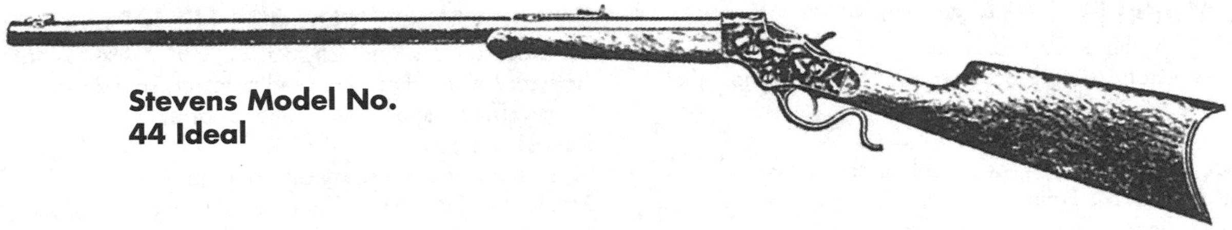
Stevens Model No. 44 Ideal

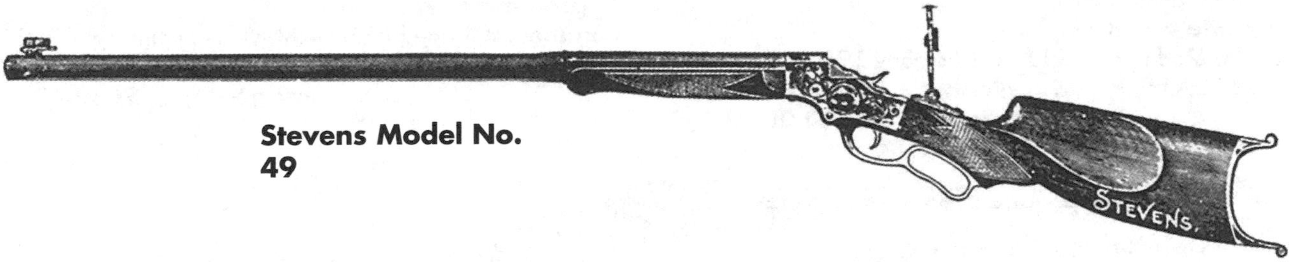

Stevens Model No. 49

Stevens Model No. 51

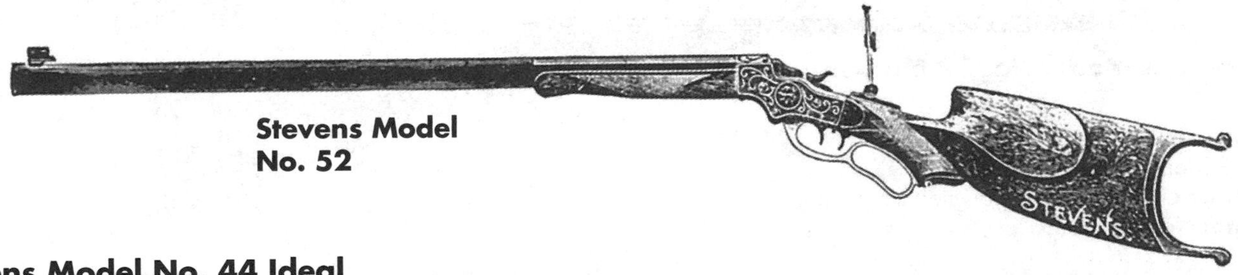

Stevens Model No. 52

Stevens Model No. 44 Ideal

Caliber: 22 long rifle; 25 RF, 25-20 SS, 32-20, 32-40, 38-55, 44-40
Action: Lever action rolling-block; exposed hammer; single-shot
Magazine: None
Barrel: 24" or 26"; round, octagon, or half octagon
Sights: Open rear, Rocky Mountain front
Stock and Forearm: Plain walnut, straight grip
Approximate wt.: 7 lbs.
Comments: Produced from the late 1890s until the early 1930s; a takedown model.

Estimated Value: **Excellent:** **$1,000.00**
Very good: **$ 800.00**

Stevens Model No. 44½ Ideal

Same as the Model 44 except it has a falling block action. Discontinued in 1916.

Estimated Value: **Excellent:** **$1,200.00**
Very good: **$ 950.00**

Stevens Model Nos. 45 to 54

Structurally the same as Model 44. They differ in engravings and finishes and are generally fancy models that bring high prices. Produced until World War I; target sights and stocks.

Estimated Value: **Excellent:** **$1,250.00 – 3,000.00**
Very good: **$1,000.00 – 2,500.00**

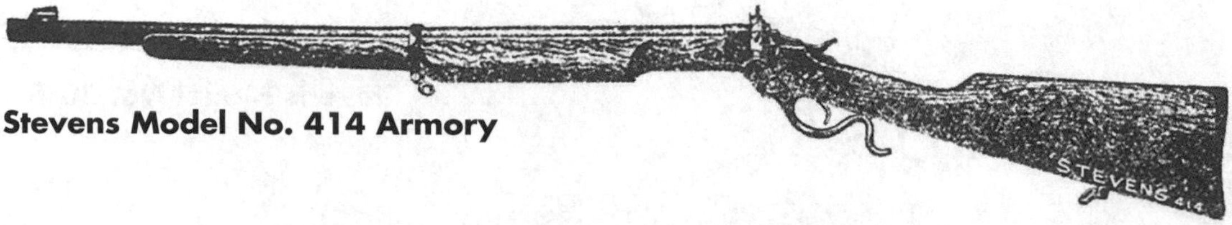

Stevens Model No. 414 Armory

Stevens Model No. 425 High Power

Stevens Model No. 414 Armory

Caliber: 22 long rifle or 22 short only
Action: Lever action rolling block; exposed hammer single-shot
Magazine: None
Barrel: 26"; heavy round
Sights: Rocky Mountain front, adjustable receiver rear
Stock and Forearm: Plain walnut straight grip, military stock, and forearms; bands; swivels
Approximate wt.: 8 lbs.
Comments: Made from 1912 until the early 1930s.

Estimated Value:	**Excellent:**	**$800.00**
	Very good:	**$640.00**

Stevens Model No. 425 High Power

Caliber: Rimless Rem. 25, 30, 32, 35; smokeless flat nose
Action: Lever action; exposed hammer; single extractor
Magazine: 5-shot tubular, under barrel
Barrel: 22"; round
Sights: Post front, adjustable sporting rear
Stock and Forearm: Plain walnut straight grip stock and forearm
Approximate wt.: 7 lbs.
Comments: Made for about five years beginning in 1911.

Estimated Value:	**Excellent:**	**$800.00**
	Very good:	**$640.00**

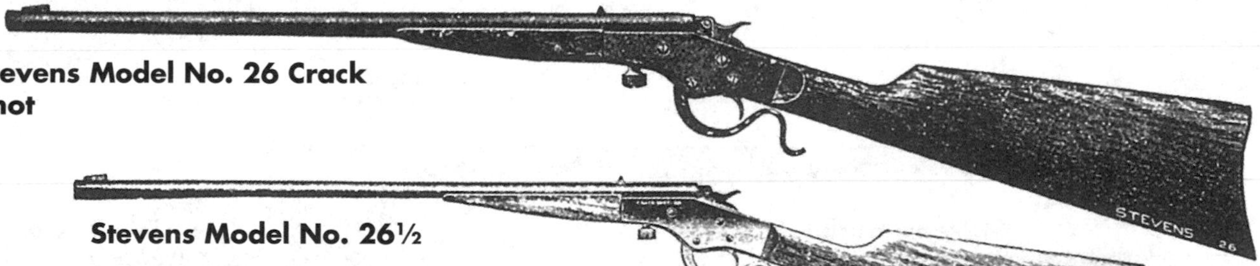

Stevens Model No. 26 Crack Shot

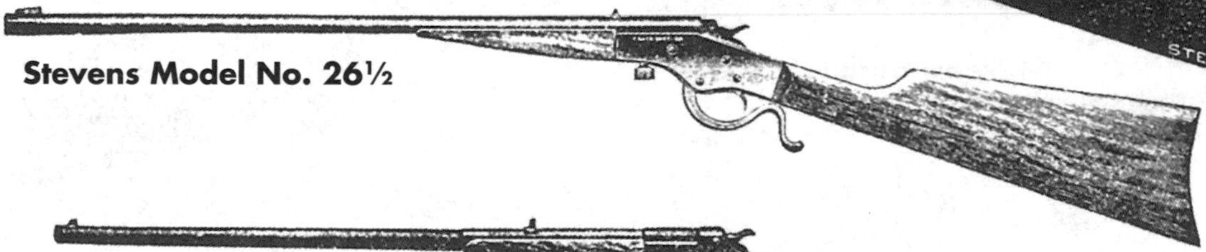

Stevens Model No. 26½

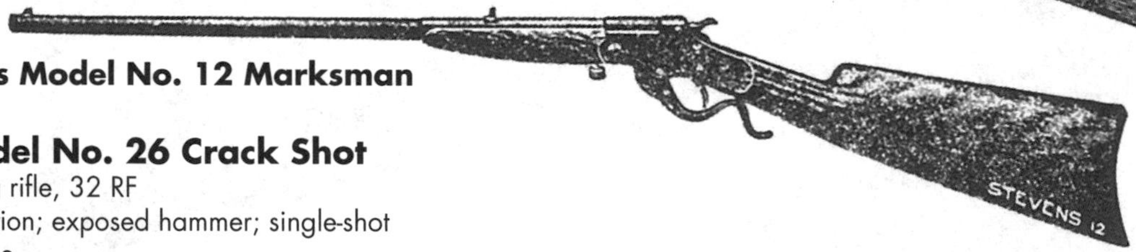

Stevens Model No. 12 Marksman

Stevens Model No. 26 Crack Shot

Caliber: 22 long rifle, 32 RF
Action: Lever action; exposed hammer; single-shot
Magazine: None
Barrel: 18", 22"
Sights: Open rear, blade front
Stock and Forearm: Plain walnut straight grip stock and tapered forearm
Approximate wt.: 3¼ to 3½ lbs.
Comments: Produced from 1913 until just prior to World War II.

Estimated Value:	**Excellent:**	**$450.00**
	Very good:	**$360.00**

Stevens Model No. 26½

Same as the Model No. 26 except: smooth bore for shot cartridges.

Estimated Value:	**Excellent:**	**$500.00**
	Very good:	**$400.00**

Stevens Model No. 12 Marksman

Caliber: 22 long rifle, 25 RF, 32 RF
Action: Lever action tip up; exposed hammer
Magazine: None, single-shot
Barrel: 20"; round
Sights: Bead front, open rear
Stock and Forearm: Plain walnut straight grip stock and short tapered forearm
Approximate wt.: 4 lbs.
Comments: Replaced the Maynard Jr. Made from 1912 to 1916.

Estimated Value:	**Excellent:**	**$425.00**
	Very good:	**$340.00**

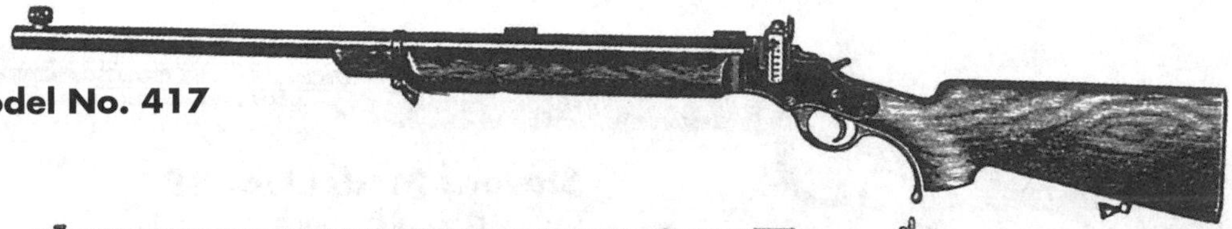

Stevens Model No. 417

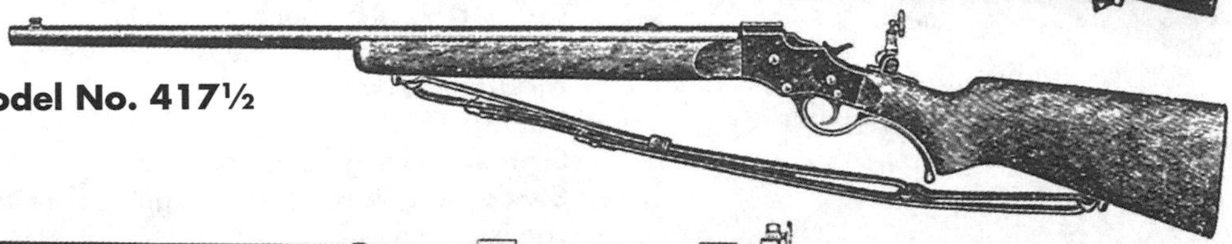

Stevens Model No. 417½

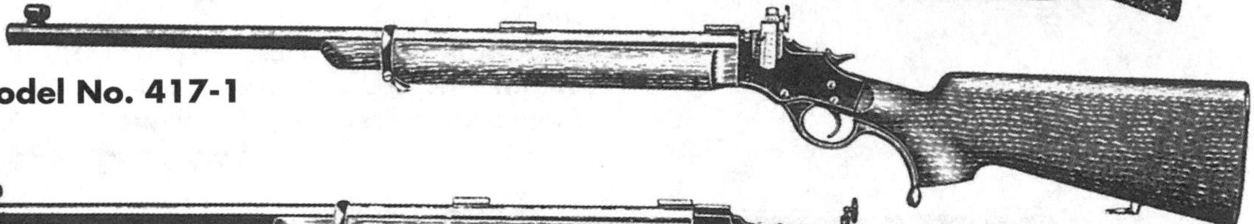

Stevens Model No. 417-1

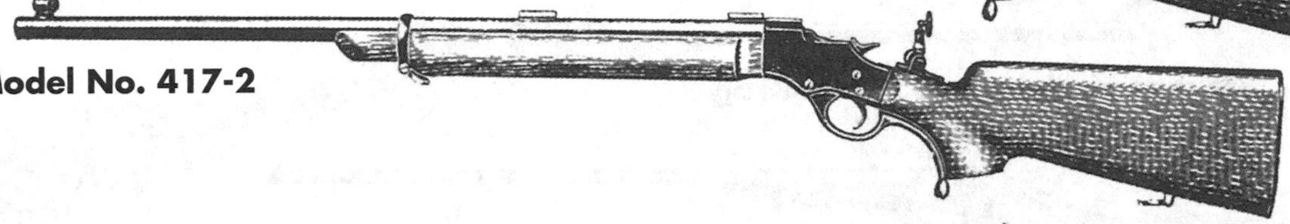

Stevens Model No. 417-2

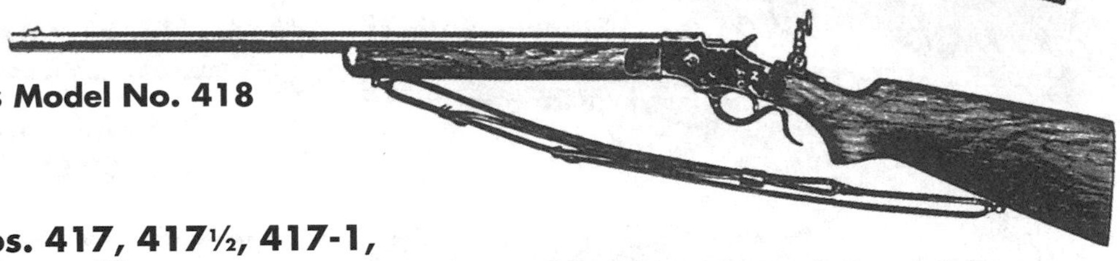

Stevens Model No. 418

Stevens Model Nos. 417, 417½, 417-1, 417-2, 417-3 Walnut Hill

Caliber: 22 long rifle; 22 WRF, 25 Stevens
Action: Lever action; exposed hammer; single-shot
Magazine: None
Barrel: 28" or 29"; heavy
Sights: 417: Lyman 52L extension rear; 417½: Lyman 144 tang peep and folding center; 417-1: Lyman 48L rear; 417-2: 144 rear; 417-3: no sights
Stock and Forearm: Plain walnut pistol grip stock and forearm; bands, swivels
Approximate wt.: 8¼ to 10½ lbs.
Comments: Made from the early 1930s until the late 1940s. Models differ in sights.

Estimated Value:	**Excellent:**	**$1,350.00**
	Very good:	**$1,075.00**

Stevens Model Nos. 418, 418½ Walnut Hill

Caliber: No. 418: 22 long rifle, 22 short; No. 418½: 22 WRF or 25 Stevens RF
Action: Lever action; exposed hammer; single-shot
Magazine: None
Barrel: 26"
Sights: Lyman 144 tang peep, blade front; 418½: Lyman 2A tang peep, bead front
Stock and Forearm: Plain walnut pistol grip stock and forearm; swivels
Approximate wt.: 6½ lbs.
Comments: Made from the early 1930s to just before World War II.

Estimated Value:	**Excellent:**	**$800.00**
	Very good:	**$640.00**

Stevens Model No. 72 Crackshot

Stevens Model No. 72 Crackshot

Caliber: 22 short, long, long rifle
Action: Lever action falling-block; single-shot
Magazine: None
Barrel: 22"; octagon
Sights: Sporting front, open rear
Stock and Forearm: Plain walnut straight grip stock and tapered forearm; case-hardened receiver
Approximate wt.: 4½ lbs.
Comments: Made from the early 1970s to 1988.

Estimated Value:	**Excellent:**	**$200.00**
	Very good:	**$160.00**

Stevens Model No. 89

Stevens Model No. 89

Caliber: 22 short, long, long rifle
Action: Lever action; exposed hammer; single-shot
Magazine: None
Barrel: 18½"; round
Sights: Sporting front, open rear
Stock and Forearm: Straight walnut stock and forearm with carbine band
Approximate wt.: 5 lbs.
Comments: Produced from the mid-1970s to the mid-1980s.

Estimated Value:	**Excellent:**	**$125.00**
	Very good:	**$100.00**

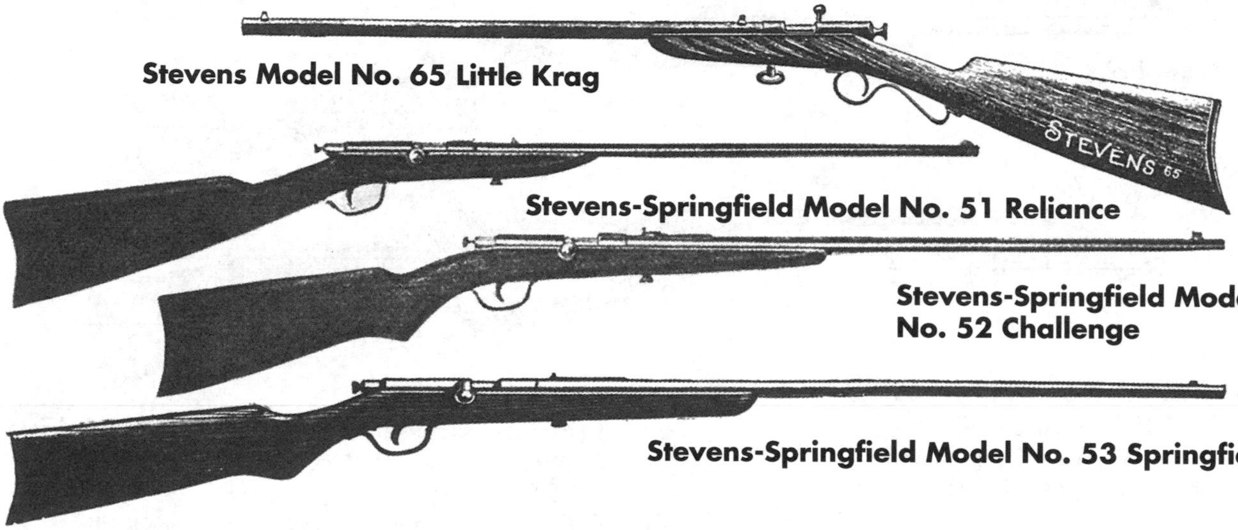

Stevens Model No. 65 Little Krag

Stevens-Springfield Model No. 51 Reliance

Stevens-Springfield Model No. 52 Challenge

Stevens-Springfield Model No. 53 Springfield Jr.

Stevens Model No. 65 Little Krag

Caliber: 22 short, long, long rifle
Action: Bolt action; single-shot
Magazine: None
Barrel: 20"; round
Sights: Bead front, fixed peep or open rear
Stock and Forearm: Plain walnut one-piece straight grip stock and forearm
Approximate wt.: 3¼ lbs.
Comments: Produced from 1903 to about 1910.

Estimated Value:	**Excellent:**	**$500.00**
	Very good:	**$400.00**

Stevens-Springfield Model No. 52 Challenge

Caliber: 22 short, long, long rifle
Action: Bolt action; single-shot
Magazine: None
Barrel: 22"; round
Sights: Bead front, adjustable sporting rear
Stock and Forearm: Plain walnut one-piece pistol grip stock and forearm
Approximate wt.: 3½ lbs.
Comments: Takedown, produced from the early 1930s to just before World War II.

Estimated Value:	**Excellent:**	**$175.00**
	Very good:	**$140.00**

Stevens-Springfield Model No. 51 Reliance

Caliber: 22 short, long, long rifle
Action: Bolt action; single-shot
Magazine: None
Barrel: 20"; round
Sights: Open rear, blade front
Stock and Forearm: Plain walnut one-piece straight grip stock and forearm
Approximate wt.: 3 lbs.
Comments: Takedown, made for about five years beginning in 1930.

Estimated Value:	**Excellent:**	**$200.00**
	Very good:	**$160.00**

Stevens-Springfield Model No. 53 Springfield Jr.

Caliber: 22 short, long, long rifle
Action: Bolt action; single-shot
Magazine: None
Barrel: 24"
Sights: Bead front, adjustable sporting rear
Stock and Forearm: Plain walnut semi-pistol grip stock and forearm
Approximate wt.: 4½ lbs.
Comments: Produced from 1930 to the late 1940s.

Estimated Value:	**Excellent:**	**$150.00**
	Very good:	**$120.00**

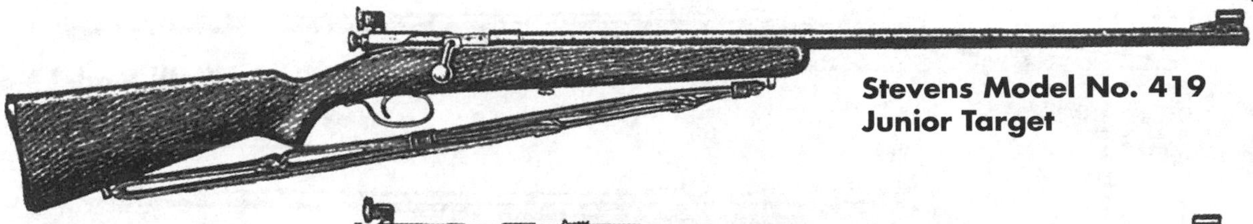

Stevens Model No. 419
Junior Target

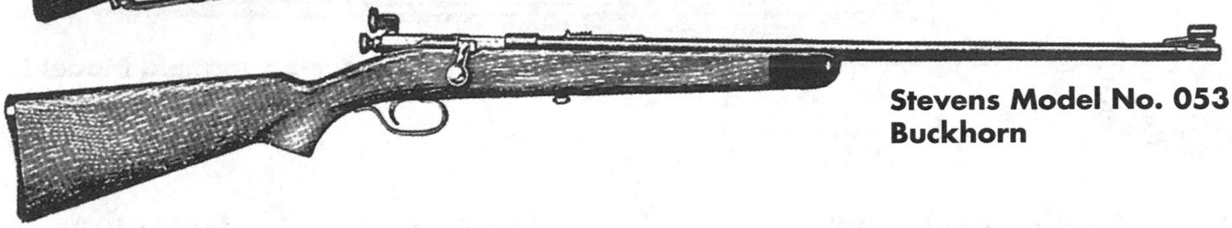

Stevens Model No. 053
Buckhorn

Stevens Model No. 419 Junior Target

Caliber: 22 short, long, long rifle
Action: Bolt action; single-shot
Magazine: None
Barrel: 26"
Sights: Blade front, peep rear
Stock and Forearm: Plain walnut pistol grip stock with grooved forearm; swivels
Approximate wt.: 5½ lbs.
Comments: Made from 1932 until 1936.

Estimated Value:	**Excellent:**	**$250.00**
	Very good:	**$200.00**

Stevens Model Nos. 53 and 053 Buckhorn

Caliber: 22 short, long, long rifle; 22WRF; 25 Stevens RF
Action: Bolt action; single-shot
Magazine: None
Barrel: 24"; blued; round
Sights: Model No. 053 hooded ramp front, open middle, peep receiver; Model 53 open rear, bead front
Stock and Forearm: Plain walnut pistol grip stock and forearm
Approximate wt.: 5½ lbs.
Comments: Made from the mid-1930s to the late 1940s.

Estimated Value:	**Excellent:**	**$200.00**
	Very good:	**$160.00**

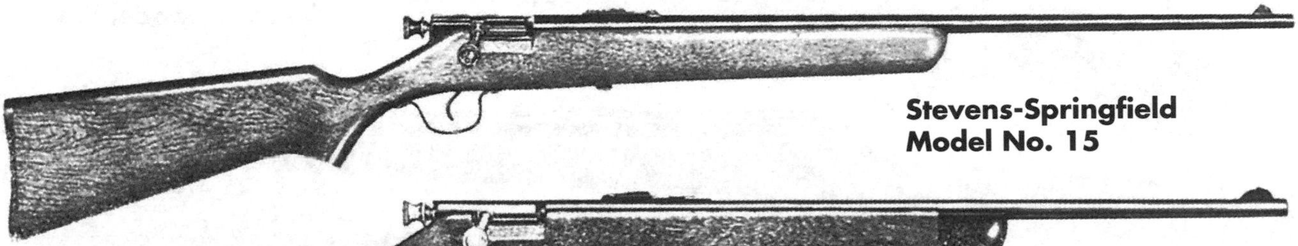

Stevens-Springfield
Model No. 15

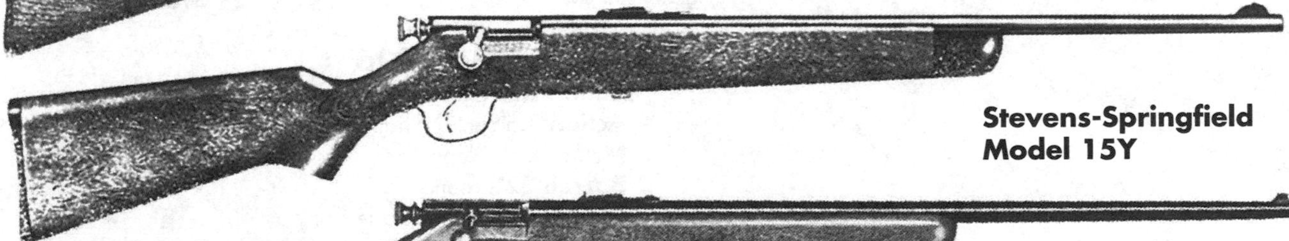

Stevens-Springfield
Model 15Y

Stevens Model No. 120

Stevens Model No. 120

Caliber: 22 short, long, long rifle
Action: Bolt action; single-shot; pull hammer
Magazine: None
Barrel: Blued; 24"; round
Sights: Blade front, adjustable rear
Stock and Forearm: Plain hardwood one-piece semi-pistol grip stock and forearm
Approximate wt.: 5 lbs.
Comments: Produced in the late 1970s to the early 1980s.

Estimated Value:	**Excellent:**	**$110.00**
	Very good:	**$ 85.00**

Stevens-Springfield Model Nos. 15, Stevens 15, and 15Y

Caliber: 22 short, long, long rifle
Action: Bolt action; single-shot
Magazine: None
Barrel: Stevens-Springfield Model No. 15 22"; Stevens 15, 24"; Stevens 15Y, 21"
Sights: Open rear; bead front
Stock and Forearm: Plain walnut pistol grip, Stevens 15Y; short butt stock, black tipped forearm
Approximate wt.: 4 to 5 lbs.
Comments: Stevens-Springfield Model No. 15 produced from the late 1930s to the late 1940s; Stevens No. 15, made from the late 1940s to the mid-1960s; Stevens 15Y, made from the late 1950s to the mid-1960s.

Estimated Value:	**Excellent:**	**$125.00**
	Very good:	**$100.00**

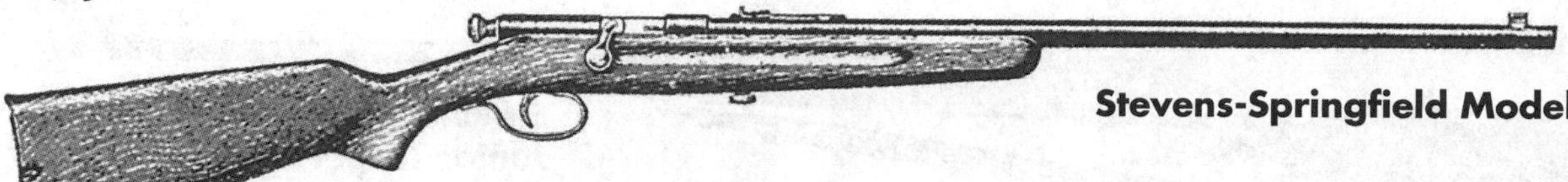

Stevens-Springfield Model No. 82

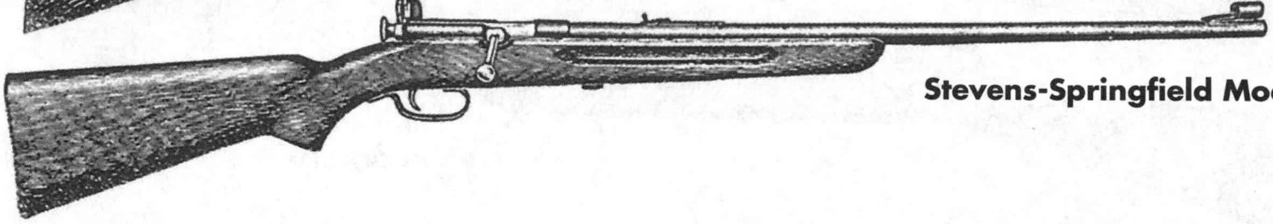

Stevens-Springfield Model No. 83

Stevens-Springfield Model No. 82
Caliber: 22 short, long, long rifle
Action: Bolt action; single-shot
Magazine: None
Barrel: 22"; round
Sights: Open rear, bead front
Stock and Forearm: Plain walnut pistol grip stock, groove in forearm
Approximate wt.: 4 lbs.
Comments: Made from the mid-1930s to 1940.
Estimated Value: **Excellent:** **$175.00**
Very good: **$140.00**

Stevens-Springfield Model No. 83
Caliber: 22 short, long, long rifle, 22 WRF, 25 Stevens RF
Action: Bolt action; single-shot
Magazine: None
Barrel: 24"; round
Sights: Peep rear, open mid, hooded ramp front
Stock and Forearm: Plain walnut pistol grip stock with groove in forearm
Approximate wt.: 4½ lbs.
Comments: Made from the mid-1930s to 1940.
Estimated Value: **Excellent:** **$175.00**
Very good: **$140.00**

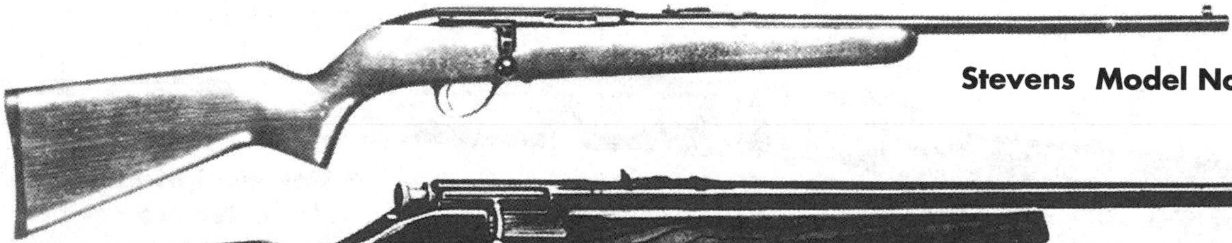

Stevens Model No. 73

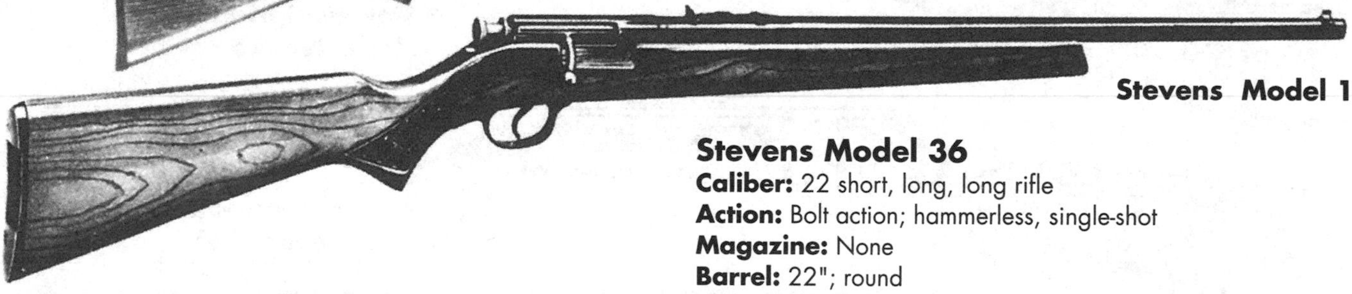

Stevens Model 125

Stevens Model 125
Caliber: 22 short, long, long rifle
Action: Bolt action; single-shot
Magazine: None
Barrel: Blued; 22"; round
Sights: Sporting front, open rear with elevator
Stock and Forearm: Checkered hardwood one-piece semi-pistol grip stock and forearm
Approximate wt.: 5 lbs.
Comments: Discontinued in the mid-1980s.
Estimated Value: **Excellent:** **$105.00**
Very good: **$ 85.00**

Stevens Model 125Y
A youth version of the Model 125 with shorter stock. Discontinued in the early 1980s.
Estimated Value: **Excellent:** **$110.00**
Very good: **$ 90.00**

Stevens Model 36
Caliber: 22 short, long, long rifle
Action: Bolt action; hammerless, single-shot
Magazine: None
Barrel: 22"; round
Sights: Open rear, blade front
Stock and Forearm: Hardwood, one-piece semi-pistol grip stock and forearm
Approximate wt.: 5 lbs.
Comments: Produced from 1984 to 1985.
Estimated Value: **Excellent:** **$100.00**
Very good: **$ 80.00**

Stevens Model Nos. 73 and 73Y
Caliber: 22 short, long, long rifle
Action: Bolt action; single-shot
Magazine: None
Barrel: 20" on Model No. 73; 18" on Model No. 73Y
Sights: Sporting front, open rear
Stock and Forearm: Plain walnut pistol grip; short stock on Model No. 73Y
Approximate wt.: Model No. 73 – 4¾ lbs.; Model No. 73Y – 4½ lbs.
Comments: Made from 1965 to the early 1980s.
Estimated Value: **Excellent:** **$100.00**
Very good: **$ 80.00**

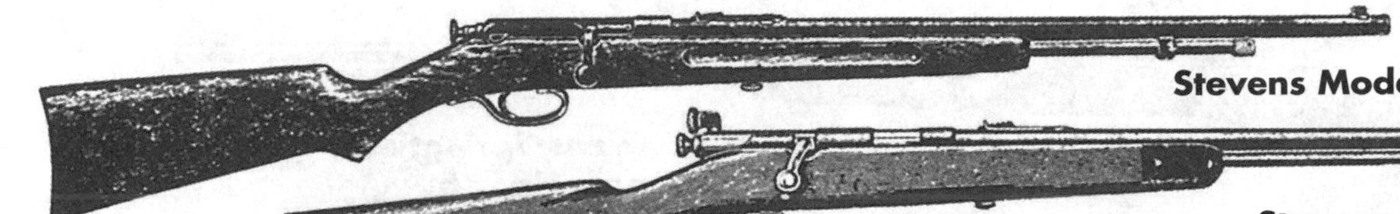

Stevens Model No. 66 Buckhorn

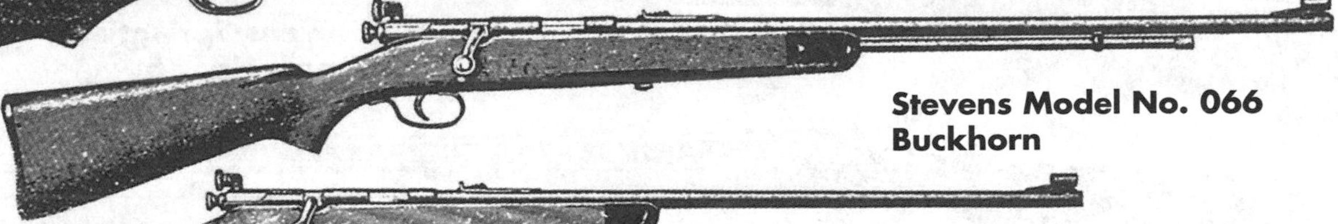

Stevens Model No. 066 Buckhorn

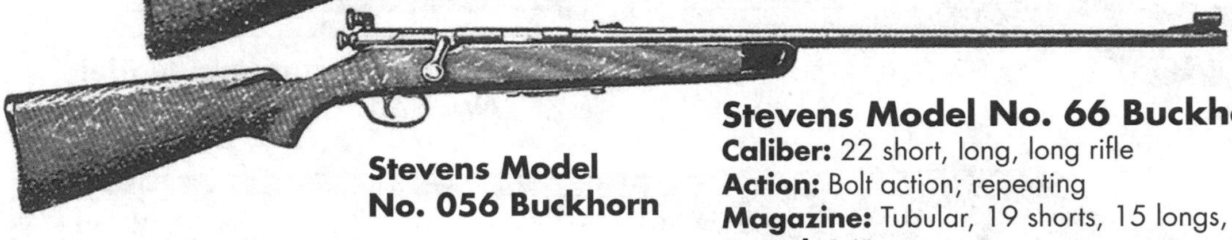

Stevens Model No. 056 Buckhorn

Stevens Model Nos. 56 and 056 Buckhorn

Caliber: 22 short, long, long rifle
Action: Bolt action; repeating
Magazine: 5-shot clip
Barrel: 24"
Sights: Model No. 56: bead front, open rear; Model No. 056 Buckhorn: hooded ramp front, open middle receiver peep
Stock and Forearm: Plain walnut pistol grip stock and black tipped forearm
Approximate wt.: 6 lbs.
Comments: Made from the mid-1930s to the late 1940s.

Estimated Value:	**Excellent:**	**$220.00**
	Very good:	**$175.00**

Stevens Model No. 66 Buckhorn

Caliber: 22 short, long, long rifle
Action: Bolt action; repeating
Magazine: Tubular, 19 shorts, 15 longs, 13 long rifles
Barrel: 24"
Sights: Open rear, bead front
Stock and Forearm: Plain walnut semi-pistol grip stock and forearm
Approximate wt.: 5 lbs.
Comments: Made from the 1920s to the late 1940s.

Estimated Value:	**Excellent:**	**$145.00**
	Very good:	**$115.00**

Stevens Model No. 066 Buckhorn

Same as the Model No. 66 except: hooded ramp front sight; open middle sight; receiver peep sight. Made from the mid-1930s until the late 1940s.

Estimated Value:	**Excellent:**	**$200.00**
	Very good:	**$160.00**

Stevens Model No. 322

Stevens Model No. 322, 322S

Caliber: 22 Hornet
Action: Bolt action; repeating
Magazine: 5-shot clip
Barrel: 21"; round
Sights: Ramp front, open rear; Model No. 322S has peep rear
Stock and Forearm: Plain walnut pistol grip stock and forearm
Approximate wt.: 6¾ lbs.
Comments: Made from the late 1940s to the early 1950s.

Estimated Value:	**Excellent:**	**$275.00**
	Very good:	**$220.00**

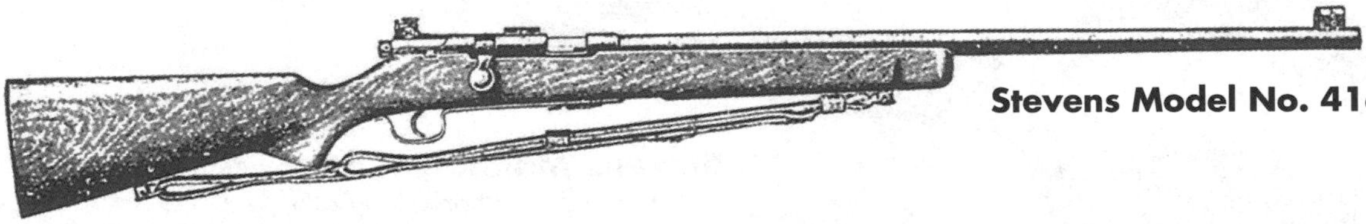

Stevens Model No. 416

Stevens Model No. 416

Caliber: 22 long rifle
Action: Bolt action; repeating
Magazine: 5-shot clip
Barrel: 26" heavy
Sights: Receiver peep, hooded ramp front
Stock and Forearm: Plain walnut pistol grip stock and forearm
Approximate wt.: 9½ lbs.
Comments: Made from the late 1930s to the late 1940s.

Estimated Value:	**Excellent:**	**$400.00**
	Very good:	**$320.00**

Stevens Model No. 325 and 325S

Caliber: 30-30
Action: Bolt action; repeating
Magazine: 3-shot clip
Barrel: 21"; round
Sights: Open rear, bead front; Model No. 325S peep rear
Stock and Forearm: Walnut pistol grip stock and forearm
Approximate wt.: 6¾ lbs.
Comments: Made from the late 1940s to the early 1950s.

Estimated Value:	**Excellent:**	**$400.00**
	Very good:	**$320.00**

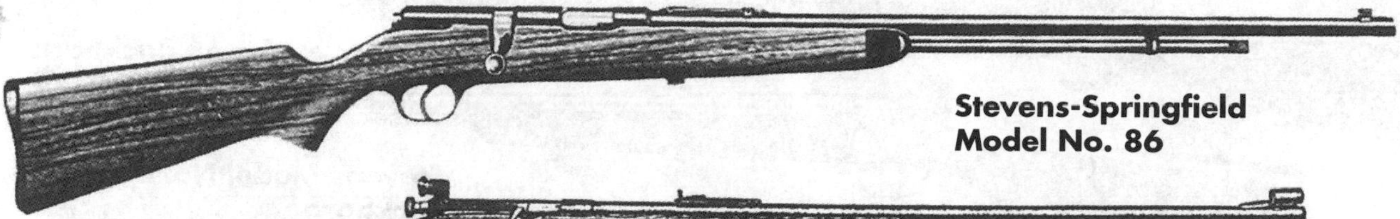

Stevens-Springfield Model No. 86

Stevens-Springfield Model No. 086

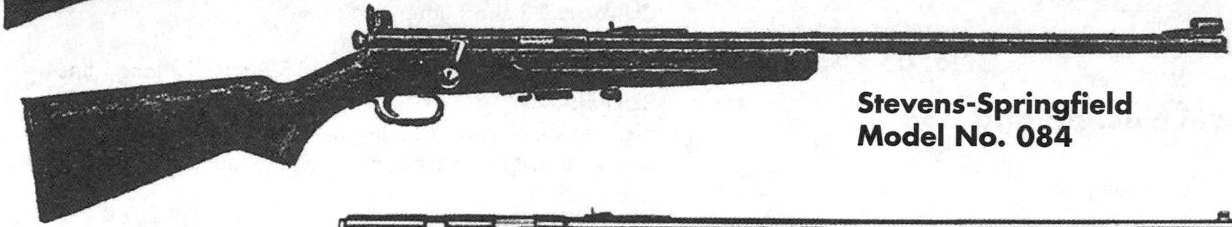

Stevens-Springfield Model No. 084

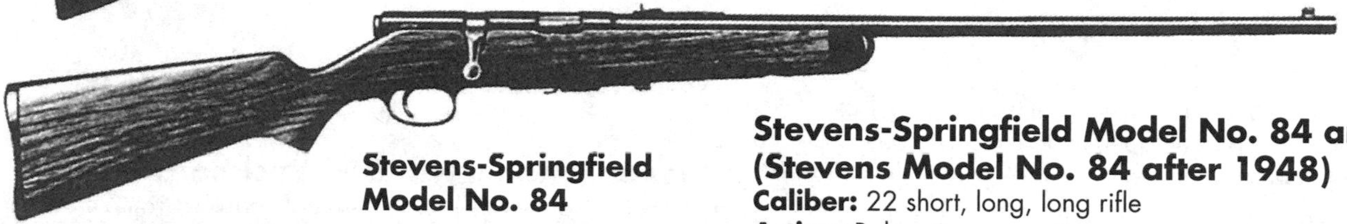

Stevens-Springfield Model No. 84

Stevens-Springfield Model No. 86, 086 (Stevens Model No. 86 after 1948)

Model No. 86 is the same as the Model No. 84 except: a tubular magazine that holds 21 shorts, 17 longs, 15 long rifles. Made from the mid-1930s until the mid-1960s. Model No. 86 Stevens or Model No. 086 Stevens is the same as the Model No. 84 or Model No. 084 Stevens except tubular magazines.

Estimated Value:	**Excellent:**	**$200.00**
	Very good:	**$160.00**

Stevens-Springfield Model No. 84 and 084 (Stevens Model No. 84 after 1948)

Caliber: 22 short, long, long rifle
Action: Bolt action; repeating
Magazine: 5-shot clip
Barrel: 24"; round
Sights: Model No. 84: bead front, open rear; Model No. 84 Stevens or Model No. 084 peep rear and hooded ramp front
Stock and Forearm: Plain walnut pistol grip stock and forearm; black tip on forearm of Model No. 84
Approximate wt.: 6 lbs.
Comments: Made from early 1940 until the mid-1960s.

Estimated Value:	**Excellent:**	**$200.00**
	Very good:	**$160.00**

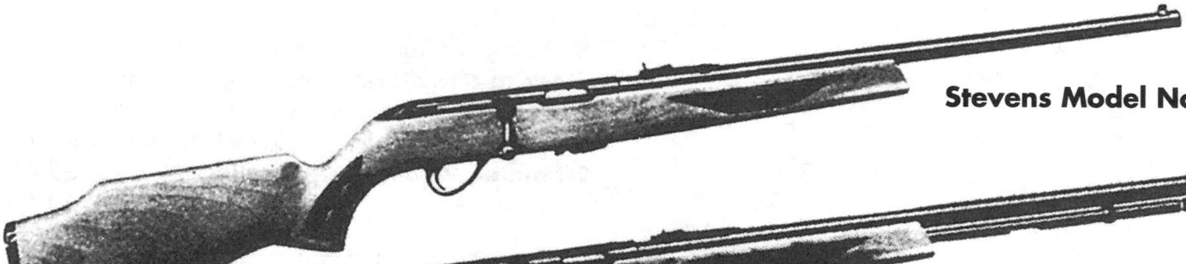

Stevens Model No. 34

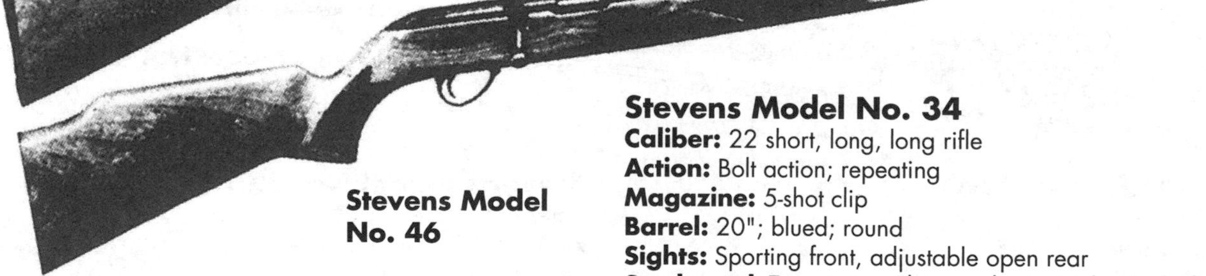

Stevens Model No. 46

Stevens Model No. 34

Caliber: 22 short, long, long rifle
Action: Bolt action; repeating
Magazine: 5-shot clip
Barrel: 20"; blued; round
Sights: Sporting front, adjustable open rear
Stock and Forearm: Plain walnut pistol grip before 1969; checkered Monte Carlo after 1969
Approximate wt.: 5½ lbs.
Comments: Made from the mid-1960s to the early 1980s.

Estimated Value:	**Excellent:**	**$120.00**
	Very good:	**$ 95.00**

Stevens Model No. 46

Similar to the Model No. 34 except tubular magazine. Discontinued in the late 1960s.

Estimated Value:	**Excellent:**	**$125.00**
	Very good:	**$100.00**

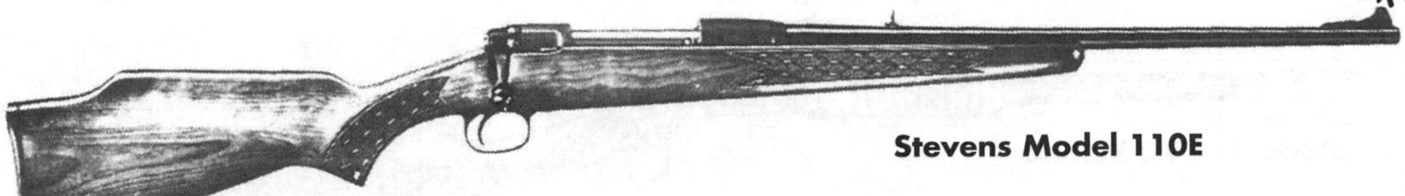

Stevens Model 110E

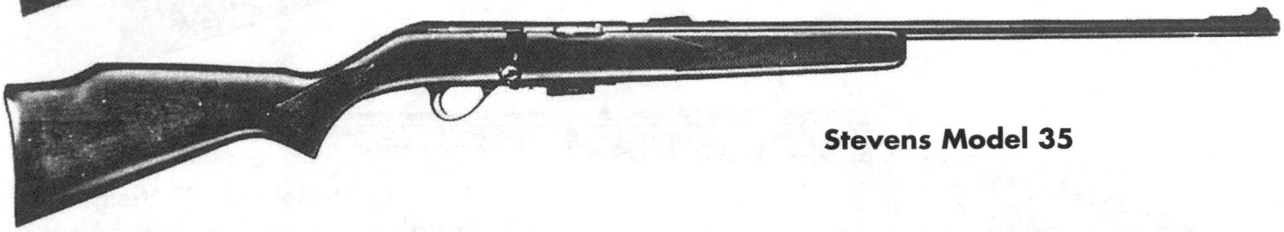

Stevens Model 35

Stevens Models 110E and 110ES

Caliber: 243, 30-06, 308
Action: Bolt action; hammerless; repeating
Magazine: 4-shot box, internal
Barrel: Blued; 22"
Sights: Ramp front, open rear; Model 110ES has 4X scope
Stock and Forearm: Checkered hardwood one-piece Monte Carlo semi-pistol grip stock and forearm
Approximate wt.: 7 lbs.
Comments: Made from the late 1970s to 1981 as Stevens; made in 1982 as Savage. Add 10% for Model 110ES.
Estimated Value: **Excellent:** **$275.00**
Very good: **$220.00**

Stevens Models 35 and 35M

Caliber: 22 short, long, long rifle
Action: Bolt action; repeating
Magazine: 4-shot detachable clip
Barrel: Blued; 22"
Sights: Ramp front, sporting rear with step elevator; grooved for scope
Stock and Forearm: Checkered hardwood Monte Carlo one-piece semi-pistol grip stock and forearm
Approximate wt.: 4¾ lbs.
Comments: Produced from 1982 to 1985.
Estimated Value: **Excellent:** **$110.00**
Very good: **$ 90.00**

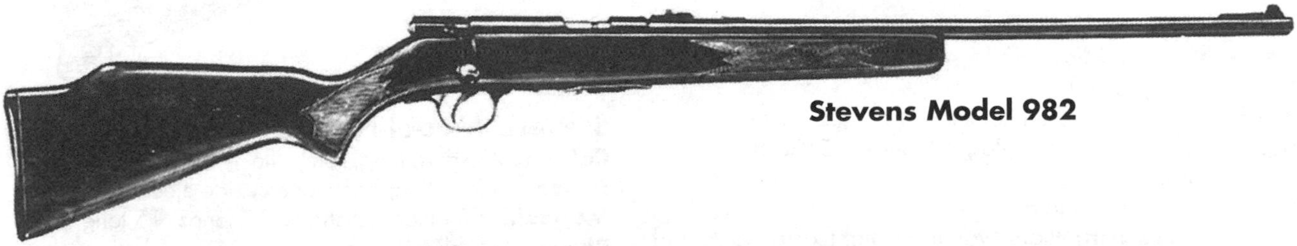

Stevens Model 982

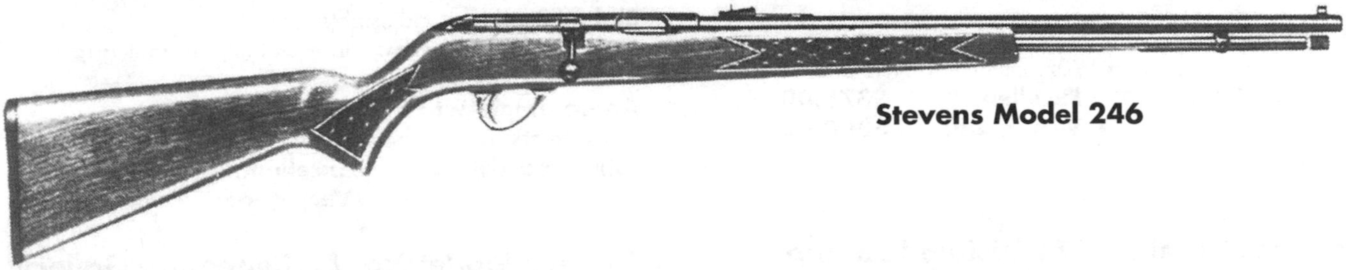

Stevens Model 246

Stevens Model 246

Caliber: 22 short, long, long rifle
Action: Bolt action; repeating
Magazine: Tubular, 22 shorts, 17 longs, 15 long rifles
Barrel: Blued; 20"
Sights: Blade front, elevator open rear
Stock and Forearm: Checkered hardwood one-piece semi-pistol grip stock and forearm
Approximate wt.: 5 lbs.
Comments: Produced in the late 1970s.
Estimated Value: **Excellent:** **$130.00**
Very good: **$105.00**

Stevens Model 982

Caliber: 22 short, long, long rifle
Action: Bolt action; repeating
Magazine: 5-shot detachable clip; 10-shot available
Barrel: Blued; 22"
Sights: Ramp front, open rear with elevator
Stock and Forearm: Checkered hardwood one-piece Monte Carlo semi-pistol grip stock and forearm
Approximate wt.: 5¾ lbs.
Comments: Advertised in 1981 only.
Estimated Value: **Excellent:** **$135.00**
Very good: **$110.00**

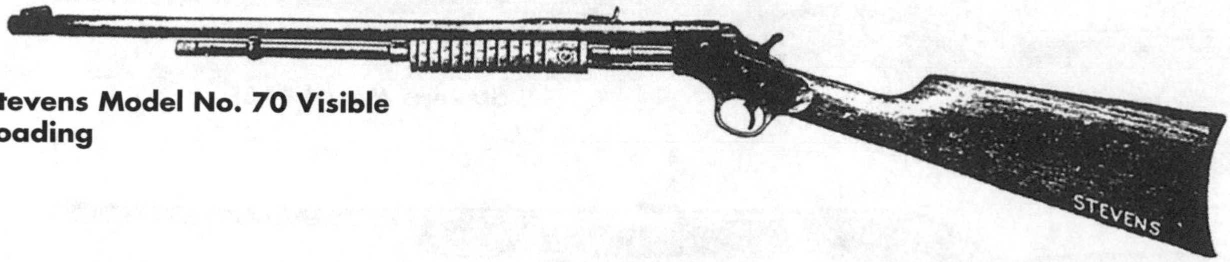

Stevens Model No. 70 Visible Loading

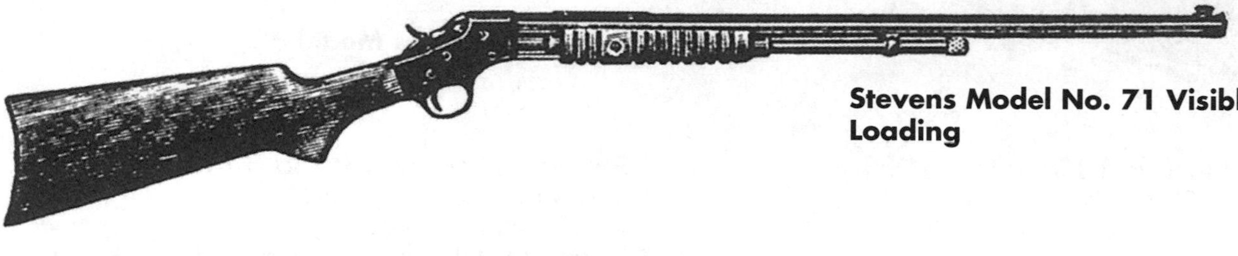

Stevens Model No. 71 Visible Loading

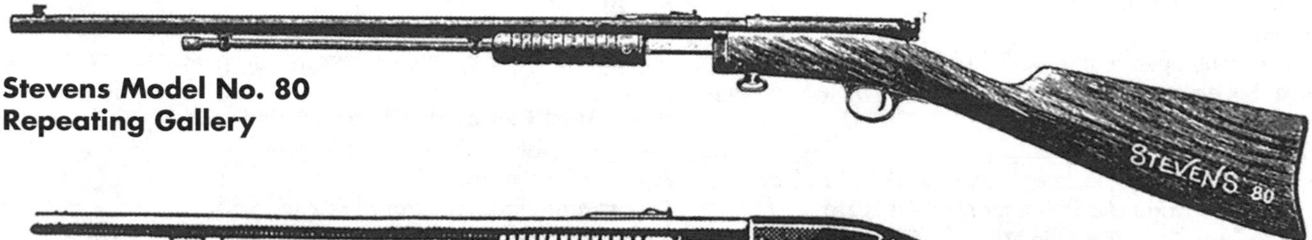

Stevens Model No. 80 Repeating Gallery

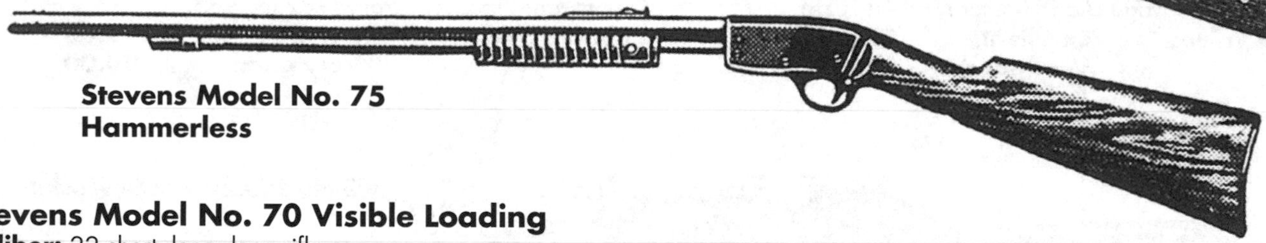

Stevens Model No. 75 Hammerless

Stevens Model No. 70 Visible Loading

Caliber: 22 short, long, long rifle
Action: Slide action; exposed hammer
Magazine: Tubular; 11 long rifles, 13 longs, 15 shorts
Barrel: 20" or 22"; round
Sights: Open rear, bead front
Stock and Forearm: Plain walnut straight grip stock and grooved slide handle
Approximate wt.: 4½ lbs.
Comments: Made from 1907 until the early 1930s.

Estimated Value:	**Excellent:**	**$375.00**
	Very good:	**$300.00**

Stevens Model No. 71 Visible Loading

Caliber: 22 short, long, long rifle
Action: Slide action; exposed hammer
Magazine: Tubular; 15 shorts, 13 longs, 11 long rifles
Barrel: 24"; octagon; blued
Sights: Bead front, adjustable flat-top sporting rear
Stock and Forearm: Plain walnut pistol grip stock and grooved slide handle
Approximate wt.: 5 lbs.
Comments: This replaced the No. 70; discontinued prior to World War II.

Estimated Value:	**Excellent:**	**$325.00**
	Very good:	**$260.00**

Stevens Model No. 75 Hammerless

Caliber: 22 short, long, long rifle
Action: Slide action; hammerless; side ejector
Magazine: Tubular, 20 shorts, 17 longs, 15 long rifles
Barrel: 24"; blued
Sights: Bead front, adjustable rear
Stock and Forearm: Plain walnut, straight grip stock and grooved slide handle
Approximate wt.: 5¼ lbs.
Comments: Made from the early 1930s until World War II.

Estimated Value:	**Excellent:**	**$300.00**
	Very good:	**$240.00**

Stevens Model No. 80 Repeating Gallery

Caliber: 22 short
Action: Slide action; hammerless
Magazine: 16-shot tubular
Barrel: 24"; round
Sights: Open rear, bead front
Stock and Forearm: Plain walnut straight grip stock and grooved forearm
Approximate wt.: 5¼ lbs.
Comments: Takedown made for about five years beginning in 1906.

Estimated Value:	**Excellent:**	**$425.00**
	Very good:	**$340.00**

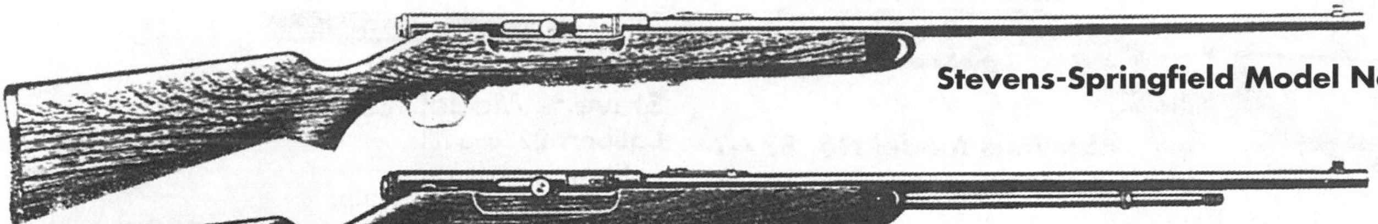

Stevens-Springfield Model No. 85

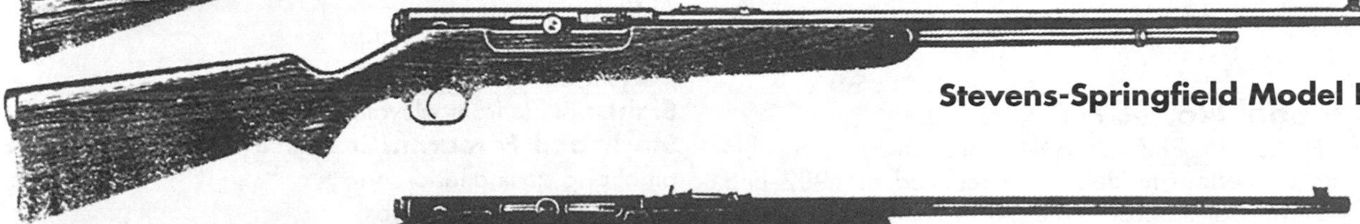

Stevens-Springfield Model No. 87

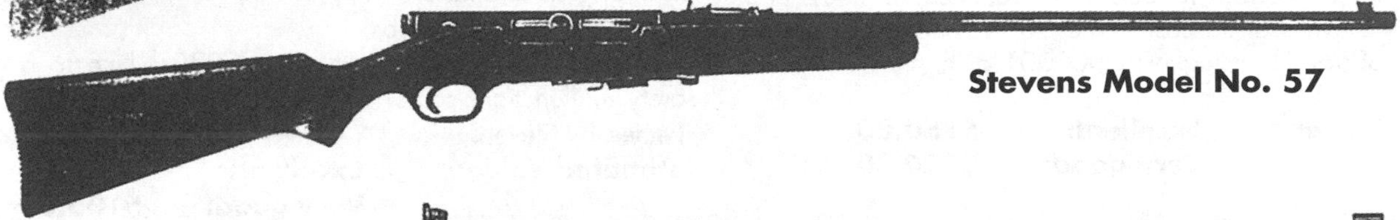

Stevens Model No. 57

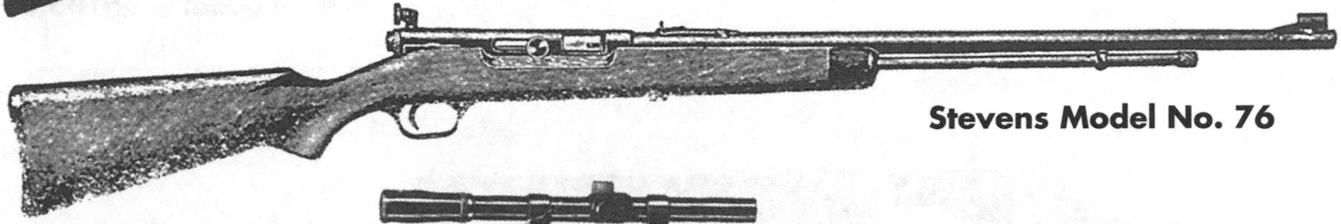

Stevens Model No. 76

Stevens Model No. 987T

Stevens-Springfield Model No. 85, 085 (Stevens Model No. 85 after 1948)

Caliber: 22 long rifle
Action: Semiautomatic; repeating
Magazine: 5-shot clip
Barrel: 24"; blued
Sights: Open rear, bead front on 85; hooded ramp front and peep rear on Model Nos. 085 and 85 Stevens
Stock and Forearm: Plain walnut pistol grip stock and forearm; 85 has black tipped forearm
Approximate wt.: 6 lbs.
Comments: Produced from the late 1930s until after World War II.

Estimated Value:	**Excellent:**	**$200.00**
	Very good:	**$160.00**

Stevens-Springfield Model No. 87, 087 (Stevens Model 87 after 1948)

Same as the No. 85, 085 except 15-shot tubular magazine.

Estimated Value:	**Excellent:**	**$200.00**
	Very good:	**$160.00**

Stevens Model No. 87 K Scout

Carbine version of Model No. 87; 20" barrel; produced until 1969.

Estimated Value:	**Excellent:**	**$200.00**
	Very good:	**$160.00**

Stevens Model Nos. 987 and 987T

Caliber: 22 long rifle
Action: Semiautomatic
Magazine: 14-shot tubular
Barrel: Blued; 20"
Sights: Ramp front, open rear with elevator; 987T has 4X scope
Stock and Forearm: Checkered hardwood, one-piece semi-pistol grip Monte Carlo stock and forearm
Approximate wt.: 6 lbs.
Comments: Produced from 1981 to 1988. Add $10.00 for scope (Model 987T).

Estimated Value:	**Excellent:**	**$120.00**
	Very good:	**$ 95.00**

Stevens Model Nos. 57 and 057

Caliber: 22 long rifle
Action: Semiautomatic; repeating
Magazine: 5-shot clip
Barrel: 24"
Sights: Open rear, bead front on Model No. 57; hooded ramp front, open middle, receiver peep on Model No. 057
Stock and Forearm: Plain walnut pistol grip stock and forearm; black tipped forearm on Model No. 57
Approximate wt.: 6 lbs.
Comments: Made from the late 1930s to the late 1940s.

Estimated Value:	**Excellent:**	**$200.00**
	Very good:	**$160.00**

Stevens Model Nos. 76 and 076

Same as Stevens Model Nos. 57 and 057 except: 15-shot tubular magazine.

Estimated Value:	**Excellent:**	**$200.00**
	Very good:	**$160.00**

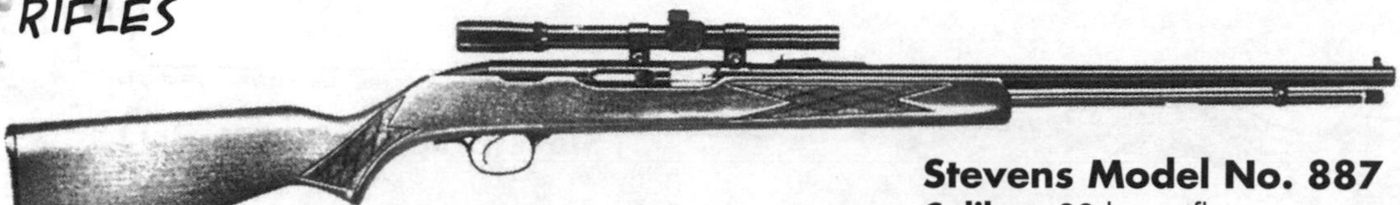

Stevens Model No. 887-T

Stevens Model No. 887

Caliber: 22 long rifle
Action: Semiautomatic
Magazine: 15-shot tubular
Barrel: Blued; 20"
Sights: Blade front, elevator open rear
Stock and Forearm: Checkered hardwood, one-piece semi-pistol grip stock and forearm
Approximate wt.: 6 lbs.
Comments: Produced in the late 1970s. Due to a possible safety malfunction, some models were recalled in 1982 and inspected by Stevens.

Estimated Value:	**Excellent:**	**$135.00**
	Very good:	**$105.00**

Stevens Model No. 887-T

Similar to the Model No. 887 with a 4X scope. Due to a possible safety malfunction certain models were recalled in 1982 and inspected by Stevens at no cost to the owner. Serial numbers recalled were B256621 or higher; C000001 or higher; D000001 or higher.

Estimated Value:	**Excellent:**	**$150.00**
	Very good:	**$120.00**

TAURUS

Taurus Model 62 Carbine

Taurus Models 62 and 62 Carbine

Caliber: 22 long rifle, 22 magnum
Action: Slide action, repeating
Magazine: 9-shot tubular
Barrel: 23" blued or stainless steel; 17" on the Model 62 Carbine
Sights: Serrated ramp front, adjustable rear
Stock and Forearm: Walnut finish hardwood, straight grip stock, and grooved slide handle
Approximate wt.: 4¾ to 5 lbs.
Comments: Introduced in 2000 in regular and shorter carbine model. Add 5% for stainless steel finish, 24% for tang sight.

Estimated Value:	**Excellent:**	**$275.00**
	Very good:	**$220.00**

Taurus Models 72 and 72 Carbine

Similar to the Model 62 and 62 Carbine except: 22 magnum caliber. Add 5% for stainless steel, 24% for tang sight.

Estimated Value:	**Excellent:**	**$275.00**
	Very good:	**$220.00**

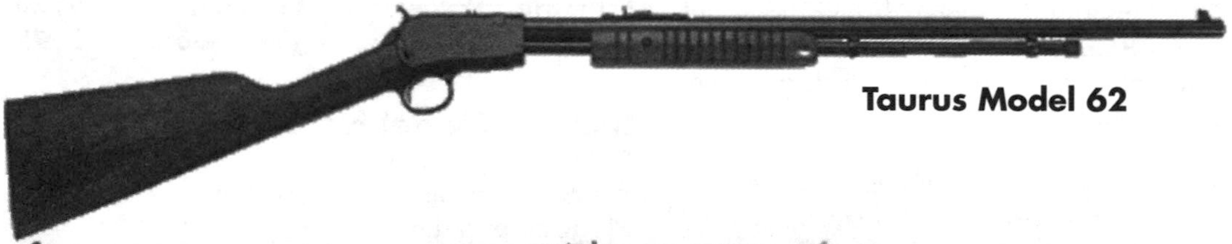

Taurus Model 62

Taurus Model 72

Taurus Model C357

Taurus Model C357

Similar to the Model 62 except: 38/357 caliber. Add 10% for stainless steel finish.

Estimated Value:	**Excellent:**	**$375.00**
	Very good:	**$300.00**

Taurus Model C45

Similar to the Model C357 except: 45 Colt caliber.

Estimated Value:	**Excellent:**	**$375.00**
	Very good:	**$300.00**

Taurus Model 63R

Taurus Model 63R-SS

Taurus Model 63R

Caliber: 22 long rifle
Action: Semiautomatic
Magazine: 10-shot tubular; load in stock
Barrel: Blued, 23"
Sights: Fixed front, adjustable rear
Stock and Forearm: Walnut finished hardwood pistol grip stock and tapered forearm.
Approximate wt.: 4½ lbs.
Comments: A reproduction of John Browning's Model 63 produced by Winchester.

Estimated Value:	**Excellent:**	**$250.00**
	Very good:	**$200.00**

Taurus Model 63R-SS

Similar to the Model 63R with stainless steel receiver and barrel; add 10% for tang sight.

Estimated Value:	**Excellent:**	**$250.00**
	Very good:	**$200.00**

THOMPSON CENTER

Thompson Center Contender Carbine

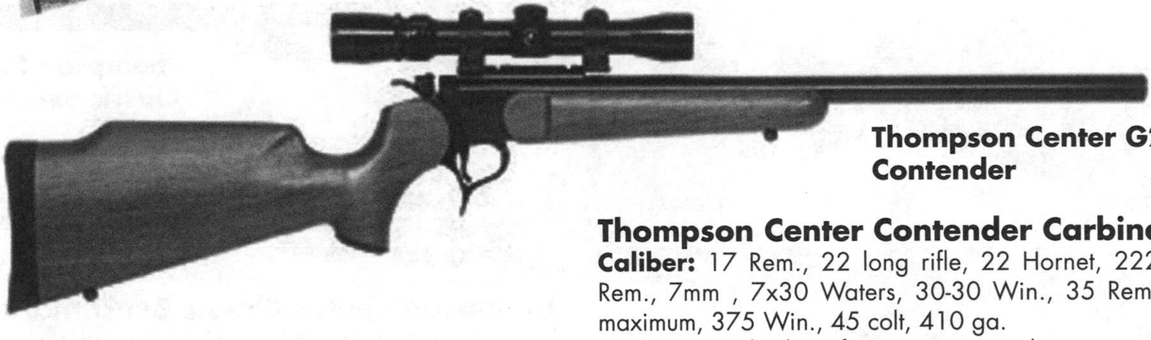

Thompson Center G2 Contender

Thompson Center Contender Carbine

Caliber: 17 Rem., 22 long rifle, 22 Hornet, 222 Rem., 223 Rem., 7mm , 7x30 Waters, 30-30 Win., 35 Rem., 357 Rem. maximum, 375 Win., 45 colt, 410 ga.
Action: Single-shot, frame accommodates any caliber interchangeable barrel, hammer adjusts
Magazine: None
Barrel: Interchangeable; 21"; 410 gauge is smooth bore with screw-in choke and ventilated rib after early 1990s
Sights: Adjustable rear; ramp front; tapped for scope mounts
Stock and Forearm: Walnut or all-weather Rynite®, pistol grip stock and forearm; recoil pad
Approximate wt.: 5¼ lbs.
Comments: Introduced in 1986. Based on the design of the popular Contender handgun. Add 48% for each additional barrel. Add 5% for ventilated rib. Add 6% for 17 Rem. Add 5% for 410 gauge.

Estimated Value:	**Excellent:**	**$425.00**
	Very good:	**$340.00**

Thompson Center SST Contender Carbine

Same as the Contender Carbine except: all stainless steel; all weather Rynite® stock; no 17 Rem. or 45 Colt calibers; add 5% for C-410 smooth bore with choke. Made in the mid-1990s.

Estimated Value:	**Excellent:**	**$450.00**
	Very good:	**$360.00**

Thompson Center G2 Contender

An updated version of the Contender Carbine; Monte Carlo stock and recoil pad. The original Contender and G2 Contender use the same barrel and forearms, but the stocks aren't the same and aren't interchangable.

Estimated Value:	**New (retail):**	**$695.00**
	Excellent:	**$520.00**
	Very good:	**$415.00**

Thompson Center Model TCR Hunter

Thompson Center Encore

Caliber: 22 Hornet, 223 Rem., 22-250 Rem., 243 Win., 25-06 Rem., 270 Win., 7mm-08 Rem., 300 Win. magnum, 308 Win., 30-06 Sprng., 45/70 Govt.
Action: Single-shot, break-open design
Magazine: None
Barrel: Interchangeable, 24" or 26" heavy barrel
Sights: Ramp front, adjustable rear
Stock and forearm: Walnut or composite Monte Carlo, pistol grip stock and forearm; rubber butt pad
Approximate wt.: $6\frac{3}{4}$ lbs.
Comments: Introduced in 2001.

Estimated Value:	**New (retail):**	**$661.00**
	Excellent:	**$495.00**
	Very good:	**$395.00**

Thompson Center Model TCR Hunter

Caliber: 22 Hornet, 222 Rem., 223 Rem., 22-250 Rem., 243 Win., 270 Win., 7mm/08, 308 Win., 30-06 Springfield, 32-40 Win., also 12 gauge rifled slug barrel (1989), 12 gauge shotgun barrel (1988) and 10 gauge shotgun barrel (1988)
Action: Top lever break-open; single-shot hammerless; adjustable single trigger
Magazine: None
Barrel: Interchangeable to select caliber or gauge; 23" light sporter barrel; $25\frac{7}{8}$" medium sporter barrel; 25" shotgun barrel; 22" rifled slug barrel
Sights: None; drilled and tapped for scope mounts; rifled slug barrel has adjustable iron sights; shotgun barrel has bead front sight
Stock and Forearm: Checkered walnut semi-pistol grip stock and grooved forearm; recoil pad
Approximate wt.: $6\frac{3}{4}$ lbs. (light sporter barrel); $7\frac{1}{4}$ lbs. (medium sporter barrel); 8 lbs. (shotgun barrel)
Comments: Produced from 1987 to the early 1990s.

Estimated Value:	**Excellent:**	**$525.00**
	Very good:	**$420.00**

Thompson Center Classic

Thompson Center Classic Benchmark

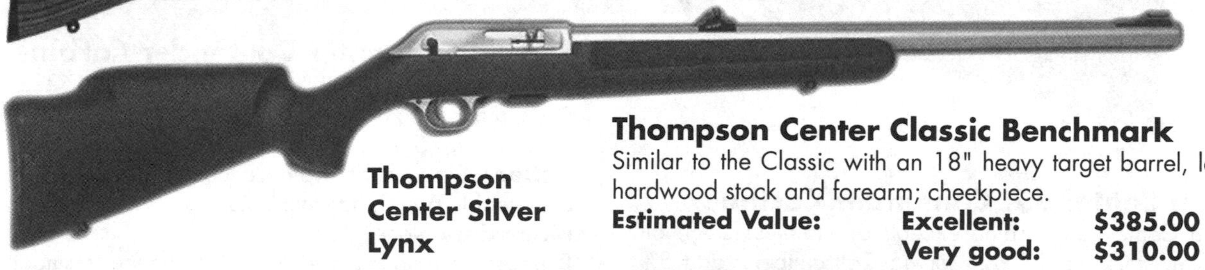

Thompson Center Silver Lynx

Thompson Center Classic

Caliber: 22 long rifle
Action: Semiautomatic
Magazine: 5-shot clip
Barrel: Blued, 22"; threaded into reciever
Sights: Ramp front, adjustable rear
Stock and Forearm: Smooth walnut, one-piece Monte Carlo stock and forearm
Approximate wt.: $5\frac{1}{2}$ lbs.
Comments: Introduced in 2003.

Estimated Value:	**Excellent:**	**$300.00**
	Very good:	**$240.00**

Thompson Center Classic Benchmark

Similar to the Classic with an 18" heavy target barrel, laminated hardwood stock and forearm; cheekpiece.

Estimated Value:	**Excellent:**	**$385.00**
	Very good:	**$310.00**

Thompson Center Silver Lynx

Caliber: 22 long rifle
Action: Semiautomatic
Magazine: 5-shot clip
Barrel: 20" stainless steel; threaded into reciever
Sights: Ramp front, adjustable rear
Stock and Forearm: Black composite, one-piece Monte Carlo stock and forearm
Approximate wt.: $5\frac{1}{2}$ lbs.
Comments: Introduced in 2003.

Estimated Value:	**Excellent:**	**$375.00**
	Very good:	**$300.00**

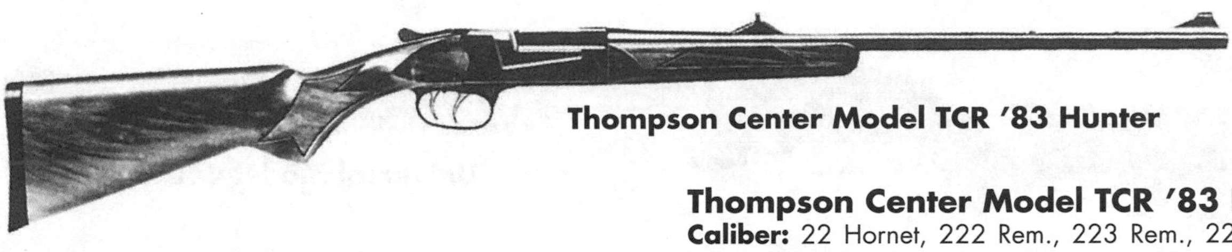

Thompson Center Model TCR '83 Hunter

Thompson Center Youth Model Carbine

Caliber: 22 long rifle, 22 Win. mag., 22 hornet, 223 Rem., 7x30 Waters, 30-30 Win., 35 Rem., 44 magnum, 45 Colt/410 gauge. The 45 Colt rifled barrel is used for 410 gauge when a detachable internal choke is screwed into the muzzle.
Action: Single-shot, frame accommodates any caliber interchangeable barrel, hammer adjusts for caliber
Magazine: None
Barrel: Interchangeable to select caliber; 16¼" barrel; 45/410 barrel has ventilated rib
Sights: Adjustable; tapped for scope mounts; 45/410 barrel has fixed rear sight and bead front
Stock and Forearm: 12" length of pull, walnut or all-weather Rynite®, pistol grip stock and forearm; recoil pad
Approximate wt.: 4½ lbs.
Comments: Introduced in 1989. Add 7% for 45/410 Model.
Estimated Value: **Excellent:** **$390.00**
Very good: **$315.00**

Thompson Center TCR Deluxe

Similar to the TCR '83 Aristocrat. Reintroduced in 1992 until 1994.
Estimated Value: **Excellent:** **$510.00**
Very good: **$410.00**

Thompson Center Model TCR '83 Hunter

Caliber: 22 Hornet, 222 Rem., 223 Rem., 22-250 Rem., 243 Win., 270 Win., 7mm Rem. magnum, 308 Win., 30-06 Springfield; caliber can be selected by replacing different caliber barrel; also 12 gauge
Action: Top lever break-open; single-shot; hammerless
Magazine: None
Barrel: Interchangeable to select caliber; 23" or 25"
Sights: Ramp front, folding leaf rear.
Stock and Forearm: Checkered walnut semi-pistol grip stock and forearm; cheekpiece; recoil pad
Approximate wt.: 6¾ lbs.
Comments: Produced from 1983 to 1987. Add 30% for each extra barrel. Replaced by Model TCR '87 Hunter.
Estimated Value: **Excellent:** **$400.00**
Very good: **$320.00**

Thompson Center Model TCR '83 Aristocrat

Similar to the TCR '83 Hunter with checkered forearm and stainless steel barrel; adjustable double set triggers. Discontinued in 1987.
Estimated Value: **Excellent:** **$420.00**
Very good: **$335.00**

UNIVERSAL

Universal Model M1 or 1000

Universal Models M1 or 1000, 1003

Similar to the U.S. M1 Carbine with a 5-shot detachable clip. Made in 30 caliber from the mid-1960s to the present. Add $50.00 for scope and detachable mount. See also Iver Johnson.
Estimated Value: **Excellent:** **$375.00**
Very good: **$300.00**

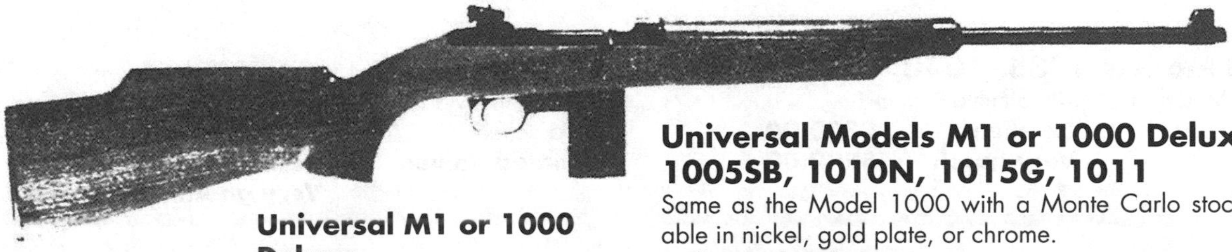

Universal M1 or 1000 Deluxe

Universal Models M1 or 1000 Deluxe, 1005SB, 1010N, 1015G, 1011

Same as the Model 1000 with a Monte Carlo stock; also available in nickel, gold plate, or chrome.
Estimated Value:

	1005SB Blue	1010N Nickel	1015G Gold	1011 Chrome
Excellent:	$300.00	$325.00	$400.00	$325.00
Very good:	$240.00	$260.00	$320.00	$260.00

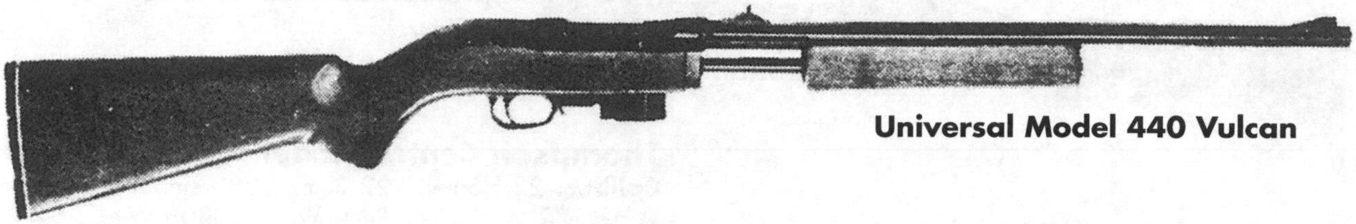

Universal Model 440 Vulcan

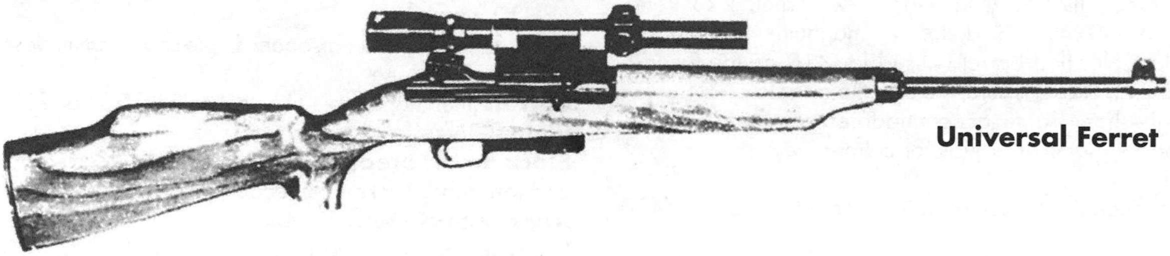

Universal Ferret

Universal Model 2200 Leatherneck

Universal Model 1020

Universal Models 1020, 1020TB, 1020TCO, and 1030

Similar to the Model 1000 with a Monte Carlo stock and a water-resistant Teflon finish in green, blue, tan, black, or gray. Currently produced as Model 1020TB (black), Model 1020TCO (green), and Model 1030 (gray).

Estimated Value:	**Excellent:**	**$350.00**
	Very good:	**$280.00**

Universal Models 1035, 1040, and 1045

Similar to the Model 1020 with a military stock.

Estimated Value:	**Excellent:**	**$300.00**
	Very good:	**$240.00**

Universal Model 1006

Similar to the Model 1005SB with stainless steel finish.

Estimated Value:	**Excellent:**	**$325.00**
	Very good:	**$260.00**

Universal Model 440 Vulcan

Caliber: 44 magnum
Action: Slide action; hammerless; repeating
Magazine: 5-shot clip
Barrel: 18¼"; carbine
Sights: Adjustable rear, ramp front with gold bead
Stock and Forearm: Walnut semi-pistol grip stock and slide handle
Approximate wt.: 6 lbs.
Comments: Made from the mid-1960s to the early 1970s.

Estimated Value:	**Excellent:**	**$300.00**
	Very good:	**$240.00**

Universal Ferret

Similar to the Model M1 with a Monte Carlo stock, no sights, and in 256 caliber.

Estimated Value:	**Excellent:**	**$300.00**
	Very good:	**$240.00**

Universal Model 2200 Leatherneck

Similar to the Model 1003 in 22 caliber. Produced from the early 1980s to the mid-1980s.

Estimated Value:	**Excellent:**	**$275.00**
	Very good:	**$220.00**

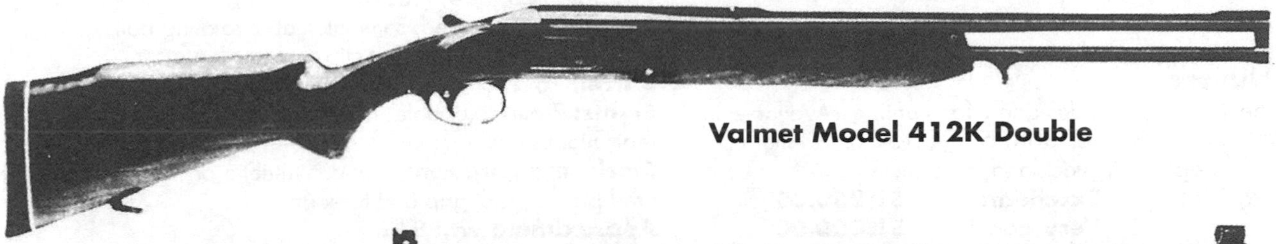

Valmet Model 412K Double

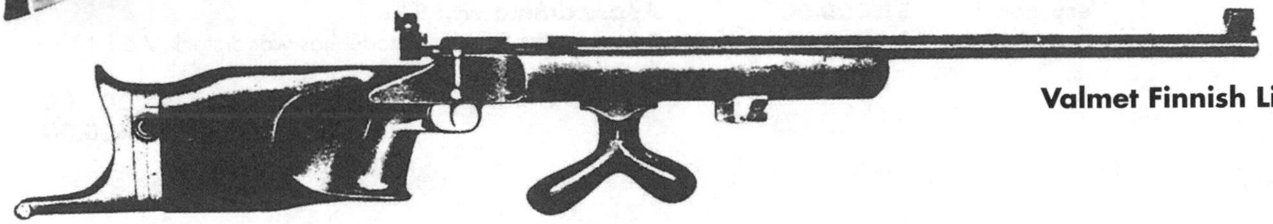

Valmet Finnish Lion

Valmet Model M-71S

Valmet Finnish Lion

Caliber: 22 long rifle
Action: Bolt action; single-shot
Magazine: None
Barrel: Blued; 29"; heavy
Sights: Extended peep rear, changeable front
Stock and Forearm: Free-rifle, pistol grip, thumbhole, one-piece stock and forearm; palm rest; swivels; Swiss butt plate
Approximate wt.: 15 lbs.
Comments: International match-type rifle; discontinued in the late 1970s.

Estimated Value:	**Excellent:**	**$725.00**
	Very good:	**$580.00**

Valmet Model 412K and 412S Double

Caliber: 243, 308, 30-06
Action: Top lever break-open, hammerless; extractors
Magazine: None
Barrel: Over and under double barrel; 24" with space between barrels
Sights: Open rear, blade front; drilled for scope
Stock and Forearm: Checkered walnut Monte Carlo pistol grip stock and forearm; recoil pad; swivels
Approximate wt.: 6½ lbs.
Comments: A double rifle produced in Finland as part of the 412 Shotgun Combination series.

Estimated Value:	**Excellent:**	**$1,750.00**
	Very good:	**$1,400.00**

Valmet 412KE Double and 412SE Double

Similar to the Model 412K Double with automatic ejectors. Introduced in the early 1980s. Calibers 375 Win. and 9.3x74 only. Discontinued in the late 1980s.

Estimated Value:	**Excellent:**	**$1,500.00**
	Very good:	**$1,200.00**

Valmet Model M-72S, M-715S, M-71S

Caliber: 223 (5.56mm)
Action: Semiautomatic, gas-operated
Magazine: 15-or 30-shot, curved detachable box
Barrel: 16½"
Sights: Open tangent rear, hooded post front; both adjustable
Stock and Forearm: Wood or reinforced resin stock; pistol grip; swivels; wood stock and forearm and plastic pistol grip on Model M-71S
Approximate wt.: 8¾ lbs.
Comments: Similar to the Model M-62S.

Estimated Value:	**Excellent:**	**$1,100.00**
	Very good:	**$ 880.00**

Valmet Model M-62S

Caliber: 7.62 x 39mm Russian
Action: Semiautomatic; gas piston, rotating bolt
Magazine: 15- or 30-shot, curved detachable box
Barrel: 16½"
Sights: Adjustable tangent peep rear, adjustable hooded post front
Stock and Forearm: Fixed metal tube or walnut stock; pistol grip; ventilated forearm
Approximate wt.: 8¾ lbs.
Comments: A powerful semiautomatic made in the mid-1970s. Add $15.00 for wood stock version.

Estimated Value:	**Excellent:**	**$1,500.00**
	Very good:	**$1,200.00**

Valmet Hunter
Similar to the Model 76 redesigned for hunting. Available in calibers: 223, 243, 30-06 or 308; 5-, 9-, 15-, or 30-shot clip. Checkered wood pistol grip stock and forearm.
Estimated Value: **Excellent:** **$1,250.00**
Very good: **$1,000.00**

Valmet Model M-76 Military
Caliber: 223, 308, 7.62x39
Action: Gas-operated, semiautomatic, rotating bolt
Magazine: 15- or 30-shot clip
Barrel: 16¾" or 20½"
Sights: Front adjustable in tunnel guard, folding leaf with peep rear; night sight
Stock and Forearm: Wood, synthetic or folding stock, checkered plastic pistol grip and forearm
Approximate wt.: 8 lbs.
Comments: Standard model has wood stock. Add 14% for synthetic stock; 16% for folding stock.
Estimated Value: **Excellent:** **$1,000.00**
Very good: **$ 800.00**

WALTHER

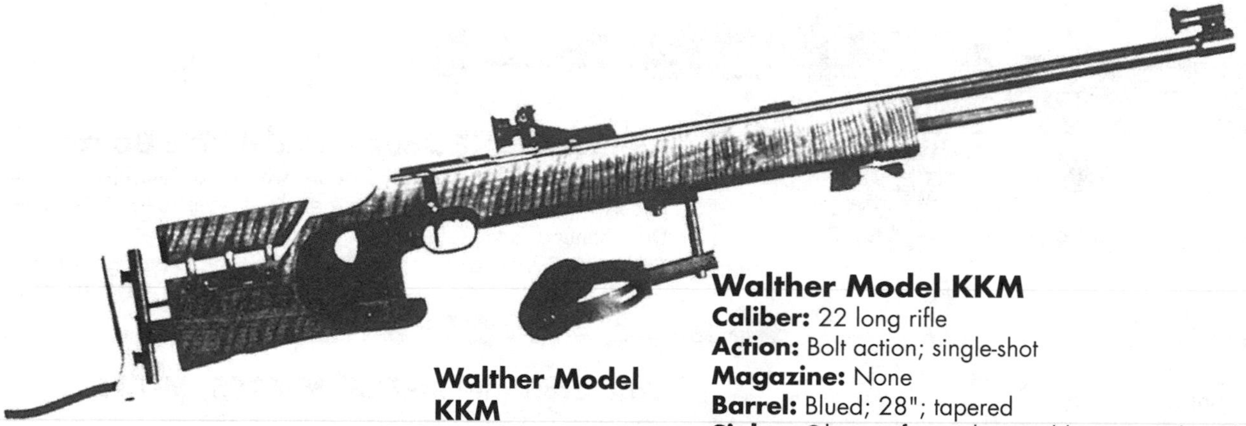

Walther Model KKM

Walther Model KKM
Caliber: 22 long rifle
Action: Bolt action; single-shot
Magazine: None
Barrel: Blued; 28"; tapered
Sights: Olympic front, changeable micro adjustable rear
Stock and Forearm: Walnut match-style with thumbhole; adjustable butt plate; heavy forearm with hand shelf; cheekpiece
Approximate wt.: 15 lbs.
Comments: A match rifle made from the 1950s to the late 1970s.
Estimated Value: **Excellent:** **$1,275.00**
Very good: **$1,025.00**

Walther Model KKJ

Walther Model KKJ
Caliber: 22 Hornet, 22 long rifle, 22 WRM
Action: Bolt action; repeating; double set trigger available
Magazine: 5-shot detachable clip
Barrel: Blued; 22½"
Sights: Adjustable rear, hooded ramp front
Stock and Forearm: Checkered walnut pistol grip stock and forearm; cheekpiece; swivels
Approximate wt.: 5½ lbs.
Comments: Made from about 1957 to late 1970s. Add $20.00 for double set trigger.
Estimated Value: **Excellent:** **$875.00**
Very good: **$700.00**

Walther Moving Target
Caliber: 22 long rifle
Action: Bolt action; single-shot
Magazine: None
Barrel: Blued; 23½"
Sights: Micro adjustable rear, globe front
Stock and Forearm: Walnut, pistol grip, thumbhole, match-type with adjustable cheekpiece and butt plate
Approximate wt.: 8¼ lbs.
Comments: A match rifle made in the 1970s.
Estimated Value: **Excellent:** **$750.00**
Very good: **$600.00**

Walther Model UIT

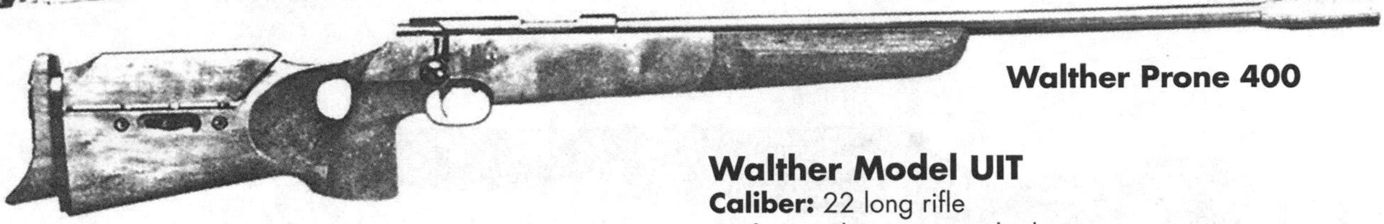

Walther Prone 400

Walther Prone 400
Similar to Model UIT with split stock and adjustable cheekpiece; thumbhole; no sights.

| Estimated Value: | Excellent: | $725.00 |
| | Very good: | $580.00 |

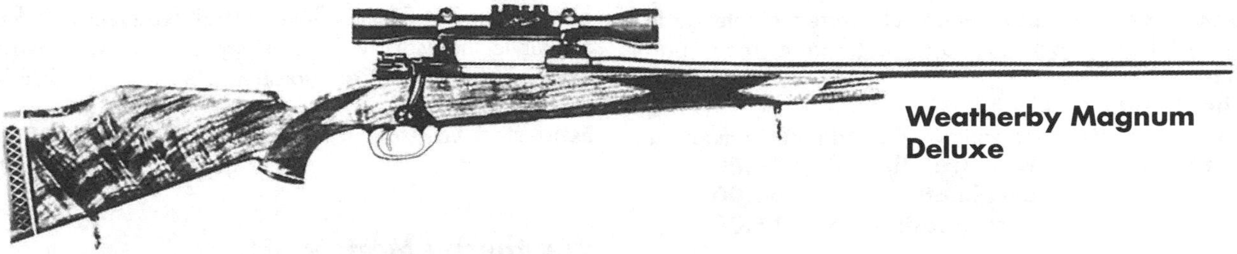

Walther Model UIT
Caliber: 22 long rifle
Action: Bolt action; single-shot
Magazine: None
Barrel: 25½"
Sights: Changeable front, micro adjustable rear
Stock and Forearm: Match-style, walnut pistol grip stock and wide forearm
Approximate wt.: 10¼ lbs.
Comments: A match rifle made from the mid-1960s into the 1980s.

| Estimated Value: | Excellent: | $1,275.00 |
| | Very good: | $1,025.00 |

WEATHERBY⊙

Weatherby Magnum Deluxe

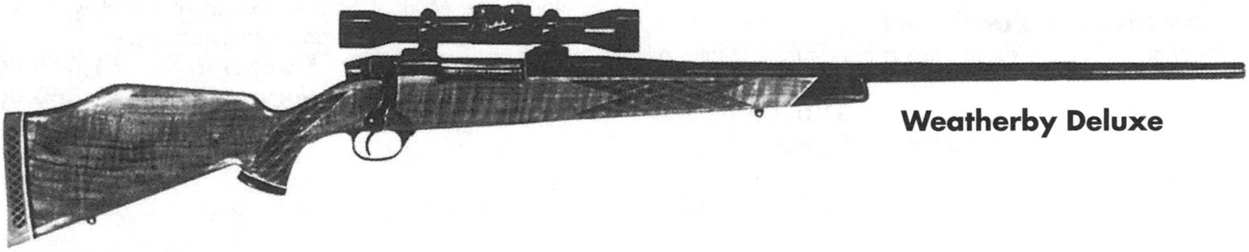

Weatherby Deluxe

Weatherby Deluxe
Similar to the Magnum Deluxe but in 270 Win. and 30-06 calibers only.

| Estimated Value: | Excellent: | $1,200.00 |
| | Very good: | $ 960.00 |

Weatherby Magnum Deluxe
Caliber: 378 mag., 300 mag., 375 mag., 7mm mag., 270 mag., 257 mag., 220 Rocket
Action: Bolt action; Mauser-type
Magazine: 3-shot
Barrel: Blued; 24"; 26" available on some calibers
Sights: None
Stock and Forearm: Checkered wood Monte Carlo one-piece pistol grip stock and tapered forearm; recoil pad; swivels; cheekpiece
Approximate wt.: 7 to 8 lbs.
Comments: Made from the late 1940s to the late 1950s.

| Estimated Value: | Excellent: | $1,675.00 |
| | Very good: | $1,350.00 |

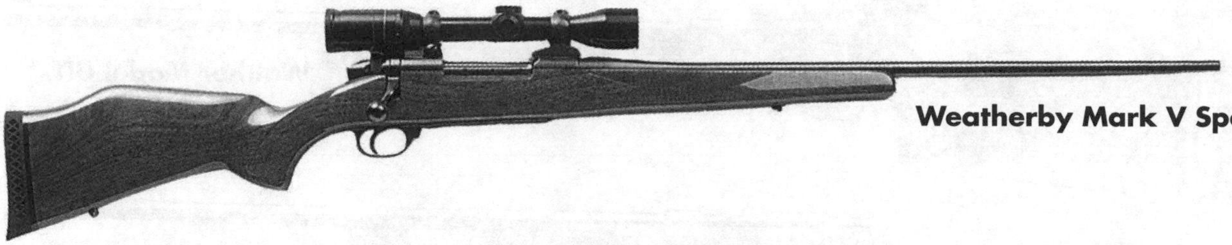

Weatherby Mark V Sporter

Weatherby Mark V Special Varmint Rifle (SVR)

Weatherby Mark V Sporter

Caliber: 22-250 Rem., .240 Wby mag., 257 Wby. mag., 270 Wby mag., 7mm Wby. mag., 7mm Rem. mag., 300 Win., 338 Win., 375 H&H, 270 Win., 30-06 Sprng., 300 Wby mag., 340 Wby. mag.
Action: Bolt action; repeating
Magazine: 3- or 4-shot box
Barrel: 22", 24" or 26"; depending on caliber; low luster blued
Sights: None
Stock and Forearm: Epoxy finish, checkered Monte Carlo, one-piece pistol grip stock and tapered forearm; recoil pad; swivel studs
Approximate wt.: 7½ to 9 lbs.
Comments: Introduced in the early 1990s. Add 5% for magnum.

Estimated Value:	**New (retail):**	**$1,529.00**
	Excellent:	**$1,150.00**
	Very good:	**$ 915.00**

Weatherby Mark V Eurosport

Similar to the Mark V Sporter except has a hand-rubbed, satin oil finish.

Estimated Value:	**Excellent:**	**$1,000.00**
	Very good:	**$ 800.00**

Weatherby Mark V Special Varmint Rifle (SVR)

Similar to the Mark V Super Predatormaster with 22" barrel; 22-250 Rem., 223 Rem. calibers; weighs 7¼ lbs.; composite stock with gray spiderweb pattern.

Estimated Value:	**Excellent:**	**$975.00**
	Very good:	**$780.00**

Weatherby Mark V Threat Response Rifle

Similar to the Mark V Special Varmint Rifle with heavy barrel; black composite stock and forearm; 223 Rem., or 308 Win. calibers.

Estimated Value:	**Excellent:**	**$1,300.00**
	Very good:	**$1,045.00**

Weatherby Mark V SLS

Similar to the Mark V Sporter except all metal work is stainless steel with matte blue finish and a laminate stock.

Estimated Value:	**Excellent:**	**$1,075.00**
	Very good:	**$ 860.00**

Weatherby Mark V Super Predatormaster

Weatherby Mark V Super Predatormaster

Similar to the Mark V Super Big Gamemaster; 24" barrel; 22-250 Rem., 223 Rem., 243., 7mm-08 Rem., 308 Win.; weighs 6¼ lbs.

Estimated Value:	**Excellent:**	**$1,350.00**
	Very good:	**$1,075.00**

Weatherby Mark V Super Big Gamemaster

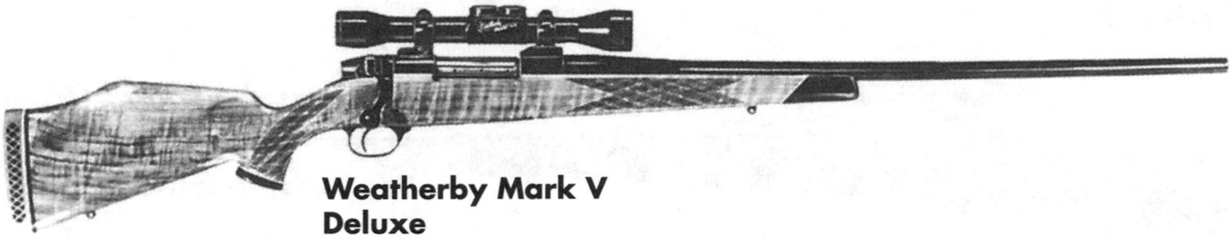

Weatherby Mark V Deluxe

Weatherby Varmintmaster

Weatherby Mark V Super Big Gamemaster

Caliber: 240 Wby mag., 25-06 Rem., 270 Win., 280 Rem., 30-06 Spfld., 257 Wby. magnum, 270 Wby magnum, 7mm Wby. magnum, 300 Wby. magnum, 7mm Rem. magnum, 300 Win. magnum
Action: Bolt action; repeating
Magazine: 5-shot box
Barrel: 24" or 26" fluted stainless steel with matte black finish
Sights: None
Stock and Forearm: Tan composite Monte carlo one-piece pistol grip stock and forearm with spiderweb pattern; Pachmayr recoil pad.
Approximate wt.: 5¾ lbs.
Comments: Introduced in 2003. Add 4% for magnum calibers.

Estimated Value:	**Excellent:**	**$1,000.00**
	Very good:	**$ 800.00**

Weatherby Mark V Euromark

Similar to the Mark V Deluxe except with hand rubbed oil-finished stock and forearm; ebony pistol grip cap and fore-end tip; all metal surfaces are matte blue. Add 6% for 378 Wby. magnum; add 17% for 416 Wby. magnum.

Estimated Value:	**Excellent:**	**$1,375.00**
	Very good:	**$1,100.00**

Weatherby Mark V Deluxe

Caliber: 22-250 Rem., 240 Wby. mag., 257 Wby. mag., 270 Wby. mag., 7mm Wby. mag., 30-06, 300 Wby. mag., 340 Wby. mag., 378 Wby. mag., 416 Wby. mag. 460 Wby. mag.
Action: Bolt action; repeating
Magazine: 3- or 4-shot, depending on caliber
Barrel: Blued; 24", 26", or 28"
Sights: None
Stock and Forearm: Checkered walnut Monte Carlo one-piece pistol grip stock and tapered forearm; recoil pad; swivels
Approximate wt.: 7¼ to 10½ lbs.
Comments: Made from the late 1950s to the present. Add 10% for 416 mag.; 6% for 378 Wby. mag.; 37% for 460 mag.

Estimated Value:	**New (retail):**	**$2,249.00**
	Excellent:	**$1,685.00**
	Very good:	**$1,350.00**

Weatherby Varmintmaster

A scaled-down version of the Mark V Deluxe in 22-250 or 224 Weatherby mag.; 24" or 26" barrel. Add 5% for Lazermark Series.

Estimated Value:	**Excellent:**	**$1,250.00**
	Very good:	**$1,000.00**

Weatherby Mark V Lazermark

Similar to the Mark V Deluxe with laser-carved oak leaf pattern instead of checkering. Add 17% for 378 Wby. mag or 416 Wby mag.

Estimated Value:	**New (retail):**	**$2,519.00**
	Excellent:	**$1,890.00**
	Very good:	**$1,510.00**

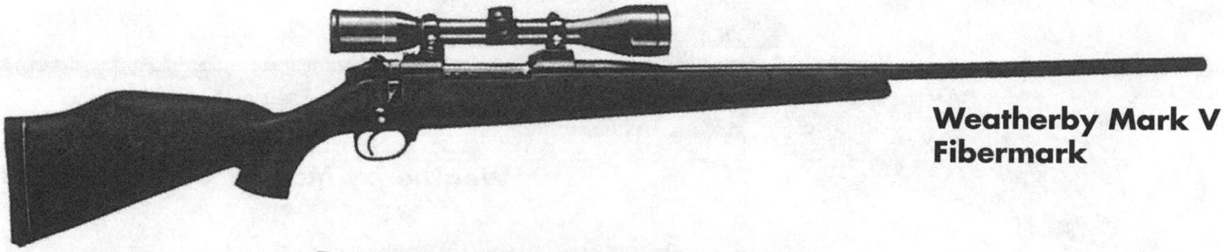

Weatherby Mark V Fibermark

Weatherby Fibermark Stainless

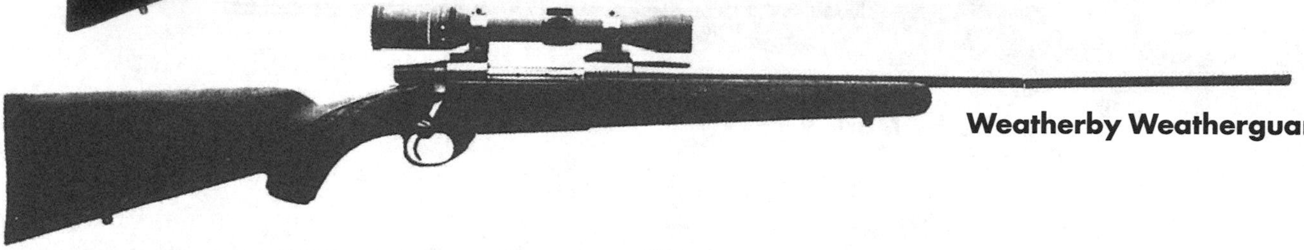

Weatherby Weatherguard

Weatherby Mark V Fibermark

Similar to the Mark V Deluxe except one-piece black fiberglass stock and forearm; weighs 7½ to 8 lbs. Produced from the mid-1980s to the early 1990s. Reintroduced in 2001. Add 25% for 30-378 Wby. magnum with 28" barrel.

Estimated Value:	**New (retail):**	**$1,469.00**
	Excellent:	**$1,100.00**
	Very good:	**$ 880.00**

Weatherby Fibermark Stainless

Similar to the Fibermark with a stainless steel finish; 24" barrel for standard calibers, 24" or 26" barrel for magnum calibers. Add 7% for magnum.

Estimated Value:	**Excellent:**	**$1,250.00**
	Very good:	**$1,000.00**

Weatherby Weatherguard

Caliber: 223 Rem., 243 Rem., 270 Win., 7mm-08 Rem., 7mm Rem. magnum, 30-06, 308 Win.
Action: Bolt action; repeating
Magazine: 4-shot (3-shot magnum), box with hinged floor plate
Barrel: 24"; blued
Sights: None, drilled and tapped for scope mounts
Stock and Forearm: Checkered synthetic composite one-piece stock and forearm, pistol grip; recoil pad, swivel studs
Approximate wt.: 7 to 8 lbs.
Comments: An all-weather gun similar to the Vanguard series.

Estimated Value:	**Excellent:**	**$525.00**
	Very good:	**$420.00**

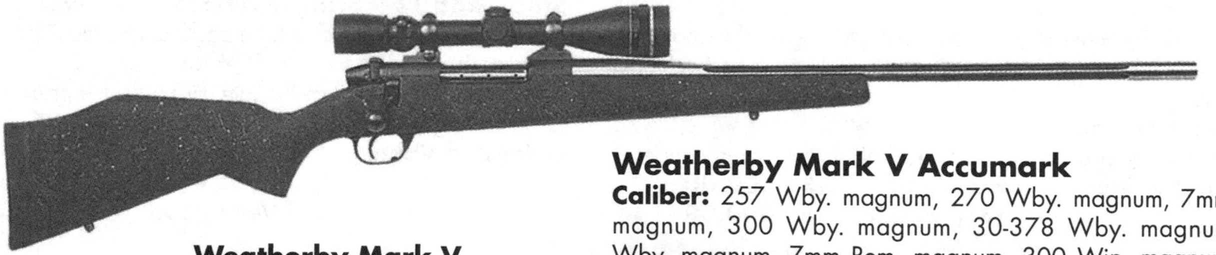

Weatherby Mark V Accumark

Weatherby Mark V Accumark

Caliber: 257 Wby. magnum, 270 Wby. magnum, 7mm Wby. magnum, 300 Wby. magnum, 30-378 Wby. magnum, 340 Wby. magnum, 7mm Rem. magnum, 300 Win. magnum; 7mm STW and 338-378 Wby. magnum added 1998
Action: Bolt action; repeating
Magazine: 3- or 4-shot box; hinged floor plate
Barrel: 26" heavy fluted stainless steel with a specially designed bedding system using an aluminum platform; 28" with 30-378 Wby. mag., or 338-378 Wby. mag.
Sights: None, drilled for scope mounts
Stock and Forearm: Synthetic, one-piece Monte Carlo stock and forearm
Approximate wt.: 8½ lbs.
Comments: Introduced in 1996; add 14% for 30-378 Wby. and/or 338-378 Wby.

Estimated Value:	**New (retail):**	**$1,909.00**
	Excellent:	**$1,430.00**
	Very good:	**$1,150.00**

Weatherby Classicmark II

Similar to the Classicmark I except: deluxe American Walnut stock and forearm with satin-finish metalwork. Right-handed version only.

Estimated Value:	**Excellent:**	**$1,450.00**
	Very good:	**$1,160.00**

Weatherby Classicmark I

Weatherby Weathermark Synthetic

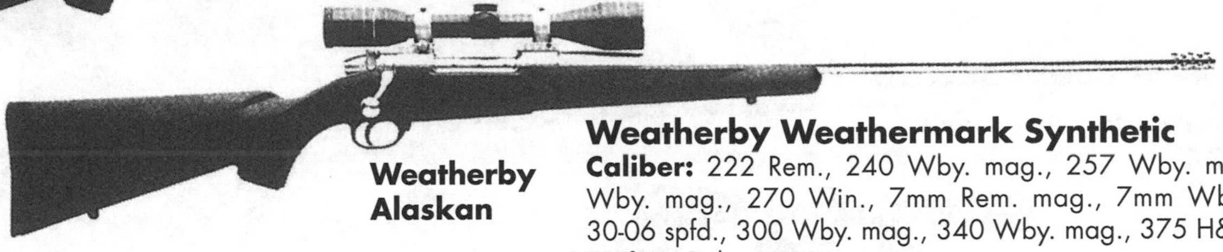

Weatherby Alaskan

Weatherby Classicmark I

Caliber: 240 Wby. mag., 257 Wby. mag., 270 Wby. mag., 270 Win., 7mm Rem. mag., 7mm Wby. mag., 30-06, 300 Wby. mag., 340 Wby. mag., 375 H&H mag., 378 Wby. mag., 416 Wby. mag., 460 Wby. mag.
Action: Bolt action; repeating
Magazine: 4-shot (3-shot mag.), box with hinged floor plate
Barrel: 22", 24", or 26"; blued
Sights: None, drilled and tapped for scope mounts
Stock and Forearm: Oil-finished, checkered walnut, Monte Carlo pistol grip, one-piece stock and forearm; recoil pad, swivel studs
Approximate wt.: 8 to 10 lbs.
Comments: Produced in the early 1990s. Add 5% to 15% for mag. calibers.

Estimated Value:	**Excellent:**	**$990.00**
	Very good:	**$790.00**

Weatherby Weathermark Synthetic

Caliber: 222 Rem., 240 Wby. mag., 257 Wby. mag., 270 Wby. mag., 270 Win., 7mm Rem. mag., 7mm Wby. mag., 30-06 spfd., 300 Wby. mag., 340 Wby. mag., 375 H&H
Action: Bolt action; repeating
Magazine: 3- or 4-shot box; hinged floor plate
Barrel: 22", 24", or 26"; blued or stainless steel
Sights: None, drilled and tapped for scope mounts
Stock and Forearm: Checkered synthetic composite one-piece pistol grip stock and forearm; recoil pad
Approximate wt.: 7 to 8 lbs.
Comments: Made in the 1990s.

Estimated Value:	**Excellent:**	**$615.00**
	Very good:	**$490.00**

Weatherby Alaskan

Similar to the Weathermark except: non-glare electroless nickel-plated finish. Made in the 1990s.

Estimated Value:	**Excellent:**	**$725.00**
	Very good:	**$580.00**

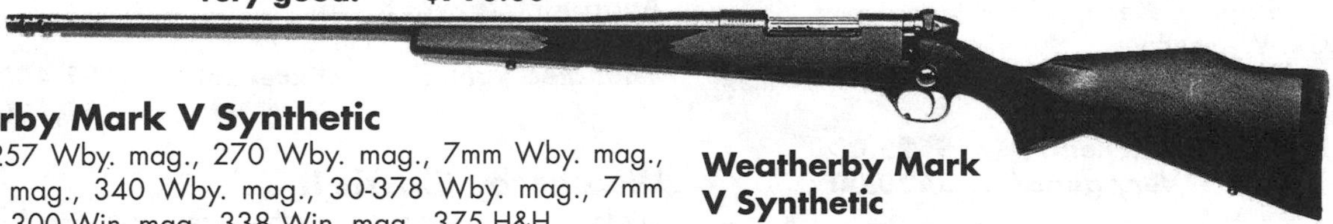

Weatherby Mark V Synthetic

Weatherby Mark V Synthetic

Caliber: 257 Wby. mag., 270 Wby. mag., 7mm Wby. mag., 300 Wby. mag., 340 Wby. mag., 30-378 Wby. mag., 7mm Rem. mag., 300 Win. mag., 338 Win. mag., 375 H&H
Action: Bolt action; repeating
Magazine: 2 or 3-shot box
Barrel: 24", 26", 28", depending on caliber; matte blue
Sights: None
Stock and Forearm: Monte Carlo, checkered one-piece injection-molded pistol grip stock and forearm; swivels; recoil pad
Approximate wt.: 8 lbs.
Comments: Add 19% for 30-378 Wby. mag. with 28" barrel.

Estimated Value:	**New (retail):**	**$1,229.00**
	Excellent:	**$ 920.00**
	Very good:	**$ 735.00**

Weatherby Mark V Fluted Stainless

Similar to the Mark V Stainless except with a fluted 24" or 26" barrel, available in 257 Wby. mag., 270 Wby. mag., 7mm Wby. mag., 300 Wby. mag., 7mm Rem. mag., and 300 Win. mag.

Estimated Value:	**Excellent:**	**$945.00**
	Very good:	**$750.00**

Weatherby Mark V Fluted Synthetic

Similar to the Mark V Synthetic with fluted 24" or 26" barrel. Available in 257 Wby. mag., 270 Wby. mag., 7mm Wby mag., 300 Wby. mag., 7mm Rem. mag., and 300 Win. mag.

Estimated Value:	**Excellent:**	**$775.00**
	Very good:	**$620.00**

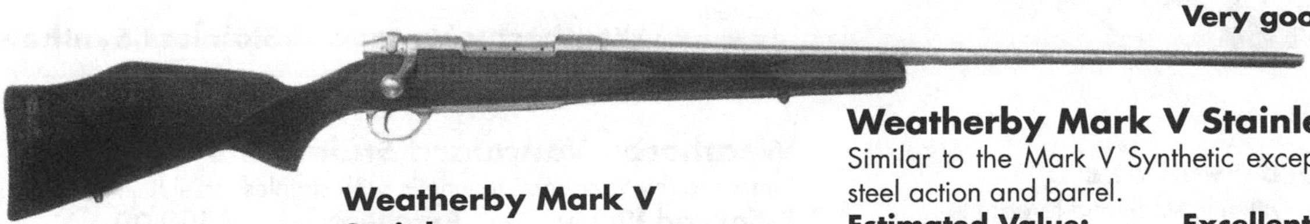

Weatherby Mark V Stainless

Weatherby Mark V Stainless

Similar to the Mark V Synthetic except with matte finish stainless steel action and barrel.

Estimated Value:	**Excellent:**	**$875.00**
	Very good:	**$700.00**

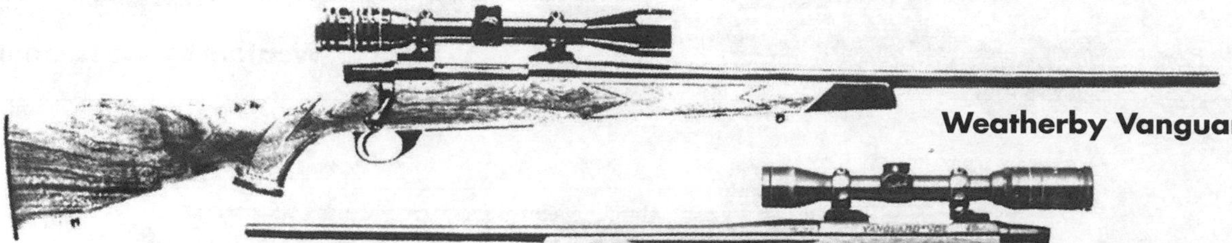

Weatherby Vanguard VGS

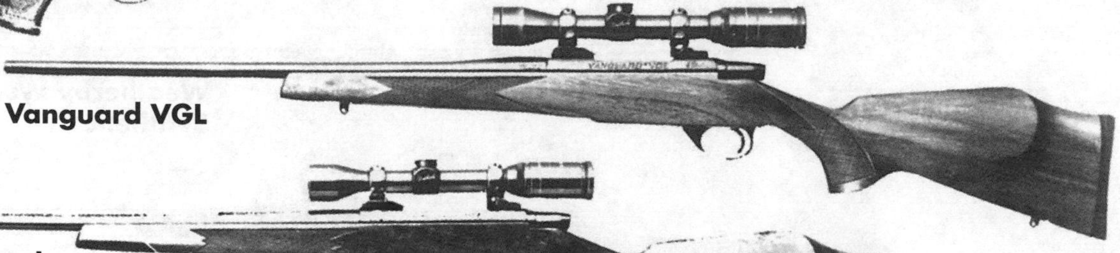

Weatherby Vanguard VGL

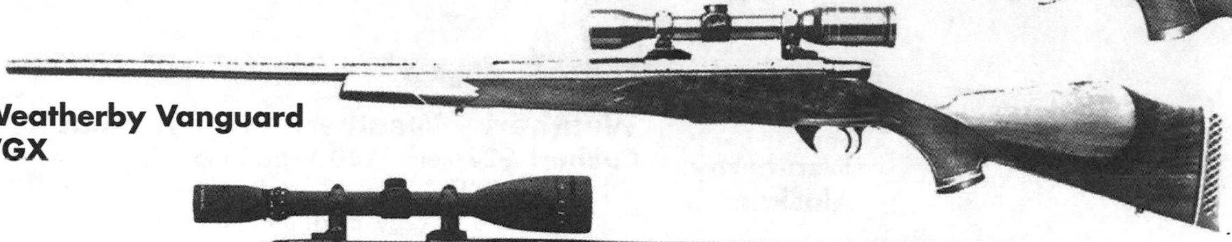

Weatherby Vanguard VGX

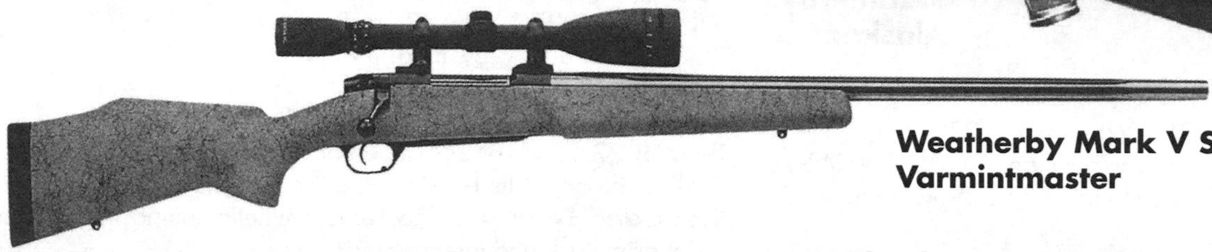

Weatherby Mark V Super Varmintmaster

Weatherby Vanguard VGX, VGS, and VGL

Caliber: 22-250, 25-06, 243, 264, 270, 30-06, 7mm Rem. mag., 300 Win. mag.
Action: Bolt action; repeating
Magazine: 5-shot (3-shot magnum), box with hinged floor plate
Barrel: Blued; 24"
Sights: None
Stock and Forearm: Checkered walnut, Monte Carlo pistol grip, one-piece stock and forearm; recoil pad, swivels; Vanguard VGX has deluxe finish
Approximate wt.: 6½ to 8 lbs.
Comments: Made from the early 1970s to the early 1990s. Add 30% for VGX. Weatherby will perform a safety upgrade on Vanguard rifles made between 1970 and 1993. Owners of these rifles are advised to contact Weatherby.

Estimated Value:	**Excellent:**	**$525.00**
	Very good:	**$420.00**

Weatherby Model Mark V Super Varmintmaster

Caliber: 223 Rem., 22-250 Rem., 220 Swift, 243 Win., 7mm-08 Rem., and 308 Win.
Action: Mark V bolt action, repeating; single-shot version available
Magazine: 5-shot box; 4-shot in 22-250 Rem.
Barrel: 22" blued; fluted
Sights: None
Stock and Forearm: Laminated Monte Carlo, one-piece pistol grip stock and beavertail forearm; black spiderweb pattern on tan finish
Approximate wt.: 8½ lbs.
Comments: Introduced in 2000.

Estimated Value:	**Excellent:**	**$1,400.00**
	Very good:	**$1,120.00**

Weatherby Classic II

Similar to the Vanguard with checkered stock and forearm; satin finish.

Estimated Value:	**Excellent:**	**$620.00**
	Very good:	**$495.00**

Weatherby Vanguard Synthetic

Weatherby Vanguard Stainless Synthetic

Weatherby Vanguard Synthetic

Similar to the Vanguard with synthetic stock and forearm.

Estimated Value:	**New (retail):**	**$419.00**
	Excellent:	**$315.00**
	Very good:	**$250.00**

Weatherby Vanguard Stainless Synthetic

Similar to the Vanguard Synthetic with stainless steel finish.

Estimated Value:	**Excellent:**	**$500.00**
	Very good:	**$400.00**

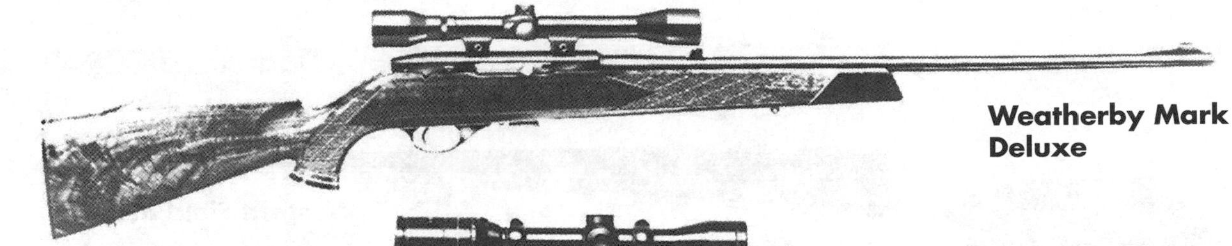

Weatherby Mark XXII Deluxe

Weatherby Vanguard Fiberguard

Weatherby Mark XXII Deluxe

Caliber: 22 long rifle
Action: Semiautomatic; hammerless
Magazine: 5- or 10-shot clip or 15-shot tubular
Barrel: Blued; 24"
Sights: Open rear, ramp front
Stock and Forearm: Checkered walnut Monte Carlo one-piece pistol grip stock and tapered forearm; swivels
Approximate wt.: 6 lbs.
Comments: Made from the mid-1960s to the early 1990s.

Estimated Value:	**New (retail):**	**$999.00**
	Excellent:	**$750.00**
	Very good:	**$600.00**

Weatherby Vanguard Fiberguard

Caliber: 223, 243, 270, 7mm Rem. mag., 30-06, 308 Win.
Action: Bolt action; repeating; short action
Magazine: 6-shot in 223; 5-shot in 243, 270, 30-06 and 308; 3-shot in 7mm Rem. magnum
Barrel: Blued; 20"
Sights: None
Stock and Forearm: A rugged, all-weather fiberglass, one-piece semi-pistol grip stock and forearm; forest green wrinkle finish with black butt pad
Approximate wt.: 6½ lbs.
Comments: Made from the mid-1980s to the early 1990s.

Estimated Value:	**Excellent:**	**$700.00**
	Very good:	**$560.00**

Weatherby Mark V Accumark Lightweight

Weatherby Mark V Sporter Lightweight

Caliber: 22-250 Rem., 243 Win., 240 Wby. mag., 25-06 Rem., 270 Win., 280 Rem., 7mm-08 Rem., 30-06 Sprg., 308 Win.
Action: Bolt action; repeating; a smaller, lighter version of Weatherby's Mark V magnum action
Magazine: 5-shot box
Barrel: 24"; round; blued
Sights: None
Stock and Forearm: Select Claro walnut, checkered Monte Carlo one-piece pistol grip stock and forearm; swivels
Approximate wt.: 6½ lbs.
Comments: A sporter rifle using a scaled-down version of Weatherby's Mark V action.

Estimated Value:	**Excellent:**	**$900.00**
	Very good:	**$720.00**

Weatherby Mark V Synthetic Lightweight

Similar to the Mark V Sporter Lightweight except has injection-molded synthetic stock, matte blue barrel. Carbine model with 20" barrel is available in 243 Win., 7mm-08 Rem., and 308 Win.

Estimated Value:	**Excellent:**	**$875.00**
	Very good:	**$700.00**

Weatherby Mark V Stainless Lightweight

Similar to the Mark V Synthetic Lightweight except action and barrel are matte-finish stainless steel. Carbine model is available with 20" barrel in 243 Win., 7mm-08 Rem., and 308 Win.

Estimated Value:	**Excellent:**	**$900.00**
	Very good:	**$720.00**

Weatherby Mark V Accumark Lightweight

Similar to the Mark V Sporter Lightweight except has a heavy contour, free-floated, 24" barrel, fluted for weight reduction and heat dissipation; hand-laminated Monte Carlo stock with gray spider-web pattern. Introduced in 1998.

Estimated Value:	**Excellent:**	**$1,025.00**
	Very good:	**$ 820.00**

Weatherby Mark V Ultra Lightweight

Similar to the Mark V Accumark Lightweight except uses metal alloys to reduce action weight; Kevlar®/fiberglass stock and forearm with Pachmayr recoil pad.

Estimated Value:	**New (retail):**	**$1,909.00**
	Excellent:	**$1,430.00**
	Very good:	**$1,150.00**

Western Field Model 732

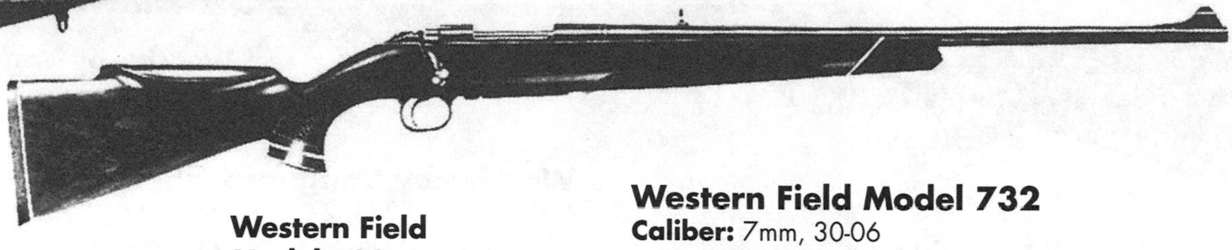

Western Field Model 730

Western Field Model 730

Similar to Model 732. Produced from the 1960s until the mid-1970s.

Estimated Value: **Excellent:** **$220.00**
Very good: **$180.00**

Western Field Model 732

Caliber: 7mm, 30-06
Action: Bolt action; repeating; hammerless
Magazine: 4- or 5-shot tubular, depending on caliber
Barrel: Blued; 22"
Sights: Leaf rear, bead front
Stock and Forearm: Checkered walnut Monte Carlo one-piece pistol grip stock and forearm; swivels
Approximate wt.: 8 lbs.
Comments: Manufactured from the 1960s into the late 1970s.
Estimated Value: **Excellent:** **$225.00**
Very good: **$180.00**

Western Field Model 780

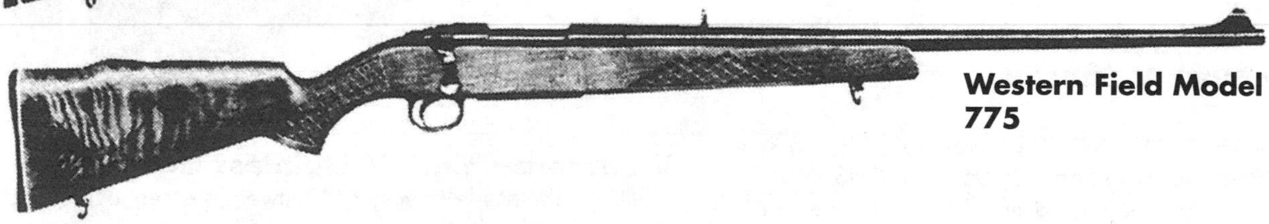

Western Field Model 775

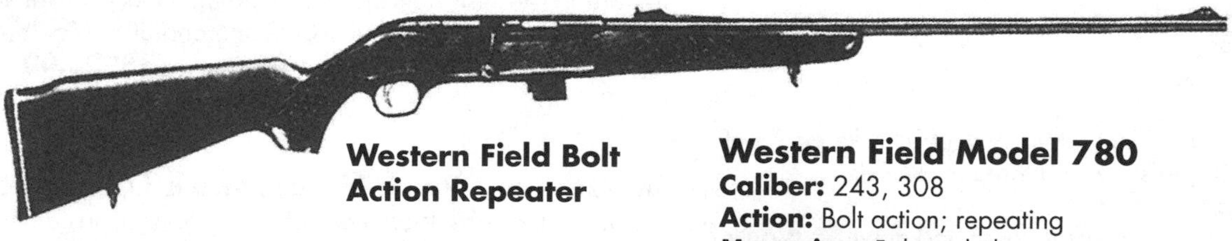

Western Field Bolt Action Repeater

Western Field Bolt Action Repeater

Caliber: 22 short, long, long rifle; 22 WMR
Action: Bolt action; repeating
Magazine: 7-shot clip in 22; 5-shot in 22 WMR
Barrel: Blued; 24"
Sights: Adjustable rear, ramp front
Stock and Forearm: Walnut one-piece pistol grip stock and forearm
Approximate wt.: 6 lbs.
Comments: Discontinued in the early 1980s. Add $5.00 for 22 WMR.
Estimated Value: **Excellent:** **$125.00**
Very good: **$105.00**

Western Field Model 780

Caliber: 243, 308
Action: Bolt action; repeating
Magazine: 5-shot tubular
Barrel: Blued; 22"
Sights: Adjustable rear, bead front
Stock and Forearm: Checkered walnut Monte Carlo one-piece pistol grip stock and forearm
Approximate wt.: 6½ lbs.
Comments: Manufactured in the 1970s.
Estimated Value: **Excellent:** **$215.00**
Very good: **$175.00**

Western Field Models 775 and 776

Similar to the Model 780; produced in the mid-1970s.

Estimated Value: **Excellent:** **$200.00**
Very good: **$155.00**

Western Field Model 842

Western Field Bolt Action

Caliber: 30-06
Action: Bolt action; repeating
Magazine: 4-shot, hinged floorplate
Barrel: Blued; 22"; round
Sights: Bead front, adjustable rear
Stock and Forearm: Smooth hardwood one-piece pistol grip stock and forearm with sling swivels
Approximate wt.: 7¾ lbs.
Comments: Made from the 1960s until the early 1980s.
Estimated Value: **Excellent:** **$200.00**
Very good: **$160.00**

Western Field Model 78 Deluxe

Caliber: 7mm mag., 30-06
Action: Bolt action
Magazine: 3-shot rotary magazine in 7mm, 4-shot in 30-06
Barrel: 24" in 7mm; 22" in 30-06
Sights: Bead front, adjustable rear
Stock and Forearm: Checkered walnut pistol grip stock and forearm; swivels
Approximate wt.: 7mm: 8¾ lbs.; 30-06: 7½ lbs.
Comments: Manufactured from the 1960s to the early 1980s.
Estimated Value: **Excellent:** **$220.00**
Very good: **$175.00**

Western Field Model 842

Caliber: 22 short, long, long rifle
Action: Bolt action; repeating
Magazine: Tubular; 18 long rifles, 20 longs, 22 shorts
Barrel: Blued; 24"
Sights: Adjustable rear, bead front
Stock and Forearm: Walnut Monte Carlo one-piece pistol grip stock and forearm
Approximate wt.: 6¼ lbs.
Comments: Manufactured from the 1960s until the mid-1970s.
Estimated Value: **Excellent:** **$120.00**
Very good: **$100.00**

Western Field Model 815

Caliber: 22 short, long, long rifle
Action: Bolt action; single-shot; hammerless
Magazine: None
Barrel: Blued; 24"
Sights: Adjustable rear, bead front
Stock and Forearm: Wood Monte Carlo one-piece pistol grip stock and forearm
Approximate wt.: 8 lbs.
Comments: Made from the 1960s until the mid-1970s.
Estimated Value: **Excellent:** **$100.00**
Very good: **$ 75.00**

Western Field Model 72

Western Field Model 72

Caliber: 30-30
Action: Lever action; exposed hammer; repeating; side ejector
Magazine: 6-shot tubular
Barrel: Blued; 18", 20"
Sights: Adjustable open rear, ramp front
Stock and Forearm: Walnut two-piece pistol grip stock and forearm; barrel band; fluted comb
Approximate wt.: 7½ lbs.
Comments: Made from the 1960s into the late 1970s.
Estimated Value: **Excellent:** **$195.00**
Very good: **$160.00**

Western Field Model 740

Similar to the Model 72 with recoil pad and 20" barrel. Produced from the 1960s until the mid-1970s.
Estimated Value: **Excellent:** **$190.00**
Very good: **$155.00**

Western Field Model 79

Caliber: 30-30
Action: Lever-action; exposed hammer; repeating; side ejection
Magazine: 6-shot tubular, side load
Barrel: Blued; 20"; round
Sights: Bead front, rear adjustable for elevation
Stock and Forearm: Smooth hardwood pistol grip stock and forearm
Approximate wt.: 7 lbs.
Comments: Made from the 1960s to the early 1980s.
Estimated Value: **Excellent:** **$200.00**
Very good: **$160.00**

Western Field Model 865

Caliber: 22 short, long, long rifle
Action: Lever-action; hammerless; repeating
Magazine: Tubular; 13 long rifles, 15 longs, 20 shorts
Barrel: Blued; 20"
Sights: Adjustable rear, bead front
Stock and Forearm: Wood Monte Carlo pistol grip stock and forearm; barrel band; swivels
Approximate wt.: 7 lbs.
Comments: Made in the mid-1970s.
Estimated Value: **Excellent:** **$135.00**
Very good: **$115.00**

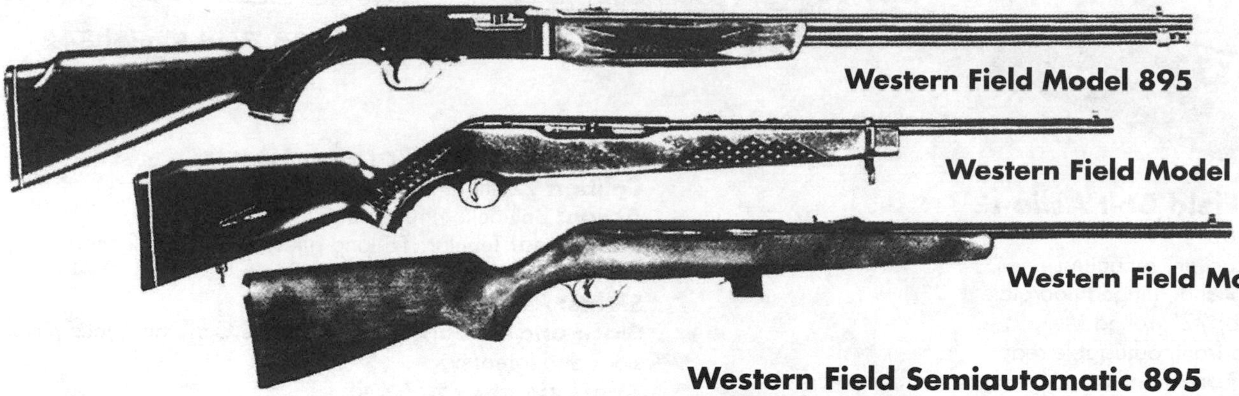

Western Field Model 895

Western Field Model 846

Western Field Model 850

Western Field Model 895
Caliber: 22 long rifle
Action: Semiautomatic; hammerless
Magazine: 18-shot tubular
Barrel: Blued; 24"
Sights: Open rear, bead front
Stock and Forearm: Checkered walnut Monte Carlo pistol grip stock and forearm
Approximate wt.: 7 lbs.
Comments: Made from the 1960s until the mid-1970s.
Estimated Value: **Excellent:** **$140.00**
Very good: **$115.00**

Western Field Model 850
Caliber: 22 long rifle
Action: Semiautomatic; hammerless
Magazine: 7-shot clip
Barrel: Blued; 18"
Sights: Adjustable rear, bead front
Stock and Forearm: Wood one-piece semi-pistol grip stock and tapered forearm
Approximate wt.: 5½ lbs.
Comments: Made from the 1960s to the mid-1970s.
Estimated Value: **Excellent:** **$140.00**
Very good: **$120.00**

Western Field Semiautomatic 895 Carbine
Caliber: 22 long rifle
Action: Semiautomatic; hammerless
Magazine: 15-shot tubular
Barrel: 21"
Sights: Blade front, rear adjustable for elevation
Stock and Forearm: Smooth hardwood one-piece pistol grip stock and forearm
Approximate wt.: 5½ lbs.
Comments: Made from the 1950s until the early 1960s.
Estimated Value: **Excellent:** **$160.00**
Very good: **$135.00**

Western Field Model 846
Caliber: 22 long rifle
Action: Semiautomatic; hammerless
Magazine: 15-shot tubular, stock load
Barrel: Blued; 18½"
Sights: Adjustable rear, bead front
Stock and Forearm: Checkered wood one-piece pistol grip stock and forearm; barrel band; swivels
Approximate wt.: 5¼ lbs.
Comments: Made from the 1960s until the mid-1970s.
Estimated Value: **Excellent:** **$150.00**
Very good: **$120.00**

WINCHESTER

Winchester Model 1900

Winchester Model 02

Winchester Model 1900
Caliber: 22 short, long
Action: Bolt action; single-shot; cocking piece
Magazine: None
Barrel: Blued; 18"; round
Sights: Open rear, blade front
Stock and Forearm: Plain one-piece straight grip stock and forearm
Approximate wt.: 3 lbs.
Comments: Made from about 1900 to 1902.
Estimated Value: **Excellent:** **$1,700.00**
Very good: **$1,350.00**

Winchester Model 02
Similar to the Model 1900 with extended trigger guard; addition of 22 long rifle and extra long. Made from about 1902 to the early 1930s.
Estimated Value: **Excellent:** **$1,000.00**
Very good: **$ 800.00**

Winchester Thumb Trigger (Model 02)

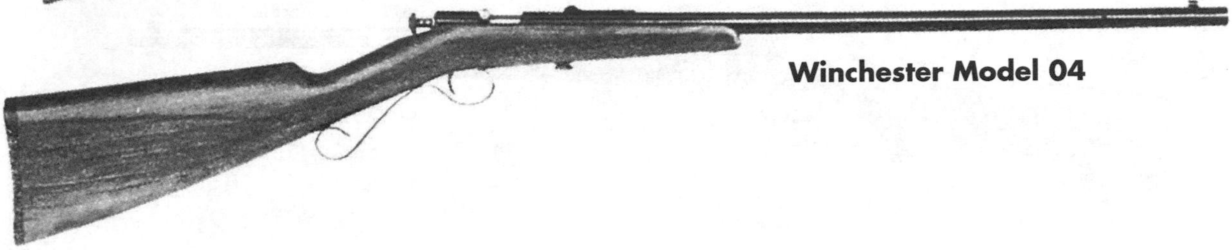

Winchester Model 04

Winchester Thumb Trigger (Model 02)

Similar to the Model 02 with no trigger. The gun is discharged by pushing a button behind the cocking piece. Made until the early 1920s.

Estimated Value:	**Excellent:**	**$1,375.00**
	Very good:	**$1,100.00**

Winchester Model 04

Similar to the Model 02 with regular trigger and a 21" barrel and lipped forearm. Made from 1904 to the early 1930s.

Estimated Value:	**Excellent:**	**$800.00**
	Very good:	**$640.00**

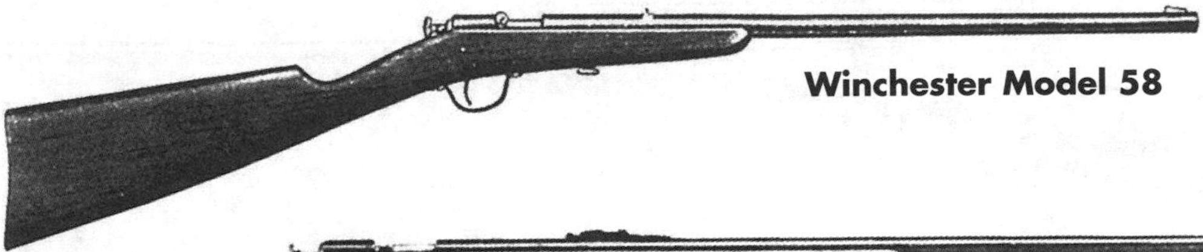

Winchester Model 58

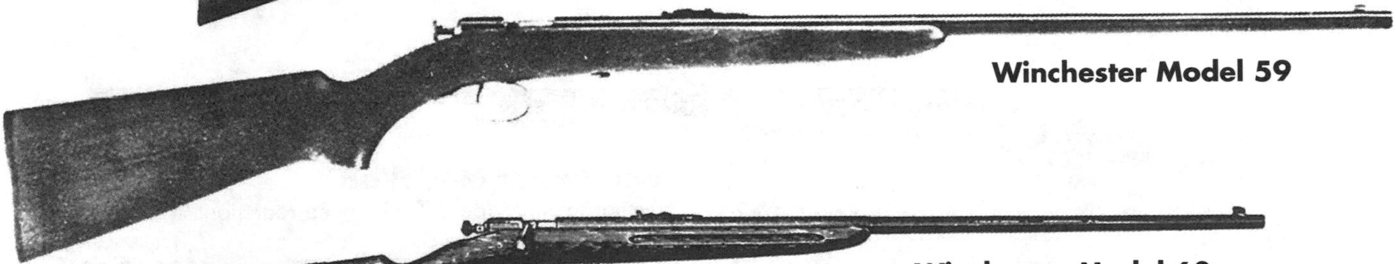

Winchester Model 59

Winchester Model 60

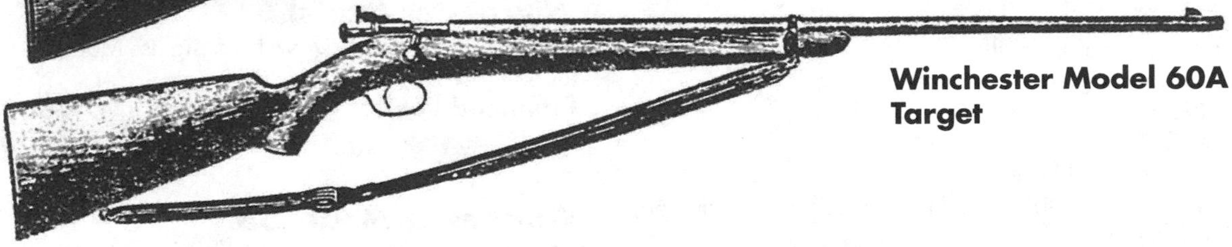

Winchester Model 60A Target

Winchester Model 58

Similar to the Model 1900 single-shot. Made from the late 1920s to the early 1930s.

Estimated Value:	**Excellent:**	**$675.00**
	Very good:	**$540.00**

Winchester Model 59

Similar to the Model 58 with a 23" barrel. Weighs about 4½ lbs. Made from about 1930 to 1931.

Estimated Value:	**Excellent:**	**$725.00**
	Very good:	**$580.00**

Winchester Model 60

Similar to the Model 59 with 23" or 27" barrel. Made from the early to the mid-1930s.

Estimated Value:	**Excellent:**	**$500.00**
	Very good:	**$400.00**

Winchester Model 60A Target

Similar to the Model 60 with special Lyman sights; swivels. Made from the early 1930s to about 1940.

Estimated Value:	**Excellent:**	**$750.00**
	Very good:	**$600.00**

Winchester Model 67

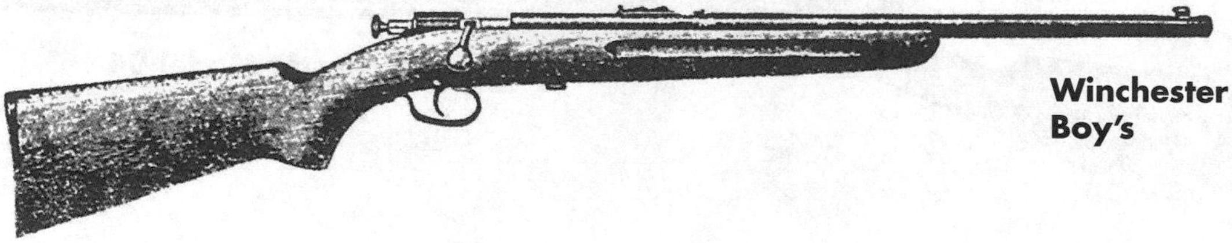

Winchester Model 67 Boy's

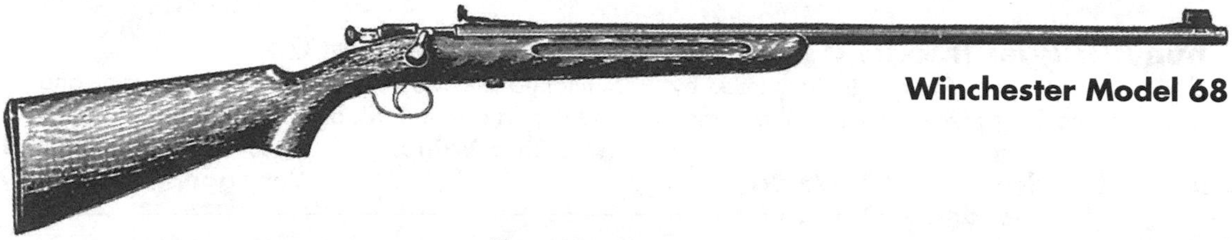

Winchester Model 68

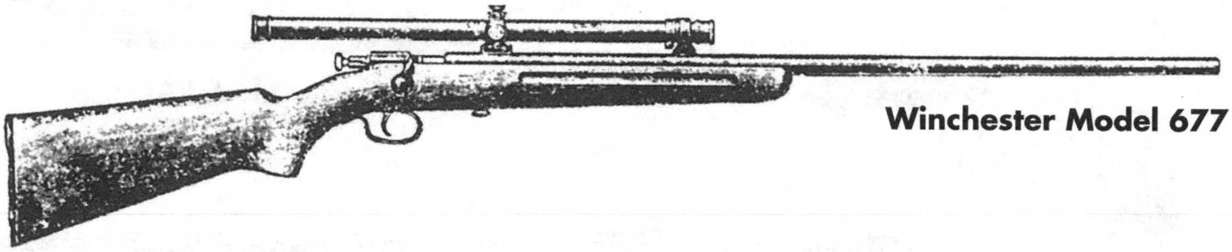

Winchester Model 677

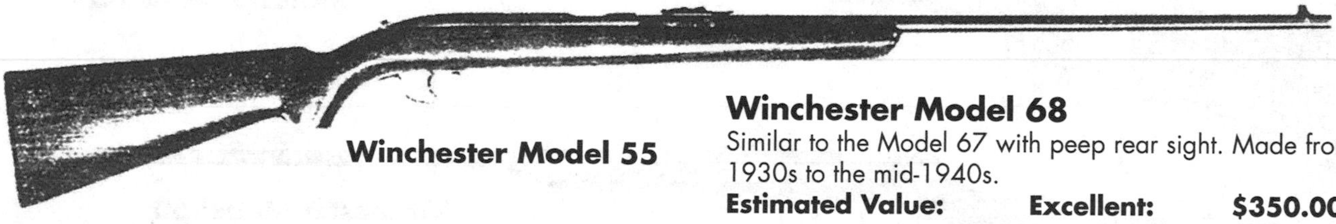

Winchester Model 55

Winchester Model 67

Caliber: 22 short, long, long rifle
Action: Bolt action; single-shot
Magazine: None
Barrel: Blued; 27"
Sights: Open rear, bead front
Stock and Forearm: Plain walnut one-piece semi-pistol grip stock and fluted forearm
Approximate wt.: 5 lbs.
Comments: Made from the mid-1930s to the early 1960s.
Estimated Value: **Excellent:** **$250.00**
Very good: **$200.00**

Winchester Model 67 Boy's

Similar to the Model 67 with a 20" barrel and youth stock.
Estimated Value: **Excellent:** **$275.00**
Very good: **$220.00**

Winchester Model 68

Similar to the Model 67 with peep rear sight. Made from the mid-1930s to the mid-1940s.
Estimated Value: **Excellent:** **$350.00**
Very good: **$280.00**

Winchester Model 677

Similar to the Model 67 with no sights. Made in the late 1930s for two years.
Estimated Value: **Excellent:** **$500.00**
Very good: **$400.00**

Winchester Model 55

Caliber: 22 short, long, long rifle
Action: Single-shot
Magazine: None
Barrel: 22"
Sights: Open rear, bead front
Stock and Forearm: Plain wood one-piece semi-pistol grip stock and forearm
Approximate wt.: 5½ lbs.
Comments: Made from the late 1950s to the early 1960s. This was the second Winchester rifle to be called the Model 55. the other was a lever action produced in the 1920s and 1930s.
Estimated Value: **Excellent:** **$300.00**
Very good: **$240.00**

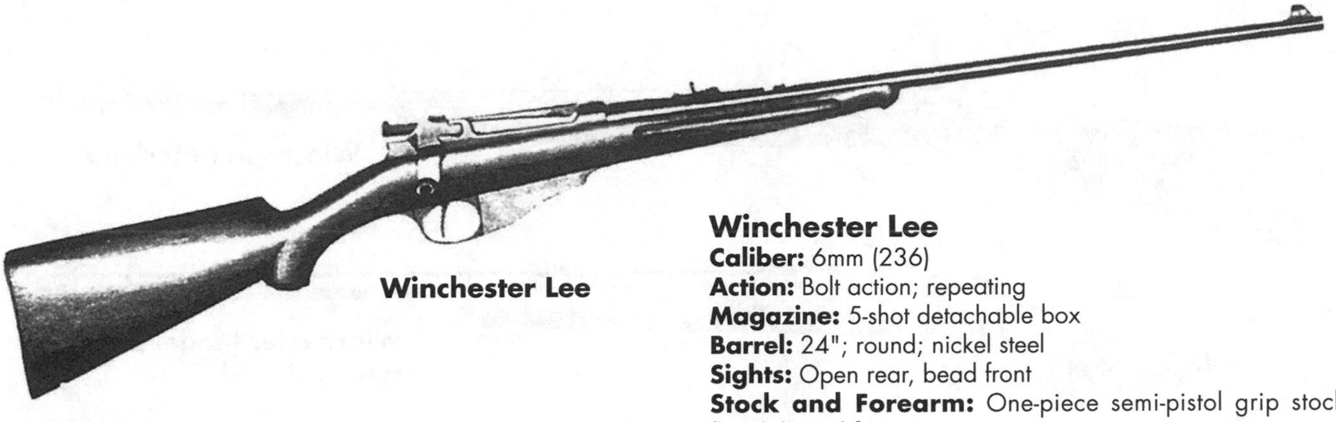

Winchester Lee

Winchester Lee

Caliber: 6mm (236)
Action: Bolt action; repeating
Magazine: 5-shot detachable box
Barrel: 24"; round; nickel steel
Sights: Open rear, bead front
Stock and Forearm: One-piece semi-pistol grip stock and fluted, lipped forearm
Approximate wt.: 7½ to 8½ lbs.
Comments: Made from the late 1890s to the early 1900s.

Estimated Value:	**Excellent:**	**$2,250.00**
	Very good:	**$1,800.00**

Winchester Lee Musket

Similar to the Winchester Lee with military sights, full-length musket forearm, 28" barrel, swivels.

Estimated Value:	**Excellent:**	**$2,500.00**
	Very good:	**$2,000.00**

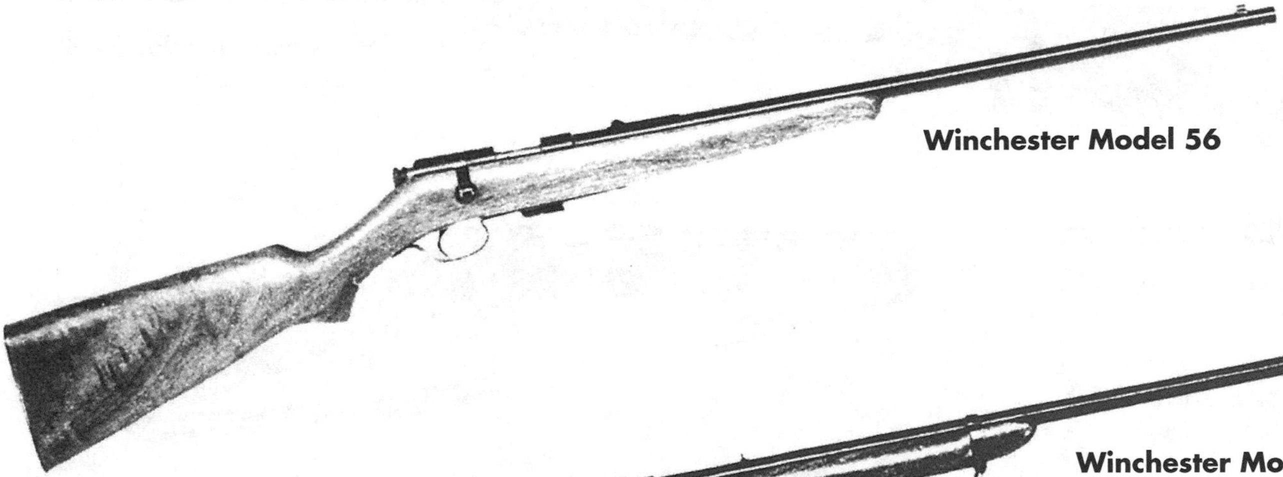

Winchester Model 56

Winchester Model 57

Winchester Model 56

Caliber: 22 short or long rifle only
Action: Bolt action; repeating
Magazine: 5- or 10-shot detachable box
Barrel: Blued; 22"
Sights: Open rear, bead front
Stock and Forearm: Plain walnut one-piece semi-pistol grip stock and lipped forearm
Approximate wt.: 5 lbs.
Comments: Made from the mid- to the late 1920s. A fancy version was available with checkered walnut stock and forearm. Priced for regular version.

Estimated Value:	**Excellent:**	**$1,200.00**
	Very good:	**$ 960.00**

Winchester Model 57

Similar to the Model 56 with longer, unlipped forearm; barrel band, swivels; special Lyman sights; target model. Made from the mid-1920s to the mid-1930s.

Estimated Value:	**Excellent:**	**$1,000.00**
	Very good:	**$ 800.00**

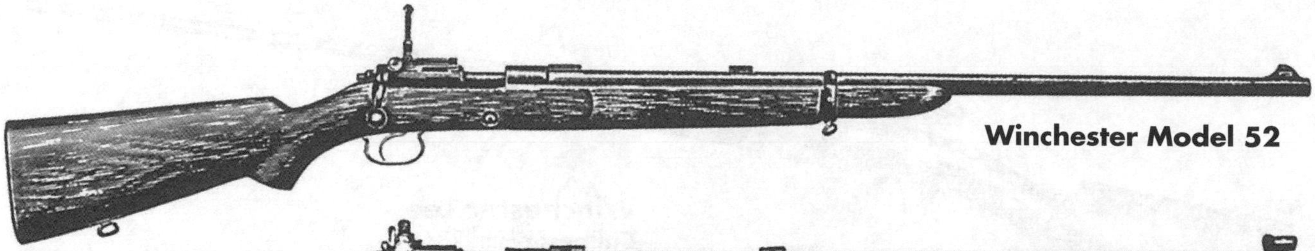

Winchester Model 52

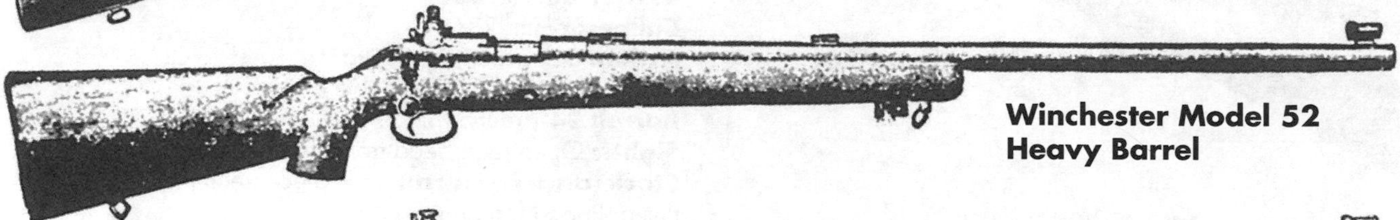

Winchester Model 52
Heavy Barrel

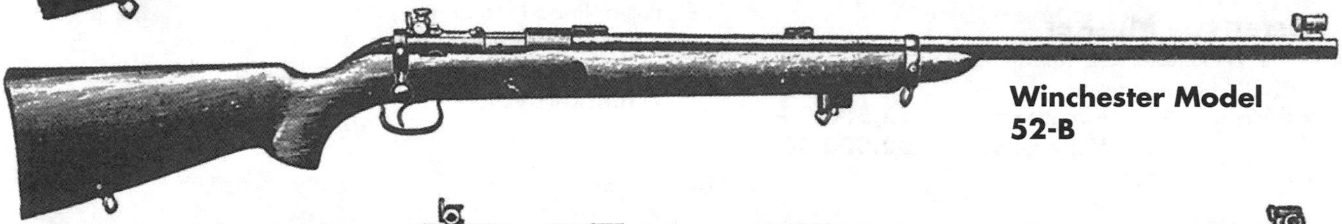

Winchester Model
52-B

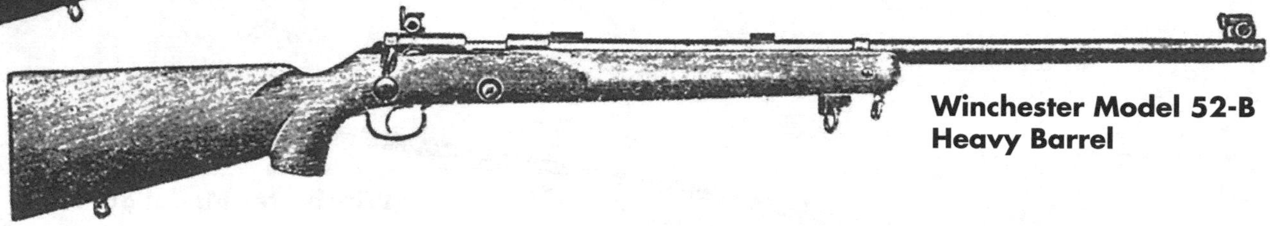

Winchester Model 52-B
Heavy Barrel

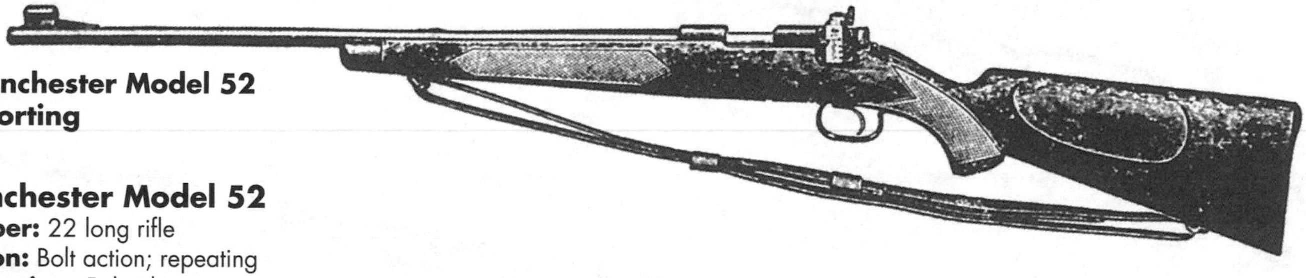

Winchester Model 52
Sporting

Winchester Model 52

Caliber: 22 long rifle
Action: Bolt action; repeating
Magazine: 5-shot box
Barrel: Blued; 28"
Sights: Peep rear, blade front
Stock and Forearm: Plain walnut one-piece pistol grip stock and forearm
Approximate wt.: 8½ lbs.
Comments: Made from about 1920 to the late 1930s.

Estimated Value:	**Excellent:**	**$1,275.00**
	Very good:	**$1,025.00**

Winchester Model 52 Heavy Barrel

Similar to the Model 52 but with a heavy barrel and special Lyman sights.

Estimated Value:	**Excellent:**	**$1,500.00**
	Very good:	**$1,200.00**

Winchester Model 52 Sporting

Similar to the Model 52 except: 24" barrel; special Lyman sights; checkering; cheekpiece. Made from the 1930s to the late 1950s.

Estimated Value:	**Excellent:**	**$3,000.00**
	Very good:	**$2,400.00**

Winchester Model 52-B

Similar to the Model 52 with improved action; high comb stock available. Made from the mid-1930s to the late 1940s.

Estimated Value:	**Excellent:**	**$1,300.00**
	Very good:	**$1,040.00**

Winchester Model 52-B Heavy Barrel

Similar to the Model 52-B with a heavy barrel.

Estimated Value:	**Excellent:**	**$1,300.00**
	Very good:	**$1,040.00**

Winchester Model 52-B Bolt Action Grade I

Similar to the Model 52-B with select walnut stock and forearm; black fore-end tip. Introduced in the late 1990s.

Estimated Value:	**Excellent:**	**$800.00**
	Very good:	**$640.00**

Winchester Model 52-B Bull Gun

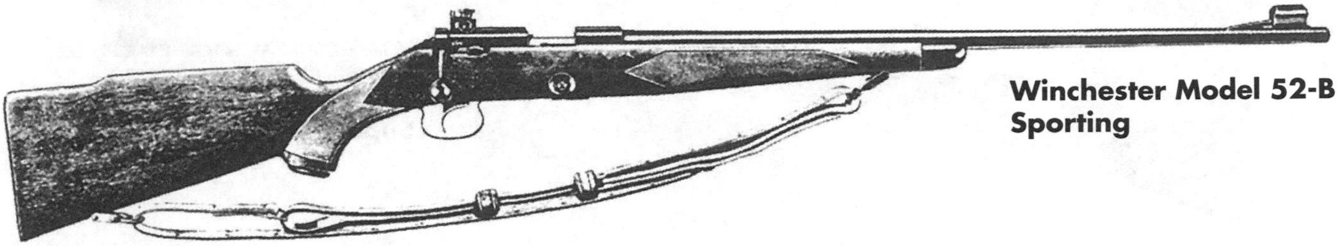

Winchester Model 52-B Sporting

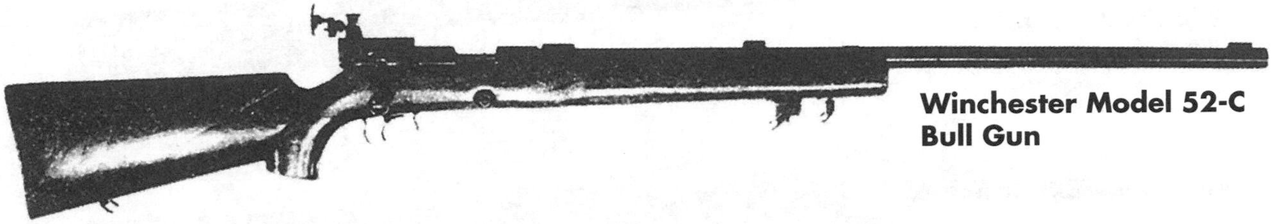

Winchester Model 52-C Bull Gun

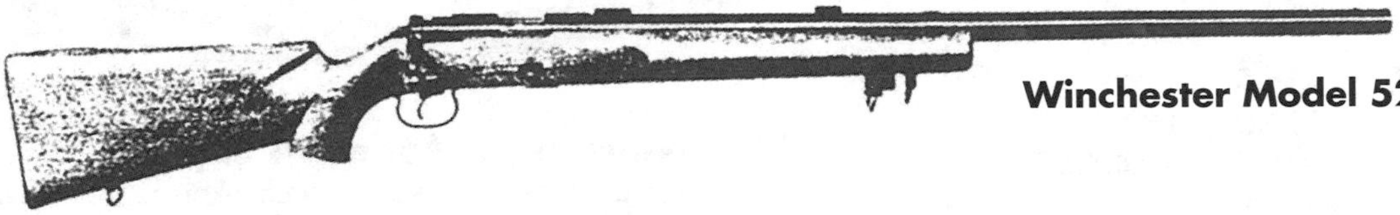

Winchester Model 52-C

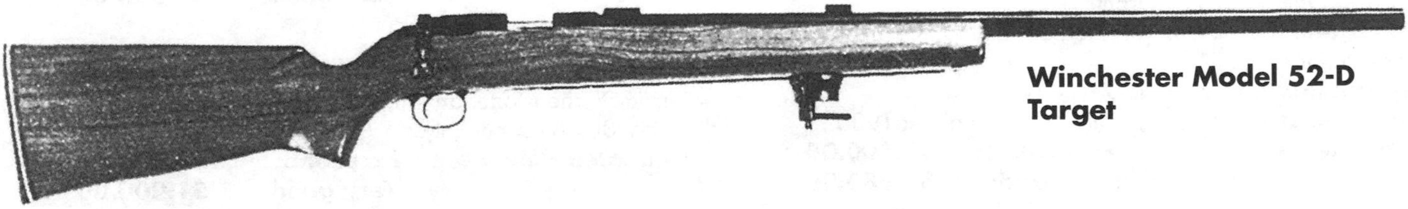

Winchester Model 52-D Target

Winchester Model 52-B Bull Gun

Similar to the Model 52-B Heavy Barrel with still heavier barrel. Weighs about 12 lbs.

Estimated Value: **Excellent:** **$1,775.00**
Very good: **$1,425.00**

Winchester Model 52-B Sporting

Similar to the Model 52 Sporting with a 52-B action. Made from the mid–1930s to the early 1960s.

Estimated Value: **Excellent:** **$3,000.00**
Very good: **$2,400.00**

Winchester Model 52-C

Similar to the Model 52-B with more improvements on the action; high comb stock. Made from the late 1940s to the early 1960s.

Estimated Value: **Excellent:** **$1,500.00**
Very good: **$1,200.00**

Winchester Model 52-C Heavy Barrel

Similar to the Model 52 Heavy Barrel with a 52-C action.

Estimated Value: **Excellent:** **$1,750.00**
Very good: **$1,400.00**

Winchester Model 52-C Bull Gun

Similar to the Model 52-B Bull Gun with a 52-C action.

Estimated Value: **Excellent:** **$1,775.00**
Very good: **$1,425.00**

Winchester Model 52-D Target

Similar to the Model 52-C except: single-shot; hand stop on fore-arm. Made from the early 1960s to the late 1970s; 22 long rifle caliber; approximate wt. 11 lbs.

Estimated Value: **Excellent:** **$1,750.00**
Very good: **$1,400.00**

Winchester Model 54 Sporting (Improved)

Winchester Model 54 Super

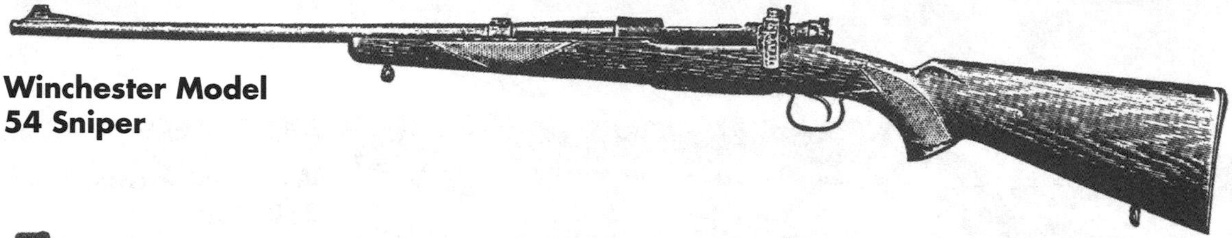

Winchester Model 54 Sniper

Winchester Model 54 National Match

Winchester Model 54

Caliber: 270, 7x57, 30-30, 30-06, 7.65x53mm, 9x57mm, 7mm, 250-3000, 22 Hornet, 220 Swift, 257 Roberts
Action: Bolt action; repeating
Magazine: 5-shot box, non-detachable
Barrel: Blued; 24"
Sights: Open rear, bead front
Stock and Forearm: Checkered walnut one-piece pistol grip stock and forearm
Approximate wt.: 7½ lbs.
Comments: Made from the mid-1920s to about 1930.

Estimated Value:	**Excellent:**	**$1,100.00**
	Very good:	**$ 880.00**

Winchester Model 54 Carbine

Similar to the Model 54 with a 20" barrel; no checkering on stock.

Estimated Value:	**Excellent:**	**$1,200.00**
	Very good:	**$ 950.00**

Winchester Model 54 Sporting (Improved)

Similar to the Model 54 with an improved action; 26" barrel; additional calibers. Made from about 1930 for six years.

Estimated Value:	**Excellent:**	**$1,000.00**
	Very good:	**$ 800.00**

Winchester Model 54 Carbine (Improved)

Similar to the Model 54 Carbine with improved action. Made from 1930 to the mid-1930s.

Estimated Value:	**Excellent:**	**$1,000.00**
	Very good:	**$ 800.00**

Winchester Model 54 Super

Similar to the Model 54 with cheekpiece; select wood; deluxe finish; swivels.

Estimated Value:	**Excellent:**	**$1,150.00**
	Very good:	**$ 925.00**

Winchester Model 54 Sniper

Similar to the Model 54 with a 26" heavy barrel; special Lyman sights; 30-06 caliber only.

Estimated Value:	**Excellent:**	**$1,500.00**
	Very good:	**$1,200.00**

Winchester Model 54 Sniper Match

Deluxe version of the Model 54 Sniper with high-quality finish.

Estimated Value:	**Excellent:**	**$1,850.00**
	Very good:	**$1,485.00**

Winchester Model 54 National Match

Similar to the Model 54 with special Lyman sights and marksman stock.

Estimated Value:	**Excellent:**	**$1,500.00**
	Very good:	**$1,200.00**

Winchester Model 54 Target

Similar to the Model 54 with 24" barrel and special Lyman sights.

Estimated Value:	**Excellent:**	**$1,350.00**
	Very good:	**$1,075.00**

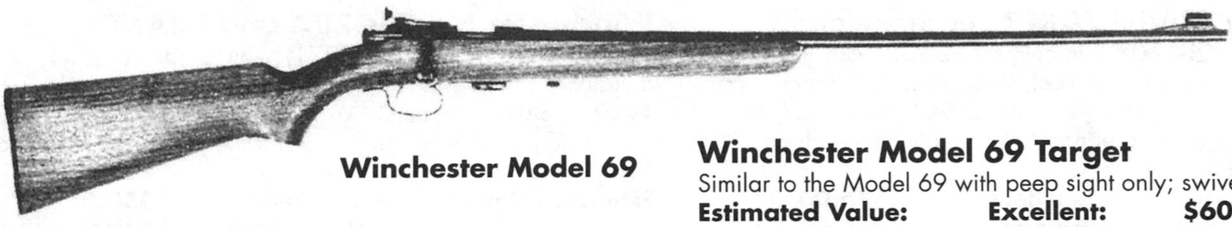

Winchester Model 69

Winchester Model 69

Caliber: 22 short, long, long rifle
Action: Bolt action; repeating
Magazine: 5- or 10-shot detachable box
Barrel: Blued; 25"
Sights: Peep or open rear, ramp front
Stock and Forearm: Plain walnut one-piece semi-pistol grip stock and forearm
Approximate wt.: 5½ lbs.
Comments: Made from the mid-1930s to the early 1960s.
Estimated Value: **Excellent:** **$425.00**
Very good: **$340.00**

Winchester Model 69 Target

Similar to the Model 69 with peep sight only; swivels.
Estimated Value: **Excellent:** **$600.00**
Very good: **$480.00**

Winchester Model 69 Match

Similar to the Model 69 Target with special Lyman sights.
Estimated Value: **Excellent:** **$550.00**
Very good: **$440.00**

Winchester Model 697

Similar to the Model 69 with no sights. Made from the late 1930s to the early 1940s.
Estimated Value: **Excellent:** **$1,000.00**
Very good: **$ 800.00**

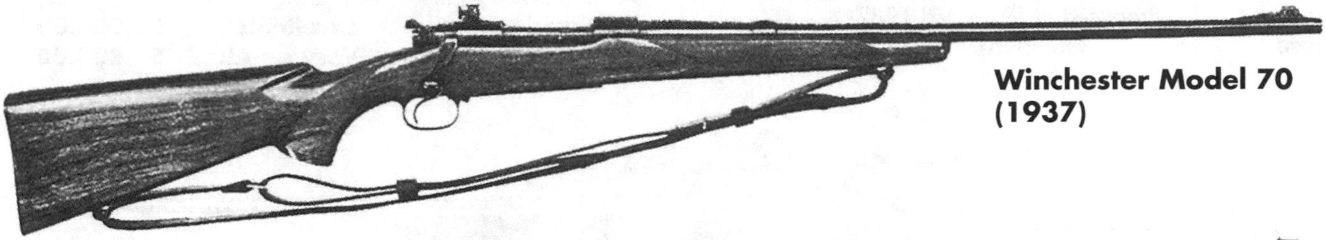

Winchester Model 70 (1937)

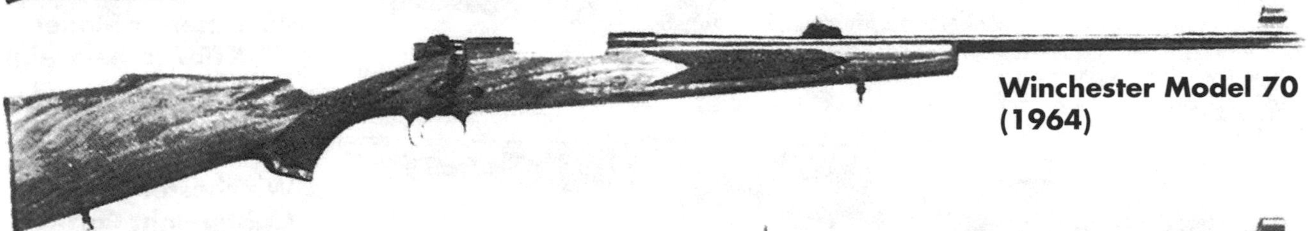

Winchester Model 70 (1964)

Winchester Model 70XTR

Winchester Model 70 (1937)

Caliber: 375 H&H mag., 300 H&H mag., 300 Win. mag., 338 win., 308 Win., 35 Rem., 358 Win., 30-06, 7x57mm, 270 Win., 257 Roberts, 250-3000, 243, 220 Swift, 22 Hornet
Action: Bolt action; repeating
Magazine: 5-shot box; 4-shot box in magnum
Barrel: Blued; 24", 25", 26"
Sights: Open rear, hooded ramp front
Stock and Forearm: Checkered walnut one-piece pistol grip stock and forearm
Approximate wt.: 7¾ lbs.
Comments: Made from about 1937 to 1963. Add $300.00 for mint, unfired condition. Add $200.00 for magnum.
Estimated Value: **Excellent:** **$1,750.00**
Very good: **$1,400.00**

Winchester Model 70 (1964)

Similar to the Model 70 (1937) except: improvements; Monte Carlo stock; swivels. Made from about 1964 to 1970; calibers 22-250, 22 Rem., 225, 243, 270, 308, 30-06.
Estimated Value: **Excellent:** **$1,000.00**
Very good: **$ 800.00**

Winchester Models 70 (1971), 70XTR (1978), and 70XTR Sporter (1983)

Similar to the Model 70 (1964) with improvements. Made from 1971 to the early 1990s. Calibers 270 Win., 30-06, 25-06 (1985), 308 Win. (1987), 243 (1988).
Estimated Value: **Excellent:** **$650.00**
Very good: **$520.00**

Winchester Model 70XTR Featherweight
Similar to the Model 70XTR in calibers 22-250, 223 (introduced in 1984); 243, 308 (short action); 270 Win., 257 Roberts, 7mm Mauser, 30-06 Springfield (standard action); recoil pad; lipped forearm; decorative checkering; 22" barrel. Produced from 1984 to the early 1990s.

Estimated Value:	**Excellent:**	**$575.00**
	Very good:	**$460.00**

Winchester Model 70XTR European Featherweight
Similar to the Model 70XTR Featherweight in caliber 6.55x55 Swedish Mauser. Produced in 1986 and 1987.

Estimated Value:	**Excellent:**	**$550.00**
	Very good:	**$440.00**

Winchester Model 70 Lightweight Carbine
Similar to the Model 70XTR Featherweight with different outward appearance; 20" barrel; calibers 270 Win., 30-06 Springfield; 22-250 Rem., 223 Rem., 243 Win., 250 Savage; 308 Win.; weighs 6 to 6¼ lbs. Produced in 1986 and 1987.

Estimated Value:	**Excellent:**	**$500.00**
	Very good:	**$400.00**

Winchester Models 70A and 70AXTR
Similar to the Model 70 (1971) with a special steel barrel; adjustable sights. Made from the early 1970s to about 1981; 4-shot or 3-shot (magnum) box magazine. Add $20.00 for 264 Win. mag., 7mm Rem. mag., or 300 Win. mag.; Police Model $10.00 less.

Estimated Value:	**Excellent:**	**$550.00**
	Very good:	**$440.00**

Winchester Model 70 Super (1937)
Similar to the Model 70 (1937) with swivels; deluxe finish; cheekpiece. Made to the early 1960s.

Estimated Value:	**Excellent:**	**$2,750.00**
	Very good:	**$2,200.00**

Winchester Model 70 Super
Similar to the Model 70 Super (1937) with recoil pad; select wood. Made from the mid-1960s to the mid-1970s.

Estimated Value:	**Excellent:**	**$1,000.00**
	Very good:	**$ 800.00**

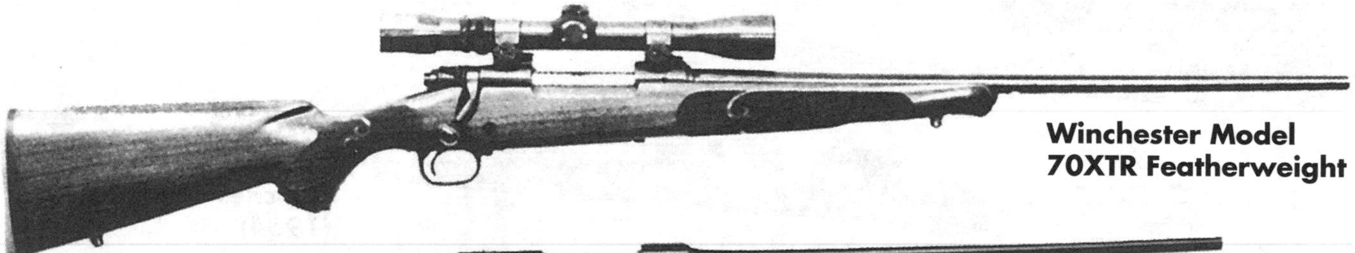
Winchester Model 70XTR Featherweight

Winchester Model 70 Lightweight Carbine

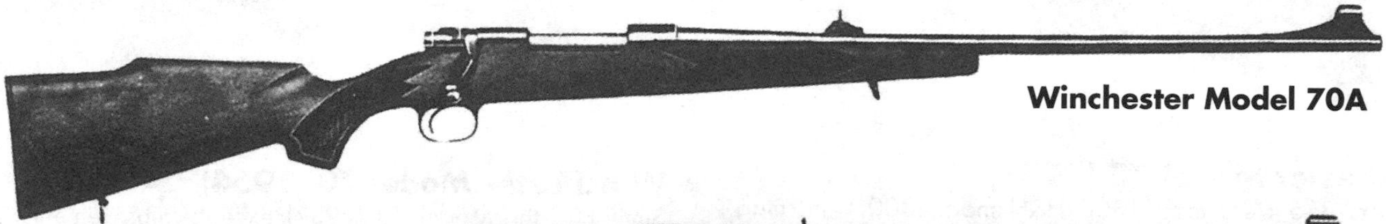
Winchester Model 70A

Winchester Model 70 Super (1937)

Winchester Model 70 Super

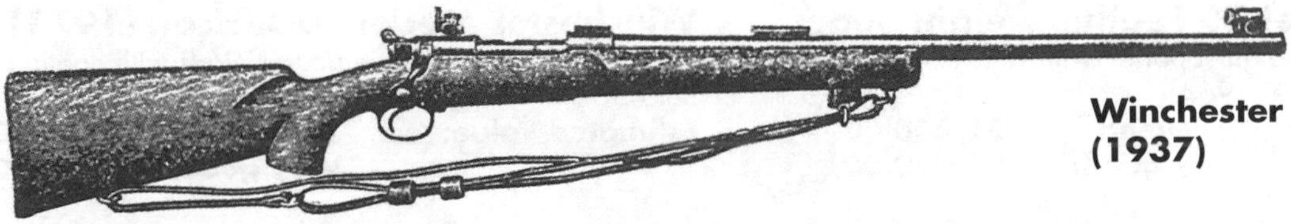

Winchester Model 70 Target (1937)

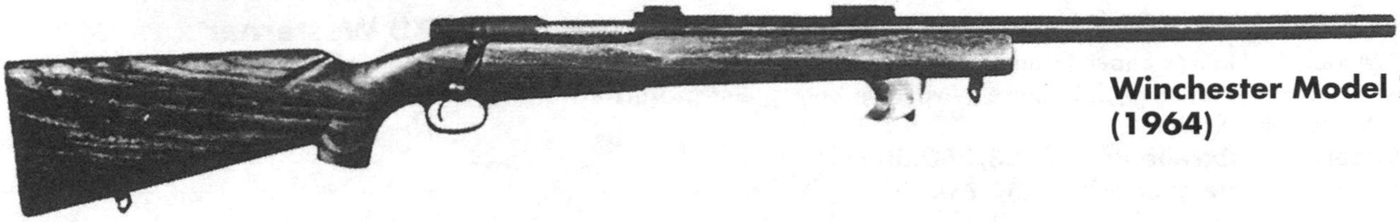

Winchester Model 70 Target (1964)

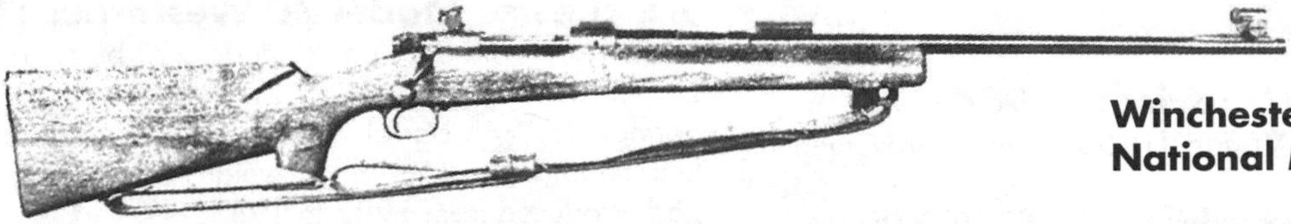

Winchester Model 70 National Match

Winchester Model 70 Mannlicher

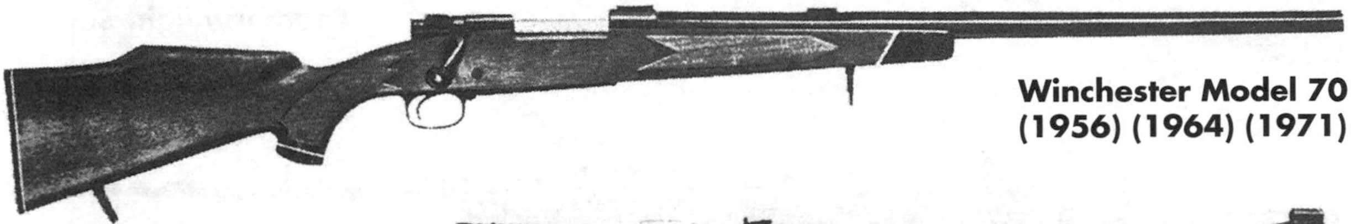

Winchester Model 70 Varmint (1956) (1964) (1971)

Winchester Model 70 Featherweight Sporter

Winchester Model 70 Target (1937)

Similar to the Model 70 (1937) with 24" barrel and improved stock. Made until about 1963.

Estimated Value: **Excellent:** **$2,000.00**
Very good: **$1,600.00**

Winchester Model 70 Target (1964 and 1971)

Similar to the Model 70 Target (1937) with aluminum hand stop. Model 1971 has minor improvements; calibers 30-06, 308 Win., or 308 Int'l Army. Add $132.00 for Int'l Army.

Estimated Value: **Excellent:** **$1,200.00**
Very good: **$ 960.00**

Winchester Model 70 National Match

Similar to the Model 70 (1937) with marksman stock in 30-06 caliber. Made from the late 1930s to the early 1960s.

Estimated Value: **Excellent:** **$1,500.00**
Very good: **$1,200.00**

Winchester Model 70 Mannlicher

Similar to the Model 70 (1964) with full-length forearm; 19" barrel; calibers 243, 270, 308, 30-06. Made to the early 1970s.

Estimated Value: **Excellent:** **$1,000.00**
Very good: **$ 800.00**

Winchester Models 70 Varmint (1956) (1964) (1971), 70XTR Varmint

Similar to the Model 70 (1937) with heavy 24" or 26" barrel. Improvements made along with other Model 70s. Calibers 222 Rem., 22-250, or 243 Win. Add 90% for pre-1964 models. Discontinued in 1988.

Estimated Value: **Excellent:** **$1,200.00**
Very good: **$ 950.00**

Winchester Model 70 Featherweight Sporter

A lightweight rifle similar to the Model 70 (1937) with improved stock. Made from the early 1950s to the 1960s.

Estimated Value: **Excellent:** **$1,500.00**
Very good: **$1,200.00**

Winchester Model 70 Featherweight Super

Similar to the Featherweight Sporter with deluxe finish; cheek-piece; swivels. Made after 1964.

Estimated Value: **Excellent:** **$1,200.00**
Very good: **$ 960.00**

Winchester Model 70 African (1956)

Similar to the Model 70 (1937) Super Grade with recoil pad; Monte Carlo stock; 3-shot magazine; 24" barrel. Available only in 458 caliber. Made until 1963.

Estimated Value: **Excellent:** **$3,250.00**
Very good: **$2,600.00**

Winchester Model 70 African (1964)

Similar to the Model 70 African (1956) with improvements. Made until 1970.

Estimated Value: **Excellent:** **$1,700.00**
Very good: **$1,350.00**

Winchester Model 70 African (1971)

Similar to the Model 70 African (1964) with floating barrel; caliber 458 Win. mag. Discontinued about 1981.

Estimated Value: **Excellent:** **$1,000.00**
Very good: **$ 800.00**

Winchester Model 70 Westerner

Similar to the Model 70 Alaskan. Made in the early 1960s.

Estimated Value: **Excellent:** **$1,200.00**
Very good: **$ 950.00**

Winchester Model 70 Westerner (1982)

Similar to the Model 70XTR with a 22" barrel and 4-shot magazine in calibers 243 Win., 270 Win., 308 Win., and 30-06 Springfield; 24" barrel and 3-shot magazine in calibers 7mm Rem. mag., 300 Win. mag.; weighs about 7½ to 7¾ lbs.; recoil pad. Produced from 1982 to 1984.

Estimated Value: **Excellent:** **$600.00**
Very good: **$480.00**

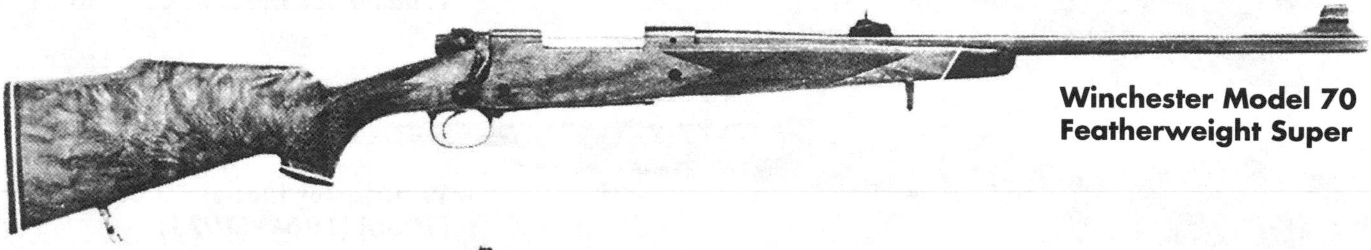

Winchester Model 70 Featherweight Super

Winchester Model 70 African (1956)

Winchester Model 70 African (1964)

Winchester Model 70 African (1971)

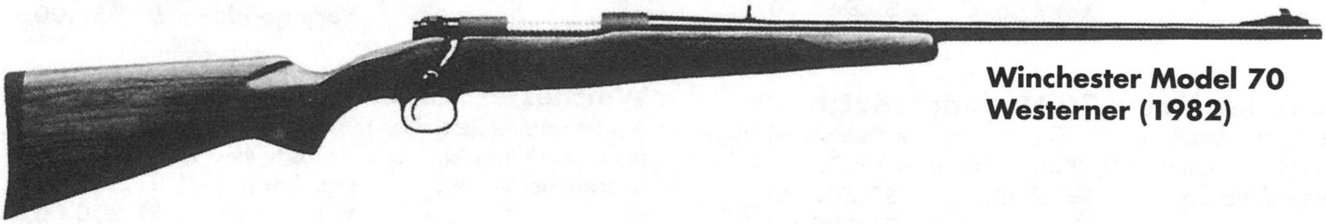

Winchester Model 70 Westerner (1982)

Winchester Model 70 Magnum (1964)

Winchester Model 70 Alaskan

Winchester Model 70 Deluxe (1964)

Winchester Model 70 Classic Super Express

Winchester Model 70 Classic Super Express and Safari Express

Same as the Model 70 Classic Sporter or Mag. with a 22" or 24" barrel in 458 Win. mag., 375 H&H mag., 416 Rem. mag. Controlled round feeding after 1993. Made from 1982 to the early 2000s.

Estimated Value:	**Excellent:**	**$1,000.00**
	Very good:	**$ 800.00**

Winchester Model 70 Deluxe (1964)

Similar to the Model 70 (1964) with Monte Carlo stock; recoil pad; deluxe features. Made from 1964 to the early 1970s.

Estimated Value:	**Excellent:**	**$875.00**
	Very good:	**$700.00**

Winchester Model 70 Alaskan

Similar to the Model 70 (1937) with 24" or 26" barrel. Made in the early 1960s.

Estimated Value:	**Excellent:**	**$1,675.00**
	Very good:	**$1,340.00**

Winchester Model 70XTR Sporter

Winchester Model 70 Winlite

Winchester Model 70 Winlite

Caliber: 270, 30-06, 7mm Rem. mag., 300 Win. mag., 300 Weatherby mag., 338 Win. mag.
Action: Bolt action; repeating
Magazine: 4-shot in 270 or 30-06; 3-shot in 7mm Rem. mag. or 338 Win. mag.
Barrel: 22" in 270 and 30-06; 24" in mag. calibers
Sights: None
Stock and Forearm: Fiberglass reinforced one-piece stock and forearm with thermoplastic bedding
Approximate wt.: 6¼ to 6¾ lbs.
Comments: Made from 1986 to 1991. Add 3% for 300 Weatherby mag.

Estimated Value:	**Excellent:**	**$600.00**
	Very good:	**$480.00**

Winchester Model 70 Magnum (1964)

Similar to the Model 70 (1964) with Monte Carlo stock; recoil pad; swivels; 3-shot magazine. Made until the early 1970s.

Estimated Value:	**Excellent:**	**$1,000.00**
	Very good:	**$ 800.00**

Winchester Model 70XTR, 70 Classic Sporter, and Classic Sporter LT

Caliber: 22-250, 223, 243, 25-06 Rem., 264 Win. mag., 270 Win., 270 Wby. mag., 300 Win mag., 338 Win. mag.; 7mm STW, 7mm Rem. mag., 300 Wby. mag., 30-06 Spfld.
Action: Bolt action; repeating; controlled round feeding after 1993
Magazine: 3-shot box
Barrel: Blued; 24" or 26"; stainless steel available in some calibers
Sights: None; drilled for scope mount
Stock and Forearm: Checkered walnut Monte Carlo one-piece pistol grip stock and forearm; recoil pad, laminated stock available
Approximate wt.: 7¾ lbs.
Comments: Produced from 1982 to 2005. Add 7% for sights; add 18% for BOSS, (Ballistic Optimizing Shooting System). Add 17% for stainless steel. Add 10% for laminated stock.

Estimated Value:	**Excellent:**	**$625.00**
	Very good:	**$500.00**

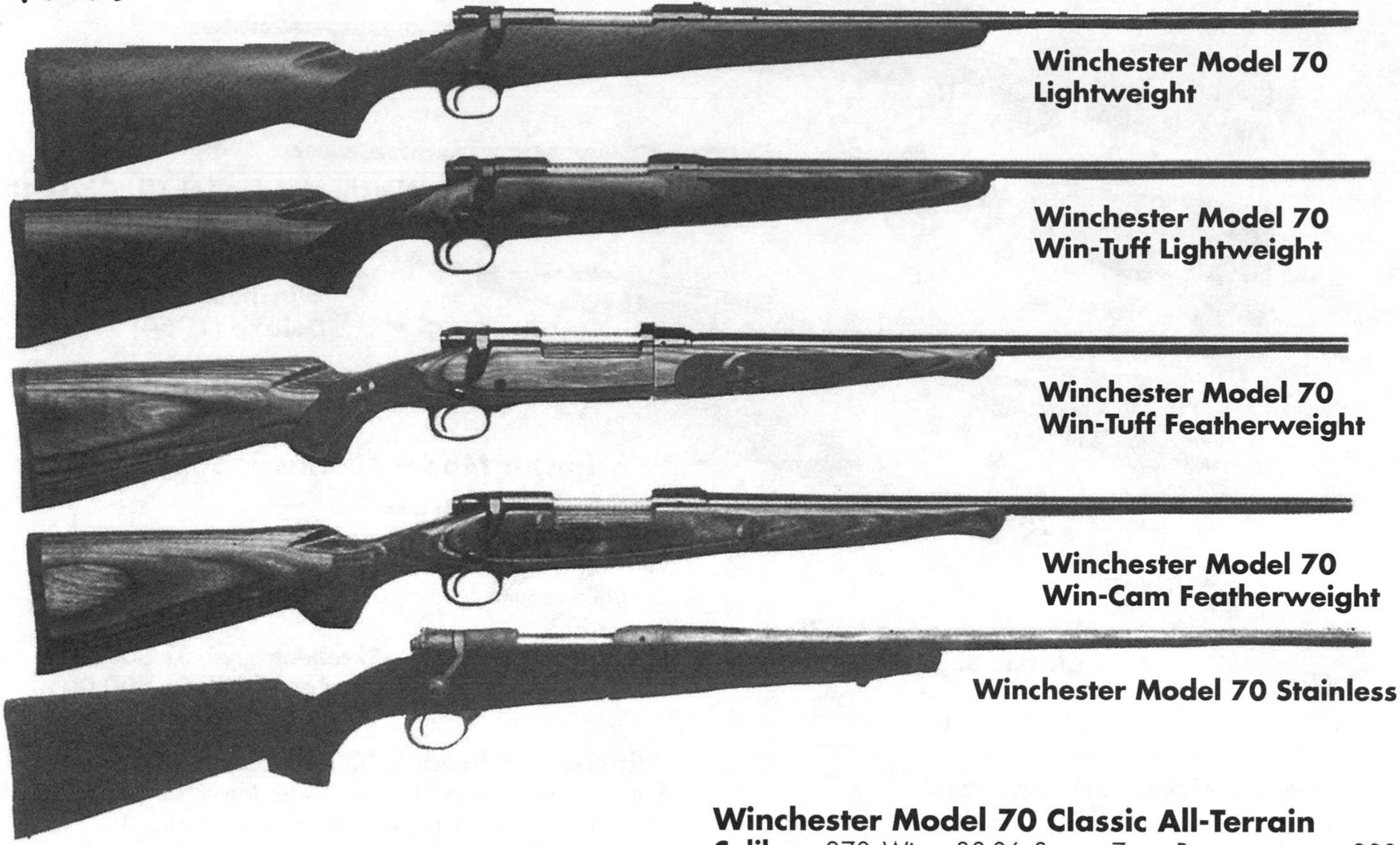
Winchester Model 70 Lightweight
Winchester Model 70 Win-Tuff Lightweight
Winchester Model 70 Win-Tuff Featherweight
Winchester Model 70 Win-Cam Featherweight
Winchester Model 70 Stainless

Winchester Model 70 Lightweight

Similar to the Model 70XTR with a 22" barrel; weighs 6¼ lbs.; calibers: 22-250 Rem., 223 Rem., 243 Win., 270 Win., 280 Win., 30-06 Spring., 308 Win.; no sights.

Estimated Value: **Excellent:** **$575.00**
Very good: **$460.00**

Winchester Model 70 Win-Tuff Lightweight

Similar to the Model 70 Lightweight with laminated stock of dye-shaded hardwoods. Available in calibers: 223 Rem., 243 Win., 270 Win., 308 Win., 30-06 Spring.; short or long action; no sights.

Estimated Value: **Excellent:** **$500.00**
Very good: **$400.00**

Winchester Model 70 Win-Tuff Featherweight

Similar to the Model 70 Featherweight with laminated stock of dye-shaded hardwood. Available in calibers: 243 Win., 270 Win., 30-06 Spring. Discontinued in 1991.

Estimated Value: **Excellent:** **$475.00**
Very good: **$380.00**

Winchester Model 70 Win-Cam Featherweight

Similar to the Model 70 Featherweight with laminated stock of green and brown camouflage. Available in 270 Win. and 30-06 Spring. Discontinued in 1991.

Estimated Value: **Excellent:** **$525.00**
Very good: **$420.00**

Winchester Model 70 Classic All-Terrain

Caliber: 270 Win., 30-06 Sprg., 7mm Rem. magnum, 300 Win. magnum
Action: Bolt action; repeating; 3-position safety
Magazine: 5-shot; 3-shot in magnum calibers
Barrel: 22", 24" stainless steel
Sights: None, drilled for scope mounts
Stock and Forearm: Checkered pistol grip, one-piece black fiberglass/graphite synthetic stock and forearm
Approximate wt.: 7¼ lbs.
Comments: Introduced in 1996; add 17% for BOSS (Ballistic Optimizing Shooting System) which is an adjustable device attached to the muzzle to control the shockwave vibrations of the barrel.

Estimated Value: **Excellent:** **$675.00**
Very good: **$540.00**

Winchester Model 70 Stainless

Caliber: 270, 30-06, 7mm Rem. mag., 300 Win. mag., 338 Win. mag.
Action: Bolt action; repeating; 3-position safety; controlled round feeding after 1993
Magazine: 5-shot; hinged floor plate
Barrel: Blued; 22", 24", or 26"
Sights: None
Stock and Forearm: Black synthetic composite impregnated with fiberglass and graphite one-piece checkered pistol grip stock and forearm; rubber recoil pad
Approximate wt.: 7¾ lbs.
Comments: Produced from 1992 to 1995; lightweight all-weather rifle.

Estimated Value: **Excellent:** **$700.00**
Very good: **$560.00**

Winchester Model 70 Super Grade

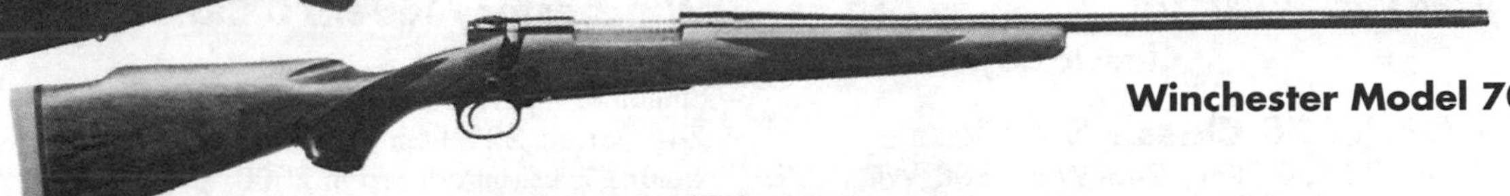

Winchester Model 70 Varmint

Winchester Model 70 Black Shadow

Winchester Models 70 Black Shadow and SuperShadow

Caliber: 270 Win., 30-06 Sprng., 7mm Rem. magnum, 300 Win. magnum, available in Winchester short magnum after 2003.
Action: Bolt action, repeating; push-feed bolt
Magazine: 5-shot; 3-shot in magnum calibers; hinged floor plate
Barrel: 24", 26" in magnum calibers; matte blue
Sights: None
Stock and forearm: Checkered composite, one-piece stock and forearm; swivels
Approximate wt.: $7\frac{1}{4}$ lbs.
Comments: Introduced in 2001. Add 6% for magnum calibers.

Estimated Value:	**Excellent:**	**$500.00**
	Very good:	**$400.00**

Winchester Model 70 Sporter DBM

Caliber: 25-06 Rem., 264 Win. mag., 270 Win., 270 Wby. mag. 30-06, 7mm Rem. mag., 300 Win. mag., 300 Wby. mag., 338 Win. mag.
Action: Bolt action; repeating
Magazine: 3-shot detachable box
Barrel: Blued; 24" or 26"
Sights: None, scope base and rings; sights optional
Stock and Forearm: Checkered walnut one-piece pistol grip stock and forearm
Approximate wt.: $7\frac{7}{8}$ lbs.
Comments: Made from 1992 to the mid-1990s. Add 6% for sights.

Estimated Value:	**Excellent:**	**$525.00**
	Very good:	**$420.00**

Winchester Model 70 Sporter Win-Tuff

Caliber: 270, 30-06, 7mm Rem. magnum, 300 Win. mag., 300 Wby. mag., 338 Win. mag.
Action: Bolt action; repeating; 3-position safety
Magazine: 5-shot in 270 and 30-06; 3-shot in magnum calibers; hinged floor plate
Barrel: 24"; blued
Sights: None
Stock and Forearm: Brown laminated checkered, one-piece stock and forearm with cheekpiece
Approximate wt.: $7\frac{7}{8}$ lbs.
Comments: Made in the early 1990s.

Estimated Value:	**Excellent:**	**$500.00**
	Very good:	**$425.00**

Winchester Models 70 Super Grade, Classic Super Grade, and Super Grade III

Caliber: 270, 30-06, 7mm Rem. mag., 300 Win. mag., 338 Win. mag.
Action: Bolt action; repeating; 3-position safety; controlled feeding after 1993
Magazine: 5-shot; 3-shot in mag.; hinged floor plate
Barrel: Blued; 24" or 26"
Sights: None, scope base and rings
Stock and Forearm: Select checkered walnut, one-piece stock and forearm, sculptured cheekpiece
Approximate wt.: $7\frac{3}{4}$ lbs.
Comments: Made from the late 1980s to the present. Add 15% for BOSS (Ballistic Optimizing Shooting System).

Estimated Value:	**New (retail):**	**$1,159.00**
	Excellent:	**$ 865.00**
	Very good:	**$ 695.00**

Winchester Model 70 SSM and Classic SM

Same as the Model 70 Stainless except: 24" or 26" barrel; black matte finish. Steel barrel and receiver; introduced in 1992. 375 H&H mag. added in 1994. Add 18% for BOSS (Ballistic Optimizing Shooting System). Discontinued in the mid-1990s.

Estimated Value:	**Excellent:**	**$700.00**
	Very good:	**$560.00**

Winchester Model 70 Varmint, 70 Heavy Varmint

Caliber: 22-250, 223, 243, 308. 220 swift (in 1994)
Action: Bolt action; repeating; 3-position safety
Magazine: 5-shot; hinged floorplate
Barrel: 26"; counter-bored heavy barrel; blued, matte, or stainless steel; fluted barrel available
Sights: None
Stock and Forearm: Checkered walnut one-piece pistol grip stock and forearm or black composite checkered matte finish stock and forearm
Approximate wt.: 9 lbs.
Comments: Made from the late 1980s to the late 1990s. Priced for stainless steel. Add 17% for fluted barrel.

Estimated Value:	**Excellent:**	**$700.00**
	Very good:	**$560.00**

Winchester Model 70 Classic Coyote Stainless

Winchester Model 70 Classic Stainless

Caliber: 223 Rem., 22-250 Rem., 243 Win., 308 Win., 270 Win., 30-06 Sprng., 7mm Rem. mag., 300 Win. mag., 300 Wby. mag., 338 Win. mag., 375 H&H
Action: Bolt action; repeating; controlled round feeding
Magazine: 3- to 5-shot box
Barrel: 22", 24" or 26"; stainless steel
Sights: None
Stock and Forearm: Black synthetic fiberglass/graphite checkered, one-piece pistol grip stock and tapered forearm; swivel studs
Approximate wt.: 7 to 7½ lbs.
Comments: Introduced in 1994; all stainless steel. Add 18% for BOSS (Ballistic Optimizing Shooting System). Add 8% for 375 H&H.

Estimated Value:	**Excellent:**	**$700.00**
	Very good:	**$560.00**

Winchester Model 70 Classic Coyote Stainless

Similar to the Model 70 Classic Stainless except: laminated stock; 24" barrel; 223 Rem., 22-250 Rem., and 243 Win. calibers; weighs 9 lbs. Introduced in 2000.

Estimated Value:	**Excellent:**	**$675.00**
	Very good:	**$540.00**

Winchester Model 70 Stealth, Stealth II

Similar to the Model 70 Classic Stainless except: heavy, 26" barrel; 223 Rem., 22-250 Rem., and 308 Win. calibers; weighs 10¾ lbs. Introduced in 2000. Winchester short magnum calibers added 2004.

Estimated Value:	**Excellent:**	**$700.00**
	Very good:	**$560.00**

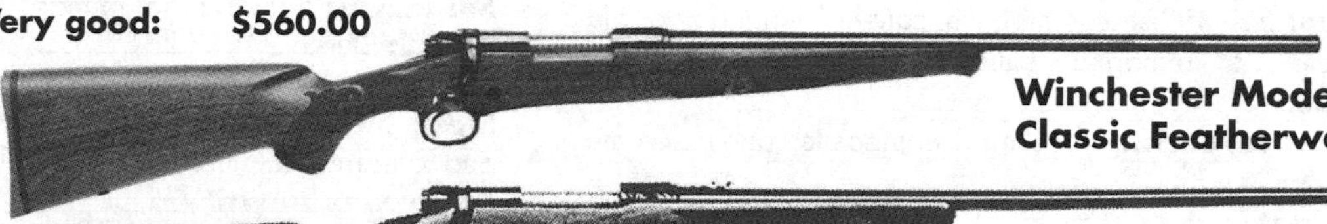

Winchester Model 70 Classic Featherweight

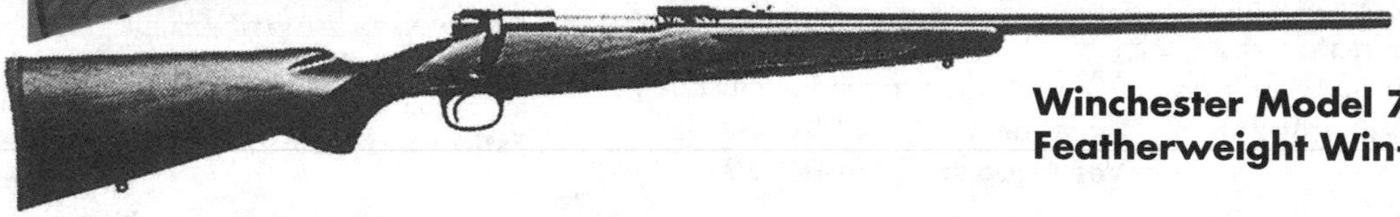

Winchester Model 70 Featherweight Win-Tuff

Winchester Model 70 Featherweight Win-Tuff

Caliber: 22-250, 223 Rem., 243 Win., 308 Win., 30-06 Spgf. calibers 65x55, 270 Win., 280 Rem. and 7mm-08 Rem. added in 1992
Action: Bolt action; repeating; 3-position safety; controlled round feeding after 1993
Magazine: 5- or 6-shot; hinged floor plate
Barrel: 22"; blued
Sights: None
Stock and Forearm: Laminated brown hardwood or walnut one-piece checkered stock and forearm with a schnabel fore-end (lipped)
Approximate wt.: 6 to 7 lbs.
Comments: Previously made in the 1980s in 243, 270, and 30-06 calibers; reintroduced in 1992 to the mid-1990s in larger selection of calibers. 223 WSSM and 243 WSSM added in 2004 (add 6%).

Estimated Value:	**Excellent:**	**$525.00**
	Very good:	**$420.00**

Winchester Model 70 Classic Compact

Similar to the Model 70 Classic Featherweight scaled down for smaller shooters; 20" barrel; 243 Win., 308 Win., 7mm-08 calibers.

Estimated Value:	**Excellent:**	**$625.00**
	Very good:	**$500.00**

Winchester Model 70 Classic Featherweight

Similar to the Model 70 Featherweight Win-Tuff except: no 6.5x55 caliber; weighs 7 to 8 lbs.; checkered walnut stock and forearm. Introduced in 1992. Controlled round feeding after 1993. Add 18% for BOSS (Ballistic Optimizing Shooting System). 223 WSSM and 243 WSSM added 2004 (add 6%).

Estimated Value:	**New (retail):**	**$799.00**
	Excellent:	**$600.00**
	Very good:	**$480.00**

Winchester Model 70 Classic Laredo

Caliber: 7mm Rem. magnum, 300 Win. magnum, 7mm STW
Action: Bolt action, repeating; 3-position safety
Magazine: 3-shot
Barrel: Blued; 26"; round
Sights: None, drilled for scope mounts
Stock and Forearm: Checkered one-piece, pistol grip stock and forearm
Approximate wt.: 7½ lbs.
Comments: Made in the late 1990s; add 15% for the BOSS (Ballistic Optimizing Shooting System). (This is used to control the shockwave pattern generated in the barrel. It consists of an attachment on the muzzle which can be adjusted.) Add 17% for fluted barrel.

Estimated Value:	**Excellent:**	**$700.00**
	Very good:	**$560.00**

Winchester Model 70 Classic, Custom Ultimate Classic

Winchester Model 70 Classic, Custom SA

Winchester Model 70 Classic, Custom SA

Same as the Model 70 Classic, Custom Ultimate Classic; available in 7mm-08 Rem., 308 Win., 358 Win., 260 Rem., 300 WSM, 450 Marlin, 270 WSM, 7mm WSM, 24" barrel; weighs 7¼ to 8¼ lbs.

Estimated Value:	**Excellent:**	**$2,500.00**
	Very good:	**$2,000.00**

Winchester Model 70 Classic, Custom Ultimate Classic

Caliber: 6.5x55 Swed., 25-06 Rem., 270 Win., 280 Rem., 30-06 Spfld., 264 Win. magnum, 7mm Rem. magnum, 7mm STW, 300 Win. magnum, 300 Wby. magnum, 338 Win. magnum, 35 Whelen, 300 Ultramag, 7mm Ultramag, 338 Ultramag
Action: Bolt action, repeating
Magazine: 5-shot detachable box
Barrel: 24" or 26" blued or stainless steel; round, fluted round, ½ octagon – ½ round, or full-tapered octagon
Sights: None, drilled and tapped for scope mounts
Stock and Forearm: Fancy grade checkered walnut one-piece pistol grip stock and forearm; recoil pad, straight cheekpiece, swivels
Approximate wt.: 7½ to 7¾ lbs.
Comments: A high-quality rifle with custom options.

Estimated Value:	**Excellent:**	**$2,700.00**
	Very good:	**$2,160.00**

Winchester Model 70 Custom Safari Express

Winchester Model 70 Classic, Custom Featherweight

Winchester Model 70 Classic, Custom Featherweight

Similar to the Model 70 Classic, Custom Ultimate Classic; 270 Win., 280 Rem., 30-06 Spfld; 22" barrel; semi-fancy American walnut with cut checkering pistol grip stock and lipped forearm; recoil pad.

Estimated Value:	**Excellent:**	**$2,500.00**
	Very good:	**$2,000.00**

Winchester Model 70 Custom Safari Express

Caliber: 375 H&H, 375 Ultramag, 404 Jeffery, 458 Lott, 458 Win. magnum, 470 Capstick
Action: Bolt action, repeating
Magazine: 3-shot box
Barrel: 22" or 24" blued
Sights: Hooded front, three-leaf express rear
Stock and Forearm: Checkered semi-fancy American walnut one-piece pistol grip stock and forearm; recoil pad
Approximate wt.: 9 to 9¼ lbs.
Comments: A heavy, high-grade hunting rifle.

Estimated Value:	**Excellent:**	**$2,700.00**
	Very good:	**$2,160.00**

Winchester Model 70 Classic, Custom Carbon

Winchester Model 70 Classic, Ultimate Shadow

Winchester Model 70 Classic, Custom Carbon

Similar to the Model 70 Classic, Custom Ultimate Classic; 25-06 Rem., 270 WSM, 7mm WSM, 300 WSM, 338 Win. magnum calibers; stainless steel barrel wrapped in high-modulus graphite epoxy for heat dissipation; lightweight composite stock; 24" or 26" barrel.

Estimated Value: **Excellent: $2,700.00**
Very good: $2,160.00

Winchester Model 70 Classic, Ultimate Shadow

Caliber: 223 WSSM, 243 WSSM, 25 WSSM, 270 WSM, 300 WSM, 7mm WSM
Action: Bolt action; repeating
Magazine: 3-shot, hinged floor plate
Barrel: 22" or 24" blued or stainless steel
Sights: None, drilled and tapped for scope mounts
Stock and Forearm: Checkered synthetic one-piece pistol grip stock and forearm with rubberized gripping surfaces; swivels; camouflage finish available
Approximate wt.: 6½ to 6¾ lbs.
Comments: Add 5% for stainless steel; 12% for camouflage.
Estimated Value: **Excellent: $800.00**
Very good: $640.00

Winchester Model 70 Custom African Express

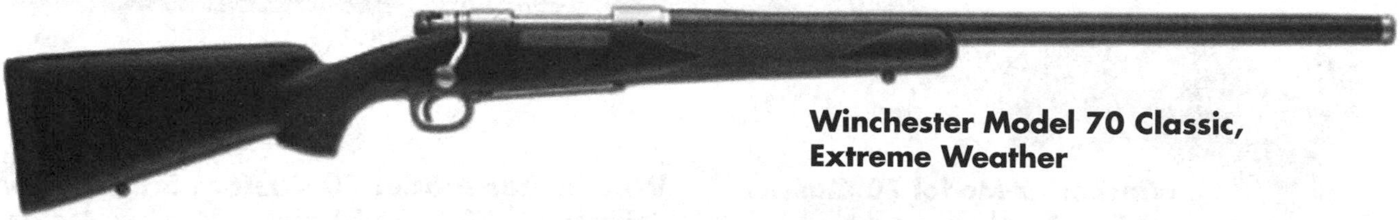

Winchester Model 70 Classic, Extreme Weather

Winchester Model 70 Custom African Express

Similar to the Model 70 Custom Safari Express in 375 H&H magnum, 416 Rem. magnum, 458 Lott, 458 Win. magnum; 4-shot magazine; hand-oiled English walnut stock and forearm.

Estimated Value: **Excellent: $3,500.00**
Very good: $2,800.00

Winchester Model 70 Classic, Extreme Weather

Similar to the Model 70 Classic, Custom Ultimate Classic; McMillan fiberglass stock with cheekpiece, all stainless steel action and barrel, Pachmayr recoil pad. 270 WSM, 30-06 Spfld, 300 Win. magnum, 300 WSM, 300 Ultramag, 308 Win., 338 Win magnum, 7mm Rem. magnum, 7mm WSM calibers; round or fluted round barrel.

Estimated Value: **Excellent: $2,000.00**
Very good: $1,600.00

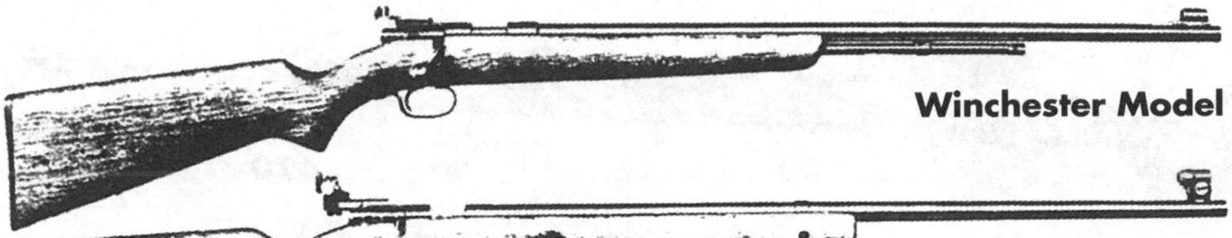

Winchester Model 72

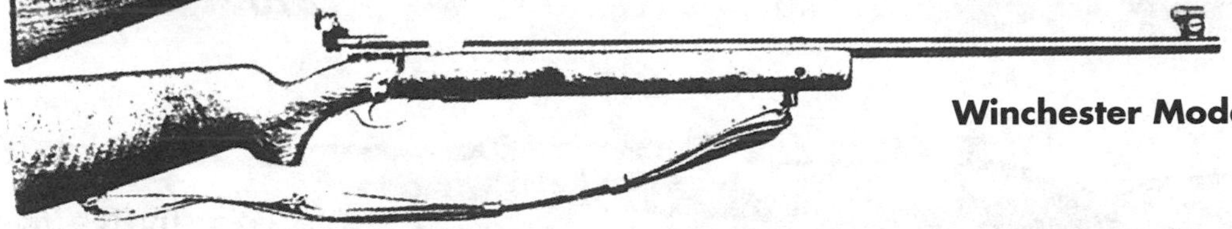

Winchester Model 75 Target

Winchester Model 75 Sporter

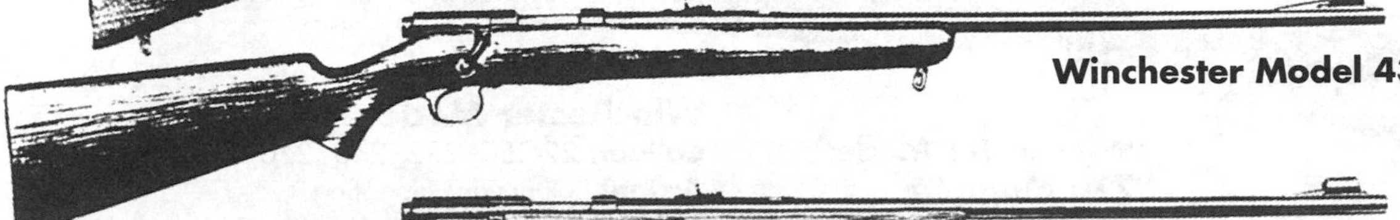

Winchester Model 43

Winchester Model 43 Special

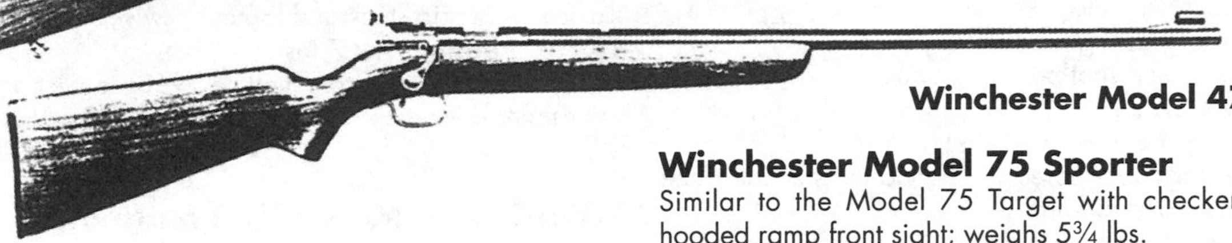

Winchester Model 47

Winchester Model 72
Caliber: 22 short, long, long rifle
Action: Bolt action; repeating
Magazine: Tubular; 15 long rifles, 16 longs, 20 shorts
Barrel: Blued; 25"
Sights: Peep or open rear, bead front
Stock and Forearm: Plain walnut one-piece semi-pistol grip stock and forearm
Approximate wt.: 5¾ lbs.
Comments: Made from the late 1930s to the late 1950s.

Estimated Value:	**Excellent:**	**$425.00**
	Very good:	**$340.00**

Winchester Model 75 Target
Caliber: 22 long rifle
Action: Bolt action; repeating
Magazine: 5- or 10-shot detachable box
Barrel: Blued; 28"
Sights: Special target sights
Stock and Forearm: Plain walnut one-piece pistol grip stock and forearm
Approximate wt.: 8¾ lbs.
Comments: Made from the late 1930s to the late 1950s.

Estimated Value:	**Excellent:**	**$1,000.00**
	Very good:	**$ 800.00**

Winchester Model 75 Sporter
Similar to the Model 75 Target with checkering; 24" barrel; hooded ramp front sight; weighs 5¾ lbs.

Estimated Value:	**Excellent:**	**$1,250.00**
	Very good:	**$1,000.00**

Winchester Model 43
Caliber: 218 Bee, 22 Hornet, 25-20, 32-30 (25-20 and 32-30 dropped in 1950)
Action: Bolt action; repeating
Magazine: 3-shot detachable
Barrel: Blued; 24"
Sights: Open rear, hooded ramp front
Stock and Forearm: Plain wood one-piece semi-pistol grip stock and forearm; swivels
Approximate wt.: 6 lbs.
Comments: Made from the late 1940s to the late 1950s.

Estimated Value:	**Excellent:**	**$725.00**
	Very good:	**$580.00**

Winchester Model 43 Special
Similar to the Model 43 with checkering and choice of open rear sight or micrometer.

Estimated Value:	**Excellent:**	**$900.00**
	Very good:	**$725.00**

Winchester Model 47
Similar to the Model 43 in 22 short, long or long rifle single-shot; 25" barrel. Made from the late 1940s to the mid-1950s.

Estimated Value:	**Excellent:**	**$425.00**
	Very good:	**$340.00**

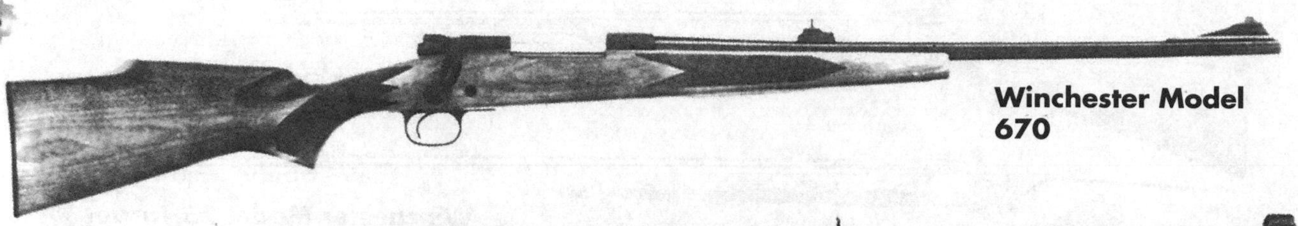

Winchester Model 670

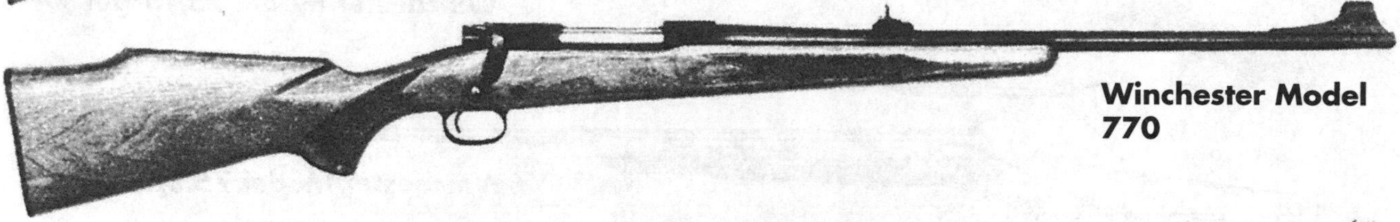

Winchester Model 770

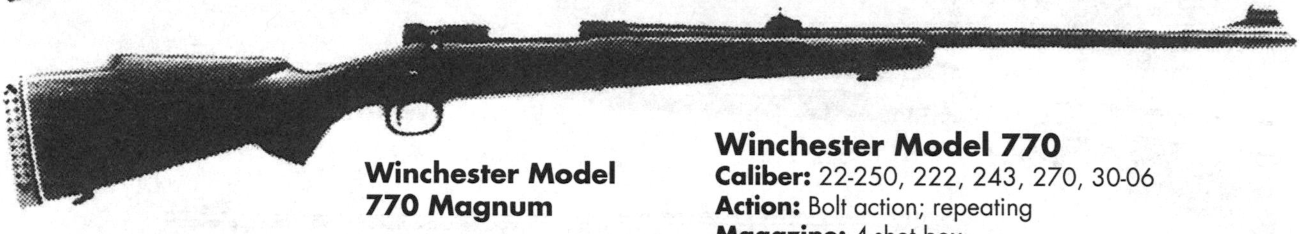

Winchester Model 770 Magnum

Winchester Model 670

Caliber: 243, 270, 30-06, 225, 243, 270, 308, 30-06 mag., 300 Win. mag., 264 Win. mag.
Action: Bolt action; repeating
Magazine: 4-shot box; 3-shot box in magnum
Barrel: Blued; 19", 22", 24"
Sights: Open rear, ramp front
Stock and Forearm: Checkered hardwood Monte Carlo one-piece pistol grip stock and forearm
Approximate wt.: 7 lbs.
Comments: Made from the mid-1960s to the late 1970s.

Estimated Value:	**Excellent:**	**$500.00**
	Very good:	**$400.00**

Winchester Model 770

Caliber: 22-250, 222, 243, 270, 30-06
Action: Bolt action; repeating
Magazine: 4-shot box
Barrel: Blued; 22"
Sights: Open rear, hooded ramp front
Stock and Forearm: Checkered walnut Monte Carlo one-piece pistol grip stock and forearm; swivels
Approximate wt.: 7 lbs.
Comments: Made from the late 1960s to the early 1970s.

Estimated Value:	**Excellent:**	**$525.00**
	Very good:	**$420.00**

Winchester Model 770 Magnum

Similar to the Model 770 in magnum with recoil pad and 24" barrel, 3-shot magazine.

Estimated Value:	**Excellent:**	**$550.00**
	Very good:	**$440.00**

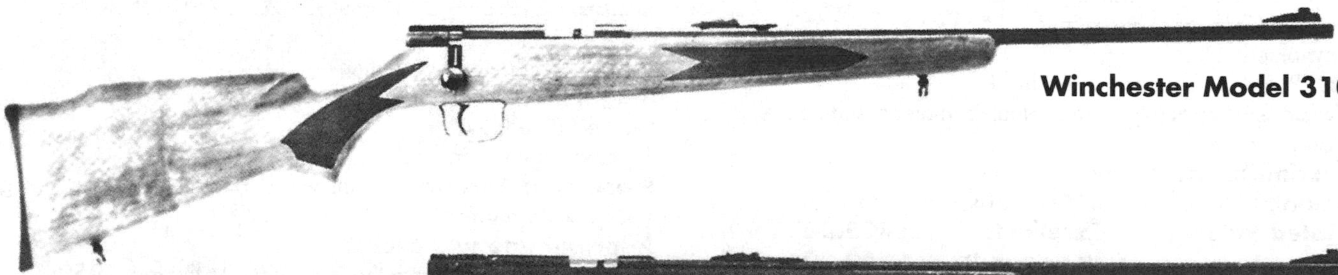

Winchester Model 310

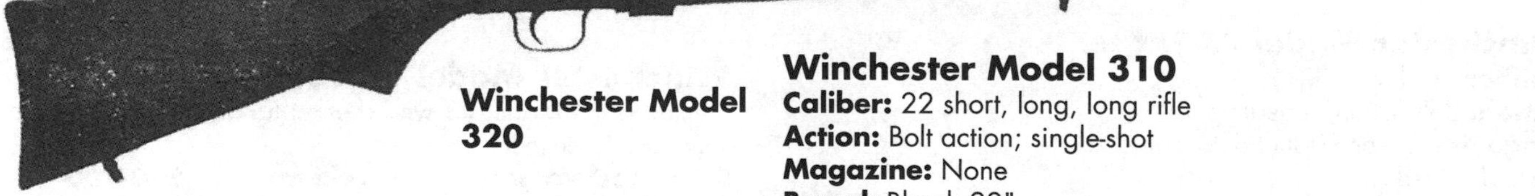

Winchester Model 320

Winchester Model 320

Similar to the Model 310 in repeating bolt action with a 5-shot clip.

Estimated Value:	**Excellent:**	**$250.00**
	Very good:	**$200.00**

Winchester Model 310

Caliber: 22 short, long, long rifle
Action: Bolt action; single-shot
Magazine: None
Barrel: Blued; 22"
Sights: Adjustable rear, ramp front
Stock and Forearm: Checkered walnut Monte Carlo one-pistol grip stock and forearm; swivels
Approximate wt.: 6 lbs.
Comments: Made from the early to the mid-1970s.

Estimated Value:	**Excellent:**	**$200.00**
	Very good:	**$160.00**

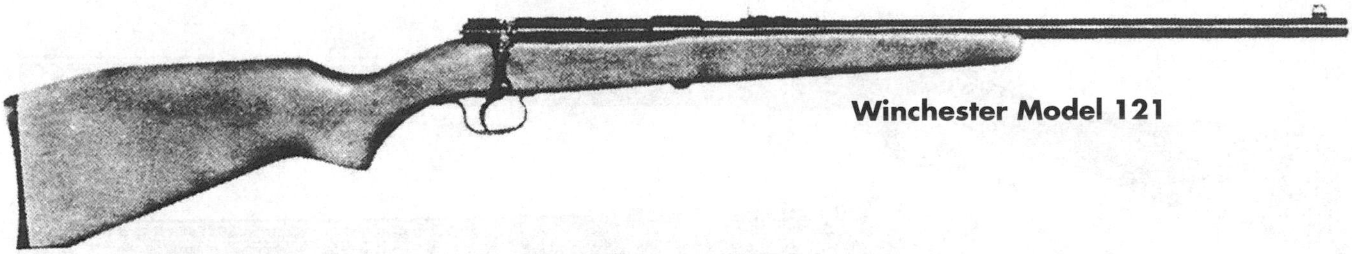

Winchester Model 121

Winchester Model 131

Winchester Model 121
Caliber: 22 short, long, long rifle
Action: Bolt action; single-shot
Magazine: None
Barrel: Blued; 20½"
Sights: Open rear, bead post front
Stock and Forearm: Plain one-piece semi-pistol grip stock and forearm
Approximate wt.: 5 lbs.
Comments: Made from the late 1960s to the early 1970s.
Estimated Value: **Excellent:** **$175.00**
Very good: **$140.00**

Winchester Model 121 Deluxe
Similar to the Model 121 with Monte Carlo stock; swivels; slightly different sights.
Estimated Value: **Excellent:** **$175.00**
Very good: **$140.00**

Winchester Model 121 Youth
Similar to the Model 121 with shorter barrel and youth stock.
Estimated Value: **Excellent:** **$160.00**
Very good: **$125.00**

Winchester Model 131
Similar to the Model 121 with semi-Monte Carlo stock; 7-shot clip magazine; bolt action repeater.
Estimated Value: **Excellent:** **$200.00**
Very good: **$160.00**

Winchester Model 141
Similar to the Model 131 with tubular magazine.
Estimated Value: **Excellent:** **$200.00**
Very good: **$160.00**

Winchester Model 70 Ranger Youth/Ladies

Winchester Ranger and Model 70 Ranger
Caliber: 223 Rem., 243 Win., 270 Win., 30-06 Sprg.
Action: Bolt action; repeating
Magazine: 4-shot
Barrel: Blued; 22"
Sights: Beaded ramp front, adjustable rear
Stock and Forearm: Plain one-piece semi-pistol grip wood stock and forearm
Approximate wt.: 7⅛ lbs.
Comments: Introduced in the mid-1980s.
Estimated Value: **Excellent:** **$390.00**
Very good: **$310.00**

Winchester Ranger Youth/Ladies, 70 Ranger Youth/Ladies and Model 70 Ranger Compact
A scaled-down bolt action (short action) carbine for young or small shooters; calibers 223 Rem., 243 Win., 7mm08 Rem., or 308 Win., 20" or 22" barrel; weighs 5¾ lbs.; beaded ramp front sight, semi-buckhorn, folding-leaf rear; plain wood, one-piece stock and forearm with swivels. Introduced in the mid-1980s.
Estimated Value: **Excellent:** **$395.00**
Very good: **$315.00**

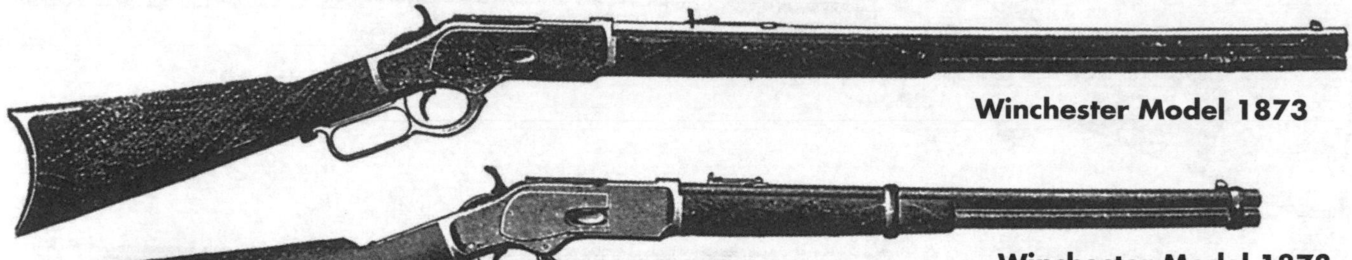

Winchester Model 1873

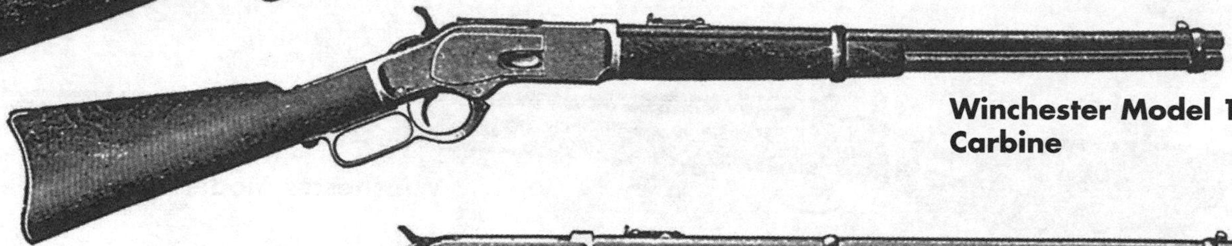

Winchester Model 1873 Carbine

Winchester Model 1886 Carbine

Winchester Model 1873

Caliber: 32-20, 38-40, 44-40
Action: Lever action; exposed hammer; repeating
Magazine: 6- or 15-shot tubular
Barrel: 24" or 26" round, octagon or half-octagon
Sights: Open rear, blade front
Stock and Forearm: Straight grip stock and forearm
Approximate wt.: 8 lbs.
Comments: Thousands of this model were sold by Winchester until 1920. Add $200.00 to $500.00 for Deluxe engraved models. Price range is for the different models i.e., 1st, 2nd, and 3rd models.

Estimated Value: **Excellent:** **$5,000.00 – 15,000.00**
Very good: **$4,000.00 – 12,000.00**

Winchester Model 1873 Carbine

Similar to the Model 1873 with a 20" barrel and 12-shot magazine. Three models made from 1873 to 1920.

Estimated Value: **Excellent:** **$6,000.00 – 16,000.00**
Very good: **$4,800.00 – 12,800.00**

Winchester Model 1873 Musket

Similar to the Model 1873 with a 30" round barrel, full-length forearm and 17-shot magazine. Three models made from 1873 to 1920.

Estimated Value: **Excellent:** **$2,500.00 – 15,000.00**
Very good: **$2,000.00 – 12,000.00**

Winchester Model 1886

Caliber: 45-70, 33 Win.; also others on early models
Action: Lever action; exposed hammer; repeating
Magazine: 4- or 8-shot tubular
Barrel: 26" round, octagon, or half-octagon
Sights: Open rear, blade front
Stock and Forearm: Plain wood straight grip stock and forearm
Approximate wt.: 7½ lbs.
Comments: Made from the mid-1880s to the mid-1930s.

Estimated Value: **Excellent:** **$7,000.00 – 15,000.00**
Very good: **$5,600.00 – 12,000.00**

Winchester Model 1886 Carbine

Similar to the Model 1886 with a 22" barrel.

Estimated Value: **Excellent:** **$10,000.00 – 17,500.00**
Very good: **$ 8,000.00 – 14,000.00**

Winchester Model 1886 Lever Action Grade I

Similar to the Model 1886 with select walnut stock and forearm. Reintroduced in the late 1990s.

Estimated Value: **Excellent:** **$825.00**
Very good: **$660.00**

Winchester Model 1886 High Grade

Similar to the Model 1886 Lever Action Grade I with engraving and highlights. Limited to 1,000 rifles.

Estimated Value: **Excellent:** **$1,500.00**
Very good: **$1,200.00**

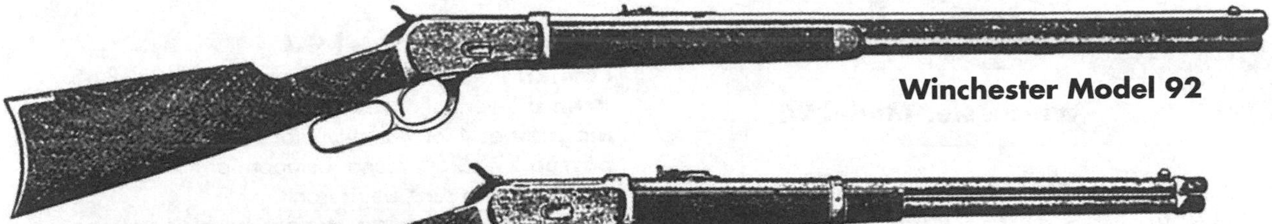

Winchester Model 92

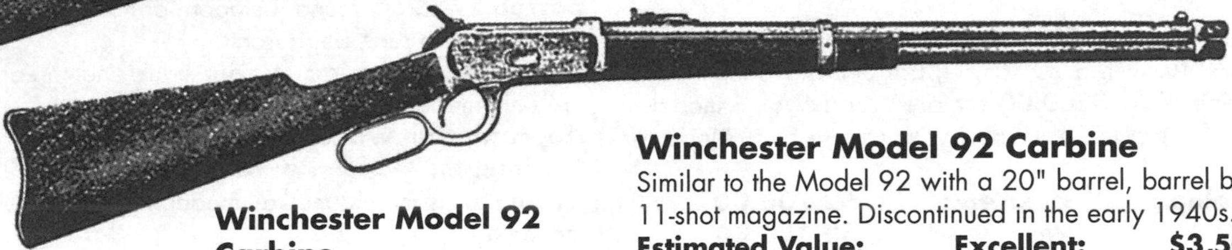

Winchester Model 92 Carbine

Winchester Model 92 Carbine

Similar to the Model 92 with a 20" barrel, barrel band and 5- or 11-shot magazine. Discontinued in the early 1940s.

Estimated Value: **Excellent:** **$3,500.00**
Very good: **$2,800.00**

Winchester Model 92

Caliber: 218 bee, 25-20, 32-30, 38-40, 44-40
Action: Lever action; exposed hammer; repeating
Magazine: 7- or 13-shot tubular
Barrel: 24"; round, octagon, or half-octagon
Sights: Open rear, bead front
Stock and Forearm: Plain walnut straight grip stock and forearm
Approximate wt.: 7 lbs.
Comments: Made from about 1892 to the early 1930s.
Estimated Value: **Excellent:** **$4,000.00**
Very good: **$3,200.00**

Winchester Model 1892 Lever Action Grade I

Similar to the Model 92 with select walnut stock and forearm. Made in the late 1990s.

Estimated Value: **Excellent:** **$625.00**
Very good: **$500.00**

Winchester Model 1892 Short Rifle

Similar to the Model 1892 Level Action Grade I except: 20" barrel; 44 magnum caliber. Introduced in the late 1990s.

Estimated Value: **Excellent:** **$575.00**
Very good: **$460.00**

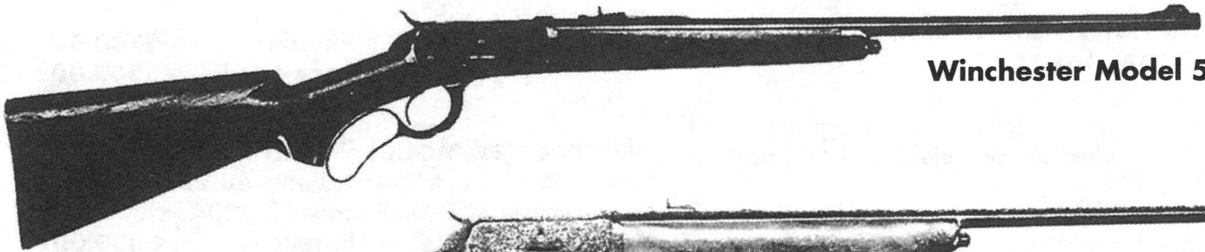

Winchester Model 53

Winchester Model 65

Winchester Model 65

Similar to the Model 53 in 25-20 and 32-30 caliber; semi-pistol grip stock; other minor improvements. Made from the early 1930s to the late 1940s.

Estimated Value: **Excellent:** **$3,000.00**
Very good: **$2,400.00**

Winchester Model 53

Similar to the Model 92 with a 6- or 7-shot magazine; 22" nickel steel barrel; choice of straight or pistol grip stock. Made from the mid-1920s to the early 1930s.

Estimated Value: **Excellent:** **$2,500.00**
Very good: **$2,000.00**

Winchester Model 65, 218 Bee

Similar to the Model 65 with peep sight and 24" barrel. Made from the late 1930s to the late 1940s.

Estimated Value: **Excellent:** **$3,200.00**
Very good: **$2,560.00**

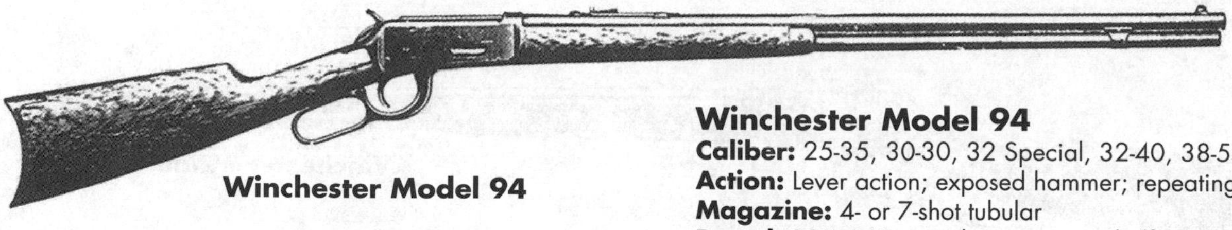

Winchester Model 94

Winchester Model 94 Carbine

Similar to Model 94 with a 20" barrel; barrel band; saddle ring, 6-shot magazine. Add $200.00 for pre-World War II models. Add $400.00 for pre-1925 Models with saddle ring. Made to the mid-1960s.

Estimated Value: **Excellent:** **$2,700.00**
Very good: **$2,150.00**

Winchester Model 94

Caliber: 25-35, 30-30, 32 Special, 32-40, 38-55
Action: Lever action; exposed hammer; repeating
Magazine: 4- or 7-shot tubular
Barrel: 22", 26"; round, octagon, or half-octagon
Sights: Open rear, bead front
Stock and Forearm: Straight stock and forearm; saddle ring on some models
Approximate wt.: 6¾ lbs.
Comments: Made from 1894 to the late 1930s. Sometimes referred to as the "Klondike" model. Add $500.00 for pre-1925 models.

Estimated Value: **Excellent:** **$3,000.00**
Very good: **$2,400.00**

Winchester Model 94 Walnut

Winchester Model 94 Trapper

Winchester Model 94 Standard, 94 Traditional, 94 Walnut

Caliber: 30-30
Action: Lever action, exposed hammer; repeating; angle-eject feature added in 1984, listed as "side eject" in 1986. Hammer stop safety added in 1992.
Magazine: 6-shot
Barrel: 20" round with barrel band
Sights: Hooded or post front, adjustable rear
Stock and Forearm: Plain or checkered walnut two-piece straight grip stock and forearm; barrel band
Approximate wt.: 6½ lbs.
Comments: Made from the mid-1960s to about 2006. Also made in calibers 44 mag., 45 Colt and 444 Marlin in the mid-1980s. 100th anniversary inscription in 1994. Deduct 8% for plain stock.

Estimated Value: **Excellent:** **$600.00**
Very good: **$480.00**

Winchester Model 94 Win-Tuff

Same as the Model 94 Standard except: laminated stock of brown dyed hardwood; hammer stop; 100th anniversary inscription in 1994. Discontinued in 1997.

Estimated Value: **Excellent:** **$375.00**
Very good: **$300.00**

Winchester Model 94 Pack Rifle

Similar to the Model 94 Walnut except: 18" barrel; checkered pistol grip stock and forearm; nosecap-style forend; ¾ magazine; removable sight hood; 30-30 Win. or 44 Rem. magnum calibers. Introduced in 2000.

Estimated Value: **Excellent:** **$700.00**
Very good: **$560.00**

Winchester Model 94 Timber Carbine

Similar to the Model 94 Pack rifle except: ported barrel; 444 Marlin caliber. 450 Marlin added in 2004.

Estimated Value: **Excellent:** **$800.00**
Very good: **$640.00**

Winchester Model 94 Antique

Similar to the Model 94 Standard with case-hardened, scroll design frame. Made from the late 1960s to 1984 in 30-30 caliber.

Estimated Value: **Excellent:** **$600.00**
Very good: **$480.00**

Winchester Model 94 Trapper

Same as the Model 94 Standard except: 16" barrel; 44 Rem. mag. and 45 Colt added in the mid-1980s, 357 added in 1992. Magazine capacity is 5-shot in 30-30 and 9-shot in 357, 44 and 45; made from 1980 to the present. 100th anniversary inscription in 1994. Add 5% for mag. caliber.

Estimated Value: **Excellent:** **$500.00**
Very good: **$400.00**

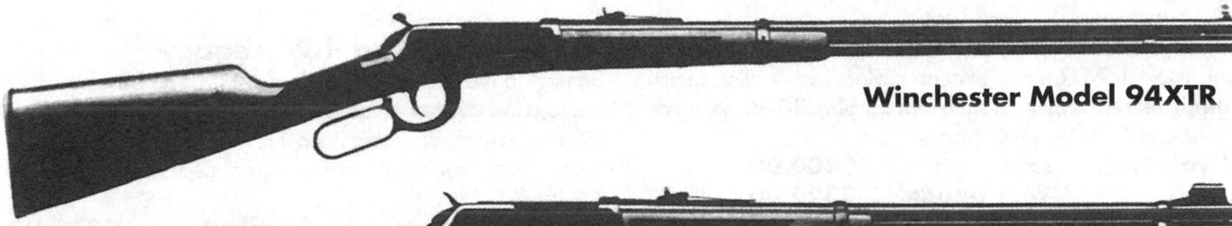

Winchester Model 94XTR

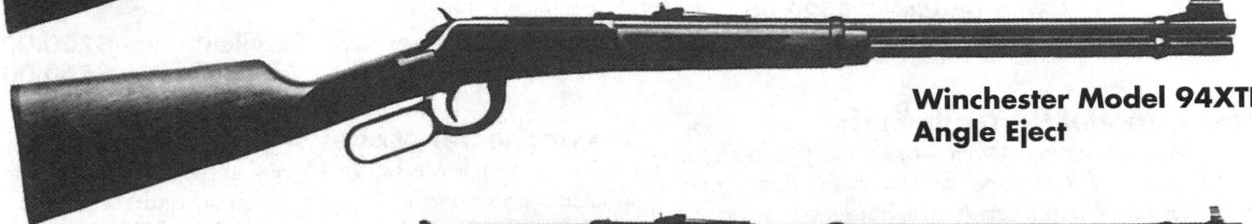

Winchester Model 94XTR Angle Eject

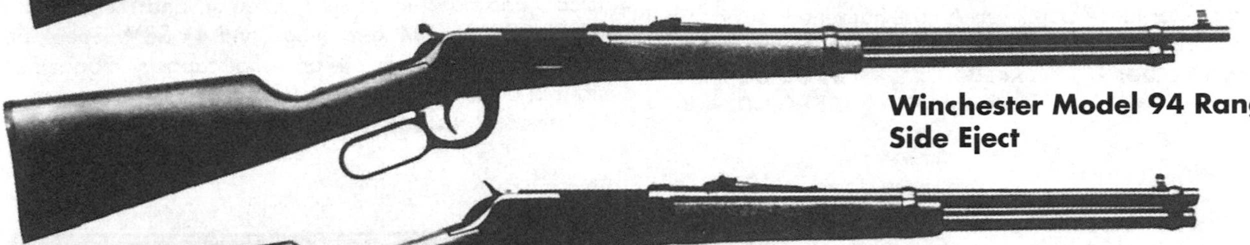

Winchester Model 94 Ranger Side Eject

Winchester Model 94 Wrangler II

Winchester Model 94XTR

Similar to the Model 94 Standard with higher grade wood, checkered stock and forearm. Made from 1979 to 1984 in 30-30 and 375 Win.; 375 Win. has recoil pad. Add 23% for 375 Win.

Estimated Value: **Excellent:** **$400.00**
Very good: **$320.00**

Winchester Model 94XTR Angle Eject

Similar to the Model 94XTR except an angle eject feature was added in 1984; in 1986 Winchester called it "side eject." Made in calibers 30-30, 7x30 Waters, 307, 356 and 357 Win.; 7x30 Waters has 7-shot magazine and 24" barrel; other models have 6-shot magazines and 20" barrels; 307, 356 and 357 calibers made from 1984 to 1986; 30-30 and 7x30 Waters made from 1984 to 1987; add 10% for 7x30 Waters.

Estimated Value: **Excellent:** **$300.00**
Very good: **$240.00**

Winchester Model 94 Side Eject

Similar to the Model 94 Standard with side eject feature; cal. 30-30, 308, 356, 375 Win. and 7x30 Waters, 6-shot mag.; recoil pad; made from 1985 to date. 32 Win. Spec. added 1992 to 1994. Add 10% for checkered stock and forearm. Hammer stop safety added in 1992. 100th anniversary inscription in 1994.

Estimated Value: **Excellent:** **$315.00**
Very good: **$250.00**

Winchester Model 94 Ranger Side Eject

Similar to the Model 94 Standard in 30-30 caliber with 5-shot magazine; blade front sight and semi-buckhorn rear; made for economy and utility; smooth wood stock and forearm with walnut finish; made from the mid-1980s to the present. 100th anniversary inscription in 1994.

Estimated Value: **Excellent:** **$285.00**
Very good: **$225.00**

Winchester Model 94 Classic Rifle or Carbine

Similar to the Model 94 Standard with select walnut stock; scroll engraving. Made from the late 1960s to the early 1970s.

Estimated Value: **Excellent:** **$295.00**
Very good: **$235.00**

Winchester Model 94 Wrangler

Same as the Model 94 Trapper except: large loop-type finger lever; roll-engraved receiver; 32 Special caliber with 5-shot magazine; no angle eject feature; made from about 1980 to 1984.

Estimated Value: **Excellent:** **$625.00**
Very good: **$500.00**

Winchester Model 94 Wrangler II

Similar to the Model 94 Wrangler in 38-55 caliber; has angle eject feature. Made from about 1984 to 1986.

Estimated Value: **Excellent:** **$500.00**
Very good: **$400.00**

Winchester Model 94 Ranger Compact

Similar to the Model 94 Ranger except scaled for smaller shooters; 16" barrel, recoil pad, post-style front sight; 30-30 Win. or 357 mag. calibers; 5- or 9-shot capacity.

Estimated Value: **Excellent:** **$400.00**
Very good: **$320.00**

Winchester Model 94 Trails End

Similar to the Model 94 Walnut with 11-shot magazine capacity; calibers: 357 mag., 44 Rem. mag. and 44 S&W Spec., and 45 Colt; add 6% for large loop lever. A case-hardened, octagon barrel version was produced in 2004 (add 70%).

Estimated Value: **Excellent:** **$700.00**
Very good: **$560.00**

Winchester Model 94 Legacy

Similar to the Model 94 Walnut with a half-pistol grip stock, fluted comb, and curved lever loop; 20" or 24" barrel; 6 to 12 capacity magazine; available in 30-30 Win., 357 mag., 45 Colt, 44 Rem. mag., 44 S&W Spec. Introduced in the late 1990s. Add 4% for 24" barrel.

Estimated Value: **Excellent:** **$700.00**
Very good: **$560.00**

Winchester Model 94 Black Shadow

Similar to the Model 94 Legacy except with composite synthetic stock, non-glare finish, fuller forearm, and recoil pad. Available in 30-30 Win., 44 Rem. mag., and 44 S&W Spec., or Big Bore model of 444 Marlin. 4- or 5-shot capacity magazine. Add 4% for Big Bore. Introduced in 1998.

Estimated Value: **Excellent:** **$400.00**
Very good: **$320.00**

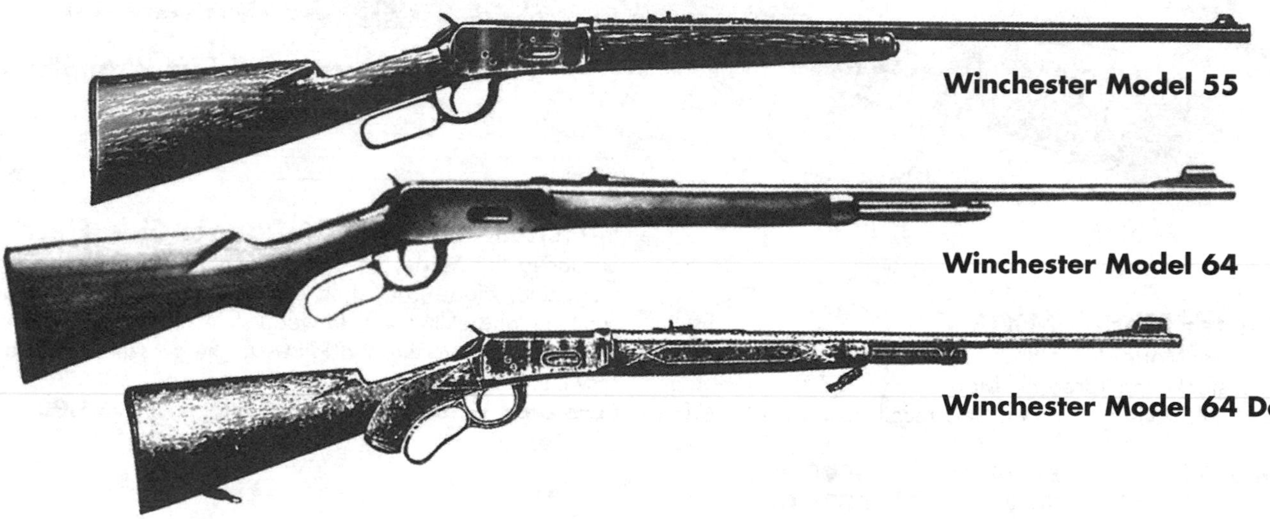

Winchester Model 55

Winchester Model 64

Winchester Model 64 Deer

Winchester Model 55

Similar to Model 94 with a 24" nickel steel barrel. Made from the mid-1920s to the early 1930s. Winchester also produced a Model 55 single-shot rifle in the 1950s.

Estimated Value: **Excellent:** **$1,300.00**
Very good: **$1,040.00**

Winchester Model 64

Similar to Models 94 and 55 with improvements; 20" or 26" barrel; available in 25-35, 30-30, 32, 219 Zipper (from 1938 – 1941). Made from the early 1930s to the late 1950s. Add $450.00 for 219 Zipper caliber.

Estimated Value: **Excellent:** **$1,000.00**
Very good: **$ 800.00**

Winchester Model 64 Deer

Similar to the Model 64 in 32 and 30-30 caliber; swivels; checkered pistol grip stock. Made from the mid-1930s to the mid-1950s.

Estimated Value: **Excellent:** **$1,200.00**
Very good: **$ 960.00**

Winchester Model 94 "Limited Edition" Centennial

Caliber: 30-30 Win.
Action: Lever action; exposed hammer; repeating; side ejector; hammer stop safety
Magazine: 5-shot (30-30); 9-shot (44) tubular
Barrel: 26"; half-round/half octagon; blued
Sights: Adjustable buckhorn rear, ramp front
Stock and Forearm: Checkered, straight, two-piece walnut stock and forearm; crescent steel butt plate and steel capped forearm
Approximate wt.: 8 lbs.
Comments: Made in 1994. 12,000 Grade I with engraving and 3,000 high grade with more elaborate engraving; add 57% for high grade.

Estimated Value: **Excellent:** **$1,275.00**
Very good: **$1,025.00**

Winchester Model 94 Wrangler Large Loop

Winchester Model 94 Big Bore

Winchester Model 94 Big Bore

Caliber: 307 Win., 356 Win., 444 Marlin added 1998
Action: Lever action, repeating; exposed hammer; hammer stop safety
Magazine: 6-shot tubular
Barrel: 20"; round; blued
Sights: Adjustable rear, hooded ramp front
Stock and Forearm: Checkered American walnut, straight grip stock and forearm; barrel band
Approximate wt.: 6½ lbs.
Comments: Introduced in the mid-1990s.

Estimated Value:	**Excellent:**	**$750.00**
	Very good:	**$600.00**

Winchester Model 94 Wrangler Large Loop

Caliber: 30-30 Win., 44 Rem. mag.
Action: Lever action; exposed hammer; repeating; side ejector; hammer stop safety; large loop finger lever
Magazine: 5-shot (30-30); 9-shot (44) tubular
Barrel: 16"; round; blued
Sights: Open front adjustable rear
Stock and Forearm: Smooth walnut straight grip stock and forearm
Approximate wt.: 6 lbs.
Comments: Made in the 1990s. Add 5% for 44 Rem. mag. 100th anniversary inscription in 1994.

Estimated Value:	**Excellent:**	**$600.00**
	Very good:	**$480.00**

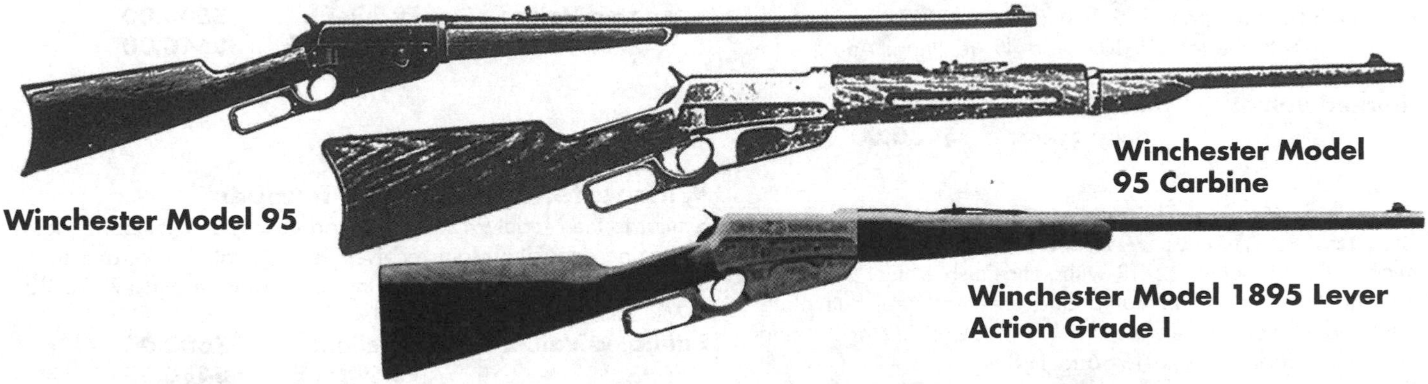

Winchester Model 95 Carbine

Winchester Model 95

Winchester Model 1895 Lever Action Grade I

Winchester Model 95

Caliber: 30-40 Krag, 30-06, 30-30, 303, 35, 405, 7.62mm, 38-72, 405 Win., 40-72.
Action: Lever action; exposed hammer; repeating
Magazine: 4-shot and 5-shot box
Barrel: 24", 26", 28"; octagon, round, or half octagon
Sights: Open rear, bead front
Stock and Forearm: Plain wood straight stock and tapered lipped forearm. A limited number was available with a pistol grip.
Approximate wt.: 8½ lbs.
Comments: Made from about 1895 to the early 1930s. A few thousand early models were built with a flat receiver; add $200.00.

Estimated Value:	**Excellent:**	**$3,500.00**
	Very good:	**$2,800.00**

Winchester Model 95 Carbine

Similar to the Model 95 with a 22" barrel.

Estimated Value:	**Excellent:**	**$3,750.00**
	Very good:	**$3,000.00**

Winchester Model 1895 Musket

Similar to the Model 95 with a 28" or 30" round nickel steel barrel; full-length forearm; barrel bands; 30-40 govt. caliber. Add $300.00 for U.S. Govt. models.

Estimated Value:	**Excellent:**	**$3,000.00**
	Very good:	**$2,400.00**

Winchester Model 1895 Lever Action Grade I

Similar to the Model 95 with select walnut stock and forearm. Reintroduced in the late 1990s.

Estimated Value:	**Excellent:**	**$870.00**
	Very good:	**$695.00**

Winchester Model 1895 High Grade

A higher quality version of the Model 1895 Lever Action Grade I.

Estimated Value:	**Excellent:**	**$1,100.00**
	Very good:	**$ 880.00**

Winchester Model 9422

Winchester Model 9422 High Grade

Winchester Models 9422, 9422XTR, 9422 Walnut, and 9422 Traditional

Caliber: 22 short, long, or long rifle; 22 magnum; 17 HMR
Action: Lever action; exposed hammer; repeating; hammer stop safety in 1992
Magazine: Tubular; 15 long rifles, 17 long, 21 shorts, 11 22 mag.
Barrel: 20"
Sights: Adjustable rear, hooded ramp front
Stock and Forearm: Plain or checkered wood straight grip stock and forearm; barrel band
Approximate wt.: 6¼ lbs.
Comments: Made from 1972 to date. 9422XTR made from the late 1970s to the late 1980s. Add 4% for mag. Add 5% for Large Loop model. Add 7% for 17 HMR.

Estimated Value:	**Excellent:**	**$600.00**
	Very good:	**$480.00**

Winchester Model 9422XTR Classic Rifle

Similar to the Model 9422XTR with satin-finish walnut pistol grip stock and forearm, fluted comb and crescent steel butt plate; curved finger lever; longer forearm; 22½" barrel; 22 or 22 magnum caliber. Produced from 1986 to 1989.

Estimated Value:	**Excellent:**	**$700.00**
	Very good:	**$560.00**

Winchester Model 9422 Win-Tuff and Win-Cam

Similar to the Model 9422 with laminated stock of brown dyed wood (Win-Tuff) or green and brown dyed wood (Win-Cam). Add 4% for magnum.

Estimated Value:	**Excellent:**	**$600.00**
	Very good:	**$480.00**

Winchester Model 9422 Legacy

Similar to the Model 9422 Walnut except with pistol grip stock and forearm, fluted comb, curved butt plate. Introduced in 1998. Add 4% for 22 mag. Add 7% for 17HMR.

Estimated Value:	**New (retail):**	**$512.00**
	Excellent:	**$385.00**
	Very good:	**$305.00**

Winchester Model 9422 High Grade

Caliber: 22 short, long, long rifle
Action: Lever action, repeating; exposed hammer; hammer stop safety
Magazine: Tubular; 21 shorts, 17 longs, or 15 long rifle
Barrel: 20½"; round, blued
Sights: Adjustable rear, hooded ramp front
Stock and Forearm: Checkered walnut, straight grip stock and forearm; barrel band
Approximate wt.: 6 lbs.
Comments: Produced in the mid-1990s, engraved receiver.

Estimated Value:	**Excellent:**	**$800.00**
	Very good:	**$640.00**

Winchester Model 9422 Trapper

Similar to the Model 9422 High Grade except: 16½" barrel; less magazine capacity; plain receiver; lesser quality stock and forearm; approximate wt: 5½ lbs. Introduced in the mid-1990s. 22 WMR caliber added 1998 (add 4%).

Estimated Value:	**Excellent:**	**$600.00**
	Very good:	**$480.00**

Winchester Model 9422 High Grade Series II

Similar to the Model 9422 High Grade. Introduced in 1998.

Estimated Value:	**Excellent:**	**$800.00**
	Very good:	**$640.00**

Winchester Model 9422 Anniversary Grade I

Similar to the Model 9422 High Grade Series II, commemorating the 25th anniversary of the Model 9422. Limited to 2,500 rifles. Made in the late 1990s.

Estimated Value:	**Excellent:**	**$750.00**
	Very good:	**$600.00**

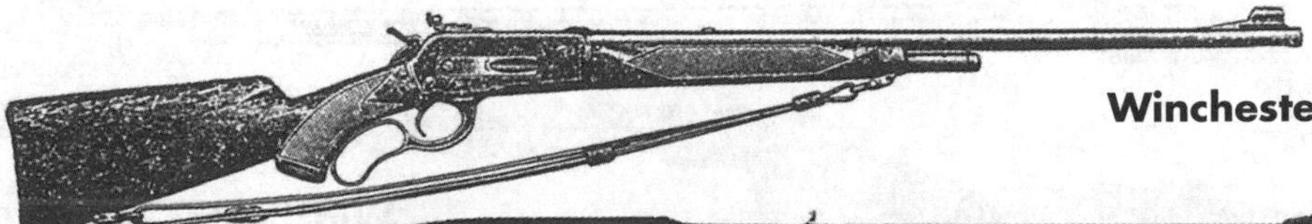

Winchester Model 71 Special

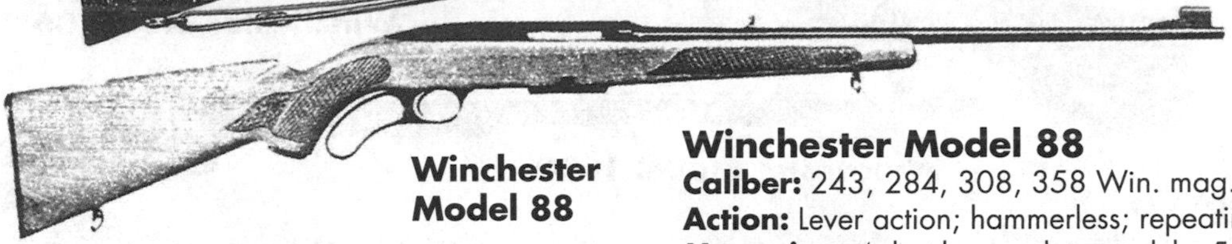

Winchester Model 88

Winchester Model 71

Caliber: 348 Win.
Action: Lever action; exposed hammer; repeating
Magazine: 4-shot tubular
Barrel: Blued; 20" or 24"
Sights: Open rear, hooded ramp front; peep sights available
Stock and Forearm: Plain or checkered walnut pistol grip stock and forearm; swivels available
Approximate wt.: 8 lbs.
Comments: Made from the mid-1930s to the late 1950s.

Estimated Value:	**Excellent:**	**$1,350.00**
	Very good:	**$1,075.00**

Winchester Model 71 Special

Similar to the Model 71 with checkering and swivels.

Estimated Value:	**Excellent:**	**$1,600.00**
	Very good:	**$1,275.00**

Winchester Model 88

Caliber: 243, 284, 308, 358 Win. mag.
Action: Lever action; hammerless; repeating
Magazine: 4-shot box on late models; 5-shot box on early models; 3-shot box in 284 caliber
Barrel: 22"
Sights: Folding leaf rear, hooded ramp front
Stock and Forearm: Checkered walnut one-piece semi-pistol grip stock and forearm; barrel band
Approximate wt.: 7¼ lbs.
Comments: Made from the mid-1950s to the mid-1970s. Add 100% for 358 Win.

Estimated Value:	**Excellent:**	**$750.00**
	Very good:	**$600.00**

Winchester Model 88 Carbine

Similar to the Model 88 with a plain stock and forearm and 19" barrel. Made from the late 1960s to the early 1970s.

Estimated Value:	**Excellent:**	**$1,000.00**
	Very good:	**$ 800.00**

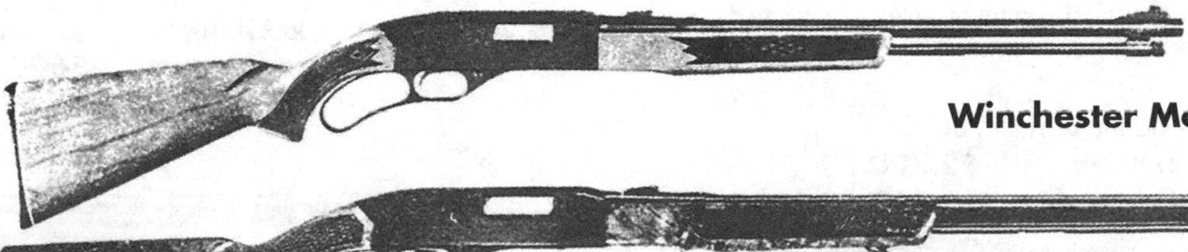

Winchester Model 250

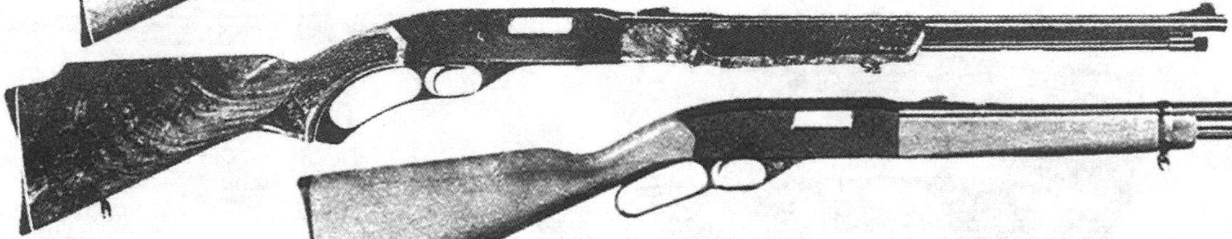

Winchester Model 250 Deluxe

Winchester Model 150

Winchester Model 250

Caliber: 22 short, long, long rifle
Action: Lever action; hammerless; repeating
Magazine: Tubular; 15 long rifles, 17 longs, 21 shorts
Barrel: Blued; 20½"
Sights: Open rear, ramp front
Stock and Forearm: Plain or checkered walnut semi-pistol grip stock and forearm
Approximate wt.: 5 lbs.
Comments: Made from the early 1960s to the mid-1970s.

Estimated Value:	**Excellent:**	**$175.00**
	Very good:	**$140.00**

Winchester Model 250 Deluxe

Similar to the Model 250 with Monte Carlo stock and swivels.

Estimated Value:	**Excellent:**	**$200.00**
	Very good:	**$160.00**

Winchester Model 255

Similar to the Model 250 in 22 magnum caliber; 11-shot magazine. Made from the mid-1960s to the early 1970s.

Estimated Value:	**Excellent:**	**$200.00**
	Very good:	**$160.00**

Winchester Model 150

Caliber: 22 short, long, long rifle
Action: Lever action; hammerless; repeating
Magazine: Tubular; 15 long rifles, 17 longs, 21 shorts
Barrel: Blued; 20½"
Sights: Open adjustable rear, blade front
Stock and Forearm: Straight stock and forearm; barrel band; alloy receiver
Approximate wt.: 5 lbs.
Comments: Made from the late 1960s to the mid-1970s.

Estimated Value:	**Excellent:**	**$175.00**
	Very good:	**$140.00**

Winchester Model 06

Winchester Model 61

Winchester Model 1890

Winchester Model 06

Caliber: 22 short, long, long rifle
Action: Slide action; exposed hammer; repeating
Magazine: Tubular; 11 long rifles, 12 longs, 15 shorts
Barrel: Blued; 20"
Sights: Open rear, bead front
Stock and Forearm: Plain wood straight stock, grooved or plain slide handle; nickel trimmed receiver and pistol grip stock available
Approximate wt.: 5 lbs.
Comments: Made from 1906 until the early 1930s.

Estimated Value:	**Excellent:**	**$2,000.00**
	Very good:	**$1,600.00**

Winchester Model 1890

Caliber: 22 short, long, long rifle
Action: Slide action; exposed hammer; repeating
Magazine: Tubular; 11 long rifles, 12 longs, 15 shorts
Barrel: 24" octagon
Sights: Open, bead front
Stock and Forearm: Plain wood straight grip stock and grooved slide handle
Approximate wt.: 5¾ lbs.
Comments: Made from 1890 to the early 1930s.

Estimated Value:	**Excellent:**	**$2,700.00**
	Very good:	**$2,160.00**

Winchester Model 61

Caliber: 22 short, long, long rifle
Action: Slide action; repeating
Magazine: Tubular; 14 long rifles, 16 longs, 20 shorts
Barrel: Blued; 24"; round or octagon
Sights: Open rear, bead front
Stock and Forearm: Plain wood semi-pistol grip stock and grooved slide handle
Approximate wt.: 5½ lbs.
Comments: Made from the early 1930s to the early 1960s. Add 30% for pre-World War II models.

Estimated Value:	**Excellent:**	**$1,000.00**
	Very good:	**$ 800.00**

Winchester Model 61 Magnum

Similar to the Model 61 in 22 magnum. Made in the early 1960s.

Estimated Value:	**Excellent:**	**$750.00**
	Very good:	**$600.00**

Winchester Model 62

Winchester Model 270

Winchester Models 62 and 62A

Caliber: 22 short, long, long rifle
Action: Slide action; exposed hammer; repeating
Magazine: Tubular; 14 long rifles, 16 longs, 20 shorts
Barrel: Blued; 23"
Sights: Open rear, blade front
Stock and Forearm: Walnut straight grip stock and grooved slide handle
Approximate wt.: 5½ lbs.
Comments: Made from the early 1930s to the late 1950s. A gallery model was available chambered for 22 shot only. It became Model 62A in the 1940s with internal improvements (deduct 30%).

Estimated Value:	**Excellent:**	**$2,000.00**
	Very good:	**$1,600.00**

Winchester Models 270 and 270 Deluxe

Caliber: 22 short, long, long rifle
Action: Slide action; repeating
Magazine: Tubular, 15 long rifles, 17 longs, 21 shorts
Barrel: 20½"
Sights: Open rear, ramp front
Stock and Forearm: Wanut pistol grip stock and slide handle; plastic available; later models checkered; Model 270 Deluxe has Monte Carlo stock
Approximate wt.: 5 lbs.
Comments: Made from the mid-1960s to the mid-1970s.

Estimated Value:	**Excellent:**	**$250.00**
	Very good:	**$200.00**

Winchester Models 275 and 275 Deluxe

Similar to the Models 270 and 270 Deluxe in 22 magnum caliber.

Estimated Value:	**Excellent:**	**$275.00**
	Very good:	**$220.00**

Winchester Model 03
Caliber: 22 short, long, long rifle
Action: Semiautomatic
Magazine: 10-shot tubular, loaded in stock
Barrel: Blued; 20"
Sights: Open rear, bead front
Stock and Forearm: Plain wood semi-pistol grip or straight stock; checkering on some models
Approximate wt.: 6 lbs.
Comments: Made from 1903 to the mid-1930s.

Estimated Value:	**Excellent:**	**$875.00**
	Very good:	**$700.00**

Winchester Model 05
Similar to the Model 03 in 32 Win. and 35 Win. caliber with a 5- or 10-shot detachable box magazine; 22" barrel. Made from 1905 to about 1920.

Estimated Value:	**Excellent:**	**$675.00**
	Very good:	**$540.00**

Winchester Model 07
Caliber: 351
Action: Semiautomatic; hammerless
Magazine: 5- or 10-shot detachable box
Barrel: Blued; 20"
Sights: Open rear, bead front
Stock and Forearm: Semi-pistol grip stock and forearm; plain wood
Approximate wt.: 7½ lbs.
Comments: Made from 1907 to the late 1950s.

Estimated Value:	**Excellent:**	**$700.00**
	Very good:	**$560.00**

Winchester Model 10
Similar to the Model 07 except: 401 caliber; 4-shot magazine. Made until the mid-1930s.

Estimated Value:	**Excellent:**	**$800.00**
	Very good:	**$640.00**

Winchester Model 63
Caliber: 22 long rifle, high speed; 22 long rifle Super X
Action: Semiautomatic
Magazine: 10-shot tubular, load in stock
Barrel: Blued; 20", 23"
Sights: Open rear, bead front
Stock and Forearm: Plain wood pistol grip stock and forearm
Approximate wt.: 5½ lbs.
Comments: Made from the early 1930s to the late 1950s.

Estimated Value:	**Excellent:**	**$2,000.00**
	Very good:	**$1,600.00**

Winchester Model 63 Grade I
Similar to the Model 63 with deep bluing and select walnut stock. Made in the late 1990s.

Estimated Value:	**Excellent:**	**$560.00**
	Very good:	**$445.00**

Winchester Model 63 High Grade
Similar to the Model 63 Grade I with engraving and gold highlights. Limited to 1,000 rifles.

Estimated Value:	**Excellent:**	**$1,000.00**
	Very good:	**$ 800.00**

Winchester Model 74
Caliber: 22 long rifle only or 22 short only
Action: Semiautomatic
Magazine: Tubular; 14 long rifles, 20 shorts; in stock
Barrel: Blued; 24"
Sights: Open rear, bead front
Stock and Forearm: Plain wood one-piece semi-pistol grip stock and forearm
Approximate wt.: 6¼ lbs.
Comments: Made from the late 1930s to the mid-1950s.

Estimated Value:	**Excellent:**	**$425.00**
	Very good:	**$340.00**

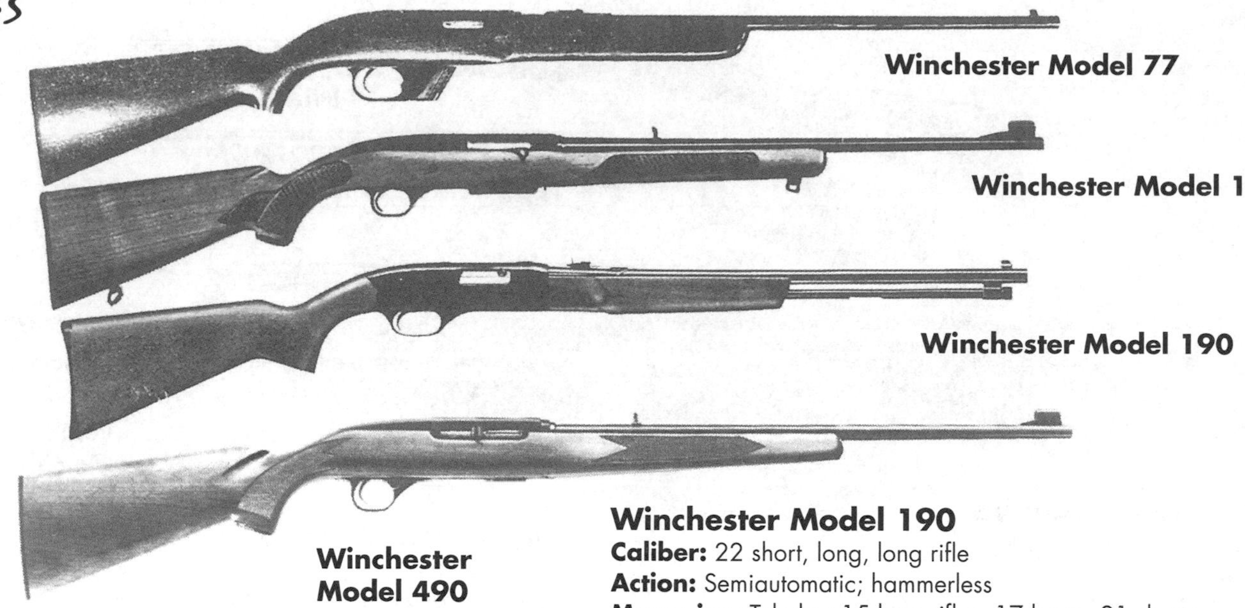

Winchester Model 77
Caliber: 22 long rifle
Action: Semiautomatic
Magazine: 8-shot detachable
Barrel: Blued; 22"
Sights: Open rear, bead front
Stock and Forearm: Plain walnut one-piece semi-pistol grip stock and forearm
Approximate wt.: 5½ lbs.
Comments: Made from the mid-1950s to the early 1960s.
Estimated Value: **Excellent:** **$400.00**
Very good: **$320.00**

Winchester Model 77 Tubular
Similar to the Model 77 with a 15-shot tubular magazine.
Estimated Value: **Excellent:** **$420.00**
Very good: **$335.00**

Winchester Model 100
Caliber: 243, 284, 308
Action: Semiautomatic, gas-operated
Magazine: 4-shot clip; 10-shot clip in 284
Barrel: Blued; 19", 22"
Sights: Open rear, hooded ramp front
Stock and Forearm: Checkered walnut one-piece stock and forearm; swivels
Approximate wt.: 7 lbs.
Comments: Made from the early 1960s to the mid-1970s. A factory recall was issued for this model in the 1990s.
Estimated Value: **Excellent:** **$500.00**
Very good: **$400.00**

Winchester Model 100 Carbine
Similar to the Model 100 with no checkering: 19" barrel; barrel bands.
Estimated Value: **Excellent:** **$600.00**
Very good: **$480.00**

Winchester Model 190
Caliber: 22 short, long, long rifle
Action: Semiautomatic; hammerless
Magazine: Tubular; 15 long rifles, 17 longs, 21 shorts
Barrel: 20½", 22"
Sights: Open rear, blade front
Stock and Forearm: Plain semi-pistol grip stock and forearm
Approximate wt.: 5 lbs.
Comments: 22 short dropped in the early 1970s; made from the mid-1960s to the late 1970s.
Estimated Value: **Excellent:** **$200.00**
Very good: **$160.00**

Winchester Model 190 Carbine
Similar to the Model 190 with a 20½" barrel; barrel band and swivels. Discontinued in the early 1970s.
Estimated Value: **Excellent:** **$200.00**
Very good: **$160.00**

Winchester Model 290
Caliber: 22 short, long, long rifle
Action: Semiautomatic
Magazine: Tubular; 15 longs, 17 long rifles, 21 shorts
Barrel: 20½"
Sights: Open rear, ramp front
Stock and Forearm: Checkered walnut pistol grip stock and forearm
Approximate wt.: 5 lbs.
Comments: Made from the mid-1960s to the mid-1970s.
Estimated Value: **Excellent:** **$225.00**
Very good: **$180.00**

Winchester Model 490
Caliber: 22 long rifle
Action: Semiautomatic
Magazine: 5-, 10-, or 15-shot clip
Barrel: Blued; 22"
Sights: Folding leaf rear, hooded ramp front
Stock and Forearm: Checkered walnut one-piece pistol grip stock and forearm
Approximate wt.: 6 lbs.
Comments: Made in the mid-1970s.
Estimated Value: **Excellent:** **$250.00**
Very good: **$200.00**

HANDGUNS

AMT Lightning Pistol
Caliber: 22 long rifle
Action: Semiautomatic, concealed hammer
Magazine: 10-shot clip
Barrel: 5" bull, 6½" tapered or bull, 8½" tapered or bull, 10" tapered or bull, 12½" tapered
Sights: Rear adjustable for windage
Finish: Stainless steel; rubber wrap-around grips
Length Overall: 9" (5" barrel)
Approximate wt.: 38 ozs. (5" bull barrel)
Comments: Made from the mid- to the late 1980s. Add 5% for 12½" barrel.

Estimated Value:	**Excellent:**	**$400.00**
	Very good:	**$320.00**

AMT Lightning Pistol

AMT Combat Government

AMT Combat and Standard Government
Caliber: 45 ACP
Action: Semiautomatic; exposed hammer; loaded chamber indicator; manual and grip safeties; adjustable target-type trigger
Magazine: 7-shot clip
Barrel: 5"
Sights: Fixed
Finish: Checkered walnut or neoprene wrap-around grips; all stainless steel construction
Length Overall: 8½"
Approximate wt.: 39 ozs.
Comments: Made from the 1970s to the late 1990s.

Estimated Value:	**Excellent:**	**$450.00**
	Very good:	**$360.00**

AMT Long Slide
Same as the AMT Combat Government except: 7" barrel; 10½" overall length; adjustable 3-dot sight system.

Estimated Value:	**Excellent:**	**$500.00**
	Very good:	**$400.00**

AMT Skipper
Same as the AMT Combat Government except: 4" barrel; 7½" overall length; 40 S&W caliber; approximate wt. 33 ozs.; adjustable sights; made from the late 1970s to about 1990.

Estimated Value:	**Excellent:**	**$400.00**
	Very good:	**$320.00**

AMT Hardballer
Same as the AMT Combat Government except: adjustable combat-type sights; serrated matte slide rib; grooved front and back straps.

Estimated Value:	**Excellent:**	**$475.00**
	Very good:	**$380.00**

AMT Backup

AMT Backup and Backup II
Caliber: 380 ACP, 22 long rifle
Action: Semiautomatic; concealed hammer; manual and grip safeties; double action only model introduced in 1992 (without grip safety)
Magazine: 5-shot clip in 380 ACP; 8-shot in 22LR
Barrel: 2½"
Sights: Fixed
Finish: Smooth or checkered wood grips; all stainless steel construction; Lexon grips on later models
Length Overall: 5"
Approximate wt.: 18 oz.
Comments: Made from the 1970s to the present. Add 6% for double action only model (Backup); 22 cal. Discontinued in the late 1980s. Reintroduced in 2005.

Estimated Value:	**Excellent:**	**$260.00**
	Very good:	**$210.00**

AMT Backup Double Action

AMT Backup Double Action
Caliber: 38 Super, 9mm, 40 S&W, and 45 ACP
Action: Semiautomatic; double action only; no manual safety
Magazine: 6-shot (38 Super or 9mm); 5-shot (40 S&W or 45ACP)
Barrel: 3"
Sights: Grooved slide type
Finish: Stainless steel, checkered fiberglass grips
Length Overall: 5¾"
Approximate wt.: 23 to 25 ozs.
Comments: Introduced in the mid-1990s.

Estimated Value:	**Excellent:**	**$365.00**
	Very good:	**$290.00**

AMT "On Duty" DA

AMT "On Duty" DA

Caliber: 9mm, 40 S&W, 45 ACP
Action: Semiautomatic; double action only with trigger disconnect thumb safety or decocker model
Magazine: 15-shot (9mm), 11-shot (40 S&W), 9-shot (45)
Barrel: 4½"
Sights: Fixed; 3-dot system
Finish: Anodized black matte; carbon fiber grips
Length Overall: 7½"
Approximate wt.: 32 ozs.
Comments: Produced from 1992 to 1995. Add 10% for 45 ACP.

Estimated Value:	**Excellent:**	**$375.00**
	Very good:	**$300.00**

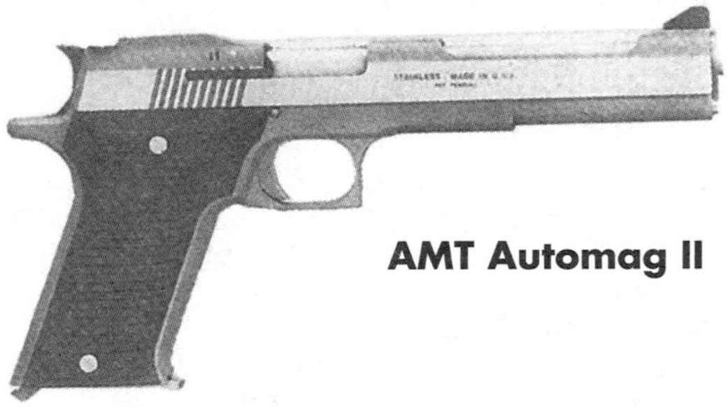

AMT Automag II

AMT Automag II

Caliber: 22 magnum
Action: Gas-assisted, single action, semiautomatic
Magazine: 9-shot clip
Barrel: 3⅜", 4½", or 6"
Sights: Adjustable front and rear
Finish: Grooved carbon-fiber grips; stainless steel
Approximate wt.: 24 to 32 ozs.
Length Overall: 6¾", 8", 9¼"
Comments: Introduced in the late 1980s; promoted as the "first and only production semiautomatic handgun in its caliber."

Estimated Value:	**Excellent:**	**$520.00**
	Very good:	**$415.00**

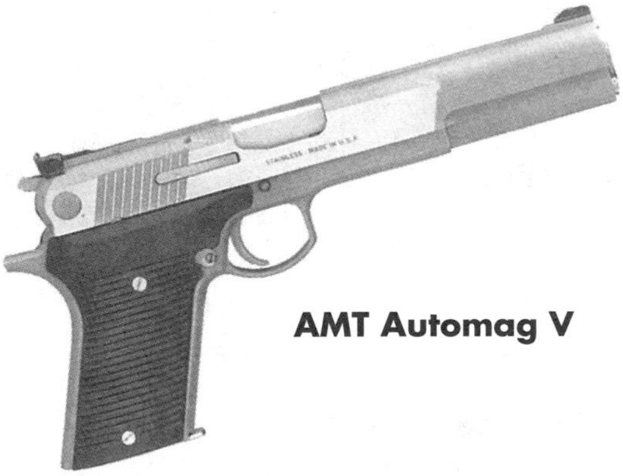

AMT Automag V

AMT Automag III

Caliber: 30 (M1 Carbine)
Action: Semiautomatic; exposed hammer
Magazine: 8-shot clip
Barrel: 6⅜"
Sights: Adjustable 3-dot system
Finish: Stainless steel; horizontally grooved carbon-fiber grips
Length Overall: 10½"
Approximate wt.: 43 ozs.
Comments: Introduced in the early 1990s.

Estimated Value:	**Excellent:**	**$500.00**
	Very good:	**$400.00**

AMT Automag IV

Similar to the Automag III except: 45 Winchester magnum caliber; weight: 46 ozs.; 7-shot clip; 6½" barrel; overall length 10½".

Estimated Value:	**Excellent:**	**$700.00**
	Very good:	**$560.00**

AMT Automag V

Similar to the Automag III except: gas venting system to reduce recoil; 50 caliber; weight 46 ozs.; 5-shot clip. Introduced in 1994; discontinued in 1996.

Estimated Value:	**Excellent:**	**$750.00**
	Very good:	**$600.00**

AMERICAN DERRINGER

American Two Barrel Derringer
Caliber: 22 S, L and LR; 22 WMR; 38 Spec.; about 60 different rifle and pistol calibers introduced in the 1980s
Action: Single action; exposed hammer; spur trigger; tip-up barrels; hammer block safety after the late 1980s
Cylinder: None; chambers in barrels; 2-shot capacity
Barrel: 3" double barrel (superposed)
Sights: Fixed
Finish: Stainless steel; rosewood, walnut, or plastic grips
Length Overall: 5"
Approximate wt.: 15 ozs., 11 ozs., or ultra light (7½ ozs.)
Comments: Made from about 1972 to 1974. Reintroduced in 1980. All stainless steel construction. Current models marked "American Derringer"; prices vary according to caliber.

Estimated Value:		
	New (retail):	$650.00 – 725.00
	Excellent:	$485.00 – 545.00
	Very good:	$390.00 – 435.00

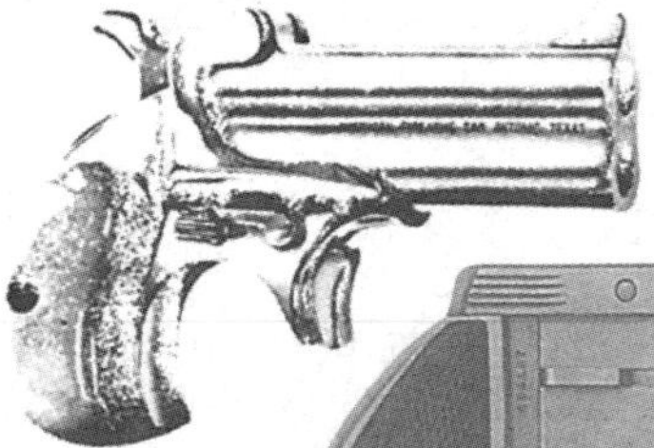

American Two Barrel Derringer

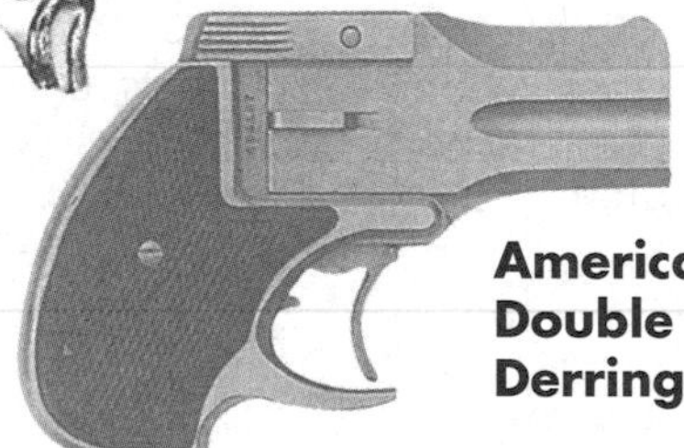

American D-38 Double Action Derringer

American 25 Automatic

American D-38 Double Action Derringer
Caliber: 22 long rifle, 22 magnum, 38 Special, 9mm Luger, 357 magnum, 40 S&W
Action: Double action only; hammerless; hammer block thumb safety
Cylinder: None; chambers in barrels; 2-shot capacity
Barrel: 3" over and under
Sights: Fixed
Finish: Satin stainless steel or blued; with aluminum grip frame; rosewood, walnut, hardwood, or black plastic grips
Length Overall: 5"
Approximate wt.: 14 ozs.
Comments: Introduced in the 1980s.

Estimated Value:		
	New (retail):	$655.00 – 705.00
	Excellent:	$490.00 – 525.00
	Very good:	$395.00 – 420.00

American 25 Automatic
Caliber: 25 ACP; 250 mag. (after 1980)
Action: Semiautomatic; concealed hammer
Magazine: 8-shot clip; 7-shot in mag.
Barrel: 2"
Sights: Fixed
Finish: Blue or stainless steel; smooth rosewood or walnut grips
Length Overall: 4½"
Approximate wt.: 15½ ozs.
Comments: Made from about 1969 to 1974; reintroduced in 1980. Early models (1969 to 1974) are marked "American Firearms." Current models (after 1980) are marked "American Derringer." Add 25% for .250 mag. Discontinued in the 1980s.

Estimated Value:	Blue	Stainless Steel
Excellent:	$350.00	$400.00
Very good:	$280.00	$320.00

American Baby Model
Similar to the 25 Automatic except 25 ACP only slightly more compact, 6-shot clip. Produced from 1982 to 1985.

Estimated Value:		
	Excellent:	$275.00
	Very good:	$225.00

ASTRA

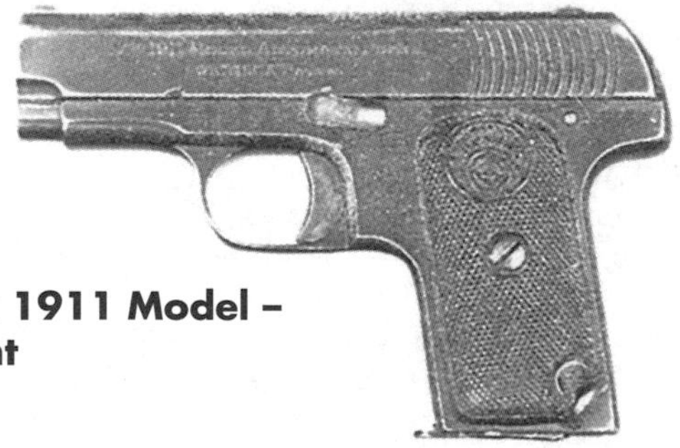

Astra 1911 Model – Patent

Astra 1911 Model – Patent
Caliber: 32 ACP (7.65 mm)
Action: Semiautomatic, concealed hammer
Magazine: 7-shot clip
Barrel: 3¼"
Sights: Fixed
Finish: Blued; checkered hard rubber grips
Length Overall: 5¾"
Approximate wt.: 29 ozs.
Comments: A Spanish copy of the Browning blowback action, probably made of trade parts. Not made by Uneta Y Compania.

Estimated Value:		
	Excellent:	$300.00
	Very good:	$240.00

Astra 1916 Model - Patent

Caliber: 32 ACP (7.65 mm)
Action: Semiautomatic, concealed hammer
Magazine: 9-shot clip
Barrel: 4"
Sights: Fixed
Finish: Blued; checkered hard rubber or wood grips
Length Overall: 6½"
Approximate wt.: 32 ozs.
Comments: A Spanish copy of the Browning blowback action, made under several trade names, probably of trade parts. Many were sold in the United States, Central America, and South America. Not made by Uneta Y Compania.

Estimated Value:	**Excellent:**	**$275.00**
	Very good:	**$220.00**

Astra 1924 Hope

Astra 1924 Hope

Caliber: 25 ACP (6.35)
Action: Semiautomatic; concealed hammer
Magazine: 6-shot clip
Barrel: 2"
Sights: Fixed
Finish: Blued; checkered rubber grips
Length Overall: 4⅓"
Approximate wt.: 12 ozs.
Comments: Some of these pistols have "HOPE" designation on the barrel.

Estimated Value:	**Excellent:**	**$325.00**
	Very good:	**$260.00**

Astra Model 400

Caliber: 9mm Bayard long; 38 ACP, 9mm Steyr, 9mm Glisenti, 9mm Luger, 9mm Browning long cartridges can be used due to chamber design
Action: Semiautomatic; concealed hammer
Magazine: 9-shot clip
Barrel: 6"
Sights: Fixed
Finish: Blued; checkered rubber grips
Length Overall: 9"
Approximate wt.: 36 ozs.
Comments: Made from 1921 until 1945 for both commercial and military use.

Estimated Value:	**Excellent:**	**$425.00**
	Very good:	**$340.00**

Astra 1915 Model – Patent

Astra 1915 Model – Patent

Caliber: 32 ACP (7.65 mm)
Action: Semiautomatic, concealed hammer
Magazine: 9-shot clip
Barrel: 3¼"
Sights: Fixed
Finish: Blued; checkered hard rubber grips
Length Overall: 5¾"
Approximate wt.: 29 ozs.
Comments: A Spanish copy of the Browning blowback action, probably made of trade parts. Not made by Uneta Y Compania.

Estimated Value:	**Excellent:**	**$250.00**
	Very good:	**$200.00**

Astra Model 300

Caliber: 380 ACP (9 mm Kurz); 32ACP
Action: Semiautomatic; concealed hammer
Magazine: 7-shot clip
Barrel: 4¼"
Sights: Fixed
Finish: Blued; checkered rubber grips
Length Overall: 6½"
Approximate wt.: 21 ozs.
Comments: This pistol was a shorter version of the Model 400 and production was started in 1922. Discontinued in 1947.

Estimated Value:	**Excellent:**	**$525.00**
	Very good:	**$420.00**

Astra Model 300

Astra Model 400

Astra Model 2000 Cub Pocket

Caliber: 22 short, 25 ACP (6.35 mm)
Action: Semiautomatic; exposed hammer
Magazine: 6-shot clip
Barrel: 2⅛"
Sights: Fixed
Finish: Blued; chrome and/or engraved, checkered grips
Length Overall: 4½"
Approximate wt.: 13 to 14 ozs.
Comments: A well-made pistol of the post-World War II period. Importation to the United States was discontinued in 1968. Add $20.00 for chrome finish.

Estimated Value:	**Excellent:**	**$300.00**
	Very good:	**$240.00**

Astra Camper Pocket

Same as Astra Cub (Model 2000) except: 22 caliber short only; 4" barrel which extends beyond front of slide; laterally adjustable rear sight. Discontinued in 1966. Add $10.00 for chrome finish.

Estimated Value:	**Excellent:**	**$275.00**
	Very good:	**$220.00**

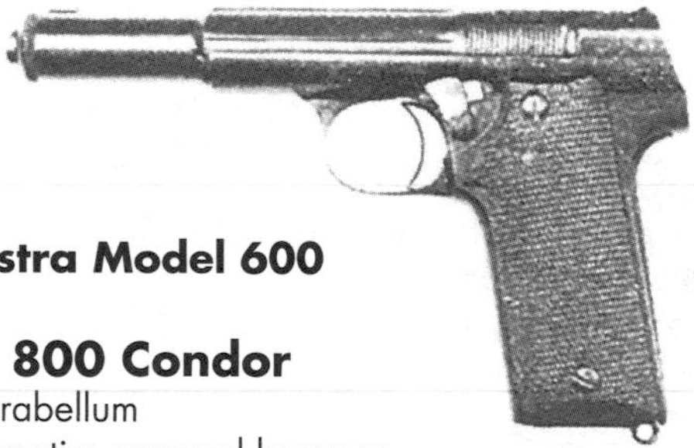

Astra Model 600

Astra Model 800 Condor

Caliber: 9mm Parabellum
Action: Semiautomatic; exposed hammer
Magazine: 8 shot clip
Barrel: 5¼"
Sights: Fixed
Finish: Blued; checkered grips
Length Overall: 8¼"
Approximate wt.: 32 ozs.
Comments: A post-war version of the Model 600 military pistol. It has a loaded chamber indicator.

Estimated Value:	**Excellent:**	**$1,275.00**
	Very good:	**$1,025.00**

Astra Model 200 Firecat

Caliber: 25 ACP (6.35mm)
Action: Semiautomatic; concealed hammer; grip safety
Magazine: 6-shot clip
Barrel: 2¼"
Sights: Fixed
Finish: Blued or chrome; plastic grips
Length Overall: 4½"
Approximate wt.: 13 ozs.
Comments: A well-machined pistol made from early 1920 to the present. It was imported to the United States from World War II until 1968. Add $10.00 for chrome finish.

Estimated Value:	**Excellent:**	**$315.00**
	Very good:	**$250.00**

Astra Model 2000 Cub Pocket

Astra Camper Pocket

Astra Model 600

Caliber: 32 ACP (7.65 mm), 9mm Luger
Action: Semiautomatic; concealed hammer
Magazine: 10-shot clip in 32 caliber; 8-shot clip in 9mm
Barrel: 5¼"
Sights: Fixed
Finish: Blued; checkered rubber or wood grips
Length Overall: 8½"
Approximate wt.: 35 ozs.
Comments: Made from 1944 to 1945 for military and police use. The 9mm was used as a substitute pistol in German military service, so some will have German acceptance marks.

Estimated Value:	**Excellent:**	**$500.00**
	Very good:	**$400.00**

Astra Model 800 Condor

Astra Model 200 Firecat

Astra Model 5000 Constable

Astra Model 5000 Constable

Caliber: 22 long rifle, 32 ACP (7.65mm) (32 discontinued), 380 ACP
Action: Double action; semiautomatic; exposed hammer with round spur
Magazine: 10-shot clip in 22 caliber long rifle, 8-shot clip in 32 ACP; 7-shot clip in 380 ACP
Barrel: 3½"; 6" on Sport model
Sights: Fixed
Finish: Blued or chrome; grooved grips; checkered on late model; plastic or wood grips
Length Overall: 6⅝" to 9⅛"
Approximate wt.: 24 to 26 ozs.
Comments: The barrel is rigidly mounted in the frame, all steel construction with hammer block safety. Add 40% for factory engraving; 7% for chrome finish; 4% for 22 cal.

Estimated Value:	**Excellent:**	**$375.00**
	Very good:	**$300.00**

Astra Model A-80, A-90

Caliber: 9mm Parabellum, 38 Super, 45 ACP
Action: Double action; semiautomatic; exposed hammer
Magazine: 14-shot clip in 9mm and 38 calibers; 8-shot clip in 45 ACP
Barrel: 3¾"
Sights: Fixed
Finish: Blued or chrome; checkered plastic grips
Length Overall: 7"
Approximate wt.: 40 ozs.
Comments: Imported from 1982 to 1990; replaced by Model A-100 in 1990. Add 10% for chrome finish.

Estimated Value:	**Excellent:**	**$375.00**
	Very good:	**$300.00**

Astra Model A-100

Astra Model A-100

Similar to the Model A-80, A-90 except: caliber 9mm, 40 S&W, or 45 ACP; re-engineered in 1993 incorporating increased magazine: 17-shot (9mm), 12-shot (40 S&W), or 9-shot (45 ACP). Add 6% for nickel finish.

Estimated Value:	**Excellent:**	**$335.00**
	Very good:	**$270.00**

Astra Model 3000

Caliber: 22 long rifle, 32 ACP, 380 ACP (9mm short)
Action: Semiautomatic; concealed hammer
Magazine: 10-shot clip in 22 caliber, 7-shot clip in 32 caliber; 6-shot clip in 380; clip
Barrel: 4"
Sights: Fixed
Finish: Blued; checkered grips
Length Overall: 6⅜"
Approximate wt.: 23 ozs.
Comments: Imported from about 1947 to 1956. Well-machined and well-finished, commercially-produced pistol. The 380 caliber has loaded chamber indicator.

Estimated Value:	**Excellent:**	**$500.00**
	Very good:	**$400.00**

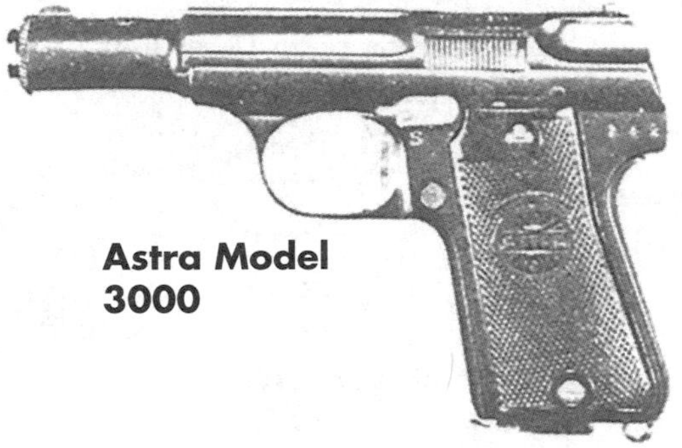

Astra Model 3000

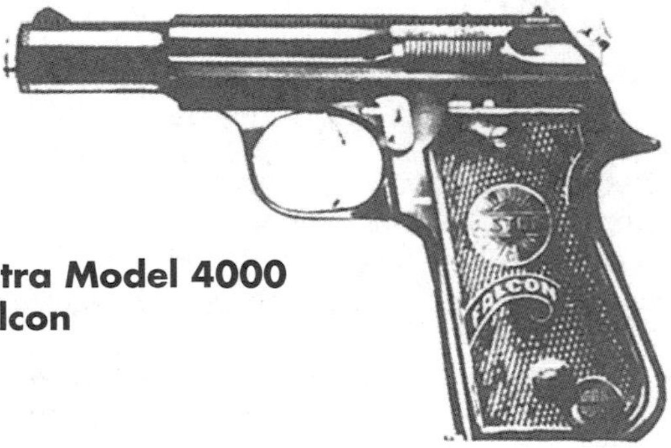

Astra Model 4000 Falcon

Astra Model 4000 Falcon

Caliber: 22 long rifle, 32 ACP (7.65mm), 380 ACP (9mm short)
Action: Semiautomatic; exposed hammer
Magazine: 10-shot clip in 22 caliber, 8-shot clip in 32 caliber; 7-shot clip in 380 caliber
Barrel: 4¼"
Sights: Fixed
Finish: Blued; checkered grips
Length Overall: 6½"
Approximate wt.: 20 to 24 ozs.
Comments: A conversion unit was available to fit the 32 caliber and 380 caliber pistols, so that 22 caliber long rifle ammunition could be used. Imported from the mid-1950s to the early 1980s. Add 75% for conversion kit.

Estimated Value:	**Excellent:**	**$500.00**
	Very good:	**$400.00**

Astra Model A-70

Caliber: 9mm Parabellum, 40 S&W
Action: Single action; semiautomatic; exposed hammer
Magazine: 8-shot clip (9mm); 7-shot clip (40 S&W)
Barrel: 3½"
Sights: Fixed
Finish: Blued or nickel; checkered plastic or rubber grips
Length Overall: 6½"
Approximate wt.: 29 ozs.
Comments: Imported in the 1990s. Add 10% for nickel finish. Add 20% for stainless steel.

Estimated Value:	**Excellent:**	**$275.00**
	Very good:	**$220.00**

Astra Model A-75

Astra Model A-75

Similar to the Model A-70 except: also caliber 45 ACP; double action with decocker; ambidextrous magazine release; approximate wt.: 34 ozs. Add 11% for 45 ACP; add 7% for nickel finish. Imported in the 1990s. Add 20% for stainless steel.

Estimated Value:	**Excellent:**	**$315.00**
	Very good:	**$250.00**

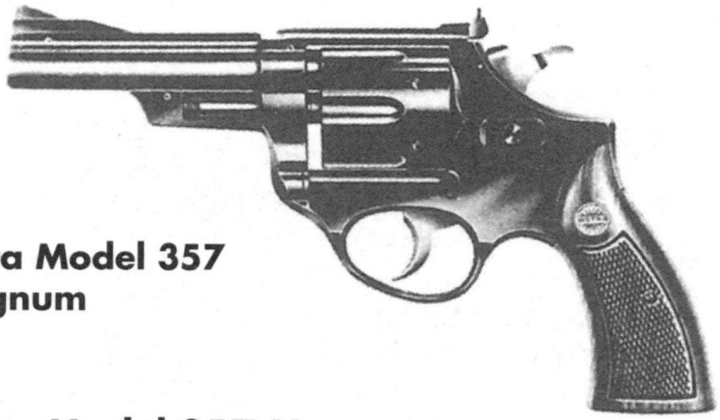

Astra Model 357 Magnum

Astra Model 357 Magnum

Caliber: 357 magnum, 38 special
Action: Double action
Cylinder: 6-shot, swing out
Barrel: 3", 4", 6", 8½" heavyweight with rib
Sights: Adjustable rear, fixed front
Finish: Blued; checkered walnut grips; stainless steel available after 1982
Length Overall: 8¼" to 13¾"
Approximate wt.: 38 to 42 ozs.
Comments: All steel construction with wide spur hammer and grooved trigger. Imported in the 1990s. Add 3% for 8½" barrel; 10% for stainless steel.

Estimated Value:	**Excellent:**	**$275.00**
	Very good:	**$220.00**

Astra Models 41 and 44

Similar to the Model 357 except 41 magnum or 44 magnum caliber; 6" or 8½" barrel. Imported in the early 1980s. Add $10.00 for 8½" barrel; Model 41 discontinued in the mid-1980s.

Estimated Value:	**Excellent:**	**$350.00**
	Very good:	**$280.00**

Astra Model 45

Similar to the Model 357 except 45 Colt or 45 ACP caliber; 6" barrel. Imported from the early 1980s to 1987.

Estimated Value:	**Excellent:**	**$350.00**
	Very good:	**$280.00**

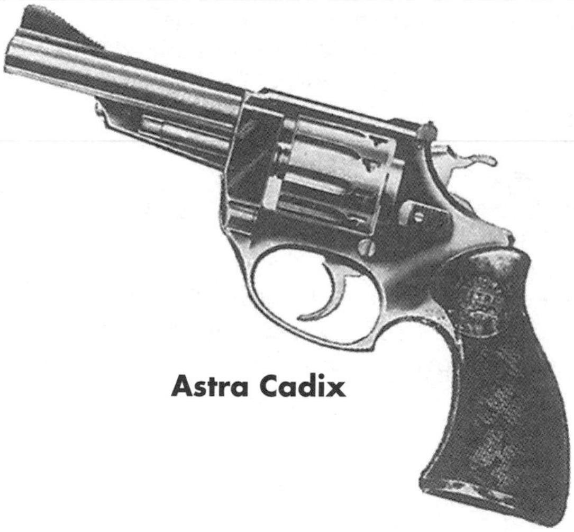

Astra Cadix

Astra Cadix

Caliber: 22 short, long and long rifle, 38 Special
Action: Double action
Cylinder: Swing-out 9-shot in 22 caliber; 5-shot in 38 Special
Barrel: 2", 4", and 6"
Sights: Adjustable rear on 4" and 6" barrel
Finish: Blued; checkered grips
Length Overall: 6½", 9", 11"
Approximate wt.: 25 to 27 ozs.
Comments: Imported from about 1960 to the late 1960s.

Estimated Value:	**Excellent:**	**$225.00**
	Very good:	**$180.00**

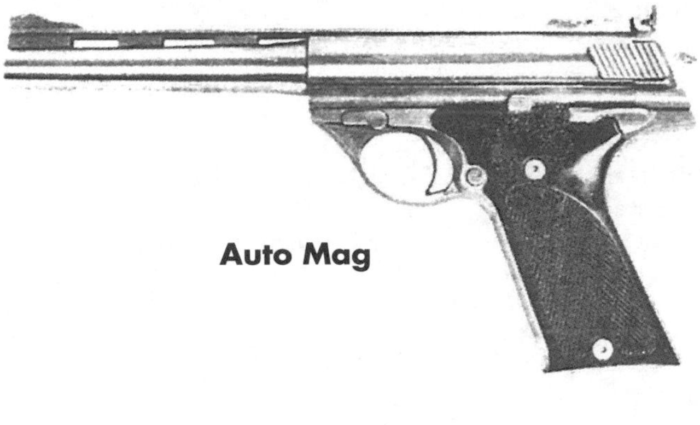

Auto Mag

Estimated Value: **Excellent:** **$1,800.00 – 2,500.00**
Very good: **$1,500.00 – 2,000.00**

Auto Mag

Caliber: 357 auto magnum or 44 auto magnum custom-loaded or hand-loaded cartridges (no commercial ammo available)
Action: Semiautomatic; exposed hammer; adjustable trigger
Magazine: 7-shot clip
Barrel: 6½" ventilated rib (44 auto mag.); 6½" or 8½" (.357 auto mag.); no rib on 8½" barrel
Sights: Ramp front sight and adjustable rear sight
Finish: Stainless steel; black polyurethane grips
Length Overall: 11½"
Approximate wt.: 60 ozs.
Comments: The most potent autoloader made. Designed by Harry Sanford, it was made by different factories (Auto Mag Corp., TDE Corp., High Standard and etc.). Requires special ammunition made from the 308 Winchester, .243, or 7.62 NATO cases. Made from about 1970 to the late 1970s. All stainless steel construction. Total production was rather small. First model called Pasadena Auto Mag. in .44 caliber only.

Bauer Stainless

Caliber: 25 ACP
Action: Single-action semiautomatic; concealed hammer
Magazine: 6-shot clip
Barrel: 2⅛"
Sights: Fixed
Finish: Heat treated stainless steel; plastic grips
Length Overall: 4"
Approximate wt.: 10 ozs.
Comments: Manufactured in the United States from about 1972 to the mid-1980s.
Estimated Value: **Excellent:** **$200.00**
Very good: **$160.00**

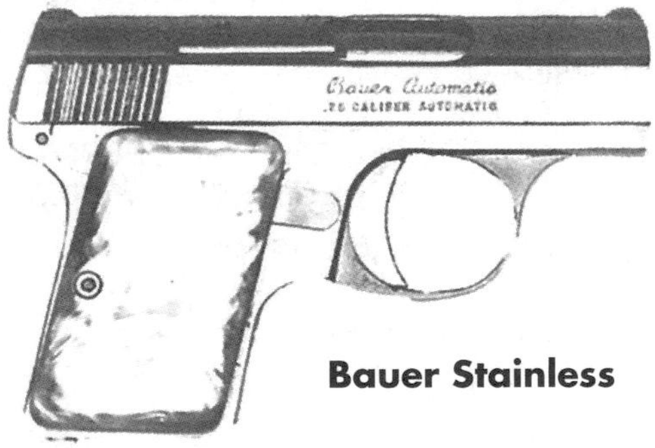

Bauer Stainless

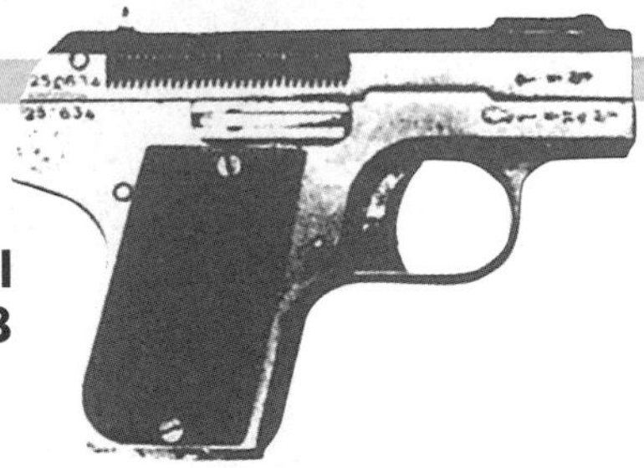

Bayard Model 1908

Bayard Model 1908

Caliber: 25 ACP (6.35 mm), 32 ACP (7.65mm), 380 ACP (9mm short)
Action: Semiautomatic; concealed hammer
Magazine: 6-shot clip
Barrel: 2¼"
Sights: Fixed
Finish: Blued; checkered grips
Length Overall: 5"
Approximate wt.: 15 to 17 ozs.
Comments: Made from basic Pieper patents of the 1900s. All calibers appear the same from a side view. Commercially sold throughout the world; one of the most compact pistols made.
Estimated Value: **Excellent:** **$275.00**
Very good: **$220.00**

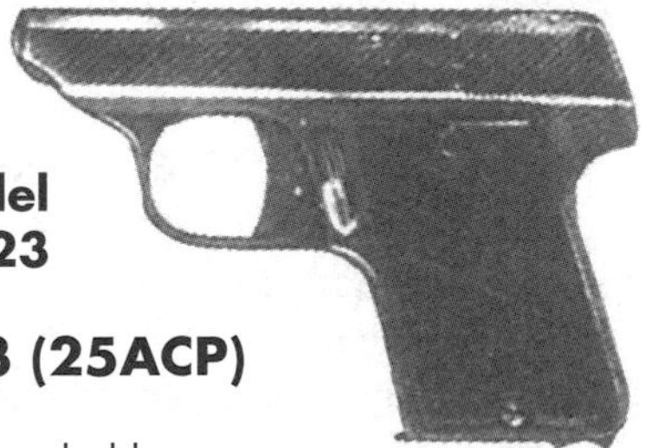

Bayard Model 1923

Bayard Model 1923 (25ACP)

Caliber: 25 ACP
Action: Semiautomatic; concealed hammer
Magazine: 6-shot clip
Barrel: 2⅛"
Sights: Fixed
Finish: Blued; checkered grips
Length Overall: 4⅓"
Approximate wt.: 12 ozs.
Comments: A Belgian variation of the Browning. This model has better construction than the Model 1908.
Estimated Value: **Excellent:** **$400.00**
Very good: **$320.00**

Bayard Model 1923 (32, 380)

Caliber: 32 ACP (7.65mm), 380 ACP (9mm short)
Action: Semiautomatic; concealed hammer
Magazine: 6-shot clip
Barrel: 3⅜"
Sights: Fixed
Finish: Blued; checkered grips
Length Overall: 5¾"
Approximate wt.: 18 to 19 ozs.
Comments: A Belgian variation of the Browning. Better construction than the Model 1908.
Estimated Value: **Excellent:** **$400.00**
Very good: **$320.00**

Bayard Model 1930

Caliber: 25 ACP (6.35mm)
Action: Semiautomatic; concealed hammer
Magazine: 6-shot clip
Barrel: 2"
Sights: Fixed
Finish: Blued; checkered grips
Length Overall: 4⅜"
Approximate wt.: 12 ozs.
Comments: A modification of the Model 1923.
Estimated Value: **Excellent:** **$300.00**
Very good: **$240.00**

BERETTA

Beretta Model 1915

Caliber: 32 ACP (7.65mm)
Action: Semiautomatic; concealed hammer
Magazine: 8-shot clip
Barrel: 3¼"
Sights: Fixed
Finish: Blued; wood or metal grips
Length Overall: 5⅞"
Approximate wt.: 20 ozs.
Comments: The earliest of the Beretta series used for military service during World War I as well as being sold commercially. Has rigid Lanyard loop on left side. Grip safety was added in 1919. Made from about 1915 to 1924.
Estimated Value: **Excellent:** **$800.00**
Very good: **$640.00**

Beretta Model 1915

Beretta Model 1919 Bantam

Caliber: 25 ACP (6.35mm)
Action: Semiautomatic; concealed hammer
Magazine: 7-shot clip
Barrel: 2½"
Sights: Fixed
Finish: Blued; wood grips
Length Overall: 4½"
Approximate wt.: 14 ozs.
Comments: Basic Beretta patent with addition of a grip safety. The front sight contour was changed prior to World War II. Importation to the United States was discontinued in 1956.
Estimated Value: **Excellent:** **$525.00**
Very good: **$420.00**

Beretta Model 1919 Bantam

Beretta Model 1923

Caliber: 9mm Luger
Action: Semiautomatic; exposed hammer
Magazine: 9-shot clip
Barrel: 4"
Sights: Fixed
Finish: Blued; wood grips
Length Overall: 6½"
Approximate wt.: 30 ozs.
Comments: Basically an Italian service pistol, but also sold commercially. A modified version of the 1915 and 1919 patents. This was the first model produced with exposed hammer. Lanyard loop on left side.
Estimated Value: **Excellent:** **$700.00**
Very good: **$560.00**

Beretta Model 1923

Beretta Model 1931

Caliber: 32 ACP (7.65mm)
Action: Semiautomatic; concealed hammer
Magazine: 7-shot clip
Barrel: 3 5/16"
Sights: Fixed
Finish: Blued; wood grips
Length Overall: 5¾"
Approximate wt.: 22 ozs.
Comments: A modified version of the Model 1923.

Estimated Value:	**Excellent:**	**$475.00**
	Very good:	**$380.00**

Beretta Model 1931

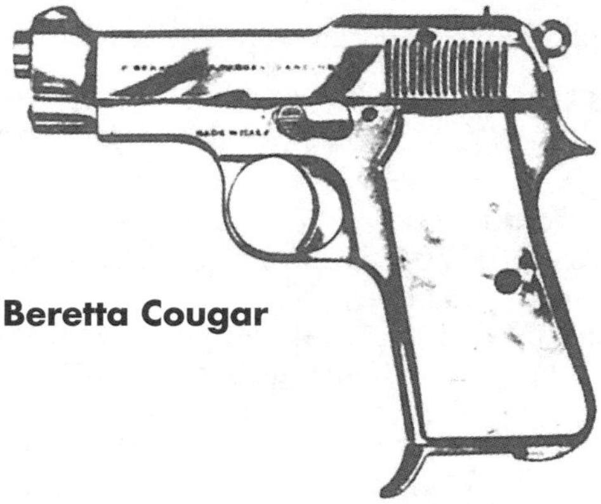

Beretta Cougar

Beretta Cougar

Caliber: 380 ACP (9mm short)
Action: Semiautomatic; exposed hammer
Magazine: 7-shot clip
Barrel: 3½"
Sights: Fixed
Finish: Blued or chrome; plastic grips
Length Overall: 6"
Approximate wt.: 22 ozs.
Comments: A post-World War II version of the Model 934 (1934). Those imported into the United States have the "Cougar" name on the pistol. Some of the later models are marked "P.B. 1966." Add $10.00 for chrome.

Estimated Value:	**Excellent:**	**$375.00**
	Very good:	**$300.00**

Beretta Model 934 (1934)

Beretta Models 934 (1934) 380 and 935 (1935) 32

Caliber: 32 ACP (7.65mm), 380 ACP (9mm short)
Action: Semiautomatic; exposed hammer
Magazine: 8-shot clip in 32; 7-shot clip in 380
Barrel: 3½"
Sights: Fixed
Finish: Blued; plastic grips
Length Overall: 6"
Approximate wt.: 22 to 24 ozs.
Comments: Official pistol of the Italian Armed Forces from 1934 until 1951 in 380 caliber. Sold commercially and used by Italian police. Lanyard loop on left side. Model 935 was discontinued in 1958.

Estimated Value:	**Excellent:**	**$450.00**
	Very good:	**$360.00**

Beretta Model 948 Plinker

Caliber: 22 long rifle
Action: Semiautomatic; exposed hammer
Magazine: 7-shot clip
Barrel: 3½", 6"
Sights: Fixed
Finish: Blued; plastic grips
Length Overall: 6" or 8½"
Approximate wt.: 16 to 18 ozs.
Comments: Made from 1948 to 1958. Similar to the 1934/35 series except: 22 caliber; aluminum alloy frame. Replaced by the "Jaguar." The 6" barrel extends about 3" beyond the slide.

Estimated Value:	**Excellent:**	**$325.00**
	Very good:	**$260.00**

Beretta Model 935 (1935)

Beretta Model 70 Puma

Caliber: 32 ACP (7.65mm); 380 ACP
Action: Semiautomatic; exposed hammer
Magazine: 7-shot clip
Barrel: 3½"
Sights: Fixed
Finish: Blued; plastic wrap-around grip
Length Overall: 6½"
Approximate wt.: 15 ozs.
Comments: Post-World War II (1946) version of the Model 935 (1935). Aluminum alloy frame was used to reduce weight. Those imported into the United States have "Puma" designation. Also made with steel frame. Discontinued. Add $15.00 for nickel finish. Made from 1960 to the mid-1980s.

Estimated Value:	**Excellent:**	**$400.00**
	Very good:	**$320.00**

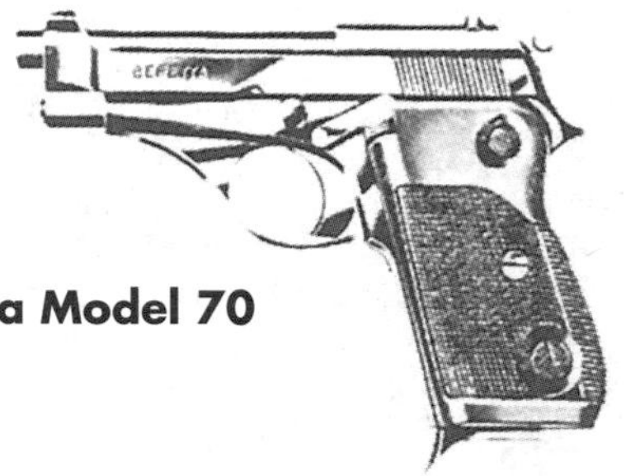

Beretta Model 70 Puma

Beretta Model 72 Jaguar

Beretta Model 70S

Beretta Model 70S

Caliber: 380 ACP (9mm short); 22 long rifle
Action: Semiautomatic; exposed hammer
Magazine: 7-shot clip in 380; 8-shot clip in 22
Barrel: 3½"
Sights: Fixed
Finish: Blued; two-piece wrap-around plastic grip
Length Overall: 6¼"
Approximate wt.: 24 ozs.
Comments: All steel compact pistol imported from Italy. Made from the late 1970s to the mid-1980s.

Estimated Value:	**Excellent:**	**$400.00**
	Very good:	**$320.00**

Beretta Model 70T

Beretta Model 70T

Caliber: 32 ACP (7.65mm)
Action: Semiautomatic; exposed hammer
Magazine: 9-shot clip
Barrel: 6"
Sights: Adjustable rear; blade front
Finish: Blued; plastic wrap-around grip
Length Overall: 9½"
Approximate wt.: 20 ozs.
Comments: Imported from Italy from 1956 to 1968. Target length barrel extends beyond front of slide.

Estimated Value:	**Excellent:**	**$425.00**
	Very good:	**$340.00**

Beretta Model 101

Same as the Model 70T except: 22 caliber long rifle; 10-shot clip. Made from 1960 to the mid-1980s.

Estimated Value:	**Excellent:**	**$300.00**
	Very good:	**$240.00**

Beretta Models 71 and 72 Jaguar

Caliber: 22 long rifle
Action: Semiautomatic; exposed hammer
Magazine: 7-shot clip
Barrel: 3½" (Model 71) and 6" (Model 72)
Sights: Fixed
Finish: Blued; wrap-around plastic grip
Length Overall: 6¼" or 8¾"
Approximate wt.: 16 to 18 ozs.
Comments: Importation to the United States started in 1956. The light weight was obtained by using aluminum alloy receiver. Similar in appearance to the Puma except the 6" barrel extends about 3" beyond the slide.

Estimated Value:	**Excellent:**	**$325.00**
	Very good:	**$260.00**

Beretta Model 949 Olympic

Beretta Model 949 Olympic, 949C

Caliber: 22 short, 22 long rifle
Action: Semiautomatic; exposed hammer
Magazine: 5-shot clip
Barrel: 8¾" with compensator muzzle brake
Sights: Rear adjustable for windage, front adjustable for elevation
Finish: Blued; checkered walnut grips with thumb rest
Length Overall: 12½"
Approximate wt.: 38 ozs.
Comments: Also called the Model 949C, it was designed for use in Olympic rapid-fire matches and designed 949LR. Made from the 1950s to the mid-1960s.

Estimated Value:	**Excellent:**	**$725.00**
	Very good:	**$580.00**

Beretta Model 951 (1951)

Caliber: 9mm Parabellum (Luger)
Action: Semiautomatic; exposed hammer
Magazine: 8-shot clip
Barrel: 4½"
Sights: Fixed
Finish: Blued; plastic wrap-around grip
Length Overall: 8"
Approximate wt.: 31 ozs.
Comments: First produced in 1950 and adopted by Italian army and navy. Has basic 1934 model features except it has aluminum alloy receiver. Also known as Brigadier model.

Estimated Value:	**Excellent:**	**$400.00**
	Very good:	**$320.00**

Beretta Minx M-2 and Model 950B

Caliber: 22 short, 25 ACP
Action: Semiautomatic; exposed hammer
Magazine: 6-shot clip
Barrel: 2½"
Sights: Fixed
Finish: Blued or nickel; plastic grips; wood grips
Length Overall: 4½"
Approximate wt.: 10 ozs.
Comments: Made from 1956 to the present. Imported from 1956 to 1968. Aluminum alloy frame with a hinged barrel that tips up. Can be used as single-shot by removing magazine and tipping up barrel to load. Reintroduced in 1979, manufactured in the United States. Add 17% for nickel finish.

Estimated Value:	**Excellent:**	**$200.00**
	Very good:	**$160.00**

Beretta Minx M-4 Model 950C

Beretta Minx M-2

Beretta Minx M-4, Model 950C, 950 BS4

Same as Minx M-2 except: 4" barrel; overall length 6"; approximate wt. 12 ozs. Add 10% for nickel finish.

Estimated Value:	**Excellent:**	**$200.00**
	Very good:	**$160.00**

Beretta Jetfire Model 950

Same as Minx M-2 except: 25 ACP (6.35mm) caliber; 8-shot clip. Add 17% for nickel finish; add 44% for engraved model with walnut grips; deduct 18% for matte finish with plastic grips; add 18% for stainless steel.

Estimated Value:	**Excellent:**	**$225.00**
	Very good:	**$180.00**

Beretta Model 951 (1951)

Beretta Model 21A Bobcat

Caliber: 22 long rifle, 25 ACP
Action: Straight blowback, double action semiautomatic
Magazine: 7-shot clip (22 caliber); 8-shot clip (25 ACP)
Barrel: 2½" tip up
Sights: Fixed
Finish: Blued; matte or nickel, alloy frame; wood or plastic grips
Length Overall: 5"
Approximate wt.: 12 ozs.
Comments: Introduced in 1984. Add 5% for nickel finish (after 1987); add 21% for engraving with wood grips; deduct 20% for matte finish.

Estimated Value:	**New (retail):**	**$335.00 - 420.00**
	Excellent:	**$250.00 - 315.00**
	Very good:	**$200.00 - 250.00**

Beretta Model 21A Bobcat

Beretta Tomcat 3032

Beretta Tomcat 3000 and 3032

Caliber: 22 long rifle, 32 (3032)
Action: Semiautomatic; double or single action, straight blowback system with tip-up barrel; exposed hammer
Magazine: 7-shot clip
Barrel: 2½" tip up
Sights: Fixed blade front, drift adjustable rear
Finish: Matte or blued with plastic or wood grips; stainless steel finish available
Length Overall: 5"
Approximate wt.: 15 ozs.
Comments: Introduced in the mid-1990s. Add 20% for blued model with wood grips; add 24% for stainless steel.

Estimated Value:	**New (retail):**	**$435.00 - 555.00**
	Excellent:	**$325.00 - 415.00**
	Very good:	**$260.00 - 335.00**

Beretta Model 76 Target

Caliber: 22 long rifle
Action: Semiautomatic; exposed hammer
Magazine: 10-shot clip
Barrel: 6"
Sights: Adjustable rear, blade front
Finish: Blued; two-piece wrap-around plastic or wood grip
Length Overall: 9½"
Approximate wt.: 35 ozs.
Comments: Imported from Italy. Competition-type heavy barrel. Add 10% for wood grips. Made from 1965 to the mid-1980s.

Estimated Value:	**Excellent:**	**$400.00**
	Very good:	**$320.00**

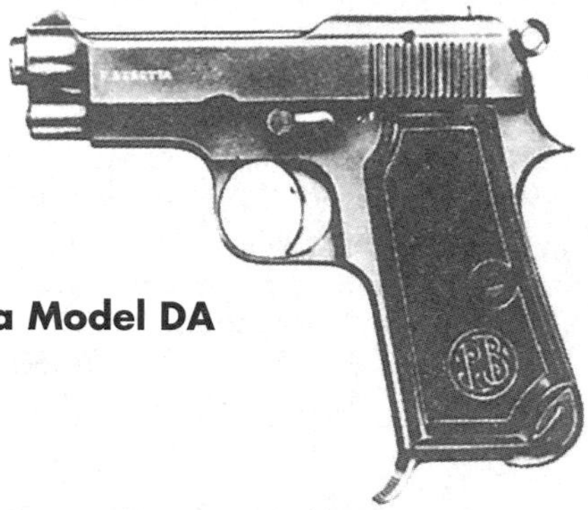

Beretta Model DA 380

Beretta Model 76 Target

Beretta Model 92SB

Caliber: 9mm Parabellum
Action: Semiautomatic; straight blowback; double action; exposed hammer
Magazine: 15-shot staggered clip
Barrel: 5"
Sights: Fixed
Finish: Blued; walnut or checkered plastic grips
Length Overall: 8½"
Approximate wt.: 34½ ozs.
Comments: Made from the early 1980s to 1986. Add 3% for wood grips.

Estimated Value:	**Excellent:**	**$500.00**
	Very good:	**$400.00**

Beretta Model 92SB Compact

Similar to the Model 92SB except 4¼" barrel; 13-shot clip; weighs 31 ozs. Add 3% for wood grips. Discontinued in 1986.

Estimated Value:	**Excellent:**	**$465.00**
	Very good:	**$375.00**

Beretta Model DA 380

Caliber: 380 ACP (9mm short)
Action: Double action; semiautomatic; exposed round spur hammer
Magazine: 13-shot staggered clip
Barrel: 3¾"
Sights: Fixed
Finish: Blued; smooth walnut grips
Length Overall: 6½"
Approximate wt.: 23 ozs.
Comments: This pistol features magazine release and safety release for either right or left hand.

Estimated Value:	**Excellent:**	**$400.00**
	Very good:	**$320.00**

Beretta Model 90

Caliber: 32 ACP (7.65mm short)
Action: Semiautomatic; straight blowback; double action; exposed hammer
Magazine: 8-shot clip
Barrel: 3½"
Sights: Fixed
Finish: Blued; contoured plastic grips
Length Overall: 6½"
Approximate wt.: 19 ozs.
Comments: Discontinued in the mid-1980s.

Estimated Value:	**Excellent:**	**$325.00**
	Very good:	**$260.00**

Beretta Models 92 and 92S

Caliber: 9mm Parabellum
Action: Semiautomatic; double and single action
Magazine: 15-shot clip
Barrel: 5"
Sights: Fixed
Finish: Blued; plastic or smooth wood grips
Length Overall: 8½"
Approximate wt.: 33 ozs.
Comments: Made from the late 1970s to the early 1980s. Add 5% for wood grips. Loaded chamber indicator.

Estimated Value:	**Excellent:**	**$500.00**
	Very good:	**$400.00**

Beretta Model 90

Beretta Model 92

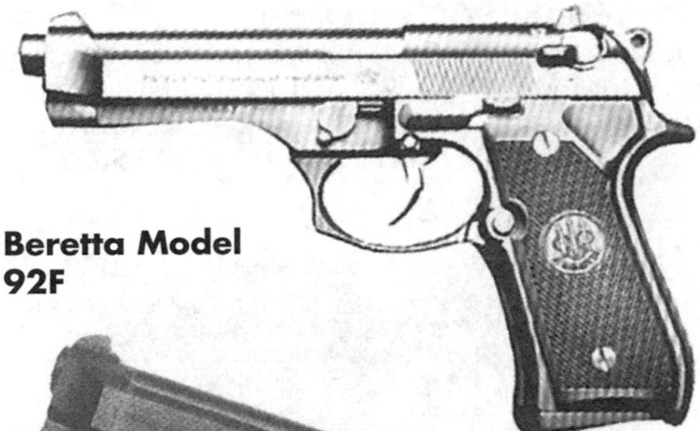

Beretta Model 92F

Beretta Model 92F Compact

Beretta Model 96

Beretta Model 92D/96D

Beretta Models 92D and 96D

Same as the Models 92DS and 96DS except: the safety lever has been eliminated. Add 4% for Model 96D (40 cal.) Introduced in 1992. Add 16% for tritium sights.

Estimated Value: **Excellent:** **$485.00**
Very good: **$385.00**

Beretta Models 92F and 92FS (after 1991)

Caliber: 9mm Parabellum
Action: Double action semiautomatic; locked breech; delayed blowback; exposed hammer; manual ambidextrous safety; large frame
Magazine: 15-shot staggered clip; 10-shot after Sept. 13, 1994
Barrel: 5"
Sights: Fixed blade front; square notched bar rear, dovetailed to slide; 3-dot sight system
Finish: Combat-style alloy frame and steel slide matte finish; or alloy frame and stainless steel; smooth or checkered plastic or wood grips
Length Overall: 8½"
Approximate wt.: 34 ozs.
Comments: Similar to the Model 92SB with improved safety features and open slide design. Adopted as the official side arm of the U.S. military in the mid-1980s. Made from 1986 to the present. Add 3% for wood grips, 21% for stainless steel, 15% for tritium sights.

Estimated Value: **New (retail):** **$799.00**
Excellent: **$600.00**
Very good: **$475.00**

Beretta Models 92F and 92FS Compact

Similar to the Model 92F with a 4¼" barrel, 13-shot clip; 10 shot clip after 1994; weighs 31 ozs. Add 3% for wood grips. Made from 1986 to present.

Estimated Value: **New (retail):** **$675.00**
Excellent: **$505.00**
Very good: **$405.00**

Beretta Models 92FS Compact Type M

Same as the Model 92FS Compact except: narrower grip, holding a single line 8-shot clip. The magazine release is not ambidextrous. Introduced in the late 1980s.

Estimated Value: **New (retail):** **$675.00**
Excellent: **$505.00**
Very good: **$405.00**

Beretta Models 96 and 96 Compact

Same as the Model 92FS except: 40 S&W caliber with 10-shot clip; the 96 Compact is the same as the Model 92FS Compact except 40 S&W caliber with 9-shot clip. Introduced in 1992. Also available in stainless steel with wood or rubber grips. Add 15% for tritium sights.

Estimated Value: **New (retail):** **$728.00**
Excellent: **$545.00**
Very good: **$435.00**

Beretta Models 92G Elite and 96G Elite

Same as the Model 92FS except: hammer drop lever does not function as a traditional safety. When the lever is released after dropping the hammer, it returns to firing position. It can be fired (double action mode for first shot) by pulling the trigger. Model 96G is 40 S&W caliber with 10-shot clip. Add 2% for Model 96G.

Estimated Value: **Excellent:** **$500.00**
Very good: **$400.00**

Beretta Models 92DS and 96DS

Same as the Model 92FS except: double action only; bobbed hammer; hammer returns to the down position after each slide cycle; safety lever. Model 96DS is 40 S&W caliber with 10-shot clip. Add 4% for 96DS. Made in the 1990s. Add 16% for tritium sights.

Estimated Value: **Excellent:** **$440.00**
Very good: **$350.00**

Beretta Model 92FS Centurion

Same as the Model 92FS except: 4¼" barrel (like the 92FS Compact) but has the 15-shot clip (like the 92FS); 10-shot clip after 1995. Introduced in 1992. Add 15% for tritium sights.

Estimated Value: **New (retail):** **$695.00**
Excellent: **$520.00**
Very good: **$415.00**

Beretta Model 96 Centurion

Same as the Model 92FS Centurion except: 40 S&W caliber with 10-shot clip. Introduced in 1992. Add 14% for tritium sights.

Estimated Value: **Excellent:** **$520.00**
Very good: **$415.00**

Beretta Model 96 Centurion

Beretta Cougar

Beretta Model 9000S

Beretta Cougar

Caliber: 9mm (8000), 40 S&W (8040), 45ACP
Action: Semiautomatic, short recoil, rotating barrel; exposed hammer; Model D has no hammer spur and is double action only; Models F and G are single or double action
Magazine: 10-shot clip
Barrel: 3½" rotating; chromium plated inside
Sights: Three-dot system with front and rear dovetailed to the slide
Finish: Matte black with checkered plastic grips
Length Overall: 7"
Approximate wt.: 32½ ozs.
Comments: Introduced in the mid-1990s. Deduct 5% for Model D.
Estimated Value: **Excellent:** **$550.00**
Very good: **$440.00**

Beretta Model 9000S

Caliber: 9mm, 40 S&W
Action: Single or double action semiautomatic; double action only model available
Magazine: 10-shot clip
Barrel: 3½" chrome lined
Sights: Adjustable, three-dot system
Finish: Polymer frame and grips
Length overall: 6"
Approximate wt.: 26 ozs.
Comments: Introduced in 2001.
Estimated Value: **Excellent:** **$425.00**
Very good: **$340.00**

Beretta Mini Cougar

Beretta Model 20

Caliber: 25 ACP
Action: Straight blowback, recoil ejector, double action semiautomatic
Magazine: 8-shot clip
Barrel: 2½" tip-up
Sights: Fixed
Finish: Blued; alloy frame, plastic or walnut grips
Length Overall: 5"
Approximate wt.: 10½ ozs.
Comments: Produced from 1984 to 1987.
Estimated Value: **Excellent:** **$225.00**
Very good: **$180.00**

Beretta Mini Cougar

Caliber: 9mm, 40 S&W, 45ACP
Action: Single or double action semiautomatic; double action only model available
Magazine: 6, 8, or 10-shot clip
Barrel: 3½"
Sights: Fixed, three-dot system
Finish: Stainless steel, plastic grips
Length overall: 6"
Approximate wt.: 27 ozs.
Comments: Introduced in 2001.
Estimated Value: **Excellent:** **$550.00**
Very good: **$440.00**

Beretta Model 81

Beretta Model 82

Caliber: 32 ACP (7.65mm)
Action: Semiautomatic; straight blowback; double action; exposed hammer; medium frame
Magazine: 9-shot clip
Barrel: 3¾"
Sights: Fixed
Finish: Blued or nickel, walnut grips
Length Overall: 6¾"
Approximate wt.: 17 ozs.
Comments: Similar to the Model 81 with a more compact grip size. Add 15% for nickel finish.

Estimated Value:	**Excellent:**	**$325.00**
	Very good:	**$260.00**

Beretta Models 83 and 83 Cheeta

Similar to the Model 82 except: 380 caliber; 4" barrel; 7-shot in-line clip; checkered plastic or walnut grips. Add 5% for walnut grips; add 8% for nickel.

Estimated Value:	**Excellent:**	**$400.00**
	Very good:	**$320.00**

Beretta Models 84 and 84 Cheeta

Similar to the Model 81 in 380 caliber (9mm short); 10- or 13-shot staggered clip; plastic grips: Add 6% for wood grips; add 13% for nickel finish with wood grips.

Estimated Value:	**New (retail):**	**$770.00**
	Excellent:	**$575.00**
	Very good:	**$460.00**

Beretta Models 85 and 85 Cheeta

Similar to the Model 82 except: 380 caliber (9mm short); 8-shot inline clip; plastic grips. Add 20% for nickel; add 7% for wood grips.

Estimated Value:	**Excellent:**	**$450.00**
	Very good:	**$360.00**

Beretta Models 86 and 86 Cheeta

Similar to the Model 85 except: tip-up barrel for loading without working the slide; wood grips.

Estimated Value:	**Excellent:**	**$475.00**
	Very good:	**$380.00**

Beretta Model 81

Caliber: 32 ACP
Action: Semiautomatic; double and single action
Magazine: 12-shot clip
Barrel: 3¾"
Sights: Fixed
Finish: Blued or nickel; plastic or smooth wood grips
Length Overall: 6¾"
Approximate wt.: 23½ ozs.
Comments: Produced in the late 1970s to about 1984. Add 3% for wood grips; add 15% for nickel finish.

Estimated Value:	**Excellent:**	**$400.00**
	Very good:	**$320.00**

Beretta Model 89

Beretta Model 86

Beretta Models 87 and 87 Cheeta

Similar to the Model 85 except: 22 long rifle; 7-shot clip. Add 4% for 6" barrel and counterweight.

Estimated Value:	**New (retail):**	**$845.00**
	Excellent:	**$635.00**
	Very good:	**$500.00**

Beretta Models 89 and 89 Gold Standard

Caliber: 22 long rifle
Action: Single-action, semiautomatic; target pistol
Magazine: 8-shot clip
Barrel: 6"
Sights: Adjustable target sights
Finish: Blued; contoured walnut grips with thumb rest
Length Overall: 9½"
Approximate wt.: 41 ozs.
Comments: Introduced in the late 1980s; discontinued in the late 1990s.

Estimated Value:	**Excellent:**	**$650.00**
	Very good:	**$520.00**

Browning Hi Power Standard

Browning 25 Pocket

Caliber: 25 ACP (6.35mm)
Action: Semiautomatic; concealed hammer
Magazine: 6-shot clip
Barrel: 2⅛"
Sights: Fixed
Finish: Blued; hard rubber grips; nickel plated, lightweight, plastic pearl grips; Renaissance engraved Nacolac pearl grips available
Length Overall: 4"
Approximate wt.: 8 to 10 ozs.
Comments: A post-World War II modification of the FN Browning Baby Automatic pistol, it was lightened and the grip safety removed. Imported into the U.S. from 1954 to 1968. Pistols imported into the U.S. and Canada usually do not have the FN trademark. Add 10% for nickel finish; add 200% for nickel-plated Renaissance engraved model (mint).

Estimated Value:	**Excellent:**	**$550.00**
	Very good:	**$440.00**

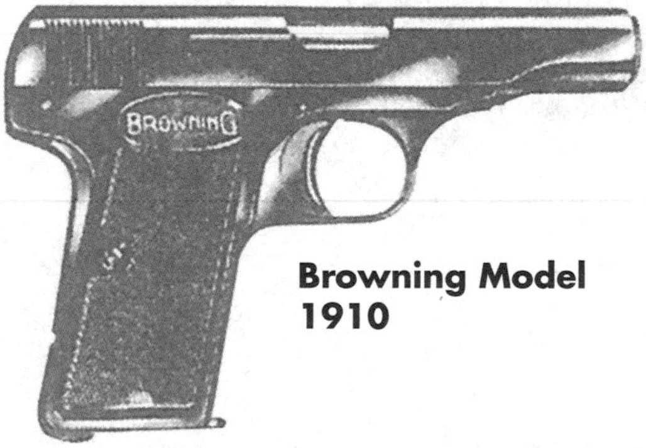

Browning Model 1910

Browning Model 1910 (1955)

Caliber: 380 ACP (9mm short), 32 ACP
Action: Semiautomatic; concealed hammer
Magazine: 6-shot clip (380 ACP) 8-shot clip (32 ACP)
Barrel: 3½"
Sights: Fixed
Finish: Blued; hard rubber grips; Renaissance engraved, Nacolac pearl grips available
Length Overall: 6"
Approximate wt.: 21 ozs.
Comments: Basic design of the 1900 model FN Browning, with the appearance streamlined and a grip safety added. Imported from 1954 to 1968. Pistols imported into the U.S. and Canada usually do not have the FN trademark. Add 200% for nickel-plated, Renaissance engraved model (mint).

Estimated Value:	**Excellent:**	**$400.00**
	Very good:	**$320.00**

Browning Hi Power Standard

Caliber: 9mm Parabellum; 40 S&W (added 1994)
Action: Semiautomatic; exposed hammer; single action
Magazine: 13-shot clip; 10-shot after 9-13-94
Barrel: 4⅝"
Sights: Fixed or adjustable rear sight
Finish: Blued; checkered walnut or molded Polymide grips; Renaissance engraved, Nacolac pearl grips available; chrome available 1982 with Packmayr grips; nickel available until 1986; matte finish with molded grips available after 1985.
Length Overall: 7¾"
Approximate wt.: 34 ozs.
Comments: Imported into the U.S. from 1954 to the present. Pistols imported into the U.S. from Belgium usually do not have FN trademark. Add 8% for adjustable sights; 10% for nickel or chrome finish; 200% for nickel-plated, Renaissance engraved (mint).

Estimated Value:	**New (retail):**	**$1,029.00**
	Excellent:	**$ 770.00**
	Very good:	**$ 615.00**

Browning Hi Power Mark III

Similar to the Hi Power except: non-glare matte, polished blue, or silver chrome finish; low profile fixed or adjustable sights; two-piece molded grips with thumbrest or walnut grips; introduced in 1991. Add 3% for silver chrome finish; add 6% for walnut grips; add 9% for adjustable sights.

Estimated Value:	**New (retail):**	**$999.00**
	Excellent:	**$750.00**
	Very good:	**$600.00**

Browning Hi Power Practical

Similar to the Hi Power except: contrasting blue slide and silver-chrome frame; wrap-around Pachmayr grips; round serrated hammer; removable front sight; add 8% for adjustable sights.

Estimated Value:	**Excellent:**	**$650.00**
	Very good:	**$520.00**

Browning Renaissance Engraved Cased Set

Contains one each of the following:

Browning 25 Automatic Pistol
Browning Model 1910 380 Automatic Pistol
Browning Model 1935 Hi Power Automatic Pistol

in a special walnut carrying case. Each pistol is nickel-plated, Renaissance engraved, with Nacolac pearl grips. Imported into the U.S. from 1954 through 1968. Price includes walnut case.

Estimated Value: Mint condition (unused): $5,000.00

Browning Hi-Power Capitan

Caliber: 9mm Parabellum
Action: Semiautomatic; exposed rounded commander-style hammer
Magazine: 10-shot clip
Barrel: 4¾"
Sights: Blade front, adjustable tangent rear
Finish: Blued; checkered walnut grips
Length Overall: 7¾"
Approximate wt.: 32 ozs.
Comments: Introduced in the 1990s. Discontinued in 2001.
Estimated Value: **Excellent:** **$575.00**
Very good: **$460.00**

Browning Challenger

Browning Challenger III

Caliber: 22 long rifle
Action: Semiautomatic; concealed hammer
Magazine: 10-shot clip
Barrel: 5½" bull barrel
Sights: Blade front, adjustable rear
Finish: Blued; smooth impregnated hardwood grips
Length Overall: 9½"
Approximate wt.: 35 ozs.
Comments: Produced from 1982 to 1986.
Estimated Value: **Excellent:** **$400.00**
Very good: **$320.00**

Browning Challenger III Sporter

Similar to the Challenger III with 6¾" round barrel. Produced from 1985 to 1987.
Estimated Value: **Excellent:** **$400.00**
Very good: **$320.00**

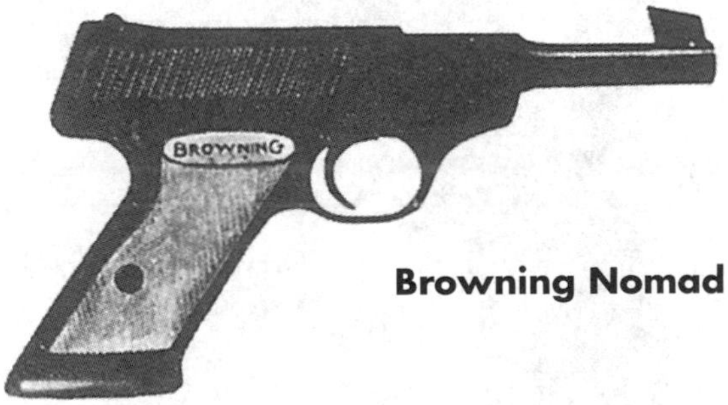

Browning Nomad

Browning Challenger

Caliber: 22 long rifle
Action: Semiautomatic; concealed hammer
Magazine: 10-shot clip
Barrel: 4½" or 6¾"
Sights: Removable blade front, adjustable rear
Finish: Blued; checkered walnut grips; gold model (gold inlaid) finely figured walnut grips; Renaissance engraved finely figured walnut grips
Length Overall: 9$\frac{3}{16}$" or 11$\frac{7}{16}$"
Approximate wt.: 36 to 38 ozs.
Comments: Blued model made from 1963 to 1974. Gold and Renaissance models introduced in 1971. All steel construction. Add 100% for gold model; add 130% for nickel-plated Renaissance engraved model (mint).
Estimated Value: **Excellent:** **$400.00**
Very good: **$320.00**

Browning Challenger II

Similar to the Challenger except 6¾" barrel only; made from about 1975 to the mid-1980s. Impregnated wood grips.
Estimated Value: **Excellent:** **$400.00**
Very good: **$320.00**

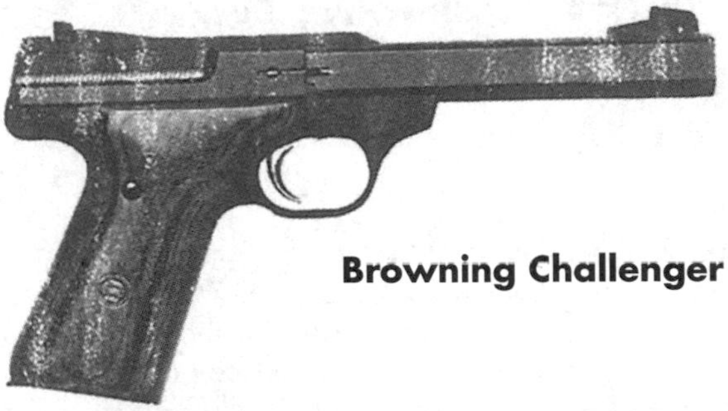

Browning Challenger III

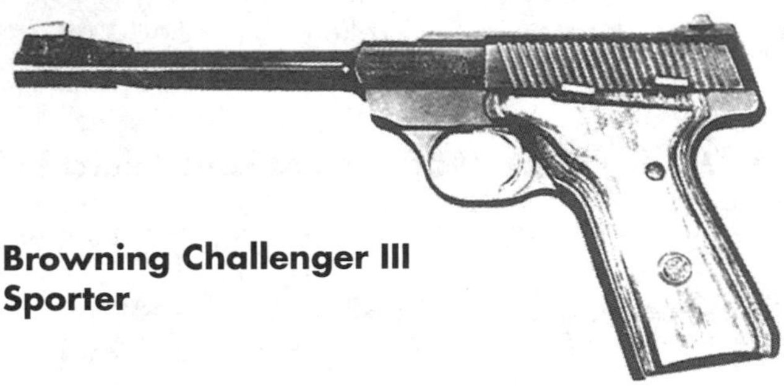

Browning Challenger III Sporter

Browning Nomad

Caliber: 22 long rifle
Action: Semiautomatic; concealed hammer
Magazine: 10-shot clip
Barrel: 4½" or 6¾"
Sights: Removable blade front, adjustable rear sight
Finish: Blued; plastic grips
Length Overall: 9" and 11¼"
Approximate wt.: 26 to 28 ozs.
Comments: Made from 1963 to 1973 with an alloy frame.
Estimated Value: **Excellent:** **$350.00**
Very good: **$280.00**

Browning Buck Mark 22 and Buck Mark Plus

Caliber: 22 long rifle
Action: Semiautomatic; blowback; concealed hammer
Magazine: 10-shot clip
Barrel: 5½" bull barrel with non-glare top
Sights: Adjustable rear, ramp front
Finish: Blued; matte except for lustre barrel sides; checkered black molded composite grips; Buck Mark Plus has deer head medallion; brass-plated trigger; laminated wood grips; nickel finish available after 1991
Length Overall: 9½"
Approximate wt.: 32 ozs.
Comments: Introduced in 1985; add 22% for Buck Mark Plus; add 18% for nickel finish.

Estimated Value:	**Excellent:**	**$250.00**
	Very good:	**$200.00**

Browning Buck Mark 22

Browning Buck Mark Bullseye

Similar to the Browning Buck Mark 22 except: 7¼" round fluted barrel; approximate wt.: 36 ozs.; rubber, laminated wood, or rosewood grips; adjustable trigger pull; introduced in 1996. Add 28% for contoured rosewood grips (target model).

Estimated Value:	**Excellent:**	**$400.00**
	Very good:	**$320.00**

Browning Buck Mark Micro and Micro Plus

Same as Buck Mark 22 except: 4" barrel; weighs 36 ozs.; overall length 8". Add 18% for nickel finish, 22% for Buck Mark Micro Plus.

Estimated Value:	**Excellent:**	**$300.00**
	Very good:	**$240.00**

Browning Pro-9 and Pro 40

Caliber: 9mm (Pro-9), 40 S&W (Pro 40)
Action: Double action, semiautomatic; exposed hammer
Magazine: 10-shot clip
Barrel: 4"
Sights: Fixed, three-dot system
Finish: Composite polymer frame and grips, stainless steel slide
Length Overall: 7¼"
Approximate wt.: 1¾ to 2 lbs.
Comments: Introduced in 2003.

Estimated Value:	**Excellent:**	**$480.00**
	Very good:	**$385.00**

Browning Buck Mark Varmint

A varmint pistol based on the Buck Mark design; 9⅞" bull barrel; full-length scope base rib; no sights; walnut grips; walnut forearm is available. Introduced in 1988; discontinued in 2000.

Estimated Value:	**Excellent:**	**$325.00**
	Very good:	**$260.00**

Browning Buck Mark 5.5 Target

Browning Buck Mark 5.5 Field and Target

Similar to the Buck Mark 22 except: 5½" heavy round barrel; with a full-length scope mount rib. Add 12% for gold or nickel Target model.

Estimated Value:	**New (retail):**	**$619.00**
	Excellent:	**$465.00**
	Very good:	**$370.00**

Browning Buck Mark Silhouette

Browning Buck Mark Silhouette and Unlimited

A silhouette-style pistol based on the Buck Mark design; 9⅞" bull barrel on the silhouette model. Unlimited has 14" barrel; hooded, adjustable sights mounted on a full-length scope rib base; walnut grips; finger groove or smooth walnut forearm. Introduced in 1988. Add 23% for Unlimited model.

Estimated Value:	**Excellent:**	**$325.00**
	Very good:	**$260.00**

Browning Pro-9, Pro 40

Browning Buck Mark Camper

Caliber: 22 long rifle
Action: Semiautomatic; blowback; concealed hammer
Magazine: 10-shot clip
Barrel: 5½" bull barrel
Sights: Adjustable target
Finish: Matte blue, nickel, or stainless tapered barrel; polymer grips
Approximate wt.: 34 ozs.
Comments: Introduced in 2000. Add 10% for nickel or stainless steel finish.

Estimated Value:	**New (retail):**	**$349.00**
	Excellent:	**$260.00**
	Very good:	**$210.00**

Browning Buck Mark Camper

Browning Buck Mark Challenge

Browning Buck Mark Challenge

Similar to the Buck Mark Camper except: lightweight tapered barrel; smaller wood grips; weighs approximately 25 ozs. Introduced in 2000.

Estimated Value:	**New (retail):**	**$429.00**
	Excellent:	**$320.00**
	Very good:	**$255.00**

Browning Buck Mark Challenge Micro

Similar to the Buck Mark Challenge except: smaller and lighter, 4" barrel. Introduced in 2000.

Estimated Value:	**Excellent:**	**$300.00**
	Very good:	**$240.00**

Browning Model BDA 380

Browning Buckmark Classic Plus

Browning Model BDM

Browning Model BDM

Caliber: 9mm Luger
Action: Semiautomatic; short recoil; double action for first shot or selector switch for double action only for all shots
Magazine: 15-shot clip; 10-shot clip after Sept. 13, 1994
Barrel: 4¾"
Sights: Adjustable rear, low-profile removable blade front
Finish: Black matte; molded wrap-around grips
Length Overall: 7¾"
Approximate wt.: 31 ozs.
Comments: Made in the 1990s.

Estimated Value:	**Excellent:**	**$460.00**
	Very good:	**$370.00**

Browning Model BDA

Caliber: 45 ACP, 9mm, 38 Super ACP
Action: Semiautomatic; exposed hammer; built-in safety block; double and single action
Magazine: 7-shot clip in 45 ACP; 9-shot clip in 9mm and 38 Super
Barrel: 4½"
Sights: Adjustable square notch rear, blade front
Finish: Blued; black checkered plastic grips
Length Overall: 7¾"
Approximate wt.: 29 ozs.
Comments: Produced from the late 1970s to 1980. Add 20% for 38 super ACP.

Estimated Value:	**Excellent:**	**$460.00**
	Very good:	**$370.00**

Browning Model BDA 380

Caliber: 380 ACP
Action: Semiautomatic; exposed hammer; double action for first shot
Magazine: 13-shot staggered row clip; 10-shot after Sept. 13, 1994
Barrel: 3¾"
Sights: Adjustable square notch rear, blade front
Finish: Blued; smooth walnut grips, bronze medallion; nickel finish available after 1981
Length Overall: 6¾"
Approximate wt.: 32 ozs.
Comments: Made from the late 1970s to the mid-1990s. Add 8% for nickel finish.

Estimated Value:	**Excellent:**	**$400.00**
	Very good:	**$320.00**

Browning Buckmark Classic Plus

Similar to the Buckmark 22 with laminated rosewood grips.

Estimated Value:	**Excellent:**	**$300.00**
	Very good:	**$240.00**

Browning Buck Mark Hunter

Similar to the Buck Mark Camper except: 7¼" barrel; hardwood grips.

Estimated Value:	**New (retail):**	**$459.00**
	Excellent:	**$345.00**
	Very good:	**$275.00**

Browning Buck Mark Hunter

Browning Buck Mark FLD Plus

Similar to the Buck Mark Classic Plus except: alloy receiver.

Estimated Value:	**Excellent:**	**$300.00**
	Very good:	**$240.00**

Browning Buck Mark FLD Plus

Browning Buck Mark FLD Plus Rosewood UDX

Similar to the Buck Mark FLD Plus except: laminated rosewood finger-groove grips.

Estimated Value:	**Excellent:**	**$335.00**
	Very good:	**$265.00**

Browning Buck Mark Standard URX

Browning Buck Mark FLD Plus Rosewood UDX

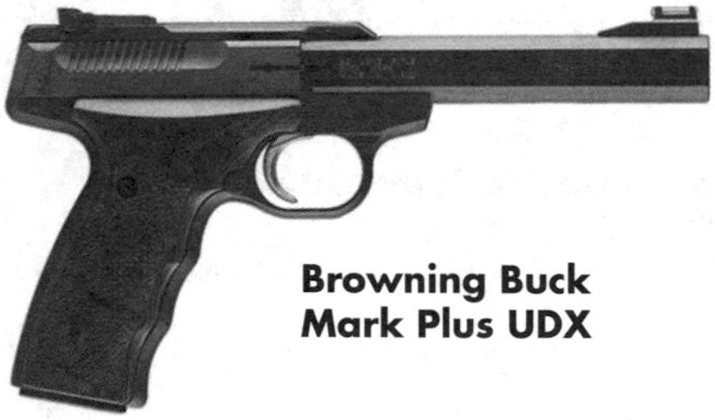

Browning Buck Mark Plus UDX

Browning Buck Mark Micro Standard URX

Browning Buck Mark Standard URX

Similar to the Buck Mark Plus except: alloy receiver; polymer finger-groove grips. Add 10% for stainless steel finish.

Estimated Value:	**New (retail):**	**$429.00**
	Excellent:	**$320.00**
	Very good:	**$255.00**

Browning Buck Mark Plus UDX

Similar to the Buck Mark Plus except: Challenger size fame and laminated walnut, finger-groove grips. Add 10% for stainless steel.

Estimated Value:	**New (retail):**	**$499.00**
	Excellent:	**$375.00**
	Very good:	**$300.00**

Browning Buck Mark Micro Standard URX

Similar to the Buck Mark Plus except: 4" barrel; alloy receiver. Add 10% for stainless steel finish.

Estimated Value:	**New (retail):**	**$429.00**
	Excellent:	**$320.00**
	Very good:	**$255.00**

Browning Medalist

Caliber: 22 long rifle
Action: Semiautomatic; concealed hammer
Magazine: 10-shot clip
Barrel: 6¾", ventilated rib
Sights: Removable blade front, adjustable micrometer rear
Finish: Blued; checkered walnut grips with thumbrest; gold model (gold inlaid) finely figured and carved walnut grips with thumb rest, Renaissance model engraved, finely figured and carved walnut grips with thumbrest
Length Overall: 11¾"
Approximate wt.: 45 ozs.
Comments: All steel construction, made from 1963 to 1974. Gold model and Renaissance model introduced in 1971. Add 80% for gold model; add 120% for nickel-plated Renaissance engraved model (mint). Price includes case and accessories.

Estimated Value:	**Excellent:**	**$750.00**
	Very good:	**$600.00**

Browning International Medalist

Browning International Medalist

Caliber: 22 long rifle
Action: Semiautomatic; hammerless
Magazine: 10-shot clip
Barrel: $5^{15}/_{16}$" heavy, counterweight
Sights: Fixed, nonreflective
Finish: Blued; wide walnut grips, adjustable hand stop
Length Overall: 11¾"
Approximate wt.: 46 ozs.
Comments: A target pistol produced in the early 1970s.

Estimated Value:	**Excellent:**	**$775.00**
	Very good:	**$620.00**

FN Browning Model 1900

Caliber: 32 ACP (7.65mm)
Action: Semiautomatic; concealed hammer
Magazine: 7-shot clip
Barrel: 4"
Sights: Fixed
Finish: Blued; hard rubber grips with FN trademark
Length Overall: 6¾"
Approximate wt.: 22 ozs.
Comments: John Browning's first commercially successful pistol. This was the beginning for the 32 automatic cartridge, which is called 7.65 Browning pistol cartridge in the rest of the world. The Model 1900 was sold commercially throughout the world and was also used by police and military in countries such as Belgium, Russia, China, and France. Made from 1900 to 1912.

Estimated Value:	**Excellent:**	**$500.00**
	Very good:	**$400.00**

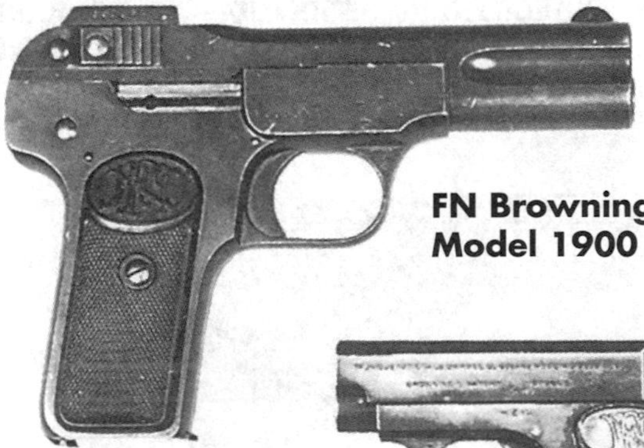

FN Browning Model 1900

FN Browning 6.35mm Vest Pocket

FN Browning Model 1903 Military

Caliber: 9mm Browning long
Action: Semiautomatic; concealed hammer
Magazine: 7-shot clip
Barrel: 5"
Sights: Fixed
Finish: Blued, hard rubber grips with FN trademark
Length Overall: 8"
Approximate wt.: 33 ozs.
Comments: Made from 1903 to 1939. Lanyard ring on left grip.

Estimated Value:	**Excellent:**	**$525.00**
	Very good:	**$420.00**

FN Browning Model 1903 Military

FN Browning 6.35mm Vest Pocket

Caliber: 25 ACP (6.35mm)
Action: Semiautomatic; concealed hammer; grip safety
Magazine: 6-shot clip
Barrel: 2"
Sights: Fixed
Finish: Blued; hard rubber grips with FN trademark
Length Overall: 4½"
Approximate wt.: 13 ozs.
Comments: Made from 1905 to 1947.

Estimated Value:	**Excellent:**	**$425.00**
	Very good:	**$340.00**

FN Browning Model 1910

FN Browning Model 1922 Military and Police

FN Browning Model 1935 Hi Power

FN Browning Model 1910

Caliber: 32 ACP (7.65mm), 380 ACP (9mm short)
Action: Semiautomatic; concealed hammer
Magazine: 7-shot clip in 32 ACP, 6-short clip in 380
Barrel: 3½"
Sights: Fixed
Finish: Blued; hard rubber grips with FN trademark
Length Overall: 6"
Approximate wt.: 21 ozs.
Comments: The basic design of the Model 1900 except it has streamlined appearance and grip safety.

Estimated Value:	**Excellent:**	**$400.00**
	Very good:	**$320.00**

FN Browning Baby

Caliber: 25 ACP (6.35mm)
Action: Semiautomatic; concealed hammer
Magazine: 6-shot clip
Barrel: 2⅛"
Sights: Fixed
Finish: Blued; hard rubber grips with FN trademark
Length Overall: 4"
Approximate wt.: 10 ozs.
Comments: Introduced in 1940. All steel construction, similar to Browning 25 Pocket Automatic Pistol, imported into U.S. from 1954 to 1968.

Estimated Value:	**Excellent:**	**$525.00**
	Very good:	**$420.00**

FN Browning Baby

FN Browning Model 1922 Military and Police

Caliber: 32 ACP (7.65mm), 380 ACP (9mm short)
Action: Semiautomatic; concealed hammer
Magazine: 9-shot clip in 32; 8-shot clip in 380
Barrel: 4½"
Sights: Fixed
Finish: Blued; hard rubber grips with FN trademark
Length Overall: 7"
Approximate wt.: 24 ozs.
Comments: Identical to the Model 1910 except it has longer grip frame, magazine, and barrel. Lanyard ring on the left grip.

Estimated Value:	**Excellent:**	**$325.00**
	Very good:	**$260.00**

FN Browning Model 1935 Hi Power

Caliber: 9mm Parabellum
Action: Semiautomatic; exposed hammer
Magazine: 13-shot staggered line clip
Barrel: 4⅝"
Sights: Fixed or adjustable
Finish: Blued or parkerized; checkered walnut or plastic grips
Length Overall: 7¾"
Approximate wt.: 34 ozs.
Comments: Production of this model by John Inglis Co. of Canada began in 1943. Some of these were produced with an alloy frame to reduce weight. Also during World War II Model 1935 was produced under German supervision for military use. The quality of the German pistol was poorer than those made before or after the war. A smaller version was also made from 1937 to 1940 with shorter barrel, slide and 10-shot clip.

Estimated Value:	**FN**	**German (superv.)**	**Canadian**
Excellent:	**$800.00**	**$600.00**	**$1,000.00**
Very good:	**$640.00**	**$480.00**	**$ 800.00**

CZ

CZ Model 22 (1922)

Caliber: 380 ACP (9mm short), 25 ACP
Action: Semiautomatic; exposed hammer with shielding on both sides
Magazine: 8-shot clip
Barrel: 3½"
Sights: Fixed
Finish: Blued
Length Overall: 6"
Approximate wt.: 22 ozs.
Comments: Made in Czechoslovakia in the 1920s.

Estimated Value:	**Excellent:**	**$500.00**
	Very good:	**$400.00**

CZ Model 22 (1922)

CZ Model 1936 Pocket

Caliber: 25 ACP (6.5mm)
Action: Double action semiautomatic; slide does not cock hammer (hammer is cocked and released by the trigger), shield exposed hammer
Magazine: 8-shot clip
Barrel: 2½"
Sights: Fixed
Finish: Blued; plastic grips
Length Overall: 4¾"
Approximate wt.: 14 ozs.
Comments: Introduced in 1936. U.S. importation discontinued in 1968.

Estimated Value:	**Excellent:**	**$400.00**
	Very good:	**$320.00**

CZ Model 1945 Pocket

Same as CZ Model 1936 except for minor modifications. Introduced in the mid-1940s. U.S. importation discontinued in 1968.

Estimated Value:	**Excellent:**	**$375.00**
	Very good:	**$300.00**

CZ Model 38 (1938)

Caliber: 380 ACP (9mm short)
Action: Double action; semiautomatic
Magazine: 9-shot clip
Barrel: 3¾"
Sights: Fixed
Finish: Blued; plastic grips
Length Overall: 7"
Approximate wt.: 28 ozs.
Comments: Imported from the late 1930s to the mid-1940s.

Estimated Value:	**Excellent:**	**$500.00**
	Very good:	**$400.00**

CZ Model 50 (1950)

Caliber: 32 ACP (7.65mm)
Action: Semiautomatic; exposed hammer; double action
Magazine: 8-shot clip
Barrel: 3⅛"
Sights: Fixed
Finish: Blued; plastic grips
Length Overall: 6½"
Approximate wt.: 25 ozs.
Comments: No longer imported into the U.S.

Estimated Value:	**Excellent:**	**$225.00**
	Very good:	**$180.00**

CZ "Duo" Pocket

Caliber: 25 ACP (6.35mm)
Action: Semiautomatic; concealed hammer
Magazine: 6-shot clip
Barrel: 2⅛"
Sights: Fixed
Finish: Blued; plastic grips
Length Overall: 4½"
Approximate wt.: 15 ozs.
Comments: Imported from the mid-1920s to the early 1960s.

Estimated Value:	**Excellent:**	**$225.00**
	Very good:	**$180.00**

CZ Model 27 (1927) Pocket

Caliber: 32 ACP (7.65mm)
Action: Semiautomatic; exposed hammer with shielding on both sides
Magazine: 8-shot clip
Barrel: 4"
Sights: Fixed
Finish: Blued; plastic grips
Length Overall: 6½"
Approximate wt.: 25 ozs.
Comments: This pistol usually bears the CZ mark, but the World War II version may have the name Bohmische Waffenfabrik on slide. Made from 1927 to 1951.

Estimated Value:	**Excellent:**	**$500.00**
	Very good:	**$400.00**

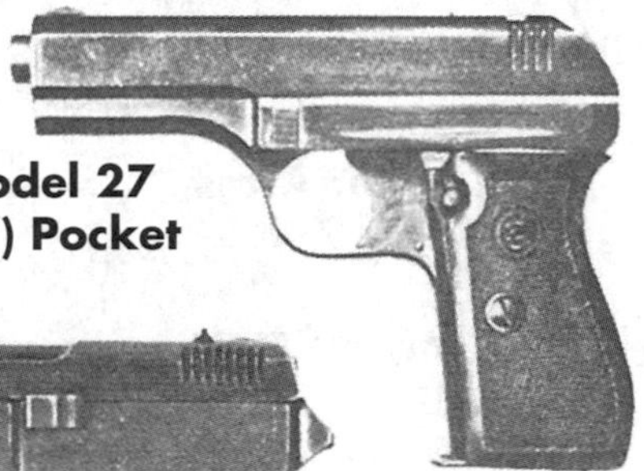

CZ Model 27 (1927) Pocket

CZ Model 38 (1938)

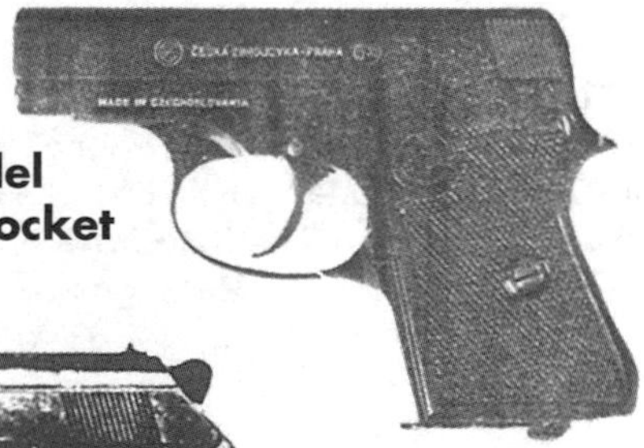

CZ Model 1945 Pocket

CZ Model 50 (1950)

CZ "Duo" Pocket

CZ Model 70

Caliber: 7.65mm (32)
Action: Semiautomatic; exposed hammer; double action
Magazine: 8-shot clip
Barrel: 3⅛"
Sights: Fixed
Finish: Blued; checkered plastic grips
Length Overall: 6½"
Approximate wt.: 25 ozs.
Comments: Produced in Czechoslovakia.

Estimated Value:	**Excellent:**	**$300.00**
	Very good:	**$240.00**

CZ Model 75, 40 S&W

Caliber: 9mm Parabellum
Action: Semiautomatic; selective double action; exposed hammer
Magazine: 15-shot clip
Barrel: 4½"
Sights: Fixed
Finish: Blued; checkered plastic grips
Length Overall: 8"
Approximate wt.: 35 ozs.
Comments: Produced in Czechoslovakia.

Estimated Value:	**Excellent:**	**$400.00**
	Very good:	**$310.00**

CHARTER ARMS

Charter Arms Model 79K

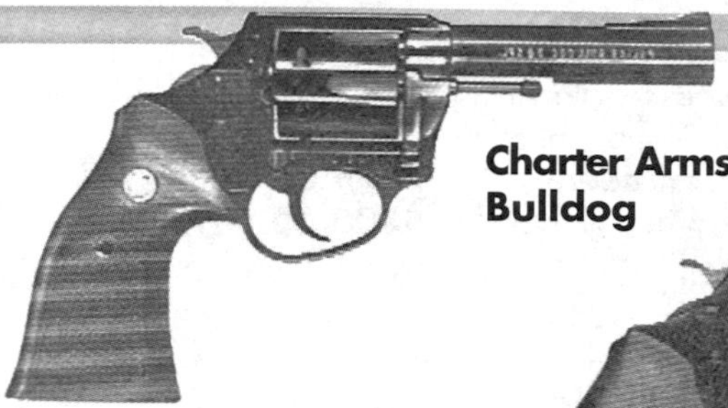

Charter Arms Bulldog

Charter Arms Police Bulldog

Charter Arms Model 79K

Caliber: 380 Auto, 32 Auto
Action: Semiautomatic; double action; exposed hammer
Magazine: 7-shot clip
Barrel: 3½"
Sights: Adjustable
Finish: Stainless steel; checkered walnut grips
Length Overall: 6½"
Approximate wt.: 24½ ozs.
Comments: Made from 1985 to 1987.

Estimated Value:	**Excellent:**	**$350.00**
	Very good:	**$280.00**

Charter Arms Model 40

Similar to the Model 79K in 22 long rifle caliber; 8-shot clip; weighs 21½ ozs. Made from 1985 to 1987.

Estimated Value:	**Excellent:**	**$300.00**
	Very good:	**$240.00**

Charter Arms Explorer II

Charter Arms Explorer II

Caliber: 22 long rifle
Action: Semiautomatic
Magazine: 8-shot clip
Barrel: 6" or 10" interchangeable
Sights: Blade front, adjustable rear
Finish: Black, semigloss textured enamel; simulated walnut grips; extra clip storage in grip; also available in silvertone
Length Overall: 13½" with 6" barrel
Approximate wt.: 27 ozs.
Comments: A survival pistol styled from the AR-7 rifle; produced from the late 1970s to 1986.

Estimated Value:	**Excellent:**	**$150.00**
	Very good:	**$120.00**

Charter Arms Police Bulldog

Caliber: 38 Special, 32 H&R Mag.
Action: Single and double action
Cylinder: 6-shot swing-out
Barrel: 2", 3½", 4"; tapered, bull, or shrouded barrel
Sights: Fixed
Finish: Blue or stainless steel; checked walnut bulldog grips, square butt grips, or neoprene grips
Length Overall: 8½"
Approximate wt.: 21 ozs.
Comments: Produced from 1976 to the early 1990s. Add 25% for stainless steel. Add 8% for barrel shroud.

Estimated Value:	**Excellent:**	**$300.00**
	Very good:	**$240.00**

Charter Arms Bulldog

Caliber: 44 Special, 357 magnum (357 mag. discontinued in mid-1980s)
Action: Single and double action; exposed regular or bobbed hammer
Cylinder: 5-shot swing-out
Barrel: 2½", 3", 4", 6" (4" and 6" discontinued in 1985)
Sights: Fixed
Finish: Blued; oil finished, checkered walnut bulldog grips or neoprene grips; stainless steel added 1982
Length Overall: 7½" (3" barrel)
Approximate wt.: 19 ozs.
Comments: Made from 1971 to the early 1990s. Reintroduced in the late 1990s. Add 20% for stainless steel. Also available with concealed hammer.

Estimated Value:	**New (retail):**	**$461.00**
	Excellent:	**$345.00**
	Very good:	**$275.00**

Charter Arms Target Bulldog

Similar to the Bulldog except: 4" barrel; shrouded ejector rod; adjustable rear sight. Made from the late 1970s to 1989. Add 5% for 44 Special. Add 20% for stainless steel.

Estimated Value: **Excellent:** **$300.00**
Very good: **$240.00**

Charter Arms Bulldog Pug, Mag Pug

Similar to the Bulldog except: 2½" barrel; 357 magnum or 44 spec.; blued, nickel, or stainless steel; shrouded ejector rod. Produced from 1986 to 1994. Add 8% for nickel; add 20% for stainless steel. Reintroduced in 2000.

Estimated Value: **New (retail):** **$441.00**
Excellent: **$330.00**
Very good: **$265.00**

Charter Arms Target Bulldog

Charter Arms Bulldog Pug

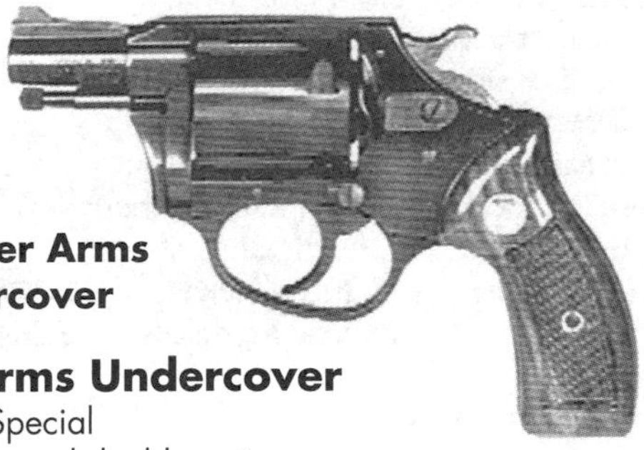

Charter Arms Undercover

Charter Arms Undercover

Caliber: 38 Special
Action: Single and double action
Cylinder: 5-shot, swing-out
Barrel: 2" or 3" (3" discontinued in 1990)
Sights: Fixed
Finish: Blued or nickel; oil finished, plain or hand-checkered walnut grips or neoprene grips; stainless steel added 1982; shrouded barrel after 1989
Length Overall: 6¼" or 7⅜"
Approximate wt.: 16 or 17 ozs.
Comments: Made from 1965 to the early 1990s; discontinued in the early 1980s; reintroduced in the late 1990s. Add 5% for nickel; 25% for stainless steel.

Estimated Value: **New (retail):** **$401.00**
Excellent: **$300.00**
Very good: **$240.00**

Charter Arms Undercoverette and Lady Blue .32

Caliber: 32 S&W long
Action: Single and double action
Cylinder: 6-shot, swing-out
Barrel: 2"
Sights: Fixed
Finish: Blued; oil finished, plain walnut grips; stainless steel available
Length Overall: 6¼"
Approximate wt.: 16½ ozs.
Comments: Made from 1970 to the early 1990s, reintroduced early 2000s; also called Undercover.

Estimated Value: **New (retail):** **$422.00**
Excellent: **$315.00**
Very good: **$250.00**

Charter Arms Bulldog Tracker

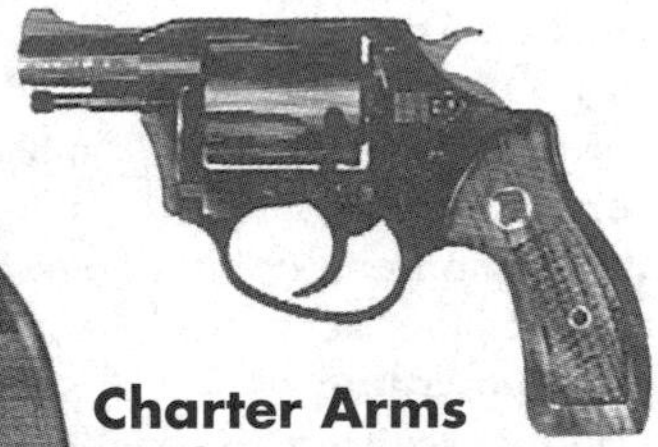

Charter Arms Undercoverette

Charter Arms Bulldog Tracker

Caliber: 357 magnum and 38 special
Action: Single and double action
Cylinder: 5-shot, swing-out
Barrel: 2½", 4", or 6" bull barrel (4" and 6" discontinued in 1989)
Sights: Adjustable rear, ramp front
Finish: Blued; checkered walnut square bull grips
Length Overall: 11"
Approximate wt.: 27½ ozs.
Comments: Produced from 1980 to the early 1990s.

Estimated Value: **Excellent:** **$300.00**
Very good: **$240.00**

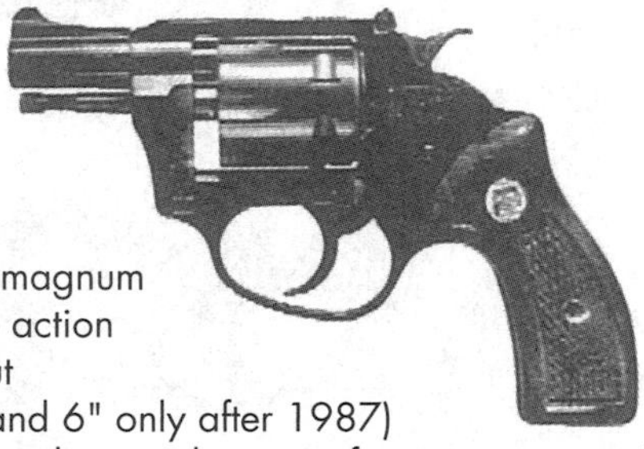

Charter Arms Pathfinder

Charter Arms Pathfinder

Caliber: 22 long rifle, 22 magnum
Action: Single and double action
Cylinder: 6-shot, swing-out
Barrel: 2", 3", or 6" (3" and 6" only after 1987)
Sights: Adjustable rear and partridge-type front on serrated ramp
Finish: Blued; oil finished, plain or hand checkered walnut grips; stainless steel after 1982
Length Overall: 7⅛" (3" barrel)
Approximate wt.: 19 ozs.
Comments: Made from 1970 to the early 1990s. Reintroduced in 2001. Add 25% for stainless steel; 10% for 6" barrel.

Estimated Value: **New (retail):** **$412.00**
Excellent: **$310.00**
Very good: **$245.00**

Charter Arms Police Bulldog 44 Special

Caliber: 44 Special
Action: Single or double, exposed hammer
Cylinder: 5-shot, swing-out, simultaneous manual ejector
Barrel: 2½" or 3½" shrouded barrel with solid rib
Sights: Snag-free front; fixed or adjustable rear
Finish: Blued or stainless steel; bulldog checkered wood or neoprene grips
Length Overall: 7" or 8"
Approximate wt.: 23 ozs.
Comments: Produced from 1990 to about 1993; add 2% for adjustable rear sight; add 12% for stainless steel.

Estimated Value:	**Excellent:**	**$300.00**
	Very good:	**$240.00**

Charter Arms Police Bulldog 357 Magnum

Caliber: 357 magnum and 38 Special
Action: Single or double, exposed hammer
Cylinder: 5-shot, swing-out, simultaneous ejector
Barrel: 4" shrouded barrel
Sights: Ramp front, adjustable rear
Finish: Stainless steel; black neoprene grips
Length Overall: 8½"
Approximate wt.: 28 ozs.
Comments: Produced from 1990 to about 1993.

Estimated Value:	**Excellent:**	**$300.00**
	Very good:	**$240.00**

Charter Arms Target Bulldog (Stainless Steel)

Charter Arms Bonnie and Clyde Set

Charter Arms Pit Bull

Charter Arms Police Bulldog 44 Special

Charter Arms Bonnie and Clyde Set

Caliber: 32 magnum (Bonnie); 38 Special (Clyde)
Action: Single and double action; exposed hammer
Cylinder: 6-shot, swing-out; fluted
Barrel: 2" shrouded barrel marked "Bonnie – 32 mag." or "Clyde – 38 spec."
Sights: Ramp front; fixed rear
Finish: Blued with smooth wood grips
Length Overall: 6½"
Approximate wt.: 21 ozs.
Comments: Each gun comes with a gun rug identified by name (Bonnie or Clyde). These guns are sold as a set. Produced from 1989 to about 1993.

Estimated Value:	**Excellent:**	**$500.00 per set**
	Very good:	**$400.00 per set**

Charter Arms Pit Bull

Caliber: 9mm
Action: Single and double, exposed hammer, regular or bobbed
Cylinder: 5-shot, swing-out, simultaneous ejector
Barrel: 2½", 3½" shrouded barrel
Sights: Fixed or adjustable
Finish: Blued or stainless steel; neoprene grips
Length Overall: 7" or 8"
Approximate wt.: 26 ozs.
Comments: Produced from 1990 to about 1993; add 2% for adjustable sights; add 8% for stainless steel.

Estimated Value:	**Excellent:**	**$325.00**
	Very good:	**$260.00**

Charter Arms Target Bulldog (Stainless Steel)

Caliber: 357 magnum and 38 Special; 44 Special; 9mm
Action: Single or double, exposed hammer
Cylinder: 5-shot, swing-out, simultaneous ejector
Barrel: 5½" shrouded barrel with ventilated rib
Sights: Ramp front; adjustable rear
Finish: Stainless steel with smooth wood target grips
Length Overall: 10"
Approximate wt.: 28 ozs.
Comments: Produced from 1990 to about 1993. Reintroduced in the early 2000s.

Estimated Value:	**New (retail):**	**$533.00**
	Excellent:	**$400.00**
	Very good:	**$320.00**

Charter Arms Pocket Target

Caliber: 22 short, long, long rifle
Action: Single and double action; exposed hammer
Cylinder: 6-shot, swing-out
Barrel: 3"
Sights: Adjustable snag-free rear, ramp front
Finish: Blued; plain grips or checkered walnut bulldog grips
Length Overall: 7⅛"
Approximate wt.: 19 ozs.
Comments: Made from the 1960s to the 1970s.
Estimated Value: **Excellent:** **$175.00**
Very good: **$140.00**

Charter Arms Pocket Target

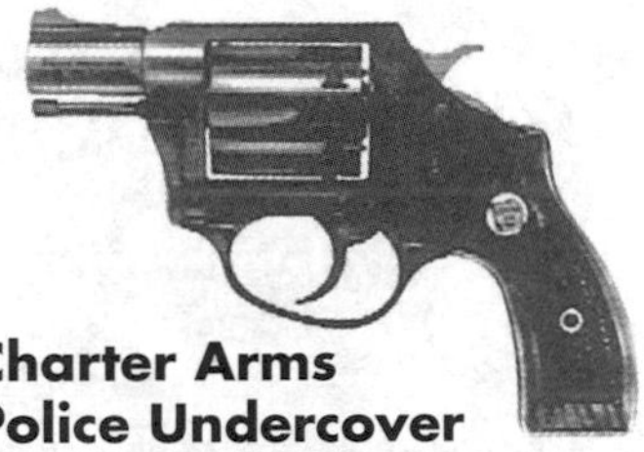

Charter Arms Police Undercover

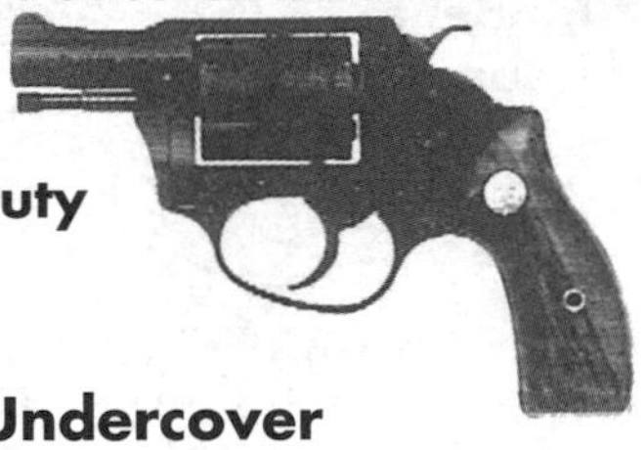

Charter Arms Off Duty

Charter Arms Off Duty

Caliber: 38 Special, 22 mag., 22LR
Action: Single and double; exposed hammer
Cylinder: 5-shot, swing-out, fluted; 6-shot in 22 cal.
Barrel: 2" (shrouded barrel after 1989)
Sights: Fixed
Finish: Flat black, nickel, or stainless steel; smooth or checkered walnut or neoprene grips
Length Overall: 6½"
Approximate wt.: 16 ozs.
Comments: Made from the mid-1980s to the mid-1990s. Add 20% for nickel; add 30% for stainless steel. Reintroduced in the early 2000s with concealed hammer.
Estimated Value: **New (retail):** **$458.00**
Excellent: **$345.00**
Very good: **$275.00**

Charter Arms Police Undercover

Caliber: 32 H&R mag., 38 Special
Action: Single and double; exposed regular or bobbed hammer
Cylinder: 6-shot, swing-out, fluted
Barrel: 2" or 4" (shrouded barrel only after 1989)
Sights: Fixed
Finish: Blued, nickel, or stainless steel; checkered walnut or neoprene grips
Length Overall: 6½"
Approximate wt.: 17½ to 20 ozs.
Comments: Introduced in 1987. Add 6% for nickel; add 12% for stainless steel.
Estimated Value: **Excellent:** **$215.00**
Very good: **$175.00**

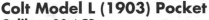

Colt Model 1900

Colt Model L (1902) Military

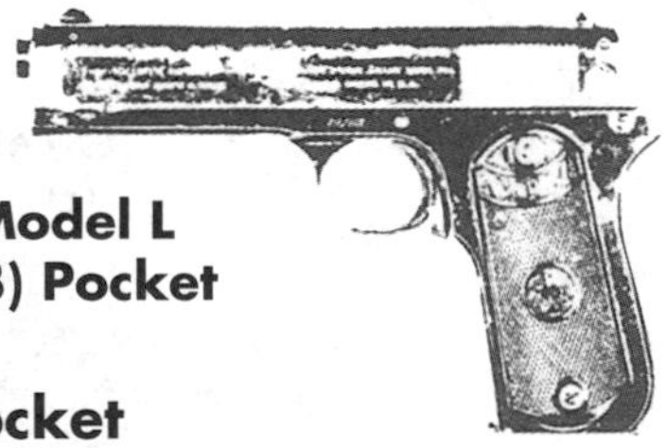

Colt Model L (1903) Pocket

Colt Model 1900

Caliber: 38 ACP
Action: Semiautomatic; exposed spur hammer
Magazine: 7-shot clip
Barrel: 6"
Sights: Fixed
Finish: Blued; plain walnut grips
Length Overall: 9"
Approximate wt.: 35 ozs.
Comments: Combination safety and rear sight. Rear sight is pressed down to block hammer from firing pin. One of the first automatic pistols made in the U.S. and first automatic pistol made by Colt. Made from 1900 to 1902. No slide lock.
Estimated Value: **Excellent:** **$4,000.00 – 7,500.00**
Very good: **$3,200.00 – 6,000.00**

Colt Model L (1902)

Similar to Colt Model 1900 except: no safety; round hammer; hard rubber grips. Made from 1902 to 1907.
Estimated Value: **Excellent:** **$3,750.00**
Very good: **$3,000.00**

Colt Model L (1902) Military

Same as Colt Model L (1902) except: longer grips (more square at bottom) with lanyard ring; 8-shot magazine; weighs 37 oz. Made from 1902 to 1928. Spur-type hammer after 1907.
Estimated Value: **Excellent:** **$2,000.00 – 5,500.00**
Very good: **$1,600.00 – 4,400.00**

Colt Model L (1903) Pocket

Caliber: 38 ACP
Action: Semiautomatic; exposed hammer
Magazine: 7-shot clip
Barrel: 4½"
Sights: Fixed
Finish: Blued; checkered hard rubber grips
Length Overall: 7½"
Approximate wt.: 31 ozs.
Comments: Made from 1903 to 1927. Round-type hammer to 1908, then changed to spur-type hammer; no slide lock or safety.
Estimated Value: **Excellent:** **$1,200.00**
Very good: **$ 960.00**

Colt Model M (32)
1st Issue Pocket

Colt Model M (32)
2nd Issue Pocket

Colt Model M (32)
3rd Issue Pocket

Colt Model M (380) 1st Issue Pocket

Caliber: 380 ACP (9 mm short)
Action: Semiautomatic
Magazine: 7-shot clip
Barrel: 3¾"
Sights: Fixed
Finish: Blued or nickel; hard rubber or checkered walnut grips
Length Overall: 6¾"
Approximate wt.: 24 ozs.
Comments: Made from 1908 to 1911. Slide lock safety and grip safety. Barrel lock bushing at muzzle.

Estimated Value:	**Excellent:**	**$750.00**
	Very good:	**$600.00**

Colt Model M (380) 2nd Issue Pocket

Similar to 1st Issue Model M (380) except: without barrel lock bushing and other minor changes. Made from 1911 to 1926. Add $200.00 for Military Model.

Estimated Value:	**Excellent:**	**$725.00**
	Very good:	**$580.00**

Colt Model M (380) 3rd Issue Pocket

Similar to 2nd Issue Model M (380) except: it has safety disconnector, which prevents cartridge in chamber from being fired if magazine is removed. Made from 1926 to 1941.

Estimated Value:	**Excellent:**	**$700.00**
	Very good:	**$560.00**

Colt Model M (380)
1st Issue Pocket

Colt Model M (380)
2nd Issue Pocket

Colt Model M (32) 1st Issue Pocket

Caliber: 32 ACP (7.65 mm short)
Action: Semiautomatic; concealed hammer
Magazine: 8-shot clip
Barrel: 3¾"
Sights: Fixed
Finish: Blued or nickel; hard rubber or checkered walnut grips
Length Overall: 6¾"
Approximate wt.: 25 ozs.
Comments: Made from 1903 to 1911. Slide lock safety and grip safety. Barrel lock bushing at muzzle.

Estimated Value:	**Excellent:**	**$775.00**
	Very good:	**$620.00**

Colt Model M (32) 2nd Issue Pocket

Similar to 1st Issue Model M (32) except: without barrel lock bushing and other minor modifications. Made from 1911 to 1926. Add $200.00 for Military Model.

Estimated Value:	**Excellent:**	**$700.00**
	Very good:	**$560.00**

Colt Model M (32) 3rd Issue Pocket

Similar to 2nd Issue Model M (32) except: safety disconnector, which prevents cartridge in chamber from being fired if magazine is removed. Made from 1926 to 1941.

Estimated Value:	**Excellent:**	**$675.00**
	Very good:	**$540.00**

Colt Model 1905 Military

Colt Model 1905 Military

Caliber: 45 ACP
Action: Semiautomatic
Magazine: 7-shot clip
Barrel: 5"
Sights: Fixed
Finish: Blued; checkered walnut grips
Length Overall: 8½"
Approximate wt.: 34 ozs.
Comments: Made from 1905 to 1912. Similar to Model 1902 38 caliber automatic pistol. First 45 caliber military automatic pistol made by Colt. Slide stop but no safety except some experimental models with short grip safety. Round hammer 1905 to 1908; after 1908 spur-type hammer. Approximately 5,000 produced. Some were fitted and equipped with a short-stock holster. These are scarce collectors' items and valued much higher.

Estimated Value:	**Excellent:**	**$5,000.00 – 7,500.00**
	Very good:	**$4,000.00 – 6,000.00**

Colt Model N Pocket

Colt Model N Pocket
Caliber: 25 ACP
Action: Semiautomatic; concealed striker instead of hammer
Magazine: 6-shot clip
Barrel: 2"
Sights: Fixed
Finish: Blued or nickel; hard rubber or checkered walnut grips
Length Overall: 4½"
Approximate wt.: 14 ozs.
Comments: Made from 1908 to 1941. Magazine safety disconnector added in 1916 (about serial number 141,000). All models have thumb safety and grip safety. Add $200.00 for Military Model; $50.00 for nickel finish.

Estimated Value:	**Excellent:**	**$575.00**
	Very good:	**$460.00**

Colt Government Model 1911
Caliber: 45 ACP
Action: Semiautomatic; exposed spur hammer
Magazine: 7-shot clip
Barrel: 5"
Sights: Fixed
Finish: Blued, nickel, and parkerized or similar finish, checkered walnut grips
Length Overall: 8½"
Approximate wt.: 39 ozs.
Comments: Slide lock, thumb safety and grip safety. Adopted as a military side arm in 1911 in U.S. Made from 1911 to 1924 with some modifications. Changed to Model 1911A1 in 1925. Military models are marked "U.S. Army," U.S. Navy," or "U.S. Marines," and "United States Property." Colt licensed other firms to produce this pistol during both World Wars. Check prices under manufacturer's name. Also check commercial model prices.

Estimated Value:	**Excellent:**	**$3,200.00 – 6,500.00**
	Very good:	**$2,550.00 – 5,200.00**

Colt Government Model 1911A1
Same as Government Model 1911 except: the grip safety tang was lengthened (to stop the hammer bite on fleshy hands); the trigger was shortened (to allow stubby fingers better control); the back strap below the grip safety was arched (for better instinctive pointing); the sights were made larger and squared (to improve sight picture). Also the grips were made of checkered walnut or plastic. The 1911A1 was introduced in 1925. Changes started about serial number 650000 in military model. Also check prices for other manufacturers' and commercial models.

Estimated Value:	**Excellent:**	**$2,500.00**
	Very good:	**$2,000.00**

Colt GI Model 1911A1
A modern production version of the 1911A1 with parkerized finish and a 7-shot clip.

Estimated Value:	**Excellent:**	**$2,500.00**
	Very good:	**$2,000.00**

Colt Commercial Model 1911
Same as Government Model 1911 except: not marked with military markings. The letter "C" is used in serial numbers. Blued or nickel finish. Made from 1911 to 1926 then changed to 1911 A1 about serial number C130000.

Estimated Value:	**Excellent:**	**$3,000.00**
	Very good:	**$2,400.00**

Colt Commercial Model 1911A1
Same as Government Model 1911 except it has same modifications as the Government Model 1911A1. Made from 1925 to 1970.

Estimated Value:	**Excellent:**	**$1,750.00**
	Very good:	**$1,400.00**

Colt Government Model 1911

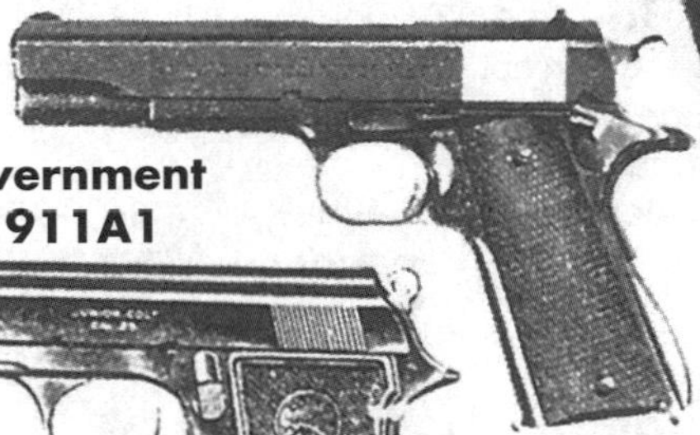

Colt Government Model 1911A1

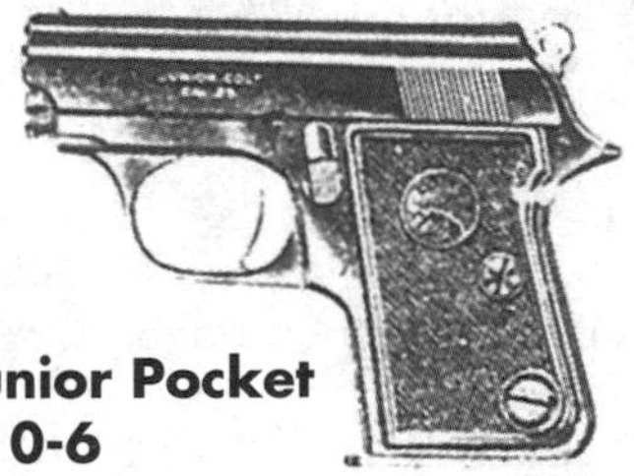

Colt Junior Pocket Model 0-6

Colt Junior Pocket Model 0-6
Caliber: 22 short, 25 ACP
Action: Semiautomatic; exposed round spur hammer
Magazine: 6-shot clip
Barrel: 2⅛"
Sights: Fixed
Finish: Blued; checkered walnut grips
Length Overall: 4½"
Approximate wt.: 13 to 14 ozs.
Comments: Made in Spain by Astra (Uneta Y Compania, Guernice, Spain) for Colt as a replacement for the Model N which was discontinued in 1941. Imported from about 1957 to 1968. Colt advertised in 1984 that many of these guns made between 1957 and 1973 were unsafe due to the firing mechanism. Colt offered to modify the pistol free and advised owners of non-modified pistols to carry the pistol with an empty chamber.

Estimated Value:	**Excellent:**	**$350.00**
	Very good:	**$280.00**

Colt 1911 (North American Arms Co.)

Same general specifications as 1911 Colt except made by North American Arms Co., in World War I period. About 100 made; company marking and serial number on slide.

Estimated Value: **Excellent:** **$15,000.00**
Very good: **$12,000.00**

Colt 1911 (Remington UMC)

Colt Super 38

Same as Colt Commercial Model 1911A1 except: caliber is 38 Super ACP; magazine is 9-shot. Made from about 1928 to 1970.

Estimated Value: **Excellent:** **$3,000.00**
Very good: **$2,400.00**

Colt Super 38 Match

Same as Colt Super except: adjustable rear sight; hand-honed action; match grade barrel. Made from about 1932 to 1940. Add 50% for adjustable sights.

Estimated Value: **Excellent:** **$4,000.00**
Very good: **$3,200.00**

Colt National Match

Same as Colt Commercial Model 1911A1 except: adjustable rear sight; hand-honed action; match grade barrel. Made from about 1932 to 1940.

Estimated Value: **Excellent:** **$3,500.00**
Very good: **$2,800.00**

Colt Service Model Ace

Similar to Colt National Match except: 22 caliber long rifle; 10-shot clip; weighs about 42 ozs. It has a "floating chamber" that makes the recoil much greater than normal 22 caliber. Made from 1938 to the mid-1940s. See Colt Ace (current).

Estimated Value: **Excellent:** **$2,000.00**
Very good: **$1,600.00**

Colt 1911 Springfield Armory N.R.A.

Same general specifications as 1911 Colt except approximately 200 were made prior to World War I and sold through the Director of Civilian Marksmanship and have N.R.A. markings on the frame.

Estimated Value: **Excellent:** **$4,000.00**
Very good: **$3,200.00**

Colt 1911 (Springfield Armory)

Same general specifications as 1911 Colt except approximately 26,000 were produced. Eagle motif and flaming bomb on frame and slide. Made in World War I period.

Estimated Value: **Excellent:** **$3,500.00**
Very good: **$2,800.00**

Colt 1911 (Remington UMC)

Same general specifications as 1911 Colt except approximately 22,000 were produced in World War I period. Inspector stamps B or E.

Estimated Value: **Excellent:** **$3,300.00**
Very good: **$2,650.00**

Colt 1911 A1 (Singer Manufacturing Co.)

Same general specifications as 1911A1 Colt except approximately 500 made; blued finished, slide marked "S.M. Co.," JKC inspector marking.

Estimated Value: **Excellent:** **$7,000.00 – 10,000.00**
Very good: **$5,600.00 – 8,000.00**

Colt 1911 A1 pistols were also produced during WWII by Union Switch and Signal Company, Remington Rand, Inc., and Ithaca Gun Company, Inc. Generally the estimated values of these pistols are about the same as the 1911 A1 pistol produced by Colt.

Colt Super 38

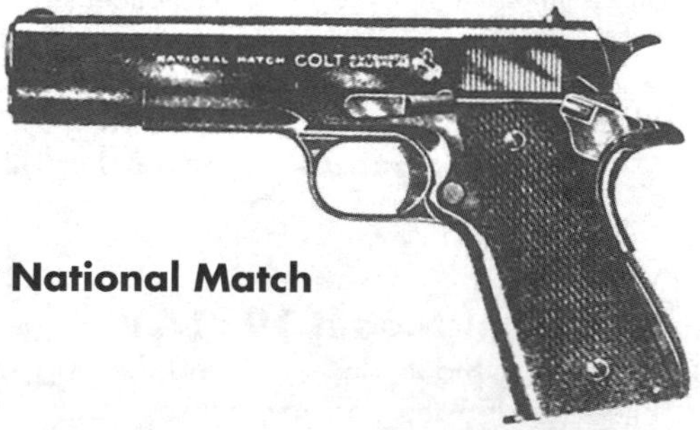

Colt National Match

Colt Service Model Ace

Colt Gold Cup National Match

Same as Colt Commercial Model 1911A1 except: hand-fitted slide; enlarged ejection port; adjustable rear sight; adjustable trigger stop; new bushing design; checkered walnut grips; match grade barrel; flat grip below safety like Model 1911. Made from about 1957 to 1970.

Estimated Value:	**Excellent:**	**$1,000.00**
	Very good:	**$ 800.00**

Colt Gold Cup Mark III National Match

Similar to Colt Gold Cup National Match except chambered for 38 Special mid-range wad cutter only. Operates with fixed barrel rather than locked breech. Made from 1960 to 1974.

Estimated Value:	**Excellent:**	**$1,000.00**
	Very good:	**$ 800.00**

Colt Gold Cup MK IV National Match (Series 70)

Caliber: 38 Special Mid-Range, 45 ACP
Action: Semiautomatic; exposed spur hammer
Magazine: 9-shot clip in 38; 7-shot in 45
Barrel: 5"
Sights: Adjustable rear for wind and elevation
Finish: Blued; checkered walnut grips with gold medallion
Length Overall: 8¾"
Approximate wt.: 39 ozs.
Comments: Arched or flat housing below grip safety. Adjustable trigger stop, hand-fitted slide, and improved barrel bushing. Made from about 1970 to the mid-1980s.

Estimated Value:	**Excellent:**	**$900.00**
	Very good:	**$720.00**

Colt Gold Cup National Match

Colt Gold Cup Mark III National Match

Colt Gold Cup MK IV National Match

Colt Gold Cup National Match MK IV/Series 80

Colt Gold Cup National Match MK IV/ Series 80

Similar to the Gold Cup MK IV National Match (Series 70) with internal improvements. Introduced in 1983; 45 caliber only; stainless steel model introduced in 1985. Add 8% for stainless steel; 14% for polished stainless steel.

Estimated Value:	**Excellent:**	**$825.00**
	Very good:	**$660.00**

Colt Gold Cup National Match MK IV/Series 70

Colt Government Model MK IV/ Series 70

Caliber: 9mm Parabellum, 38 Super ACP, 45 ACP
Action: Semiautomatic; exposed spur hammer
Magazine: 9-shot clip in 9mm and 38; 7-shot in 45
Barrel: 5"
Sights: Fixed
Finish: Blued or nickel; smooth or checkered walnut grips
Length Overall: 8½"
Approximate wt.: 38 to 39 ozs.
Comments: Made from about 1970 to the mid-1980s. Add $15.00 for 38 Super; $5.00 for 9mm; $25.00 for nickel finish. Reintroduced in 45 ACP.

Estimated Value:	**New (retail):**	**$1,000.00**
	Excellent:	**$ 750.00**
	Very good:	**$ 600.00**

Colt Government Model MK IV/Series 80

Similar to the MK IV Series 70 with internal improvements. Introduced in 1983. Calibers 9mm., 38 Super and 45 ACP; add 8% for nickel finish (discontinued); add 8% for stainless steel; 17% for polished stainless steel; 45 ACP and 38 Super Cals. only after 1995.

Estimated Value:	**Excellent:**	**$700.00**
	Very good:	**$560.00**

Colt Combat Government Model/Series 80

Similar to the Government MK IV/Series 80 with undercut front sight, outline rear sight, Colt Pachmayr grips and other slight variations. Produced from 1984 to 1987.

Estimated Value: **Excellent:** **$600.00**
Very good: **$480.00**

Colt 380 Government MK IV/Series 80

A "scaled-down" version of the Colt Government Model MK IV Series 80 in 380 ACP caliber; with round spur hammer; 3¼" barrel, weighs 21¾ ozs., overall length 6⅛". Introduced in 1984. Add 7% for stainless steel; add 14% for nickel.

Estimated Value: **Excellent:** **$525.00**
Very good: **$420.00**

Colt 380 Government MK IV/Series 80

Colt 380 Government Pocketlite

Colt 380 Government Pocketlite

Similar to the 380 Government Model MK IV/Series 80 with alloy receiver. Weighs 15 ozs. Add 7% for stainless steel.

Estimated Value: **Excellent:** **$600.00**
Very good: **$480.00**

Colt MK IV/Series 80 Officer's ACP

Caliber: 45 ACP
Action: Semiautomatic; exposed round spur hammer
Magazine: 6-shot clip
Barrel: 3½"
Sights: Fixed with dovetail rear
Finish: Non-glare matte blue; blue or stainless steel (1986); checkered wood grips; polished stainless steel (1988)
Length Overall: 7¼"
Approximate wt.: 24 ozs. (lightweight); 34 ozs. (steel)
Comments: A compact 45 ACP pistol about 1¼" shorter than the regular Colt Government models. Available in lightweight aluminum alloy or steel models. Add 8% for stainless steel. Add 15% for polished stainless steel.

Estimated Value: **Excellent:** **$750.00**
Very good: **$600.00**

Colt Officer's Model MK IV/Series 80 Concealed Carry

Similar to the MK IV/Series 80 Officer's ACP except with stainless steel commander slide and lightweight blue receiver. Introduced in 1998.

Estimated Value: **Excellent:** **$800.00**
Very good: **$640.00**

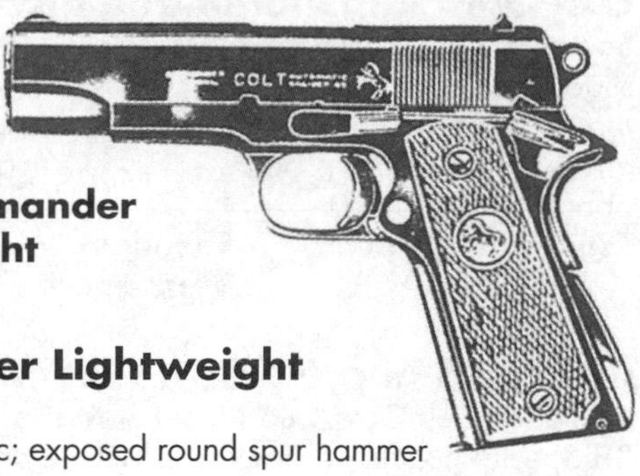

Colt Commander Lightweight

Colt Commander Lightweight

Caliber: 45 ACP
Action: Semiautomatic; exposed round spur hammer
Magazine: 7-shot clip
Barrel: 4¼"
Sights: Fixed
Finish: Blued; checkered or smooth walnut grips
Length Overall: 7¾"
Approximate wt.: 27 ozs.
Comments: Same design as Govt. 1911A1 model except shorter and lighter; rounded hammer. Aluminum alloy receiver and frame. Made from 1949 to the mid-1980s. An all-steel model was introduced in 1971 known as Combat Commander.

Estimated Value: **Excellent:** **$600.00**
Very good: **$480.00**

Colt Combat Commander LW MK IV/ Series 80

Similar to the Lightweight Commander with internal improvements. Introduced in 1983. Caliber 45 ACP; blued.

Estimated Value: **Excellent:** **$600.00**
Very good: **$480.00**

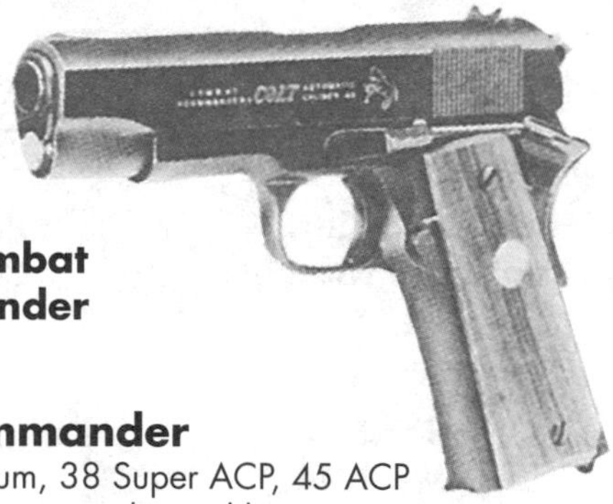

Colt Combat Commander

Colt Combat Commander

Caliber: 9mm Parabellum, 38 Super ACP, 45 ACP
Action: Semiautomatic; exposed round hammer
Magazine: 9-shot clip in 9mm and 38 Super; 7-shot clip in 45 ACP
Barrel: 4¼"
Sights: Fixed
Finish: Blued or nickel (in 45 caliber only); checkered walnut grips
Length Overall: 7⅝"
Approximate wt.: 37 ozs.
Comments: Same design as Government 1911A1 model except: shorter and lighter; rounded hammer; made from about 1971 to the mid-1980s with all steel frame and flat or arched mainspring housing. Add $5.00 for 9mm; $20.00 for nickel finish.

Estimated Value: **Excellent:** **$575.00**
Very good: **$460.00**

Colt Combat Commander MK IV/ Series 80

Colt Combat Commander MK IV/Series 80

Similar to the Combat Commander with internal improvements; introduced in 1983. Calibers 9mm, 38 Super and 45 ACP; add 8% for nickel finish; stainless steel finish (introduced in 1990). 9mm dropped in 1995.

Estimated Value: **Excellent:** **$700.00**
Very good: **$560.00**

Colt 1991 A1 MK IV/Series 80

Colt 1991 A1 MK IV/Series 80

Caliber: 45 ACP
Action: Semiautomatic; exposed spur or round spur hammer; single action
Magazine: 7-shot clip (5" and 4½" barrel models); 6-shot clip (3½" compact model)
Barrel: 3½" (compact model); 4½" (combat model); 5" (regular model)
Sights: High profile; fixed
Finish: Parkerized matte; stainless steel matte (1994); black composition grips
Length Overall: 7¼", 7¾", and 8½"
Approximate wt.: 34, 36, and 38 ozs.
Comments: A modern version of the 1911 GI service 45 in three sizes; regular model introduced in 1991; combat and compact models introduced in 1994. Add 10% for stainless steel.

Estimated Value: **New (retail):** **$925.00**
Excellent: **$695.00**
Very good: **$555.00**

Colt Special Combat Government

Similar to the 1991 A1 MK IV/Series 80 except: 5" barrel only; checkered wood grips; perforated trigger; elongated hammer; 8-shot clip; hard chrome finish. Introduced in 1999.

Estimated Value: **New (retail):** **$1,800.00**
Excellent: **$1,350.00**
Very good: **$1,075.00**

Colt MK IV/Series 80 Mustang 380

Caliber: 380 ACP
Action: Semiautomatic; exposed round spur hammer
Magazine: 5-shot clip
Barrel: 2¾"
Sights: Fixed, with dovetail rear
Finish: Blued; nickel, electroless nickel or stainless steel; composition grips
Length Overall: 5½"
Approximate wt.: 18½ ozs.
Comments: A small, compact pistol introduced in 1986. Add 12% for nickel and 7% for electroless nickel. Add 7% for stainless steel.

Estimated Value: **Excellent:** **$575.00**
Very good: **$460.00**

Colt MK IV/Series 80 Mustang Plus II

Similar to the Mustang 380 but combines the full grip length of the Colt Government Model with the shorter compact barrel and slide of the Mustang. Introduced in 1988. Add 7% for stainless steel (added in 1990).

Estimated Value: **Excellent:** **$600.00**
Very good: **$480.00**

Colt MK IV/Series 80 Mustang Pocketlite

Similar to the MK IV/Series 80 Mustang 380 with an alloy receiver; weighs 12½ ozs. Introduced in 1988. Add 7% for stainless steel or nickel.

Estimated Value: **Excellent:** **$600.00**
Very good: **$480.00**

Colt MK IV/Series 80 Mustang 380

Colt MK IV/Series 80 Mustang Plus II

Colt Delta Elite

Colt Delta Elite, MK IV/Series 80

Caliber: 10mm
Action: Semiautomatic; exposed round hammer; long trigger
Magazine: 7-shot clip
Barrel: 5"
Sights: Fixed, white dot
Finish: Blued; black neoprene "pebbled" wrap-around combat-style grips with Colt Delta medallion; stainless steel available in the late 1980s
Length Overall: 8½"
Approximate wt.: 38 ozs.
Comments: Redesigned and re-engineered Colt Government for the 10mm cartridge. Introduced in 1987; discontinued in the late 1990s. Add 8% for stainless steel; 28% for Gold Cup model.

Estimated Value:	**Excellent:**	**$875.00**
	Very good:	**$700.00**

Colt Double Eagle Series 90

Caliber: 45 ACP, 10mm, 9mm; 38 Super (added in 1992)
Action: Double action semiautomatic with exposed combat-style rounded hammer. A decocking lever allows the hammer to be decocked with a round in the chamber without using the trigger. The firing pin remains locked during this sequence.
Magazine: 8-shot clip
Barrel: 5"
Sights: Fixed, white dot; adjustable sights available
Finish: Matte stainless steel; checkered Xenoy grips.
Length Overall: 8½"
Approximate wt.: 39 ozs.
Comments: Introduced in 1990; discontinued in the late 1990s. Add 3% for 10mm; add 4% for adjustable sights. 45 ACP only after 1995.

Estimated Value:	**Excellent:**	**$750.00**
	Very good:	**$600.00**

Colt Double Eagle Officer's Model

Similar to the Double Eagle with 3½" barrel, stainless steel or blued finish. Add 10% for stainless steel.

Estimated Value:	**Excellent:**	**$800.00**
	Very good:	**$640.00**

Colt Double Eagle Combat Commander

Similar to the Double Eagle in 45ACP or 40 S&W caliber; 4¼" barrel.

Estimated Value:	**Excellent:**	**$825.00**
	Very good:	**$660.00**

Colt Combat Elite

Caliber: 45 ACP; 38 Super (added in 1993)
Action: Semiautomatic; exposed round combat hammer
Magazine: 7-shot clip
Barrel: 5"
Sights: Fixed, white dot sights
Finish: Matte stainless steel receiver with blue carbon steel slide and internal working parts; black neoprene "pebbled" wrap-around combat-style grips
Length Overall: 8½"
Approximate wt.: 38 ozs.
Comments: Introduced in the late 1980s; designed for combat-style match shooters; dropped in the late 1990s.

Estimated Value:	**Excellent:**	**$850.00**
	Very good:	**$680.00**

Colt Combat Elite

Colt Double Eagle Series 90

Colt Double Eagle Officer's Model

Colt Series 90 Pony

Caliber: 380 Auto
Action: Double action, semiautomatic; bobbed hammer
Magazine: 6-shot clip
Barrel: 2¾"
Sights: Fixed
Finish: Stainless steel, black composite grips
Length Overall: 5½"
Approximate wt.: 19 ozs.
Comments: Made in the late 1990s.

Estimated Value:	**Excellent:**	**$600.00**
	Very good:	**$480.00**

Colt Series 90 Pony Pocketlite

Similar to the Series 90 Pony except with alloy receiver; weighs 13 ozs.

Estimated Value:	**Excellent:**	**$600.00**
	Very good:	**$480.00**

Colt Defender
Caliber: 45 ACP
Action: Semiautomatic
Magazine: 6-shot clip
Barrel: 3"
Sights: Fixed, white dot sights
Finish: Matte blue or stainless steel; wrap-around composite grips
Length Overall: 7"
Approximate wt.: 34 ozs.
Comments: Introduced in 1998.

Estimated Value:	**New (retail):**	**$999.00**
	Excellent:	**$750.00**
	Very good:	**$600.00**

Colt Defender

Colt Ace (Later)
Caliber: 22 long rifle
Action: Semiautomatic; exposed spur hammer
Magazine: 10-shot clip
Barrel: 5"
Sights: Fixed rear, ramp-style front
Finish: Blued; checkered walnut grips
Length Overall: 8⅜"
Approximate wt.: 42 ozs.
Comments: A full-size automatic similar to the Colt Government MK IV/Series 70 in 22 long rifle. Produced from 1979 to the mid-1980s. Also see Colt Service Model Ace.

Estimated Value:	**Excellent:**	**$600.00**
	Very good:	**$480.00**

Colt Woodsman Target Model (1st Issue)
Caliber: 22 long rifle (regular velocity)
Action: Semiautomatic; concealed hammer
Magazine: 10-shot clip
Barrel: 6½"
Sights: Adjustable
Finish: Blued; checkered walnut grips
Length Overall: 10½"
Approximate wt.: 28 ozs.
Comments: This model was not strong enough for high-speed cartridges, until a strong heat-treated housing was produced about serial number 83790. Thumb safety only. Made from about 1915 to 1932.

Estimated Value:	**Excellent:**	**$1,250.00**
	Very good:	**$1,000.00**

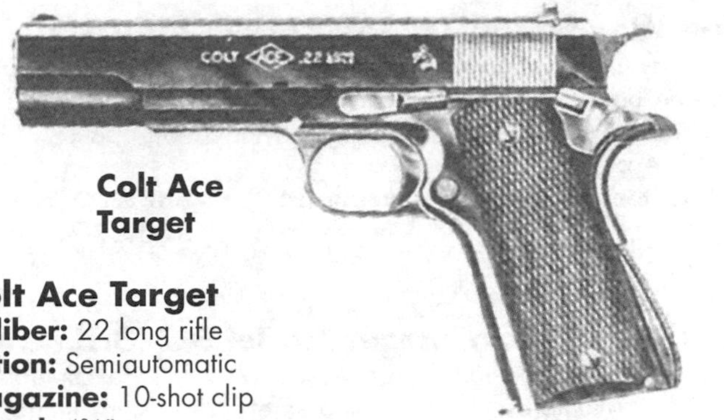

Colt Ace Target

Colt Ace Target
Caliber: 22 long rifle
Action: Semiautomatic
Magazine: 10-shot clip
Barrel: 4¾"
Sights: Adjustable rear sight
Finish: Blued; checkered walnut or plastic grips
Length Overall: 8¼"
Approximate wt.: 38 ozs.
Comments: Similar in appearance to the 1911 A1 with the same safety features. Made from about 1931 to 1941.

Estimated Value:	**Excellent:**	**$1,500.00**
	Very good:	**$1,200.00**

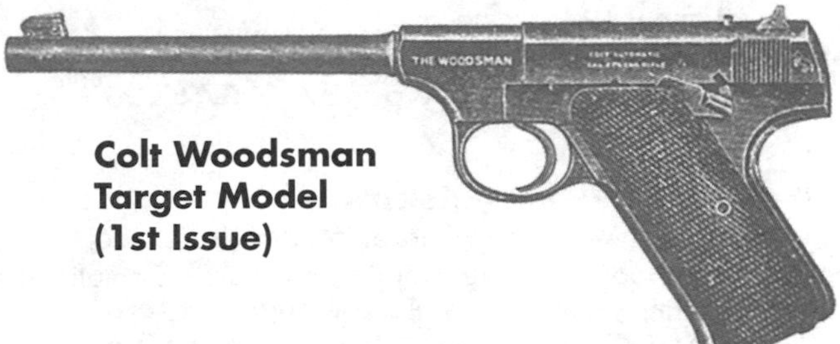

Colt Woodsman Target Model (1st Issue)

Colt Woodsman Sport Model (1st Issue)
Caliber: 22 long rifle
Action: Semiautomatic; concealed hammer
Magazine: 10-shot clip
Barrel: 4½" tapered barrel
Sights: Adjustable
Finish: Blued; checkered walnut grips
Length Overall: 8½"
Approximate wt.: 27 ozs.
Comments: Same as Colt Woodsman Target Model (2nd Issue) except shorter. Made from about 1933 to the late 1940s.

Estimated Value:	**Excellent:**	**$1,250.00**
	Very good:	**$1,000.00**

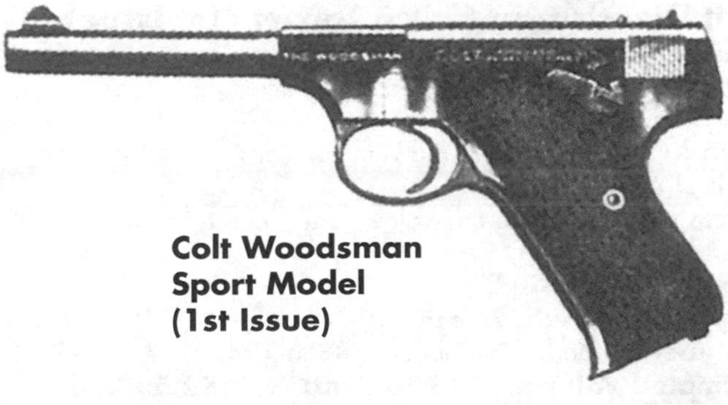

Colt Woodsman Sport Model (1st Issue)

Colt Woodsman Target Model (2nd Issue)

Same as Colt Woodsman Target Model 1st Issue except heavier tapered barrel and stronger housing for using either the 22 long rifle regular or high-speed cartridges. Made from about 1932 to 1945. Approximate wt. is 29 ozs.

Estimated Value: **Excellent:** **$875.00**
Very good: **$700.00**

Colt Woodsman Target Model S-2 (3rd Issue)

Same as Colt Woodsman Target Model (2nd Issue) except longer grips with thumbrest, larger thumb safety; slide stop; magazine disconnector; slide stays open when magazine is empty; checkered walnut or plastic grips. Approximate wt. is 32 ozs. Made from 1948 to the late 1970s.

Estimated Value: **Excellent:** **$800.00**
Very good: **$640.00**

Colt Woodsman Sport Model S-1 (2nd Issue)

Same as Colt Woodsman Target Model S-2 (3rd Issue) except 4½" barrel, 9" overall length; approximate weight is 30 ozs. Made from about 1948 to the late 1970s.

Estimated Value: **Excellent:** **$900.00**
Very good: **$720.00**

Colt Model S-4 Targetsman

Similar to Colt Woodsman Target Model (3rd Issue) except cheaper made adjustable rear sight and lacks automatic slide stop. Made from about 1959 to the late 1970s.

Estimated Value: **Excellent:** **$625.00**
Very good: **$500.00**

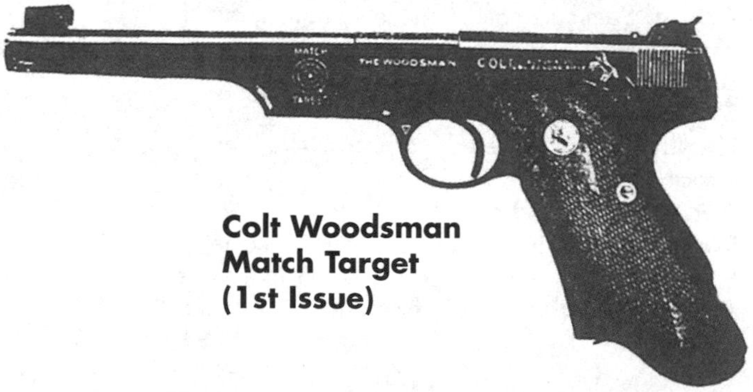

Colt Woodsman Match Target (1st Issue)

Colt Woodsman Match Target (1st Issue)

Caliber: 22 long rifle
Action: Semiautomatic; concealed hammer
Magazine: 10-shot clip
Barrel: 6½"; slightly tapered with flat sides
Sights: Adjustable rear
Finish: Blued; checkered walnut, one-piece grip with extended sides
Length Overall: 11"
Approximate wt.: 36 ozs.
Comments: Made from about 1938 to 1942.
Estimated Value: **Excellent:** **$2,500.00**
Very good: **$2,000.00**

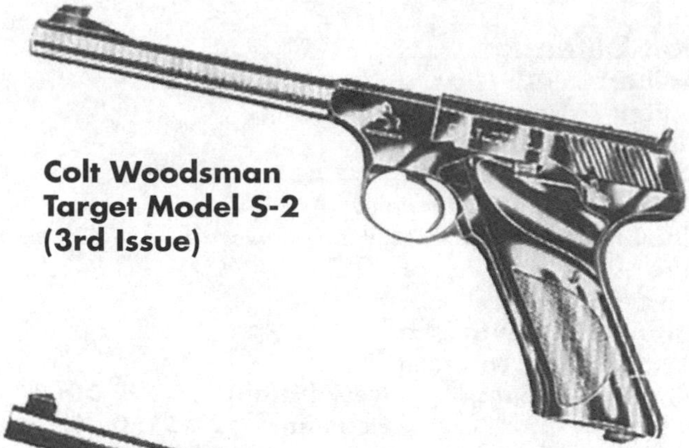

Colt Woodsman Target Model S-2 (3rd Issue)

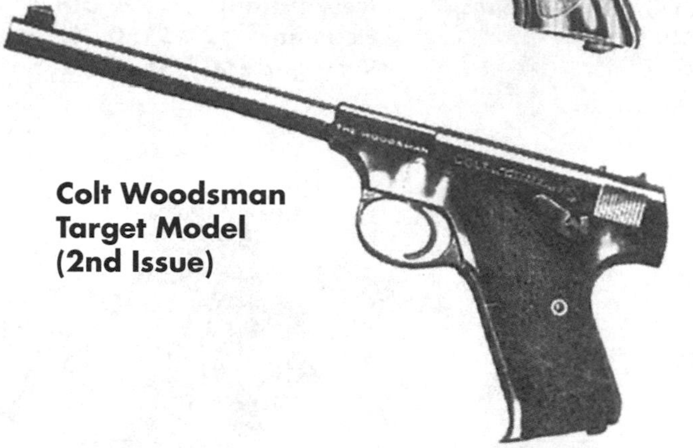

Colt Woodsman Target Model (2nd Issue)

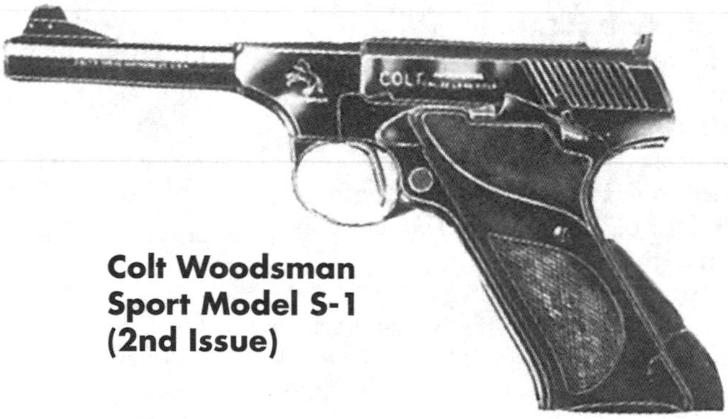

Colt Woodsman Sport Model S-1 (2nd Issue)

Colt Model S-4 Targetsman

Colt Woodsman Match Target Model S-3

Colt Woodsman Match Target Model S-3

Caliber: 22 long rifle
Action: Semiautomatic; concealed hammer
Magazine: 10-shot clip
Barrel: 4½", 6"
Sights: Adjustable rear
Finish: Blued; checkered walnut grips with thumbrest
Length Overall: 9", 10½"
Approximate wt.: 36 to 39 ozs.
Comments: Made from about 1948 to the late 1970s. Flat sided weight added to full length of barrel. It has a slide stop and magazine safety.

Estimated Value:	**Excellent:**	**$900.00**
	Very good:	**$720.00**

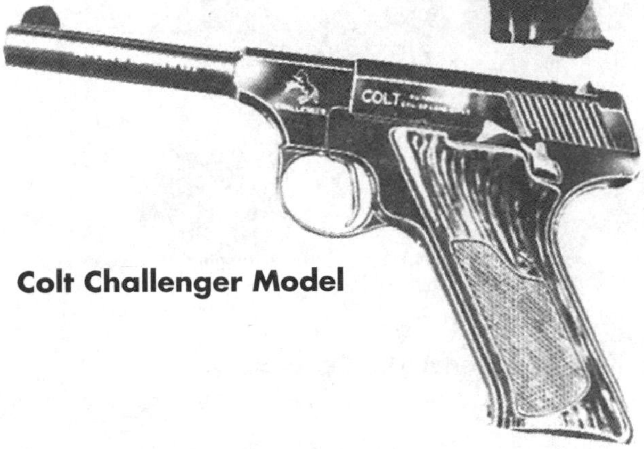

Colt Challenger Model

Colt Challenger Model

Caliber: 22 long rifle
Action: Semiautomatic; concealed hammer
Magazine: 10-shot clip
Barrel: 4½", 6"
Sights: Fixed
Finish: Blued; checkered plastic grips
Length Overall: 9", 10½"
Approximate wt.: 30 to 32 ozs. (depending on length)
Comments: Same basic design as Colt Woodsman Target Model (3rd Issue) except slide doesn't stay open when magazine is empty; no magazine safety. Made from about 1950 to 1955.

Estimated Value:	**Excellent:**	**$625.00**
	Very good:	**$500.00**

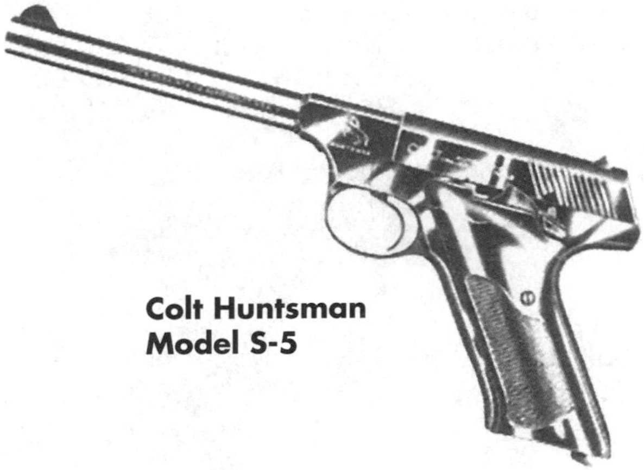

Colt Huntsman Model S-5

Colt Huntsman Model S-5

Caliber: 22 long rifle
Action: Semiautomatic; concealed hammer
Magazine: 10-shot clip
Barrel: 4½", 6"
Sights: Fixed
Finish: Blued; checkered walnut grips
Length Overall: 9", 10½"
Approximate wt.: 31 to 32 ozs.
Comments: Made from about 1955 to the 1970s.

Estimated Value:	**Excellent:**	**$625.00**
	Very good:	**$500.00**

Colt 22 Semi-Auto

Caliber: 22 long rifle
Action: Semiautomatic; concealed hammer; factory adjusted trigger travel on target model
Magazine: 10-shot clip
Barrel: 4½" or 6" (target model); bull barrel with ventilated sighting rib; counter bored at muzzle; elevated scope mount on target model
Sights: Fixed; adjustable rear and removable front on target model
Finish: Matte stainless steel; black composite monogrip
Length Overall: 8⅝" or 10⅝"
Approximate wt.: 33½ to 40½ ozs.
Comments: Made in the mid-1990s; add 50% for target model (adjustable trigger travel, 6" bull barrel, adjustable sights, target ventilated rib, and scope mount rail).

Estimated Value:	**Excellent:**	**$250.00**
	Very good:	**$200.00**

Colt 22 Semi-Auto

Colt XSE Government

Caliber: 45 ACP
Action: Single action, semiautomatic; exposed hammer
Magazine: 8-shot clip
Barrel: 5"
Sights: White dot front and rear
Finish: Blued or brushed stainless steel; double diamond rosewood grips; aluminum trigger
Length Overall: 8½"
Approximate wt.: 39 ozs.
Comments: Introduced in 2003.

Estimated Value:	**New (retail):**	**$1,250.00**
	Excellent:	**$ 935.00**
	Very good:	**$ 750.00**

Colt XSE Government

Colt XSE Commander

Similar to the XSE Government with 4¼" barrel; 7¾" overall length; brushed stainless steel finish.

Estimated Value:	**New (retail):**	**$1,250.00**
	Excellent:	**$ 935.00**
	Very good:	**$ 750.00**

Colt XSE Commander

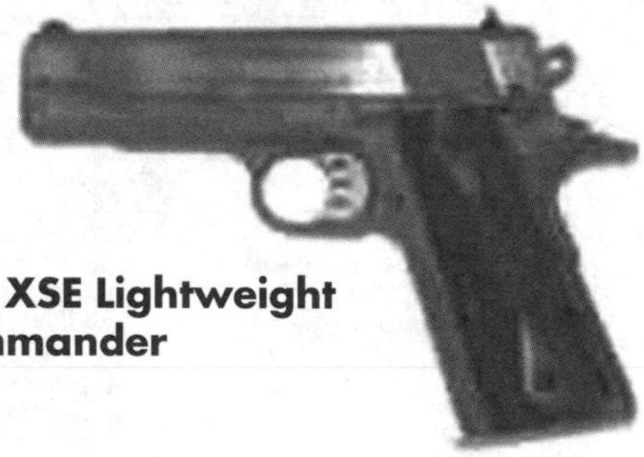

Colt XSE Lightweight Commander

Colt XSE Lightweight Commander

Similar to the XSE Commander with aluminum frame and Teflon-coated receiver.

Estimated Value:	**New (retail):**	**$1,250.00**
	Excellent:	**$ 935.00**
	Very good:	**$ 750.00**

Colt Single Action Army

The Colt Single Action Army is the gun most associated with the settling of the American West. Sometimes referred to as the Peacemaker or the Frontier, the revolver was manufactured from the early 1870s until just before World War II. A new generation was released in the 1950s. Over 30 caliber specifications have been noted for this handgun, from 22 rimfire to 455 and 476. Many were manufactured in 45 Colt, 44-40, 38-40, and 32-20. It was produced for both black powder and smokeless powder cartridges. The guns were produced in barrel lengths of 2½" and longer, with the most common lengths being 4¾", 5½", and 7½". Finishes available for the Colt S.A.A. range from blue and case hardening to nickel, with more exotic finishes sometimes surfacing. Varying degrees of finish from plain to slight engraving to extensive engraving have been recorded as either factory decorated or after-market design. Grips can be found in walnut, hard rubber, ivory, pearl, and stag in varying degrees of carving and design. Grips could be designated from the factory or purchased separately from gun dealers. These guns are highly desirable collectors' items bringing, in some cases, many thousands of dollars and so the buyer should be especially careful of mismatched parts, hybrids, and out-and-out fakes. Certain celebrity or historical associations could also drive the price up considerably. The buyer should be aware of unwarranted claims and require documentation in these cases. Later production Colt Singe Action Army revolvers can be found at the end of the Colt revolver section.

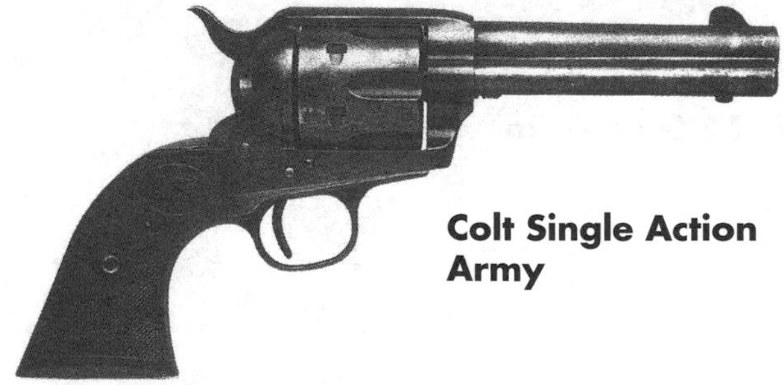

Colt Single Action Army

Colt Single Action Army

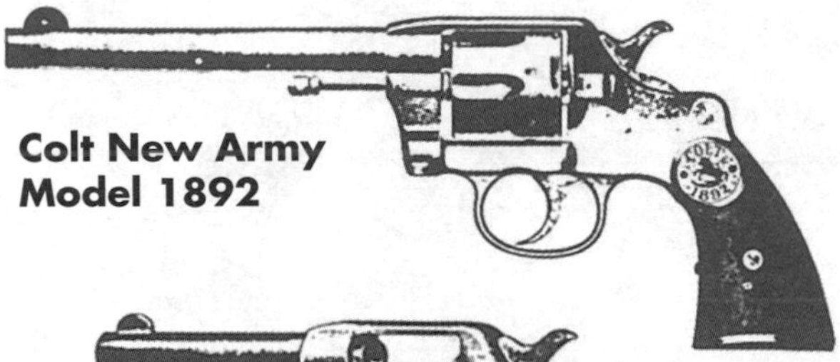

Colt New Army Model 1892

Colt New Navy Model 1892

Colt New Army Model 1892

Caliber: 38 Colt short and long, 41 Colt short and long, 38 Special added in 1904, 32-30 added in 1905
Action: Single or double action
Cylinder: 6-shot; ⅔ fluted; swing-out; simultaneous hand ejector
Barrel: 3", 4½", 6"
Sights: Fixed
Finish: Blued or nickel; hard rubber or walnut grips
Length Overall: 8¼" to 11¼"
Approximate wt.: 29 to 32 ozs.
Comments: Made from 1892 to 1908. Lanyard swivel attached to butt in 1901. All calibers on 41 caliber frame.
Estimated Value: **Excellent:** **$1,750.00**
Very good: **$1,400.00**

Colt New Navy Model 1892

Similar to Colt New Army Model 1892 except has double cylinder notches and locking bolt. Sometimes called New Army 2nd issue.
Estimated Value: **Excellent:** **$2,250.00**
Very good: **$1,800.00**

Colt Army Model 1903

Same as Colt New Army Model 1892 except modified grip design (smaller and shaped better); bore is slightly smaller in each caliber to increase accuracy.
Estimated Value: **Excellent:** **$1,500.00**
Very good: **$1,200.00**

Colt Double Action Army Model

Caliber: 32-20, 38-40, 44-40, 45 Colt
Action: Single or double action
Cylinder: 6-shot; ⅔ fluted; side load
Barrel: 3½" and 4" without side rod ejector; 4¾", 5½", and 7½" with the side rod ejector
Sights: Fixed
Finish: Blued or nickel; hard rubber or checkered walnut grips
Length Overall: 8½" to 12½"
Approximate wt.: 35 to 39 ozs.
Comments: Made from about 1877 to 1910. Lanyard loop in butt; also called "Double Action Frontier."
Estimated Value: **Excellent:** **$4,000.00**
Very good: **$3,200.00**

Colt Lightning Model

Caliber: 38 centerfire, 41 centerfire
Action: Single or double action
Cylinder: 6-shot; ⅔ fluted; side load; loading gate
Barrel: 2½", 3½", 4½", 6"
Sights: Fixed
Finish: Blued or nickel; hard rubber bird's-head grips
Length Overall: 7½" to 11"
Approximate wt.: 26 to 30 ozs.
Comments: Made from about 1877 to 1912 with and without side rod ejector. This was the first double action revolver made by Colt.
Estimated Value: **Excellent:** **$3,000.00**
Very good: **$2,400.00**

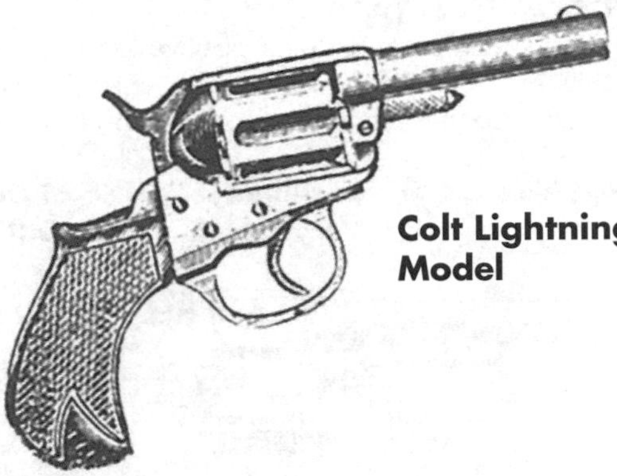

Colt Lightning Model

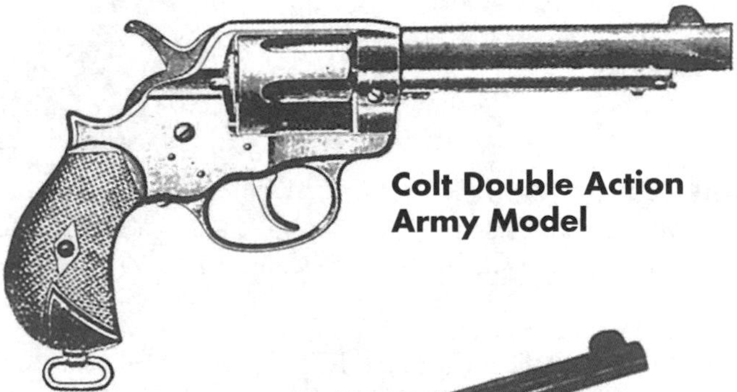

Colt Double Action Army Model

Colt Army Model 1903

Colt Double Action Philippine Model

Same as Colt Double Action Army Model except larger trigger guard and trigger. It was made originally for the army in Alaska but was sent to the Philippines instead.
Estimated Value: **Excellent:** **$4,500.00**
Very good: **$3,600.00**

Colt New Pocket

Caliber: 32 short and long Colt
Action: Single or double action
Cylinder: 6-shot; swing-out; simultaneous ejector
Barrel: 2½", 3½", 6"
Sights: Fixed
Finish: Blued or nickel; hard rubber grips
Length Overall: 6½" to 10½"
Approximate wt.: 15 to 18 ozs.
Comments: Made from about 1895 to 1905.
Estimated Value: **Excellent:** **$400.00 – 750.00**
Very good: **$320.00 – 600.00**

Colt Pocket Positive

Similar to the New Pocket with the positive locking system of the Police Positive; 32 short and long S&W cartridges or 32 Colt Police Positive. Made from the early 1900s to just prior to World War II.

Estimated Value: **Excellent:** **$625.00**
Very good: **$500.00**

Colt New Police

Colt Bisley Model

Caliber: 32 long centerfire, 32-20 WCF, 38 long Colt CF, 38-40 WCF, 41 long Colt CF, 44 S&W Russian, 44-40 WCF, 45 Colt, 455 Eley
Action: Single action
Cylinder: 6-shot; fluted; side load
Barrel: 4¾", 5½", 7½" with side rod ejector
Sights: Fixed
Finish: Blued with case-hardened frame and hammer; checkered hard rubber grips
Length Overall: 10¼" to 13"
Approximate wt.: 36 to 40 ozs.
Comments: Developed from the original Single Action Army Revolver by changing the trigger, hammer, and grips. Made from 1897 to 1912.
Estimated Value: **Excellent:** **$2,000.00 – 7,500.00**
Very good: **$1,600.00 – 6,000.00**

Colt Bisley Flat-Top Model

Similar to the Colt Bisley Model except: frame over the cylinder has a flat top; the longer barrel models were referred to as target models; wood and ivory grips as well as hard rubber; target adjustable sights or regular fixed sights. Short barrel models sometimes referred to as the Pocket Bisley. It usually had fixed sights and no side rod ejector.

Estimated Value: **Excellent:** **$3,500.00 – 15,000.00**
Very good: **$2,800.00 – 12,000.00**

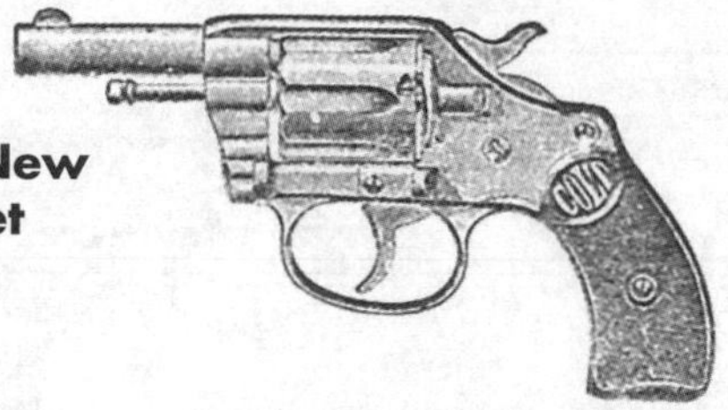

Colt New Pocket

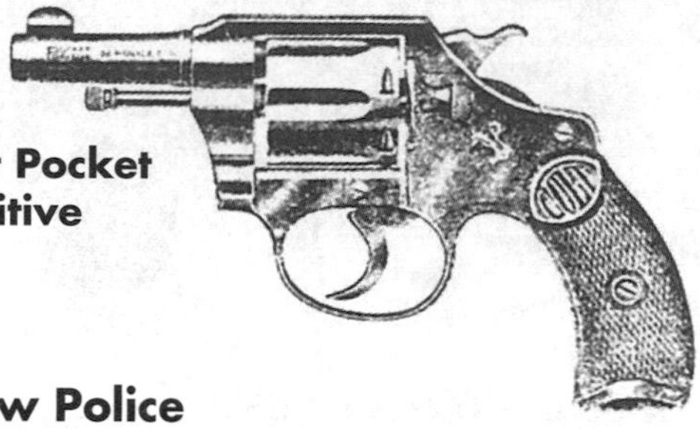

Colt Pocket Positive

Colt New Police

Caliber: 32 Colt short and long, 32 Colt New Police (S&W long)
Action: Single or double action
Cylinder: 6-shot; swing-out; simultaneous ejector
Barrel: 2½", 4", 6"
Sights: Fixed
Finish: Blued or nickel; hard rubber grips
Length Overall: 6½" to 10½"
Approximate wt.: 16 to 18 ozs.
Comments: Built on same frame as New Pocket except larger grips. Made from about 1896 to 1905.
Estimated Value: **Excellent:** **$500.00 – 975.00**
Very good: **$400.00 – 780.00**

Colt New Police Target

Same as Colt New Police except: 6" barrel only; blued finish and target sights. This is a target version of the New Police Model, made from 1896 to 1905.

Estimated Value: **Excellent:** **$1,375.00**
Very good: **$1,100.00**

Colt Bisley Model

Colt Bisley Flat-Top Model

Colt New Service

Caliber: 38 special, 357 magnum (introduced about 1936), 38-40, 44-40, 44 Russian, 44 Special, 45 ACP, 45 Colt, 450 Eley, 455 Eley, and 476 Eley
Action: Single or double action
Cylinder: 6-shot; swing-out; simultaneous ejector
Barrel: 4", 5", 6" in 357 and 38 Special; 4½", 5½", 7½" in other calibers; 4½" in 45 ACP (Model 1917 Revolver made for U.S. government during World War II)
Sights: Fixed
Finish: Blued or nickel; checkered walnut grips
Length Overall: 9¼" to 12¾"
Approximate wt.: 39 to 44 ozs.
Comments: Made from about 1898 to 1942. The above calibers were made sometime during this period.

Estimated Value:	**Excellent:**	**$1,200.00**
	Very good:	**$ 960.00**

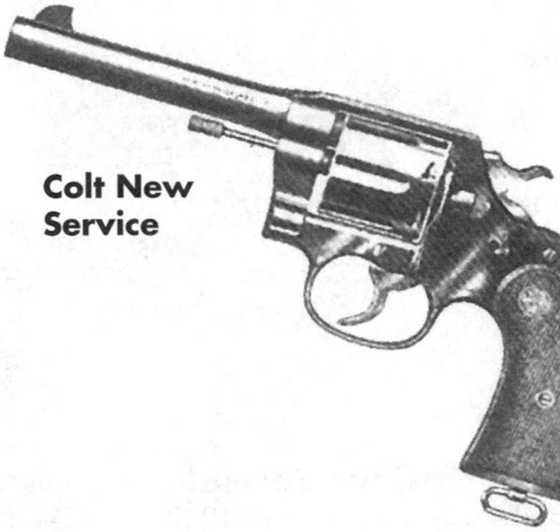

Colt New Service

Colt New Service Target

Caliber: Originally made for 44 Russian, 450 Eley, 455 Eley, and 476 Eley. Later calibers were made for 44 Special, 45 Colt, and 45 ACP
Action: Single or double action
Cylinder: 6-shot; swing-out; simultaneous ejector
Barrel: 6" and 7"
Sights: Adjustable target sights
Finish: Blued; checkered walnut grips
Length Overall: 11¼" to 12¾"
Approximate wt.: 40 to 42 ozs.
Comments: A target version of the New Service revolver with hand-finished action. Made from about 1900 to 1939.

Estimated Value:	**Excellent:**	**$1,500.00**
	Very good:	**$1,200.00**

Colt New Service Target

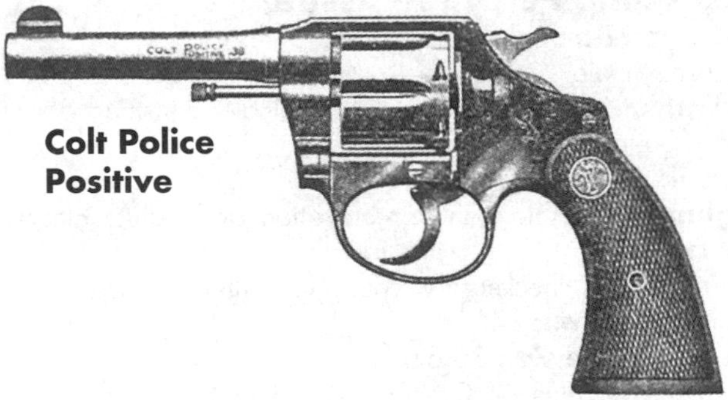

Colt Police Positive

Colt Police Positive Target

Colt Police Positive

Caliber: 32 short and long Colt (discontinued in 1915), 32 Colt New Police (32 S&W long), 38 New Police (38 S&W long)
Action: Single or double action
Cylinder: 6-shot; swing-out; simultaneous ejector
Barrel: 2½", 4", 5", and 6"
Sights: Fixed
Finish: Blued or nickel; hard rubber or checkered walnut grips
Length Overall: 6½" to 10½"
Approximate wt.: 18 to 22 ozs.
Comments: This is an improved version of the New Police with the Positive Lock feature which prevents the firing pin from contacting the cartridge until the trigger is pulled. Made from 1905 to 1943.

Estimated Value:	**Excellent:**	**$500.00**
	Very good:	**$400.00**

Colt Police Positive Target

Same as the Colt Police Positive except 22 caliber long rifle from 1910 to 1932 and 22 long rifle regular or high-speed after 1932, 22 Winchester rim fire from 1910 to 1935; blued finish; 6" barrel only; adjustable target sights; checkered walnut grips. Approximate wt. is 22 to 26 ozs.

Estimated Value:	**Excellent:**	**$650.00**
	Very good:	**$520.00**

Colt Marine Corps Model 1905

Colt Police Positive Special

Caliber: 32-20 (discontinued in 1942), 32 New Police (S&W long), 38 Special
Action: Single or double action
Cylinder: 6-shot; swing-out; simultaneous ejector
Barrel: 4", 5", 6"
Sights: Fixed
Finish: Blued or nickel; checkered rubber, plastic, or walnut grips
Length Overall: 8¾" to 10¾"
Approximate wt.: 23 to 28 ozs.
Comments: Made from about 1907 to the 1970s.
Estimated Value: **Excellent:** **$575.00**
Very good: **$460.00**

Colt Officer's Model Target (1st Issue)

Caliber: 38 special
Action: Single or double action
Cylinder: 6-shot; ⅔ fluted; swing-out; simultaneous ejector
Barrel: 6"
Sights: Adjustable
Finish: Blued; checkered walnut grips
Length Overall: 10½"
Approximate wt.: 34 ozs.
Comments: Hand-finished action. Made from about 1904 to 1908.
Estimated Value: **Excellent:** **$1,200.00**
Very good: **$ 960.00**

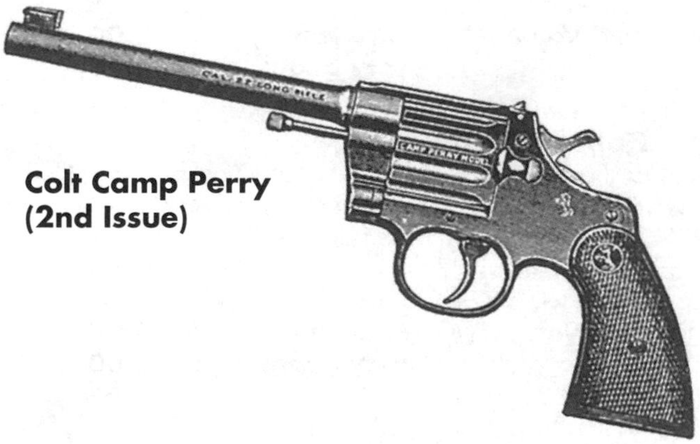

Colt Camp Perry (2nd Issue)

Colt Marine Corps Model 1905

Caliber: 38 Colt short and long
Action: Single or double action
Cylinder: 6-shot; ⅔ fluted; swing-out; simultaneous hand ejector
Barrel: 6"
Sights: Fixed
Finish: Blued or nickel; hard rubber or walnut grips
Length Overall: 10½"
Approximate wt.: 32 ozs.
Comments: Made from 1905 to 1908. Lanyard ring in butt; grip is smaller and more rounded at the butt than the Army or Navy Models. Sometimes called Model 1907.
Estimated Value: **Excellent:** **$3,500.00**
Very good: **$2,800.00**

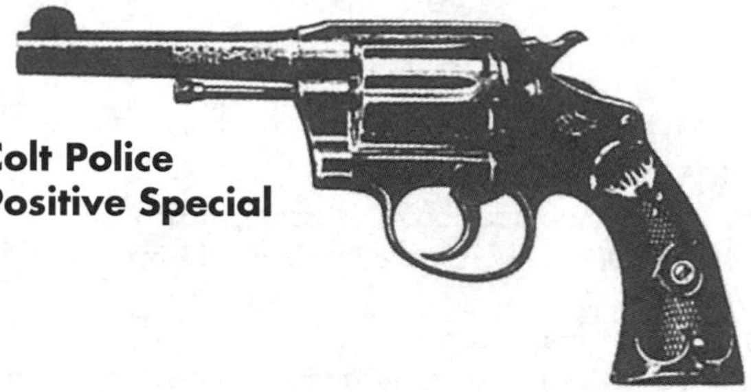

Colt Police Positive Special

Colt Officer's Model Taret (1st Issue)

Colt Camp Perry (1st Issue)

Caliber: 22 short, long, long rifle
Action: Single
Cylinder: 1-shot; swing-out flat steel block instead of cylinder with rod ejector
Barrel: 10"
Sights: Adjustable front for elevation and adjustable rear for windage
Finish: Blued; checkered walnut grips with medallion
Length Overall: 14"
Approximate wt.: 35 oz.
Comments: Built on Officer's Model frame. Made from about 1926 to 1934.
Estimated Value: **Excellent:** **$2,750.00**
Very good: **$2,200.00**

Colt Camp Perry (2nd Issue)

Same as 1st Issue except: 8" barrel (heavier); shorter hammer fall; overall length 12"; approximate wt. 34 ozs., chamber is recessed for cartridge head to make it safe to use 22 long rifle high-speed cartridges. Made from about 1934 to 1941.
Estimated Value: **Excellent:** **$2,500.00**
Very good: **$2,000.00**

Colt New Service Model 1909

Caliber: 32-20, 38 Special, 38-40, 42 Colt short and long, 44 Russian, 44-40, 45 Colt
Action: Single or double action
Cylinder: 6-shot; ⅔ fluted; swing-out; simultaneous hand ejector
Barrel: 4", 4½", 5", 6"
Sights: Fixed
Finish: Blued or nickel; hard rubber or walnut grips
Length Overall: 9¼" to 11¼"
Approximate wt.: 32 to 34 ozs.
Comments: Made from 1909 to 1928. Adopted by U.S. armed forces from 1909 to 1911 (Automatic became standard side-arm). Also called "Army Special."

Estimated Value:	**Excellent:**	**$1,150.00**
	Very good:	**$ 925.00**

Colt New Service Model 1909

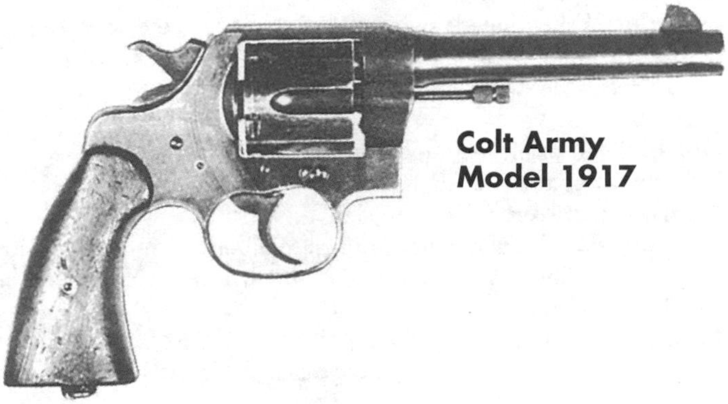

Colt Army Model 1917

Colt Officer's Model Target (2nd Issue)

Colt Army Model 1917

Caliber: 45 ACP or 45 ACP rim cartridges
Action: Single or double action
Cylinder: 6-shot; fluted; swing-out; simultaneous hand ejector; used semi-circular clips to hold rimless case of 45 ACP
Barrel: 5½" round tapered
Sights: Fixed
Finish: Blued; oiled-finished walnut grips
Length Overall: 10¾"
Approximate wt.: 40 ozs.
Comments: Made from about 1917 to 1928.

Estimated Value:	**Excellent:**	**$1,250.00**
	Very good:	**$1,000.00**

Colt Officer's Model Target (2nd Issue)

Caliber: 22 long rifle (regular) 1930 – 32; 22 long rifle (high-speed) 1932 – 49; 32 Police Positive 1932 – 42; 38 Special 1908 – 49
Action: Single or double action
Cylinder: 6-shot; ⅔ fluted; swing-out; simultaneous hand ejector
Barrel: 6" in 22 caliber and 32 Police Positive; 4", 4½", 5", 6" and 7½" in 38 Special
Sights: Adjustable rear
Finish: Blued; checkered walnut grips
Length Overall: 9¼" to 12¾"
Approximate wt.: 32 to 40 ozs.
Comments: Hand-finished action, tapered barrel. Made from about 1908 to 1949.

Estimated Value:	**Excellent:**	**$975.00**
	Very good:	**$780.00**

Colt Banker's Special

Caliber: 22 short, long, long rifle (regular or high-speed); 38 New Police (S&W long)
Action: Single or double action
Cylinder: 6-shot; swing-out; simultaneous ejector
Barrel: 2"
Sights: Fixed
Finish: Blued; checkered walnut grips
Length Overall: 6½"
Approximate wt.: 19 to 23 ozs.
Comments: Same as Police Positive except 2" barrel only and rounded grip after 1933. Made from about 1928 to 1940.

Estimated Value:	**22 Cal.**	**38 Cal.**
Excellent:	**$1,975.00**	**$1,350.00**
Very good:	**$1,580.00**	**$1,080.00**

Colt Banker's Special

Colt Shooting Master

Caliber: 38 Special, 357 magnum (introduced in 1936), 44 Special, 45 ACP, 45 Colt
Action: Single or double action
Cylinder: 6-shot; swing-out; simultaneous ejector
Barrel: 6"
Sights: Adjustable target sight
Finish: Blued; checkered walnut grips
Length Overall: 11¼"
Approximate wt.: 42 to 44 ozs.
Comments: A deluxe target revolver based on the New Service revolver. Made from about 1932 to 1940.

Estimated Value:	**Excellent:**	**$1,275.00**
	Very good:	**$1,020.00**

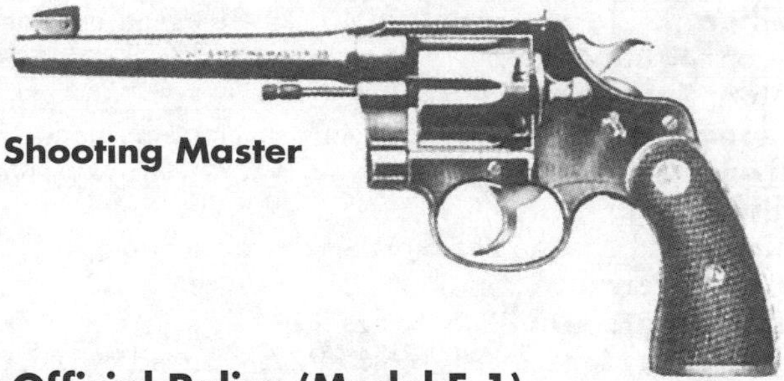

Colt Shooting Master

Colt Detective Special

Colt Commando Special

Colt Detective Special

Caliber: 32 New Police (S&W long), 38 Special
Action: Single or double action
Cylinder: 6-shot; swing-out; simultaneous ejector
Barrel: 2" and 3"
Sights: Fixed
Finish: Blued or nickel; checkered walnut grips with rounded or square butt
Length Overall: 6¾" to 7¾"
Approximate wt.: 21 oz.
Comments: Made from about 1926 to 1987. Available with or without hammer shroud. Add 10% for nickel finish.

Estimated Value:	**Excellent:**	**$725.00**
	Very good:	**$580.00**

Colt Commando Special

Similar to the Detective Special with matte finish and rubber grips. Produced from 1984 to 1987.

Estimated Value:	**Excellent:**	**$700.00**
	Very good:	**$560.00**

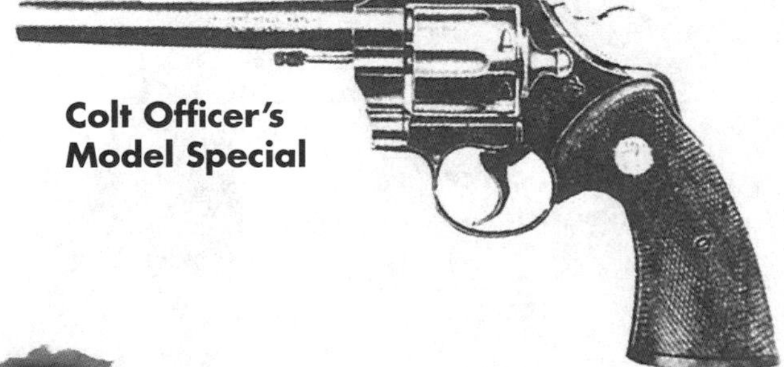

Colt Officer's Model Special

Colt Official Police (Model E-1)

Caliber: 22 long rifle (regular) introduced in 1930; 22 long rifle (high-speed) introduced in 1932; 32-30 made from about 1928 to 1942; 38 Special made from 1928 to 1969; 41 long Colt made from 1928 to 1930
Action: Single or double action
Cylinder: 6-shot; fluted; swing-out; simultaneous ejector
Barrel: 4" and 6" in 22 caliber; 4", 5" and 6" in 32-20; 2", 4", 5" and 6" in 41 caliber
Sights: Fixed
Finish: Blued or nickel; checkered walnut or plastic grips
Length Overall: 7¼" to 11¼"
Approximate wt.: 30 to 38 ozs.
Comments: 41 caliber frame in all calibers. A refined version of the New Service Model 1909 which was discontinued in 1928. Made from about 1928 to 1970.

Estimated Value:	**Excellent:**	**$575.00**
	Very good:	**$460.00**

Colt Commando

Similar to Colt Official Police (Model E-1) except made to government specifications in 38 Special only; sandblasted blue finish; produced for the government during WWII. Made from 1942 to 1945.

Estimated Value:	**Excellent:**	**$600.00**
	Very good:	**$480.00**

Colt Commando

Colt Officer's Model Special

Caliber: 22 long rifle (regular and high-speed); 38 Special
Action: Single or double action
Cylinder: 6-shot, ⅔ fluted; swing-out; simultaneous ejector
Barrel: 6"
Sights: Adjustable for windage and elevation
Finish: Blued; checkered plastic grips
Length Overall: 11¼"
Approximate wt.: 42 ozs. in 22 caliber, 38 ozs. in 38 caliber
Comments: Replaced the Officer's Model Target (2nd issue) as target arm; heavier non-tapered barrel and redesigned hammer. Made from 1949 to 1953.

Estimated Value:	**Excellent:**	**$600.00**
	Very good:	**$480.00**

Colt Cobra Model D-3

Caliber: 22 S, L, LR; 32 New Police; 38 Special
Action: Single or double action
Cylinder: 6-shot, ⅔ fluted; swing-out; simultaneous ejector
Barrel: 2", 3", 4" and 5"
Sights: Fixed
Finish: Blued or nickel; checkered walnut grips
Length Overall: 6⅝" to 9⅝"
Approximate wt.: 16 to 22 ozs.
Comments: Frame is made of a light alloy, but cylinder is steel. Made from 1950 to late 1970. Add 10% for nickel finish.

Estimated Value:	**Excellent:**	**$600.00**
	Very good:	**$480.00**

Colt Agent Model D-4

Caliber: 38 Special
Action: Single or double action
Cylinder: 6-shot, swing-out; simultaneous ejector
Barrel: 2"
Sights: Fixed
Finish: Blued; checkered walnut grips
Length Overall: 6¾"
Approximate wt.: 14 ozs.
Comments: Frame made of lightweight alloy. Made from the early 1960s to the late 1970s. Also available with hammer shroud.

Estimated Value:	**Excellent:**	**$550.00**
	Very good:	**$440.00**

Colt Agent Light Weight

Similar to the Detective Special with matte finish; 2" barrel; approximate wt. is 17 ozs.; produced in the mid-1980s.

Estimated Value:	**Excellent:**	**$525.00**
	Very good:	**$420.00**

Colt Air Crewman Special

Caliber: 38 Special
Action: Single or double action
Cylinder: 6-shot, swing-out; simultaneous ejector; aluminum alloy
Barrel: 2"
Sights: Fixed
Finish: Blued; checkered walnut grips
Length Overall: 6¾"
Approximate wt.: 14 ozs.
Comments: A rare lightweight special revolver developed by Colt at the request of U.S. Air Force during the Korean War. They were recalled in 1960.

Estimated Value:	**Excellent:**	**$4,000.00**
	Very good:	**$3,200.00**

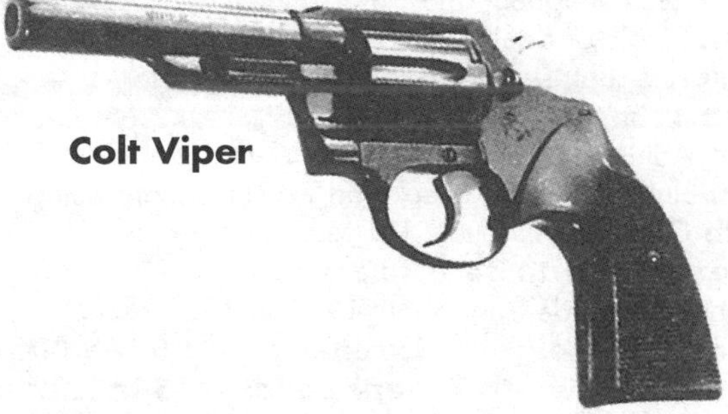

Colt Viper

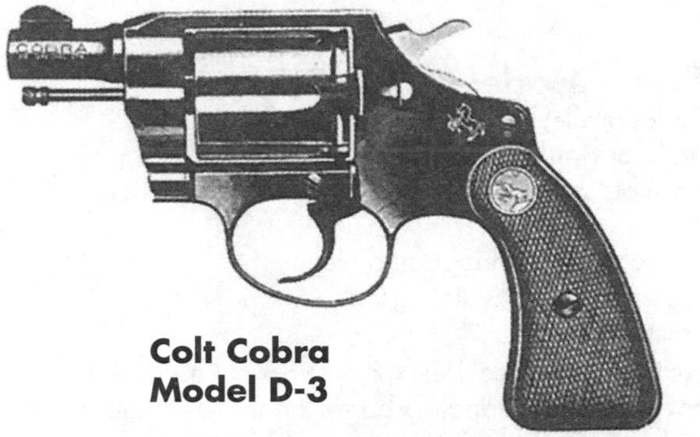

Colt Cobra Model D-3

Colt Agent Model D-4

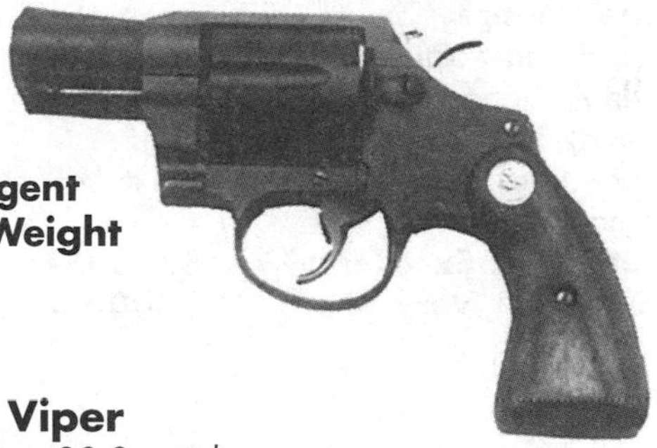

Colt Agent Light Weight

Colt Viper

Caliber: 38 Special
Action: Single or double action
Cylinder: 6-shot, swing-out
Barrel: 4"
Sights: Fixed rear, ramp front
Finish: Blued or nickel; checkered walnut wrap-around grips
Length Overall: 8⅝"
Approximate wt.: 20 ozs.
Comments: Lightweight aluminum alloy frame, shrouded ejector rod. Made in the late 1970s. Add $20.00 for nickel model.

Estimated Value:	**Excellent:**	**$600.00**
	Very good:	**$480.00**

Colt Border Patrol

Caliber: 38 Special
Action: Single or double action
Cylinder: 6-shot, swing-out; simultaneous ejector
Barrel: 4"
Sights: Fixed; Baughman quick draw front sight
Finish: Blued; checkered walnut grips
Length Overall: 8¾"
Approximate wt.: 34 ozs.
Comments: In 1952 about 400 were produced for a branch of the U.S. Treasury department. The barrel is marked on the left side, "Colt Border Patrol."

Estimated Value:	**Excellent:**	**$4,500.00**
	Very good:	**$3,600.00**

Colt Officer's Model Match

Caliber: 22 long rifle, 38 Special
Action: Single or double action
Cylinder: 6-shot; swing-out; simultaneous ejector; ⅔ fluted
Barrel: 6"
Sights: Adjustable for windage and elevation
Finish: Blued; checkered walnut grips
Length Overall: 11¼"
Approximate wt.: 22 caliber, 42 ozs; 38 caliber, 38 ozs.
Comments: Has heavy tapered barrel and wide hammer spur. Made from about 1953 to 1970.

Estimated Value:	**Excellent:**	**$700.00**
	Very good:	**$560.00**

Colt Officer's Model Match

Colt (.357) Three Fifty Seven

Colt (.357) Three Fifty Seven

Caliber: 357 magnum and 38 Special
Action: Single or double action
Cylinder: 6-shot; swing-out; simultaneous ejector
Barrel: 4" and 6"
Sights: Adjustable rear sight
Finish: Blued; checkered walnut grips
Length Overall: 9¼" and 11¼"
Approximate wt.: 36 to 39 ozs.
Comments: Made from about 1953 to 1962. It was replaced by the Trooper Model.

Estimated Value:	**Excellent:**	**$600.00**
	Very good:	**$480.00**

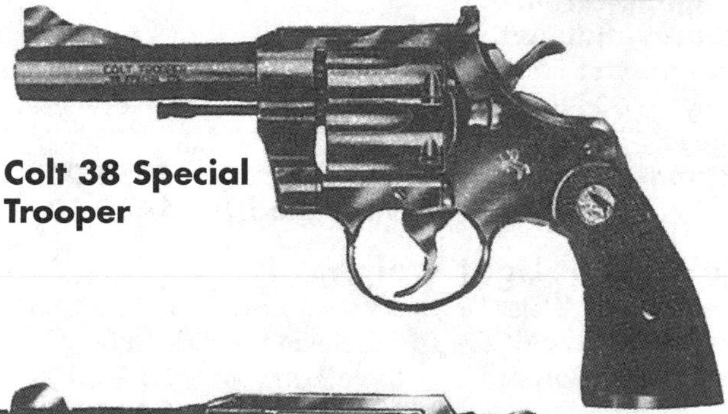

Colt 38 Special Trooper

Colt 38 Special Trooper

Caliber: 22, 38 Special
Action: Single or double action
Cylinder: 6-shot; swing-out; simultaneous ejector;
Barrel: 4" and 6"
Sights: Adjustable rear and quick-draw front
Finish: Blued or nickel; checkered walnut square butt grips
Length Overall: 9¼" and 11¼"
Approximate wt.: 36 to 43 ozs.
Comments: Made from about 1953 to 1962.

Estimated Value:	**Excellent:**	**$575.00**
	Very good:	**$460.00**

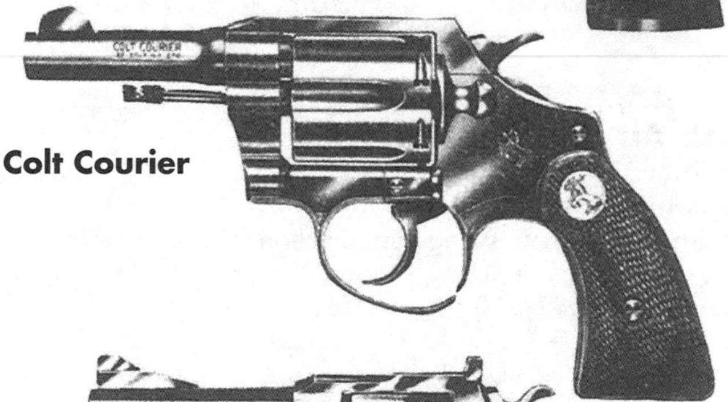

Colt Courier

Colt Courier

Caliber: 22 short, long, long rifle, 32 New Police (S&W long)
Action: Single or double action
Cylinder: 6-shot; swing-out; simultaneous ejector; made of lightweight alloy
Barrel: 3"
Sights: Fixed
Finish: Dual tone blue; checkered plastic grips
Length Overall: 7½"
Approximate wt.: 14 to 20 ozs.
Comments: Frame and cylinder made of lightweight alloy. Made in 1954 and 1955 only.

Estimated Value:	**Excellent:**	**$1,275.00**
	Very good:	**$1,020.00**

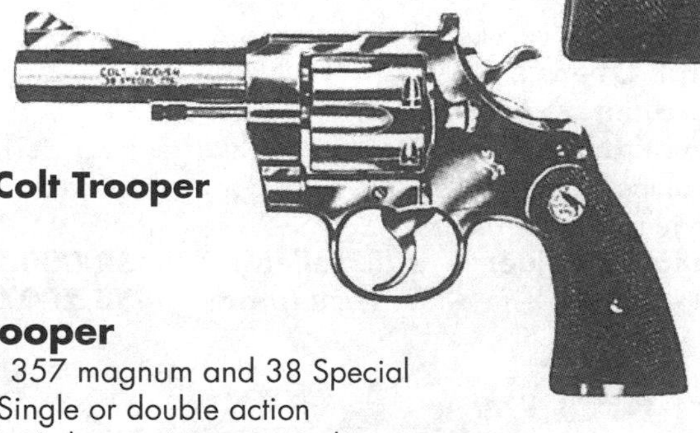

Colt Trooper

Colt Trooper

Caliber: 357 magnum and 38 Special
Action: Single or double action
Cylinder: 6-shot; swing-out; simultaneous ejector
Barrel: 4" or 6"
Sights: Adjustable rear and quick draw front
Finish: Blued or nickel; checkered walnut, square butt grips
Length Overall: 9¼" to 11¼"
Approximate wt.: 34 to 38 ozs.
Comments: Made from about 1953 to 1969.

Estimated Value:	**Excellent:**	**$575.00**
	Very good:	**$460.00**

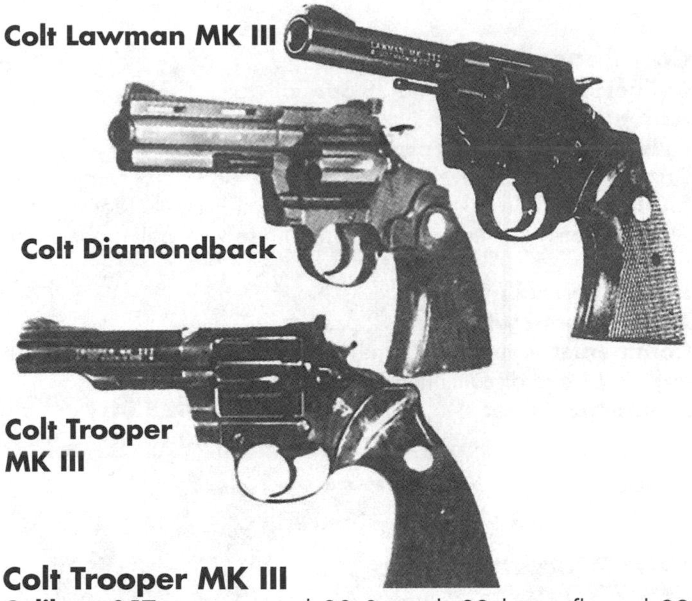

Colt Lawman MK III

Colt Diamondback

Colt Trooper MK III

Colt Trooper MK III

Caliber: 357 magnum and 38 Special; 22 long rifle and 22 WMR added in 1979
Action: Single or double action
Cylinder: 6-shot; swing-out; simultaneous ejector
Barrel: 4", 6", 8" in 1980
Sights: Adjustable rear
Finish: Blued or nickel; checkered walnut grips; non-glare electroless plating available after 1981 (Colt-guard)
Length Overall: 9½", 11¼", and 13½"
Approximate wt.: 39 to 42 ozs.
Comments: Made from about 1969 to the mid-1980s; wide target-type trigger and hammer. Add $20.00 for nickel; add $7.00 for 8" barrel.

Estimated Value:	**Excellent:**	**$425.00**
	Very good:	**$340.00**

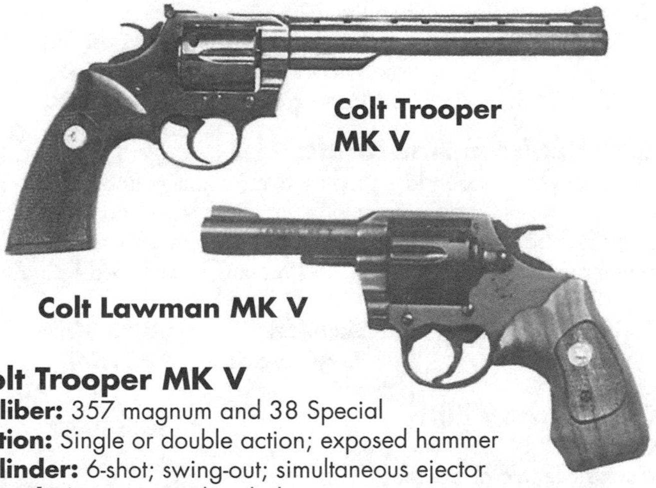

Colt Trooper MK V

Colt Lawman MK V

Colt Trooper MK V

Caliber: 357 magnum and 38 Special
Action: Single or double action; exposed hammer
Cylinder: 6-shot; swing-out; simultaneous ejector
Barrel: 4" or 6" ventilated rib
Sights: Red insert front, adjustable rear
Finish: Blued, nickel, or non-glare electroless plating (Colt-guard); checkered walnut grips
Length Overall: 9½" to 11½"
Approximate wt.: 39 to 45 ozs.
Comments: A medium frame revolver with inner and outer improvements on the Trooper MK III. Produced from 1982 to 1987. Add 9% for nickel finish.

Estimated Value:	**Excellent:**	**$500.00**
	Very good:	**$400.00**

Colt Diamondback

Caliber: 22, 22 long rifle, 38 Special
Action: Single or double
Cylinder: 6-shot; swing-out; simultaneous ejector
Barrel: 2½", 4", 6" ventilated rib; 2½" dropped in the late 1970s
Sights: Adjustable rear
Finish: Blued or nickel; checkered walnut square butt grips
Length Overall: 7½", 9"
Approximate wt.: 26 to 32 ozs.
Comments: Made from 1967 to 1987. Add 10% for nickel finish.

Estimated Value:	**Excellent:**	**$700.00**
	Very good:	**$560.00**

Colt Lawman MK III

Caliber: 357 magnum and 38 Special
Action: Single or double action
Cylinder: 6-shot; swing-out; simultaneous ejector
Barrel: 2" or 4"
Sights: Fixed
Finish: Blued or nickel; checkered walnut grips; non-glare electroless plating available after 1981 (Colt-guard)
Length Overall: 7¼", 9¼"
Approximate wt.: 36 to 39 ozs.
Comments: Made in the 1970s and the early 1980s. Add 10% for nickel finish.

Estimated Value:	**Excellent:**	**$500.00**
	Very good:	**$400.00**

Colt Lawman MK V

Similar to the Trooper MK V except: 2" or 4" solid rib barrel; fixed sights. Add 10% for nickel finish. Discontinued in the mid-1980s.

Estimated Value:	**Excellent:**	**$400.00**
	Very good:	**$320.00**

Colt DS-II

Caliber: 38 Special
Action: Double action revolver
Cylinder: 6-shot; swing-out; simultaneous ejector
Barrel: 2"
Sights: Fixed, ramp front
Finish: Stainless steel, checkered rubber grips
Length Overall: 7½"
Approximate wt.: 21 ozs.
Comments: Made in the late 1990s.

Estimated Value:	**Excellent:**	**$450.00**
	Very good:	**$360.00**

Colt .38 SF-VI

Caliber: 38 Special
Action: Single or double action; exposed hammer
Cylinder: 6-shot; swing-out; simultaneous ejector; fluted
Barrel: 2" or 4"; ejector rod shroud
Sights: Ramp front, grooved frame rear
Finish: Blued or stainless steel; black neoprene round butt grips
Length Overall: 7" or 9"
Approximate wt.: 21 to 25 ozs.
Comments: A smooth action similar to the Python; made in the late 1990s.

Estimated Value:	**Excellent:**	**$425.00**
	Very good:	**$340.00**

Colt King Cobra

Caliber: 357 magnum; 38 Special
Action: Single or double action
Cylinder: 6-shot; swing-out; simultaneous ejector
Barrel: 2½", 4", 6", or 8"; 4" or 6" after 1995
Sights: Red ramp front with white outline adjustable rear
Finish: Blued, matte stainless steel, or bright polished stainless steel, black rubber combat grips
Length Overall: 8", 9", 11", or 13"; 9" or 11" after 1995
Approximate wt.: 36, 42, 46 or 48 ozs.; 42 to 46 ozs. (1995)
Comments: Introduced in 1989. It has a full-length contoured ejector rod housing and a solid barrel rib. Stainless steel only after 1995; discontinued in 2000.

Estimated Value:	**Excellent:**	**$600.00**
	Very good:	**$480.00**

Colt Model I-3 Python, New Police Python, Python

Caliber: 357 magnum, 38 Special; 22 long rifle and 22 WMR available in 1981 only
Action: Single or double action
Cylinder: 6-shot; swing-out; simultaneous ejector
Barrel: 2½", 3", 4", 6", or 8" after 1980; ventilated rib
Sights: Blade front, adjustable rear (for windage and elevation). Red insert in front sight in 1980s
Finish: Blued or nickel; checkered walnut target grips; also rubber grips in 1980s; non-glare electroless plating and stainless steel in 1980s
Length Overall: 7¼" to 13¼"
Approximate wt.: 39 to 44 ozs.
Comments: Made from about 1955 to the late 1990s. Add 16% for black stainless steel; add 11% for stainless steel; add 4% for nickel finish.

Estimated Value:	**Excellent:**	**$1,000.00**
	Very good:	**$ 800.00**

Colt Official Police MK III

Caliber: 38 Special
Action: Single or double
Cylinder: 6-shot; swing-out; simultaneous ejector
Barrel: 4", 5", 6"
Sights: Fixed
Finish: Blued; checkered walnut square butt grips
Length Overall: 9¼", 10¼", 11¼"
Approximate wt.: 34 to 36 ozs.
Comments: Made from about 1970 to the late 1970s.

Estimated Value:	**Excellent:**	**$500.00**
	Very good:	**$400.00**

Colt Official Police MK III

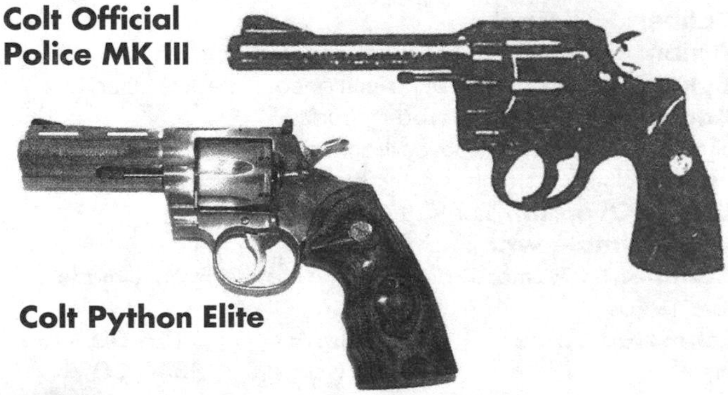

Colt Python Elite

Colt Peacekeeper

Caliber: 357 magnum and 38 Special
Action: Single or double action
Cylinder: 6-shot; swing-out; simultaneous ejector
Barrel: 4" or 6" with ventilated rib and short ejector shroud
Sights: Red insert front and white outline adjustable rear
Finish: Non-glare matte blue combat finish with Colt rubber combat grips
Length Overall: 9" or 11"
Approximate wt.: 38 or 42 ozs.
Comments: A medium frame 357 magnum introduced in the mid-1980s and discontinued in 1988.

Estimated Value:	**Excellent:**	**$425.00**
	Very good:	**$340.00**

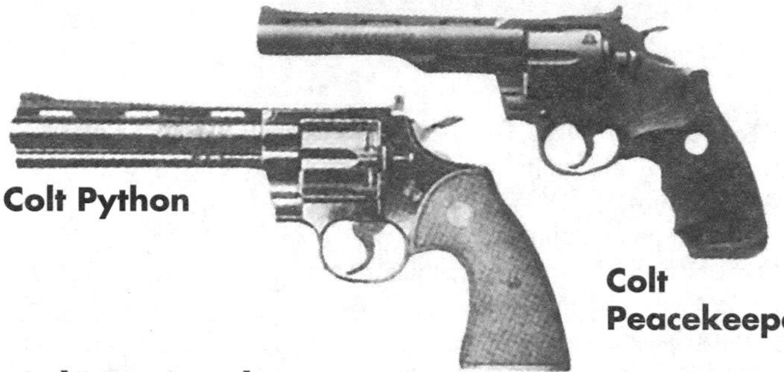

Colt Python

Colt Peacekeeper

Colt Anaconda

Caliber: 44 mag., 44 Special; 45 Colt (added in 1994)
Action: Single or double action
Cylinder: 6-shot; swing-out; simultaneous ejector
Barrel: 4", 6", or 8"; ventilated rib
Sights: Red ramp front, white outline adjustable rear
Finish: Matte stainless steel; rubber combat grips
Length Overall: 9" to 13¼"
Approximate wt.: 47 to 59 ozs.
Comments: Introduced in the 1990s.

Estimated Value:	**New (retail):**	**$1,100.00**
	Excellent:	**$ 825.00**
	Very good:	**$ 660.00**

Colt Realtree Anaconda

Same as the Anaconda except: 44 magnum caliber or 44 Special; 8" barrel; gray camouflage finish on exposed metal (Realtree); combat-style or Hogue monogrip; scope and scope mounts optional; add 35% for scope and mounts; introduced in the mid-1990s.

Estimated Value:	**Excellent:**	**$875.00**
	Very good:	**$700.00**

Colt Python Elite

Caliber: 357 magnum
Action: Single or double
Cylinder: 6-shot swing-out, simultaneous ejector
Barrel: 4" or 6"; ventilated ribs
Sights: Red ramp front, white outline adjustable rear
Finish: Blued or brushed stainless steel; walnut finger-groove grips
Length Overall: 11½" to 13½"
Approximate wt.: 40 to 44 ozs.
Comments: An updated version of the Colt Python.

Estimated Value:	**New (retail):**	**$1,250.00**
	Excellent:	**$ 935.00**
	Very good:	**$ 750.00**

Colt Single Action Army

Caliber: 357 magnum, 38 Special, 44 Special, 45 Colt
Action: Single action
Cylinder: 6-shot; side load; loading gate; under barrel ejector rod
Barrel: 4¾", 5½", and 7½"
Sights: Fixed
Finish: Blued with case-hardened frame; composite rubber grips; nickel with checkered walnut grips
Length Overall: 10⅛" to 12⅞"
Approximate wt.: 37 to 43 ozs.
Comments: A revival of the Single Action Army Revolver, which was discontinued in 1941. The serial numbers start at 1001 SA. The letters SA were added to the serial numbers when production was resumed. Made from about 1955 to the mid-1980s. Add 4% for a 7½" barrel; add 12% for nickel finish.

Estimated Value:	**Excellent:**	**$2,000.00**
	Very good:	**$1,600.00**

Colt New Frontier, Single Action Army

Colt New Frontier, Single Action Army

This is the same handgun as the Colt Single Action Army revolver except frame is flat topped; finish is high polished; ramp front sight and adjustable rear sight (wind and elevation); blued and case-hardened finish; smooth walnut grips. This is a target version of the SA Army, made from about 1961 to the mid-1980s in 44-40, 44 Spec., and 45 Colt caliber only. Add $20.00 for 7½" barrel.

Estimated Value:	**Excellent:**	**$1,200.00**
	Very good:	**$ 960.00**

Colt Frontier Scout

Caliber: 22 and 22 WRF (interchangeable cylinder)
Action: Single action
Cylinder: 6-shot side load; loading gate; under barrel ejector rod
Barrel: 4¾" or 9½" (Buntline Scout)
Sights: Fixed
Finish: Blued or nickel; plastic or wood grips
Length Overall: $9\frac{5}{16}$" to 14¼"
Approximate wt.: 24 to 34 ozs.
Comments: Single Action Army replica ¾-scale size in 22 caliber. Made with bright alloy frame and blued steel frame from about 1958 to 1972. Add $50.00 for interchangeable cylinder; $10.00 for nickel finish; $10.00 for Buntline Scout.

Estimated Value:	**Excellent:**	**$425.00**
	Very good:	**$340.00**

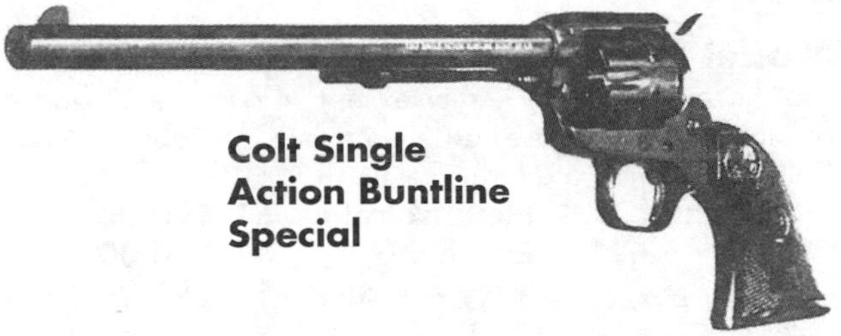

Colt Single Action Buntline Special

Colt New Frontier Buntline Special

Same as the Colt New Frontier (1961 Model) except: 45 caliber only; 12" barrel; 17½" overall; weighs 42 ozs. Made from 1962 to 1967.

Estimated Value:	**Excellent:**	**$2,500.00**
	Very good:	**$2,000.00**

Colt Single Action Buntline Special

This is basically the same revolver as the Colt Single Action Army Revolver (1955 Model) except it is 45 Colt caliber only. The barrel is 12"; the gun has an overall length of 17½"; weighs about 42 ozs. It was made from about 1957 until 1975. Available again in 1980. Add 15% for nickel finish. 44 Special available after 1981.

Estimated Value:	**Excellent:**	**$2,500.00**
	Very good:	**$2,000.00**

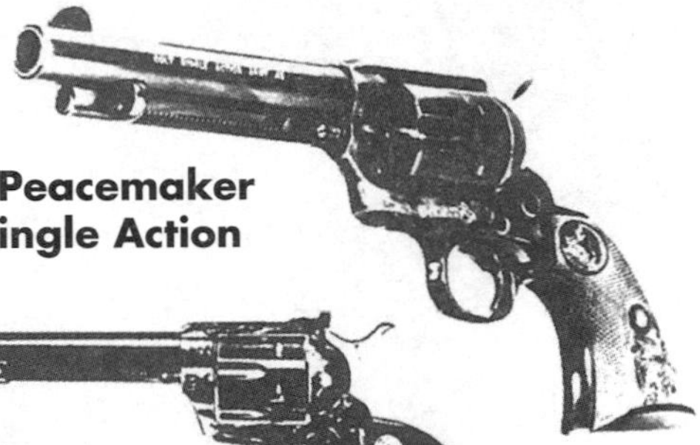

Colt Peacemaker 22 Single Action

Colt New Frontier

Colt Peacemaker 22 Single Action

Caliber: 22, 22 WRF when equipped with dual cylinder
Action: Single
Cylinder: 6-shot side load; loading gate; under barrel ejector rod
Barrel: 4¾", 6", and 7½"
Sights: Fixed
Finish: Blued barrel and cylinder; case-hardened frame; black composite rubber grips
Length Overall: $9\frac{5}{16}$" to 12¾"
Approximate wt.: 29 to 33 ozs.
Comments: All steel, 22 caliber version of the 45 caliber Peacemaker. Made from 1972 to the late 1970s. Add $6.00 for 7½" barrel.

Estimated Value:	**Excellent:**	**$400.00**
	Very good:	**$320.00**

Colt New Frontier

Same as the Colt Peacemaker 22 SA except equipped with a ramp front sight and adjustable rear sight; flat top frame. Reintroduced in 1982, produced until 1986.

Estimated Value:	**Excellent:**	**$375.00**
	Very good:	**$300.00**

Colt Model P Single Action Army

Similar to the Single Action Army except: 4¾" or 5½" barrel; nickel or blue with color case-hardened finish; available in 44-40 or 45 Colt caliber. Add 5% for nickel finish.

Estimated Value:	**New (retail):**	**$1,590.00**
	Excellent:	**$1,190.00**
	Very good:	**$ 950.00**

Colt Cowboy

An economical version of the Model P Single Action Army. 45 Colt caliber; blued with color case-hardened finish. Introduced in 2000.

Estimated Value:	**Excellent:**	**$600.00**
	Very good:	**$480.00**

DARDICK

Dardick Magazine Pistol

Dardick Magazine Pistol

David Dardick developed a handgun, which resembles an automatic pistol, around a new type of cartridge called the "tround." The tround has a triangular case made of plastic. For the 38 caliber, the primer, powder, and bullets are loaded into the tround. The 22 caliber cartridges are simply placed in a plastic tround to adapt them to the feeding system. The firing pin position is changed to rimfire by manually turning a screw in the frame. The basic gun will shoot 22 caliber or 38 caliber by changing the barrel. The feeding system uses a three-legged star wheel which moves from magazine to firing position and dumps rounds through an opening on the right side. The feeding system is moved 120° with each pull of the trigger. The magazine is loaded by placing trounds in singly or by using 10-shot stripper clips. Production was started in 1959 in Hamden, Connecticut, and ceased in 1960. All facilities, guns, and parts were auctioned to Numrich Arms in 1960. Approximately 40 guns were produced. The gun was made in three models and a rifle conversion kit. All models were made with two barrels (22 and 38 caliber). Dardick 1100 (11-shot); Dardick 1500 (15-shot); Dardick 2000 (20-shot). Prices double if rifle conversion kit is included.

Estimated Value:

Pistol with 22 and 38 caliber barrels

Excellent:	**$1,000.00**
Very good:	**$ 800.00**

DESERT EAGLE (MAGNUM RESEARCH, INC.)

Desert Eagle, Mark I and Mark VII

Caliber: 357 mag. (in early 1980s); 44 mag. (in 1986); 41 mag. (in 1989); 50 Action Express mag. (1992) (6" barrel only)
Action: Gas-operated semiautomatic; single action (double action in 1992); exposed hammer; rotating locking bolt
Magazine: 9-shot clip (357 mag.); 8-shot clip (41 and 44 mag.); 7-shot clip (50 mag.)
Barrel: 6" standard; 10" or 14" available
Sights: Combat-style or target-style with adjustable rear
Finish: Black oxide; satin nickel; bright nickel; or blued; wraparound rubber grips; alloy or stainless steel frame
Length Overall: 10½", 14½", or 18½"
Approximate wt.: 48 to 59 ozs. (alloy frame); 58 to 70 ozs. (steel or stainless steel)
Comments: Add 18% for 50 mag.; add 14% for 41 mag; add 6% for stainless steel frame; add 20% for 10" or 14" barrel.

Estimated Value:	**Excellent:**	**$1,020.00**
	Very good:	**$ 815.00**

Desert Eagle Mark I

Magnum Research Desert Eagle Mark XIX System

Caliber: 357 magnum; 44 magnum; 50AE
Action: Gas-operated semiautomatic; double action; exposed hammer; rotating locking bolt
Magazine: 9-shot clip (357); 8-shot clip (44); 7-shot clip (50)
Barrel: 6" or 10"
Sights: Adjustable rear, ramp front
Finish: Black oxide; other finishes available; alloy, steel, or stainless steel frame
Length Overall: 10½" or 14½"
Approximate wt.: 48 to 60 ozs.
Comments: Introduced in 1996; the XIX System consists of a basic platform to which different caliber barrel, slide, and clip can be attached to provide different calibers with the same pistol. Add 8% for 10" barrel. Add 15% for 44 magnum.

Estimated Value:	New (retail):	$1,563.00
	Excellent:	$1,175.00
	Very good:	$ 935.00

Magnum Research Baby Eagle

Caliber: 9 mm, 41AE, 40 S&W
Action: Semiautomatic, single or double action; exposed hammer; decocking safety
Magazine: 10-shot clip
Barrel: 3½" or 3¾"
Sights: Combat style
Finish: Black oxide; other finishes available
Length Overall: 7" to 8¼"
Approximate wt.: 38 ozs.
Comments: Introduced in 1992, discontinued in the late 1990s; reintroduced in 1999.

Estimated Value:	Excellent:	$420.00
	Very good:	$335.00

Magnum Research Mountain Eagle

Magnum Research Mountain Eagle

Caliber: 22 long rifle
Action: Semiautomatic, single action
Magazine: 15-shot clip, 10-shot after September 1994
Barrel: 4½", 6", or 8"; polymer and steel barrel
Sights: Adjustable rear, ramp front
Finish: Black oxide; black, one-piece injection molded grips
Length Overall: 8½" to 12¼"
Approximate wt.: 19 to 23 ozs.
Comments: Introduced in 1992, discontinued in the late 1990s. Add 40% for Target Model (8" barrel); add 20% for 6" barrel.

Estimated Value:	Excellent:	$200.00
	Very good:	$160.00

Magnum Research Desert Eagle Mark XIX System

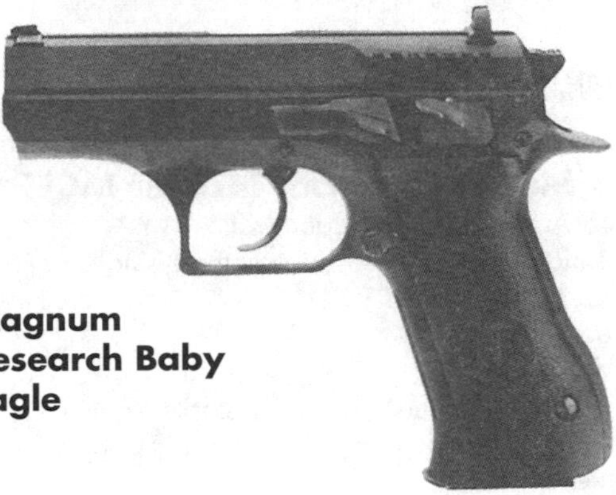

Magnum Research Baby Eagle

Magnum Research Lone Eagle SSP-91

Caliber: Almost any caliber from 22 long rifle to 444 Marlin available
Action: Single-shot, interchangeable actions of different calibers can be snapped into place on the high-tech polymer stock assembly
Magazine: None
Barrel: 10"
Sights: Adjustable rear, ramp front
Finish: Black oxide; other finishes available; polymer stock and action bed
Length Overall: 15⅛"
Approximate wt.: 65 to 72 ozs.
Comments: Introduced in 1992. Barreled action assemblies bring approximately $319.00 for each caliber in black oxide finish. Priced for stock assembly and one-barreled action assembly.

Estimated Value:	Excellent:	$350.00
	Very good:	$280.00

Magnum Research Lone Eagle SSP-91

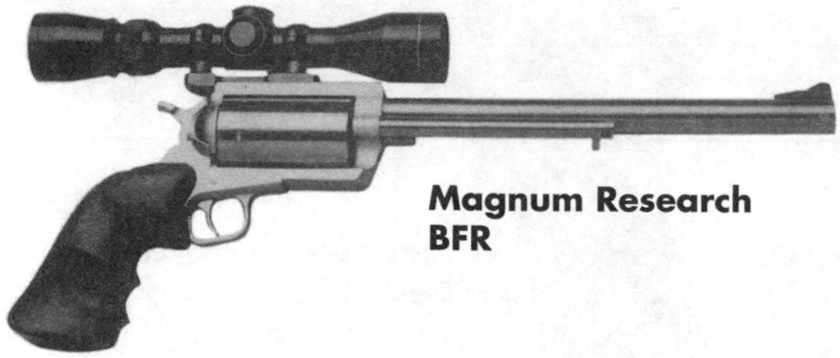

Magnum Research BFR

Magnum Research BFR

Caliber: 22 Hornet, 45 Colt, 45-70, 444 Marlin, 450 Marlin, 454 Casull, 480 Ruger, 475 Linebaugh
Action: Single action
Cylinder: Smooth, 6-shot; 5-shot in some calibers
Barrel: 6½", 7½", or 10"
Sights: Adjustable rear, ramp front
Finish: Stainless steel; checkered rubber or walnut grips; finger-grooved grips available
Length overall: 10" to 14½"
Approximate wt.: 48 to 64 ozs.
Comments: Introduced in 2001.
Estimated Value: **New (retail):** **$929.00**
Excellent: **$695.00**
Very good: **$555.00**

DETONICS

Detonics Mark I, Combat Master MC-1

Caliber: 45 ACP; 9mm; 38 Super ACP
Action: Semiautomatic; exposed hammer; single action; thumb safety
Magazine: 6-shot clip
Barrel: 3¼"
Sights: Fixed; some models have adjustable sights
Finish: Polished blue, matte blue; walnut grips
Length Overall: 6¾"
Approximate wt.: 29 ozs.
Comments: A lightweight compact combat pistol made from the late 1970s to the early 1990s.
Estimated Value: **Excellent:** **$690.00**
Very good: **$550.00**

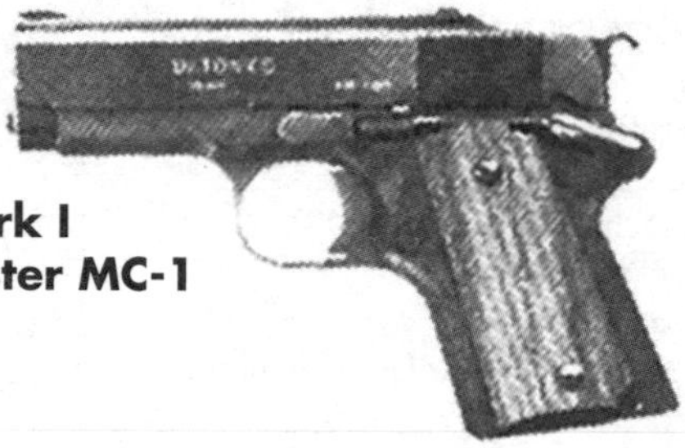

Detonics Mark I Combat Master MC-1

Detonics Mark V, Combat Master

Similar to the Mark I except matte stainless steel finish. Discontinued in 1985.
Estimated Value: **Excellent:** **$700.00**
Very good: **$560.00**

Detonics Mark VI, Combat Master

Similar to the Mark V with polished stainless steel finish. Discontinued in the early 1990s.
Estimated Value: **Excellent:** **$675.00**
Very good: **$540.00**

Detonics Scoremaster

Similar to the Combat Master with a 5" or 6" barrel, 7- or 8-shot clip; 45 ACP or 451 Detonics magnum. Add 4% for 6" barrel. Discontinued in the early 1990s.
Estimated Value: **Excellent:** **$1,000.00**
Very good: **$ 800.00**

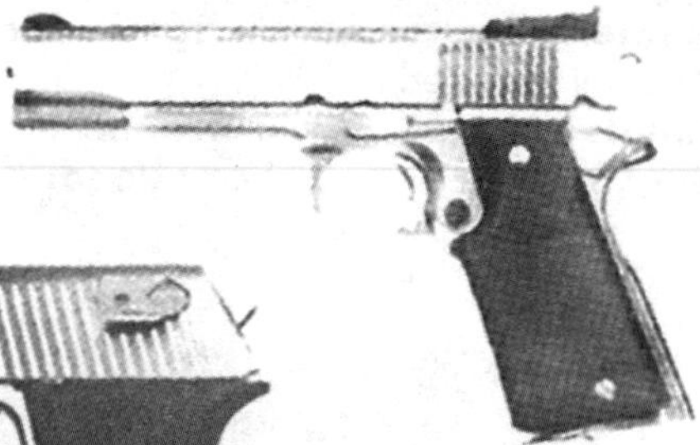

Detonics Scoremaster

Detonics Service Master

Similar to the Combat Master except slightly longer and heavier, Millett sights, dull finish. Discontinued in the mid-1980s.
Estimated Value: **Excellent:** **$750.00**
Very good: **$600.00**

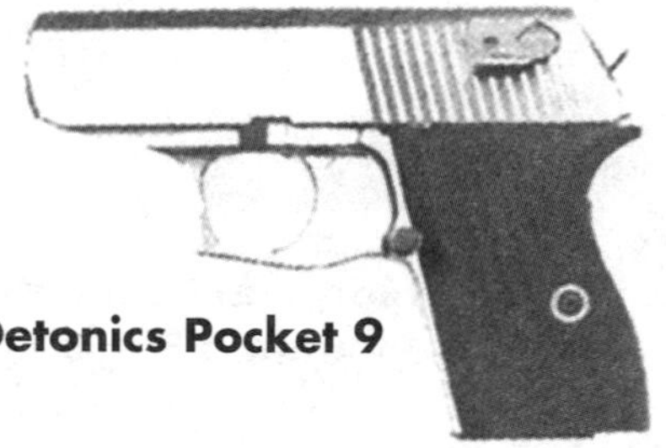

Detonics Pocket 9

Detonics Pocket 9

Caliber: 9mm
Action: Double and single action, blowback; semiautomatic
Magazine: 6-shot clip
Barrel: 3"
Sights: Fixed
Finish: Matte finish stainless steel, hooked and serrated trigger guard
Length Overall: 5¾"
Approximate wt.: 26 ozs.
Comments: Produced in the mid-1980s.
Estimated Value: **Excellent:** **$400.00**
Very good: **$320.00**

Fiala Single-shot Magazine Pistol

Caliber: 22 short, long, long rifle
Action: Hand-operated slide action to chamber cartridge, cock striker and eject empty case
Magazine: 10-shot clip
Barrel: 3", 7½", 20"
Sights: Target sight (adjustable rear sight)
Finish: Blued; plain wood grips
Length Overall: 6¾", 11¼", or 23¾"
Approximate wt.: 27 to 44 ozs.
Comments: Produced from about 1920 to 1923. A rare American pistol which has the appearance of an automatic pistol. A shoulder stock was supplied for use with the 20" barrel.

Fiala Single-shot Magazine Pistol

Estimated Value:

	Pistol with 3" and 7½" barrel	Pistol with all 3 barrels, shoulder stock and case
Excellent:	**$1,000.00**	**$2,000.00**
Very good:	**$ 880.00**	**$1,600.00**

Glocks 17, 17L, and 19

Caliber: 9mm Luger
Action: Recoil-operated semiautomatic; double action only; concealed hammer
Magazine: 17-shot clip (17 and 17L); 15-shot clip (19); or an optional 19- or 17-shot clip; 10-shot clips in USA after 9-13-94
Barrel: 4" (19); 4½" (17); 6" (17L)
Sights: Fixed (service model) or adjustable rear (sport model)
Finish: Space-age polymer and machined steel
Length Overall: 7½" (17); 9" (17L); 7" (19)
Approximate wt.: 23 ozs. (17L); 21 ozs. (19)
Comments: Introduced in 1983. Standard sidearm of Austrian Armed Forces in 1985. The 17L has cut-away slide top with ported barrel. Add 5% for 17L; add 5% for adjustable sights.

Estimated Value:	**New (retail):**	**$641.00**
	Excellent:	**$480.00**
	Very good:	**$385.00**

Glock 17

Glock 20

Glocks 20 and 21

Similar to the Glock 19 except: Calibers 10mm (15-shot Glock 20) and 45 ACP (13-shot Glock 21); 10-shot clips in USA after 9-13-94; 4½" barrel; add 5% for adjustable sights.

Estimated Value:	**New (retail):**	**$700.00**
	Excellent:	**$525.00**
	Very good:	**$420.00**

Glocks 29 and 30

Similar to Models 20 and 21 except: subcompact with a 3¾" barrel. 29 is 10 mm., 30 is 45 ACP. Add 5% for adjustable sights.

Estimated Value:	**New (retail):**	**$700.00**
	Excellent:	**$525.00**
	Very good:	**$420.00**

Glocks 22 and 23

Similar to Glocks 20 and 21 except: 40 S&W caliber; Glock 22 has 13-shot clip with 4½" barrel and Glock 23 has 15-shot clip with 4" barrel. 10-shot clips after 9-13-94; add 5% for adjustable sights.

Estimated Value: **New (retail):** **$641.00**
Excellent: **$480.00**
Very good: **$385.00**

Glock 24

Glocks 24 and 24C

Similar to Glock 17L with 6" barrel except: ported or unported barrel in 40 S&W caliber; approximate wt.: 27 ozs.; add 5% for adjustable sights; add 6% for ported barrel (Glock 24C); 10-shot clip in USA. Introduced in 1994.

Estimated Value: **Excellent:** **$620.00**
Very good: **$500.00**

Glock 26 and 27

Caliber: 9mm Luger (26); 40 S&W (27)
Action: Recoil-operated semiautomatic; double action only; concealed hammer
Magazine: 10-shot clip (26); 9-shot clip (27)
Barrel: 3½"
Sights: Fixed or adjustable
Finish: Space-age polymer and machined steel
Length Overall: 6¼"
Approximate wt.: 20 ozs.
Comments: Introduced in the mid-1990s; add 5% for adjustable sights.

Estimated Value: **New (retail):** **$641.00**
Excellent: **$480.00**
Very good: **$385.00**

Glock 34 and 35

Caliber: 9mm (34); 40 S&W (35)
Action: Recoil-operated semiautomatic; concealed hammer
Magazine: 10-shot clip
Barrel: 5¼"
Sights: Adjustable target
Finish: Matte blue; polymer grips
Length Overall: 8½"
Approximate wt.: 27 ozs.
Comments: Introduced in 2000.

Estimated Value: **New (retail):** **$775.00**
Excellent: **$580.00**
Very good: **$465.00**

Glock 31

Glock 31

Caliber: 357 SIG
Action: Recoil-operated semiautomatic, single or double action
Magazine: 10-shot clip
Barrel: 4½"; ported barrel available
Sights: Fixed; adjustable sights available
Finish: Polymer and machined steel
Length overall: 9"
Approximate wt.: 26 ozs.
Comments: Add 4% for adjustable sights or ported barrel.

Estimated Value: **New (retail):** **$619.00**
Excellent: **$465.00**
Very good: **$370.00**

Glock 32

Similar to Glock 31 except: smaller and more compact; 4" barrel; weighs 24 ozs. Add 4% for adjustable sights or ported barrel.

Estimated Value: **New (retail):** **$619.00**
Excellent: **$465.00**
Very good: **$370.00**

Glock 33

Similar to Glock 31 except: a subcompact model with 3½" barrel; weighs 20 ozs. Add 4% for adjustable sights.

Estimated Value: **New (retail):** **$619.00**
Excellent: **$465.00**
Very good: **$370.00**

Glock 36

Similar to Glock 21 except: a subcompact version with 3¾" barrel; weighs 22 ozs. Add 4% for adjustable sights.

Estimated Value: **New (retail):** **$668.00**
Excellent: **$500.00**
Very good: **$400.00**

Glock 36

Great Western Frontier

Great Western Double Barrel Derringer

Caliber: 38 Special; 38 S&W
Action: Single, double barrel; tip up to eject and load
Cylinder: None; barrels chambered for cartridges
Barrel: Superposed 3" double
Sights: Fixed
Finish: Blued; checkered plastic grips
Length Overall: 4⅞"
Approximate wt.: 14 ozs.
Comments: Replica of the Remington Double Derringer. Made from about 1952 to 1962.

Estimated Value:	**Excellent:**	**$400.00**
	Very good:	**$320.00**

Great Western Frontier

Caliber: 22 short, long, long rifle, 32-20; 357 magnum, 38 Special, 44-40; 44 magnum, 44 Special, 45 Colt
Action: Single, hand ejector
Cylinder: 6-shot; fluted
Barrel: 4¾", 5½", 7½" round barrel with ejector housing under barrel
Sights: Blade front; groove in top strap for rear sight
Finish: Blued; imitation stag grips
Length Overall: 10⅜" to 13⅛"
Approximate wt.: 38 to 42 ozs.
Comments: Replica of the Colt Single Action revolver. Made from about 1951 to 1962. Values of these revolvers vary due to the poor quality of the early models. After 1955 they were also available in unassembled kit form. Values for factory-made models.

Estimated Value:	**Excellent:**	**$500.00**
	Very good:	**$400.00**

H & R Self Loading 25

Caliber: 25 ACP
Action: Semiautomatic; concealed hammer
Magazine: 6-shot clip
Barrel: 2"
Sights: None
Finish: Blued; hard rubber grips
Length Overall: 4½"
Approximate wt.: 13 ozs.
Comments: Approximately 20,000 made from about 1912 to 1915.

Estimated Value:	**Excellent:**	**$400.00**
	Very good:	**$320.00**

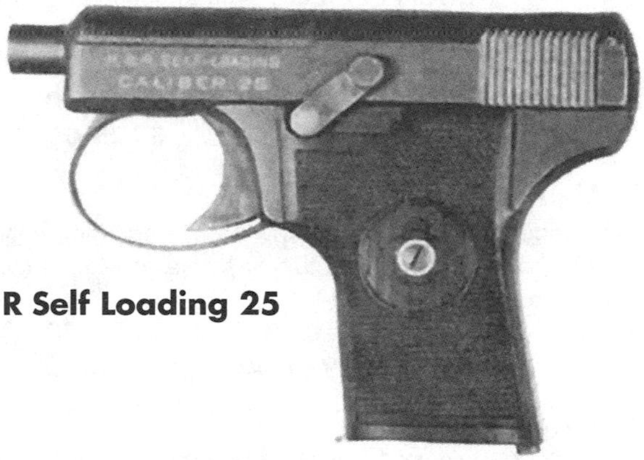

H & R Self Loading 25

H & R Self Loading 32

H & R Self Loading 32

Caliber: 32 ACP
Action: Semiautomatic; concealed hammer; grip safety
Magazine: 8-shot clip
Barrel: 3½"
Sights: Fixed
Finish: Blued; hard rubber grips
Length Overall: 6½"
Approximate wt.: 22 ozs.
Comments: A modified Webley and Scott design. Approximately 40,000 produced from about 1916 to 1939.

Estimated Value:	**Excellent:**	**$425.00**
	Very good:	**$340.00**

H & R American

H & R Model 4

H & R Model 4

Caliber: 32 S&W, 32 S&W long, 38 S&W
Action: Double and single; exposed hammer; solid frame; side load
Cylinder: 6-shot in 32 caliber, 5-shot in 38 caliber, removable cylinder
Barrel: 2½", 4½", or 6" hexagon barrel
Sights: Fixed
Finish: Blued or nickel; hard rubber grips
Length Overall: 6½" to 10"
Approximate wt.: 14 to 18 ozs.
Comments: Made from about 1904 to 1941.
Estimated Value: **Excellent:** **$150.00**
Very good: **$120.00**

H & R Model 5

Similar to Model 4 except: 32 S&W caliber only; smaller frame and cylinder (5-shot); weighs 10 to 12 ozs. Produced from about 1905 to 1939.
Estimated Value: **Excellent:** **$160.00**
Very good: **$125.00**

H & R Model 6

Similar to Model 5 except: 22 short, long, long rifle; 7-shot cylinder; minor change in shape of top of frame at rear of cylinder. Made from about 1906 to 1941.
Estimated Value: **Excellent:** **$150.00**
Very good: **$120.00**

H & R Trapper Model

Same as Model 6 except 6" barrel, checkered square butt walnut grips. Made from about 1924 to 1942.
Estimated Value: **Excellent:** **$275.00**
Very good: **$220.00**

H & R Hunter Model (1926)

Same as Trapper Model except 10" barrel, weighs 18 ozs. Made from about 1926 to 1930.
Estimated Value: **Excellent:** **$300.00**
Very good: **$240.00**

H & R Hunter Model (1930)

Similar to Hunter Model (1926) except: larger frame; 9-shot safety cylinder (recessed chambers); weighs 26 ozs. Made from about 1930 to 1941.
Estimated Value: **Excellent:** **$300.00**
Very good: **$240.00**

H & R American

Caliber: S&W, 32 S&W long; 38 S&W
Action: Single or double; exposed hammer; solid frame; side load
Cylinder: 6-shot in 32 caliber; 5-shot in 38 caliber; removable cylinder
Barrel: 2½", 4½", or 6" hexagon barrel
Sights: Fixed
Finish: Blued or nickel; hard rubber round butt grips
Length Overall: 6½" to 9¾"
Approximate wt.: 14 to 16 ozs.
Comments: Made from about 1883 to 1941.
Estimated Value: **Excellent:** **$125.00**
Very good: **$100.00**

H & R Young American

Caliber: 22 short, long, long rifle, 32 S&W short
Action: Single or double; exposed hammer; solid frame; side load
Cylinder: 7-shot in 22 caliber; 5-shot in 32 caliber; removable cylinder
Barrel: 2", 4½", or 6" hexagon barrel
Sights: Fixed
Finish: Blued or nickel; hard rubber round butt grips
Length Overall: 5½" to 9¾"
Approximate wt.: 10 to 12 ozs.
Comments: Made from about 1885 to 1941.
Estimated Value: **Excellent:** **$130.00**
Very good: **$105.00**

H & R Vest Pocket

Same as H & R Young American except 1⅛" barrel only; double action only; no spur on hammer; approximate wt. 8 ozs. Produced from about 1891 to 1941.
Estimated Value: **Excellent:** **$125.00**
Very good: **$100.00**

H & R Young American

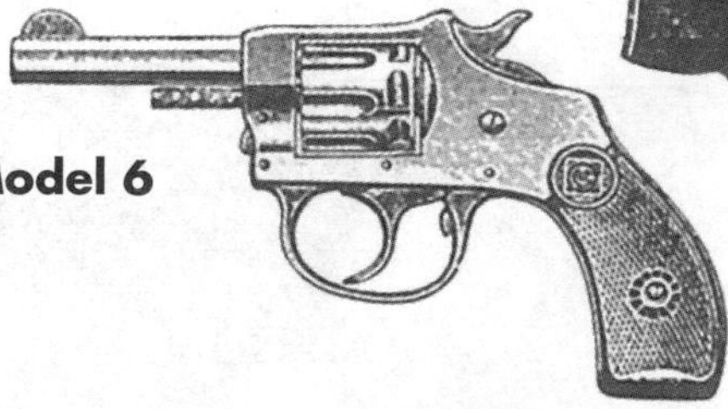

H & R Model 6

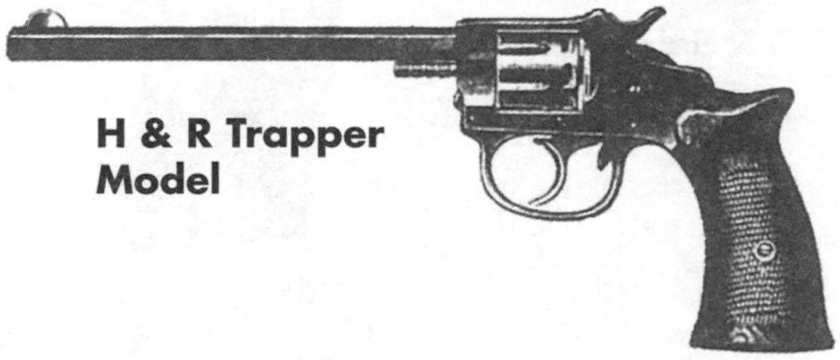

H & R Trapper Model

H & R Automatic Ejecting Revolver

Caliber: 32 S&W, 32 S&W long; 38 S&W
Action: Single or double; exposed hammer; hinged frame; top break
Cylinder: 6-shot in 32 caliber; 5-shot in 38 caliber; simultaneous automatic ejector
Barrel: 3¼", 4", 5", or 6" round barrel with rib
Sights: Fixed
Finish: Blued or nickel; hard rubber round butt grips
Length Overall: 7¼" to 10"
Approximate wt.: 15 to 18 ozs.
Comments: Made from about 1891 to 1941.

Estimated Value:	**Excellent:**	**$140.00**
	Very good:	**$115.00**

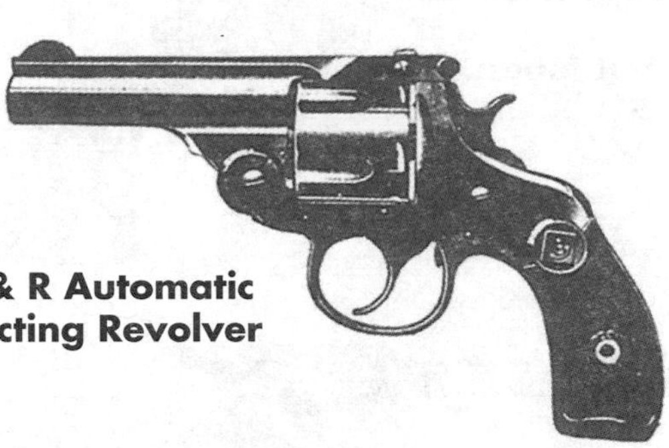

H & R Automatic Ejecting Revolver

H & R Model 50

Same as the Automatic Ejecting Revolver except: double action only; concealed hammer; frame completely encloses hammer area. Made from about 1899 to 1941.

Estimated Value:	**Excellent:**	**$150.00**
	Very good:	**$120.00**

H & R Model 50

H & R Premier

Caliber: 22 short, long, long rifle, 32 S&W
Action: Single or double; exposed hammer; small hinged frame; top break
Cylinder: 7-shot in 22 caliber; 5-shot in 32 caliber; simultaneous automatic ejector
Barrel: 2", 3", 4", 5", or 6" round ribbed barrel
Sights: Fixed
Finish: Blued or nickel; hard rubber round butt grips
Length Overall: 5¾" to 9¾"
Approximate wt.: 12 to 16 ozs.
Comments: Made from about 1895 to 1941.

Estimated Value:	**Excellent:**	**$150.00**
	Very good:	**$120.00**

H & R Premier

H & R Model 40

Same as the Premier except double action only; concealed hammer; frame completely encloses hammer area. Made from about 1899 to 1941.

Estimated Value:	**Excellent:**	**$160.00**
	Very good:	**$125.00**

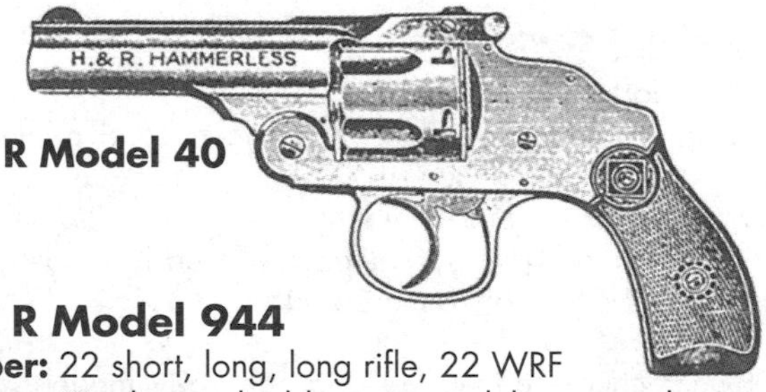

H & R Model 40

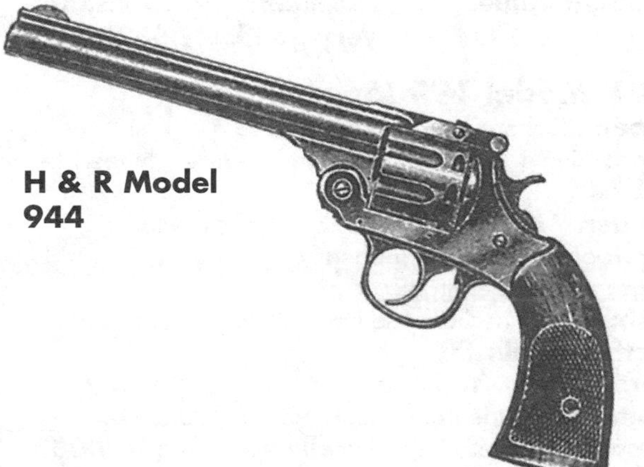

H & R Model 944

H & R Model 944

Caliber: 22 short, long, long rifle, 22 WRF
Action: Single or double; exposed hammer; heavy hinged frame; top break
Cylinder: 9-shot; simultaneous automatic ejector
Barrel: 6" round ribbed barrel
Sights: Fixed
Finish: Blued; checkered square butt walnut grips
Length Overall: 10"
Approximate wt.: 24 ozs.
Comments: Produced from about 1925 to 1930.

Estimated Value:	**Excellent:**	**$150.00**
	Very good:	**$120.00**

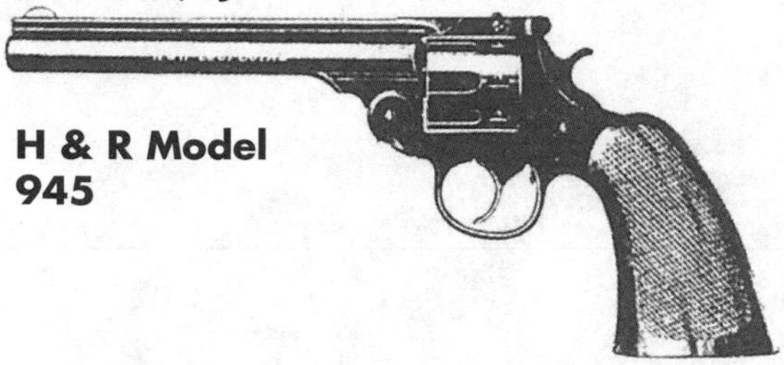

H & R Model 945

H& R Model 922

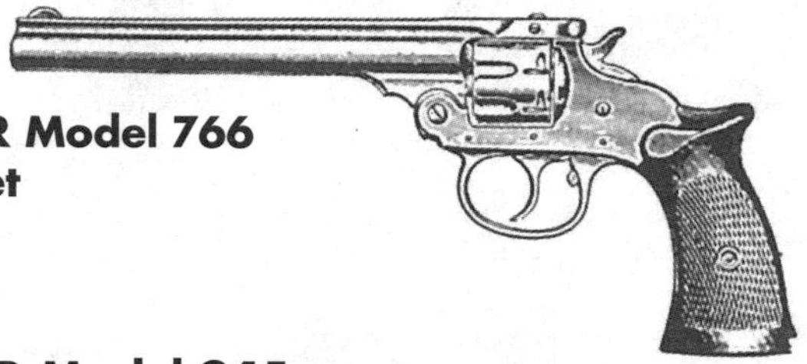

H & R Model 766 Target

H & R Model 945

Same as the Model 944 except safety cylinder (recessed chambers). Made from about 1929 to 1941.

Estimated Value: **Excellent:** **$165.00**
Very good: **$135.00**

H & R Model 955

Same as the Model 945 except: 10" barrel; approximate weight is 28 ozs. Made from about 1929 to 1941.

Estimated Value: **Excellent:** **$160.00**
Very good: **$130.00**

H & R Model 922

Caliber: 22 short, long, long rifle
Action: Single or double; exposed hammer; solid frame; side load
Cylinder: 9-shot removable cylinder
Barrel: 4", 6", or 10" octagon barrel in early models, later models had 2½", 4", or 6" round barrel
Sights: Fixed
Finish: Blued; checkered walnut grips on early models; plastic grips on later models
Length Overall: 8¼" to 14¼"
Approximate wt.: 20 to 26 ozs.
Comments: Made from about 1929 to the 1970s.
Estimated Value: **Excellent:** **$125.00**
Very good: **$100.00**

H & R Model 923

Same as the Model 922 except nickel finish. Made from about 1930 to the late 1970s.

Estimated Value: **Excellent:** **$140.00**
Very good: **$110.00**

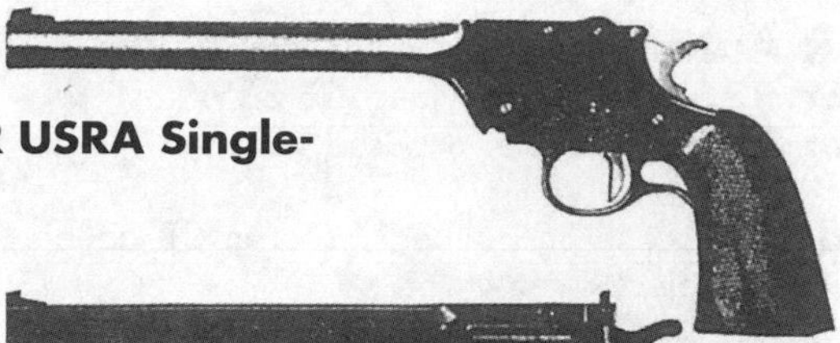

H & R USRA Single-shot

H & R Model 199 (Sportsman)

H & R Model 766 Target

Caliber: 22 short, long, long rifle, 22 WRF
Action: Single or double; exposed hammer; small hinged frame; top break
Cylinder: 7-shot; simultaneous automatic ejector
Barrel: 6" round barrel
Sights: Fixed
Finish: Blued; checkered square butt walnut grips
Length Overall: 10"
Approximate wt.: 16 ozs.
Comments: Made from about 1926 to 1936.
Estimated Value: **Excellent:** **$160.00**
Very good: **$130.00**

H & R Ultra Sportsman

Caliber: 22 short, long, long rifle, 22 WRF
Action: Single or double; exposed hammer; top break
Cylinder: 9-shot; simultaneous automatic ejector
Barrel: 6" round barrel
Sights: Adjustable target sights
Finish: Blued; checkered square butt walnut grips
Length Overall: 10"
Approximate wt.: 30 ozs.
Comments: Heavy frame; short cylinder; wide hammer spur. Made from about 1928 to 1938.
Estimated Value: **Excellent:** **$225.00**
Very good: **$180.00**

H & R USRA Single-shot

Same as the Ultra Sportsman except single-shot only (no cylinder); cartridge chamber in barrel; barrel fills in cylinder space; 7", 8", or 10" barrel lengths; approximate wt.: 29 to 31 ozs. Made from about 1928 to 1943.

Estimated Value: **Excellent:** **$475.00**
Very good: **$380.00**

H & R Model 199 (Sportsman)

Caliber: 22 short, long, long rifle
Action: Single or double; exposed hammer; hinged frame; top break
Cylinder: 9-shot; simultaneous automatic ejector
Barrel: 6" round barrel, ribbed
Sights: Adjustable target
Finish: Blued; checkered square butt walnut grips
Length Overall: 11"
Approximate wt.: 27 ozs.
Comments: Made from about 1931 to 1951.
Estimated Value: **Excellent:** **$165.00**
Very good: **$135.00**

H & R Defender 38

Similar to the Model 199 Sportsman except: 38 S&W caliber; 4" or 6" barrel; fixed sights, plastic grips. Made from about 1933 to 1946.

Estimated Value: **Excellent:** **$145.00**
Very good: **$115.00**

H & R Model 299 New Defender

Similar to the Model 199 Sportsman except 2" barrel; 61/4" overall length. Made from about 1936 to 1941.

Estimated Value: **Excellent:** **$135.00**
Very good: **$110.00**

H & R Model 999 (Deluxe Sportsman)

Same as the Model 199 Sportsman except: redesigned hammer and barrel rib. Made from 1951 to 1986. 32 caliber (6-shot) with 4" barrel available after 1978. Produced in 22 caliber in early 1990s.

Estimated Value: **Excellent:** **$300.00**
Very good: **$240.00**

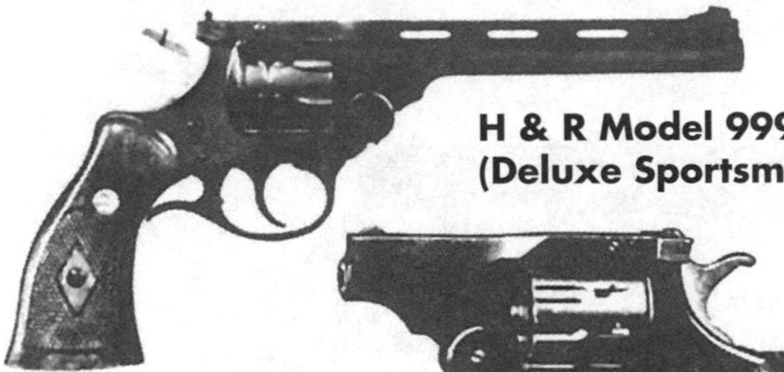

H & R Model 999 (Deluxe Sportsman)

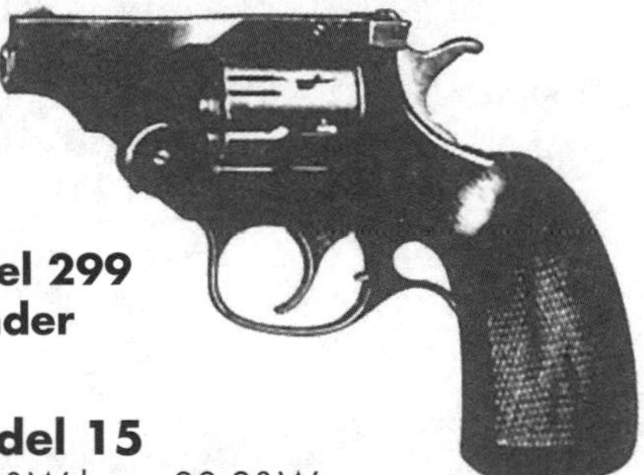

H & R Model 299 New Defender

H & R Bobby Model 15

Caliber: 32 S&W, 32 S&W long, 38 S&W
Action: Single or double; exposed hammer; hinged frame; top break
Cylinder: 6-shot in 32 caliber, 5-shot in 38 caliber; simultaneous automatic ejector
Barrel: 4" round, ribbed
Sights: Fixed
Finish: Blued; checkered square butt walnut grips
Length Overall: 9"
Approximate wt.: 23 ozs.
Comments: Made from about 1941 to 1943.
Estimated Value: **Excellent:** **$235.00**
Very good: **$190.00**

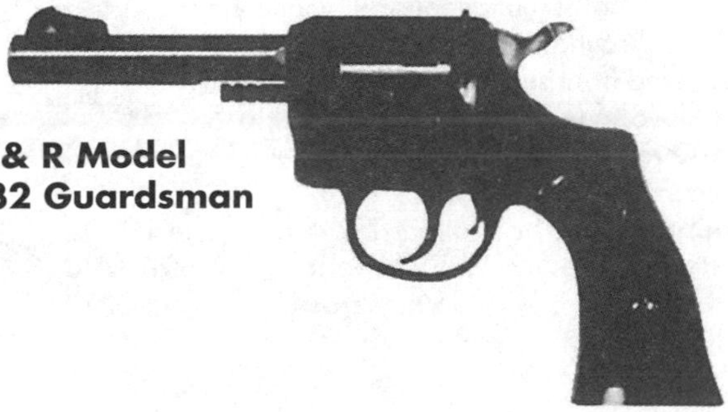

H & R Model 732 Guardsman

H & R Model 929 Side-Kick

H & R Model 632

H & R Models 929 and 930 Side-Kick

Caliber: 22 short, long, long rifle
Action: Single or double; exposed hammer; solid frame
Cylinder: 9-shot swing-out; simultaneous manual ejector
Barrel: 2½", 4", or 6" round, ribbed
Sights: 2½" has fixed sights; 4" and 6" have windage adjustable rear sights
Finish: Blued; checkered plastic grips; walnut grips available after 1982
Length Overall: 6¾" to 10¼"
Approximate wt.: 22 to 28 ozs.
Comments: Made from about 1956 to 1986. Reintroduced in 1990s with 4" barrel. Add $15.00 for walnut grips. Model 930 has nickel finish. Add 10% for nickel finish.
Estimated Value: **Excellent:** **$150.00**
Very good: **$120.00**

H & R Models 632 and 633

Caliber: 32 S&W, 32 S&W long
Action: Single or double; exposed hammer; solid frame
Cylinder: 6-shot
Barrel: 2½" or 4" round
Sights: Fixed
Finish: Blued or nickel (633); checkered tenite grips
Length Overall: 6¾" to 8¼"
Approximate wt.: 19 to 21 oz.
Comments: 2½" barrel model has round butt grips. Made from about 1946 to 1986. Model 633 has nickel finish. Add 10% for nickel finish. Made from the early 1950s to the mid-1980s.
Estimated Value: **Excellent:** **$135.00**
Very good: **$110.00**

H & R Models 732 and 733 Guardsman

Caliber: 32 S&W, 32 S&W long, 32 H & R magnum
Action: Single or double; exposed hammer; solid frame
Cylinder: 6-shot swing-out; simultaneous manual ejector
Barrel: 2½" or 4" round
Sights: Fixed
Finish: Blued or nickel; checkered plastic grips; walnut grips available after 1982
Length Overall: 6¾" to 8¼"
Approximate wt.: 23 to 26 ozs.
Comments: Made from about 1958 to 1986. Add 10% for walnut grips. Model 733 has nickel finish. Add 10% for nickel finish.
Estimated Value: **Excellent:** **$150.00**
Very good: **$120.00**

H & R Models 622 and 623

Caliber: 22 short, long, long rifle
Action: Single or double; exposed hammer; solid frame; side load
Cylinder: 6-shot removable
Barrel: 2½", 4", 6" round
Sights: Fixed
Finish: Blued or nickel; checkered plastic grips
Length Overall: 6¾" to 10¼"
Approximate wt.: 24 to 28 ozs.
Comments: Made from about 1957 to 1986. Model 623 has nickel finish. Add 10% for nickel finish.

Estimated Value:	**Excellent:**	**$145.00**
	Very good:	**$115.00**

H & R Model 642

Similar to the Model 622 in 22 WMR caliber; 2½" or 4" barrel. Discontinued in 1983.

Estimated Value:	**Excellent:**	**$145.00**
	Very good:	**$115.00**

H & R Models 939 and 940 Ultra Side-Kick

Caliber: 22 short, long, long rifle
Action: Single or double; exposed hammer; solid frame
Cylinder: 9-shot swing-out; simultaneous manual ejector
Barrel: 6" ventilated rib target barrel; bull barrel on 940
Sights: Ramp front; adjustable rear sight
Finish: Blued; checkered walnut grips with thumbrest
Length Overall: 10½"
Approximate wt.: 33 ozs.
Comments: Made from about 1958 to the 1980s. Reintroduced in the 1990s as 939 Premier; discontinued in 2000.

Estimated Value:	**Excellent:**	**$215.00**
	Very good:	**$175.00**

H & R Model 903

Similar to the Model 939 with a solid heavy flat side barrel and adjustable sights. Produced from 1980 to 1984.

Estimated Value:	**Excellent:**	**$145.00**
	Very good:	**$115.00**

H & R Model 603

Similar to the Model 903 in 22 magnum. Made from the early to the mid-1980s.

Estimated Value:	**Excellent:**	**$160.00**
	Very good:	**$125.00**

H & R Model 904 and 905

Similar to the Model 903 with a 4" or 6" heavy round barrel. Blue satin finish available after 1982 (Model 904). Model 905 has nickel finish. Add 10% for nickel finish. Made in the early 1980s.

Estimated Value:	**Excellent:**	**$160.00**
	Very good:	**$125.00**

H & R Model 604

Similar to the Model 904 in 22 magnum.

Estimated Value:	**Excellent:**	**$200.00**
	Very good:	**$160.00**

H & R Model 622

H & R Models 900 and 901

Caliber: 22 short, long, long rifle
Action: Single or double; exposed hammer; solid frame; side load
Cylinder: 9-shot removable
Barrel: 2½", 4", or 6"
Sights: Fixed
Finish: Blued; checkered plastic grips
Length Overall: 6½" to 10"
Approximate wt.: 23 to 26 ozs.
Comments: Made from about 1962 to 1973. Model 901 has nickel finish. Add 10% for nickel finish.

Estimated Value:	**Excellent:**	**$145.00**
	Very good:	**$115.00**

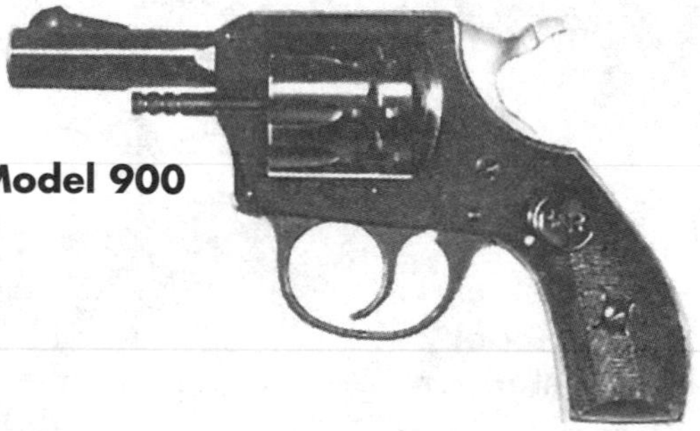

H & R Model 900

H & R Model 939 Ultra Side-Kick

H & R Model 925 Defender

Caliber: 38 S&W
Action: Single or double; exposed hammer; hinged frame; top break
Cylinder: 5-shot; simultaneous automatic ejector
Barrel: 2½" round, ribbed
Sights: Fixed front sight; adjustable rear sight
Finish: Blued; one-piece wrap-around grip
Length Overall: 6¾"
Approximate wt.: 22 ozs.
Comments: Made from about 1964 to the late 1970s.

Estimated Value:	**Excellent:**	**$200.00**
	Very good:	**$160.00**

H & R Model 949 Forty-Niner

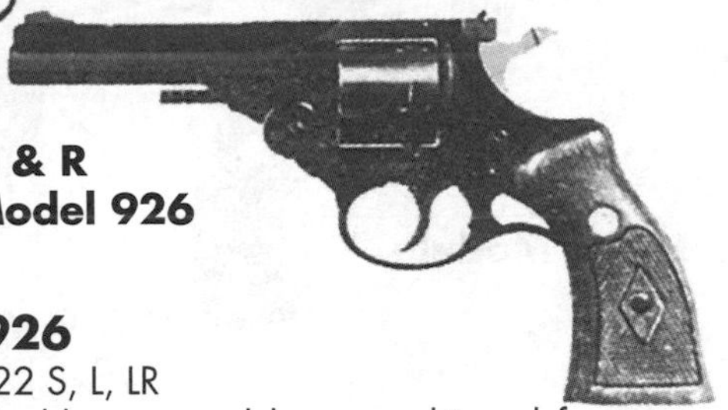

H & R Model 926

H & R Model 926

Caliber: 38 S&W; 22 S, L, LR
Action: Single or double; exposed hammer; hinged frame; top break
Cylinder: 5-shot in 38 cal.; 9-shot in 22 cal.
Barrel: 4"
Sights: Adjustable rear sight
Finish: Blued; checkered plastic square butt grips
Length Overall: 8¼"
Approximate wt.: 31 ozs.
Comments: Made from about 1972 to the late 1970s.

Estimated Value:	**Excellent:**	**$145.00**
	Very good:	**$115.00**

H & R Model 649 Convertible

H & R Model 666 Convertible

H & R Model 666 Convertible

Caliber: 22 short, long, long rifle, 22 magnum (WMR) with extra interchangeable cylinder
Action: Single or double; exposed hammer; solid frame; side load
Cylinder: 6-shot removable; extra interchangeable cylinder so either cartridge can be used
Barrel: 6" round
Sights: Fixed
Finish: Blued; black cycolac, square butt grips
Length Overall: 10¼"
Approximate wt.: 28 ozs.
Comments: Made from about 1975 to the late 1970s.

Estimated Value:	**Excellent:**	**$145.00**
	Very good:	**$115.00**

H & R Model 676 Convertible

Similar to the Model 649 Convertible except: 4½", 5½", 7½", or 12" barrel; blued barrel with antique color case-hardened frame; finger rest at back of trigger guard. Discontinued in the early 1980s. Add 12% for 12" barrel.

Estimated Value:	**Excellent:**	**$150.00**
	Very good:	**$120.00**

H & R Model 686 Convertible

Similar to the Model 676 with ramp front sight, adjustable rear sight. Add $20.00 for 12" barrel.

Estimated Value:	**Excellent:**	**$160.00**
	Very good:	**$125.00**

H & R Models 949 and 950 Forty-Niner

Caliber: 22 short, long, long rifle
Action: Single or double; exposed hammer; solid frame; side load and ejector
Cylinder: 9-shot
Barrel: 5½" or 7½" round
Sights: Blade front; adjustable rear sights
Finish: Blued; smooth walnut, one-piece, western-style grips; case colored frame
Length Overall: 10¼" to 12¼"
Approximate wt.: 36 oz. to 38 ozs.
Comments: Made from about 1959 to 1986. Reintroduced in the 1990s. The Model 950 has nickel finish. Add 10% for nickel finish.

Estimated Value:	**Excellent:**	**$200.00**
	Very good:	**$160.00**

H & R Model 976

Similar to the Model 949 with 7½" barrel, case-hardened frame. Add $20.00 for nickel finish. Discontinued in the early 1980s.

Estimated Value:	**Excellent:**	**$175.00**
	Very good:	**$140.00**

H & R Models 649 and 650 Convertible

Caliber: 22 short, long, long rifle, 22 magnum (WMR) with extra interchangeable cylinder
Action: Single or double; exposed hammer; solid frame; side load and ejector
Cylinder: 6-shot removable cylinder; single manual ejector; extra interchangeable cylinder
Barrel: 5½" or 7½" round barrel; ejector rod housing under barrel
Sights: Blade front; adjustable rear sights
Finish: Blued barrel; satin finish frame; smooth western-style walnut grips
Length Overall: 10¼"
Approximate wt.: 32 ozs.
Comments: Western-style; made from about 1975 to 1986. Model 650 has nickel finish. Add 10% for nickel finish.

Estimated Value:	**Excellent:**	**$150.00**
	Very good:	**$120.00**

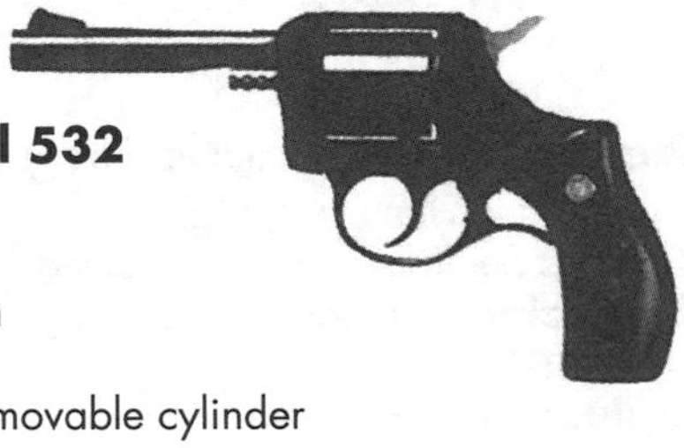

H & R Model 532

H & R Model 532

Caliber: 32 H & R magnum
Action: Single or double
Cylinder: 5-shot pull-pin removable cylinder
Barrel: 2¼", 4" round
Sights: Fixed
Finish: Blued; smooth walnut grips
Length Overall: 6¾" to 8¼"
Approximate wt.: 20 to 25 ozs.
Comments: Introduced in 1984 for the new H & R magnum caliber. Discontinued in 1986.

Estimated Value:	**Excellent:**	**$200.00**
	Very good:	**$160.00**

H & R Model 504

Caliber: 32 H & R magnum
Action: Single or double; swing-out cylinder; exposed hammer
Cylinder: 5-shot swing-out
Barrel: 3", 4", 6" target bull
Sights: Blade front; rear adjustable for windage and elevation
Finish: Blued; smooth walnut grips, round or square butt
Length Overall: 7½" to 10"
Approximate wt.: 29 to 35 ozs.
Comments: Introduced in 1984 for the new H & R magnum caliber. Discontinued in 1986.
Estimated Value: **Excellent:** **$200.00**
Very good: **$160.00**

H & R Model 504

H & R Model 829

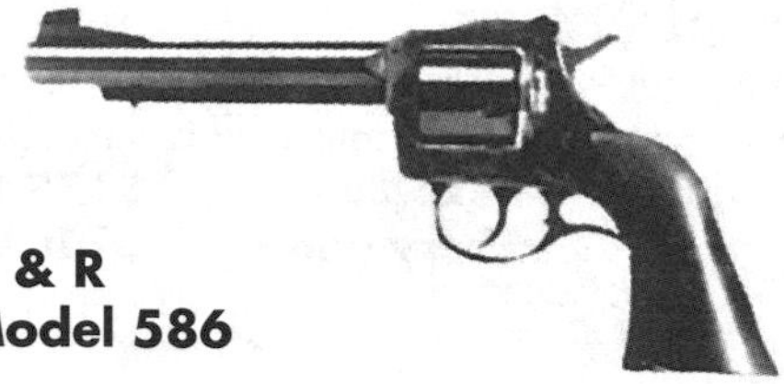

H & R Model 586

H & R Model 586

Caliber: 32 H & R magnum
Action: Single or double; side loading and ejector
Cylinder: 5-shot removable
Barrel: 4½", 5½", 7½", 10" round
Sights: Ramp and blade front, rear adjustable for windage and elevation
Finish: Blued; case-hardened frame; hardwood grips
Length Overall: 10¼" (5½" barrel)
Approximate wt.: 30 to 38 ozs.
Comments: Introduced in 1984 for the new 32 H & R magnum caliber. Discontinued in 1986.
Estimated Value: **Excellent:** **$200.00**
Very good: **$160.00**

H & R Model 829 and 830

Caliber: 22 long rifle
Action: Single or double; exposed hammer
Cylinder: 9-shot swing-out
Barrel: 3" bull barrel
Sights: Ramp front, adjustable rear
Finish: Blued or nickel; smooth walnut grips
Length Overall: 7¼"
Approximate wt.: 27 ozs.
Comments: Produced from 1981 to 1984. Model 830 has nickel finish. Add 10% for nickel finish.
Estimated Value: **Excellent:** **$135.00**
Very good: **$110.00**

H & R Model 826

Similar to the Model 829 in 22 magnum caliber.
Estimated Value: **Excellent:** **$150.00**
Very good: **$120.00**

H & R Model 832 and 833

Similar to the Model 829 in 32 caliber. Made from 1982 to 1984. Model 833 has nickel finish. Add 10% for nickel finish.
Estimated Value: **Excellent:** **$145.00**
Very good: **$115.00**

HARTFORD

Hartford Automatic Target

Caliber: 22 long rifle
Action: Semiautomatic; concealed hammer
Magazine: 10-shot clip
Barrel: 6¾"
Sights: Fixed front; rear sight dovetailed in slide
Finish: Blued; black rubber grips
Length Overall: 10¾"
Approximate wt.: 32 ozs.
Comments: Made from about 1929 to 1930. Similar in appearance to Colt Woodsman and High Standard Model B Automatic Pistol. Rights and properties of Hartford Arms were sold to High Standard Mfg. Co. in 1932.
Estimated Value: **Excellent:** **$600.00**
Very good: **$480.00**

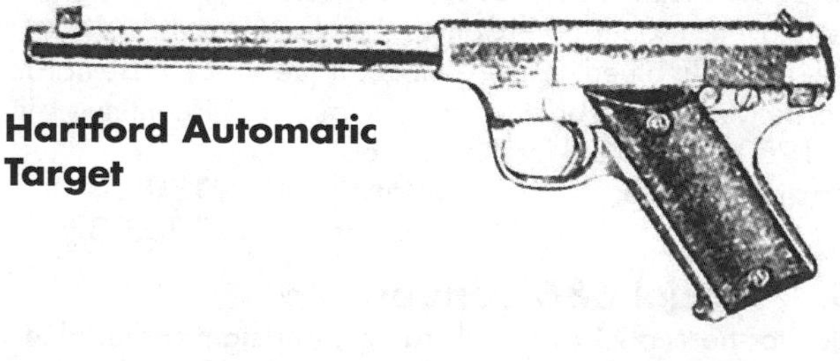

Hartford Automatic Target

Hartford Repeating Pistol

Caliber: 22 long rifle
Action: Manual operation of slide after each shot to eject cartridge and feed another cartridge from magazine to chamber; concealed hammer
Magazine: 10-shot clip
Barrel: 6¾"
Sights: Fixed front; rear sight dovetailed in slide
Finish: Blued; black rubber grips
Length Overall: 10¾"
Approximate wt.: 31 ozs.
Comments: Made from about 1929 to 1930.

Estimated Value:	**Excellent:**	**$525.00**
	Very good:	**$420.00**

Hartford Single-shot

Caliber: 22 long rifle
Action: Single action, hand-operated, concealed hammer, single-shot
Magazine: None
Barrel: 6¾"
Sights: Fixed front; rear sight dovetailed in slide
Finish: Matte finish on slide and frame; blued barrel; black rubber or walnut grips
Length Overall: 10¾"
Approximate wt.: 37 ozs.
Comments: Made from about 1929 to 1930.

Estimated Value:	**Excellent:**	**$550.00**
	Very good:	**$440.00**

Heckler & Koch Model P7 (M-8, M-10, M-13 & K-3)

Caliber: 9mm Parabellum (M-8 and M13); 380 ACP (K-3) added in 1988; 40 S&W (M-10) added in 1991
Action: Recoil-operated semiautomatic; concealed hammer; contains a unique system of cocking by squeezing front of grips, uncocking by releasing; also double action
Magazine: 8-shot clip (M-8 and K-3); 10-shot clip (M-10); 13-shot clip (M-13); 10-shot clip after Sept. 13, 1994
Barrel: 4⅛"
Sights: Fixed
Finish: Blued or nickel; black grips
Length Overall: 6½"
Approximate wt.: 33½ ozs.
Comments: Made in West Germany. Introduced in 1982; add 19% for M-10; add 21% for M-13.

Estimated Value:	**Excellent:**	**$1,115.00**
	Very good:	**$ 895.00**

Heckler & Koch Model P9S

Heckler & Koch Model P9S

Caliber: 9mm Parabellum; 45 ACP
Action: Semiautomatic; concealed hammer; cocking lever
Magazine: 9-shot clip (9mm); 7-shot clip in 45 ACP
Barrel: 4"
Sights: Fixed; blade front, square notch rear
Finish: Blued; black plastic grips; wood combat grips available
Length Overall: 7½"
Approximate wt.: 28 to 31 ozs.
Comments: Made in West Germany. Discontinued in 1989.

Estimated Value:	**Excellent:**	**$650.00**
	Very good:	**$520.00**

Heckler & Koch Model P9S Competition

Similar to the Model P9S Target with both 4" and 5½" barrels, 2 slides, wood competition grips, and plastic grips, all packed in a special case. 9mm only.

Estimated Value:	**Excellent:**	**$950.00**
	Very good:	**$760.00**

Heckler & Koch Model P9S Target

Similar to the Model P9S with adjustable trigger, trigger stop, and adjustable rear sight; 5½" barrel available.

Estimated Value:	**Excellent:**	**$800.00**
	Very good:	**$640.00**

Heckler & Koch Model HK4

Heckler & Koch Model HK4

Caliber: 380; Conversion kits available for calibers 38, 25, and 22 long rifle
Action: Semiautomatic; double action; exposed hammer spur
Magazine: 7-shot clip
Barrel: 3⅜"
Sights: Fixed; blade front, notch rear; nonreflective
Finish: Blued; black plactic grips; grip extension on clip
Length Overall: 6"
Approximate wt.: 17 ozs.
Comments: Discontinued in the mid-1980s. Add 100% for all three conversion kits.

Estimated Value:	**Excellent:**	**$400.00**
	Very good:	**$320.00**

Heckler & Koch Model VP70Z

Caliber: 9mm
Action: Semiautomatic; blowback, recoil-operated; double action only; hammerless
Magazine: Double stacked 18-shot clip
Barrel: 4½"
Sights: Fixed; ramp front, notched rear
Finish: Blued; black plastic grips; solid plastic receiver
Length Overall: 8"
Approximate wt.: 29 ozs.
Comments: A pistol with few moving parts, designed for the outdoorsman. Discontinued in the mid-1980s.

Estimated Value:	**Excellent:**	**$450.00**
	Very good:	**$360.00**

Heckler & Koch Model USP 9, USP 40 and USP 45

Caliber: 9mm (USP 9), 40 S&W (USP 40); 45 ACP (USP 45)
Action: Semiautomatic; double action and single action or double action only; manual safety, decocking lever, or no decocking lever; about 10 variations of actions to select from; exposed or bobbed hammer
Magazine: 13-shot clip (USP 40); 15-shot clip (USP 9); 10-shot clip after Sept. 13, 1994
Barrel: 4⅛" steel barrel; 6"
Sights: Fixed three-dot sight system; tritium sights optional
Finish: One-piece milled steel slide; "HE" finish to resist corrosion; metal reinforced polymer frame and integral non-slip grip with stippling and cross-hatched grooves; stainless steel available in 1996
Length Overall: 7¾"
Approximate wt.: 26 to 28 ozs.
Comments: Introduced in 1993. Add 10% for stainless steel; add 10% for cal. 45 ACP.

Estimated Value:	**New (retail):**	**$859.00**
	Excellent:	**$645.00**
	Very good:	**$515.00**

Heckler & Koch Mark 23

Heckler & Koch Mark 23

Caliber: 45 ACP
Action: Short recoil, single or double action semiautomatic
Magazine: 10-shot clip
Barrel: 5¾"
Sights: Blade front, adjustable rear; three-dot system
Finish: Blued, synthetic grips
Length overall: 10"
Approximate wt.: 41 ozs.
Comments: Introduced in 2001.

Estimated Value:	**New (retail):**	**$2,500.00**
	Excellent:	**$1,875.00**
	Very good:	**$1,500.00**

Heckler & Koch USP Compact

Similar to the USP except: 3½" or 3¾" barrel; smaller, compact size. Add 11% for stainless steel, 5% for 45 ACP caliber.

Estimated Value:	**New (retail):**	**$859.00**
	Excellent:	**$645.00**
	Very good:	**$515.00**

HIGH STANDARD

High Standard Model B

Caliber: 22 long rifle
Action: Semiautomatic; concealed hammer; thumb safety
Magazine: 10-shot clip
Barrel: 4½" or 6¾"
Sights: Fixed
Finish: Blued; hard rubber grips
Length Overall: 8½" and 10¾"
Approximate wt.: 30 to 34 ozs.
Comments: Produced from about 1931 to 1942.

Estimated Value:	**Excellent:**	**$550.00**
	Very good:	**$440.00**

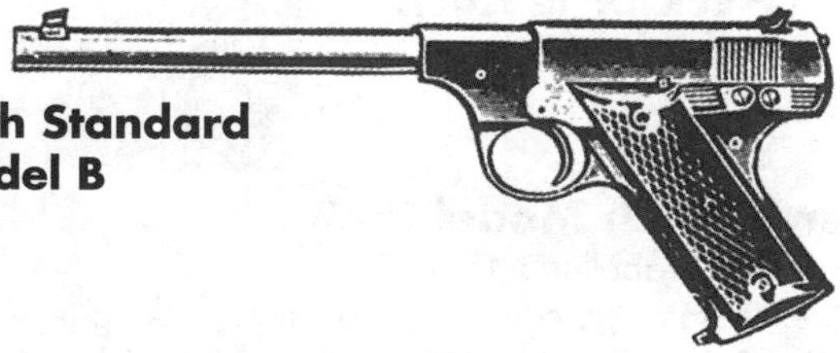

High Standard Model B

High Standard Model HB

Same as Model B except exposed hammer and no thumb safety. Made from about 1932 to 1942. Produced after World War II with a safety. Add 20% for pre-war model.

Estimated Value:	**Excellent:**	**$650.00**
	Very good:	**$520.00**

High Standard Model A

Caliber: 22 long rifle
Action: Semiautomatic; concealed hammer; thumb safety
Magazine: 10-shot clip
Barrel: 4½" or 6¾"
Sights: Adjustable target sights
Finish: Blued; checkered walnut grips
Length Overall: 9¼" and 11¼"
Approximate wt.: 34 to 36 ozs.
Comments: Made from about 1937 to 1942.

Estimated Value:	**Excellent:**	**$875.00**
	Very good:	**$700.00**

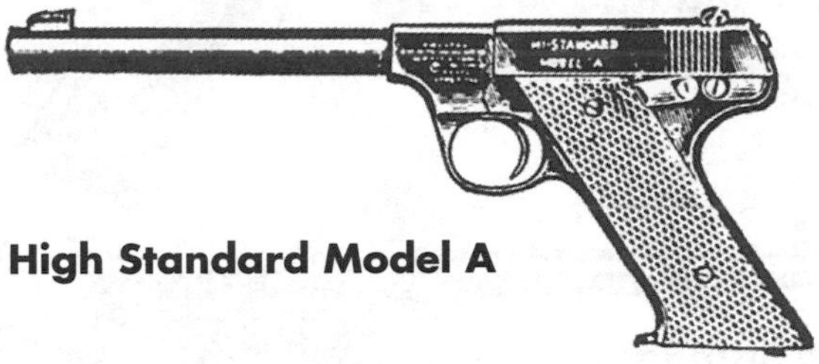

High Standard Model A

High Standard Model SB

Same as the Model B except 6¾" smooth bore for shooting 22 long rifle shot cartridges. Produced in 1939 in very limited quantities.

Estimated Value:	**Excellent:**	**$3,000.00**
	Very good:	**$2,400.00**

High Standard Model C

Same as the Model B except chambered for 22-short cartridges. Made from about 1932 to 1942.

Estimated Value:	**Excellent:**	**$800.00**
	Very good:	**$640.00**

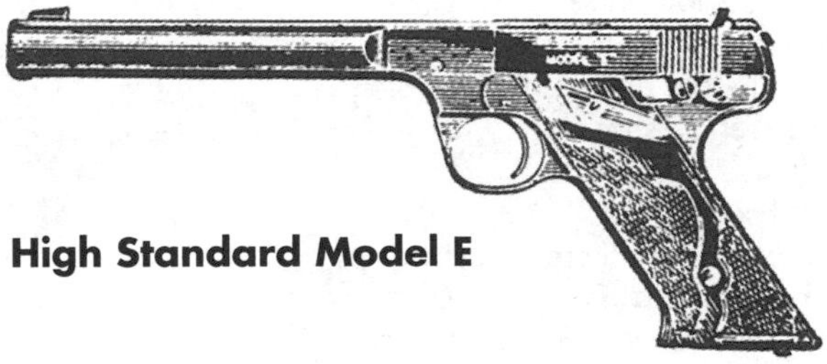

High Standard Model E

High Standard Model HA

Same as the Model A except exposed hammer spur and no thumb safety.

Estimated Value:	**Excellent:**	**$1,300.00**
	Very good:	**$1,040.00**

High Standard Model D

Same as the Model A except heavier barrel; approximate wt.: 37 to 40 ozs., depending on barrel length.

Estimated Value:	**Excellent:**	**$800.00**
	Very good:	**$640.00**

High Standard Model HD

High Standard Model HD

Same as the Model D except exposed hammer spur and no thumb safety.

Estimated Value:	**Excellent:**	**$1,300.00**
	Very good:	**$1,040.00**

High Standard Model HDM or HD Military

Same as the Model HD except it has thumb safety. Made from about 1941 to 1947, stamped "U.S. Property."

Estimated Value:	**Excellent:**	**$750.00**
	Very good:	**$600.00**

High Standard Model HD Military (Postwar)

Same as the Model HDM except it is not stamped "U.S. Property." Made from about 1946 to 1951 (post-World War II model).

Estimated Value:	**Excellent:**	**$600.00**
	Very good:	**$480.00**

High Standard Model E

Similar to the Model A except extra heavy barrel; thumbrest grips. Approximate wt.: 39 to 42 ozs.

Estimated Value:	**Excellent:**	**$1,300.00**
	Very good:	**$1,040.00**

High Standard Model HE

Same as the Model E except exposed hammer spur and no thumb safety.

Estimated Value:	**Excellent:**	**$1,700.00**
	Very good:	**$1,360.00**

High Standard Model G-B

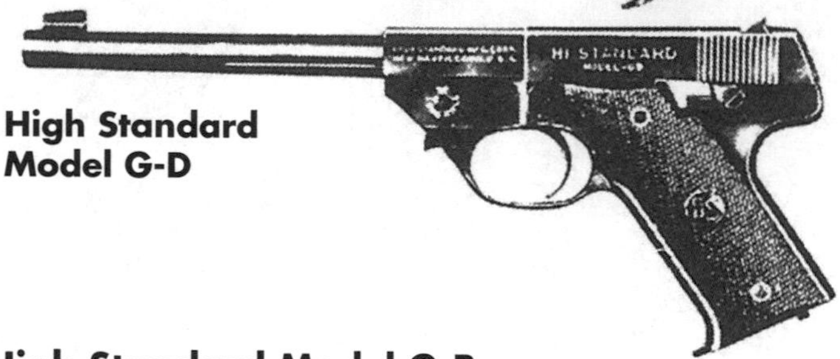

High Standard Model G-D

High Standard Model G-B

Caliber: 22 long rifle
Action: Semiautomatic; concealed hammer; takedown model; interchangeable barrels; thumb safety
Magazine: 10-shot clip
Barrel: 4½" or 6¾"
Sights: Fixed
Finish: Blued; checkered plastic grips
Length Overall: 8½" and 10¾"
Approximate wt.: 34 to 36 ozs.
Comments: Made from about 1948 to 1951. Add 25% if pistol has both barrels.

Estimated Value:	**Excellent:**	**$525.00**
	Very good:	**$425.00**

High Standard Model G-D

Same as the Model G-B except: adjustable target sights; checkered walnut grips; approximate wt.: 38 to 40 ozs.; length overall about 9¼" to 11½". Add 25% if pistol has both barrels.

Estimated Value:	**Excellent:**	**$850.00**
	Very good:	**$680.00**

High Standard Model G-E

Same as the Model G-D except: heavy barrel; thumbrest; walnut grips; approximate wt.: 42 to 44 ozs. Add 25% if pistol has both barrels. Made from the late 1940s to the early 1950s.

Estimated Value:	**Excellent:**	**$1,100.00**
	Very good:	**$ 880.00**

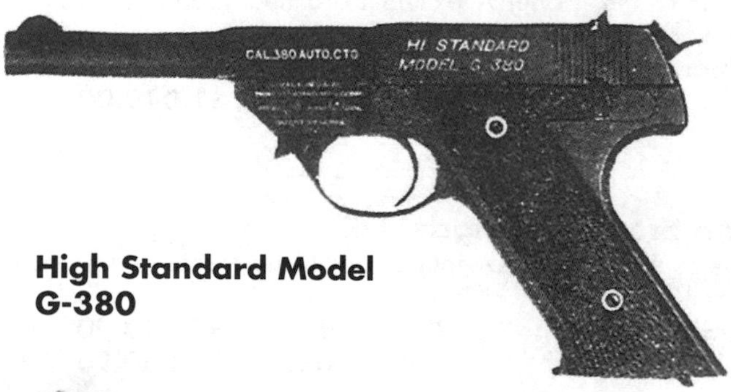

High Standard Model G-380

High Standard Olympic 1st Model

Same as the Model G-E except 22 short caliber; light alloy slide; made from about 1950 to 1951; approximate wt.: 38 to 40 ozs. Add 20% if pistol has both barrels.

Estimated Value:	**Excellent:**	**$1,300.00**
	Very good:	**$1,050.00**

High Standard Olympic 2nd Model

Same as Olympic 1st Model except: thumb safety located at center top of left grip; plastic grips with thumbrest; produced from about 1951 to 1958. Add 20% if pistol has both barrels.

Estimated Value:	**Excellent:**	**$1,000.00**
	Very good:	**$ 800.00**

High Standard Olympic 1st Model

High Standard Olympic 2nd Model

High Standard Model G-380

Caliber: 380 ACP
Action: Semiautomatic; exposed hammer spur; thumb safety; barrel takedown model
Magazine: 6-shot clip; bottom release
Barrel: 5"
Sights: Fixed; blade front and notched rear
Finish: Blued; checkered plastic grips
Length Overall: 9"
Approximate wt.: 40 ozs.
Comments: First of the barrel takedown models produced by High Standard. Made from about 1944 to 1950.

Estimated Value:	**Excellent:**	**$700.00**
	Very good:	**$560.00**

High Standard Olympic ISU

High Standard Olympic ISU
Caliber: 22 short
Action: Semiautomatic; concealed hammer; wide target trigger; anti-backlash trigger adjustment
Magazine: 10-shot clip
Barrel: 5½" bull barrel (1963 to 1966); 8" tapered barrel (1958 to 1964); 6¾" tapered barrel (1958 to the present); integral stabilizer and 2 removable weights
Sights: Ramp front; adjustable rear
Finish: Blued; checkered walnut grips with thumbrests
Length Overall: 11¼" (6¾" barrel)
Approximate wt.: 40 to 41 ozs.
Comments: Meets International Shooting Union regulations; left- or right-handed grips; regular High Standard-style grip or the squared military-style grip; military style has rear sight frame mounted. Made from about 1958 to the late 1970s.

Estimated Value:	**Excellent:**	**$1,175.00**
	Very good:	**$ 940.00**

High Standard Olympic Military
Caliber: 22 short
Action: Semiautomatic; concealed hammer
Magazine: 5-shot clip
Barrel: 5½" bull barrel
Sights: Adjustable rear, ramp front; drilled and tapped for scope mount
Finish: Blued aluminum alloy slide and carbon steel frame
Length Overall: 11½"
Approximate wt.: 44 ozs.
Comments: Reintroduced in the 1990s. Add 10% for sights.

Estimated Value:	**Excellent:**	**$800.00**
	Very good:	**$640.00**

High Standard Olympic RF (Rapid Fire)
Similar to the Olympic Military except: matte finish; 4" barrel; integral muzzle brake and forward mounted compensator; ventilated rib; adjustable trigger; special international grips; introduced in 1996.

Estimated Value:	**Excellent:**	**$1,750.00**
	Very good:	**$1,400.00**

High Standard Sport-King 1st Model
Caliber: 22 long rifle
Action: Semiautomatic; concealed hammer; takedown model with interchangeable barrel; thumb safety at top center of left grip
Magazine: 10-shot clip
Barrel: 4½" and/or 6¾"
Sights: Fixed
Finish: Blued; checkered plastic grips with thumbrest
Length Overall: 9", 11¼"
Approximate wt.: 36 to 39 ozs.
Comments: Made from about 1951 to 1958. Add 25% for pistol with both barrels.

Estimated Value:	**Excellent:**	**$425.00**
	Very good:	**$340.00**

High Standard Sport-King 2nd Model
Similar to Sport-King 1st Model except: made from about 1958 to 1965; interior changes; interchangeable barrels; blue or nickel finish; weighs 39 to 42 ozs. Add $15.00 for nickel finish. Reintroduced in the early 1980s to 1985 and again in the 1990s. Slightly different grip style. Add 25% for both barrels.

Estimated Value:	**Excellent**	**$450.00**
	Very good:	**$360.00**

High Standard Lightweight Sport-King
Same as Sport-King 1st Model except: made from about 1954 to 1965; aluminum alloy frame; weighs 28 to 30 ozs. Add 25% for pistol with both barrels.

Estimated Value:	**Excellent:**	**$425.00**
	Very good:	**$340.00**

High Standard Flite-King 1st Model
Same as Sport-King 1st Model except: made from about 1953 to 1958; aluminum alloy frame and slide; weighs 24 to 26 ozs.; 22 short caliber only. Add 25% for pistol with both barrels.

Estimated Value:	**Excellent:**	**$500.00**
	Very good:	**$400.00**

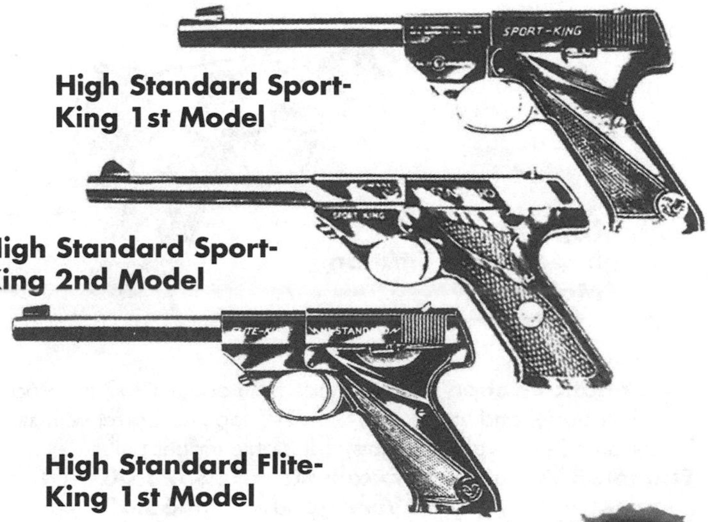

High Standard Sport-King 1st Model

High Standard Sport-King 2nd Model

High Standard Flite-King 1st Model

High Standard Flite-King 2nd Model

Same as Sport-King 1st Model Automatic except: made from about 1958 to 1965; all steel construction; 22 short caliber only. Add 25% for pistol with both barrels.

Estimated Value: **Excellent:** **$500.00**
Very good: **$400.00**

High Standard Field-King

High Standard Field-King

Same as Sport-King 1st Model except: adjustable target sights; 6¾" heavy barrel; weighs about 44 ozs.

Estimated Value: **Excellent:** **$525.00**
Very good: **$420.00**

High Standard Supermatic Standard Citation and Military Citation Model

High Standard Supermatic Series

Caliber: 22 long rifle
Action: Semiautomatic; concealed hammer; thumb safety; take-down model with interchangeable barrels
Magazine: 10-shot clip
Barrel: 4½", 5½", 6¾" 7¼", 8", 10"
Sights: Ramp front, adjustable rear
Finish: Blued; checkered plastic or checkered wood grips with or without thumb rest
Length Overall: 9¼" to 14¾"
Approximate wt.: 40 to 46 ozs.
Comments: The 5¼" barrels are heavy (bull) barrels and the 7¼" barrels are heavy (bull) fluted barrels.

Standard Supermatic Model manufactured from about 1951 to 1958; 4¼" and 6¾" interchangeable barrels. Add 25% for pistols with both barrels.

Estimated Value: **Excellent:** **$600.00**
Very good: **$480.00**

Supermatic Tournament Model made from about 1958 to 1963; 5½" bull barrel and/or 6¾" regular barrel with stabilizer and 2 removable weights; adjustable trigger pull. Add 20% for pistol with both barrels. Reintroduced in the 1990s.

Estimated Value: **Excellent:** **$600.00**
Very good: **$480.00**

High Standard Supermatic Citation Model

Supermatic Citation Model made from about 1959 to 1966; 5½" bull barrel and/or 6¾", 8", or 10" tapered barrel with stabilizer and 2 removable weights; adjustable trigger pull.

Estimated Value: **Excellent:** **$575.00**
Very good: **$460.00**

Supermatic Citation, Military or Citation II made from about 1965 to 1985; 5½" heavy (bull) or 7¼" heavy fluted barrel with military grip or standard grip. 5½" or 7¼" slabbed barrel in 1984 (Citation II). Dropped in 1984; reintroduced in 1990s with 5½" barrel.

Estimated Value:: **Excellent:** **$525.00**
Very good: **$420.00**

High Standard Citation MS (Metallic Silhouette)

Same as the Supermatic Citation except: 10" barrel; matte blue finish; RPM sights; approximate wt.: 49 ozs.; length overall: 14"; introduced in 1996.

Estimated Value: **Excellent:** **$625.00**
Very good: **$500.00**

Supermatic Trophy Citation made from about 1959 to 1966; 5½" bull barrel or 7¼" heavy fluted barrel.

Estimated Value: **Excellent:** **$650.00**
Very good: **$520.00**

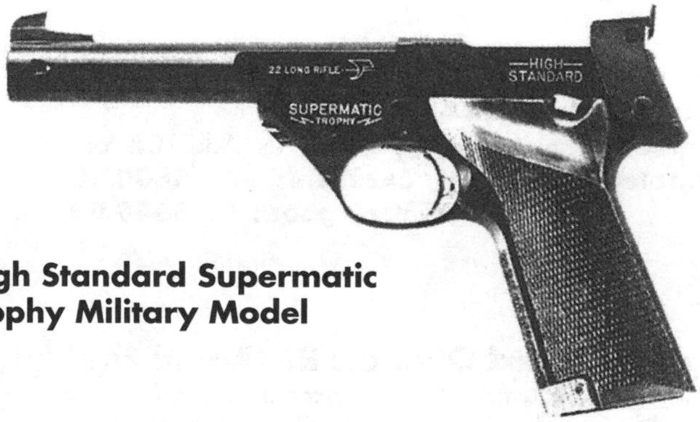

High Standard Supermatic Trophy Military Model

Supermatic Trophy Military Model manufactured from about 1965 to 1985; 5½" bull barrel or 7¼" fluted barrel with square military-style grip; adjustable trigger pull. Add 20% for both barrels.

Estimated Value: **Excellent:** **$800.00**
Very good: **$640.00**

High Standard Dura-Matic

Caliber: 22 long rifle
Action: Semiautomatic; concealed hammer; takedown interchangeable barrels model
Magazine: 10-shot clip
Barrel: 4½", 6½"
Sights: Fixed
Finish: Blued; checkered plastic grips
Length Overall: 8⅞", 10⅞"
Approximate wt.: 33 to 35 ozs.
Comments: Manufactured from about 1954 to 1969.

Estimated Value:	**Excellent:**	**$325.00**
	Very good:	**$260.00**

High Standard Dura-Matic

High Standard Plinker

Caliber: 22 long rifle
Action: Semiautomatic; concealed hammer
Magazine: 10-shot clip
Barrel: 4½", 6½"
Sights: Fixed
Finish: Blued; checkered plastic grips
Length Overall: 9" to 11"
Approximate wt.: 28 to 30 ozs.
Comments: Made from about 1971 to 1974.

Estimated Value:	**Excellent:**	**$300.00**
	Very good:	**$240.00**

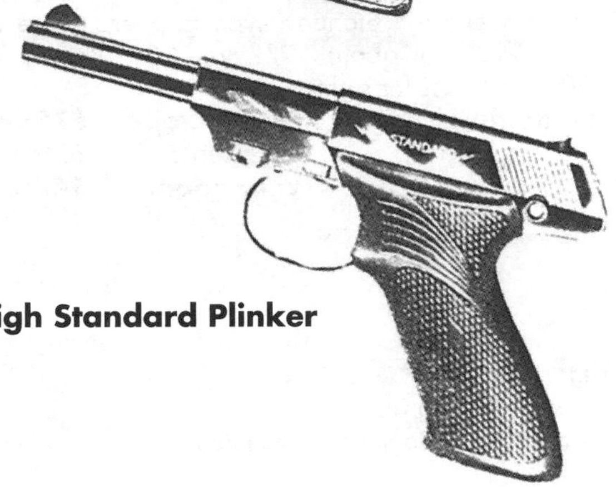

High Standard Plinker

High Standard Trophy

High Standard Supermatic Trophy

Caliber: 22 long rifle
Action: Semiautomatic; concealed hammer; adjustable trigger pull
Magazine: 10-shot clip
Barrel: 5½" or 7¼"; bull or fluted barrel
Sights: Adjustable; drilled and tapped for scope mount
Finish: Blued; checkered wood grips
Length Overall: 9½" or 11¼"
Approximate wt.: 44 ozs.
Comments: Reintroduced in the 1990s; add 10% for 7¼" barrel or sights.

Estimated Value:	**New (retail):**	**$785.00**
	Excellent:	**$590.00**
	Very good:	**$470.00**

High Standard Sharpshooter and Survival Pack

Caliber: 22 long rifle
Action: Semiautomatic; concealed hammer
Magazine: 10-shot clip
Barrel: 5½" bull barrel
Sights: Ramp front; adjustable rear
Finish: Blued; checkered walnut grips; nickel available after 1982
Length Overall: 10¼"
Approximate wt.: 42 ozs.
Comments: Made from about 1971 to 1985. A survival pack consisting of a nickel pistol; extra magazine and canvas case after 1982. Add 25% for complete pack.

Estimated Value:	**Excellent:**	**$525.00**
	Very good:	**$420.00**

High Standard Sharpshooter

High Standard Victor

Caliber: 22 long rifle
Action: Semiautomatic; concealed hammer; interchangeable barrel
Magazine: 10-shot clip
Barrel: 4½" or 5½" with solid or aluminum ventilated rib and barrel weights
Sights: Ramp front; adjustable rear; drilled and tapped for scope
Finish: Blued; checkered walnut grips with thumbrest; later models have some gold-plated parts
Length Overall: 8¾", 9¾"
Approximate wt.: 38 to 42 ozs.
Comments: High Standard-type grip or square military-type grip. Made from about 1972 to 1985. Reintroduced in the 1990s. Add 10% for sights.

Estimated Value:	**New (retail):**	**$785.00**
	Excellent:	**$590.00**
	Very good:	**$470.00**

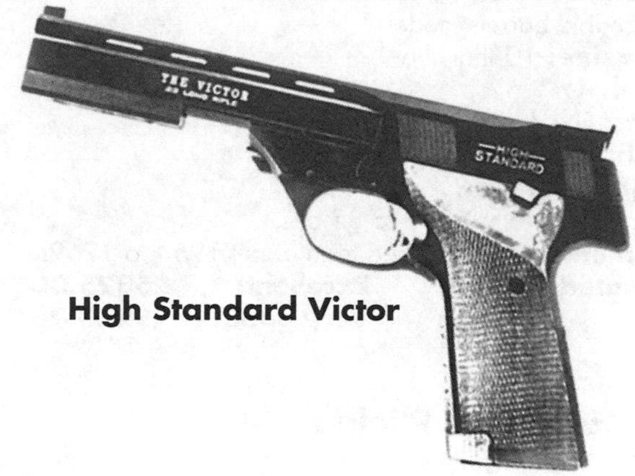

High Standard Victor

High Standard 10-X

Caliber: 22 long rifle
Action: Semiautomatic; concealed hammer; adjustable target trigger
Magazine: 10-shot clip; 2 extra (standard)
Barrel: 5½" bull barrel
Sights: Blade front, adjustable rear mounted independent of slide
Finish: Nonreflective blue; checkered walnut military grip; components hand-picked and fitted by gunsmith; gunsmith's initials located under left grip
Length Overall: 10¼"
Approximate wt.: 42 ozs.
Comments: A custom competition gun, introduced in the 1980s.

Estimated Value:	**Excellent:**	**$1,750.00**
	Very good:	**$1,400.00**

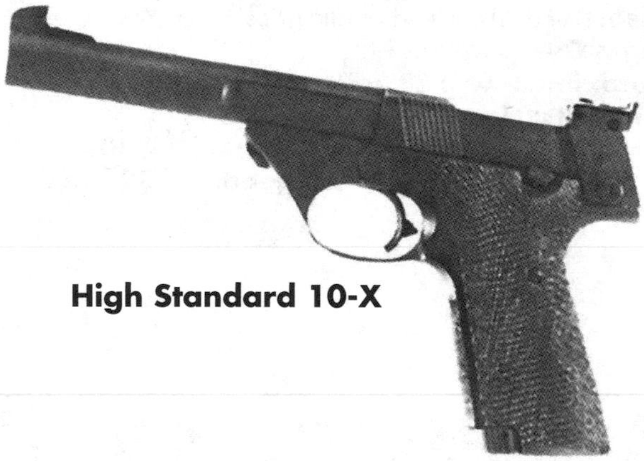
High Standard 10-X

High Standard Model 1911 GI

Caliber: 45 ACP
Action: Single action, semiautomatic; exposed hammer
Magazine: 7-shot clip
Barrel: 5"
Sights: Fixed
Finish: Parkerized with checkered walnut grips
Length overall: 8½"
Approximate wt.: 39 ozs.
Comments: Similar to the Colt 1911A1. Introduced in 2001.

Estimated Value:	**Excellent:**	**$450.00**
	Very good:	**$360.00**

High Standard Model 1911 Crusader

Similar to the Model 1911 GI except: available in 45 ACP or 38 Super calibers; blued, stainless steel, or "TuTone" finish. Add 6% for 38 Super (9 shot clip). Add 2% for "TuTone" finish; 3% for stainless steel.

Estimated Value:	**Excellent:**	**$500.00**
	Very good:	**$400.00**

High Standard Model 1911 Crusader Combat

Similar to the Model 1911 Crusader except: 4¼" barrel. Add 2% for "TuTone" finish, 3% for stainless steel.

Estimated Value: **Excellent:** **$500.00**
Very good: **$400.00**

High Standard Model 1911 G-Man

Similar to the Model 1911 Crusader except: Teflon finish; 8-shot clip.

Estimated Value: **Excellent:** **$950.00**
Very good: **$760.00**

High Standard Sentinel

Caliber: 22 short, long, long rifle
Action: Single or double; solid frame
Cylinder: 9-shot swing-out; simultaneous manual ejector
Barrel: 3", 4", 6"
Sights: Fixed
Finish: Blued or nickel; checkered plastic grips
Length Overall: 8" to 11"
Approximate wt.: 18 to 24 ozs.
Comments: Made from about 1954 to 1974; aluminum alloy frame.

Estimated Value: **Excellent:** **$200.00**
Very good: **$160.00**

High Standard Sentinel Deluxe

Same as Sentinel Revolver except adjustable rear sight; checkered square butt walnut grips; wide trigger; 4" or 6" only; made from about 1965 to 1974.

Estimated Value: **Excellent:** **$250.00**
Very good: **$200.00**

High Standard Sentinel Imperial

Same as Sentinel revolver except ramp front sight; black or nickel finish; checkered square butt walnut grips. Made from about 1961 to 1965.

Estimated Value: **Excellent:** **$250.00**
Very good: **$200.00**

High Standard Model 1911 Supermatic Trophy Match

Similar to the Model 1911 GI except: stainless steel finish; 5" or 6" barrel; adjustable sights.

Estimated Value: **Excellent:** **$900.00**
Very good: **$725.00**

High Standard Model 1911 Camp Perry Model

Similar to the Model 1911 Supermatic Trophy Match except: 5" barrel only; blued finish.

Estimated Value: **Excellent:** **$620.00**
Very good: **$500.00**

High Standard Sentinel

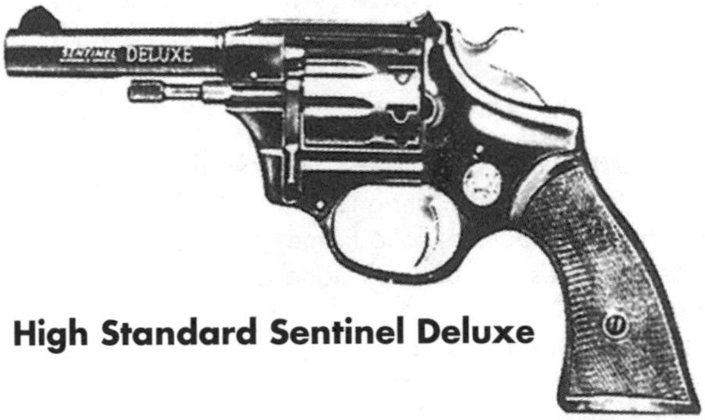

High Standard Sentinel Deluxe

High Standard Sentinel Imperial

High Standard Sentinel Snub

Same as Sentinel revolver except 2$\frac{3}{8}$" barrel only; overall length 7$\frac{1}{2}$"; weighs 15 ozs.; checkered plastic bird's head grip (round butt). Made from about 1956 to 1974. Some were made in pink, turquoise, and gold colored finish as well as blue and nickel.

Estimated Value: **Excellent:** **$275.00**
Very good: **$220.00**

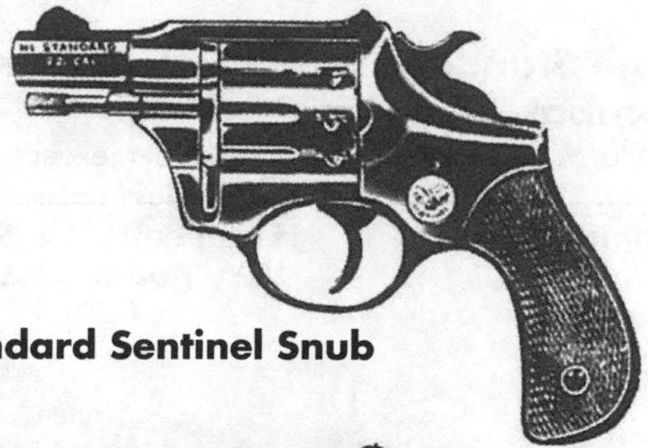

High Standard Sentinel Snub

High Standard Sentinel Mark I

Caliber: 22 short, long, long rifle
Action: Single or double; solid frame
Cylinder: 9-shot swing-out; simultaneous manual ejector
Barrel: 2", 4"
Sights: Ramp front; fixed or adjustable rear
Finish: Blued or nickel; smooth walnut grips
Length Overall: 7", 9"
Approximate wt.: 28 to 30 ozs.
Comments: A completely redesigned and improved all-steel version of the 22 caliber Sentinel. Made from about 1974 to the late 1970s. Add $10.00 for nickel finish; add $10.00 for adjustable rear sight.

Estimated Value: **Excellent:** **$230.00**
Very good: **$185.00**

High Standard Sentinel Mark IV

High Standard Sentinel Mark IV

Same as Sentinel Mark I except 22 magnum only. Add $10.00 for nickel finish or adjustable rear sight.

Estimated Value: **Excellent:** **$225.00**
Very good: **$180.00**

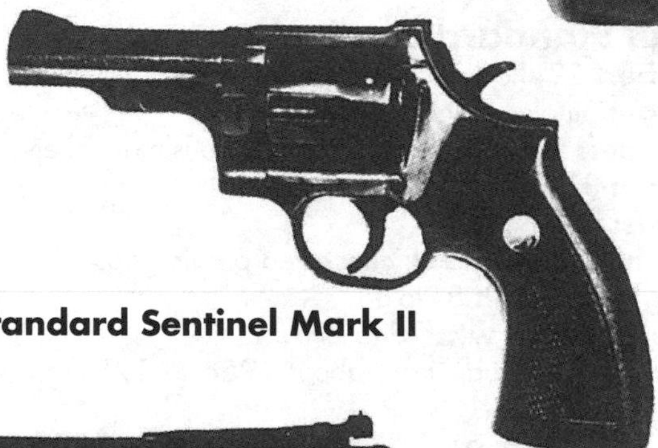

High Standard Sentinel Mark II

High Standard Sentinel Mark II

Caliber: 38 Special, 357 magnum
Action: Single or double; solid frame
Cylinder: 6-shot swing-out; simultaneous manual ejector
Barrel: 2$\frac{1}{2}$", 4", 6"
Sights: Fixed rear; ramp front
Finish: Blued; checkered walnut grips
Length Overall: 7$\frac{1}{2}$" to 11"
Approximate wt.: 38 to 40 ozs.
Comments: Heavy duty all-steel revolver. Made from about 1974 to the late 1970s.

Estimated Value: **Excellent:** **$300.00**
Very good: **$240.00**

High Standard Sentinel Mark III

High Standard Sentinel Mark III

Same as Sentinel Mark II except deluxe trophy blue finish; checkered walnut wrap-around grips; checkered back strap; adjustable rear sight.

Estimated Value: **Excellent:** **$335.00**
Very good: **$265.00**

High Standard Sentinel New Model

High Standard Sentinel New Model

Similar to the Sentinel with 22 caliber cylinder and interchangeable 22 magnum cylinder. Available with 2" or 4" barrel. Reintroduced in 1982 to 1985. Add $20.00 for extra cylinder.

Estimated Value: **Excellent:** **$225.00**
Very good: **$180.00**

High Standard Longhorn
Caliber: 22 short, long, long rifle
Action: Single or double; solid frame
Cylinder: 9-shot swing-out; simultaneous manual ejector
Barrel: 4½" or 5½" (1961 to 1966); 9½" (1971 to present); dummy ejector housing under barrel
Sights: Blade front; fixed or adjustable rear
Finish: Blued; plastic grips; walnut grips on 9½" barrel model
Length Overall: 10", 11", 15"
Approximate wt.: 26 to 32 ozs.
Comments: Aluminum alloy frame (about 1961 to 1971). Steel frame (about 1971 to 1985).

Estimated Value:	**Excellent:**	**$325.00**
	Very good:	**$260.00**

High Standard Longhorn Combination
Similar to Longhorn revolver except extra interchangeable cylinder in 22 magnum caliber; 9½" barrel only; smooth walnut grips. Made from about 1971 to 1985.

Estimated Value:	**Excellent:**	**$350.00**
	Very good:	**$280.00**

High Standard Kit Gun
Caliber: 22 short, long, long rifle
Action: Single or double; solid frame
Cylinder: 9-shot swing-out; simultaneous manual ejector
Barrel: 4"
Sights: Ramp front; adjustable rear
Finish: Blued; checkered walnut grips
Length Overall: 9"
Approximate wt.: 19 ozs.
Comments: Aluminum alloy frame. Made from about 1970 to 1973.

Estimated Value:	**Excellent:**	**$250.00**
	Very good:	**$200.00**

High Standard Double Nine
Caliber: 22 short, long, long rifle
Action: Single or double; solid frame
Cylinder: 9-shot swing-out; simultaneous manual ejector
Barrel: 5½"; dummy ejector housing under barrel
Sights: Blade front; fixed or adjustable rear
Finish: Blued or nickel; plastic grips
Length Overall: 11"
Approximate wt.: 28 ozs.
Comments: Aluminum alloy frame (about 1958 to 1971); a western style of the Sentinel revolvers. Steel frame from about 1971 to 1985. Add $10.00 for nickel finish.

Estimated Value:	**Excellent:**	**$300.00**
	Very good:	**$240.00**

High Standard Double Nine Combination
Same as Double Nine revolver except: extra interchangeable cylinder in 22 magnum caliber; smooth walnut grip; made from about 1971 to 1985; steel frame; weighs 32 ozs. Add $10.00 for nickel finish.

Estimated Value:	**Excellent:**	**$325.00**
	Very good:	**$260.00**

High Standard Natchez
Similar to Double Nine revolver except 4½" barrel only; 10" overall length; weighs 32 ozs.; blued finish only; plastic ivory bird's head grips. Made from about 1961 to 1966.

Estimated Value:	**Excellent:**	**$375.00**
	Very good:	**$300.00**

High Standard Posse
Similar to Double Nine revolver except 3½" barrel without dummy ejector housing; 9" overall length; weighs 24 ozs.; brass trigger guard and grip frame; blued finish only; smooth walnut grips. Made from about 1961 to 1966.

Estimated Value:	**Excellent:**	**$275.00**
	Very good:	**$220.00**

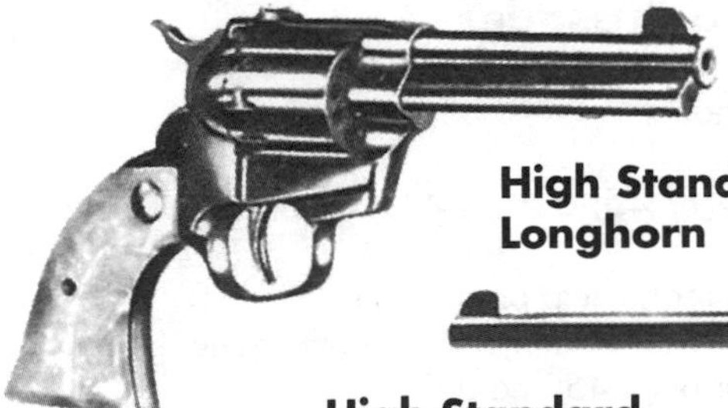
High Standard Longhorn

High Standard Longhorn Combination

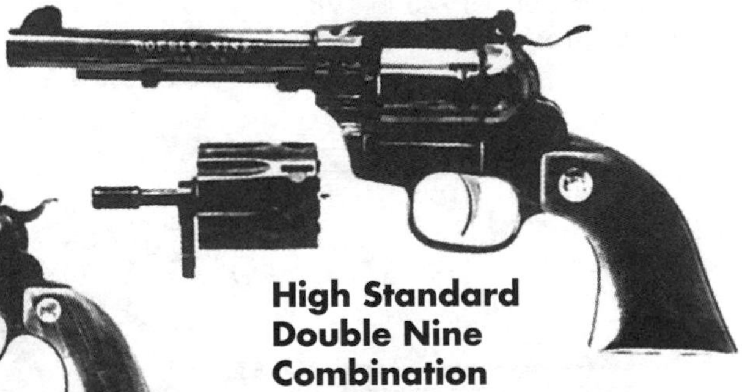
High Standard Double Nine Combination

High Standard Double Nine

High Standard Posse

High Standard Natchez

High Standard Hombre

Caliber: 22 short, long, long rifle
Action: Single or double; solid frame
Cylinder: 9-shot swing-out; simultaneous ejector
Barrel: 4½"
Sights: Blade front; adjustable rear
Finish: Blued or nickel; smooth walnut grip
Length Overall: 10"
Approximate wt.: 26 ozs.
Comments: Steel frame; manufactured from about 1972 to 1974. Add $10.00 for nickel finish.

Estimated Value:	**Excellent:**	**$300.00**
	Very good:	**$240.00**

High Standard Durango

Caliber: 22 short, long, long rifle
Action: Single or double; solid frame
Cylinder: 9-shot swing-out; simultaneous ejector
Barrel: 4½", 5½"; dummy ejector housing under barrel
Sights: Blade front; adjustable rear
Finish: Blued or nickel; smooth walnut grip
Length Overall: 10", 11"
Approximate wt.: 25 to 27 ozs.
Comments: Made from about 1972 to 1975.

Estimated Value:	**Excellent:**	**$275.00**
	Very good:	**$220.00**

High Standard High Sierra Combination

Caliber: 22 short, long, long rifle and 22 magnum
Action: Single or double; solid frame
Cylinder: 9-shot swing-out; two interchangeable cylinders (22 cal. and 22 mag. cal.)
Barrel: 7" octagonal
Sights: Blade front; adjustable rear
Finish: Blued; smooth walnut grip
Length Overall: 12½"
Comments: Steel frame; gold-plated trigger guard and backstrap. Made from about 1973 to 1985.

Estimated Value:	**Excellent:**	**$350.00**
	Very good:	**$280.00**

High Standard Camp Gun

High Standard Crusader

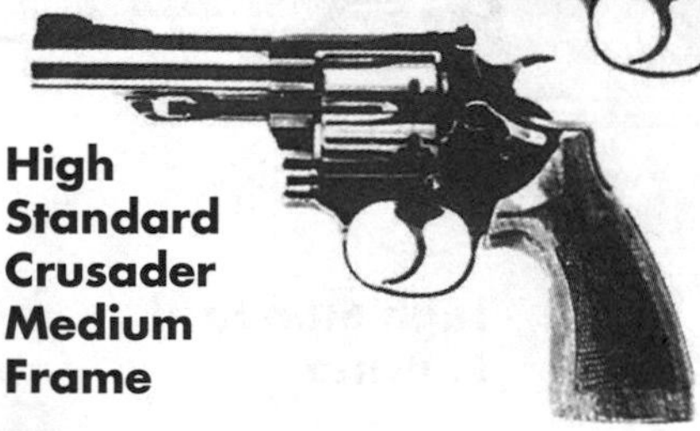

High Standard Crusader Medium Frame

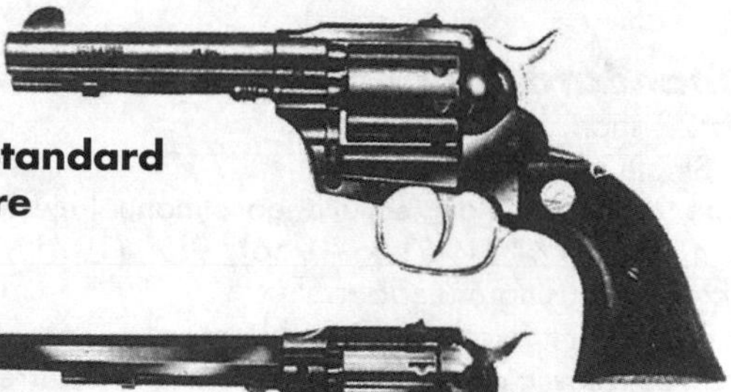

High Standard Hombre

High Standard Durango

High Standard High Sierra Combination

High Standard Camp Gun

Caliber: 22 short, long, long rifle and 22 magnum
Action: Single or double; solid frame; simultaneous ejector
Cylinder: 9-shot swing-out
Barrel: 6"
Sights: Ramp front; adjustable rear
Finish: Blued; checkered walnut grip
Length Overall: 11"
Approximate wt.: 28 ozs.
Comments: Made from about 1975 to the late 1970s. Add $10.00 for 22 magnum caliber. Reintroduced in 1982 to 1985.

Estimated Value:	**Excellent:**	**$225.00**
	Very good:	**$180.00**

High Standard Crusader

Caliber: 44 magnum, 45 Colt, 357 magnum
Action: Single or double
Cylinder: 6-shot
Barrel: 4½" in 44 or 45; 6½" in 44, 45, or 357; 8⅜" in 44, 45, or 357
Sights: Adjustable rear, ramp blade front
Finish: Blued; shrouded ejector rod; smooth walnut grips in 44; checkered walnut grips in 45 and 357
Length Overall: 9⅞" to 14"
Approximate wt.: 43 to 52 ozs.
Comments: A large frame handgun made from about the late 1970s to the early 1980s. Add $5.00 for 6½" barrel; add $12.00 for 8⅜" barrel.

Estimated Value:	**Excellent:**	**$800.00**
	Very good:	**$640.00**

High Standard Crusader Medium Frame

Similar to the Crusader in 357 magnum only; 4½" or 6½" barrel; weight is 40 to 42 ozs.; a smaller version of the Crusader. Add $7.00 for 6½" barrel.

Estimated Value:	**Excellent:**	**$450.00**
	Very good:	**$360.00**

High Standard Derringer

Caliber: 22 short, long, long rifle (1962 to the present); 22 magnum rim fire (1963 to the present)
Action: Double; concealed hammer; hammer block safety; front of trigger guard cut away
Cylinder: None; 2-shot chambers in barrels
Barrel: 3½" double barrel (superposed); duel ejection; cartridge chamber in each barrel
Sights: Fixed
Finish: Blued or nickel; plastic grips (1962 to the present); gold-plated presentation model in walnut case (1965 to 1966); electroless nickel finish and walnut grips after 1982
Length Overall: 5"
Approximate wt.: 11 ozs.
Comments: Steel barrels; aluminum alloy frame. Made from about 1962 to 1985.

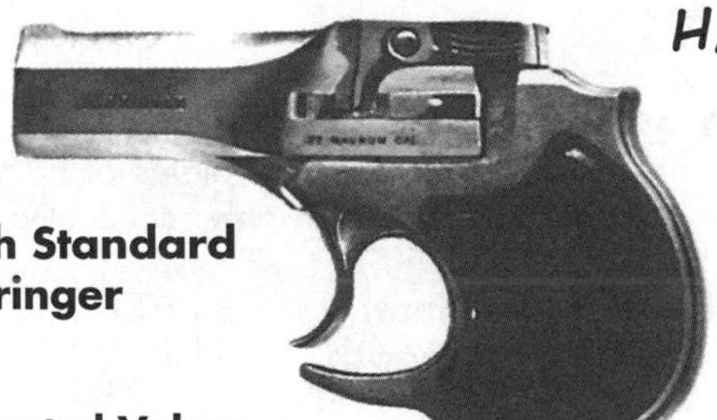

High Standard Derringer

Estimated Value:

	Blued	Nickel	Electro. Nickel
Excellent:	**$250.00**	**$190.00**	**$250.00**
Very good:	**$150.00**	**$150.00**	**$150.00**

Gold presentation models with case in unused condition (with consecutive numbers):
1-Derringer $500.00
2-Derringer $1,100.00

Iver Johnson X300 Pony and PO 380

Caliber: 380 ACP
Action: Single action; semiautomatic; exposed hammer
Magazine: 6-shot clip
Barrel: 3"
Sights: Adjustable rear, blade front
Finish: Blued, nickel, or military; checkered or smooth walnut grips; stainless steel in 1990 only
Length Overall: 6"
Approximate wt.: 20 ozs.
Comments: Add 5% for nickel finish; add 15% for stainless steel; made from 1984 to 1990.
Estimated Value: **Excellent:** **$285.00**
Very good: **$235.00**

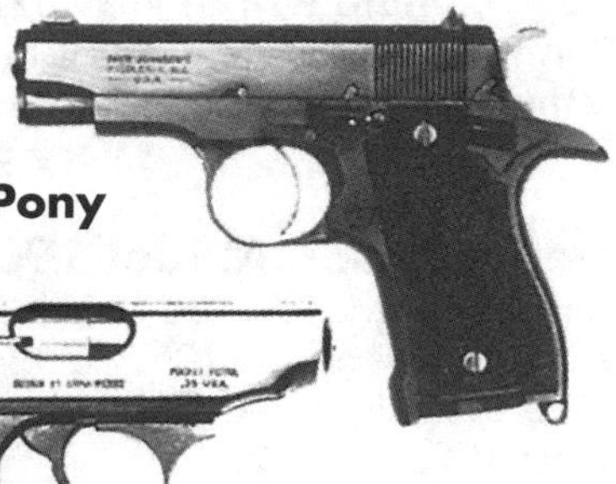

Iver Johnson X300 Pony

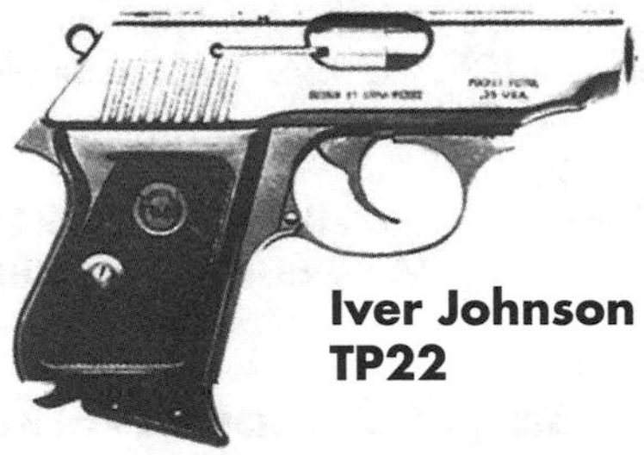

Iver Johnson Model TP22

Iver Johnson Models TP22 and TP25

Caliber: 22 long rifle (TP22); 25 ACP (TP25)
Action: Double action; semiautomatic; exposed hammer
Magazine: 7-shot clip
Barrel: 3"
Sights: Fixed
Finish: Blued, nickel; plastic grips; finger extension on clip
Length Overall: 5½"
Approximate wt.: 15 ozs.
Comments: Made from 1982 to 1991. Add 8% for nickel.
Estimated Value: **Excellent:** **$200.00**
Very good: **$160.00**

Iver Johnson Trailsman

Caliber: 22 long rifle
Action: Semiautomatic, concealed hammer
Magazine: 10 shot clip
Barrel: 4½" or 6"
Sights: Fixed
Finish: Blued; checkered plastic or smooth hardwood grips
Length Overall: 9" to 11"
Approximate wt.: 28 to 30 ozs.
Comments: Produced from 1984 to 1987. Add 10% for high polish with hardwood grips.
Estimated Value: **Excellent:** **$220.00**
Very good: **$180.00**

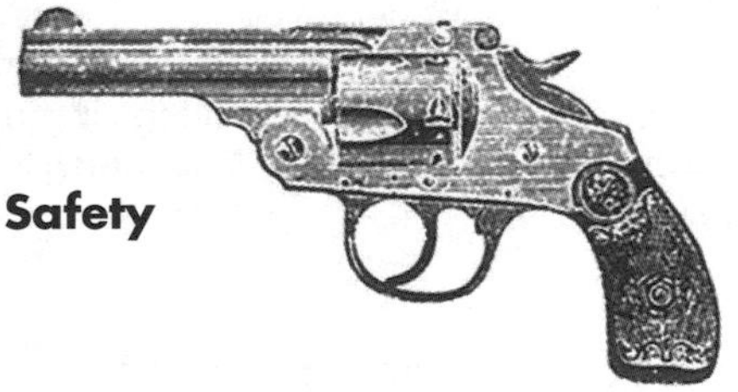

Iver Johnson Safety Hammer

Iver Johnson Safety Hammer

Caliber: 22 S, L & LR; 32 S&W; 32 S&W long; and 38 S&W black powder
Action: Single or double; exposed hammer; hinged frame; top break style; simultaneous ejector; heavier frame on 32 and 38 caliber
Cylinder: 7-shot in 22 caliber; 6-shot in 32 caliber; 5-shot in 38 caliber
Barrel: 2", 3", 3¼", 4", 5", 6"; round barrel with solid rib
Sights: Fixed
Finish: Blued or nickel; rubber or wood grips; round or square butt
Length Overall: 6¾" to 10¾" depending on barrel length
Approximate wt.: 14 to 21 ozs. depending on caliber and barrel length
Comments: Made from about 1892 to 1950 with some improvements and minor changes.
Estimated Value: **Excellent:** **$200.00**
Very good: **$160.00**

Iver Johnson Safety Hammerless

Same as Safety Hammer model except side plates of frame extended to enclose hammer; double action only; concealed hammer. Made from about 1895 to 1950.

Estimated Value: **Excellent:** **$150.00**
Very good: **$120.00**

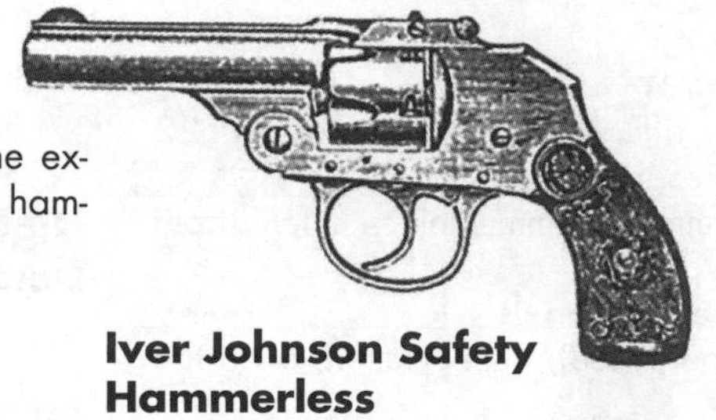

Iver Johnson Safety Hammerless

Iver Johnson Model 1900

Caliber: 22 short, long, long rifle, 32 S&W, 32 S&W long, 38 S&W
Action: Single or double; exposed hammer; solid frame; side load
Cylinder: 7-shot in 22 caliber; 6-shot in 32 caliber; 5-shot in 38 caliber; removable cylinder
Barrel: 2½", 4½", 6"; octagon barrel
Sights: Fixed
Finish: Blued or nickel; hard rubber grips
Length Overall: 7" to 10¾" depending on barrel length
Approximate wt.: 11 to 19 ozs.
Comments: Made from about 1900 to the mid-1940s.
Estimated Value: **Excellent:** **$200.00**
Very good: **$160.00**

Iver Johnson Model 1900

Iver Johnson Model 1900 Target

Same as the Model 1900 except 22 caliber only; 6" or 9" barrel length; length overall 10¾" to 13¾"; approximate weight is 22 to 26 ozs.; checkered walnut grips; blued finish only. Made from about 1925 to 1942.

Estimated Value: **Excellent:** **$225.00**
Very good: **$180.00**

Iver Johnson Target 9-Shot Revolver

Similar to the Model 1900 Target except 9-shot cylinder; 6" or 10" barrel; 10¾" to 14¾" length overall; weighs 24 to 28 ozs. Introduced about 1929 and discontinued in the mid-1940s.

Estimated Value: **Excellent:** **$175.00**
Very good: **$140.00**

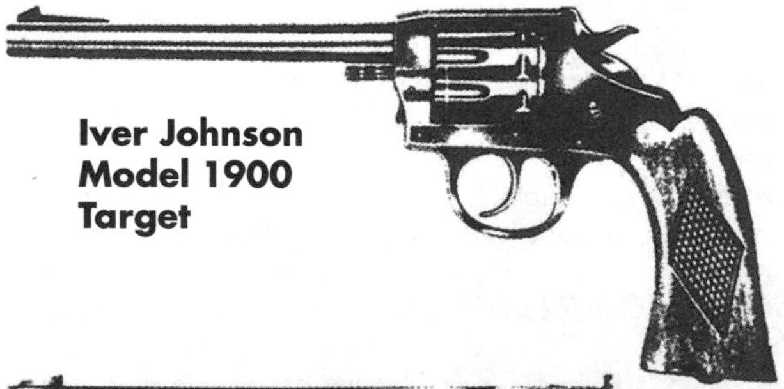

Iver Johnson Model 1900 Target

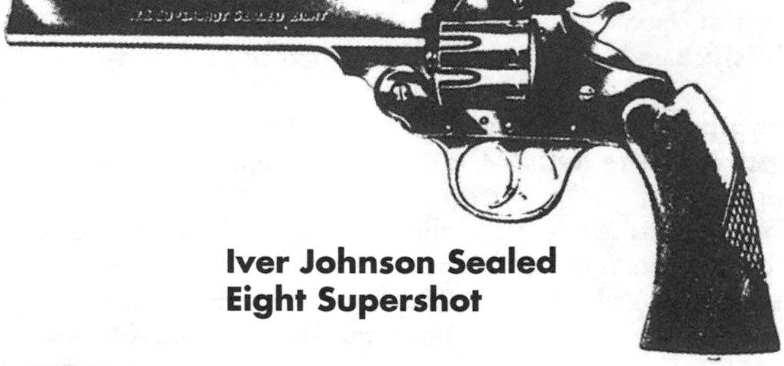

Iver Johnson Sealed Eight Supershot

Iver Johnson Supershot

Caliber: 22 short, long, long rifle
Action: Single or double; exposed hammer; hinged frame; top break style; simultaneous ejector
Cylinder: 7-shot; 9-shot
Barrel: 6"; round barrel with solid rib on top
Sights: Fixed
Finish: Blued; checkered walnut grips (one piece)
Length Overall: 10¾"
Approximate wt.: 25 ozs.
Comments: Some have adjustable finger rests behind trigger guards. Made from about 1929 to 1950.
Estimated Value: **Excellent:** **$200.00**
Very good: **$160.00**

Iver Johnson Sealed Eight Supershot

Similar to Supershot revolver except: 8-shot recessed cylinder; adjustable rear sight; for cartridge head; 10" barrel length; 10¾" to 14¾" over. Made from about 1931 to 1957.

Estimated Value: **Excellent:** **$200.00**
Very good: **$160.00**

Iver Johnson Sealed Eight Target

Caliber: 22 short, long, long rifle
Action: Single or double; exposed hammer; solid frame; side load
Cylinder: 8-shot; cylinder recessed for cartridge head; removable
Barrel: 6", 10"; octagon barrel
Sights: Fixed
Finish: Blued; checkered walnut grips (one piece)
Length Overall: 10¾"; 14¾"
Approximate wt.: 24 to 28 ozs.
Comments: Made from about 1931 to 1957.
Estimated Value: **Excellent:** **$175.00**
Very good: **$140.00**

Iver Johnson Sealed Eight Target

Iver Johnson Sealed Eight Protector

Caliber: 22 short, long, long rifle
Action: Single or double; exposed hammer; hinged frame; top break style; simultaneous ejector
Cylinder: 8-shot; cylinder recessed for cartridge head
Barrel: 2½"
Sights: Fixed
Finish: Blued; checkered walnut grips
Length Overall: 7½"
Approximate wt.: 20 ozs.
Comments: Some have adjustable finger rests behind trigger guards. Made from about 1933 to the late 1940s.

Estimated Value:	**Excellent:**	**$225.00**
	Very good:	**$180.00**

Iver Johnson Sealed Eight Protector

Iver Johnson Champion

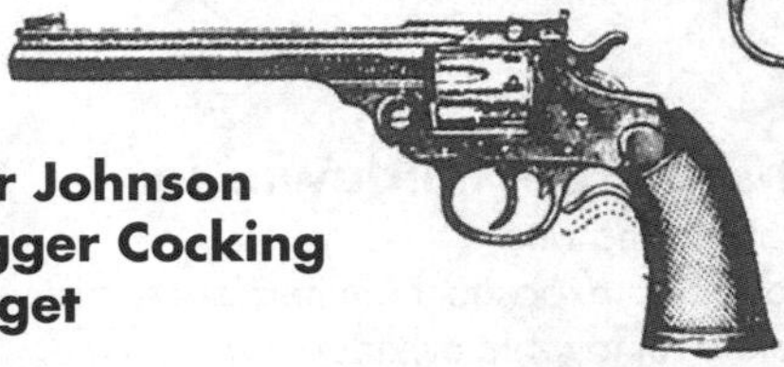

Iver Johnson Trigger Cocking Target

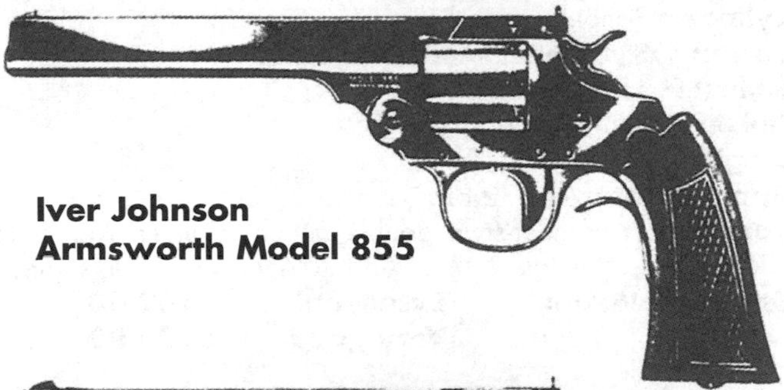

Iver Johnson Armsworth Model 855

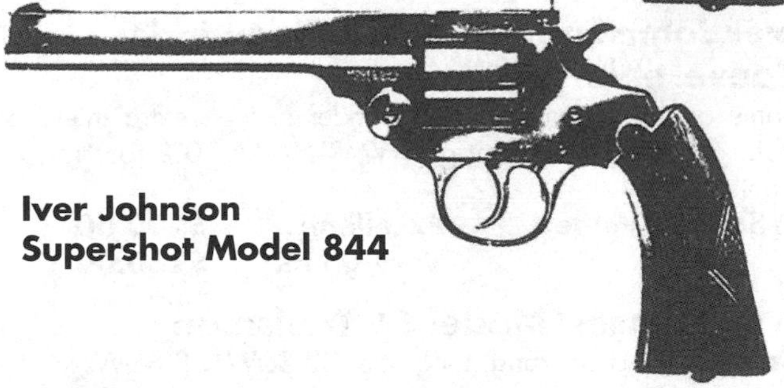

Iver Johnson Supershot Model 844

Iver Johnson Model 55S Cadet

Caliber: 22 short, long, long rifle, 32, 38
Action: Single or double; solid frame; exposed hammer; side load
Cylinder: 8-shot in 22 caliber; 5-shot in 32 and 38 caliber; removable cylinder
Barrel: 2½"
Sights: Fixed
Finish: Blued; plastic round butt grips
Length Overall: 7"
Approximate wt.: 24 ozs.
Comments: Made from about 1954 to 1961.

Estimated Value:	**Excellent:**	**$200.00**
	Very good:	**$160.00**

Iver Johnson Champion

Caliber: 22 short, long, long rifle
Action: Single; exposed hammer; hinged frame; top-break style; simultaneous ejector
Cylinder: 8-shot; cylinder recessed for cartridge head
Barrel: 6"
Sights: Adjustable target sights
Finish: Blued; checkered walnut grips (one piece)
Length Overall: 10¾"
Approximate wt.: 28 ozs.
Comments: Made from about 1938 to 1948. Adjustable finger rests behind trigger guards.

Estimated Value:	**Excellent:**	**$350.00**
	Very good:	**$275.00**

Iver Johnson Trigger Cocking Target

Same as Champion Revolver except the trigger cocks the hammer on the first pull, then releases the hammer to fire the revolver on the second pull. Made from about 1940 to 1947.

Estimated Value:	**Excellent:**	**$365.00**
	Very good:	**$290.00**

Iver Johnson Armsworth Model 855

Caliber: 22 short, long, long rifle
Action: Single; exposed hammer; hinged frame; top break style; simultaneous ejector
Cylinder: 8-shot; cylinder recessed for cartridge head
Barrel: 6"
Sights: Adjustable front and rear sights
Finish: Blued; checkered walnut grips (one piece)
Length Overall: 10¾"
Approximate wt.: 30 ozs.
Comments: Adjustable finger rests behind trigger guards. Made from about 1954 to 1957.

Estimated Value:	**Excellent:**	**$175.00**
	Very good:	**$140.00**

Iver Johnson Supershot Model 844

Similar to Armsworth Model 855 except double and single action; 4½" or 6" barrel lengths; 9¼" to 10¾" overall length. Introduced about 1955, discontinued about 1957.

Estimated Value:	**Excellent:**	**$200.00**
	Very good:	**$160.00**

Iver Johnson Model 55S Cadet

Iver Johnson Model 55 S-A Cadet

Similar to the Model 55S Cadet except addition of loading gate about 1962; also in calibers 22 WMR and 38 Special. Made from about 1962 to the late 1970s.

Estimated Value: **Excellent:** **$225.00**
Very good: **$180.00**

Iver Johnson Model 55

Caliber: 22 short, long, long rifle
Action: Single or double; exposed hammer; solid frame; side load
Cylinder: 8-shot; chambers recessed for cartridge head; removable cylinder; unfluted cylinder
Barrel: 4½", 6"
Sights: Fixed
Finish: Blued; checkered walnut grips
Length Overall: 9¼" to 10¾"
Approximate wt.: 22 to 24 ozs.
Comments: Made from about 1955 to 1961.
Estimated Value: **Excellent:** **$145.00**
Very good: **$115.00**

Iver Johnson Model 55A Target

Same as the Model 55 Revolver except: fluted cylinder; loading gate; checkered plastic grips. Introduced about 1962. Made until the late 1970s.

Estimated Value: **Excellent:** **$175.00**
Very good: **$140.00**

Iver Johnson Model 57

Same as the Model 55 revolver except: adjustable front and rear sights; checkered plastic grips. Made from about 1955 to 1961.

Estimated Value: **Excellent:** **$150.00**
Very good: **$120.00**

Iver Johnson Model 57A Target

Same as the Model 55 revolver except: fluted cylinder; adjustable front and rear sights; checkered plastic grips; loading gate. Produced about 1962 to the mid-1970s.

Estimated Value: **Excellent:** **$160.00**
Very good: **$125.00**

Iver Johnson Model 57A Target

Iver Johnson Model 66 Trailsman

Iver Johnson Model 55 S-A Cadet

Iver Johnson Model 50A Sidewinder

Iver Johnson Model 50A Sidewinder

Caliber: 22 short, long, long rifle
Action: Single or double; exposed hammer; solid frame; side load with loading gates; removable cylinder
Cylinder: 8-shot; recessed chambers
Barrel: 4½", 6"; ejector rod under barrel
Sights: Fixed or adjustable
Finish: Blued; plastic grips
Length Overall: 9¾", 11¼"
Approximate wt.: 32 ozs.
Comments: Frontier-style double action revolver. Made from about 1961 to the late 1970s. Add 20% for adjustable sights.
Estimated Value: **Excellent:** **$160.00**
Very good: **$125.00**

Iver Johnson Model 50A Sidewinder Convertible

Same as the Model 50A Sidewinder except: extra interchangeable cylinder for 22 mag. (WMR). Add 10% for adjustable sights.

Estimated Value: **Excellent:** **$200.00**
Very good: **$160.00**

Iver Johnson Model 66 Trailsman

Caliber: 22 short, long, long rifle; 32 S&W; 38 S&W
Action: Single or double; exposed hammer; hinged frame; top break style; simultaneous manual ejector under barrel; rebounding type hammer
Cylinder: 8-shot in 22 caliber; 5-shot in 32 and 38 caliber; recessed chambers
Barrel: 2¾", 6", rib on top of barrel
Sights: Adjustable
Finish: Blued; checkered walnut or plastic grip; round butt on 2¾" barrel; square butt on 6" barrel
Length Overall: 7", 11"
Approximate wt.: 28 to 32 ozs.
Comments: 2¾" barrel model from about 1961 to 1971; 6" barrel made from about 1958 to 1975.
Estimated Value: **Excellent:** **$200.00**
Very good: **$160.00**

Iver Johnson Model 67 Viking

Same as the Model 66 Trailsman except: hammer safety device; 4½" or 6" barrel lengths. Made from about 1964 to 1975.

Estimated Value: **Excellent:** **$225.00**
Very good: **$180.00**

Iver Johnson Model 67S Viking

Same as the Model 67 except: 2¾" barrel lengths; overall length 7"; approximate weight is 25 ozs.

Estimated Value: **Excellent:** **$250.00**
Very good: **$200.00**

Iver Johnson Bulldog

Caliber: 22 short, long, long rifle; 38 Special
Action: Single or double; exposed hammer; solid frame; side load with loading gate
Cylinder: 8-shot in 22 caliber; 5-shot in 38 caliber recessed chambers
Barrel: 2½", 4", heavy duty ribbed
Sights: Adjustable
Finish: Blued; plastic grips; round or square butt
Length Overall: 6½", 9"
Approximate wt.: 26 to 30 ozs.
Comments: Made from about 1974 to the late 1970s. Add $2.00 for 4" barrel; $10.00 for 38 caliber.

Estimated Value: **Excellent:** **$160.00**
Very good: **$125.00**

Iver Johnson Cattleman Trail Blazer

Caliber: 22 short, long, long rifle; 22 magnum (WMR)
Action: Single action; solid frame; exposed hammer; side load with loading gate
Cylinder: 6-shot; 2 interchangeable cylinders
Barrel: 5½", 6", manual ejector rod under barrel
Sights: Ramp front; adjustable rear
Finish: Blued; case-hardened frame, brass backstrap and trigger guard; smooth walnut grip
Length Overall: 11¼" to 12¼"
Approximate wt.: 38 to 40 ozs.
Comments: Made from about 1974 to the late 1970s. Price includes both cylinders.

Estimated Value: **Excellent:** **$250.00**
Very good: **$200.00**

Iver Johnson Cattleman Buckhorn Buntline

Iver Johnson Cattleman Magnum

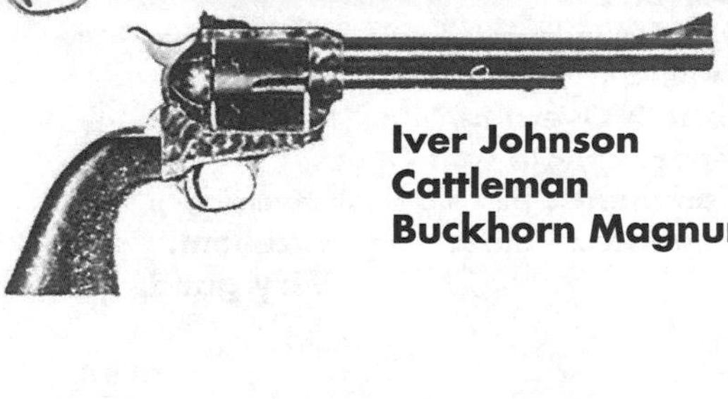

Iver Johnson Cattleman Buckhorn Magnum

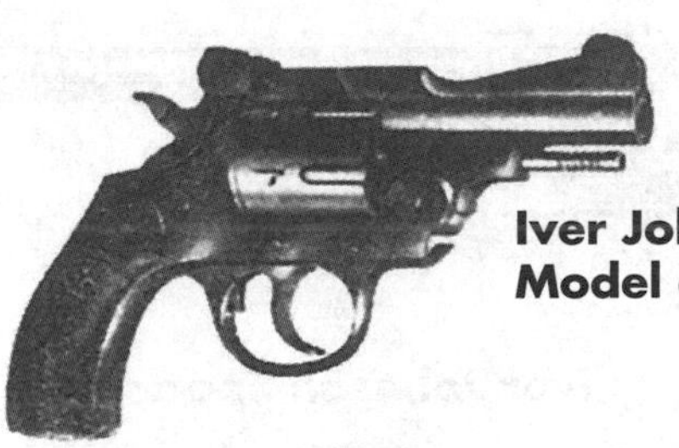

Iver Johnson Model 67S Viking

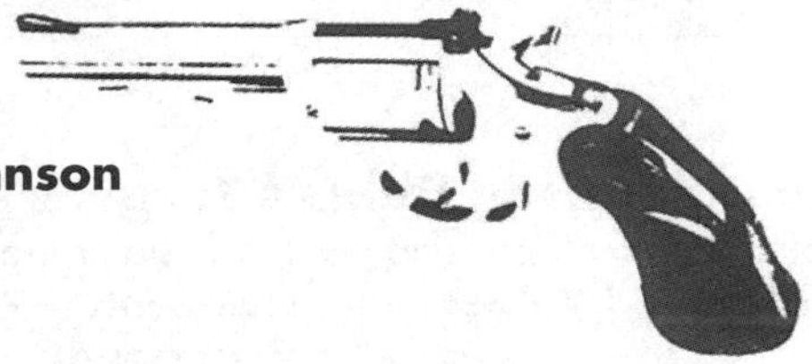

Iver Johnson Bulldog

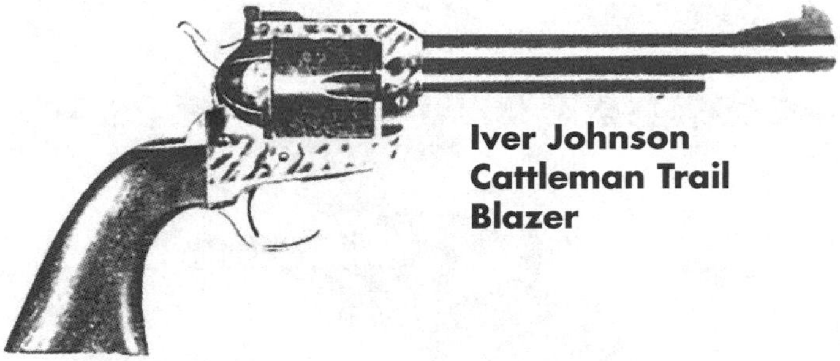

Iver Johnson Cattleman Trail Blazer

Iver Johnson Cattleman Magnum

Caliber: 357 mag. and 38 Spec.; 45 long Colt; 44 mag. and 44 Spec.
Action: Single; solid frame; exposed hammer; side load with loading gate
Cylinder: 6-shot
Barrel: 4¾", 5½", 7½" (357 mag. and 44 LC); 4¾", 6", 7½" (44 mag.); manual ejector rod under barrel
Sights: Fixed
Finish: Blued; case-hardened frame, brass backstrap and trigger guard; smooth walnut grip
Length Overall: 10½" to 13¼"
Approximate wt.: 38 to 46 ozs.
Comments: Made from about 1974 to the early 1980s. Add 12% for 44 mag.

Estimated Value: **Excellent:** **$285.00**
Very good: **$225.00**

Iver Johnson Cattleman Buckhorn Magnum

Same as the Cattleman Magnum except: ramp front sight and adjustable rear sight. Add 10% for 12" barrel; 10% for 44 mag.

Estimated Value: **Excellent:** **$325.00**
Very good: **$260.00**

Iver Johnson Cattleman Buckhorn Buntline

Same as the Cattleman Buckhorn Magnum except: 18" barrel length only; grip backstrap is cut for shoulder stock attachment; smooth walnut attachable shoulder stock; overall length without shoulder stock 24" and with shoulder stock 36½"; approximate weight is 56 ozs. without shoulder stock; shoulder stock weight is approximately 30 ozs. Prices include stock. Add 8% for 44 mag.

Estimated Value: **Excellent:** **$450.00**
Very good: **$360.00**

Iver Johnson Sportsman

Iver Johnson Rookie

Caliber: 38 Special
Action: Single or double
Cylinder: 5-shot; fluted
Barrel: 4"
Sights: Fixed
Finish: Blued or nickel; plastic grips
Length Overall: 9"
Approximate wt.: 29 ozs.
Comments: Made from the mid- to the late 1970s.
Estimated Value: **Excellent:** **$165.00**
Very good: **$135.00**

Iver Johnson Deluxe Target

Similar to the Sportsman with adjustable sights.
Estimated Value: **Excellent:** **$175.00**
Very good: **$140.00**

Iver Johnson Sportsman

Similar to the Rookie in 22 long rifle caliber; 4¾" or 6" barrel; blued finish; made in the mid-1970s.
Estimated Value: **Excellent:** **$150.00**
Very good: **$120.00**

JAPANESE

Type 26 Japanese

Type 26 Japanese

Caliber: 9mm rimmed pistol
Action: Double only; top break; hammer without cocking spur
Magazine: 6-shot; automatic ejector
Barrel: 4¾"
Sights: Blade front; "V" notch rear
Finish: Blued; checkered one-piece round grip
Length Overall: 9½"
Approximate wt.: 32 ozs.
Comments: Made from about 1893 to 1924.
Estimated Value: **Excellent:** **$1,000.00**
Very good: **$ 800.00**

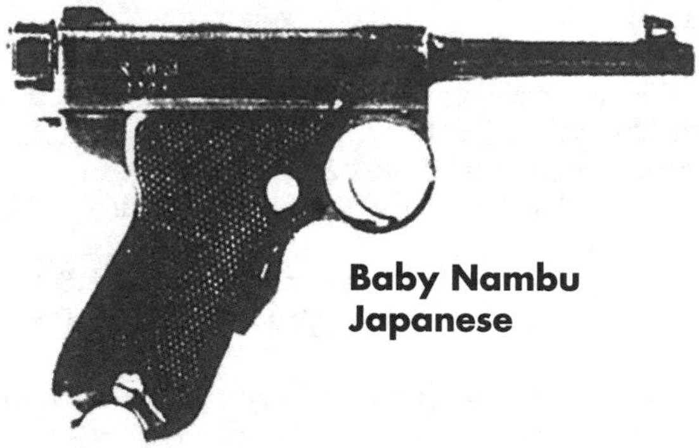

Baby Nambu Japanese

1904 Nambu Japanese

Caliber: 8mm bottle-necked Japanese
Action: Semiautomatic; grip safety below trigger guard
Magazine: 8-shot chip
Barrel: 4¾"
Sights: Barleycorn front; notched tangent rear
Finish: Blued; checkered wood grips
Length Overall: 8¾"
Approximate wt.: 32 ozs.
Comments: Made from about 1904 to 1925. Usually has a slot cut in rear of grip to accommodate shoulder stock holster. Add 10% for shoulder stock holster.
Estimated Value: **Excellent:** **$1,750.00**
Very good: **$1,400.00**

Nambu Type 14 Japanese

Caliber: 8mm bottle-necked Japanese
Action: Semiautomatic; manual safety
Magazine: 8-shot chip
Barrel: 4¾"
Sights: Barleycorn front; undercut notch rear
Finish: Blued; grooved wood grips
Length Overall: 9"
Approximate wt.: 32 ozs.
Comments: A modified form of the 1904 Nambu introduced about 1925 and produced until about 1945.
Estimated Value: **Excellent:** **$1,100.00**
Very good: **$ 880.00**

Baby Nambu Japanese

Caliber: 7mm bottle-necked Japanese cartridge
Action: Semiautomatic; grip safety below trigger guard
Magazine: 7-shot chip
Barrel: 3¼"
Sights: Barleycorn front; "V" notch rear
Finish: Blued; checkered wood grips
Length Overall: 7¼"
Approximate wt.: 24 ozs.
Comments: This is a smaller version of the 1904 Nambu.
Estimated Value: **Excellent:** **$3,000.00**
Very good: **$2,400.00**

Modified Nambu Type 14 Japanese
Similar to the 1904 Nambu except it has enlarged trigger guard to allow use of heavy gloves and a spring mounted in lower front of grip to hold magazine more securely.

Estimated Value:	**Excellent:**	**$1,100.00**
	Very good:	**$ 880.00**

Type 57 New Nambu Japanese

Type 57B New Nambu Japanese

Type 94 Japanese
Caliber: 8mm bottle-necked Japanese
Action: Semiautomatic
Magazine: 6-shot clip
Barrel: 3¾"
Sights: Barleycorn front; square notch rear
Finish: Blued; checkered grips
Length Overall: 7¼"
Approximate wt.: 28 ozs.
Comments: Made from about 1937 to 1945. Made for export but was used as a service pistol during World War II. Most show evidence of poor manufacture, and can be fired accidentally without pulling the trigger.

Estimated Value:	**Excellent:**	**$875.00**
	Very good:	**$700.00**

Type 57 New Nambu Japanese
Caliber: 9mm Parabellum; 45 ACP
Action: Semiautomatic; recoil-operated
Magazine: 8-shot clip
Barrel: 4½"
Sights: Fixed
Finish: Blued; checkered grips
Length Overall: 7¾"
Approximate wt.: 28 ozs.
Comments: A modified copy of the U.S. 1911 A1 produced by the firm of Shin Chuo Kogyo K.K. since World War II. Magazine catch at bottom of grip; doesn't have the grip safety.

Estimated Value:	**Excellent:**	**$600.00**
	Very good:	**$480.00**

Type 57B New Nambu Japanese
Caliber: 32 ACP (7.65mm Browning)
Action: Semiautomatic; blowback-operated
Magazine: 8-shot clip
Barrel: 3"
Sights: Fixed
Finish: Blued; checkered grips
Length Overall: 6¼"
Approximate wt.: 20 ozs.
Comments: A modified copy of the Browning M1910 pistol produced by the firm of Shin Chuo Kogyo K.K. after World War II.

Estimated Value:	**Excellent:**	**$600.00**
	Very good:	**$480.00**

KIMBER

Kimber Custom II

Kimber Custom II
Caliber: 45 ACP
Action: Semiautomatic; exposed rounded spur hammer
Magazine: 7-shot clip
Barrel: 5"
Sights: Fixed, low profile
Finish: Matte black steel, aluminum trigger; black synthetic double diamond grips
Length Overall: 8¾"
Approximate wt.: 38 ozs.
Comments: A modern version of the popular 1911 A1 Colt design with improved features.

Estimated Value:	**New (retail):**	**$828.00**
	Excellent:	**$620.00**
	Very good:	**$495.00**

Kimber Custom II Target

Kimber Custom II TLE

Kimber Custom II TLE/RL

Kimber Warrior

Kimber Desert Warrior

Kimber Custom II Target

Similar to the Custom II except with Kimber adjustable sights.

Estimated Value: **New (retail):** **$942.00**
Excellent: **$700.00**
Very good: **$565.00**

Kimber Custom II TLE

Similar to the Custom II except with Meprolight Tritium 3-dot night sights; frame has rontstrap checkering; available with matte black or stainless steel finish (add 15%).

Estimated Value: **New (retail):** **$1,044.00**
Excellent: **$ 785.00**
Very good: **$ 625.00**

Kimber Custom II TLE/RL

Similar to the Custom II TLE (LG). Add 10% for stainless steel finish.

Estimated Value: **New (retail):** **$1,139.00**
Excellent: **$ 855.00**
Very good: **$ 685.00**

Kimber Custom II TLE (LG)

Similar to the Custom II TLE except with tactical gray crimson trace lazergrips.

Estimated Value: **Excellent:** **$940.00**
Very good: **$750.00**

Kimber Warrior

Caliber: 45 ACP
Action: Semiautomatic; exposed rounded spur hammer
Magazine: 7-shot clip
Barrel: 5"
Sights: Tactical wedge, Tritium night sights
Finish: Matte black steel, tactical grips
Length Overall: 8¾"
Approximate wt.: 39 ozs.
Comments: A 45 caliber match grade pistol based on improvements of Colt's popular 1911 A1 model.

Estimated Value: **New (retail):** **$1,441.00**
Excellent: **$1,080.00**
Very good: **$ 810.00**

Kimber Desert Warrior

Similar to the Warrior except with Kimber's Dark Earth finish.

Estimated Value: **New (retail):** **$1,458.00**
Excellent: **$1,095.00**
Very good: **$ 875.00**

Kimber Royal II

Kimber Royal II

Caliber: 45 ACP
Action: Semiautomatic; exposed rounded spur hammer
Magazine: 7-shot clip
Barrel: 5"
Sights: Fixed, low profile
Finish: Blued; checkered rosewood double diamond grips, aluminum trigger
Length Overall: 8¾"
Approximate wt.: 38 ozs.
Comments: A modern version of the popular 1911 A1 Colt design with improved features.

Estimated Value:	**New (retail):**	**$1,013.00**
	Excellent:	**$ 760.00**
	Very good:	**$ 600.00**

Kimber Stainless II

Kimber Stainless II

Similar to the Royal II except with stainless steel finish; available with high polish finish in 38 Super caliber (add 19%) or 9mm caliber; available with night sights (add 16%).

Estimated Value:	**New (retail):**	**$964.00**
	Excellent:	**$725.00**
	Very good:	**$575.00**

Kimber Stainless Target II

Kimber Stainless Target II

Similar to the Stainless II except with Kimber adjustable sights; available in calibers 45 ACP, 38 Super, 9mm, or 10mm.

Estimated Value:	**New (retail):**	**$1,068.00**
	Excellent:	**$ 800.00**
	Very good:	**$ 640.00**

Kimber Gold Match II

Kimber Gold Match II

Caliber: 45 ACP
Action: Semiautomatic; exposed rounded spur hammer
Magazine: 8-shot clip
Barrel: 5" oversize, custom fitted
Sights: Adjustable
Finish: High-polish blued; checkered rosewood double diamond grips
Length Overall: 8¾"
Approximate wt.: 38 ozs.
Comments: Kimber's improved version of Colt's National Match based on the 1911 design.

Estimated Value:	**New (retail):**	**$1,345.00**
	Excellent:	**$1,010.00**
	Very good:	**$ 805.00**

Kimber Gold Match II Stainless

Kimber Gold Match II Stainless

Similar to the Gold Match II except stainless steel finish; available in 9mm or 45 ACP calibers; add 2% for 9mm.

Estimated Value:	**New (retail):**	**$1,519.00**
	Excellent:	**$1,140.00**
	Very good:	**$ 910.00**

Kimber Team Match II

Kimber Team Match II

Similar to the Gold Match II Stainless except with satin silver stainless steel finish; laminated, checkered-design grips; available in 45 ACP or 38 Super calibers; add 3% for 38 Super.

Estimated Value:	**New (retail):**	**$1,535.00**
	Excellent:	**$1,150.00**
	Very good:	**$ 920.00**

Kimber Compact Stainless II

Kimber Compact Stainless II

Caliber: 45 ACP
Action: Semiautomatic; exposed rounded spur hammer
Magazine: 7-shot clip
Barrel: 4"
Sights: Fixed, low profile
Finish: Satin stainless steel; checkered black synthetic double diamond grips
Length Overall: 7¾"
Approximate wt.: 34 ozs.
Comments: A compact pistol based on the popular Colt 1911 A1 design.

Estimated Value:	**New (retail):**	**$1,009.00**
	Excellent:	**$ 755.00**
	Very good:	**$ 605.00**

Kimber Pro Carry II

Kimber Pro Carry II

Caliber: 45 ACP; 9mm
Action: Semiautomatic; exposed rounded spur hammer
Magazine: 7-shot clip
Barrel: 4"
Sights: Fixed, low profile; night sights available
Finish: Matte black aluminum frame and steel slide; checkered black synthetic double diamond grips
Length Overall: 7¾"
Approximate wt.: 28 ozs.
Comments: A lightweight, aluminum-frame pistol similar to the Compact II. Add 4% for 9mm; 13% for night sights.

Estimated Value:	**New (retail):**	**$888.00**
	Excellent:	**$665.00**
	Very good:	**$530.00**

Kimber Pro Carry II Stainless

Similar to the Pro Carry II except with satin silver finish and stainless steel slide; add 3% for 9mm, 12% for night sights.

Estimated Value:	**New (retail):**	**$979.00**
	Excellent:	**$735.00**
	Very good:	**$585.00**

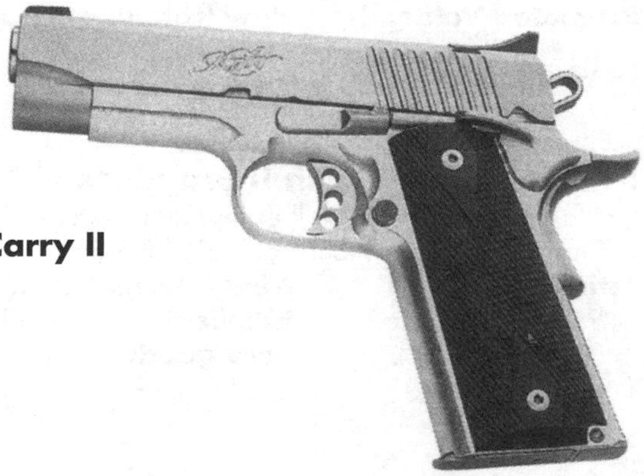

Kimber Pro Carry II Stainless

Kimber Pro Carry II Stainless (LG)

Similar to the Pro Carry II Stainless except with tactical gray, crimson trace lasergrips.

Estimated Value:	**Excellent:**	**$900.00**
	Very good:	**$720.00**

Kimber Pro Carry HD II

Kimber Pro TLE II

Kimber Pro TLE II (LG)

Kimber Pro TLE II RL

Kimber Ultra Carry II

Kimber Ultra Carry II/Night Sights (LG)

Kimber Pro Carry HD II

Similar to the Pro Carry II Stainless except with stainless steel frame; available in 45 ACP or 38 super calibers (add 4% for 38 Super).

Estimated Value:	**New (retail):**	**$1,008.00**
	Excellent:	**$ 755.00**
	Very good:	**$ 605.00**

Kimber Pro TLE II

Caliber: 45 ACP
Action: Semiautomatic; exposed rounded spur hammer
Magazine: 7-shot clip
Barrel: 4" bull
Sights: Meprolight Tritium 3-dot night sights, fixed
Finish: Matte black steel, aluminum trigger; checkered black synthetic double diamond grips
Length Overall: 7¾"
Approximate wt.: 35 ozs.
Comments: Similar to the rest of the Pro Carry II line with Tritium night sights.

Estimated Value:	**New (retail):**	**$1,102.00**
	Excellent:	**$ 825.00**
	Very good:	**$ 660.00**

Kimber Pro TLE II (LG)

Similar to the Pro TLE II except with tactical gray crimson trace lasergrips.

Estimated Value:	**Excellent:**	**$955.00**
	Very good:	**$765.00**

Kimber Pro TLE II RL

Similar to the Pro TLE II except with tactical rail frame.

Estimated Value:	**New (retail):**	**$1,197.00**
	Excellent:	**$ 895.00**
	Very good:	**$ 720.00**

Kimber Pro TLE II RL Stainless

Similar to the Pro TLE II RL except with satin silver stainless steel finish.

Estimated Value:	**New (retail):**	**$1,322.00**
	Excellent:	**$ 990.00**
	Very good:	**$ 795.00**

Kimber Ultra Carry II

Caliber: 45 ACP
Action: Semiautomatic; exposed rounded spur hammer
Magazine: 7-shot clip
Barrel: 3"
Sights: Fixed, low profile
Finish: Matte black aluminum frame with steel slide; checkered black synthetic double diamond grips
Length Overall: 6¾"
Approximate wt.: 25 ozs.
Comments: A compact lightweight carry version based on the Colt 1911 A1 design.

Estimated Value:	**New (retail):**	**$888.00**
	Excellent:	**$665.00**
	Very good:	**$530.00**

Kimber Ultra Carry II/Night Sights (LG)

Similar to the Ultra Carry II except with Meprolight Tritium 3-dot night sights and tactical gray crimson trace lasergrips.

Estimated Value:	**New (retail):**	**$1,346.00**
	Excellent:	**$1,010.00**
	Very good:	**$ 805.00**

Kimber Tactical Ultra II

Kimber Tactical Pro II

Kimber Tactical Custom II

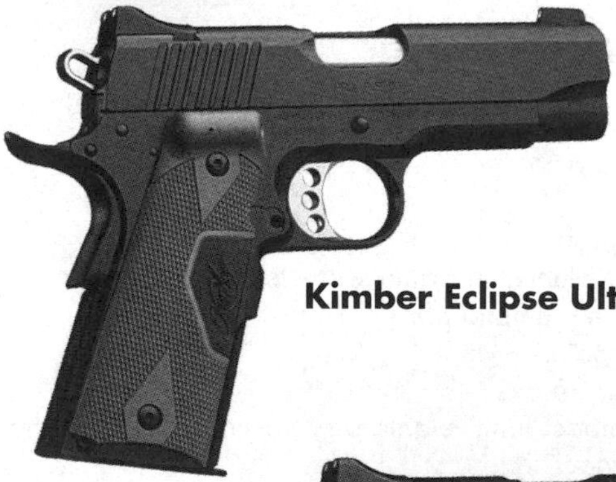

Kimber Eclipse Ultra II

Kimber Eclipse Pro II

Kimber Ultra Carry II Stainless

Similar to the Ultra Carry II except with satin silver finish frame and stainless steel slide; 9mm or 45 ACP calibers (add 5% for 9mm).

Estimated Value:	**New (retail):**	**$1,210.00**
	Excellent:	**$ 905.00**
	Very good:	**$ 725.00**

Kimber Tactical Ultra II

Caliber: 45 ACP
Action: Semiautomatic; exposed rounded spur hammer
Magazine: 7-shot clip
Barrel: 3"
Sights: Meprolight Tritium 3-dot night sights, fixed
Finish: Matte gray aluminum, matte black steel slide; checkered, laminated double diamond grips
Length Overall: 6¾"
Approximate wt.: 25 ozs.
Comments: Lightweight, compact pistol based on the Colt 1911 A1 design.

Estimated Value:	**New (retail):**	**$1,250.00**
	Excellent:	**$ 935.00**
	Very good:	**$ 750.00**

Kimber Tactical Pro II

Similar to the Tactical Ultra II except with a 4" barrel; weighs 28 oz., 7¾" overall length; also available in 9mm caliber (add 3%).

Estimated Value:	**New (retail):**	**$1,250.00**
	Excellent:	**$ 935.00**
	Very good:	**$ 750.00**

Kimber Tactical Custom II

Similar to the Tactical Ultra II except with a 5" barrel; weighs 31 oz.; 8¾" overall length.

Estimated Value:	**New (retail):**	**$1,250.00**
	Excellent:	**$ 935.00**
	Very good:	**$ 750.00**

Kimber Eclipse Ultra II

Caliber: 45 ACP
Action: Semiautomatic; exposed rounded spur hammer
Magazine: 7-shot clip
Barrel: 3"
Sights: Meprolight Tritium 3-dot night sights, fixed
Finish: Brush-polished stainless steel; checkered, laminated double diamond grips
Length Overall: 6¾"
Approximate wt.: 31 ozs.
Comments: Similar to Kimber's Tactical series except with a stainless steel frame and slide.

Estimated Value:	**New (retail):**	**$1,236.00**
	Excellent:	**$ 925.00**
	Very good:	**$ 740.00**

Kimber Eclipse Pro II

Similar to the Eclipse Ultra II except with a 4" barrel; weighs 35 oz.; 7¾" overall length.

Estimated Value:	**New (retail):**	**$1,236.00**
	Excellent:	**$ 925.00**
	Very good:	**$ 740.00**

Kimber Eclipse Pro Target II

Kimber Eclipse Pro Target II

Similar to the Eclipse Pro II except with adjustable sights.

Estimated Value:	**New (retail):**	**$1,345.00**
	Excellent:	**$1,010.00**
	Very good:	**$ 805.00**

Kimber Eclipse Custom II

Kimber Eclipse Custom II

Similar to the Eclipse Pro II except with a 5" barrel; weighs 38 oz.; 8¾" overall length; also available in 10mm caliber (add 3%).

Estimated Value:	**New (retail):**	**$1,250.00**
	Excellent:	**$ 935.00**
	Very good:	**$ 750.00**

Kimber Eclipse Target II

Kimber Eclipse Target II

Similar to the Eclipse Custom II except with adjustable sights.

Estimated Value:	**New (retail):**	**$1,345.00**
	Excellent:	**$1,010.00**
	Very good:	**$ 805.00**

Kimber SIS Ultra

Caliber: 45 ACP
Action: Semiautomatic; exposed rounded spur hammer
Magazine: 7-shot clip
Barrel: 3"
Sights: Tritium fixed SIS night sights
Finish: Matte gray stainless steel frame and slide; stippled black laminated grips
Length Overall: 6¾"
Approximate wt.: 31 ozs.
Comments: Designed by Kimber in conjunction with the Los Angeles Police Department's Special Investigation Unit.

Estimated Value:	**Excellent:**	**$985.00**
	Very good:	**$790.00**

Kimber SIS Ultra

Kimber SIS Pro

Similar to the SIS Ultra except with a 4" barrel; weighs 35 oz.; 7¾" overall length.

Estimated Value:	**Excellent:**	**$985.00**
	Very good:	**$790.00**

Kimber SIS Custom

Similar to the SIS Ultra except with a 5" barrel; 8-shot clip; weighs 38 oz.; 8¾" overall length.

Estimated Value:	**Excellent:**	**$985.00**
	Very good:	**$790.00**

Kimber SIS Pro

Kimber SIS Custom

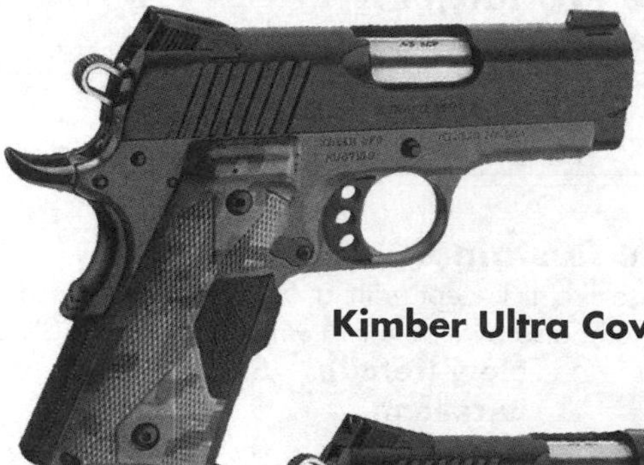

Kimber Ultra Covert II

Kimber Pro Covert II

Kimber Custom Covert II

Kimber Ultra Aegis II

Kimber Pro Aegis II

Kimber Custom Aegis II

Kimber Ultra Covert II

Caliber: 45 ACP
Action: Semiautomatic; exposed rounded spur hammer
Magazine: 7-shot clip
Barrel: 3"
Sights: Tactical Wedge Tritium night sights, fixed
Finish: Desert tan aluminum frame, matte black slide; synthetic camouflage crimson trace lasergrips
Length Overall: 6¾"
Approximate wt.: 25 ozs.
Comments: Lightweight compact pistol based on the Colt 1911A1 design.

Estimated Value:	**New (retail):**	**$1,603.00**
	Excellent:	**$1,200.00**
	Very good:	**$ 960.00**

Kimber Pro Covert II

Similar to the Ultra Covert II except with a 4" barrel; weighs 28 oz.; 7¾" overall length.

Estimated Value:	**New (retail):**	**$1,603.00**
	Excellent:	**$1,200.00**
	Very good:	**$ 960.00**

Kimber Custom Covert II

Similar to the Ultra Covert II except with a 5" barrel; weighs 31 oz.; 8¾" overall length.

Estimated Value:	**New (retail):**	**$1,603.00**
	Excellent:	**$1,200.00**
	Very good:	**$ 960.00**

Kimber Ultra Aegis II

Caliber: 9mm
Action: Semiautomatic; bobbed hammer
Magazine: 8-shot clip
Barrel: 3"
Sights: Tactical Wedge Tritium night sights, fixed
Finish: Satin silver aluminum frame and matte black steel slide; fluted rosewood grips
Length Overall: 6¾"
Approximate wt.: 25 ozs.
Comments: A lightweight, compact 9mm pistol based on the Colt 1911 A1 design.

Estimated Value:	**New (retail):**	**$1,277.00**
	Excellent:	**$ 950.00**
	Very good:	**$ 765.00**

Kimber Pro Aegis II

Similar to the Ultra Aegis II except with a 4" barrel; weighs 28 oz.; 7¾" overall length.

Estimated Value:	**New (retail):**	**$1,277.00**
	Excellent:	**$ 955.00**
	Very good:	**$ 765.00**

Kimber Custom Aegis II

Similar to the Ultra Aegis II except with a 5" barrel; weighs 31 oz.; 8¾" overall length.

Estimated Value:	**New (retail):**	**$1,277.00**
	Excellent:	**$ 995.00**
	Very good:	**$ 765.00**

Kimber Ultra CDP II

Kimber Compact CDP II

Kimber Pro CDP II

Kimber Custom CDP II

Kimber Ultra Raptor II

Kimber Pro Raptor II

Kimber Ultra CDP II

Caliber: 45 ACP, 9mm
Action: Semiautomatic; exposed rounded spur hammer
Magazine: 7-shot clip
Barrel: 3"
Sights: Meprolight Tritium 3-dot night sights, fixed
Finish: Matte black aluminum frame and satin silver stainless steel slide; checkered rosewood double diamond grips
Length Overall: 6¾"
Approximate wt.: 25 ozs.
Comments: A personal defense pistol based on the Colt 1911 A1 design; add 3% for 9mm caliber.

Estimated Value:	**New (retail):**	**$1,318.00**
	Excellent:	**$ 990.00**
	Very good:	**$ 790.00**

Kimber Compact CDP II

Similar to the Ultra CDP II except with a 4" barrel; 45 ACP only; weighs 27 oz.; 7¾" overall length.

Estimated Value:	**New (retail):**	**$1,318.00**
	Excellent:	**$ 990.00**
	Very good:	**$ 790.00**

Kimber Pro CDP II

Similar to the Compact CDP II; weighs 28 oz.

Estimated Value:	**New (retail):**	**$1,318.00**
	Excellent:	**$ 990.00**
	Very good:	**$ 790.00**

Kimber Custom CDP II

Similar to the Ultra CDP II except with a 5" barrel; 45 ACP only; weighs 31 oz.; 8¾" overall length.

Estimated Value:	**New (retail):**	**$1,318.00**
	Excellent:	**$ 990.00**
	Very good:	**$ 790.00**

Kimber Ultra Raptor II

Caliber: 45 ACP
Action: Semiautomatic; exposed rounded spur hammer
Magazine: 7-shot clip
Barrel: 3"
Sights: Tactical Wedge Tritium night sights, fixed
Finish: Matte black aluminum frame and steel slide with scaled serrations; scale-pattern zebra wood grips
Length Overall: 6¾"
Approximate wt.: 25 ozs.
Comments: One of Kimber's "custom shop" pistols based on the Colt 1911 A1 design.

Estimated Value:	**New (retail):**	**$1,248.00**
	Excellent:	**$ 935.00**
	Very good:	**$ 700.00**

Kimber Pro Raptor II

Similar to the Ultra Raptor II except with a steel frame; 4" barrel; 8-shot clip; weighs 35 oz.; 7¾" overall length.

Estimated Value:	**New (retail):**	**$1,248.00**
	Excellent:	**$ 935.00**
	Very good:	**$ 750.00**

Kimber Raptor II

Kimber Raptor II

Similar to the Pro Raptor II except with a 5" barrel; weighs 38 oz.; 8¾" overall length.

Estimated Value:	**New (retail):**	**$1,379.00**
	Excellent:	**$1,035.00**
	Very good:	**$ 825.00**

Kimber Raptor II Stainless

Kimber Raptor II Stainless

Similar to the Raptor II except with a brushed-polished stainless steel finish.

Estimated Value:	**New (retail):**	**$1,359.00**
	Excellent:	**$1,020.00**
	Very good:	**$ 815.00**

Kimber Grand Raptor II

Similar to the Raptor II Stainless except with a brushed-polished stainless steel slide and high-polish stainless steel frame.

Estimated Value:	**New (retail):**	**$1,587.00**
	Excellent:	**$1,190.00**
	Very good:	**$ 950.00**

Kimber Grand Raptor II

Kimber Ultra RCP II

Caliber: 45 ACP
Action: Semiautomatic; bobbed hammer
Magazine: 7-shot clip
Barrel: 3"
Sights: Sight trough
Finish: Matte black aluminum frame and steel slide; smooth, fluted synthetic grips
Length Overall: 6¾"
Approximate wt.: 25 ozs.
Comments: A lightweight, compact pistol based on the Colt 1911 A1 design.

Estimated Value:	**New (retail):**	**$1,299.00**
	Excellent:	**$ 975.00**
	Very good:	**$ 780.00**

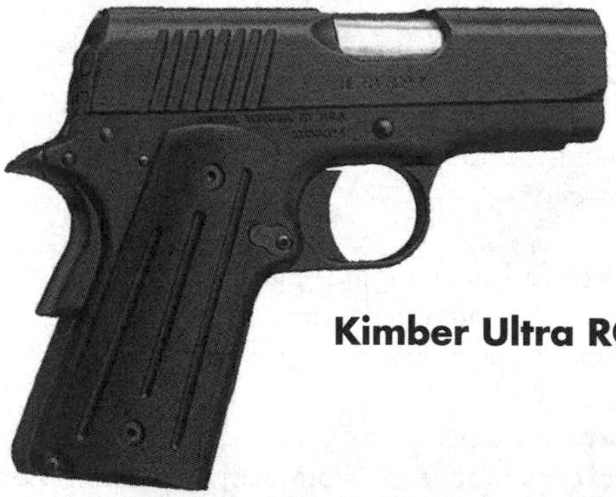

Kimber Ultra RCP II

Kimber Gold Combat II

Kimber Gold Combat II

Caliber: 45 ACP
Action: Semiautomatic; exposed rounded spur hammer
Magazine: 8-shot clip
Barrel: 5"
Sights: Meprolight Tritium 3-dot night sights, fixed
Finish: Matte black steel; checkered rosewood double diamond grips; synthetic grips after 2008
Length Overall: 8¾"
Approximate wt.: 39 ozs.
Comments: A full sized 45 ACP produced in Kimber's "custom shop" and based on the Colt 1911 A1 design.

Estimated Value:	**New (retail):**	**$2,223.00**
	Excellent:	**$1,665.00**
	Very good:	**$1,335.00**

Kimber Rimfire Target

Kimber Rimfire Target

Caliber: 22 long rifle
Action: Semiautomatic; exposed rounded spur hammer
Magazine: 10-shot clip
Barrel: 5"
Sights: Adjustable
Finish: Matte black or silver aluminum frame and slide; black checkered synthetic double diamond grips
Length Overall: 8¾"
Approximate wt.: 23 ozs.
Comments: A large frame 22 caliber pistol based on the Colt 1911 A1 design.

Estimated Value:	**New (retail):**	**$834.00**
	Excellent:	**$625.00**
	Very good:	**$500.00**

Kimber Rimfire Super

Kimber Rimfire Super

Similar to the Rimfire Target except with a satin silver-finish frame and matte black slide; checkered rosewood double diamond grips.

Estimated Value:	**New (retail):**	**$1,172.00**
	Excellent:	**$ 880.00**
	Very good:	**$ 705.00**

LIGNOSE

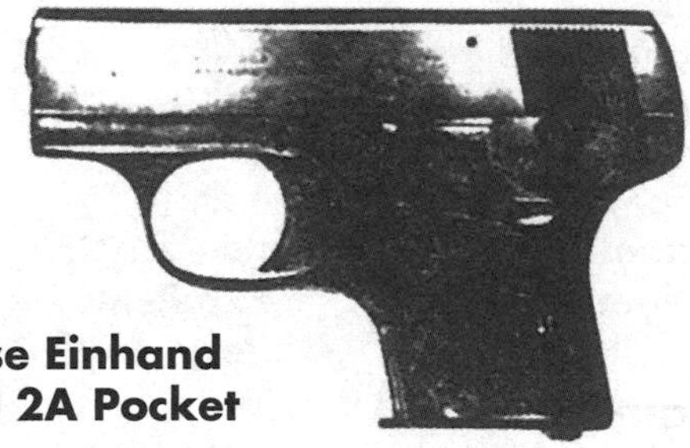

Lignose Einhand Model 2A Pocket

Lignose Model 2 Pocket

Lignose Model 2 Pocket

Caliber: 25 ACP (6.35mm)
Action: Semiautomatic; concealed hammer, thumb safety at top rear of left grip
Magazine: 6-shot clip
Barrel: 2⅛"
Sights: Fixed
Finish: Blued; checkered hard rubber grips
Length Overall: 4¾"
Approximate wt.: 15 ozs.
Comments: Operation principle based on the 1906 Browning 25 caliber automatic pocket pistol; made from about 1920 to the late 1920s. Made in Germany. Early models marked "Bergmann."

Estimated Value:	**Excellent:**	**$425.00**
	Very good:	**$340.00**

Lignose Einhand Model 2A Pocket

Similar specifications as the Model 2 except designed for one-hand operation, hence the name Einhand (one hand). Slide can be retracted to load and cock hammer, by using the trigger finger to pull back the front part of the trigger guard.

Estimated Value:	**Excellent:**	**$700.00**
	Very good:	**$560.00**

Lignose Einhand Model 3A Pocket

Same as the Model 2A except longer grip and uses 9-shot clip.

Estimated Value:	**Excellent:**	**$825.00**
	Very good:	**$660.00**

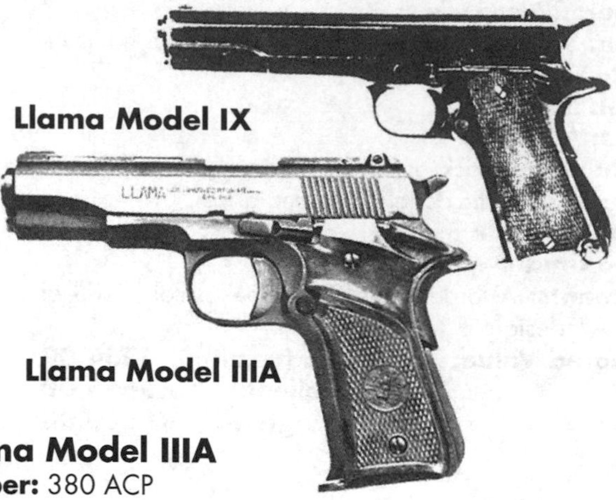

Llama Model IX

Llama Model IIIA

Llama Model IIIA

Caliber: 380 ACP
Action: Semiautomatic; manual and grip safety; exposed hammer
Magazine: 7-shot clip
Barrel: 3¾"
Sights: Partridge front; adjustable rear
Finish: Blued, chrome, chrome engraved; plastic or polymer grips
Length Overall: 6¼"
Approximate wt.: 24 ozs.
Comments: Imported from about 1951 to 2000. Ventilated rib on top of slide. Add 18% for chrome; $50.00 for engraving.
Estimated Value: **Excellent:** **$275.00**
Very good: **$220.00**

Llama Model VIII

Caliber: 9mm Luger, 38 Super ACP
Action: Semiautomatic; manual and grip safety; exposed hammer
Magazine: 9-shot clip
Barrel: 5"
Sights: Fixed front; adjustable rear
Finish: Blued, chrome, chrome engraved; checkered wood or simulated pearl grips
Length Overall: 8½"
Approximate wt.: 39 ozs.
Comments: Imported from about 1953 to the late 1970s. Add 15% for chrome; 30% for engraved; 20% for engraving.
Estimated Value: **Excellent:** **$310.00**
Very good: **$245.00**

Llama Model XI

Caliber: 9mm Luger
Action: Semiautomatic; manual safety; no grip safety; round exposed hammer
Magazine: 8-shot clip
Barrel: 4⅞"
Sights: Fixed
Finish: Blued, chrome; checkered plastic grips with modified thumbrest
Length Overall: 8"
Approximate wt.: 34 ozs.
Comments: Imported from about 1951 to the late 1970s, with some minor modifications. Add 15% for chrome. Add 15% for engraving.
Estimated Value: **Excellent:** **$325.00**
Very good: **$260.00**

Llama Model IX

Caliber: 45 ACP, 9mm, 38 super
Action: Semiautomatic; locked breech; exposed hammer; manual safety
Magazine: 7-shot clip
Barrel: 5"
Sights: Fixed
Finish: Blued, checkered walnut grips
Length Overall: 8½"
Approximate wt.: 39 ozs.
Comments: Imported from about 1936 to 1952.
Estimated Value: **Excellent:** **$325.00**
Very good: **$260.00**

Llama Model IXA

Similar to the Model IX except 45 ACP only; ventilated rib on slide; modified and improved version; also in chrome and chrome engraved finish. Imported from about 1952 to the late 1970s. Add 15% for chrome; 30% for chrome engraved.
Estimated Value: **Excellent:** **$335.00**
Very good: **$265.00**

Llama Standard Automatic Large Frame

Similar to the Model IXA except 13 shot clip and plain slide. Add 25% for chrome finish; discontinued.
Estimated Value: **Excellent:** **$275.00**
Very good: **$220.00**

Llama Model I

Caliber: 32 ACP (7.65mm)
Action: Semiautomatic; blowback-type; exposed hammer
Magazine: 8-shot clip
Barrel: 4"
Sights: Fixed
Finish: Blued, wood grips
Length Overall: 6½"
Approximate wt.: 25 ozs.
Comments: Imported from about 1935 to 1941.
Estimated Value: **Excellent:** **$250.00**
Very good: **$200.00**

Llama Model II

Similar to the Model I except 7-shot clip; caliber 380 ACP (9mm short). Made from about 1935 to 1941.
Estimated Value: **Excellent:** **$260.00**
Very good: **$210.00**

Llama Model III

A modified version of the Model II. Imported from about 1947 to 1954.
Estimated Value: **Excellent:** **$275.00**
Very good: **$220.00**

Llama Model XI

Llama Model XV

Caliber: 22 long rifle
Action: Semiautomatic; blowback-type; exposed hammer; grip and manual safety
Magazine: 9-shot clip
Barrel: 3¹¹⁄₁₆" ventilated rib
Sights: Partridge type, fixed
Finish: Blued, chrome, chrome engraved; checkered wood grips
Length Overall: 6¼"
Approximate wt.: 18 ozs.
Comments: A smaller version of the 1911 A1 Colt 45 ACP. Imported from about 1955 to the late 1970s. Add 15% for chrome; 30% for engraved.
Estimated Value: **Excellent:** **$300.00**
Very good: **$240.00**

Llama Model XA

Same as the Model XV except caliber 32 ACP; 8-shot clip. Add 15% for chrome.
Estimated Value: **Excellent:** **$300.00**
Very good: **$240.00**

Llama Standard Automatic Small Frame

Similar to Models XV, XA and IIIA except: 22 LR and 380 calibers; plain slide. Add 35% for chrome finish.
Estimated Value: **Excellent:** **$225.00**
Very good: **$180.00**

Llama Standard Automatic Compact and Mini-Max

Similar to the Large Frame Model but scaled down; 9mm, 40 S&W, or 45 ACP caliber; walnut or teakwood grips; 7- or 10-shot clip; 34 to 37 oz.; 4" barrel. Introduced in 1987. Add 12% for chrome finish; add 18% for stainless steel.
Estimated Value: **Excellent:** **$325.00**
Very good: **$260.00**

Llama Model XV

Llama Omni

Caliber: 9mm Parabellum, 45 auto
Action: Semiautomatic; double action; exposed hammer
Magazine: 13-shot clip in 9mm; 7-shot clip in 45
Barrel: 5"
Sights: Ramp blade front; adjustable rear
Finish: Blued; checkered plastic grips
Length Overall: 7½"
Approximate wt.: 30 ozs.
Comments: Imported from 1982 to 1988.
Estimated Value: **Excellent:** **$425.00**
Very good: **$340.00**

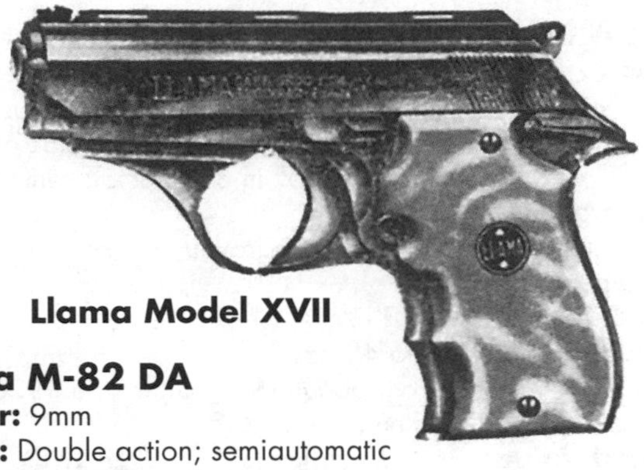

Llama Model XVII

Llama M-82 DA

Caliber: 9mm
Action: Double action; semiautomatic
Magazine: 15-shot clip
Barrel: 4¼"
Sights: Fixed front, adjustable rear
Finish: Blued, matte black polymer grips
Length Overall: 7¾"
Approximate wt.: 39 ozs.
Comments: Imported in the late 1980s and the early 1990s.
Estimated Value: **Excellent:** **$600.00**
Very good: **$480.00**

Llama Model XVII

Caliber: 22 short
Action: Semiautomatic; exposed hammer with round spur; manual safety
Magazine: 6-shot clip
Barrel: 2⅜"
Sights: Fixed
Finish: Blued, chrome; plastic grips
Length Overall: 4½"
Approximate wt.: 14 ozs.
Comments: No longer imported into U.S. because of 1968 gun control law. Also known as Executive Model. Add 10% for chrome.
Estimated Value: **Excellent:** **$250.00**
Very good: **$200.00**

Llama Model XVIII

Same as the Model XVII except 32 ACP caliber only; no longer imported into U.S. Add 10% for chrome.
Estimated Value: **Excellent:** **$240.00**
Very good: **$190.00**

Llama Max-I

Caliber: 45 ACP, 9mm
Action: Semiautomatic; exposed spur hammer; grip safety; single action
Magazine: 7-shot clip
Barrel: 4¼" (compact model); 5½" (large frame model)
Sights: Fixed; three-dot combat style
Finish: Non-glare combat matte; satin finish chrome; smooth rubber grips
Length Overall: 7⅞" (compact model); 8½" (large frame model)
Approximate wt.: 34 to 36 ozs.
Comments: Imported in the 1990s. Add 14% for chrome. Add 40% for compensator model.
Estimated Value: **Excellent:** **$300.00**
Very good: **$240.00**

Llama Martial

Caliber: 22 short, long, long rifle; 38 Special
Action: Double or single action; solid frame; simultaneous ejector
Cylinder: 6-shot swing-out with thumb latch on left side of frame
Barrel: 6" in 22 caliber; 4" and 6" in 38 Special; ventilated rib
Sights: Target
Finish: Blued, chrome, chrome engraved; checkered wood or simulated pearl grips
Length Overall: 9¼" to 11¼"
Approximate wt.: 35 to 40 ozs.
Comments: Imported from about 1969 to the late 1970s. Add 10% for chrome; 15% for engraved.

Estimated Value:	**Excellent:**	**$285.00**
	Very good:	**$225.00**

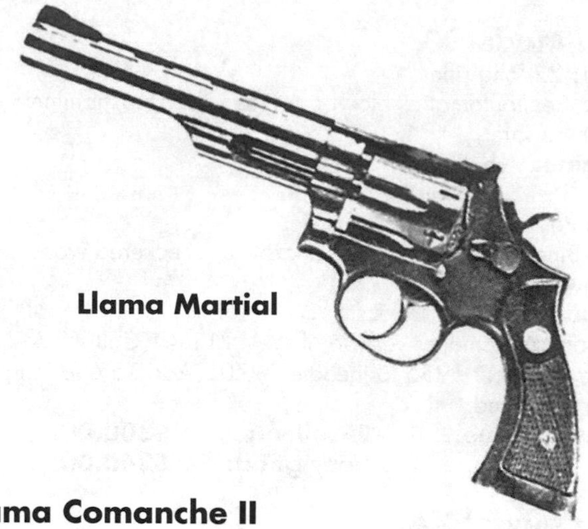

Llama Martial

Llama Comanche I

Caliber: 22 short, long, long rifle
Action: Double or single action; simultaneous hand ejector; solid frame
Cylinder: 6-shot swing-out with thumb latch on left side of frame
Barrel: 6" with ventilated rib
Sights: Ramp front; adjustable rear
Finish: Blued; checkered walnut target grips
Length Overall: 9¼"
Approximate wt.: 36 ozs.
Comments: Imported from about 1978 to the mid-1980s. Add 10% for chrome.

Estimated Value:	**Excellent:**	**$300.00**
	Very good:	**$240.00**

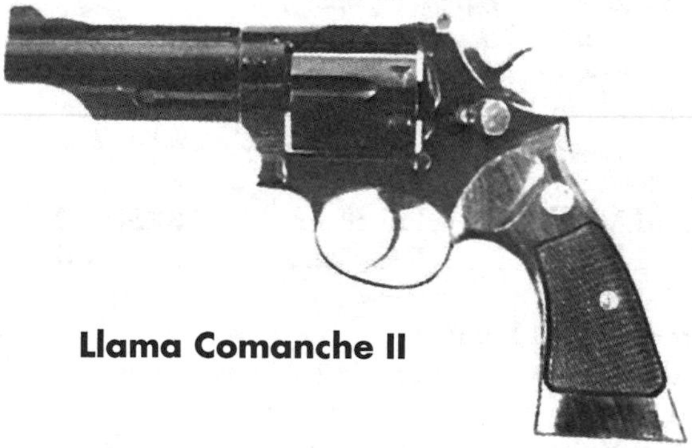

Llama Comanche II

Llama Comanche II

Similar to the Comanche I in 38 Special with a 4" or 6" barrel. Imported from 1973 to the 1980s.

Estimated Value:	**Excellent:**	**$245.00**
	Very good:	**$195.00**

Llama Comanche III

Similar to the Comanche II in 357 magnum caliber. Add 17% for satin chrome finish.

Estimated Value:	**Excellent:**	**$300.00**
	Very good:	**$240.00**

Llama Super Comanche, Super Comanche IV

A heavier version of the Comanche in 44 mag.; 6" barrel; 8½" barrel available after the early 1980s.

Estimated Value:	**Excellent:**	**$325.00**
	Very good:	**$260.00**

Llama Super Comanche V

Similar to the Super Comanche IV except 357 caliber. This heavy frame revolver has 4", 6", and 8½" barrel. Produced in the 1980s and the early 1990s.

Estimated Value:	**Excellent:**	**$300.00**
	Very good:	**$240.00**

MAB

MAB Model A

Caliber: 25 ACP (6.35mm)
Action: Semiautomatic; concealed hammer; manual safety; blowback design
Magazine: 6-shot clip
Barrel: 2½"
Sights: Fixed front; no rear
Finish: Blued; checkered hard rubber or plastic grips
Length Overall: 4½"
Approximate wt.: 18 ozs.
Comments: Resembles Browning Model 1906 vest pocket pistol. Production started about 1924, imported into U.S. as WAC Model A or Le Defendeur. Importation stopped in 1968.

Estimated Value:	**Excellent:**	**$250.00**
	Very good:	**$200.00**

MAB Model B

Similar to the Model A except top part of front section of slide cut away for empty cartridges to eject at top. Made from about 1932 to 1966 (never imported into U.S.).

Estimated Value:	**Excellent:**	**$235.00**
	Very good:	**$185.00**

MAB Model C

Caliber: 32 ACP, 380 ACP
Action: Semiautomatic; concealed hammer; grip safety and manual safety
Magazine: 7-shot clip in 32 ACP; 6-shot clip in 380 ACP
Barrel: 3¼"
Sights: Fixed
Finish: Blued; checkered hard rubber grips
Length Overall: 6¼"
Approximate wt.: 23 ozs.
Comments: Production started about 1933. Importation into U.S. stopped in 1968.

Estimated Value:	**Excellent:**	**$300.00**
	Very good:	**$240.00**

MAB Model E

Caliber: 25 ACP (6.35mm)
Action: Semiautomatic; concealed hammer; manual safety and grip safety
Magazine: 10-shot clip
Barrel: 4"
Sights: Fixed
Finish: Blued; checkered plastic grips
Length Overall: 7"
Approximate wt.: 24 ozs.
Comments: Production started about 1949; importation into U.S. discontinued in 1968. Imported into U.S. as WAC Model E.

Estimated Value:	**Excellent:**	**$375.00**
	Very good:	**$300.00**

MAB Model F

Caliber: 22 long rifle
Action: Semiautomatic; concealed hammer; manual safety; blowback design
Magazine: 9-shot clip
Barrel: 4½", 6", 7"
Sights: Fixed
Finish: Blued; checkered grips
Length Overall: 8½" to 11"
Approximate wt.: 23 ozs.
Comments: Production began in 1950. Imported into U.S. under WAC trademark. Importation stopped in 1968.

Estimated Value:	**Excellent:**	**$400.00**
	Very good:	**$320.00**

MAB Model R

MAB Model D

Caliber: 32 ACP, 380 ACP
Action: Semiautomatic; concealed hammer; grip safety and manual safety
Magazine: 9-shot clip in 32 ACP, 8-shot clip in 380 ACP
Barrel: 4"
Sights: Fixed
Finish: Blued; checkered hard rubber grips
Length Overall: 7"
Approximate wt.: 25 ozs.
Comments: Imported into U.S. as WAC Model D or MAB Le Gendarme; production started about 1932; importation discontinued in 1968.

Estimated Value:	**Excellent:**	**$350.00**
	Very good:	**$280.00**

MAB Model E

MAB Model P-15

Caliber: 9mm Parabellum
Action: Semiautomatic; exposed hammer with round spur; recoil operated with locking breech; manual safety
Magazine: 8-shot clip; 15-shot staggered row clip
Barrel: 4½"
Sights: Blade front; notch rear
Finish: Blued; checkered grips
Length Overall: 8"
Approximate wt.: 25 ozs.
Comments: Bears a resemblance to the Browning Model 1935.

Estimated Value:	**Excellent:**	**$450.00**
	Very good:	**$360.00**

MAB Model R

Caliber: 22 long rifle; 32 ACP, 380 ACP, 9mm Parabellum
Action: Semiautomatic; exposed hammer; manual safety
Magazine: 9-shot clip in 22 caliber; 8-shot clip in 32 ACP; 7-shot clip in 380 ACP, 7- or 14-shot clip in 9mm
Barrel: 4½" or 7½" (22); 4" in other calibers
Sights: Fixed
Finish: Blued; checkered grips
Length Overall: 7" to 10½"
Approximate wt.: 25 ozs.
Comments: This model was never imported into the U.S.

Estimated Value:	**Excellent:**	**$325.00**
	Very good:	**$260.00**

Mauser WTP Model 1 Vest Pocket

Caliber: 25 ACP
Action: Semiautomatic; concealed hammer
Magazine: 6-shot clip
Barrel: 2⅜"
Sights: Fixed
Finish: Blued; hard rubber grips
Length Overall: 4¼"
Approximate wt.: 12 ozs.
Comments: Made from about 1923 to 1939.

Estimated Value:	**Excellent:**	**$600.00**
	Very good:	**$480.00**

Mauser WTP Model 2 Vest Pocket

Similar to the Model 1 except: curved back strap and trigger guard; smaller size (2" barrel, about 4" overall length); approximate weight is 10 ozs. Made from about 1939 to 1942 and from about 1950 until importation into U.S. discontinued in 1968.

Estimated Value:	**Excellent:**	**$550.00**
	Very good:	**$440.00**

Mauser Automatic Pocket

Caliber: 25 ACP, 32 ACP
Action: Semiautomatic; concealed hammer
Magazine: 9-shot clip in 25 ACP, 8-shot clip in 32 ACP
Barrel: 3" on 25 ACP; 3½" on 32 ACP
Sights: Fixed
Finish: Blued; checkered walnut or hard rubber grips
Length Overall: 5½" on 25 ACP; 6" on 32 ACP
Approximate wt.: 22 ozs.
Comments: 25 ACP model made from about 1910 to 1939. 32 ACP model made from about 1914 to 1934.

Estimated Value:	**Excellent:**	**$475.00**
	Very good:	**$380.00**

Mauser Model 1934 Pocket

Mauser Model 1934 Pocket

Similar to the Automatic Pocket Pistol except larger one-piece wooden wrap-around grip which covered the back strap. Made from about 1934 to 1939. 32 ACP only.

Estimated Value:	**Excellent:**	**$500.00**
	Very good:	**$400.00**

Mauser WTP Model 2 Vest Pocket

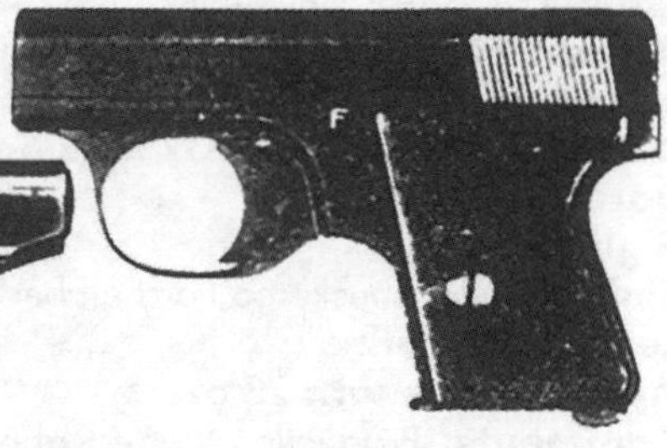

Mauser Model HSC Pocket Pistol

Mauser Model HSC Pocket Pistol

Caliber: 32 ACP, 380 ACP
Action: Semiautomatic; double action; exposed hammer
Magazine: 8-shot clip
Barrel: 3⅜"
Sights: Fixed
Finish: Blued or nickel; checkered wood grips
Length Overall: 6¼"
Approximate wt.: 21 ozs.
Comments: Made from about 1938 to World War II and from about 1968 to the late 1980s (deduct 25% for later model). Add 5% for nickel finish.

Estimated Value:	**Excellent:**	**$800.00**
	Very good:	**$640.00**

Mauser Military Model (Broomhandle Mauser)

Caliber: 7.63 Mauser; 9mm Parabellum (during World War I marked with a large figure "9" cut in the wood grip), 9mm Mauser
Action: Semiautomatic; exposed hammer; selective fire introduced in 1930 – selective lever on "N" operated as normal semiautomatic and on "R" operated as a machine pistol with fully automatic fire
Magazine: 5- to 10-shot box magazine standard; 5- to 20-shot magazine on selective fire models
Barrel: 5½" standard; also manufactured with other barrel lengths
Sights: Adjustable for elevation
Finish: Blued; checkered wood, serrated wood, carved wood, smooth wood, or hard rubber grips
Length Overall: 12" with 5½" barrel
Approximate wt.: 43 ozs. with 5½" barrel
Comments: Made from about 1896 to 1918 and from about 1922 to 1937 with minor changes and improvements. Also produced with a shoulder stock holster (wood).

Estimated Value:	**Excellent:**	**$7,000.00 – 15,000.00**
	Very good:	**$5,600.00 – 12,000.00**

Mauser Military Model (Broomhandle Mauser)

Mitchell Arms Citation II and Trophy II

Caliber: 22 long rifle
Action: Single action semiautomatic; push-button barrel change; concealed hammer; thumb safety
Magazine: 10-shot clip
Barrel: 5½" or 7¼" fluted
Sights: Ramp front; adjustable rear on frame-mounted bridge
Finish: Stainless steel; checkered walnut grips with thumbrest
Length Overall: 10¼" to 12½"
Approximate wt.: 42 to 44 ozs.
Comments: Made in the mid-1990s; based on the High Standard Supermatic Series. Add 6% for the Trophy II Model.

Estimated Value:	**Excellent:**	**$375.00**
	Very good:	**$300.00**

Mitchell Arms Olympic ISU II

Caliber: 22 long rifle; 22 short (not interchangeable)
Action: Single action semiautomatic; concealed hammer; adjustable trigger; changeable barrel button
Magazine: 10-shot clip
Barrel: 6¾" tapered; integral stabilizer and two removable weights
Sights: Ramp front; frame mounted bridge for adjustable rear sight; drilled and tapped for scope mount
Finish: Stainless steel; checkered grips with thumbrest; stippled front and rear grip frame
Length Overall: 11¼"
Approximate wt.: 40 ozs.
Comments: Made in the mid-1990s; see High Standard Olympic ISU.

Estimated Value:	**Excellent:**	**$525.00**
	Very good:	**$420.00**

Mitchell Arms Victor II

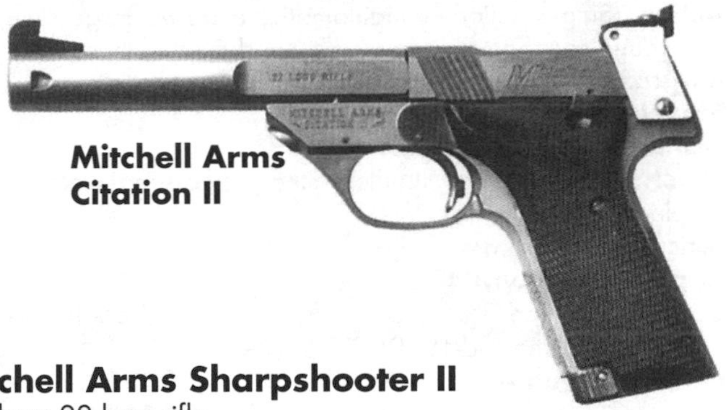

Mitchell Arms Citation II

Mitchell Arms Sharpshooter II

Caliber: 22 long rifle
Action: Single action semiautomatic; push-button barrel change; concealed hammer; thumb safety
Magazine: 10-shot clip
Barrel: 5½" bull barrel
Sights: Ramp front; adjustable rear
Finish: Stainless steel; checkered walnut grips
Length Overall: 10¼"
Approximate wt.: 42 ozs.
Comments: Made in the mid-1990s.

Estimated Value:	**Excellent:**	**$325.00**
	Very good:	**$260.00**

Mitchell Arms Sport King II

Caliber: 22 long rifle
Action: Single action semiautomatic; push-button barrel change; concealed hammer; thumb safety
Magazine: 10-shot clip
Barrel: 4½" or 6¾"
Sights: Ramp front; adjustable rear
Finish: Stainless steel; checkered plastic grips
Length Overall: 9" or 11¼"
Approximate wt.: 36 to 39 ozs.
Comments: Made in the mid-1990s.

Estimated Value:	**Excellent:**	**$250.00**
	Very good:	**$200.00**

Mitchell Arms Victor II

Caliber: 22 long rifle
Action: Single action semiautomatic; push-button barrel change; concealed hammer; thumb safety
Magazine: 10-shot clip
Barrel: 4½" or 5½"; ventilated rib, solid rib, or Weaver rib
Sights: Adjustable target sights
Finish: Stainless steel; checkered walnut grips with thumbrest; stippled grip frame in front and rear; gold-plated trigger, safety, magazine release, slide lock, and gold-filled markings
Length Overall: 9" or 11¼"
Approximate wt.: 36 to 39 ozs.
Comments: Made in the mid-1990s. Same as the High Standard Victor; add 5% for Solid Rib model; add 14% for Weaver rib model.

Estimated Value:	**Excellent:**	**$500.00**
	Very good:	**$400.00**

Mitchell Arms Signature Series '94 (Standard Model)

Caliber: 45 ACP
Action: Single action semiautomatic; exposed target-style skeleton round spur hammer; grip safety and manual thumb safety
Magazine: 8-shot clip; beveled magazine well
Barrel: 5"; low profile rib on slide
Sights: Fixed or adjustable
Finish: Blued steel or stainless steel; checkered walnut grips; stippled grip frame
Length Overall: 8½"
Approximate wt.: 40 ozs.
Comments: Add 8% for adjustable sights; add 6% for stainless steel. Made in the mid-1990s.

Estimated Value:	**Excellent:**	**$425.00**
	Very good:	**$340.00**

Mitchell Arms Signature Series '94 (Wide Body)

Same as Standard Model except: wider grip frame to accommodate the staggered 13-shot clip; smooth walnut grips; add 6% for adjustable sights; add 5% for stainless steel finish.

Estimated Value:	**Excellent:**	**$510.00**
	Very good:	**$405.00**

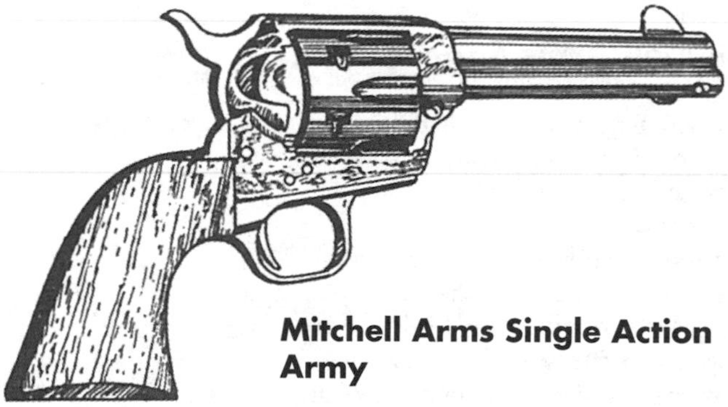

Mitchell Arms Single Action Army

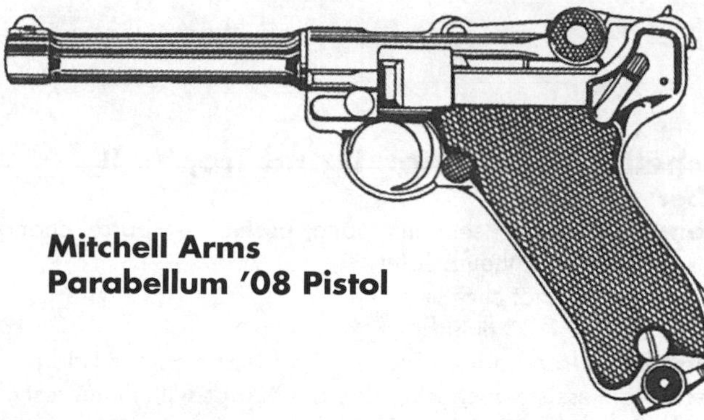

Mitchell Arms Parabellum '08 Pistol

Mitchell Arms Parabellum '08 Pistol

Caliber: 9mm Luger
Action: Single action semiautomatic; patterned after the German 9mm Luger pistol
Magazine: 7-shot clip
Barrel: 5"; round
Sights: Fixed
Finish: Stainless steel, checkered grips
Length Overall: 10"
Approximate wt.: 36 ozs.
Comments: Made in the mid-1990s.

Estimated Value:	**Excellent:**	**$450.00**
	Very good:	**$360.00**

Mitchell Arms Single Action Army

Caliber: 357 magnum and 38 Special; 45 Colt; 45 ACP
Action: Single action; exposed hammer; side load
Cylinder: 6-shot with loading gate
Barrel: 4¾"; 5½", or 7½"; ejector rod
Sights: Fixed; blade front, notched rear
Finish: Blued or nickel; walnut grips
Length Overall: 10"
Approximate wt.: 36 ozs.
Comments: Patterned after the Colt Single Action Army Revolver. Add 10% for nickel finish. Add 20% for extra cylinder in 45 ACP. Made in the mid-1990s.

Estimated Value:	**Excellent:**	**$300.00**
	Very good:	**$240.00**

NEW ENGLAND

New England Standard Revolver-22

Caliber: 22 short, long, or long rifle; 22 Win. magnum
Action: Single or double; exposed hammer; solid frame
Cylinder: 9-shot 22 short, long, or long rifle; 6-shot in 22 magnum; swing-out, simultaneous manual ejector
Barrel: 2½" or 4"
Sights: Blade front; fixed rear (groove in frame)
Finish: Blued or nickel; hardwood, walnut finish smooth grips
Length Overall: 7" (2½" barrel), 8½" (4" barrel)
Approximate wt.: 26 ozs.
Comments: Introduced in 1989. Add 10% for nickel finish.

Estimated Value:	**Excellent:**	**$125.00**
	Very good:	**$100.00**

New England Standard Revolver-32 H&R Magnum

New England Standard Revolver-32 H&R Mag.

Same as the Standard Revolver-22 except 32 H&R magnum caliber only; 5-shot cylinder; approximate weight: 25 ozs. Introduced in 1989. Add 10% for nickel finish.

Estimated Value:	**Excellent:**	**$135.00**
	Very good:	**$110.00**

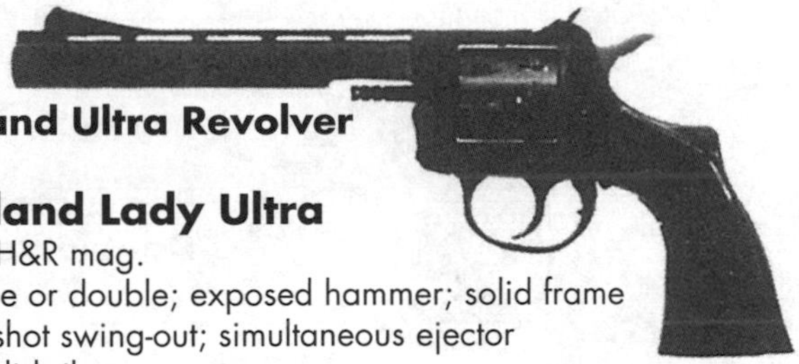

New England Ultra Revolver

New England Lady Ultra
Caliber: 32 H&R mag.
Action: Single or double; exposed hammer; solid frame
Cylinder: 5-shot swing-out; simultaneous ejector
Barrel: 3" solid rib
Sights: Blade front; adjustable rear
Finish: Blued; smooth wood grips
Length Overall: 7¼"
Approximate wt.: 31 ozs.
Comments: Introduced in the early 1990s.

Estimated Value:	**Excellent:**	**$125.00**
	Very good:	**$100.00**

New England Ultra Revolver
Caliber: 22 S, L, or LR; 22 Win. mag.; 32 H&R mag
Action: Single or double; exposed hammer; swing-out cylinder
Cylinder: 9-shot; (22 S, L, or LR); 6-shot (22 mag.); 5-shot (32 H&R mag.); simultaneous manual ejector
Barrel: 3" or 6"; with solid rib
Sights: Blade front; adjustable rear
Finish: Blued; hardwood, walnut finish smooth grips
Length Overall: 7⅝" (3" barrel); 10⅝" (6" barrel)
Approximate wt.: 31 to 36 ozs.
Comments: Introduced in 1990. Add 5% for 32 mag.

Estimated Value:	**Excellent:**	**$130.00**
	Very good:	**$105.00**

NORTH AMERICAN ARMS

North American Arms (Mini Revolver)
Caliber: 22 short; 22 long rifle (1976); 22 mag. (1978), 17 mach, 17HMR
Action: Single action; exposed hammer; spur trigger; solid frame
Cylinder: 5-shot; removable cylinder; available with two cylinders (22 long rifle and 22 mag.)
Barrel: 1⅛", 1⅝", 2½", 4"
Sights: Blade front; fixed rear
Finish: Stainless steel; polycarbonate round butt (bird head) grips
Length Overall: 4" to 8", depending on barrel length and caliber
Approximate wt.: 4 to 6 ozs.
Comments: Made from about 1975 to the present. Add 10% for 22 mag.; 30% for revolver with both cylinders; add 65% for 4" barrel.

Estimated Value:	**New (retail):**	**$199.00**
	Excellent:	**$150.00**
	Very good:	**$120.00**

North American Black Widow
Similar to the Mini Revolver except: adjustable sights, heavy ventilated rib barrel; black rubber grips.

Estimated Value:	**New (retail):**	**$259.00**
	Excellent:	**$195.00**
	Very good:	**$155.00**

North American Guardian
Caliber: 32 ACP, 380 ACP
Action: Recoil-operated semiautomatic; concealed hammer; double action only
Cylinder: 6-shot clip
Barrel: 2", 2½"
Sights: Fixed
Finish: Stainless steel; black or gold titanium; polymer grips
Length Overall: 4"
Approximate wt.: 15 ozs.
Comments: Introduced in 2000. Add 10% for 380ACP.

Estimated Value:	**New (retail):**	**$409.00**
	Excellent:	**$305.00**
	Very good:	**$245.00**

North American Arms (Mini Revolver)

REMINGTON

Remington Model 1891, Single-Shot Target
Caliber: 22, 25, 32RF, 32 S&W CF
Action: Single
Cylinder: None; single-shot with rolling breech block for rimfire or centerfire calibers
Barrel: 8", 10", 12"; half octagon
Sights: Dovetail, German silver front and adjustable "V" notch rifle rear
Finish: Blued barrel; case-hardened frame; oil finished walnut grips and fore-end
Length Overall: 12" to 16" depending on barrel length
Approximate wt.: 40 to 45 ozs.

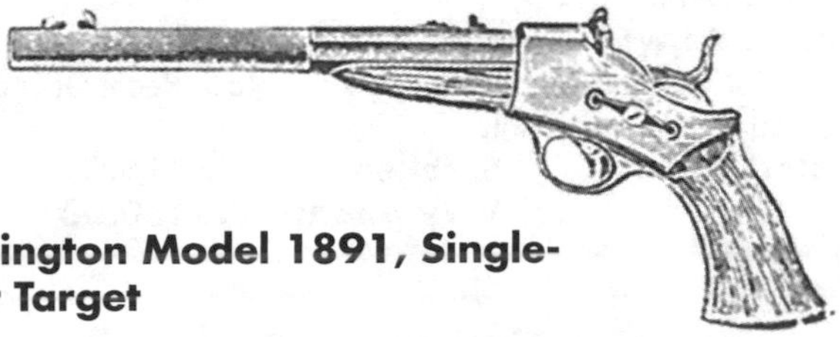

Remington Model 1891, Single-Shot Target

Comments: Made from about 1891 to 1900 in light target calibers. Serial number on side of frame under grip. Less than 200 made.

Estimated Value:	**Excellent:**	**$2,000.00 – 4,000.00**
	Very good:	**$1,600.00 – 3,200.00**

Remington 41 Caliber Double Derringer

Caliber: 41 caliber rimfire
Action: Single; visible hammer with safety position; sheath trigger; manual extractor
Cylinder: None; 2-shot double barrels
Barrel: 3" superposed double barrels; ribbed top barrel; barrels swing up to load and extract cartridges
Sights: Blade front; groove in frame rear
Finish: Blued or nickel plated; plain or engraved; round butt grips made of metal, walnut, rosewood, hard rubber, ivory, or pearl
Length Overall: 4⅞"
Approximate wt.: 11 ozs.
Comments: Approximately 132,000 were produced from about 1866 to 1935. Serial numbers were repeated on these pistols, so the best way to estimate the age of a pistol is by the markings. They were marked as follows:
1866 – 1869: no extractors; left side of barrel E. REMINGTON & SONS, ILION, N.Y.; right side of barrel ELLIOT'S PATENT DEC. 12, 1865
1869 – 1880: left side of barrel: ELLIOT'S PATENT DEC. 12 1865; right side of barrel: E. REMINGTON & SONS, ILION, N.Y.
1880 – 1888: barrel rib top: E. REMINGTON & SONS, ILION N.Y. ELLIOT'S PATENT DEC. 12th 1865
1888 – 1910: barrel rib top: REMINGTON ARMS CO. ILION N.Y.
1910 – 1935: barrel rib top: REMINGTON ARMS U.M.C. CO. ILION, N.Y.
In 1934 the Double Derringer was called Model No. 95.
Estimated Values:

Plain models	**Excellent:**	**$2,000.00 – 4,000.00**
	Very good:	**$1,600.00 – 3,200.00**
Presentation models	**Excellent:**	**$3,000.00 – 5,000.00**
	Very good:	**$2,400.00 – 4,000.00**

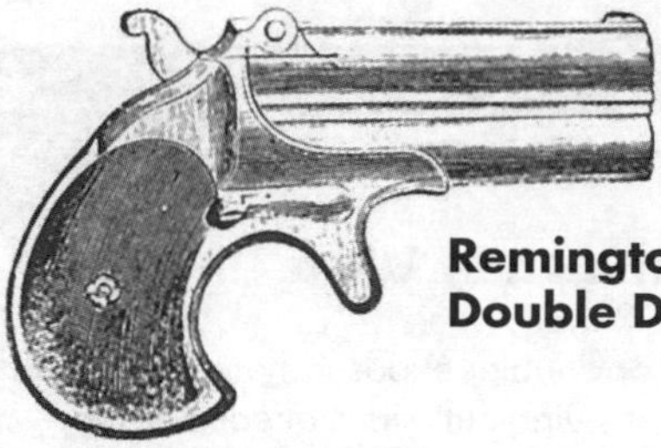
Remington 41 Caliber Double Derringer

Remington Model 1901, De-Luxe (S-S) Target

Caliber: 22 short, long, long rifle, 44 Russian CF
Action: Single
Cylinder: None; single-shot with rolling breech block for rimfire or centerfire calibers
Barrel: 9" round; 10" half octagon
Sights: Ivory bead front; adjustable "V" rear
Finish: Blued barrel and frame; checkered walnut grips and fore-end
Length Overall: 13" to 14"
Approximate wt.: 36 to 44 ozs.
Comments: Made from about 1901 to 1909. Approximately 1,000 produced.

Estimated Value:	**Excellent:**	**$2,000.00 – 4,000.00**
	Very good:	**$1,600.00 – 3,200.00**

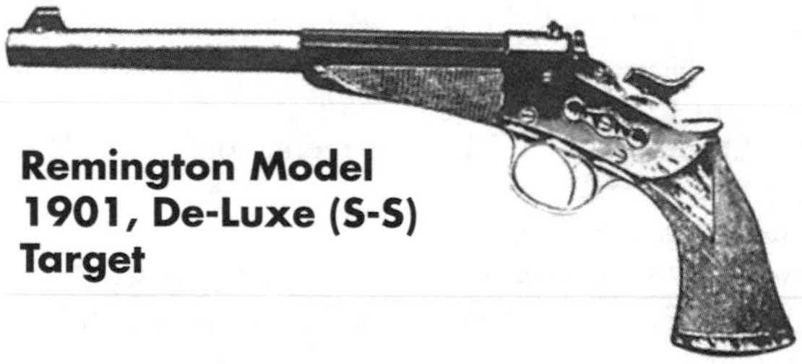
Remington Model 1901, De-Luxe (S-S) Target

Remington Model XP-100 Long Range

Caliber: 221 Remington "Fire Ball"
Action: Bolt action; single-shot; thumb safety
Cylinder: None
Barrel: 10½" round steel with ventilated rib
Sights: Blade front; adjustable rear
Finish: Blued with bright polished bolt and handle; brown checkered nylon (Zytel) one-piece grip and fore-end; fore-end has cavity for adding balance weights
Length Overall: 16¾"
Approximate wt.: 60 ozs.
Comments: Made from about 1963 to 1986. Receiver is drilled and tapped for scope mount.

Estimated Value:	**Excellent:**	**$575.00**
	Very good:	**$460.00**

Remington Model XP-100 Long Range

Remington Model XP-100 Silhouette

Similar to the Model XP-100 Long Range except: 10½" or 14½" plain barrel; 7mm Benchrest Rem. caliber; walnut or Zytel (nylon) stock; adjustable sights; produced from 1980 to the 1990s.

Estimated Value:	**Excellent:**	**$500.00**
	Very good:	**$400.00**

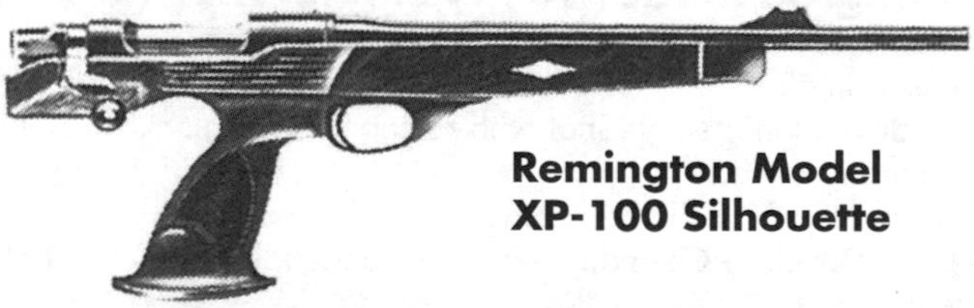
Remington Model XP-100 Silhouette

Remington Model XP-100 Varmint Special

Similar to the XP-100 Silhouette in 223 Rem. caliber. Zytel (nylon) stock; introduced in 1988.

Estimated Value:	**Excellent:**	**$450.00**
	Very good:	**$360.00**

Remington Model XP-100 Hunter

Caliber: 22-250 (Introduced in the mid-1990s), 223 Rem., 260 Rem. (Introduced in the mid-1990s), 7mm-08 Rem. (dropped in the mid-1990s), 35 Rem.
Action: Bolt action; single-shot
Cylinder: None
Barrel: 14½" plain; drilled and tapped for scope
Sights: None
Finish: Blued; laminated wood, one-piece stock
Length Overall: 21"
Approximate wt.: 4½ lbs.
Comments: Made in the 1990s.
Estimated Value: **Excellent:** **$575.00**
Very good: **$460.00**

Remington Model XP-100 Hunter

Remington Experimental 45 Caliber

An estimated value hasn't been placed on this pistol since it is not known how many were produced or how they were marked. They were similar to the Remington Model 51 Automatic Pistol except: in 45 caliber, larger and had an exposed spur hammer. They were made for U.S. Government test purposes about 1917.

Remington US Models 1911 and 1911 A1

These were pistols made by Remington, on the Colt Patent, for the U.S. Government during World War I and World War II. See Colt Government Model 1911 and 1911 A1 for prices.

Remington Model 51

Caliber: 32 ACP, 380 ACP
Action: Semiautomatic; concealed hammer
Magazine: 8-shot clip in 32 caliber; 7-shot clip in 380 caliber
Barrel: 3¼"
Sights: Fixed
Finish: Blued; hard rubber grips
Length Overall: 6⅝"
Approximate wt.: 20 ozs.
Comments: Made from about 1920 to 1934. Approximately 69,000 were produced in 32 and 380 calibers.
Estimated Value: **Excellent:** **$650.00**
Very good: **$525.00**

ROSSI

Rossi Models M68 and M88

Caliber: 38 Special
Action: Double or single; exposed hammer
Cylinder: 5-shot fluted, swing-out
Barrel: 2" or 3"; partially shrouded ejector rod
Sights: Fixed; ramp front, low profile rear
Finish: Blued or nickel (M68); stainless steel (M-88); checkered wood or rubber combat style grips
Length Overall: 6½" to 7½"
Approximate wt.: 21 to 23 ozs.
Comments: Introduced in the 1980s. Add 4% for nickel finish; add 18% for stainless steel.
Estimated Value: **Excellent:** **$170.00**
Very good: **$135.00**

Rossi Model M68 & M88

Rossi Models M515 and M518

Caliber: 22 mag. (M515); 22 short, long, and long rifle (M518)
Action: Double or single; exposed hammer
Cylinder: 6-shot fluted, swing-out
Barrel: 4"; partially shrouded ejector rod; solid rib
Sights: Ramp front with red insert; adjustable rear
Finish: All stainless steel; checkered wood or wrap-around rubber combat grips
Length Overall: 9"
Approximate wt.: 30 ozs.
Comments: Introduced in 1994. Add 6% for 22 magnum (Model M515).
Estimated Value: **Excellent:** **$215.00**
Very good: **$175.00**

Rossi Models M720 and M720 Hammerless

Caliber: 44 Special
Action: Double or single on exposed hammer model; double only on shrouded hammer model
Cylinder: 5-shot fluted, swing-out
Barrel: 3"; shrouded ejector rod; solid rib
Sights: Ramp front with red insert; adjustable rear; fixed square notch rear on hammerless model
Finish: Stainless steel; rubber wrap around combat grips
Length Overall: 8"
Approximate wt.: 28 ozs.
Comments: Hammerless model introduced in 1994.
Estimated Value: **Excellent:** **$235.00**
Very good: **$190.00**

Rossi Model M851

Caliber: 38 Special
Action: Double or single; exposed hammer
Cylinder: 6-shot, swing-out
Barrel: 4"; shrouded ejector rod; ventilated rib
Sights: Ramp front with red insert; adjustable rear
Finish: Stainless steel; checkered wood grips
Length Overall: 9"
Approximate wt.: 35 ozs.
Comments: Introduced in the late 1980s.

Estimated Value:	**Excellent:**	**$205.00**
	Very good:	**$165.00**

Rossi Model 351

Rossi Model 851

Rossi Model M851

Rossi Models 351 and 851

Caliber: 38 Special +P
Action: Double or single, exposed hammer
Cylinder: 6-shot swing-out
Barrel: 2" (Model 351); 4" (Model 851)
Sights: Ramp front, fixed rear; adjustable rear on Model 851
Finish: Blued or stainless steel: wrap-around rubber grips
Length overall: 7½" to 9½"
Approximate wt.: 24 to 38 ozs.
Comments: Add 15% for stainless steel finish.

Estimated Value:	**New (retail):**	**$389.00**
	Excellent:	**$290.00**
	Very good:	**$235.00**

Rossi Model M971

Rossi Models 461 and 462

Caliber: 357 mag., 38 Special +P
Action: Double or single, exposed hammer
Cylinder: 6-shot swing-out
Barrel: 2", shroud under barrel
Sights: Ramp front, fixed rear
Finish: Blued carbon steel (Model 461); stainless steel (Model 462); rubber, wrap-around grips
Length overall: 6½"
Approximate wt.: 26 ozs.
Comments: Add 15% for stainless steel finish (Model 462).

Estimated Value:	**New (retail):**	**$389.00**
	Excellent:	**$290.00**
	Very good:	**$235.00**

Rossi Model M971

Caliber: 357 magnum and 38 Special
Action: Double or single; exposed hammer
Cylinder: 6-shot, swing-out
Barrel: 2½", 4", or 6", shrouded ejector rod; solid rib
Sights: Ramp front with red insert; adjustable rear
Finish: Blued (4" only); stainless steel in all barrel lengths; checkered wood or rubber combat grips
Length Overall: 8¼", 9¼", or 11¼"
Approximate wt.: 22, 36, or 41 ozs.
Comments: Add 12% for stainless steel.

Estimated Value:	**Excellent:**	**$215.00**
	Very good:	**$175.00**

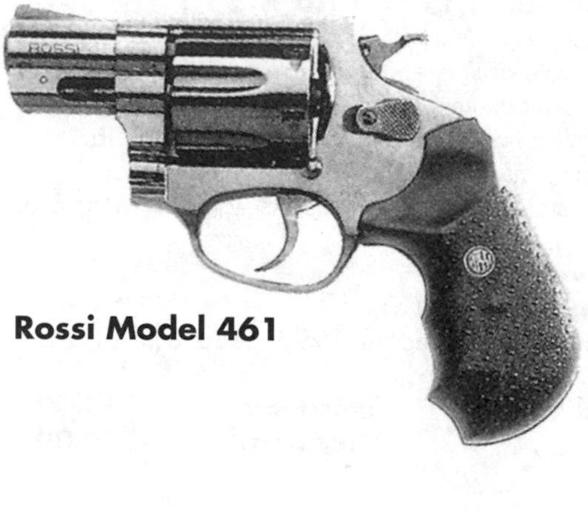

Rossi Model 461

Ruger Standard Automatic

Ruger Standard Automatic

Caliber: 22 long rifle
Action: Semiautomatic; concealed hammer; thumb safety
Magazine: 9-shot clip
Barrel: 4¾" or 6"; tapered round barrel
Sights: Partridge-type front; dovetail rear
Finish: Blued; checkered walnut or hard rubber grips
Length Overall: 8¾", 10"
Approximate wt.: 36 to 38 ozs.
Comments: Made from about 1949 to 1982. (Sturm Ruger Company was formed about 1949.) Red eagle insignia on grip used until 1951, then changed to black eagle insignia, after death of Alex Sturm. Add 160% for red eagle insignia on grip (pre-1951).

Estimated Value:	**Excellent:**	**$325.00**
	Very good:	**$260.00**

Ruger Mark I Bull Barrel Target

Ruger Mark II Standard Automatic

Similar to the Standard Automatic except: blued or stainless steel; internal improvements; 10-shot clip; slight difference in rear receiver design; 4¾" or 6" round tapered barrel. Introduced in 1982. Add 31% for stainless steel.

Estimated Value:	**Excellent:**	**$350.00**
	Very good:	**$280.00**

Ruger Mark II Target

Ruger Mark I Target

Ruger Mark I Target

Similar to Ruger Standard Automatic except adjustable sights; 6⅞" tapered barrel only. Made from about 1950 to 1982.

Estimated Value:	**Excellent:**	**$500.00**
	Very good:	**$400.00**

Ruger Mark II Target

Similar to the Mark II Standard Automatic with adjustable sights. 5½", 6⅞, or 10" tapered barrel. Introduced in 1982. Add 19% for stainless steel.

Estimated Value:	**Excellent:**	**$300.00**
	Very good:	**$240.00**

Ruger Mark I Bull Barrel Target

Similar to Ruger Mark I Target Pistol except barrel length 5½"; overall length 9½"; untapered heavier barrel. Made from about 1963 to 1982.

Estimated Value:	**Excellent:**	**$525.00**
	Very good:	**$420.00**

Ruger Mark II Bull Barrel Target

Similar to the Mark II Target with 4", 5½", or 6⅞" bull barrel. Introduced in 1982. Also 10" bull barrel introduced in 1983. Add 20% for stainless steel.

Estimated Value:	**Excellent:**	**$325.00**
	Very good:	**$260.00**

Ruger Mark II Bull Barrel Target

Ruger 22/45

Ruger Mark II Government

Similar to the Mark II Bull Barrel with a 6⅞" bull barrel. Add 20% for stainless steel.

Estimated Value:	**Excellent:**	**$350.00**
	Very good:	**$280.00**

Ruger 22/45

Similar to the Mark II 22 models except: 4¾" and 5¼" tapered barrel or 5½" bull barrel; 400 series stainless steel; approximate weight: 28 to 35 ozs.; injection moulded grip and trigger guard; frame of Zytel, a fiberglass reinforced composite; the grip angle and magazine latch almost identical to the Colt 1911 Model 45 ACP; fixed or adjustable sights; add 18% for 5¼" or 5½" barrel with adjustable sights. Add 10% for stainless steel.

Estimated Value:	**Excellent:**	**$225.00**
	Very good:	**$180.00**

Important safety warning to owners of Ruger P85 models made between 1987 and 1990. If the firing pin is broken, these pistols may fire when the safety/decock lever is depressed. Contact Sturm, Ruger, and Company, Prescott, Arizona 1-800-424-1886 to schedule factory modification.

Ruger Model P85

Caliber: 9mm
Action: Double action, recoil-operated, semiautomatic, ambidextrous safety
Magazine: 15-shot, staggered detachable
Barrel: 4½"
Sights: Fixed
Finish: Blued or stainless steel; grooved plastic grips with Ruger insignia
Length Overall: 8"
Approximate wt.: 32 ozs.
Comments: A compact combat pistol; made from 1987 to 1990. Add 10% for extra magazine and high impact molded case. Add 12% for stainless steel.

Estimated Value:	**Excellent:**	**$325.00**
	Very good:	**$260.00**

Ruger Model P85 Mk II

Same as the Model P85 except: new features and field-tested refinements, such as changes to the safety mechanism to prevent firing during decocking, even in the event of a broken firing pin. Introduced in 1990. Add 10% for stainless steel. Discontinued in 1993.

Estimated Value:	**Excellent:**	**$350.00**
	Very good:	**$280.00**

Ruger Model P85

Ruger Model P89

Similar to the Model P85 MK II except: decocking lever or regular safety. Introduced in 1991. Also available in double action only with spurless hammer. Add 10% for stainless steel.

Estimated Value:	**Excellent:**	**$355.00**
	Very good:	**$285.00**

Ruger Model P94

Ruger Model P90, KP90

Similar to the Model P85 MK II except: 45 ACP; 7-shot clip; regular safety or decocking lever; blued or stainless steel. Introduced in 1992. Add 7% for stainless steel (Model KP90).

Estimated Value:	**New (retail):**	**$591.00**
	Excellent:	**$445.00**
	Very good:	**$355.00**

Ruger Model P89

Ruger Model P91

Similar to the Model P85 MK II except: 40 S&W; 11-shot clip; stainless steel only; no external safety lever; decocking lever or double action only; double action only has spurless hammer.

Estimated Value:	**Excellent:**	**$350.00**
	Very good:	**$280.00**

Ruger Model P93

Similar to the Model P91 except: 15-shot clip; 9mm; 4" barrel; blued or stainless steel with decocking lever or double action only; double action only has spurless hammer. Introduced in 1993. Add 23% for stainless steel.

Estimated Value:	**Excellent:**	**$350.00**
	Very good:	**$280.00**

Ruger Model P94, KP94

Similar to the Model P93 except: 4½" barrel; overall length 7½"; approximate wt.: 33 ozs.; 9mm 15-shot or 40 S&W 11-shot; blued or stainless steel; slightly larger than the Model P93; fixed white dot sights; it has a tilting barrel link like the Colt M1911A1; available in the following models: double action with regular safety; decocking lever; and double action only spurless hammer. Add 23% for stainless steel (Model KP94).

Estimated Value:	**Excellent:**	**$350.00**
	Very good:	**$280.00**

Ruger Model P95

Similar to the Model P94 except: 9mm caliber only; 4" barrel. Add 30% for stainless steel finish.

Estimated Value:	**New (retail):**	**$393.00**
	Excellent:	**$295.00**
	Very good:	**$235.00**

Ruger Model P95

Ruger Model P97, P97D

Similar to the Model P95 except: 45ACP caliber. P97D is decock only.

Estimated Value:	**Excellent:**	**$345.00**
	Very good:	**$275.00**

Ruger GP-100 Double-Action Revolver

Caliber: 357 mag. or 38 Special
Action: Double and single; solid frame; exposed hammer
Cylinder: 6-shot; swing-out; simultaneous ejector
Barrel: 3", 4", or 6" heavy barrel with ejector rod shroud
Sights: Fixed or changeable front; fixed or adjustable rear
Finish: Blued or stainless steel; with a cushioned grip system. A newly designed skeleton-type grip frame is used. The grips are rubber with polished wood inserts.
Length Overall: $8\frac{3}{8}$" or $11\frac{3}{8}$"
Approximate wt.: 36 to 46 ozs.
Comments: Introduced in 1986. Add 8% for stainless steel. Add 4% for adjustable sights.

Estimated Value:	**New (retail):**	**$634.00**
	Excellent:	**$475.00**
	Very good:	**$380.00**

Ruger Model SP 101

Caliber: 9mm; 357 mag. and 38 Spl.; 32 H&R; 22 S, L, or LR
Action: Single and double; exposed hammer, or spurless hammer
Cylinder: 5-shot (9mm, 357 mag. and38 Spl.); 6-shot (22 and 32 H&R caliber); swing-out
Barrel: 2" or $3\frac{1}{16}$" (38 Special); 2" or 4" (22 caliber); shrouded ejector rod
Sights: Ramp front; fixed rear; 22 has adjustable rear
Finish: Stainless steel except grips and sights; rubber grips with polished inserts
Length Overall: $7\frac{1}{2}$" to $9\frac{1}{2}$"
Approximate wt.: 25 to 27 ozs. (38 Spl, 9mm and 357 mag.); 32 oz. (22 and 32 H&R)
Comments: Introduced in 1990.

Estimated Value:	**New (retail):**	**$607.00**
	Excellent:	**$455.00**
	Very good:	**$365.00**

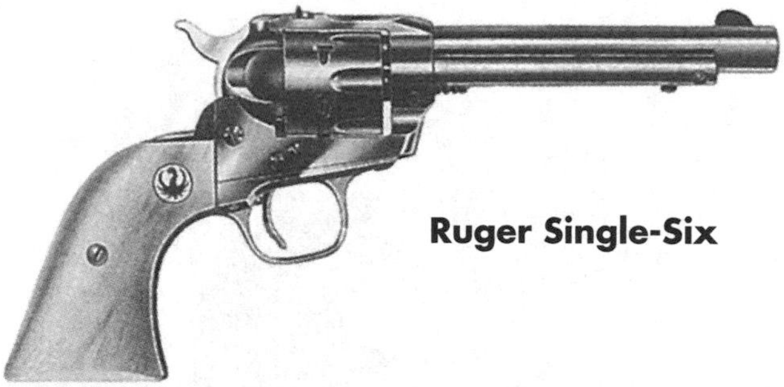

Ruger Single-Six

Ruger New Model Single-Six 32 H&R

Caliber: 32 H&R
Action: Single, solid frame with loading gate
Cylinder: 6-shot, half-fluted, loading gate
Barrel: $4\frac{5}{8}$"; ejector rod under barrel
Sights: Fixed; blade front, notch rear
Finish: Blued, case-hardened frame or stainless steel; hardwood or simulated ivory grips
Length overall: 10"
Approximate wt.: 34 ozs.
Comments: Similar to the Single-Six with internal improvements.

Estimated Value:	**Excellent:**	**$500.00**
	Very good:	**$400.00**

Ruger GP-100 Double-Action Revolver

In 1982 Ruger announced the production of a Single Action Conversion Kit that could be fitted on any "Old Model" Ruger Single Action revolver. This innovation, fitted at the factory, would give the old model a "transfer bar"-type mechanism by replacing a few key parts in the revolver. This would provide a safer handling single action. Unless it can be verified that the conversion has been made at the factory, all "Old Model" Single Action revolvers should be handled as such with caution.

Ruger Single-Six

Caliber: 22 short, long, long rifle, 22 WMR (after 1959)
Action: Single; solid frame with loading gate
Cylinder: 6-shot half-fluted; flat loading gate from 1954 to 1957 then changed to fit the contour of the frame
Barrel: $4\frac{5}{8}$", $5\frac{1}{2}$", $6\frac{1}{2}$", $9\frac{1}{2}$"; ejector rod under barrel
Sights: Blade front; rear sight dovetailed and can be tapped to left or right
Finish: Blued; checkered hard rubber or smooth walnut grips
Length Overall: 10", $10\frac{7}{8}$", $11\frac{7}{8}$", $14\frac{7}{8}$"
Approximate wt.: 32 to 36 ozs.
Comments: The grip frame is made of aluminum alloy and the frame is made of chrome molybdenum steel; produced from about 1953 to 1973. Add $150.00 for flat loading gate.

Estimated Value:	**Excellent:**	**$600.00**
	Very good:	**$480.00**

Ruger Lightweight Single-Six

Same as the Ruger Single-Six except: made for 22 short, long and long rifle only; $4\frac{7}{8}$" barrel; 10" overall length; weighs 23 ozs.; cylinder and frame made of lightweight alloy. Produced from about 1956 to 1958.

Estimated Value:	**Excellent:**	**$475.00**
	Very good:	**$380.00**

Ruger Convertible Single-Six

Same as the Ruger Single-Six revolver except: furnished with two cylinders – one chambered for 22 and the other chambered for 22 WMR. Manufactured from about 1961 to 1973. Prices for gun with both cylinders.

Estimated Value:	**Excellent:**	**$625.00**
	Very good:	**$500.00**

Ruger Convertible Super Single-Six

Same as the Ruger Single-Six revolver except: ramp front sight; adjustable rear sight with protective ribs on frame to protect rear sight. Made from about 1964 to 1973. Priced for gun with both cylinders.

Estimated Value:	**Excellent:**	**$575.00**
	Very good:	**$460.00**

Ruger New Model Super Single-Six Convertible

Similar to the Ruger Convertible Super Single-Six except: adjustable sights; improved version featuring wide trigger; heavy stronger lock works; transfer bar firing pin protector; new interlocking mechanism; other improvements. Made from about 1973 to 2005. 22 LR and 22 WMR cylinders.

Estimated Value: **Excellent:** **$325.00**
Very good: **$260.00**

Ruger New Model Super Single-Six Convertible Stainless Steel

Same as the Ruger New Model Super Single-Six Convertible Revolver except: all stainless steel construction except sights (blued). 5½" or 6½" barrel only. Made from about 1976 to 2005. Priced for gun with both cylinders.

Estimated Value: **Excellent:** **$375.00**
Very good: **$300.00**

Ruger New Model Super Single-Six 32 Magnum

Ruger Blackhawk 357 Convertible

Ruger Vaquero

Caliber: 357 magnum 45 long Colt (1993); 44-40 (1994); 44 mag. (1994)
Action: Single; solid frame with loading gate
Cylinder: 6-shot; fluted
Barrel: 4⅝", 5½", or 7½" in 45 long Colt and 44-40 calibers; 5½", or 7½" in 44 mag.; ejector rod
Sights: Fixed; blade front and groove in frame for rear
Finish: Blued with color case finish on frame or high-gloss stainless steel; smooth rosewood grips
Length Overall: 10¼" to 13⅛"
Approximate wt.: 39 to 41 ozs.
Comments: Introduced in 1993. Blued or stainless steel same price. Add 8% for simulated ivory grips.

Estimated Value: **New (retail):** **$679.00**
Excellent: **$510.00**
Very good: **$405.00**

Ruger Bisley Vaquero

Similar to the Vaquero except: Bisley-style frame and grips; available with 4⅝" or 5½" barrel. Add 6% for stainless steel finish.

Estimated Value: **Excellent:** **$450.00**
Very good: **$360.00**

Ruger New Model Super Single-Six Convertible

Ruger New Model Super Single-Six Convertible Stainless Steel

Ruger New Model Super Single-Six 32 Mag.

Caliber: 32 H&R; also handles 32 S&W and 32 S&W long
Action: Single; solid frame with loading gate
Cylinder: 6-shot; heavy fluted cylinder
Barrel: 4¾", 5½", 6½", or 9½"; ejector rod
Sights: Ramp front, adjustable rear
Finish: Blued; smooth walnut grips
Length Overall: 9⅞" to 14⅞"
Approximate wt.: 32 to 36 ozs.
Comments: Introduced in 1986 to bridge the gap between the 22 caliber and 38 caliber revolvers.

Estimated Value: **Excellent:** **$375.00**
Very good: **$300.00**

Ruger Blackhawk 357 Magnum

Caliber: 357 magnum and 38 Special interchangeably
Action: Single; solid frame with loading gate
Cylinder: 6-shot
Barrel: 4⅝", 6½"; round barrel with ejector rod under barrel
Sights: Ramp front; adjustable rear sight
Finish: Blued; checkered hard rubber or smooth walnut wood grips
Length Overall: 10⅛"; 12"
Approximate wt.: 35 to 40 ozs.
Comments: Made from about 1955 to 1973. In 1961 the frame was modified to a heavier frame with integral ribs on top to protect rear sight and slight grip alterations to improve the comfort of the "hold."

Estimated Value:	**Pre-1961**	**Post-1961**
Excellent:	**$475.00**	**$525.00**
Very good:	**$380.00**	**$420.00**

Ruger Blackhawk 357 Convertible

Same as the Ruger Blackhawk 357 Magnum Revolver except fitted with extra interchangeable cylinder for 9mm Parabellum cartridges. Manufactured from about 1967 to 1973.

Estimated Value: **Excellent:** **$550.00**
Very good: **$440.00**

Ruger Bird's Head Vaquero

Similar to the Ruger Vaquero; Black Micarta bird's head grips, 4½" barrel.

Estimated Value: **Excellent:** **$475.00**
Very good: **$380.00**

Ruger New Model Blackhawk

Similar to the Ruger Blackhawk 357 except: improved version featuring wide trigger; stronger lock works; transfer bar firing pin protector; new interlocking mechanism; other improvements. Made from about 1973 to present in 30 carbine, 357 mag., 41 mag. and 45 long Colt. Available with 4⅝", 5½", 6½", and 7½" barrel.

Estimated Value:	**New (retail):**	**$557.00**
	Excellent:	**$415.00**
	Very good:	**$335.00**

Ruger Stainless Steel New Model Blackhawk

Same as the Ruger New Model Blackhawk except: stainless steel construction except sights (blued). Made from about 1976 to the present.

Estimated Value:	**New (retail):**	**$681.00**
	Excellent:	**$510.00**
	Very good:	**$410.00**

Ruger New Model Blackhawk Convertible

Same as the Ruger New Model Blackhawk except: fitted with extra interchangeable cylinder for 357 magnum and 9mm Parabellum cartridges from about 1973 to the present; 45 Colt and 45 ACP cartridges from about 1973 to present; blued finish.

Estimated Value:	**New (retail):**	**$636.00**
	Excellent:	**$475.00**
	Very good:	**$380.00**

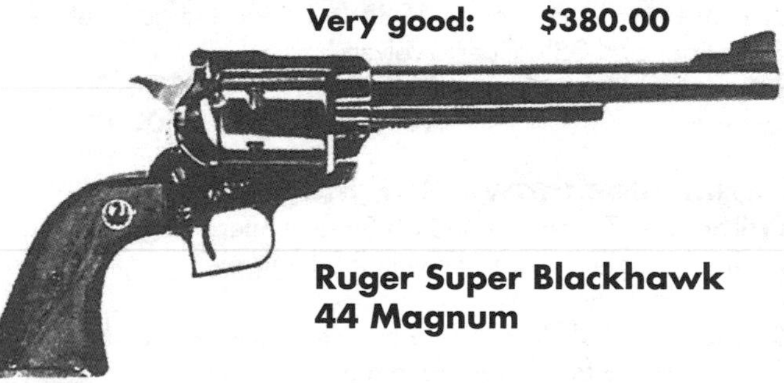

Ruger Super Blackhawk 44 Magnum

Ruger Super Blackhawk 44 Magnum

Caliber: 44 mag. and 44 S&W Special (interchangeably)
Action: Single; solid frame with loading gate
Cylinder: 6-shot; heavy non-fluted cylinder
Barrel: 7½"; ejector rod
Sights: Ramp front; adjustable rear sight
Finish: Blued; smooth walnut wood grips; square back trigger guard
Length Overall: 13⅜"
Approximate wt.: 48 ozs.
Comments: Produced from about 1959 to 1973.

Estimated Value:	**Excellent:**	**$525.00**
	Very good:	**$420.00**

Ruger New Model Super Blackhawk 44 Mag.

Similar to the Super Blackhawk 44 Mag. except: improved version, featuring stronger lock works; transfer bar firing pin protector; new interlocking mechanism; blued or stainless steel; 5½", 7½" or 10½" barrel; other improvements. Made from about 1973 to the present. Add 10% for stainless steel; 2% for 10½" barrel.

Estimated Value:	**New (retail):**	**$670.00**
	Excellent:	**$500.00**
	Very good:	**$400.00**

Ruger New Model Blackhawk

Ruger Stainless Steel New Model Blackhawk

Ruger Blackhawk 44 Magnum

Caliber: 44 magnum and 44 S&W Special interchangeably
Action: Single; solid frame with loading gate
Cylinder: 6-shot; heavy fluted cylinder
Barrel: 6½"; ejector rod under barrel
Sights: Ramp front; adjustable rear sight
Finish: Blued; smooth walnut grips
Length Overall: 12½"
Approximate wt.: 40 ozs.
Comments: Produced from about 1956 to 1962.

Estimated Value:	**Excellent:**	**$575.00**
	Very good:	**$460.00**

Ruger Blackhawk 41 Magnum

Caliber: 41 magnum
Action: Single; solid frame with loading gate
Cylinder: 6-shot
Barrel: 4⅝", 6½" with ejector rod
Sights: Ramp front; adjustable rear sight
Finish: Blued; smooth walnut grips
Length Overall: 10¾"; 12⅛"
Approximate wt.: 35 to 38 ozs.
Comments: Produced from about 1965 to 1973.

Estimated Value:	**Excellent:**	**$525.00**
	Very good:	**$420.00**

Ruger Blackhawk 30 Caliber

Caliber: 30 U.S. Carbine (M1)
Action: Single; solid frame with loading gate
Cylinder: 6-shot
Barrel: 7½" with ejector rod
Sights: Ramp front; adjustable rear sight
Finish: Blued; smooth walnut wood grips
Length Overall: 13⅛"
Approximate wt.: 39 ozs.
Comments: Made from about 1950 to 1973. A good companion handgun for the M1 carbine (30 caliber).

Estimated Value:	**Excellent:**	**$500.00**
	Very good:	**$400.00**

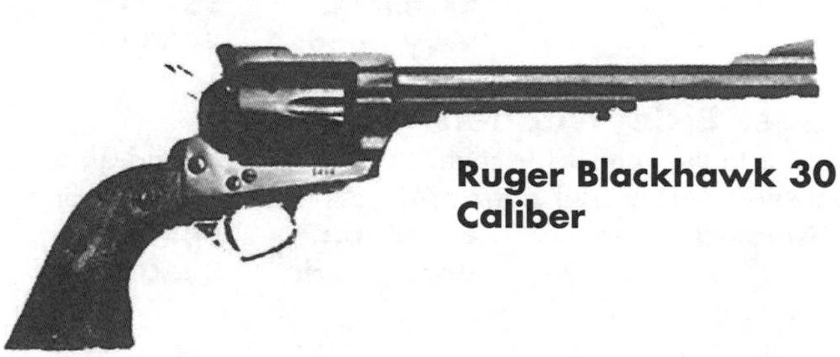

Ruger Blackhawk 30 Caliber

Ruger Blackhawk 45 Caliber
Caliber: 45 long Colt
Action: Single; solid frame with loading gate
Cylinder: 6-shot
Barrel: 4⅝", 7½" round barrel with ejector rod under barrel
Sights: Ramp front; adjustable rear sight
Finish: Blued; smooth walnut grips
Length Overall: 10⅛"; 13⅛"
Approximate wt.: 38 to 40 ozs.
Comments: Made from the late 1960s to 1973. Replaced by the New Model Blackhawk in 1973.

Estimated Value:	**Excellent:**	**$525.00**
	Very good:	**$420.00**

Ruger Redhawk
Caliber: 357 mag.; 41 mag.; 44 mag.; 45 long Colt
Action: Double and single; solid frame; exposed hammer
Cylinder: 6-shot swing-out; simultaneous ejector
Barrel: 5½", 7½", shrouded ejector rod under barrel
Sights: Adjustable rear, blade front
Finish: Stainless steel; blued model added in 1986; checkered or smooth walnut grips
Length Overall: 11", 13"
Approximate wt.: 52 ozs.
Comments: A heavy frame 44 mag. revolver introduced in 1979. 357 mag. and 41 mag. added in 1984. Add 13% for stainless steel; 8% for scope rings; 357 mag. dropped in 1986. 41 mag. dropped in 1992.

Estimated Value:	**New (retail):**	**$887.00**
	Excellent:	**$665.00**
	Very good:	**$530.00**

Ruger Super Redhawk
Caliber: 44 magnum, .44 Special, 454 Casull, 45 Colt and 480 Ruger
Action: Double and single
Cylinder: 6-shot swing-out; simultaneous ejector; fluted cylinder
Barrel: 7½" or 9½"
Sights: Ramp front base with interchangeable insert sight blades; adjustable white outline square notch rear
Finish: Stainless steel; cushioned grip system. A skeleton-type grip frame features rubber panels with Goncalo Alves panel inserts.
Length Overall: 13" or 15"
Approximate wt.: 56 ozs.
Comments: Introduced in 1987. Add 18% for 454 Casull, 45 Colt and 480 Ruger.

Estimated Value:	**New (retail):**	**$942.00**
	Excellent:	**$700.00**
	Very good:	**$560.00**

Ruger Police Service-Six

Ruger Blackhawk 45 Caliber Convertible
Same as Blackhawk 45 Caliber revolver except: fitted with extra interchangeable cylinder for 45 ACP cartridges. Made from about 1970 to 1973. Replaced by New Model Blackhawk in 1973.

Estimated Value:	**Excellent:**	**$500.00**
	Very good:	**$400.00**

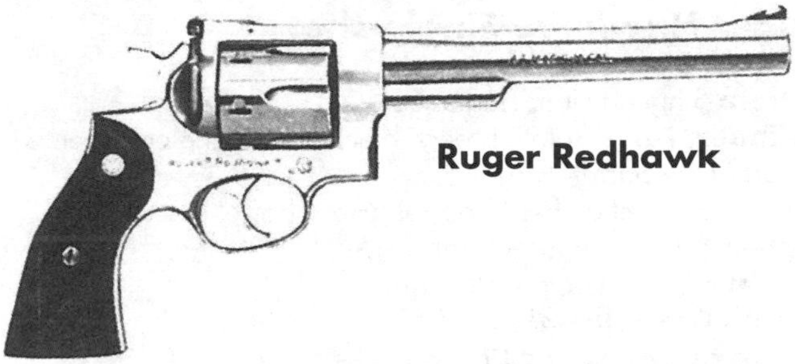

Ruger Redhawk

Ruger Security-Six 357 Magnum

Ruger Security-Six 357 Magnum
Caliber: 357 magnum, 38 Special
Action: Double and single; solid frame; exposed hammer
Cylinder: 6-shot; simultaneous ejector
Barrel: 2¾", 4", 6"
Sights: Adjustable
Finish: Blued or stainless steel; square butt, checkered walnut grips
Length Overall: 8", 9¼", 11"
Approximate wt.: 32 to 35 ozs.
Comments: Made from 1972 to the mid-1980s. A solid frame revolver with swing-out cylinder. Stainless steel model made from about 1975 to the mid-1980s. Add 9% for stainless steel.

Estimated Value:	**Excellent:**	**$325.00**
	Very good:	**$260.00**

Ruger Speed-Six
Similar to the Security-Six 357 Magnum revolver except: round butt style grips and in calibers 9mm Parabellum, 38 Special and 357 magnum. Fixed sights only. Made from about 1975 to 1989. Add $16.00 for 9mm; add 9% for stainless steel. 9mm dropped in the mid-1980s.

Estimated Value:	**Excellent:**	**$325.00**
	Very good:	**$260.00**

Ruger Service-Six and Police Service-Six
Similar to the Speed-Six revolver except: square butt style grips. Made from about 1976 to 1989. Add 8% for 9mm; add 8% for stainless steel. 9mm dropped in the mid-1980s. Called Police Service-Six after 1987.

Estimated Value:	**Excellent:**	**$325.00**
	Very good:	**$260.00**

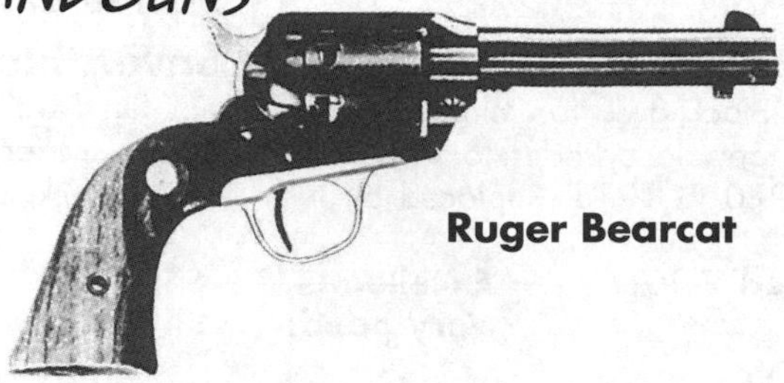

Ruger Bearcat

Ruger Hawkeye Single-shot
Caliber: 256 mag.
Action: Single action; single-shot
Cylinder: None; rotate breech block to load the chamber, which is part of the barrel
Barrel: 8½"; chamber in barrel; under barrel ejector rod
Sights: Adjustable target sights
Finish: Blued; smooth walnut grips
Length Overall: 14½"
Approximate wt.: 44 ozs.
Comments: The Hawkeye is built on the Ruger 44 mag. frame and resembles a revolver in appearance. Made from about 1963 to 1966.

Estimated Value:	**Excellent:**	**$2,000.00**
	Very good:	**$1,600.00**

Ruger New Bearcat (Convertible)
Caliber: 22 short, long or long rifle; 22WMR
Action: Single; solid frame with loading gate
Cylinder: 6-shot; non-fluted, roll-engraved; each gun is fitted with two cylinders (regular 22 and 22 mag.)
Barrel: 4" round with ejector rod
Sights: Fixed; blade front; groove in frame for rear
Finish: Blued or high gloss stainless steel; smooth walnut or rosewood grips
Length Overall: 9¼"
Approximate wt.: 28 ozs.
Comments: All steel construction; reintroduced in 1994; add 9% for stainless steel.

Estimated Value:	**New (retail):**	**$516.00**
	Excellent:	**$385.00**
	Very good:	**$310.00**

Ruger New Model Bisley
Caliber: 22 long rifle or 32 H&R mag. in small frame; 357 mag., 41 mag., 44 mag., or 45 long Colt in large frame
Action: Single; solid frame with loading gate
Cylinder: 6-shot fluted or non-fluted cylinder with or without roll engraving
Barrel: 6½" small frame, 7½" large frame; ejector rod under barrel
Sights: Ramp front, adjustable or fixed rear
Finish: Blued; smooth wood grips
Length Overall: 11½" frame, 13" large frame
Approximate wt.: 41 ozs. small frame, 48 ozs. large frame
Comments: Introduced in 1985 and 1986. Based on the Ruger single action design with a longer, different-angle grip similar to the old Colt Bisley revolvers; 32 caliber discontinued 2001.

Estimated Value:		**Small Frame**	**Large Frame**
	New (retail):		**$703.00**
	Excellent:	**$400.00**	**$525.00**
	Very good:	**$320.00**	**$420.00**

Ruger Bearcat
Caliber: 22 short, long or long rifle
Action: Single; solid frame with loading gate
Cylinder: 6-shot; non-fluted, engraved
Barrel: 4" round with ejector rod
Sights: Fixed
Finish: Blued; smooth walnut grips
Length Overall: 8⅞"
Approximate wt.: 17 ozs.
Comments: Alloy frame; coil springs and non-fluted engraved cylinder. Manufactured from about 1958 to 1972.

Estimated Value:	**Excellent:**	**$525.00**
	Very good:	**$420.00**

Ruger Super Bearcat
Same as the Ruger Bearcat revolver except all steel construction and made from about 1971 to 1975.

Estimated Value:	**Excellent:**	**$550.00**
	Very good:	**$440.00**

SAUER

Sauer 1913 (Old Model)

Sauer 1930 Model

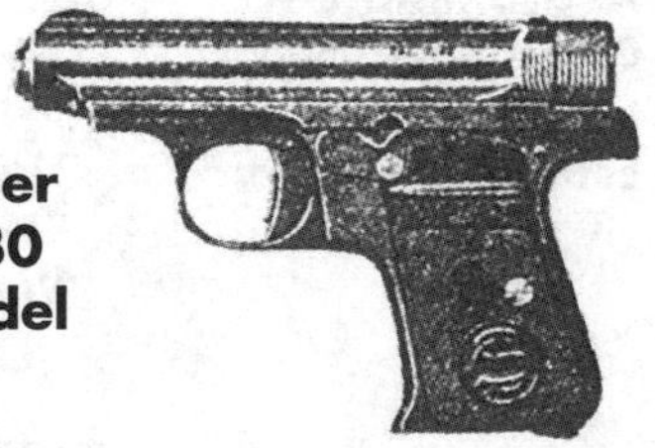

Sauer 1913 (Old Model)
Caliber: 32 ACP (7.65mm); 25 ACP (6.35mm)
Action: Semiautomatic; concealed hammer
Magazine: 7-shot clip
Barrel: 3"
Sights: Fixed
Finish: Blued; checkered hard rubber grips
Length Overall: 5⅞"
Approximate wt.: 32 ozs.
Comments: Made from about 1913 to 1930.

Estimated Value:	**Excellent:**	**$1,200.00**
	Very good:	**$ 960.00**

Sauer 1930 Model
Similar to the Sauer 1913 (Old Model) except improved version with main difference being the improved grip design which provides a better hold; some models made with indicator pins to show when they were cocked; some models made with alloy slide and receiver (approximately 15 ozs.) Made from about 1930 to 1938.

Estimated Value:	**Excellent:**	**$600.00**
	Very good:	**$480.00**

Sauer WTM Pocket
Caliber: 25 ACP (6.35mm)
Action: Semiautomatic; concealed hammer
Magazine: 6-shot clip
Barrel: 2½"
Sights: Fixed
Finish: Blued; checkered hard rubber grips
Length Overall: 4⅛"
Approximate wt.: 18 ozs.
Comments: Made from about 1924 to 1928. Fluted slide with top ejection port.

Estimated Value:	**Excellent:**	**$425.00**
	Very good:	**$340.00**

Sauer 1938 Model (Model H)

Sauer 1928 Model Pocket
Similar to the Sauer WTM Pocket Pistol except: smaller in size, 2" barrel and about 3⅞" overall length. Made from about 1928 to 1938.

Estimated Value:	**Excellent:**	**$425.00**
	Very good:	**$340.00**

Sauer 1938 Model (Model H)
Caliber: 32 ACP (7.65mm); 380 ACP; 22 LR
Action: Semiautomatic; double action; concealed hammer; lever on left side permitted hammer to be cocked or uncocked by the thumb; also could be fired by pulling trigger in double action style
Magazine: 7-shot clip
Barrel: 3¼"
Sights: Fixed
Finish: Blued; checkered plastic grips
Length Overall: 6¼"
Approximate wt.: 26 ozs.
Comments: Some models made with alloy slide (approximately 18 ozs. in weight); wartime models (WWII) inferior to earlier models. Made from about 1938 to 1944. Add 50% for 22 caliber.

Estimated Value:	**pre-war**	**wartime**
Excellent:	**$600.00**	**$500.00**
Very good:	**$480.00**	**$400.00**

SAVAGE

Savage Model 1905 Military Type
Caliber: 45 ACP
Action: Semiautomatic; blowback design, grip safety; exposed cocking lever
Magazine: 8-shot clip
Barrel: 5¼"
Sights: Fixed
Finish: Blued; checkered walnut grips
Length Overall: 9"
Approximate wt.: 36 ozs.
Comments: Approximately 200 were produced from about 1908 to 1911 and sold to U.S. Government Ordnance Dept. for tests, but lost to competition.

Estimated Value:	**Excellent:**	**$7,000.00 – 10,000.00**
	Very good:	**$5,600.00 – 8,000.00**

Savage Model 1907

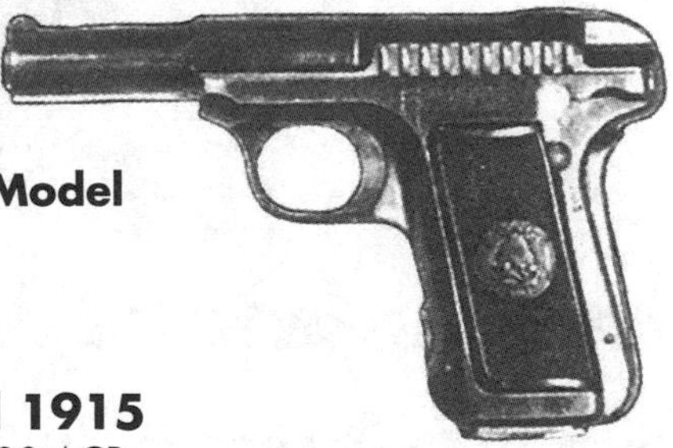

Savage Model 1915

Savage Model 1907
Caliber: 32 ACP, 380 ACP (after 1912)
Action: Semiautomatic; exposed rounded or spur cocking lever
Magazine: 10-shot in 32 caliber, 9-shot in 380 caliber
Barrel: 3¾" in 32 caliber; 9-shot in 380 caliber
Sights: Fixed
Finish: Blued; metal, hard rubber, or wood grips
Length Overall: 6½" (32 caliber); 7" (380 caliber)
Approximate wt.: 20 ozs.
Comments: Manufactured from about 1908 to 1920, with improvements and some changes in 1909, 1914, and 1918. Some military models with Lanyard loop were made of the 1912 variety and sold from 1915 to 1917.

Estimated Value:	**Excellent:**	**$500.00**
	Very good:	**$400.00**

Savage Model 1915
Caliber: 32 ACP, 380 ACP
Action: Semiautomatic; concealed hammer
Magazine: 10-shot in 32 caliber, 9-shot in 380 caliber
Barrel: 3¾" (caliber); 4¼" (380 caliber)
Sights: Fixed
Finish: Blued; hard rubber grips
Length Overall: 6½" (32 caliber), 7" (380 caliber)
Approximate wt.: 22 ozs.
Comments: Manufactured from about 1915 to 1917. Approximately 6,500 were produced in 32 caliber and approximately 2,350 were produced in 380 caliber.

Estimated Value:	**Excellent:**	**$650.00**
	Very good:	**$520.00**

Savage Model 1917

Caliber: 32 ACP, 380 ACP
Action: Semiautomatic; exposed spur cocking lever; thumb safety
Magazine: 10-shot clip in 32; 9-shot clip in 380, wider magazine than previous models to allow for cartridges to be staggered in a double row
Barrel: 3¾" in 32; 7" in 380
Sights: Fixed
Finish: Blued; hard rubber grips
Length Overall: 6½" in 32, 7" in 380
Approximate wt.: 24 ozs.
Comments: Made from about 1918 to 1928. Approximately 28,000 made in 32 caliber and 126,000 in 380 caliber. Wide frame and flared grips and the slide has small vertical gripping serrations.

Estimated Value:	**Excellent:**	**$375.00**
	Very good:	**$300.00**

Savage Model 1917

Savage Model 101 Single-shot

Savage Model 101 Single-shot

Caliber: 22 short, long, long rifle
Action: Single; single-shot
Cylinder: None; the false cylinder is the chamber part of the barrel
Barrel: 5½" alloy steel; swings out to load; ejector rod under barrel
Sights: Blade front; notched-bar rear
Finish: Blued barrel; painted one-piece aluminum alloy frame; compressed impregnated wood grips
Length Overall: 9½"
Approximate wt.: 20 ozs.
Comments: A single-shot pistol built to resemble a single-action frontier revolver. Made from about 1960 to 1968.

Estimated Value:	**Excellent:**	**$235.00**
	Very good:	**$185.00**

SHERIDAN

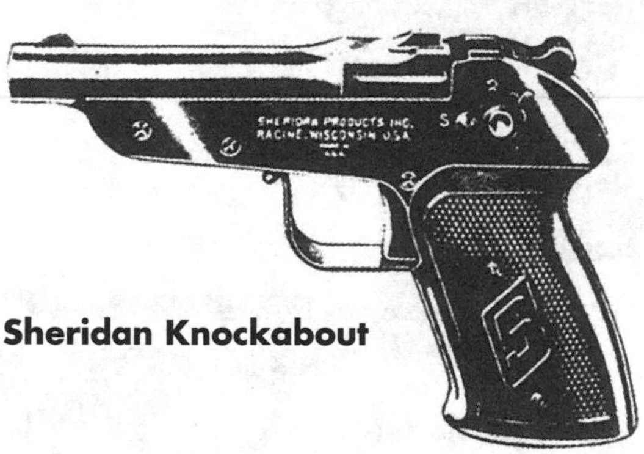

Sheridan Knockabout

Sheridan Knockabout

Caliber: 22 short, long, long rifle
Action: Single; exposed hammer; single-shot
Magazine: None
Barrel: 5½"; tip up barrel
Sights: Fixed
Finish: Blued; checkered plastic grips
Length Overall: 6¾"
Approximate wt.: 21 ozs.
Comments: An inexpensive single-shot pistol which resembles an automatic pistol. Made from about 1953 to 1962. Approximately 20,000 produced.

Estimated Value:	**Excellent:**	**$300.00**
	Very good:	**$240.00**

SMITH + WESSON

Smith & Wesson 1891 Single-shot Target Pistol

Caliber: 22 short, long, long rifle
Action: Single; exposed hammer; hinged frame (top break); single-shot
Cylinder: None
Barrel: 10"
Sights: Adjustable target
Finish: Blued; hard rubber square butt grips
Length Overall: 13½"
Approximate wt.: 25 ozs.
Comments: Made from about 1891 to 1905.

Estimated Value:	**Excellent:**	**$1,000.00**
	Very good:	**$ 800.00**

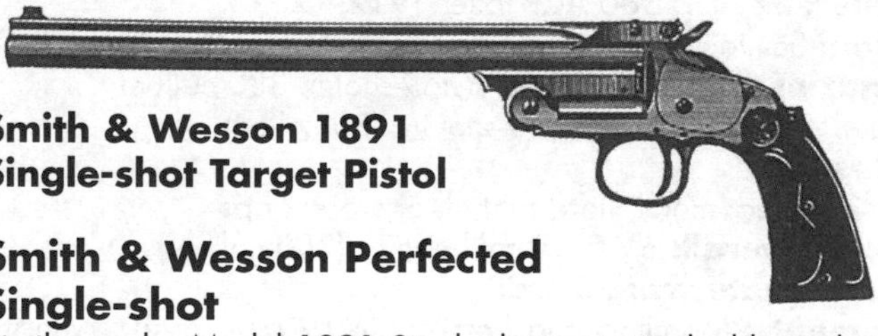

Smith & Wesson 1891 Single-shot Target Pistol

Smith & Wesson Perfected Single-shot

Similar to the Model 1891 Single-shot except: double and single action; checkered square butt walnut grips; made from about 1909 to 1923; the U.S. Olympic team of 1920 used this pistol, therefore it is sometimes designated "Olympic Model." Add $150.00 for Olympic Models.

Estimated Value:	**Excellent:**	**$1,200.00**
	Very good:	**$ 960.00**

Smith & Wesson Straightline

Caliber: 22 short, long, long rifle
Action: Single; exposed striker (hammer); single-shot
Magazine: None
Barrel: 10"; cartridge chamber in barrel; barrel pivots to the left to eject and load
Sights: Target sights
Finish: Blued; walnut grips
Length Overall: 11½"
Approximate wt.: 35 ozs.
Comments: Pistol resembles automatic pistol in appearance; sold with metal case, screwdriver, and cleaning rod. Made from about 1925 to 1937. Add $100.00 for original case and accessories.

Estimated Value:	**Excellent:**	**$2,000.00**
	Very good:	**$1,600.00**

Smith & Wesson Model 32 Automatic

Smith & Wesson Model 39

Smith & Wesson Model 59

Smith & Wesson Model 39

Caliber: 9mm (Parabellum) Luger
Action: Semiautomatic; double action; exposed hammer; thumb safety
Magazine: 8-shot clip
Barrel: 4"
Sights: Ramp front; rear adjustable for windage
Finish: Blued or nickel; checkered walnut grips
Length Overall: 7½"
Approximate wt.: 28 ozs.
Comments: Made from about 1954 to 1982. Normally pistol has aluminum alloy frame; approximately 925 pistols were produced with steel frames sometime prior to 1966. Add $25.00 for nickel finish. Replaced by S&W Model 439.

Estimated Value:	**Alloy Frame**	**Steel Frame**
Excellent:	**$425.00**	**$1,250.00**
Very good:	**$340.00**	**$1,000.00**

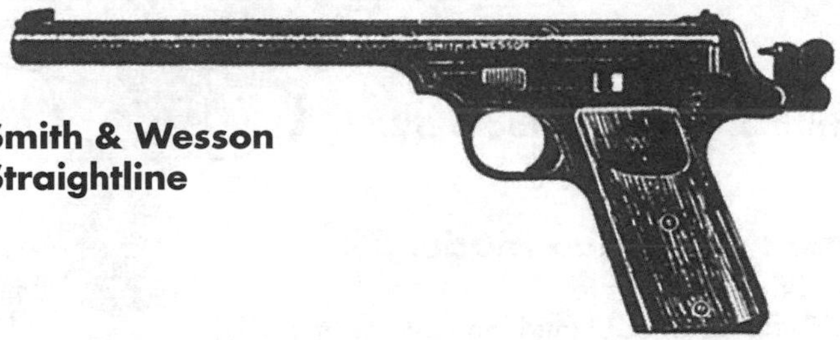

Smith & Wesson Straightline

Smith & Wesson Model 32 Automatic

Caliber: 32 ACP
Action: Semiautomatic; concealed hammer; grip safety located in front of grip below trigger guard
Magazine: 7-shot clip
Barrel: 3½"; barrel is fixed to the frame; the slide fits into guides on the barrel
Sights: Fixed
Finish: Blued; smooth walnut grips
Length Overall: 6½"
Approximate wt.: 24 ozs.
Comments: Serial numbers are a separate series beginning at number 1. Approximately 958 were produced from about 1924 to 1937.

Estimated Value:	**Excellent:**	**$2,250.00**
	Very good:	**$1,800.00**

Smith & Wesson Model 35 Automatic

Caliber: 35 S&W automatic
Action: Semiautomatic; concealed hammer; grip safety located in front of grip below trigger guard; manual safety at rear of left grip
Magazine: 7-shot clip
Barrel: 3½"; barrel hinged to rear of frame
Sights: Fixed
Finish: Blued or nickel; smooth walnut grips
Length Overall: 6½"
Approximate wt.: 22 ozs.
Comments: Serial numbers are a separate series beginning at number 1. Approximately 8,350 were produced from about 1913 to 1921.

Estimated Value:	**Excellent:**	**$775.00**
	Very good:	**$620.00**

Smith & Wesson Model 59

Caliber: 9mm (Parabellum) Luger
Action: Semiautomatic; double action; exposed hammer; thumb safety
Magazine: 14-shot staggered column clip
Barrel: 4"
Sights: Ramp front; rear adjustable for windage
Finish: Blued or nickel; checkered molded nylon grips
Length Overall: 7½"
Approximate wt.: 28 ozs.
Comments: Similar to the Model 39 except: straight back grip; grip is wider to accommodate the staggered column magazine. Made from about 1973 to 1982. Add 8% for nickel. Replaced by S&W Model 459.

Estimated Value:	**Excellent:**	**$475.00**
	Very good:	**$380.00**

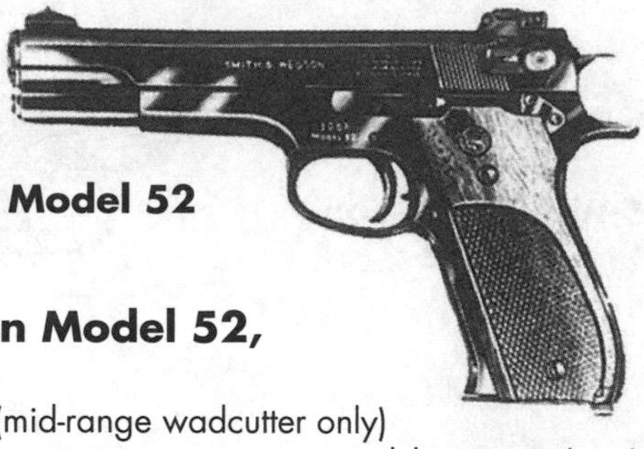

Smith & Wesson Model 52

Smith & Wesson Model 52, 38 Master

Caliber: 38 Special (mid-range wadcutter only)
Action: Single action; semiautomatic; exposed hammer; thumb safety
Magazine: 5-shot clip
Barrel: 5"
Sights: Adjustable rear sight and ramp front
Finish: Blued; checkered walnut grips
Length Overall: 8⅞"
Approximate wt.: 42 ozs.
Comments: Made from about 1961 to 1993.

Estimated Value:	**Excellent:**	**$800.00**
	Very good:	**$640.00**

Smith & Wesson Model 439

Smith & Wesson Model 439

Caliber: 9mm (Parabellum) Luger
Action: Semiautomatic; double action; exposed hammer; thumb safety
Magazine: 8-shot clip
Barrel: 4"
Sights: Serrated ramp front; rear adjustable or fixed
Finish: Blued or nickel; checkered walnut grips with S&W monogram
Length Overall: 7½"
Approximate wt.: 30 ozs.
Comments: The frame is constructed of aluminum alloy. It is similar to Model 39 except with improved extraction system. Made from about 1981 to 1989. Add 8% for nickel finish.

Estimated Value:	**Excellent:**	**$425.00**
	Very good:	**$340.00**

Smith & Wesson Model 539

Similar to the Model 439 except the frame is constructed of steel and the weight is about 36 ozs.; made from about 1981 to the mid-1980s. Add 8% for nickel finish.

Estimated Value:	**Excellent:**	**$450.00**
	Very good:	**$360.00**

Smith & Wesson Model 639

Similar to the Model 439 except satin stainless steel finish. Approximate wt.: 36 ozs. Add 4% for adjustable rear sight. Made from 1984 to 1989.

Estimated Value:	**Excellent:**	**$475.00**
	Very good:	**$380.00**

Smith & Wesson Model 459

Caliber: 9mm (Parabellum) Luger
Action: Semiautomatic; double action
Magazine: 14-shot staggered clip
Barrel: 4"
Sights: Serrated ramp front sight; rear adjustable for windage and elevation or fixed
Finish: Blued or nickel; checkered high-impact molded nylon grips
Length Overall: 7½"
Approximate wt.: 30 ozs.
Comments: The frame is constructed of aluminum alloy; the grip back is straight; the grip is thick to accommodate the staggered column magazine; it has an improved extraction system. Nickel finish discontinued in the late 1980s. Add 4% for adjustable rear sight. Made from 1981 to 1989.

Estimated Value:	**Excellent:**	**$475.00**
	Very good:	**$380.00**

Smith & Wesson Model 559

Similar to the Model 459 except the frame is steel and the weight is approximately 40 ozs. Made from about 1981 to the mid-1980s. Add 7% for nickel finish.

Estimated Value:	**Excellent:**	**$475.00**
	Very good:	**$380.00**

Smith & Wesson Model 659

Similar to the Model 459 except: satin stainless steel finish. Approximate wt.: 40 ozs. Add 4% for adjustable rear sight. Made from 1984 to 1989.

Estimated Value:	**Excellent:**	**$465.00**
	Very good:	**$375.00**

Smith & Wesson Model 459

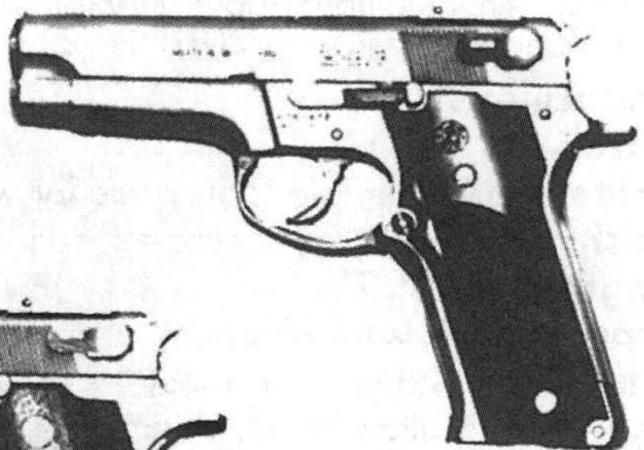

Smith & Wesson Model 659

Smith & Wesson Model 639

Smith & Wesson Model 745

Caliber: 45 ACP
Action: Single action; semiautomatic; adjustable trigger stop
Magazine: 8-shot clip
Barrel: 5"
Sights: Ramp front, square notch rear, adjustable for windage
Finish: Stainless steel frame; blued carbon steel slide, hammer, trigger, sights; checkered walnut grips
Length Overall: $8\frac{5}{8}$"
Approximate wt.: $38\frac{3}{4}$ ozs.
Comments: Introduced in 1987. Discontinued in 1990.

Estimated Value:	**Excellent:**	**$625.00**
	Very good:	**$500.00**

Smith & Wesson Model 469

Caliber: 9mm (Parabellum) Luger
Action: Double action; semiautomatic; exposed bobbed hammer
Magazine: 12-shot clip
Barrel: $3\frac{1}{2}$"
Sights: Serrated ramp front, square notch rear
Finish: Blued; pebble grain molded Debrin grips; aluminum alloy frame
Length Overall: $6\frac{7}{8}$"
Approximate wt.: 26 ozs.
Comments: Made from 1984 to 1989.

Estimated Value:	**Excellent:**	**$400.00**
	Very good:	**$320.00**

Smith & Wesson Model 669

Same as the Model 469 except barrel and slide are stainless steel. Made from the mid-1980s to 1989.

Estimated Value:	**Excellent:**	**$450.00**
	Very good:	**$360.00**

Smith & Wesson Model 3904

Caliber: 9mm
Action: Double action, semiautomatic with exposed hammer and ambidextrous safety
Magazine: 8-shot clip
Barrel: 4"
Sights: Post front with white dot, fixed or micrometer adjustable rear with two white dots
Finish: Blued; aluminum alloy frame, carbon steel slide; Debrin one-piece wrap-around grips with curved back strap
Length Overall: $7\frac{1}{2}$"
Approximate wt.: 28 ozs.
Comments: Made from 1989 to 1991. Add 5% for adjustable rear sight.

Estimated Value:	**Excellent:**	**$450.00**
	Very good:	**$360.00**

Smith & Wesson Model 3906

Same as the Model 3904 except stainless steel. Add $4\frac{1}{2}$% for adjustable rear sight.

Estimated Value:	**Excellent:**	**$500.00**
	Very good:	**$400.00**

Smith & Wesson Model 645

Caliber: 45 ACP
Action: Double action; semiautomatic; exposed hammer
Magazine: 8-shot clip
Barrel: 5"
Sights: Red-ramp front, fixed white-outline rear
Finish: Stainless steel; checkered high-impact **molded nylon grips**
Length Overall: $8\frac{5}{8}$"
Approximate wt.: 38 ozs.
Comments: Made from the mid-1980s to 1989.

Estimated Value:	**Excellent:**	**$475.00**
	Very good:	**$380.00**

Smith & Wesson Model 645

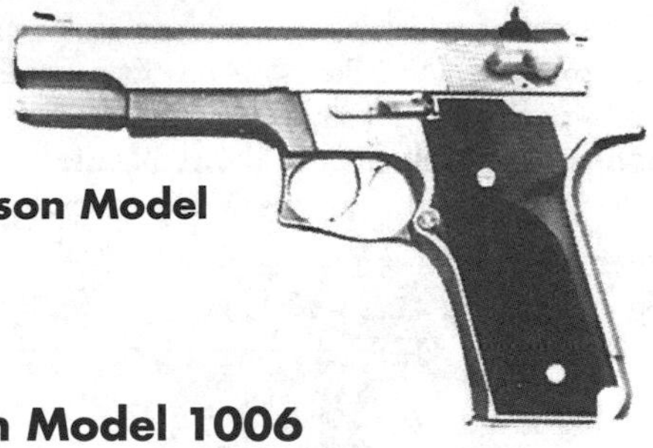

Smith & Wesson Model 469

Smith & Wesson Model 1006

Caliber: 10mm
Action: Double action; semiautomatic, exposed hammer, ambidextrous safety
Magazine: 9-shot clip
Barrel: 5"
Sights: Post front with white dot, fixed rear with two white dots or adjustable rear with white dots
Finish: Stainless steel, Debrin one-piece wrap-around grips with straight back strap
Length Overall: $8\frac{1}{2}$"
Approximate wt.: 38 ozs.
Comments: Produced from 1990 to 1993. Add 4% for adjustable rear sight.

Estimated Value:	**Excellent:**	**$575.00**
	Very good:	**$460.00**

Smith & Wesson Model 3904

Smith & Wesson Model 5903

Caliber: 9mm Luger Parabellum
Action: Double action, semiautomatic, ambidextrous safety, exposed hammer
Magazine: 15-shot clip; 10-shot clip after 9-13-94
Barrel: 4"
Sights: Post front with white dot, fixed or micrometer adjustable rear with two white dots
Finish: Stainless steel slide with aluminum alloy frame; Debrin one-piece wrap-around grips; curved back strap
Length Overall: 7½"
Approximate wt.: 29 ozs.
Comments: Introduced in 1990. Add 5% for adjustable rear sight.

Estimated Value:	**Excellent:**	**$550.00**
	Very good:	**$440.00**

Smith & Wesson Model 5904

Same as the Model 5903 except: blued finish; carbon steel slide. Approximate wt.: 27 ozs. Introduced in 1989. Add 5% for adjustable rear sight. Discontinued in 1997.

Estimated Value:	**Excellent:**	**$515.00**
	Very good:	**$410.00**

Smith & Wesson Model 5906

Same as the Model 5903 except: stainless steel slide and frame; approximate wt.: 38 ozs.; Add 5% for adjustable rear sight. Add 15% for fixed night sights.

Estimated Value:	**Excellent:**	**$500.00**
	Very good:	**$400.00**

Smith & Wesson Model 3914

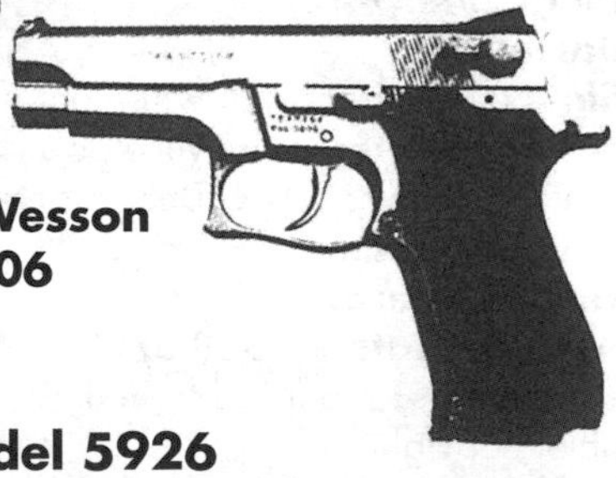

Smith & Wesson Model 5906

Smith & Wesson Model 5926

Similar to the Model 5903 except: fixed sights only; stainless steel slide and frame; no safety lever, it uses a decocking lever to lower the hammer from the cocked position (this permits the pistol to be fired double action without moving a safety lever). Produced from 1991 to 1993.

Estimated Value:	**Excellent:**	**$550.00**
	Very good:	**$440.00**

Smith & Wesson Model 5946

Same as the Model 5926 except: no decocking lever; it can only be fired double action for each shot; the hammer is bobbed. Introduced in 1991.

Estimated Value:	**Excellent:**	**$500.00**
	Very good:	**$400.00**

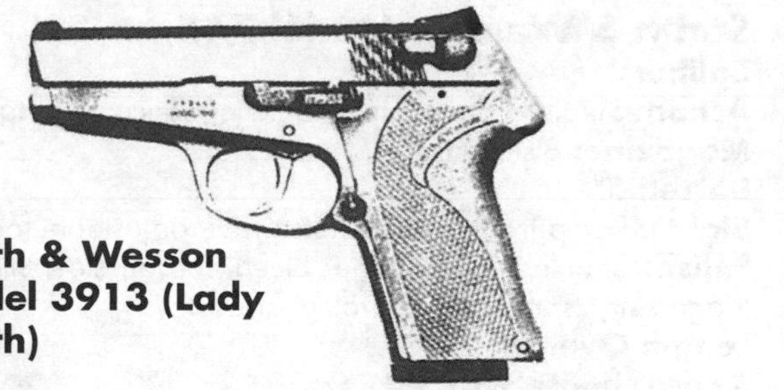

Smith & Wesson Model 3913 (Lady Smith)

Smith & Wesson Models 3913 and 3913 LS (Lady Smith)

Caliber: 9mm Luger Parabellum
Action: Double action, semiautomatic with bobbed hammer and ambidextrous safety
Magazine: 8-shot clip
Barrel: 3½"
Sights: Post front with white dot front sight, fixed rear with two white dots
Finish: Stainless steel slide; black Debrin one-piece wrap-around grips
Length Overall: 6¾"
Approximate wt.: 25 ozs.
Comments: Introduced in 1989. Model 3913 LS is a small, compact double action 9mm automatic specially designed for female shooters; add 3% for Model 3913 LS.

Estimated Value:	**Excellent:**	**$655.00**
	Very good:	**$525.00**

Smith & Wesson Model 3914

Similar to the Model 3913 (Lady Smith) except: blued finish carbon steel slide and alloy frame with gray Debrin one-piece wrap-around grips. Produced from 1989 to 1993.

Estimated Value:	**Excellent:**	**$500.00**
	Very good:	**$400.00**

Smith & Wesson Models 3953 and 3954

Same as Models 3913 and 3914 except: double action only for each shot; no safety lever; Model 3953 has stainless steel slide and alloy frame. Model 3954 has blued finish with carbon steel slide and alloy frame. Add 11% for stainless steel slide (Model 3953). Introduced in 1991. Model 3954 discontinued in 1993.

Estimated Value:	**Excellent:**	**$525.00**
	Very good:	**$400.00**

Smith & Wesson Model 6904

Caliber: 9mm Luger Parabellum
Action: Double action, semiautomatic; exposed bobbed hammer; ambidextrous safety
Magazine: 12-shot clip; 10-shot after Sept. 13, 1994
Barrel: 3½"
Sights: Post front with white dot; fixed rear with two white dots
Finish: Blued, carbon steel slide with aluminum alloy frame; Debrin one-piece wrap-around grips with curved backstrap
Length Overall: 6⅞"
Approximate wt.: 27 ozs.
Comments: Produced from 1989 to 1997.

Estimated Value:	**Excellent:**	**$475.00**
	Very good:	**$380.00**

Smith & Wesson Model 6906
Same as the Model 6904 except stainless steel slide with aluminum alloy frame. Introduced in 1989. Add 16% for night sights (1992).

Estimated Value:	**Excellent:**	**$525.00**
	Very good:	**$420.00**

Smith & Wesson Model 6946
Same as the Model 6906 except: double action only for each shot; no safety lever; introduced in 1991.

Estimated Value:	**Excellent:**	**$525.00**
	Very good:	**$420.00**

Smith & Wesson Model 1066
Similar to the Model 6906 except: 4¼" barrel; overall length is approximately 7¾"; fixed sights.

Estimated Value:	**Excellent:**	**$525.00**
	Very good:	**$420.00**

Smith & Wesson Model 1076
Same as the Model 1066 except: decocking lever; no safety lever.

Estimated Value:	**Excellent:**	**$525.00**
	Very good:	**$420.00**

Smith & Wesson Model 1086
Same as the Model 1066 except: double action only for all shots; bobbed hammer; no decocking lever; no safety lever.

Estimated Value:	**Excellent:**	**$500.00**
	Very good:	**$400.00**

Smith & Wesson Model 4006

Smith & Wesson Model 4006
Caliber: 40 S&W
Action: Double action, semiautomatic; exposed hammer; ambidextrous safety
Magazine: 11-shot clip; 10-shot after 9-13-94
Barrel: 4"
Sights: Post with white dot front; fixed or adjustable rear with two white dots
Finish: Stainless steel slide and frame; Debrin one-piece wraparound straight backstrap grips
Length Overall: 7½"
Approximate wt.: 30 ozs.
Comments: Introduced in 1990. Add 4% for adjustable sights. Add 15% for fixed night sights (1992).

Estimated Value:	**Excellent:**	**$525.00**
	Very good:	**$420.00**

Smith & Wesson Model 6906

Smith & Wesson Model 4026
Same as the Model 4006 except: it has a decocking lever to lower the hammer; no safety lever.

Estimated Value:	**Excellent:**	**$550.00**
	Very good:	**$440.00**

Smith & Wesson Model 4046
Same as the Model 4006 except: double action only for each shot; no safety lever; bobbed hammer; add 15% for fixed night sights. Introduced in 1991.

Estimated Value:	**Excellent:**	**$600.00**
	Very good:	**$480.00**

Smith & Wesson Models 4003 and 4004
Same as the Model 4006 except: Model 4003 has aluminum alloy frame and stainless steel slide; Model 4004 has aluminum alloy frame and carbon steel slide with blued finish. Add 7% for stainless steel slide (Model 4003). Model 4004 discontinued in 1995.

Estimated Value:	**Excellent:**	**$525.00**
	Very good:	**$420.00**

Smith & Wesson Models 4043 and 4044
Same as Models 4003 and 4004 except: double action only with bobbed hammer; no safety lever. Introduced in 1992. Model 4044 discontinued in 1995.

Estimated Value:	**Excellent:**	**$700.00**
	Very good:	**$560.00**

Smith & Wesson Models 4053 and 4054
Same as Models 4043 and 4044 except: more compact; 3½" barrel; approximately 7" overall. Introduced in 1992; Model 4054 discontinued in 1995.

Estimated Value:	**Excellent:**	**$550.00**
	Very good:	**$440.00**

Smith & Wesson Models 4013 and 4014
Same as Models 4003 and 4004 except: more compact; 3½" barrel; overall length is approximately 7"; Model 4013 has stainless steel slide and alloy frame; Model 4014 has blued finish with carbon steel slide and alloy frame. Introduced in 1992. Model 4014 discontinued in 1997.

Estimated Value:	**Excellent:**	**$765.00**
	Very good:	**$610.00**

Smith & Wesson Model 4516

Caliber: 45 ACP
Action: Double action, semiautomatic, exposed hammer; ambidextrous safety
Magazine: 7-shot clip
Barrel: 3¾"
Sights: Post front with white dot; fixed rear with two white dots
Finish: Stainless steel frame and slide with Debrin one-piece wrap-around grips
Length Overall: 7¼"
Approximate wt.: 35 ozs.
Comments: A compact 45 automatic; produced from 1989 to 1997.

Estimated Value:	**Excellent:**	**$550.00**
	Very good:	**$440.00**

Smith & Wesson Model 915

Caliber: 9mm
Action: Double or single; exposed hammer
Magazine: 15-shot clip
Barrel: 4"
Sights: Fixed
Finish: Blued; carbon steel slide and alloy frame; checkered composite straight-back strap grips
Length Overall: 7½"
Approximate wt.: 29 ozs.
Comments: Produced in the early 1990s.

Estimated Value:	**Excellent:**	**$375.00**
	Very good:	**$300.00**

Smith & Wesson Model 411

Similar to the Model 915 except: 40 S&W caliber; 11-shot clip; approximate wt.: 30 ozs. Produced in the early 1990s.

Estimated Value:	**Excellent:**	**$425.00**
	Very good:	**$340.00**

Smith & Wesson Model 915

Smith & Wesson Model 908

Smith & Wesson Model 909, 910

Smith & Wesson Model 4506

Smith & Wesson Model 4506

Caliber: 45 ACP
Action: Double action, semiautomatic; exposed hammer, ambidextrous safety
Magazine: 8-shot clip
Barrel: 5"
Sights: Post front with white dot; fixed or micrometer adjustable rear with two white dots
Finish: Stainless steel frame and slide with Debrin one-piece wrap-around grips
Length Overall: 8½"
Approximate wt.: 39 ozs.
Comments: Made in the late 1980s and the 1990s. Add 4% for adjustable rear sight.

Estimated Value:	**Excellent:**	**$600.00**
	Very good:	**$480.00**

Smith & Wesson Model 4576

Same as the Model 4506 except: more compact; 4¼" barrel; approximate overall length is 7¾"; decocking lever; no safety lever.

Estimated Value:	**Excellent:**	**$625.00**
	Very good:	**$500.00**

Smith & Wesson Model 4566

Same as the Model 4506 except: 4¼" barrel; approximate overall length 7¾"; more compact; introduced in 1990.

Estimated Value:	**Excellent:**	**$625.00**
	Very good:	**$500.00**

Smith & Wesson Model 4586

Same as the Model 4576 except: double action only for all shots; no decocking lever; no safety lever. Introduced in 1991.

Estimated Value:	**Excellent:**	**$625.00**
	Very good:	**$500.00**

Smith & Wesson Models 908, 909, and 910

Caliber: 9mm
Action: Double action, semiautomatic; 908 has bobbed hammer, 909 and 910 have exposed hammer
Magazine: 8-shot clip (908), 9-shot clip (909), 10-shot staggered clip (910)
Barrel: 3½" (908), 4" (909 and 910)
Sights: Fixed white dot
Finish: Blued; carbon steel or stainless steel slide and alloy frame; 908 has straight back strap; 909 and 910 have curved back strap
Length Overall: 6⅞" (908); 7⅜" (909 and 910)
Approximate wt.: 30 ozs.
Comments: Model 908 was introduced in 1996; Models 909 and 910 were introduced in the early 1990s; Model 909 was discontinued in the late 1990s. Add 4% for stainless steel.

Estimated Value:	**New (retail):**	**$679.00**
	Excellent:	**$510.00**
	Very good:	**$405.00**

Smith & Wesson Models 2213 and 2214
Caliber: 22 long rifle
Action: Single action, semiautomatic; concealed hammer
Magazine: 8-shot clip
Barrel: 3"
Sights: Fixed sights with white dots
Finish: Model 2213 has stainless steel slide with alloy frame. Model 2214 is blued carbon steel slide with alloy frame.
Length Overall: 7"
Approximate wt.: 18 ozs.
Comments: Made in the 1990s. Add 17% for stainless steel (2213).
Estimated Value: **Excellent: $250.00**
Very good: $200.00

Smith & Wesson Model 61 Escort
Caliber: 22 long rifle
Action: Semiautomatic; concealed hammer; thumb safety
Magazine: 5-shot clip
Barrel: 2⅛"
Sights: Fixed
Finish: Blued or nickel; checkered plastic grips
Length Overall: 4¾"
Approximate wt.: 14 ozs.
Comments: Made from about 1970 to 1973. Add $15.00 for nickel finish.
Estimated Value: **Excellent: $300.00**
Very good: $240.00

Smith & Wesson Model 410
Caliber: 40 S&W
Action: Double action, semiautomatic; exposed hammer
Magazine: 10-shot clip
Barrel: 4"
Sights: Fixed white dot
Finish: Blued; carbon steel or stainless steel slide and alloy frame
Length Overall: 7½"
Approximate wt.: 30 ozs.
Comments: Introduced in 1996. Add 3% for stainless steel; 30% for Crimson Trace Lazergrips.
Estimated Value: **Excellent: $500.00**
Very good: $400.00

Smith & Wesson Model 41

Smith & Wesson Model 46

Smith & Wesson Model 457

Smith & Wesson Model 410

Smith & Wesson Model 457
Caliber: 45 ACP
Action: Double action, semiautomatic, bobbed hammer
Magazine: 7-shot clip
Barrel: 3¾"
Sights: Fixed white dot
Finish: Matte blue; alloy frame and carbon steel or stainless steel slide; straight back strap grip
Length Overall: 7¼"
Approximate wt.: 30 ozs.
Comments: Introduced in 1996. Add 3% for stainless steel.
Estimated Value: **Excellent: $510.00**
Very good: $410.00

Smith & Wesson Models 4513TSW and 4553TSW
Caliber: 45 ACP
Action: Double action only, semiautomatic, bobbed hammer (4553TSW); straight back strap grip. Single action (4513TSW).
Magazine: 6-shot clip
Barrel: 3¾"
Sights: White dot front, 2-dot low mount rear
Finish: Aluminum alloy/stainless steel; satin finish
Length Overall: 6⅞"
Approximate wt.: 29 ozs.
Comments: Introduced in the 1990s.
Estimated Value: **Excellent: $600.00**
Very good: $480.00

Smith & Wesson Model 41
Caliber: 22 short or 22 long rifle (not interchangeable)
Action: Single action; semiautomatic; concealed hammer; thumb safety
Magazine: 12-shot clip; 10-shot after 9-13-94
Barrel: 5½" heavy barrel or 7" regular barrel
Sights: Adjustable micrometer rear; Partridge front
Finish: Blued; checkered walnut grips with thumbrest
Length Overall: 9" to 10½"
Approximate wt.: 40 to 44 ozs.
Comments: Made from about 1957 to the present. At present made for 22 long rifle only.
Estimated Value: **New (retail): $1,288.00**
Excellent: $ 965.00
Very good: $ 775.00

Smith & Wesson Model 46
Similar to the Model 41 except: 22 long rifle caliber only; plastic grips with thumbrest. Made from about 1957 to 1966.
Estimated Value: **Excellent: $650.00**
Very good: $520.00

Smith & Wesson Model 422

Caliber: 22 long rifle
Action: Single action; semiautomatic; concealed hammer.
Magazine: 12-shot clip; 10-shot clip after 9-13-94
Barrel: 4½" or 6" barrel
Sights: Fixed sights; adjustable sights on target model
Finish: Blued; aluminum frame, carbon steel slide; plastic grips on field; checkered walnut on target
Length Overall: 7½" or 9"
Approximate wt.: 22 to 23 ozs.
Comments: Introduced in 1987; add 25% for target sights.

Estimated Value:	**Excellent:**	**$250.00**
	Very good:	**$200.00**

Smith & Wesson Model 622

Same as the Model 422 except stainless steel slide and aluminum alloy frame. Introduced in 1990. Add 20% for target sights. Add 9% for ventilated rib.

Estimated Value:	**Excellent:**	**$275.00**
	Very good:	**$220.00**

Smith & Wesson Model 2206

Same as the Model 422 except: stainless steel slide and frame; 6" barrel. Introduced in 1990. Add 12% for target model.

Estimated Value:	**Excellent:**	**$325.00**
	Very good:	**$260.00**

Smith & Wesson Model 22A Sport Series

Caliber: 22 long rifle
Action: Single action, semiautomatic; concealed hammer
Magazine: 10-shot clip
Barrel: 4", 5½", 5½" bull, 7"
Sights: Partridge front; adjustable rear
Finish: Black, two-piece polymer or wooden grips; aluminum alloy/stainless steel
Length Overall: 8" to 11"
Approximate wt.: 28 to 39 ozs.
Comments: Introduced in the late 1990s. Add 11% for 5½" barrel, 25% for 7" barrel, 40% for 5½" bull barrel, 32% for stainless bull barrel.

Estimated Value:	**New (retail):**	**$324.00**
	Excellent:	**$245.00**
	Very good:	**$195.00**

Smith & Wesson Model 22S Sport Series

Same as the Model 22A except: stainless steel, no 4" barrel model; add 10% for 7" barrel, 16% for bull with synthetic grips, 21% for bull with Dymondwood grips.

Estimated Value:	**Excellent:**	**$310.00**
	Very good:	**$250.00**

Smith & Wesson Model 22A Sport Series

Smith & Wesson Sigma Series SW380

Smith & Wesson Sigma Series SW380

Caliber: 380 ACP
Action: Double action only, semiautomatic; concealed hammer
Magazine: 6-shot clip
Barrel: 3"
Sights: Post front, gutter type rear
Finish: Back; one-piece grip and polymer frame
Length Overall: 6"
Approximate wt.: 14 ozs.
Comments: Introduced in 1995, a small, lightweight concealable pistol.

Estimated Value:	**Excellent:**	**$300.00**
	Very good:	**$240.00**

Smith & Wesson Sigma Series SW9C & SW40C

Caliber: 9mm (SW9C) or 40 S&W (SW40C)
Action: Double action only, semiautomatic; concealed hammer
Magazine: 10-shot clip
Barrel: 4"
Sights: White dot, optional night sights
Finish: Black; one-piece grip and polymer frame
Length Overall: 7¼"
Approximate wt.: 26 ozs.
Comments: Made in the mid- to the late 1990s. Deduct 29% without night sights.

Estimated Value:	**Excellent:**	**$425.00**
	Very good:	**$340.00**

Smith & Wesson Sigma Series SW9C

Smith & Wesson Sigma Series SW9F

Smith & Wesson Sigma Series SW9F and W40F

Caliber: 9mm (SW9F) or 40 S&W (SW40F)
Action: Double action only, semiautomatic; concealed hammer
Magazine: 10-shot clip
Barrel: 4½"
Sights: White dot, optional night sights
Finish: Matte blue; one-piece grip and polymer frame; carbon steel slide
Length Overall: 7¾"
Approximate wt.: 26 ozs.
Comments: Introduced in the early 1990s. SW9F discontinued in 1997.

Estimated Value:	**Excellent:**	**$450.00**
	Very good:	**$360.00**

Smith & Wesson Sigma SW9P, SW40P

Smith & Wesson Sigma SW9P, SW40P

Caliber: 9mm (SW9P) or 40 S&W (SW40P)
Action: Double action only, concealed hammer, semiautomatic
Magazine: 10-shot clip
Barrel: 4"
Sights: White dot sight system
Finish: Compact black "Melonite" polymer frame and grips; stainless steel slide and barrel
Length Overall: 7¼"
Approximate wt.: 24½ oz.
Comments: Similar to the other Smith & Wesson Sigma series pistols.

Estimated Value:	**Excellent:**	**$375.00**
	Very good:	**$300.00**

Smith & Wesson Model SW1911

Smith & Wesson Model SW1911

Caliber: 45ACP
Action: Single-action, semiautomatic; exposed hammer
Magazine: 8-shot clip
Barrel: 5"
Sights: White dot sight system
Finish: Stainless steel; rubber grips
Length Overall: 8½"
Approximate wt.: 39 oz.
Comments: An updated and improved handgun based on John Browning's 1911 design.

Estimated Value:	**New (retail):**	**$1,169.00**
	Excellent:	**$ 875.00**
	Very good:	**$ 700.00**

Smith & Wesson Sigma SW9G, SW40G

Smith & Wesson Sigma SW9G, SW40G

Similar to the SW9P, SW40P, with the Nato Green "Melonite" finish.

Estimated Value:	**Excellent:**	**$375.00**
	Very good:	**$300.00**

Smith & Wesson Sigma SW9VE, SW40VE

Similar to the SW9P, SW40P, without the "Melonite" finish.

Estimated Value:	**New (retail):**	**$490.00**
	Excellent:	**$365.00**
	Very good:	**$295.00**

Smith & Wesson Sigma SW9VE, SW40VE

Smith & Wesson Sigma Series SW9M, SW9V & SW40V

Caliber: 9mm (SW9M, SW9V) or 40 S&W (SW40V)
Action: Double action only, semiautomatic; concealed hammer
Magazine: 7-shot clip (SW9M); 10-shot clip (SW9V, SW40V)
Barrel: 3½" (SW9M); 4" (SW9V, SW40V)
Sights: Front sight post (SW9M); white dot (SW9V, SW40V); rear sight fixed channel (SW9M); fixed two-dot (SW9V, SW 40V)
Finish: Black-polymer/carbon (SW9M); black or gray polymer/ stainless steel (SW9V, SW40V)
Length Overall: 6¼" (SW9M), 7¼" (SW9V, SW40V)
Approximate wt.: 18 ozs. (SW9M); 25 ozs. (SW9V, SW40V)
Comments: Made in the 1990s.

Estimated Value:	**Excellent:**	**$325.00**
	Very good:	**$260.00**

Smith & Wesson
Chief's Special CS9,
CS40, CS45

Smith & Wesson Chief's Special CS9, CS40, and CS45

Caliber: 9mm (CS9), 40 (CS40), 45ACP (CS45)
Action: Double action, semiautomatic
Magazine: 7-shot clip, 6-shot clip in 45ACP
Barrel: 3" (CS9), 3¼" (CS40, CS45)
Sights: White dot sights front and rear
Finish: Aluminum alloy and stainless steel; wrap-around rubber grips
Length Overall: 6¼" to 6½"
Approximate wt.: 20½ to 23½ oz.
Comments: A compact frame pistol made of aluminum alloy and stainless steel. Add 6% for 45ACP (CS45).

Estimated Value:	**Excellent:**	**$525.00**
	Very good:	**$420.00**

Smith & Wesson
Model 4040 PD

Smith & Wesson Model 4040 PD

Caliber: 40 S&W
Action: Double action, semiautomatic
Magazine: 7-shot clip
Barrel: 3½"
Sights: White dot sight system
Finish: Matte black, scandium alloy and steel; rubber grips
Length Overall: 6½"
Approximate wt.: 25½ oz.
Comments: A compact pistol made of scandium alloy and steel. Introduced in 2003.

Estimated Value:	**Excellent:**	**$575.00**
	Very good:	**$460.00**

Smith & Wesson
Model SW99

Smith & Wesson Model SW99

Caliber: 9mm, 40 S&W, 45ACP, 9mm or 40 S&W in compact frame
Action: Double action semiautomatic; decocking button
Magazine: 10-shot clip, 9-shot clip in 45ACP, 8- or 10-shot in compact frame
Barrel: 4", 4⅛", 4¼"; 3½" in compact frame
Sights: White dot front, adjustable dot rear
Finish: Polymer frame with adjustable grip sizes; full or compact frame
Length Overall: 7⅛" to 7½"; 6½" compact frame
Approximate wt.: 25 to 25½ oz.; 22½ to 23 oz. compact frame
Comments: A polymer frame compact or full-size pistol produced as a collaboration between Smith & Wesson and Karl Walther. Add 15% for full size frame.

Estimated Value:	**Excellent:**	**$525.00**
	Very good:	**$420.00**

Smith & Wesson
Model 3913TSW

Smith & Wesson Models 3913TSW and 3953TSW

Caliber: 9mm Parabellum
Action: Double action, semiautomatic (3913TSW); double action only (3953TSW); bobbed hammer
Magazine: 7-shot clip
Barrel: 3½"
Sights: White dot front; two-dot lo-mount rear
Finish: Satin or aluminum alloy stainless steel
Length Overall: 6½"
Approximate wt.: 25 ozs.
Comments: Introduced in the 1990s.

Estimated Value:	**Excellent:**	**$570.00**
	Very good:	**$450.00**

Smith & Wesson No. 3
Single Action New Model

Smith & Wesson No. 3 Single Action New Model

Caliber: 44 S&W Russian centerfire
Action: Single; exposed hammer; hinged frame (top-break); simultaneous automatic ejector
Cylinder: 6-shot
Barrel: 4", 5", 6", 6½", 7½", or 8" ribbed
Sights: Fixed or target
Finish: Blued or nickel; round butt, hard rubber or checkered walnut grips
Length Overall: 9" to 13"
Approximate wt.: 36 to 40 ozs.
Comments: An improved version of the S&W Russian single action revolver. Approximately 36,000 were manufactured from about 1878 to 1908. Sometimes called Single Action Russian Model.
Estimated Value: Excellent: $3,000.00 – 6,000.00
Very good: $2,500.00 – 5,000.00

Smith & Wesson No. 3
New Model Double Action

Smith & Wesson No. 3 New Model Double Action

Same as No. 3 Single Action New Model except: double and single action; 4", 5", 6" and 6½" barrel; overall length 9" to 11½"; sometimes listed as S&W 1881 Navy Revolver; rear of trigger guard is square. Made from 1881 to 1908.
Estimated Value: Excellent: $750.00 – 1,500.00
Very good: $600.00 – 1,200.00

Smith & Wesson Model 4013TSW & 4053TSW

Caliber: 40 S&W
Action: Double action, semiautomatic (4013TSW); double action only (4053TSW); bobbed hammer
Magazine: 9-shot clip
Barrel: 3½"
Sights: White dot front; two-dot low-mount rear
Finish: Satin or aluminum alloy stainless steel
Length Overall: 6½"
Approximate wt.: 27 ozs.
Comments: Introduced in the 1990s.
Estimated Value: Excellent: $600.00
Very good: $480.00

Smith & Wesson Double Action 44 Wesson Favorite

Similar to the No. 3 Single Action New Model except: double and single action; 5" barrel only; lighter barrel and frame. Made from about 1882 to 1883 (approximately 1,200 produced).
Estimated Value: Excellent: $2,500.00 – 5,000.00
Very good: $2,000.00 – 4,000.00

Smith & Wesson 32 Double Action

Caliber: 32 S&W centerfire
Action: Single and double; hinged frame (top break)
Cylinder: 5-shot; simultaneous ejector
Barrel: 3" 1880 – 1882; 3", 3½", 6", 8", 10" 1882 – 1909; 3", 3½", 6" 1909 – 1919
Sights: Fixed
Finish: Blued or nickel; round butt, hard rubber grips
Length Overall: 7¼" to 14¼"
Approximate wt.: 23 to 28 ozs.
Comments: Made from about 1880 to 1919 in five modifications or issues; rear of trigger guard is square.
Estimated Value:

Issue	Dates	Quantity	Excellent	Very good
1st	1880	less than 100	$3,500.00	$3,000.00
2nd	1880 – 1882	22,000	$ 500.00	$ 400.00
3rd	1882 – 1889	21,200	$ 525.00	$ 420.00
4th	1889 – 1909	239,500	$ 300.00	$ 240.00
5th	1909 – 1919	44,600	$ 450.00	$ 360.00

Smith & Wesson Safety Model Double Action

Caliber: 32 S&W, 38 S&W
Action: Double only; concealed hammer with frame enclosing it; hinged frame; top break style; grip safety on rear of grip frame
Cylinder: 5-shot; simultaneous ejector
Barrel: 2", 3", or 3½" in 32 caliber; 2", 3¼", 4", 5", or 6" in 38 caliber; rib on top
Sights: Fixed
Finish: Blued or nickel; hard rubber or checkered walnut grips
Length Overall: 5¾" to 9¾"
Approximate wt.: 15 to 20 ozs.
Comments: Sometimes listed as the Safety Hammerless, New Department Model. Made from about 1887 to 1941. About five changes and improvements were made from 1887 to 1940.
Estimated Value: Excellent: $700.00
Very good: $560.00

Smith & Wesson Perfected 38

Caliber: 38 S&W centerfire
Action: Single and double; exposed hammer; hinged frame (top break; but also has side latch)
Cylinder: 5-shot; simultaneous ejector
Barrel: 3¼", 4", 5", and 6"
Sights: Fixed
Finish: Blued or nickel; round butt, hard rubber grip
Length Overall: 7½" to 10¼"
Approximate wt.: 24 to 30 ozs.
Comments: Similar to earlier 38 double action revolvers except: heavier frame; a side latch along with the top latch; improved lock work. Approximately 58,400 were produced from about 1909 to 1920.

Estimated Value:	**Excellent:**	**$625.00**
	Very good:	**$500.00**

Smith & Wesson Single Action Target

Caliber: 32-44 S&W, 38-44 S&W
Action: Single; exposed hammer; hinged frame (top break)
Cylinder: 6-shot; simultaneous ejector
Barrel: 6½"
Sights: Target
Finish: Blued or nickel; round butt; hard rubber or checkered walnut grips
Length Overall: 11"
Approximate wt.: 38 to 40 ozs.
Comments: One of the first handguns to prove that a short-barrel arm could be a really accurate weapon. Made from 1887 to 1910.

Estimated Value:	**Excellent:**	**$3,500.00**
	Very good:	**$2,800.00**

Smith & Wesson 1891 Single Action

Smith & Wesson 38 Double Action

Caliber: 38 S&W
Action: Single and double; exposed hammer; hinged frame; top break; back of trigger guard squared
Cylinder: 5-shot; simultaneous ejector
Barrel: 3¼", 4", 5", 6"
Sights: Fixed
Finish: Blued or nickel; round butt; hard rubber grips
Length Overall: 7½" to 10¼"
Approximate wt.: 20 to 24 ozs.
Comments: Made from about 1880 to 1910 with some improvements and minor changes.

Estimated Value:	**Excellent:**	**$700.00**
	Very good:	**$560.00**

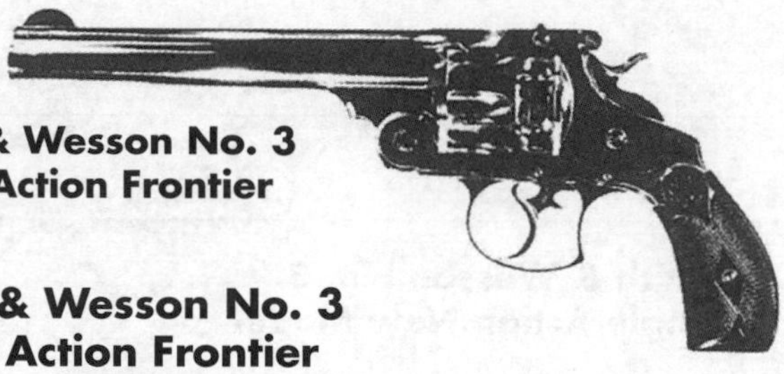

Smith & Wesson No. 3 Single Action Frontier

Smith & Wesson No. 3 Single Action Frontier

Caliber: 44-40 Winchester rifle cartridge
Action: Single; exposed hammer; hinged frame (top break)
Cylinder: 6-shot; simultaneous automatic ejector
Barrel: 4", 5", and 6½"
Sights: Fixed or target
Finish: Blued or nickel; round butt, hard rubber or checkered walnut grips
Length Overall: 8½" to 11"
Approximate wt.: 38 to 42 ozs.
Comments: Approximately 2,000 manufactured from about 1885 to 1908.

Estimated Value:	**Excellent:**	**$7,000.00**
	Very good:	**$5,600.00**

Smith & Wesson Double Action Frontier

Similar to the No. 3 Single Action Frontier except: double and single action; rear of trigger guard is square. Made from about 1886 to 1908 (approximately 15,000 were produced).

Estimated Value:	**Excellent:**	**$1,800.00**
	Very good:	**$1,440.00**

Smith & Wesson 1891 Single Action

Caliber: 38 S&W centerfire
Action: Single; exposed hammer; hinged frame (top-break)
Cylinder: 5-shot; simultaneous ejector
Barrel: 3¼", 4", 5" and 6"
Sights: Fixed
Finish: Blued or nickel; round butt, hard rubber grips
Length Overall: 6¾" to 9½"
Approximate wt.: 34 to 38 ozs. (depending on barrel length)
Comments: This revolver was also available with an accessory single-shot target barrel in 22 caliber, 32 caliber, or 38 caliber; and 6", 8", and 10" lengths. Made from 1891 to 1911.

Estimated Value:

	Revolver	**Revolver and single-shot barrel**
Excellent:	**$1,200.00**	**$1,750.00**
Very good:	**$ 960.00**	**$1,400.00**

Smith & Wesson Model 3 Schofield

Caliber: 45 Schofield
Action: Single action, hinged frame (top break) repeating
Cylinder: 6-shot, simultaneous automatic ejector
Barrel: 7"
Sights: Half moon post front, fixed notch rear
Finish: Polished blue with case-hardened trigger and hammer; smooth walnut grips
Length overall: 12½"
Approximate wt.: 40 ozs.
Comments: A modern production version of the Smith & Wesson Schofield. Introduced in 2001.

Estimated Value:	**Excellent:**	**$1,000.00**
	Very good:	**$ 800.00**

Smith & Wesson Model M Hand Ejector

Caliber: 22 short, long, long rifle
Action: Double and single; exposed hammer; solid frame.
Cylinder: 9-shot; swing-out, simultaneous manual ejector
Barrel: 2¼" (1902 to 1911); 3", 3½" (1906 to 1911), or 6" (1911 to 1921)
Sights: Fixed or adjustable (available after 1911)
Finish: Blued or nickel; checkered hard rubber round butt grips (1902 to 1911); checkered hard rubber square butt grips (1911 to 1921)
Length Overall: 5¾" to 10½"
Approximate wt.: 10 to 14 ozs.
Comments: Cylinder latch release on left side of frame from 1902 to 1906; cylinder latch under barrel from 1906 to 1921. Made from about 1902 to 1921, sometimes called Lady Smith.

Estimated Value:	**Excellent:**	**$725.00**
	Very good:	**$580.00**

Smith & Wesson Model 1 32 Hand Ejector

Caliber: 32 S&W long
Action: Single and double; exposed hammer; first Smith & Wesson solid frame revolver; longer top strap over cylinder than later models
Cylinder: 6-shot; swing-out; simultaneous manual ejector
Barrel: 3¼", 4¼", or 6"
Sights: Fixed
Finish: Blued or nickel; round butt; hard rubber grips
Length Overall: 8" to 10¾"
Approximate wt.: 20 to 24 ozs.
Comments: First model produced by Smith & Wesson with solid frame and swing-out cylinder. Made from about 1896 to 1903. Approximately 19,712 were produced.

Estimated Value:	**Excellent:**	**$675.00**
	Very good:	**$540.00**

Smith & Wesson Model 30 Hand Ejector

Smith & Wesson Model 30 Hand Ejector

Caliber: 32 S&W and 32 S&W long
Action: Single and double; exposed hammer; solid frame
Cylinder: 6-shot swing-out; simultaneous manual ejector; cylinder release on left side of frame
Barrel: 2" (1949 to 1975); 3", 4", 6"
Sights: Fixed
Finish: Blued or nickel; checkered hard rubber or checkered walnut round butt grips
Length Overall: 6" to 10"
Approximate wt.: 16 to 20 ozs.
Comments: Made from about 1903 to 1975 with many improvements and minor changes over the years.

Estimated Value:	**Excellent:**	**$425.00**
	Very good:	**$340.00**

Smith & Wesson Model M Hand Ejector

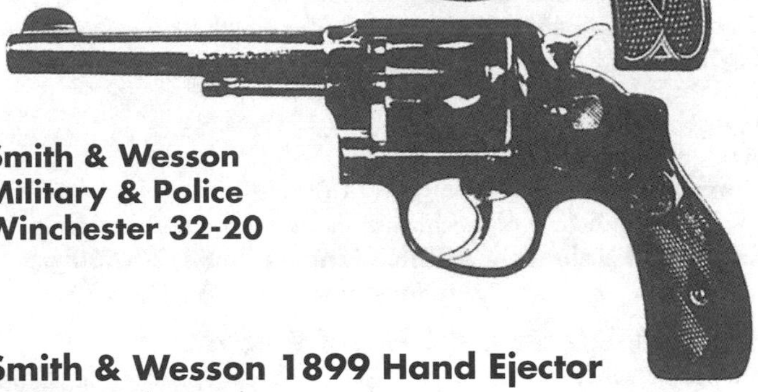

Smith & Wesson Military & Police Winchester 32-20

Smith & Wesson 1899 Hand Ejector

Caliber: 38 long Colt
Action: Double and single; exposed hammer; solid frame
Cylinder: 6-shot; swing-out; simultaneous manual ejector; cylinder release on side of frame
Barrel: 4", 5", 6", or 6½"
Sights: Fixed
Finish: Blued or nickel; checkered hard rubber or walnut round butt grips
Length Overall: 9" to 11½"
Approximate wt.: 22 to 25 ozs.
Comments: Made for police, army, navy and commercial use; forerunner of the military and police models. Made from about 1899 to 1902 (approximately 21,000 produced). Army and navy versions have Lanyard swivel in butt and 6" or 6½" barrel lengths.

Estimated Value:	**Excellent:**	**$725.00**
	Very good:	**$580.00**

Smith & Wesson Military and Police Winchester 32-20

Similar to the Model 1899 except: caliber 32-20 only; some improvements and changes over the years produced from about 1899 to 1940.

Estimated Value:	**Excellent:**	**$725.00**
	Very good:	**$580.00**

Smith & Wesson Mexican Model

Caliber: 38 S&W centerfire
Action: Single; exposed hammer; hinged frame (top break); spur trigger
Cylinder: 5-shot; simultaneous ejector
Barrel: 3¼", 4", 5", and 6"
Sights: Fixed
Finish: Blued or nickel; round butt, hard rubber grips
Length Overall: 7¾" to 10½"
Approximate wt.: 34 to 38 ozs.
Comments: Similar to the Model 1891 except: it has a spur trigger; doesn't have half-cock notch on the hammer. Approximately 2,000 manufactured from about 1891 to 1911.

Estimated Value: Excellent:	**$3,000.00 – 4,000.00**
Very good:	**$2,400.00 – 3,200.00**

Smith & Wesson New Century Triple Lock

Caliber: 44 S&W Special, 450 Eley, 45 Colt, or 455 Mark II British
Action: Single and double; exposed hammer; solid frame
Cylinder: 6-shot swing-out; simultaneous hand ejector; called triple lock because of lock on cylinder crane as well as the usual locks under barrel and at rear of cylinder
Barrel: 4", 5", 6½", 7½" tapered round
Sights: Fixed
Finish: Blued or nickel; checkered walnut grips
Length Overall: 9¼" to 12¾"
Approximate wt.: 36 to 41 ozs.
Comments: Approximately 20,000 made from about 1908 to 1915; about 5,000 of these were made for the British army.
Estimated Value: **Excellent:** **$1,200.00**
Very good: **$ 960.00**

Smith & Wesson 44 Hand Ejector

Similar to the New Century Triple Lock except: cylinder crane lock eliminated; 44 Smith & Wesson Special, 44 Smith & Wesson Russian, or 45 Colt calibers; 45 Colt caliber made in 6½" barrel only; other calibers in 4", 5", 6" lengths. Made from about 1915 to 1937.
Estimated Value: **Excellent:** **$1,250.00**
Very good: **$1,000.00**

Smith & Wesson 22/32 Target

Caliber: 22 short, long, long rifle
Action: Single and double; exposed hammer; solid frame
Cylinder: 6-shot swing-out; recessed chamber (1935 to 1953); cylinder release on left side of frame
Barrel: 6"
Sights: Adjustable target sights
Finish: Blued; checkered square butt walnut grips
Length Overall: 10½"
Approximate wt.: 24 ozs.
Comments: Frame design similar to Model 30 hand ejector model. Made from about 1911 to 1953.
Estimated Value: **Excellent:** **$700.00**
Very good: **$560.00**

Smith & Wesson 22/32 1935 Kit Gun

Same as the 22/32 Target except: 4" barrel; overall length 8"; weighs about 21 ozs.; round butt grips. Made from about 1935 to 1953.
Estimated Value: **Excellent:** **$550.00**
Very good: **$440.00**

Smith & Wesson Model 51 1960 22/32 Kit Gun

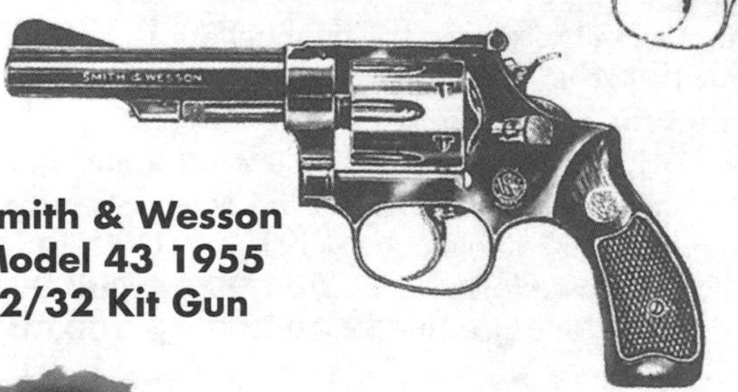

Smith & Wesson Model 43 1955 22/32 Kit Gun

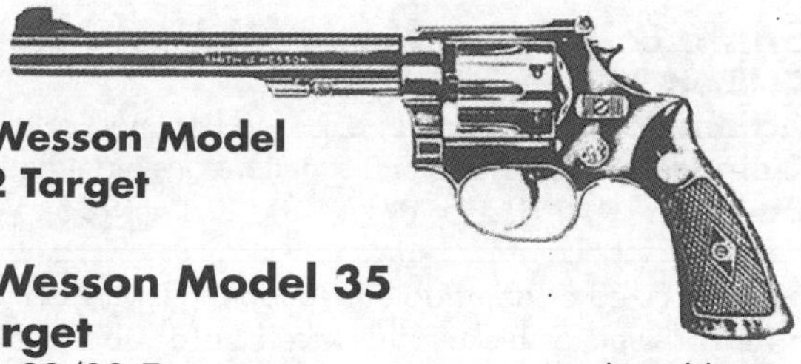

Smith & Wesson Model 35 22/32 Target

Smith & Wesson Model 35 22/32 Target

Similar to the 22/32 Target except: newer type adjustable rear sight; S&W magna-type target grips; weighs about 25 ozs. Made from about 1953 to 1974.
Estimated Value: **Excellent:** **$575.00**
Very good: **$460.00**

Smith & Wesson Model 34 1953 22/32 Kit Gun

Similar to the 22/32 Kit Gun except: 2" or 4" barrel; round or square butt grips; blued or nickel finish. Made from about 1953 to 1992. Nickel finish discontinued in the late 1980s.
Estimated Value: **Excellent:** **$425.00**
Very good: **$340.00**

Smith & Wesson Model 43 1955 22/32 Kit Gun

Same as the Model 34 1953 22/32 Kit Gun except: 3½" barrel only; lighter alloy frame; weighs approximately 15 ozs.; square butt grips. Made from about 1954 to 1974.
Estimated Value: **Excellent:** **$550.00**
Very good: **$440.00**

Smith & Wesson Model 51 1960 22/32 Kit Gun

Same as the Model 43 1953 22/32 Kit Gun except: chambered for 22 magnum only; all steel construction; weighs approximately 24 ozs. Made from about 1960 to 1974.
Estimated Value: **Excellent:** **$600.00**
Very good: **$480.00**

Smith & Wesson 1917 Army

Caliber: 45 auto rim cartridge; 45 ACP (by using two 3-round steel half-moon clips to hold the cartridge heads)
Action: Single and double; exposed hammer; solid frame
Cylinder: 6-shot swing-out; simultaneous manual ejector; release on left side of frame
Barrel: 5½"
Sights: Fixed
Finish: Blued; smooth or checkered square butt walnut grips
Length Overall: 10¾"
Approximate wt.: 37 ozs.
Comments: Approximately 175,000 made for the U.S. Government from about 1917 to 1919. Then made for commercial sale from about 1919 to 1941. U.S. Government models had a dull blue finish and smooth grips.

Estimated Value:	**Military**	**Commercial**
Excellent:	**$750.00**	**$675.00**
Very good:	**$600.00**	**$540.00**

Smith & Wesson Model 22 1950 Army

Similar to the 1917 Army except: made after World War II; minor changes. Made from about 1950 to 1967.
Estimated Value: **Excellent:** **$1,200.00**
Very good: **$ 960.00**

Smith & Wesson 1926 Model 44 Military

Caliber: 44 S&W Special
Action: Single and double; exposed hammer
Cylinder: 6-shot swing-out; simultaneous manual ejector; cylinder release on left side of frame
Barrel: 3¼", 4", 5", 6½"
Sights: Fixed
Finish: Blued or nickel; checkered square butt walnut grips
Length Overall: 9¼" to 11¾"
Approximate wt.: 40 ozs.
Comments: Made from about 1926 to 1941.

Estimated Value:	**Excellent:**	**$975.00**
	Very good:	**$780.00**

Smith & Wesson 1926 Model 44 Target

Same as the 1926 Model Military except: 6½" barrel; adjustable target sights; blued finish only. Made from about 1926 to 1941.

Estimated Value:	**Excellent:**	**$1,300.00**
	Very good:	**$1,045.00**

Smith & Wesson Model 21 1950 44 Military

Similar to the 1926 Model Military revolver except: made after World War II; minor changes. Made from about 1950 to 1967.

Estimated Value:	**Excellent:**	**$2,000.00**
	Very good:	**$1,600.00**

Smith & Wesson Model 24 1950 44 Target

Similar to the 1926 Model 44 Target except: 4" or 6½" barrel; made after World War II; minor changes; ribbed barrel. Made from about 1950 to 1967. There was a limited edition run of 7,500 in the mid-1980s.

Estimated Value:	**Excellent:**	**$1,100.00**
	Very good:	**$ 880.00**

Smith & Wesson Model 624 44 Special

Similar to the Model 24, 1950 44 Target Revolver except stainless steel. Produced only in the mid-1980s. Add 3% for 6½" barrel.

Estimated Value:	**Excellent:**	**$700.00**
	Very good:	**$560.00**

Smith & Wesson Model 24 1950 44 Target

Smith & Wesson Model 25 1955 Target

Smith & Wesson 1926 Model 44 Military

Smith & Wesson 1926 Model 44 Target

Smith & Wesson Model 21 1950 44 Military

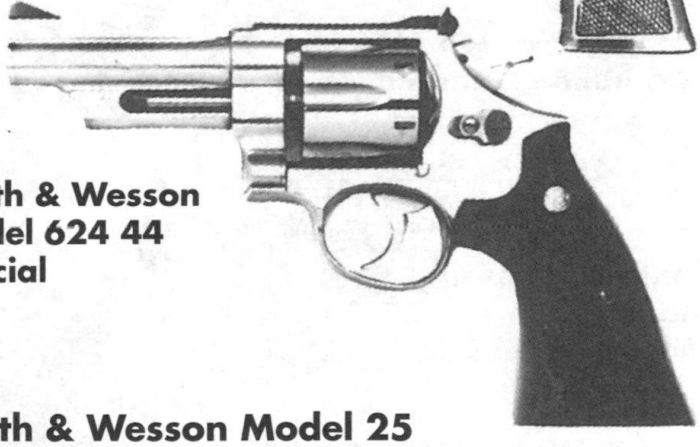

Smith & Wesson Model 624 44 Special

Smith & Wesson Model 25

Caliber: 45 ACP; 45 long Colt
Action: Single and double; exposed hammer; solid frame
Cylinder: 6-shot swing-out; simultaneous manual ejector; cylinder release on left side
Barrel: 4", 6", 8⅜"
Sights: Red ramp front; micrometer click rear adjustable for windage and elevation
Finish: Blued or nickel; checkered Goncolo Alves target grips
Length Overall: 9⅜" to 13¾"
Approximate wt.: 44 to 52 ozs.
Comments: This revolver is built on the large N frame. Made from about 1955 to 1992. Add 3% for 8⅜" barrel, add 9% for presentation box. Nickel finish discontinued in the late 1980s.

Estimated Value:	**Excellent:**	**$1,200.00**
	Very good:	**$ 960.00**

Smith & Wesson Model 25 1955 Target

Similar to the Model 25 except 6" barrel only; blued finish; 45 ACP caliber; ⅛" plain partridge front sight; add 9% for presentation box.

Estimated Value:	**Excellent:**	**$800.00**
	Very good:	**$640.00**

Smith & Wesson Model 20 Heavy Duty

Caliber: 38 Special
Action: Single and double; exposed hammer; solid frame
Cylinder: 6-shot swing-out; simultaneous ejector; release on left side of frame
Barrel: 4", 5", 6½"
Sights: Fixed
Finish: Blued or nickel; checkered square butt walnut grips
Length Overall: 9⅜" to 11⅞"
Approximate wt.: 38 to 41 ozs.
Comments: Made from about 1930 to 1967. Add 75% for pre-WWII models.

Estimated Value:	**Excellent:**	**$825.00**
	Very good:	**$660.00**

Smith & Wesson Model 23 Outdoorsman Revolver

Similar to the Model 20 Heavy Duty except: target version; 6½" barrel only; ribbed barrel after 1950; approximate wt.: 42 ozs.; blued finish; adjustable target sights. Made from about 1930 to 1967.

Estimated Value:	**Excellent:**	**$950.00**
	Very good:	**$760.00**

Smith & Wesson Model 64 Military and Police

Smith & Wesson Model 12 Military & Police Airweight

Smith & Wesson Model 64 Military & Police

Same as the Model 10 Military and Police except: satin finish stainless steel. Made from about 1972 to the present. Add 1% for 3" or 4" barrel; add 5% for 38+P caliber.

Estimated Value:	**New (retail):**	**$782.00**
	Excellent:	**$585.00**
	Very good:	**$470.00**

Smith & Wesson Model 12 Military & Police Airweight

Same as the Model 10 Military and Police except: light alloy frame; 2" or 4" barrel; approximate wt.: 28 ozs. Made from about 1952 to the late 1980s.

Estimated Value:	**Excellent:**	**$475.00**
	Very good:	**$380.00**

Smith & Wesson K-32 Target

Similar to the S&W 38 Military and Police Target except: caliber 32 S&W; 32 S&W long; and 32 Colt New Police; heavy barrel; approximate wt.: 34 ozs. Made from about 1940 to 1941.

Estimated Value:	**Excellent:**	**$1,200.00**
	Very good:	**$ 960.00**

Smith & Wesson Model 20 Heavy Duty

Smith & Wesson Military & Police

Caliber: 38 Special
Action: Single and double; exposed hammer; solid frame
Cylinder: 6-shot swing-out; simultaneous ejector; release on left side of frame
Barrel: 2" (after 1933); 4", 5", 6", 6½" (1902 – 1915)
Sights: Fixed
Finish: Blued or nickel; checkered hard rubber or checkered walnut round or square butt grips
Length Overall: 7" to 11½"
Approximate wt.: 26 to 32 ozs.
Comments: Made from about 1902 to 1942 with improvements and minor changes. Basic frame is known as S&W K frame. Add 5% for nickel finish. Also known as 1902 Model and 1905 Model M&P.

Estimated Value:	**Excellent:**	**$425.00**
	Very good:	**$340.00**

Smith & Wesson Model 10 Military & Police

Caliber: 38 Special
Action: Double and single; exposed hammer; solid frame
Cylinder: 6-shot swing-out: simultaneous manual ejector
Barrel: 2", 3", or 4"
Sights: Fixed
Finish: Blued or nickel: square or round butt checkered walnut grips
Length Overall: 7" to 9½"
Approximate wt.: 28 to 34 ozs.
Comments: Made from about 1948 to the present. Add 4% for nickel finish; blued only in the 1990s.

Estimated Value:	**New (retail):**	**$758.00**
	Excellent:	**$565.00**
	Very good:	**$455.00**

Smith & Wesson Victory Model

Same as the Model 10 Military and Police except: sand blasted or brushed parkerized finish; 4" barrel; smooth square butt grips with Lanyard ring; made from about 1941 to 1946 for the U.S. Government during World War II; 38 Special caliber; Some 38-200 caliber with 5" barrel were made for the British forces.

Estimated Value:	**Excellent:**	**$575.00**
	Very good:	**$460.00**

Smith & Wesson 38 Military & Police Target

Same as the Model 10 Military and Police except: 6" barrel only; approximate wt.: 33 ozs.; checkered walnut grips; adjustable target sights. Made from about 1924 to 1941.

Estimated Value:	**Excellent:**	**$600.00**
	Very good:	**$480.00**

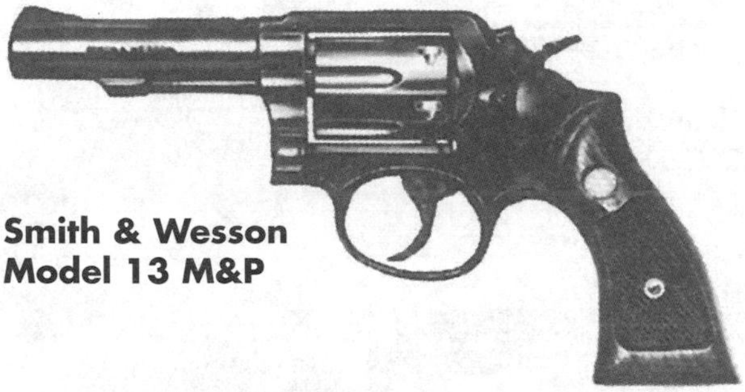

Smith & Wesson Model 13 M&P

Smith & Wesson Model 13 M&P

Similar to the Model 10 Military and Police except 357 mag. caliber and 3" or 4" heavy barrel.

Estimated Value: **Excellent:** **$500.00**
Very good: **$400.00**

Smith & Wesson Model 65 M&P

Similar to the Model 13 except: satin stainless steel finish; 3" or 4" barrel.

Estimated Value: **Excellent:** **$400.00**
Very good: **$320.00**

Smith & Wesson Model 65 Lady Smith

Similar to the Model 65 M&P except: 3" barrel; round butt rosewood grips; includes soft side Lady Smith case; glass bead finished stainless steel. Introduced in 1992.

Estimated Value: **Excellent:** **$400.00**
Very good: **$320.00**

Smith & Wesson Model 27 357 Mag.

Smith & Wesson Model 28 Highway Patrolman

Smith & Wesson Model 27 357 Mag.

Caliber: 357 mag. and 38 Special
Action: Single and double; exposed hammer; solid frame
Cylinder: 6-shot swing-out; simultaneous manual ejector
Barrel: 3½", 5", 6", 6½", 8⅜" ribbed
Sights: Ramp front, adjustable rear
Finish: Blued or nickel; checkered walnut grips
Length Overall: 7⅞" to 14¼"
Approximate wt.: 42 to 49 ozs.
Comments: Made from about 1935 to the mid-1990s. Made from 1935 to 1938 on special orders. Add 2% for 8⅜" barrel. Add $40.00 for presentation box.

Estimated Value: **Excellent:** **$500.00**
Very good: **$400.00**

Smith & Wesson Model 28 Highway Patrolman

Similar to the Model 27 357 Mag. except: 4" or 6" barrel; ramp front sight and adjustable rear sight; blued finish. Made from about 1954 to the late 1980s. Add 10% for target grips.

Estimated Value: **Excellent:** **$575.00**
Very good: **$460.00**

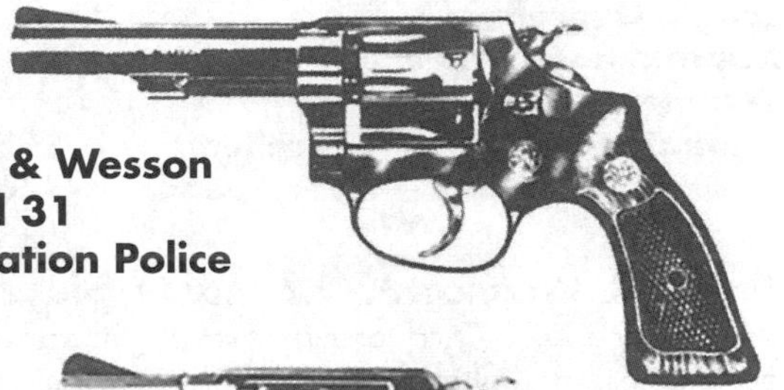

Smith & Wesson Model 31 Regulation Police

Smith & Wesson Model 32 Terrier

Smith & Wesson Model 31 Regulation Police

Caliber: 32 Smith & Wesson Long, 32 Colt New Police
Action: Single and double; exposed hammer; solid frame
Cylinder: 6-shot swing-out; simultaneous manual ejector; release on left side of frame
Barrel: 2" (1949 to the present); 3", 3¼", 4", 4¼", 6"
Sights: Fixed
Finish: Blued or nickel; checkered square butt walnut grips
Length Overall: 6½" to 10½"
Approximate wt.: 17 to 20 ozs.
Comments: Made from about 1917 to 1992. Nickel finish discontinued in the early 1980s.

Estimated Value: **Excellent:** **$425.00**
Very good: **$340.00**

Smith & Wesson Regulation Police Target

Similar to the Smith & Wesson Model 31 Regulation Police except: 6" barrel only; adjustable target sights; blued finish. Made from about 1917 to 1940.

Estimated Value: **Excellent:** **$500.00**
Very good: **$400.00**

Smith & Wesson Model 33 Regulation Police Revolver

Same as the Smith & Wesson Model 31 Regulation Police except: 38 caliber S&W and 38 Colt New Police; 5-shot cylinder. Made from about 1917 to 1974.

Estimated Value: **Excellent:** **$400.00**
Very good: **$320.00**

Smith & Wesson Model 32 Terrier

Similar to the Model 33 Regulation Police except: 2" barrel only; 6½" overall length. Made from about 1936 to 1974.

Estimated Value: **Excellent:** **$400.00**
Very good: **$320.00**

Smith & Wesson Model K-22 Outdoorsman

Caliber: 22 short, long, long rifle
Action: Single and double; exposed hammer; solid frame
Cylinder: 6-shot swing-out; simultaneous manual ejector
Barrel: 6"
Sights: Fixed or target sights
Finish: Blued or nickel; checkered walnut grips
Length Overall: 11½"
Approximate wt.: 35 ozs.
Comments: Made from about 1931 to 1942.
Estimated Value: **Excellent:** **$950.00**
Very good: **$760.00**

Smith & Wesson K-22 Masterpiece

Same as the K-22 Outdoorsman except: improved version; better adjustable rear sight; short cocking action; antibacklash trigger; made from about 1942 to 1947.
Estimated Value: **Excellent:** **$1,000.00**
Very good: **$ 800.00**

Smith & Wesson Model 14 K-38 Masterpiece

Caliber: 38 Special
Action: Single or double; or single action only; exposed hammer; solid frame
Cylinder: 6-shot swing-out; simultaneous manual ejector; release on left side of frame
Barrel: 6" or 8⅜"; 6" only after the mid-1980s
Sights: Partridge front; click adjustable rear
Finish: Blued; checkered square butt walnut grips or Hogue rubber grips
Length Overall: 11⅛" or 13½"
Approximate wt.: 36 to 38 ozs.
Comments: Made from about 1947 to 2000. Add $10.00 for 8⅜" barrel; $40.00 for target accessories.
Estimated Value: **Excellent:** **$575.00**
Very good: **$640.00**

Smith & Wesson Model 14 Single Action

Similar to the Model 14 K-38 Masterpiece except: single action; 6" barrel only.
Estimated Value: **Excellent:** **$600.00**
Very good: **$480.00**

Smith & Wesson Model 16 K-32 Masterpiece

Same as the Model 14 K-38 Masterpiece except: 32 S&W long and 32 Colt Police caliber; 6" barrel only; double and single action. Made from about 1947 to 1974.
Estimated Value: **Excellent:** **$1,275.00**
Very good: **$1,020.00**

Smith & Wesson Model 14 K-38 Masterpiece

Smith & Wesson Model K-22 Outdoorsman

Smith & Wesson Model 14 Single Action

Smith & Wesson Model 16 K-32 Masterpiece

Smith & Wesson Model 15 38 Combat Masterpiece

Same as the Model 14 K-38 Masterpiece except: 2", 4", 6", or 8⅜" barrel; approximate wt.: 30 to 39 ozs.; quick draw front sight; blued or nickel finish; double and single action. Made from about 1950 to the present. Add 7% for nickel finish (discontinued in the late 1980s); 3% for 8⅜" barrel (discontinued in 1989). 4" barrel only after 1990.
Estimated Value: **Excellent:** **$500.00**
Very good: **$400.00**

Smith & Wesson Model 67 38 Combat Masterpiece

Same as the Model 15 38 combat Masterpiece except: 4" barrel only; satin finish stainless steel construction. Introduced in 1972.
Estimated Value: **New (retail):** **$845.00**
Excellent: **$635.00**
Very good: **$500.00**

Smith & Wesson Model 19 357 Combat Magnum

Same as the Model 15 38 Combat Masterpiece except: 2½", 4", or 6" barrel; caliber 357 magnum or 38 Special; round or square butt. Made from about 1956 to present. Add 2% for square butt target stocks, 6% for target sights. Add 2% for 4" barrel.
Estimated Value: **Excellent:** **$475.00**
Very good: **$380.00**

Smith & Wesson Model 66 357 Combat Magnum

Same as the Model 19 357 Combat Magnum except: satin finish stainless steel. Produced from about 1972 to present. Add 12% for target accessories; 2% for target sights; 1% for 4" or 6" barrel.
Estimated Value: **Excellent:** **$400.00**
Very good: **$320.00**

Smith & Wesson Model 617 K-22 Masterpiece

Smith & Wesson Model 17 K-22 Masterpiece

Smith & Wesson Model 17 K-22 Masterpiece

Same as the Model 14 K-38 Masterpiece except: 22 short, long, long rifle caliber; 6" or 8⅜" barrel. Made from about 1947 to 1996; approximate wt.: 40 ozs. Add 3% for 8⅜" barrel; 9% for target trigger and hammer. Full-length ejector housing added in 1989.

Estimated Value: **Excellent:** **$525.00**
Very good: **$420.00**

Smith & Wesson Model 18 Combat Masterpiece

Same as the Model 17 K-22 Masterpiece except: 4" barrel; length overall 9⅛"; approximate wt. 38 ozs. Made from 1950 to the mid-1980s. Add 10% for target trigger and hammer.

Estimated Value: **Excellent:** **$600.00**
Very good: **$480.00**

Smith & Wesson Model 48 Masterpiece Magnum

Same as the Model 17 K-22 Masterpiece except: chambered for 22 magnum. Introduced in 1959.

Estimated Value: **Excellent:** **$500.00**
Very good: **$400.00**

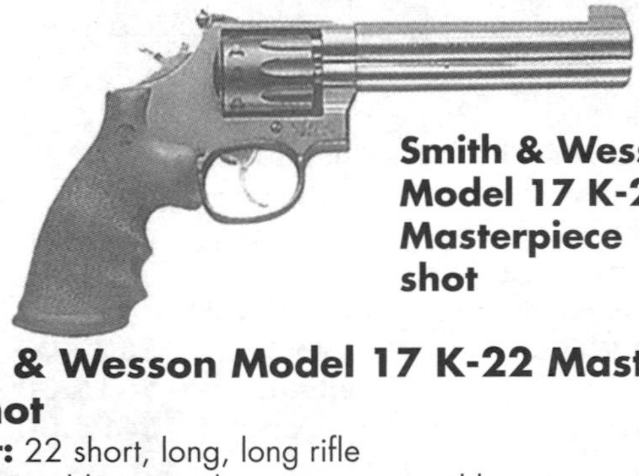

Smith & Wesson Model 17 K-22 Masterpiece 10-shot

Smith & Wesson Model 17 K-22 Masterpiece 10-Shot

Caliber: 22 short, long, long rifle
Action: Double or single action; exposed hammer; solid frame
Cylinder: 10-shot; swing-out
Barrel: 6", carbon steel
Sights: Ramp front, adjustable rear
Finish: Blued; Hogue rubber grips
Length Overall: 11⅛"
Approximate wt.: 42 ozs.
Comments: Made in the mid- to the late 1990s.

Estimated Value: **Excellent:** **$375.00**
Very good: **$300.00**

Smith & Wesson Model 617 K-22 Masterpiece

Caliber: 22 short, long and long rifle
Action: Single and double action; exposed hammer; solid frame
Cylinder: 6-shot swing-out; simultaneous manual ejector
Barrel: 4", 6", 8⅜"; full-length ejector shroud
Sights: Ramp front and micrometer adjustable rear
Finish: Stainless steel; square butt Goncalo Alves grips
Length Overall: 9⅛", 11⅛", 13½"
Approximate wt.: 42, 48, and 54 ozs.
Comments: Introduced in 1990. Add 3% for 8⅜" barrel; add 6% for target trigger and hammer.

Estimated Value: **New (retail):** **$940.00**
Excellent: **$700.00**
Very good: **$560.00**

Smith & Wesson Model 648

Same as the Model 617 except: 6" barrel, 22 mag caliber. Produced in the early 1990s.

Estimated Value: **Excellent:** **$475.00**
Very good: **$380.00**

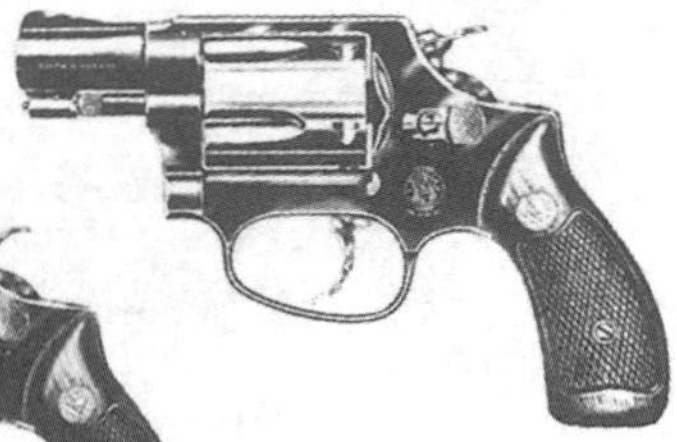

Smith & Wesson Model 36 Chief's Special

Smith & Wesson Model 37 Airweight

Smith & Wesson Model 36 Chief's Special

Caliber: 38 Special
Action: Single and double; exposed hammer; solid frame
Cylinder: 5-shot swing-out; simultaneous manual ejector
Barrel: 2" or 3"
Sights: Fixed
Finish: Blued or nickel; round or square butt, checkered walnut grips
Length Overall: 6½" to 7¾"
Approximate wt.: 19 to 20 ozs.
Comments: Made from about 1950 to 2000. Add 4% for nickel finish.

Estimated Value: **Excellent:** **$350.00**
Very good: **$280.00**

Smith & Wesson Model 37 and 637 Airweight Chief's Special

Same as the Model 36 Chief's Special except: light alloy frame; approximate wt.: 13 to 14 ozs. Made from about 1954 to the present. Add 4% for nickel finish or stainless steel (637).

Estimated Value: **New (retail):** **$640.00**
Excellent: **$480.00**
Very good: **$385.00**

Smith & Wesson Model 638 Airweight

Similar to the Model 637 Airweight except it has a "Bodyguard" frame and shrouded hammer.

Estimated Value: **New (retail):** **$640.00**
Excellent: **$480.00**
Very good: **$385.00**

Smith & Wesson Model 60 Chief's Special Stainless

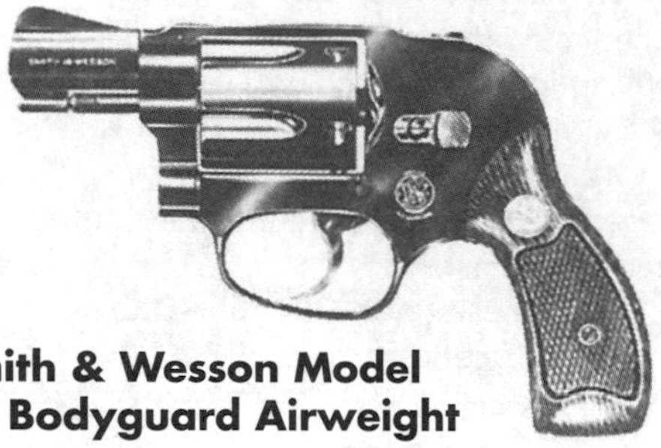

Smith & Wesson Model 38 Bodyguard Airweight

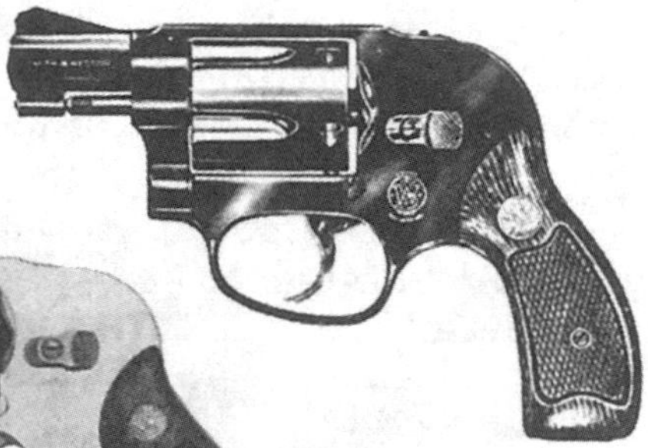

Smith & Wesson Model 49 Bodyguard

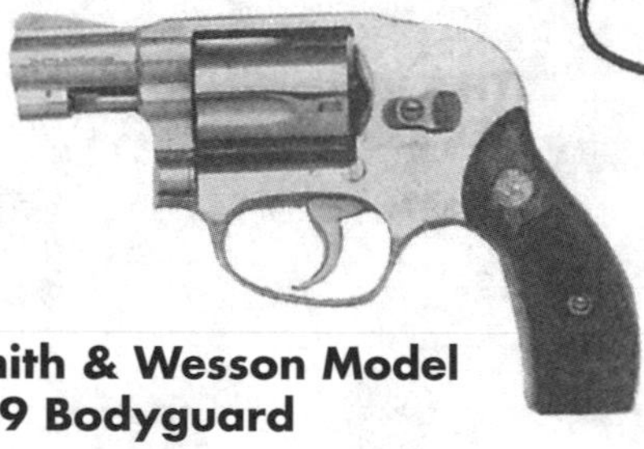

Smith & Wesson Model 649 Bodyguard

Smith & Wesson Model 60 Chief's Special Stainless (38)

Same as the Model 36 Chief's Special except: satin finish stainless steel; round butt grip; approximate wt.: 20 ozs.

Estimated Value: **Excellent:** **$420.00**
Very good: **$335.00**

Smith & Wesson Model 38 Bodyguard Airweight

Same as the Model 36 Chief's Special except: light alloy frame; shrouded hammer; approximate wt.: 15 ozs.; 2" barrel only. Introduced in 1955. Add 3% for nickel finish.

Estimated Value: **Excellent:** **$375.00**
Very good: **$300.00**

Smith & Wesson Model 49 Bodyguard

Same as the Model 38 Bodyguard Airweight except: steel frame; approximate wt.: 21 ozs. Made from about 1959 to the present. Nickel finish discontinued in the late 1980s.

Estimated Value: **Excellent:** **$500.00**
Very good: **$400.00**

Smith & Wesson Model 649 Bodyguard

Same as the Model 49 Bodyguard except: stainless steel; calibers: 38 S&W Spec., 38 S&W Spec. +P, 357 mag.

Estimated Value: **New (retail):** **$822.00**
Excellent: **$615.00**
Very good: **$495.00**

Smith & Wesson Model 36 Lady Smith

Caliber: 38 special
Action: Single and double action with exposed hammer; solid frame
Cylinder: 5-shot swing-out; simultaneous manual ejector
Barrel: 2", 3" heavy barrel
Sights: Serrated front; fixed notch rear
Finish: Blued; 2" barrel has smooth wood grips; 3" heavy barrel has smooth wood combat-style grips
Length Overall: 6¼" (2" barrel); 7⅜" (3" barrel)
Approximate wt.: 20 ozs. (2" barrel); 23 ozs. (3" barrel)
Comments: Introduced in 1989.
Estimated Value: **Excellent:** **$500.00**
Very good: **$400.00**

Smith & Wesson Model 60 Lady Smith

Same as the Model 36 Lady Smith except: all stainless steel; 2" barrel. Introduced in 1989.

Estimated Value: **New (retail):** **$822.00**
Excellent: **$615.00**
Very good: **$495.00**

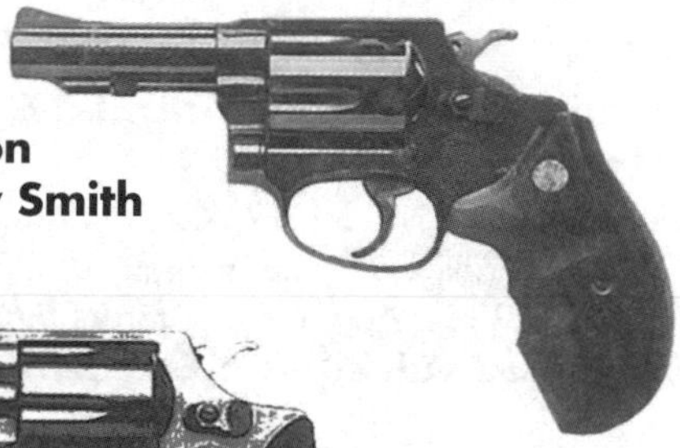

Smith & Wesson Model 36 Lady Smith

Smith & Wesson Model 60 Lady Smith

Smith & Wesson Model 60 357 Mag Chief's Special

Caliber: 357 magnum or 38 Special
Action: Double or single action; exposed hammer
Cylinder: 5-shot; swing-out
Barrel: 2⅛" or 3"
Sights: Black ramp front, fixed notch rear
Finish: Stainless steel; Uncle Mike's combat grip
Length Overall: 6 5/16"
Approximate wt.: 24 ozs.
Comments: Introduced in 1996 (357 caliber).
Estimated Value: **New (retail):** **$822.00**
Excellent: **$615.00**
Very good: **$495.00**

Smith & Wesson Model 60 357 Mag Chief's Special

Smith & Wesson Model 40 Centennial Hammerless

Smith & Wesson Model 42 Centennial Airweight

Smith & Wesson Model 40 Centennial Hammerless

Same as the Model 36 Chief's Special except: concealed hammer; frame extends over hammer area; 2" barrel; double action only; grip safety located on rear of grip. Made from about 1952 to 1974.

Estimated Value:	**Excellent:**	**$525.00**
	Very good:	**$420.00**

Smith & Wesson Model 42 Centennial Airweight

Same as the Model 40 Centennial except: light alloy frame; approximate wt.: 13 ozs. Made from about 1954 to 1974.

Estimated Value:	**Excellent:**	**$425.00**
	Very good:	**$340.00**

Smith & Wesson Model 940 Centennial

Caliber: 9mm
Action: Double action only; enclosed hammer; no grip safety
Cylinder: 5-shot swing-out; simultaneous manual ejector
Barrel: 2" or 3"
Sights: Fixed; ramp front, square notch rear
Finish: Stainless steel; round butt combat grips
Length Overall: 6½" to 7½"
Approximate wt.: 23 to 24 ozs.
Comments: Introduced in 1991; 2" barrel only after 1993.

Estimated Value:	**Excellent:**	**$500.00**
	Very good:	**$400.00**

Smith & Wesson Model 442 Centennial Airweight

Caliber: 38 Special
Action: Double action only; enclosed hammer; no grip safety; alloy frame
Cylinder: 5-shot swing-out; simultaneous manual ejector
Barrel: 2"
Sights: Fixed; ramp front, square notch rear
Finish: Blued or nickel; round butt grips
Length Overall: 6½"
Approximate wt.: 16 ozs.
Comments: Introduced in the 1990s; add 3% for nickel finish.

Estimated Value:	**New (retail):**	**$616.00**
	Excellent:	**$460.00**
	Very good:	**$370.00**

Smith & Wesson Model 642 Centennial Airweight

Similar to the Model 442 Centennial Airweight except: stainless steel; 2" or 3" barrel; approximate wt.: 16 or 17 ozs.

Estimated Value:	**New (retail)**	**$616.00**
	Excellent:	**$460.00**
	Very good:	**$370.00**

Smith & Wesson Model 642 LS (Lady Smith)

Same as the Model 642 Centennial Airweight except: 2" barrel; price includes softside carrying case.

Estimated Value:	**New (retail):**	**$806.00**
	Excellent:	**$605.00**
	Very good:	**$480.00**

Smith & Wesson Model 642 Centennial Airweight

Smith & Wesson Model 640 Centennial

Caliber: 357 magnum or 38 Special
Action: Double action only; concealed hammer; solid frame
Cylinder: 5-shot swing-out; simultaneous manual ejector
Barrel: 1⅞" or 2⅞"
Sights: Ramp front; fixed square notch rear
Finish: Stainless steel with smooth Goncalo Alves round butt grips, or Uncle Mike's Combat grips
Length Overall: 6½"
Approximate wt.: 20 ozs.
Comments: Introduced in 1990.

Estimated Value:	**New (retail):**	**$822.00**
	Excellent:	**$615.00**
	Very good:	**$495.00**

Smith & Wesson Model 57 41 Mag.

Caliber: 41 magnum
Action: Single and double; exposed hammer; solid frame
Cylinder: 6-shot swing-out; simultaneous manual ejector; release on left side of frame
Barrel: 4", 6", or 8⅜"
Sights: Ramp front, adjustable rear
Finish: Blued or nickel (discontinued in the late 1980s); checkered walnut grips
Length Overall: 9⅜" to 13¾"
Approximate wt.: 38 to 42 ozs.
Comments: Made from about 1964 to 1993. Add 4% for 8⅜" barrel; $40.00 for presentation box.

Estimated Value:	**Excellent:**	**$425.00**
	Very good:	**$340.00**

Smith & Wesson Model 657 41 Mag.

Similar to the Model 57 41 Mag. except: stainless steel; Hogue rubber combat grips. Introduced in the mid-1980s. Add 4% for 8⅜" barrel.

Estimated Value:	**Excellent:**	**$600.00**
	Very good:	**$480.00**

Smith & Wesson Model 58 Military & Police

Similar to the Model 57 41 magnum except: 4" barrel only; fixed sights; no rib on barrel. Made from about 1964 to the late 1970s. Add $10.00 for nickel finish.

Estimated Value: **Excellent:** **$600.00**
Very good: **$480.00**

Smith & Wesson Model 58 Military and Police

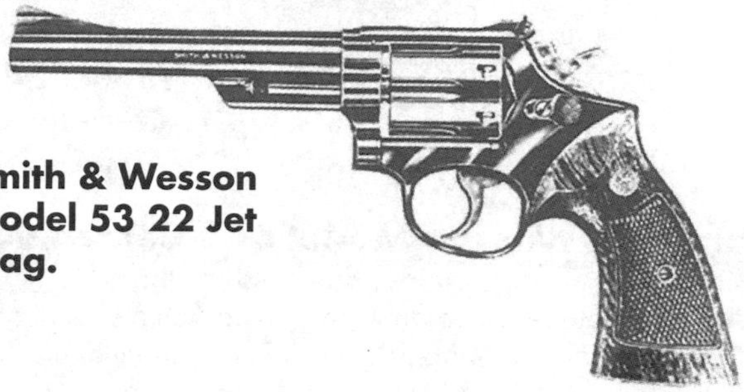

Smith & Wesson Model 53 22 Jet Mag.

Smith & Wesson Model 53 22 Jet Mag.

Caliber: 22 Rem. Jet centerfire or 22 S, L, or LR by using chamber inserts and repositioning floating firing pin on hammer
Action: Single and double; exposed hammer; solid frame
Cylinder: 6-shot swing-out; simultaneous manual ejector
Barrel: 4", 6", or 8⅜"
Sights: Ramp front; adjustable rear
Finish: Blued; checkered walnut target grips
Length Overall: 9¼" to 13⅝"
Approximate wt.: 38 to 42 ozs.
Comments: Made from about 1961 to 1974. Could be fitted with regular 22 caliber cylinder. Add $100.00 for extra cylinder.
Estimated Value: **Excellent:** **$725.00**
Very good: **$580.00**

Smith & Wesson Model 29 44 Magnum

Caliber: 44 magnum and 44 Special
Action: Single and double; exposed hammer; solid frame
Cylinder: 6-shot swing-out; simultaneous manual ejector; release on left side of frame
Barrel: 4", 6", 8⅝", or 10⅝" ribbed; 6" or 8⅜" only after early 1990s
Sights: Ramp front; adjustable rear
Finish: Blued or nickel: checkered wood grips
Length Overall: 9⅜" to 13¾"
Approximate wt.: 44 to 49 ozs.
Comments: Made from about 1956 to 2000. Add 2% for 8⅜" or nickel finish; add 11% for 10⅝" barrel; add $40.00 for presentation box.
Estimated Value: **Excellent:** **$975.00**
Very good: **$780.00**

Smith & Wesson Model 629 44 Mag.

Same as the Model 29 44 mag. except: satin stainless steel finish. Add 3% for 8⅜" barrel; add $40.00 for presentation box. 10⅝" barrel not available.

Estimated Value: **Excellent:** **$575.00**
Very good: **$460.00**

Smith & Wesson Model 29 Classic 44 Magnum

Similar to the Model 29 44 Magnum except: 5", 6", or 8⅝" barrel; full lug barrel; interchangeable front sight. Add 2% for 8⅝" barrel.

Estimated Value: **New (retail):** **$1,280.00**
Excellent: **$ 960.00**
Very good: **$ 765.00**

Smith & Wesson Model 629 Classic

Similar to the Model 29 Classic 44 Mag. except: stainless steel construction. Introduced in 1990.

Estimated Value: **New (retail):** **$1,114.00**
Excellent: **$ 835.00**
Very good: **$ 665.00**

Smith & Wesson Model 29 Classic DX

Similar to the Model 29 Classic 44 mag. except: combat grips. Add 2% for 8⅝" barrel. Produced in the early 1990s.

Estimated Value: **Excellent:** **$650.00**
Very good: **$520.00**

Smith & Wesson Model 629 Classic DX

Similar to the Model 29 Classic DX except: stainless steel. Add 3% for 8⅝" barrel. Introduced in 1990.

Estimated Value: **Excellent:** **$625.00**
Very good: **$500.00**

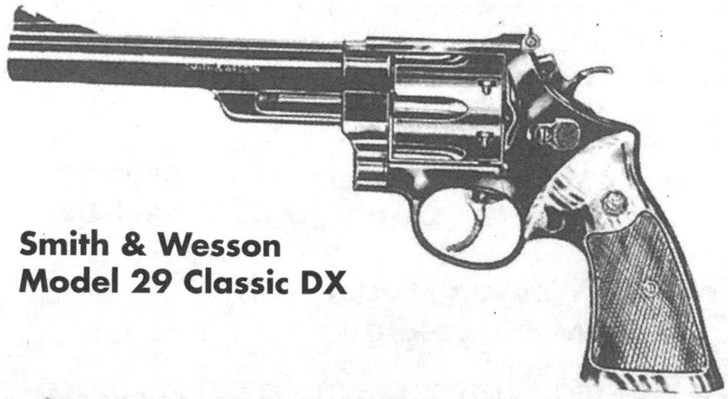

Smith & Wesson Model 29 Classic DX

Smith & Wesson Model 629 Classic

Smith & Wesson Model 581 Distinguished Service Mag.

Caliber: 357 mag. and 38 Special
Action: Single and double; exposed hammer; solid frame
Cylinder: 6-shot swing-out; simultaneous manual ejector;
Barrel: 4" or 6" heavy barrel with full-length ejector rod shroud; 4" barrel only after the mid-1980s
Sights: Serrated ramp front, fixed rear
Finish: Blued or nickel; checkered walnut magna service grips
Length Overall: 9¾" to 11¾"
Approximate wt.: 42 to 44 ozs.
Comments: Smith & Wesson's new "L" frame revolver. It is slightly larger than the "K" frame which permits it to accommodate a sturdier cylinder. Introduced in 1982. Nickel finish discontinued in the late 1980s.

Estimated Value:	**Excellent:**	**$425.00**
	Very good:	**$340.00**

Smith & Wesson Model 681 Distinguished Service Mag.

Similar to the Model 581 except: satin stainless steel finish; 4" barrel only.

Estimated Value:	**Excellent:**	**$475.00**
	Very good:	**$380.00**

Smith & Wesson Model 586 Distinguished Combat Mag.

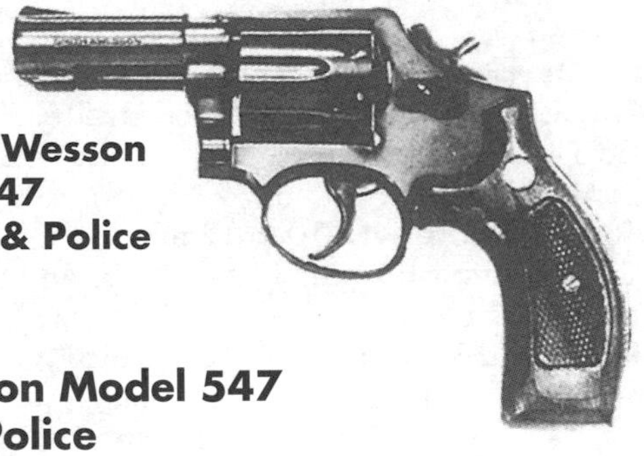

Smith & Wesson Model 547 Military & Police

Smith & Wesson Model 547 Military and Police

Caliber: 9mm Parabellum
Action: Single and double; exposed hammer; solid frame
Cylinder: 6-shot swing-out; simultaneous manual ejector; release on left side of frame
Barrel: 3" or 4" heavy barrel
Sights: Fixed rear, serrated ramp front
Finish: Blued; checkered walnut round butt grips with 3" barrel and square butt with 4" barrel
Length Overall: 8¼" to 9¼"
Approximate wt.: 32 to 34 ozs.
Comments: A 9mm revolver built on a "K" frame that features a unique new extraction system for positive extraction of the 9mm cartridge. Made from about 1981 to the mid-1980s.

Estimated Value:	**Excellent:**	**$425.00**
	Very good:	**$340.00**

Smith & Wesson Model 610

Caliber: 10mm
Action: Single and double; exposed hammer; solid frame
Cylinder: 6-shot swing-out; simultaneous manual ejector, unfluted
Barrel: 6½"
Sights: Interchangeable front, micrometer adjustable rear
Finish: Stainless steel; Hogue rubber combat grips
Length Overall: 12"
Approximate wt.: 52 ozs.
Comments: Introduced in the 1990s.

Estimated Value:	**Excellent:**	**$575.00**
	Very good:	**$460.00**

Smith & Wesson Model 625

Caliber: 45 ACP
Action: Single and double; exposed hammer; solid frame
Cylinder: 6-shot swing-out; simultaneous manual ejector
Barrel: 3", 4", 5"; full-length ejector housing under barrel
Sights: Serrated black ramp front and micrometer adjustable rear
Finish: Stainless steel; Pachmayr Gripper round butt grips
Length Overall: 8⅜", 9⅜", 10⅜"
Approximate wt.: 41, 43, and 46 ozs.
Comments: Introduced in 1989.

Estimated Value:	**New (retail):**	**$1,106.00**
	Excellent:	**$ 830.00**
	Very good:	**$ 660.00**

Smith & Wesson Model 586 Distinguished Combat Magnum

Caliber: 357 mag. and 38 Special
Action: Single and double; exposed hammer; solid frame
Cylinder: 6-shot swing-out; simultaneous manual ejector; cylinder release on left side
Barrel: 4", 6", or 8⅜" heavy barrel with a full-length ejector shroud; 8⅜" barrel discontinued in 1991
Sights: Red ramp front, micrometer click rear adjustable for windage and elevation
Finish: Blue or nickel; checkered Goncalo Alves grips
Length Overall: 9¾" to 13¾"
Approximate wt.: 42 to 46 ozs.
Comments: S and W's new "L" frame revolver; slightly larger than the "K" frame which permits it to accommodate a sturdier cylinder; introduced in 1982. Add 3% for nickel finish; 9% for adjustable front sight; 5% for 8⅜" barrel.

Estimated Value:	**Excellent:**	**$450.00**
	Very good:	**$360.00**

Smith & Wesson Model 686 Distinguished Combat Magnum

Similar to the Model 586 except: satin stainless steel. Add 2% for target grips; 7% for adjustable front sight; 5% for 8⅜" barrel. Also available with 2½" barrel. A Power Port model is available (686PP) with an integral recoil compensator (add 12%).

Estimated Value:	**Excellent:**	**$525.00**
	Very good:	**$420.00**

Smith & Wesson Model 686 Plus

Smith & Wesson Model 686 Plus

Caliber: 357 magnum or 38 Special, 38+p
Action: Double or single action
Cylinder: 7-shot
Barrel: 2½", 4", or 6", full lug
Sights: Red ramp front, adjustable blade rear
Finish: Stainless steel; Hogue rubber grip
Length Overall: 7½", 9½", or 12"
Approximate wt.: 35 to 45 ozs.
Comments: Introduced in 1996. Add 3% for 4" barrel, 5% for 6" barrel.
Estimated Value: **Excellent:** **$545.00**
Very good: **$435.00**

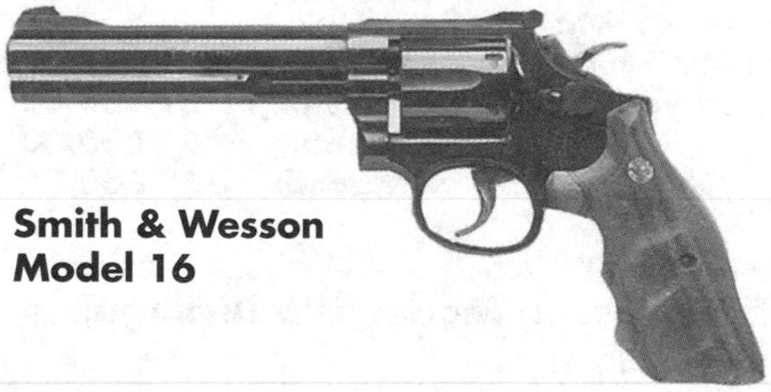

Smith & Wesson Model 16

Smith & Wesson Model 16

Caliber: 32 mag. and 32 S&W
Action: Single and double; exposed hammer; solid frame
Cylinder: 6-shot swing-out; simultaneous manual ejector
Barrel: 4", 6", $8\frac{3}{8}$"; full-length ejector rod housing.
Sights: Ramp front sight; S&W micrometer adjustable rear
Finish: Blued with square butt Goncalo Alves combat style grips
Length Overall: $9\frac{1}{8}$" (4 barrel); $11\frac{1}{8}$" (6" barrel); 13½" ($8\frac{3}{8}$" barrel)
Approximate wt.: 42, 47, and 54 ozs.
Comments: Produced from 1989 to 1994. Add 3% for 6" barrel; add 4% for $8\frac{3}{8}$" barrel; add 7% for target trigger and target hammer. 6" barrel only after 1991.
Estimated Value: **Excellent:** **$600.00**
Very good: **$480.00**

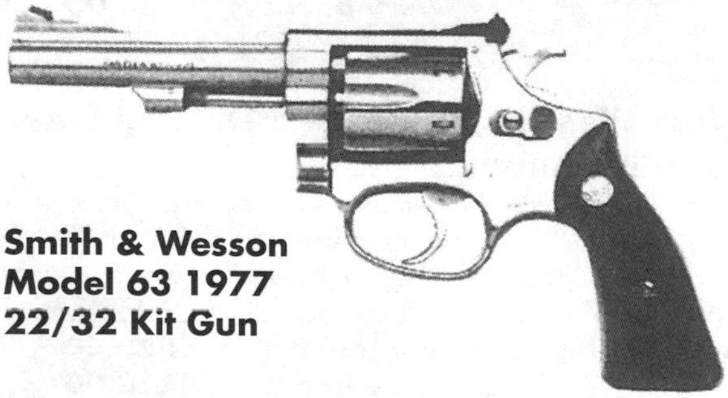

Smith & Wesson Model 63 1977 22/32 Kit Gun

Smith & Wesson Model 696

Caliber: 44 S&W Special
Action: Double or single action; exposed hammer; solid frame
Cylinder: 5-shot; swing-out, fluted
Barrel: 3"
Sights: Red ramp front, adjustable white outline rear
Finish: Stainless steel, Uncle Mike's Combat grips
Length Overall: 8¼"
Approximate wt.: 36 ozs.
Comments: Introduced in the late 1990s.
Estimated Value: **Excellent:** **$600.00**
Very good: **$480.00**

Smith & Wesson Model 696

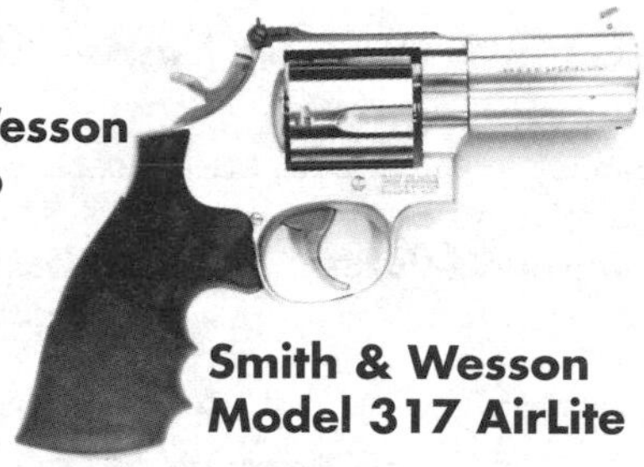

Smith & Wesson Model 317 AirLite

Smith & Wesson Model 317 AirLite and 317 Kit Gun

Caliber: 22 short, long, long rifle
Action: Double or single action; exposed hammer; solid frame
Cylinder: 8-shot; swing-out, fluted
Barrel: $1\frac{7}{8}$" or 3" (Kit Gun)
Sights: Pinned black ramp front, adjustable rear
Finish: Aluminum alloy/carbon steel or stainless steel; Clear Cote finish; Dymondwood boot or Uncle Mike's Combat grips
Length Overall: $6\frac{7}{8}$" or 7½"
Approximate wt.: 10 to 12 ozs.
Comments: Introduced in the 1990s. Add 8% for Dymondwood grips or 3" barrel.
Estimated Value: **New (retail):** **$790.00**
Excellent: **$590.00**
Very good: **$475.00**

Smith & Wesson Model 63 1977 22/32 Kit Gun

Caliber: 22 S, L, or LR
Action: Single and double; exposed hammer
Cylinder: 6-shot swing-out
Barrel: 2" or 4"
Sights: Adjustable micrometer square notch rear, red ramp front
Finish: Satin stainless steel; checkered walnut grips
Length Overall: $9\frac{3}{8}$"
Approximate wt.: 24½ ozs.
Comments: Made from 1977 to 2000.
Estimated Value: **Excellent:** **$350.00**
Very good: **$280.00**

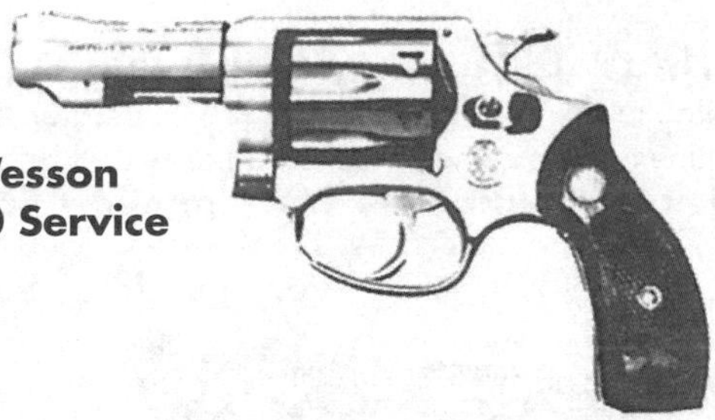

Smith & Wesson Model 650 Service Kit Gun

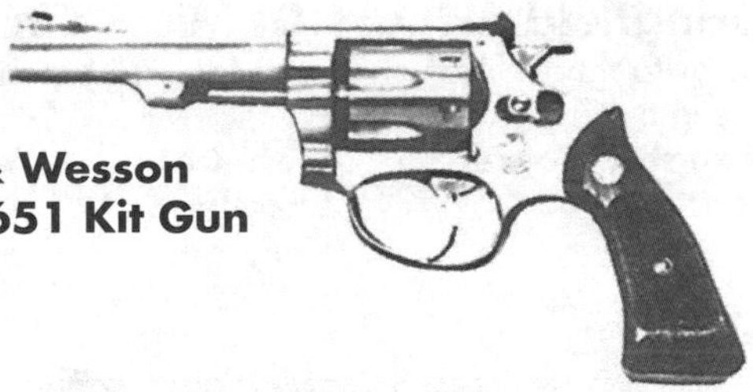

Smith & Wesson Model 651 Kit Gun

Smith & Wesson Model 650 Service Kit Gun

Caliber: 22 magnum
Action: Single and double action, exposed hammer
Cylinder: 6-shot swing-out, simultaneous ejector
Barrel: 3" heavy barrel
Sights: Serrated ramp front, fixed square notch rear
Finish: Satin stainless steel; checkered walnut round butt grips
Length Overall: 7"
Approximate wt.: 23½ ozs.
Comments: A "J" frame revolver produced in the mid-1980s.

Estimated Value:	**Excellent:**	**$425.00**
	Very good:	**$340.00**

Smith & Wesson Model 651 Kit Gun

Caliber: 22 mag.
Action: Double and single, exposed hammer
Clynder: 6-shot swing-out, simultaneous ejector
Barrel: 4"
Sights: Red ramp front, adjustable micrometer click rear
Finish: Satin stainless steel; checkered walnut square butt grips
Length Overall: 8⅜"
Approximate wt.: 24½ ozs.
Comments: A "J" frame revolver produced from the mid-1980s to 2000.

Estimated Value:	**Excellent:**	**$425.00**
	Very good:	**$340.00**

SPRINGFIELD ARMORY

Springfield Armory GI 45 Full Size

Springfield Armory GI Champion

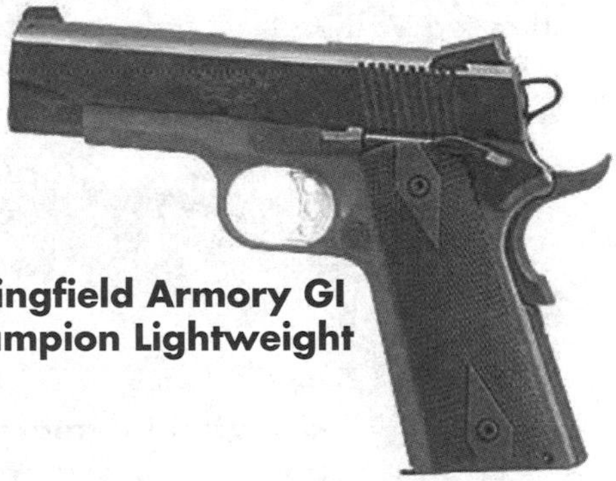

Springfield Armory GI Champion Lightweight

Springfield Armory GI 45 Full Size

Caliber: 45 ACP
Action: Semiautomatic, exposed spur hammer
Magazine: 7-shot clip
Barrel: 5" steel, parkerized
Sights: Low profile military
Finish: Parkerized steel, checkered hardwood grips engraved "US"; stainless steel available; olive drab steel available; matte black with black polymer grips available
Length overall: 8½"
Approximate wt.: 39 oz.
Comments: Based on John Browning's 1911 design. Add 8% for stainless steel, 9% for matte black.

Estimated Value:	**New (retail):**	**$643.00**
	Excellent:	**$480.00**
	Very good:	**$385.00**

Springfield Armory GI Champion

Similar to the GI 45 Full Size except 4" barrel, overall length 7½"; weighs 7 oz.

Estimated Value:	**New (retail):**	**$643.00**
	Excellent:	**$480.00**
	Very good:	**$385.00**

Springfield Armory GI Champion Lightweight

Similar to the GI Champion except: frame is forged aluminum alloy with anodized black hard coat; weighs 30 oz.

Estimated Value:	**New (retail):**	**$643.00**
	Excellent:	**$480.00**
	Very good:	**$385.00**

Springfield Armory GI Micro Compact

Similar to the GI 45 Full Size except: 3" barrel; 6-shot clip; overall length 6½"; weighs 33 oz.

Estimated Value: **New (retail):** **$693.00**
Excellent: **$520.00**
Very good: **$415.00**

Springfield Armory GI Micro Compact

Springfield Armory Mil-Spec

Caliber: 45 ACP
Action: Semiautomatic, exposed spur hammer
Magazine: 7-shot clip
Barrel: 5" stainless steel
Sights: Fixed combat, 3-dot
Finish: Parkerized forged steel frame and slide with checkered hardwood or black plastic grips; stainless steel finish available
Length overall: 8½"
Approximate wt.: 39 oz.
Comments: Similar to the GI series but with improvements and cosmetic differences. Add 9% for stainless steel finish.

Estimated Value: **New (retail):** **$753.00**
Excellent: **$565.00**
Very good: **$450.00**

Springfield Armory Loaded Full-Size MC Operator

Springfield Armory Loaded Full-Size MC Operator

Caliber: 45 ACP
Action: Semiautomatic, exposed spur hammer
Magazine: 7-shot clip
Barrel: 5" stainless steel
Sights: Low profile combat rear, dovetail front
Finish: Forged steel; olive drab Armory Kote frame; black Armory Kote slide; Pachmayr wraparound grips.
Length overall: 8½"
Approximate wt.: 42 oz.
Comments: The Operator has a light-mounting rail forged directly into the frame.

Estimated Value: **New (retail):** **$1,387.00**
Excellent: **$1,040.00**
Very good: **$ 830.00**

Springfield Armory Lightweight Operator

Similar to the Loaded Full-Size MC Operator except: anodized aluminum alloy frame; checkered hardwood grips; weighs 34 oz.

Estimated Value: **New (retail):** **$643.00**
Excellent: **$480.00**
Very good: **$385.00**

Springfield Armory Lightweight Operator

Springfield Armory Lightweight Champion Operator

Springfield Armory Lightweight Champion Operator

Similar to the Lightweight Operator except: 4" barrel; weighs 31 oz.; 7½" overall lengh.

Estimated Value: **New (retail):** **$643.00**
Excellent: **$480.00**
Very good: **$385.00**

Springfield Armory Loaded Full-Size Trophy Match

Springfield Armory Loaded Full-Size Trophy Match

Caliber: 45 ACP
Action: Semiautomatic, exposed spur hammer
Magazine: 7-shot clip
Barrel: 5" stainless steel
Sights: Adjustable low profile rear, dovetail front, target
Finish: Polished stainless steel flats with matte rounds; checkered hardwood grips
Length overall: 8½"
Approximate wt.: 40 oz.
Comments: Designed with competition features for match use.

Estimated Value: **New (retail):** **$1,605.00**
Excellent: **$1,200.00**
Very good: **$ 960.00**

Springfield Armory TRP

Springfield Armory TRP

Caliber: 45 ACP
Action: Semiautomatic, exposed spur hammer
Magazine: 7-shot clip
Barrel: 5" stainless steel barrel
Sights: Fixed low profile combat rear, dovetail front
Finish: Forged steel frame with black Armory Kote, black composite grips; stainless steel available
Length overall: 8½"
Approximate wt.: 42 oz.
Comments: Designed around the specifications of the FBI contract pistol, the TRP-PRO Model.

Estimated Value:	**New (retail):**	**$1,777.00**
	Excellent:	**$1,332.00**
	Very good:	**$1,065.00**

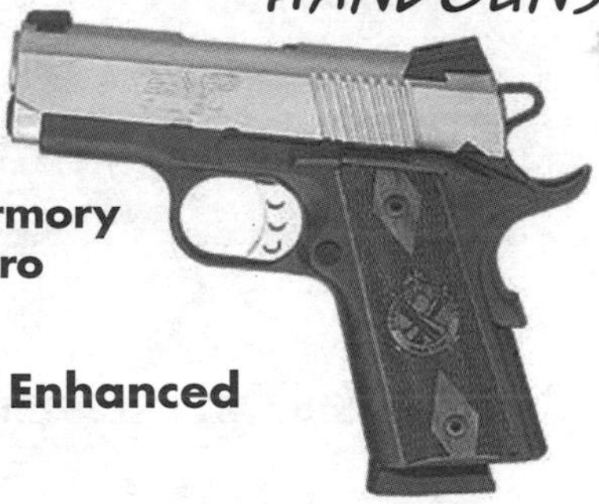

Springfield Armory Enhanced Micro Pistol EMP

Springfield Armory Enhanced Micro Pistol EMP

Caliber: 9 x 19 mm; 40
Action: Semiautomatic, exposed spur hammer
Magazine: 9-shot clip with slam pad; 8-shot in 40 caliber
Barrel: 3" stainless steel
Sights: Fixed low profile combat rear, dovetail front
Finish: Forged aluminum alloy with black hardcoat anodized finish; checkered hardwood grips
Length overall: 6½"
Approximate wt.: 26 oz.; 33 oz. in 40 caliber
Comments: A short action, 1911-style pistol.

Estimated Value:	**New (retail):**	**$1,345.00**
	Excellent:	**$1,000.00**
	Very good:	**$ 800.00**

STAR

Star Model 1919 Pocket

Caliber: 25 ACP (6.35mm)
Action: Semiautomatic; exposed hammer
Magazine: 8-shot clip
Barrel: 2⅝"
Sights: Fixed
Finish: Blued; checkered walnut grips
Length Overall: 4⅞"
Approximate wt.: 16 ozs.
Comments: Made from about 1919 to 1934. Distinguished by the safety at the top rear of the slide.

Estimated Value:	**Excellent:**	**$300.00**
	Very good:	**$240.00**

Star Model CO Pocket

Improved version of the 1919 Model; safety in front of left grip rather than top rear of slide; plastic grips; some engraved nickel-plated models produced. Made from about 1934 to 1957. Add $20.00 for engraved nickel model.

Estimated Value:	**Excellent:**	**$275.00**
	Very good:	**$220.00**

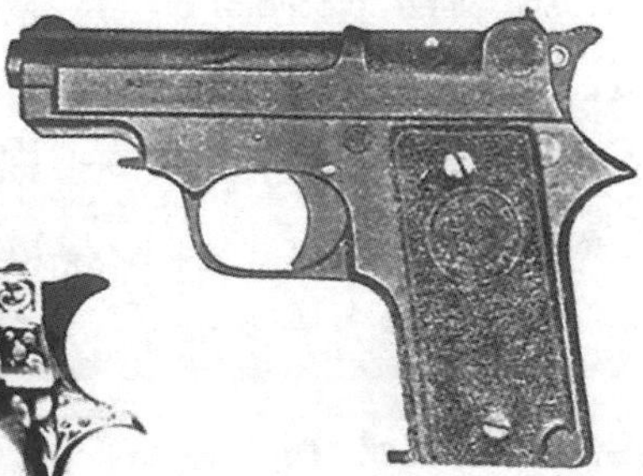

Star Model 1919 Pocket

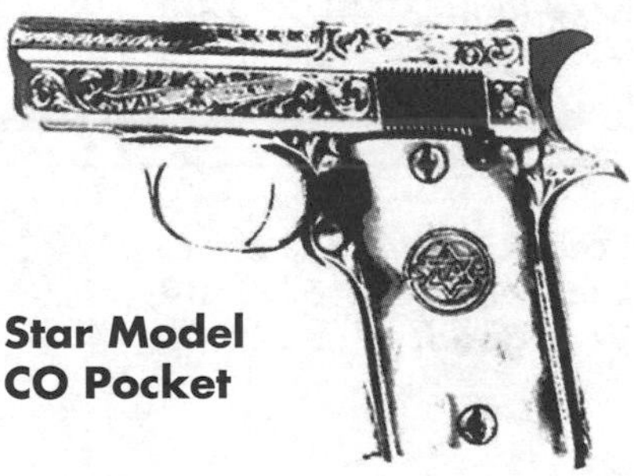

Star Model CO Pocket

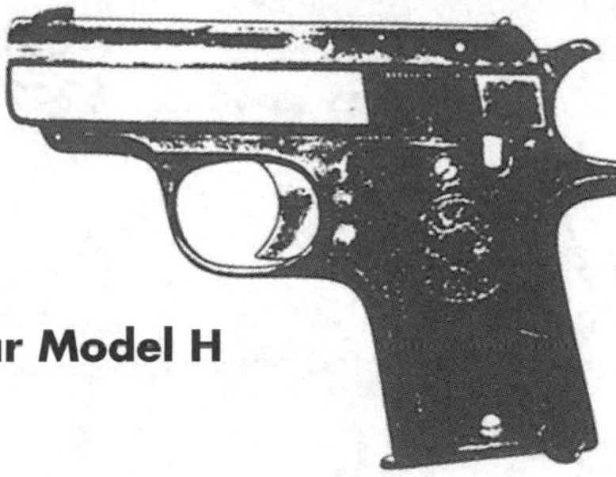

Star Model H

Star Model H

Similar to the Model CO pistol except: caliber 32 ACP; 9-shot clip; approximate wt.: 20 ozs. Made from about 1934 to 1941.

Estimated Value:	**Excellent:**	**$275.00**
	Very good:	**$220.00**

Star Model HN

Same as the Model H except: caliber 380 ACP; 6-shot clip.

Estimated Value:	**Excellent:**	**$300.00**
	Very good:	**$240.00**

Star Model E Pocket

Caliber: 25 ACP (6.35mm)
Action: Semiautomatic; exposed hammer
Magazine: 6-shot clip
Barrel: 2"
Sights: Fixed
Finish: Blued; checkered grips
Length Overall: 4"
Approximate wt.: 10 ozs.
Comments: Small compact pocket pistol; safety located in front of left grip; no longer in production.

Estimated Value:	**Excellent:**	**$225.00**
	Very good:	**$180.00**

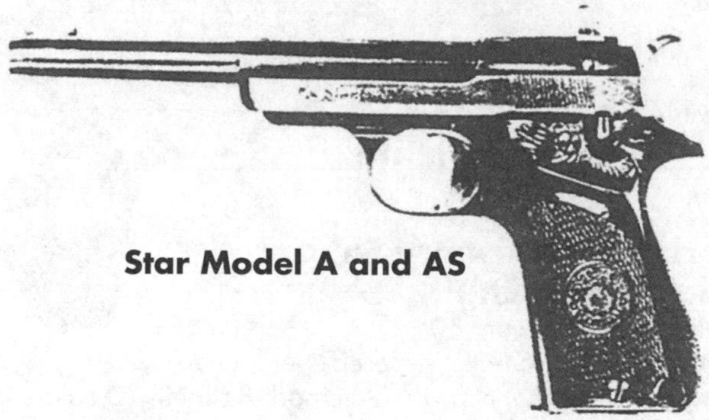

Star Model A and AS

Star Model B Super
Caliber: 9mm Parabellum
Action: Semiautomatic; exposed hammer
Magazine: 8-shot clip
Barrel: 5"
Sights: Blade front; fixed rear
Finish: Blued; all steel
Length Overall: 8¾"
Approximate wt.: 38 ozs.
Comments: Imported from the 1970s to the early 1990s; an improved version of Model B with loaded chamber indicator; refined takedown and reassembly system; a high visability white dot sighting system. Add 9% for nickel finish.
| **Estimated Value:** | **Excellent:** | **$300.00** |
| | **Very good:** | **$240.00** |

Star Model F and FR
Caliber: 22 long rifle
Action: Semiautomatic; exposed hammer; manual safety at top rear of left grip
Magazine: 10-shot clip
Barrel: 4¼" (regular); 6" and 7" on Sport and Target models
Sights: Fixed; adjustable on Sport and Target models
Finish: Blued, chromed, or chromed engraved; plastic grips
Length Overall: 7¼" to 10"
Approximate wt.: 24 to 32 ozs.
Comments: Model F made from about 1942 to 1968. Model FR is an improved version made from about 1968 to the late 1970s. Add $10.00 for chrome model.
| **Estimated Value:** | **Excellent:** | **$300.00** |
| | **Very good:** | **$240.00** |

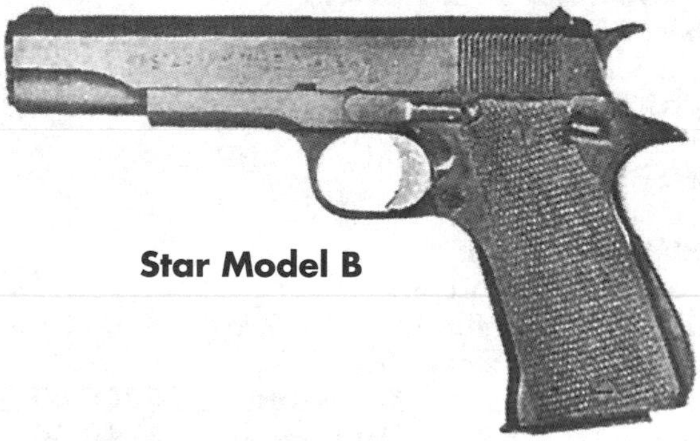

Star Model F and FR

Star Model A and AS
Caliber: 9mm Luger, 9mm Bergman, 9mm Largo, 38 Super auto
Action: Semiautomatic; exposed hammer
Magazine: 8-shot clip
Barrel: 5"
Sights: Fixed
Finish: Blued; checkered walnut grips
Length Overall: 8"
Approximate wt.: 35 ozs.
Comments: This handgun resembles the 1911 A1 Colt. Made from about 1924 to the late 1970s.
| **Estimated Value:** | **Excellent:** | **$400.00** |
| | **Very good:** | **$320.00** |

Star Model B
Similar to the Model A except: barrel lengths 4¼" or 6½"; caliber 9mm Parabellum only. Made from about 1924 to 1976.
| **Estimated Value:** | **Excellent:** | **$375.00** |
| | **Very good:** | **$300.00** |

Star Model B

Star Model I (Police Model)
Caliber: 32 ACP
Action: Semiautomatic; exposed hammer
Magazine: 9-shot clip
Barrel: 4¾"
Sights: Fixed
Finish: Blued; plastic grips
Length Overall: 7½"
Approximate wt.: 25 ozs.
Comments: Made from about 1934 to 1945; never imported into the U.S.
| **Estimated Value:** | **Excellent:** | **$275.00** |
| | **Very good:** | **$220.00** |

Star Model IN
Same as the Model I except: caliber 380 ACP; 8-shot clip.
| **Estimated Value:** | **Excellent:** | **$275.00** |
| | **Very good:** | **$220.00** |

Star Model Super Star

Star Model M (Military)
Caliber: 380 ACP; 9mm Luger; 9mm Bergmann, 38 ACP, 45 ACP
Action: Semiautomatic; exposed hammer; manual safety
Magazine: 7-shot clip in 45 caliber, 8-shot clip in all other calibers
Barrel: 5"
Sights: Fixed
Finish: Blued; checkered grips
Length Overall: 8½"
Approximate wt.: 36 ozs.
Comments: A modified version of the U.S. Government Colt 1911 45 automatic, made from about 1935. Not imported into the U.S.
Estimated Value: Excellent: $300.00
 Very good: $240.00

Star Model Super Star
Same as the Model M except: 38 Super ACP, 9mm Parabellum and 38 ACP only; addition of disarming bolt; improved sights; magazine safety; indicator for number of unfired cartridges. Made from about 1942 to 1954.
Estimated Value: Excellent: $400.00
 Very good: $320.00

Star Model 31P and 31PK
Caliber: 9mm Parabellum, 40 S&W
Action: Double action, semiautomatic; exposed hammer; ambidextrous safety and decocking lever
Magazine: 15-shot clip
Barrel: 3¾"
Sights: Blade front; adjustable rear
Finish: 31P has all-steel construction in blued or Starvel finish; 31PK has alloy frame in blued finish only
Length Overall: 7¾"
Approximate wt.: 39½ ozs. (31P), 30 ozs. (31PK)
Comments: Imported from 1990 to 1995. Add 6% for all-weather Starvel finish; 10% for 40 S&W.
Estimated Value: Excellent: $350.00
 Very good: $280.00

Star Megastar
Caliber: 10 mm, 45 ACP
Action: Double action, semiautomatic; exposed hammer; ambidextrous safety
Magazine: 12-shot clip, 10-shot in USA after 9-13-94
Barrel: 4½"
Sights: Combat-style triple dot system; fully adjustable rear sight
Finish: All-steel blued or all-weather Starvel finish; rubber grips
Length Overall: 8½"
Approximate wt.: 47½ ozs.
Comments: Imported from 1992 to 1995. Add 5% for Starvel finish.
Estimated Value: Excellent: $400.00
 Very good: $320.00

Star Firestar M-40, M-43, and M-45
Caliber: 9mm (M43); 40 S&W (M-40); 45 ACP (M-45)
Action: Double action, semiautomatic; exposed hammer; ambidextrous safety
Magazine: 7-shot clip (M-43), 6-shot in 40 or 45 caliber
Barrel: 3½"
Sights: Combat-style triple dot system; fully adjustable rear sight
Finish: All-steel blued or all-weather Starvel finish
Length Overall: 6½"
Approximate wt.: 30½ ozs.
Comments: Made in 1990. Add 6% for Starvel finish; add 5% for 40 caliber; add 9% for 45 caliber.
Estimated Value: Excellent: $385.00
 Very good: $305.00

Star Firestar

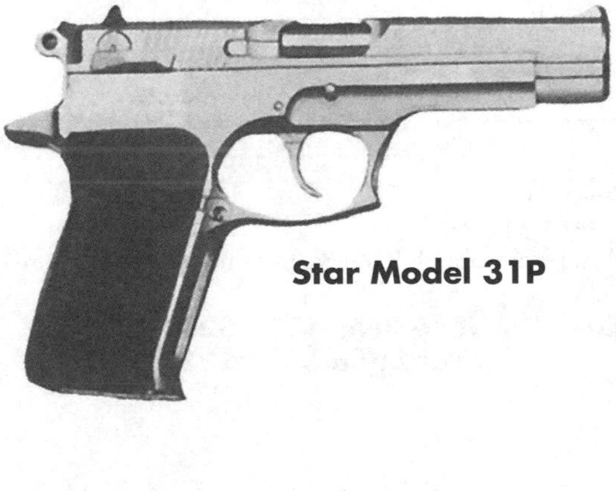

Star Model 31P

Star Model S
Caliber: 38 ACP
Action: Semiautomatic; exposed hammer; thumb safety
Magazine: 7-shot clip
Barrel: 4"
Sights: Fixed
Finish: Blued or chromed; engraved; plastic grips
Length Overall: 6½"
Approximate wt.: 20 ozs.
Comments: A scaled-down modification of the Colt 1911 45 Automatic. Imported from about 1941 to 1968.

Estimated Value:	**Excellent:**	**$235.00**
	Very good:	**$190.00**

Star Model SI
Same as the Model S except: caliber 32 ACP; 8-shot clip.

Estimated Value:	**Excellent:**	**$200.00**
	Very good:	**$160.00**

Star Model Super S
Same as the Model S except: addition of disarming bolt; improved luminous sights; magazine safety; indicator for number of unfired cartridges. Discontinued in 1954.

Estimated Value:	**Excellent:**	**$260.00**
	Very good:	**$210.00**

Star Model Super SI
Same as the Model Super S except: 32 ACP; 8-shot clip.

Estimated Value:	**Excellent:**	**$240.00**
	Very good:	**$190.00**

Star Model Super S

Star Model Super SI

Star Model Super SM
Caliber: 380 ACP
Action: Semiautomatic; exposed hammer; thumb safety
Magazine: 9-shot clip
Barrel: 4"
Sights: Blade front; rear adjustable for windage
Finish: Blued or chrome; checkered wood grips
Length Overall: 6¾"
Approximate wt.: 21 ozs.
Comments: Made from about 1970 to the late 1970s. Add 4% for chrome model.

Estimated Value:	**Excellent:**	**$280.00**
	Very good:	**$225.00**

Star Model DK (Starfire)
Caliber: 380 ACP
Action: Semiautomatic; exposed hammer; thumb safety
Magazine: 6-shot clip
Barrel: 5"
Sights: Fixed
Finish: Blued; checkered plastic grips
Length Overall: 5½"
Approximate wt.: 16 ozs.
Comments: Imported from about 1958 to the late 1960s.

Estimated Value:	**Excellent:**	**$300.00**
	Very good:	**$240.00**

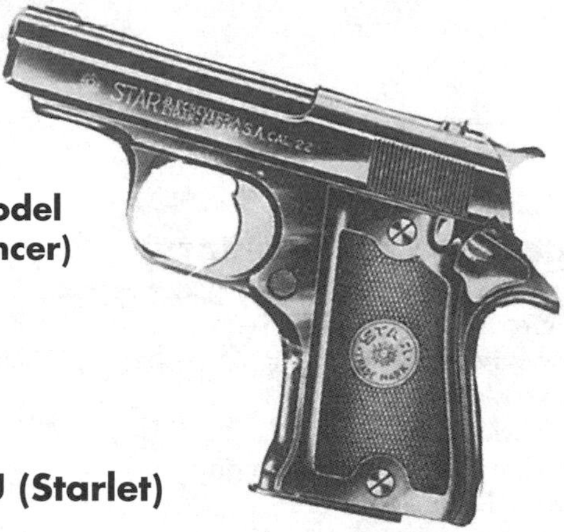

Star Model HK (Lancer)

Star Model CU (Starlet)
Caliber: 25 ACP
Action: Semiautomatic; exposed hammer
Magazine: 8-shot clip
Barrel: 2⅜"
Sights: Fixed
Finish: Blued or chromed slide; black, gray, gold, blue, or green receiver; checkered plastic grips
Length Overall: 4¾"
Approximate wt.: 12 ozs.
Comments: Imported from about 1957 to 1968. Manual safety catch at top rear of left grip. Alloy frame.

Estimated Value:	**Excellent:**	**$240.00**
	Very good:	**$190.00**

Star Model HK (Lancer)
Basically the same as the Model CU Starlet except: caliber 22 long rifle; 3" barrel; 5½" overall length. Imported from the mid-1950s to the late 1960s.

Estimated Value:	**Excellent:**	**$215.00**
	Very good:	**$170.00**

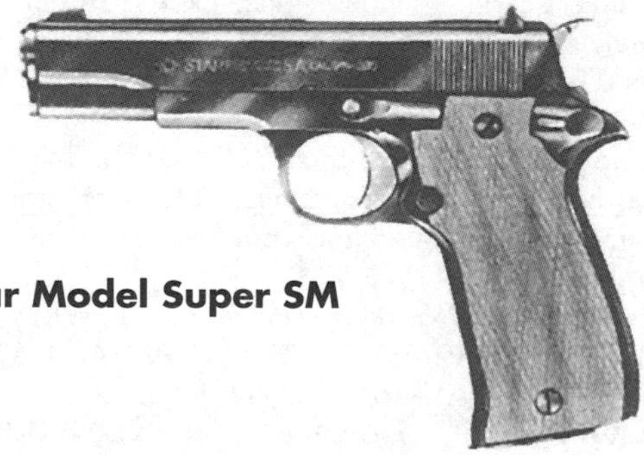

Star Model Super SM

Star Model 28

Caliber: 9mm Parabellum
Action: Semiautomatic; double action; exposed hammer
Magazine: 15-shot clip
Barrel: 4¼"
Sights: Notched partridge front, adjustable rear
Finish: Blued; checkered plastic grips
Length Overall: 8"
Approximate wt.: 40 ozs.
Comments: Imported from 1982 to 1985.

Estimated Value:	**Excellent:**	**$375.00**
	Very good:	**$300.00**

Star Model 30PK

An improved version of the Model 28 with alloy frame and slightly shorter; 15-shot clip; combat-style trigger guard.

Estimated Value:	**Excellent:**	**$390.00**
	Very good:	**$315.00**

Star Model 30 M

Similar to the Model 30PK with steel frame and better sight plane.

Estimated Value:	**Excellent:**	**$375.00**
	Very good:	**$300.00**

Star Model BM

Star Model BKS

Star Model BKS, BKM

Caliber: 9mm Parabellum
Action: Semiautomatic; exposed hammer; manual thumb safety
Magazine: 8-shot clip
Barrel: 4½"
Sights: Fixed
Finish: Blued; chrome; checkered walnut grips
Length Overall: 7¼"
Approximate wt.: 26 ozs.
Comments: Imported from about 1970 to the early 1990s. Alloy frame; resembles Colt 1911. Add 4% for chrome model.

Estimated Value:	**Excellent:**	**$250.00**
	Very good:	**$200.00**

Star Model BM

Similar to the Model BKM without alloy frame, weighs 35 ozs. Add $15.00 for chrome finish; add 13% for Starvel weather-resistant finish.

Estimated Value:	**Excellent:**	**$275.00**
	Very good:	**$220.00**

Star Model PD

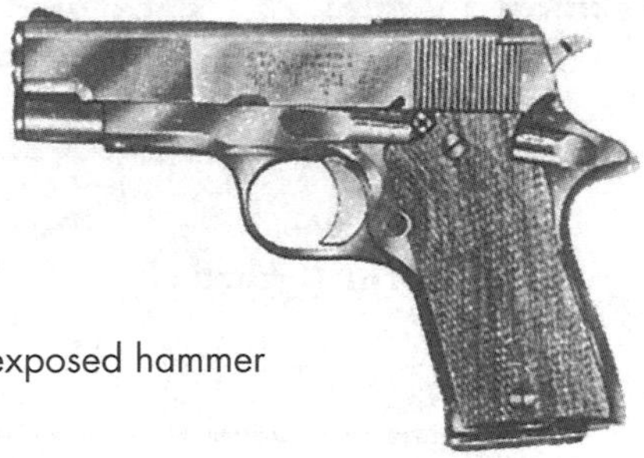

Star Model PD

Caliber: 45 ACP
Action: Semiautomatic; exposed hammer
Magazine: 6-shot clip
Barrel: 4"
Sights: Ramp front; adjustable rear
Finish: Blued; chrome available until the early 1980s; checkered wood grips; Starvel weather-resistant finish available in 1990
Length Overall: 7"
Approximate wt.: 25 ozs.
Comments: Imported from about 1975 to the early 1990s. Add 3% for chrome model; add 10% for Starvel finish.

Estimated Value:	**Excellent:**	**$400.00**
	Very good:	**$320.00**

STERLING

Sterling Model 283

Sterling Model 283

Caliber: 22 long rifle
Action: Semiautomatic; exposed hammer; adjustable trigger and a rear lock safety
Magazine: 10-shot clip
Barrel: 4½", 6", or 8" heavy bull barrel
Sights: Blade front; click adjustable rear
Finish: Blued; checkered plastic grips
Length Overall: 9", 10½", or 12½"
Approximate wt.: 36 to 40 ozs.
Comments: All-steel construction. Made from about 1970 to 1972. Also known as Target 30 Model.

Estimated Value:	**Excellent:**	**$225.00**
	Very good:	**$180.00**

Sterling Model 284

Same as the Model 283 automatic pistol except: lighter tapered barrel, also know as Target 300L Model. Made from about 1970 to 1972.

Estimated Value: Excellent: $250.00
 Very good: $200.00

Sterling Model 285

Same as the Model 283 automatic pistol except: ramp front sight, fixed rear sight; made in 4½" heavy barrel only; non-adjustable trigger. Made from about 1970 to 1972. Also known as Husky Model.

Estimated Value: Excellent: $225.00
 Very good: $180.00

Sterling Model 286

Same as the Model 283 automatic pistol except: ramp front sight, fixed rear sight; made in 4½" and 6" tapered barrel only; non-adjustable trigger. Also known as Trapper Model. Made from about 1970 to 1972.

Estimated Value: Excellent: $225.00
 Very good: $180.00

Sterling Model 285

Sterling Model 286

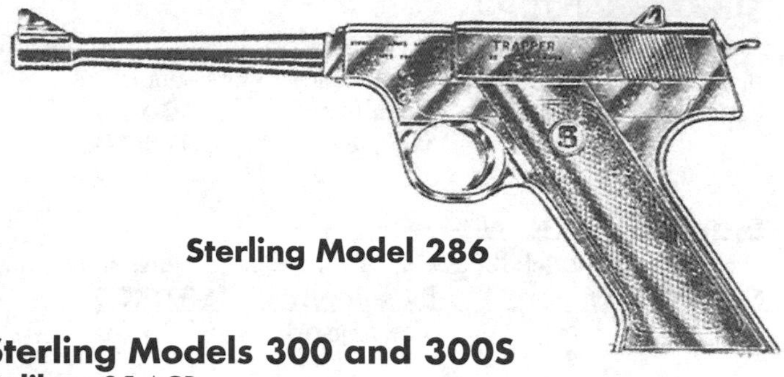

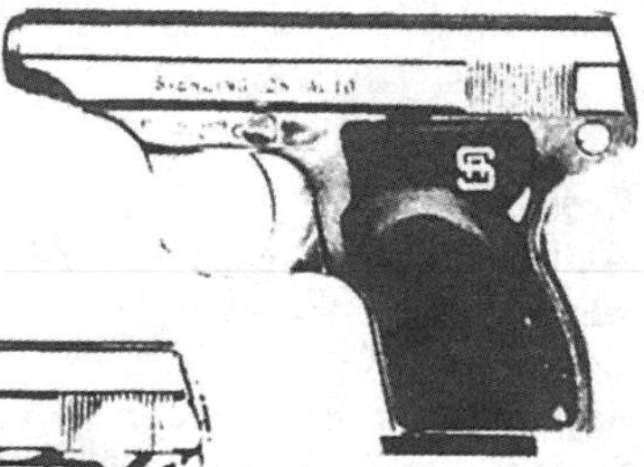

Sterling Model 300

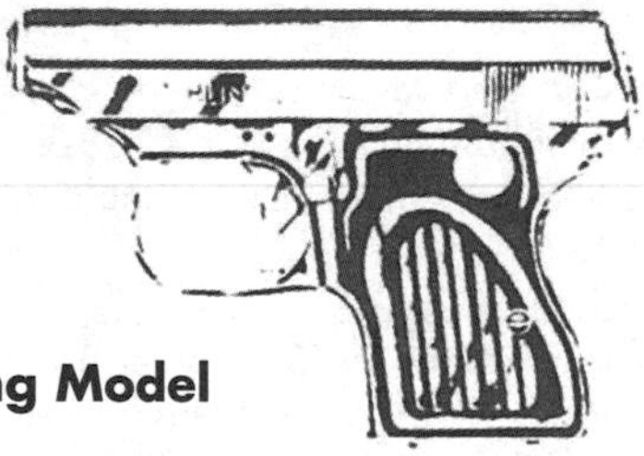

Sterling Model 302

Sterling Model 400 Automatic Pistol

Caliber: 380 ACP
Action: Semiautomatic; double action; exposed hammer; safety locks firing pin
Magazine: 6-shot clip
Barrel: 3½"
Sights: Ramp front, adjustable rear
Finish: Blued or nickel; checkered grips
Length Overall: 6½"
Approximate wt.: 24 ozs.
Comments: All-steel construction. Made from about 1973 to the late 1970s. Replaced by MK II 400. Add 10% for nickel finish.

Estimated Value: Excellent: $225.00
 Very good: $180.00

Sterling MK II 400 and MK II 400S

Similar to Model 400 except streamlined and lightweight, 32 ACP. Add 5% for nickel finish; 15% for stainless steel (MK II 400S).

Estimated Value: Excellent: $275.00
 Very good: $220.00

Sterling Models 300 and 300S

Caliber: 25 ACP
Action: Semiautomatic blowback action; concealed hammer
Magazine: 6-shot clip
Barrel: 2½"
Sights: None
Finish: Blued, nickel, or stainless steel (after 1975) with Cycolac grips
Length Overall: 4½"
Approximate wt.: 13 ozs.
Comments: All-steel construction. Made from about 1972 to the mid-1980s. Add 10% for nickel finish; 20% for stainless steel.

Estimated Value: Excellent: $200.00
 Very good: $160.00

Sterling Models 302 and 302S

Same as the Model 300 Automatic Pistol except caliber 22 long rifle. Model 302S is stainless steel; add 20% for stainless steel.

Estimated Value: Excellent: $200.00
 Very good: $160.00

Sterling MK II 400

Sterling Model 402
Similar to the Model 400 Automatic Pistol except: caliber 22 long rifle, 8-shot clip magazine. Made from about 1973 to 1975. Add $10.00 for nickel finish.
Estimated Value: **Excellent:** **$200.00**
Very good: **$160.00**

Sterling Model 402 MK II, 402S MK II
Similar to the MK II 400 in 32 ACP caliber. Model 402S MK II is stainless steel; add 15%.
Estimated Value: **Excellent:** **$250.00**
Very good: **$200.00**

Sterling Model 400S
Similar to the Model 400 except constructed of stainless steel. Made from about 1976 to the late 1970s.
Estimated Value: **Excellent:** **$275.00**
Very good: **$220.00**

Sterling Model X Caliber
Caliber: 22 S, L and LR; 22 mag.; 357 mag.; 44 mag.
Action: Single-action; single-shot
Magazine: None
Barrel: 8" or 20" heavy octagonal; a caliber change is made by changing barrel
Sights: Ramp front, adjustable rear; tapped for scope mounts
Finish: Blued; smooth wood, finger-grooved grips and small lipped forearm
Length Overall: 13" with 8" barrel
Approximate wt.: 54 to 62 ozs.
Comments: A silhouette-style, single-shot pistol with interchangeable barrels for caliber change. Add 50% for each additional barrel.
Estimated Value: **Excellent:** **$325.00**
Very good: **$260.00**

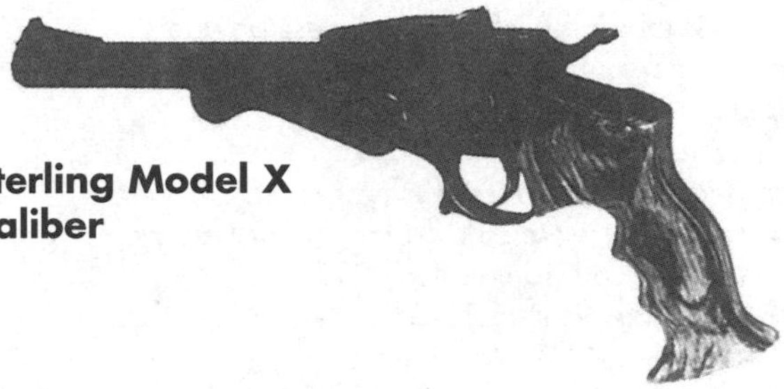

Sterling Model X Caliber

STEVENS

Stevens Tip-Up Pocket
Caliber: 22 short, 30 RF (to 1902)
Action: Single with sheath trigger (spur)
Cylinder: None; single-shot with tip-up barrel
Barrel: 3½"; part octagon
Sights: Blade front; notch in frame rear
Finish: Blued barrel; nickel-plated frame to 1912; blued frame after 1912; varnished walnut square butt grips
Length Overall: 6¼"
Approximate wt.: 10 ozs.
Comments: Made from about 1888 to 1915. Marked "J Stevens A. and T. Co."
Estimated Value: **Excellent:** **$425.00**
Very good: **$340.00**

Stevens Diamond Target
Caliber: 22 RF long rifle (black power 1888 to 1912); 22 long rifle (smokeless powder 1912 to 1915)
Action: Single; sheath trigger (spur)
Cylinder: None; single-shot with tip-up
Barrel: 6", 10"; part octagon
Sights: Globe or bead front; peep or adjustable rear
Finish: Blued barrel; nickel-plated iron frame to 1912; varnished long walnut square grips
Length Overall: 9½" to 13½"
Approximate wt.: 10 to 13 ozs.
Comments: Made from about 1888 to 1915. Marked "J. Stevens A. and T. Co." Approximately 132,000 produced.
Estimated Value: **Excellent:** **$375.00**
Very good: **$300.00**

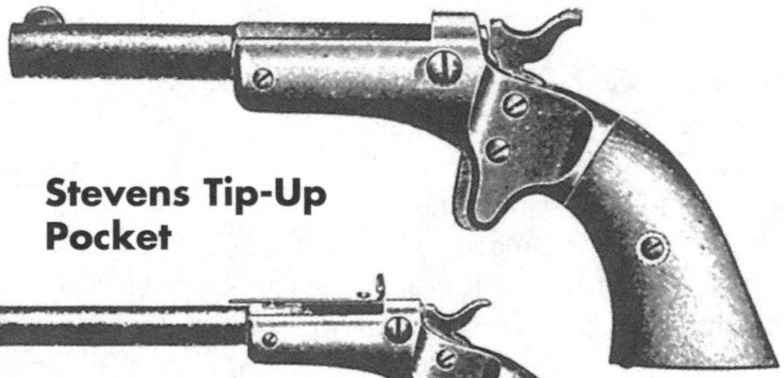

Stevens Tip-Up Pocket

Stevens Diamond Target

Stevens Hunter's Pet
Caliber: 22 long rifle, 25 RF, 32 RF, 38 long RF, 44 long RF, 38-40, 44-40, 38-35, 44-50, 24 gauge
Action: Single with sheath trigger (spur)
Cylinder: None; single-shot with pivoted barrel
Barrel: 18", 20", 22", or 24" octagon and half octagon
Sights: Adjustable for elevation; also some had Stevens' Vernier peep sight attached to back strap
Finish: Blued barrel; nickel-plated frame and detachable skeleton stock; smooth, varnished walnut, square butt grips
Length Overall: 22" to 28"
Approximate wt.: 5¾ lbs.
Comments: Serial numbers in 4,000 to 13,000 range. Approximately 8,000 produced from about 1888 to 1907.
Estimated Value: **Excellent:** **$600.00**
Very good: **$480.00**

Stevens Lord Gallery
Caliber: 22 long rifle, 25 RF (smokeless powder)
Action: Single; tip-up barrel
Magazine: None; single-shot
Barrel: Octagon breech; 6", 8", 10"
Sights: Bead front; stepped elevator rear
Finish: Blued barrel; plated frame; varnished walnut grips with base butt cap; blued frame after 1912
Length Overall: 9¼" to 13¼"
Approximate wt.: 24 to 28 ozs.
Comments: Made from about 1907 to 1915. Marked "J Stevens A. and T. Co."
Estimated Value: **Excellent:** **$400.00**
Very good: **$320.00**

Stevens Off-Hand 1907 – 1915
Caliber: 22 long rifle, 25 RF, smokeless powder
Action: Single, tip-up barrel
Cylinder: None; single-shot
Barrel: Octagon breech; 6", 8", 10"
Sights: Bead front; stepped elevator rear
Finish: Blued barrel; plated frame; varnished walnut grips with base butt cap; blued frame after 1912
Length Overall: 9¼" to 13¼"
Approximate wt.: 24 to 28 ozs.
Comments: Made from about 1907 to 1915. Marked "J. Stevens A. and T. Co."
Estimated Value: **Excellent:** **$425.00**
Very good: **$340.00**

Stevens Off-Hand 1923 – 1939
Caliber: 22 long rifle
Action: Single; tip-up barrel
Cylinder: None; single-shot
Barrel: Octagon breech; 6", 8", 20", 12¼"
Sights: Bead front; rear adjustable for elevation
Finish: Blued barrel and frame, also plated frame; walnut grips with butt cap
Length Overall: 9¼" to 15½"
Approximate wt.: 24 to 34 ozs.
Comments: Made from about the mid-1920s to the late 1930s.
Estimated Value: **Excellent:** **$400.00**
Very good: **$320.00**

Stevens Off-Hand 410
Caliber: 410 gauge (2½")
Action: Single; tip-up barrel
Cylinder: None; single-shot
Barrel: Octagon breech; choked 8" or 12¼" barrel
Sights: Shotgun front sight
Finish: Blued barrel and frame, also plated frame; walnut grips with butt cap
Length Overall: 11¼" to 15½"
Approximate wt.: 23 to 25 ozs.
Comments: Made from about 1925 to 1935. Marked "J Stevens Arms Company."
Estimated Value: **Excellent:** **$400.00**
Very good: **$320.00**

Stevens Lord Gallery

Stevens Off-Hand 1907 – 1915

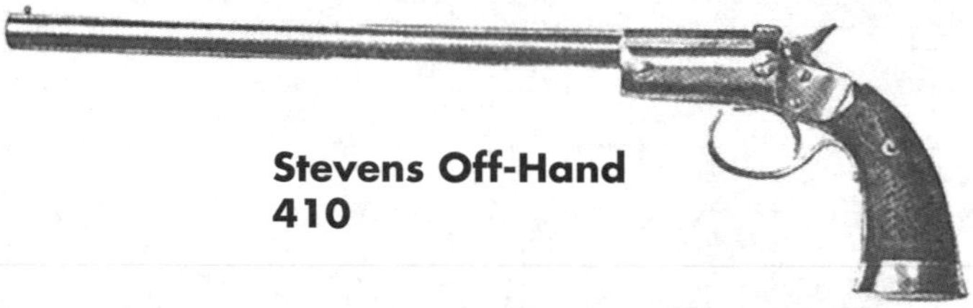
Stevens Off-Hand 410

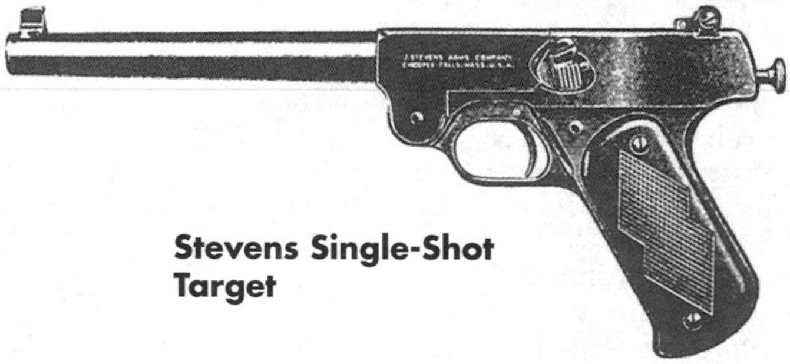
Stevens Single-Shot Target

Stevens Single-Shot Target
Caliber: 22 long rifle
Action: Single; tip up barrel; round knurled cocking piece
Cylinder: None; single-shot
Barrel: Round, 8"
Sights: Partridge front; adjustable windage rear
Finish: Blued (blackish blue color); black composition checkered grips
Length Overall: 11½"
Approximate wt.: 37 ozs.
Comments: A single-shot target pistol with configuration of an automatic pistol. Made from about 1919 to 1942. Approximately 10,000 produced. The 1919 pistols had serial numbers from 1 to approximately 5,000 range with "Pat. App'd For" on barrel. After 1920 marked "Pat'd April 27, 1920." All pistols marked "J. Stevens Arms Company."
Estimated Value: **Excellent:** **$425.00**
Very good: **$340.00**

Roth-Steyr Self-Loading Pistol

Caliber: 8mm Roth-Steyr
Action: Semiautomatic concealed striker; locked breech design uses rotation of barrel by cam action to unlock barrel when fired; the striker is cocked by the recoil, but the trigger action has to pull it further back before it will release to fire.
Magazine: 10-shot non-detachable; usually loaded by a charger from the top
Barrel: 5⅛"
Sights: Fixed
Finish: Blued; checkered wood grips
Length Overall: 9⅛"
Approximate wt.: 36 lbs.
Comments: Adopted by the Austro-Hungarian Cavalry in 1907. This is one of the earliest forms of successful locked-breech pistols.
Estimated Value: **Excellent:** **$1,000.00**
Very good: **$ 800.00**

Steyr Model 1909 Pocket Automatic Pistol

Caliber: 32 ACP
Action: Semiautomatic; concealed hammer; blowback action; early models have no extractor (empty case is blown out by gas after the breech-block is pushed open by firing); barrel can be tipped down for cleaning, using as a single-shot pistol, or for removing unfired cartridges
Magazine: 7-shot clip
Barrel: 3½"
Sights: Fixed
Finish: Blued; checkered wood grips
Length Overall: 6½"
Approximate wt.: 23 ozs.
Comments: Made in both Austria and Belgium. The Austrian variety was a finer pistol from the standpoint of manufacture and reliability. Add $30.00 for later model with extractor.
Estimated Value: **Excellent:** **$375.00**
Very good: **$300.00**

Steyr-Solothurn Pocket Model Automatic Pistol

Similar to the Steyr Model 1909 except: a modified version; uses extractors to remove empty cases; production started about 1934 from Solothurn factory in Switzerland.
Estimated Value: **Excellent:** **$300.00**
Very good: **$240.00**

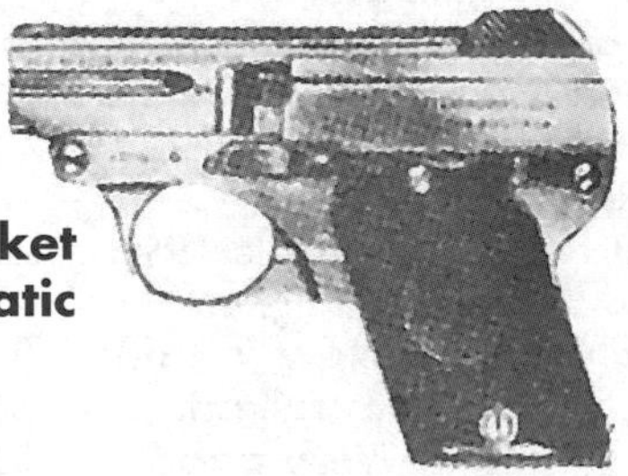

Steyr Vest Pocket (Baby) Automatic Pistol

Steyr Vest Pocket (Baby) Automatic Pistol

Caliber: 25 ACP
Action: Semiautomatic; concealed hammer; blowback action; early models have no extractor (empty case is blown out by gas after the breech block is pushed open by firing); barrel can be tipped down for cleaning, using as a single-shot pistol, or for removing unfired cartridges
Magazine: 6-shot clip
Barrel: 2"
Sights: Fixed
Finish: Blued; hard rubber checkered grips
Length Overall: 4½"
Approximate wt.: 12 ozs.
Comments: First manufactured about 1908. Add $10.00 for later model with extractor.
Estimated Value: **Excellent:** **$500.00**
Very good: **$400.00**

Steyr Model 1912 Military

Caliber: 9mm Steyr
Action: Semiautomatic; exposed hammer; short recoil; locked breech action (barrel rotates to unlock breech when gun is fired)
Magazine: 8-shot non-detachable; loaded from top singly or by using a strip clip
Barrel: 5"
Sights: Fixed
Finish: Blued; checkered wood grips
Length Overall: 8½"
Approximate wt.: 33 ozs.
Comments: Made from about 1911 until after World War I; also referred to as Model 1911 or Steyr-Hahn; adopted by the Austro-Hungarian Army in 1912.
Estimated Value: **Excellent:** **$2,000.00**
Very good: **$1,600.00**

Steyr Nazi-Proofed

Same as the Steyr Model 1912 except: converted to fire the 9mm Luger cartridge during World War II and marked "P-08" on left side of slide.
Estimated Value: **Excellent:** **$1,200.00**
Very good: **$ 960.00**

Steyr Model GB

Caliber: 9mm Parabellum
Action: Gas delayed blowback action, semiautomatic, double action
Magazine: 18-shot clip
Barrel: 5½"
Sights: Fixed
Finish: Black crinkled with blued slide; plastic checkered grips and trigger guard
Length Overall: 8½"
Approximate wt.: 39 ozs.
Comments: Imported in the mid-1980s.
Estimated Value: **Excellent:** **$700.00**
Very good: **$560.00**

Taurus Model PT-58

Taurus Model 58, PT-58

Caliber: 380 ACP
Action: Semiautomatic; double action; exposed round spur hammer
Magazine: 12-shot staggered clip; 10-shot after 9-13-94
Barrel: 4"
Sights: Blade front, notched bar rear
Finish: Blued; stainless steel, or satin nickel; smooth walnut grips
Length Overall: 7"
Approximate wt.: 30 ozs.
Comments: Made in Brazil; introduced in 1988; add 5% for satin nickel finish; add 10% for stainless steel.

Estimated Value:	**Excellent:**	**$300.00**
	Very good:	**$240.00**

Taurus Model PT 100

Taurus Model PT 100 and PT 101

Caliber: 40 S&W
Action: Double action only; semiautomatic; ambidextrous safety
Magazine: 11-shot clip; 10-shot after 9-13-94
Barrel: 5"
Sights: Fixed (PT 100); adj. rear, 3-dot combat (PT 101)
Finish: Blued, satin nickel, or satin stainless steel; Brazilian hardwood grips; rosewood or mother-of-pearl grips available
Length Overall: 8½"
Approximate wt.: 34 ozs.
Comments: Introduced in 1992. Add 8% for nickel (discontinued in 2001); add 10% for stainless steel; add 11% for adjustable sights.

Estimated Value:	**New (retail):**	**$589.00**
	Excellent:	**$440.00**
	Very good:	**$355.00**

Taurus Model PT 92 AF and PT 99 AF

Caliber: 9mm Parabellum
Action: Semiautomatic, double action; exposed round spur hammer
Magazine: 15-shot clip; 10-shot after 9-13-94
Barrel: 5"
Sights: Blade front, notched bar rear (PT 92 AF); blade front, micrometer adjustable rear (PT 99 AF)
Finish: Blued or satin nickel; smooth walnut grips; stainless steel available after 1992; rosewood or mother-of-pearl grips available.
Length Overall: 8½"
Approximate wt.: 34 ozs.
Comments: Made in Brazil. Add 4% for adjustable sights; add 3% for stainless steel.

Estimated Value:	**Excellent:**	**$400.00**
	Very good:	**$320.00**

Taurus Model 92 AFC

Taurus Model 92 AFC

A compact version of the Model PT 92 AF; 4" barrel; 13-shot clip; 10-shot after 9-13-94. Add 8% for nickel finish; add 14% for stainless steel.

Estimated Value:	**Excellent:**	**$350.00**
	Very good:	**$280.00**

Taurus Model PT 92 AF

Taurus Model PT 111

Caliber: 9mm
Action: Semiautomatic; double action only
Magazine: 10-shot clip
Barrel: 3⅛"
Sights: Fixed; night sights available
Finish: Blued or stainless steel, black polymer frame; checkered rubber grip panels; titanium finish available
Length Overall: 5¼"
Approximate wt.: 19 ozs.
Comments: Introduced in the late 1990s. Add 2% for stainless steel finish. Add 17% for night sights.

Estimated Value:	**New (retail):**	**$441.00**
	Excellent:	**$330.00**
	Very good:	**$265.00**

Taurus Model PT 132, PT 138, PT 140, PT 145

Similar to the Model PT 111 except: 380 ACP (PT 138), 40 S&W (PT 140), or 45 ACP (PT 145) caliber. Introduced in 2000. Add 6% for stainless steel finish. Add 7% for PT 140, 15% for PT 145. Add 17% for night sights.

Estimated Value: **New (retail):** **$441.00**
Excellent: **$330.00**
Very good: **$265.00**

Taurus Model PT 940 and PT 945

Caliber: 40 S&W (PT 940); 45 ACP (PT 945)
Action: Semiautomatic; double action; exposed round spur hammer; last shot hold-open; manual ambidextrous hammer-drop safety
Magazine: 9-shot clip (PT 940); 8-shot clip (PT 945)
Barrel: 4½"
Sights: Fixed; three-dot combat; night sights available
Finish: Blued or stainless steel; hardwood or Santoprene II grips; rosewood or mother-of-pearl grips available
Length Overall: 7½"
Approximate wt.: 30 ozs.
Comments: Introduced in the mid-1990s. Made in Brazil; add 3% for stainless steel; add 14% for night sights; add 6% for 45 ACP (945).

Estimated Value: **Excellent:** **$400.00**
Very good: **$320.00**

Taurus Model PT 957

Similar to the Model PT 940 except: 357 caliber. Add 5% for stainless steel finish.

Estimated Value: **Excellent:** **$375.00**
Very good: **$300.00**

Taurus Model PT 22 and PT 25

Taurus Model PT 22 and PT 25

Caliber: 22 long rifle (PT 22); 25 ACP (PT 25)
Action: Double action only; semiautomatic; tip-up barrel
Magazine: 9-shot clip (PT 22), 8-shot clip (PT 25)
Barrel: 2¾" tip-up
Sights: Fixed
Finish: Blued or nickel; smooth Brazilian hardwood grips; several finishes added in 2005
Length Overall: 5¼"
Approximate wt.: 12¼ ozs.
Comments: Introduced in 1992. Add 8% for gold trim with rosewood grips.

Estimated Value: **New (retail):** **$262.00**
Excellent: **$195.00**
Very good: **$160.00**

Taurus Model PT 138

Taurus Model PT 945

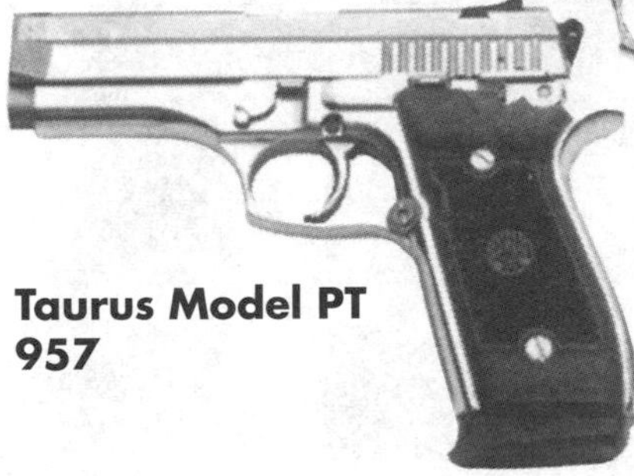

Taurus Model PT 957

Taurus Model PT 400

Similar to the Model PT 945 except: 400 Corbon caliber; ported barrel. Add 3% for stainless steel finish.

Estimated Value: **Excellent:** **$375.00**
Very good: **$300.00**

Taurus Model PT 908

Caliber: 9mm Parabellum
Action: Semiautomatic; double action; exposed round spur hammer; last shot hold-open; manual hammer-drop safety
Magazine: 8-shot clip
Barrel: 3¾"
Sights: Fixed; 3-dot combat
Finish: Blued or stainless steel; rubber grips
Length Overall: 7"
Approximate wt.: 30 ozs.
Comments: Introduced in 1993. Made in Brazil; add 9% for stainless steel.

Estimated Value: **Excellent:** **$325.00**
Very good: **$260.00**

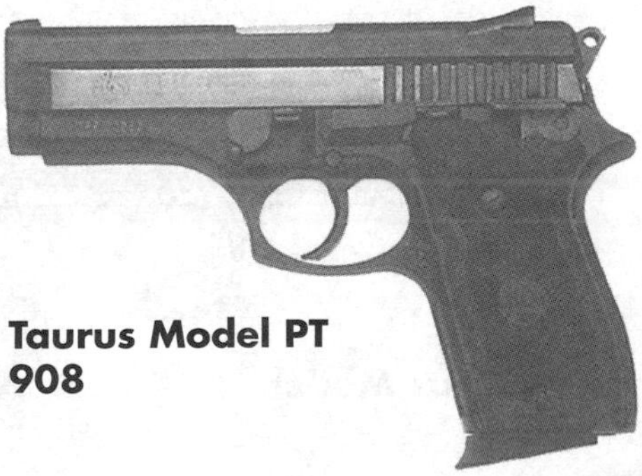

Taurus Model PT 908

Taurus Model PT 938

Caliber: 380 ACP
Action: Double action; semiautomatic; ambidextrous safety
Magazine: 10-shot clip
Barrel: 3¾" tip-up
Sights: Fixed
Finish: Blued or stainless steel, forged alloy frame, black checkered rubber grips
Length Overall: 5¼"
Approximate wt.: 27 ozs.
Comments: Introduced in the late 1990s. Add 6% for stainless steel finish.

Estimated Value:	**Excellent:**	**$350.00**
	Very good:	**$280.00**

Taurus PT 938

Taurus Model 1911

Taurus Model 1911

Caliber: 45 ACP
Action: Double action, semiautomatic; exposed hammer
Magazine: 8-shot clip
Barrel: 5"
Sights: Adjustable rear, blade front
Finish: Blued; checkered wood grips; stainless steel available
Length overall: 8¾"
Approx. wt.: 32 oz.
Comments: Add 3% for stainless steel.

Estimated Value:	**New (retail):**	**$757.00**
	Excellent:	**$565.00**
	Very good:	**$455.00**

Taurus Model 24/7

Taurus Model PT 909

Caliber: 9 mm
Action: Double action, semiautomatic; exposed hammer
Magazine: 17-shot clip
Barrel: 4"
Sights: Fixed
Finish: Blued; steel/alloy construction; checkered rubber grips
Length overall: 8¼ "
Approx. wt.: 28 oz.
Comments: Add 3% for stainless steel.

Estimated Value:	**Excellent:**	**$400.00**
	Very good:	**$320.00**

Taurus Model PT 909

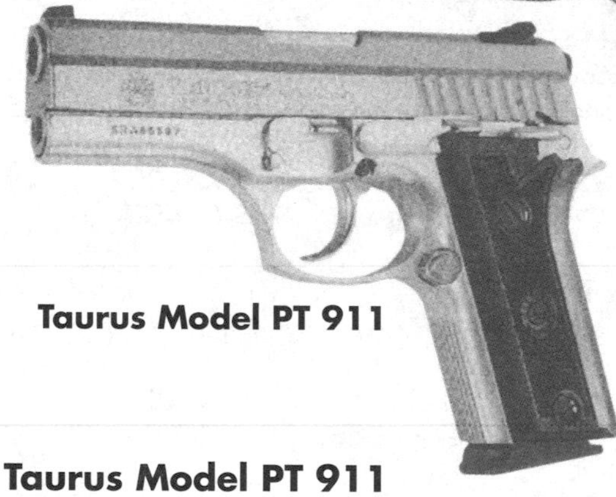

Taurus Model PT 911

Taurus Model PT 911

Caliber: 9mm
Action: Semiautomatic; ambidextrous safety
Magazine: 10-shot clip
Barrel: 3¾"
Sights: Fixed
Finish: Blued or stainless steel; black Santoprene grips
Length Overall: 6"
Approximate wt.: 28 ozs.
Comments: Introduced in the late 1990s. Add 4% for stainless steel.

Estimated Value:	**New (retail):**	**$757.00**
	Excellent:	**$565.00**
	Very good:	**$455.00**

Taurus Model 24/7

Caliber: 9mm, 40 S&W, 45ACP
Action: Double action only, concealed hammer
Cylinder: 10-shot clip
Barrel: 4"
Sights: Fixed dot system sights
Finish: Blued; polymer steel or polymer stainless steel; rubber ribbed overlay grips
Length Overall: 6½"
Approximate wt.: 27½ ozs.
Comments: Add 10% for stainless steel.

Estimated Value:	**Excellent:**	**$350.00**
	Very good:	**$280.00**

Taurus Model 745 Millennium Pro Compact

Taurus Model 745 Millennium Pro Compact

Caliber: 45 ACP
Action: Double action, semiautomatic; exposed hammer
Magazine: 6-shot clip
Barrel: 3¼"
Sights: Fixed
Finish: Polymer/steel construction; checkered polymer grips
Length overall: 6⅛"
Approx. wt.: 20 oz.
Comments: Add 3% for stainless steel.

Estimated Value:	**Excellent:**	**$315.00**
	Very good:	**$250.00**

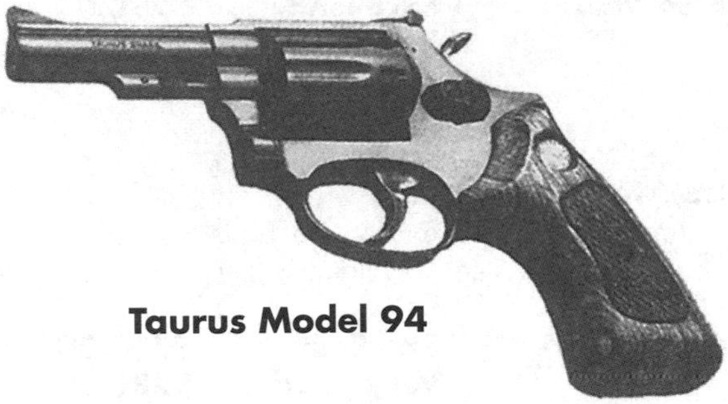

Taurus Model 94

Taurus Model 94 and 941

Caliber: 22 short, long and long rifle (Model 94); 22 magnum (Model 941)
Action: Single and double; exposed hammer
Cylinder: 9-shot (Model 94); 8-shot (Model 941)
Barrel: 2", 3", or 4" heavy, solid rib; Model 941 has ejector shroud under barrel; 5" barrel added in 1996.
Sights: Fixed; ramp front, adjustable rear
Finish: Blued or stainless steel; checkered hardwood or rubber grips
Length Overall: 6¾", 8¼", or 9¼"
Approximate wt.: 24 to 28 ozs.
Comments: Made in Brazil; add 8% for Model 941; add 16% for stainless steel.

Estimated Value:	**New (retail):**	**$405.00**
	Excellent:	**$305.00**
	Very good:	**$245.00**

Taurus Model 731

Taurus Model 731

Caliber: 32 H&R magnum, 32 S&W
Action: Double or single action; exposed hammer
Cylinder: 6-shot swing-out
Barrel: 2" heavy, solid rib, ejector shroud; ported barrel
Sights: Serrated ramp front, fixed rear
Finish: Stainless steel; black Santoprene grips; titanium available
Length Overall: 7½"
Approximate wt.: 29 ozs.
Comments: Introduced in the late 1990s. Add 20% for titanium.

Estimated Value:	**New (retail):**	**$514.00**
	Excellent:	**$385.00**
	Very good:	**$305.00**

Taurus Model 73 and 741

Caliber: 32 H&R magnum
Action: Single and double action; exposed hammer
Cylinder: 6-shot, swing-out; simultaneous ejector
Barrel: 3" or 4" heavy barrel
Sights: Fixed or adjustable sights
Finish: Blue, satin nickel, or stainless steel
Length Overall: 7¾" or 8¾"
Approximate wt.: 20 ozs.
Comments: Produced in Brazil. Add 10% for satin nickel; add 35% for stainless steel.

Estimated Value:	**Excellent:**	**$240.00**
	Very good:	**$190.00**

Taurus Model 76 and 761

Similar to Models 73 and 741 except: blued finish only, 6" barrel.

Estimated Value:	**Excellent:**	**$220.00**
	Very good:	**$175.00**

Taurus Model 65

Taurus Model 66

Taurus Model 65

Caliber: 357 mag. and 38 Spl.
Action: Single and double action; exposed hammer
Cylinder: 6-shot swing-out, simultaneous ejector
Barrel: 2½" or 4" heavy barrel
Sights: Fixed; ramp front, square notch rear
Finish: Royal blue, satin nickel, or stainless steel; checkered walnut or rubber grips
Length Overall: 8½" or 9½"
Approximate wt.: 34 ozs.
Comments: Currently produced in Brazil. Add 5% for satin nickel finish. Add 24% for stainless steel.

Estimated Value:	**New (retail):**	**$441.00**
	Excellent:	**$330.00**
	Very good:	**$265.00**

Taurus Model 66

Similar to the Model 65 except: 2½", 4", and 6" barrel lengths; serrated ramp front sight and micrometer adjustable rear; blued, satin nickel or stainless steel; checkered walnut target grip on 6"; add 5% for satin nickel finish; add 24% for stainless steel. Silhouette model with 12" barrel available (add 5%).

Estimated Value:	**New (retail):**	**$493.00**
	Excellent:	**$370.00**
	Very good:	**$295.00**

Taurus Model 669 and 689

Same as the Model 66 except: 4" or 6" barrel; full ejector rod shroud; blued or stainless steel only; introduced in 1988. Add 24% for stainless steel. Model 689 has ventilated rib (add 4%).

Estimated Value:	**Excellent:**	**$275.00**
	Very good:	**$220.00**

Taurus Model 445 and 445T

Caliber: 44 Special
Action: Double or single action; exposed or concealed hammer; double action only model available.
Cylinder: 5-shot swing-out
Barrel: 2" heavy, solid rib, ported on Model 445T
Sights: Serrated ramp front, notched rear
Finish: Blued or stainless steel; spectrum blue or gold titanium; rubber grips
Length Overall: 7½"
Approximate wt.: 29 ozs.
Comments: Introduced in the late 1990s; Model 445T introduced in 2000; add 15% for stainless steel; add 85% for 445T.

Estimated Value:	**Excellent:**	**$290.00**
	Very good:	**$235.00**

Taurus Model 450

Similar to the Model 445 except: 45 Long Colt caliber; ported barrel; blue, stainless steel, or titanium finish. Add 25% for titanium.

Estimated Value:	**Excellent:**	**$350.00**
	Very good:	**$280.00**

Taurus Model 415

Similar to the Model 445 except: 41 magnum caliber; stainless steel, blue, or titanium finish. Ported barrel on titanium model. Add 25% for titanium.

Estimated Value:	**Excellent:**	**$400.00**
	Very good:	**$320.00**

Taurus Model 817

Caliber: 38 Special +P
Action: Double or single, exposed hammer
Cylinder: 7-shot swing-out
Barrel: 2"; ported barrel available
Sights: Fixed ramp front, notched rear
Finish: Blued or stainless steel; rubber grips
Length overall: 7½"
Approximate wt.: 21 ozs.
Comments: Add 5% for ported barrel; 12% for stainless steel finish.

Estimated Value:	**New (retail):**	**$459.00**
	Excellent:	**$345.00**
	Very good:	**$275.00**

Taurus Model 425 Tracker

Caliber: 41 Magnum
Action: Double and single action; exposed hammer
Cylinder: 7-shot, swing-out
Barrel: 4" ported
Sights: Adjustable
Finish: Matte stainless steel or gray titanium; rubber grips
Length Overall: 9½"
Approximate wt.: 34 ozs.
Comments: Introduced in 2000. Add 35% for titanium finish.

Estimated Value:	**New (retail):**	**$597.00**
	Excellent:	**$450.00**
	Very good:	**$360.00**

Taurus Model 627 Tracker

Taurus Model 627 Tracker

Similar to the Model 425 Tracker except: 357 magnum caiber; add 35% for titanium finish.

Estimated Value:	**New (retail):**	**$600.00**
	Excellent:	**$450.00**
	Very good:	**$360.00**

Taurus Model 455 Tracker

Similar to the Model 425 Tracker except: 45ACP caliber; 2", 4", or 6½" barrel.

Estimated Value:	**Excellent:**	**$395.00**
	Very good:	**$320.00**

Taurus Model 460 Tracker

Similar to the Model 425 Tracker except: 45 Colt caliber; 4" or 6½" ported barrel only.

Estimated Value:	**Excellent:**	**$395.00**
	Very good:	**$320.00**

Taurus Model 971 Tracker

Taurus Models 970 Tracker and 971 Tracker

Similar to the Model 425 Tracker except: 22 long rifle or 22 magnum calibers; 6½" barrel only. Add 4% for magnum. Model 971 is 22 magnum.

Estimated Value:	**New (retail):**	**$472.00**
	Excellent:	**$355.00**
	Very good:	**$285.00**

Taurus Model 17 Tracker

Similar to the Model 970 Tracker except: 17HMR caliber.

Estimated Value:	**Excellent:**	**$350.00**
	Very good:	**$280.00**

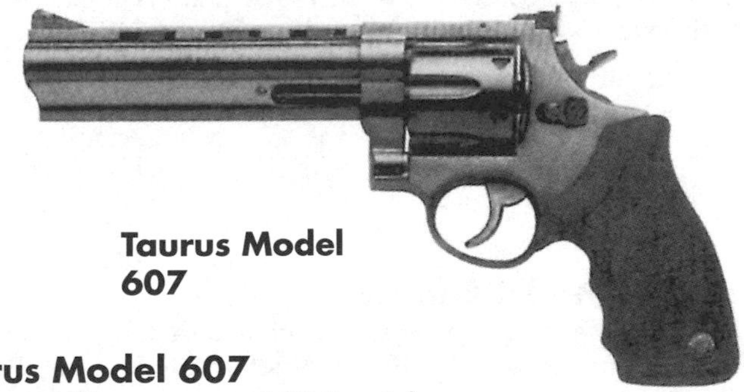

Taurus Model 607

Taurus Model 607

Caliber: 357 magnum and 38 Special
Action: Double or single action; exposed hammer
Cylinder: 7-shot; swing-out
Barrel: 4" heavy, solid rib; 6½" heavy, ventilated rib; integral compensator
Sights: Adjustable rear and serrated ramp front
Finish: Blued or stainless steel; Santoprene grips
Length Overall: 9½" to 11½"
Approximate wt.: 30 to 32 ozs.
Comments: Introduced in the mid-1990s; add 15% for stainless steel; add 4% for ventilated rib.

Estimated Value:	**Excellent:**	**$350.00**
	Very good:	**$280.00**

Taurus Model 608

Taurus Model 608

Same as the Model 607 except: 8-shot cylinder; introduced in 1996; add 15% for stainless steel; add 4% for ventilated rib or ported barrel.

Estimated Value:	**New (retail):**	**$615.00**
	Excellent:	**$460.00**
	Very good:	**$370.00**

Taurus Model 454 Raging Bull

Caliber: 454 Casull
Action: Double or single action; exposed hammer
Cylinder: 5-shot swing-out
Barrel: 6½" or 8⅜" extra heavy, ventilated rib, ported
Sights: Partridge front, micrometer click, adjustable rear
Finish: Blued or stainless steel; black Santoprene grips
Length Overall: 10" to 14"
Approximate wt.: 53 ozs.
Comments: Introduced in the late 1990s; add 7% for stainless steel.

Estimated Value:	**New (retail):**	**$923.00**
	Excellent:	**$690.00**
	Very good:	**$550.00**

Taurus Model 444 Raging Bull

Same as the Model 454 except chambered for 44 magnum caliber. Introduced in 1998. Add 9% for stainless steel. Titanium alloy frame available.

Estimated Value:	**New (retail):**	**$711.00**
	Excellent:	**$533.00**
	Very good:	**$425.00**

Taurus Model 480 Raging Bull

Taurus Model 480 Raging Bull

Similar to the Model 454 Raging Bull in 480 Ruger caliber; 5", 6", or 8" barrel.

Estimated Value:	**Excellent:**	**$480.00**
	Very good:	**$385.00**

Taurus Model 22H Raging Hornet

Taurus Model 22H Raging Hornet

Caliber: 22 Hornet
Action: Single and double action; exposed hammer
Cylinder: 8-shot, swing-out
Barrel: 10" ventilated rib
Sights: Adjustable; scope mount base installed
Finish: Matte stainless steel; black rubber grips
Length Overall: 14½"
Approximate wt.: 50 ozs.
Comments: Introduced in 2000.

Estimated Value:	**Excellent:**	**$675.00**
	Very good:	**$540.00**

Taurus Model 218 Raging Bee

Similar to the Model 22H Raging Hornet except; 218 Bee caliber.

Estimated Value:	**Excellent:**	**$725.00**
	Very good:	**$580.00**

Taurus Model Raging 30

Similar to the Model 22H Raging Hornet except: 30 Carbine caliber; full-moon clips included.

Estimated Value:	**Excellent:**	**$675.00**
	Very good:	**$540.00**

Taurus Model 416 Raging Bull

Taurus Model 416 Raging Bull

Similar to the Model 444 Raging Bull except: 41 magnum caliber; 6½" barrel only.

Estimated Value: **New (retail): $780.00**
Excellent: $585.00
Very good: $470.00

Taurus Model 606CH

Taurus Model 606, 606CH

Caliber: 357 magnum and 38 Special
Action: Double or single action; exposed or concealed hammer (606CH)
Cylinder: 6-shot swing-out
Barrel: 2" heavy, solid rib, ejector shroud; ported barrel available
Sights: Serrated ramp front, notched rear
Finish: Blued or stainless steel; black Santoprene grips
Length Overall: 7½"
Approximate wt.: 29 ozs.
Comments: Introduced in the late 1990s; add 16% for stainless steel; add 6% for ported barrel.

Estimated Value: **Excellent: $300.00**
Very good: $240.00

Taurus Model 606

Taurus Model 650 CIA

Similar to the Model 606CH except hammerless only. Add 10% for stainless steel.

Estimated Value: **New (retail): $456.00**
Excellent: $340.00
Very good: $270.00

Taurus Model 617

Taurus Model 617

Caliber: 357 magnum and 38 Special
Action: Double or single action; exposed or concealed hammer
Cylinder: 7-shot swing-out
Barrel: 2" heavy, solid rib, ejector shroud; ported barrel available
Sights: Serrated ramp front, notched rear
Finish: Blued or stainless steel; black Santoprene grips
Length Overall: 7½"
Approximate wt.: 29 ozs.
Comments: Introduced in the late 1990s; add 13% for stainless steel; add 5% for concealed hammer.

Estimated Value: **New (retail): $459.00**
Excellent: $345.00
Very good: $275.00

Taurus Model 617T

Similar to the Model 617 except: ported barrel; titanium finish.

Estimated Value: **Excellent: $530.00**
Very good: $425.00

Taurus Model 851

Similar to the Model 651 in 38 Special caliber only. Available with blued finish, Ultralite alloy frame (add 8%), shadow gray titanium (add 40%), stainless steel (add 12%), Ultra-lite alloy stainless steel (add 19%), Ultralite alloy titanium (add 39%), and spectrum blue titanium (add 50%).

Estimated Value:	**New (retail):**	**$433.00**
	Excellent:	**$325.00**
	Very good:	**$260.00**

Taurus Model 851

Taurus Models 80 and 82

Caliber: 38 Special
Action: Single or double action; exposed hammer
Cylinder: 6-shot swing-out; simultaneous ejector
Barrel: 3" or 4"; standard barrel (80); heavy barrel (82)
Sights: Fixed
Finish: Blued, satin nickel, or stainless steel; checkered walnut or rubber grips
Length Overall: 8⅛" or 9⅛"
Approximate wt.: 30 ozs. (Model 80); 34 ozs. (Model 82)
Comments: Made in Brazil. Add 6½% for satin nickel finish. Add 16% for stainless steel. Model 80 discontinued in 2001.

Estimated Value:	**New (retail):**	**$424.00**
	Excellent:	**$320.00**
	Very good:	**$255.00**

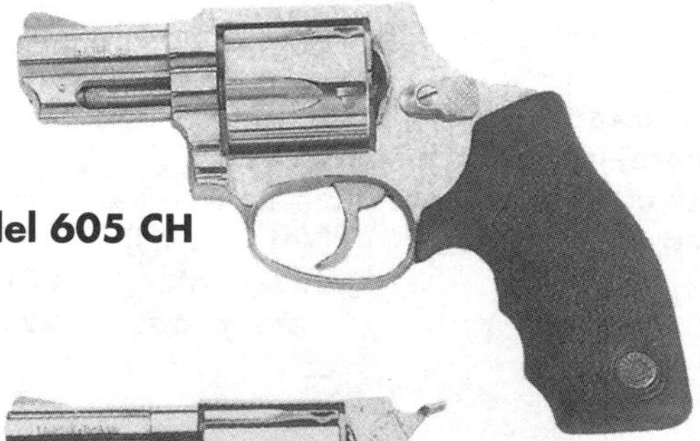

Taurus Model 605 CH

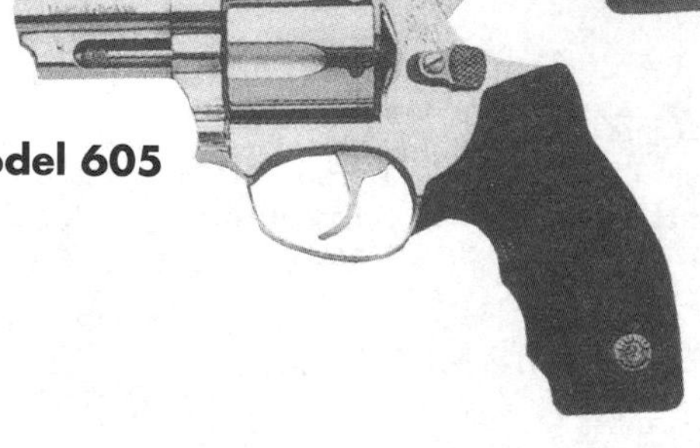

Taurus Model 605

Taurus Model 651 Protector

Caliber: 357 magnum, 38 Special
Action: Double or single; shrouded hammer
Cylinder: 5-shot swing-out; simultaneous manual ejector
Barrel: 2" ported
Sights: Fixed
Finish: Blued; shadow gray titanium or matte stainless steel; rubber grips
Length Overall: 6½"
Approximate wt.: 25 ozs.
Comments: Add 12% for stainless steel; add 35% for titanium (discontinued 2010).

Estimated Value:	**New (retail):**	**$433.00**
	Excellent:	**$325.00**
	Very good:	**$260.00**

Taurus Model 651 Protector

Taurus Model 80

Taurus Model 605

Caliber: 357 magnum and 38 Special
Action: Double or single action; exposed hammer
Cylinder: 5-shot swingout
Barrel: 2¼" or 3" heavy, solid rib
Sights: Fixed; notched rear and serrated ramp front
Finish: Blued or stainless steel; Santoprene grips
Length Overall: 7½" to 8¼"
Approximate wt.: 25 to 30 ozs.
Comments: Introduced in the mid-1990s; add 16% for stainless steel. Add 6% for ported barrel.

Estimated Value:	**New (retail):**	**$424.00**
	Excellent:	**$320.00**
	Very good:	**$255.00**

Taurus Model 83

Similar to the Model 82 except: 4" heavy barrel only; ramp front sight and micrometer adjustable rear sight. Add 5% for satin nickel finish. Add 18% for stainless steel.

Estimated Value:	**Excellent:**	**$235.00**
	Very good:	**$185.00**

Taurus Model 605CH

Same as the Model 605 except: concealed hammer; 2¼" barrel only; add 20% for stainless steel; double action only. Discontinued in 1997.

Estimated Value:	**Excellent:**	**$280.00**
	Very good:	**$225.00**

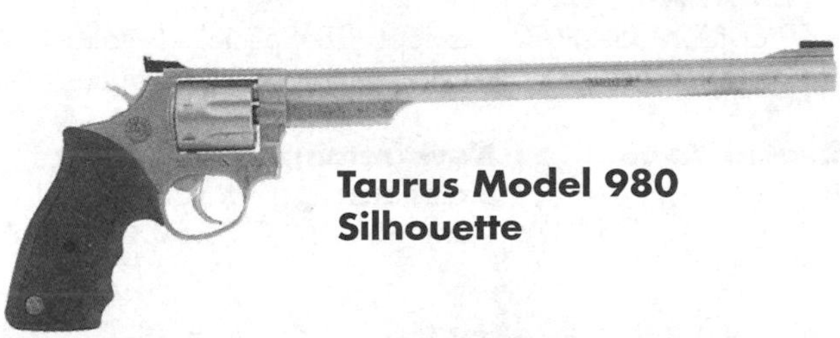

Taurus Model 980 Silhouette

Taurus Model 980 Silhouette and 981 Silhouette

Caliber: 22 long rifle; 22 magnum (981)
Action: Double or single, exposed hammer; repeating
Cylinder: 7-shot swingout
Barrel: 12"
Sights: Serrated ramp front, adjustable rear
Finish: Blued or matte stainless steel; rubber grips
Length overall: 16½"
Approximate wt.: 57 ozs.
Comments: Introduced in 2001. Add 3% for Model 981.

Estimated Value:	**Excellent:**	**$575.00**
	Very good:	**$460.00**

Taurus Model 17 Silhouette

Similar to the Model 980 Silhouette except: 17HMR caliber.

Estimated Value:	**Excellent:**	**$575.00**
	Very good:	**$460.00**

Taurus Model 218 Silhouette

Similar to the Model 980 Silhouette except: 218 Bee caliber.

Estimated Value:	**Excellent:**	**$600.00**
	Very good:	**$480.00**

Taurus Model 86 Target

Taurus Model 86 and 96 Target

Caliber: 38 Special (86); 22 S, L, or LR (96)
Action: Single or double; exposed hammer
Cylinder: 6-shot swingout; simultaneous ejector
Barrel: 6"
Sights: Partridge-type front; micrometer adjustable rear
Finish: Blued; checkered walnut target grip
Length Overall: 11¼"
Approximate wt.: 34 ozs.
Comments: Produced in Brazil. Model 86 dropped in the mid-1990s.

Estimated Value:	**Excellent:**	**$290.00**
	Very good:	**$235.00**

Taurus Model 905CH

Similar to the Model 905 with concealed hammer; double action only; add 12% for stainless steel.

Estimated Value:	**Excellent:**	**$300.00**
	Very good:	**$240.00**

Taurus Model 431 and 441

Caliber: 44 Special
Action: Single or double; exposed hammer
Cylinder: 5-shot swing-out
Barrel: 3" or 4" (Model 431); 3", 4", or 6" (Model 441); heavy solid rib and ejector shroud
Sights: Fixed (Model 431); Partridge front, adjustable rear (Model 441)
Finish: Blued or stainless steel; checkered hardwood grips
Length Overall: 8¼" or 11¼"
Approximate wt.: 34 to 40 ozs.
Comments: Made in Brazil; add 9% for Model 441 (adj. sights); add 24% for stainless steel.

Estimated Value:	**Excellent:**	**$200.00**
	Very good:	**$160.00**

Taurus Model 44

Caliber: 44 magnum or 44 Special
Action: Single or double; exposed hammer
Cylinder: 6-shot swing-out
Barrel: 4", 6½", or 8⅜"; heavy solid rib on 4"; ventilated rib on other models
Sights: Ramp front, adjustable rear
Finish: Blued or stainless steel; hardwood or rubber grips
Length Overall: 9¾" or 14"
Approximate wt.: 44 to 57 ozs.
Comments: Made in Brazil; add 5% for 6½" or 8⅜" barrel; add 15% for stainless steel. Introduced in 1994.

Estimated Value:	**Excellent:**	**$450.00**
	Very good:	**$360.00**

Taurus Model 44

Taurus Model 905

Taurus Model 905

Caliber: 9mm
Action: Double or single
Cylinder: 5-shot swing-out; simultaneous manual ejector
Barrel: 2"
Sights: Fixed
Finish: Blued; Ultralite alloy stainless steel, stainless steel; rubber grips
Length Overall: 6½"
Approximate wt.: 25 ozs.
Comments: add 8% for Ultralite alloy stainless steel, add 12% for stainless steel.

Estimated Value:	**New (retail):**	**$433.00**
	Excellent:	**$325.00**
	Very good:	**$260.00**

Taurus Model 85

Taurus Model 85, 85CH

Caliber: 38 Special
Action: Single or double action; exposed or concealed hammer
Cylinder: 5-shot swingout, simultaneous ejector
Barrel: 2" or 3" heavy barrel
Sights: Fixed; serrated ramp front, notch rear
Finish: Royal blue, satin nickel, or stainless steel; rosewood or rubber grips; titanium available
Length Overall: 6½" or 7½"
Approximate wt.: 21 ozs.
Comments: Produced in Brazil. Add 7% for satin nickel finish. Add 22% for stainless steel. Add 7% for ported barrel. Add 40% for titanium.

Estimated Value:	**Excellent:**	**$280.00**
	Very good:	**$225.00**

Taurus Model 850

Similar to the Model 85CH except: 38 Special +P caliber; rubber grips; blued, stainless steel (add 13%), or titanium finish (add 50%).

Estimated Value:	**New (retail):**	**$433.00**
	Excellent:	**$325.00**
	Very good:	**$260.00**

Taurus Model 85CH

Taurus Model 85CH

Same as the Model 85 except: 2" barrel; concealed hammer; double action only. Add 22% for stainless steel; add 40% for titanium alloy.

Estimated Value:	**Excellent:**	**$295.00**
	Very good:	**$235.00**

THOMPSON CENTER

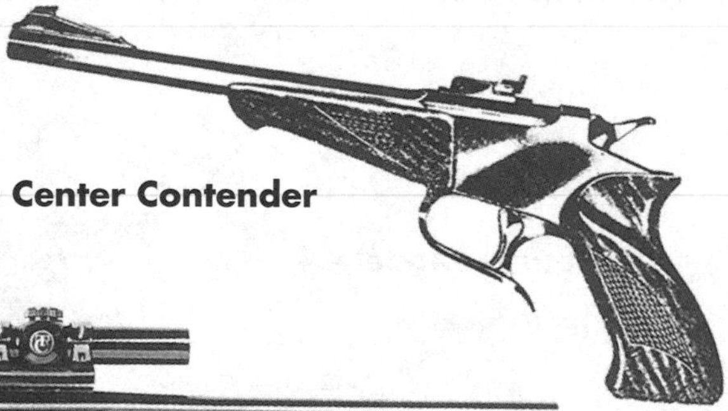

Thompson Center Contender

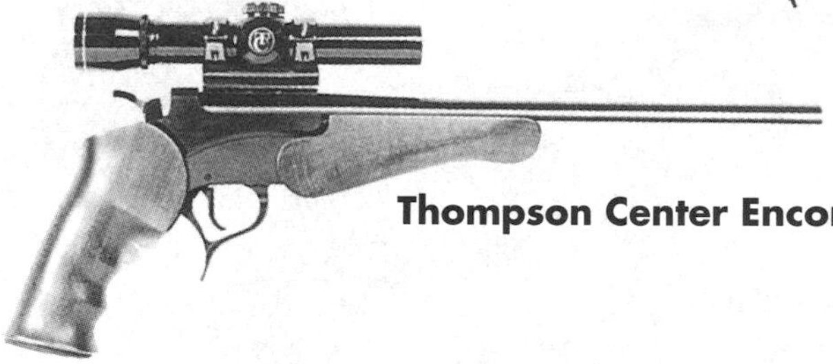

Thompson Center Encore

Thompson Center Encore

Caliber: 15 calibers available from 22 to 480 Ruger
Action: Single-shot, break-open; spur hammer
Magazine: None
Barrel: Interchangeable barrels: 12" or 15" with ventilated rib
Sights: Ramp front, adjustable rear
Finish: Blued or stainless steel; walnut or rubber grips and forearm
Length overall: 16" to 18"
Approximate wt.: 64 to 72 ozs.
Comments: Similar to the Contender. Introduced in 2000. Add 10% for stainless steel finish.

Estimated Value:	**New (retail):**	**$649.00**
	Excellent:	**$485.00**
	Very good:	**$390.00**

Thompson Center Contender

Caliber: 22 S, L, or LR to 45-70 Govt.; over the years approximately 35 to 40 calibers were made including some wildcat calibers. Presently made in 18 calibers: 22 long rifle, 22 Win. mag., 22 Hornet, 222 Rem., 223 Rem., 270 Rem., 7mm TCU, 7x30 Waters, 30-30 Win., 32-20 Win., 357 mag., 357 Rem. maximum, 35 Rem., 10mm auto, 44 mag., 445 Super mag.; 45-70 Govt., and 45 Colt/410 gauge
Action: Single action with adjustable trigger; the frame will accommodate any caliber barrel and the hammer adjusts to rim fire or centerfire ammunition
Cylinder: None; single-shot
Barrel: 8¾" (discontinued in the early 1980s), 10" and 14" (introduced in the late 1970s), 16¼" (introduced in 1990). Octagon or round; regular or bull barrel; plain or ventilated rib; the 45 Colt/410 gauge barrel has a removable internal choke to use for 410 gauge shot shells; blued or stainless steel
Sights: Ramp front; adjustable rear; ventilated rib has fixed sights
Finish: Blued or stainless steel frame; checkered or smooth walnut grip and fore-end
Length Overall: 12½" to 20"
Approximate wt.: 38 to 60 ozs.
Comments: Made from about 1967 to 2001. Add 3% for internal choke or vent. rib. Add 4% for 16" barrel. Add 3% for stainless steel barrel. Add 11% for stainless steel barrel and frame.

Estimated Value:	**Excellent:**	**$375.00**
	Very good:	**$300.00**

Thompson Center Contender Armour Alloy II

Similar to the Contender except the parts and barrels are not interchangeable with the standard model Contender. It has a special Armour Alloy II non-glare satin finish. Made in the following calibers: 22 long rifle, 223 Rem., 357 magnum, 357 Rem. maximum, 44 magnum, 7mm TCU, 7x30 Waters, 30-30 Win., 35 Rem., 45 Colt/410 gauge. The 45 Colt/410 gauge has a removable internal choke to use with regular 410 gauge shot shells in 10" bull barrel or ventilated rib barrel. All other calibers use 10" bull barrel or 14" bull barrel. Introduced in 1986 and discontinued in 1990. Add 5% for ventilated rib with internal choke. Add 3% for 14" barrel.

Estimated Value: **Excellent:** **$320.00**
Very good: **$260.00**

Thompson Center Contender Hunter

Caliber: 223 Rem., 7x30 Waters, 30-30 Win., 375 Win., 35 Rem., 44 mag., 45-70 Govt.
Action: Single action; adjustable trigger; break open
Cylinder: None; single-shot
Barrel: 12" or 14" round; T/C Muzzle Tamer to reduce muzzle jump and recoil; blued or stainless steel
Sights: 2.5x T/C scope with lighted duplex reticle
Finish: Blued or stainless steel frame; smooth walnut grip and fore-end; grip has rubber insert to cushion recoil; QD swivels and nylon sling
Length Overall: 16"
Approximate wt.: 65 ozs.
Comments: Introduced in 1990. Add 2% for stainless steel barrel; add 4% for stainless steel barrel and frame.
Estimated Value: **Excellent:** **$600.00**
Very good: **$480.00**

WALTHER

Walther Model 1 Vest Pocket

Caliber: 25 ACP
Action: Semiautomatic; concealed hammer
Magazine: 6-shot clip
Barrel: 2"
Sights: Fixed
Finish: Blued; checkered hard rubber grips
Length Overall: 4¼"
Approximate wt.: 10 ozs.
Comments: Top section of slide is cut away from behind front sight to breech block face. Made from about 1908 to 1912.
Estimated Value: **Excellent:** **$750.00**
Very good: **$600.00**

Walther Model 2 Vest Pocket

Similar to the Model 1 except: slide fully encloses the barrel; ejector port right side of slide; overall length is 4¼"; approximate weight is 12 ozs. Made from about 1909 to 1915.

Estimated Value: **Excellent:** **$775.00**
Very good: **$625.00**

Walther Model 4 Pocket

Similar to the Model 3 except: larger in overall size; 3½" barrel; 6" overall; longer grip; 8-shot clip; a slide extension is connected to the forward end of the slide. Made from about 1910 to 1918.

Estimated Value: **Excellent:** **$600.00**
Very good: **$480.00**

Walther Model 3 Pocket

Caliber: 32 ACP
Action: Semiautomatic; concealed hammer
Magazine: 6-shot clip
Barrel: 2⅝"
Sights: Fixed
Finish: Blued; checkered hard rubber grips
Length Overall: 5"
Approximate wt.: 17 ozs.
Comments: Made from about 1910 to 1918; ejector port in left side of slide.
Estimated Value: **Excellent:** **$1,200.00**
Very good: **$ 960.00**

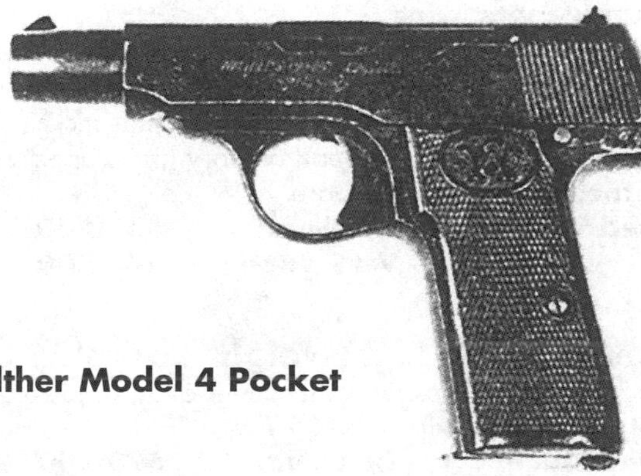

Walther Model 4 Pocket

Walther Model 5 Vest Pocket Pistol
Similar to the Model 2 except: improved version with a better finish. Made from about 1913 to 1920.

Estimated Value: **Excellent:** **$500.00**
Very good: **$400.00**

Walther Model 6
Caliber: 9mm Parabellum
Action: Semiautomatic; concealed hammer
Magazine: 8-shot clip
Barrel: 4¾"
Sights: Fixed
Finish: Blued; hard rubber grips
Length Overall: 8⅛"
Approximate wt.: 33 ozs.
Comments: Made from about 1915 to 1917.
Estimated Value: **Excellent:** **$4,500.00**
Very good: **$3,600.00**

Walther Model 7 Pocket
Caliber: 25 ACP
Action: Semiautomatic; concealed hammer
Magazine: 8-shot clip
Barrel: 3"
Sights: Fixed
Finish: Blued; checkered hard rubber grips
Length Overall: 5¼"
Approximate wt.: 13 ozs.
Comments: Introduced in 1917, discontinued in 1918. Ejector port on right side of slide.
Estimated Value: **Excellent:** **$525.00**
Very good: **$420.00**

Walther Model 8 Pocket
Caliber: 25 ACP
Action: Semiautomatic; concealed hammer
Magazine: 8-shot clip
Barrel: 2⅞"
Sights: Fixed
Finish: Blued; checkered plastic grips
Length Overall: 5⅛"
Approximate wt.: 13 ozs.
Comments: Made from about 1920 to 1945. Earlier models had takedown catch but later models used trigger guard as slide lock; a variety of special styles were made such as nickel- or gold-plated, engraved finishes with pearl or ivory grips. Special plated and engraved styles are worth more.
Estimated Value: **Excellent:** **$550.00**
Very good: **$440.00**

Walther Model 8 Lightweight Pocket
Same as the Model 8 except: aluminum alloy used for frame, making it lighter; approximate wt.: 9 ozs.
Estimated Value: **Excellent:** **$700.00**
Very good: **$560.00**

Walther Model 9 Vest Pocket
Caliber: 25 ACP
Action: Semiautomatic; concealed hammer
Magazine: 6-shot clip
Barrel: 2"
Sights: Fixed
Finish: Blued; checkered plastic grips
Length Overall: 4"
Approximate wt.: 9½ ozs.
Comments: Made from about 1921 to 1945; a variety of special styles were made such as nickel- or gold-plated engraved finishes with pearl or ivory grips; top section of slide from front sight to breech block face is cut away. Special plated and engraved styles are worth more.
Estimated Value: **Excellent:** **$750.00**
Very good: **$600.00**

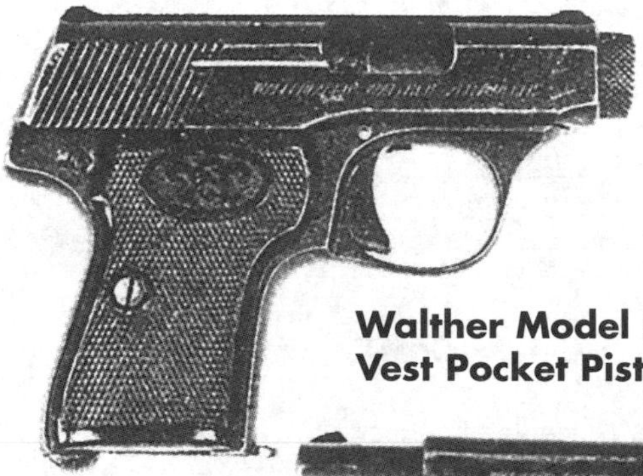

Walther Model 5 Vest Pocket Pistol

Walther Model 7 Pocket

Walther Model 9 Vest Pocket

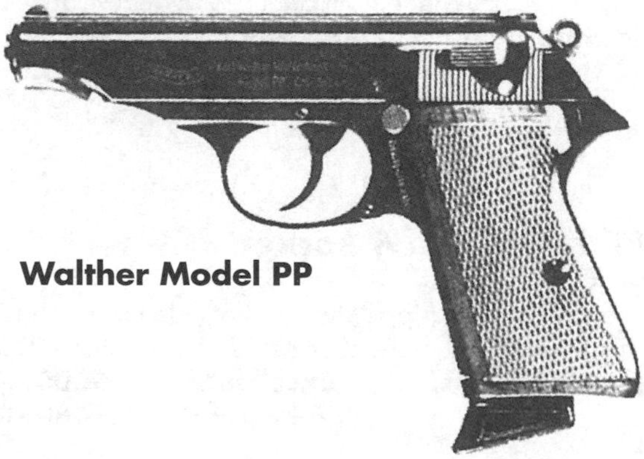

Walther Model PP

Walther Model PP

Caliber: 22 long rifle, 25 ACP, 32 ACP, or 380 ACP
Action: Semiautomatic; double action; exposed hammer; thumb safety that drops the hammer on blocked firing pin
Magazine: 8-shot clip
Barrel: 3¾"
Sights: Fixed
Finish: Blued; checkered plastic or checkered wood grips; steel back strap
Length Overall: 6 9/16"
Approximate wt.: 24 ozs.
Comments: Made from about 1929 to 1945; also nickel-, silver-, and gold-plated engraved models with ivory and pearl grips were produced; first commercially successful double action automatic pistol; initially made in 32 ACP but later made in 22, 25 and 380 calibers; the centerfire calibers were made with and without a signal pin to indicate a round in the chamber; World War II models had poorer finish and workmanship. Special plated and engraved models are worth more.

Estimated Value:	Regular Model	WWII Model
Excellent:	$600.00	$700.00
Very good:	$480.00	$560.00

Walther Model PPK

Same as the Model PP except: 3¼" barrel; 5 5/16" overall length; 7-shot magazine; approximate wt.: 19 ozs.; one-piece wrap-around grip. Made from about 1931 to 1945.

Estimated Value:	Regular Model	WWII Model
Excellent:	$650.00	$750.00
Very good:	$525.00	$600.00

Walther Model PPK

Walther Models PP and PPK Lightweight

Same as Models PP and PPK except lighter in weight due to aluminum alloy frame.

Estimated Value: **Excellent:** **$875.00**
Very good: **$700.00**

Walther Model PPK/S (West German)

Same as Model PPK except: larger size to meet U.S. Treasury Dept. specifications in 1968; uses the slide and barrel of PPK Model mounted on the PP Model frame; overall length about 6"; 8-shot magazine.

Estimated Value: **Excellent:** **$575.00**
Very good: **$460.00**

Walther Model PP (West German)

Same as the pre-World War II Model PP except: produced in West Germany from about 1955 to the present. Add 50% for 32 or 380 ACP.

Estimated Value: **Excellent:** **$778.00**
Very good: **$625.00**

Walther Model PPK Auto

Same as the pre-World War II Model PPK except: produced in West Germany from about 1955. Importation into U.S. discontinued in 1968 due to size restrictions imposed by the U.S. Treasury Department.

Estimated Value: **Excellent:** **$500.00**
Very good: **$400.00**

Walther Model PPK Lightweight

Same as the Model PPK except: lighter in weight due to use of aluminum alloy frame and not made in 380 caliber. Importation discontinued in 1968.

Estimated Value: **Excellent:** **$500.00**
Very good: **$400.00**

Walther Model PPK American

Similar to the Model PPK except: manufactured in the United States in blue or stainless steel. Introduced in 1986.

Estimated Value: **New (retail):** **$626.00**
Excellent: **$470.00**
Very good: **$375.00**

Walther Model PPK/S American

Caliber: 380 ACP
Action: Semiautomatic; double action; exposed hammer
Magazine: 7-shot clip
Barrel: 3¼"
Sights: Fixed
Finish: Blued or stainless steel; plastic grips
Length Overall: 6"
Approximate wt.: 23 ozs.
Comments: An American-built model of the Walther PPK/S, introduced in the late 1970s.

Estimated Value:	**New (retail):**	**$626.00**
	Excellent:	**$470.00**
	Very good:	**$375.00**

Walther Model P-5

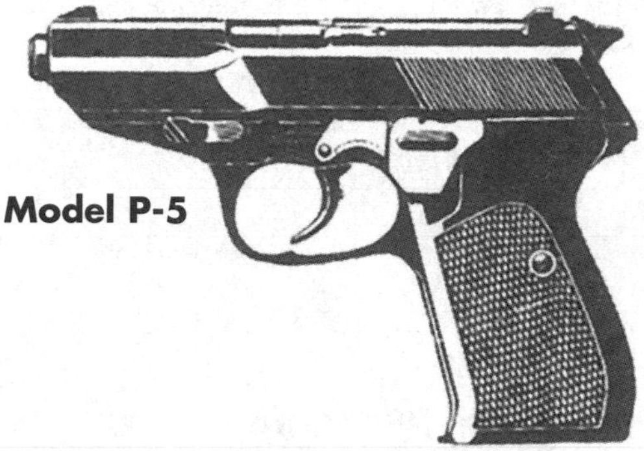

Walther Model P-5 (West German)

Caliber: 9mm Parabellum
Action: Semiautomatic; double action; exposed hammer
Magazine: 8-shot clip
Barrel: 3½" or 3"
Sights: Adjustable rear, blade front
Finish: Blued; plastic grips
Length Overall: 7"
Approximate wt.: 28 ozs.
Comments: Introduced in 1980.

Estimated Value:	**Excellent:**	**$700.00**
	Very good:	**$560.00**

Walther Model HP

Caliber: 9mm Parabellum
Action: Semiautomatic; double action; exposed hammer
Magazine: 8-shot clip
Barrel: 5"
Sights: Fixed
Finish: Blued; checkered walnut or plastic grips
Length Overall: 8⅜"
Approximate wt.: 35 ozs.
Comments: Well-made pistol, produced from about 1937 to 1945.

Estimated Value:	**Excellent:**	**$1,500.00**
	Very good:	**$1,200.00**

Walther P-38 Military

Similar to the Model HP except: modified version of the Model HP adopted as the official German service arm in 1938 and produced until about 1945. A poorer quality mass-produced military pistol; some of the wartime models were of very loose fit and very rough finish.

Estimated Value:	**Excellent:**	**$1,000.00**
	Very good:	**$ 800.00**

Walther P-38 (West German)

Same as the P-38 Military Model except: improved workmanship; use of aluminum alloy in construction of frame; calibers 22 long rifle, 30 Luger and 9mm Parabellum; approximate wt.: 28 ozs.; add 11% for 22 caliber.

Estimated Value:	**Excellent:**	**$550.00**
	Very good:	**$440.00**

Walther Model P88 (West German)

Caliber: 9mm Parabellum
Action: Double action, semiautomatic; exposed hammer
Magazine: 15-shot clip; 10-shot clip in U.S. after 9-13-94
Barrel: 4"
Sights: Rear adjustable for windage and elevation
Finish: Blued, non-reflective matte finish; alloy frame; black plastic grips
Length Overall: 7⅜"
Approximate wt.: 31½" ozs.
Comments: A combat-style handgun designed for ambidextrous use. Introduced in 1987. Produced in West Germany.

Estimated Value:	**Excellent:**	**$1,000.00**
	Very good:	**$ 800.00**

Walther Model P-38 K

Similar to the Model P-38 IV with a 2¾" barrel.

Estimated Value:	**Excellent:**	**$750.00**
	Very good:	**$600.00**

Walther Model P-38 IV

Similar to the P-38 with strengthened slide, no dust cover, and steel reinforced frame; adjustable rear sight.

Estimated Value:	**Excellent:**	**$700.00**
	Very good:	**$560.00**

Walther Model TPH

Caliber: 22 long rifle; 25 ACP
Action: Semiautomatic, exposed hammer
Magazine: 6-shot clip, with finger extension
Barrel: 2¼"
Sights: Fixed
Finish: Blue or stainless steel; black plastic grips
Length Overall: 5⅜"
Approximate wt.: 14 ozs.
Comments: A scaled-down version of the Model PP-PPK series in 22 long rifle; 25 ACP added in 1992. Introduced in the late 1980s.

Estimated Value:	**Excellent:**	**$650.00**
	Very good:	**$520.00**

Walther Model P99 and P990

Caliber: 9mm, 40 S&W
Action: Double or single action, semiautomatic; double action only model (P990) available
Magazine: 10-shot clip
Barrel: 4"
Sights: Interchangeable front, adjustable rear
Finish: Polymer frame and grips with a variety of slide color finishes; engraving available
Length overall: 8"
Approximate wt.: 25 ozs.
Comments: Price is for standard model. Engraved models are considerably more expensive.

Estimated Value:	**New (retail):**	**$825.00**
	Excellent:	**$615.00**
	Very good:	**$495.00**

Walther Model P22

Caliber: 22 long rifle
Action: Double or single action, semiautomatic
Magazine: 10-shot clip
Barrel: 3½" or 5"
Sights: Three-dot system with adjustable rear
Finish: Polymer frame and grips
Length overall: 7" to 8½"
Approximate wt.: 19½ to 23 ozs.
Comments: Add 8% for 5" barrel.

Estimated Value:	**New (retail):**	**$375.00**
	Excellent:	**$280.00**
	Very good:	**$225.00**

WEBLEY

Webley 1906 Model Vest Pocket

Caliber: 25 ACP
Action: Semiautomatic; exposed hammer; grip safety in front of grip
Magazine: 6-shot clip
Barrel: 2⅛"
Sights: None
Finish: Blued; checkered hard rubber grips
Length Overall: 4¾"
Approximate wt.: 12 ozs.
Comments: Made from about 1906 to 1940.

Estimated Value:	**Excellent:**	**$400.00**
	Very good:	**$320.00**

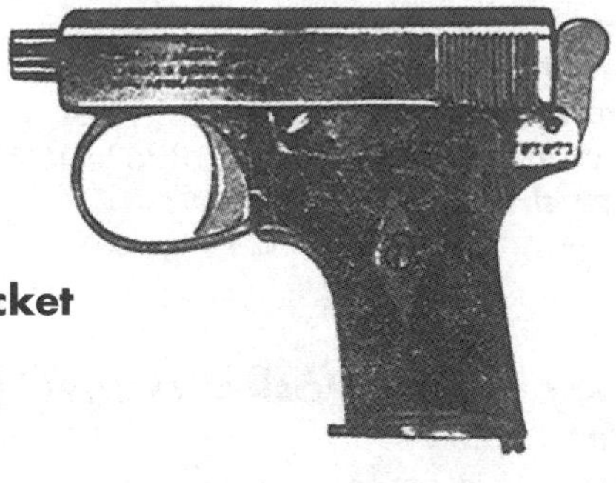

Webley 1906 Model Vest Pocket

Webley & Scott 1909 Model Vest Pocket

Similar to the 1906 except: ejector port in top of slide; concealed hammer; has fixed front and rear sights. Made from about 1909 to 1940.

Estimated Value:	**Excellent:**	**$900.00**
	Very good:	**$725.00**

Webley & Scott 9mm Military and Police

Caliber: 9mm Browning long
Action: Semiautomatic; exposed hammer; grip safety
Magazine: 8-shot clip
Barrel: 5¼"
Sights: Fixed
Finish: Blued; checkered plastic grips
Length Overall: 8"
Approximate wt.: 32 ozs.
Comments: Made from about 1909 to 1930.

Estimated Value:	**Excellent:**	**$800.00**
	Very good:	**$640.00**

Webley & Scott 9mm Military and Police

Webley & Scott Mark I

Caliber: 455 Webley self-loading
Action: Semiautomatic; exposed hammer; grip safety
Magazine: 7-shot clip
Barrel: 5"
Sights: Fixed front; movable rear
Finish: Blued; checkered hard rubber or checkered walnut grips
Length Overall: 8½"
Approximate wt.: 39 ozs.
Comments: Adopted by the British Royal Navy and Marines in 1913. Made from about 1911 to 1931.

Estimated Value:	**Excellent:**	**$1,000.00**
	Very good:	**$ 800.00**

Webley & Scott Mark I No. 2
Similar to the Mark I except: a slightly different version with fitted shoulder stock and adjustable rear sight; issued to the British Royal Flying Corps in 1915. Prices for gun with shoulder stock.
Estimated Value: **Excellent:** **$1,500.00**
Very good: **$1,200.00**

Webley & Scott 38
Similar to the Mark I except: a smaller modified version with concealed hammer; 8-shot magazine; 38 ACP caliber. Made from about 1910 to 1930.
Estimated Value: **Excellent:** **$600.00**
Very good: **$480.00**

Webley & Scott 1909 Model Single-shot Target

Webley & Scott 1909 Model Single-Shot Target
Caliber: 22 short, long, long rifle
Action: Single action; exposed hammer; hinged frame; tip-up barrel; trigger guard also barrel release
Cylinder: None; single-shot; chamber in barrel
Barrel: 10" round
Sights: Fixed; later models have adjustable rear sight
Finish: Blued; hard rubber or wood grips
Length Overall: 15"
Approximate wt.: 35 ozs.
Comments: Target pistol. Made from about 1909 to 1965 with improvements.
Estimated Value: **Excellent:** **$400.00**
Very good: **$320.00**

Webley & Scott 1906 Model Police
Caliber: 32 ACP; 380 ACP
Action: Semiautomatic; exposed hammer
Magazine: 8-shot clip in 32 ACP, 7-shot clip in 380 ACP
Barrel: 3½"
Sights: Fixed; police version has rear sight and civilian model has a groove for rear sight
Finish: Blued; checkered hard rubber grips
Length Overall: 6¼"
Approximate wt.: 20 ozs.
Comments: Made from about 1905 to 1940; with or without grip safety.
Estimated Value: **Excellent:** **$375.00**
Very good: **$300.00**

Webley & Scott 1911 Model Single-shot
Caliber: 22 short, long, long rifle
Action: Manually operated slide to chamber cartridge; exposed hammer
Magazine: None; single-shot
Barrel: 4½" or 9"
Sights: Adjustable
Finish: Blued; checkered hard rubber grips
Length Overall: 6¼" to 10¾"
Approximate wt.: 20 to 24 ozs.
Comments: Has the appearance of automatic pistol; built on the 32 caliber frame; made for police training arm; some had removable wooden shoulder stocks. Made from about 1925 to 1927 with only a few hundred being produced. Priced with shoulder stock.
Estimated Value: **Excellent:** **$550.00**
Very good: **$440.00**

Webley & Scott Match Invader Single-shot Target
Similar to the 1909 Model Single-shot Target except: also in caliber 32 S&W long, 38S&W or 38 Special; approximate wt.: 33 ozs. Made from about 1952 to 1965.
Estimated Value: **Excellent:** **$475.00**
Very good: **$380.00**

Webley & Scott Mark III Government Model
Caliber: 450, 455, or 476 Webley
Action: Single or double; exposed hammer; hinged frame; top break; simultaneous ejector
Cylinder: 6-shot
Barrel: 4", 6", 7½"
Sights: Fixed, also adjustable rear
Finish: Blued; hard rubber or wood grips
Length Overall: 9¼" to 12¾"
Approximate wt.: 36 to 40 ozs.
Comments: Made from about 1896 to 1928.
Estimated Value: **Excellent:** **$700.00**
Very good: **$560.00**

Webley & Scott Pocket Model Hammerless
Caliber: 32 S&W
Action: Double action; concealed hammer; hinged frame; top break; simultaneous ejector
Cylinder: 6-shot
Barrel: 3½"
Sights: Fixed
Finish: Blued; hard rubber or wood grips
Length Overall: 6½"
Approximate wt.: 18 ozs.
Comments: The hammer is enclosed by the frame. Made from about 1898 to 1940.
Estimated Value: **Excellent:** **$450.00**
Very good: **$360.00**

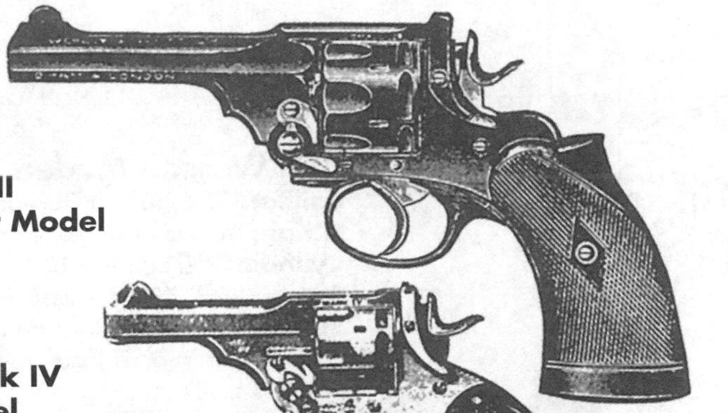

**Webley &
Scott Mark III
Government Model**

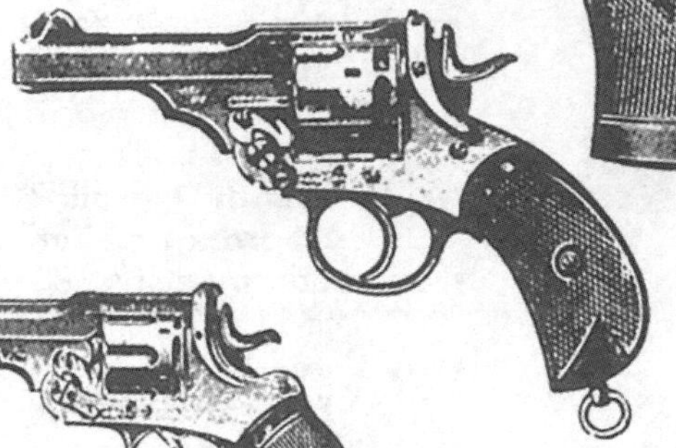

**Webley Mark IV
Pocket Model**

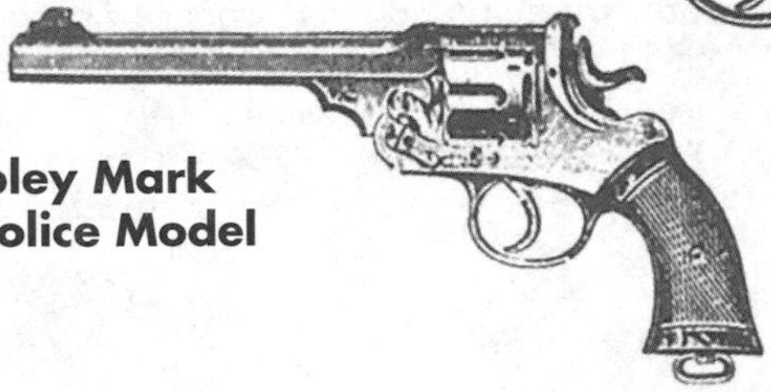

**Webley Mark
IV Police Model**

Webley Mark IV Pocket Model
Similar to the Mark IV Police Model except: calibers 32 S&W, 32 S&W long, or 38 S&W; barrel length: 3"; approximate wt.: 24 ozs.; overall length: 7⅛".

Estimated Value: Excellent: **$450.00**
 Very good: **$360.00**

Webley Mark IV Target Model
Similar to the Mark IV Police Model except: caliber 22 short, long, long rifle only; adjustable rear sight; barrel length 6"; approximate wt.: 32 ozs. Made from about 1931 to 1968.

Estimated Value: Excellent: **$800.00**
 Very good: **$640.00**

Webley & Scott Mark III Police
Caliber: 38 S&W
Action: Single or double; exposed hammer; hinged frame; top break simultaneous ejector
Cylinder: 6-shot
Barrel: 3", 4", 5"
Sights: Fixed or adjustable rear
Finish: Blued; checkered hard rubber or walnut grips
Length Overall: 8¼" to 10¼"
Approximate wt.: 19 to 22 ozs.
Comments: Made from about 1897 to 1945.

Estimated Value: Excellent: **$800.00**
 Very good: **$640.00**

Webley & Scott Police & Civilian Pocket
Similar to the Pocket Model Hammerless except: exposed hammer; double and single action. Made from about 1901 to 1940.

Estimated Value: Excellent: **$325.00**
 Very good: **$260.00**

Webley Mark IV Police Model
Caliber: 38 S&W
Action: Single or double; exposed hammer; hinged frame; top break; simultaneous ejector
Cylinder: 6-shot
Barrel: 4", 5", 6"
Sights: Fixed or adjustable
Finish: Blued; checkered walnut or plastic grips
Length Overall: 8⅛" to 10⅛"
Approximate wt.: 24 to 29 ozs.
Comments: Made from about 1927 to the present.

Estimated Value: Excellent: **$450.00**
 Very good: **$360.00**

Webley Mark IV War Model
Similar to the Mark IV Police Model except: made during World War II (from about 1940 to 1945); poor finish and fitting.

Estimated Value: Excellent: **$450.00**
 Very good: **$360.00**

Webley Mark VI British Service
Caliber: 455 Webley
Action: Single or double; hinged frame; top-break; simultaneous ejector
Cylinder: 6-shot
Barrel: 4", 6", 7½"
Sights: Fixed
Finish: Blued; checkered hard rubber or wood grips
Length Overall: 9¼" to 12¾"
Approximate wt.: 34 to 39 ozs.
Comments: Made from about 1915 to 1928.

Estimated Value: Excellent: **$600.00**
 Very good: **$480.00**

Webley Police Mark VI Target
Similar to the Mark VI British except: caliber 22 short, long, long rifle; barrel length 6" only; target sights; approximate wt.: 40 ozs.

Estimated Value: Excellent: **$500.00**
 Very good: **$400.00**

Dan Wesson Model 12

Dan Wesson Model 11

Dan Wesson Model 11
Caliber: 357 magnum or 38 Special (interchangeable)
Action: Double or single; exposed hammer; simultaneous ejector
Cylinder: 6-shot; swingout
Barrel: 2½", 4", 6"; interchangeable barrels
Sights: Ramp front; fixed rear
Finish: Blued; one-piece changeable walnut grip
Length Overall: 7¾" to 11¼"
Approximate wt.: 36 to 40 ozs.
Comments: Made from about 1970 to 1974. Barrels and barrel cover (shroud) can be changed quickly by means of a recessed barrel nut; also one-piece grip readily changeable to option styles.
Estimated Value: Excellent: $300.00
 Very good: $240.00

Dan Wesson Model 12
Same as the Model 11 except target model with adjustable rear sight.
Estimated Value: Excellent: $325.00
 Very good: $260.00

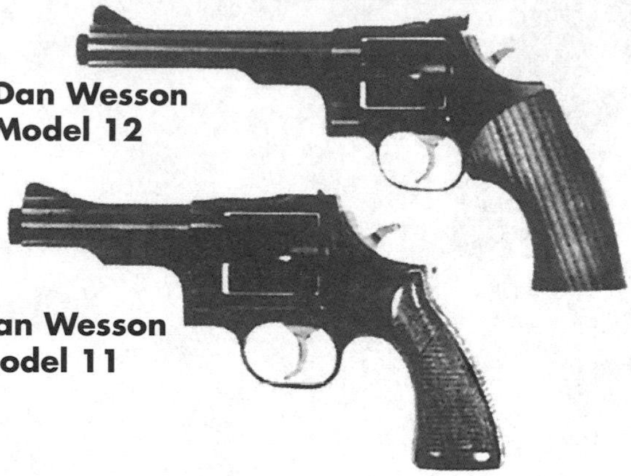

Dan Wesson Model 15-2

Dan Wesson Models 14, 14-2, and 714
Caliber: 357 mag. or 38 Special (interchangeable)
Action: Double or single; exposed hammer
Cylinder: 6-shot; swingout
Barrel: 2½", 4", 6"; interchangeable barrels
Sights: Ramp front; fixed rear
Finish: Blued; one-piece walnut grip; satin blue available; 714 stainless steel
Length Overall: 7¾" to 13¼"
Approximate wt.: 36 to 42 ozs.
Comments: Made from about 1973 to the late 1970s. A modified version of the Model 22. Price increases with barrel length. Add 15% for stainless steel (714).
Estimated Value: Excellent: $350.00 – 400.00
 Very good: $280.00 – 320.00

Dan Wesson Models 8-2 and 708
Similar to the Model 14 except 38 caliber only. Add $15.00 for bright blue finish (8-2B) (discontinued in 1987); add 15% for stainless steel (708).
Estimated Value: Excellent: $275.00 – 325.00
 Very good: $220.00 – 260.00

Dan Wesson Model 14

Dan Wesson Models 15-2 and 715
Caliber: 357 magnum or 38 Special (interchangeable)
Action: Double or single; exposed hammer
Cylinder: 6-shot; swingout; simultaneous ejector
Barrel: 2½", 4", 6", 8", 10", 12", 15" interchangeable barrels
Sights: Interchangeable colored front sight blade; adjustable rear sight with white outline
Finish: Blued; checkered wood target grips; Model 715 is stainless steel
Length Overall: 7¾" to 13¼"
Approximate wt.: 32 to 42 ozs.
Comments: Made from about 1975 to the late 1980s. Price increases with barrel length. Add 9% for stainless steel (Model 715).
Estimated Value: Excellent: $500.00 – 600.00
 Very good: $400.00 – 480.00

Dan Wesson Model 9-2

Dan Wesson Models 9-2 and 709

Similar to the Model 15-2 except 38 caliber only. No 12" or 15" barrel. Add 9% for stainless steel (Model 709).

Estimated Value: **Excellent:** **$300.00 – 450.00**
Very good: **$240.00 – 360.00**

Dan Wesson Models 9-2V and 709-V

Similar to the Model 9-2 with ventilated rib. Price increases with barrel length. Add 12% for stainless steel (Model 709-V).

Estimated Value: **Excellent:** **$325.00 – 450.00**
Very good: **$260.00 – 375.00**

Dan Wesson Models 9-2VH and 709-VH

Similar to the Model 9-2 with heavier bull barrel and ventilated rib. Prices increases with barrel length. Add 10% for stainless steel (Model 709-VH).

Estimated Value: **Excellent:** **$425.00 – 500.00**
Very good: **$340.00 – 400.00**

Dan Wesson Model 15

Similar to the Model 14 except adjustable rear sight. Made from about 1973 to 1976.

Estimated Value: **Excellent:** **$300.00**
Very good: **$240.00**

Dan Wesson Model 15-2H

Same as the Model 15-2 except it has a heavier bull barrel. A special-order item after 1981.

Estimated Value: **Excellent:** **$400.00**
Very good: **$320.00**

Dan Wesson Model 15-2H

Dan Wesson Models 15-2V and 715-V

Same as the Model 15-2 except it has ventilated rib. Add 9% for stainless steel (Model 715-V).

Estimated Value: **Excellent:** **$425.00 – 525.00**
Very good: **$340.00 – 420.00**

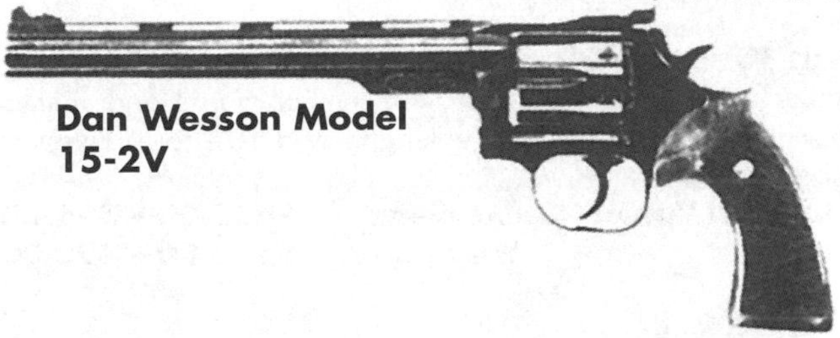

Dan Wesson Model 15-2V

Dan Wesson Model 15-2VH

Dan Wesson Models 15-2VH and 715-VH

Same as the Model 15-2 except: heavier bull barrel with ventilated rib. Add 12% for stainless steel (Model 715-VH).

Estimated Value: **Excellent:** **$500.00 – 600.00**
Very good: **$400.00 – 480.00**

Dan Wesson Model 22V

Dan Wesson Models 22M-VH and 722M-VH

Similar to the Model 22-VH except: 22 mag. caliber. Add 10% for stainless steel finish (Model 722M-VH).

Estimated Value: **Excellent:** **$425.00 – 525.00**
Very good: **$340.00 – 420.00**

Dan Wesson Models 22 and 722

Similar to the Model 15-2 except: 22 caliber. Introduced in the late 1970s. Not available with 12" or 15" barrel. Price increases with barrel length. Add 12% for stainless steel (Model 722).

Estimated Value: **Excellent:** **$500.00 – 600.00**
Very good: **$400.00 – 480.00**

Dan Wesson Models 22M and 722M

Similar to the Model 22 except: 22 mag. caliber. Add 10% for stainless steel finish (Model 722M).

Estimated Value: **Excellent:** **$475.00 – 550.00**
Very good: **$380.00 – 440.00**

Dan Wesson Models 22V and 722-V

Similar to the Model 22 except: ventilated rib. Price increases with barrel length. Add 12% for stainless steel (Model 722-V).

Estimated Value: **Excellent:** **$375.00 – 475.00**
Very good: **$300.00 – 380.00**

Dan Wesson Models 22-VH and 722-VH

Similar to the Model 22 with heavier bull barrel and ventilated rib. Price increases with barrel length. Add 10% for stainless steel (Model 722-VH).

Estimated Value: **Excellent:** **$425.00 - 525.00**
Very good: **$340.00 - 420.00**

Dan Wesson Models 22M-V and 722M-V

Similar to the Model 22-V except: 22 mag. caliber. Add 10% for stainless steel finish (Model 722M-V).

Estimated Value: **Excellent:** **$425.00 - 525.00**
Very good: **$340.00 - 420.00**

Dan Wesson Model 73220

Dan Wesson Models 3220 and 73220

Similar to the Model 22 except: 32-20 caliber. Model 73220 has stainless steel finish.

Estimated Value: **Excellent:** **$450.00 - 545.00**
Very good: **$360.00 - 435.00**

Dan Wesson Model 732

Dan Wesson Models 32 and 732

Similar to the Model 15-2 except: 32 mag. caliber; 2½", 4", 6", or 8" barrel. Introduced in the mid-1980s. Add 9% for stainless steel (Model 732).

Estimated Value: **Excellent:** **$475.00 - 550.00**
Very good: **$380.00 - 440.00**

Dan Wesson Models 32-V and 732-V

Similar to the Model 32 with ventilated rib. Add 9% for stainless steel (Model 732-V).

Estimated Value: **Excellent:** **$400.00 - 500.00**
Very good: **$320.00 - 400.00**

Dan Wesson Models 32-VH and 732-VH

Similar to the Model 32 with ventilated rib, heavy barrel. Add 9% for stainless steel (Model 732-VH).

Estimated Value: **Excellent:** **$400.00 - 500.00**
Very good: **$320.00 - 400.00**

Dan Wesson Models 40-V and 740-V 357 Super Magnum

Caliber: 357 Maximum
Action: Double and single; exposed hammer
Cylinder: 6-shot; swingout; fluted
Barrel: 4", 6", 8", or 10"; interchangeable barrels; ventilated rib
Sights: Interchangeable colored front sight blade, adjustable interchangeable rear
Finish: Blued; smooth grips; stainless steel (Model 740-V)
Length Overall: 14½" with 8" barrel
Approximate wt.: 59 to 62 ozs.
Comments: Introduced in the mid-1980s. Comes with an extra barrel. Price increases with barrel length. Add 13% for stainless steel.

Estimated Value: **Excellent:** **$475.00 - 550.00**
Very good: **$380.00 - 440.00**

Dan Wesson Models 40-V8S and 740-V8S

Similar to the Model 40-V except: slotted barrel shroud; 8" barrel only; extra barrel included; weighs 64 ozs. Add 10% for stainless steel (Model 740-V8S).

Estimated Value: **Excellent:** **$450.00**
Very good: **$360.00**

Dan Wesson Models 40-VH and 740-VH

Similar to the Model 40-V with heavy barrel; extra barrel included. Add $60.00 for stainless steel (Model 740-VH).

Estimated Value: **Excellent:** **$400.00 - 500.00**
Very good: **$320.00 - 400.00**

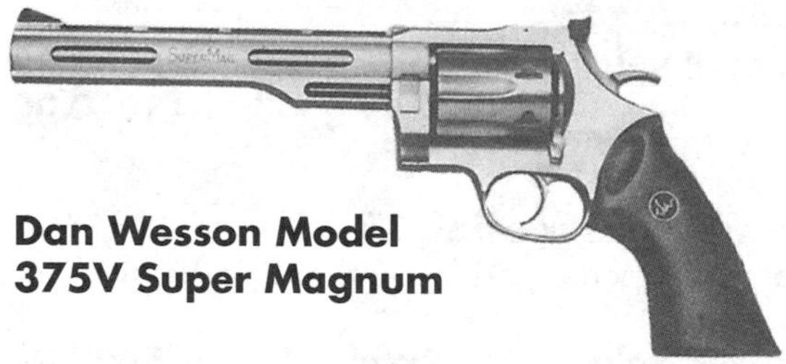

Dan Wesson Model 375V Super Magnum

Dan Wesson Model 375V Super Magnum

Similar to the Model 40V except: 375 mag. caliber.

Estimated Value: **Excellent:** **$400.00 - 500.00**
Very good: **$320.00 - 400.00**

Dan Wesson Model 375-V8S Super Magnum

Similar to the Model 375V except: slotted barrel shroud and 8" barrel.

Estimated Value: **Excellent:** **$475.00**
Very good: **$380.00**

Dan Wesson Model 375-VH Super Magnum

Similar to the Model 375V except: ventilated rib shroud and heavy barrel.

Estimated Value: **Excellent:** **$400.00 - 525.00**
Very good: **$320.00 - 420.00**

Dan Wesson Model 44-V

Dan Wesson Models 44-V and 744-V

Caliber: 44 mag. and 44 Special (jacketed only)
Action: Single and double, exposed hammer, wide hammer and trigger
Cylinder: 6-shot; swingout; simultaneous ejector
Barrel: 4", 6", 8", 10" interchangeable barrel; ventilated rib
Sights: Interchangeable colored front sight blade, adjustable rear with white outline
Finish: Blued; smooth or checkered walnut grips with thumb flute; stainless steel (Model 744-V)
Length Overall: 12" with 6" barrel
Approximate wt.: 48 to 63 ozs.
Comments: Introduced in the early 1980s. Price increases with barrel length. Add 17% for stainless steel (Model 744-V).

Estimated Value:	**Excellent:**	**$425.00 – 575.00**
	Very good:	**$340.00 – 460.00**

Dan Wesson Models 41-V and 741-V

Similar to the Model 44-V except: 41 mag. caliber.

Estimated Value:	**Excellent:**	**$600.00 – 675.00**
	Very good:	**$480.00 – 540.00**

Dan Wesson Models 44-VH and 744-VH

Similar to the Model 44-V except: heavier bull barrel. Price increases with barrel length.

Estimated Value:	**Excellent:**	**$600.00 – 675.00**
	Very good:	**$480.00 – 540.00**

Dan Wesson Models 41-VH and 741-VH

Similar to the Model 44-VH in 41 magnum caliber. Add 11% for stainless steel finish (Model 741-VH).

Estimated Value:	**Excellent:**	**$525.00 – 575.00**
	Very good:	**$420.00 – 460.00**

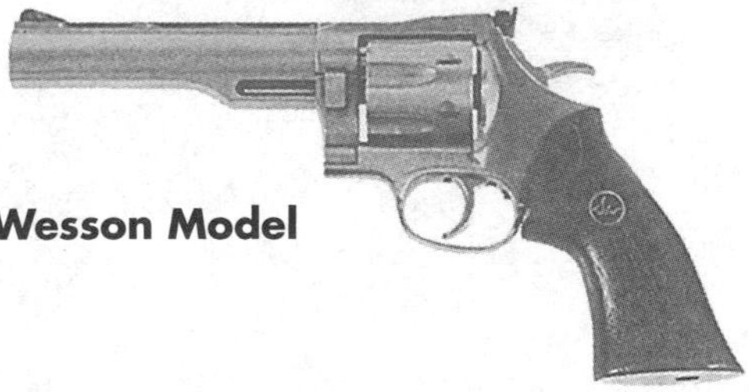

Dan Wesson Model 41-V

Dan Wesson Models 45-V and 745-V

Caliber: 45 Colt
Action: Single and double, exposed hammer, wide hammer and trigger
Cylinder: 6-shot; swingout; simultaneous ejector
Barrel: 4", 6", 8", or 10" ventilated rib shroud
Sights: Interchangeable colored front sight blade
Finish: Blued; smooth walnut grips; stainless steel (Model 745-V)
Length Overall: 12" with 6" barrel
Approximate wt.: 48 to 63 ozs.
Comments: Introduced in 1988. Price increases with barrel length.

Estimated Value:	**Excellent:**	**$600.00 – 675.00**
	Very good:	**$480.00 – 540.00**

Dan Wesson Models 45-VH and 745-VH

Similar to the Model 45-V with heavier bull barrel. Price increases with barrel length. Add 17% for stainless steel (Model 745-VH).

Estimated Value:	**Excellent:**	**$525.00 – 675.00**
	Very good:	**$420.00 – 540.00**

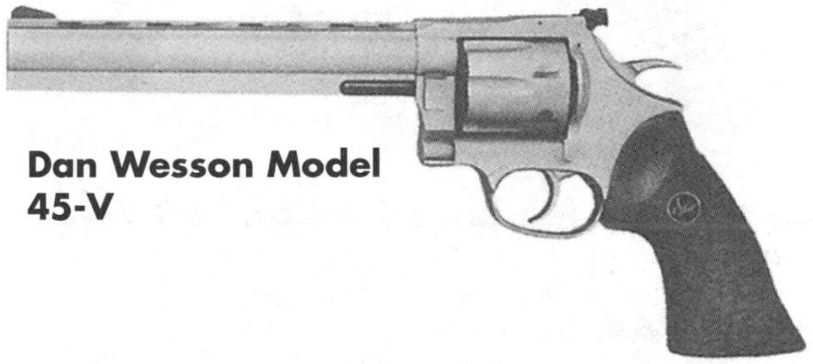

Dan Wesson Model 45-V

Dan Wesson Models 360 and 7360

Similar to the Model 45V except: 360DW caliber. Model 7360 has stainless steel finish.

Estimated Value:	**Excellent:**	**$575.00 – 665.00**
	Very good:	**$460.00 – 535.00**

Dan Wesson Models 445VH and 7445VH

Same as the Models 445V and 7445V except: ventilated heavy rib shroud. Made in the 1990s. Add 2% per inch of barrel over 4".

Estimated Value:	**Excellent:**	**$500.00**
	Very good:	**$400.00**

Dan Wesson Models 460 and 7460

Similar to the Model 45V except: 45ACP caliber. Model 7460 has stainless steel finish.

Estimated Value:	**Excellent:**	**$575.00 – 665.00**
	Very good:	**$460.00 – 535.00**

Dan Wesson Models 40 and 740

Similar to the Model 44V except: 357 Maxi/Super magnum caliber. Model 740 has stainless steel finish.

Estimated Value:	**Excellent:**	**$695.00 – 785.00**
	Very good:	**$550.00 – 625.00**

Dan Wesson Model 714

Dan Wesson Models 414 and 714

Similar to the Model 44V except: 414 Super magnum caliber. Model 714 has stainless steel finish.

Estimated Value:	**Excellent:**	**$695.00 – 785.00**
	Very good:	**$550.00 – 625.00**

Dan Wesson Model
FB 44

Dan Wesson Model
445V

Dan Wesson Models FB 44 and FB 744

Caliber: 44 magnum and 44 Special
Action: Double or single; exposed hammer
Cylinder: 6-shot swing-out
Barrel: 4", 5", 6", or 8"
Sights: Red ramp front, adjustable rear
Finish: Blued or brushed stainless steel (FB 744); Hogue finger grooved rubber grips
Length Overall: 9¾" to 13¾"
Approximate wt.: 50 to 66 ozs.
Comments: Made in the 1990s; add 10% for stainless steel (Model FB 744); add 1% per inch for barrel length over 4".

Estimated Value:	**Excellent:**	**$500.00**
	Very good:	**$400.00**

Dan Wesson Model
FB-14

Dan Wesson Models FB-14 and FB-714

Caliber: 357 magnum and 38 Special
Action: Double or single; exposed hammer
Cylinder: 6-shot swing-out
Barrel: 2½" or 4"; fixed
Sights: Fixed
Finish: Blued or stainless steel (ModelFB-714); smooth wood grips
Length Overall: 8¼" to 9¾"
Approximate wt.: 36 to 40 ozs.
Comments: Made in the early 1990s; add 8% for stainless steel (Model FB-714); add 2% for 4" barrel.

Estimated Value:	**Excellent:**	**$325.00**
	Very good:	**$260.00**

Dan Wesson Model 445V and 7445V

Caliber: 445 Supermag
Action: Double or single; exposed hammer
Cylinder: 6-shot swing-out
Barrel: 4", 6", 8", or 10"; interchangeable; ventilated rib shroud
Sights: Interchangeable colored blade front; adjustable rear
Finish: Blued or stainless steel (Model 7445V); smooth wood grips
Length Overall: 10" to 16"
Approximate wt.: 50 to 64 ozs.
Comments: Made from the early to the late 1990s.

Estimated Value:	**Excellent:**	**$695.00 – 785.00**
	Very good:	**$550.00 – 630.00**

Dan Wesson Models FB-15 and FB-715

Same as the Models FB-14 and FB-714 except: 3", 4", 5", or 6" barrel; adjustable rear sight; add 8% for stainless steel (Model FB-715); add 2% per inch of barrel length over 3".

Estimated Value:	**Excellent:**	**$320.00**
	Very good:	**$255.00**

Dan Wesson
Model 738P

Dan Wesson Model 738P

Caliber: 38 Special +P
Action: Double or single; exposed hammer
Cylinder: 5-shot swing-out
Barrel: 2" fixed
Sights: Fixed
Finish: Stainless steel, wood or rubber grips
Length Overall: 6½"
Approximate wt.: 24½ ozs.
Comments: Made from the early to the mid-1990s.

Estimated Value:	**Excellent:**	**$325.00**
	Very good:	**$260.00**

ACKNOWLEDGMENTS

Thank you to the companies included for the use of catalogs, advertisements, and promotional material.

A special thanks to the following gun manufacturers for additional photos, information, and assistance: Beretta Arms Co., Inc. for material on Beretta handguns and shotguns; Travis Hall of Browning for material on Browning handguns, rifles, and shotguns; Charter Arms Corporation for material on Charter Arms handguns; Colt Industries, Firearms Division, for material on Colt handguns and rifles; Commercial Trading Imports, Inc. for material on Baikal shotguns; Jennifer Harding of Harrington & Richardson, Inc. for material on Harrington & Richardson handguns, rifles, and shotguns and New England firearms; Heckler & Koch for material on Heckler & Koch rifles and handguns; Interarms for material on Mark X rifles, Valmet rifles, Whitworth rifles, Walther handguns and rifles, Star handguns, and Astra handguns; Ithaca Gun Co. for material on Ithaca shotguns; Iver Johnson Arms, Inc. for material on Iver Johnson handguns; Kleinguenther, Inc. for materials on Kleinguenther rifles; Mannlicher for materials on Mannlicher rifles and shotguns; Diana Morin of Marlin for material on Marlin and Marlin-Glenfield rifles and shotguns; Joe Koziel of O.F. Mossberg and Sons, Inc. for material on Mossberg and New Haven rifles and shotguns; Remington for material on Remington rifles, shotguns, and handguns; Richland Arms Co. for material on Richland shotguns; Tom Mihalek of Savage Arms for material on Savage rifles and shotguns, Stevens rifles and shotguns, Fox shotguns, and Anschutz rifles; Sears, Roebuck and Co. for material on Sears rifles and shotguns and Ted Williams rifles and shotguns; Smith and Wesson for material on Smith & Wesson handguns, rifles, and shotguns; Speer Inc. Advertising for material on Mossberg firearms; Sterling Arms Corporation for material on Sterling handguns; Sturm, Ruger and Co. for material on Ruger handguns, rifles, and shotguns; Universal Firearms for material on Universal rifles; Adam Weatherby of Weatherby, Inc. for material on Weatherby rifles and shotguns; Winchester-Western for material on Winchester rifles and shotguns; U.S. Repeating Arms for material on Winchester rifles and shotguns.

Petersen Publishing Company for the use of the following photographs from *Guns and Ammo Annual*, 1977, 1982, and *Hunting Annual* 1983:

Shotguns:

Beretta BL4, 680 Trap, 685, MKII Trap, GR-2; 410, AL-2; Bernardelli Game Cock; Browning Super Light, Citori Trap, B-SS, BPS, 2000; Charles Daly Field III, Auto Superior; Fox FA-1; Franchi Standard; Harrington & Richardson 176, 1212; Ithaca 37 Standard, 37 DV Deluxe, 37 Bicentennial, 51 Deluxe Trap, 51 Magnum, 51 Deerslayer; Mannlicher Oxford, Mossberg 500 ATP8, 500 AHTD, Slugster, Richland 200; Smith & Wesson 916, 1000, 3000; Valmet 412K; Weatherby Orion, Athena, 92, 82; Winchester 1200 Defender

Rifles:

Anschutz 1422D, 520/61; Browning BAR; Harrington & Richardson 750; Heckler & Koch 770, 940; Mossberg 321K, 341, 353, 800, 810; New Haven 453T; Remington 541 S, 700 ADL; Salo Classic, Safari; Stevens 35, 125; Valmet 412, M62/S, M71/S; Walther KKJ, KKM, UIT, Moving Target; Winchester 70 XTR Featherweight, 70 Western, 70XTR Sporter Magnum, Super Xpress

Handguns:

Beretta 951; Browning Challenger II, Challenger III; Charter Arms Explorer II, Bulldog Tracker; Colt S-4 Targetsman, Target S-3; Dan Wesson 9-2, 44V; Heckler & Koch HK4, P9S; Iver Johnson TP22; Llama Comanche; Ruger Redhawk; Smith and Wesson 30, 1953 22/32, 25-1955, 10, 31, 27, 28, 58, 38, 547 M and P, 586; Sterling MKII 400

Stackpole Books for the use of the following photographs from W.H.B. Smith's *Book of Pistols and Revolvers* and *Book of Rifles*: Astra 1911 Patent, 1915 Patent, 1924, 300, 600, 400; Bayard 1908, 1923, 1930; Beretta 1915, 1923, 1931; Browning, FN, 1900, 1903 Military, 1910, 1922; CZ 22, 1945; Colt 1900, 1902, 1905, Model M, 1911; Fiala Single-shot; Harrington & Richardson 32; Japanese Military pistols; Lignose 2A, 2 Pocket; MAB C; Mauser 2; Sauer 1913, WTM, H; Savage 1907, 1915, 1917; Smith & Wesson 32 and 35, No. 3 Frontier, Doubled Action Frontier, Military and Police 32-20, New Century; Star 1919; Steyr Solothurn, Vest Pocket; Walther 5, 4, 7, 9; Webley & Scott 1906, Mark I; Military rifles